Civilization

PAST & PRESENT

Civilization
PAST & PRESENT

Ninth Edition

Volume 1 To 1650

Palmira Brummett
UNIVERSITY OF TENNESSEE

Robert B. Edgar
HOWARD UNIVERSITY

Neil J. Hackett
OKLAHOMA STATE UNIVERSITY

George F. Jewsbury
CENTRE D'ÉTUDES DU MONDE RUSSE
ÉCOLE DES HAUTES ÉTUDES EN SCIENCES SOCIALES

Alastair M. Taylor
EMERITUS, QUEENS UNIVERSITY

Nels M. Bailkey
EMERITUS, TULANE UNIVERSITY

Clyde J. Lewis
EMERITUS, EASTERN KENTUCKY UNIVERSITY

T. Walter Wallbank (Late)

An imprint of Addison Wesley Longman, Inc.

New York • Reading, Massachusetts • Menlo Park, California • Harlow, England
Don Mills, Ontario • Sydney • Mexico City • Madrid • Amsterdam

Editor in Chief: Priscilla McGeehon
Director of Development: Betty Slack
Developmental Editor: Barbara A. Conover
Executive Marketing Manager: Sue Westmoreland
Supplements Editor: Joy Hilgendorf
Project Manager: Ellen MacElree
Design Manager: John Callahan
Cover and Text Designer: John Callahan
Cover Photograph: *Head of a Wild Young Girl (Leda)* by Leonardo da Vinci, courtesy of Super Stock.
Art Studio: Mapping Specialists Limited
Photo Researcher: PhotoSearch, Inc.
Electronic Production Specialist: Sarah Johnson
Electronic Page Makeup: York Graphic Services
Printer and Binder: Von Hoffmann Press
Cover Printer: The Lehigh Press, Inc.

For permission to use copyrighted material, grateful acknowledgment is made to the copyright holders on pp. C-1–C-5, which are hereby made part of this copyright page.

Please visit our website at http://www.awlonline.com

ISBN 0-321-00529-5
ISBN 0-321-00531-7 (Volume One)
ISBN 0-321-00533-3 (Volume Two)

12345678910—VH—0302010099

Brief Contents

Detailed Contents

*Each chapter ends with a Conclusion, Suggestions for Reading, Suggestions for Web Browsing, and Notes.

Documents

Maps

Discovery Through Maps

To the Instructor

The ninth edition of *Civilization Past & Present* continues to present a survey of world history, treating the development and growth of civilization not as a unique European experience but as a global one through which all the great culture systems have interacted to produce the present-day world. This edition includes all the elements of history—social, economic, political, military, religious, aesthetic, legal, and technological—to illustrate that global interaction.

The authors acknowledge that for our predominantly Western audience, an appreciation of their civilization is an essential aim of education, but this alone is no longer adequate. With the accelerating tempo of developments in business, communication, and technology, every day each part of the world is brought into closer contact with other parts: economic and political events that happen in even the most remote corner of the world affect each of us individually.

Changes to Organization and Content

The ninth edition maintains the strengths that have made *Civilization Past & Present* a highly respected textbook. As they revised, the authors used the latest historical scholarship and profited from many helpful suggestions from both adopters of the text and reviewers. Maintained throughout the text is a consistent writing style and level of presentation seldom found in multiauthored texts. In addition, the text introduces two new authors: Palmira Brummett of the University of Tennessee writes about Islam and West and South Asia, and Robert B. Edgar of Howard University provides coverage of Africa. While the ninth edition retains the basic organization and approach of its predecessors, all chapters have been reviewed and revised in light of the globalization of a rapidly changing world. Without increasing the number of chapters, the authors have carefully evaluated, revised, and rewritten chapters to provide balanced coverage of all parts of the world throughout history.

The new edition features the following specific changes:

- Chapter 1, on prelithic to neolithic societies, has been rewritten to reflect recent scholarship in prehistory.

- Chapter 2, "Early Civilizations: The Near East and Western Asia," is a new chapter featuring substantial information on Nubia.
- Chapter 5, "Classical China: From Origins to Empire, Prehistory to 220 c.e.," is a new, full chapter on early Chinese history.
- Chapter 6, "Ancient India: From Origins to 300 c.e.," is a new, full chapter on the early history of India.
- Chapter 10, "Islam: From Its Origins to 1300," rewritten by our scholar-author on Middle Eastern studies, offers expanded discussion of early Islam.
- Chapter 11, "The African Genesis: African Civilizations to 1500," rewritten by our scholar-author on African studies, features expanded coverage of early African history.
- Chapter 12, "The Growth and Spread of Asian Culture, 300–1300," has been updated and expanded.
- Chapter 13, "The Americas to 1492," includes a new section on the Amerindians of North America, in addition to already strong coverage of Central and South American civilizations.
- Chapter 15, "The Christian Reformations and the Emergence of the Modern Political System: Faith and State in Europe, 1517–1648," provides an improved analysis of the interrelationship of religious and political developments.
- Chapter 17, "The Islamic Gunpowder Empires, 1300–1650," is a newly written chapter.
- Chapter 18, "Ming China and National Development in Korea, Japan, and Southeast Asia, 1300–1650," provides coverage of these Asian civilizations.
- Chapter 19, "From Absolutism to the Old Regime: Centralized Power in Europe, 1648–1774," is reorganized and features expanded treatment of the origins and crises of central power.
- Chapter 20, "Limited Central Power in the Capitalist World, 1600–1789," emphasizes the interrelationship between decentralized political power and the world market.
- Chapter 21, "The Scientific Revolution and the Enlightenment: New Ideas and Their Consequences," discusses the interaction of scientific discovery and new political and social thought

and the consequence of that fusion in enlightened despotism and the American Revolution.

- Chapter 22, "The French and Napoleonic Revolutions and Their Impact on Europe and the Americas, 1789–1825," illustrates the impact of the quarter century of French dominance and its role in introducing the modern world.
- Chapter 23, "Africa, Asia, and European Penetration, 1650–1815," newly written and expanded, presents the European advances from a global rather than a Eurocentric view.
- Chapter 24, "Foundations of Western Dominance: Industrial, Scientific, Technological, Business, and Cultural Developments, 1815–1914," provides an enhanced overview of the material and of the intellectual forces fueling the Industrial Revolution and a century of European domination.
- Chapter 25, "The Politics of Ideas in the Western World, 1815–1861," and Chapter 26, "Power Politics in the West, 1861–1914," consider Western political developments in two stages: the politics of ideology to 1861 and the politics of Realpolitik to 1914.
- Chapter 27, "Africa and the Middle East, 1800–1914," an entirely new chapter, gives an account of non-Western affairs of that century from a non-Western point of view.
- Chapter 28, "Four Faces of Nineteenth-Century Imperialism," offers an analysis of the various forms of Western colonialism.
- Chapter 29, "The Perils of 'Progress': Middle-Class Thought and the Failure of European Diplomacy, 1878–1914," is a study of the complacency, misreading of science, and racism that permitted Europeans to ignore ticking time bombs such as the crisis in the Balkans.
- Chapter 30, "Winning the War and Losing the Peace: The Democracies, 1914–1939," discusses the end of the liberal dream in Europe after the disaster of World War I.
- Chapter 32, "Emerging National Movements in Asia and Africa, 1920s to 1950s," a new chapter, offers expanded treatment of Asia and Africa during the period between World Wars I and II.
- The final three chapters, Chapter 34, "The Cold War and After: Russia and Eastern Europe, 1945–1999," Chapter 35, "The 'Developed World' Since 1945," and Chapter 36, "The Developing World: The Struggle for Survival," have all been updated and expanded to reflect events of the late 1990s.

New Split

The split for the two-volume edition has changed: Volume 1, To 1650, contains Chapters 1–18; Volume 2, From 1300, contains Chapters 14–36. The start of Volume 2 has been moved back to accommodate courses that cover material beginning earlier than 1650.

Pedagogical Features

The text has been developed with the dual purpose of helping students acquire a solid knowledge of past events and, equally important, of helping them think more constructively about the significance of those events for the complex times in which we now live. A number of pedagogical features—some well tested in earlier editions and a number of new ones—will assist students in achieving these goals.

New

Full-Color Format: The full-color format design of the ninth edition is intended to make *Civilization Past & Present* more "user-friendly" to its readers. *Photographs:* The text's more than 500 photos, most in full color, have been carefully selected to present a mix of Western and non-Western images. Special care has been taken to include images illustrating the lifestyles and contributions of women for all eras and areas. *Maps:* The use of full color allows students more readily to see distinctions on the more than 120 maps in the text. Some maps make clear the nature of a single distinctive event; others illustrate larger trends. The caption accompanying each map highlights the significance of the map and its relevance to a specific text topic.

Discovery Through Maps: A special new feature focusing on primary maps in each chapter offers a unique historical view—be it local, city, country, world, or constellation— of the way in which a particular culture looked at the world at a particular time. For example, a 4000-year-old Chinese map shows the major facts of life for the time: rivers and where they run, mountains, and provinces that paid tribute to the emperor; while an elaborate seventeenth-century map of Amsterdam makes clear that it was the Golden Age not only for the Netherlands but also for the Dutch cartographers who depicted its world.

Part Opening Essays: New essays at the beginning of each part relate the various chapters one to the other and emphasize thematic development within the book. These essays allow students to take stock of where they have been in their study of global history and to discover where the flow of history will take them.

Suggested Web Sites: Following the Suggestions for Reading is a listing of Web sites related to major topics of the chapter, offering access to differing interpretations, images, sounds, and discussion groups.

Chronology Tables: Short chronology tables within the chapter narrative allow the reader a quick recap of the important events or trends of a specific period.

Revised

Excerpts from Primary Source Documents: These excerpts from original sources represent a mix of the best of the old and a strengthening of the new, particularly non-Western documents. The selections have been chosen to give a variety of testimonies—political, economic, legal, religious, artistic, social, and popular—to show students the kinds of materials historians use to understand and interpret the past.

Chapter Opening Pages: Redesigned chapter opening pages feature an illustration relevant to the chapter topics, a chapter outline, and a streamlined, easy-to-read time line of key events that are discussed in the chapter.

Suggestions for Reading: Detailed annotated bibliographies list general interpretations, monographs, and collections of source materials that students can consult to expand their understanding of a particular topic or to prepare reports and papers.

Pronunciation Guide: The general index at the back of the text includes a pronunciation for most proper names. Students should find it easy, as well as helpful, to look up the correct pronunciation of the names and places they encounter in the text. The index also provides pronunciation guides for unfamiliar, difficult, or foreign words.

The ninth edition of *Civilization Past & Present* is a thorough revision in both its text narrative and its pedagogical features. It is intended to provide the reader with an understanding of the legacies of past eras and to illuminate the way in which the study of world history gives insights into the genesis, nature, and direction of our global civilization. The need for this kind of perspective has never been greater.

For Qualified College Adopters: Supplements for Instructors

Annotated Instructor's Edition by Paul Bischoff of Oklahoma State University. This unique edition helps instructors cover cultures and periods outside their areas of expertise with teaching suggestions, project ideas, chapter comparisons, additional background, and suggestions for further reading. It is an especially valuable resource for both new instructors and more experienced faculty in search of new ideas and for all professors who struggle to teach cultures outside their areas of expertise.

Brummett Online, http://www.awlonline.com/brummett, by Richard Rothaus of St. Cloud State University. This course companion provides text-specific resources for students and instructors and includes our on-line syllabus manager. Students will find it easy to learn and study with the chapter outlines, self-testing programs, Web activities, primary sources, Internet links, and glossary. Instructors will love it for the teaching ideas and aids, on-line images, links, and syllabus manager.

Instructor's Resource Manual revised by Patricia Ali of Morris College. This collection of resources includes chapter outlines, definitions, discussion suggestions, critical thinking exercises, term paper and essay topics, and audiovisual suggestions. It also includes special *African Perspectives* essays by Robert Edgar and *Genocide in History* essays by George Jewsbury.

Brummett Presentation Maker These easy-to-customize PowerPoint slides outline key points of each chapter of the text and are available as transparency masters and on dual platform CD-ROM and Windows or Macintosh disks.

Guide to Teaching World History by Palmira Brummett of the University of Tennessee at Knoxville. This new guide offers explanations of major issues and themes in world history, sample syllabi and instructions on how to create a manageable syllabus, ideas for cross-cultural and cross-temporal connections, a pronunciation guide, and tips on getting through all the material.

Test Bank and Test Generator by Susan Hellert of the University of Wisconsin at Platteville. This easy-to-customize test bank presents a wealth of multiple-choice, true-false, short-answer, and essay questions.

Discovering World History Through Maps and Views Overhead Transparency Acetates by Gerald Danzer of the University of Illinois at Chicago. This unique resource contains more than 100 full-color acetates of beautiful reference maps, source maps, urban plans, views, photos, art, and building diagrams.

Longman World History Atlas Overhead Transparency Acetates These acetates are available to instructors who select the *Longman World History Atlas* for their students.

Overhead Transparency Acetates to Accompany *Civilization Past & Present* These text-specific acetates are available to all adopters.

IRC World History Videodisk Instructional Resources Corporation's library of 2400 still images, 71 historical maps, and 12 narrative section overviews is especially flexible for classroom lectures and presentations.

Historical Newsreel Video This 90-minute video contains newsreel excerpts examining U.S. involvement in world affairs over the past 60 years.

Longman-Penguin Putnam Inc. Value Bundles Students and professors alike will love the value and quality of the Penguin books offered at a deep discount when bundled with *Civilization Past & Present,* Ninth Edition.

Supplements for Students

Interactive Edition CD-ROM This new CD-ROM is an electronic version of the text that contains the entire text, maps, and charts, as well as photos, glossary, and electronic student study guide. Its easy-to-use navigation makes it simple to search by topic or name, take notes on-line, and link to the Internet.

Brummett Online, http://www.awlonline.com/brummett, by Richard Rothaus of St. Cloud State University. This course companion provides text-specific resources for students and instructors and includes our on-line syllabus manager. Students will find it easy to learn and study with the chapter outlines, self-testing programs, Web activities, primary sources, Internet links, and glossary. Instructors will love it for the teaching ideas and aids, on-line images, Web links, and syllabus manager.

Student Study Guide in two volumes: Volume 1 (Chapters 1–18) and Volume 2 (Chapters 14–36) prepared by Sterling Kernek and David G. Egler of Western Illinois University, and Melvin Lyttaker III of Southeastern Community College. Each chapter includes chapter overviews, lists of themes and concepts, map exercises, multiple-choice practice tests, and critical thinking and essay questions.

StudyWizard Computerized Tutorial prepared by Paul George of Miami-Dade Community College. This interactive program features chapter outlines and multiple-choice, true-false, and short-answer questions. It also contains a glossary and gives users immediate test scores and answer explanations.

Everything You Need to Know About *Civilization Past & Present* This is a concise guide to the textbook's organization, pedagogy, themes, and special features.

Everything You Need to Know About Your History Course by Sandra Mathews-Lamb of Nebraska Wesleyan University. This guide helps students succeed in history courses by describing good techniques for taking notes, researching and writing papers, reading primary and secondary sources, reading maps, charts, and graphs, taking exams, learning from lectures, and using the textbook.

Guide to Internet and Advanced Media Resources for World History, Second Edition, by Richard Rothaus of St. Cloud State University. This guide shows students how to make the most of the Internet in their world history course and includes a comprehensive listing of Web resources for all areas of world history.

Documents in World History, Second Edition, edited by Peter N. Stearns et al. This two-volume collection of primary sources makes history come to life with first-hand accounts from all areas of the world.

World History Map Workbooks, Second Edition, by Glee Wilson of Kent State University. This two-volume workbook includes over 80 maps accompanied by a contextual overview and exercises in making, reading, and understanding maps. The exercises teach the locations of and relationships among various countries.

Longman World History Atlas This full-color, easy-to-read atlas contains 56 maps designed especially for the world history course. It is free when bundled with the text.

Longman World History Series These books focus on the world historical significance of a particular movement, experience, or interaction. Concise and inexpensive, they bring the global connections and consequences of these events to the fore, showing students how events that happened long ago or far away can still affect them.

Environmentalism: A Global History by Ramachandra Guha. Discusses the global and interconnected nature of the environmental movement from the Romantics to today with clear language and organization.

Colonial Encounters in the Age of High Imperialism by Scott B. Cook of the Rhode Island School of Design. Examines the world-transforming experience of Western imperialism from 1870 to 1914, focusing specifically on Belgium and the Congo, the United States and Hawaii, and Britain and India.

Timelink: World History Computerized Atlas by William Hamblin of Brigham Young University. A highly graphic, Hypercard-based computerized atlas and historical geography tutorial for Macintosh computers.

Acknowledgments

We are most grateful to the following reviewers who gave generously of their time and knowledge to provide thoughtful evaluations and many helpful suggestions for the revision of this edition.

Wayne Ackerson
Salisbury State University

Joseph Appiah
J. Sargeant Reynolds Community College

Mark C. Bartusis
Northern State University

Mauricio Borrero
St. John's University

Demoral Davis
Jackson State University

Paul George
Miami-Community College, Dade

David Gleason
Armstrong Atlantic State University

Christopher Guthrie
Tarleton State University

Janine Hartman
University of Cincinnati

Thomas Hegarty
University of Tampa

David Hill
McHenry County College

Thomas Howell
Louisiana College

Clark Hultquist
University of Montevallo

Daniel R. Kazmer
Georgetown University

Teresa Lafer
Pennsylvania State University

Robert McCormick
Newman University

David A. Meier
Dickinson State University

David Owusu-Ansah
James Madison University

George Pesely
Austin-Peay State

Charles Risher
Montreat College

Bill Schell
Murray State University

Paul J. Smith
Haverford College

Edward Tabri
Columbus State Community College

Joseph A. Tomberlin
Valdosta State University

Chris Warren
Copiah-Lincoln Community College

Mary Watrous
Washington State University

David L. White
Appalachian State University

We also thank the many conscientious reviewers who reviewed previous editions of this book.

Jay Pascal Anglin
University of Southern Mississippi

Joel Berlatsky
Wilkes College

Jackie R. Booker
Kent State University

Darwin F. Bostwick
Old Dominion University

Robert F. Brinson, Jr.
Santa Fe Community College

Robert H. Buchanan
Adams State College

Michael L. Carrafiello
East Carolina University

James O. Catron, Jr.
North Florida Junior College

William H. Cobb
East Carolina University

J. L. Collins
Allan Hancock College

J. R. Crawford
Montreat-Anderson College

Edward R. Crowther
Adams State College

Lawrence J. Daly
Bowling Green State University

William Edward Ezzell
DeKalb College–Central Campus

John D. Fair
Auburn University at Montgomery

Robert B. Florian
Salem-Teikyo University

Nels W. Forde
University of Nebraska

Joseph T. Fuhrmann
Murray State University

Robert J. Gentry
University of Southwestern Louisiana

Jeffrey S. Hamilton
Old Dominion University

Donald E. Harpster
College of St. Joseph

Gordon K. Harrington
Weber State University

J. Drew Harrington
Western Kentucky University

Geoff Haywood
Beaver College

Conrad C. Holcomb, Jr.
Surry Community College

Roger L. Jungmeyer
Lincoln University of Missouri

Bernard Kiernan
Concord College

Michael L. Krenn
University of Miami

Harral E. Landry
Texas Women's University

Marsha K. Marks
Alabama A&M University

Caroline T. Marshall
James Madison University

Eleanor McCluskey
Broward Community College

Arlin Migliazzo
Whitworth College

William C. Moose
Mitchell Community College

Wayne Morris
Lees-McRae College

John G. Muncie
East Stroudsburg University

Sr. Jeannette Plante, CSC
Notre Dame College

Norman Pollock
Old Dominion University

J. Graham Provan
Millikin University

George B. Pruden, Jr.
Armstrong State College

John D. Ramsbottom
Northeast Missouri State University

Ruth Richard
College of Lake County

Hugh I. Rodgers
Columbus College

Patrick J. Rollins
Old Dominion University

Chad Ronnander
University of Minnesota

Barry T. Ryan
Westmont College

Louis E. Schmier
Valdosta State College

William M. Simpson
Louisiana College

Barbara G. Sniffen
University of Wisconsin-Oshkosh

Lawrence Squeri
East Stroudsburg University

Terrence S. Sullivan
University of Nebraska at Omaha

Gordon L. Teffeteller
Valdosta State College

Malcolm R. Thorp
Brigham Young University

Helen M. Tierney
University of Wisconsin-Platteville

Leslie Tischauser
Prairie State College

Arthur L. Tolson
Southern University

Thomas Dwight Veve
Dalton College

John R. Willertz
Saginaw Valley State University

To the Student

We set two goals for ourselves when we wrote *Civilization Past & Present.* The first is to provide you with an understanding of the contributions of past eras in all parts of the globe to the shaping of subsequent events. The second is to illuminate the way in which the study of world history gives us insights into the genesis, nature, and direction of our own civilization.

These are challenging tasks. However, given the globalization of all aspects of our lives, they are essential. When economies in East Asia are in a state of crisis, the impact is felt on Wall Street. The culture of the New World—especially music and movies—has spread around the globe. When tragedies occur in the Balkans, we are all affected. Long gone are the days when an occurrence that took place far away could be isolated.

Now you are taking a course in world history to understand the development of the cultures of the world—cultures that are coming together to form a multifaceted world civilization. Understanding how and why other civilizations have chosen differing routes to their future, you can gain an understanding of why your part of civilization has succeeded or failed in attaining its potential. With an understanding of world history, you will be able to respond more knowledgeably to the changes through which you will live and make informed choices as a world citizen.

History is the study of change over time. A historian is a person who focuses on one aspect of changes in the past, poses questions about why a particular event has taken place, proposes answers—hypotheses—and tests those hypotheses against the evidence—all of the evidence. We do not expect you to be historians at this point in your career—to form your own hypotheses and write monographs. We have written this book, however, to enable you to study change over time in seven major chronological stages:

- Part 1, "The Ancient World," takes you from prehistory to the development of civilizations in Africa, Southwest Asia, South Asia, and East Asia to the third century of this era.
- Part 2, "The Middle Ages," studies the formative stages of the world's peoples at this pivotal time. Here we examine the establishment of the political, religious, social, and cultural frameworks that would characterize Europe, Southwest Asia, Africa, Asia, and the Americas to the fifteenth century.
- Part 3, "The Transition to Modern Times," examines the impact of new intellectual frameworks, new modes of technology, and new economic systems in the world to the middle of the seventeenth century.
- Part 4, "The Rising European Tide," traces the interrelated burst of political, economic, scientific, and ideological energy that propelled the European continent to prominence by the end of the eighteenth century.
- Part 5, "The Century of Western Dominance," concentrates on the West's ascendency during the nineteenth century. The wave of technological, scientific, business, and intellectual exploration swept over, but did not overwhelm, the non-Western world.
- Part 6, "The New Thirty Years' War," discusses the end of the liberal dream during the three decades that witnessed the bloody catastrophes of the two world wars, the advent of authoritarian states, and the horrors of the Holocaust and nuclear weapons.
- Part 7, "From Bipolar Ideology to Global Competition," discusses the globalization of the world since 1945, first as part of the bipolar conflict known as the Cold War and then with the economic unification of the world and its vast disparity between the very rich and the extremely poor.

The authors have included a number of tools to help you on your voyage through this text. At the beginning of each part, a brief **essay** summarizes the major events and accomplishments occurring in its time frame and relates the chapters, and their world regions, to each other. These essays will give you a helpful overall perspective of the chapters included in each part.

As you begin the chapter, take five or ten minutes to look at the **chapter opening pages.** These two pages at the beginning of each chapter telegraph what is to come: a photo conceptualizes the main themes of the chapter, and a chapter outline and a time line allow you to fix beginning and end points in this part of your trip. Take time to read the introduction and then thumb to the end of the chapter to read the conclusion. Next, go through the chapter reading only the main and secondary headlines. Finally, return to the beginning of the chapter and start to read—knowing in advance where you have come from and which way you are going.

Within each chapter we offer you other tools to gain an understanding of the past. Events take place in a location, and each location has particular features that affect what will happen. Thus the text includes more than 120 four-color **maps,** each with its own explanatory caption. Some maps are designed to make clear the nature of a single distinctive event; others illustrate larger trends.

Different civilizations have different visions of themselves and their place in the world. The **Discovery Through Maps** boxes will give you a notion of the way that various cultures in the world have seen themselves and their relation to the rest of the globe. For example, in "A Korean-Centered View of the World," dating from around 1600, Japan shrivels away to a distant, tiny archipelago; and the labeling of non-Western areas of "An American View of the World in the 1820s" makes American intolerance toward the non-Western world immediately clear.

We also include two or more excerpts from **primary source documents** in each chapter. These excerpts from original sources offer you a window into the way that the people of the time expressed themselves. The documents cover a variety of viewpoints: political, economic, legal, religious, social, artistic, and popular. As examples, an ancient Roman text gives advice on how to "Avoid Enticements into the Snares of Love"; in "Louis XIV to His Son," the Sun King of France instructs his son, a young man who never does become king; and in "That Was No Brother," two documents— one by an African chief and the other by the English explorer Henry Morton Stanley—give two very different perceptions of the same battle.

Short **chronology tables** within the chapter narrative will give you a quick view of the important events in a specific period.

The text's 500 **photos,** most in full color, give balanced pictorial coverage of all parts of the world. They enhance the reading of each chapter by giving additional context and bringing the matters under discussion to life. For this edition, we have paid special attention in these photos to the lifestyles and contributions of women.

After you have finished each chapter you will find two features to help you prepare a paper or project, or simply to learn more about a particular topic. The annotated bibliographies of **suggestions for reading** indicate useful general studies, monographs, and source materials. Also provided is a list of **suggested Web sites** to allow you to hook up to databases, sounds, images, or discussion groups dealing with the topics under consideration.

Finally, you will encounter numerous terms and names in your reading. The **pronunciation key** in the index will help you pronounce these often perplexing words. Say the words aloud so that you will become familiar with how the words sound as well as how they look.

Prologue

Perspective on Humanity

If the time span of our planet—now estimated at some 5 billion years—were telescoped into a single year, the first eight months would be devoid of any life. The next two months would be taken up with plant and very primitive animal forms, and not until well into December would any mammals appear. In this "year," members of *Homo erectus,* our ancient predecessors, would mount the global stage only between 10 and 11 P.M. on December 31. And how has the human species spent that brief allotment? Most of it—the equivalent of more than half a million years— has been given over to making tools out of stone. The revolutionary changeover from food-hunting nomads to farmers who raised grain and domesticated animals would occur in the last 60 seconds. And into that final minute would be crowded all of humanity's other accomplishments so far: the use of metal; the creation of civilizations; the mastery of the oceans; and the harnessing of steam, then gas, electricity, oil, and, finally, nuclear energy. Brief though it has been, humanity's time on the globe reveals a rich tapestry of science, industry, religion, and art. This accumulated experience of the human species is our *history.*

Past and Present

As we read and learn about early societies and their members, we discover them to be very different from us and the world in which we live. Yet we are linked by more than curiosity to our ancient predecessors. Why? Because we are of the same species, and we share a fundamental commonality that connects present with past: the human-environment nexus. It is the dynamic interplay of environmental factors and human activities that accounts for the process known as history. The biological continuity of our species, coupled with humanity's unflagging inventiveness, has enabled each generation to build on the experiences and contributions of its forebears so that continuity and change in human affairs proceed together.

The Universal Culture Pattern

In the interplay of humans with their environment and fellow beings, certain fundamental needs are always present. Six needs, common to people at all times and in all places, form the basis of a "universal culture pattern":

1. *The need to survive.* Men and women must have food, shelter, clothing, and the means to provide for their offsprings' survival.
2. *The need for social organization.* For people to make a living, raise families, and maintain order, a social structure is essential. Views about the relative importance of the group and the individual within it may vary with any such social structure.
3. *The need for stability and protection.* From earliest times, communities have had to keep peace among their members, defend themselves against external attack, and protect community assets.
4. *The need for knowledge and learning.* Since earliest times, humankind has transmitted knowledge acquired through experience, first orally, then by means of writing systems, and now by electronic means as well. As societies grow more complex, there is increasing need to preserve knowledge and transmit it through education to as many people as possible.
5. *The need for self-expression.* People responded creatively to their environment even before the days when they decorated the walls of Paleolithic caves with paintings of the animals they hunted. The arts appear to have a lineage as old as human experience.
6. *The need for religious expression.* Equally old is humanity's attempt to answer the "why" of its existence. What early peoples considered supernatural in their environment could often, at a later time, be explained by science in terms of natural phenomena. Yet today, no less than in archaic times, men and women continue to search for answers to the ultimate questions of existence.

Culture Change and Culture Lag

When people in a group behave similarly and share the same institutions and ways of life, they can be said to have a common *culture.* Throughout this text we will be looking at a number of different cultures, some of which are designated as *civilizations.* (If all societies have culture, then civilization is a particular *kind* of culture.) "A culture is the way of life of a human group; it includes all the learned and standardized forms of behavior which one uses and others in one's group expect and recognize. . . . Civilization is that kind of culture which includes the use of writing, the presence of cities and of wide political organization, and the development of occupational specialization."[1]

Cultures are never wholly static or wholly isolated. A particular culture may have an individuality that sets it off sharply from other cultures, but invariably it has been influenced by external contacts. Such contacts may be either peaceful or warlike, and they meet with varying degrees of acceptance. Through these contacts occurs the process of culture *diffusion*. Geography, too, has profoundly influenced the development of cultures, although we should not exaggerate its importance. Environmental influences tend to become less marked as people gain technological skill and mastery over the land. The domestication of animals and cereals, for example, took place in both the Old and New Worlds, but the animals and grains were different because of dissimilar ecological factors. Invention is another important source of culture change, although it is not clear to what extent external physical contact is required in the process of invention. However, men and women in different times and places have reached similar solutions to the challenges posed by their respective environments—resulting in the phenomenon known as *parallel invention*.

Some parts of a culture pattern change more rapidly than others, so that one institution sometimes becomes outmoded in relation to others in a single society. When different parts of a society fail to mesh harmoniously, the condition is often called *culture lag*. Numerous examples of this lag could be cited: the exploitation of child laborers during the nineteenth century, the failure to allow women to vote until the twentieth century, and the tragedy of hunger in the midst of plenty.

Past and Present as Prologue

What can the past and present—as history—suggest to us for tomorrow's world? Changes in the physical and social environments will probably accelerate as a result of continued technological innovation. These changes can result in increased disequilibrium and tensions among the various segments comprising the universal culture pattern—in other words, in increased culture lag.

Has the past anything to tell the future about the consequences of cultural disequilibrium—anything that we might profitably use in present-day planning for the decades ahead? Because our planet and its resources are finite, at some point a society must expect to shift progressively from exponential growth toward an overall global equilibrium. By that term, we mean the setting of maximal levels on the number of humans who can inhabit this planet with an assured minimal standard of life and on the exploitation of the earth's resources required to provide that standard. Otherwise, environmental disaster on an unprecedented scale could result in the decades ahead. Past and present conjoin to alert us to the need to engage in new forms of planning for the years ahead and also to the need to rethink our existing social goals and value systems. We need as long and as accurate a perspective as possible to make realistic analyses and to take the appropriate actions to improve our quality of life.

The "How" of History

History is the record of the past actions of humankind, based on surviving evidence. History shows that all patterns and problems in human affairs are the products of a complex process of growth. By shedding light on that process, history provides a means for us to benefit from human experience.

History as a Science

There is more than one way to treat the past. In dealing with the American or Russian Revolution or the Meiji Restoration, for example, the historian may describe events in narrative form or, instead, analyze general causes and compare stages with the patterns of similar events in other countries. Unlike the scientist, who attempts to verify hypotheses by repeating experiments under controlled conditions in the laboratory and to classify phenomena in a general group or category, the historian has to pay special attention to the *uniqueness* of data, because each event takes place at a particular time and in a particular place. And since that time is now past, the historian cannot verify conclusions by duplicating the circumstances in which the event occurred.

Nevertheless, historians insist that history be written as "scientifically" as possible and that evidence be analyzed with the same objective attitude employed by scientists examining natural phenomena. This scientific spirit requires historians to handle evidence according to established rules of historical analysis, to recognize biases and attempt to eliminate their effects, and to draw only such conclusions as the evidence seems to warrant.

The Historical Method

To meet these requirements, historians have evolved the "historical method." The first step is the search for *sources*, which may be material remains, oral traditions, pictorial data, or written records. From the source the historian must infer the facts. This process has two parts. *External criticism* tests the genuineness of the source. *Internal criticism* evaluates the source to ascertain the author's meaning and the accuracy of the work.

The final step in the historical method is *synthesis*. Here the historian must determine which factors in a given situation are most relevant to the purpose at hand, since obviously one cannot include everything that occurred. This delicate process of selection underscores the role that subjectivity plays in the writing of history. Furthermore, the more complex the events involved, the more crucial the historian's judgment becomes.[2]

Periodization

Can we really categorize history as "ancient," "medieval," or "modern"? Clearly, what is "modern" in the twentieth century will conceivably be considered "medieval" in the twenty-fifth century and eventually "ancient" in the thirty-fifth century. Yet not to break up the account would be akin to reading this book without the benefit of parts, chapters, paragraphs, or even separate sentences. Like time itself, history would then become a ceaseless flow of consciousness and events. To simplify the task and to manage materials more easily, the historian divides time into periods. The divisions chosen and the lines drawn reveal the distinctive way in which the historian regards the past.

The "Why" of History

The historian seeks to describe not only *what* has happened and *how* it happened but also *why* society undergoes change. Any search of this kind raises a number of fundamental questions: the impact of long-term geographical, economic, and social forces; the role of the individual; the power of the group in the extent to which events are unique or, conversely, can fit into patterns; and the problem of progress in human affairs. The answers vary with different philosophical views of the universe and the human role therein.

People who hold the teleological view see in history the guidance of a Divine Will, directing human destinies according to a cosmic purpose. Other thinkers have exalted the role of the individual in the historical process, contending that major figures chiefly determined the course of human events. Opponents of this thesis argue that history is determined by "forces" and "laws" and by the actions of entire societies. Sociologists approach history primarily by analyzing the origins, institutions, and functions of groups. Economists tend to look at the historical record from the standpoint of group action and especially the impact of economic forces.

To Karl Marx irresistible economic forces governed human beings and determined the trend of events. Marx contended that the shift from one economic stage to another—such as the shift from feudalism to capitalism—is attained by upheavals, or revolutions, which occur because the class controlling the methods of production eventually resists further progress in order to maintain its vested interests.

Numerous other attempts have been made to explain societal processes according to a set of principles. Writing at the time of World War I, the German Oswald Spengler maintained that civilizations were like organisms; each grew with the "superb aimlessness" of a flower and passed through a cycle of spring, summer, autumn, and winter. Charles Darwin's evolutionary hypothesis made a strong impact on nineteenth-century thought and gave rise to the concept that the principle of "survival of the fittest" must also apply to human societies. This line of thought—known as social Darwinism—raises social and ethical questions of major importance.

Does history obey impersonal laws and forces so that its course is inevitable? Or, at the other extreme, since every event is a unique act, is history simply the record of unforeseen and unrelated episodes? Can this apparent dilemma be avoided? We believe it can. Although all events are, in various respects, unique, they also contain elements that invite comparison. The comparative approach permits us to seek relationships between historical phenomena and to group them into movements or patterns or civilizations. We eschew any "theory" of history, preferring to see merit in a number of basic concepts. These include the effects of physical environment on social organization and institutions; the roles played by economic, political, and religious factors; and the individual impact exerted by men and women occupying key positions in various societies.

The Challenge of History

Progress and growth are continuous factors. They depend on, and contribute to, the maintenance of peace and security, the peaceful settlement of international disputes, and worldwide improvement in economic and social standards. Surely an indispensable step toward solving contemporary humanity's dilemma—technology without the requisite control and power without commensurate wisdom—must be a better understanding of how the world and its people came to be what they are today. Only by understanding the past can we assess both the perils and the opportunities of the present—and move courageously and compassionately into the future.

Notes

1. David G. Mandelbaum, "Concepts of Civilization and Culture," *Encyclopaedia Britannica,* 1967 ed., Vol. 5, p. 831A.

2. See P. Gardiner, *The Nature of Historical Explanation* (London: Oxford University Press, 1952), p. 98.

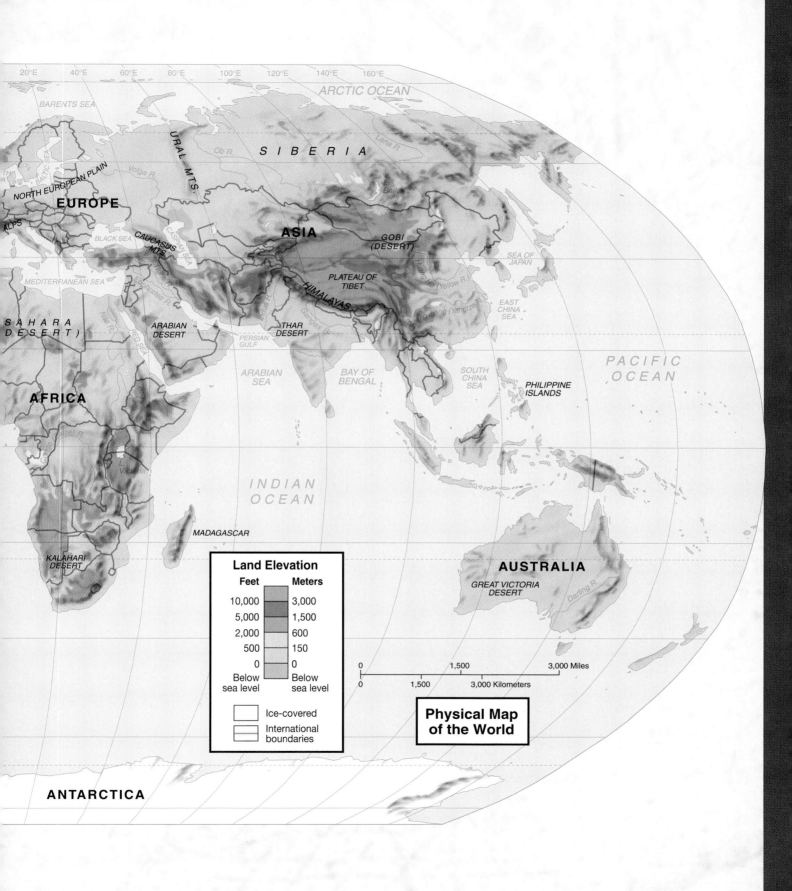

ARCTIC OCEAN

BARENTS SEA

SIBERIA

Ob R.

Lena R.

URAL MTS.

NORTH EUROPEAN PLAIN

Volga R.

EUROPE

BALTIC SEA

ASIA

GOBI
(DESERT)

SEA OF
JAPAN

ALPS

BLACK SEA

CAUCASUS
MTS.

CASPIAN SEA

Huang He (Yellow R.)

MEDITERRANEAN SEA

Euphrates R.

PLATEAU OF
TIBET

HIMALAYAS

Chang Jiang (Yangtze R.)

EAST
CHINA
SEA

SAHARA
DESERT)

Nile R.

RED SEA

ARABIAN
DESERT

Indus R.

Ganges

THAR
DESERT

Tigris R.

PERSIAN
GULF

ARABIAN
SEA

BAY OF
BENGAL

SOUTH
CHINA
SEA

PACIFIC
OCEAN

AFRICA

PHILIPPINE
ISLANDS

INDIAN
OCEAN

Victoria

MADAGASCAR

AUSTRALIA

KALAHARI
DESERT

GREAT VICTORIA
DESERT

Darling R.

Land Elevation

Feet		Meters
10,000		3,000
5,000		1,500
2,000		600
500		150
0		0
Below sea level		Below sea level

☐ Ice-covered

▨ International boundaries

0   1,500   3,000 Miles

0   1,500   3,000 Kilometers

Physical Map
of the World

ANTARCTICA

Civilization

PAST & PRESENT

The Ancient World

The origin and age of the universe may never be known precisely, but modern scientists believe that our world has been circling the sun for 5 billion years. During that incredibly long time, the earth changed from a gaseous to a liquid and finally to a solid state, waters formed on the earth's shell, and in their depths life took form. Remains of early humanlike creatures unearthed in Africa may be 3 to 4 million years old. The time span from those remote days to about 3500 B.C.E. is usually referred to as *prehistoric* or *preliterate* times. By far the greatest part of that time span was taken up by the human struggle for survival—a struggle in which human beings learned to shape crude tools from stone, make fire, and domesticate plants and animals.

The stage was now set for a progressively rapid extension of human control over the environment. We find the first civilizations widely scattered along the banks of rivers. Mesopotamia straddled the Tigris and the Euphrates; Egypt and Nubia stretched along the Nile; China expanded eastward from the region of the Wei and the Huang Ho; India arose along the Indus and the Ganges. Prolific in their gifts to the human race and so dynamic that two of them—China and India—have retained unbroken continuity to our own day, these civilizations possessed similarities at least as arresting as their differences. In all four, political systems developed, crafts flourished and commerce expanded, calendars and systems of writing were invented, art and literature of extraordinary beauty were created, and religions and philosophies came into being to satisfy people's inner yearnings.

Indebted to the Egyptians and Mesopotamians, Minoan and Mycenaean Greece fashioned a wealthy, sophisticated, commercial culture. Much of this Aegean civilization—the first advanced culture to appear in Europe—was destroyed by the end of the second millennium B.C.E., but enough remained to serve as the foundation for Greek civilization. Insatiably curious about their world, the Greeks enjoyed a freedom of thought and expression unknown in earlier societies. Their fierce passion to remain independent, however, was too often unrestrained. The failure of the Greek city-states to find a workable basis for cooperation doomed them to political disaster. Although the conquest of the city-states by King Philip of Macedonia ended the Hellenic Age, the influence of the Greeks was destined to increase. The establishment of a vast empire in the Near East by Philip's son, Alexander the Great, ushered in the Hellenistic Age and the widespread diffusion of Greek culture.

Meanwhile, a new power—Rome—had been developing on the Italian peninsula. After five centuries of modest growth, this city-state embarked on a career of unprecedented expansion. The splendor of Roman arms was matched by skill in administration, wisdom in law, and ingenuity in the practical arts of engineering and communication. These talents and abilities enabled the Romans to erect a Mediterranean empire, which survived until the fifth century C.E. Probably the greatest achievement of the Roman Empire was the skillful governing of a diversity of cultures within a political unity. To the Romans we owe a debt for preserving and disseminating classical culture, for the legacy of Greco-Roman culture is the foundation of Western civilization.

Despite often cataclysmic disasters during its formative period, China pursued ambitious innovations in all aspects of its society, from philosophy to economics. Throughout China the state established a theoretical focus toward the amelioration of social evils and the relief of distress. This was the ever-changing product of two of the main ingredients in the Chinese tradition—Confucianism, with its concern for a humane society, and Legalism, with its stress on the power of the state, always modified by the underlying, unified civilization. And by means of this civilization China was able to erect a fundamental frame of identity in which all other activities took place.

During India's formative age, three major religions were evolving on the subcontinent. Hinduism became the dominant social and religious force in India, with its notions of *dharma* allocated by caste. Jainism fostered the notion of *ahimsa* (nonviolence), which would play a powerful role in the twentieth-century Indian independence movement. Buddhism challenged the Brahmin order and spread beyond the frontiers of India, ultimately to become a world religion. India today is the heir of one of the longest-living civilizations in the world, one that has produced a set of religious, philosophical, and literary traditions that endures up to the present day.

Now let us survey the glorious classical age of civilization.

Prehistoric art in Los Toldos Cave, Argentina, includes representations of deer and hands. Archaeologists have dated the art to around 15,000 B.C.E.

Prelithic to Neolithic Societies

In the Beginning . . .

Today we speak about the advent of a new millennium and its significance. But what happened in the preceding thousands of years to shape our existence and direct our present and future actions? Without some knowledge of the opening chapter of the human story—just when and where our ancestors came to exist—we have no sense of how human history began.

This introductory chapter provides an overview of the longest period in which our ancestors existed on the planet, a time when they developed the basic tools and forms of social structure and behavior on which all succeeding cultures would build. Indeed, our Stone Age ancestors created the plot and tenuous story line that we continue both to follow and to expand, with novel twists and creative additions.

The Development of Humankind

Did God create humanity "in his own image," or was our species itself the product of physical change and adaptation neither more nor less than the rocks, plants, and animals of this planet? The controversy surrounding the theory of human evolution continues into the third millennium of the Common Era, although with decreasing intensity as more fossil evidence comes to light. Of course, the fossil record can probably never be complete, and paleontologists have only skeletal

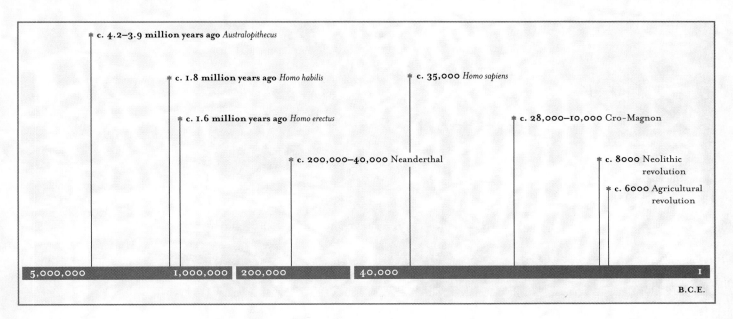

- c. 4.2–3.9 million years ago *Australopithecus*
- c. 1.8 million years ago *Homo habilis*
- c. 1.6 million years ago *Homo erectus*
- c. 200,000–40,000 Neanderthal
- c. 35,000 *Homo sapiens*
- c. 28,000–10,000 Cro-Magnon
- c. 8000 Neolithic revolution
- c. 6000 Agricultural revolution

5,000,000 1,000,000 200,000 40,000 I

B.C.E.

remains (usually partial ones) to analyze. Nevertheless, the evidence for evolution appears overwhelming, but the theory does not preclude the presence of a guiding intelligence ultimately responsible for the progressive development of organic life from simple to more complex forms, culminating in the intelligence and creativity of our own species.

According to the theory of evolution, humans belong to the Primate order, which also includes the lemurs, tarsiers, monkeys, and apes. The primates possess a similar skeletal structure, their hands and feet can grasp and retain objects, and compared with other creatures, they have a relatively large brain, excellent stereoscopic vision, and a mediocre sense of smell. The earliest primates, living perhaps 60 million years ago, were small mouselike creatures resembling the modern tree shrew that inhabited trees and hunted insects at night. Their way of life encouraged the development of mobile thumbs, flexible forelimbs, keen eyesight, and eye-hand coordination. Many species of these first primates became extinct, but tarsierlike and lemurlike types survived and became the ancestors of higher forms of primates.

As we can see from the geological table below, important developments occurred among the primates during the Tertiary period. In the Oligocene epoch, different lines of monkeys evolved, as well as primitive forms of anthropoid apes; in the next epoch, the Miocene, the ape family grew in size and variety and spread over much of Africa, Asia, and Europe. Before the end of this epoch (that is, no later than 28 million years ago), a development of the first magnitude occurred when the ape family became differentiated. One line evolved into the tree-dwelling apes, while the second led to ground-dwelling types known as hominids, or what we may arbitrarily call *prehumans* or *protohumans*. In time these prehumans learned to walk upright, their legs grew longer than their arms, and their hands—no longer required for locomotion—became more dexterous. Most important, the prehuman head gradually shifted toward a more upright position, rendering superfluous much of the muscle at the back of the neck. This development favored the progressive expansion of the brain, which in turn ultimately led to modern "thinking man" *(Homo sapiens)*, the only survivor of the many-branched hominid tree.

Development of the Genus *Homo*

No conclusive fossil evidence bearing on prehuman evolution during the Pliocene epoch, which followed the Miocene, has yet been found. However, the Pleistocene epoch provides us with increasing data on the dynamic development of our genus, *Homo*. Remains of the Australopithecines ("southern apes") who lived

Geological Time Chart and Development of Primates

Epoch	Millions of Years Ago	First Primates to Appear
Quaternary Period		
Holocene	Present	
Pleistocene	0.01–3[*]	
Glacial phase: 4		*Homo sapiens,* Neanderthal Man
3		*Homo erectus; Homo ergaster*
2		
1		*Homo habilis; Australopithecus* ("Lucy")
Tertiary Period		
Pliocene	3–12	
Miocene	12–28	Apelike forms
Oligocene	28–40	Monkeys
Eocene	40–60	Earliest primates: tarsierlike and lemurlike types

[*]The Pleistocene epoch probably lasted 2 to 3 million years and ended about 10,000 years ago.

in Africa were discovered in 1924. No more than 4 feet in height, *Australopithecus* had an erect posture but an apelike brain, with a cranial volume measuring no more than 500 cubic centimeters.

Over the past 40 years, our knowledge of hominids and their relation to the genus *Homo* has been growing rapidly. In December 1998 the world learned of the discovery in South Africa of a skeleton that could rewrite human history. Some 20 miles northwest of Johannesburg, in a limestone cave, paleontologists discovered a fossilized hominid 4 feet tall and some 3.5 million years old. Described as "probably the most momentous paleoanthropological find ever made in Africa," its virtually complete remains provide uniquely detailed information on the transition from ape to human. This Australopithecine hominid had heels adapted for standing upright, walked on two legs, and used distended big toes to climb trees. Once the entire fossil has been fully examined, the ratio of brain size to the rest of its body will help determine if the specimen is a direct ancestor of humans.[1]

The first representative of the genus *Homo*, which was to succeed the Australopithecines, had been discovered in 1960 by Louis S. B. Leakey at Olduvai Gorge in Tanzania at a site some 1.75 million years old. His find was less than 5 feet tall, weighed less than 100 pounds, walked erect, had a well-developed thumb, and had a cranial capacity of 656 cubic centimeters (considerably more than *Australopithecus*). Significantly, these fossil remains were found in association with crude tools—rocks cracked and flaked into shapes used to cut meat killed by lions and leopards. Leakey named his find *Homo habilis* ("skillful man").

The succeeding millennia were notable for changes in body structure and for complexifying the number of species in the human fossil record. In 1984 paleontologists discovered in northern Kenya a species recognizably like our own, as illustrated by a remarkably complete 1.6 million–year–old skeleton known as the Turkana Boy. These humans possessed an essentially modern body structure and gait and long and slender limbs, had brains double the size of those of apes (though not much above half the modern human average), and were capable of growing to 6 feet tall. The Boy and his relatives were initially assigned to a new and more advanced species, *Homo erectus*, but distinctive differences in braincase construction have given them a separate status, *Homo ergaster*.

Evidence of *Homo erectus* was discovered in 1891 in Java (Java Man) and in 1927 in China (Peking Man). Since the 1950s, many *Homo erectus* fossils, dating back at least 1.6 million years, have also been uncovered in Africa. *Erectus* was the first species of *Homo* to migrate out of Africa, into the Near East

Hominid footprints at Laetoli, Tanzania, document a child walking northward in the footsteps of a bipedal adult.

and Europe and eventually to the Pacific Ocean—probably, it is conjectured, because they were active hunters of wild game and sought ever-larger ranges. Recent evidence indicates that *Homo erectus* possibly took no more than 100,000 years to reach Java from Africa. Its members had a cranial volume larger than *Homo habilis* but much less than modern humans, whose brain capacity averages between 1300 and 1600 cubic centimeters. They were about 5 feet 6 inches tall and had heavy brows and a receding forehead. They developed the ability to control and use fire, a major step in mastering the environment and extending human habitation into colder latitudes—and this skill set humans apart from the rest of the natural world. They also perfected the first major standardized all-purpose tool, the hand ax, made by striking flakes from a flint stone that had been hardened in fire to make it flake easily. Its cutting edge could be as effective as steel for cutting meat. The hand ax remained a favored tool long after the extinction of *Homo erectus*, which occurred well before the end of the Pleistocene epoch, and the gradual emergence of modern humans, *Homo sapiens*.

From about 200,000 to 40,000 years ago, during the last ice age, the Neanderthals were the principal inhabitants of Europe and adjacent parts of Asia and Africa. Named after the Neander Valley in western Germany where their remains were unearthed, they were the first specimens of fossil humans to be

Aerial view of Olduvai Gorge in Tanzania, the site of findings by Mary and Louis S. B. Leakey, including the first representative fossils of the genus Homo.

found. Somewhat taller than 5 feet, the Neanderthals had sloping foreheads with prominent brow ridges and thickset bodies. They invented a variety of specialized stone tools and adapted to extreme cold by using fire, wearing furs, and living in caves and rock shelters. With their stone-tipped spears, they became able hunters.

Despite a brain size averaging slightly larger than our own, Neanderthals were long considered to be brutish, dimwitted, slouching creatures—the stereotypical "cave man" of modern cartoonists. Were they a subspecies of *Homo sapiens* or a separate species? Recent mitochondrial DNA testing of an arm bone from a Neanderthal skeleton (found in the Neander Valley in 1857) showed very little overlap with the DNA of *Homo sapiens*. The conclusion is that *Homo sapiens* and Neanderthals may have had a common ancestor, but the Neanderthals are definitely not a subspecies of *Homo sapiens*. Yet their similarities are noteworthy. If a Neanderthal "could be reincarnated and placed in a New York subway—provided he was bathed, shaved, and dressed in modern clothing—it is doubtful whether he would attract any more attention than some of its other denizens."[2]

The culminating phase of the development of the genus *Homo* occurred some 40,000 years ago when the Cro-Magnons replaced the Neanderthals in Europe. What happened to the latter can only be conjectured. Named after the locality in southern France where their bones were first unearthed in 1868, Cro-Magnon skeletons are virtually indistinguishable from human skeletons of today. Skillfully made flints and bone tools, along with polychrome paintings found on the walls of caves, reflect an advanced culture. By 20,000 B.C.E. Cro-Magnon and other representatives of *Homo sapiens* inhabited Europe, Asia, Africa, and Australia and had migrated across the Bering Strait into North America. Today there is but one existing species of the genus *Homo*.

Preliterate Cultures and Societies

In many respects we humans are eclipsed in physical endowments by numerous other creatures—in an all-species Olympic Games, we might never qualify for a medal. We cannot compete with the strength of the elephant or the speed of the antelope on land or any number of animals that live in the sea. Our ability to defy gravity is dwarfed by insects that can jump farther and higher in terms of their size, to say nothing of birds whose specialized structures enable them to fly and to soar. Nor can we claim to have the acute sight of a hawk. However, in certain particulars humans are biologically superior to other inhabitants of the earth. What are the essential attributes that enable our species to forge far ahead of all others? Erect posture is certainly one characteristic. Although other primates also possess opposable thumbs, in humans the thumb is longer and more powerful than in apes and monkeys, making it ideal for purposive action, such as making tools, where manual dexterity is mainly of cerebral origin. And although apes and monkeys have eyes capable of stereoscopic and color vision, apparently only humankind has the capacity for close visual attention.

Refined vision and manual dexterity result not solely from our muscular apparatus but in large part from our finely attuned nervous system. This nervous system, in which the brain is the vital hub, has enabled humans to outdo all other animals in both adjusting to our immediate environment and progressively modifying it to our own needs and goals. So significant are the size and multiple capabilities of the human brain as a factor differentiating us from other primates that it has been termed the "organ of civilization."

Human intelligence is also unique because of the quality this intelligence displays. It enables humans to reason and apply imagination and to make tools to a set and regular pattern. At the same time, we should recognize that many animals are also capable of solving problems in adjusting to their environments and display imagination in the process. Furthermore, some nonhuman primates are tool users or even engage in patterned tool manufacture. For example, chimpanzee bands in East Africa have been observed to make more than five types of tools, with the young learning how to fashion them by copying from their mothers.[3] But even though these primates can make tools, they lack a type of intelligence and imagination that functions by means of symbols, which seems to be unique to our species.

Like other creatures, humans possess a practical intelligence by which to make meaningful responses to the environment. In addition, however, we have the capability of both thinking and communicating symbolically. The principle of symbolism operates so as to give everything a name and to make its functioning universally applicable rather than restrict it to local or particular cases. A symbol is not only universal but also versatile, since the same meaning can be expressed in various languages or in different contexts with the same language. By means of this capability to engage in symbolic thought and communication, humankind has created patterns of behavior and learning that can be termed *culture*. Compared with other animals, we live also in a symbolic universe, with its new dimension of reality. "Language, myth, art, and religion are parts of this universe. They are the varied threads which weave the symbolic net, the tangled web of human experience. All human progress in thought and experience refines upon and strengthens this net."[4]

Dawn of Paleolithic Cultures

Benjamin Franklin is credited with first defining human beings as "toolmaking animals." Yet this attribute is based on a tradition that began in the Pleistocene epoch when a distinct evolution occurred in the use and manufacture of tools among hominids. Australopithecine sites in South Africa indicate that while these contemporaries of early *Homo* may not have fashioned tools, they at least made use of objects as improvised tools or weapons. Improvisation would have played an important role also among the first humans—even as today some Native Australians carve wooden implements with naturally fractured stone pieces.

At this early stage we find *eoliths* ("dawn stones"), odd bits of stone picked up to perform an immediate job. This simple utilization of what was at hand has been described as the first of three major steps in the formative history of toolmaking. The second stage consisted of *fashioning*, the haphazard preparation of a tool as need arose. The third step was *standardization*, the making of implements according to certain set traditions.[5] It is with this third stage that we see the importance of symbolic thought in creating patterns of learning and behavior—as illustrated by the Acheulean hand ax, whose design was so uniform that specimens from southern Africa, Kenya, South India, and England's Thames Valley are nearly identical.

Since the fashioning of tools by striking pieces of rock with other stones was the most distinctive feature of humankind's earliest societies, the first stage in its cultural development is known as the Paleolithic, or Old Stone, Age. Strictly speaking, *Paleolithic* is a cultural and not a chronological term. In fact, much of our knowledge of Paleolithic culture comes from groups surviving into modern times—for example, indigenous peoples in the rain forests of Brazil. From an economic standpoint, the Paleolithic is also a food-collecting stage, when humans hunted, fished, and collected wild fruits, nuts, and berries on which to survive.

Let us consider a technological phenomenon associated with the invention and development of computers. Many of the first machines filled an entire room, and their capabilities were unreliable and limited. But scientists progressively miniaturized them while increasing their reliability and specialized capabilities. This is but the latest example of a phenomenon that recurs through the history of technology and began with the invention and subsequent sophistication of tools in Stone Age cultures.

At first, toolmaking was haphazard and associated with pebble tools, made of split pebbles or shattered chunks of stone the size of one's fist or a bit larger. Such occasional toolmaking has been substantiated by finds in early Pleistocene geological beds in Africa, including the Olduvai Gorge. Standardized toolmaking resulted in better-made pebble tools with sharp edges. Found at the Lake Rudolph site in East Africa, some 600 knifelike tools carefully fashioned from smooth volcanic rock date back 2.6 million years. Another early tradition occurred in East and South Asia, where Peking Man made standardized

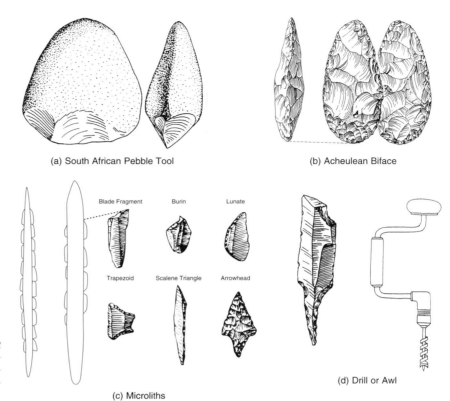

(a) South African Pebble Tool

(b) Acheulean Biface

Blade Fragment Burin Lunate

Trapezoid Scalene Triangle Arrowhead

(c) Microliths

(d) Drill or Awl

As human beings faced an ever-expanding set of challenges to their existence, they invented even more sophisticated tools, as evidenced by these examples of Paleolithic toolmaking.

chopper tools: broad heavy scrapers or cleavers and tools with an adzlike cutting edge.

The next standardized cultural tradition comprises core-biface tools. Here the implements are large pear-shaped pieces, made by flaking a stone slab around its edges from both sides. This produces a pointed core tool trimmed flat on the two opposite sides, or faces. The resulting hand ax (though the term may give an erroneous impression because to us an ax is not a pointed tool) was the first major standardized, all-purpose implement, equipped with two sharp cutting edges and employed probably as a hunter's knife as well as for chopping, cutting, scraping, and digging up grubs and roots. Hand axes, typified by the Acheulean tool industries in Europe, are associated with *Homo erectus*. They were "the predominant tool of a cultural tradition which not only spread over nearly one-fifth of the land area of the globe, but persisted for more than a hundred thousand years."[6]

Middle and Late Paleolithic Cultures

From about 70,000 to 35,000 years ago, the European and western Asian landscape was inhabited by Neanderthals who, as mentioned earlier, learned to adapt themselves to colder climatic conditions by living in caves and rock shelters. Their toolmaking industries involved the rudimentary beginnings of spe-

cialized tools and weapons. For example, the Neanderthals made side-scrapers, small heart-shaped hand axes, and invented stone-tipped spears to hunt their quarry.

About 35,000 B.C.E. the middle Paleolithic in Europe gave way to late Paleolithic cultures. By the end of the glacial phases, around 10,000 years ago, humans had inhabited Europe, western Asia, Africa, and Australia—and subsequently migrated into the Americas. *Homo sapiens*'s technology was marked by a wide range of new specialized tools and weapons. These included blade tools—narrow, parallel-sided flakes. The degree of toolmaking sophistication that had now been reached is marked by the invention of tools whose primary purpose was to make other tools. Noteworthy was the burin, shaped like a chisel, which worked bone, antlers, ivory, and wood into implements for particular purposes. The fashioning of small, specialized flints, known as *microliths*, represent a compact use of materials—indeed, the ancestor of present-day technological miniaturization. In late Paleolithic cultures, too, we find humans "taking to the air" by applying mechanical principles to the movement of weapons and tools. Throwers were made to launch spears; these worked on the lever principle and increased the propelling power of a hunter's arm. Late in this period, the bow was also invented, probably in North Africa. "It was the first means of concentrating muscular energy for the propulsion of an arrow, but it was soon discovered that it also provided a means of twirling a stick, and this led to the invention of the rotary drill."[7]

To withstand the cold weather, late Paleolithic peoples fashioned garments from sewn skins—bone needles with eyes, belt fashioners, and even buttons have been found in their sites—and they erected the first manmade buildings in areas where natural caves did not exist. The reindeer and mammoth hunters of what is present-day Russia lived in tents and huts made of hides and brush or in communal houses partially sunk into the ground with a mammoth's ribs for roof supports. There is also evidence that coal was used for fuel.

A special achievement of late Paleolithic cultures was their aesthetic expression. In 1879 a Spanish nobleman named Sautuola discovered a long procession of magnificently drawn bison on the ceiling of a cave on his Altamira estate in northern Spain. Archaeologists scoffed at Sautuola's discovery: the paintings were "too modern" and "too realistic." In a few years, however, Sautuola was vindicated with the discovery of more than a hundred Cro-Magnon caves in Spain and France, dating from about 28,000 to 10,000 B.C.E. In those caves were found animated paintings of bison, reindeer, primitive horses, and other animals, colored in shades of black, red, yellow, and brown.

Cave art rivals that of civilized artists not only stylistically but also as an expression of significant human experience. Universal in appeal, the drawings reflect a complete dependence on game animals and success in hunting them. By drawing pictures of food animals—sometimes shown pregnant or pierced by spears and arrows—the artists may have believed that they could wield a magical power over the spirits of animals to ensure their multiplication. "A clue to the meaning of cave art can perhaps be obtained from the famous dancing figure found in Les Trois Frères in the Ariège. . . . It is a painting in black of a bearded figure wearing a mask and antlers of a red deer, the skin of a horse or wolf and a long, bushy tail. The suggestion that the dance was part of a magic ritual is inescapable."[8] Paleolithic artists also chiseled pictures on rock and bone and modeled figures out of clay.

Mesolithic, or Transitional, Cultures

Sweeping climatic changes that ended the fourth glacial phase initiated the Holocene, or Recent, epoch. With the final retreat of glaciers about 10,000 years B.C.E, alterations in the sea level greatly changed coastlines, and dense forests replaced areas in Europe marked previously by sparse vegetation, or tundra. Because of their highly specialized adaptation to cold weather, the reindeer moved north, and the hairy mammoth and other animals hunted by late Paleolithic peoples became extinct. The savannas of the Near East and North Africa were transformed into deserts dotted with occasional oases.

Humans adjusted to postglacial conditions by developing new cultures called Mesolithic, or Transitional. In Europe, many of these Mesolithic groups

The Conception of Space in Primeval Art

Primeval art never places objects in an immediate surrounding. Primeval art has no background. This is apparent in such large murals as the ceiling of Altamira as well as the small ritual objects of *art mobilier*. It is inherent in the prehistoric conception of space: all linear directions have equal right, and likewise all surfaces, whether they be regular or irregular. They can be tilted at any angle to the horizon throughout the entire 360-degree range. Animals that to us appear to be standing on their heads do not appear inverted to the eye of primeval man, because they existed, as it were, in space free from forces of gravity. . . .

The complete freedom and independence of vision of primeval art has never since been attained. It was its distinguishing characteristic. In our sense, there was no up and no down, no above and no below. Whether an animal appeared in a vertical position or in any other position was irrelevant to the eye of pre-historic man. Nor was there a clear distinction or separation of one object from another. . . . Violent juxtaposition in size as well as in time were accepted as a matter of course. All was displayed within an eternal present, the perpetual interflow of today, yesterday, and tomorrow. . . .

Whether one looks at the Hall of the Hieroglyphs of Pech-Merle, with its intertwining figurations, or at the Altamira ceiling, with its powerful sequence of animals intimately associated with undecipherable symbols, the space conception of primeval art remains the same. It is not chaos. It approaches rather to the order of the stars, which move about in endless space, unconfined and universal in their relations.

From Sigfried Giedion, *The Eternal Present: The Beginnings of Art*, Bollingen Series 35.6.1 (New York: Pantheon Books, 1962), pp. 532–538.

lived along the coasts, fishing, seal-hunting, and gathering shellfish. Whereas Paleolithic peoples lived a largely nomadic life, Mesolithic groups followed a semisedentary existence, as attested by the large mounds of seashells and other debris, known as *kitchen middens*, found in Denmark and elsewhere along the Baltic seacoast. Other Mesolithic peoples lived inland, where in the plentiful forests they chopped wood with stone axes equipped with handles, made bows and arrows for hunting, and devised such forms of transport as skis, sleds, and dugout canoes. To provide propulsion for these sleds, our Mesolithic forebears domesticated the dog—the first of the many animals brought into a special symbiotic relationship with humans.

Mesolithic peoples were not able to produce their own food supply. However, while some groups retained the traditional food-gathering pattern of existence in Europe, Africa, and Australia, others—in southwestern Asia, for example—augmented their food resources with edible grasses that they found growing seasonally. Here a significant transition began to take place: the shift toward a food-producing economy, associated with the Neolithic Age. Paleolithic and Mesolithic peoples were hunters and fishers; our Neolithic ancestors were also farmers and herdsmen. The overall result comprised what has been described as the "first economic revolution"—and in the view of some scholars, perhaps the most far-reaching breakthrough in the ever-dynamic relationship of our species with its physical environment.

The Neolithic Revolution and the Advent of Agriculture

Neolithic cultures are usually characterized by the cultivation of grains, domestication of animals, pottery making, and use of polished stone tools (hence the name Neolithic, or New Stone, Age applied to these cultures). Actually, all four characteristics are not always present in a given Neolithic culture. Furthermore, certain advances usually associated with the Neolithic had been anticipated by Mesolithic groups (such as the domestication of dogs). Like *Paleolithic, Neolithic* is a technological and economic stage rather than an age or chronological period. For example, whereas Neolithic settlements in the Near East date back some 9000 years, the domestication of animals in Britain did not occur until thousands of years later.

Remains of a community dating to between 8000 and 6000 B.C.E.—older than any previously known settlement—have been unearthed at Jericho. Whereas early farming settlements were mainly small villages of 100 or 200 people, Jericho's location at an oasis enabled it to occupy an area of 74 acres, and it was protected by an enclosing fortification wall as early as 7000 B.C.E.[9] Farming was possible because wild grains grew well there, and the local spring provided a continuous source of water.

Some authorities hold, however, that agriculture originated not at oases but in sites, such as Jarmo and Hassuna, in the mountainous uplands of what is now northern Iraq. Jarmo's 250 people lived in 20 mud-walled houses, reaped their grain with stone sickles, stored their food in stone bowls, and possessed domesticated goats, sheep, and dogs. Later levels of settlement contain evidence of domesticated pigs and clay pottery. The many tools made of obsidian, a volcanic rock from beds 300 miles away, indicate that a primitive form of commerce must have existed.

The wild ancestors of wheat and barley are thought to be highland forms—rainfall was greater there than on the arid lowlands—and wildlife was abundant. Neolithic farmers generally settled near a reliable water supply and combined agriculture with additional sources of food. The domestication of animals provided ready food, clothing, and transport. Tending herds instead of having to hunt them made a more settled existence possible. In southern Asia, in turn, water buffalo and elephants were domesticated, as were the llama and alpaca in the Peruvian highlands.

The best-preserved early village so far uncovered is Çatal Hüyük in southern Turkey, first excavated in 1961. This 32-acre site, occupied shortly before 6000 B.C.E., contains some of the most advanced features of Neolithic culture: pottery, woven textiles, mud-brick houses, shrines honoring a mother goddess, and plastered walls decorated with murals and carved reliefs.

Domestic Skills, Economic and Social Changes

Neolithic artisans ground and polished stones to produce axes, adzes, and chisels with strong and sharp cutting edges. They devised methods for drilling holes in stone, used boulders for grinding grain, and made stone bowls for storage. These stone artifacts show a much greater interest in design than had previously been the case. Moreover, when Neolithic peoples ceased to roam in search of food, they were better able to make pottery in quantity and to decorate it with geometric designs. Clothing and baskets had been fashioned in pre-Neolithic cultures, but the pattern of Neolithic life gave women more time to develop skills in the domestic arts. Similarly, Neolithic men paid more attention to the art of constructing shelters than their semisedentary Mesolithic forebears did. In Europe, where wood was abundant, rectangular timber houses were constructed; some had two rooms, a gabled roof, and walls of split saplings.

Discovery Through Maps

Oldest Known Map: Çatal Hüyük

This wall painting is perhaps the oldest known map. It is also, for modern viewers, one of the most easily understood ancient maps. It is a city plan painted on two walls of a room in a Neolithic community in south-central Anatolia, near what is still the major land route in Turkey between Europe and the Near East. Radiocarbon dating has placed the image around 6200 B.C.E. It is a very large figure, nearly 9 feet wide.

By the 1960s archaeologists had uncovered 139 rooms in the complex and decided that at least 40 were used for special rites, probably of a religious nature. One of these special rooms, whose walls had often been replastered, contained this large image featuring rows of boxlike shapes. Archaeologists were amazed at the similarity between their own carefully drawn site maps and the painting on the wall. It soon became apparent that the Neolithic image was a map of the community or perhaps of the town that immediately preceded the one the dig was uncovering.

A great deal of information can be gleaned from this map:

- The town site was on a slope, with rows of houses or buildings set on graded terraces.
- The rectangular buildings and the streets set at right angles provide a gridiron look that has characterized much town planning throughout history.
- The elongated, or linear, pattern of the settlement may reflect an orientation to a major road.
- The large figure that looks like a mountain with two peaks beyond the town is, no doubt, Hasan Dǎg, a volcano that was active until about 2000 B.C.E. The volcano was the source of the obsidian that was the basis of the settlement's wealth. The glassy, volcanic rock was used for making cutting tools, knives, scrapers, weapons, jewelry, ornaments, and a variety of other artifacts.

The complete map contains about 80 rooms or buildings, somewhat fewer structures than were found in the actual town that was excavated. Since the wall was replastered several times, perhaps the map was "updated." Or it may have served a ceremonial purpose for which the absolute accuracy of a civic map was unnecessary.

Remains found near Swiss lakes show that even on soft, swampy earth the builders could erect houses by placing them on wooden foundations or on piles sunk into the ground.

Neolithic cultures brought profound economic and social changes. Paleolithic and Mesolithic peoples could not develop any permanent settlements or accumulate an excess of food, whereas a food-producing economy was radically different. By cultivating plants and breeding stock, villagers could now add to the food traditionally acquired by hunting. As a consequence, they greatly increased their

control over the external environment. Also, a food-producing way of life that required permanent settlements enabled larger populations to be sustained. Any food surplus could be put aside for planting the following year's crops or was available to trade for commodities not produced locally. In addition, this food surplus helped support specialists who could now engage full time in toolmaking and other crafts.

Inevitably, the culture pattern was becoming more complex and interdependent. Within the community, a division of labor existed between the sexes. While the men made the tools and weapons, tended the herds, hunted, and built the dwellings, the women grew and prepared the food, wove baskets, fashioned clothing and pottery, and reared the young. Social anthropologists have found a strong correlation between communal ownership and female rights and high status, on the one hand, and individual ownership and male dominance, on the other. The first of these connections existed in early Neolithic times, as reflected in a social order in which descent was matrilineal (through the mother's line) and domicile was matrilocal (the husband lived with his wife's family or clan). "Indeed, it is tempting to be convinced that the earliest Neolithic societies throughout their range in time and space gave woman the highest status she has ever known. The way of life and its values, the skills demanded, were ideally suited to her."[10]

Each Neolithic village was largely self-supporting, growing its own food and using local materials for its tools, weapons, and houses. Because the people in Neolithic settlements had only limited contacts with the outside world, each village tended to develop its own localized culture. This condition of isolation permitted two types of settlement at different cultural and technological stages—a Mesolithic and a Neolithic, for example—to coexist for centuries with little interchange and consequently few modifications in their respective patterns of living.

The Neolithic revolution spread from its regional origins to the Balkan Peninsula by 5000 B.C.E., to Egypt and central Europe by 4000 B.C.E., and to Britain and northwestern India by 3000 B.C.E. The Neolithic cultures of western and northeastern Africa, Mesoamerica, and the Andes are later independent developments; cultural transference between the Near East and China is now doubted.

Preliterate Thought and Customs

Perhaps it is natural for most of us, living in a highly complex urban and mechanized society, to assume that preliterate peoples, ancient or modern, would possess few laws, little education, and only the simplest codes of conduct. But this is far from true. The organization of preliterate societies may have been as complex as our own. Rules regarding the role of parents, the treatment of children, the punishment of evildoers, the conduct of business, the worship of divine beings, and the conventions of eating and recreation have existed for scores of millennia, along with methods to influence or coerce individual members of society to do the "correct thing."

We cannot know with certainty about features of early peoples that are not apparent from the remains of tools and other objects. But we can speculate about these preliterate cultures by applying the conclusions that anthropologists have drawn from studies of present-day nonliterate societies. Yet a word of caution is necessary. That the general level of technological development in a modern-day nonliterate society appears to be similar to the stage reached in an ancient one does not mean that all aspects of the two cultures are comparable. Furthermore, it is often dif-

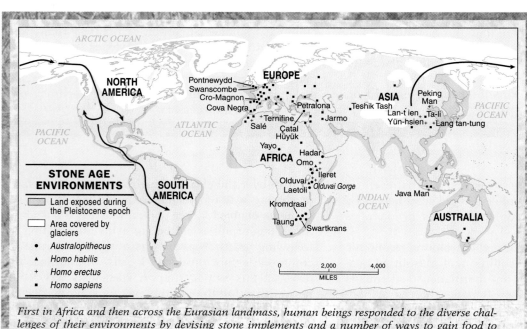

First in Africa and then across the Eurasian landmass, human beings responded to the diverse challenges of their environments by devising stone implements and a number of ways to gain food to assure their survival.

ficult to measure to what degree modern nonliterate societies have been affected by literate ones.

Forms of Social Organization

Among all peoples, past and present, the basic social unit appears to be the *elementary family*—parents and their offspring. Anthropologists cannot be certain what marriage customs were prevalent in the earliest societies, but monogamy was probably most common. The *extended family*—an individual family together with a circle of related persons who usually trace their descent through their mothers and are bound together by mutual loyalty—is often found in primitive social groupings. The extended family strengthens the elementary unit both in obtaining food and in protecting its members against other groups. Land is communally owned but allocated to separate families. Because of its economic and social advantages, this form of organization probably existed in ancient times.

A third preliterate social unit is the *clan*—a group of individuals within a community who believe that they have a common ancestor and therefore are "of one blood, of one soul." A clan is patrilineal if its members trace their relationship through the male line, matrilineal if through the female. Many preliterate peoples identify their clans by a *totem*—an animal or some natural object—that is revered and made the subject for amulets of various sorts. Nearly everyone is acquainted with the totem poles made by the Indians of British Columbia and Alaska. Forms of totemism in modern-day society include the insignia worn by a particular military unit, the emblems of such organizations as the Elks and Moose, and animal mascots used by college football teams.

A fourth grouping among some preliterate peoples is the *tribe*. This term lacks a precise definition, but it may be thought of as a community characterized by a common speech or distinctive dialect, a common cultural heritage, and a specific inhabited territory. Group loyalty is a strong trait among members of a tribe, and it is often accompanied by contempt for the peoples and customs of other communities.

Collective Responsibility in Law and Government

In preliterate societies, ethical behavior consists of not violating custom. The close relationships that exist in extended families and clans encourage conformity. Justice among individuals of a primitive group is synonymous with maintaining equilibrium. If one person steals another's property, the economic equilibrium has been disturbed. Such a theft constitutes a wrong against the victim; but where modern legal procedure calls for punishment of the thief, in these societies justice is achieved by a settlement between the injured person and the thief. If the latter restores what has been stolen or its equivalent, the victim is satisfied and the thief is not punished. More serious offenses, like murder and wounding, are also private matters, to be avenged by the next of kin on the principle of "an eye for an eye." Certain acts, however, are considered dangerous to the whole group and require punishment by the entire community. Treason, witchcraft, and incest are typical offenses in this category. Such acts cannot be settled by compensation; the punishment meted out is usually death. If a clan member gets into trouble too often, others will regard that person as a social nuisance and an economic liability, to be banished from the group or even executed.

Scholars theorize that in food-gathering and the earliest food-producing societies, as in nonliterate societies today, the governing political body was small and egalitarian. The adults participated in the decisions of the group, with special deference being paid to the views of older tribal members because of their greater experience and knowledge of the community's traditions and ceremonies. Serious decisions, such as going to war or electing a chief, required the consent of a general assembly of all adult males. The elected chief of the tribe was pledged to rule in accordance with custom and in consultation with the council of elders. Because of the strong element of representation present, this early form of government has been called "primitive democracy." Among more advanced food-producing communities, however, government tended to fall increasingly under the control of the richest members. In time there emerged strong individuals claiming political and religious leadership; we shall encounter them in the following chapters on early civilizations.

Religion and Magic

Perhaps the strongest single force in the life of preliterate peoples, past and present, is religion. Religious sensibilities apparently originated in feelings of awe that arose as our ancestors became conscious of the universe about them. Awe and wonder led to the belief, usually called *animism*, that life exists in everything in nature—winds, stones, trees, animals, and humans themselves. A natural extension is a belief in the existence of spirits separable from material bodies. Many spirits became objects of reverence, the human spirit being among the first. Neanderthal people placed food and implements alongside their carefully buried dead, an indication that they believed in an afterlife and treated their forebears with affection and respect.

We know also that late Paleolithic people revered the spirits of the animals they hunted for food, as

Stone Age fertility figurines have been throught the world. Shown here are three examples dating from around 25,000 B.C.E.: the limestone Venus of Willendorf, a mammoth ivory carving from Russia, and the ivory Venus of Lespugue.

well as the spirit of fertility on which both human and animal life depended. Such reverence was associated with totemism and in particular with the worship of a fertility deity, the Earth Mother (or Mother Goddess), who is known to us from many carved and modeled female figures with exaggerated sexual features. These fertility figurines have been excavated from Stone Age sites all over the world.

At Çatal Hüyük, 33 representations of the Mother Goddess have been found, but only eight of a god. The latter represented either the son of the goddess or her consort. The relative scarcity of male deities, together with evidence that the cult of the goddess was administered by priestesses rather than by priests, supports the view that women occupied a central position in Neolithic society.

Closely associated with primitive religion is the practice of magic. In addition to revering spirits, primitive people wanted to compel them to provide favors. For this purpose they employed magic. They turned to shamans to ward off droughts, famines, floods, and plagues through what they believed to be magic powers of communication with the spirits.

Neolithic "Science"

Traditionally, magic has been regarded as diametrically opposed to science. The former claims supernatural powers over natural forces, whereas the latter rejects any such determinism and studies natural phenomena by open-ended methods in its search for general laws. Yet as scholars are increasingly recognizing, both preliterate peoples and scientists believe that nature is orderly and that what is immediately apprehended by the senses can be systematically

classified. For example, the Hanunóo of the Philippines have recorded 461 animal types and have classified insect forms into 108 named categories, including 13 for ants and termites. They have more than 150 terms for the parts and properties of plants, which provide categories for "discussing the hundreds of characteristics which differentiate plant types and often indicate significant features of medicinal or nutritional value."[11]

Examples like these can be found in Stone Age societies all over the world. They point to the overall conclusion that the efforts of these "primitive" investigators and classifiers were not directed solely to economic or "useful" ends. Rather, plants and animals were deemed to be of value and interest in their own right, in turn inspiring a desire for knowledge for its own sake. The great contributions of Stone Age men and women—domestication of plants and animals, invention of tools, pottery, and weaving—involved centuries of methodical observation and often-repeated experiments. "This thirst for objective knowledge is one of the most neglected aspects of the thought of people we call 'primitive.' Even if it is rarely directed toward facts of the same level as those with which modern science is concerned, it implies comparable intellectual application and methods of observation. In both cases the universe is an object of thought at least as much as it is a means of satisfying needs."[12]

Further indications of the desire by early people to acquire knowledge have been provided by studies of Neolithic large stone monuments *(megaliths)*. The megalithic complex of Stonehenge in England has traditionally been considered a religious structure. However, an American astronomer, aided by a computer, found an "astonishing" number of correlations between the alignments of recognized Stonehenge positions—stones, holes, mounds—and the solar and lunar positions around 1500 B.C.E., when Stonehenge was built.[13] This knowledge would assist in developing a more accurate calendar, particularly useful when it came to planting crops.

The construction of Neolithic astronomical structures had occurred long before Stonehenge. Ancient sandstone monuments in southern Egypt indicate that their builders possessed a surprisingly complex knowledge of geometry and astronomy. These monuments are between 5000 and 7000 years old and represent the earliest known astronomical complex. A satellite survey of the Nabta Playa depression shows slabs in various configurations, including a circle that would have allowed the inhabitants to anticipate sunrise during the summer solstice. The ceremonial complex has alignments to cardinal and solstitial directions, while five alignments within the playa deposits radiate outward from megalithic structures, which may have served funerary purposes. The area would

Skara Brae in the Orkney Islands is an excellent example of a late Neolithic settlement that dates from 1500 B.C.E.

have been partly submerged by monsoon floodwaters during rainy seasons at the time; this placement suggests that the site may have been primarily "an expression of the interconnections between sun, water, death, and the fertile earth."[14]

Conclusion

Scientists and religionists have long debated who or what was responsible for the origin of our universe. Although evidence for evolution appears overwhelming, the theory does not preclude the presence of a guiding intelligence responsible for both the universe's creation and our planet's geological and biological development, culminating in the intelligence and behavior of our own species. During vast geological ages, organic life developed from single-celled organisms to multicelled creatures of extraordinary complexity. The earliest primates appeared in the Tertiary period. During the Oligocene epoch, different lines of monkeys and primitive forms of anthropoid apes evolved. Before the end of the Miocene epoch, one line of apes developed into tree-dwellers; another led to the ground-dwelling hominids, or prehumans. A considerable gap exists in our knowledge of prehuman development during the following Pliocene epoch.

The Pleistocene epoch provides us with rich data on the evolution of the genus *Homo.* In Africa emerged an apelike hominid, *Australopithecus,* that is not in modern mankind's line of descent. There was also *Homo habilis,* associated with the earliest

making of tools. Next appeared the *Homo erectus* group, including both Java Man and Peking Man, followed by Neanderthal Man and *Homo sapiens.* With their ability to think and communicate in symbolic terms, coupled with a toolmaking capability, early humans began, slowly but progressively, to acquire control over their terrestrial environment and in so doing to lay the foundations for the technological order so dominant in our lives today.

Thus paralleling its biological evolution began the first great period of humankind's cultural evolution, called the Paleolithic, or Old Stone, Age. We have seen how our ancestors' toolmaking capability advanced from reliance on very simple implements—such as the standardized, all-purpose hand ax, in use for 100,000 years or longer—to ever more specialized and sophisticated tools and techniques of operation. This technological evolution enabled *Homo* in turn to move into and adapt to different environments, whether the higher latitudes of Eurasia and North America, the rain forests of Southeast Asia, or the deserts of Australia. By the end of the last glacial phase, our forebears had spread over most of the world, and in the postglacial period they developed a semisedentary form of existence as found in the Mesolithic, or Transitional, cultures.

Paleolithic and Mesolithic cultures had food-gathering economies. Then, perhaps around 10,000 years ago, the Neolithic, or New Stone, Age emerged with the appearance of food-producing communities in western Asia and elsewhere. Neolithic cultures are usually characterized by the cultivation of grains, the domestication of animals, pottery making, and the fashioning of polished stone tools. These advances occurred in various places on earth and at different times. The revolutionary change from a food-gathering to a food-producing type of economy made possible the next stage in humankind's cultural evolution, riverine civilizations.

Suggestions for Reading

For a comprehensive and attractively written account of the human fossil record, the evolution of the human brain and cognitive powers, and the significance of lithic art, see Ian Tattersall, *Becoming Human: Evolution and Human Uniqueness* (Harcourt Brace, 1998); this might also be read in conjunction with Donald C. Johanson and Blake Edgar, *From Lucy to Language* (Simon & Schuster, 1996).

Delta Willis, *The Hominid Gang: Behind the Scenes in the Search for Human Origins* (Viking, 1989), is a popular account of the state of the art of human paleontology. Brian Fagan, *World Prehistory: A Brief Introduction* (HarperCollins, 1993), and J. Cowlett, *Ascent to Civilization: The Archeology of Early Man* (Knopf, 1984), are brief conventional accounts. See also Richard E. Leakey, *The Making of Mankind* (Michael Joseph, 1981); an interesting account of the life and work of his father, Louis S. B. Leakey, discoverer of *Homo habilis,* is found in the elder Leakey's book *By the Evidence: Memoirs, 1932–1951* (Harcourt Brace, 1974).

On genetic research and human origins, see Robert Shapiro, *The Human Blueprint: The Race to Unlock the Secret of Our Genetic Script* (St. Martin's Press, 1991). On human evolution and the spread of humankind from Africa to the rest of the world, see Noel T. Boaz, *Eco Homo: How the Human Being Emerged from the Cataclysmic History of the World* (HarperCollins, 1997); Jared Diamond, *The Third Chimpanzee: The Evolution and Future of the Human Animal* (HarperCollins, 1992); Roger Lewin, *Bones of Contention: Controversies in the Search for Human Origins* (Simon & Schuster, 1987); Christopher Stringer and Robin McKie, *African Exodus: The Origins of Modern Humanity* (Henry Holt, 1997); and Alan Walker and Pat Shipman, *The Wisdom of the Bones: In Search of Human Origins* (Knopf, 1996).

Two works dealing with the origins of toolmaking in a broad cultural matrix are Kenneth P. Oakley, "Skill as a Human Possession," in *A History of Technology,* Vol. 1 (Clarendon Press, 1956), and Robert J. Braidwood, *Prehistoric Men* (Scott, Foresman, 1967); both are well illustrated with pictures of lithic implements, from pebble tools to microliths. For two accounts of perhaps the most famous of all megaliths, see Rodney Castleden, *The Making of Stonehenge* (Routledge, 1993), and Gerald S. Hawkins and John B. White, *Stonehenge Decoded* (Dell, 1966). An interesting and informative analysis of an early key Neolithic settlement is found in James Mellaart, *Çatal Hüyük: A Neolithic Town in Anatolia* (McGraw-Hill, 1967). On early communities, see Tim Megarry, *Society in Prehistory: The Origins of Human Culture* (New York University Press, 1995), and Jared Diamond, *Guns, Germs, and Steel: The Fates of Human Societies* (Norton, 1997).

Fundamental forms of expression in primeval art, symbolization, the role of animals, depiction of the human figure (including fertility figurines), and the conception of space in prehistory are dealt with in detail in Sigfried Giedion's profusely illustrated book *The Eternal Present: The Beginnings of Art* (Pantheon, 1962). For a study of religious concepts in Stone Age art and their influence on European thought, see Gertrude Rachel Levy, *The Gate of Horn* (Faber & Faber, 1948). The role and significance of the Earth Mother cult in lithic cultures is analyzed and illustrated in Erich Neumann, *The Great Mother: An Analysis of the Archetype* (Pantheon, 1963), and perceived within a feminist critique in the opening chapters of Riane Eisler, *The Chalice and the Blade: Our History, Our Future* (Harper & Row, 1987). On religion and rock art, see David Lewis-Williams and Thomas Dowson, *Images of Power: Understanding Bushman Rock Art* (Southern Book Publishers, 1989), and David Lewis-Williams, *Believing and Seeing: Symbolic Meanings in Southern San Rock Paintings* (Academic Press, 1981).

Suggestions for Web Browsing

Fossil Hominids: Mary Leakey
http://www.talkorigins.org/faqs/homs/mleakey.html/

Discussion, with images, of the life and findings of one of the twentieth century's most famous archaeologists. Links to husband Louis Leakey, son Richard Leakey, Olduvai Gorge, and fossil findings.

Human Prehistory: An Exhibition
http://users.hol.gr/~dilos/prehis.htm

Walk through six rooms of text and vivid images that discuss the works of Lyell, Huxley, and Darwin; the first humans; the first human creations; the first villages, including Çatal Hüyük; and artworks of Neolithic Greece.

Chauvet Cave
http://www.culture.fr/culture/arcnat/chuvet/en/gvpda-d.htm

A French government site on a major discovery of prehistoric cave art. Contains information about the findings and many views of cave paintings at both this location and others in France.

Neanderthal Museum
http://www.neanderthal.de/

Site of a German museum whose goals are to maintain and popularize the cultural heritage of the Neanderthals.

Notes

1. BBC World Service, Dec. 10, 1998.
2. Richard E. Leakey, *The Making of Mankind* (London: Michael Joseph, 1981), p. 148.
3. See Jane Goodall, "Chimpanzees on the Gombe Stream Reserve," in *Primate Behavior,* ed. Irven De Vore et al. (New York: Holt, Rinehart and Winston, 1965), pp. 425–473.
4. Ernst Cassirer, *An Essay on Man: An Introduction to a Philosophy of Human Culture* (New Haven, Conn.: Yale University Press, 1965), pp. 24–25.
5. Robert J. Braidwood, *Prehistoric Men,* 7th ed. (Chicago: Scott, Foresman, 1967), p. 34.
6. Kenneth P. Oakley, "Skill as a Human Possession," in *A History of Technology,* Vol. 1 (Oxford: Clarendon Press, 1956), p. 25.
7. Ibid., p. 33.
8. Stuart Piggott, ed., *The Dawn of Civilization* (London: Thames & Hudson, 1961), p. 28.

9. Colin Renfrew, "The Emergence of Civilization," in *The Encyclopedia of Ancient Civilizations*, ed. Arthur Cotterell (New York: Viking, 1980), p. 13.

10. Jacquetta Hawkes and Leonard Woolley, "History of Mankind: Cultural and Scientific Development," in *Prehistory and the Beginnings of Civilization*, Vol. 1 (Paris: UNESCO, 1963), p. 264. For more on the status of women in Neolithic cultures, see Riane Eisler, *The Chalice and the Blade: Our History, Our Future* (San Francisco: Harper & Row, 1987), ch. 1.

11. Harold C. Conklin, *The Relation of Hanunóo Culture to the Plant World*, doctoral dissertation, Yale University, 1954 (microfilm), p. 97.

12. Claude Lévi-Strauss, *The Savage Mind* (Chicago: University of Chicago Press, 1970), p. 3.

13. Gerald S. Hawkins and John B. White, *Stonehenge Decoded* (New York: Dell, 1966), pp. 117–118, cited approvingly in Jacques Briard, *The Bronze Age in Barbarian Europe: From the Megaliths to the Celts*, trans. Mary Turton (Boston: Routledge & Kegan Paul, 1979).

14. Rob Stein, *Archaeology: Astronomical Structures in Ancient Egypt* (Washington, D.C.: Washington Post Company, 1998); J. M. Malville, F. Wendorf, A. A. Mazar, and R. Schild, "Megaliths and Neolithic Astronomy in Southern Egypt," *Nature*, April 2, 1998.

Head of a bull (c. 2430 B.C.E.) fashioned of lapis lazuli, this finely made creature decorated a lyre, which was found in the Royal Cemetery at Ur.

Early Civilizations
The Near East and Western Asia

Historians do not agree on how best to define the term *civilization*. But most would accept the view that a civilization is a culture that has attained a degree of complexity, characterized by urban life. In other words, a civilization is a culture capable of sustaining a great number of specialists to cope with the economic, social, political, and religious needs of a large social unit. Other hallmarks of civilization are a system of writing (originating from the need to keep records), monumental architecture in place of simple buildings, and art that is not merely decorative, like that on Neolithic pottery, but is representative of people and their activities. All these characteristics of civilization first appeared together in the southern part of Mesopotamia, the land called Sumer.

Mesopotamia: The First Civilization

Around 6000 B.C.E., after the agricultural revolution had begun to spread from its place of origin on the northern fringes of the Fertile Crescent, an area of rich soil stretching northeast from the Nile River to the Tigris in what is now northern Iraq and then southeast to the Persian Gulf, Neolithic farmers started filtering into the Fertile Crescent itself. Although this broad plain received insufficient regular rainfall to support agriculture, the eastern section benefited from the Tigris and

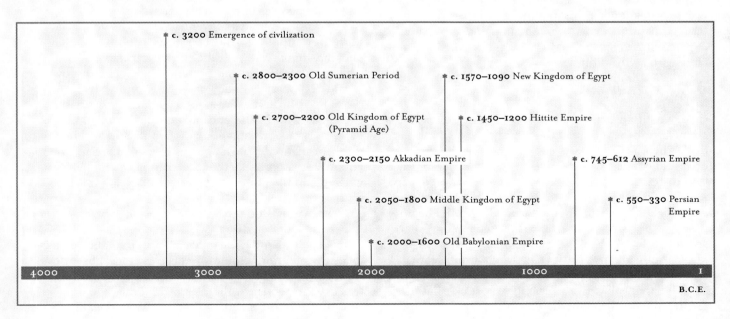

c. 3200 Emergence of civilization

c. 2800–2300 Old Sumerian Period

c. 1570–1090 New Kingdom of Egypt

c. 2700–2200 Old Kingdom of Egypt (Pyramid Age)

c. 1450–1200 Hittite Empire

c. 2300–2150 Akkadian Empire

c. 745–612 Assyrian Empire

c. 2050–1800 Middle Kingdom of Egypt

c. 550–330 Persian Empire

c. 2000–1600 Old Babylonian Empire

4000 3000 2000 1000 I

B.C.E.

Early Sumer and Akkad

c. 3200–2800 B.C.E.	Protoliterate period in Sumer
c. 2800–2300 B.C.E.	Old Sumerian period
c. 2370–2315 B.C.E.	Reign of Sargon of Akkad
c. 2300–2150 B.C.E.	Akkadian dominance
c. 2150–2000 B.C.E.	Neo-Sumerian period
c. 2000–1600 B.C.E.	Old Babylonian period
c. 1792–1750 B.C.E.	Reign of Hammurabi
c. 1595 B.C.E.	Sack of Babylon by Hittites

Euphrates Rivers as sources of irrigation. Known to the Greeks as Mesopotamia (Greek for "between the rivers"), the lower reaches of this plain, beginning near the point where the two rivers nearly converge, was called Babylonia. Babylonia included two geographical areas—Akkad in the north and Sumer, the delta of this river system, in the south.

Broken by river channels teeming with fish and refertilized frequently by alluvial silt laid down by uncontrolled floods, Sumer had tremendous agricultural potential if the environmental problems could be solved: swamps had to be drained, canals had to be dug to bring water to remote fields, and safeguards had to be constructed against flooding. In the course of the several successive cultural phases that followed the arrival of the first Neolithic farmers, these and other related problems were solved by cooperative effort. Between 3500 and 3100 B.C.E. the foundations were established for a type of economy and social order markedly different from anything previously known. This far more complex culture, based on large urban centers populated by interdependent and specialized workers, is what we associate with civilization.

Prelude to Civilization

Late Neolithic artisans discovered how to extract copper from oxide ores by heating them with charcoal. Then, about 3100 B.C.E., metal workers discovered that copper was improved by the addition of tin. The resulting alloy, bronze, was harder than copper and provided a sharper cutting edge. Thus the advent of civilization in Sumer is associated with the beginning of the Bronze Age, and this technology soon spread to Egypt, Europe, and Asia. The Bronze Age lasted until about 1200 B.C.E., when iron weapons and tools began to replace those made of bronze.

The first plow was probably a stick that the farmer pulled through the soil by a rope. In time,

however, domesticated cattle were harnessed to drag the plow. Yoked, harnessed oxen pulled plows in the Mesopotamian soil by 3000 B.C.E.

Since the Mesopotamian plain had no stone, no metals, and no timber except its soft palm trees, these materials had to be transported from Syria and Asia Minor. Water transport down the Tigris and Euphrates assisted this process. The oldest sailing boat known is represented by a model found in a Sumerian grave of about 3500 B.C.E. Soon after this date, wheeled vehicles appear in the form of war chariots drawn by donkeys.

Another important invention was the potter's wheel, first used in Sumer soon after 3500 B.C.E. Earlier, people had fashioned pots by molding or coiling clay by hand, but now a symmetrical product could be produced in a much shorter time. A pivoted clay disk heavy enough to revolve from its own momentum, the potter's wheel has been called the first true mechanical device.

The Emergence of Civilization in Sumer, c. 3200–2800 B.C.E.

By 3200 B.C.E. the population of Sumer had increased to the point where people were living in cities and had developed the majority of the characteristics of a civilization. Because these included the first evidence of writing, this first phase of Sumerian civilization, to about 2800 B.C.E., is called the Protoliterate period.

The Sumerian language is not related to Semitic or Indo-European, the major language families that appear later in the Near East. The original home of the Semitic-speaking peoples may have been the Arabian peninsula, and the Indo-Europeans seem to have migrated from regions around the Black and Caspian Seas. A third, much smaller language family, sometimes called Hamitic, included the Egyptians and other peoples of northeastern Africa.

Certain technical inventions of Protoliterate Sumer eventually made their way to both the Nile and the Indus valleys. Chief among these were the wheeled vehicle and the potter's wheel. The discovery in Egypt of cylinder seals similar in shape to those used in Sumer attests to contact between the two areas toward the end of the fourth millennium B.C.E. Certain early Egyptian art motifs and architectural forms are also thought to be of Sumerian origin. And it is probable that the example of Sumerian writing stimulated the Egyptians to develop a script of their own.

The symbols on the oldest Sumerian clay tablets, the world's first writing, were pictures of concrete things such as a person's face, a sheep, a star, or a measure of grain. Some of these pictographs also represented ideas; for example, the picture of a foot was used to represent the idea of walking, and a picture of a mouth joined to that for water meant "to

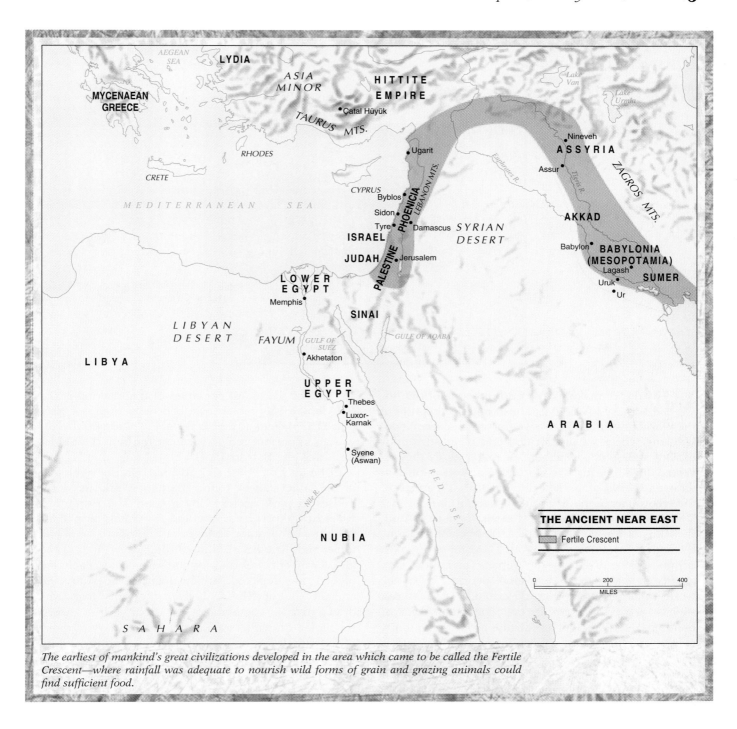

The earliest of mankind's great civilizations developed in the area which came to be called the Fertile Crescent—where rainfall was adequate to nourish wild forms of grain and grazing animals could find sufficient food.

drink." This early pictographic writing developed into phonetic (or syllabic) writing when the scribes realized that a sign could represent a sound as well as an object or idea. Thus the personal name Kuraka could be written by combining the pictographs for mountain *(kur)*, water *(a)*, and mouth *(ka)*. By 2800 B.C.E. the use of syllabic writing had reduced the number of Sumerian signs from nearly 2000 to 600.

When writing, Mesopotamian scribes used a reed stylus to make wedge-shaped impressions in soft clay tablets. This *cuneiform* system of writing (from the Latin *cuneus*, "wedge") was adopted by many other peoples of the Near East, including the Babylonians, the Assyrians, the Hittites, and the Persians.

The Old Sumerian Period, c. 2800–2300 B.C.E.

By 2800 B.C.E. the Sumerian cities had fully emerged into complex civilizations. This first historical age, called the Old Sumerian period, was characterized by constant warfare as each city attempted to protect or

Discovery Through Maps
Map of Nippur

Why do we make maps? Certainly one of the primary reasons is to establish one's perception of the world graphically—to give ourselves a security of knowing where we are located and what surrounds us. Our ancestors probably made maps before they invented any other form of written communication. But dating very old maps is a difficult task, for much of the record has been lost to the ravages of time.

Many of the world's oldest maps come to us from the ruins of Mesopotamia and from ancient Anatolia, the region now known as Turkey. These maps are most commonly engraved on clay tablets, and most vary greatly in scale—from very small perceptions of the world to larger inscriptions describing local features, such as a particular city or even individual fields or buildings. Scholars still are unsure as to the antiquity of many of these early efforts at cartography; dates given for some Mesopotamian maps may vary by as much as 1500 years, and the interpretation of their contents, size, symbols, and even colors differs widely.

One of the oldest examples of mapmaking is the Babylonian clay tablet inscribed with a map of Nippur. That ancient city, near the old capital of Babylon, was an important religious center for both the Sumerians and the Babylonians, who believed that Nippur was the holy city of their god Enlil. On the right side of the tablet can be found the temple and its storehouses, a park enclosed by a wall. The Euphrates River runs through the city, and two canals branch off from it—one leading to fields on the right side of the tablet and the other running through the center of the city. A wall encloses the city, and seven gates, each one named, are depicted. Archaeologists who study the ancient site of Nippur believe that this map was drawn to scale—if so, this tablet is our earliest known town plan drawn to such scale. The primary purpose of the map is not known, although a good possibility is that the map was intended to help in repairing the defenses of the city's walls.

enlarge its land and guarantee its access to water and irrigation. Each city-state was a theocracy, for the chief local god was believed to be the actual ruler. The god's earthly representative was the *ensi*, the high priest and city governor, who acted as the god's caretaker in both religious and civil functions. Though given the power to act for the god by virtue of being the human agent or the divine ruler, the ensi was not himself considered a divine being.

The ensis were powerful and sometimes autocratic rulers. Most familiar is the semilegendary Gilgamesh, ruler of Uruk about 2700 B.C.E., who is

known only from several epic tales. Like all Sumerian monarchs, Gilgamesh had to contend with the frequent opposition of the nobility who sat in his council. "The nobles of Uruk are gloomy in their chambers," begins the *Epic of Gilgamesh*, because "day and night is unbridled his [Gilgamesh's] arrogance." They appeal to the gods to create a hero who will be a "match" for Gilgamesh: "Let them contend, that Uruk may have peace." This tactic fails when the two heroes, after fighting to a draw, become fast friends. In another epic tale, Gilgamesh is able to overcome the refusal of his council to approve his decision not to submit to the ensi of Kish. He appeals to "the convened assembly of the men of his city," who readily support him: "Do not submit to the house of Kish, let us smite it with weapons."[1]

Early Sumerian society was highly collectivized, with the temples of the city god and subordinate deities assuming a central role. "Each temple owned lands which formed the estate of its divine owners. Each citizen belonged to one of the temples, and the whole of a temple community—the officials and priests, herdsmen and fishermen, gardeners, craftsmen, stonecutters, merchants, and even slaves—was referred to as 'the people of the god *X.*'"[2] The part of the temple land called "common" was worked by all members of the community, while the remaining land was divided among the citizens for their support at a rental of from one-third to one-sixth of the crop. Priests and temple administrators, however, held rent-free lands.

In addition to the temple lands, a considerable part of a city's territory originally consisted of land collectively owned by clans, kinship groups comprising a number of extended families. By 2600 B.C.E. these clan lands were becoming the private property of great landowners called *lugals* (literally, "great men"). Deeds of sale record the transfer of clan lands to private owners in return for substantial payments in copper to a few clan leaders and insignificant grants of food to the remaining clan members. These private estates were worked by "clients" whose status resembled that of the dependents of the temples.

In time, priests, administrators, and ensis began usurping temple land and other property and oppressing the common people. Their arrogance frequently led to the rise of despots who came to power on a wave of popular discontent. Since these despots were usually lugals, the term *lugal* became a political title and is generally translated as "king."

The Sumerian lugals made the general welfare their major concern. Best known is Urukagina, who declared himself lugal of Lagash near the end of the Old Sumerian period and ended the rule of priests and "powerful men," each of whom, he claimed, was guilty of acting "for his own benefit." Urukagina's inscriptions describe his many reforms and conclude: "He freed the inhabitants of Lagash from usury, burdensome controls, hunger, theft, murder, and seizure [of their property and persons]. He established freedom. The widow and the orphan were no longer at the mercy of the powerful man."[3]

The Sumerians, like their Mesopotamian successors, made extensive use of the institution of slavery, and slaves are recorded to have worked in many capacities—as farm and urban laborers, as servants in homes and temples, and in civic positions, such as in public administration. In certain cities, slaves accounted for 40 to 50 percent of the population. Slaves in Mesopotamia were not without rights, and in many cases they were treated with care. Slavery was not based on racial characteristics or cultural differences; people of the same culture became enslaved through conquest or to pay off debt. Perhaps because of the possibility that any city-state might be overtaken and its residents enslaved at the whims of the gods, the treatment of slaves in Mesopotamia seems generally to have been more humane than at other times and places in human history.

The Akkadian Period, c. 2300–2150 B.C.E.

Immediately north of Sumer lay the narrow region of Akkad, inhabited by Semites who had adopted much of Sumerian culture. Appearing late in the fourth millennium B.C.E., the Akkadians were among the earliest of the Semitic peoples who migrated into Mesopotamia from Arabia. A generation after Urukagina, Sargon I (2370–2315 B.C.E.),* an outstanding Akkadian ruler, conquered Sumer and went on to establish an empire that extended from the Persian Gulf almost to the Mediterranean Sea.

Very proud of his lower-class origins, Sargon boasted that his humble, unwed mother had been forced to abandon him: "She set me in a basket of rushes . . . [and] cast me into the river." Rescued and brought up by a gardener, Sargon rose to power through the army. As lugal, Sargon looked after the welfare of the lower classes and aided the rising class of private merchants. At the merchants' request, he once sent his army to far-off Asia Minor to protect a colony of them from interference by a local ruler. We are told that Sargon "did not sleep" in his efforts to promote prosperity and that in this new free enterprise economy, trade moved as freely "as the Tigris where it flows into the sea, . . . all lands lie in peace, their inhabitants prosperous and contented."[4]

Sargon's successors, however, were unable either to repel the attacks of less civilized mountain peoples or to overcome the desire for independence of the priest-dominated Sumerian cities. As a result, the dynasty founded by Sargon collapsed about 2150 B.C.E.

The Neo-Sumerian Period, c. 2150–2000 B.C.E.

Order and prosperity were restored by the lugals of the Third Dynasty of Ur. By creating a highly centralized administration in Sumer and Akkad, these rulers solved the problem of internal rebellion that had been of such concern for Sargon and his successors. The formerly temple-dominated cities became provinces administered by closely regulated governors. Religion became an arm of the state: the high priests were state appointees, and the temple economic organization was used as the state's agent in

Akkadian art is noted for its realism, perhaps best illustrated by this life-size head, cast in bronze, found at Nineveh and often conjectured to be Sargon. The head was deliberately mutilated in antiquity.

rigidly controlling the newly developing free enterprise economy that Sargon had encouraged.

At the head of this bureaucratic state stood the lugal of Ur, now considered a living god and celebrated in hymns as a heaven-sent authority who "brings splendor to the land, . . . savior of orphans whose misery he relieves, . . . the vigilant shepherd who conducts the people unto cooling shade."[5] Much of what we call social legislation was passed by these "vigilant shepherds." Their objective was the righting of wrongs that were not covered by the old customary law (*nig-ge-na*, "truth"), because the prologue to the law code of Ur-Nammu, founder of the dynasty, declared that it was the king's purpose to see that "the orphan did not fall a prey to the wealthy" and that "the man of one shekel did not fall a prey to the man of one mina [sixty shekels]."[6]

Disaster struck Ur about 2000 B.C.E., when Elamites from what is now Iran destroyed the city. The Sumerians were never again a dominant element politically, but their culture persisted as the foundation for all subsequent civilizations in the Tigris-Euphrates valley.

For more than two centuries following the destruction of Ur, disunity and warfare again plagued

Mesopotamia, along with economic stress, inflation, and acute hardship for the lower classes. Merchants, however, used the absence of state controls to become full-fledged capitalists who amassed fortunes that they invested in banking operations and land. The stronger local rulers of the period freed the poor from debt slavery and issued a variety of reform laws best illustrated by the legislation of Hammurabi.

The Old Babylonian Period, c. 2000–1600 B.C.E.

Semitic Amorites (from the Sumerian word *Amurru*, "West"), under the rule of their king, Hammurabi (c. 1792–1750 B.C.E.) of Babylon in Akkad, brought most of Mesopotamia under one rule by 1760 B.C.E. Hammurabi was a successful warrior who succeeded in expanding and securing Babylon's military power north into Assyria and south into Sumer.

Hammurabi is best known for his code of nearly 300 laws whose stated objective was "to cause justice to prevail in the land, to destroy the wicked and evil, to prevent the strong from oppressing the weak, . . . and to further the welfare of the people."[7] Hammurabi's legislation reestablished a state-controlled economy in which merchants were required to obtain a "royal permit," interest was limited to 20 percent, and prices were set for basic commodities and for fees charged by physicians, veterinarians, and builders. Minimum wages were established, and debt slavery was limited to three years. Other laws protected wives and children; but a wife who had "set her face to go out and play the part of a fool, neglect her house, belittle her husband" could be divorced without alimony, or the husband could take another wife and force the first to remain as a servant. Unless a son committed some grave offense, his father could not disinherit him. If the state failed to maintain law and order, the victim of that failure received compensation from the state: the value of the property stolen, or one mina of silver to the relatives of a murder victim.

Punishments were graded in their severity; the higher the guilty party on the social scale, the more severe the penalty. If an upper-class person, for example, knocked out the tooth of a social equal, his tooth would be knocked out; but if he did the same to a commoner, he paid a fine.

In the epilogue to the code, Hammurabi eloquently summed up his efforts to provide social justice for his people:

Let any oppressed man, who has a cause, come before my image as king of righteousness! Let him read the inscription on my monument! Let him give heed to my weighty words! And may my monument enlighten him as to his cause and may he understand his case! May he set his heart at ease! (and he will exclaim): "Hammurabi indeed is a ruler who is like a real father to his people. . . ."[8]

The Babylonians achieved little that today can accurately be called pure science. They did observe nature and collect data, which is the first requirement of science; but to explain natural phenomena, they did not go beyond the formulation of myths that defined things in terms of the unpredictable whims of the gods. The sun, moon, and five visible planets were thought to be gods who were able to influence human lives; accordingly, their movements were watched, recorded, and interpreted. Thus was born the pseudoscience of astrology.

Literature and Religion

The Babylonians took over from the Sumerians a body of literature ranging from heroic epics that compare favorably with the *Iliad* and the *Odyssey* to wisdom writings that have their counterparts in the Hebrew Old Testament. The Sumerian *Epic of Gilgamesh* recounts the exploits of the heroic ruler of Uruk who lived about 2700 B.C.E. Like all early folk epics, it reflects the values of a heroic age. The supreme value is the fame achieved through the performance of heroic deeds. After Gilgamesh slays the fierce Bull of Heaven, the "lyre maidens" of Uruk chant:

> *Who is most splendid among the heroes?*
> *Who is most glorious among men?*
> *Gilgamesh is most splendid among the heroes,*
> *Gilgamesh is most glorious among men.*

Since what these heroic heroes fear most is death, which replaces a glorious life on earth with a dismal existence in the House of Dust, "where dust is their fare and clay their food," the epic's central theme is Gilgamesh's hope for everlasting life. He seeks out and questions Utnapishtim, who was granted eternal life because he saved all living creatures from a great flood. (Utnapishtim's story has numerous similarities with the Hebrew account of Noah and the Flood.) But Gilgamesh's quest is hopeless, and he is so informed on several occasions:

> *Gilgamesh, whither rovest thou?*
> *The life thou pursuest thou shalt not find.*
> *When the gods created mankind,*
> *Death for mankind they set aside,*
> *Life in their own hands retaining.*
> *Thou, Gilgamesh, let full be thy belly.*
> *Make thou merry by day and by night.*
> *Of each day make thou a feast of rejoicing,*
> *Day and night dance thou and play! . . .*
> *Pay heed to the little one that holds on to thy hand,*
> *Let thy spouse delight in thy bosom!*
> *For this is the task of mankind!*[9]

The ancient Mesopotamians never progressed beyond this early view that immortality is reserved for the gods. Unlike the Egyptians, they did not go on

This scene is atop the nearly 8-foot stele, now in the Louvre, on which Hammurabi's code of laws is inscribed. It shows the self-styled "king of justice" saluting Shamash, the god of justice, who extends to him a rod and a ring, the symbols of royal authority.

Mathematics and Science

Building on the work of the Sumerians, the Babylonians made advances in arithmetic, geometry, and algebra. For ease of computation with both whole numbers and fractions, they compiled tables for multiplication and division and for square and cube roots. They knew how to solve linear and quadratic equations, and their knowledge of geometry included the theorem later formulated by the Greek philosopher Pythagoras: the square of the hypotenuse of a right-angled triangle is equal to the sum of the squares of the other two sides. They took over the Sumerian sexagismal system of counting based on the unit 60. This system is still used today in computing divisions of time and angles. They also adopted the Sumerian principle of place-value notation that gave numbers a value according to their position in a series. To represent zero, they employed the character for "not," which is the same as our "naught," still used orally for "zero."

to develop a belief in an attractive life after death as a reward for good behavior on earth. They did come to believe in divine rewards for moral conduct, but these were rewards to be enjoyed in this life—increased worldly goods, numerous offspring, long life. Thus they celebrated the sun-god Shamash in hymns that proclaimed that "the honest merchant . . . is pleasing to Shamash, and he will prolong his life. He will enlarge his family, gain wealth . . . and his descendants will never fail." The dishonest merchant, by contrast "is disappointed in the matter of profit and loses his capital."[10]

The ethical content of Babylonian religion was largely lost when the numerous priesthoods—more than 30 different types of priests and priestesses are known—became preoccupied with an elaborate set of rituals, particularly those designed to ward off evil demons and divine the future. Good deeds, the priests insisted, could not protect a person from demons that have the power to make their part-human and part-animal bodies invisible:

> *Doors and bolts do not stop them;*
> *High walls and thick walls they cross like waves;*
> *They leap from house to house . . . ;*
> *Under the doors they slip like serpents.[11]*

While one large class of priests provided amulets inscribed with incantations and magic formulas to exorcise demons, another group dealt with divining the future. Almost anything could be viewed as an omen, but most popular were dreams, the movements of birds and animals, the internal organs of sacrificed animals, the shape taken by oil poured on the surface of water, the casting of lots, and astronomical phenomena. Some of these methods of divination have survived virtually unchanged through the ages.

Ancient Egypt

c. 3100 B.C.E.	Menes unites Upper Egypt
c. 2700 B.C.E.	Construction of Step Pyramid
c. 1720 B.C.E.	Hyksos conquer Egypt
c. 1600 B.C.E.	Oldest medical text
c. 1479–1458 B.C.E.	Regency of Queen Hatshepsut
c. 1458–1436 B.C.E.	Reign of Thutmose III
c. 1363–1347 B.C.E.	Reign of Amenhotep IV (Akhenaton)
c. 1290–1224 B.C.E.	Reign of Ramses II
c. 700s B.C.E.	Conquest of Egypt by Kush

The End of an Era

The pattern of disunity and warfare, all too familiar in Mesopotamia, reasserted itself following Hammurabi's death. In 1595 B.C.E. the Hittites, an Indo-European people who had established themselves in Asia Minor, mounted a daring raid down the Euphrates, sacking Babylon and destroying the weakened dynasty of Hammurabi. The swift success of the Hittite raid was made possible by a new means of waging war: the use of lightweight chariots drawn by horses instead of donkeys or oxen. The next five centuries in Mesopotamia were an age of disorder about which little is known; nevertheless, the cultural heritage left by the Sumerians and Babylonians survived. Meanwhile, in a neighboring river valley, another civilization had emerged.

Egypt: Gift of the Nile

Egypt, one of Africa's earliest civilizations, is literally "the gift of the [Nile] river," as the ancient Greek historian Herodotus observed. The Nile River stretches for 4100 miles, but it is its last valley, extending 750 miles from the First Cataract to the Nile Delta, that was the heartland of Egyptian civilization. Egyptians called the Nile valley Kemet ("the black land") because its soils were renewed annually by the rich black silt deposited by the floodwaters of the Blue Nile and the Atbara, rivers descending from the Ethiopian highlands. Unlike the unpredictable floods of Mesopotamia, the Nile's floods rose and fell with unusual precision, reaching Aswan by late June and peaking in September before beginning to subside. The perennial key to successful farming was controlling the Nile by diverting its floodwaters along the 10- to 20-mile-wide floodplain for irrigation. Egyptian farmers achieved this by building an elaborate network of dikes and canals.

Predynastic Egypt

By 4800 B.C.E. the earliest farming communities began to appear in the western Nile Delta and spread to the rest of Egypt over the next eight centuries. Recognizing the advantages of creating larger social groupings and the need to cushion themselves from the impact of droughts, floods, and plagues, farming communities started banding together to form regional chiefdoms. Two distinct kingdoms gradually emerged. Lower Egypt comprised the broad Nile Delta north of Memphis, and Upper Egypt extended southward along the narrow Nile valley as far as the First Cataract, a rocky stretch of rapids that disrupted the flow of the river, at Aswan. Each kingdom contained about a score of districts (later called *nomes*) that had formerly been ruled by independent chieftains.

The Predynastic period ended soon after 3100 B.C.E. when King Menes united Upper Egypt and started gradually incorporating Lower Egypt into a new kingdom with its capital at Memphis. This period has become known as the First Dynasty, and it marks the beginning of one of the longest-lasting civilizations in history, flourishing for 3000 years.

The Old Kingdom, c. 2700–2200 B.C.E.

The kings of the Third through Sixth Dynasties—the period called the Old Kingdom or Pyramid Age—firmly established order and stability, as well as the basic elements of Egyptian civilization. The nobility lost its independence, and all power was centered in the king, or *pharaoh* (*per-ao*, "great house," originally signified the royal palace but during the New Kingdom began to refer to the king). The king had a character both divine and human. Considered a god, he also represented humans before the gods. As the god of Egypt, the king, with his relatives, owned extensive tracts of land (from which he made frequent grants to temples, royal funerary cults, and private persons) and received the surplus from the crops produced on the huge royal estates. This surplus supported a large corps of specialists—administrators, priests, scribes, artists, artisans, and merchants—who labored in the service of the pharaoh. The people's welfare was thought to rest on absolute devotion to the god-king. "If you want to know what to do in life," advised one Egyptian writer, "cling to the pharaoh and be loyal." As a consequence, Egyptians felt a sense of security that was rare in Mesopotamia.

The belief that the pharaoh was divine led to the practice of mummification and the construction of colossal tombs—*pyramids*—to preserve the pharaoh's embalmed body for eternity. The ritual of mummification was believed to restore vigor and activity to the dead pharaoh; it was his passport to eternity. "You live again, you live again forever, here you are young once more forever." The pyramid tombs, especially those of the Fourth Dynasty at Giza near Memphis, which are the most celebrated of all ancient monuments, reflect the great power and wealth of the Old Kingdom pharaohs. Although pyramid construction was ordinarily concentrated during the four months of the year when the land was flooded by the Nile, the Egyptian masses performed it primarily as an act of fidelity to their god-king, on whom the security and prosperity of Egypt depended.

Security and prosperity came to an end late in the Sixth Dynasty. The burden of building and maintaining pyramid tombs for each new king exhausted the state. The Nile floods failed and crops were di-

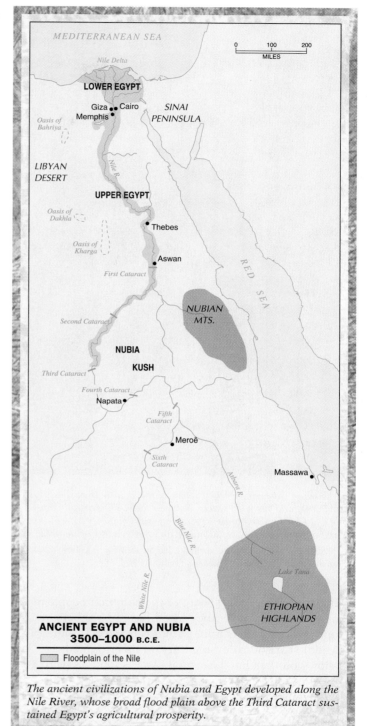

ANCIENT EGYPT AND NUBIA 3500–1000 B.C.E.

▭ Floodplain of the Nile

The ancient civilizations of Nubia and Egypt developed along the Nile River, whose broad flood plain above the Third Cataract sustained Egypt's agricultural prosperity.

minished, yet taxes were increased. As the state and its god-king lost credibility, provincial rulers assumed the prerogatives of the pharaohs, including the claim to immortality, and districts became independent.

For about a century and a half, known as the First Intermediate Period (c. 2200–2050 B.C.E.), the central authority of the pharaoh weakened as civil war raged among contenders for the throne and local rulers reasserted themselves. Outsiders raided and

Menkaure (Mycerinus), the builder of the Fourth Dynasty's third pyramid, and his wife, Queen Kamerernebly. The portrait statues of Old Kingdom pharaohs express a classical maturity of technique and of content—dignity, authority, and the certainty of eternal life.

Pair Statue of Mycerinus and Queen Kha-merer-nebty II, Egypt, Dynasty IV, Giza, Valley Temple of Mycerinus. Museum of Fine Arts, Boston, Harvard-Museum Expedition, 11.1738.

infiltrated the land. The lot of the common people became unbearable as they faced famine, robbery, and oppression. "All happiness has vanished," related a Middle Kingdom commentary on this troubled era. "I show you the land in turmoil. . . . Each man's heart is for himself. . . . A man sits with his back turned, while one slays another."[12]

The Middle Kingdom, c. 2050–1800 B.C.E.

Stability was restored by the pharaohs of the Eleventh and Twelfth Dynasties, who reunited the kingdom and ruled from Thebes for a century. Stressing their role as watchful shepherds of the people, the Middle Kingdom pharaohs promoted the welfare of the downtrodden. One of them claimed, "I gave to the beggar and brought up the orphan. I gave success to the poor as to the wealthy."[13] The pharaohs of the Twelfth Dynasty revived the building of pyramids as

well as the construction of public works. The largest of these, a drainage and irrigation project in the marshy Fayum district south of Memphis, resulted in the reclamation of thousands of acres of arable land. Moreover, a concession gave a wider group of people the right to have their bodies mummified and erect private tombs and thereby, like the pharaohs and the nobility, to enjoy immortality.

During the Thirteenth Dynasty, the Hyksos ("rulers of foreign lands"), a Semitic people from western Asia, assumed power over much of Egypt. The Hyksos are often portrayed as invaders who conquered Egypt around 1720 B.C.E., but now it is understood that the Hyksos migrated into Lower Egypt during the Middle Kingdom and established trading networks. During the Second Intermediate Period (c. 1800–1570 B.C.E.), they took advantage of weaknesses in the Egyptian state and gradually took control over all of Lower Egypt and many parts of Upper Egypt. The Hyksos did not sweep aside Egyptian institutions and culture. They adapted to existing Egyptian government structures, copied architectural styles and the hieroglyphic ("sacred carvings") system of writing, and incorporated Egyptian cults into their religious pantheon. The Hyksos army also introduced new weaponry to the Egyptians: the horse-drawn chariot and bronze weapons such as the curved sword and body armor and helmets.

The New Kingdom or Empire, c. 1570–1090 B.C.E.

Hyksos rule over Egypt lasted several centuries before a resurgent Egyptian dynasty based at Thebes challenged it. To nationalistic Egyptians, the Hyksos conquest was a great humiliation imposed on them by detestable barbarians. The Egyptian prince of Thebes proclaimed, "No man can settle down, when despoiled by the taxes of the Asiatics. I will grapple with him, that I may rip open his belly! My wish is to save Egypt and to smite the Asiatics!"[14] Adopting the new weapons introduced by their rulers, the Egyptians expelled the Hyksos and pursued them into Palestine. The pharaohs of the Eighteenth Dynasty, who reunited Egypt and founded the New Kingdom, made Palestine the nucleus of an Egyptian empire in western Asia.

The outstanding representative of this aggressive state was Thutmose III. Thutmose II had married his half-sister, Hatshepsut, but when their union failed to produce a male heir, Thutmose II fathered Thutmose III with a concubine. When Thutmose II died in 1479 B.C.E., Thutmose was still a child, and Hatshepsut was to act as co-regent until he came of age. However, she had her own ambitions. Supported by the powerful priests of the sun-god Amon, Hatshepsut proclaimed herself "king" and legitimized her succession by claiming that she was the designated successor and depicting herself as a daughter of Amon in many of her statues and helmets—sometimes even sporting the royal beard! She adopted all the customary royal titles.

Thutmose III had to wait for more than two decades before he assumed the throne on his own. Toward the end of his reign, he ordered Hatshepsut's name and inscriptions erased, her reliefs effaced, and her statues broken and thrown into a quarry. Historians still speculate whether he was expressing his anger at Hatshepsut or promoting his own accomplishments. This "Napoleon of Egypt," as Thutmose III has been called, is most noted for leading his army on 17 campaigns as far as Syria, where he set up his boundary markers on the banks of the Euphrates, called by the Egyptians "the river that runs backwards." Under his sway, Thutmose III allowed the existing rulers of conquered states to remain on their thrones, but their sons were taken as hostages to Egypt, where they were brought up, thoroughly Egyptianized, and eventually sent home to succeed their fathers as loyal vassals of Egyptian rule. Thutmose III erected *obelisks*—tall, pointed shafts of stone—to commemorate his reign and to record his wish that "his name might endure throughout the future forever and ever." Four of his obelisks survived in Egypt and today adorn the cities of Istanbul, Rome, London, and New York.

The Egyptian Empire reached its peak under Amenhotep III (c. 1402–1363 B.C.E.). The restored capital at Thebes, with its temples built for the sun-god Amon east of the Nile at Luxor and Karnak, became the most magnificent city in the world. Tribute flowed in from conquered lands, and relations were expanded with Asia and the Mediterranean. To improve ties, the kings of Mitanni and Babylonia offered daughters in marriage to Amenhotep III. In return, they asked the pharaoh for gold, "for gold is as common as dust in your land."

During the reign of the succeeding pharaoh, Amenhotep IV (c. 1363–1347 B.C.E.), however, the empire went into a sharp decline as the result of an internal struggle between the pharaoh and the powerful and wealthy priests of Amon, "king of the gods." The pharaoh undertook to revolutionize Egypt's religion by proclaiming the worship of the sun's disk, Aton, in place of Amon and all the other deities. Often called the first monotheist (although, as Aton's son, the pharaoh was also a god and he, not Aton, was worshipped by the Egyptians), Amenhotep changed his name to Akhenaton ("agreeable to Aton"), left Amon's city to found a new capital (Akhetaton), and concentrated on religious reform. Most of Egypt's tributary princes in Asia defected when their appeals for aid against invaders went unheeded. At home the Amon priesthood encouraged dissension. When Akhenaton died, his 9-year-old brother, Tutankhamen ("King Tut," c. 1347–1338 B.C.E.)—now best remembered for his small but richly furnished tomb, discovered in 1922—returned to the worship of Amon and to Memphis, where he

Sections of a wall painting from the tomb chapel of the treasurer Sebekhotep at Thebes show Nubians presenting gold nuggets and rings to King Thutmose IV. The painting dates from around 1400 B.C.E.

The largest of the colossal columns of the Hypostyle Hall of the temple of Karnak rise more than 70 feet and are more than 20 feet in diameter.

came under the influence of the priests of Amon. At this point the generals of the army took control of Egypt.

One of the new army leaders founded the Nineteenth Dynasty (c. 1305–1200 B.C.E.), which sought to reestablish Egyptian control over Palestine and Syria. The result was a long struggle with the Hittites, who in the meantime had pushed south from Asia Minor into Syria. This struggle reached a climax in the reign of Ramses II (c. 1290–1224 B.C.E.), the pharaoh of the Hebrew Exodus from Egypt under Moses (although Moses is not mentioned in Egyptian records). Ramses II regained Palestine, but when he failed to dislodge the Hittites from Syria, he agreed to a treaty. Its strikingly modern character is revealed in clauses providing for nonaggression, mutual assistance, and extradition of fugitives.

The long reign of Ramses II was one of Egypt's last periods of national grandeur. The number and size of Ramses' monuments rival those of the Pyramid Age. Outstanding among them are the great Hypostyle Hall, built for Amon at Karnak, and the temple at Abu Simbel in Nubia, with its four colossal statues of Ramses, which has been raised to save it from inundation by the waters of the High Dam at

Aswan. After Ramses II, royal authority gradually decayed as the power of the priests of Amon rose.

Third Intermediate Period, 1090–332 B.C.E.

The Third Intermediate Period was another period of transition in which the Amon priesthood at Thebes became so strong that the high priest was able to found his own dynasty and to rule over Upper Egypt. At the same time, merchant princes set up a dynasty of their own in the Delta. Libyans from the west moved into central Egypt, where in 940 B.C.E. they established a dynasty whose founder, Shoshenq, was a contemporary of King Solomon of Israel. Two centuries later, Egypt was conquered by the rulers of the kingdom of Kush, who established the Twenty-Fifth Dynasty. Kush's rule came to an end around 670 B.C.E. when the Assyrians of Mesopotamia made Egypt a province of their empire.

Egypt enjoyed a brief reprise of revived glory during the Twenty-Sixth Dynasty (c. 663–525 B.C.E.), which expelled the Assyrians with the aid of Greek mercenaries. The revival of ancient artistic and literary forms proved to be one of the most creative periods in Egyptian history. After attempts to expand into Syria were blocked by Nebuchadnezzar's Babylonians, Egypt's rulers concentrated on expanding their commercial linkages throughout the region. To achieve this end, Pharaoh Necho II (c. 610–595 B.C.E.) created the first Egyptian navy. He encouraged the Greeks to establish trading colonies in the Nile Delta; he put 12,000 laborers to work, digging a canal between the Nile mouth and the Red Sea (it was completed later by the Persians); and he commissioned a Phoenician expedition to search for new African trade routes.

Egypt passed under Persian rule in 525 B.C.E. but was able to regain its independence in 404 B.C.E. After three brief dynasties, Egypt again fell under the Persians before coming within the domain of Alexander the Great.

Nubia and the Kingdom of Kush

Egypt's most enduring relationship was with its neighbor to the south, Nubia, an area that stretches almost 900 miles from the town of Aswan to Khartoum, the point where the Blue and White Niles converge. The Nile gave Nubian civilization a distinctive character but in ways different from those in Egypt. As the Nile flows northward, its course is interrupted six times by cataracts that served as barriers to river traffic and Nubia's commercial contacts with Egypt. Moreover, the Nile did not contribute significantly to Nubia's agricultural life. The Nile's floodplain is about 2 miles wide, and many sections of the land are barren.

Emerging around 4000 B.C.E., the earliest Nubian culture was made up of hunters, fishermen, farmers, and seminomadic pastoralists. This culture was distinguished for its highly skilled sculptures, ceramics, and clay figurines. Nubia also developed a healthy trade with Egypt. Nubia exchanged animals and animal hides, incense, timber, gold, rare gems, and ebony and ivory for Egyptian honey, cloth, pearls, copper chisels, and alabaster vases.

After a centralized state emerged in Egypt, Egyptian dynasties regarded Nubia as a source of raw materials and slaves and made several attempts to colonize Nubia. During Egypt's First Intermediate Period, Egyptian soldiers invaded Lower Nubia (between the First and Second Cataracts) and built 11 fortresses with imposing names such as "Subduing the Oasis-Dwellers" and "Warding Off the Bow-Men." This state of hostility did not prevent Nubians from marrying into Egyptian royal families and the Egyptian state and army from recruiting Nubian administrators and archers.

Around 2300–2100 B.C.E. a new group of people, most likely herders from desert areas west of the Nile, migrated into Nubia. Around 1600 B.C.E. Egyptian records began referring to a "kingdom of Kush" that was centered in a fertile area of the Nile around the Third Cataract. Kush's capital was at Kerma, an urban center renowned for its sophisticated temples and palaces. Although the basis of Kush's society was agriculture and animal husbandry, Kush engaged in extensive trade with Egypt to the north and African societies to the south and east.

When the Hyksos dominated Egypt, Kushites regained control of Lower Nubia. After expelling the Hyksos, Egyptian forces reasserted their dominion over northern Nubia as far south as the Fourth Cataract, including Kerma. For the next four centuries, Egyptian administrators exploited Nubian gold to finance military campaigns in Asia and created an "Egyptianized" Nubian elite that adopted Egyptian deities and ritual and burial practices.

Kush did not regain its autonomy until the eighth century B.C.E., when a new line of rulers established themselves at Meroë in a fertile stretch of the Nile between the Fifth and Sixth Cataracts. The high point of Kush's power came a short time later. Taking advantage of strife in Egypt, the armies of Kush's King Piye swept through Egypt, conquering territory as far north as the Nile Delta. Although Piye proclaimed himself pharaoh over Egypt and Nubia, he allowed local rulers in Egypt a measure of independence. His successor, Shabaqo, was not so benign. He brought Egypt under the direct control of Kush. He and the three pharaohs who succeeded him estab-

lished the Twenty-Fifth Dynasty, which ruled Kush and Egypt for the next half century until they were forced to retreat following an Assyrian invasion.

Kush remained in existence until 400 C.E., when it was absorbed into the Ethiopian kingdom of Aksum. Around the second century B.C.E. Kush's rulers started recording their royal annals in a script that was part hieroglyphics and part shorthand cursive script. To this day, this language has not been translated.

Egyptian Society and Economy

Although most Egyptians were virtual serfs subject to forced labor, class stratification was not rigid, and people of merit could rise to a higher rank in the service of the pharaoh. The best avenue for advancement was education. The pharaoh's administration needed many scribes, and young men were urged to attend a scribal school. "Be a scribe, who is freed from forced labor, and protected from all work. . . . He directeth every work that is in this land." Yet then as now, the education of a young man was beset with pitfalls. "I am told thou forsakest writing, that thou givest thyself up to pleasures; thou goest from street to street, where it smelleth of beer, to destruction. Beer, it scareth man from thee, it sendeth thy soul to perdition."[15]

Compared with the Greeks and Romans, Egyptian women enjoyed more rights, although their status at all levels of society was generally lower than that of men. Few women could qualify as scribes and thus were largely excluded from administrative positions. However, women could serve as temple priestesses, musicians, gardeners, farmers, and bakers. Some royal women, because of their positions as wives or mothers of pharaohs, had great influence in royal courts. Business and legal documents show that women shared many of the economic and legal rights of men. Women generally had rights to own, buy, sell, and inherit property without reliance on male legal guardians, to engage in business deals, to make wills, and to testify in court.

The economy of Egypt was dominated by the divine pharaoh and his state, which owned most of the land and monopolized its commerce and industry. Because of the Nile and the proximity to the Mediterranean and Red Seas, most of Egypt's trade was carried out by ships. Boats regularly plied up and down the Nile, which, unlike the Tigris and the Euphrates, is easily navigable in both directions up to the First Cataract at Aswan. The current carries ships downstream, and the prevailing north wind enables them to sail upstream easily. Trade reached its height during the empire (c. 1570–1090 B.C.E.), when commerce traveled along four main routes: the Nile River to and from the south; the Red Sea, which was connected by

Many tomb paintings depict everyday life in Egypt. Here two servants pick figs at the tomb of Khnumhotpes at Bani Hasan.

caravan to the Nile bend near Thebes; a caravan route to Mesopotamia and southern Syria; and the Mediterranean Sea, connecting northern Syria, Cyprus, Crete, and Greece with the Nile Delta. Egypt's indispensable exports were timber, copper, tin, and olive oil, paid for with gold from its rich mines, linens, wheat, and papyrus rolls made from reeds—the preferred writing materials of the ancient world (the word *paper* is derived from the Greek *papyros*).

Egyptian Religion

During the Old Kingdom, Egyptian religion was lacking in ethical content. Relations between people and gods were based on material, not moral, considerations—the gods were thought to reward those who brought them gifts of sacrifice. But widespread suffering during the First Intermediate Period led to a revolution in religious thought. It was now believed that instead of sacrificial offerings, the gods were interested in good characters and love for one's fellows: "More acceptable [to the gods] is the character of one upright of heart than the ox of the evildoer. . . . Give the love of thyself to the whole world, a good character is a remembrance."[16]

Osiris, the mythical fertility god of the Nile whose death and resurrection explained the annual rise and fall of the river, became the center of Egypt's most popular religious cult when the new emphasis on moral character was combined with the supreme reward of an attractive afterlife. "Do justice whilst

thou endurest upon earth," people were told. "A man remains over after death, and his deeds are placed beside him in heaps. However, existence yonder is for eternity. . . . He who reaches it without wrongdoing shall exist yonder like a god."[17] The original premoral nature myth told how Osiris had been murdered by Seth, his brother, who cut the victim's body into many pieces and scattered them around Egypt. When Isis, his bereaved widow, collected all the pieces and wrapped them in linen, Osiris was resurrected, the Nile floods resumed, and vegetation revived. The moralized Osiris cult taught that Seth was the god of evil, that Osiris was the first mummy, and that every mummified Egyptian could become another Osiris, capable of resurrection from the dead and a blessed eternal life.

However, only a soul free of sin would be permitted to live forever in what was described as the "Field of the Blessed, an ideal land where there is no wailing and nothing evil, where barley grows four cubits high . . . ; where, even better, one has to do no work in the field oneself, but can let others take care of it."[18] In a ceremony called "counting up character," Osiris weighed the heart of the deceased against the Feather of Truth. If the heart was heavy with sin and outweighed the Feather of Truth, a horrible creature devoured it. During the empire the priesthood of Osiris became corrupt and claimed that it knew clever methods of surviving the soul testing, even if a person's heart were heavy with sin. Charms and magical prayers and formulas were sold to the living as insurance policies guaranteeing them a happy out-

In this scene from the Book of the Dead, a princess stands in the Hall of Judgment in the Underworld before a set of scales on which the jackal-headed god Anubis weighs her heart against the Feather of Truth. The baboonlike god Thoth records the result.

come in the judgment before Osiris. They constitute much of what is known as the Book of the Dead, which was placed in the tomb.

Mathematics and Science

The Egyptians were much less skilled in mathematics than the Mesopotamians. Their arithmetic was limited to addition and subtraction, which also served them when they needed to multiply and divide. They could cope with only simple algebra, but they did have considerable knowledge of practical geometry; the obliteration of field boundaries by the annual flooding of the Nile made the measurement of land a necessity. A knowledge of geometry was also essential in computing the dimensions of ramps for raising stones during the construction of pyramids. In these and other engineering projects the Egyptians were superior to their Mesopotamian contemporaries. Like the Mesopotamians, the Egyptians acquired a "necessary" technology without developing a truly scientific method. Yet what has been called the oldest known scientific treatise (c. 1600 B.C.E.) was composed during the New Kingdom. Its author, possibly a military surgeon or a doctor who treated pyramid-building laborers, described cases of dislocations and broken bones and recommended treatments or, in the case of more serious complications, nothing at all. In advising the physician to "measure for the heart" that "speaks" in various parts of the body, he

recognized the importance of the pulse and speculated about the circulation of the blood. Other medical writings considered a range of ailments, from pregnancy complications to hippopotamus bites. To Egyptian practitioners, the causes of medical conditions had to be dealt with holistically on a spiritual as well as a physical level. Thus they prescribed a combination of medicines, rituals, magical spells, and amulets.

The Old Kingdom also produced the world's first known solar calendar, the direct ancestor of our own. In order to plan their farming operations in accordance with the annual flooding of the Nile, the Egyptians kept records and discovered that the average period between floods was 365 days. They observed that the Nile flood coincided with the annual appearance of the Dog Star (Sirius) on the eastern horizon at dawn, and they soon associated the two phenomena. They also calculated that since the year was six hours short, an extra day had to be added every four years.

Monumentalism in Architecture

Because of their impressive, enduring tombs and temples, the Egyptians have been called the greatest builders in history. The earliest tomb was the mud-brick Arab *mastaba*, so called because of its resemblance to a low bench. By the beginning of the Third Dynasty, stone began to replace brick, and an architectural genius named Imhotep, now honored as the "father of architecture in stone," constructed the first pyramid by piling six huge stone mastabas one on top of the other. Adjoining this Step Pyramid was a temple complex whose stone columns were not freestanding but attached to a wall, as though the architect were tentatively feeling his way in the use of the new medium.

The most celebrated of the true pyramids were built for the Fourth Dynasty pharaohs Khufu, Khafre, and Menkaure. Khufu's pyramid, the largest of the three, covers 13 acres and originally rose 481 feet. It is composed of 2.3 million limestone bricks, some weighing 15 tons and all pushed and pulled into place by human muscle. This stupendous monument was built without mortar, yet some of the stones were so perfectly fitted that a knife cannot be inserted in the joints. The Old Kingdom's 80 pyramids are a striking expression of Egyptian civilization. Their dignity and massiveness reflect the religious basis of Egyptian society—the dogma that the king was a god who owned the nation and that serving him was the most important task of the people.

Just as the glory and serenity of the Old Kingdom can be seen in its pyramids, constructed as an act of loyalty by its subjects, so the power and wealth of the empire survive in the Amon temples at Thebes, made possible by the booty and tribute of conquest. On the east side of the Nile were built the magnificent temples of Karnak and Luxor. The Hypostyle Hall of the temple of Karnak, built by Ramses II, is larger than the cathedral of Notre Dame in Paris. Its forest of 134 columns is arranged in 16 rows, with the roof over the two broader central aisles raised to allow the en-

try of light. This technique was later used in Roman basilicas and in Christian churches.

Sculpture and Painting

Egyptian art was essentially religious. Tomb paintings and relief sculpture depict the everyday activities that the deceased wished to continue enjoying in the afterlife, and statues glorify the god-kings in all their serenity and eternity. Since religious art is inherently conservative, Egyptian art seldom departed from the classical tradition established during the vigorous and self-assured Old Kingdom. Sculptors idealized and standardized their subjects, and the human figure is shown either looking directly ahead or in profile, with a rigidity very much in keeping with the austere architectural settings of the statues.

Yet on two occasions an unprecedented realism appeared in Egyptian sculpture. The faces of some of the Middle Kingdom rulers appear drawn and weary, seemingly reflecting the burden of reconstructing Egypt after the collapse of the Old Kingdom. An even greater realism is seen in the portraits of Akhenaton and his queen, Nefertiti, which continued into the following reign of Tutankhamen. The pharaoh's brooding countenance is realistically portrayed, as is his ungainly paunch and his happy but far from godlike family life as he holds one of his young daughters on his knee or munches on a bone. The "heretic" pharaoh, who insisted on what he called "truth" in religion, seems also to have insisted on truth in art.

Painting shows the same precision and mastery of technique that are evident in sculpture. No attempt was made to show objects in perspective, and the scenes

The Step Pyramid (Third Dynasty, c. 2700 B.C.E.) was the first pyramid built of stone. The few remaining columns of the adjoining temple, also the first to be constructed of stone, are fluted to resemble the bundles of mud-smeared reeds that were formerly used as building materials.

The brooding and careworn countenance of this Middle Kingdom, pharaoh King Sesostris III, contrasts sharply with the confidence and vitality that characterize the portrait statues of Old Kingdom pharaohs.

This famous painted bust of Queen Nefertiti ("the beautiful one has come"), the wife and sister of Akhenaton, illustrates why she has been called "the most beautiful woman in history." Despite her dreamy expression, she had a forceful personality. She ultimately broke with her husband and moved out of the palace to another part of the capital.

seem flat. The effect of distance was conveyed by making objects in a series or by putting one object above another. Another convention employed was to depict everything from its most characteristic angle. Often the head, arms, and legs were shown in side view while the eyes, shoulders, and chest were shown in front view.

Writing and Literary Texts

In Egypt, as in Sumer, writing began with pictures. But unlike the Mesopotamian signs, the Egyptian hieroglyphics remained primarily pictorial. At first the hieroglyphics represented only objects, but later they came to stand for ideas and syllables. Early in the Old Kingdom the Egyptians took the further step of using alphabetical characters for 24 consonant sounds. Although they also continued to use the old pictographic and syllabic signs, the use of sound symbols had far-reaching consequences. It influenced their Semitic neighbors in Syria to produce an alphabet that, in its Phoenician form, became the forerunner of our own.

Among the earliest Egyptian literary works are the Pyramid Texts, a collection of magic spells and ritual texts inscribed on the walls of the burial chambers of Old Kingdom pharaohs. Their recurrent theme is an affirmation that the dead pharaoh is really a god and that no obstacle can prevent him from joining his fellow gods in the heavens.

Old Kingdom literature went on to achieve a classical maturity of style and content—it stresses a "truth" that is "everlasting." Hence *The Instructions of Ptah-hotep*, addressed to the author's sons, insists that "it is the strength of truth that it endures long, and a man can say, 'I learned it from my father.'" Ptah-hotep's maxims stress the values and virtues that are important in fostering positive human relationships. To him, honesty is a good policy because it will gain one wealth and position, while affairs with other men's wives is a bad policy because it will impede one's path to success in life.[19]

The troubled times that followed the collapse of the Old Kingdom produced the highly personal writings of the First Intermediate Period and the Middle Kingdom. They contain protests against the ills of the day, demands for social justice, and praise for a new value, romantic love, as a means of forgetting misery. The universal appeal of this literature is illustrated by the following lines from a love poem in which the beloved is called "sister."

I behold how my sister cometh, and my heart is in
  gladness.
Mine arms open wide to embrace her; my heart exul-
  teth within me; for my lady has come to me. . . .
She kisseth me, she openeth her lips to me; then am I
  joyful even without beer.[20]

A notable example of Egyptian literature is Akhenaton's *Hymn to the Sun,* which is similar in spirit to Psalm 104 in the Old Testament ("O Lord, how manifold are thy works!"). A few lines indicate its lyric beauty and its conception of one omnipotent and beneficent Creator:

Splendid you rise in heaven's lightland,
O living Aton, creator of life! . . .
How many are your deeds,
Though hidden from sight;
O Sole God beside whom there is none!
You made the earth as you wished, you alone.[21]

The Hittites,
c. 2000–1200 B.C.E.

Except for a brief mention in the Old Testament (Uriah the Hittite, for example, whose wife, Bathsheba, had an affair with King David), very little was known about the Hittites until archaeologists began to unearth the remains of their civilization in Asia Minor in 1906. By 1920 Hittite writing had been deciphered, and it proved to be the earliest example of a written Indo-European language. The Hittites are thought to have entered Asia Minor from the north about 2000 B.C.E., and their superior military ability—particularly demonstrated by the horse-drawn chariot—enabled them to conquer the native people of central Asia Minor.

The kings of the early Hittite kingdom were aggressive monarchs who were frequently at odds with their nobles and were unable to establish an orderly succession to the throne. One early Hittite king tells how his grandfather's choice of his son as heir to the throne was "spurned" by "the leading citizens," and he goes on to warn his own son "not [to] relax," for otherwise "it will mean the same old mischief."[22]

The Hittite Empire

After 1450 B.C.E. a series of energetic Hittite kings succeeded in ending the "old mischief" of their nobles and created a more powerful government and an empire that included Syria, which had been left virtually undefended by the Egyptian pharaoh Akhenaton. Ramses II moved north from Palestine in an unsuccessful attempt to reconquer the region. Ambushed and forced back to Palestine after a bloody battle, Ramses agreed to a treaty of "good peace and good brotherhood" with the Hittites in 1269 B.C.E. The Hittites may have been eager for peace with Egypt because of the threat posed by a new movement of Indo-European peoples. Many survivors of the resulting upheavals, which possibly included the fall of Troy (c. 1150 B.C.E.), fled by sea seeking new lands to plunder or settle. Collectively known as the Sea Peoples, these uprooted people included Philistines, Sicilians, Sardinians, and Etruscans. They left their names in the areas where they eventually settled. The collapse of the Hittite Empire, shortly after 1200 B.C.E., was partially a result of these migrations.

Hittite Civilization

The Hittite state under the empire was based on the models of the older monarchies of Mesopotamia and Egypt. The king claimed to represent the sun-god and was deified after death. The nobles held large estates granted by the king and in return provided warriors, who were armed increasingly with iron weapons. The Hittites were among the first people to manufacture iron weapons and use them effectively. Not until after 1200 B.C.E. did iron metallurgy become widespread throughout the eastern Mediterranean area.

The Hittites adopted the Mesopotamian cuneiform script, together with some works of Babylonian literature. While their law code showed some similarity to the code of Hammurabi, it differed in prescribing more humane punishments. Instead of retaliation ("an eye for an eye"), the Hittite code made greater use of restitution and compensation.

The Hittites left their mark primarily as intermediaries. Their skills in metalworking, especially in iron, were passed quickly to their neighbors. Not especially creative in the formulation of law or literature and art, they borrowed extensively from other cultures and in turn passed their knowledge on to others, in particular to the neighboring Phrygians, Lydians, and Greeks.

The Era of Small States,
c. 1200–700 B.C.E.

After 1200 B.C.E., with the Hittite Empire destroyed and Egypt in decline, the Semitic peoples of Syria and Palestine were able to assert their territorial claims in the power vacuum created by the weakness of the dominant states. For nearly 500 years, until they were conquered by the Assyrians, these peoples played a significant role in history.

The Phoenicians

Phoenicians is a name the Greeks gave to those Canaanites who lived along the Mediterranean coast

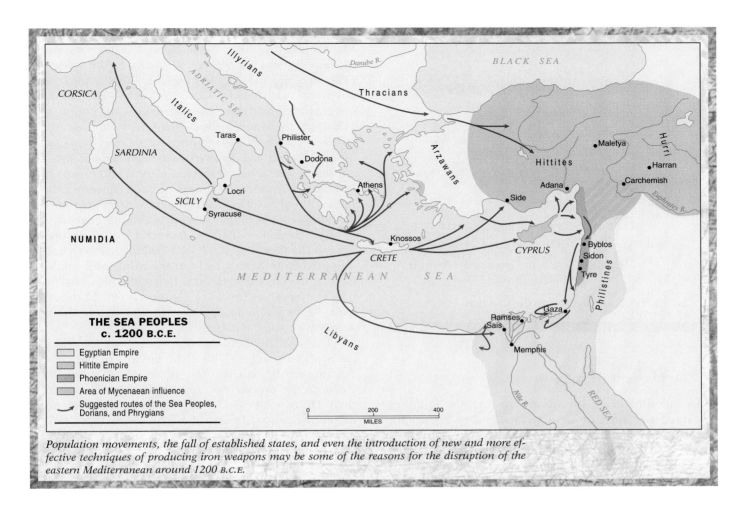

Population movements, the fall of established states, and even the introduction of new and more effective techniques of producing iron weapons may be some of the reasons for the disruption of the eastern Mediterranean around 1200 B.C.E.

of Syria, an area that is today Lebanon. Hemmed in by the Lebanon Mountains to the east, the Phoenicians turned to the sea for their livelihood and empire and by the eleventh century B.C.E. had become the Mediterranean's greatest traders, shipbuilders, navigators, and colonizers before the Greeks. To obtain silver and copper from Spain and tin from Britain, they established Gades (Cadiz) on the Atlantic coast of Spain. Carthage, one of a number of Phoenician trading posts on the shores of the Mediterranean, was destined to become Rome's chief rival in the third century B.C.E.

Although the Phoenicians were essentially traders, their home cities—notably Tyre, Sidon, and Byblos—also produced manufactured goods. Their most famous export was woolen cloth dyed with the purple dye obtained from shellfish found along their coast. They were also skilled makers of furniture (made from the famous cedars of Lebanon), metalware, glassware, and jewelry. The Greeks called Egyptian papyrus rolls *biblia* ("books") because Byblos was the shipping point for this widely used writing material; later the Hebrew and Christian Scriptures were called "the Book" (Bible).

Culturally, the Phoenicians were not particularly original. They left behind no literature and little innovative art. Yet they made one of the greatest contributions to human progress, the perfection of the alphabet, which, along with the Babylonian sexagesimal system of notation, they carried westward. Between 1800 and 1600 B.C.E. various Canaanite peoples, influenced by Egypt's semialphabetical writing, started to evolve a simplified method of writing. The Phoenician alphabet of 22 consonant symbols (the Greeks later added signs for vowels) is related to the 30-character alphabet of Ugarit, a Canaanite city, which was destroyed about 1200 B.C.E. by the raiding Sea Peoples.

The half-dozen Phoenician cities never united to form a strong state, and in the second half of the eighth century B.C.E. all but Tyre were conquered by the Assyrians. When Tyre finally fell to the Chaldeans in 571 B.C.E., the Hebrew prophet Ezekiel spoke what reads like an epitaph to the once great role played by the Phoenicians:

When your wares came from the seas, you satisfied many peoples; with your abundant wealth and merchandise, you enriched the kings of the earth. Now you are wrecked by the seas, in the depths of the waters; your merchandise and all your crew have sunk with you. (Ezekiel 27:33–34)

The Hebrew Kingdoms

In war, diplomacy, inventions, and art, the Hebrews contributed little of great significance to history; in religion and ethics, however, their contribution to world civilization was tremendous. Out of their experience grew three great religions: Judaism, Christianity, and Islam.

Much of Hebrew experience is recorded in the Holy Writ of Israel (the Old Testament), whose present content was approved about 90 C.E. by a council of rabbis. As a work of literature it is outstanding; but it is more than that. "It is Israel's life story—a story that cannot be told adequately apart from the conviction that God had called this people in his grace, separated them from the nations for a special responsibility, and commissioned them with the task of being his servant in the accomplishment of his purpose."[23]

The biblical account of the history of the Hebrews (later called Israelites and then Jews) begins with the patriarchal clan leader Abraham, called in Genesis 14:13 "the Hebrew" (a nomad or wanderer). About 1800 B.C.E. Abraham led his people out of Ur in Sumer, where they had settled for a time in their wanderings, and eventually they arrived in the land of Canaan, later called Palestine.

About 1550 B.C.E., driven by famine, some Hebrews followed Abraham's great-grandson Joseph, son of Israel (also called Jacob), into Egypt. Joseph's rise to power in Egypt, and the hospitable reception of his people there, is attributed to the presence of the largely Semitic Hyksos, who had conquered Egypt about 1720 B.C.E. Following the expulsion of the Hyksos by the pharaohs of the Eighteenth Dy-

nasty, the Hebrews were enslaved by the Egyptians. Shortly after 1300 B.C.E. a Hebrew leader named Moses led them out of bondage and into the wilderness of Sinai, where they entered into a pact or covenant with their God, Yahweh. The Sinai Covenant bound the people as a whole—the nation of Israel, as they now called themselves—to worship Yahweh before all other gods and to obey his Law (Torah). In return, Yahweh made the Israelites his chosen people, whom he would protect and to whom he granted Canaan, the Promised Land "flowing with milk and honey." The history of Israel from this time on is the account of the working out of this covenant.

The Israelites had to contend for Palestine against the Canaanites, whose Semitic ancestors had migrated from Arabia early in the third millennium B.C.E. Joined by other Hebrew tribes already in Palestine, the Israelites formed a confederacy of 12 tribes, led by leaders called *judges*, and in time succeeded in subjugating the Canaanites.

The decisive battle in 1125 B.C.E. at Megiddo, called Armageddon ("Hill of Megiddo") in the New Testament of the Christian Bible, owed much to Deborah the prophetess, who "judged Israel at that time" (Judges 4:4). God ordered Deborah, already famous throughout Israel for her wisdom, to accompany the discouraged war leaders and stir them to victory. For this reason she has been called the Hebrew Joan of Arc.

The vigorous and decisive role played by Deborah and other Israelite women (Moses' sister Miriam, for example) reflects the great influence of women in early Israel. Genesis describes the two sexes as being equal and necessary for human livelihood: "So God created mankind in his image, . . . male and female he created them. And God blessed them and said to them, 'Be fruitful and multiply and fill the earth and subdue it [together]'" (1:27–28). And in the Song of Songs the maiden and the youth share equally in the desire and expression of love; there is no sense of subordination of one to the other. But the continuing dangers that faced the nation led to the creation of a strong centralized monarchy, and with it came male domination and female subordination. Deborah was the last recorded Israelite woman who played an obvious and public leadership role.

Soon after the Canaanites were defeated, a far more formidable opponent appeared. The Philistines, one of the Sea Peoples who had tried unsuccessfully to invade Egypt and from whom the name *Palestine* comes, settled along the coast about 1175 B.C.E. Aided by the use of iron weapons, which were new to the region and the Hebrews, the Philistines captured the Ark of the Covenant, the sacred chest described as having mysterious powers, in which Moses had placed stone tablets inscribed with the Ten Commandments entrusted to him by Yahweh. By the mid-

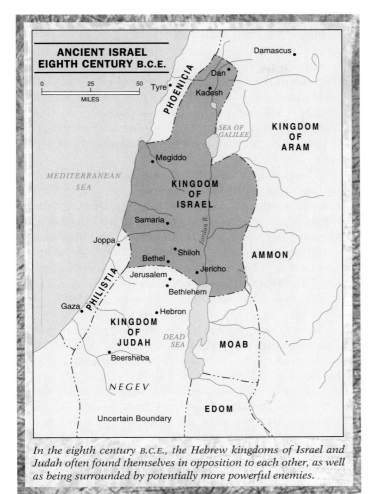

ANCIENT ISRAEL
EIGHTH CENTURY B.C.E.

In the eighth century B.C.E., the Hebrew kingdoms of Israel and Judah often found themselves in opposition to each other, as well as being surrounded by potentially more powerful enemies.

dle of the eleventh century B.C.E. the Philistines were well on their way to dominating the entire land.

Lacking central authority, the loose 12-tribe confederacy of Israel could not cope with the Philistine danger. "Give us a king to govern us," the people demanded, "that we also may be like all the nations, and that our king may govern us and go before us and fight our battles" (1 Samuel 8:6, 20). This move was strongly opposed by the conservative upper class, led by the prophet-judge Samuel. He warned the assembled Israelites that if they set up a king they would reject the "rule of God" and suffer divine disapproval. He predicted that a king would subject them to despotic tyranny. But the Israelite assembly rejected Samuel's advice and elected Saul as their first king. At that point "the Lord said to Samuel, 'Hearken to the voice of the people in all that they say to you; for they have not rejected you, but they have rejected me from being king over them'" (1 Samuel 8:7). This statement appears to have been a grudging concession on God's part, like that of a father who allows his wayward son to learn from experience the folly of his ways.

Saul's reign (c. 1020–1000 B.C.E.) was not successful. Continuously undercut by the conservatives led by Samuel and overshadowed by the fame of the boy hero David, who had slain the Philistine giant Goliath in single combat, Saul made no attempt to transform Israel into a centralized state. He collected no taxes, and his army was composed of volunteers. A victim also of his own unsteady and moody nature, Saul finally committed suicide after an unsuccessful battle with the Philistines.

Saul's successor, the popular David (c. 1000–961 B.C.E.), not only restricted the Philistines to a narrow coastal strip but also became the ruler of the largest state in the ancient history of the area, stretching from the Euphrates to the Gulf of Aqaba. David also wrested Jerusalem from the Canaanites and made it the private domain of his royal court, separate from the existing 12 tribes. His popularity was enhanced when he deposited the recovered Ark of the Covenant in his royal chapel, to which he attached a priesthood. The priests in turn proclaimed that God had made a special covenant with David as "the Lord's servant" and with the throne of David through all generations to come.

David's work was completed by his son Solomon (961–922 B.C.E.), under whom Israel reached its high point of worldly power and splendor as a powerful monarchy. In the words of the Bible:

Solomon ruled over all the kingdoms from the Euphrates to the land of the Philistines and to the border of Egypt; they brought tribute and served Solomon all the days of his life. . . . And Judah and Israel dwelt in safety, from Dan even to Beersheba, every man under his vine and under his fig tree, all the days of Solomon. . . . And God gave Solomon wisdom and understanding beyond measure, and largeness of mind. . . .

Now the weight of gold that came to Solomon in one year was six hundred and sixty-six talents of gold, besides that which came from the traders and from the traffic of the merchants, and from all the kings of Arabia and from the governors of the land. . . . The king also made a great ivory throne, and overlaid it with the finest gold. (1 Kings 5:1, 5, 9; 10:14–15, 18)

But the price of Solomon's vast bureaucracy, building projects (especially the palace complex and the Temple at Jerusalem), standing army (1400 chariots and 12,000 horses), and harem (700 wives and 300 concubines) was great. High taxes, forced labor, and the loss of tribal independence led to dissension. The Old Testament attributed this dissension to Solomon's feeble old age:

For when Solomon was old, his wives turned away his heart after other gods; and his heart was not wholly true to the Lord his God, as was the heart of David his father. . . . Therefore the Lord said to Solomon, "Since . . . you have not kept my covenant and my statutes, which I have commanded you, I will surely tear the kingdom from you . . . ." (1 Kings 11:4, 11)

When Solomon died in 922 B.C.E., the kingdom split in two—Israel in the north and Judah in the south. These two weak kingdoms were in no position to defend themselves when new, powerful empires rose again in Mesopotamia. In 722 B.C.E. the Assyrians captured Samaria, the capital of the northern kingdom, taking 27,290 Israelites into captivity (the famous "ten lost tribes" of Israel; two remained in the southern kingdom) and settling foreign peoples in their place. The resulting population, called Samaritans, was ethnically, culturally, and religiously mixed, as well as politically incapacitated.

The southern kingdom of Judah held out until 586 B.C.E., when Nebuchadnezzar, Chaldean ruler of Babylon, destroyed Jerusalem and carried away an estimated 15,000 captives; "none remained, except the poorest people of the land" (2 Kings 24:14). Thus began the famous Babylonian Captivity of the Jews (Judeans), which lasted until 538 B.C.E. when Cyrus, the king of Persia, having conquered Babylon, allowed them to return to Jerusalem, where they rebuilt the Temple destroyed by Nebuchadnezzar.

Generally peaceful Persian rule was followed by that of the Hellenistic Greeks and Romans. Then from 66 to 70 C.E. the Jews rebelled against Rome, and Jerusalem was largely destroyed in the savage fighting that resulted. The Jews were again driven into exile, known as the Diaspora (Greek for "scattering").

Hebrew Religion

From the time of Abraham, the Hebrews worshipped one god, a stern, warlike tribal deity whose name, Yahweh (Jehovah), was first revealed to Moses. Yahweh differed from the many Near Eastern nature gods in being completely separate from the physical universe that he had created. This view of Yahweh as the creator of all things everywhere eventually led to the monotheistic belief that Yahweh was the sole God in the universe.

After their entrance into Palestine, many Hebrews adopted the fertility dieties of the Canaanites as well as the luxurious Canaanite manner of living. As a result, prophets arose who "spoke for" Yahweh (*prophētēs* is Greek for "to speak"), insisting on strict adherence to the Sinai Covenant and condemning the "whoring" after other gods, the selfish pursuit of wealth, and the growth of social injustice.

Between 750 and 550 B.C.E. appeared a series of great prophets who wrote down their messages. They sought to purge the religion of Israel of all corrupting influences and to refine the concept of Yahweh. As summed up by Micah (c. 750 B.C.E.) in a statement often cited as the essence of all higher religions, "He has shown you, O man, what is good; and what does the Lord require of you but to do justice, and to love kindness, and to walk humbly with your God?" (Micah 6:8). Micah's contemporary, the shepherd-prophet Amos, stressed the need for social justice: "Thus saith the Lord: . . . [the rich and powerful] sell the righteous for silver, and the needy for a pair of sandals. They trample the head of the poor into the dust of the earth, and turn aside the way of the afflicted . . . so that they have profaned my holy name" (Amos 2:6–7).

The prophets viewed the course of Hebrew history as being governed by the sovereign will of Yahweh, seeing the Assyrians and the Chaldeans as "the rod of Yahweh's anger" to punish his stubborn, wayward people. They also developed the idea of a coming Messiah (the "anointed one" of God), a descendant of King David. As "a king in righteousness," the Messiah would begin a reign of peace and justice. This ideal would stir the hopes of Jews for centuries.

Among the greatest of the Hebrew prophets are Jeremiah and the anonymous Second Isaiah, so called because his message was incorporated into the Book of Isaiah (chapters 40–55). Jeremiah witnessed the events that led to Nebuchadnezzar's destruction of Jerusalem and the Temple and to the Babylonian Captivity of the Jews. He prepared the people for these disasters by affirming that Yahweh would forgive their sins and restore "a remnant" of his people by proclaiming a "new covenant." The old Sinai Covenant had been between Yahweh and the nation, which no longer existed. It had become overlaid with ritual and ceremony and centered in the Temple, which had been destroyed. The new covenant was between Yahweh and each individual; religion was now a matter of one's own heart and conscience, and both the nation and the Temple were considered unnecessary. Second Isaiah, who lived at the end of the Babylonian Captivity, capped the work of his predecessors by proclaiming Israel to be Yahweh's "righteous servant," purified and enlightened by suffering and ready to guide the world to the worship of the one, eternal, supreme God. Thus the Jews who returned from the Captivity were provided a renewed faith in their destiny and a new understanding of their religion that would gain strength through the centuries.

The Aramaeans

Closely related to the Hebrews were the Aramaeans, who occupied Syria east of the Lebanon Mountains. The most important of their little kingdoms was centered on Damascus, one of the oldest continuously inhabited cities in the world. The Aramaeans dominated the camel caravan trade connecting Mesopotamia, Phoenicia, and Egypt and

Assyria

c. 1350 B.C.E.	Assyrian rise to power
704–681 B.C.E.	Military power at height
669–626 B.C.E.	Reign of Ashurbanipal
612 B.C.E.	Fall of Nineveh

continued to do so even after Damascus fell to the Assyrians in 732 B.C.E. The Aramaic language, which used an alphabet similar to the Phoenician, became the international language of the Near East. In Judea it was more commonly spoken than Hebrew among the lower classes and was used by Jesus and his disciples.

Later Empires of Western Asia, c. 700–500 B.C.E.

By 700 B.C.E. the era of small states had ended with the emergence of the Assyrian Empire. The two great contributions of the Assyrians were the forcible unification of weak, unstable nations and the establishment of an efficient imperial organization.

The Assyrian Empire

For two centuries before 700 B.C.E. the Assyrians had been attempting to transform the growing economic unity of the Near East—evidenced by Solomon's trading operations and even more by the activities of Aramaean merchants—into political unity. The Assyrian move to dominate the Mediterranean began in the ninth century B.C.E. and after a period of weakness was resumed in the eighth century, when they also took over Babylon. By 671 B.C.E. the Assyrians had annexed Egypt and were the masters of the entire Fertile Crescent.

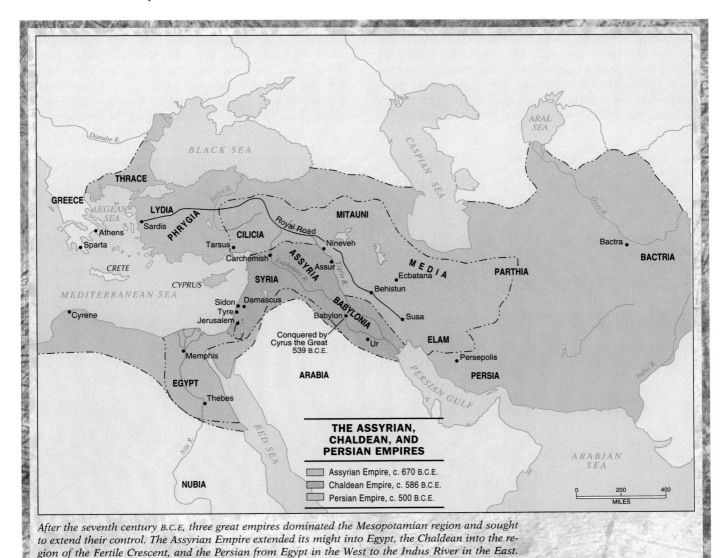

THE ASSYRIAN, CHALDEAN, AND PERSIAN EMPIRES

- Assyrian Empire, c. 670 B.C.E.
- Chaldean Empire, c. 586 B.C.E.
- Persian Empire, c. 500 B.C.E.

After the seventh century B.C.E, three great empires dominated the Mesopotamian region and sought to extend their control. The Assyrian Empire extended its might into Egypt, the Chaldean into the region of the Fertile Crescent, and the Persian from Egypt in the West to the Indus River in the East.

A Semitic people long established in the hilly region of the upper Tigris, the Assyrians had experienced a thousand years of constant warfare. But their matchless army was only one of several factors that explain the success of Assyrian imperialism: a policy of calculated terrorism, an efficient system of political administration, and the support of the commercial classes that wanted political stability and unrestricted trade over large areas.

The Assyrian army, with its chariots, mounted cavalry, and sophisticated siege engines, was the most powerful yet seen in the ancient world. Neither troops nor walls could long resist the Assyrians, whose military might seemed unstoppable. Conquered peoples were held firmly in control by systematic policies designed to terrorize. A typical statement from the Assyrian royal inscriptions reads: "From some I cut off their noses, their ears and their fingers, of many I put out the eyes. . . . I bound their heads to tree trunks round about the city."[24] Mass deportations, like that of the Israelites, were employed as an effective means of destroying national feeling.

The well-coordinated Assyrian system of political administration was another factor in the success of the empire. Conquered lands became provinces ruled by governors who exercised extensive military, judicial, and financial powers. Their chief tasks were to ensure the regular collection of tribute (payments demanded by the conquerors) and the raising of troops for the permanent army that eventually replaced the native militia of sturdy Assyrian peasants. An efficient system of communications carried the "king's word" to the governors as well as the latter's reports to the royal court—including one prophetic dispatch reading: "The king knows that all lands hate us." Nevertheless, the Assyrians must be credited with laying the foundations for some elements of the later more humane administrative systems of their successors, the Persians and Alexander the Great of Macedonia.

Assyrian Culture

The Assyrians borrowed from the cultures of other peoples and unified the elements into a new product. This is evident in Assyrian architecture and sculpture, the work of subject artisans and artists. Both arts glorified the power of the Assyrian king. The palace, serving as both residence and administrative center, replaced the temple as the characteristic architectural form. A feature of Assyrian palace architecture was the structural use of the arch and the column, both borrowed from Babylonia. Palaces were decorated with splendid relief sculptures that glorified the king as warrior and hunter. Assyrian sculptors were especially skilled in portraying realistically the ferocity and agony of charging and dying lions.

This ancient Assyrian statue, "The Dying Lion," is an example of a common theme in royal Assyrian sculpture. The prowess of the Assyrian king as hunter and leader was often emphasized through such artistic themes.

Assyrian kings were interested in preserving written as well as pictorial records of their reigns, and King Ashurbanipal (669–626 B.C.E.) left a record of his great efforts in collecting the literary heritage of Sumer and Babylon. The 22,000 clay tablets found in the ruins of his palace at Nineveh provided modern scholars with their first direct knowledge of the bulk of this literature, which included the Sumerian *Epic of Gilgamesh*.

Downfall of the Assyrian Empire

Revolt against Assyrian terror and tribute was inevitable when Assyria's strength weakened and effective opposition to Assyrian terror arose. By the middle of the seventh century B.C.E. the Assyrians had been decimated by wars, and the Assyrian kings had to use unreliable mercenary troops and conscripted subject peoples. Egypt regained its independence under the Twenty-Sixth Dynasty, and the Medes to the north refused to pay further tribute. The Chaldeans, a new group of Semites who had migrated into Babylonia, revolted in 626 B.C.E. In 612 B.C.E. they joined the Medes in destroying Nineveh, the Assyrian capital. From one end of the Fertile Crescent to the other, people rejoiced: "Nineveh is laid waste; who will bemoan her? . . . All who hear the news of you clap their hands over you. For upon whom has not come your unceasing evil?" (Nahum 3:7, 19).

The Lydians and the Medes

The fall of Assyria left four states to struggle over the crumbs of empire: Chaldea and Egypt fought over Syria and Palestine, and Media and Lydia clashed over eastern Asia Minor.

After the collapse of the Hittite Empire about 1200 B.C.E., the Lydians had followed the Phrygians, whose last king was the legendary Midas, who died around 680 B.C.E., in establishing a kingdom in western Asia Minor. When Assyria fell, the Lydians expanded eastward until stopped by the Medes at the Halys River. Lydia profited from being in control of part of the commercial land route between Mesopotamia and the Aegean and from the possession of valuable gold-bearing streams. About 675 B.C.E. the Lydians invented coinage, which replaced the silver bars in general use up to that time. Lydia's most famous king was Croesus, and the phrase "rich as Croesus" is a reminder of Lydia's legendary wealth. With the king's defeat by the Persians in 547 B.C.E., Lydia ceased to exist as an independent state.

The Medes were an Indo-European people who by 1000 B.C.E. had established themselves on the Iranian plateau east of Assyria. By the seventh century B.C.E. they had created a strong kingdom with Ecbatana as its capital and with the Persians, their kinsmen to the south, as their subjects. Following the collapse of Assyria, the Medes expanded into Armenia and eastern Asia Minor, but their short-lived empire ended in 550 B.C.E. when they, too, were absorbed by the Persians.

The Chaldean (Neo-Babylonian) Empire

While the Median kingdom controlled the highland region, the Chaldeans, with their capital at Babylon, were masters of the Fertile Crescent. Nebuchadnezzar, who had become king of the Chaldeans in 604 B.C.E., raised Babylonia to another epoch of brilliance after more than a thousand years of eclipse. By defeating the Egyptians in Syria, Nebuchadnezzar ended their hopes of re-creating their empire. As we have seen, he destroyed Jerusalem in 586 B.C.E. and took thousands of captured Jews to Babylonia.

Nebuchadnezzar rebuilt Babylon, making it the largest and most impressive city of its day. The tremendous city walls were wide enough at the top to have rows of small houses on either side. In the center of Babylon ran the famous Procession Street, which passed through the Ishtar Gate. This arch, which was adorned with brilliant tile animals, is the best remaining example of Babylonian architecture. The immense palace of Nebuchadnezzar towered terrace upon terrace, each decorated with masses of ferns, flowers, and trees. These roof gardens, the famous Hanging Gardens of Babylon, were so beautiful that they were regarded by the Greeks as one of the seven wonders of the ancient world.

Nebuchadnezzar also rebuilt the great temple-tower, or *ziggurat* (a Sumerian invention), the biblical "Tower of Babel," which the Greek historian Herodotus described a century later as

> *a tower of solid masonry, a furlong [220 yards] in length and breadth, upon which was raised a second tower, and on that a third, and so on up to eight. The ascent to the top is on the outside, by a path which winds round all the towers.*[25]

Nebuchadnezzar was the last great Mesopotamian ruler, and Chaldean power quickly crumbled after his death in 562 B.C.E. Chaldean priests, whose interests included political intrigue as well as astrology, continually undermined the monarchy. Finally, in 539 B.C.E. they opened the gates of Babylon to Cyrus the Persian, allowing him to add Babylon to his impressive new empire.

The Persian Empire

Cyrus the Persian was the greatest conqueror in the history of the ancient Near East. In 550 B.C.E. he

The brilliantly glazed bricks of the Ishtar Gate suggest the splendor of the Neo-Babylonian Empire during the reign of Nebuchadnezzar (604–562 B.C.E.). Adorning the brick is a stately procession of realistic-looking bulls and fantastic dragons, which feature a serpent's head and tail, a lion's body and forelegs, and a falcon's hind legs. Separately molded and glazed bricks were used to form the animals, which appear in raised relief on the gate.

ended Persian subjugation to the Medes by capturing Ecbatana and ending the Median dynasty. The Medes readily accepted their vigorous new ruler, who soon demonstrated that he deserved to be called "the Great." When King Croesus of Lydia moved across the Halys River in 547 B.C.E. to pick up some of the pieces of the collapsed Median Empire, Cyrus defeated him and annexed Lydia, including Greek cities on the coast of Asia Minor that were under Lydia's nominal control. Then he turned his attention eastward, establishing his power as far as the frontier of India. Babylon and its empire were next on his list. After Cyrus died, his son Cambyses (530–522 B.C.E.) conquered Egypt. The next ruler, Darius I (522–486

B.C.E.), added the Punjab region in India and Thrace in Europe. He also began a conflict with the Greeks that continued intermittently for more than 150 years until the Persians were conquered by Alexander the Great. Long before this event, the Persian nobility had forgotten Cyrus the Great's answer to their suggestion that they "leave this small and barren country of ours" and move to fertile Babylonia:

> *Do so if you wish, but if you do, be ready to find yourselves no longer governors but governed; for soft lands breed soft men; it does not happen that the same land brings forth wonderful crops and good fighting men.*[26]

Persian Government

Built on the Assyrian model, the Persian administrative system was far more efficient and humane. The empire was divided into 20 *satrapies*, or provinces, each ruled by a governor called a *satrap*. To check the satraps, a secretary and a military official representing the "Great King, King of Kings" were installed in every province. Also, special inspectors, "the Eyes and Ears of the King," traveled throughout the realm.

Imperial post roads connected the important cities. Along the Royal Road between Sardis and Susa there was a post station every 14 miles, where the king's couriers could obtain fresh horses, enabling them to cover the 1600-mile route in a week.

Persia

c. 600 B.C.E.	Union under Achaemenid kings
559–530 B.C.E.	Reign of Cyrus the Great
550 B.C.E.	Conquest of Median Empire
539 B.C.E.	Conquest of Babylon
530–522 B.C.E.	Reign of Cambyses
522–486 B.C.E.	Reign of Darius I

The Majesty of Darius the Great: A Persian Royal Inscription

The Persian kings ruled their vast empire with absolute authority. But the power of the king had to be used in a responsible and ethical manner and in agreement with the purposes of the great god of the Persians, Ahura-Mazda. The following inscription was intended to show the Persian people that the king was able and powerful but also just and honorable.

A great god is Ahuramazda who created this excellent work which one sees; who created happiness for man; who bestowed wisdom and energy upon Darius the king. Says Darius the king: by the favour of Ahuramazda I am of such a kind that I am a friend to what is right, I am no friend to what is wrong. It is not my wish that to the weak is done wrong because of the mighty, it is not my wish that the weak is hurt because of the mighty, that the mighty is hurt because of the weak. What is right, that is my wish. I am no friend of the man who is a follower of the lie. I am not hot-tempered. When I feel anger rising, I keep that under control by my thinking power. I control firmly my impulses. The man who co-operates, him do I reward according to his co-operation. He who

does harm, him I punish according to the damage. It is not my wish that a man does harm, it is certainly not my wish that a man if he causes damage be not punished. What a man says against a man, that does not convince me, until I have heard testimony(?) from both parties. What a man does or performs according to his powers, satisfies me, therewith I am satisfied and it gives me great pleasure and I am very satisfied and I give much to faithful men.

I am trained with both hands and feet. As a horseman I am a good horseman. As a bowman I am a good bowman, both afoot and on horseback. As a spearman I am a good spearman, both afoot and on horseback. And the skills which Ahuramazda has bestowed upon me and I have had the strength to use them, by the favour of Ahuramazda, what has been done by me, I have done with these skills which Ahuramazda has bestowed upon me.

From B. Gharib, "A Newly Found Inscription of Xerxes," *Franica Antiqua*, 1968, as quoted in Amélie Kuhrt, *The Ancient Near East: c. 3000–330 B.C.*, Vol. 2 (London: Routledge, 1995), p. 681.

"Nothing mortal travels so fast as these Persian messengers," wrote Herodotus. "These men will not be hindered . . . , either by snow, or rain, or heat, or by the darkness of night."[27]

The Persian Empire was the first to attempt to govern many different racial groups on the principle of equal responsibilities and rights for all peoples. So long as subjects paid their taxes and kept the peace, the king did not interfere with local religion, customs, or trade. Indeed, Darius was called "the shopkeeper" because he stimulated trade by introducing a uniform system of gold and silver coinage on the Lydian model.

Persian Religion and Art

The humaneness of the Persian rulers may have stemmed from the ethical religion founded by the prophet Zoroaster, who lived in the early sixth century B.C.E. Zoroaster attempted to replace what he called "the lie"—ritualistic, idol-worshiping cults and their Magi priests—with a religion centered on the sole god Ahura-Mazda ("Wise Lord"). This "father of Justice" demanded "good thoughts of the mind, good deeds of the hand, and good words of the tongue" from those who would attain paradise (a

Persian word). This new higher religion made little progress until first Darius and then the Magi adopted it. The Magi revived many old gods as lesser deities, added much ritual, and replaced monotheism with dualism by transforming what Zoroaster had called the principle or spirit of evil into the powerful god Ahriman (the model for the Jewish Satan), the rival of Ahura-Mazda, "between which each man must choose for himself." The complicated evolution of Zoroastrianism is revealed in its holy book, the Avesta ("The Law"), assembled in its present form between the fourth and sixth centuries C.E. Zoroastrian eschatology—the "doctrine of final things" such as the resurrection of the dead and a last judgment—influenced later Judaism. Following the Muslim conquest of Persia in the seventh century C.E., Zoroastrianism died out in its homeland. It exists today among the Parsees in India and in scattered communities worldwide.

In art the Persians borrowed largely from their predecessors in the Fertile Crescent, particularly the Assyrians. Their most important contribution was in palace architecture, the best remains of which are at Persepolis. Built on a high terrace, the royal residence was reached by a grand stairway faced with beautiful reliefs. Instead of the warfare and violence that characterized Assyrian sculpture, these reliefs

This scene, on a Greek vase (c. 330 B.C.E.), depicts King Darius (center) listening to his advisers as they confer on the eve of the battle of Marathon, which the Persians lost to the Greeks in 490 B.C.E.

depict hundreds of soldiers, courtiers, and representatives of 23 nations of the empire bringing gifts to the king for the festival of the new year.

Conclusion

Historians have determined that civilization—interdependent urban living—developed in Mesopotamia and Egypt in the second half of the fourth millennium B.C.E. Both of these civilizations originated in river valleys: one by the Tigris and Euphrates and one by the Nile. In each instance, the complex society we call a civilization was the result of organized and cooperative efforts that were necessary to make the rivers useful to humans living along them.

Mesopotamian civilization originated in the land called Sumer. The achievements of the Sumerians served as a foundation for later Mesopotamian civilizations established by Semitic peoples migrating into the river valleys. The most significant of these

later Semitic civilizations was the Babylonian Empire ruled by Hammurabi. Babylon was sacked by the Indo-European Hittites of Asia Minor, who went on to duel with Egypt over control of Syria and Palestine.

In Egypt a great civilization arose on the banks of the Nile, a civilization both monumental and timeless. The temples and tombs of the Egyptian monarchs were designed to endure forever and to preserve the satisfying and stable existence of this world into eternity. Egypt centered on the absolute rule of the pharaohs—god-kings who eventually extended their domain from Nubia to the Euphrates River.

By 1200 B.C.E. the great Near Eastern empires—Babylonian, Egyptian, and Hittite—had weakened, allowing the Semitic peoples of Syria and Palestine more opportunity to make their own cultural contributions, the most significant being the ethical monotheism of the Hebrews. Political diversity was ended by the rise of the Assyrian Empire, which unified all of the ancient Near East for the first time. After the fall of Assyria, the Chaldean Nebuchadnezzar constructed a new Babylonian Empire, but it was soon engulfed by the expansion of Persia. Stretching from India to Europe, the Persian Empire gave the Near East its greatest extension and power.

The achievements of these early civilizations would become the inheritance of the Greeks and eventually the Romans. Much of the social and cultural legacy of the ancient Near East remains preserved in the fabric of those Mediterranean societies, which rose to political and cultural prominence after the first civilizations declined in vitality.

Suggestions for Reading

Amélie Kuhrt, *The Ancient Near East*, 2 vols. (Routledge, 1995), is an outstanding overview. William W. Hallo and William Kelly Simpson, *The Ancient Near East: A History* (Harcourt Brace, 1998), is also excellent. See also Charles A. Burney, *From Village to Empire: An Introduction to Near Eastern Archaeology* (Phaidon, 1977), and Michael Roaf, *Cultural Atlas of Mesopotamia and the Ancient Near East* (Facts on File, 1990).

Nicholas Postgate, *Early Mesopotamia: Economy and Society at the Dawn of History* (Routledge, 1994), is a most valuable survey. See also Georges Roux, *Ancient Iraq*, 3rd ed. (Penguin, 1992); Samuel N. Kramer, *The Sumerians: Their History, Culture, and Character* (University of Chicago Press, 1971), and the same author's excellent *History Begins at Sumer* (University of Pennsylvania Press, 1981). Joan Oates, *Babylon* (Thames & Hudson, 1979); H. W. F. Saggs, *The Greatness That Was Babylon* (Hawthorne Books, 1962); and Mare van de Mieroop, *The Ancient Mesopotamian City* (Oxford University Press, 1997), are other good sources.

Henri Frankfort et al., *The Intellectual Adventure of Ancient Man* (University of Chicago Press, 1946), is a highly regarded interpretation of Mesopotamian, Egyptian, and Hebrew thought. See also Thorkild Jacobsen, *The Treasures of Darkness:*

A History of Mesopotamian Religion (Yale University Press, 1976).

Survey histories of Egyptian history include Nicolas Grimal, *A History of Ancient Egypt*, trans. Ian Shaw (Blackwell, 1992); *The Cambridge Ancient History* (Cambridge University Press, 1970–1997); Barry J. Kemp, *Ancient Egypt: Anatomy of a Civilization* (Routledge, 1989); Bruce Trigger et al., *Ancient Egypt: A Social History* (Cambridge University Press, 1983); T. G. H. James, *An Introduction to Ancient Egypt* (Harper & Row, 1990); Stephen Quirke and Jeffrey Spencer, eds., *The British Museum Book of Ancient Egypt* (Thames & Hudson, 1992); Guillemette Andrew, *Egypt in the Age of the Pyramids* (Cornell University Press, 1997); Sergio Donadoni, ed., *The Egyptians* (University of Chicago Press, 1997); and Ian Shaw and Paul Nicholson, *The Dictionary of Ancient Egypt* (Abrams, 1995). The position of women in Egyptian society is covered in Gay Robins, *Women in Ancient Egypt* (Harvard University Press, 1993); Barbara Patterson, *Women in Ancient Egypt* (St. Martin's Press, 1991); and Joyce Tyldesley, *Daughters of Isis: Women of Ancient Egypt* (Viking, 1994).

Selections of Egyptian literature are presented in John Foster, *Echoes of Egyptian Voices: An Anthology of Ancient Egyptian Poetry* (University of Oklahoma Press, 1992); R. B. Parkinson, trans. and ed., *Voices from Ancient Egypt: An Anthology of Middle Kingdom Writings* (University of Oklahoma Press, 1991); and Miriam Lichtheim, *Ancient Egyptian Literature*, 3 vols. (University of California Press, 1975).

The history of Nubia and the kingdom of Kush is examined in Derek Welsby, *The Kingdom of Kush* (Wiener, 1998); Stanley Burstein, ed., *Ancient African Civilizations: Kush and Axum* (Wiener, 1998); David O'Connor, *Ancient Nubia: Egypt's Rival in Africa* (University of Pennsylvania Press, 1993); P. L. Shinnie, *Ancient Nubia* (Kegan Paul, 1996); John Taylor, *Egypt and Nubia* (Harvard University Press, 1991); and William Y. Adams, *Nubia: Corridor to Africa* (Princeton University Press, 1977).

For Syrian art, see Harvey Weiss, ed., *Ebla to Damascus: Art and Architecture of Ancient Syria* (Smithsonian Institution, 1985). O. R. Gurney, *The Hittites*, 2nd ed. (Penguin, 1980) is an excellent work. See also Trevor Bryce, *The Kingdom of the Hittites* (Oxford University Press, 1998). Gerhard Herm, *The Phoenicians: The Purple Empire of the Ancient World*, trans. Caroline Hillier (Morrow, 1975), and Nancy K. Sandars, *The Sea Peoples: Warriors of the Ancient Mediterranean, 1250–1150 B.C.* (Thames & Hudson, 1978), are excellent accounts of the seafaring peoples of the Near East.

David J. Goldberg and John D. Rayner, *The Jewish People: Their History and Their Religion* (Viking, 1987), and Harry M. Orlinsky, *Ancient Israel* (Cornell University Press, 1960), are succinct overviews. Excellent longer surveys are Bernhard W. Anderson, *Understanding the Old Testament*, 4th ed. (Prentice Hall, 1986); Michael Grant, *The History of Ancient Israel* (Macmillan, 1984); and John Bright, *A History of Israel*, 3rd ed. (Westminster, 1981).

A. T. Olmstead's *History of Assyria* (Scribner, 1923) and *History of the Persian Empire* (Phoenix, 1948) are the standard accounts. See also Rustom Masani, *Zoroastrianism: The Religion of the Good Life* (Macmillan, 1968); Richard Frye, *The Heritage of Persia* (Mazda Publishing, 1993); and Jean-Louis Huot, *Persia: From the Origins to the Achaemenids* (World, 1965).

On ancient Near Eastern art and architecture, see Seton Lloyd, *The Art of the Ancient Near East* (Oxford University Press, 1961); Henri Frankfort, *The Art and Architecture of the Ancient Orient* (Penguin, 1978); Pierre Amiet, *Art of the Ancient Near East* (Abrams, 1980); and Ann C. Gunter, ed., *Investigating Artistic Environments in the Ancient Near East* (Smithsonian Institution, 1990).

For significant source readings, see James B. Pritchard, ed., *The Ancient Near East: An Anthology of Texts and Pictures* (Princeton University Press, 1958).

Suggestions for Web Browsing

Oriental Institute Virtual Museum
http://www.oi.uchicago.edu/OI/MUS/QTVR96/QTVR96.html

An integral part of the University of Chicago's Oriental Institute, the Oriental Institute Museum offers a virtual showcase of the history, art, and archaeology of the ancient Near East.

Life in Early Mesopotamia
http://www.hum.ku.dk/cni/mashnaqa/index.html

This site offers glimpses into a recent archaeological expedition to Tell Mashnaqa, a settlement nearly 7000 years old. Images of finds and of archaeologists at work.

Hammurabi
http://home.echo-on.net/~smithda/hammurabi.html

A short biography of Hammurabi, in addition to a discussion of the legal concepts he espoused in his code and a virtual recreation of the Hanging Gardens of Babylon.

Egyptian Museum
http://www.idsc.gov.eg/culture/egy_mus.htm

Web site of the Egyptian Museum in Cairo, highlighting images of accessories and jewelry, sculptures, furniture, mummies, and written documents of ancient Egypt from the museum's enormous collection.

Museums of the Vatican: Gregorian Egyptian Museum
http://christusrex.org/www1/vaticano/EG-Egiziano.html

The Vatican Museum's Egyptian Museum provides images and descriptions of many of the significant objects in one of the world's best ancient Egyptian museums.

Nubia: The Land Upriver
http://www.library.nwu.edu/class/history/B94/B94nubia.html

The geography and early history of the Nubian peoples, from prehistoric times to the kingdom of Kush.

Creative Impulse: Mesopotamia
http://history.evansville.net/meso.html

The University of Evansville's impressive site on all things about ancient Mesopotamia—images and documents on various aspects of Mesopotamia's ancient civilizations.

World Cultures: Mesopotamia and Persia
http://www.wsu.edu:8080/~dee/MESO/PERSIANS.HTM

This site gives valuable information on the influence of geography on early Persian civilization, reviews Persian military history, and discusses the importance of Persian religion.

Notes

1. "Gilgamesh and Agga," in Samuel N. Kramer, *The Sumerians: Their History, Culture, and Character* (Chicago: University of Chicago Press, 1971), pp. 187–190.
2. Henri Frankfort, *The Birth of Civilization in the Near East* (London: Williams & Norgate, 1951), p. 60.
3. "The Reforms of Urukagina," in Nels M. Bailkey, ed., *Readings in Ancient History: Thought and Experience from Gilgamesh to St. Augustine*, 4th ed. (Lexington, Mass.: Heath, 1992), p. 21.

4. Adam Falkenstein and W. von Soden, *Sumerische und Akkadische Hymnen und Gebete* (Zurich: Artemis-Verlag, 1953), p. 188. For a partial translation and full discussion of this text, see Samuel N. Kramer, *History Begins at Sumer* (Garden City, N.Y.: Doubleday/Anchor Books, 1959), pp. 228–232.

5. H. de Genouillac, trans., in *Revue d'Assyriologe* 25 (Paris, 1928), p. 148.

6. Quoted in Kramer, *History Begins at Sumer,* p. 53.

7. R. F. Harper, *The Code of Hammurabi* (Chicago: University of Chicago Press, 1904), p. 3.

8. Ibid., p. 101.

9. From *Epic of Gilgamesh,* trans. E. A. Speiser, in *Ancient Near Eastern Texts Relating to the Old Testament,* 2nd ed., ed. James B. Pritchard (Princeton, N.J.: Princeton University Press, 1955), p. 90.

10. Bailkey, *Readings in Ancient History,* p. 29.

11. Quoted in Sabatino Moscati, *The Face of the Ancient Orient* (Garden City, N.Y.: Doubleday/Anchor Books, 1962), p. 71.

12. Miriam Lichtheim, *Ancient Egyptian Literature,* Vol. 1 (Berkeley: University of California Press, 1975), pp. 141–142.

13. John A. Wilson, *The Burden of Egypt* (Chicago: University of Chicago Press, 1951), p. 117.

14. Ibid., p. 164.

15. Adolf Erman, *The Literature of the Ancient Egyptians,* trans. Aylward M. Blackman (London: Methuen, 1927), pp. 190, 196, 197.

16. "The Instruction of Meri-ka-Re," in Wilson, *The Burden of Egypt,* p. 120.

17. Ibid., p. 119.

18. Quoted in George Steindorff and George Hoyingen-Huene. *Egypt* (Locust Valley, N.Y.: Augustin, 1943), p. 23.

19. Bailkey, *Readings in Ancient History,* pp. 39–43.

20. George Steindorff and Keith E. Steel, *When Egypt Ruled the East* (Chicago: University of Chicago Press, 1942), p. 125.

21. Miriam Lichtheim, *Ancient Egyptian Literature,* Vol. 2 (Berkeley: University of California Press, 1975), pp. 96, 98.

22. O. R. Gurney, *The Hittites* (New York: Penguin, 1932), p. 172.

23. Bernhard W. Anderson, *Understanding the Old Testament,* 2nd ed. (Englewood Cliffs, N.J.: Prentice Hall, 1966), p. 559.

24. Daniel D. Luckenbill, *Ancient Records of Assyria and Babylonia,* Vol. 1 (Chicago: University of Chicago Press, 1926), p. 147.

25. Herodotus, *History of the Persian Wars,* 1.181.

26. Ibid., 9.122.

27. Ibid., 8.88.

3

The theater at Delphi, where the god Apollo was thought to speak to the Greeks by taking over the body of his priestess.

The Greek Achievement

Minoan, Mycenaean, Hellenic, and Hellenistic Civilizations

Chapter Contents

S carred by time, weather, and modern pollution, the ruins of the Athenian Acropolis today stand under a smog-laden sky and overlook the trees and buildings of a bustling modern city sprawled beneath. These ruins are striking symbols of a great civilization whose principal center was Athens.

In the fifth century B.C.E. the temples and statues of the Acropolis were new and gleaming, fresh from the hands of confident architects and sculptors. Five hundred years later, when Greece was a province of the Roman Empire, they still impressed the writer Plutarch:

The works . . . are wonderful; they were quickly created and they have lasted for ages. In beauty each one appeared venerable as soon as it was finished, but in freshness and vigor it looks even now new and lately built. They bloom with an eternal freshness that seems untouched by time, as though they had been inspired by an unfading spirit of youth.[1]

Today the Acropolis no longer appears to be "untouched by time"; yet for us no less than for Plutarch, ancient Athens and the civilization that was centered there has retained an "eternal freshness." Greece's accomplishments were to prove enduring. Its magnificent intellectual and artistic legacy would provide much of the cultural heritage of Western civilization. And when we look at the Greek experience as a whole—political, economic, social, religious, and cultural—we can see the great impact of the ancient Greeks on the development of civilization in the West.

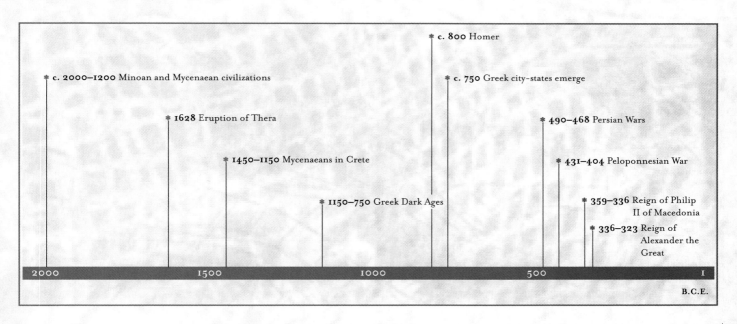

- c. 800 Homer
- c. 2000–1200 Minoan and Mycenaean civilizations
- c. 750 Greek city-states emerge
- 1628 Eruption of Thera
- 490–468 Persian Wars
- 1450–1150 Mycenaeans in Crete
- 431–404 Peloponnesian War
- 1150–750 Greek Dark Ages
- 359–336 Reign of Philip II of Macedonia
- 336–323 Reign of Alexander the Great

2000   1500   1000   500   I

B.C.E.

Minoan and Mycenaean Civilizations, c. 2000—1200 B.C.E.

Classical Greek civilization was preceded by two advanced cultures on the lands surrounding the Aegean Sea. Minoan civilization came into full flower about 2000 B.C.E.; Mycenaean civilization seems to have exerted its greatest power between 1450 and 1200 B.C.E. And both civilizations appear to have collapsed suddenly following 1200 B.C.E.

Preclassical Greece

c. 2000–1200 B.C.E.	Minoan and Mycenaean civilizations
1628 B.C.E.	Eruption of Thera
1450–1150 B.C.E.	Mycenaeans in Crete
1150–750 B.C.E.	Greek Dark Ages

The Minoans

The first of these early cultures of the Aegean area to develop is now referred to as Minoan, after the legendary King Minos of Crete. Crete was the center of Minoan civilization, which spread to the Aegean Islands, the coast of Asia Minor, and mainland Greece. A narrow, 160-mile-long island, Crete served as a stepping-stone between Europe, Asia, and Africa.

Stimulated by immigrants from Asia Minor and by economic and cultural contacts with Mesopotamia, Egypt, and more southern Africa, a brilliant civilization emerged here by 2000 B.C.E.

Minoan prosperity was based on large-scale trade that ranged from Sicily, Greece, and Asia Minor to Syria and Africa. The Minoans employed the first ships capable of long voyages over the open sea.

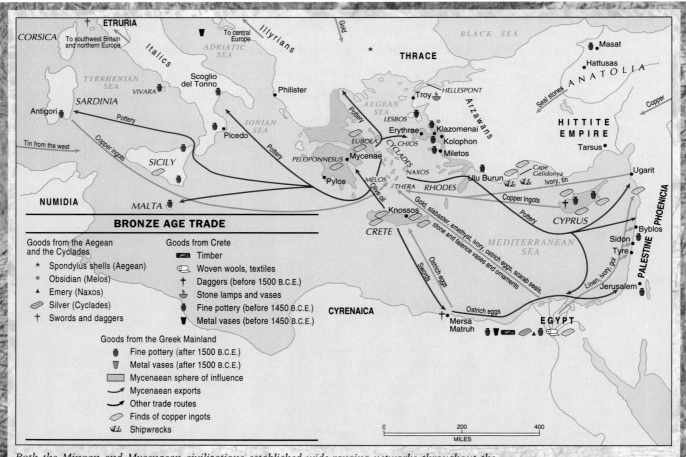

Both the Minoan and Mycenaean civilizations established wide-ranging networks throughout the Mediterranean. Evidence of trading contacts from as far away as Kush (south of Egypt) and Afghanistan has been found in Aegean Bronze Age archaeological sites.

Chief exports were olive oil, wine, metalware, and magnificent pottery. This trade was the monopoly of an efficient bureaucratic government under a powerful ruler whose administrative records were written on clay tablets, first in a form of picture writing (hieroglyphic) and later in a script known as Linear A, whose 87 signs represented syllables. As neither script has been deciphered, our knowledge of Minoan civilization is incomplete and imprecise; most of it is derived from the material remains—walls, temples, houses, and pottery and tablet fragments—uncovered by archaeologists.

The spectacular discoveries of the English archaeologist Sir Arthur Evans a century ago first brought to light this impressive civilization, whose existence had previously only been hinted at in the epics of Homer and in Greek legends such as that of the Minotaur, half bull and half man, who devoured young men and women sent as tribute from Greece. Between 1900 and 1905 Evans excavated the ruins of a great palace at Knossos, the dominant city in Crete after 1700 B.C.E. Rising at least three stories high and sprawling over nearly 6 acres, this "Palace of Minos," built of brick and limestone and employing unusual downward-tapering columns of wood, was a maze of royal apartments, storerooms, corridors, open courtyards, and broad stairways. Equipped with running water, the palace had a sanitation system that surpassed anything else constructed in Europe until Roman times. Walls were painted with elaborate frescoes in which the Minoans appear as a happy, peaceful people with a pronounced liking for dancing, festivals, and athletic contests. Women are shown enjoying a freedom and dignity unknown elsewhere in the ancient Near East or classical Greece. They are not secluded in the home but are seen sitting with men and taking an equal part in public festivities—even as athletes and bullfighters. Their dresses are very elaborate, with bright patterns and colors, pleats, puffed sleeves, and flounces. Bodices are open in front to the waist, and hair is elaborately fashioned with ringlets over the forehead and around the ears.

One of the most notable features of Minoan culture was its art, unrestrained and full of rhythmic motion. Art seems to have been an essential part of everyday life and not, as in the ancient Near East, an adjunct to religion and the state. What little is known of Minoan religion also contrasts sharply with other religious patterns in the Near East: there were no great temples, powerful priesthoods, or large cult statues of the gods. The principal deity was probably a Mother Goddess; her importance reflected the important position held by women in Minoan society. A number of recovered statuettes show her dressed like a fashionable Minoan woman with flounced skirts; a tightly laced, low-cut bodice; and elaborately arranged hair. She was perhaps the early inspiration for such later Greek goddesses as Athena, Demeter, and Aphrodite.

The Mycenaeans

About 2000 B.C.E. or shortly thereafter, the first Indo-European Greek tribes, collectively called Achaeans, entered Greece, where they absorbed the earlier settlers and ruled from fortified citadels at Mycenae, Pylos, Athens, and other sites in the south of Greece. By 1600 B.C.E. the Achaeans—or Mycenaeans, as they are usually called—had adopted much of the advanced culture of the Minoans. However, unlike the Minoans, the Mycenaeans seemed to have been a

The queen's chamber of the Palace of Minos at Knossos on Crete had walls decorated with frescoes of frolicking fish and dolphins.

In contrast to some of the rigid and grandiose Mesopotamian and Egyptian statues, those of the Minoans were small and animated. This little priestess holds snakes, possibly reflecting Minoan religious rituals.

more warlike people and sailed the seas as raiders as well as traders. Mycenaean women adopted Minoan fashions and added a variety of sumptuous jewelry, from bracelets to earrings.

Some of the wealth accumulated by the kings of Mycenae—the greatest single hoard of gold, silver, and ivory objects found anywhere before the discovery of Tutankhamen's tomb—was unearthed in 1876 by Heinrich Schliemann, a few years after his sensational discoveries at Troy. The royal palace on the acropolis, or citadel, of Mycenae had well-proportioned audience rooms and apartments, fresco-lined walls, floors of painted stucco, and large storerooms. Impressive also were the royal "beehive" tombs, constructed of cut stone and covered with earth, near the citadel.

The expansive force of Mycenaean civilization led to the planting of colonies in the eastern Mediterranean (Hittite sources refer to Achaeans in Asia Minor) and even to the conquest of Knossos about 1450

B.C.E. This Mycenaean takeover was made possible by the destruction of the mazelike palace at Knossos by fire, perhaps the aftermath of an earthquake. Minoan dominance in the Aegean and prosperity on Crete had already been lessened by the devastation caused by the catastrophic eruption of the volcanic island of Thera (modern Santorini), 80 miles north of Crete, and a massive tidal wave that may have struck the northern shore of the island at a height of nearly half a mile. Archaeologists and volcanologists now place this great eruption in 1628 B.C.E., but the resulting damage to structures, crops, and the merchant fleet of the Minoans may have contributed to making the civilization vulnerable to Mycenaean raids. The palace at Knossos was rebuilt by the Mycenaeans only to be destroyed about 1380 B.C.E. by earthquake and fire, and the center of civilization in the Aegean shifted to the Greek mainland.

Much about the specifics of Minoan-Mycenaean relations was unclear until after 1952, when a young English architect, Michael Ventris, startled the scholarly world by deciphering a late type of Minoan script known as Linear B, many examples of which had been found by Evans at Knossos and by later archaeologists at mainland Greek sites such as Pylos, Mycenae, and Thebes. When Linear B turned out to be an early form of Greek written in syllabic characters, it followed that the rulers of Knossos after 1450 B.C.E. must have been Achaean Greeks who had adopted the Minoan script to write their own language.

The Linear B texts, which are administrative documents and inventories, add greatly to our knowledge of Mycenaean life. The Mycenaean centers were fortified palaces and administrative offices and not, as in Crete, true cities. The bulk of the population lived in scattered villages where they worked either communal land or land held by nobles or kings. The nobles were under the close control of the kings, whose administrative records were kept daily by a large number of scribes. Prominent in these records are details of the disbursement of grain and wine as wages and the collection of taxes in kind. The most important item of income was olive oil, the major article in the wide-ranging Mycenaean trade, which was operated as a royal monopoly. Perhaps it was their role as merchant adventurers that led the Achaean kings about 1250 B.C.E. to launch an expedition against Troy to eliminate a powerful commercial rival.

Troy, Site of Homer's *Iliad*

The city of Troy occupied a strategic position on the Hellespont (the strait from the Aegean to the Black Sea, now known as the Dardanelles). In this location, Troy could command both sea traffic through the straits and land routes between Asia and Europe. For many years scholars thought this city existed only in the epic poems of Homer. Heinrich Schliemann (1822–1890), a German romantic dreamer and amateur archaeologist, believed otherwise. As a youth he had read Homer's *Iliad*, and he became firmly convinced that Troy had actually existed. At the age of 48, having made a fortune in the California gold rush and in worldwide trade, Schliemann retired from business to prove that his dreams of ancient Troy's existence were true.

In 1870 Schliemann began excavations at the legendary site of Troy, where he unearthed nine buried cities, built one on top of the other. He discovered a treasure of golden earrings, hairpins, and bracelets in the second city (Troy II), which led him to believe that this was the city of Homer's epics. Excavations in the 1930s, however, showed that Troy II had been destroyed about 2200 B.C.E., far too early to have been the scene of the Trojan War. Scholars now believe that Troy VI or VII was probably the city made famous by Homer.

Neither the view that Troy was the victim of commercial rivalry nor the other widely held theory that it was destroyed by Achaean pirates seeking wealth corresponds to Homer's view that the Trojan War was caused by the abduction of Helen, queen of Sparta, by the Trojan prince Paris. Led by Agamemnon, king of Mycenae, the wrathful Achaeans besieged Troy for ten long years. Homer's *Iliad* deals only with a few weeks during the tenth year of the siege.

The Fall of Mycenaean Civilization

Greek traditions recorded that around 1200 B.C.E. a new wave of Greek invaders, materially aided by weapons made of iron instead of bronze, invaded Greece from the north and conquered the Mycenaean strongholds. These newcomers may have followed in the wake of the devastation caused by raiding Sea Peoples (see Chapter 2); some archaeologists suggest that invasions of new peoples caused less damage to Mycenaean sites than did revolts of the lower classes against their powerful and autocratic overlords. First of the Mycenaean strongholds to fall was Pylos, whose Linear B archives contain numerous references to quickly undertaken preparations to meet military emergencies. We find orders directing women and children to places of safety; instructions to armorers, "rowers," and food suppliers; and a report titled "How the Watchers Are Guarding the Coastal Regions."[2] The preparations were in vain, however. Pylos was sacked and burned, and all of the other major Mycenaean citadels were likewise destroyed.

In 1876, when Heinrich Schliemann found this gold death mask at Mycenae, he excitedly telegraphed a friend: "I have looked upon the face of Agamemnon." The mask, however, dates from about 1500 B.C.E., nearly three centuries before the Trojan War, during which Agamemnon is said to have reigned.

The Rise of Hellenic Civilization, c. 1150–500 B.C.E.

The four centuries from around 1150 to 750 B.C.E., the Greek Dark Ages, were marked by drastic depopulation and the disappearance of the major characteristics of Mycenaean civilization—centralized and bureaucratic administration, wide-ranging commerce, sophisticated art forms, monumental architecture, and writing. Although the fall of Mycenaean civilization was a catastrophic event, the passing of the Mycenaeans eventually gave rise to the development of a new and different civilization, the Hellenic. Hellenic civilization derives its name from the Greek god Hellen, who is credited with bringing humans to first inhabit Greece (Greeks ancient and modern call their country Hellas).

The Influence of Geography

Geographical factors played an important part in shaping the events of Greek history. The numerous mountain ranges that crisscross the peninsula, which is about the size of the state of Maine, severely restricted internal communication and led to the development of fiercely independent city-states and the reluctance of the Greeks to unite into a single nation. The mountains cover two-thirds of the peninsula, and along the west coast they come close to the sea,

The Development of Hellenic Civilization

c. 1150–c. 750 B.C.E.	Greek "Dark Ages"
c. 800–750 B.C.E.	Establishment of the Greek *polis* (city-state)
c. 750–550 B.C.E.	Great age of Greek colonization
c. 650 B.C.E.	Age of Greek tyrants Helot revolt in Sparta
c. 600 B.C.E.	Coinage introduced in Greece
594 B.C.E.	Solon named sole archon in Athens
c. 560 B.C.E.	Pisistratus is tyrant in Athens
508–502 B.C.E.	Cleisthenes establishes democracy in Athens

leaving few harbors or arable plains. Elsewhere the deeply indented coast provides many natural harbors. A narrow isthmus at the Gulf of Corinth made southern Greece almost an island—in fact, it was called the Peloponnesus ("Pelop's island"). The jagged coastline and the many islands offshore stimulated seagoing trade, and the rocky soil (less than a fifth of Greece is arable) and few natural resources encouraged the Greeks to establish colonies abroad.

The Homeric Age

Most of our information about the Greek Dark Ages is derived from the epics put in written form around 750 B.C.E. and attributed to a supposedly blind Ionian poet named Homer. Controversy surrounds the question of Homer's existence and whether he alone or several poets composed the *Iliad* and the *Odyssey.* The Homeric epics retain something of the material side of the Mycenaean period, handed down to Homer's time by a continuous oral tradition. But in terms of the details of political, economic, and social life, the religious beliefs and practices, and the ideals that gave meaning to life, the poet could only describe what was familiar to him in his own age, probably soon after 800 B.C.E.

The values held by Homer to give meaning to life in the Homeric Age were predominantly heroic values—the strength, skill, and valor of the dominating warrior. Such was the earliest meaning of *aretē*, "excellence" or "virtue," a key term whose meaning changed as values changed during the course of Greek culture. To obtain *aretē*—defined by one

Homeric hero as "to fight ever in the forefront and outdo my companions"—and the undying fame that was its reward, men welcomed hardship, struggle, and even death. Honor, like fame, was a measure of *aretē*, and the greatest of human tragedies was the denial of honor due to a great warrior. Homer makes such a denial the theme of the *Iliad:* "The ruinous wrath of Achilles that brought countless ills upon the Achaeans" when Achilles, insulted by Agamemnon, withdraws from battle.

The Homeric king was essentially a war leader, hardly more than a leader among his companions, fellow nobles who sat in his council to advise him and to check any attempt he might make to exercise arbitrary power. There was also a popular assembly of all arms-bearing men, whose consent was needed whenever a crisis occurred, such as war or the election of a new king.

Society was clearly aristocratic—only the *aristoi* ("best") possessed *aretē*—and the common man was reprimanded and beaten when he dared to question his superiors. Yet the commoners had certain political rights as members of the popular assembly.

The economy was a simple, self-sufficient agricultural system in which private ownership of land replaced the collective group ownership of Mycenaean times. One Homeric hero states that as a reward for leadership and heroism, he holds "a large estate by the banks of the river Zanthus, fair with orchard lawns and wheat-growing land."[3] The Greek word for "large estate" is *temenos*, a "cutting," which apparently indicates that the estate had been "cut out" of the common land.

From Oligarchy to Tyranny

The *polis*, or city-state—the political unit consisting of the city and its people—did not exist in the Greek Dark Ages. The nucleus of every polis was the high, fortified site, the *acropolis*, where people could take refuge from attack. In time this defensive center took on added significance as the focus of political and religious life. When commerce revived in the eighth and seventh centuries B.C.E., a trading center (*agora*) developed below the acropolis. The two areas and the surrounding territory, usually smaller than a modern county, formed the polis (the plural is *poleis*), from which our word *politics* is derived.

The political development of the polis was so rich and varied that it is difficult to think of a form of government not experienced—and given a lasting name—by the Greeks: monarchy, oligarchy, tyranny, and democracy.

By the middle of the eighth century B.C.E., the nobles, who wished to share in the authority exercised by monarchs, had taken over the government of most city-states, ushering in an age of aristocracy ("govern-

Greek civilization flourished in the mountainous lands of the eastern Mediterranean. Mainland Greece lacked arable land and navigable rivers, but its extensive coastline and fine harbors drew the Greeks to the sea for sustenance and commerce.

ment by the best") or oligarchy ("government by the few," a limited number of aristocrats). Exercising their superior power, the nobles in many locations abolished the popular assembly, acquired a monopoly of the best land, reduced many commoners to virtual serfdom, and forced others to seek a living on rocky, barren soil.

The hard lot of common people under aristocracy or oligarchy is recorded in the poet Hesiod's *Works and Days* (c. 700 B.C.E.). A commoner who had been cheated out of his parcel of land by his evil brother in league with "bribe-swallowing" aristocratic judges, Hesiod was the prophet of a moralized conception of the gods and a new age of social justice. To establish a just society, Hesiod argued, people must learn to pursue moderation (*sophrosyne*) in all things—apparently the first written expression of this famous Greek ideal—and realize that "far-seeing" Zeus and the other gods punish evildoers and reward the righteous. In contrast to Homer, with his aristocratic heroes, Hesiod defined human excellence, or *arete*, in a way to make it attainable by common people. Its essential ingredients were righteousness and

work—honest work in competition with one's fellows being a desirable goal. "Gods and men hate him who lives without work," Hesiod insisted. "His nature is like the drones who sit idle and eat the labor of the bees." Furthermore, "work is no shame, but idleness is a shame," and "esteem," "glory," and "riches" follow work.[4]

Hesiod's newly written ideals of moderation and justice were slow to take root. Often the poor found relief only by emigrating overseas. As Plato later noted, the wealthy promoted colonization as a safety valve to ward off a threatened political and economic explosion:

> *When men who have nothing, and are in want of food, show a disposition to follow their leaders in an attack on the property of the rich—these, who are the natural plague of the state, are sent away by the legislator in a friendly spirit as far as he is able; and this dismissal of them is euphemistically termed a colony.*[5]

From 750 to 550 B.C.E. the Greeks planted colonies throughout much of the Mediterranean world. Colonies were founded along the northern coast of the Aegean and around the Black Sea. So many Greeks migrated to southern Italy and eastern Sicily that the region became known as *Magna Graecia*, Great Greece. Colonies were also founded as far west as present-day France—at Massilia (modern Marseilles), for example—and Spain and on parts of the African coast. Unique was Naucratis in Egypt, not a true colony but a trading post whose residents gained extraterritorial rights (their own magistrates and law courts) from the Egyptians.

In time colonization lessened some of Greece's economic and social problems. By 600 B.C.E. economic progress and the use of coined money, probably inspired by the Lydians, had created the beginnings of a middle class. The Greek poleis gradually became "industrialized" as a result of concentrating on the production of specialized goods—vases, metal products, textiles, olive oil, and wine—for export in exchange for food and raw materials. But before this economic revolution was completed, the continuing land hunger of the poor and landless contributed to a political revolution.

After 650 B.C.E. rulers known as *tyrants* seized power in many Greek states and, supported by both the desperately poor and the rising merchant classes, took the reins of government from the nobility. They were supported also by a new heavily armed infantry force (the hoplite phalanx), composed of middle-class citizens wealthy enough to furnish their own equipment. These tyrants (the word meant simply "one who usurps power" and did not at first have to-day's connotation of brutality) sometimes distributed land to the landless poor and, by promoting further colonization, trade, and industry, increased economic development and generally made their poleis better places to live for all residents.

Athens to 500 B.C.E.

Athens and Sparta, the two city-states destined to dominate the political history of Greece during the classical period (the fifth century B.C.E. and most of the fourth), underwent markedly different courses of development during the period prior to 500 B.C.E. Whereas the political, economic, and social evolution of Athens was typical of most Greek states, Sparta's development produced a unique way of life that elicited the wonder and often the admiration of other Greeks.

In Athens during the seventh century B.C.E., the council of nobles became supreme. The popular assembly rarely met, and the king's authority was replaced by that of nine magistrates, called *archons* ("rulers"), chosen annually by the aristocratic council to exercise the king's civil, military, and religious powers. While the nobles on their large estates prospered, the small farmers and sharecroppers suffered. Bad years forced them to borrow seed from their rich neighbors, and when they were unable to repay their debts, they were sold into slavery. To the small farmers' clamor for the cancellation of debts and the end to debt slavery was added the voice of the landless for the redistribution of land.

A sixth-century B.C.E. oil container produced in Corinth. Corinthian pottery was the most popular of all such work for over 200 years, and many examples of it are found throughout the Mediterranean region.

When the Athenian nobles finally realized that their failure to address the cry for reform might result in the rise of a tyrant, they agreed to the policy of compromise advocated by the aristocrat Solon. In 594 B.C.E. Solon was made sole archon, with broad authority to revise the constitution of Athens in order to avoid class conflict. Inspired by the ideals of moderation and justice promoted by Hesiod a century earlier, Solon instituted middle-of-the-road reforms that have made his name a byword for wise statesmanship.

For the lower classes, Solon agreed to canceling all debts and forbidding future debt slavery, but he rejected as too radical the demand for the redivision of the land. His long-range solution to the economic problem was to seek full employment by stimulating trade and industry. To achieve this goal, Solon required fathers to teach their sons a trade, granted citizenship to foreign artisans and merchants who settled in Athens, and encouraged the intensive production of wine and olive oil for export.

Moderation also characterized Solon's political reforms—the common people were granted important political rights, but not complete equality. Although laws continued to originate in the new aristocratic Council of Four Hundred, they now had to be ratified by the popular assembly, which Solon revived. And since wealth, not birth, became the qualification for membership in the new council and for the archonships, wealthy commoners could acquire full political equality. Furthermore, the assembly could now act as a court to hear appeals from the decisions of the archons and to try the archons for misdeeds in office.

Unfortunately, Solon's moderate reforms did not completely satisfy the rich or the poor. The poor had received neither land nor full political equality, while the nobles thought Solon a radical who had betrayed his class. Deeply discouraged, Solon described what is too often the lot of moderate reformers: "Formerly their eyes sparkled when they saw me; now they coldly scorn me, no longer friends but enemies."[6]

Solon had warned the Athenians to accept his reforms unless "the people in its ignorance comes into the power of a tyrant." He lived to see his prediction fulfilled. In 560 B.C.E., after a period of anarchy, Pisistratus, a military hero and champion of the commoners, seized power as tyrant. He addressed the economic problem by banishing many nobles, whose lands he distributed among the poor, and by promoting commerce and industry. Together with extensive public works and the patronage of culture—starting Athens on the road to cultural leadership in Greece—these reforms gave rise to a popular saying that "life under Pisistratus was paradise on earth."

Pisistratus was succeeded by his two sons, one of whom was assassinated and the other exiled after he became tyrannical in the modern sense of the word. When the nobles, aided by a Spartan army, took the opportunity to restore aristocracy, a noble named Cleisthenes temporarily seized power and resisted Spartan interference. From 508 to 502 B.C.E. Cleisthenes put through constitutional reforms that greatly reduced the remaining power of the nobility. He disregarded the old noble-dominated tribes and created ten new ones, each embracing citizens of all classes from widely scattered districts. The popular assembly soon acquired the right to initiate legislation and became the sovereign power in the state; there could be no appeal from its decisions. The new democratic Council of Five Hundred, selected by lot from the ten tribes, advised the assembly and supervised the administrative actions of the archons. Cleisthenes' final reform was the peculiar institution of *ostracism*, an annual referendum in which a quorum of citizens could vote to exile for ten years any individual thought to be a threat to the new Athenian democracy. (A quorum consisted of 6000 of the 50,000 male citizens over the age of 18. The average attendance at an Athenian assembly, whose ordinary meetings were held every ten days, was about 5000.) By 500 B.C.E. the Athenian polis had established a form of democratic government more thorough than in any other city in the ancient world.

Sparta to 500 B.C.E.

Like many other Greek city-states, Sparta had moved from monarchy to oligarchy when the nobles installed five annual aristocratic magistrates, called *ephors* ("overseers"), to supervise the kings' activities. Instead of sending out colonists to solve the common problems of overpopulation and land hunger, the Spartan oligarchs turned to a simpler solution: the conquest of their Greek neighbors in Messenia, who were forced to become state slaves *(helots)*. Around 650 B.C.E., however, the Messenians revolted, and it took nearly 20 years to crush the uprising, during which the aristocrats were forced to seek the aid of the Spartan commoners. In return, the nobles agreed to the commoners' demand for land division and political equality. Private ownership of land was abolished, and the land was divided equally among the 9000 Spartan citizens. In addition, the nobles established a popular assembly of all Spartan citizens with the right to elect the ephors and to approve or veto the proposals of the 30-member Council of Elders. While the Athenian state required only two years of military training for young men, the Spartan system—traditionally attributed to a legendary lawgiver named Lycurgus—was designed to make every Spartan man a professional soldier and to keep him in a constant state of readiness for war, especially the ever-present danger of a helot revolt. To this end,

No Adulterers in Sparta

Adultery was regarded among them as an impossible crime. A story is told of a very old Spartan named Geradas, who, when asked by a stranger what was done to adulterers in Sparta, answered, "Stranger, there are no adulterers among us." "And if there were one?" asked the stranger. "Then," said Geradas, "he would have to pay as compensation a bull big enough to stand on Mount Taygetus and drink from the river Eurotas." The stranger, astonished, asked, "Where can you find so big a bull?" "Where can you find an adulterer in Sparta?" answered Geradas.

From Plutarch, *Lives*, "Lycurgus," 15.

Sparta's totalitarian state enforced absolute subordination of the individual to its will.

State officials examined all newborn children, and any found sickly or deformed were abandoned to die. At the age of 7 a boy was taken from his family and placed in the charge of state educators, who taught him to bear hardship, endure discipline, and devote his life to the state. At 20 the young Spartan enrolled in the army and lived in barracks, where he contributed food from his allotment of land granted by the state and worked by helots. At 30 he was allowed to marry, but he continued to live in barracks, sneaking back to visit his wife only at night. Finally, at 60, he was released from the army and could live at home with his family.

This lifelong discipline produced formidable soldiers and inspired them with the spirit of obedience and respect for Spartan law. Plutarch reports in his biography of Lycurgus that Spartan training "accustomed the citizens to have neither the will nor the ability to lead a private life, but, like bees, to be organic parts of their community, clinging together around their leader, forgetting themselves in their enthusiastic patriotism, and belonging wholly to their country."[7]

Although many Greeks admired the Spartan way of life, the typical Spartan was an unsophisticated, uncultured fighting machine who exaggerated his masculinity, took few baths, and spoke few words. According to Plutarch, "When one of them was invited to hear a man imitate a nightingale, he answered, 'I have heard the original.'" Plutarch's description of their marriages is equally revealing:

Their marriage custom was for the husband to carry off his bride by force. They did not carry off little immature girls, but grown-up women who were ripe for marriage. After the bride had been carried off, . . . the bridegroom . . . comes into the room, unties her girdle, and takes her to himself. After spending a short time with her, he returns composedly to his usual quarters to sleep with the other young men. And so he continues afterwards, passing his days with his companions and visiting his wife by stealth, feeling ashamed and afraid that some one in the house might hear him. . . . This went on for a long time, and some even had children born to them before they ever saw their wives by daylight.[8]

Spartan girls also received state training in order to become healthy mothers of warrior sons. Clad in short tunics, which other Greeks thought immodest, they engaged in running, wrestling, and throwing the discus and javelin. As their men marched off to war, Spartan women bade them a laconic farewell (Laconia was the Spartan homeland): "Come back *with* your shield—or *on* it." Plutarch also reports that the Spartans

did away with all seclusion and retirement for women, and ordained that girls, no less than boys, should go naked in processions, and dance and sing at festivals in the presence of the young men. . . . This nakedness of the maidens had in it nothing disgraceful. It was done modestly, not licentiously, and it produced habits of simplicity and taught them to desire good health and beauty of body, and to love honor and courage no less than the men. This it was that made them speak and think as Gorgo, the wife of Leonidas, is said to have done. Some foreign lady, it seems, said to her, "You Spartan women are the only ones who rule men." She answered, "Yes, for we are the only ones who give birth to men."[9]

While Sparta developed the finest military machine in Greece, it remained backward culturally and economically. Trade and travel were prohibited because the city fathers feared that foreign ideas might threaten Spartan discipline. Sparta is a classic example of how intellectual stagnation accompanies rigid social conformity and military regimentation.

To provide additional assurance that its helots remained uncontaminated by democratic ideas, Sparta allied itself with oligarchic parties in other Peloponnesian states and aided them in suppressing their democratic opponents. The resulting Spartan League of oligarchic states, in operation by the end of the

Bronze statuette of a Spartan girl exercising (c. 500 B.C.E.).

sixth century B.C.E., was shortly to be opposed by an Athenian-led union of democratic states.

Unity and Strife in the Hellenic World, 500–336 B.C.E.

The leaders of a Greek economic and cultural revival after 750 B.C.E. were the Ionian Greeks, descendants of Mycenaeans who had fled the so-called Dorian invaders and settled the Aegean coast of Asia Minor, its offshore islands, and the mainland region of Attica, whose major city was Athens. Influenced by contacts with Phoenician traders (from whom they borrowed the alphabet in the eighth century B.C.E.) and neighboring Lydia and Egypt, the Ionians became innovators in art, science, philosophy, and literature; they were said to have "first kindled the torch of Hellenism." Ionian creativity was also evident in their commercial ventures, which spread throughout the Aegean region. It was especially because of their economic prosperity that they became the first of the Greeks to face threats from the great powers of the Near East.

The Persian Wars

When the Persians conquered Lydia in 547 B.C.E., they also took over Ionia, which had been under moderate Lydian rule. In open opposition to their Persian-appointed tyrants, the Ionian cities revolted in 499 B.C.E., established democratic regimes, and appealed to the Athenians, who were also Ionians, for aid. Athens sent 20 ships—token help, but far too few to prevail over the Persians. By 494 B.C.E. the Persian king Darius I had crushed the revolt, burning the Greek polis of Miletus in revenge.

Darius knew that Ionia was insecure as long as Athens remained free to incite the Ionian Greeks to revolt again. Thus in 490 B.C.E. a Persian force of about 20,000 infantry and cavalry sailed across the Aegean, conquering Greek island states in their path, and finally encamped on the plain of Marathon near Athens. Darius's aim of forcing the Athenians to accept the exiled son of Pisistratus as a pro-Persian tyrant was ended when the Athenian army, half the size of the Persian, won an overwhelming victory, slaying 6400 of the invaders while losing only 192.

The battle of Marathon was one of the most decisive in history. It destroyed the belief in Persian invincibility and demonstrated, according to the Greek historian Herodotus, that "free men fight better than slaves." Ten years later the Greeks were forced to prepare for a new Persian invasion under Xerxes, Darius's successor, whose objective was the subjection of all of Greece. Athens now had 200 warships, the largest fleet in Greece, and Sparta had agreed to head a defensive alliance of 31 states.

The Persian army was too huge to be transported by ship. Crossing the swift-flowing, mile-wide Hellespont near Troy on two pontoon bridges—a notable feat of engineering—the army marched along the Aegean coast accompanied by a great fleet carrying provisions. The Spartans wanted to abandon all of Greece except the Peloponnesus to the invaders but finally agreed to a holding action at the narrow pass of Thermopylae. Here 300 Spartans and a few

Persian Wars

before c. 540 B.C.E.	Persian control of Greek cities in Asia Minor
499–495 B.C.E.	Rebellion of Greek cities in Asia Minor
490 B.C.E.	Battle of Marathon
480–479 B.C.E.	Xerxes' invasion of Greece
480 B.C.E.	Battles of Thermopylae and Salamis
479 B.C.E.	Battles of Plataea

All of the eastern Mediterranean became involved in the war between Athens and Sparta. The Spartans, surrounded by Athens's growing power, concluded that they had to go to war to prevent eventual Athenian dominance.

thousand other Greeks held back the Persians for three days until the Persians discovered a mountain path to the rear of the Greek position. The Spartans fought magnificently until all were slain, together with 700 other Greeks. The Spartan dead were immortalized on a monument erected at the pass: "Go tell the Spartans, you who pass us by, that here, obedient to their laws, we lie."

The Persians then sacked Athens, whose inhabitants had been evacuated, for they placed their faith in "wooden walls"—their fleet. Their faith was not misplaced; in the Bay of Salamis the Greek fleet, largely Athenian, turned the tide of victory with the shout: "On, sons of the Greeks! Set free your country, set your children free, your wives, the temples of your country's gods, your fathers' tombs; now they are all at stake." With 200 of his 350 ships destroyed and his lines of communication cut, Xerxes had no alternative but to retreat to Asia, although he left a strong force in Greece. The following summer (479 B.C.E.) the Greek army, with the Spartan army in the forefront, defeated the Persian force at Plataea, and Greece was for the time being safe from invasion.

Culmination of Athenian Democracy

The part they played in the Greek victory over the mighty Persian Empire exhilarated the Athenians and gave them the confidence and energy that made them the leaders of the Greek world during most of the remainder of the fifth century B.C.E. During this period, known as the Golden Age of Greece, the Athenians "attempted more and achieved more in a wider variety of fields than any nation great or small has ever attempted or achieved in a similar space of time."[10]

For more than 30 years (461–429 B.C.E.) during this period, the great statesman Pericles guided Athenian policy. In Pericles' time actual executive power no longer resided in the archons, who were chosen by lot, but in a board of ten elected generals. The generals urged the popular assembly to adopt specific measures, and the success or failure of their policies determined whether they would be reelected at the end of their annual term. Pericles failed in re-election only once, and so great was his influence on the Athenians that, in the words of his contemporary, the historian Thucydides, "what was in name a democracy was virtually a government by its greatest citizen."[11]

To enable even the poorest citizen to participate in government, Pericles extended payment to jurors (a panel of 6000 citizens chosen annually by lot) and to members of the assembly. Although his conservative opponents called this political bribery, Pericles insisted that it was essential to the success of democracy:

> Our constitution is named a democracy, because it is in the hands not of the few but of the many. . . . [Athenians] do not allow absorption in their own various affairs to interfere with their knowledge of the city's. We differ from other states in regarding the man who holds aloof from public life not as "quiet" but as useless; we decide or debate, carefully and in person, all matters of policy, holding, not that words and deeds go ill together, but that acts are foredoomed to failure when undertaken undiscussed."[12]

Athenian Society

The majority of the inhabitants of Athens, however, were not recognized as participating citizens. Women, slaves, and resident aliens were denied citizenship and had no voice in the government. Legally, women were first the property of their fathers and then of their husbands. They could not possess property in their own name or, as the law expressly stated, "make a contract about anything worth more than a bushel of barley."

Athens was distinctly a man's world. A wife's function was to bear children and manage the home, where she was restricted to the women's quarters when her husband entertained his friends. Men did not marry until they were about 30, and they usually married girls half their age. Marriages were normally arranged by the families, and prospective brides and bridegrooms seldom met before their marriage was arranged. Families were rather small, and infanticide, usually by exposure, of unwanted infants (especially girls) was practiced as a primitive form of population control. The average life expectancy was little more than 30 years, but if one were able to survive childhood, a longer life could be anticipated.

Athenian society allowed a double moral standard, and the sexual activity of a husband outside of marriage was not a matter for negative public comment. An acceptable social institution intended to serve the needs and desires of upper-class Athenian men was that of the female "companions" *(hetaerae)*. They were normally resident aliens and therefore not subject to the social restrictions imposed on Athenian women. A few of the *hetaerae*, such as Aspasia, the mistress and later wife of Pericles, were cultivated women who entertained at gatherings frequented by Athenian political and cultural leaders. Generally speaking, however, champions of the social emancipation of Athenian women were almost nonexistent, and the women themselves accepted their status. Aside from a few cases in which wives murdered their husbands (usually by poison), married life seems to have been stable and peaceful. Attic (Athenian) gravestones in particular attest to the love spouses felt for one another. The tie to their children was strong, and the community set high store by the honor owed by sons and daughters to their parents.

Homosexuality was an acceptable form of social conduct for Athenian men during certain periods of their lives. A sexual relationship between a mature man and a young boy just before the youth attained puberty was common practice. This relationship was viewed as pedagogical—a rite of initiation into adult society—and such relationships were most common among Athenian soldiers. However, male homosexuality that continued into the years when Athenians were expected to marry and produce children, as well as homosexual prostitution at any time, was not socially acceptable. Such relationships were regarded as unnatural, and the Athenian government issued strong legal prohibitions against them.

In fifth-century Athens it is estimated that one out of every four persons was a slave. Some were war captives and others were children of slaves, but most came from outside Greece through slave dealers. No large slave gangs were employed on plantations, as they were on later Roman estates and state labor projects. Small landowners owned one or more slaves, who worked in the fields alongside their masters. Those who owned many slaves—one rich Athenian owned a thousand—hired them out to private individuals or to the state, where they worked beside Athenian citizens and received the same wages.

Other slaves were taught a trade and set up in business. They were allowed to keep one-sixth of their wages, and many of them were able to purchase their freedom. Although a very few voices argued that slavery was contrary to nature and that all people were equal, the Greek world as a whole agreed with Aristotle that some people—non-Greeks in particular—were incapable of full human reason; thus they were by nature slaves who needed the guidance of a master.

Athenian Imperialism

The Greek victory over Persia had been made possible by a temporary cooperation of leading Greek city-states, but that unity quickly dissolved after the war when Sparta, fearful of helot rebellion at home, recalled its troops and resumed its policy of isolation. Because the Persians still ruled the Ionian cities and another invasion of Greece seemed possible, Athens in 478 B.C.E. invited the city-states bordering the Aegean to form a defensive alliance called the Delian League. To maintain a 200-ship navy that would police the seas, each state was assessed ships or money in proportion to its wealth. From the beginning, Athens dominated the league. Since almost all of the 173 member states paid their assessments in money, which Athens was eager to collect, the Athenians furnished the necessary ships by building them to Athenian specifications in Athenian harbors, with cash collected from their allies.

By 468 B.C.E., after the Ionian cities had been set free and the Persian fleet had been destroyed, various league members thought it unnecessary to continue league membership. In putting down all attempts to withdraw from the league, the Athenians were motivated to a certain extent by the fear that the Persian danger still existed but mainly by the desire to maintain and protect the large free trade area necessary for Greek—and especially Athenian—commerce and industry. The Athenians created an empire because they dared not disband the Delian League. By aiding in the suppression of local aristocratic factions within its subject states and at times imposing democratic governments on the allied states, Athens both eased the task of controlling its empire and emerged as the leader of a union of democratic states.

To many Greeks—above all to the members of the oligarchic Spartan League and the suppressed aristocratic factions within the Athenian Empire—Athens had become a "tyrant city" and an "enslaver of Greek liberties." Pericles, however, justified Athenian imperialism on the grounds that it brought "freedom"—freedom from fear and want to the Greek world:

> We secure our friends not by accepting favors but by doing them. . . . We are alone among mankind in doing men benefits, not on calculations of self-interest, but in the fearless confidence of freedom. In a word, I claim that our city as a whole is an education to Greece.[13]

The Peloponnesian War

In 431 B.C.E. the Peloponnesian War broke out between the Spartan League and the Athenian Empire. Although commercial rivalry between Athens and Sparta's major ally, Corinth, was an important factor, the conflict is a classic example of how fear can generate a war unwanted by either side. The contemporary historian Thucydides wrote, "The real but unavowed cause I consider to have been the growth of the power of Athens, and the alarm which it inspired in Lacedaemon [Sparta]; this made war inevitable."[14] Several incidents served to ignite the underlying tension, and Sparta finally felt it necessary to declare war on the "aggressors."

Sparta's hope for victory lay in its army's ability to besiege Athens and destroy the crops in the Athenian countryside. Pericles, for his part, relied on Athens's unrivaled navy to import sufficient food and to harass its enemies' coasts. Fate took a hand in this game, however. In the second year of the war a plague, probably an outbreak of typhus, killed a third of the Athenian population, including Pericles. His death was a great blow to Athens, for leadership of the government passed to leaders of lesser vision and talent. In the words of Thucydides:

> Pericles, by his rank, ability, and known integrity, was able to exercise an independent control over the masses—to lead them instead of being led by them. . . . With his successors it was different. More on a level with one another, and each grasping at supremacy, they ended by committing even the conduct of state affairs to the whims of the multitude. This, as might have been expected in a great imperial state, produced a host of blunders.[15]

These blunders would lead Thucydides to conclude that "a democracy is incapable of [running an] empire."[16]

Eight more years of indecisive warfare ended in 421 B.C.E. with a compromise peace. During the succeeding period Athenian imperialism manifested itself in its worst form through the actions of Pericles' less able successors. In 416 B.C.E. an expedition embarked for Melos, a neutral Aegean island, to force it to join the Athenian Empire. Thucydides reports the Athenian argument used to justify their obvious imperialism:

> We believe that Heaven, and we know that men, by a natural law, always rule where they are stronger. We did not make that law, nor were we the first to act on it; we found it existing, and it will exist forever, after we are gone; and we know that you and anyone else as strong as we are would do as we do.[17]

The Athenians executed all Melians of military age and sold the women and children into slavery.

The war was resumed in 415 B.C.E. with an Athenian expedition against Syracuse, the major Greek state in Sicily, that ended in complete disaster. Acting on the invitation of states that feared Syracusan expansion, the Athenians hoped to add Sicily to their empire and so become powerful enough "to rule the whole of the Greek world."[18] But bad luck and incompetent leadership resulted in the destruction of two Athenian fleets and a large army by the Syracusans, who were also supported by Sparta. The war dragged on until 404 B.C.E., when Athens capitulated after its last fleet was destroyed by a Spartan fleet built with money received from Persia in exchange for possession of the Greek cities in Ionia. At home, Athens had been weakened by the plots and schemes of oligarchic politicians to whom Sparta now turned over the government. The once great city-state was also stripped of its empire, its fleet, the defense walls that led to the port, and its army and navy.

Aftermath of the War

Anarchy and depression were the political and economic legacies of the Peloponnesian War. Having ended the "tyranny" of Athens over Greece, the Spartans substituted their own form of rule that made the Athenian Empire's seem mild in comparison. Everywhere democracies were replaced by oligarchies supported by Spartan troops. The bloody regimes of these unimaginative oligarchs soon led to successful democratic revolutions at Athens and elsewhere. As one of their generals admitted, the Spartans did not know how to govern free people. Incessant warfare between a bewildering series of shifting alliances became typical of the fourth century B.C.E. Some alliances were even financed by Persia, which wanted to keep Greece disunited and weak.

Political instability in turn contributed to the economic and social ills that plagued Greece during this period. Commerce and industry lagged, and the unemployed who did not go abroad as soldiers of fortune supported authoritarian leaders and their radical schemes for the redivision of wealth. The wealthy, for their part, became increasingly reactionary and uncompromising. Most intellectuals—including Plato and Aristotle—lost faith in democracy and joined with the wealthy in looking for "a champion powerful in action" who would bring order and security to Greece. They found him, finally, in the person of the king of Macedonia.

The Macedonian Unification of Greece

To the north of Greece lay Macedonia, inhabited by hardy peasants, powerful nobles, and weak kings who were related to the Greeks. Macedonia had just emerged as a centralized, powerful state under their young and brilliant King Philip II (359–336 B.C.E.), who created the most formidable army yet known by joining the well-trained Macedonian cavalry of nobles with the hoplite infantry used by the Greeks. In his youth, Philip had been a hostage at Thebes, where he acquired an appreciation of Greek culture, an understanding of Greek political weakness, and a desire to win for Macedonia a place of honor in the Hellenic world. After unifying all of his home country—including a string of Greek colonies that had been established along its coast during the earlier centuries of Macedonia's weakness—Philip turned to the Greek city-states, whose wars afforded him the opportunity first to intervene and then to dominate.

Forensic facial reconstruction of Philip II, father of Alexander the Great, based on remains of his skull found in his tomb in Macedonia. The king had suffered an arrow wound to the eye during battle.

Demosthenes, a great Athenian orator and champion of democracy, warned in vain that "democracies and dictators cannot exist together" and urged the Athenians and other Greeks to stop Philip before it was too late. Ultimately, Athens and Thebes did act to stop Philip's advance, but their combined forces were shattered at Chaeronea in 338 B.C.E. Philip then forced the Greeks to form a league in which each state, while retaining self-government, swore to "make war upon him who violates the general peace" and to furnish Philip with men and supplies for a campaign against Persia. Two years later, before setting out for Asia Minor, Philip was assassinated by a noble with a personal grudge, leaving the war against Persia as a legacy for his gifted son Alexander.

Incapable of finding a solution to the anarchy that tore their world to shreds, the Greeks ended as political failures and at the mercy of a great outside power, first Macedonia and later Rome. They retained their cultural leadership, however, and the culture of the new Hellenistic Age and its successor, the world of Rome, was to be largely Greek.

The Greek Genius

The Greeks were the first to formulate many of the Western world's fundamental concepts in politics, philosophy, science, and art. How was it that a relatively small number of people could leave such a great legacy to later civilizations? The definitive answer may always elude historians, but a good part of the explanation may lie in environmental and social factors.

Unlike the Near Eastern monarchies, the polis was not governed by a "divine" ruler, nor were the thoughts and activities of its citizens limited by powerful priesthoods. Many Greeks, and most notably the Athenians, were fond of good conversation and loved debate and argument. As late as the first century C.E., St. Paul was welcomed by the Athenians because they "liked to spend all their time telling and listening to the latest new thing" (Acts 17:21).

The Greek Character

The Greeks felt a need to discover order and meaning both in nature and in human life. This outlook pro-duced exceptional results in science, philosophy, and the arts. Beginning with Hesiod, the Greeks stressed the virtue of *sophrosynē* (moderation, self-control) as the key to happiness and fulfillment in life. Its opposite was *hubris*, meaning pride, arrogance, and unbridled ambition. The result of human excess and the basic cause of personal misfortune and social injustice, hubris invariably provoked *nemesis*, or retribution. According to the Greeks, an unavoidable law would cause the downfall or disgrace of anyone guilty of hubris. The Athenian dramatists employed this theme in their tragedies, and Herodotus attributed the Persian defeat by the Greeks to Xerxes' overpowering pride, for "Zeus tolerates pride in none but himself."[19]

The Greeks had all the human frailties and failings—at times they were irrational, vindictive, and cruel. But at their best they were guided by the ideals that permeate their intellectual and artistic legacy. The philosopher Protagoras is credited with the statement, "Man is the measure of all things"—a saying that sums up the humanistic character of Greek thought and art.

Greek Religious Development

Early Greek religion, like almost all early religious expressions, abounded in gods and goddesses who personified the forces of nature. Zeus, sky-god and wielder of thunderbolts, ruled the world from Mount Olympus in nearby Thessaly with the aid of lesser deities, many of whom were his children. His power was limited only by the mysterious decrees of Fate. Homer's gods act like humans, capable of evil deeds, favoritism, and jealousy, differing from ordinary people only in their immortality. Zeus was often the undignified victim of the plots of his wife, Hera, and other deities, and he asserted his authority through threats of violence. Hades, the place of the dead, was a subterranean land of dust and darkness, and Achilles, as Homer tells us in the *Odyssey,* would prefer to be a slave on earth than a king in Hades.

By the time of Hesiod (c. 700 B.C.E.), a religious reformation had begun that changed the vengeful and capricious gods of Homer into more sophisticated dispensers of justice who rewarded the good and punished the wicked. Zeus's stature was increased when he was newly identified as the source of Fate, which was no longer considered a separate mysterious power. And from the famous oracle at Delphi the voice of Zeus's son Apollo urged all Greeks to follow the ideal of moderation: "Nothing in excess" and "Know thyself" (meaning "know your limitations").

A century after Hesiod, the Orphic and Eleusinian mystery cults emerged as a type of Greek higher religion. Their initiates *(mystae)* were promised salvation in an afterlife of bliss in Elysium, formerly the

---

Classical Greek Literature and Culture

c. 800 B.C.E.	Homer
c. 700–480 B.C.E.	Archaic period of Greek art
c. 700 B.C.E.	Hesiod, *Works and Days*
c. 600 B.C.E.	Thales of Miletus, "father of philosophy"
525–456 B.C.E.	Aeschylus
c. 496–406 B.C.E.	Sophocles
c. 484–c. 425 B.C.E.	Herodotus, "father of history"
c. 480–406 B.C.E.	Euripides
c. 470–399 B.C.E.	Socrates
460–400 B.C.E.	Thucydides
c. 445–385 B.C.E.	Aristophanes
427–347 B.C.E.	Plato
c. 420 B.C.E.	Hippocrates' medical school
384–322 B.C.E.	Aristotle
342–270 B.C.E.	Epicurus
c. 336–c. 264 B.C.E.	Zeno

home after death of a few heroes only. The basis of the Orphic cult was an old myth about Dionysus, a son of Zeus, who was killed and eaten by the evil Titans before Zeus arrived on the scene and burned them to ashes with his lightning bolts. Orpheus, a legendary figure, taught that Zeus then created man from the Titans' ashes. Human nature, therefore, is composed of two distinct and opposing elements: the evil titanic element (the body) and the divine Dionysian element (the soul). Death, which frees the divine soul from the evil body, is therefore to be welcomed. "Happy and blessed one!" reads a typical Orphic tomb inscription. "Thou shalt be god instead of mortal."

Early Greek Philosophy

What the Greeks were the first to call *philosophy* ("love of wisdom") arose from their curiosity about nature. The early Greek philosophers were called *physikoi* ("physicists") because their main interest was the investigation of the physical world. ("It is according to their wonder," wrote Aristotle, "that men begin to philosophize, pursuing science in order to know.") Only later, beginning with Socrates, would the chief concern of philosophy be not natural science but *ethics*—how people ought to act in light of moral principles.

The Mesopotamians, as noted in Chapter 2, were skilled observers of astronomical phenomena, which, like the Greeks, they attributed to the action of the gods. The early Greek philosophers, beginning with Thales of Miletus around 600 B.C.E., changed the course of human knowledge by insisting that the phenomena of the universe could be explained by natural rather than supernatural causes. This rejection of mythological explanations and the use of reason to explain natural phenomena have been called the "Greek miracle."

Called the "father of philosophy," Thales speculated on the nature of the basic substance of which everything in the universe is composed. He concluded that it was water, which exists in different states and is indispensable to the maintenance and growth of organisms. Thales' successors in Ionia proposed elements other than water as this primal substance in the universe. One called it the "boundless," apparently a general concept for matter; another proposed "air," out of which all things come by a process of "rarefying and condensing"; a third asserted that fire was the "most mobile, most transformable, most active, most life-giving" element. This search for a material substance as the first principle or cause of all things culminated two centuries after Thales in the atomic theory of Democritus (c. 460–370 B.C.E.). To Democritus, reality was the mechanical motion of indivisible atoms, which differed in shape, size, position, and arrangement but not in quality. Moving about continuously, atoms combined to create objects.

While these and other early Greek philosophers were proposing some form of matter as the basic element in nature, Pythagoras of Samos (c. 582–500 B.C.E.) countered with the profoundly significant idea that the "nature of things" was something nonmaterial: numbers. By experimenting with a vibrating chord, Pythagoras discovered that musical harmony is based on arithmetical proportions, and he intuitively concluded that the universe was constructed of numbers and their relationships. His mystical, nonmaterial interpretation of nature, together with his belief that the human body was distinct from the soul, greatly influenced Plato.

An important result of early Greek philosophical speculation was the undermining of conventional beliefs and traditions. In religion, for example, Anaximander argued that thunder and lightning were caused by blasts of wind and not by Zeus's thunderbolts. Xenophanes went on to ridicule the traditional view of the gods: "If oxen and lions had hands, . . . they would make portraits and statues of their gods in their own image."

The eroding of traditional beliefs was intensified during the last half of the fifth century B.C.E. by the activity of professional teachers, called Sophists ("intellectuals"). They taught a variety of subjects—the nucleus of our present arts and sciences—which they claimed would lead to material success. The most popular subject was *rhetoric*, the art of persuasion, or how to take either side of an argument. The Sophists tried to put all conventional beliefs to the test of rational criticism. Concluding that truth was relative, they denied the existence of universal standards to guide human actions.

Socrates, a Martyr to Truth

A contemporary of the early Sophists but opposed to their conclusions was the Athenian Socrates (c. 470–399 B.C.E.). Like the Sophists, Socrates turned from concern with the gods to human affairs; in the words of the Roman statesman Cicero, Socrates was "the first to call philosophy down from the heavens and to set her in the cities of men, bringing her into their homes and compelling her to ask questions about life and morality and things good and evil." But unlike the Sophists, Socrates believed that by asking meaningful questions and subjecting the answers to logical analysis, agreement could be reached about ethical standards and rules of conduct. And so he would question passersby in his function of "midwife assisting in the birth of correct ideas" (to use his own figure of speech). Taking as his motto the famous inscription on the temple of Apollo at Delphi,

"Know thyself," he insisted that "the unexamined life is not worth living." To Socrates, human excellence or virtue *(aretē)* is not Homer's heroic action or simply Hesiod's moral character but intellectual activity—knowledge. Evil and error are the result of ignorance.

In time Socrates' quest for truth led to his undoing. The Athenians, unnerved by their defeat in the Peloponnesian War and viewing Socrates as just another subversive Sophist, arrested him "because he does not believe in the gods recognized by the state . . . and . . . because he corrupts the youth." By a slim majority, a jury of citizens condemned Socrates to die, a fate he accepted without bitterness and with a last request:

> *When my sons are grown up, I would ask you, my friends, to punish them, and I would have you trouble them, as I have troubled you, if they seem to care about riches, or anything, more than about virtue; or if they pretend to be something when they are really nothing, then reprove them, as I have reproved you, for not caring about that for which they ought to care, and thinking that they are something when they are really nothing. And if you do this, both I and my sons will have received justice at your hands.[20]*

Plato and His Theory of Ideas

After Socrates' death, philosophical leadership passed to his most famous disciple, Plato (427–347 B.C.E.). Like Socrates, Plato believed that truth exists, but only in the realm of thought, the spiritual world of ideas or forms. Such universal truths as beauty, good, and justice exist apart from the material world, and the beauty, good, and justice encountered in the world of the senses are only imperfect reflections of eternal and changeless ideas. The task for humans is to come to know the true reality—the eternal ideas—behind these imperfect reflections. Only the soul, and the "soul's pilot," reason, can accomplish this goal, for the human soul is spiritual and immortal, and in its prenatal state it existed "beyond the heavens" where "true Being dwells."[21]

Disillusioned with the democracy that had led Athens to ruin in the Peloponnesian War and that had condemned Socrates to death, Plato put forward his concept of an ideal state in the *Republic,* the first systematic work on political science. The state's basic function, founded on the idea of justice, was the satisfaction of the common good. Plato described a kind of "spiritualized Sparta" in which the state regulated every aspect of life, including thought. Accordingly, poets and forms of music considered unworthy were banished from the state. Private property was abolished on the grounds that it bred selfishness. Plato believed there was no essential difference between men and women; therefore, women received the

same education and held the same occupations as men, including "the art of war, which they must practice like men."[22] Individuals belonged to one of three classes and found happiness only through their contribution to the community: workers by producing the necessities of life, warriors by guarding the state, and philosophers by ruling in the best interests of all the people.

Plato founded the Academy in Athens, the famous school that existed from about 388 B.C.E. until 529 C.E., when it was closed by the Christian emperor Justinian. Here Plato taught and encouraged his students, whom he expected to become the intellectual elite who would go forth and reform society.

Aristotle, the Encyclopedic Philosopher

Plato's greatest pupil was Aristotle (384–322 B.C.E.), who set up his own school, the Lyceum, at Athens. Reacting against the otherworldly tendencies of Plato's thought, Aristotle insisted that ideas have no separate existence apart from the material world; knowledge of universal ideas is the result of the painstaking collection and organization of particular facts. Aristotle's Lyceum, accordingly, became a center for the analysis of data from many branches of learning.

Today, Aristotle's most significant works are the *Ethics* and the *Politics.* They deal with what he called the "philosophy of human affairs," whose object is the acquisition and maintenance of human happiness. Two kinds of virtue *(aretē),* intellectual and moral, which produce two types of happiness, are described in the *Ethics.* Intellectual virtue is the product of reason, and only such people as philosophers and scientists ever attain it. Much more important for the good of society is moral virtue—virtues of character, such as justice, bravery, and temperance—which is the product less of reason than of habit and thus can be acquired by all. In this connection Aristotle introduced his "doctrine of the mean" as a guide for good conduct. He considered all moral virtues to be means between extremes; courage, for example, is the mean between cowardice and rashness. In the *Politics* Aristotle viewed the state as necessary "for the sake of the good life," because its laws and educational system provide the most effective training needed for the attainment of moral virtue and hence happiness. Thus to Aristotle, the viewpoint popular today that the state stands in opposition to the individual would be unthinkable.

There have probably been few geniuses whose interests were as widespread as Aristotle's. He investigated such diverse fields as biology (his minute observations include the life cycle of the gnat), mathematics, astronomy, physics, literary criticism (the concept of *catharsis*—art as a release of emotion), rhetoric, logic (deductive and inductive), politics (he

Aristotle Criticizes Communism

Aristotle foreshadows the failure of communist regimes.

Next let us consider what should be our arrangements about property: should the citizens of the perfect state have their possessions in common or not? . . .

There is always a difficulty in men living together and having things in common, but especially in their having common property. . . .

The present arrangement, if improved as it might be by good customs and laws, would be far better, and would have the advantages of both systems. Property should be in a certain sense common, but, as a general rule, private; for, when every one has a distinct interest, men will not complain of one another and they will make more progress, because every one will be attending to his own business. . . .

. . . Again, how immeasurably greater is the pleasure, when a man feels a thing to be his own; for the love of self is a feeling implanted by nature and not given in vain, although selfishness is rightly censured; this, however, is not the mere love of self, but the love of self in excess, like the miser's love of money; for all, or almost all, men love money, and other such objects in a measure. And further, there is the greatest pleasure in doing a kindness or service to friends or guests or companions, which can only be rendered when a man has private property. The advantage is lost by the excessive unification of the state. . . . No one, when men have all things in common, will any longer set an example of liberality or do any liberal action; for liberality consists in the use which is made of property.

[Communistic] legislation may have a specious appearance of benevolence; men readily listen to it, and are easily induced to believe that in some wonderful manner everybody will become everybody's friend, especially when some one is heard denouncing the evils now existing in states, . . . which are said to arise out of the possession of private property. These evils, however, are due to a very different cause—the wickedness of human nature.

. . . The error of Socrates [i.e., Plato] must be attributed to the false notion of unity from which he starts. Unity there should be, both of the family and of the state, but in some respects only. For there is a point at which a state may attain such a degree of unity as to be no longer a state, or at which, without actually ceasing to exist, it will become an inferior state, like harmony passing into unison, or rhythm which has been reduced to a single foot. The state, as I was saying, is a plurality, which should be united and made into a community by education. . . . Let us remember that we should not disregard the experience of ages.

From Aristotle, *Politics*, trans. Benjamin Jowett (Oxford: Clarendon Press, 1908), pp. 60–64.

---

analyzed 158 Greek and foreign constitutions), ethics, and metaphysics. His knowledge was so encyclopedic that there is hardly a college course today that does not take note of what Aristotle had to say on the subject. Although his works on natural science are now little more than historical curiosities, they held a place of undisputed authority until the scientific revolution of the sixteenth and seventeenth centuries. But in no important sense are his humanistic studies, such as the *Ethics* and the *Politics*, out of date.

Medicine

Superstitions about the human body blocked the development of medical science until 420 B.C.E., when Hippocrates, the "father of medicine," founded a school in which he emphasized the value of observation and the careful interpretation of symptoms. Such modern medical terms as *crisis*, *acute*, and *chronic* were first used by Hippocrates. He was firmly convinced that disease resulted from natural, not supernatural, causes. Writing of epilepsy, considered at the time a "sacred" or supernaturally inspired sickness, one Hippocratic writer observed:

It seems to me that this disease is no more divine than any other. It has a natural cause just as other diseases have. Men think it supernatural because they do not understand it. But if they called everything supernatural which they do not understand, why, there would be no end of such thing![23]

The Hippocratic school also gave medicine a sense of service to humanity that it has never lost. All members took the famous Hippocratic Oath, still in use today. One section states: "I will adopt the regimen which in my best judgment is beneficial to my patients, and not for their injury or for any wrongful purpose. I will not give poison to anyone, though I be asked . . . nor will I procure abortion."[24]

Despite their empirical approach, the Hippocratic school adopted the theory that the body contained four liquids or *humors*—blood, phlegm, black bile, and yellow bile—whose proper balance was the basis of health. This doctrine was to impede medical progress until modern times.

The Writing of History

If history is defined as an honest attempt to find out what happened and then to explain why it happened, Herodotus of Halicarnassus (c. 484–c. 425 B.C.E.) deserves to be called the "father of history." In his highly entertaining history of the Persian Wars, he identified the clash of two distinct civilizations, the Hellenic and the Near Eastern. His portrayal of both the Greeks and the Persians was in most cases highly impartial, but his fondness for a good story often led him to include tall tales in his work. As he stated more than once, "My duty is to report what has been said, but I do not have to believe it."

The first truly scientific historian was Thucydides (460–400 B.C.E.), who wrote a notably objective account of the Peloponnesian War. Although Thucydides was a contemporary of the events and a loyal Athenian, a reader can scarcely detect whether he favored Athens or Sparta. Thucydides believed that his history would become "an everlasting possession" for those who desire a clear picture of what has happened and, human nature being as it is, what is likely to be repeated in the future. His belief was based on his remarkable ability to analyze and explain human behavior. (Three examples were quoted in our account of the Peloponnesian War on p. 66.) In describing the character and purpose of his work, Thucydides probably had Herodotus in mind:

The absence of romance in my history will, I fear, detract somewhat from its interest; but I shall be content if it is judged useful by those inquirers who desire an exact knowledge of the past as an aid to the interpretation of the future, which will according to human nature recur in much the same way. My history has been composed to be an everlasting possession, not the show-piece of an hour.[25]

Hellenic Poetry and Drama

Greek literary periods can be classified according to the dominant poetic forms that reflect particular stages of cultural development in Greece. First came the time of great epics, followed by periods in which lyric poetry and then drama flourished.

Sometime during the eighth century B.C.E. in Ionia, the *Iliad* and the *Odyssey*, the two great epics attributed to Homer, were set down in their present form. The *Iliad*, describing the clash of arms between the Greeks and Trojans "on the ringing plains of windy Troy," glorifies heroic bravery and physical strength against a background of divine intervention in human affairs. The *Odyssey*, relating the adventure-filled wanderings of Odysseus on his return to Greece after Troy's fall, places less stress on divine intervention and more on the cool resourcefulness of the hero in escaping from danger and in regaining his kingdom. These stirring epics have provided inspiration and source material for generations of poets in the Western world.

As Greek society continued to develop and seek new varieties of artistic expression, a new type of poetry, written to be sung to the accompaniment of a small stringed instrument called a lyre, became popular among the Ionian Greeks. Unlike Homer, authors of this lyric poetry sang not of legendary events but of present delights and sorrows. This new note, personal and passionate, can be seen in the following examples, in which the contrast between the new values of what is called the Greek Renaissance and those of Homer's heroic age is sharply clear. Unlike Homer's heroes, Archilochus of Paros (seventh century B.C.E) unashamedly throws away his shield and runs from the battlefield:

My trusty shield adorns some Thracian foe;
I left it in a bush—not as I would!
But I have saved my life; so let it go.
Soon I will get another just as good.[26]

And in contrast to Homer's view of an unromantic, purely physical attraction between Paris and the abducted Helen ("He led the way to the couch and the lady followed willingly"), Sappho of Lesbos (sixth century B.C.E.), one of the first and greatest of all female poets, saw Helen as the helpless, unresisting victim of romantic love:

Did not Helen, who was queen of mortal
beauty, choose as first among mankind
the very scourge of Trojan honor?
Haunted by Love, she forgot kinsmen,
her own dear child, and wandered off to a remote
* country.*
Weak and fitful woman bending before any man![27]

Drama (also in verse) developed from the religious rites of Dionysus (son of Zeus from an affair with the daughter of the king of Tyre) in which a large chorus and its leader sang and danced. Thespis, a contemporary of Solon, added an actor called the "answerer" (*hypocrites*, the origin of our word *hypocrite*) to converse with the chorus and its leader. This innovation made dramatic dialogue possible. By the fifth century B.C.E. in Athens, two distinct forms, tragedy and comedy, had evolved. Borrowing from the old familiar legends of gods and heroes for their

Discovery Through Maps

The World According to Herodotus, c. 450 B.C.E.

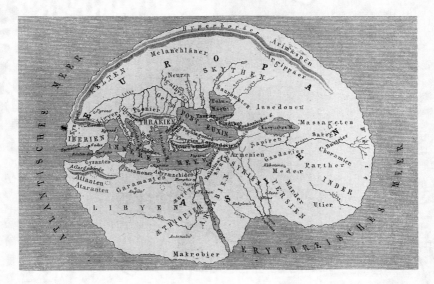

This map depicts the known world at the time of the Greek historian Herodotus, who lived and worked around 450–425 B.C.E. The map is a modern rendition of what we know Herodotus thought to be the world, as described in his writings, the *Histories*. The *Histories* was written to describe the events and circumstances that led the Greeks and the Persians to engage in war—a war that Herodotus believed changed the direction of human history. To understand why these two great powers came to conflict, the historian believed he would have to examine the origins, geographical setting, culture, and traditions of the whole empire of the Persians, as well as the background of the Greek city-states. The *Histories* became not just a listing of chronological events but an exploration of geography, sociology, and anthropology as well.

We are certain that Herodotus himself traveled extensively throughout his world in order to learn firsthand of the people he described. Most of his geographical knowledge came from his own observations or from interviews with the people he met. He seems to have believed that the earth was a flat disk, although he must have been familiar with contemporary theories that the world might be a sphere. He differed from most of his contemporaries in not picturing Europe, Africa (which he called Libya), and Asia as approximately the same size. He described Europe as being as long as both Asia and Africa put together. And yet Herodotus did not travel to the farthest reaches of the continent but relied on accounts of others; he knew nothing of the existence of Britain or Scandinavia, for example, and he did not know if Europe was surrounded by water to the west or north. His knowledge of Asia was limited to the lands of the Persian Empire. He knew that the Caspian Sea was an inland sea and not, as most of his contemporaries believed, a sea that emptied into the band of ocean that encircled the earth. He also knew that Africa was surrounded by water—a fact that the geographer Ptolemy missed 500 years later.

plots, the tragedians reinterpreted them from the point of view of the values and problems of their own times.

In reworking the old legends of the heroic age, Aeschylus (525–456 B.C.E.) attempted to spread the new values being presented about Greek religion, first expressed by Hesiod, by showing how following the old unsophisticated beliefs leads to suffering. In his trilogy, the *Oresteia*, for example, he concerned himself with hubris as applied to the murder of the hero Agamemnon by his queen following his return from the Trojan War. Aeschylus then proceeded to work out its ramifications—murder piled on murder until people through suffering learn to substitute the moral law of Zeus for the primitive law of the blood feud. Like the prophets of Israel, Aeschylus taught that while "sin brings misery," misery in turn leads to wisdom:

Aristophanes on the Shortcomings of Athenian Democracy

In *The Frogs,* Aristophanes exhorts the Athenians to elect better-quality leaders.

[The leader of the chorus comes forward and addresses the audience.]

We chorus folk two privileges prize:
To amuse you, citizens, and to advise.
So, mid the fun that marks this sacred day,
We'll put on serious looks, and say our say. . . .
But if we choose to strut and put on airs
While Athens founders in a sea of cares,
In days to come, when history is penned,
They'll say we must have gone clean round the
  bend. . . .
I'll tell you what I think about the way
This city treats her soundest men today:
By a coincidence more sad than funny,
It's very like the way we treat our money.
The noble silver drachma, that of old
We were so proud of, and the recent gold,
Coins that rang true, clean-stamped and worth their
  weight

Throughout the world, have ceased to circulate.
Instead, the purses of Athenian shoppers
Are full of shoddy silver-plated coppers.
Just so, when men are needed by the nation,
The best have been withdrawn from circulation.
Men of good birth and breeding, men of parts,
Well schooled in wrestling and in gentler arts,
These we abuse, and trust instead to knaves,
Newcomers, aliens, copper-pated slaves,
All rascals—honestly, what men to choose!
There was a time when you'd have scorned to use
Men so debased, so far beyond the pale,
Even as scapegoats to be dragged from jail
And flogged to death outside the city gate.
My foolish friends, change now, it's not too late!
Try the good ones again: if they succeed,
You will have proved that you have sense indeed.

From Aristophanes, *The Frogs and Other Plays,* trans. David Barrett (Baltimore: Penguin, 1964), pp. 181–183.

Zeus the Guide, who made man turn
Thought-ward, Zeus, who did ordain
Man by Suffering shall Learn.
So the heart of him, again
Aching with remembered pain,
Bleeds and sleepeth not, until
Wisdom comes against his will.[28]

A generation later, Sophocles (c. 496–406 B.C.E.) largely abandoned Aeschylus's concern for the working out of divine justice and concentrated on character. To Sophocles, a certain amount of suffering was inevitable in life. No one is perfect; even in the best people there is a tragic flaw that causes them to make mistakes. Sophocles dwelled mainly on the way in which human beings react to suffering. Like his contemporary, the sculptor Phidias, Sophocles viewed humans as ideal creatures—"Many are the wonders of the world, and none so wonderful as Man"—and he displayed human greatness by depicting people experiencing great tragedy without whimpering. It has been said that to Sophocles—and to Shakespeare—"tragedy is essentially an expression, not of despair, but of the triumph over despair and of confidence in the value of human life."[29]

Euripides (c. 480–406 B.C.E.), the last of the great Athenian tragedians, reflects the rationalism and critical spirit of the late fifth century B.C.E. Gone is Sophocles' idealized view of humanity. To Euripides, human life was pathetic, and the ways of the gods were ridiculous. His recurrent theme was "Since life began, hath there in God's eye stood one happy man?"

For this he has been called the "poet of the world's grief." Euripides has also been called the first psychologist, for he looked deep into the human soul and described what he saw with intense realism. His *Medea,* for example, is a startling and moving account of a woman's exploitation and her retaliatory rage. When Medea's overly ambitious husband discards her for a young heiress, she kills her children out of a bitter hatred that is the dark side of her once passionate love:

He, even he,
Whom to know well was all the world to me,
The man I loved, hath proved most evil. Oh,
Of all things upon earth that bleed and grow,
A herb most bruised is woman.
. . . but once spoil her of her right
In man's love, and there moves, I warn thee well,
No bloodier spirit between heaven and hell.[30]

Far more than those of Aeschylus or even Sophocles, the themes of Euripides still remain relevant to the modern world.

Comedies were bawdy and spirited. There were no libel laws in Athens, and Aristophanes (c. 445–385 B.C.E.), the famous comic-dramatist and a conservative in outlook, brilliantly satirized Athenian democracy as a mob led by demagogues, the Sophists (among whom he included Socrates) as subversive, and Euripides as an underminer of civic spirit and traditional faith. Another favorite object of Aristophanes' satire was the youth of Athens; in the following lines from *The Wasps,* they are lampooned by the chorus of old men:

Yes, we may be poor old crocks,
But the whiteness of our locks
Does the City better credit, I would say,
Than the ringlets and the fashions
And the pederastic passions
Of the namby-pamby youngsters of today.[31]

Hellenic Architecture

During the archaic period of Greek art (c. 700–480 B.C.E.), architecture flourished in Ionia, Greece, and the Greek colonies in Sicily and southern Italy. Reflecting the prosperity produced by colonization, large stone temples were constructed. Their form may have developed from wooden structures that had been influenced by the remains of Mycenaean palaces or perhaps Egyptian temples.

The classical phase of Greek architecture reached its zenith in Athens during the second half of the fifth century B.C.E. The Parthenon, the Erechtheum, and the other temples on the Acropolis in Athens exhibit the highly developed features that make Greek structures so pleasing to the eye. All relationships, such as column spacing and height and the slight curvature of floor and roof lines, were calculated and executed with remarkable precision to achieve a perfect balance, both structurally and visually. The three orders, or styles, usually identified by the characteristics of the columns, were the Doric, which was used in the Parthenon; the Ionic, seen in the Erechtheum; and the later and more ornate Corinthian.

Greek temples afford an interesting comparison with those of Egypt. Whereas the Egyptian temple was enclosed by walls and only priests and royalty could

An ornate capital of the third Greek order, the Corinthian, which was more popular with the Hellenistic Greeks and the Romans.

In the Parthenon, great care was taken to design a perfect building, both structurally and visually. The topics of the Doric columns lean toward the center, and the columns are more widely spaced in the middle of each row than at the ends. All these refinements create an illusion of perfect regularity that would be lacking if the parts were actually regular. Sculpture adorned the triangular gables and part of the frieze just below the gables; another sculptured frieze ran around the walls inside the colonnade. The whole building was once painted in bright colors.

These statues illustrate the three major phases of Greek art. The kouros *("youth") statue (c. 540 B.C.E.) on the left is typically archaic, the statue of the warrior has all the characteristics of classical art, and the Laocoön group on the right illustrates the striving for effect of much of postclassical Hellenistic sculpture. This last statue depicts the legend that Laocoön and his two sons were strangled by a huge snake sent by Apollo as punishment for warning the unbelieving Trojans about the Trojan horse, a device used by the Greeks to gain entrance to Troy and destroy the city.*

Kouros, Statue of a youth, c. 610–600 B.C.E. The Metropolitan Museum of Art, New York. Fletcher Fund, 1932. (32.11.1). Photograph © 1993 The Metropolitan Museum of Art.

enter its inner rooms, the Greek temple was open, with a colonnade porch and an inside room containing a statue of the god or goddess. Sacrifice and ritual took place outside the temple, where the altar was placed.

Other types of buildings, notably the theaters, stadiums, and gymnasiums, also express the Greek spirit and way of life. In the open-air theaters, the circular shape of the spectators' sections and the plan of the orchestra section set a style that has survived to the present day.

Hellenic Sculpture and Pottery

Greek sculpture is usually described as having passed through three stages of development: the archaic period, the classical, and the Hellenistic. Greek sculpture of the archaic period, although crude in its representation of human anatomy, has the freshness and liveliness of youth. Influenced partly by Egyptian models, the statues of nude youths and draped maidens usually stand stiffly with clenched fists and with one foot thrust awkwardly forward. The fixed smile and formalized treatment of hair and drapery also reveal the sculptors' struggle to master the technique of their art.

The mastery of technique by 480 B.C.E. brought in the classical period of fifth-century Greek sculpture, whose principles of harmony and proportion have shaped the course of Western art. Sculpture from this period displays both the end of technical immaturity and the beginning of idealization of the human form, which reached its culmination in the dignity and poise of Phidias's figures in the continu-

ous frieze and pediments of the Parthenon. Carved with restraint and "calm exaltation," the frieze represents the citizens of Athens participating in a procession in honor of their patron goddess, Athena, which took place every four years.

The more relaxed nature of fourth-century B.C.E. Hellenic sculpture, while still considered classical, lacks some of the grandeur and dignity of fifth-century art. Charm, grace, and individuality characterize the work of Praxiteles, the most famous sculptor of the century. These qualities can be seen in his flowing statues of the god Hermes holding the young Dionysus and of Aphrodite stepping into her bath.

The making of pottery, the oldest Greek art, started at the beginning of the Greek Dark Ages (c. 1150 B.C.E.) with crude imitations of late Mycenaean forms. Soon the old Mycenaean patterns were replaced by abstract geometrical designs. With the coming of the archaic period came paintings of scenes from mythology and daily life. We can get an idea of what Greek painting, now lost, must have been like from surviving Greek pottery and mosaics.

The Hellenistic Age, 336–30 B.C.E.

The Hellenistic Age is the three-century period from Alexander the Great to Augustus, the first of the Roman emperors, who completed Rome's domination of the Mediterranean world by adding Egypt to Rome's empire in 30 B.C.E. The Hellenistic Age was

Macedonia and Alexander

359–336 B.C.E.	Reign of Philip II
338 B.C.E.	Philip conquers Greek city-states
336–323 B.C.E.	Reign of Alexander the Great
334 B.C.E.	Alexander invades Persian Empire
331 B.C.E.	Final battle at Gaugamela
327 B.C.E.	Alexander enters India
323 B.C.E.	Alexander dies

a period of economic expansion, cosmopolitanism, striking intellectual and artistic achievements, and the wide distribution of Greek culture.

Alexander the Great

When Philip of Macedonia was assassinated in 336 B.C.E., his authority was claimed by his 20-year-old son Alexander, who proved himself a resolute king from the very beginning of his reign by gaining the support of the Macedonian nobles, even though some of them suspected the young man of being involved in Philip's murder. Alexander persuaded his father's old generals and comrades to swear their loyalty to him and proceeded to demand the loyalty of the Greek League, which had been founded by his father. When the Greek city of Thebes responded to a rumor

that Alexander had been killed in battle in the north by rebelling against the Macedonians, Alexander marched his army quickly to the south and ruthlessly crushed the city, selling its remaining inhabitants into slavery. The Greeks were horrified at such brutal action, but a lesson was learned, and few states dared consider rebellion in the years ahead.

Alexander was one of history's most remarkable individuals. Of average height and looks for a Macedonian, he nevertheless impressed his contemporaries as a gifted athlete, a charismatic personality, and a natural leader. Both his father, Philip, and his mother, Olympias, a princess from Illyria, were strong influences on him. Philip earned his son's respect as a king and a general, and Olympias was a forceful woman who wished great things for her son and who constantly assured the boy that his true father was not Philip but the god Zeus.

Having been tutored by Aristotle, Alexander was aware of the glories of Hellenic culture and wished to be the fulfillment of the Greek ideal. Reveling in the heroic deeds of the *Iliad*, which he always kept at his bedside, Alexander saw himself as a new Achilles waging war against barbarians when he planned to complete his father's plans to avenge the Persian attacks on Greece by conquering the Persian Empire. In 334 B.C.E. he set out with an army of 35,000 soldiers recruited from Macedonia and the Greek League. In quick succession he subdued Asia Minor, Syria, and Palestine, defeating the Persians in two great battles. He marched into Egypt, where the Egyptians welcomed him as a deliverer from their Persian masters and recognized the Macedonian as pharaoh, the living god-king of Egypt.

Alexander the Great in his first battle against Darius III in 333 B.C.E. This detail, from a late Hellenistic mosaic at Pompeii, is based on a Greek painting made around 300 B.C.E.

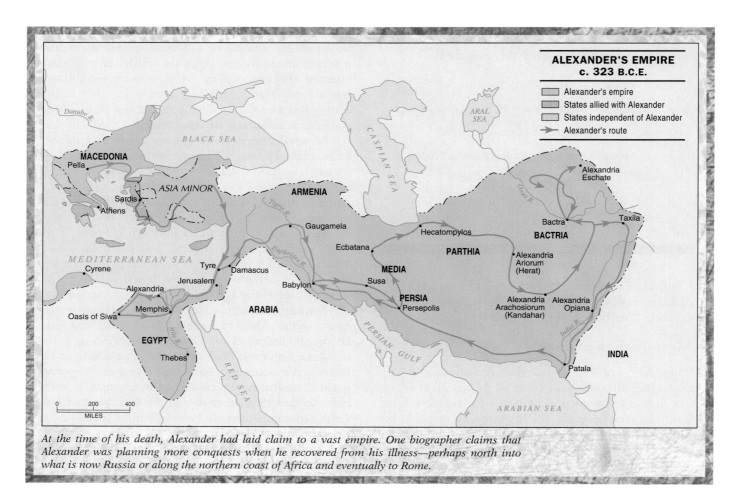

ALEXANDER'S EMPIRE
c. 323 B.C.E.

- Alexander's empire
- States allied with Alexander
- States independent of Alexander
- → Alexander's route

At the time of his death, Alexander had laid claim to a vast empire. One biographer claims that Alexander was planning more conquests when he recovered from his illness—perhaps north into what is now Russia or along the northern coast of Africa and eventually to Rome.

Greatly impressed with Egypt and its traditions, Alexander wished to spend more time there. But Darius III, the Persian king, was gathering one more great army to oppose the invader, and Alexander marched into Mesopotamia to meet the Persian armies for a final battle. In 331 B.C.E., at Gaugamela, near the ancient city of Nineveh, the Macedonians defeated the Persians. Darius III was executed by his own relatives as he fled, and Alexander became Great King of the Persian Empire. Alexander led his victorious troops to the ancient Persian capital city of Persepolis, but his campaigns did not end there. He wished to demand the loyalty of all Persian lands and to extend the great empire. He led his troops north through Media, then south and east into present-day Afghanistan, finally venturing as far east as the rich river valleys of India. There his weary and frightened soldiers, many of whom had been away from home for more than ten years, forced him to turn back.

In 323 B.C.E. Alexander fell ill with a mysterious fever. Perhaps he had contracted malaria in India; perhaps he fell victim to his accumulated battle wounds; perhaps his years of heavy drinking had taken their toll; perhaps, as rumor had it, he had been slowly poisoned by his enemies in the Macedonian camp. Whatever the case, after a short illness, and without designating an heir to his empire, Alexander died in Babylon at the age of 32.

Alexander the Great is a puzzling figure to modern historians. Some view him as a ruthless conqueror who never lost a battle and a despot who ordered even his fellow Macedonians to prostrate themselves in his presence. Others, however, influenced by Greek and Roman writers and perhaps by their own idealism, picture him as a farsighted visionary hoping to unite East and West in one world and seeking the eventual "brotherhood of man" by establishing universal equality through a common Greek culture.

Some of Alexander's military and administrative policies sought to unify the lands he conquered and to promote what he himself called "concord and partnership in the empire" between easterners and westerners. He blended Persians with Greeks and Macedonians in his army and administration; he founded numerous cities—70, according to tradition—in the East and settled many of his followers in them; and he married two oriental princesses and encouraged his officers and men to take foreign wives. Finally, for perhaps egotistical and certainly for political reasons, he ordered the Greek city-states to accord him "divine honors."

Alexander was a remarkable blend of the romantic idealist and the practical realist, contrasting traits that he inherited from his parents. His mother, Olympias, who practiced the rites of the cult of Dionysus and claimed to be a descendant of the Greek hero Achilles, instilled in her son a consciousness of a divine mission that drove him onward, even to seeking the end of the earth beyond India. From his father he inherited his remarkable abilities as military commander, expert diplomat, and able political administrator. Alexander was a self-confident idealist who was excited by challenges, but meeting those challenges forced him to take actions that were practical and pragmatic. For example, he could not merely conquer the Great King of Persia; he had to act as his successor as well. Alexander ruled for only 13 years, but in many ways the world was never the same again.

The Division of Alexander's Empire

With the Greeks now masters of the ancient Near East, a new and distinctly cosmopolitan period in their history and culture began—the Hellenistic ("Greek-like") Age. For several decades following Alexander's sudden death, his generals rivaled each other for the spoils of empire. Three major Hellenistic kingdoms emerged and maintained an uneasy balance of power until the Roman conquests of the second and first centuries B.C.E.: Egypt, ruled by Alexander's friend and general Ptolemy and his successors; Asia, comprising most of the remaining provinces of the Persian Empire and held together with great difficulty by the dynasty founded by Seleucus; and Macedonia and Greece, ruled by the descendants of Antigonus the One-Eyed.

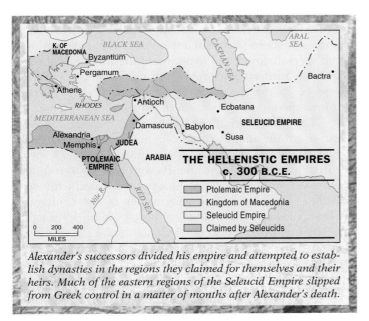

Alexander's successors divided his empire and attempted to establish dynasties in the regions they claimed for themselves and their heirs. Much of the eastern regions of the Seleucid Empire slipped from Greek control in a matter of months after Alexander's death.

While the Antigonids in Macedonia followed the model of Alexander's father, Philip, in ruling as national kings selected by the army, the Ptolemies ruled Egypt as divine pharaohs, and some of the Seleucids attempted to have themselves recognized as "saviors" and "benefactors" of their subjects. Ptolemaic and Seleucid administrations were centralized in bureaucracies staffed mainly by Greeks, an arrangement that created a vast gulf between rulers and ruled:

> *"What a mob!" [the Greek poet Theocritus has a Greek woman residing in Alexandria say to her friend]. "They're like ants, no one can count them. Ptolemy, you've done many good things.... No more hoods creep up on you nowadays and do you in—an old Egyptian habit. The tricks those scoundrels used to play! They're all alike—dirty, lazy, good-for-nothings!"[32]*

Plagued by native revolts, dynastic troubles, and civil war, the Hellenistic kingdoms eventually began to crumble. Macedonia lost effective control of Greece by 250 B.C.E. when Athens asserted its independence and most of the other Greek states resisted Macedonian domination by forming two federal leagues, the Achaean and the Aetolian. Their constitutions have long commanded the attention of students of federal unions, including the writers of the United States Constitution.

The eastern reaches of Alexander's empire—India, Bactria, and Parthia—gradually broke out of Seleucid control. Pergamum, in northwestern Asia Minor, renounced its allegiance to the Seleucids and became an independent kingdom famous for its artists and scholars. In 200 B.C.E. the new power of Rome entered the scene, and by 30 B.C.E. Rome had annexed all but the last remaining Hellenistic state, Egypt; in that very year Cleopatra, the last reigning member of the dynasty founded by Ptolemy, was captured by the Romans and committed suicide.

Hellenistic Economy and Society

The Hellenistic Age was a time of economic expansion and social change. In the wake of Alexander's conquests, thousands of Greeks moved eastward to begin a new era of Greek colonization, ending the long economic depression that followed the breakup of the Athenian Empire. An economic union of East and West permitted the free flow of trade, and prosperity was stimulated further when Alexander put into circulation huge amounts of Persian gold and silver and introduced a uniform coinage. The result was a much larger and more affluent middle class than had existed previously. The condition of the poor, however, was made worse by rising prices.

By the third century B.C.E. the center of trade had shifted from Greece to the Near East. Largest of the

Hellenistic cities, and much larger than any cities in Greece itself, were Antioch, in northern Syria, and Alexandria, in Egypt. The riches of India, Persia, Arabia, and the Fertile Crescent were brought by sea and land to these Mediterranean ports.

Alexandria outdistanced all other Hellenistic cities as a commercial center. Its merchants supplied the ancient world with wheat, linen, papyrus, glass, and jewelry. Boasting a population of nearly a million, the city had a double harbor in which a great lighthouse, judged one of the wonders of the ancient world, rose to a height estimated at 370 feet. Its busy streets were filled with a mixture of peoples—Greeks, Macedonians, Jews, and Egyptians. As in all other Hellenistic cities in the Near East, the privileged Greeks and Macedonians were at the top of the social scale and the mass of natives at the bottom; the large Jewish population lived apart and was allowed a large degree of self-government. Labor was so cheap that slavery hardly existed in Hellenistic Egypt. As a consequence, worker-organized strikes were frequent.

Hellenistic Philosophy

Developments in philosophical thought reflected the changed conditions of the Hellenistic Age. With the growing loss of political freedom and the common condition of internal disorder, philosophers concerned themselves less with the reform of society and more with the attainment of happiness for the individual. "There is no point in saving the Greeks" is the way one Hellenistic philosopher summed up the new outlook, quite in contrast to that of Socrates, Plato, and Aristotle. This emphasis on peace of mind for the individual living in an insecure world led to the rise of four principal schools of Hellenistic philosophy, all of which had their start at Athens.

The Skeptics and Cynics reflected most clearly the doubts and misgivings of the times. The Skeptics hoped to achieve freedom from anxiety by denying the possibility of finding truth. The wise, they argued, will suspend judgment and not preach to others because they have learned that sensory experience, the only source of knowledge, is deceptive. The Skeptics were like modern pragmatists in substituting probability for certainty and insisting that even the probable must be tested by experience and exposed to the possibility of contradiction. To drive the point home, they were famous for arguing both sides of the same question.

To make their point, the Cynics carried this negativism further; their ideal was nonattachment to the values and conventions of society. Cynic philosophers, including Diogenes, wandered from city to city, calling for the public to pursue a nonconformist concept of *aretē:* "Look at me, I am without house or city, property or slave. I sleep on the ground. I have no wife, no children. What do I lack? Am I not without distress or fear? Am I not free?"[33]

More practical and popular were Epicureanism and Stoicism. The Athenian Epicurus (342–270 B.C.E.) taught that happiness could be achieved simply by freeing the body from pain and the mind from fear—particularly the fear of death. To reach this dual goal, people must avoid bodily excesses, including sensual pleasures, and accept the scientific teaching of Democritus that both body and soul are composed of atoms that fall apart at death. Beyond death there is no existence and nothing to fear. Epicurus maintained that the finest pleasures are intellectual and that the gods do not concern themselves with humans but spend their time pursuing true pleasure like good Epicureans.

The Stoics, followers of Zeno (c. 336–c. 264 B.C.E.), a Semite who settled in Athens, argued in contrast to Epicureanism that the universe is controlled by some power—variously called destiny, reason, natural law, providence, or God—that determines everything that happens. Fortified by this knowledge, wise Stoics conform their will to the "world will" and "stoically" accept whatever part fortune gives to them in the drama of life. The Epicurean retreated from worldly responsibilities, but the Stoic urged participation. Stoicism's stern sense of duty and belief in the equality of all people under a single ruling force made it particularly attractive to the Roman conquerors of the ancient world.

Science and Mathematics

The Greek concern for rational, impartial inquiry reached its highest level in the Hellenistic period, particularly in Alexandria, where the Ptolemies subsidized a great research institute, the Museum, and a library of more than half a million books. Emphasizing specialization and experimentation and enriched by Near Eastern astronomy and mathematics, Greek science in the third century B.C.E. achieved results unmatched until early modern times.

The expansion of geographical knowledge resulting from Alexander's conquests inspired scientists to make accurate maps and to estimate the size of the earth, which had been identified as a globe through observation of its shadow in a lunar eclipse. Eratosthenes, the outstanding geographer of the century, drew parallels of latitude and longitude on his map of the inhabited world and calculated the circumference of the globe (within 1 percent, an error of 195 miles) by measuring the difference in the angles of the noonday sun's shadows at Aswan and Alexandria. In astronomy, Aristarchus put forward the radical theory that the earth rotates on its axis and moves in an orbit around the sun. Most of his contemporaries adhered, however, to the prevailing geocentric theory, which stated that the earth was stationary and the sun revolved around it. Not only was this view supported by the powerful authority of Aristotle, but it also seemed to explain all the known facts of celestial motion. This was particularly true after Hipparchus in the next century added the new idea of *epicycles*—each planet revolves in its own small orbit while moving around the earth. Aristarchus's heliocentric theory was forgotten until the sixteenth century C.E., when it was revived by Copernicus.

Mathematics also made great advances in the third century B.C.E. Euclid systematized the theorems of plane and solid geometry, and Archimedes of Syracuse, who had studied at Alexandria, calculated the value of *pi*, invented a terminology for expressing numbers up to any magnitude, and established the rudiments of calculus. Archimedes also discovered specific gravity by noticing that he displaced water when submerged in his bath. And despite his dislike for making practical use of his knowledge, he invented the compound pulley, the windlass, and the endless screw for raising water.

The Hellenistic Greeks also extended the advances in medicine made earlier by Hippocrates and his school. By dissecting bodies of dead criminals, they were able to trace the outlines of the nervous system, to understand the principle of the circulation of the blood, and to ascertain that the brain, not the heart, is the true center of consciousness.

Hellenistic Art and Literature

The host of new cities that sprang up in Hellenistic times served as a tremendous impetus to new developments and experiments in architecture. The new cities benefited from town planning; the streets were laid out on a rectangular grid. The great public buildings were elaborate and highly ornamented; this was an age that preferred the ornate Corinthian column to the simpler Doric and Ionic styles of decoration.

Hellenistic sculptors continued and intensified the realistic, dramatic, and emotional approach that began to appear in late classical sculpture. Supported by rulers and other rich patrons in such affluent cities as Alexandria, Antioch, Rhodes, and Pergamum, they displayed their technical virtuosity by representing violent scenes, writhing forms, and dramatic poses, all with a realism that could make stone simulate flesh. Like most postclassical art, little evidence remained of the balance and restraint of classical Greek sculpture. The famous Laocoön group, with its twisted poses, contorted faces, and swollen muscles, stands in obvious contrast to the works of classical Greece seeking balance, harmony, and restraint.

In this second-century B.C.E. marble sculpture found on the island of Delos, Aphrodite defends herself with her sandal against the unwanted advances of the lecherous god Pan. The goddess is assisted by the winged god Eros (Cupid).

The quality of literature from the Hellenistic Age was generally inferior to that of the Hellenic Age. Scholarship flourished, and we are in debt for the preservation of much of Greek classical literature to the subsidized scholars at the Alexandrine library—"fatted fowls in a coop," as a Skeptic philosopher called them. They composed epics in imitation of Homer (one new feature was romantic love, not found in Homer), long poems on dreary subjects like the weather, and short, witty epigrams—all in a highly polished style. These sophisticated scholars also invented a new type of romantic, escapist literature: pastoral poetry extolling the unspoiled life and loves of shepherds and their rustic love interests. (Later both Roman and modern poets and painters would adopt this Hellenistic tradition of celebrating the charms of unsophisticated country life.) The best of the new poetry was written at Alexandria in the third century B.C.E. by Theocritus, who also composed very realistic poetry. The following short example, written by a contemporary, illustrates its character and appeal:

> *Would that my father had taught me the craft of a*
> *keeper of sheep,*
> *For so in the shade of the elm tree, or under the rocks*
> *on the steep,*
> *Piping on reeds I had sat, and had lulled my sorrow to*
> *sleep.*[34]

The Hellenistic Contribution

The greatest contribution of the Hellenistic Age was the diffusion of Greek culture throughout the ancient East and the newly rising Roman West. In the East, the cities that Alexander and his successors built were the agents for spreading Hellenistic culture from the Aegean Sea to India. Literate Asians learned Greek to facilitate trade and to read Greek literature. In Judea, upper-class Jews built Greek theaters and gymnasiums and adopted Greek speech, dress, and names.

For a time the Seleucid Empire provided the peace and economic stability necessary to ensure the partial Hellenization of a vast area. But with an insufficient number of Greeks to colonize so large an area as the Near East, the Greek cities remained only islands in an Asian ocean. As time passed, this ocean encroached more and more on the Hellenized outposts.

The gradual weakening of the loosely knit Seleucid Empire eventually resulted in the creation of independent kingdoms on the edge of the Hellenistic world. In the middle of the third century, a nomad chieftain founded the kingdom of Parthia, situated between the Seleucid and Bactrian kingdoms. Claiming to be the heirs of the more ancient Persians, the Parthians expanded until by 130 B.C.E. they had wrested Babylonia from the Seleucids. Although Parthia was essentially a native Iranian state, its inhabitants absorbed some Hellenistic culture. Cut off from Seleucid rule by the Parthian kingdom, Bactria also became independent. Its Greek rulers, descendants of Alexander's veterans, controlled the caravan route to India and issued some of the most beautiful of Greek coins. In 183 B.C.E. the Bactrians crossed into India and conquered the province of Gandhara. One result of the conquest was a strong Greek influence on Indian art (see Chapter 6).

In the history of Western civilization, there is little of greater significance than Rome's absorption of Greek civilization and its transference of that heritage to later European culture. The stage on which this story began was the cosmopolitan Hellenistic Age, which "longed and strove for *Homonoia*, Concord between man and man . . . [and] proclaimed a conception of the world as One Great City."[35] The process by which the Roman West was Hellenized will be described in the next chapter.

Conclusion

The two most important centers of the Aegean maritime civilization were Knossos, on the island of Crete, and Mycenae, on the Greek mainland. Aegean civilization reached its highest development first in Crete (2000–1450 B.C.E.), where these island dwellers fashioned a sophisticated urban culture, drawing on original creativity as well as influences from the Near East and Africa. After 1450 B.C.E. the center of Aegean culture shifted to Mycenae. The Mycenaean dominance lasted until nearly 1100 B.C.E., when migrations of peoples and possibly internal revolt ended their control, bringing about yet more migrations and displacement that probably forced the Mycenaeans eastward to Ionia and Asia Minor. There, and on the Greek mainland, fiercely independent city-states evolved a distinctly Hellenic culture that was to come to full fruition in the Hellenic Age (eighth to fourth centuries B.C.E.).

The Greek achievement reached its zenith in fifth-century B.C.E. Athens. During that time, the Athenians saved Greece from conquest by Persia and went on to unify most of Greece under their leadership. During its short existence, the Athenian Empire brought peace and prosperity to the Greek world. Athens also made itself the center of Greece's Golden Age of art, literature, and philosophy. We can therefore understand the assessment made by Pericles: "I claim that our city as a whole is an education to Greece."[36]

We can also paraphrase Pericles' statement and say that the history of Greece as a whole is an education to us. All aspects of Greek civilization—political, economic, social, cultural, and religious—appear to have gone through a complete development. (For example, is there any form of government that the Greeks did not experience?) With an understanding of Greek civilization from its beginning in the Greek Middle Ages, we are better able to understand European civilization from its beginning in the Middle Ages. We will also be inclined to say of Greek history what Thucydides said of his *History of the Peloponnesian War:* that it can be "judged useful by those inquirers who desire an exact knowledge of the past as an aid to the interpretation of the future, which will according to human nature recur in much the same way."[37]

Fortunately for the Greeks, and for us, Philip II of Macedonia, who conquered the city-states and ended their independence, sincerely admired Hellenic culture—an admiration shared by his son, Alexander the Great. It was the ambitious and charismatic Alexander who conquered the Near East and set up the empire that was eventually carved into three great successor states at the time of Alexander's death. The Hellenistic Age, which began with those successor states, was a period of economic expansion, cosmopolitanism, striking intellectual and artistic achievements, and the wide diffusion of Greek culture.

Suggestions for Reading

John Boardman, Jasper Griffin, and Oswyn Murray, eds., *The Oxford History of the Classical World* (Oxford University Press, 1986); Alan Samuel, *Promise of the West: The Greek World, Rome, and Judaism* (Routledge, 1988); and Peter Green, *Classical Bearings: Interpreting Ancient History and Culture* (Thames & Hudson, 1990), are valuable treatments.

Paul MacKendrick, *The Greek Stones Speak: The Story of Archaeology in Greek Lands,* 2nd ed. (Norton, 1981), is a popular account of the great archaeological discoveries in the Aegean area. See also Rodney Castleden, *Minoans: Life in Bronze Age Crete* (Routledge, 1990); Michael Wood, *In Search of the Trojan War* (New American Library, 1985); William McDonald and Carol Thomas, *Progress into the Past: The Rediscovery of Mycenaean Civilization* (Indiana University Press, 1990); Emily Vermeule, *Greece in the Bronze Age* (University of Chicago Press, 1972); Chester G. Starr, *The Origins of Greek Civilization, 1100–650 B.C.* (Knopf, 1961); Carl William Blegen, *Troy and Trojans* (Praeger, 1963); and A. J. B. Wace, *Mycenae* (Princeton University Press, 1949). Mary Renault, *The King Must Die* (Bantam, 1974), is an absorbing novel set in Mycenaean times.

John V. A. Fine, *The Ancient Greeks: A Critical History* (Belknap/Harvard University Press, 1983); A. R. Burn, *The Pelican History of Greece* (Penguin, 1966); M. I. Finley, *The Ancient Greeks: An Introduction to Their Life and Thoughts* (Viking, 1963); and Antony Andrewes, *The Greeks* (Norton, 1978), are valuable analyses. J. B. Bury and Russell Meiggs, *A History of Greece to the Death of Alexander the Great,* 4th ed. (St. Martin's Press, 1975), is a standard detailed history. M. I. Finley, *The World of Odysseus,* 2nd ed. (Viking, 1977), is excellent on the historical value of Homer. On the transition from oligarchy to democracy, see Antony Andrewes, *The Greek Tyrants* (Humanities Press, 1956), and W. G. Forrest, *The Emergence of Greek Democracy, 800–400 B.C.* (McGraw-Hill, 1966).

Valuable special studies on politics, economics, and society include A. R. Burn, *Persia and the Greeks: The Defense of the West, 546–478 B.C.,* 2nd ed. (Stanford University Press, 1984); Humphrey Mitchell, *Sparta* (Cambridge University Press, 1952); A. H. M. Jones, *Athenian Democracy* (Johns Hopkins University Press, 1986); Michel M. Austin and Pierre Vidal-Naquet, *Economic and Social History of Ancient Greece* (University of California Press, 1979); John Boardman, *The Greeks Overseas: Their Early Colonies and Trade,* 3rd ed. (Thames & Hudson, 1982); Russell Meiggs, *The Athenian Empire* (Oxford University Press, 1980); Cyril E. Robinson, *Everyday Life in Ancient Greece* (Greenwood Press, 1978); Frank Frost, *Greek Society,* 3rd ed. (Heath, 1987); M. I. Finley, *Ancient Slavery and Modern Ideology* (Penguin, 1983); H. A. Harris, *Sport in Greece and Rome* (Cornell University Press, 1972); K. J. Dover, *Greek Homosexuality,* 2nd ed. (MJF Books, 1997); and Chester G. Starr, *The Influence of Sea Power in Ancient History* (Oxford University Press, 1989). Martin Bernal, *Black Athena: The Afroasiatic Roots of Classical Civilization,* 2 vols. (Rutgers University Press, 1987, 1991), claims that Greek civilization had African and Near Eastern origins. For some critical reviews, see the *Journal of Mediterranean Archaeology,* vol. 3, no. 2 (June 1990).

Sarah Pomeroy, *Goddesses, Whores, Wives, and Slaves: Women in Classical Antiquity* (Schocken, 1976), is a short popular account. Bonnie S. Anderson and Judith P. Zinsser, *A History of Their Own: Women in Europe from Prehistory to the Present,* Vol. 1 (Harper & Row, 1988), and Mary Kinnear, *Daughters of Time: Women in the Western Tradition* (University of Michigan Press, 1982), are outstanding studies. See also Eva Cantarella, *Pandora's Daughters: The Role and Status of Women in Greek and Roman Antiquity* (Johns Hopkins University Press, 1988).

Edith Hamilton, *The Greek Way* (Norton, 1930), is a popular appreciation of Hellenic literature. Werner Jaeger, *Paideia: The Ideals of Greek Culture,* 2nd ed., Vol. 1: *Archaic Greece: The Mind of Athens* (Oxford University Press, 1986), has been called "the most illuminating work on Greece." See also Albin Lesky, *A History of Greek Literature* (Hackett, 1996).

Walter Burkert, *Greek Religion* (Harvard University Press, 1985), is a standard work. See also Walter F. Otto, *The Homeric Gods: The Spiritual Significance of Greek Religion* (Octagon Books, 1978); Michael Grant, *Myths of the Greeks and Romans* (Meridian, 1995); A. W. H. Adkins, *Moral Values and Political Behavior in Ancient Greece: From Homer to the End of the Fifth Century* (Norton, 1972); Eric R. Dodds, *The Greeks and the Irrational* (University of California Press, 1983); and Joseph Fontenrose, *The Delphic Oracle, Its Responses and Operations* (University of California Press, 1978).

Good introductions to Greek philosophy and science include W. K. C. Guthrie, *The Greek Philosophers from Thales to Aristotle* (Routledge, 1989); Francis M. Cornford, *Before and After Socrates* (Cambridge University Press, n.d.); G. E. R. Lloyd, *Early Greek Science: Thales to Aristotle* (Norton, 1970); G. E. R. Lloyd, *Greek Science After Aristotle* (Norton, 1973); and Erwin H. Ackerknecht, *A Short History of Medicine,* rev. ed. (Johns Hopkins University Press, 1982).

J. J. Pollitt, *Art and Experience in Classical Greece* (Cambridge University Press, 1972), is outstanding. See also Blanche R. Brown, *Anticlassicism in Greek Sculpture of the Fourth Century B.C.* (New York University Press, 1973); R. M. Cook, *Greek Art: Its Development, Character and Influence* (Penguin, 1991); A. W. Lawrence, *Greek Architecture,* 5th ed. (Yale University Press, 1996); Margarete Bieber, *The Sculpture of the Hellenistic Age,* 2nd ed. (Hacker, 1980); and Graham Ley, *A Short Introduction to the Ancient Greek Theater* (University of Chicago Press, 1991).

William W. Tarn, *Hellenistic Civilisation,* 3rd ed. (Methuen, 1966), is a detailed survey. See also F. W. Walbank, *The Hellenistic World* (Harvard University Press, 1982); John Onians, *Art and Thought in the Hellenistic Age: The Greek World View, 350–50 B.C.* (Thames & Hudson, 1979); and A. A. Long, *Hellenistic Philosophy: Stoics, Epicureans, Sceptics,* 2nd ed. (University of California Press, 1986). On the career and motives of Alexander the Great, see the biographies by Peter Green (Praeger, 1970), Ulrich Wilcken (Norton, 1932), J. R. Hamilton (University of Pittsburgh Press, 1974), and William W. Tarn (Beacon Press, 1948).

Suggestions for Web Browsing

Minoan Palaces
http://dilos.com/region/crete/minoan_pictures.html

Images and text from major Minoan archaeological sites, including Knossos.

Ancient Greek World
http://www.museum.upenn.edu/Greek_World/Intro.html

A presentation by the University of Pennsylvania Museum of Archaeology and Anthropology. Text and museum artifacts tell the vivid story of life in ancient Greece: land and time; daily life, economy, religion, and death.

Perseus Project
http://www.perseus.tufts.edu/

An impressive compilation of information on Greek art, architecture, and literature. One of the most useful but also scholarly sites dealing with ancient Greece.

Vatican Museum: Greek Collection
http://christusrex.org/www1/vaticano/GP-Profano.html

The excellent works in the Vatican's Greek collection are displayed and discussed in this outstanding site.

Daily Life in Ancient Greece
http://members.aol.com/Donnclass/Greeklife.html

A wonderfully entertaining site on ancient Greek life—gives a feel for what life would be like in a variety of Greek city-states.

Women's Life in Greece and Rome
http://www.uky.edu/ArtsSciences/Classics/wlgr/wlgr-index.html

Details about the private life and legal status of women, in addition to biographies of prominent women of ancient Rome.

Diotima: Women and Gender in the Ancient World
http://www.uky.edu/ArtsSciences/Classics/gender.html

An excellent site for information on women in ancient Greece—their political influence, occupations, dress, diet. A great range of information.

Alexander the Great
http://www.erc.msstate.edu/~vkire/faq/history/11.3.html

Web page detailing the life of the king of Macedonia and conqueror of the Persian Empire. Text and images describe his early life, ascension to the throne, major battles, travels, and death.

Ancient Olympics
http://olympics.tufts.edu/

Compare ancient and modern Olympic sports and read about the Olympic athletes who were famous in those earlier times.

Notes

1. Plutarch, *Lives*, "Pericles," 13.
2. See Leonard R. Palmer, *Mycenaeans and Minoans: Aegean Prehistory in the Light of the Linear B Tablets* (New York: Knopf, 1961), ch. 5.
3. Homer, *Iliad*, 12.360.
4. Quoted in Werner Jaeger, *Paideia: The Ideals of Greek Culture*, Vol. 1: *Archaic Greece: The Mind of Athens* (New York: Oxford University Press, 1939), p. 70.
5. Plato, *Laws* 5.735.
6. Plutarch, *Lives*, "Solon," 16.
7. Plutarch, *Lives*, "Lycurgus," 15.
8. Ibid.
9. Ibid.
10. Cyril E. Robinson, *Hellas: A Short History of Ancient Greece* (Boston: Beacon Press, 1955), p. 68.
11. Thucydides, *History of the Peloponnesian War* 2.65.
12. Ibid., 2.37, 40.
13. Ibid., 2.40, 41.
14. Ibid., 1.23.
15. Ibid., 2.65.
16. Ibid., 3.37.
17. Ibid., 5.105.
18. Ibid., 6.90.
19. Herodotus, *History of the Persian Wars* 7.10.
20. Plato, *Apology* 41.
21. Plato, *Phaedrus* 247.
22. Plato, *Republic* 451.
23. Quoted in Max Cary and T. J. Haarhoff, *Life and Thought in the Greek and Roman World*, 5th ed. (London: Methuen, 1959), p. 192.
24. Quoted in A. R. Burn, *The Pelican History of Greece* (Baltimore: Penguin, 1966), p. 272.
25. Thucydides, *History of the Peloponnesian War* 1.22.
26. Quoted in A. R. Burn, *The Lyric Age of Greece* (New York: St. Martin's Press, 1960), p. 166.
27. Sappho, "To Anaktoria," trans. Willis Barnstone, ll. 6–13, in *Sappho* (New York: Anchor Books, 1965).
28. Aeschylus, *Agamemnon*, in *Ten Greek Plays*, trans. Gilbert Murray, ed. Lane Cooper (New York: Oxford University Press, 1929), p. 96.
29. Joseph Wood Krutch, *The Modern Temper* (New York: Harcourt Brace, 1956), p. 84.
30. Euripides, *Medea*, in *Ten Greek Plays*, pp. 320, 321.
31. Aristophanes, *The Wasps*, ll. 1065–1070, in *The Frogs and Other Plays*, trans. David Barrett (Baltimore: Penguin, 1964), p. 77.
32. Theocritus, *Idyl* 15, trans. Nels M. Bailkey.
33. Quoted in I. E. S. Edwards and John Boardman, eds., *The Cambridge Ancient History*, Vol. 11 (Cambridge: Cambridge University Press, 1936), p. 696.
34. Moschus, *Idyl* 9, trans. Andrew Lang.
35. Gilbert Murray, *Hellenism and the Modern World* (Boston: Beacon Press, 1953), pp. 56–57.
36. Thucydides, *History of the Peloponnesian War* 2.41.
37. Ibid., 1.22.

The ruins of the Roman Carthage in modern Tunisia stand today as memorials to the splendor and might of Rome in its glory. Carthage, once the greatest rival to Rome's advance, gave way to conquest and was rebuilt under Roman dominance.

Roman Civilization

The Roman World, 509 B.C.E.—568 C.E.

Chapter Contents

As the Athenians saw the symbol of their city-state's democracy and culture in the Acropolis, so the Romans viewed the Forum as the symbol of world dominance. Temples were to be found there, but in contrast to the Acropolis, the Forum was dominated by secular buildings—meetinghouses used for judicial, financial, and other sorts of public business; the Senate House; the nearby Colosseum, used for gladiatorial shows; and the great palaces of the emperors rising on the neighboring Palatine Hill. While the Acropolis was crowned with statues to Athena, the Forum was adorned with triumphal arches and columns commemorating military conquests. Rome was the capital of a world-state, extending from Britain to the Euphrates, and its citizens were proud of their imperial position.

Although the buildings in the Forum appear Greek in style, they are more monumental and immense. Here, then, are two clues in understanding the Romans: they borrowed much from others, especially the Greeks, and often they modified what they took. The Romans replaced the chaos of the Hellenistic Age with law and order and embraced the intellectual and artistic legacy of the conquered Greeks. As Rome's empire expanded, this legacy was spread westward throughout most of Europe.

Throughout a history that led from a simple farming community in the plain of Latium to a strong state that became the master of the Mediterranean world as well as of Gaul, Britain, and parts of Germany, the Romans met one challenge

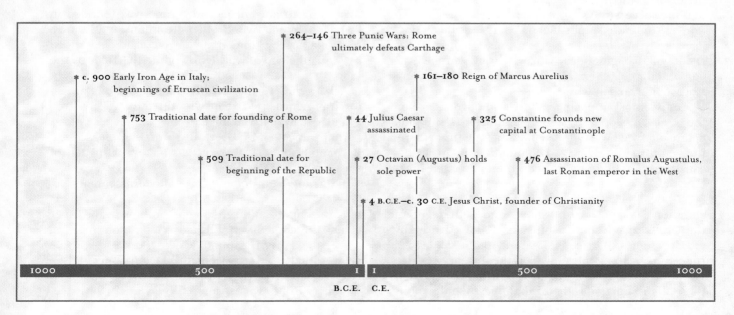

264–146 Three Punic Wars: Rome ultimately defeats Carthage

c. 900 Early Iron Age in Italy; beginnings of Etruscan civilization

161–180 Reign of Marcus Aurelius

753 Traditional date for founding of Rome

44 Julius Caesar assassinated

325 Constantine founds new capital at Constantinople

509 Traditional date for beginning of the Republic

27 Octavian (Augustus) holds sole power

476 Assassination of Romulus Augustulus, last Roman emperor in the West

4 B.C.E.–c. 30 C.E. Jesus Christ, founder of Christianity

| 1000 | 500 | I | I | 500 | 1000 |

B.C.E.   C.E.

after another with practicality and efficiency. In the company of its marching legions went engineers and architects, so that today, scattered throughout the lands that once were part of the Roman world, the remains of roads, walls, baths, basilicas, amphitheaters, and aqueducts survive as symbols of the Roman contribution to Western civilization.

Rome to 509 B.C.E.

The history of Rome extends from 753 B.C.E., the traditional date for the founding of the city by Romulus, Rome's legendary first king, to 568 C.E., shortly after the death of Justinian. The first period in this span of more than a thousand years ended in 509 B.C.E. with the expulsion of the Etruscan monarch Tarquin the Proud, the seventh and last of Rome's kings, and the establishment of an aristocratic republic.

Geography and Early Settlers of Italy

Geography did much to shape the course of events in Italy. The Italian peninsula is 600 miles long and about four times the size of Greece, or two-thirds that of California. A great mountainous backbone, the Apennine range, runs almost the entire length of the peninsula. But the land is not so rugged as in Greece, and the mountains do not constitute a formidable barrier to political unification. Unlike in Greece, a network of roads could be built to link the regions. Furthermore, the plain of Latium and its major city, Rome, occupied a strategic position. It was relatively easy to defend, and once the Romans had begun to establish themselves as successful conquerors, they occupied a central position on the peninsula, which made it difficult for their enemies to unite successfully against them. The strategic position of Rome was duplicated on a larger scale by Italy itself. Italy juts into the Mediterranean almost in the center of that great sea. Once Italy was unified, its commanding position aided it in dominating the entire Mediterranean world.

Italy's most imposing valleys and harbors are on the western slopes of the Apennines. The Italian peninsula faced west, not east. For a long time, therefore, culture in Italy lagged behind that of Greece because cultural contact between the two peoples was long delayed.

Both Greeks and Romans were offshoots of a common Indo-European stock, and settlement of the Greek and Italian peninsulas followed broadly parallel stages. Between 2000 and 1000 B.C.E., when Indo-European peoples invaded the Aegean world, a western wing of this nomadic migration filtered into the Italian peninsula, then inhabited by indigenous

Neolithic tribes. The first invaders, skilled in the use of copper and bronze, settled in the Po valley. Another wave of Indo-Europeans, equipped with iron weapons and tools, followed; in time the newer and older settlers intermingled and spread throughout the peninsula. One group, the Latins, settled in the plain of Latium, in the lower valley of the Tiber River.

As the Iron Age dawned in the western Mediterranean, the cultures of Italy became increasingly significant. During the ninth century B.C.E. the Etruscans established a dominant culture throughout much of Italy. The exact origin of the Etruscans remains uncertain. Some experts believe them to have been a non-Indo-European people who came to Italy by sea from Asia Minor. Others believe that their origin is explained through a rapid and creative growth of already resident iron-using peoples in northern Italy. Perhaps a combination of the two explanations is most likely—that native creativity fueled by contact with immigrants from the East resulted in a distinctly aggressive and creative culture. Expanding from the west coast up to the Po valley and south to the Bay of Naples, the Etruscans organized the backward Italic peoples into a loose confederation of Etruscan-dominated city-states.

After 750 B.C.E. Greek colonists migrated to southern Italy and Sicily, where they served as a protective buffer against powerful and prosperous Carthage, a Phoenician colony established in North Africa about 800 B.C.E. Yet the future was not to belong to these various invaders but to an insignificant village on the Tiber River, then in the shadows of Etruscan expansion. This was Rome, destined to be ruler of the ancient world.

Rome's Origins

According to ancient legend, Rome was founded in 753 B.C.E. by the twin brothers Romulus and Remus, sons of a nearby king's daughter who had been raped by Mars, the god of war. Thrown into the Tiber by the king, they were rescued and suckled by a she-wolf. Other legends further related that Romulus's ancestor was Aeneas, a Trojan who after the fall of Troy founded a settlement in Latium. The Aeneas story, perhaps invented by Greek mythmakers, pleased the Romans because it linked their history with that of the Greeks.

Turning from fable to fact, modern scholars believe that in the eighth century B.C.E. the inhabitants of some small Latin settlements on hills in the Tiber valley united and established a common meeting place, the Forum, around which the city of Rome grew. Situated at a convenient place for fording the river and protected from invaders by the hills and marshes, Rome was strategically located. Neverthe-

The Italian peninsula has little arable land and few navigable rivers and is crisscrossed with mountains. The Romans' ability to impose unity on this fragmented "boot" attests to their military and cultural strength and determination.

less, the expanding Etruscans conquered Rome about 625 B.C.E., and under their direction Rome became an important city-state.

Some features of Etruscan culture were original contributions; some were borrowed from the Greek colonies in southern Italy, and much of these, including the alphabet, was passed on to the Romans. (Etruscan writing can be read phonetically, but it is still not completely understood.) From their Etruscan overlords, the Romans acquired some of their gods and the practice of prophesying by examining animal entrails and observing the flight of birds. From the conquerors, too, the conquered learned the art of building (especially the arch), the practice of making statues of their gods, and the staging of gladiatorial combats. Even the name *Roma* appears to be an Etruscan word.

The Roman Monarchy, 753–509 B.C.E.

Rome's political growth followed a line of development similar to that of the Greek city-states: monarchy of the sort described by Homer, oligarchy, democracy, and, finally, the permanent dictatorship of the Roman emperors. For reasons that are both clear and instructive, in moving from oligarchy to democracy the Romans succeeded in avoiding the intermediate stage of tyranny.

The executive power, both civil and military, of Rome's seven kings (the last three were Etruscans) was called the *imperium*, which was symbolized by an ax bound in a bundle of rods *(fasces)*. In the twentieth century C.E. the fasces provided both the symbol and the name for Italian dictator Benito Mussolini's political creed, *fascism*.

Etruscan tombs were often elaborately painted with scenes of feasting and entertainment. On this tomb youths celebrate with music and wine.

Although the imperium was officially conferred on the monarch by a popular assembly made up of all arms-bearing citizens, the king turned for advice to a council of nobles called the Senate. Senators held their positions for life, and they and their families belonged to the *patrician* class, the fathers of the state (*pater* means "father"). The other class of Romans, the *plebeians,* or commoners, included small farmers, artisans, and many clients, or dependents, of patrician landowners.

In 509 B.C.E. the patricians overthrew the Etruscan monarchy and established an aristocratic form of government, known as the Republic.

The Early Republic, 509–133 B.C.E.: Domestic Affairs

The history of the Roman Republic can be divided into two distinct periods. During the first, from 509 to 133 B.C.E., two themes are dominant: a constitutional change from aristocracy to democracy, the result of the gradual extension of political and social equality to the plebeian lower class; and the expansion of Rome, first in Italy and then in the Mediterranean area.

Establishment of the Republic

In 509 B.C.E. the patricians forced out the last Etruscan king, Tarquin the Proud (Tarquinius Superbus), claiming he had acted despotically. (According to the Roman historian Livy, Tarquin was called "the Proud" because he "was the first king of Rome to break the established tradition of consulting the Senate on all matters of public business, and to govern by the mere authority of himself and his household.")[1] The patricians replaced the monarchy with an aristocracy they called a *republic* (*res publica,* "commonwealth"). The imperium was transferred to two new magistrates, called *consuls.* Elected annually from the patrician class, the consuls invariably exercised power in the interest of that class. In the event of war or serious domestic emergency, an "extraordinary" magistrate called *dictator* could be substituted for the two consuls, but he was given absolute power for six months only. The popular assembly was retained because the patricians could control it by means of their plebeian clients who, in return for a livelihood, voted as their patrons directed them.

Struggle for Equal Rights

For more than two centuries following the establishment of the Republic, the plebeians struggled for political and social equality. Outright civil war was avoided by the willingness, however reluctant and delayed, of the patricians to accept the demands of the plebeians. This largely explains why it was unnecessary for the plebeians to resort to tyrants to help them gain their goals, as had happened in the Greek city-states, or to revolt. Much of the plebeians' success in this struggle was due to their having been granted the right to organize themselves as a corporate body capable of collective action. This concession, granted by the Senate early in the fifth century B.C.E. after the plebeians threatened to leave Rome and found a city elsewhere, established a sort of state within a state known as the *Concilium Plebis* ("gathering of the plebeians"), which was presided over by plebeian leaders called *tribunes* and could pass *plebiscites* ("plebeian decrees") that were binding only on the plebeian community. The tribunes also received the right to stop unjust or oppressive acts of the patrician consuls and Senate by uttering the word *veto* ("I forbid").

The next major concession was in the field of law. Because the consuls often interpreted Rome's unwritten customary law to suit patrician interests, the plebeians demanded that it be written down and made available for all to see. As a result, about 450 B.C.E. the law was inscribed on a dozen tablets of bronze and set up publicly in the Forum. This Law of the Twelve Tables was the first landmark in the long history of Roman law, and Roman schoolchildren were required to memorize it.

In time the plebeians acquired other fundamental rights and safeguards: the rights to appeal a death sentence imposed by a consul and to be retried before the popular assembly were secured; marriage between patricians and plebeians, prohibited by the Law of the Twelve Tables, was legalized; and the enslavement of citizens for debt was abolished.

That their service in the Roman army was indispensable to the patricians greatly increased the plebeians' bargaining position in the state. Since Rome was almost constantly at war during these years, the patrician leaders of the state were more ready to accommodate plebeian demands than to face the possibility of a withdrawal of military participation by the commoners.

Little by little the plebeians acquired more power in the government. In 367 B.C.E. one consulship was reserved for the plebeians, and before the end of the century plebeians were eligible to hold other important magistracies that the patricians had created in the meantime. Among these new offices, whose powers had originally been held by the consuls, were the *praetor* (in charge of the administration of justice), *quaestor* (treasurer), and *censor* (supervisor of public morals and the letting of state contracts).

The long struggle for equality ended in 287 B.C.E. when the Concilium Plebis was recognized as a constitutional body, which then became known as the Tribal Assembly, and its plebiscites became laws *(leges)* binding on all citizens, patricians as well as plebeians. The Roman Republic was technically a democracy, although in actual practice a senatorial aristocracy of noble patricians and rich plebeians continued to control the state. Having gained political and social equality, the plebeians were usually willing to allow the more experienced Senate to run the government from this time until 133 B.C.E., a period of almost constant warfare.

After 287 B.C.E. conflict in Roman society gradually assumed a new form. Before this time, the issue of greatest domestic importance had primarily been social and political inequality between the classes of patricians and plebeians. After equality was achieved, many rich plebeians were elected to the highest offices and became members of an expanded senatorial aristocracy. The new Roman "establishment" was prepared to guard its privileges even more fiercely than the old patricians had done. This fact became evident in 133 B.C.E. when a popular leader, Tiberius Gracchus, arose to challenge the establishment. But

This statue of a patrician with busts of his ancestors dates from either the first century B.C.E. or the first century C.E. The patricians were the aristocracy of Rome, and during the later Republic they came increasingly into conflict with senators and generals who took the part of the plebeians.

by this time the Roman populace had lost many of the characteristics that the citizens of the early Republic had demonstrated.

Society and Religion

The most important unit of early Roman society was the family. The power of the family father *(pater familias)* was absolute, and strict discipline was imposed to instill in children the virtues to which the Romans attached particular importance—loyalty, courage, self-control, and respect for laws and ancestral customs. The Romans of the early Republic were stern, hardworking, and practical. Cato the Elder (d. 149 B.C.E.), for example, took inspiration from frequent visits to view the small farm and humble cottage of a former consul who,

> though he had become the greatest of Romans, had subdued the most warlike nations, and driven Pyrrhus out of Italy, nevertheless tilled this little patch of ground with his own hands and occupied this cottage, after three triumphs. Here it was that the ambassadors of the Samnites once found him seated at his hearth cooking turnips, and offered him much gold; but he dismissed them, saying that a man whom such a meal satisfied had no need of gold.[2]

In contrast to the frequency of divorce in the late Republic, marriage in the early Republic was viewed as a lifelong union; patrician marriages were usually arranged between families and were undertaken primarily for the creation of children, but on many occasions such unions resulted in mutual affection between husband and wife. An early epitaph from the second century B.C.E. reads:

> Stranger, what I say is short, stay and read. Here is the unbeautiful grave of a beautiful woman. Her parents named her Claudia. She loved her husband with her whole heart. She bore two sons: one of whom she left alive on earth, the other she buried in the earth. Her speech was gay, but her bearing seemly. She kept the home. She made the wool. I have spoken. Go away.[3]

The religion of the early Romans had as yet little or no connection with ethics, and views concerning life after death were very vague. Religious practices were confined to placating the spirits *(numina)* of the family and the state by the repetition of complicated formulas, or spells. Mispronunciation of even a single syllable was enough to cause the spell to lose its power. Under Etruscan influence the major spirits were personified. The sky-spirit Jupiter became the patron god of Rome; Mars, spirit of vegetation, became god of war; and Janus, whose temple doors remained open when the army was away at war, was originally the spirit of the city gate.

Although early Roman religion had little to do with morals, it had much to do with morale. It strengthened family solidarity and enhanced a patriotic devotion to the state and its gods. But the early Romans' respect for hard work, frugality, and family and state gods was to be challenged by the effects of Rome's expansion in Italy and over much of the Mediterranean area during the early Republic.

The Early Republic, 509–133 B.C.E.: Foreign Affairs

The growth of Rome from a small city-state to the dominant power in the Mediterranean world in less than 400 years (509–133 B.C.E.) was a remarkable achievement. Roman expansion was not deliberately planned; rather, it was the result of dealing with unsettled conditions, first in Italy and then abroad, which were thought to threaten Rome's security. Rome always claimed that its wars were defensive, waged to protect itself from potentially hostile neighbors.

By 270 B.C.E. the first phase of Roman expansion had been accomplished. Ringed by hostile peoples—Etruscans in the north, land-hungry hill tribes in central Italy, and Greeks in the south—Rome subdued them all after long, determined effort and found itself master of all Italy south of the Po valley. In the process the Romans developed the administrative skills and traits of character—both fair-mindedness and ruthlessness—that would lead to the acquisition of an empire with possessions on three continents by 133 B.C.E.

Roman Conquest of Italy

Soon after driving out their Etruscan overlords in 509 B.C.E., Rome and the Latin League, composed of

---

The Early Wars of Rome

509 B.C.E.	Etruscans expelled from Rome
390 B.C.E.	Gauls attack and plunder Rome
338 B.C.E.	Rome emerges victor in wars with members of the Latin League
264–241 B.C.E.	Rome wins Sicily in First Punic War
218–201 B.C.E.	Rome defeats Hannibal in Second Punic War
149–146 B.C.E.	Carthage destroyed in Third Punic War

Livy: Horatius at the Bridge

Livy relates how one man saved Rome from reconquest by the Etruscans, about 506 B.C.E.

On the approach of the Etruscan army, the Romans abandoned their farmsteads and moved into the city. Garrisons were posted. In some sections the city walls seemed sufficient protection, in others the barrier of the Tiber. The most vulnerable point was the wooden bridge, and the Etruscans would have crossed it and forced an entrance into the city, had it not been for the courage of one man, Horatius Cocles—that great soldier whom the fortune of Rome gave to be her shield on that day of peril.... Proudly [Horatius] took his stand at the outer end of the bridge; conspicuous amongst the rout of fugitives, sword and shield ready for action, he prepared himself for close combat, one man against an army. The advancing enemy paused in sheer astonishment at such reckless courage. Two other men, Spurius Lartius and Titus Herminius, both aristocrats with a fine military record, were ashamed to leave Horatius alone, and with their support he won through the first few minutes of desperate danger. Soon, however, he forced them to save themselves and leave him; for little was now left of the bridge, and the demolition squads were calling them back before it was too late. Once more Horatius stood alone; with defiance in his eyes he confronted the Etruscan chivalry, challenging one after another to single combat, and mocking them all as tyrants' slaves who, careless of their own liberty, were coming to destroy the liberty of others. For a while they hung back, each waiting for his neighbour to make the first move, until shame at the unequal battle drove them to action, and with a fierce cry they hurled their spears at the solitary figure which barred their way. Horatius caught the missiles on his shield and, resolute as ever, straddled the bridge and held his ground. The Etruscans moved forward, and would have thrust him aside by the sheer weight of numbers, but their advance was suddenly checked by the crash of the falling bridge and the simultaneous shout of triumph from the Roman soldiers who had done their work in time. The Etruscans could only stare in bewilderment as Horatius, with a prayer to Father Tiber to bless him and his sword, plunged fully armed into the water and swam, through the missiles which fell thick about him, safely to the other side where his friends were waiting to receive him. It was a noble piece of work—legendary, maybe, but destined to be celebrated in story through the years to come.

From Livy, *The Early History of Rome*, trans. Aubrey de Sélincourt (Hammondsworth, England: Penguin, 1960), bk. 2, ch. 10.

---

other Latin peoples in Latium, entered into a defensive alliance against the Etruscans. This new combination was so successful that by the beginning of the fourth century B.C.E. it had become the chief power in central Italy. But at this time (390 B.C.E.) a major disaster almost ended the history of Rome. A raiding army of Celts, called Gauls by the Romans, invaded Italy from central Europe, wiped out the Roman army, and almost destroyed the city by fire. The elderly members of the Senate, according to the traditional account, sat awaiting their fate with quiet dignity before they were massacred. Only a garrison on the Capitoline Hill held out under siege. After seven months and the receipt of a huge ransom in gold, the Gauls withdrew. The stubborn Romans rebuilt their city and protected it with a stone wall, part of which still stands. They also remodeled their army by replacing the solid line of fixed spears of the phalanx formation, borrowed from the Etruscans and Greeks, with much more maneuverable small units of 120 men, called *maniples*, armed with javelins instead of spears. It would be 800 years before another barbarian army would be able to conquer the city of Rome.

The Latin League grew alarmed at Rome's increasing strength, and war broke out between the former allies. Upon Rome's victory in 338 B.C.E. the league was dissolved, and the Latin cities were forced to sign individual treaties with Rome. Thus the same year that saw the domination of Macedonia over Greece also saw the rise of a new power in Italy.

Border clashes with aggressive mountain tribes of Samnium led to three fiercely fought Samnite wars and the extension of Rome's frontiers to the Greek colonies in southern Italy by 290 B.C.E. Fearing Roman conquest, the Greeks prepared for war and called in the mercenary army of the Greek king, Pyrrhus of Epirus, who dreamed of becoming a second Alexander the Great. Pyrrhus's war elephants, unknown in Italy, twice routed the Romans, but at so heavy a cost that such a triumph is still called a "Pyrrhic victory." When a third battle failed to persuade the Romans to make peace, Pyrrhus is reported to have remarked, "The discipline of these barbarians is not barbarous," and returned to his homeland. By 270 B.C.E. the Roman army had subdued the Greek city-states in southern Italy.

Treatment of Conquered Peoples

Instead of slaughtering or enslaving their defeated foes in Italy, the Romans treated them fairly, in time creating a strong loyalty to Rome throughout the peninsula. Roman citizenship was a prized possession that was not extended to all peoples in Italy until the first century B.C.E. Most defeated states were required to sign a treaty of alliance with Rome, which bound them to accept Rome's foreign policy and to supply troops for the Roman army. No tribute was required, and each allied state retained local self-government. Rome did, however, annex about one-fifth of the conquered lands, on which nearly 30 colonies were established by 250 B.C.E.

The First Punic War

After 270 B.C.E. only Carthage remained as Rome's rival in the West. Much more wealthy and populous than Rome, with a magnificent navy that controlled the western Mediterranean and with a domain that included the northern coast of Africa, Sardinia, Corsica, western Sicily, and much of Spain, Carthage seemed more than a match for Rome. But Carthage was governed by a commercial oligarchy, which hired mercenaries to do its fighting. In the long run, the lack of a loyal body of citizens and allies, such as Rome had, proved to be Carthage's fatal weakness.

The First Punic War (from *punicus*, Latin for "Phoenician") broke out in 264 B.C.E. when Rome attempted to throw out a Carthaginian force that had occupied Messina, on the northeastern tip of Sicily, just across from Roman Italy. According to Polybius, a Hellenistic Greek historian, the Romans "felt it was absolutely necessary not to let Messina fall, or allow the Carthaginians to secure what would be like a bridge to enable them to cross into Italy."[4] Rome and its Italian allies lost more than 500 ships in naval engagements and storms before Carthage asked for peace in 241 B.C.E. (The Romans won only after they had invented the *corvus*, or "crow," a boarding bridge at the bow of a ship that, when lowered, turned a naval battle into a land battle.) Sicily, Sardinia, and Corsica were annexed as the first acquisitions in Rome's overseas empire, regulated and taxed—in contrast to Rome's allies in Italy—by Roman officials called *governors*.

The Contest with Hannibal

Stunned by its defeat, Carthage concentrated on enlarging its empire in Spain. Rome's determination to prevent this led to the greatest and most difficult war in Roman history. While both powers sought a position of advantage, a young Carthaginian general, Hannibal, precipitated the Second Punic War by attacking Saguntum, a Spanish town claimed by Rome as an ally. Rome declared war, and Hannibal, seizing the initiative, in 218 B.C.E. led an army of about 40,000 men, 9000 cavalry troops, and a detachment of African elephants across the Alps into Italy. Although the crossing had cost him nearly half of his men and all but one of his elephants, Hannibal defeated the Romans three times within three years.

Hannibal's forces never matched those of the Romans in numbers. At Cannae, for example, where Hannibal won his greatest victory, some 70,000 Romans were wiped out by nearly 50,000 Carthaginians. On the whole, Rome's allies remained loyal in spite of these losses—testimony to Rome's fair and statesmanlike treatment of its Italian subjects. Because the Romans controlled the seas, Hannibal received little aid from Carthage. As a result, Hannibal was unable to inflict a mortal blow against the Romans.

The Romans finally produced a general, Scipio, who was Hannibal's match in military strategy and who was bold enough to invade Africa. Asked to return home after 15 years spent on Italian soil, Hannibal clashed with Scipio's legions at Zama, where the Carthaginians suffered a complete defeat. The power of Carthage was broken forever by a harsh treaty imposed in 201 B.C.E. Carthage was forced to pay a huge war indemnity, disarm its forces, and turn Spain over to the Romans. Hannibal fled to the Seleucid Empire, where he stirred up anti-Roman sentiment.

Roman Intervention in the East

The defeat of Carthage left Rome free to turn eastward and deal with King Philip V of Macedonia. Fearful of the new power that had risen in the west, Philip had allied himself with Hannibal during the darkest days of the Second Punic War. (He sent no aid, however, because of an uprising in Greece.) Now, in 200 B.C.E., Rome was ready to act, following an appeal from Pergamum and Rhodes for aid in protecting the smaller Hellenistic states from Philip, who was advancing in the Aegean, and from the Seleucid emperor, who was moving into Asia Minor. The heavy Macedonian phalanxes were no match for the mobile Roman legions, and in 197 B.C.E. Philip was soundly defeated in Macedonia. His dreams of empire were ended when Rome deprived him of his warships and military bases in Greece. The Romans then proclaimed the independence of Greece and were praised as liberators by the grateful Greeks. According to the Roman historian Livy:

There was one people in the world which would fight for others' liberties at its own cost, to its own peril,

Hannibal's Character

The Roman historian Livy wrote the following character sketch of the great Carthaginian leader Hannibal. In Livy's brief profile, both the respect and the hatred the Romans held for their formidable enemy are quite obvious.

Hannibal was sent to Spain, where the troops received him with unanimous enthusiasm, the old soldiers feeling that in the person of this young man Hamilcar himself was restored to them. In the features and expression of the son's face they saw the father once again, the same vigour in his look, the same fire in his eyes. Very soon he no longer needed to rely upon his father's memory to make himself beloved and obeyed: his own qualities were sufficient. Power to command and readiness to obey are rare associates; but in Hannibal they were perfectly united, and their union made him as much valued by his commander as by his men. . . . Reckless in courting danger, he showed superb tactical ability once it was upon him. Indefatigable both physically and mentally, he could endure with equal ease excessive heat or excessive cold; he ate and drank not to flatter his appetites but only so much as would sustain his bodily strength. His time for waking, like his time for sleeping, was never determined by daylight or darkness: when his work was done, then, and then only, he rested, without need, moreover, of silence or a soft bed to woo sleep to his eyes. Often he was seen lying in his cloak on the bare ground amongst the common soldiers on sentry or picket duty. His accoutrement, like the horses he rode, was always conspicuous, but not his clothes, which were like those of any other officer of his rank and standing. Mounted or unmounted he was unequalled as a fighting man, always the first to attack, the last to leave the field. So much for his virtues—and they were great; but no less great were his faults: inhuman cruelty, a more than Punic perfidy, a total disregard of truth, honour, and religion, of the sanctity of an oath and of all that other men hold sacred. Such was the complex character of the man . . . doing and seeing everything which could help to equip him as a great military leader.

From Livy, *History of Rome*, 21.4, in Livy, *The War with Hannibal*, trans. Aubrey de Sélincourt (New York: Penguin, 1986).

---

and with its own toil, not limiting its guaranties of freedom to its neighbors, to men of the immediate vicinity, or to countries that lay close at hand, but ready to cross the sea that there might be no unjust empire anywhere and that everywhere justice, right, and law might prevail.[5]

A few years later Rome declared war on the Seleucid emperor, who had moved into Greece, urged on by Hannibal and a few greedy Greek states that resented Rome's refusal to dismember Macedonia. The Romans forced the emperor to leave Greece and Asia Minor, pay a huge indemnity, and give up his warships and war elephants. The Seleucids were checked again in 168 B.C.E. when a Roman ultimatum halted their invasion of Egypt. A Roman envoy met the advancing Seleucid army and, drawing a ring in the sand around the emperor, demanded that he decide on war or peace with Rome before stepping out of it. Egypt was declared a Roman protectorate. A year later Rome supported the Jews in their successful revolt against the Seleucids by addressing this message to the Seleucid ruler: "Wherefore hast thou made thy yoke heavy upon our friends and confederates the Jews? If therefore they complain any more against thee, we will do them justice, and fight with thee by sea and by land" (1 Maccabees 9:31–32).

Most of the East was now a Roman protectorate, the result of a policy—revealed again in Rome's action in stopping Seleucid aggression—in which Roman self-interest was combined with idealism. But Roman idealism turned sour when anti-Romanism became widespread in Greece, particularly among the poorer classes, who resented Rome's support of conservative governments and the status quo in general. The new policy was clearly revealed in 146 B.C.E. when, after many Greeks had supported an attempted Macedonian revival, Rome destroyed Corinth, a hotbed of anti-Romanism, as an object lesson. The Romans also supported the oligarchic factions in all Greek states and placed Greece under the watchful eye of the governor of Macedonia, which had been made a Roman province two years earlier. The idealistic Roman was fast becoming an ugly Roman.

Destruction of Carthage

In the West, meanwhile, Rome's hardening policy led to suspicion of Carthage's reviving prosperity and to a demand by Roman extremists for war—*Carthago delenda est* ("Carthage must be obliterated"). Obviously provoking the Third Punic War, the Romans besieged Carthage, which resisted heroically for

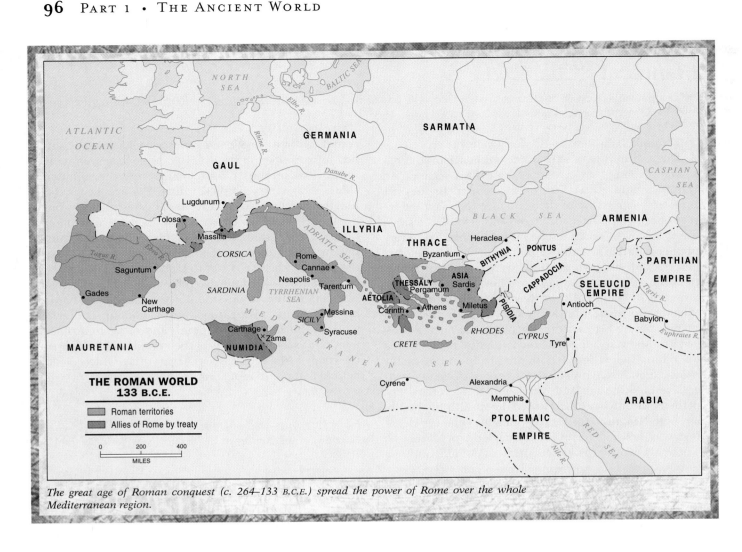

The great age of Roman conquest (c. 264–133 B.C.E.) spread the power of Rome over the whole Mediterranean region.

three years. They destroyed the city in 146 B.C.E., the same year they destroyed Corinth, and annexed the territory as a province.

Rome, Supreme in the Ancient World

In 133 B.C.E. Rome acquired its first province in Asia when the king of Pergamum, dying without an heir, left his kingdom to Rome. Apparently he feared that the discontented masses would revolt after his death unless Rome, with its reputation for maintaining law and order in the interest of the propertied classes, took over. Rome accepted the bequest and then spent the next three years suppressing a revolution of the poorer classes in the new province, called Asia. With provinces on three continents—Europe, Africa, and Asia—the once obscure Roman Republic was now supreme in the ancient world.

The Late Republic, 133–30 B.C.E.

The century following 133 B.C.E., during which Rome's frontiers reached the Euphrates and the Rhine, witnessed the failure of the Republic to solve problems generated in part by the acquisition of an empire. These years serve as a good example of the failure of a democracy and its replacement by a dictatorship. The experience of the late Republic illustrates Thucydides' verdict that a democracy is incapable of running an empire. Athens kept its democracy but lost its empire; Rome would keep its empire and lose its democracy.

Effects of Roman Expansion

The political history of Rome thus far has consisted of two dominant themes: the gradual extension of equal rights for all male citizens and the expansion of Roman dominion over the Mediterranean world. Largely as a result of this expansion, Rome faced critical social and economic problems by the middle of the second century B.C.E.

One of the most pressing problems was the decline in the number of small landowners, whose spirit and devotion had made Rome great. Burdened by frequent military service, their farms and buildings destroyed by Hannibal, and unable to

The Late Republic

133–123 B.C.E.	Reform movement of the Gracchi
88–82 B.C.E.	First Civil War (Marius vs. Sulla)
58–49 B.C.E.	Caesar conquers Gaul
49–45 B.C.E.	Second Civil War (Pompey vs. Caesar)
44 B.C.E.	Caesar assassinated
31 B.C.E.	Third Civil War (Octavian vs. Antony)
27 B.C.E.	Octavian (Augustus) becomes ruler of Rome

compete with the cheap grain imported from the new Roman province of Sicily, small farmers sold out and moved to the great city. Here they joined the unemployed and discontented *proletariat,* so called because their only contribution was *proles,* "children." The proletariat comprised a majority of the citizens in the city.

At the same time, improved farming methods learned from the Greeks and Carthaginians encouraged rich aristocrats to buy more and more land. Abandoning the cultivation of grain, they introduced large-scale scientific production of olive oil and wine, sheep and cattle. This change was especially profitable because an abundance of cheap slaves from conquered territory was available to work on the estates. These large slave plantations, called *latifundia,* were now common in many parts of Italy.

The land problem was further complicated by the government's practice of leasing part of the territory acquired in the conquest of the Italian peninsula to anyone willing to pay a percentage of the crop or animals raised on it. Only the wealthy could afford to lease large tracts of this public land, and in time they treated it as if it were their own property. Plebeian protests led to an attempt to limit the holdings of a single individual to 320 acres of public land, but the law enacted for that purpose was never enforced.

Corruption in the government was another mark of the growing weakness of the Roman Republic. Provincial officials took advantage of the opportunity to engage in graft for great profit, and a new sort of Roman businessmen scrambled selfishly for the profitable state contracts to supply the armies, collect taxes and loan money in the provinces, and lease state-owned mines and forests. An early example of corrupt business practices occurred during the Second Punic War. According to Livy, "Two scoundrels, taking advantage of the assumption by the state of all risks from tempest in the case of goods carried by sea

to armies in the field," fabricated false accounts of shipwrecks. "Their method was to load small and more or less worthless cargoes into old, rotten vessels, sink them at sea . . . , and then, in reporting the loss, enormously exaggerate the value of the cargoes." When the swindle was reported to the Senate, it took no action because it "did not wish at a time of such national danger to make enemies of the capitalists."[6]

Although in theory the government was a democracy, in practice it remained a senatorial oligarchy. Wars tend to strengthen the executive power in a state, and in Rome the Senate traditionally had such power. Even the tribunes, guardians of the people's rights, became for the most part puppets of the Senate. By the middle of the second century B.C.E. the government was in the hands of a wealthy, self-serving Senate, which became increasingly incapable of coping with the problems of governing a world-state. Ordinary citizens were for the most part impoverished and landless, and Rome swarmed with fortune hunters, imported slaves, unemployed farmers, and discontented war veterans. The poverty of the many, coupled with the great wealth of the few, hastened the decay of the old Roman traits of discipline, simplicity, and respect for authority. The next century (133–30 B.C.E.) saw Rome torn apart by internal conflict, which led to the establishment of a permanent dictatorship and the end of the Republic.

Reform Movement of the Gracchi

An awareness of Rome's profound social and economic problems led to the reform program of an idealistic and ambitious young aristocrat named Tiberius Gracchus. His reforming spirit was partly the product of the newly imported philosophical learning of Greece and an awareness that the old Roman character and way of life were fast slipping away. He sought to arrest Roman decline by restoring the backbone of the old Roman society, the small landowner. Supported by a faction of senators, Tiberius was elected tribune for the year 133 B.C.E. at the age of 29.

Tiberius proposed to the Tribal Assembly that the act limiting the holding of public land to 320 acres per citizen, plus 160 acres for each of two grown-up sons, be reenacted. Much of the public land would in the future continue to be held by the present occupants and their heirs as private property, but the rest was to be taken back and granted to the poor in small plots of 9 to 18 acres. The recipients were to pay a small rent and could not sell their holdings. In his address to the assembly Tiberius noted that

it is with lying lips that their commanders exhort the soldiers in their battles to defend sepulchres and shrines from the enemy; . . . they fight and die to support others in wealth and luxury, and though they are styled masters of the world, they have not a single clod of earth that is their own.[7]

When it became evident that the Tribal Assembly would adopt Tiberius's proposal, the Senate persuaded one of the other tribunes to veto the measure. On the ground that a tribune who opposed the will of the people had no right to his office, Tiberius took a fateful—and, the Senate claimed, unconstitutional—step by having the assembly depose the tribune in question. The agrarian bill was then passed.

To ensure the implementation of his agrarian reform, Tiberius again violated custom by standing for reelection in the Tribal Assembly after completing his one-year term. Claiming that he sought to make himself king, partisans of the Senate murdered Tiberius and 300 of his followers. The Republic's failure at this point to solve its problems without bloodshed stands in striking contrast to its earlier history of peaceful reform.

Tiberius's work was taken up by his younger brother, Gaius Gracchus, who was elected tribune for 123 B.C.E. In addition to the allocation of public land to the poor, Gaius proposed establishing Roman colonies in southern Italy and in Africa—his enemies said near the site of Carthage. To protect the poor against speculation in the grain market (especially in times of famine), Gaius committed the government to the purchase, storage, and subsequent distribution of wheat to the urban masses at about half the actual market price. Unfortunately, what Gaius intended as a relief measure later became a dole, whereby nearly free food was distributed—all too often for the advancement of astute politicians—to the entire proletariat.

Another of Gaius's proposals would have granted citizenship to Rome's Italian allies, who felt they were being mistreated by Roman officials. This proposal cost Gaius the support of the Roman proletariat, which did not wish to share the privileges of citizenship or share its control of the Tribal Assembly. Consequently, in 121 B.C.E. Gaius failed to be reelected to a third term as tribune when his opponents packed the Tribal Assembly with their followers on election day, and the Senate again resorted to force. It decreed what is today called martial law by authorizing the consuls to take any action deemed necessary "to protect the state and suppress the tyrants." Three thousand of Gaius's followers were killed in rioting or arrested and executed, a fate Gaius avoided by committing suicide.

The Senate had shown that it had no intention of initiating needed domestic reforms or of allowing others to do so, and the Gracchi's deaths were ominous signals of the way the Republic would decide its internal disputes in the future.

In foreign affairs as well, the Senate soon demonstrated ineptness. Rome was forced to grant citizenship to its Italian allies after the Senate's failure to deal with their grievances pushed them into open revolt (90–88 B.C.E.). Other shortsighted actions led to the first of the three civil wars that assisted in the destruction of the Republic.

The First Civil War: Marius Versus Sulla

Between 111 and 105 B.C.E. Roman armies, dispatched by the Senate and commanded by senators, failed to protect Roman business interests in Numidia, a kingdom in North Africa allied to Rome. Nor were they able to prevent Germanic tribes from overrunning southern Gaul, then a Roman province, and threatening Italy itself. Accusing the Senate of neglect and incompetence in directing Rome's foreign affairs, the Roman commercial class and common people joined together to elect Gaius Marius consul in 107 B.C.E., and the Tribal Assembly commissioned him to raise an army to put down the foreign danger. Marius first pacified North Africa and then crushed the first German threat to Rome. In the process he created a new-style Roman army that was destined to play a major role in the turbulent history of the late Republic.

Unlike the old Roman army, which was composed of conscripts who owned their own land and thought of themselves as loyal citizens of the Republic, the new army created by Marius was recruited from landless citizens for long terms of service. These professional soldiers identified their own interests with those of their commanders, to whom they swore loyalty and looked to for bonuses of land and money, since the Senate refused their requests for such support. Thus the character of the army changed from a militia of draftees to a career service in which loyalty to the state was replaced with loyalty to the commander. Ambitious generals were in a position to use their military power to seize the government.

In 88 B.C.E. the king of Pontus, in Asia Minor, encouraged by growing anti-Roman sentiment in the province of Asia and in Greece caused by corrupt governors, tax collectors, and moneylenders, declared war on Rome. The Senate ordered Cornelius Sulla, an able general and a strong supporter of the Senate's authority, to march east and restore order. As a countermove, the Tribal Assembly chose Marius for the eastern command. In effect both the Senate and the Tribal Assembly, whose power the Gracchi had revived, claimed to be the ultimate authority in the state. The result was the first of a series of civil wars between rival generals, each claiming to champion the cause of either the Senate or the Tribal Assembly. The first civil war ended in a complete victory for Sulla, who in 82 B.C.E. was appointed by the Senate to the seldom employed special office of dictator, not for a maximum of six months but for an unlimited term as "dictator for the revision of the constitution."

Sulla intended to restore the preeminence of the Senate. He drastically reduced the powers of the tribunes and the Tribal Assembly, giving the Senate virtually complete control of all legislation. Having massacred several thousand of the opposition, Sulla was convinced that his constitutional improvements would be permanent, and in 79 B.C.E. he voluntarily resigned his dictatorship and retired from public life. His reactionary changes, however, were not to last.

The Second Civil War: Pompey Versus Caesar

The first of the civil wars and its aftermath increased both division and discontent in the state and fueled the ambitions of younger individuals eager for personal power. The first of these men to come forward was Pompey, who had won fame as a military leader. In 70 B.C.E. he was elected consul. Although he was a former supporter of Sulla, he won popularity with the commoners by repealing Sulla's laws limiting the power of the tribunes and the Tribal Assembly. Pompey then put an end to disorder in the East caused by piracy (the result of the Senate's neglect of the Roman navy), the continuing threats of the king of Pontus, and the political uncertainty caused by the collapse of the Seleucid Empire. New Roman provinces and client states set up by Pompey brought order eastward as far as the Euphrates. These included the province of Syria—the last remnant of the once vast Seleucid Empire—and the client state of Judea, supervised by the governor of Syria.

Still another ambitious and able leader made his major impact in 59 B.C.E. Julius Caesar allied himself politically with Pompey and was elected consul. Following his consulship, Caesar spent nine years conquering Gaul, under the pretext of protecting the Gauls from the Germans across the Rhine. He accumulated a fortune in plunder and trained a loyal army of veterans. During his absence from Rome, he kept his name before the citizens by publishing an attractively written account of his military feats, *Commentaries on the Gallic War.*

Caesar's conquest of Gaul was to have tremendous consequences for the course of Western civilization, for its inhabitants quickly assimilated Roman culture. Consequently, when the Roman Empire collapsed in the West in the fifth century C.E., Romanized Gaul (France) ultimately took its place as a center of medieval civilization.

Fearful of Caesar's growing power, Pompey associated himself with the Senate in order to ruin him. When the Senate demanded in 49 B.C.E. that Caesar

disband his army, he crossed the Rubicon, the river in northern Italy that formed the boundary of his province. By crossing the Rubicon—a phrase employed today for any step that commits a person to a given course of action—Caesar in effect declared war on Pompey and the Senate. He marched on Rome while Pompey and most of the Senate fled to Greece, where Caesar defeated them at Pharsalus in 48 B.C.E. "They would have it so" was Caesar's curt comment as he walked among the Roman dead after the battle. Pompey was killed in Egypt when he sought refuge there, but the last Pompeian army was not defeated until 45 B.C.E. (After one battle, Caesar sent a friend a three-word letter: *Veni, vidi, vici*—"I came, I saw, I conquered.")

As he assumed the title of "dictator for the administration of public affairs," Caesar initiated far-reaching reforms. He granted citizenship to the Gauls and packed the Senate with many new non-Italian members, in this way making it a more truly representative body as well as a rubber stamp for his policies. In the interest of the poorer citizens, he reduced debts, inaugurated a public works program, established colonies outside Italy, and decreed that one-third of the laborers on the slave-worked estates in Italy be persons of free birth. As a result, he was able to reduce from 320,000 to 150,000 the number of people in the city of Rome receiving free grain. (The population of Rome is estimated to have been 500,000.) His most enduring act was the reform of the calendar in the light of Egyptian knowledge; with minor changes, this calendar of 365¼ days is still in use today.

Caesar realized that the Republic was dead. In his own words, "The Republic is merely a name, without form or substance." He believed that only intelligent autocratic leadership could save Rome from continued civil war and collapse. But Caesar inspired the hatred of many, particularly those who viewed him as a tyrant who had destroyed the Republic. On the Ides (fifteenth day) of March, 44 B.C.E., a group of conspirators, led by Brutus and other ex-Pompeians whom Caesar had pardoned, stabbed him to death in the Senate, and Rome was once more drawn into conflict.

Caesar's assassins had been offended by certain of his actions that seemed to fall just short of monarchy—his purple robe, the statues erected in his honor, the coins bearing his portrait—and they assumed that with his death the Republic would be restored to its traditional status. But the people of Rome remained unmoved by the conspirators' cry of "Liberty! Freedom! Tyranny is dead!" The majority of them were prepared to accept a successor to Caesar whose power and position stopped just short of a royal title. The real question was, who was to be Caesar's successor?

The Third Civil War: Antony Versus Octavian

Following Caesar's death, his 18-year-old grand-nephew and heir, Octavian, allied himself with Caesar's chief lieutenant, Mark Antony, against the conspirators and the Senate. The conspirators' armies were routed, and Cicero, a renowned orator and champion of the Senate, was put to death for his hostility toward Antony. Then for more than a decade Octavian and Antony exercised dictatorial power and divided the Roman world between them. But the ambitions of each man proved too great for the alliance to endure.

Antony, who took charge of the eastern half of the empire, became completely infatuated with Cleopatra, the last of the Egyptian Ptolemies. He even went so far as to transfer Roman territories to her control. Octavian took advantage of Antony's blunders to propagandize Rome and Italy against Antony and his foreign lover queen "with her polluted crew of creatures foul with lust." The resulting struggle was portrayed by Octavian as a war between the Roman West and the "oriental" East. When Octavian's fleet met Antony's near Actium in Greece, first Cleopatra and then Antony deserted the battle and fled to Egypt. There Antony committed suicide, as Cleopatra did soon afterward when Alexandria was captured in 30 B.C.E.

The Early Empire, 30 B.C.E.–180 C.E.

At the end of a century of civil violence, Rome was at last united under one leader, Octavian, who was hailed by the grateful Romans as the "father of his country." The Republic gave way to the permanent dictatorship of the empire, and two centuries of imperial greatness, known as the *Pax Romana* ("Roman Peace"), followed.

Reconstruction Under Augustus

Following his triumphal return to Rome, Octavian in 27 B.C.E. announced that he would "restore the Republic." But he did so only outwardly by blending republican institutions with his own strong personal leadership. He consulted the Senate on important issues, allowed it to retain control over Italy and half of the provinces, and gave it the legislative functions of the nearly unused Tribal Assembly. The Senate in return bestowed on Octavian the title *Augustus* ("The Revered," a title previously used for gods), by which he was known thereafter.

During the rest of his 45-year rule, Augustus never again held the office of dictator, and he seldom held the consulship. Where, then, did his strength lie? Throughout his career he kept the powers of a tribune, which gave him the right to initiate legislation and to veto the legislative and administrative acts of others. He also kept for himself the governorship of the frontier provinces, where the armies were stationed. Augustus's nearly total control of the army meant that his power could not be successfully challenged. From his military title, *imperator* ("victorious general"), is derived our modern term *emperor.*

Augustus thus effected a compromise "between the need for a monarchical head of the empire and the sentiment which enshrined Rome's republican constitution in the minds of his contemporaries."[8] He preferred the modest title of *princeps*, "first citizen" or "leader," which he felt best described his position, and his form of disguised dictatorship is therefore known as the Principate. At the beginning of the empire, then, political power was ostensibly divided between the princeps and the senatorial aristocrats. This arrangement was continued by most of Augustus's successors during the next two centuries.

Seeking to efface the scars of more than a century of civil strife, Augustus concentrated on internal reform. He did annex Egypt and extend the Roman frontier to the Danube as a defense against barbarian invasions, but he failed in an attempt to conquer Germany up to the Elbe River. As a result of this failure, the Germans were never Romanized, like the Celts of Gaul and Spain, and the boundary between their language and the Roman-based Romance languages of France and Spain is still the Rhine.

Augustus also sought to cure a sick society—to end the mood of utter hopelessness felt by many concerned Romans, among them the poet Horace:

Time corrupts all. What has it not made worse?
Our grandfathers sired feebler children; theirs
Were weaker still—ourselves; and now our curse
Must be to breed even more degenerate heirs.[9]

Through legislation and propaganda, Augustus sought with some success to check moral and social decline and revive the old Roman ideals and traditions. He rebuilt deteriorated temples, revived old priesthoods, and restored religious festivals. He attempted to reestablish the integrity of the family by legislating against adultery, the chief grounds for divorce, which had become quite common during the late Republic. A permanent court was set up to prosecute adulterous wives and their lovers. Among those found guilty and banished from Rome were Augustus's own daughter and granddaughter. Finally, to disarm the gangs that had been terrorizing citizens, he outlawed the carrying of daggers.

Augustus greatly reduced the corruption and exploitation that had flourished in the late Republic by creating a well-paid civil service, open to all classes. He also established a permanent standing army, stationed in the frontier provinces and kept out of politics. More than 40 colonies of retired soldiers were founded throughout the empire; among them were Palermo in Sicily, Patras in Greece, and Baalbek in Syria.

Augustus's reforms also gave rise to a new optimism and patriotism that were reflected in the art and literature of the Augustan Age (discussed later in this chapter).

The Julio-Claudian and Flavian Emperors

Augustus was followed by four descendants from among his family, the line of the Julio-Claudians, who ruled from 14 to 68 C.E. Augustus's stepson Tiberius, whom the Senate accepted as his successor, and Claudius were fairly efficient and devoted rulers; in Claudius's reign the Roman occupation of Britain began in 43 C.E. The other two rulers of this imperial line disregarded the appearance that they were only the first among all citizens: Caligula was a madman who demanded to be worshipped as a god and toyed with the idea of having his favorite horse elected to high office in Rome; Nero was infamous for his immorality, the murder of his wife and his mother, and his persecution of Christians in Rome. (See Chapter 7 for a discussion of the rise and spread of Christianity.)

In 64 C.E. a great fire raged for nine days, destroying more than half of the capital. The Roman historian Tacitus has left us a vivid account of how Nero made the unpopular Christians scapegoats for the fire:

> *Large numbers . . . were condemned—not so much for incendiarism as for their anti-social tendencies. Their deaths were made farcical. Dressed in wild animals' skins, they were torn to pieces by dogs, or crucified, or made into torches to be ignited after dark. . . . Nero provided his Gardens for the spectacle, and exhibited displays in the Circus. . . . Despite their guilt as Christians, and the ruthless punishment it deserved, the victims were pitied. For it was felt they were being sacrificed to one man's brutality rather than to the national interest.*[10]

The Julio-Claudian line ended in 68 C.E. when Nero, declared a public enemy by the Senate and facing army revolts, committed suicide. In the following year four emperors were proclaimed by rival armies, with Vespasian the final victor. For nearly 30 years (69–96 C.E.) the Flavian dynasty (Vespasian followed by his two sons, Titus and Domitian) provided the empire with effective but autocratic rule. The fiction of republican institutions gave way to a scarcely veiled monarchy as the Flavians openly treated the office of emperor as theirs by right of conquest and inheritance.

The Antonines: "Five Good Emperors"

An end to autocracy and a return to the Augustan principle of an administration of equals—emperor and Senate—characterized the rule of the Antonine emperors (96–180 C.E.), under whom the empire reached the height of its prosperity and power. Selected on the basis of proven ability, these "good emperors" succeeded, according to Tacitus, in establishing "the rare happiness of times, when we may think what we please, and express what we think."[11] Two of these emperors are especially worthy of note.

Hadrian reigned from 117 to 138 C.E. His first important act was to stabilize the boundaries of the empire. He gave up as indefensible recently conquered Armenia and Mesopotamia and erected protective walls in Germany and Britain, the latter an imposing structure of stone 20 feet high. Hadrian traveled extensively, inspecting almost every province of the empire. New cities were founded, old ones were restored, and many public works were constructed, among them the famous Pantheon, still standing in Rome.

The last of the "five good emperors" was Marcus Aurelius, who ruled from 161 to 180 C.E. He preferred the study of philosophy and the quiet contemplation of his books to the blood and brutality of the battlefield. Yet he was repeatedly troubled by the invasions of the Parthians from the east and Germans from across the Danube. While engaged in his Germanic campaigns, he wrote his *Meditations*, a collection of personal thoughts notable for its lofty Stoic idealism and love of humanity. Ironically, the Stoic manner in which Christian martyrs accepted death did not impress him:

> *What an admirable soul that is which is ready, if at any moment it must be separated from the body. . . . This readiness must come from a man's own judgment, not from mere obstinacy, as with the Christians, but with reason and dignity if it is to persuade another, and without tragic show.*[12]

Like a good Stoic, Marcus Aurelius died at his post at Vindobona (Vienna); at Rome his equestrian statue still stands on the Capitoline Hill.

The Pax Romana

In its finest period, the empire was a vast area stretching from Britain to the Euphrates and containing

The villa of the emperor Hadrian at Tivoli, a short distance away from Rome's congestion. Hadrian had the villa landscaped and decorated with replicas of famous Greek and oriental monuments.

The praetorian guard, the emperors' elite bodyguards, are shown here in a relief carving from Rome.

more than 100 million people. It was welded together into what Pliny the Elder, in the first century C.E., termed the "immense majesty of the Roman Peace." Writing during the rule of Augustus, the Roman poet Virgil was the spokesman for what enlightened Romans felt to be the mission of Rome:

> Others, doubtless, will mould lifelike bronze with greater delicacy, will win from marble the look of life, will plead cases better, chart the motions of the sky with the rod and foretell the risings of the stars. You, O Roman, remember to rule the nations with might. This will be your genius—to impose the way of peace, to spare the conquered and crush the proud.[13]

Non-Romans were equally conscious of the rich benefits derived from the Pax Romana, which began with Augustus and reached its fullest development under the Five Good Emperors. They welcomed the peace, prosperity, and administrative efficiency of the empire. Cities increased in number and were largely self-governed by their own upper-class magistrates and senates. In the mid-second century C.E., a Greek orator declared that the Romans "have linked together the nations of the world in one great family."[14]

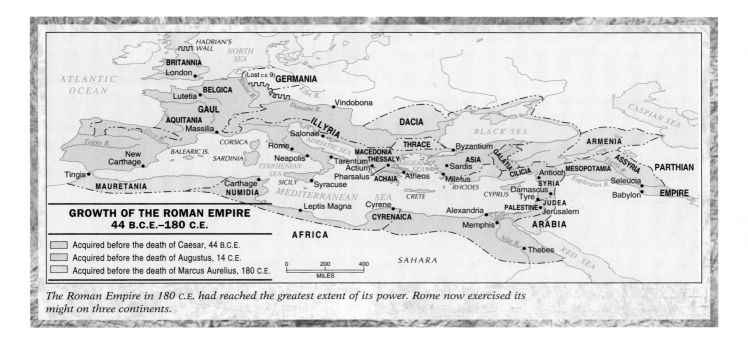

GROWTH OF THE ROMAN EMPIRE
44 B.C.E.–180 C.E.

- Acquired before the death of Caesar, 44 B.C.E.
- Acquired before the death of Augustus, 14 C.E.
- Acquired before the death of Marcus Aurelius, 180 C.E.

The Roman Empire in 180 C.E. had reached the greatest extent of its power. Rome now exercised its might on three continents.

The "True Democracy" of the Roman Empire

At the head of this huge world-state stood the emperor, its defender and symbol of unity as well as an object of worship. "The whole world speaks in unison," proclaimed the same Greek orator, "more distinctly than a chorus; and so well does it harmonize under this director-in-chief that it joins in praying this empire may last for all time."[15] The major theme of the many accounts written to celebrate the generally enlightened government of the Principate was that liberty had been exchanged for order and prosperity. The empire was said to represent a new kind of democracy: "the true democracy and the freedom that does not fail," "a democracy under the one man that can rule and govern best." The last century of the Republic, by contrast, exhibited

> the evils found in every democracy. . . . The cause is the multitude of our population and the magnitude of the business of our government; for the population embraces men of every kind, . . . and the business of the state has become so vast that it can be administered only with the greatest difficulty.[16]

Economic Prosperity

Rome's unification of the ancient world had far-reaching economic consequences. The Pax Romana was responsible for the elimination of tolls and other artificial barriers, the suppression of piracy and lawlessness, and the establishment of a reliable coinage. Such factors, in addition to the longest period of peace the West has ever enjoyed, explain in large measure the great expansion of commerce that occurred in the first and second centuries C.E. Industry was also stimulated, but its expansion was limited since wealth remained concentrated and no mass market for industrial goods was created. Industry remained organized on a small-shop basis, with producers widely scattered, resulting in self-sufficiency.

The economy of the empire remained basically agricultural, and huge estates, the *latifundia*, prospered. On these tracts, usually belonging to absentee owners, large numbers of *coloni*, free tenants, tilled the soil as sharecroppers. The *coloni* were replacing slave labor, which was becoming increasingly hard to secure with the disappearance of the flow of war captives.

Early Evidence of Economic Stagnation

Late in the first century C.E. the first sign of economic stagnation appeared in Italy. Italian agriculture began to suffer from overproduction as a result of the loss of Italy's markets for wine and olive oil in Roman Gaul, Spain, and North Africa, which were becoming self-sufficient in those products. To aid the Italian wine producers, the Flavian emperor Domitian created an artificial scarcity by forbidding the planting of new vineyards in Italy and by ordering half the existing vineyards in the provinces to be plowed under. A century later the Five Good Emperors sought to solve the continuing problem of overproduction in Italy by subsidizing the buying power of consumers. Loans at 5 percent interest were made to ailing landowners, with the interest to be paid into the treasuries of Italian municipalities and earmarked "for girls and boys of needy parents to be supported at public expense." This system of state subsidies was soon extended to the provinces.

Also contributing to Roman economic stagnation was the continuing drain of money to the East for the purchase of such luxury goods as silks and spices and the failure of city governments within the empire to keep their finances in order, thus making it necessary for the imperial government to intervene. As an official sent by one of the Five Good Emperors to investigate the fiscal troubles of some cities in Asia Minor reported:

> Many sums of money are detained in private hands for a variety of reasons, and in addition some are disbursed for quite illegitimate expenditures. . . . The city of Nicomedia, my lord, has expended 3,329,000 sesterces on an aqueduct, which has been abandoned still unfinished and has even been torn down. Again they disbursed 200,000 sesterces for another aqueduct, but this, too, has been abandoned. So now, after throwing away all that money they must make a new expenditure in order to have water.[17]

Such early evidence of declining prosperity foreshadowed the economic crisis of the third century C.E., when political anarchy and monetary inflation caused the economy of the empire to collapse (see Chapter 7).

Rome, Imperial Capital

At the hub of the sprawling empire was Rome, with close to a million inhabitants. Augustus boasted that he had found a city of brick and had left it one of marble. Nonetheless, Rome presented a great contrast of magnificence and slums, of splendid public buildings and poorly constructed tenements, which often collapsed or caught fire. The crowded narrow streets, lined with apartment houses and swarming with all manner of people, are described by the satirist Juvenal early in the second century C.E.:

> . . . Hurry as I may, I am blocked
> By a surging crowd in front, while a vast mass
> Of people crushes onto me from behind.
> One with his elbow punches me, another
> With a hard litter-pole; one bangs a beam
> Against my head, a wine-cask someone else.
> With mud my legs are plastered; from all sides
> Huge feet trample upon me, and a soldier's
> Hobnails are firmly planted on my toes.[18]

Social Life

At the top of the social order were the old senatorial families who lived as absentee owners of huge es-

A typically furnished bedroom in a villa near Pompeii (first century B.C.E.) illustrates the Roman view of domestic comfort. Though sparsely furnished, the room retains an elegant atmosphere, created in part by the elaborate murals and intricate mosaic floor pavement.

tates and left commerce and finance to a large and wealthy middle class. In contrast to the tenements of the poor, the homes of the rich were palatial, as revealed by excavations at Pompeii, which was buried and so preserved by the eruption of the volcano Vesuvius in 79 C.E. These elaborate villas contained courts and gardens with fountains, rooms with marble walls, mosaics on the floors, and numerous frescoes and other works of art. An interesting feature of Roman furniture was the abundance of couches and the scarcity of chairs. People usually reclined, even at meals.

The lower classes in the cities found a refuge from the dullness of their existence in social clubs, or guilds, called *collegia*, each comprising the workers of one trade. The activity of the collegia did not center on economic goals, like modern trade unions, but on the worship of a god and on feasts, celebrations, and decent burials for members.

The living conditions of slaves varied greatly. Those in domestic service were often treated humanely, with their years of efficient service frequently rewarded by emancipation. Nor was it uncommon for freed slaves to rise to positions of significance in business, letters, and the imperial service. However, conditions among slaves on the large estates could be indescribably harsh. Beginning with Augustus, however, numerous enactments protected slaves from mistreatment; Hadrian, for example, forbade private prisons and the killing of a slave without judicial approval.

Recreation played a key role in Roman social life. Both rich and poor were exceedingly fond of their public baths, which in the capital alone numbered 800 during the early days of the empire. The baths served the same purpose as modern-day athletic clubs. The larger baths contained enclosed gardens, promenades, gymnasiums, libraries, and famous works of art as well as a sequence of cleansing rooms through which one moved—the sweat room, the warm room where sweat was scraped off by a slave (soap was unknown), the tepid room for cooling off, and the invigorating cold bath. Another popular room was the lavatory, with its long row of marble toilets equipped with comfortable arm rests. Here Romans liked to sit and chat for an hour or more.

Footraces, boxing, and wrestling were minor sports; chariot racing and gladiatorial contests were the chief amusements. The cry for "bread and circuses" reached such proportions that by the first century C.E. the Roman calendar had as many as 100 days set aside as holidays, the majority of which were given over to games furnished at public expense. The most spectacular sport was chariot racing. The largest of six racecourses at Rome was the

A fresco portrait of a young woman from Pompeii. She seems to be caught in thought as she prepares to make an entry in her diary.

Circus Maximus, a huge marble-faced structure seating about 150,000 spectators. The games, which included as many as 24 races each day, were presided over by the emperor or his representative. The crowds bet furiously on their favorite charioteers, whose fame equaled that of the sports heroes of our own day.

Of equal or greater popularity were the gladiatorial contests, organized by both emperors and private promoters as regular features on the amusement calendar. These cruel spectacles, which have no exact counterpart in any other civilization, were held in arenas, the largest and most famous of which was the Colosseum, opened in 80 C.E. The contests took various forms. Ferocious animals were pitted against armed combatants or occasionally even against unarmed men and women who had been condemned to death. Another type of contest was the fight to the death between gladiators, generally equipped with different types of weapons but matched on equal terms. It was not uncommon for the life of a defeated gladiator who had fought courageously to be spared at the request of the spectators. Although many Romans considered these bloodletting contests barbaric, they continued until the fifth century, when Christianity forbade them.

A mosaic from the third century B.C.E. depicting gladiators. Introduced to Rome by the Etruscans, gladiatorial contests grew in popularity and cruelty as Rome grew older.

The Roman Crisis of the Third Century

In the third century C.E., internal anarchy and foreign invasion drastically transformed the Roman Empire. Augustus's constitutional monarchy in which the emperor shared power with the Senate changed to a despotic absolute monarchy in which the emperors made no attempt to hide the fact that they were backed by the military and would tolerate no senatorial influence. By the late third century, the emperor was no longer adressed as *princeps*, "first among equals," but as *dominus et deus*, "lord and god." The Principate had been replaced by the absolute rule known as the Dominate.

The transformation of the Roman Empire in the third century was foreshadowed by the reign of Commodus, who in 180 C.E. began a 12-year rule characterized by incompetence, corruption, cruelty, and neglect of affairs of state. He was strangled in 192, and civil war followed for a year until the establishment of the Severan dynasty (193–235). The Severan dynasty was intimidated by the military, just as the Principate had been. After 235, when the last member of the Severan dynasty was murdered by his own troops, 50 years of bloody civil wars, Germanic invasions, and new foreign threats ensued. Of the 26 men who claimed the title of emperor during this time, only one died a natural death.

Equally deadly to the well-being of the empire as military anarchy and foreign invasions was prolonged economic decline. The economy became static, inflation set in, and the concentration of land ownership in the hands of the few destroyed the small farming classes. The *latifundia*, with their fortified villas, grew as the number of *coloni* grew. As the rural tax base declined, chaotic conditions took their toll on trade, and by the end of the period the government refused to accept its own money for taxes and required payment in goods and services.

A much needed reconstruction of the empire was accomplished by Diocletian (285–305), a rough-hewn soldier and shrewd administrator. To increase the strength of the government, he completed the trend toward an autocracy of an oriental type featuring the Senate in a diminished role. He attempted to restructure the empire to ensure better government and an

The Roman Empire

14–68 C.E.	Period of the Julio-Claudian emperors
64 C.E.	Rome destroyed by fire; Emperor Nero attributes fire to Christians
69–96 C.E.	Period of the Flavian emperors
79 C.E.	Mount Vesuvius erupts, destroying Pompeii
96–180 C.E.	Period of the Antonine emperors
313 C.E.	Emperor Constantine issues Edict of Milan; Christians free to worship
378 C.E.	Battle of Adrianople; Germanic invasions into Roman Empire begin
395 C.E.	Roman Empire divided into eastern and western empires
476 C.E.	Last Roman emperor in the West assassinated

efficient succession scheme. Diocletian also tried to stop the economic decay of the empire by issuing new coins based on silver and gold and by imposing a freeze on prices and wages.

His succession scheme collapsed when Constantine (306–337) overcame his rivals to take power. He believed that the Christian God helped him during a battle for the city of Rome, and in return he actively supported Christianity by issuing in 313 the Edict of Milan, an order which decreed that Christianity would be tolerated throughout the empire. He continued the basic trends of Diocletian's work to ensure the production of essential goods and services as well as the collection of taxes. He imposed decrees tying people and their children to the same occupation in the same place. Most important, he moved the capital to the site of the old Greek colony of Byzantium (renaming it Constantinople). By doing so he in effect left Rome open to the attacks of the advancing Germanic peoples but ensured the continuation of Roman government in a new, safer location.

The Germanic Tribes

Waves of restless and diverse Germanic tribes were drawn into the power vacuum created during the two centuries of Rome's decline. While the westernmost German tribes (Franks, Angles, and Saxons) had achieved a settled agricultural life in the third and early fourth centuries, the Goths, Vandals, and Lombards remained largely nomadic.

The economic and legal practices of the Germanic tribes set them apart from the Romans. They engaged in so little commerce that cattle, rather than money, sufficed as a measure of value. A basic factor behind Germanic restlessness seems to have been land hunger. Their numbers were increasing, much of their land was forest and swamp, and their agricultural methods were inefficient. In an effort to eliminate blood feuds, the tribal law codes of the Germans encouraged the payment of compensation as an alternative for an aggrieved kin or family seeking vengeance. For the infliction of specific injuries, a stipulated payment, termed a *bot,* was required. The amount of compensation varied according to the severity of the crime and the social position of the victim.

Lack of written laws made it necessary to hold trials to determine guilt or innocence. A person standing trial could produce oath-helpers who would swear to his innocence. If unable to obtain oath-helpers, the accused was subjected to trial by ordeal, of which there were three kinds. In the first, the defendant had to lift a small stone out of a vessel of boiling water; unless his scalded arm healed within a prescribed number of days, he was judged guilty. In the second, he had to walk blindfolded and barefoot across a floor on which lay pieces of red-hot metal; success in avoiding the metal was a sign of inno-

cence. In the third, the bound defendant was thrown into a stream; if he sank he was innocent, but if he floated he was guilty because water was considered a divine element that would not accept a guilty person. Trial by ordeal lasted until the thirteenth century, when it was outlawed by Pope Innocent III and various secular rulers.

According to the Roman historian Tacitus, the Germans were notorious as heavy drinkers and gamblers, but Tacitus praised their courage, respect for women, and freedom from many Roman vices. A favorite amusement was listening to the tribal bards recite old tales of heroes and gods. Each warrior leader had a retinue of followers who were linked to him by personal loyalty. The war band—*comitatus* in Latin—had an important bearing on the origin of medieval feudalism, which was based on a similar personal bond between knights and their feudal lords. The heroic values associated with the *comitatus* also continued into the Middle Ages, where they formed the basis of the value system of the feudal nobility.

During the many centuries that the Romans and Germans faced each other across the Rhine-Danube frontier, there was much contact—peaceful as well as warlike—between the two peoples. Roman trade reached into German territory, and Germans entered the Roman Empire as slaves. During the troubled third century, many Germans were invited to settle on vacated lands within the empire or to serve in the Roman legions. By the fourth century the bulk of the Roman army and its generals in the west were German.

The Germans beyond the frontiers were kept in check by force of arms, by frontier walls, by diplomacy and gifts, and by playing off one tribe against another. In the last decades of the fourth century, however, these methods proved insufficient to prevent a series of great new invasions.

The Germanic Invasions

The impetus behind the increasing German activity on the frontiers in the late fourth century was the approach of the Huns. These nomads, superb horsemen and fighters from central Asia, had plundered and slain their Asian neighbors for centuries. In 372 they crossed the Volga and soon subjugated the easternmost Germanic tribe, the Ostrogoths. Terrified at the prospect of being conquered, the Visigoths, who found themselves next in the path of the advancing Huns, petitioned the Romans to allow them to settle as allies inside the empire. Permission was granted, and in 376 the entire tribe of Visigoths crossed the Danube into Roman territory. But soon corrupt Roman officials cheated and mistreated them, and the proud Germanic tribe went on a rampage. Valens, the East Roman emperor, tried to stop them, but he lost both his army and his life in the battle of Adrianople in 378.

Adrianople has been described as one of history's decisive battles, since it destroyed the legend of the invincibility of the Roman legions and ushered in a century and a half of chaos. For a few years the emperor Theodosius I held back the Visigoths, but after his death in 395 they began to migrate and pillage under their leader, Alaric. He invaded Italy, and in 410 his followers sacked Rome. The weak West Roman emperor ceded southern Gaul to the Visigoths, who soon expanded into Spain. Their Spanish kingdom lasted until the Muslim conquest of the eighth century.

To counter Alaric's threat to Italy, the Romans had withdrawn most of their troops from the Rhine frontier in 406 and from Britain the following year. A flood of Germanic tribes soon surged across the unguarded frontiers. The Vandals pushed their way through Gaul to Spain and, after pressure from the Visigoths, moved on to Africa, the granary of the empire. In 455 a Vandal raiding force sailed over from Africa, and Rome was sacked a second time. Meanwhile the Burgundians settled in the Rhone valley, the Franks gradually spread across Gaul, and the Angles, Saxons, and Jutes invaded Britain. Although each of these tribes set up a German-ruled kingdom within the confines of the empire, only the Franks in Gaul and the Angles and Sax-

ons in Britain managed to establish kingdoms that lasted longer than a few generations.

Meanwhile the Huns pushed farther into Europe. Led by Attila, the "scourge of God," the mounted nomads crossed the Rhine in 451. The remaining Roman forces in Gaul, joined by the Visigoths, defeated the Huns near Troyes. Attila then plundered northern Italy and planned to take Rome, but disease, lack of supplies, and the dramatic appeal of Pope Leo I, whose actions brought great prestige to the papacy, caused him to return to the plains of eastern Europe. The Huns' threat disintegrated after 453, when Attila died on the night of his marriage to a Germanic princess.

The End of the West Roman Empire, 395–568 C.E.

After the death of Theodosius I in 395, the Roman Empire was divided between his two sons. The decline of Roman rule in the West was hastened as a series of weakened emperors abandoned Rome and sought safety behind the marshes at the northern Italian city of Ravenna. The leaders of the imperial

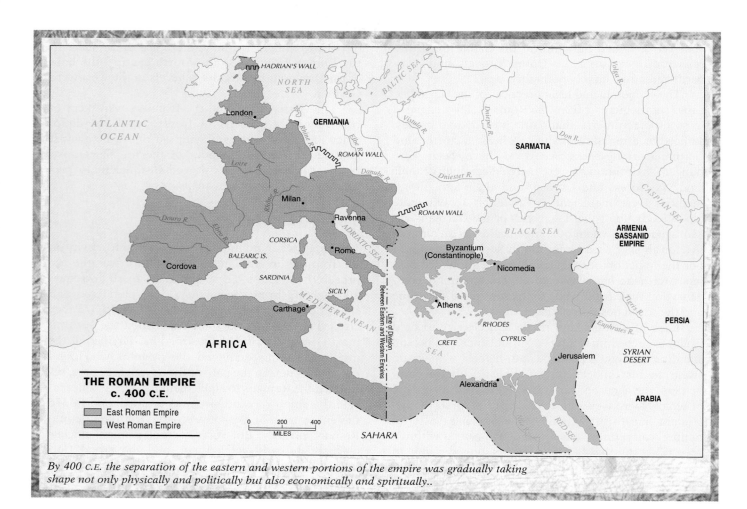

By 400 C.E. the separation of the eastern and western portions of the empire was gradually taking shape not only physically and politically but also economically and spiritually..

army, whose ranks were now mainly German, exercised the real power.

In 475 Orestes, the German commander of the troops, forced the Senate to elect his young son Romulus Augustulus ("Little Augustus") emperor in the West. The following year another German commander, Odovacar, killed Orestes. Seeing no reason to continue the powerless imperial line in the West, he deposed Romulus Augustulus and named himself head of the government. The deposition of this boy, who ironically bore the names of the legendary founder of Rome and the founder of the empire, marks the traditional "fall" of the Roman Empire.

The disintegration of the Huns' empire following the death of Attila freed the Ostrogoths to migrate as other tribes were doing. Under their energetic king, Theodoric (c. 454–526), the Ostrogoths were moved into action. Theodoric accepted a commission from the emperor in Constantinople to reimpose imperial authority over Italy, now in Odovacar's hands. In 488 Theodoric led his people into the Italian peninsula, where, after hard fighting, Odovacar sued for peace. After Odovacar was treacherously murdered, Theodoric established a strong Ostrogothic kingdom in Italy with its capital at Ravenna. Because he appreci-

ated the culture he had seen at Constantinople, Theodoric maintained classical culture on a high level. Following his death without a male heir in 526, civil war broke out in Italy, paving the way for a 20-year war of reconquest (535–555) by the armies of the East Roman emperor, Justinian. Italy was ravaged from end to end by the fighting, and the classical civilization that Theodoric had carefully preserved was in large part destroyed.

In 568, three years after the death of Justinian, the last wave of Germanic invaders, the Lombards, reputed to have been the most brutal and fierce of all the Germans, poured into Italy. The emperor in the East held on to southern Italy, as well as Ravenna and Venice, and the pope became virtual ruler of Rome. Not until the late nineteenth century would Italy again be united under one government.

The Roman Contribution

Unlike the Greeks, the Romans were not greatly interested in abstract thought. They constructed no original system of philosophy, invented no major new literary forms, and made no outstanding scientific

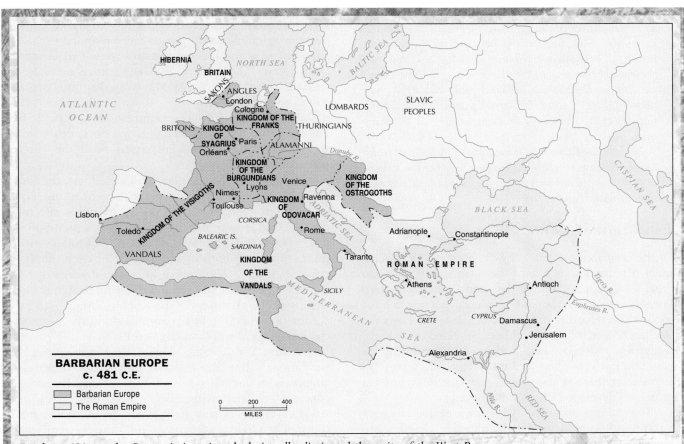

By about 481 C.E. the Germanic invasions had virtually eliminated the unity of the West Roman Empire, but the fate of the East was quite different.

discoveries. They excelled in the art of government. The Romans created a workable world-state and developed a skill in administration, law, and practical affairs. The Pax Romana was fashioned and maintained by a people who were, on the whole, conscious of their responsibilities to others.

The Roman Spirit

The Roman spirit was composed of many factors. Never completely forgotten was the tradition of plain living that stemmed from Rome's early history as a nation of farmers. Geography was another factor; for centuries the Romans faced the need to conquer or be conquered, and they had to stress discipline and duty to the state. But the Roman spirit also had another side. It could be arrogant and cruel, and its sense of justice was often untempered with mercy. In 84 C.E., a Scottish chieftain is reported to have said of his Roman conquerors, "To robbery, slaughter, plunder, they give the lying name of empire; they create a desert and call it peace."[19]

Rome's answer to such criticism was delivered a few years earlier by a Roman general to some tribes in Gaul that had revolted after the infamous emperor Nero had arrested some of their leaders:

Gaul always had its petty kingdoms and internecine wars, until you submitted to our authority. We, though so often provoked, have used the right of conquest to burden you only with the cost of maintaining peace. . . . You often command our legions. You rule these and other provinces. There is no privilege, no exclusion. . . . Endure the passions and rapacity of your masters, just as you bear barren seasons . . . and other natural evils. There will be vices as long as there are men. But they are not perpetual. . . .

Should the Roman be driven out . . . what can result but wars between all these nations? . . . Let the lessons of fortune . . . teach you not to prefer rebellion and ruin to submission and safety.[20]

Evolution of Roman Law

Of the contributions made by the Romans in government, Roman law is one of the most significant. Two great legal systems, Roman law and English common law, still remain the foundation of legal systems in most modern Western nations. Roman law is the basis for the law codes of Italy, France, Scotland, the Latin American countries, and Louisiana. Where English common law is used, as in the United States (except in Louisiana), there is also a basic heritage of great legal principles developed by ancient Roman jurists.

Roman law evolved slowly over a period of about a thousand years. At first, as in all early societies, the law was unwritten custom, handed down from a remote past, and harsh in its judgments. As noted earlier, in the fifth century B.C.E. this law was put in writing in the Law of the Twelve Tables, as the result of plebeian demand. During the remainder of the Republic the body of Roman law (*jus civile*, "law of the citizen") was enlarged by legislation passed by the Senate and the assembly and by judicial interpretation of existing law to meet new conditions. By the second century C.E. the emperor had become the sole source of law, a responsibility he entrusted to scholars "skilled in the law" (*jurisprudentes*). These scholars stuck fast to the principle of equity ("Follow the beneficial interpretation"; "Letter of law is height of injustice") and to Stoic philosophy with its concept of a "law of nature" (*jus naturale*) common to all people and assessable by human reason. As a result, the power of the father over the family was weakened, women gained control over their property, and the principle that an accused person was innocent until proven guilty was established. Finally, in the sixth century C.E. the enormous bulk of Roman law from all sources was codified and so preserved for the future.

Roman Engineering and Architecture

The empire's needs required a communication system of paved roads and bridges as well as huge public buildings and aqueducts. As road builders, the Romans surpassed all previous peoples. Constructed of layers of stone and gravel according to sound engineering principles, their roads were planned for the use of armies and messengers and were kept in constant repair. The earliest and best-known main Roman highway was the Appian Way. Running from Rome to the Bay of Naples, it was built about 300 B.C.E. to facilitate Rome's expansion southward. It has been said that the speed of travel possible on Roman highways was not surpassed until the early nineteenth century.

In designing their bridges and aqueducts, the Romans placed a series of stone arches next to one another to provide mutual support. At times several tiers of arches were used, one above the other. Fourteen aqueducts, stretching a total of 265 miles, supplied some 50 gallons of water daily for each inhabitant of Rome. They were proudly described by Rome's superintendent of aqueducts as "a signal testimony to the greatness of the Roman Empire," to be contrasted with "the idle pyramids or all the useless, though famous, works of the Greeks."[21]

At first the Romans copied Etruscan architectural models, but later they combined basic Greek elements with distinctly Roman innovations. By using concrete—a Roman invention—faced with brick or stone, they developed new methods for enclosing space. The Greeks' static post-and-lintel system was replaced by the more dynamic techniques of vaulting derived from the arch, borrowed from the Etruscans.

This splendid aqueduct, built under Augustus, spans the Gard River near Nîmes, in southern France. Its three massive tiers of arches are both majestic and beautiful. The topmost level served as a road.

Heavy concrete barrel vaults, cross (or groin) vaults, and domes—all so solid that they exerted no sidewise thrust—made possible the vast interiors that distinguish Roman architecture. The barrel vault was essentially a series of connected arches resembling a tunnel, and the cross vault consisted of two barrel vaults intersecting at right angles. The largest Roman domed structure is the Pantheon, the oldest important roofed building in the world that is still intact. As its name indicates, it was dedicated to "all the gods" by the emperor Hadrian as a symbol of the union of Greeks and Romans on equal terms. The massive dome rests on thick round walls of poured concrete with no window openings to weaken them. The only light enters through a great hole, 30 feet wide, at the top of the dome. The size of the dome remained unsurpassed until the twentieth century.

The typical Roman basilica, which served as a social and commercial center and as a law court, was not domed or vaulted. It was a rectangular structure with a light wooden ceiling held up by rows of columns that divided the interior into a central nave and side aisles. The roof over the nave was raised to admit light, creating a clerestory like that found in the temple at Karnak, in Egypt. The Roman basilica would eventually evolve into the Christian church.

Roman buildings were built to last, and their size, grandeur, and decorative richness aptly symbolized the proud imperial spirit of Rome. Whereas the Greeks evolved the temple, theater, and stadium, the Romans contributed the triumphal arch, bath, basilica, amphitheater, and multistoried apartment house.

Perhaps the most famous Roman building is the Colosseum, a huge amphitheater about $\frac{1}{4}$ mile around on the outside and with a seating capacity of about 45,000. On the exterior, its arches are decorated with Doric, Ionic, and Corinthian columns.

Sculpture and Painting

After the conquest of Greece, many Romans acquired a passion for Greek art. The homes of the wealthy were filled with statues, either brought to Rome as plunder or copied in Greece and shipped to Rome in great number.

Although strongly influenced by Etruscan and Greek models, the Romans developed a distinctive sculpture of their own, particularly portrait sculpture, which was remarkably realistic. Their skill in portraiture probably originated in the early practice of making and preserving wax images of the heads of important deceased family members. During the Principate, portraiture and relief sculpture tended to idealize the likenesses of the emperors. The Romans developed a great fund of decorative motifs, such as

Marble representation of a dying Gallic woman and her husband committing suicide rather than be taken prisoner by the Romans. The Romans regarded the Gauls as courageous but unsophisticated in politics and culture.

cupids, garlands of flowers, and scrolls of various patterns, which are still used today.

What little Roman painting has been preserved clearly reflects the influence of Hellenistic Greek models. The Romans were particularly skilled in producing floor mosaics—often copies of Hellenistic paintings—and in painting frescoes. The frescoes still to be seen in Pompeii and elsewhere show that the artists drew objects in clear though idealized perspective.

Literary Rome

In literature as in art, the Romans turned to the Greeks for their models. Roman epic, dramatic, and lyric poetry forms were usually written in conscious imitation of the Greek masterpieces. Although Latin literature is for the most part inferior to its Greek models, it remains one of the world's great literatures largely because of its influence on medieval, Renaissance, and modern culture.

Formal Latin literature did not begin until the mid-third century B.C.E. when a Greek slave named Livius Andronicus translated Homer's *Odyssey* and several Greek plays into Latin. By the end of the same century the first of a series of Latin epics dealing with Rome's past was composed. Only a few fragments have survived.

The oldest examples of Latin literature to survive intact are the 21 comedies of Plautus (c. 254–184 B.C.E.), which were adapted from Hellenistic Greek originals but with many Roman allusions, colloquialisms, and customs added. Plautus's comedies are bawdy and vigorously humorous, and their rollicking plots of illicit love and sarcastic characters such as a nagging wife ("Look at you! Gadding about, reeking of scent; you ought to know better, at your time of life"), timid husband ("But dear, I was only helping a friend buy a bottle of perfume"), lovelorn youth, clever slave, and swashbuckling soldier reveal the level of culture and taste in early Rome. The works of Plautus suggest many of the types that modern comedy has assumed, including farce, burlesque, and comedy of manners.

The Golden and Silver Ages of Latin Literature

Latin literature came of age in the first century B.C.E., when an outpouring of intellectual effort coincided with the last years of the Republic. This period marks the first half of the Golden Age of Latin literature, known as the Ciceronian period because of the stature of Marcus Tullius Cicero (106–43 B.C.E.), the greatest master of Latin prose and an outstanding intellectual force in Roman history.

Acclaimed as the greatest orator of his day, Cicero found time during his busy public life to write

The Golden and Silver Ages of Latin Literature, c. 100 B.C.E.–138 C.E.	
106–43 B.C.E.	Cicero: Orations and letters
c. 87–54 B.C.E.	Catullus: Poems and epigrams
c. 99–55 B.C.E.	Lucretius: Philosophical poem *On the Nature of Things*
70–19 B.C.E.	Virgil: Epic poem *Aeneid*
65–8 B.C.E.	Horace: Poems
43 B.C.E.–17 C.E.	Ovid: *The Art of Love; Metamorphoses*
59 B.C.E.–17 C.E.	Livy: *History of Rome*
c. 55 B.C.E.–117 C.E.	Tacitus: *Annals, Histories, Agricula*
c. 50 B.C.E.–127 C.E.	Juvenal: *Satires*
c. 46–c. 126 C.E.	Plutarch: *Parallel Lives*

extensively on philosophy, political theory, and rhetoric. Some 900 of his letters survive. Together with 58 speeches, they give us insight into Cicero's personality as well as life in the late Republic. Cicero also made a rich contribution by passing on to the Romans and to later ages much of Greek thought—especially that of Plato and the Stoics—and at the same time interpreting philosophical concepts from the standpoint of a Roman intellectual and practical man of affairs. He did more than any other Roman to make Latin a great literary language.

Two notable poets of the Ciceronian period were Catullus and Lucretius. Catullus (c. 87–54 B.C.E.) was a socially active young man who wrote highly personal lyric poetry. His best-known poems are addressed to "Lesbia," an unprincipled noblewoman ten years his senior with whom he carried on a tempestuous affair: "I hate and love—the why I cannot tell, / But by my tortures know the fact too well."[22]

Catullus's contemporary Lucretius (c. 99–55 B.C.E.) found in the philosophy of Epicurus an antidote to his profound disillusionment with his fellow citizens who, he wrote, "in their greed of gain . . . amass a fortune out of civil bloodshed: piling wealth on wealth, they heap carnage on carnage. With heartless glee they welcome a brother's tragic death."[23]

Augustus provided the Roman world with a stability and confidence that encouraged a further outpouring of literary creativity. The second phase of the Golden Age of Latin literature, the Augustan Age, was notable particularly for its excellent poetry. Virgil (70–19 B.C.E.) is considered the greatest of all Roman poets. His masterpiece, a great national epic called the *Aeneid*, glorifies the work of Augustus and eloquently asserts Rome's destiny to conquer and rule the world. Using Homer's *Odyssey* as his model, Virgil recounted the fortunes of Aeneas, the legendary founder of the Latin people, who came from burning Troy to Italy. Throughout the *Aeneid* runs Virgil's deep and enthusiastic patriotism—but at a price: unlike Homer's resourceful and spirited Odysseus, Virgil's Aeneas is decidedly wooden, a piece of imperial symbolism about as animated as a triumphal arch. He abruptly leaves Carthage where the queen, Dido, has fallen passionately in love with him (Virgil is adept at describing the emotions of romantic love, a value unknown in Homer); he must stop "idling and fiddling" around in Africa and hurry on to fulfill his "high destiny" in Italy. As he puts out to sea he tells the weeping Dido, "God's will, not mine, says 'Italy.'"[24] (One can understand why some Romans would claim that Carthaginian outrage over Aeneas's treatment of Dido led to the Punic Wars.)

As the most noted poet after the death of Virgil, Horace (65–8 B.C.E.) often sincerely praised the emperor's achievements:

> *Now Parthia fears the fist of Rome, the fasces*
> *Potent on land and sea; now the once haughty*
> *Ambassadors from the Caspian and the Indus*
> *Sue for a soft reply.*
> *Now Faith and Peace and Honor and old-fashioned*
> *Conscience and unremembered Virtue venture*
> *To walk again, and with them blessed Plenty,*
> *Pouring her brimming horn.*[25]

Most of Horace's poetry, however, is concerned with everyday human interests and moods, and succeeding generations up to the present have been attracted by his serene outlook on life:

> *Happy the man, and happy he alone,*
> *He, who can call today his own:*
> *He who secure within, can say,*
> *Tomorrow do thy worst, for I have lived today.*[26]

Quite a different sort of poet was Ovid (43 B.C.E.–17 C.E.). His preference for themes of sensual love in his *Art of Love* and other poems ("There she stood, faultless beauty in front of me, naked") caused Augustus to exile him to the shores of the Black Sea, Rome's equivalent to Communist Russia's Siberia. But Ovid was also a first-rate storyteller, and it is largely through his *Metamorphoses*, a witty verse collection of Greek stories about the life of the gods—not neglecting their love lives—that classical mythology was transmitted to the modern world.

The literature of the Silver Age, the period between the deaths of Augustus and Hadrian (14–138 C.E.), substituted a more critical and negative spirit for the patriotism and optimism of the Augustan Age. Despite a great emphasis on artificial stylistic devices, the Silver Age was memorable for its moral emphasis, seen in Tacitus, Plutarch, Seneca, and especially Juvenal (c. 50 B.C.E.–127 C.E.), who has been called the greatest satiric poet who ever lived. With moral indignation and bitter irony he attacked the shortcomings of Roman society: the common people of the city, no longer having votes to sell, are interested only in free "bread and circuses"; a good woman is a "rare bird," as "uncommon as a black swan," but "worse still is the well-read menace" who "with antiquarian zeal quotes poets I've never heard of."[27]

The Writing of History

Two Roman historians produced notable works during the Golden and Silver Ages. The first, Livy (59 B.C.E.–17 C.E.), was a contemporary of Virgil. His immense *History of Rome*, like the latter's *Aeneid*, is of epic proportions and glorifies Rome's conquests and ancestral ways. By assembling the legends and traditions of early Roman history and folding them into a continuous narrative, Livy, like Virgil, intended to advance Augustus's program of moral and social regeneration. He praised the virtues of the ancient Romans and sought to draw moral lessons from an idealized past:

> *What chiefly makes the study of history wholesome and profitable is this, that you behold the lessons of every kind of experience set forth as on a conspicuous monument; from these you may choose for yourself and for your own state what to imitate, from these mark for avoidance what is shameful in the conception and shameful in the result.*[28]

Tacitus (55–117 C.E.), like his contemporary Juvenal, was concerned with improving society. In his *Germania* he contrasted the life of the idealized, simple Germanic tribes with the corrupt and immoral existence of the Roman upper classes. In the *Annals* and *Histories* he used his vivid, epigrammatic prose to depict the shortcomings of the emperors and their courts from the death of Augustus to 96 C.E. Tacitus idealized the earlier Republic, and because he viewed the emperors as tyrants, he could not do justice to the positive contributions of imperial government.

The most famous Greek author in the empire was Plutarch (c. 46–c. 126 C.E.). He lectured on philosophy in Rome before retiring to his small hometown to pursue research on the outstanding figures in Roman and Greek history in order to discover what qualities make people great or unworthy. His *Parallel Lives*, containing 46 biographies of famous Greeks and Romans arranged in pairs for the purpose of comparison, is one of the great readable classics of world literature. Because many of the sources Plutarch used have been lost, his *Lives* is a mine of valuable information for the historian.

Lucretius: "Avoid Enticement into the Snares of Love"

Epicurean philosophers regarded love as one of many vain pursuits that lead to unhappiness. "By clinging to it," Lucretius writes, "you assure yourself of heartsickness and pain."

To avoid enticement into the snares of love is not so difficult as, once entrapped, to escape out of the toils and snap the tenacious knots of Venus. And yet, be you never so tightly entangled and embrangled, you can still free yourself from the curse unless you stand in the way of your own freedom. First, you should concentrate on all the faults of mind or body of her whom you covet and sigh for. For men often behave as though blinded by love and credit the beloved with charms to which she has no valid title. How often do we see blemished and unsightly women basking in a lover's adoration! . . . A sallow wench is acclaimed as a nut-brown maid. A sluttish slattern is admired for her "sweet disorder." Her eyes are never green, but grey as Athene's. If she is stringy and woody, she is lithe as a gazelle. A stunted runt is a sprite, a sheer delight from top to toe. A clumsy giantess is "a daughter of the gods divinely tall." She has an impediment in her speech—a charming lisp, of course. She's as mute as a stockfish—what modesty! A waspish, fiery-tempered scold—she "burns with a gem-like flame." She becomes "svelte" and "willowy" when she is almost too skinny to live; "delicate" when she is half-dead with coughing. Her breasts are swollen and protuberant: she is "Ceres suckling Bacchus." Her nose is snub—"a Faun," then, or "a child of the Satyrs." Her lips bulge: she is "all kiss." It would be a wearisome task to run through the whole catalogue. But suppose her face in fact is all that could be desired and the charm of Venus radiates from her whole body. Even so, there are still others. Even so, we lived without her before.

From Lucretius, *On the Nature of the Universe*, trans. Ronald Latham (Harmondsworth, England: Penguin, 1951), bk. 4, ll. 1146 ff.

Religion and Philosophy

The turmoil of the late Republic helped erode the traditions, values, and religion of earlier Rome. For spiritual satisfaction and salvation, many Romans turned increasingly to the mystery cults of Greece (see Chapter 3) or the Near East. Among the latter were Cybele, the Great Mother, and the Egyptian Isis, who attracted the greatest number of women followers. A faithful mother herself, she extended a mother's arms to the weary of this world:

> Behold, I am come; thy weeping and prayer hath moved me to succor thee. . . . Thou shalt live blessed in this world . . . and when after thine allotted span of life . . . thou as a dweller in the Elysian Fields shalt worship me as one that hath been favorable to thee.[29]

The more intellectually sophisticated of Romans turned to Greek philosophy, particularly Epicureanism and Stoicism, for meaning. As young men, both Virgil and Horace embraced Epicureanism, but Lucretius was the most important Roman interpreter of this philosophy. In *On the Nature of Things*, Lucretius followed Epicurus in basing his explanation of the "nature of things" on materialism and atomism. He called on people to free themselves from the fear of death—which was drawing them to the emotional mystery religions of Greece and the East—since souls, like bodies, are composed of atoms that fall apart when death comes: "What has this bugbear Death to frighten man / If souls can die, as well as bodies can?"[30] Lucretius exhorted his readers to seek pleasure in the study of philosophy and not in material gain or such sensual excitements as love.

More in line with Roman taste, especially in the days of the empire, was Stoicism. The emphasis of Roman Stoicism was on living a just life, constancy to duty, courage in adversity, and service to humanity. Stoic influence had a humanizing effect on Roman law by introducing such concepts as the law of nature and the brotherhood of all, including slaves. The law of nature, as defined by Cicero, "is not a product of human thought, nor is it any enactment of peoples, but something eternal which rules the whole universe by its wisdom in command and prohibition." It is the source of "the rational principles on which our laws must be based."[31]

One of the outstanding Roman Stoics was Seneca (4 B.C.E.–65 C.E.), Nero's tutor and a writer of moral essays and tragedies. He was regarded with high favor by the leaders of the early Christian church, for his Stoicism, like that of the ex-slave Epictetus (d. 135 C.E.) and the emperor Marcus Aurelius, had the appearance of a religious creed. He stressed an all-wise Providence, or God, and believed that each person possessed a spark of the divine:

Discovery Through Maps

The Farnese Atlas

In this Roman sculpture from the first century C.E., now in the Archaeological Museum in Naples, the Greek god Atlas is represented as supporting a heavenly globe inscribed with the symbols for the Roman constellations. Atlas was credited by both the Greeks and the Romans not only with supporting the heavens but also with working out the "science" of astrology and discovering the spherical nature of the stars. He is represented in this sculpture as supporting the vault of the sky, which surrounds the earth.

Atlas was said to be one of the Titans, a race of gods who dominated the heavens and earth and whose dominance was threatened by another race of god, the Olympians. The gigantic god reigned over a great kingdom located in the west—Atlantis, larger than Europe and Africa combined, graced with beautiful temples, palaces, homes, and gardens. Atlas ruled Atlantis with wisdom and justice; he also knew all the secrets of the seas and the heavens. But the race of Olympians grew jealous and sent a great deluge, which destroyed Atlantis. Atlas survived and joined his brothers in rebellion against the Olympians. They were defeated, and the god Zeus, leader of the Olympic gods, spared Atlas's life but condemned him to bear the burden of supporting the heavens on his shoulders for all eternity. The Romans, firm believers in the influence of the heavens on human activities, made Atlas a popular subject of painting and sculpture.

God is near you, he is with you, he is within you. This is what I mean, Lucilius: a holy spirit dwells within us, one who marks our good and bad deeds, and is our guardian. . . . No man can be good without the help of God.[32]

Christians assumed that Seneca must have been influenced by St. Paul during the latter's stay in Rome. By 400 C.E. a fictitious collection of letters between the two was being circulated.

Science in the Roman Empire

The Romans had little scientific curiosity, but by putting the findings of Hellenistic science to practical use, they became masters in engineering, applied medicine, and public health.

The Romans pioneered in public health service and developed the extensive practice of *hydrotherapy,* the use of mineral baths for healing. Beginning in the early empire, doctors were employed in infirmaries where soldiers, officials, and the poor could obtain free medical care. Great aqueducts and admirable drainage systems also indicate Roman concern for public health.

Characteristic of their utilitarian approach to science was their interest in amassing large encyclopedias. The most important of these was the *Natural History,* compiled by Pliny the Elder (23–79 C.E), an enthusiastic collector of all kinds of scientific odds and ends. In writing his massive work, Pliny is reputed to have read more than 2000 books. The result is an intriguing mixture of fact and fable thrown together with scarcely any method of classification. Nevertheless, it was the most widely read work on science during the empire and the early Middle Ages.

Pliny was well aware of the lack of creative scientific activity in his day. "In these glad times of peace," he wrote, "no addition whatever is being made to knowledge by means of original research, and in fact even the discoveries of our predecessors are not being thoroughly studied." To Pliny, the cause of this state of affairs was "blind engrossment with avarice," and he cited this example: "Now that every sea has been opened up . . . , an immense multitude goes on voyages—but their object is profit not knowledge."[33] Pliny himself was suffocated by a rain of hot ashes while observing the eruption of Mount Vesuvius near Pompeii, an awesome event that killed roughly 2000 people and was described by Pliny's nephew: "Many lifted up their hands to the gods, but a great number believed there were no gods, and that this night was to be the world's last, eternal one."[34]

The last great scientific minds of the ancient world were two Greeks, Claudius Ptolemy and Galen, both of whom lived in the second century C.E. Ptolemy resided at Alexandria, where he became celebrated as a geographer, astronomer, and mathematician. His maps show a comparatively accurate knowledge of a broad section of the known world, and he used an excellent projection system. But he exaggerated the size of Asia, an error that influenced Columbus to underestimate the width of the Atlantic and to set sail from Spain in search of Asia. His work on astronomy, usually called the *Almagest* ("The Great Work") from the title of the Arabic translation, presented the geocentric (earth-centered) view of the universe that prevailed until the sixteenth century. In mathematics, Ptolemy's work in improving and developing trigonometry became the basis for modern knowledge of the subject.

Galen, born in Pergamum, in Asia Minor, was a physician for a school of gladiators. His fame spread, and he was called to Rome, where he became physician to the emperor Marcus Aurelius. Galen was responsible for notable advances in physiology and anatomy; for example, he was the first to explain the mechanism of respiration. Forbidden by the Roman government to dissect human bodies, Galen experimented with animals and demonstrated that an excised heart can continue to beat outside the body and that injuries to one side of the brain produce effects in the opposite side of the body.

Galen's account of how he discovered the cause of a Roman woman's chronic insomnia shows that he was aware of the psychosomatic factor in illness: he noted that the lady's pulse "suddenly became extremely irregular" whenever the name of a famous actor was mentioned. "Now what was it that escaped the notice of previous physicians when examining the aforesaid woman?" Galen wrote. "They have no clear conception of how the body tends to be affected by mental conditions."[35] Galen's medical encyclopedia, in which he summarized the medical knowledge of antiquity, remained the standard authority until the sixteenth century.

Conclusion

The story of Rome's rise from an insignificant and unsophisticated village along the banks of the Tiber to the mighty capital of an empire that included most of western Europe, the Mediterranean area, and the Near East will always remain one of the most fascinating stories in world history. Rome's expansion was accompanied by much devastation and suffering, yet it was less disastrous than continued international anarchy would have been.

Through the Roman achievement of a single empire and a cosmopolitan culture, the Greek legacy was preserved, synthesized, and disseminated—and the Romans were able to make important advances of their own. They excelled in political theory, governmental administration, and jurisprudence. Whereas the Greeks were individualistic, the Romans put a higher value on conformity, and their essentially conservative and judicious character more than compensated for their lack of creativity.

Rome's greatest achievement was the establishment of peace and prosperity over a vast area for long periods under a stable and acceptable government. The Roman citizens who accomplished this task were characterized by Livy, Rome's great historian at the end of the Republican period, in words that anticipate what modern Americans have often said of themselves:

> *I hope that my passion for Rome's past has not impaired my judgment; for I do honestly believe that no country has ever been greater or purer than ours or richer in good citizens and noble deeds; none has been free for so many generations from the vices of avarice and luxury; nowhere have thrift and plain living been for so long held in such esteem.*[36]

Suggestions for Reading

Kare Christ, *The Romans: An Introduction to Their History and Civilization* (University of California Press, 1984), and Michael Grant, *History of Rome* (Scribner, 1979), are highly recommended general accounts. Also excellent are Donald R. Dudley, *The Civilization of Rome* (Mentor, 1960); Reginald H. Barrow, *The Romans* (Penguin, 1975); T. J. Cornell, *The Beginnings of Rome* (Routledge, 1995); and Peter D. Arnott, *The Romans and Their World* (St. Martin's Press, 1970). Max Cary and Howard H. Scullard, *A History of Rome: Down to the Reign of Constantine*, 3rd ed. (St. Martin's Press, 1976), is an outstanding account.

Massimo Pallotino, *The Etruscans*, rev. ed. (Penguin, 1975), and Emeline Hill Richardson, *The Etruscans: Their Art and Civilization* (University of Chicago Press, 1964), are excellent works. See also Michael Grant, *The Etruscans* (Scribner, 1981); Paul MacKendrick, *The Mute Stones Speak: The Story of Archaelogy in Italy* (Norton, 1976); and Alexandre Grandazzi, *The Foundation of Rome: Myth and History* (Cornell University Press, 1997).

Recommended special studies are Serge Lancel, *Carthage: A History* (Oxford University Press, 1997); Robert Malcolm Errington, *The Dawn of Empire: Rome's Rise to World Power* (Cornell University Press, 1972); William V. Harris, *War and Imperialism in Republican Rome, 327–70 B.C.* (Oxford University Press, 1978), which argues that Rome was deliberately imperialistic; Edward Luttwak, *The Grand Strategy of the Roman Empire* (Johns Hopkins University Press, 1977), a groundbreaking work of military history; Ramsay MacMullen, *The Enemies of the Roman Order: Treason, Unrest, and Alienation in the Empire* (Routledge, 1993); David Stockton, *The Gracchi* (Oxford University Press, 1979); Matthias Gelzer, *Caesar: Politician and Statesman* (Harvard University Press, 1985); Lily R. Taylor, *Party Politics in the Age of Caesar* (University of California Press, 1961); Ronald Syme, *The Roman Revolution* (Oxford University Press, 1939); P. A. Brunt, *Social Conflicts in the Roman Republic* (Norton, 1974); Arnold Hugh Martin Jones, *Augustus* (Norton, 1972); Fergus Millar, *The Emperor in the Roman World, 31 B.C.–A.D. 337* (Cornell University Press, 1977); Averil Cameron, *The Later Roman Empire* (Harvard University Press, 1993); William K. Klingaman, *The First Century: Emperors, Gods, and Everyman* (HarperCollins, 1990); and Olga Tellegen-Couperus, *A Short History of Roman Law* (Routledge, 1993).

Michael Grant, *Cities of Vesuvius: Pompeii and Herculaneum* (Penguin, 1978), re-creates the daily life of these buried cities. See also Claude Nicolet, *The World of the Citizen in Republican Rome* (University of California Press, 1980); John E. Stambaugh, *The Ancient Roman City* (Johns Hopkins University Press, 1988); John P. V. D. Balsdon, *Life and Leisure in Ancient Rome* (McGraw-Hill, 1969), and *Roman Women: Their History and Habits* (Knopf, 1975); Mary Lefkowitz and Maureen Fant, eds., *Women's Life in Greece and Rome: A Source Book in Translation*, rev. ed. (Johns Hopkins University Press, 1992); Keith Bradley, *Slavery and Society in Rome* (Cambridge University Press, 1994) and *Discovering the Roman Family* (Oxford University Press, 1991); Henry Charles Boren, *Roman Society: A Social, Economic, and Cultural History*, 2nd ed. (Heath, 1992); Florence Dupont, *Daily Life in Ancient Rome* (Oxford University Press, 1992); Beryl Rawson, ed., *The Family in Ancient Rome: New Perspectives* (Cornell University Press, 1986); Judith Hallett, *Fathers and Daughters in Roman Society* (Princeton University Press, 1984); Harold B. Mattingly, *The Man in the Roman Street* (Norton, 1966); and Michael Grant, *The Jews in the Roman World* (Scribner, 1973). Roland Auguet, *Cruelty and Civilization: The Roman Games* (Routledge, 1994), and Carlin Barton, *The Sorrows of the Ancient Romans* (Princeton University Press, 1993), both deal with games and gladiatorial combats.

Other books of interest are Martin L. Clarke, *The Roman Mind: Studies in the History of Thought from Cicero to Marcus Aurelius* (Norton, 1968); Chester G. Starr, *Civilization and the Caesars: The Intellectual Revolution in the Roman Empire* (Cornell University Press, 1954); Max Ludwig Wolfram Laistner, *The Greater Roman Historians* (University of California Press, 1963); Stanley Frederick Bonner, *Education in Ancient Rome* (University of California Press, 1978); John G. Landels, *Engineering in the Ancient World* (University of California Press, 1978); Martin Henig, ed., *A Handbook of Roman Art* (Oxford University Press, 1983); Mortimer Wheeler, *Roman Art and Architecture* (Thames & Hudson, 1985); Herbert Jennings Rose, *Religion in Greece and Rome* (Harper Torchbooks, 1959); and Robert Turcan, *The Cults of the Roman Empire* (Oxford University Press, 1996).

Recommended historical novels are Winifred Bryher, *Coin of Carthage* (Harvest, 1965); Thornton Wilder, *The Ides of March* (Avon, 1975); John Williams, *Augustus* (Penguin, 1979); Robert Graves, *I Claudius* (Vintage, 1977); Marguerite Yourcenar, *Memoirs of Hadrian* (Modern Library, 1984); Lindsey Davis, *Time to Depart* (Warner, 1995); and a continuing series of novels dealing with the Roman Republic by Colleen McCullough, beginning with *The First Man in Rome* (Morrow, 1990).

Suggestions for Web Browsing

Museums of the Vatican: Gregorian Estruscan Museum
http://christusrex.org/www1/vaticano/ET1-Etrusco.html
http://christusrex.org/www1/vaticano/ET2-Etrusco.html
Two sites within the extensive pages of the Museums of the Vatican offer numerous images from the Etruscan period.

Timeline
http://www.exovedate.com/ancient_timeline_one.html
The history of ancient Rome, with a chronological index and links to Internet resources. Emphasis is placed on the roles of women in ancient times.

Roman Empire
http://library.advanced.org/10805/rome/html
The history of the empire is illustrated through maps and time lines. Examinations of the sources of our knowledge through Roman writers is emphasized. An extensive history of ancient Rome.

Online Encyclopedia of the Roman Empire
http://www.salve.edu/~dmaaiom/deimprom.html
A massive site emphasizing the study of Roman history through coins and through maps of the empire.

Pompeii Forum Project
http://jefferson.village.virginia.edu/pompeii/forummap.htmp
Constructed by historians and archaeologists from the University of Virginia, this site examines ancient Pompeii through a variety of photographs.

Vesuvius
http://volcano.und.nodak.edu
A beautiful exploration of Mount Vesuvius in ancient Rome and as it appears today. Speculation on the next eruption as well.

Pompeii
http://www.tulane.edu/lester/text/Western.Architect/Pompeii/Pompeii.html
One hundred images from this Tulane University site provide a virtual tour of ancient Pompeii.

Women's Life in Greece and Rome
http://www.uky/edu/ArtsSciences/Classics/wlgr/wlgr-index.html
Details about the private life and legal status of women, in addition to biographies of prominent women of ancient Rome.

Roman Art and Architecture
http://harpy.uccs.edu/roman/html/romarch.html
A collection of images of Roman architecture.

Notes

1. Livy, *History of Rome*, 1.51, trans. Aubrey de Sélincourt, in *Livy: The Early History of Rome* (Baltimore: Penguin, 1988), p. 89.
2. Plutarch, *Lives*, "Cato the Elder," 2.2, trans. Bernadotte Perrin, Loeb Classical Library, Vol. 47 (Cambridge, Mass.: Harvard University Press, 1948), p. 307.
3. Quoted in Donald R. Dudley, *The Civilization of Rome* (New York: New American Library, 1962), p. 21.
4. Polybius, *Histories* 1.10, trans. Evelyn S. Shuckburgh, in *The Histories of Polybius*, Vol. I (Bloomington: University of Indiana Press, 1962), p. 10.
5. Livy, *Roman History* 33, trans. E. T. Sage, Loeb Classical Library, Vol. 9 (Cambridge, Mass.: Harvard University Press, 1979), p. 367.
6. Livy, *Roman History* 25.3, trans. Aubrey de Sélincourt, in *Livy: The War with Hannibal* (Baltimore: Penguin, 1965), p. 296.
7. Plutarch, *Lives*, "Tiberius Gracchus" 9.5, trans. Bernadotte Perrin, Loeb Classical Library, Vol. 10 (Cambridge, Mass.: Harvard University Press, 1948), pp. 165, 167.
8. Mason Hammond, *City-State and World State in Greek and Roman Political Theory Until Augustus* (Cambridge, Mass.: Harvard University Press, 1951), p. 153.
9. Horace, *Odes* 3.6, trans. James Michie, in *The Odes of Horace* (Indianapolis: Bobbs-Merrill, 1965), p. 138.
10. Tacitus, *Annals* 15:44, trans. Michael Grant (Baltimore: Penguin, 1959), p. 354.
11. Tacitus, *History* 1.1, trans. Alfread S. Church and William S. Brodribb, *The Complete Works of Tacitus* (New York: Random House, 1992), p. 420.
12. Marcus Aurelius, *Meditations* 11.3, trans. A. S. L. Farquarson, in *The Meditations of the Emperor Marcus Antoninus* Vol. I, (Oxford: Oxford University Press, 1944), p. 217.
13. Virgil, *Aeneid* 6.847–853, in Naphtali Lewis and Meyer Reinhold, eds., *Roman Civilization: Selected Readings*, Vol. 2 (New York: Columbia University Press, 1955), p. 23.
14. Aelius Aristides, *To Rome*, Oration 26, trans. S. Levin (Glencoe, Ill.: Free Press, 1950), p. 126.
15. Ibid., p. 126.
16. The advice of Maecenas, Rome's richest capitalist, to Augustus in Dio Cassius, *Roman History* 52, 14–15, trans. Earnest Cary, Loeb Classical Library, Vol. 6 (Cambridge, Mass.: Harvard University Press, 1925), pp. 109 ff.
17. Pliny the Younger, *Letters* 10.17a, in Naphtali Lewis and Meyer Reinhold, eds., *Roman Civilization: Selected Readings*, Vol. 2 (New York: Columbia University Press, 1955), p. 342.
18. Juvenal, *Satires* 3, in R. C. Trevelyan, *Translations from Horace, Juvenal, and Montaigne* (New York: Cambridge University Press, 1941), p. 129.
19. Tacitus, *Agricola* 30.
20. Tacitus, *Histories* 4. 74.
21. Frontinus, quoted in Michael Grant, *The World of Rome* (New York: New American Library, 1960), p. 298.
22. Catullus, *Carmen* 85, trans. Theodore Martin.
23. Lucretius, *On the Nature of the Universe* 3.70, trans. Ronald Latham (Baltimore: Penguin, 1951), p. 98.
24. Virgil, *Aeneid* 4.1, trans. C. Day Lewis.
25. Horace, "The Centennial Hymn," trans. James Michie, in *The Odes of Horace* (Indianapolis: Bobbs-Merrill, 1965), p. 227.
26. Horace, *Odes* 3.29, trans. John Dryden.
27. Juvenal, *Satires* 6, trans by Peter Green, in *The Sixteen Satires* (Baltimore: Penguin, 1974), p. 146.
28. Livy, *History of Rome* 1.10, trans. B. O. Foster, Loeb Classical Library, Vol. 1, (Cambridge, Mass.: Harvard University Press, 1976), p. 7.
29. Apuleius, *The Golden Ass* 5–6, in Nels Bailkey, *Readings in Ancient History: Thought and Experience from Gilgamesh to St. Augustine*, 4th ed. (Lexington, Mass.: Heath, 1992), p. 441.
30. Lucretius, *On The Nature of the Universe* 1.95, trans. Ronald Latham (Baltimore: Penguin, 1951), p. 30.
31. Cicero, *De Legibus* 1.4. 14–6.20.
32. Seneca, *Epistles* 41, quoted in Chester G. Starr, *Civilization and the Caesars: The Intellectual Revolution in the Roman Empire* (New York: Norton, 1965), p. 228.
33. Pliny, *Natural History* 2.14.117–118, trans. H. Rackham, Loeb Classical Library, Vol. 1 (Cambridge, Mass.: Harvard University Press, 1989), pp. 259, 261.
34. Pliny the Younger, *Letters* 6.16–20.
35. Galen, "On Prognosis," in Thomas W. Africa, *Rome and the Caesars* (New York: Wiley, 1965), p. 217.
36. Livy, *Roman History* 1.1, trans. Aubrey de Sélincourt, in *Livy: The Early History of Rome* (Baltimore: Penguin, 1960), p. 34.

The tombs of the First Emperor, 210 B.C.E., have yielded most of the surviving art from that period in China. The more than 6000 figures, including these terra cotta warriors, were not discovered until 1974 in one of the greatest archeological discoveries in history.

Classical China

From Origins to Empire, Prehistory to 220 C.E.

Chapter Contents

As in other parts of the world, there were tool-using humanoids some 600,000 to 800,000 years ago on the Chinese subcontinent. They lived in a vast watershed drained by three river systems that rise close together on the high Tibetan plateau and flow eastward to the Pacific. Three mountain systems also rise in the west, diminishing in altitude as they slope eastward between the river systems. The Huang Ho (Yellow River), traditionally known as "China's Sorrow" because of the misery caused by its periodic flooding, crosses the North China plain. In this area, the original homeland of Chinese culture, the climate is like that of western Europe, with an agriculture based on wheat and millet. The Yangtze River and its valley form the second river system. South of this valley lie the subtropical rice-growing, silk, and tea lands of South China, the home of ancient cultures that were destroyed or transformed by Chinese expansion from the north. Here the Hsi (West) River, converging on present-day Guangzhou (Canton), forms the third major river system.

Within the Chinese subcontinent, geographers have identified at least eight different ecosystems, ranging from the semitropical southeast, receiving more than 4 feet of rain each year, to the desertlike northwest, which gets less than 4 inches of rain annually. Separated by mountains, deserts, and seas from the rest of the world, the Chinese developed independent of the other world centers and spread a unified culture along the river valleys over a greater land area than any other civilization. The same geographical context of easily penetrated frontiers and a fragmented land gave the Chinese a legacy of political disunity.

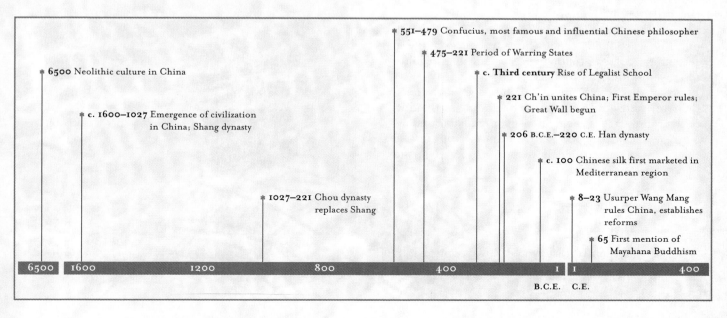

* 551–479 Confucius, most famous and influential Chinese philosopher

* 475–221 Period of Warring States

* c. **Third century** Rise of Legalist School

* 6500 Neolithic culture in China

* 221 Ch'in unites China; First Emperor rules; Great Wall begun

* c. 1600–1027 Emergence of civilization in China; Shang dynasty

* 206 B.C.E.–220 C.E. Han dynasty

* c. 100 Chinese silk first marketed in Mediterranean region

* 1027–221 Chou dynasty replaces Shang

* 8–23 Usurper Wang Mang rules China, establishes reforms

* 65 First mention of Mayahana Buddhism

6500   1600   1200   800   400   I | I   400

B.C.E.   C.E.

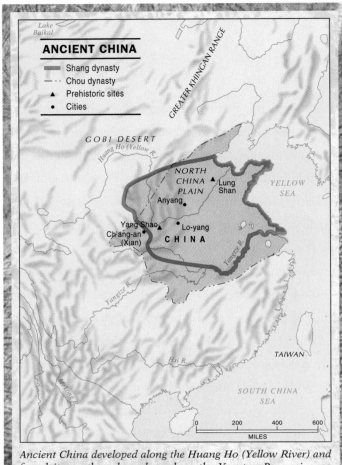

ANCIENT CHINA

— Shang dynasty
- - - Chou dynasty
▲ Prehistoric sites
• Cities

Ancient China developed along the Huang Ho (Yellow River) and found its southern boundary along the Yangtze. Possessing no major geographical barriers to invasion along its northern, western, and southern borders, the country was open to attack.

6500 B.C.E. In each region, climate and rainfall dictated which crops could be grown. Each crop imposed its own demands on settlement patterns and land use, especially the need to find artificial means of raising water in the south and the use of horses and other pastoral animals in the north. The evidence indicates that China's Neolithic culture, which domesticated the pig, cultivated millet, and produced silk, originated independent of that in the Near East.

The people of China's last Neolithic culture, called Lung Shan, lived in walled towns throughout North China. The walls of their towns, located along the rivers, sheltered the townfolk from aggressive bands of nomadic Chinese, living in a horse-raising economy, who remained in the foothills and plains. While the towns made institutional and technological advances, especially in the area of defense, the nomadic bands created their own effective weapons. The tension between the settled communities and the invading bands had a decisive effect on the development of Chinese civilization and politics.

The Chinese Neolithic urban centers shared the commercial and religious activities of other world Neolithic centers. But in China the consistent outside threat led to the development of a military elite to defend the population and ultimately the establishment of a system of war leaders who would become kings. The fabled Hsia dynasty actually existed and flourished for some three centuries before it was replaced by the Shang in the seventeenth century B.C.E.

Despite China's huge size—larger than the United States—the threat of invasion from the north was always present. Invaders brought challenges that altered the development of China's civilization and introduced important political concepts. But throughout this vast land, the Chinese pursued a life of settled agriculture, following a system that began in the seventh millennium B.C.E.

New discoveries reveal a unified civilization in the river valleys as early as the beginning of the third millennium B.C.E. Archaeologists have also found evidence of common political life and writing earlier than 1750 B.C.E., which have proved that dynasties once thought legendary actually did exist.

Neolithic China

A series of recently discovered sites confirms the presence of Neolithic settlements in China around

Neolithic bowls, c. 8000–2000 B.C.E. These Neolithic bowls testify to the advanced craftmanship of "preliterate" times.

The Creation of China, to the Fifth Century B.C.E.

Shang was originally the name of a dominant tribe whose leaders replaced the Hsia as the overlords of the tribal leaders in North China. From the archaeological evidence of their capitals it is evident that the kings, victorious war leaders, had enormous power. They could demand the work of a large number of laborers and craftsmen to build their palaces and tombs. The most important testimony to Shang rule were the walled, protected cities to which the less powerful tribal leaders had to come to pay tribute. As their political and military fortunes varied, the rulers moved their capitals frequently during the six centuries of Shang rule (c. 1600–1027 B.C.E.). The last capital was at modern Anyang.

China's Bronze Age began about 2000 B.C.E., and during the Shang dynasty the Chinese developed a sophisticated bronze metallurgy. They used bronze to make elaborate ceremonial and drinking vessels (the Shang leaders were notorious for their drinking bouts) and weapons. Not only were the bronze productions practical, but they were also works of art with both incised and high-relief designs.

The Shang people used a system of writing so advanced that it probably originated before their rule, under the Hsia, although no earlier documents have yet been found. It was based on 3000 pictographic characters, some of which are still in use today. These characters stand for individual words rather than sounds and consist of recognizable representations of everyday objects and ideographs expressing ideas such as walking. The Chinese were the only people in East Asia to devise their own, original written language; the Chinese pictographs and ideographs served as the foundation for the written languages of other people in East Asia, including the Koreans and the Japanese.

Most Shang writing is found on thousands of "oracle bones," fragments of animal bones and tortoise shells. Usually, these contained written questions for the ancestral spirits, who were believed to be closely tied to their living descendants as members of the family group. The living would ask the dead such questions as "Will the king's child be a son?" and "If we raise an army of 3000 men to drive *X* away from *Y*, will we succeed?" The shell or bone would then be heated in a fire, and the resulting cracks would be interpreted as an answer to the question.

Later, as the state and its activities grew more complex, the kings had to oversee not only fighting but also taxing and governing. The leaders needed to record their decisions and to transmit them to their often distant subjects. These tasks were done by scribes, who became increasingly useful to the kings. Later the

Preimperial History	
before 1600 B.C.E.	Hsia (Xia)
c. 1600–1027 B.C.E.	Shang
1027–770 B.C.E.	Western Chou (Zhou) (traditional)
770–221 B.C.E.	Eastern Chou (Zhou)
770–476 B.C.E.	Spring and Autumn period
475–221 B.C.E.	Warring States period

scribes would grow in power to become trusted officials who would defend the monarch's power when the kings were off fighting the almost continual wars.

Religion played the key connective role in the maintenance of social order. The hereditary kings that ruled Shang China acted as the sole link between the people and the chief forces in the spirit world. The kings had limited earthly political power because they were compelled by tradition to rule with the consent of the "Council of Great and Small." But only the king could worship and make humble petitions for favors to the chief deity in heaven (the *T'ien*), considered the ancestor of the king's own clan. The oracle bones reveal that the kings often appealed to the ancestral spirits in order to overcome the opposition of the

This bronze mask was discovered at Anyang, in eastern China, in the tomb of a ruler of the Shang dynasty, one of the earliest periods of Chinese history for which we have archaeological evidence.

Council. Unlike the common people, the kings and nobles had recorded ancestors and belonged to a clan. They were the descendants in the male line from a common ancestor whom they worshipped. To win the aid or avoid the displeasure of the spirits, both animals and humans (prisoners of war) were sacrificed, and a beerlike liquor was poured on the ground.

The lesser levels of society each had their local gods, to whom requests to guarantee good harvests and long life were addressed. The peasants belonged to no clans, and there is no evidence that they worshipped their ancestors. Instead, their gods were the fundamental forces of nature, such as rivers, mountains, earth, wind, rain, and the stars and planets.

During the Shang period a special group of Chinese became skilled in the use of magic, with which they attempted to manipulate the two conflicting forces of the world. They called these two opposed but complementary forces *yang* and *yin*. *Yang* was associated with the sun and all things male, strong, warm, and active. *Yin* was associated with the moon and all things female, dark, cold, weak, and passive. In later ages Chinese philosophers—all male—would employ these concepts to require the obedience and passivity that was expected of women.

The power of the kings and nobles rested on their ownership of the land, their monopoly of bronze metallurgy, their chariots, and the kings' religious functions. We can see proof of the power of the Shang kings and their nobles in their imposing buildings, military superiority, and tombs. They often entered into battle across North China and for centuries gained victory by using chariots, a potent technological advantage. After death, they were buried in sumptuous tombs along with their chariots and still-living servants and war captives.

Peasants might be legally free but had little mobility. They rarely owned land and worked plots periodically assigned to them by royal and noble landowners. They collectively cultivated the fields retained by their lords. Farming methods were primitive, not having advanced beyond the Neolithic level. Bronze was used for weapons, not tools or implements, and the peasants continued to reap wheat and millet with stone sickles and till their allotted fields with wooden plows.

The Chou Dynasty: The "Feudal" Age

Shortly after 1030 B.C.E. the Chou (Zhou) tribe came out of the west and overthrew the Shang dynasty, who, the Chou charged, had failed to rule fairly and benevolently. The Chou leader announced that the god of heaven *(T'ien)* had given him a mandate to replace the Shang. This was more than a convenient justification of the seizure of power. It introduced a new aspect of Chinese thought: that the cosmos is ruled by an impersonal and all-powerful Heaven, which sits in judgment over the human ruler, who continues to be the link between Heaven's commands and human fate.

The Chou was a powerful western frontier tribe that took advantage of the opportunities of the wealth and increasing weakness of Shang rule, much as the Macedonians would be drawn into Greece 500 years later. Given their military strength, the other Chinese tribes wisely switched their loyalty to the Chou, who went on to establish a dynasty that lasted for almost 900 years (c. 1027–221 B.C.E.), the longest in Chinese history.

Spread out over most of North China and the Yangtze valley, the very size of the Chou domain made it impossible to be ruled directly from the center. The Chou kings set up what Europeans two millennia later would call a feudal system of government (see Chapter 9). In this system the kings gave local authority and land to relatives and powerful nobles. These 50 or so people entered into a type of contract with the king in which they would hold their land and authority dependent on the king's will: in return they were to fight for him. Sometimes these subordinates (later called *vassals*) received hereditary power and property; others might have to have the contract renewed with each new generation or monarch. Under this system, peasants and women had little or no standing.

The early Chou kings were strong leaders who kept the allegiance of their vassals while fighting off attacks on the frontiers. However, after two centuries, complacency set in, and a succession of weak kings led to a reduction in the central throne's power: taking advantage of advances in military technology, the vassals became more independent.

By the eighth century B.C.E. the vassals no longer went to the Chou capital for investiture by the Son of Heaven, the title the Chou king had adopted. As the Chou monarchs became weaker, court officials increased their influence. Under the feudal politics of the Chou, bureaucratic documentation became ever more complex, as the center had to define its relations with the more than 50 major dependencies and continually changing foreign contacts. The kings' scribes, clerks, and officials wrote the documents that defined hierarchy and order and mastered the political precedents that the military men needed to exercise legitimate authority. As the state became more complex, the qualifications for state servants became more specific. Now the officials of the state, along with the nobles, could gain rank, land, wealth, and an assured future for their family.

The remnants of Chou royal power disappeared completely in 771 B.C.E. when an alliance of disloyal vassals and barbarians destroyed the capital and killed the king. Part of the royal family managed to escape eastward to Lo-yang, however, where the dynasty survived for another five centuries (until around 250 B.C.E.) doing little more than performing state religious rituals as the Sons of Heaven. Seven of the stronger feudal princes gradually conquered their weaker neighbors. In the process they assumed the title *wang* ("king"), formerly used only by the Chou ruler, and began to end the feudal rights of their own vassals and establish centralized bureaucracies.

Warfare among these emerging centralized states was incessant, particularly during the two and one-half centuries known as the period of Warring States (475–221 B.C.E.). By 221 B.C.E. the ruler of the Ch'in, the most advanced of the seven Warring States, had conquered all of his rivals and established a unified empire of which he was the absolute ruler.

The art of horseback riding, common among the nomads of central Asia, greatly influenced later Chou China. In response to the threat of mounted nomads, rulers of the Warring States period began constructing increasingly complex defensive walls. Inside China itself, the swifter and more mobile cavalry replaced the chariots, and the infantry adapted to new conditions by wearing tunics and trousers adopted from the nomads.

Chou Economy and Society

Despite its political instability, the Chou period is unrivaled by any later period in Chinese history for its material and cultural progress. These developments led the Chinese to emphasize the vast difference between their own high civilization and the nomadic ways of the "barbarians" beyond their frontiers. This distinction was proudly kept until the twentieth century, as the Chinese belief in their cultural superiority came to be viewed by non-Chinese as insufferably arrogant.

During the sixth century B.C.E. the Chinese mastered the use of iron and mass-produced cast iron objects from molds, which were in wide use by the end of the third century B.C.E. (The first successful European attempts at casting iron were not made until the end of the Middle Ages.) The ox-drawn iron-tipped plow, together with the use of manure and the growth of large-scale irrigation and water-control projects, led to a more dependable and productive food supply and greater population growth.

The Chou understood the necessity to build canals to improve their realm's economy and communication. The canals made it possible to move food and useful items dependably over long distances. Commerce and wealth grew rapidly. At the beginning of the Chou dynasty, brightly colored shells, bolts of silk, and ingots of precious metals were used as forms of exchange; by the end of the dynasty, small round copper coins with square holes had taken their place.

Under the Chou dynasty, merchant and artisan classes played an economically prominent, if not socially recognized, role as wealth spread beyond the nobles and court servants. Indicative of the rise in the general economic level, chopsticks and finely lacquered objects, today universally considered as symbols of Chinese and East Asian culture, were in general use by the end of the period.

Bronze vessels, such as this one from the early tenth century B.C.E., were designed to contain water, wine, meat, or grain used during the sacrificial rites in which the Shang and Chou prayed to the spirits of their ancestors. Animals were a common motif of ritual bronzes.

bols of Chinese and East Asian culture, were in general use by the end of the period.

Social divisions and consciousness became highly developed under Chou political feudalism and remained until modern times. During the first half of the Chou era, the king and the aristocracy became increasingly separated from the mass of the people on the basis of land ownership and family descent. The social hierarchy came to be more precisely defined, for centuries locking people into their particular social stratum with little or no hope of "moving up."

The core units of aristocratic society were the elementary family, the extended family, and the clan, held together by patriarchal authority and ancestor worship. Marriages were formally arranged unions between families. The customs of the nobles can be compared in only the most general way to those of Europe's feudal nobility, especially when the Chou system began to fall apart (see Chapter 9).

Social changes came with the weakening of the Chou in the fifth century B.C.E. and the division of the land between the remnants of the Chou and a number of independent principalities. With the weakening of the political center, the rigid social hierarchy changed. Money played a more important role, and land came more and more to be transferred by either sale or purchase and less and less by hereditary transfer from generation to generation of the nobility. Once land, the prime measure of wealth and status, could be bought and sold, the rich of whatever rank could become part of the economic, if not social, elites. It can be argued that these changes did not constitute true social mobility, but it did signal the end of the political feudalism of the early Chou and the social system that accompanied it.

This economic and political transformation threatened the traditional, idealized hierarchy. Teachers and philosophers, longing for the "good old days" of social stability, played an important role in defining and teaching the values that would dominate Chinese society into the twentieth century. They found a willing audience among the people who had the most to gain from order and hierarchy, the clerks and officials who increased their influence, wealth, and legal privileges during the Chou dynasty.

One of the social values that emerged during this time was that society was held together by a complex code of what Europeans would later call chivalry, *li*, practiced in both war and peace. It symbolized the traits of the most noble warrior, and men in the elite classes devoted years to its mastery. As Chou China disintegrated, the early kings came to be seen as the most ideal and most representative part of the system. At a time when disorder and social upheaval dominated the land, this nostalgia for the imagined past led to the conceptualizing of an entire hierarchical social order developed around an idealized monarch, with each inferior in the descending scale owing respect and obedience to his superior. Referred to in Chinese chronicles as the *Spring and Autumn Annals*, this schema is the justification for order and discipline. As we will see, Confucius and his disciples codified the rules of how a just society should function during a time of strife.

The peasant masses stood outside of this feudal hierarchy. They were economically subjected to control by "an interlocking oligarchy of government officials, landed gentry, and rural moneylenders," although they remained "legally free to buy and sell land or change their occupation." Unfortunately, they were "bound to the land they cultivated by a number of economic factors."[1] They were in effect tied to their villages—the great majority of the population worked as tenants of noble landholders or moneylenders, paying one-tenth of their crop as rent. Despite the increased agricultural production resulting from large-scale irrigation and the ox-drawn iron-tipped plow, the peasants had difficulty eking out an existence. Some were forced into debt slavery. A major problem in the Chinese economy, evident by late Chou times, was that the majority of farmers worked fields so small that they could not produce a crop surplus to tide them over periods of scarcity. Their poverty drove them even further down in the Chinese social structure.

The Philosophical Schools

The continual battles among the feudal lords during the period of Warring States (475–221 B.C.E.) destroyed the relative stability of the Shang and early Chou dynasties. The values and habits based on the traditions of an orderly society disappeared from Chinese life. In the next three centuries, some great teachers and philosophers thought deeply about the nature of humanity and the problems of society. They created a range of philosophies on "how man should live" that went from the extremes of living for society to living for one's own soul. These teachers and philosophers have shaped Chinese society ever since.

Confucianism: Rationalized Hierarchy

The first, most famous, and certainly most influential Chinese philosopher and teacher was K'ung-fu-tzu ("Master K'ung, the Sage," 551–479 B.C.E.), known in the West as Confucius after Jesuit missionaries to China in the seventeenth century latinized his name. He was just one in a line of teachers who tried to explain the universe and his people's role in it. Unlike some thinkers in the West, the Chinese teachers and thinkers did not spend as much time on abstract concepts—there are no Chinese equivalents of Plato or Aristotle. Only a few teachers "felt called to identify a system that lay behind the operation of the universe; others were moved to formulate a means of sustaining the corporate life of a community, . . . even supporting the rule of a government." Their thoughts "concerned the behavior of man to man and the organization of his government, rather than the framework within which concepts should be defined."[2]

Confucius's disciples believed that their master composed or edited the Five Confucian Classics—two books of history and one book each on poetry, divination (predicting the future through supernatural means), and ceremonies—which were in large part a product of the early Chou period. But the only work that can be accurately attributed to Confucius is the *Analects* ("Selected Sayings"), a collection of his responses to his disciples' questions.

Confucius, who belonged to the lower aristocracy of a minor state, Lu, was more or less a contemporary of the Buddha in India, Zoroaster in Persia, and the early philosophers of Greece. Like the Buddha and Zoroaster, Confucius lived in a troubled time—an age of political and social turmoil—and his prime concern, like theirs, was the improvement of society and the maintenance of order. To achieve this goal, Confucius did not look to the gods and spirits for assistance; he accepted the existence of Heaven *(T'ien)* and spirits, but he insisted it was more important "to know the essential duties of man living in a society of men." "We don't know yet how to serve men," he said; "how can we know about serving the spirits?" And, "we don't yet know about life, so how can we know about death?" He advised a ruler to "respect the ghosts and spirits but keep them at a distance" and "devote yourself to the proper demands of the people." Confucius and his disciples tried to freeze a social hierarchy into an ethical

Through the ages, Confucius became idealized as the genial authority to whom one could look for instruction on "how man should live."

framework, to stabilize society into a complex network of respect bestowed and respect expected, whether between father and son or between ruler and noble.

This goal was more than an academic exercise. It was a response to a time in which violence between communities and a breakdown of tradition within communities threatened the Chinese civilization. Teachers and philosophers sought to explain to their students and followers a way to understand that the disorder in which they lived was part of a larger, eternal scheme, that there was an "operation of the world," "an integrated system" that "brought about the movement seen in the heavens and on earth." Further,

> *Kings and emperors who wished to establish a permanent regime that their sons and grandsons would inherit relied on intellectual support to demonstrate that their call for obedience and exercise of temporal power were legitimate. Theories of empire and statecraft . . . provide for an acceptable explanation of how a monarch had received his charge to rule.[3]*

Thus during this period of the Warring States,

> *it was becoming desirable, or even necessary, to place the requirements of an ordered, civilized society within*

the framework of the single organic universe and to prescribe ideal forms of conduct that would distinguish Chinese from those less fortunate mortals who lived beyond the pale.[4]

Confucius filled the need for the definition of this "single organic universe." He believed that the improvement of society was the responsibility of the ruler and that the quality of government depended on the ruler's moral character: "The way *(Tao)* of learning to be great consists in shining with the illustrious power of moral personality, in making a new people, in abiding in the highest goodness." Confucius's definition of the Tao as "moral personality" and the "highest goodness" was in decided contrast to the old premoral Tao, in which gods and spirits, propitiated by offerings and ritual, regulated human life for good or ill. Above all, Confucius's "new way" meant a concern for the rights of others, the adherence to a type of Golden Rule: when a disciple asked, "Is there any saying that one can act on all day, every day?" Confucius replied, "Perhaps the saying about consideration: 'Never do to others what you would not like them to do to you.'"

Although Confucius called himself "a transmitter and not a creator," his redefinition of Tao and his teachings produced an ethical program for this world, by this world. He was, in effect, putting new wine into old bottles. He did the same thing with two other key terms, *li* and *chün-tzu*. *Li*, meaning "honorable behavior," was the chivalric code of the constantly fighting *chün-tzu*, the hereditary feudal "noblemen" of the Chou period. As refined and reinterpreted by Confucius, *li* came to embody such ethical virtues as righteousness and love for one's fellow humans. The *chün-tzu*, under the influence of the new definition of *li*, became "noble men," or "gentlemen," whose social origins were not important. As Confucius said, "The noble man understands what is right; the inferior man understands what is profitable." Confucius's teachings have had a greater and longer-lasting influence on China, and much of East Asia, than those of any other philosopher.

Taoism: Intuitive Mysticism

A second philosophical reaction to the troubled times of the late Chou period was the teaching of Lao-tzu ("Old Master"), a semilegendary figure who was believed to have been a contemporary of Confucius. As with Confucius, the key term in Lao-tzu's teaching is *Tao*, from which his philosophy takes its name. But whereas Confucius defined Tao as a rational standard of ethics in human affairs, Lao-tzu gave it a metaphysical, transcendental meaning: the course of nature, the natural and inevitable, all-regulating order of the universe.

The goal of Taoism, like that of Confucianism, is a happy life. Lao-tzu believed that this goal could be achieved by living a life in conformity with nature, retiring from the chaos and evils of contemporary Warring States society and shunning human institutions and

Mencius on Human Nature

Lao Tzu said: "The nature of man may be likened to a swift current of water: you lead it eastward and it will flow to the east; you lead it westward and it will flow to the west. Human nature is neither disposed to good nor to evil, just as water is neither disposed to east nor west." Mencius replied: "It is true that water is neither disposed to east nor west, but is it neither disposed to flowing upward nor downward? The tendency of human nature to do good is like that of water to flow downward. There is no man who does not tend to do good; there is no water that does not flow downward. Now you may strike water and make it splash over your forehead, or you may even force it up the hills. But is this in the nature of water? It is of course due to the force of circumstances. Similarly, man may be brought to do evil, and that is because the same is done to his nature."

From W. Theodore de Bary, ed., *Sources of Chinese Tradition* (New York: Columbia University Press, 1960), pp. 102–103.

opinions as unnatural and artificial "outside things." Thus at the heart of Taoist thought is the concept of *wu-wei*, or "nonaction"—a manner of living that, like nature itself, is nonassertive and spontaneous. Lao-tzu pointed out that in nature all things work silently; they fulfill their function, and after they reach their bloom, they return to their origins. Unlike Confucius's ideal gentleman, who is constantly involved in society in order to preserve and better it, Lao-tzu's sage is a private person, an individualist, accepting life's burdens.

Taoism is a revolt not only against society but also against the intellect's limitations. Intuition, not reason, is the source of true knowledge; and books, Taoists said, are "the dregs and refuse of the ancients." One of the most famous Taoist philosophers, Chuang-tzu (fourth century B.C.E.), who made fun of Confucianists as tiresome busybodies, even questioned the reality of the world of the senses. He said that he once dreamed that he was a butterfly, "flying about enjoying itself." When he awakened he was confused: "I do not know whether I was Chuang-tzu dreaming that I was a butterfly, or whether now I am a butterfly dreaming that I am Chuang-tzu."

Anecdotes and allegories abound in Taoist literature, as in all mystical teachings that deal with subjects that are difficult to put into words. (As the Taoists put it, "The one who knows does not speak, and the one who speaks does not know.") But Taoist mysticism is more philosophical than religious. It does not aim to extinguish the personality through the union with the Absolute or God. Rather, its aim is to teach how one can obtain happiness in this world by living a simple life in harmony with nature.

Confucianism and Taoism became the two major philosophies that shaped Chinese thought and civilization. Although these rival schools frequently sniped at each other, they never became mutually exclusive outlooks on life. Taoist intuition complemented Confucian rationalism; during the centuries to come, Chinese were often Confucianists in their social relations and Taoists in their private life.

Mencius's Contribution to Confucianism

The man whose work was largely responsible for the emergence of Confucianism as the most widely accepted philosophy in China was Mencius, or Meng-tzu (372–289 B.C.E.). Born a century after the death of Confucius, Mencius added important new dimensions to Confucian thought in two areas: human nature and government.

Whereas Confucius had only implied that human nature is good, Mencius emphatically insisted that all people are innately good and tend to seek the good just as water tends to run downhill. But unless people strive to preserve and develop their innate goodness, which is the source of righteous conduct, it can be corrupted by the bad practices and ideas existing in the environment. Mencius taught that the opposite of righteous conduct is selfishness, and he attacked the extreme individualism of the Taoists as a form of selfishness. He held that "all men are brothers."

The second area in which Mencius elaborated on Confucius's teaching was politics. Mencius and his followers emphasized the key role of traditions and memories as a guide to life. In their lessons they distinguished between good kings, who ruled benevolently, and the rulers of his day (the period of Warring States), who governed by force and spread violence and disorder. Because good rulers of the past were guided by ethical standards, he said, they behaved benevolently toward the people and provided for their well-being. Unlike Confucius, who did not question the right of hereditary kings to rule, Mencius said that the people have a right to rebel against bad rulers and even kill them if necessary, because they have lost the "mandate of Heaven."

As we have seen, this concept had been used by the Chou to justify their revolt against the Shang. On that occasion the concept had a religious meaning, being connected with the worship of Heaven, who supported the ruler as the Son of Heaven. Mencius,

Legalism: The Theories of Han Fei Tzu (d. 233 B.C.E.)

When the sage rules the state, he does not count on people doing good of themselves, but employs such measures as will keep them from doing any evil. If he counts on people doing good of themselves, there will not be enough such people to be numbered by the tens in the whole country. But if he employs such measures as will keep them from doing evil, then the entire state can be brought up to a uniform standard. Inasmuch as the administrator has to consider the many but disregard the few, he does not busy himself with morals but with laws.

. . . Therefore, the intelligent ruler upholds solid facts and discards useless frills. He does not speak about deeds of humanity and righteousness, and he does not listen to the words of learned men.

Those who are ignorant about government insistently say: "Win the hearts of the people." If order could be procured by winning the hearts of the people, then even the wise ministers Yi Yin and Kuan Chung would be of no use. For all that the ruler would need to do would be just to listen to the people. Actually, the intelligence of the people is not to be relied upon any more than the mind of a baby. If the baby does not have his head shaved, his sores will recur; if he does not have his boil cut open, his illness will go from bad to worse. However, in order to shave his head or open the boil someone has to hold the baby while the affectionate mother is performing the work, and yet he keeps crying and yelling incessantly. The baby does not understand that suffering a small pain is the way to obtain a great benefit.

. . . The sage considers the conditions of the times . . . and governs the people accordingly. Thus though penalties are light, it is not due to charity; though punishment is heavy, it is not due to cruelty. Whatever is done is done in accordance with the circumstances of the age. Therefore circumstances go according to their time, and the course of action is planned in accordance with the circumstances.

. . . Now take a young fellow who is a bad character. His parents may get angry at him, but he never makes any change. The villagers may reprove him, but he is not moved. His teachers and elders may admonish him, but he never reforms. The love of his parents, the efforts of the villagers, and the wisdom of his teachers and elders—all the three excellent disciplines are applied to him, and yet not even a hair on his shins is altered. It is only after the district magistrate sends out his soldiers and in the name of the law searches for wicked individuals that the young man becomes afraid and changes his ways and alters his deeds. So while the love of parents is not sufficient to discipline the children, the severe penalties of the district magistrate are. This is because men become naturally spoiled by love, but are submissive to authority. . . .

That being so, rewards should be rich and certain so that the people will be attracted by them; punishments should be severe and definite so that the people will fear them; and laws should be uniform and steadfast so that the people will be familiar with them. Consequently, the sovereign should show no wavering in bestowing rewards and grant no pardon in administering punishments, and he should add honor to rewards and disgrace to punishments—when this is done, then both the worthy and the unworthy will want to exert themselves.

From W. Theodore de Bary, ed., *Sources of Chinese Tradition* (New York: Columbia University Press, 1960), pp. 141–147.

however, secularized and humanized the "mandate of Heaven" by equating it with the people: "Heaven hears as the people hear; Heaven sees as the people see." By redefining the concept in this way, Mencius made the welfare of the people the ultimate standard for judging government. Indeed, he even told rulers to their faces that the people were more important than the rulers were. Mencius did believe that all people were morally equal and that the ruler needed the consent of the people, but he was clearly the advocate of benevolent monarchy rather than popular democracy.

Legalism

By the end of the Warring States period in the third century B.C.E., as the Ch'in arose in western China, another body of thought emerged. It came to be called the School of Law, or Legalism. It had no single founder, as Confucianism and Taoism did, nor was it ever a school in the sense of a teacher leading disciples. What it did have in common with Confucianism and Taoism was the desire to establish stability in an age of turmoil, to strengthen the king at the expense of all other elements of society.

The Legalists emphasized the importance of harsh and inflexible law as the only means of achieving an orderly and prosperous society. They believed that human nature was basically bad and that people acted virtuously only when forced to do so. Therefore, they argued for an elaborate system of laws defining fixed penalties for each offense, with no exceptions for rank, class, or circumstances. Judges were not to use their own conscience in estimating the gravity of the crime and arbitrarily deciding on the punishment. Their task was solely to define the crime correctly; the punishment was provided automatically by the code of law.

Since the enforcement of law required a strong state, the immediate goal of the Legalists was to enhance the power of the ruler at the expense of other elements, particularly the nobility. Their ultimate goal was the creation of a centralized state strong enough to unify all China and end the chaos of the Warring States period. The unification of China in 221 B.C.E. by the Ch'in was largely the result of putting Legalist ideas of government into practice.

The First Chinese Empire

Two dynasties, the Ch'in (Qin) and the Han, unified China and created a centralized empire. The Ch'in dynasty collapsed soon after the death of its founder, but the Han lasted for more than four centuries. Together these dynasties transformed China, but the changes were the culmination of earlier developments during the Warring States period.

Rise of Legalist Ch'in

Throughout the Warring States period there was a widely shared hope that a king would unite China and inaugurate a great new age of peace and stability. Whereas the Confucians believed that such a king would accomplish the task by means of his outstanding moral virtue, the Legalists substituted overwhelming might as the essential element of effective government. The political philosophy of the Legalists—who liked to sum up and justify their doctrine in the two words "It works"—triumphed, and no state became more adept at practicing that pragmatic philosophy than the Ch'in.

The rise to preeminence of the Ch'in state began in 352 B.C.E., when its ruler selected Lord Shang, a man imbued with Legalist principles, to be chief minister. Recognizing that the growth of Ch'in power depended on a more efficient and centralized bureaucratic structure than could exist under feudalism, Lord Shang undermined the old hereditary nobility by creating a new aristocracy based on military merit. He also introduced a universal draft beginning at approximately age 15. As a result, chariot and cavalry warfare, in which the nobility had played the leading role, was replaced in importance by masses of peasant infantry equipped with iron weapons.

Economically, Lord Shang further weakened the old landowning nobility by abolishing the peasants' attachment to the land and granting them ownership of the plots they tilled. Thereafter the liberated peasants paid taxes directly to the local state, thus increasing its wealth and power. These reforms made Ch'in the most powerful of the Warring States.

The Early Empires

221–206 B.C.E.	Ch'in (Qin)
206 B.C.E.–8 C.E.	Earlier (Western) Han
8–23 C.E.	Reign of Wang Mang
23–220 C.E.	Later (Eastern) Han

China United

Nearly a century after Lord Shang, another Legalist prime minister helped the king of Ch'in prepare and carry out the conquest of the other Warring States, bring an end to the powerless Chou dynasty in 256 B.C.E., and unite China in 221 B.C.E. The king then declared himself the "First August Supreme Ruler" *(Shih Huang-ti)* of China, or First Emperor, as his new title is usually translated—a title that would endure until 1911. He also enlarged China—a name derived from the word *Ch'in*—by conquests in the south as far as the South China Sea. He stated that his dynasty would last 10,000 generations; it lasted 15 years.

The First Emperor moved the leading members of the old nobility to the capital, where they could be closely watched. To block rebellion, he ordered the entire civilian population to surrender its weapons to the state. A single harsh legal code, which replaced all local laws, was so detailed in its provisions that it was said to have been like "a fishing net through which even the smallest fish cannot slip out." The population was organized into groups of ten families, and each person was held responsible for the actions of all the members of the group. This structure ensured that all crimes would be reported; it also increased loyalty to the state at the expense of loyalty to the family.

The entire realm, which extended into South China and Vietnam, was divided into 48 provinces, administrative units drawn to erase traditional feudal units and to assist direct rule by the emperor's centrally controlled civil and military appointees. To destroy the source of the aristocracy's power and to permit the emperor's agents to tax every farmer's harvest, private ownership of land by peasants, promoted a century earlier in the state of Ch'in by Lord Shang, was decreed for all of China. Thus the Ch'in Empire reflected emerging social forces at work in China—the peasants freed from serfdom, the merchants eager to increase their wealth within a larger political area, and the new military and administrative upper class.

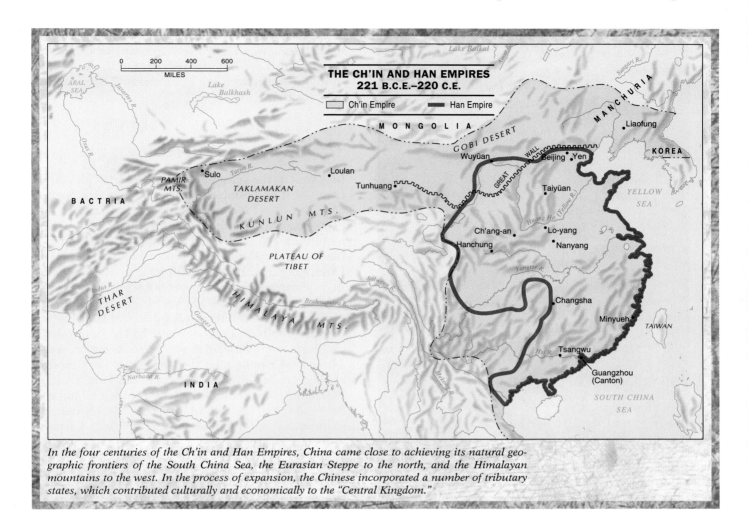

In the four centuries of the Ch'in and Han Empires, China came close to achieving its natural geographic frontiers of the South China Sea, the Eurasian Steppe to the north, and the Himalayan mountains to the west. In the process of expansion, the Chinese incorporated a number of tributary states, which contributed culturally and economically to the "Central Kingdom."

Among the many public works of the First Emperor's short reign—all constructed by forced labor—were 4000 miles of highways and thousands of miles of canals and waterways, one of which connected the Yangtze to the Hsi River and Guangzhou. The written language was standardized, as were weights and measures and even the length of axles so that cart wheels would fit the grooves cut in the highways. Although the First Emperor, like some Warring States rulers before him, built walls to impede the incursion of nomadic tribes from central Asia, it is no longer believed that he built the 1400-mile Great Wall of China. In its present form the Great Wall was mainly the work of the sixteenth-century Ming dynasty.[5]

The First Emperor tried to enforce intellectual conformity and to cast the Ch'in Legalist system as the only natural political order. He suppressed all other schools of thought, especially the Confucians, who idealized Chou feudalism by stressing the obedience of sons to their fathers, of nobles to the lord, and of lords to the king. To break the hold of the past,

the emperor put into effect a Legalist proposal requiring that all privately owned books reflecting past traditions be burned and that "all . . . who raise their voice against the present government in the name of antiquity be beheaded together with their families." He created a new cultural elite of state-appointed teachers who would give an approved reading of the traditions and lessons of history. This set in motion the precedent that "imperial governments would henceforth insist that approved texts and suitable interpretations would be used for this purpose and that teaching would be conducted along recognized lines."[6]

Near the Ch'in capital at Ch'ang-an (Xian), the First Emperor employed over half a million laborers to construct a huge mound tomb for himself and, nearby, three large pits filled with life-size terra cotta figures of his imperial guard. The mausoleum has not been excavated, but the partial excavation of the pits revealed some 7500 soldiers aligned in military formation. Amazingly, each head is a personal portrait—no two faces are alike.

Representations of the First Emperor's army, such as this life-size terra cotta (literally "baked earth") warrior found in his tomb, testify to the grandeur of his reign.

When the First Emperor died in 210 B.C.E. while on one of his frequent tours of inspection, he was succeeded by an inept son who was unable to control the rivalry among his father's chief aides. Ch'in policies had alienated not only the intellectuals and the old nobility but also the peasants, who were subjected to ruinous taxation and forced labor. Rebel armies rose in every province of the empire, some led by peasants, others by aristocrats. Anarchy followed, and by 206 B.C.E. the Ch'in dynasty had disappeared. But the Chinese Empire itself, which Ch'in created, would last for more than 2000 years (until 1912, when China became a republic), the longest-lived political institution in world history.

At issue in the fighting that continued for another four years was not only the question of succession to the throne but also the form of government. The peasant and aristocratic leaders, first allied against Ch'in, became engaged in a ruthless civil war. The aristocrats sought to restore the oligarchic feu-

dalism of pre-Ch'in times. Their opponents, whose main leader was Liu Pang, a peasant who had become a Ch'in general, desired a centralized state. In this contest between the old order and the new, the new was the victor.

The Han Dynasty:
The Empire Consolidated

In 206 B.C.E. the peasant Liu Pang defeated his aristocratic rival and established the Han dynasty. Named after the Han River, a tributary of the Yangtze, the new dynasty had its capital at Ch'ang-an. It lasted for more than 400 years and is traditionally divided into two parts: the Earlier Han (206 B.C.E.–8 C.E.) and the Later Han (23–220 C.E.), with its capital at Lo-yang. In time and importance, the Han corresponded to the late Roman Republic and early Roman Empire; ethnic Chinese still call themselves "men of Han."

The empire and power sought by Liu Pang and his successors were those of the Ch'in, but they succeeded where the Ch'in had failed because they were moderate and gradual in their approach. Liu Pang reestablished for a time some of the vassal kingdoms and feudal states in regions distant from the capital. He reduced peasant discontent by momentarily lowering

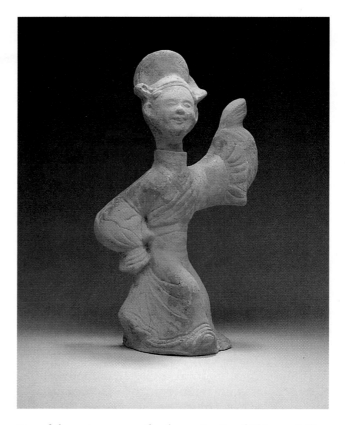

One of the major reasons for the continuity of Chinese civilizations through the millennia is the role played by women in perpetuating the value structure and passing it on to the next generation.

taxes and reducing forced labor. Later, around 100 B.C.E., the Han established a road system that made it possible for a person to go from Beijing to Guangzhou on foot in 56 days, or 32 days on horseback.

But the masterstroke of the Han emperors was to enlist the support of the Confucian intellectuals. They provided the empire with an ideology that would last until 1912, replacing the Ch'in's extreme legalistic ideology of harsh punishment and terror. The emperors recognized that an educated bureaucracy was necessary for governing so vast an empire. To appeal to the scholar-gentry (the landowner-bureaucrats), they lifted the ban on the Confucian classics and other Chou literature, and the way was open for a revival of intellectual life that had been suppressed under the Ch'in. The result was called Han Confucianism.

In accordance with Legalist principles, now tempered by Confucian insistence on the ethical basis of government, the Han emperors established administrative organs staffed by a salaried bureaucracy with as many as 20 levels to rule their empire. Talented men entered government service through an examination system based on the Confucian classics. Confucius's emphasis on loyalty as the most important duty—son to father within the family, minister to king within the state—pleased the Han and all later emperors. The highest level of bureaucracy made positions hereditary in the family.

The examinations were theoretically open to all Chinese men except merchants. (The Han inherited both the Confucian bias against trade as an unvirtuous striving for profit and the Legalist suspicion of merchants, who put their own interests ahead of those of the state and society.) The bureaucrats came from the landlord class because wealth was necessary to obtain the education needed to pass the examinations. Consequently, the earlier division of Chinese society between aristocrats and peasants became a division between peasants and landowner-bureaucrats.

Wu Ti and the Pax Sinica

After 60 years of consolidation, the Han Empire reached its greatest extent and development during the long reign of Wu Ti ("Martial Emperor"), from 141 to 87 B.C.E. To accomplish his goal of territorial expansion, he raised the peasants' taxes but not those of the great landowners, who remained virtually exempt from taxation. In addition, he increased the amount of labor and military service the peasants were forced to contribute to the state. Further, he imposed a state monopoly on the sale of iron and salt and banned the export of metal goods and female stock animals.

In conventional wisdom, people came to be placed in one of four vocations, in descending order: scholars, farmers, craftsmen, and tradesmen. This was more of a social than an economic arrangement. The merchants worked closely with the farmers and craftsmen to sell everything from food and alcoholic beverages to wagons and hardware. Trade and manufacturing became essential elements of communal life. Even though merchants were social inferiors, they became richer than individuals in the other castes. The traditional officials resented them more and more but could not block them because the tradesmen's wealth grew from their trade in what could be called daily goods. In fact, the state found trade to be useful in buying off the invading steppe tribes.

The Martial Emperor justified his expansionist policies in terms of self-defense against Mongolian nomads, the Hsiung-nu, known later to the West as the Huns. Their attacks had caused the First Emperor to construct a wall to obstruct their raiding cavalry. To outflank the nomads in the west, Wu Ti extended the wall and annexed a large corridor extending through the Tarim River basin of central Asia to the Pamir Mountains, close to Bactria. This corridor has ever since remained a part of China.

Wu Ti failed in an attempt to form an alliance with the Scythians in Bactria, but his envoy's report of the interest shown in Chinese silks by the peoples of the area was the beginning of a commercial exchange between China and the West. This trade brought great profits to Chinese merchants and their colleagues in the West.

Wu Ti also outflanked the Hsiung-nu in the east by the conquest of southern Manchuria and northern Korea. In addition, he completed the conquest of South China, begun by the Ch'in, and he added northern Vietnam to the Chinese Empire. Chinese settlers moved into all the conquered lands. As the armies of the Roman Republic were laying the foundation of the Pax Romana in the West, the Martial Emperor was establishing a Pax Sinica ("Chinese Peace") in the East.

Han Decline

Wu Ti's conquests led to a fiscal crisis. As costs increased, taxes increased, and the peasants' burdens led them to revolt once again. The central government had to rely more and more on local military commanders and great landowners for control of the population, giving them great power and prestige at its own expense. This cycle of decline after an initial period of increasing prosperity and power has been the pattern of all Chinese dynasties. During the Han this "dynastic cycle," as Western historians of China call it, led after Wu Ti's death to a succession of mediocre rulers and a temporary usurpation of the throne (8–23 C.E.) that divided the Earlier from the Later Han.

The usurper, Wang Mang, the Confucian chief minister of the court, united Confucian ethics with Legalist practice. Like his contemporary in the West, the Roman emperor Augustus, his goal was the rejuvenation of society by employing the power of the state. By Wang Mang's day the number of large tax-free estates had greatly increased while the number of taxpaying peasant holdings had declined. This inequity was a by-product of the private land ownership that under the Ch'in had replaced the old communal use of the land. Rich officials and merchants were able to acquire the lands of impoverished peasant-owners, who became tenants paying exorbitant rents.

More and more peasants fell behind in their rents and were forced to sell themselves or their children into debt slavery. To remedy this situation and increase the government's tax income, Wang Mang abolished debt slavery and decreed that the land was the property of the nation and should be portioned out to peasant families, who would pay taxes on their allotments.

Wang Mang also tried to solve the long-standing issue of inflation. This problem had greatly increased after Wu Ti found himself in financial difficulties, debased the coinage, and set maximum prices for basic commodities. Wang Mang tried to stabilize prices by a program called "leveling" in which the government bought surplus commodities when prices fell and sold them when scarcity caused prices to rise. (In 1938 a chance reading of Wang Mang's leveling proposal inspired the "ever-normal granary" program of the American New Deal.)[7]

Wang Mang's remarkable reform program failed. As is the case with so many radical changes, the conservative bureaucracy was unequal to the difficult administrative task. The powerful landowners rebelled against the ruler who proposed to confiscate their land. Although Wang Mang rescinded his reforms, he was killed by the rebels in 23 C.E. The conflict of landlordship and tenancy, along with the concentration of power of great families, became—and remained—a major problem in Chinese history.

The Later Han dynasty never reached the heights of its predecessors. Warlords who were members of the rich landowner class seized more and more power, and widespread peasant rebellions (one band was led by "Mother Lu," a woman skilled in witchcraft) sapped the state's resources. Surviving in name only during its last 30 years, the Han dynasty ended in 220, when the throne was usurped by the son of a famous warlord. Three and a half centuries of disunity and turbulence followed—the longest period of strife in China's long history, often called China's Middle Ages, as in Europe after the fall of the Roman Empire. But China eventually succeeded where Europe failed: in 589 the Sui dynasty united China again. With a few exceptions, it has remained united to this day.

In the Confucian hierarchy, tradespeople ranked at the bottom of the social scale. Yet as economic and political conditions changed in the second and first centuries B.C.E., they came to play a prominent role.

Han Scholarship, Art, and Technology

Politically and culturally, the relation of the Han to the Chou paralleled that of ancient Rome to Greece. Politically, the disunity of Greece and the Chou was followed by the imperial unity and administrative genius of the Romans and the Han. Culturally, just as the Romans owed a great debt to the Greeks, so did the Han to the Chou. Furthermore, Greek and Chou intellectual creativity was not matched by the Romans and the Han.

Scholarship flourished under the Han, but it was mainly concerned with collecting and interpreting the classics of Chinese thought produced in the Chou period. As the basis of education for prospective bureaucrats, Wu Ti established an imperial university in 124 B.C.E.; a century later it had about 3000 students. The Han scholars venerated Confucius, who moved in the popular imagination from being a teacher, a man like any other, to the ideal thinker and a being regarded as in some ways divine. Confucianism became the official philosophy of the state. Great respect for learning, together with the system of civil service examinations based on the Five Confucian Classics, became fundamental characteristics of Chinese civilization.

Han scholars started another scholarly tradition with their historical writings. Their antiquarian interest in researching the past produced a comprehensive history of China, the *Historical Records (Shih Chi).* This huge and highly detailed work of 130 chapters begins with the Hsia dynasty and discusses the Han emperors and the reign of Wu Ti. Scholars appreciate the work's freedom from superstition and its careful weighing of the evidence. Proof of its independent nature can be seen in the fact that Wu Ti castrated the book's author for defending a general that Wu Ti had dismissed. In the Later Han a scholar wrote the *History of the Han,* about the Earlier Han, and thereafter it became customary for each dynasty to write the official history of its immediate predecessor.

A fundamental belief of Chinese historiography is that "during the period of remotest antiquity a golden age existed of sage-rulers who governed a happy and contented people." There is no "beginning" for Chinese historians, such as Christ for the Christian world or the Hegira for the Muslims. "Events are dated either according to their occurrence within a recurring sixty-year cycle (with each year having its own appellation) or according to their position within the reigns of successive rulers."[8] The Chinese believed that the successes and failures of the past provided guidance for one's own time and for the future. As stated in the *Historical Records,* "Events of the past, if not forgotten, are teachings about the future." The state-sponsored Chinese historians wrote to affirm the intimate and unchanging and essential link—the emperor—between the heavenly order and politics, caught up in a predictable cycle. By contrast, Greek historians such as Herodotus and Thucydides wrote "to face and reconcile themselves to the fact that . . . permanence is impossible" and change is necessary in human affairs.[9]

Archaeological investigation was used as an aid to the writing of history. One scholar anticipated modern archaeologists by more than a thousand years in classifying human history by "ages": "stone" (Old Stone Age), "jade" (New Stone Age), "bronze," and "the present age" when "weapons are made of iron."[10]

Another monument to Han scholarship was the world's first dictionary, *Shuo Wen* ("Words Explained"), produced during Wu Ti's reign. It listed the meaning and pronunciation of more than 9000 Chinese characters.

In contrast to Han scholarship, Han art was clearly creative. The largely decorative art of the past, which served a religious purpose, was replaced by a realistic pictorial art (foreshadowed earlier by the individually sculpted soldiers buried near the First Emperor's tomb) portraying ordinary life. The result was the first great Chinese flowering of sculpture, both in relief and in the round. Some of the finest examples of this realistic secular art are the models of the tall and spirited horses that Wu Ti imported from Bactria. The Han greatly admired these proud "celestial" and "blood-sweating" horses from the West, and their artists brilliantly captured the beasts' high spirit.

This bronze horse is a masterpiece in fluidity and motion. The artist who produced it at the beginning of the Common Era understood the musculature, coordination, and spirit that enable horses to achieve great speed. In this work of art, the only contact the horse has with the earth is the right rear hoof, which is placed on a flying swallow.

This brocade mitten, dating from the first or second century C.E., was unearthed in 1959 from a site in Sinkiang.

During the Han period China surpassed the level of technological development in the rest of the world. Notable inventions included a primitive seismograph capable of indicating earthquakes several hundred miles away; the use of water power to grind grain and to operate a piston bellows for iron smelting; the horse collar, which greatly increased the pulling power of horses; paper made from cloth rags, which replaced cumbersome bamboo strips and expensive silk cloth as a writing surface; and the humble but extremely useful wheelbarrow. By the end of the first century B.C.E., the Han Chinese had recognized sunspots and accurately determined the length of the calendar year, an example of the high level gained in their mathematical and observational astronomy.[11]

Popular Taoism and Buddhism

By the time the First Emperor united China and ended the Warring States period in 221 B.C.E., a popular form of Taoism had emerged. Popular Taoism was a religion of spirits and magic that provided the spiritual comfort not found in the abstract philosophical nature of Taoism or Confucianism. Its goals were long life and personal immortality. These goals were to be achieved not so much as a reward for ethical conduct but through magical charms and spells and by drinking an "elixir of immortality." The search for such an elixir, which was thought to contain the vital forces of nature, led to an emphasis on diet and to the culinary excellence for which the Chinese are famous.

Popular Taoism also became a way to express peasant discontent. In 184 C.E., in one of many such uprisings throughout China's history, the Yellow Turbans led a widespread peasant revolt inspired by Taoist followers of the now-deified Lao-tzu. Over 300,000 rebels destroyed much of China and greatly contributed to the anarchy that fatally weakened the Later Han dynasty.

The breakdown of the political and social order during the Later Han also produced an upsurge in philosophical Taoism. Educated Chinese began to turn inward in their thinking, discouraged with Confucianism and its concern for society.

Mahayana Buddhism, first mentioned in China in 65 C.E., provided another answer to the need for religious assurance. It was brought to China by missionaries and traders through central Asia. About 148 C.E. a Buddhist missionary established a center for the translation of Buddhist writings into Chinese at the Later Han capital. However, relatively few Chinese were attracted to the religion during this period. Buddhism's great attraction of converts and influence on Chinese culture came after the fall of the Han dynasty, when renewed political turmoil made its emphasis on otherworldly salvation appealing to the great majority of Chinese.

China and Foreign Trade

Chinese leaders had ambivalent feelings about trade with foreigners. On the one hand, they did not want to provide them with the means to become richer or the technology to become stronger. But to ensure stability on the northern frontier and with their central Asian neighbors, the Chinese engaged in trade, especially in silk. In return they received the horses and woolen goods they needed. Although this trade directly contradicted the belief in the need for self-sufficiency, the government began to actively promote the silk business in the first century B.C.E. Some of the caravans carrying silk reached the Mediterranean basin via middlemen along the Silk Road.

In 138 B.C.E. the Han emperor Wu Ti sent an envoy to Bactria to seek allies against the Hsiung-nu. Although the envoy failed to secure an alliance, the information he brought back amounted to the Chinese discovery of western Eurasia. Intrigued above all by his envoy's report indicating great interest in

Discovery Through Maps

An Ancient Chinese Map

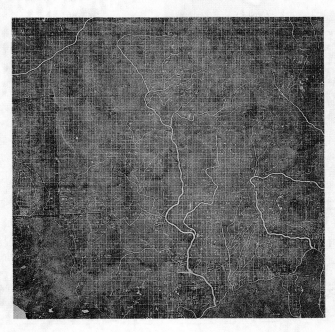

Young civilizations, like young human beings, tend to concentrate solely on themselves, with little idea of the outside world beyond their immediate surroundings. A sense of context can be gained only with experience, wisdom, and—sometimes—humility. The person who made this ancient map had little idea of what lay beyond but revealed considerable knowledge of what is in the center.

Because we are used to a level of great precision, thanks to modern cartography, it is easy to overlook the subtlety of this map. Where are the longitude and latitude lines? Which way is north? What is the scale of this map—how can we know distances from place to place? This 4000-year-old map shows us the three major facts of life for the time: rivers and where they run, mountains, and provinces that paid tribute to the emperor.

As we saw in Chapter 2, rivers served as the centers for the developments of the great civilizations after the Neolithic era. They provided transportation, food, fertilization for lands during the annual floods, and—unfortunately—access for invaders. This map shows the Huang Ho (Yellow) and the Yangtze, not as we would recognize them from a map, but as they must have looked to someone traveling along them without any reference to a larger context. It is an interesting experience to try to draw a map of the world as we know it from the paths we actually traverse and not from the majesty and exactitude of a satellite-verified image. After attempting such an exercise, we can appreciate even more this ancient map of China.

Chinese silks and his description of the magnificent horses, Wu Ti resolved to open trade relations with his western neighbors. His armies pushed across the Pamir Mountains to a location close to Alexandria Eschate (Khojend), founded by Alexander the Great as the northern limit of his empire. Shortly after 100 B.C.E. silk began arriving in the Mediterranean basin, conveyed by the Parthians. Wealthy private merchants carried on this trade, which required large outlays of capital. They organized their cargoes into

caravans of shaggy packhorses and two-humped Bactrian camels. When the Chinese soon moved back across the Pamirs, the Kushans of India became their middlemen, selling the silk to the Parthians and later to Western merchants coming by sea to India.

It was not until about 120 C.E. that the Parthians allowed some Western merchants to cross their land. The information they brought back about the Chinese was used by Ptolemy in constructing his map of the world. During the first and second centuries

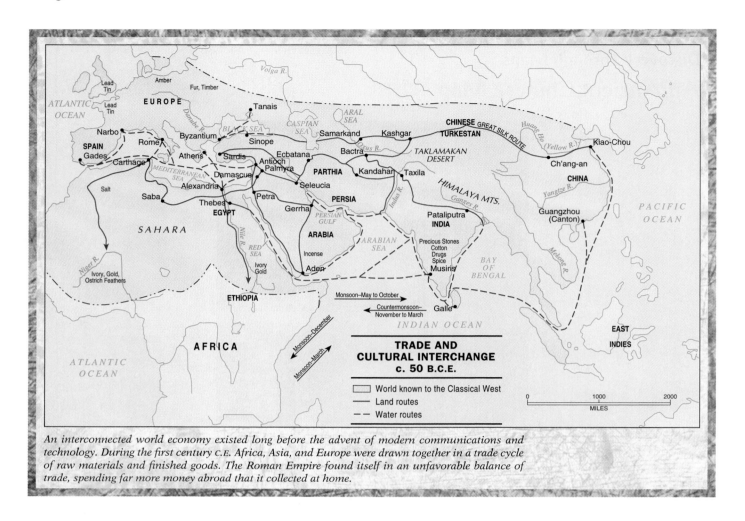

An interconnected world economy existed long before the advent of modern communications and technology. During the first century C.E. Africa, Asia, and Europe were drawn together in a trade cycle of raw materials and finished goods. The Roman Empire found itself in an unfavorable balance of trade, spending far more money abroad that it collected at home.

C.E.—the prosperous years of the Pax Romana—the peoples of the Roman Empire had a voracious appetite for Chinese silk, which the Romans believed was produced from the leaves of trees and which was sold in the market quarter of Rome. In 166 C.E., according to the Chinese *History of the Later Han Dynasty*, some merchants from Ta Ch'in ("Great Ch'in," the Chinese name for Rome), claiming to represent "King Antun" (the emperor Marcus Aurelius Antoninus), arrived in South China by sea across the Bay of Bengal and around the Malay peninsula.

To satisfy the Roman world's insatiable appetite for luxury goods, trade with the East grew immensely in the first two centuries of the Common Era. But because such Roman exports as wool, linen, glass, and metalware to the East did not match in value Rome's imports of silk, spices, perfumes, gems, and other luxuries, the West suffered seriously from an adverse balance of trade. Gold and silver had to be continually exported to Asia. Late in the first century C.E., Pliny estimated that China and Arabia drained away annually at least 100 million sesterces (the daily wage of an unskilled Roman laborer was 4 sesterces).

For the Chinese, trade with what would come to be Europe was the least important aspect during the Han dynasty and continued to be so until the nineteenth century. During the Han there would be no close ties between China and the West. Indochina, Korea, Japan, India, and the lands to the north all came together in the next millennium to form the first global trading zone, in conjunction with the Arab markets, and to enrich and stimulate China.[12]

Conclusion

Despite often cataclysmic disasters during their formative period, the Chinese did not lose their relish for life. They reacted to human suffering not by pursuing a long and arduous religious quest but by instituting ambitious innovations in all aspects of society, from philosophy to economics. Throughout, the power of the state retained its theoretical focus toward the amelioration of social evils and the relief of distress. This was the ever-changing product of two of the main ingredients in the Chinese tradition—Confucianism, with its concern for a humane society, and Legalism, with its stress on the power of the state, always modified by the underlying, unified civilization.

And that unified civilization did for China what the Judeo-Christian tradition with its ethical monotheism, Greece with its individual pursuit of truth and beauty, and Rome with its laws and institutions did for Europe—erect the fundamental frame of identity, in which all other activities take place.

Suggestions for Reading

John K. Fairbank, *China: A New History* (Harvard University Press, 1992), is an up-to-date survey by an eminent authority. Among other general histories of China are Witold Rodzinski, *The Walled Kingdom: A History of China from Antiquity to the Present* (Free Press, 1984); Jacques Gernet, *A History of Chinese Civilization,* 2nd ed. (Cambridge University Press, 1982); Arthur Cotterell, *China: A Concise Cultural History* (Murray, 1988); and John K. Fairbank, *China: Tradition and Transformation,* rev. ed. (Houghton Mifflin, 1989). For insightful contributions on a variety of topics in Chinese history, see Derk Bodde, *Essays on Chinese Civilization* (Princeton University Press, 1981).

For a brilliant series of interpretations on Chinese civilization, see Michael Loewe, *The Pride That Was China* (St. Martin's Press, 1990). Arthur Waldron, *The Great Wall of China: From History to Myth* (Cambridge University Press, 1990), cuts through popular views of the wall (both Chinese and Western) and presents a multifaceted study of the importance of walls in China and their construction.

Fuller accounts of the periods covered in this chapter are Michael Loewe and Denis C. Twitchett, eds., *The Ch'in and Han Empires, 221 B.C.–A.D. 220* (Cambridge University Press, 1986); Kwang-Chih Chang, *The Archaeology of Ancient China,* 4th ed. (Yale University Press, 1987), and *Shang Civilization* (Yale University Press, 1982); René Grousset, *The Rise and Splendour of the Chinese Empire* (Bles, 1952); and Michael Loewe, *Everyday Life in Early Imperial China* (Harper & Row, 1965). Arthur Cotterell, *The First Emperor of China: The Greatest Archaeological Find of Our Time* (Holt, Rinehart and Winston, 1981), is a well-illustrated popular account of the founder of the Ch'in dynasty and the archaeological discoveries at his tomb.

Benjamin Schwartz, *The World of Thought in Ancient China* (Harvard University Press, 1985), is an authoritative fresh view. See also Frederick W. Mote, *Intellectual Foundations of China,* 2nd ed. (McGraw-Hill, 1989); Fung Yulan, *A Short History of Chinese Philosophy* (Free Press, 1966); Arthur Waley, *Three Ways of Thought in Ancient China* (Stanford University Press, 1983); and Marcel Granet, *The Religion of the Chinese People* (Harper Torchbooks, 1975). W. Theodore de Bary, ed., *Sources of Chinese Tradition* (Columbia University Press, 1960), is an outstanding collection of translations with valuable commentaries. On science and invention, see Robert Temple, *The Ge-*nius of China: 3,000 Years of Science, Discovery, and Invention* (Simon & Schuster, 1986), and Christopher Cullen, *Astronomy and Mathematics in Ancient China: The Zhou bi su an jing* (Cambridge University Press, 1996). On the fine arts, see Michael Sullivan, *The Arts of China,* 3rd ed. (University of California Press, 1984), and Wen Fong, ed., *The Great Bronze Age of China* (Metropolitan Museum of Art/Knopf, 1980).

Robert E. Wheeler, *Rome Beyond the Imperial Frontiers* (Greenwood, 1972) is a study of Rome's trade with the East. See also L. Boulnois, *The Silk Road* (Allen & Unwin, 1963).

Suggestions for Web Browsing

Ancient Dynasties
http:// www-chaos.umd.edu/history/ancient1.html
Images and text present a view of early China, from prehistory to the era of the Warring States, 221 B.C.E.

China the Beautiful
http://www.chinapage.com/chinese.html
Extensive site exploring the art, calligraphy, poetry, literature, and music of China throughout its lengthy history.

Ancient China
http://www.wsu.edu:8080/~dee/ANCCHINA/ANCCHINA.HTM
Chinese history from 4000 to 256 B.C.E., with details about philosophy and culture.

Notes

1. Derk Bodde, "Feudalism in China," in *Essays on Chinese Civilization,* ed. Charles Le Blanc and Dorothy Borei (Princeton, N.J.: Princeton University Press, 1981), pp. 85–86.
2. Michael Loewe, *The Pride That Was China* (New York: St. Martin's Press, 1990), pp. 98–99.
3. Ibid., p. 99.
4. Ibid.
5. Arthur Waldron, *The Great Wall of China: From History to Myth* (Cambridge: Cambridge University Press, 1990).
6. Loewe, *Pride That Was China,* p. 106.
7. W. Theodore de Bary, *East Asian Civilizations: A Dialogue in Five Stages* (Cambridge, Mass.: Harvard University Press, 1988), p. 19.
8. Bodde, "Feudalism," pp. 154, 245.
9. R. G. Collingwood, *The Idea of History* (New York: Galaxy Books, 1956), p. 22.
10. Kwang-Chih Chang, *The Archaeology of Ancient China,* 4th ed. (New Haven, Conn.: Yale University Press, 1987), p. 5.
11. Christopher Cullen, *Astronomy and Mathematics in Ancient China: The Zhou bi su an jing* (Cambridge: Cambridge University Press, 1996).
12. See Loewe, *Pride That Was China,* ch. 18.

Indian stone carving showing Buddists worshipping the site be-neath the Bodhi tree, where the Buddha gained Enlightenment (Bodhi).

Adoration of the Bodhi Tree, India, Amaravati Satavahana period, 2nd century. Stone relief, 80 × 57.1 cm. The Cleveland Museum of Art, Purchase from J. H. Wade Fund, 1970.43

Ancient India

From Origins to 300 C.E.

Chapter Contents

The Indian subcontinent since ancient times has functioned as a matrix for networks of trade and culture. It has been the target of conquerors and empire builders and the origination point of philosophical and artistic trends that have radiated outward along the land-based routes linking Asia with Europe and the seaborne routes connecting South Asia to Africa, the Middle East, Southeast Asia, and East Asia. The civilizations of classical India have had a profound effect that endures to this day on the arts, literature, religion, and philosophical beliefs of the world.

The subcontinent called India was a land of sometimes dense settlement as early as the Stone Age, dating back 500,000 years. An area diverse in climate, geography, language, and ethnicity, it was a primarily village-based agricultural society and remains so today. In the ancient times discussed here, India produced an extensive riverine civilization in the northwest that ultimately declined, absorbed tribes of immigrating Indo-Europeans (Aryans) who became dominant, generated a second wave of urbanization in the east that matured into a vast empire embracing most of the subcontinent, and again absorbed several waves of invasion and immigration from the northwest. Synthesizing the social ideas and the philosophical and religious beliefs and practices of the immigrant Indo-Europeans and the indigenous Dravidians, India developed three major religious traditions during this time, Hinduism, Jainism, and Buddhism, the last of which spread far beyond the bounds of India to become a pan-Asian and today global religion.

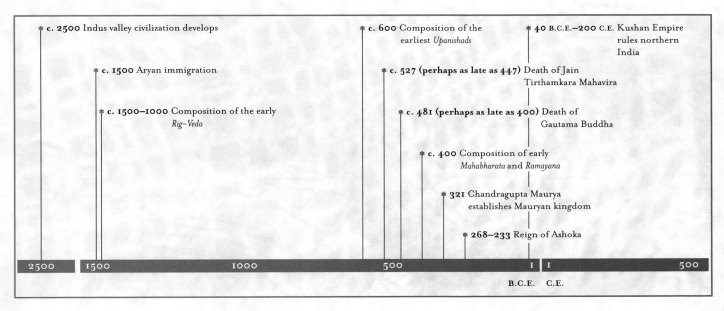

c. 2500 Indus valley civilization develops

c. 1500 Aryan immigration

c. 1500–1000 Composition of the early *Rig-Veda*

c. 600 Composition of the earliest *Upanishads*

c. 527 (perhaps as late as 447) Death of Jain Tirthamkara Mahavira

c. 481 (perhaps as late as 400) Death of Gautama Buddha

c. 400 Composition of early *Mahabharata* and *Ramayana*

321 Chandragupta Maurya establishes Mauryan kingdom

268–233 Reign of Ashoka

40 B.C.E.–200 C.E. Kushan Empire rules northern India

| 2500 | 1500 | 1000 | 500 | I | I | 500 |

B.C.E.   C.E.

India comprises an area comparable to Europe in size and internal diversity. And like Europe, the regions and peoples of India came to be roughly divided into two major language groups, the Indo-European in the north and the Dravidian in the south; each group embraces a number of separate languages. In the centuries between 1500 B.C.E. and 300 C.E. the emerging Hindu cultural synthesis gave the subcontinent a general cultural unity similar to the unity afforded to Europe by the spread of the Christian religion in the first millennium C.E.

In this chapter we trace the important threads of Indian history to the third century C.E., a time when the Pax Romana in the West was coming to an end and when India was poised for the rise of another great empire in the north, the classical Hindu empire of the Guptas. This period was the formative age of Indian civilization, when its basic institutions and cultural patterns were determined.

Early India

Sometime before 2500 B.C.E. a counterpart of the civilizations that had emerged along the Tigris and Euphrates and the Nile appeared along the Indus River in India. Among its major cities, Mohenjo-Daro, located north of Karachi in present-day Pakistan, is believed to have been one of the largest Bronze Age cities of the world. Around the time that the Indus valley civilization collapsed, the Indo-European migrants known as Aryans began to move into the subcontinent from the Iranian plateau (about 1500 B.C.E.). The Aryans became the dominant social and cultural group in the subcontinent, though they assimilated much from the indigenous peoples of northern India. Their Vedic religion, cultivated by their seers and priests (Brahmins), became the foundation for much of the later cultural development of the entire subcontinent.

Geography of India

The term *India* is used here to refer to the entire subcontinent, an area encompassing the modern nations of Pakistan, India, Nepal, Bhutan, Bangladesh, and Sri Lanka. It is a large, irregular diamond, the lower sides of which are bounded by the warm waters of the Indian Ocean and the upper sides of which are bounded by the mountain walls of the Himalayas on the north and several smaller ranges on the west. The highest mountains in the world, the Himalayas, and their western counterparts divide India from the rest of Asia, making it a discrete subcontinent. Through the Khyber Pass and other mountain passes in the northwest and across the Indian Ocean have come the armed conquerors, restless tribes, merchants,

and travelers who did much to shape India's turbulent history.

In addition to the northern mountain belt, which shields India from arctic winds, the subcontinent comprises two other major geographical regions. In the north is the great plain (which came to be known as Hindustan after the Muslim invasions), extending from the Indus valley to the Bay of Bengal. It spans the watersheds of two great river systems, the Indus and the Ganges, which have their sources in the Himalayas. South of this great plain, and separated from it in the west by the Vindhya mountain range, rises a semiarid plateau, the Deccan ("southland"). This plateau rises up about 2000 feet above sea level in the Western Ghats ("steps") along India's western peninsular coast and then slopes gently downward to the shallow Eastern Ghats along India's eastern ocean shore.

India's climate and the rhythms of Indian life are governed by the dry northeast monsoon wind of the winter and the wet southwest monsoon wind of the summer. Most parts of India receive most of their rainfall during the summer and autumn months of the southwest monsoon, which blows in from the Arabian Sea. The Western Ghats cause the summer monsoon to drop most of its rain on the thin Malabar Coast, making it one of the wettest areas of the globe but also giving much of the western Deccan its semi-

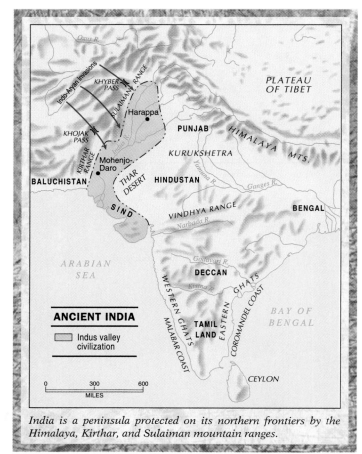

India is a peninsula protected on its northern frontiers by the Himalaya, Kirthar, and Sulaiman mountain ranges.

arid climate. The eastern side of the Deccan fares better from the summer monsoon.

It is in western Hindustan, now part of the state of Pakistan, that India's earliest civilization arose. This area is made up of an alluvial plain (called the Punjab, "land of the five rivers") watered by the upper Indus and its tributaries and the region of the lower Indus (called Sind, from *sindhu*, meaning "river," and the origin of the terms *Hindu* and *India*).

The Indus Civilization, c. 2500–1500 B.C.E.

The rise of civilization in the Indus valley around 2500 B.C.E. duplicated what had occurred in Mesopotamia nearly a thousand years earlier. In both areas Neolithic farmers lived in food-producing villages situated on the hilly flanks of large river valleys. These settlements spread out along the river valleys, capitalizing on their abundant water and fertile soil. Here they developed the more complex way of life we call a civilization. Some of these farming villages had grown into large cities with as many as 40,000 inhabitants by 2300 B.C.E. Excavations of two of these cities, Mohenjo-Daro in Sind and Harappa in the Punjab, have provided much of our knowledge of the Indus valley civilization, but its sites were widely dispersed across the whole of northwestern India. Reaching its height in the centuries around 2000 B.C.E., the Indus valley civilization produced highly organized towns and uniform weights, measures, and pottery.

Although Mohenjo-Daro and Harappa were 400 miles apart, the Indus River made possible the main-tenance of a uniform administration and economy over the entire area. The cities were carefully planned, with straight paved streets intersecting at right angles and an elaborate drainage system with underground channels. The spacious two-storied houses of the well-to-do contained bathrooms and were constructed with the same type of baked bricks used for roads. A script employing some 400 pictographic signs has not yet been deciphered. The only known use of the script was on engraved stamp-seals, which may have been used for identification or to mark property.

The economy of the Indus civilization, like that of Mesopotamia and Egypt, was based on irrigation farming. Wheat and barley were the chief crops, and the state collected these grains as taxes and stored them in huge granaries. The importance of agriculture explains the presence of numerous mother goddess figurines, representing fertility. Such figures are also found in various forms throughout the Mediterranean world. For the first known time in world history, chickens were domesticated as a food source during the Indus civilization, and cotton was grown and used in making textiles. The spinning and weaving of cotton remains one of the subcontinent's chief industries.

Copper and bronze were used for tools and weapons, but the rarity of weapons suggests that warfare was uncommon. Trade was sufficiently well organized to obtain needed raw materials—copper, tin, silver, gold, and timber—from the mountain regions to the west. There is also evidence of active trade contacts with Mesopotamia, some 1500 miles to the west, as early as 2300 B.C.E. (the time of Sargon of Akkad).

The ruins at Mohenjo-Daro are still impressive more than four millennia after the city was established.

For centuries the Indus valley civilization flourished. Excavations at Mohenjo-Daro, however, show clearly that decline set in about 1700 B.C.E., when a series of great floods caused by earthquakes altered the course of the Indus and apparently severely affected the settlements along it. Harappa to the north appears to have suffered a similar fate. The invaders who came through the northwest passes around 1500 B.C.E. may have contributed to the disappearance of the Indus valley civilization, but their role in that process is unclear.

The Aryan Immigration and the Early Vedic Age, 1500–1000 B.C.E.

The semibarbaric migrants, who called themselves Aryas ("noble people," to distinguish themselves from the indigenous people), moved through the mountain passes onto the Indus plains. They spoke an early form of Sanskrit, an Indo-European language, and formed the easternmost wave of the great Indo-European migrations of the second millennium B.C.E., whose profound effects on the ancient world we have noted in earlier chapters. The Aryans were basically a pastoral people who counted their wealth in cattle, but they were also effective warriors whose leaders fought from horse-drawn chariots.

In the first five or six centuries after their arrival in India, the Aryans moved slowly eastward, settled throughout the Punjab, took up agriculture from the indigenous peoples, and came to dominate the whole area socially and culturally. Indigenous populations of the subcontinent, the majority of whom may well have belonged to the ethnolinguistic group called Dravidian, were either conquered and assimilated by the Aryans or driven south into the Deccan. The Aryans referred to these darker-skinned but more civilized people as *Dasas*, "savages," a term that later came to mean "slaves."

During these centuries the Aryans worshipped their gods with sacrificial rituals that were accompanied by specially composed "verses of praise and adoration," *ric* verses, which would be recited together in "hymns." The *ric* verses and the hymns they made up were regarded as the sacred compositions of inspired seers (the Brahmins), who could see the gods and understood their ways and were thus able to compose verses that could influence the gods to favor and bless Aryan men and their families. Over a thousand such hymns were gathered together in the *Rig-Veda*, a collection that has been memorized and used in worship continuously for over three thousand years. (*Veda* means "knowledge," a reference to the Brahmin's knowing all the hymns by memory.) Thanks to the *Rig-Veda* we know more about the Aryans than we know about their Indus civilization predecessors, for whom only archaeological evidence survives.

The early Aryan religion involved making sacrificial offerings of grain, cakes, dairy products, and animals to the gods, who embodied and controlled the forces of what we today call "nature," in return for

Excavations at Mohenjo-Daro have unearthed mother goddess figurines and stamp seals. The female figure, with her elaborate headdress, may well be a symbol of fertility. The seal shown below features a humped Indian bull. Such figures, suggesting male potency, were prominent in Indus art. The writing on the seals, a pictographic script employing about 250 symbols and 400 characters, remains undeciphered.

Rig-Veda: Creation and the Kinds of Men

The Purusha Sutra of the *Rig-Veda* provides the first suggestion in ancient Vedic texts of the notion of the *varnas,* the idea that humankind is divided into four classes and their differences are based in Creation itself. The four classes are priests *(Brahmins),* rulers and warriors *(Rajanyas* or *Kshatriyas),* herders and merchants *(Vaishyas),* and the low-class workers or servants *(Shudras).* Purusha (the "primordial cosmic man") serves as the victim in the cosmic sacrifice from which the universe originates.

The sacrificial victim, namely Purusha, born at the very beginning, they [the gods] sprinkled with sacred water upon the sacrificial grass. With him as oblation, the gods performed the sacrifice, and also the *Sadhyas* [a class of semidivine beings] and the *rishis* [ancient seers].

From that wholly offered sacrificial oblation were born the verses and the sacred chants. . . . From it the horses were born and also those animals who have double rows of teeth; cows were born from it, from it were born goats and sheep.

When they divided Purusha, in how many different portions did they arrange him? What became of his mouth, what of his two arms? What were his two thighs and his two feet called?

His mouth became the brahmin; his arms were made into the rajanya; his two thighs the vaishyas; from his two feet the shudra was born.

The moon was born from his mind, from the eye the sun was born; from the mouth Indra and Agni [Vedic gods], from the breath the wind was born.

From the navel was the atmosphere created, from the head the heaven issued forth; from the two feet was born the earth and the quarters [the cardinal directions] from the ear. Thus did they fashion the worlds.

. . . With this sacrificial oblation did the gods offer the sacrifice. These were the first norms [dharma] of sacrifice. These greatnesses reached to the sky wherein live the ancient *Sadhyas* and gods.

From Ainslie T. Embree, ed., *Sources of Indian Tradition,* Vol. 1, 2nd ed. (New York: Columbia University Press, 1988), pp. 18–19.

such material gains as long life, health, many offspring, victory in war, and life in the "bright place in the sky" (heaven). The god worshipped most in the *Rig-Veda* was Indra, storm-god and patron of warriors, who is described as leading the Aryans in destroying the forts of the Dasas. Virile and boisterous, Indra personified the heroic virtues of the Aryan warrior aristocracy as he drove his chariot across the sky, wielded his thunderbolts, ate the meat of sacrificed bulls and buffaloes by the score, and quaffed entire lakes of the stimulating ritual drink *soma.*

Next to Indra in popularity was Agni, the benevolent god of fire, who performed many services for the mobile Aryans, not least of which was conveying their ritual offerings up to the other gods. Another major Aryan god was Varuna, the sky-god. Viewed as the king of the gods, he lived in a great palace in the heavens where one of his associates was a sun-god, Mitra, known as Mithras to the Persians and, a thousand years later, widely worshipped in the Roman Empire. Varuna was the guardian of *rita,* the "right order of things." *Rita* is both the cosmic law of nature (the regularity of the seasons, for example) and the customary tribal law of the Aryans.

The *Rig-Veda* is the earliest surviving Indo-European work of literature, and it gives some insight into the institutions and ideas of the Early Vedic Age. Each tribe was headed by a war leader called *raja,* a word closely related to the Latin word for king, *rex.* (Latin and Sanskrit are both Indo-European languages.) Like the early kings of Sumer, Greece, and Rome, the *raja* was only the first among equals. Two tribal assemblies, one a small council of the great men of the tribe and the other a larger gathering of the heads of families, approved his accession to office and advised him on important matters.

The hymns in the *Rig-Veda* mention three social classes, the Brahmins, the Kshatriyas (nobility), and the Vaishyas (commoners). Aryan peoples elsewhere, such as the Romans and the Celts, seem to have had a similar social structure. A fourth class, the Shudras, the non-Aryan conquered population of workers and serfs, was then added at the bottom of the social scale. In one of the later hymns of the *Rig-Veda,* these four social classes are mapped out on the body of the Cosmic Man, Purusha.

The Later Vedic Age, c. 1000–600 B.C.E.

Most of our knowledge about the years between 1000 and 500 B.C.E. derives from two great bodies of literature: religious texts the Brahmins composed during this period—three later *Vedas,* Vedic ritual encyclopedias called *Brahmanas,* and the early *Upanishads,* Brahmin texts teaching a mystical way to gain personal beatitude—and various texts composed in the bustling new period that displaced the Vedic age, including the early texts of Buddhism, a new anti-Brahmin and anti-Vedic religion; a manual on royal government called the *Arthashastra;* and two epics that first articulated the religious and cultural synthesis that is called Hinduism today, the *Mahabharata* and the *Ramayana.* All these texts tell us a great deal about religious and philosophical thought during this time, but what we know of this period's political, social, and economic institutions we must glean from religious texts or infer from the convergence of the archaeological record with the later texts.

By about 1000 B.C.E. the Aryans had occupied the critical territory that lies between the Indus watershed and the Ganges watershed. During the Later Vedic Age they continued their movement both to the east, passing into the Doab ("land of two rivers") between the Yamuna and the Ganges and on down the Ganges valley, and to the south, toward the Vindhya Mountains. The area between the two watersheds came to be known as Kurukshetra ("the field of King Kuru"), and it became the sacred heartland of the Aryans in the Later Vedic Age. Kurukshetra was the site of the fabled Bharata war (the story of which is told in the *Mahabharata*), and many other battles critical to the history of India over the next 3000 years were fought in this vicinity. The sense of space, particularly sacred space, is very important in Indian thought; and the ways such spaces have been articulated remain a critical factor in Indian politics today (see Chapter 36).

This era seems to have been a golden age for the Brahmins and their Vedic religion. During this period some of the hymns of the *Rig-Veda* were set to melodies (called *samans*) collected in a separate *Veda* called the *Sama-Veda.* Other parts of the *Rig-Veda* were formed into the prayers of the *Yajur-Veda.* Different families of Brahmins would specialize in learning one or the other of these three *Vedas;* spectacularly large *soma* sacrifices developed that employed Brahmins of each kind. A fourth *Veda,* the *Atharva-Veda,* was formed from a large collection of sacred formulas that, when correctly uttered, were supposed to solve many of life's mundane problems: baldness, impotence, skin rashes, and so on.

As the number of Brahmin priests and *Vedas* increased, the focus of Vedic religion shifted from the gods to the power of the sacrifice itself, and especially to the holy energy contained in the sacred words of the different Vedic songs, chants, recitations, and prayers. The Brahmins' perfect singing or chanting of Vedic verses (now called *mantras*) came to be regarded as the embodiment of the sacred energy at the heart of the ritual—the energy, called *brahman,* that kept the world going, the energy that had brought the world into being.

The Brahmins composed, now in prose rather than verse, a whole new kind of text, the *Brahmanas,* which explained the philosophy of the rituals and the background meaning and use of the Vedic mantras

employed in the rituals. During the Early Vedic Age sacrifice had been a means of influencing the gods in favor of the offerer; now in the later Vedic Age the Brahmins regarded sacrifices to the gods as working automatically to produce the good results people wanted, provided that the ritual was performed exactly right. The sacrifices brought long life, many sons, victory over one's enemies, general prosperity, and heaven; they made the world a good place for all beings. Since only the priests possessed the knowledge to perform the complex and lengthy rites of sacrifice (a few of which could last for months), and since the slightest variation in ritual was thought to bring harm to the people and the land, the Brahmins gained great prestige and power.

By the beginning of the Later Vedic Age the Aryans had acquired iron metallurgy, which may have reached India via the Middle East. As in other parts of the world, iron-based tools and weapons increased the potential for agricultural exploitation of the land and made warriors with access to the technology more deadly and effective. These developments set the stage for the development in the eastern Ganges valley of cities, territory-based kingdoms, standing armies, and stronger institutions of kingship. Although some Indian kingdoms in this period were oligarchic republics, most were ruled by rajas, *maharajas* ("great kings"), or *samrajas* ("universal kings," as some called themselves). Despite the preservation of advisory councils of nobles and priests, the kings' powers were greater than those of the tribal leaders of the earlier period. They now lived in palaces and collected taxes—in the form of goods from the villages—in order to sustain their courts and armies. The cities that arose were often administrative centers connected with a palace, and some were also commercial centers.

Dramatic Developments in Religion and Culture, 600–320 B.C.E.

Out of all these new political and economic developments came dramatic cultural changes that after 600 B.C.E. elevated an entirely different kind of religion to highest status and eventually gave rise to whole new religions that challenged Brahmin hegemony and created important new institutions. The first of these developments was the composition of the earliest *Upanishads* around 600 B.C.E. The second was the rise of the new non-Vedic, even anti-Vedic, monastic religions of Jainism and Buddhism sometime in the fifth century B.C.E.

Around 600 B.C.E. a radical minority of Brahmins embraced ascetic and mystical religious ideas and practices (early forms of *yoga,* "spiritual discipline," usually involving some kind of meditation) that ultimately rejected the goals and means of Vedic ritual religion and the settled village and family life that Vedic religion presumed. Some of these radical mystics recorded the *Upanishads,* which taught "secret, mystical understandings" of the human body, the breath, the mind, and the soul. The most important of these understandings was the assertion that the light of consciousness within a person was nothing less than the undiluted energy of *brahman,* the eternal, sacred creative energy that is the source and the end of all that exists (tantamount to God in monotheistic religions).

Most of the *Upanishads* taught that all things that exist—from the most sublime ideas a person could think to the hardest, densest, crudest forms of matter—came from brahman and eventually returned to brahman, which is the only permanent reality. Beyond these ideas, the *Upanishads* taught a way for ethically pure, worthy persons (usually only Aryans, but not necessarily just Brahmins) to immerse themselves into brahman, which the *Upanishads* described as unsurpassably blissful. These ideas gained great power after their presentation in the *Upanishads;* a relatively tiny minority of people followed this yoga (most Aryans continued to avail themselves of Brahmin priests and Vedic rituals), but the basic ideas, values, and meditative techniques came to be regarded as the supreme form of Brahmin religion.

In addition to these mystical ideas, the *Upanishads* introduced the idea of the transmigration of the soul, which was entirely new in Brahmin thought. (Some scholars have speculated that this idea was part of the culture of some of the indigenous Indians, but there is no solid evidence of this.) As with most other Indo-European peoples, the Vedic Brahmins had thought that people live only once and that the fate of their soul is determined in that one

life. (The same general idea is found in all three of the Western Abrahamic religions, Judaism, Christianity, and Islam.) Vedic Aryans hoped to live up in the heavens with the sky-gods after their death. In the *Brahmanas,* the idea was put forward that a person's deeds (especially ethically significant deeds, and sacrificial offerings in particular) stayed with him or her in the form of an unseen power that would act after that person's death and condition the fate of the departed soul. A deed or action was called *karman* in Sanskrit, and the unseen power of past deeds was called *karman* as well (*karma* in contemporary English).

The latest *Brahmana* texts sometimes express a fear that people "die again"—the accumulation of their good works, their good karma, supports them in heaven when they die, but the karma gets used up keeping the soul in heaven, and the soul then "dies" again, in heaven. This fear leads directly to the idea that when the soul dies in heaven, it descends to earth, reincarnated in another body. This new person lives and dies, and the soul goes to heaven once again, if the earthly actions of this latest lifetime have been good (that is, if they conformed with the law, or *dharma,* as revealed in the *Vedas*). Bad deeds, bad karma, lead the soul to hell.

Eventually, rebirth in subhuman forms of life was seen as a natural consequence of violating dharma; after living a life as some kind of animal, a soul automatically moves up the ladder of life forms toward an eventual human incarnation because animals cannot violate dharma. The rebirth of the soul in a new body is called *samsara,* and the *Upanishads* regarded continual, unending samsara as a dreary prospect. The *Upanishads* taught that good deeds, including Vedic rituals, could do nothing more for a person than provide a temporary spell in heaven between incarnations. Bad deeds, of course, had far more unpleasant consequences; but worse than either hell or heaven was the prospect of living, acting, and dying over and over, forever without end. In the face of this bleak prospect, the *Upanishads* said the only truly good thing to do is try to escape perpetual samsara (escape from samsara was called *moksha*) and gain the immortality of reimmersing oneself in *brahman.* Gaining moksha involves permanently escaping from karma, from samsara, and from all the pain and suffering encountered in countless lives. According to the *Upanishads,* the only effective way to gain moksha is to accomplish the reimmersion of oneself into brahman. By permanently immersing oneself in brahman through meditation, a person dissolves the soul back into the holy oneness that is its ultimate source and end. The soul has "returned home"—its journey through samsara is over.

The *Upanishads* depict the first Indian gurus wandering in the forests as ascetics; there they

The Jains on the Souls in All Things

The Jains, like the Buddhists, believe in conquering desire as a way of achieving Enlightenment and escaping from the cyle of rebirth. But the Jains emphasize the existence of souls in all living things. All beings experience pleasure, pain, terror, and unhappiness. Hence Jain texts reveal a heightened sensitivity to the pain man can inflict by harming all things, animate and inanimate. This verse passage is taken from a Jain text depicting the speech of a prince trying to persuade his parents to allow him to take up a life of religion.

From clubs and knives, stakes and maces, breaking
    my limbs,
An infinite number of times I have suffered without
    hope.
By keen edged razors, by knives and shears,
Many times I have been drawn and quartered, torn
    apart and skinned.
Helpless in snares and traps, a deer,
    I have been caught and bound and fastened, and
    often I have been killed.
A helpless fish, I have been caught with hooks and
    nets;
An infinite number of times I have been killed and
    scraped, split and gutted.
A bird, I have been caught by hawks or trapped in
    nets,
Or held fast by birdlime, and I have been killed an
    infinite number of times.

A tree, with axes and adzes by the carpenters
An infinite number of times I have been felled,
    stripped of my bark, cut up, and sawn into
    planks.
As iron, with hammer and tongs by blacksmiths
An infinite number of times I have been struck
    and beaten, split and filed. . . .
Ever afraid, trembling in pain and suffering,
I have felt the utmost sorrow and agony. . . .
In every kind of existence I have suffered
Pains that have scarcely known reprieve for a
    moment.

From Ainslie T. Embree, ed., *Sources of Indian Tradition*, Vol. 1, 2nd ed. (New York: Columbia University Press, 1988), pp. 62–63.

meditated and taught their disciples. One of them summed up their quest as follows:

From the unreal lead me to the real!
From darkness lead me to light!
From death lead me to immortality!

The Jains, Defenders of All Beings

One of the two non-Vedic religions that emerged in this period, Jainism, is the "most Indian" religion of India. The Jains contributed to all of India (and today to the rest of the world) the unique ethical claim that the most important duty of a person is to cause no harm or pain to any being that can feel pain (this ethical value is called *ahimsa*, "nonviolence"). The Jains made this duty the center of their ideal of ethical behavior. The Buddhists readily agreed with the Jains about ahimsa, and they too stressed its central importance. Many, but not all, Brahmins and their followers eventually did likewise.

The most significant figure in Jain belief is Mahavira, the faith's last great teacher. His name means "the greatest of fierce, tough, heroic men" (*vira* is related to such English words as *virile*). He is called the Jina ("victor," "conqueror"), and his followers are called Jainas (those who "follow the Jina"), hence the

Western name Jainism for the religion as a whole. According to Jain tradition, Mahavira was a Kshatriya prince who at the age of 30 renounced the world—his home and family and all property and status that went with them.

For over a dozen years Mahavira followed the teachings of the earlier religious teacher Parshvanatha, whom Jainism regards as the twenty-third of the *tirthamkaras* ("ford-makers," who aid their followers in crossing the swirling flood of *samsara*, the cycle of rebirth). For these 12 years Mahavira wandered naked from place to place, lived on handouts, engaged in meditation, debated with other men also on holy quests, observed celibacy, and engaged in various painful ascetic practices in order to purify his *jiva* ("soul") of past karma. Nudity was a form of asceticism because it invited the painful ridicule of ordinary people. In his thirteenth year of asceticism Mahavira escaped the bondage of all his past karma.

Mahavira gained a great reputation as a wise and holy man, attracting many followers. At the age of 80 he died after deliberately seating himself in the posture of meditation with the intention of never moving again. This deliberate form of death by inaction is seen not as an act of suicide but as the most heroic and ascetic form of nonaction humanly possible. For those whose souls are still fouled with karma, this mode of death was regarded as highly purifying, and many Jain saints have died this way throughout history.

The Jains accept the reality of samsara and karma and regard moksha to be the only sensible goal to pursue in life; but their way of pursuing moksha was very different from that of the Brahmins of the *Upanishads*. The path to moksha that Mahavira preached centers on the practice of asceticism, although one does not have to practice the most rigorous forms to be considered a pious Jain. To gain moksha a Jain must sooner or later, in this life or a future life, renounce the world and become a wandering monk or nun. But a person may be a pious lay Jaina, supporting the monks and nuns with handouts of food, clothing, and shelter and living a life that conforms to the Jain ethic (which emphasizes nonviolence but also forbids liquor, sex outside of marriage, lying, and stealing) until he or she is convinced that the time for renunciation has come. The practice of nudity gradually died out over the centuries.

Jainism places a special emphasis on the idea that all beings (including plants, insects, and minerals) have souls and experience pain. Thus causing pain to any other sentient beings is the biggest source of the worst possible karma. Jain texts, for example, explain in graphic detail the suffering caused to the tiny beings living in wood when it is cast upon the fire. While it is inevitable that a believer will cause pain (by drinking water and the beings that are in it, for example), a person should avoid such destructive acts as much as possible. Jains who practice their faith most rigorously gently sweep the path before them with a broom as they walk, to avoid stepping on living things; they may tie cloths over their mouths to avoid inhaling any small creatures in the air.

Mahavira was the final tirthamkara of the current age of the world. Jains believe he was the twenty-fourth and last great tirthamkara in a long series of wise and powerful men who had shown people how to purify their souls and permanently separate them from the evils of perpetual samsara. Mahavira lived in the sixth or fifth century B.C.E. Jains believe he died in 527 B.C.E., but modern, non-Jain historians believe that date is too early.

In connection with their belief that Mahavira was only the last of twenty-four tirthamkaras, Jains believe that time revolves in endless cycles like a great cosmic wheel. In every era tirthamkaras like Mahavira are born to teach the doctrines of Jainism to humanity. Every era consists of millions of years. The Jains also believe that when a soul gains moksha and escapes the cycle of rebirth forever, it ascends to the topmost point of the universe, where it exists in complete purity forever. This differs dramatically from the idea of the *Upanishads* that every individual's soul is completely submerged into brahman, the single "soul" of the whole universe.

Socially, Jainism rejected the sacredness of the *Vedas* and thereby rejected the social stratification that assigned preeminence to the Brahmins. Interestingly, Jainism was the first Indian religion formally to allow women to become renouncers and pursue moksha as nuns. With some reluctance the Buddha belatedly allowed Buddhist laywomen to become nuns; and although some Hindu women did renounce the world from time to time, the Hindu dharma (Sacred Law) never formally sanctioned their doing so.

In the centuries after Mahavira the number of Jains has always been significant but never tremendously large. In spite of always being a minority religion in India, however, the Jains have consistently exerted greater influence than their numbers would lead anyone to expect. By 300 B.C.E. Jainism had gained significant political recognition in various kingdoms of North and South India. Also, because the ethics of their religion basically forbade farming for pious lay followers of the Jina (because tilling the soil kills so many small creatures), lay Jains were usually merchants living in cities. Lay Jains often became wealthy and often poured much of their wealth into the support of their religion. As a result, the Jain religion has contributed a great number of learned Jain scholars and libraries to India's cultural history.

The Middle Way of Gautama Buddha

About the same time that Mahavira lived, another ascetic and monastic religion arose in northern India. This religion, Buddhism, became tremendously popular and important in India and remained influential there for many centuries. It also spread outside India to all of Asia and today continues its expansion around the globe. Buddhism had some basic similarities to Jainism, but its root ideas were profoundly different. Both religions derive from the life and teachings of a great man; both stress the humanity of their teacher and do not rely on gods or divine rites to pursue the highest goal of life; both developed extensive monastic institutions in which many celibate men and women lived in spiritual communities, supported by a devoted laity. But there is a very archaic quality to many Jain doctrines, due probably to the fact that the Jain religion was never taken up by people outside of India. Buddhist doctrines, by contrast, seem very modern in certain ways, which may in part account for Buddhism's appeal to non-Indian peoples, including Europeans and Americans in the twentieth century.

Whereas Jainism stresses purification of the soul and ascetic pain and its leader is described in military terms as a "great hero" and "victor," Buddhism's founder was a man whose leadership was the result of his "waking up," having his understanding boosted to a higher level of insight. The word *buddha* means basically "someone who has awakened from sleep." Buddhists see the Buddha's Great Awakening (*Bodhi*) as the greatest discovery of the truth of life that has ever been made. As Jains follow Mahavira's soldierly example, Buddhists seek to use the Buddha's example and his teachings so that they too may wake up and realize the benefits of Awakening (often also called Enlightenment).

The man who became the Buddha was born Siddhartha Gautama, a prince of the Shakyas, whose small oligarchic state was located at the foot of the Himalayas. As with many of the world's great figures, the traditional accounts of the Buddha's life contain many legends and miracles. Accordingly, Gautama was conceived when his mother dreamed one night that a white elephant entered her right side. Later the baby was born from her right side, and right after birth the baby stood up and announced that this would be his last life. Seers predicted that Gautama would become either a great king or a great sage who would see four special sights of human suffering—a sick man, an old man, a dead man, and an ascetic holy man seeking to escape suffering—after which he would renounce the world and discover a way to relieve the world's suffering. The traditions tell us that Gautama's father, King Shuddodana, raised him in bounteous luxury and went to great lengths to prevent the prince from ever seeing the sick, the old, or the dead.

In the prince's twenty-ninth year, however, all his father's protections proved vain in the face of fate: on three separate occasions the prince happened to see a sick man, an old man, and a dead man. He was deeply moved and troubled to learn, from his chariot driver, that all people suffer these ghastly problems. He then happened to see a wandering ascetic who was in quest of moksha, and this encounter made him think very deeply about pursuing freedom from life's suffering himself. To his father's great disappointment, Gautama decided to follow that ascetic's example. He renounced his wealth and position, forsaking his wife and child.

Gautama studied meditation for a year with two different teachers, abandoning both after a while because their doctrines were not sufficient. Then, like Mahavira, he took up the most painful and demanding forms of asceticism and practiced them with great determination and devotion. Gautama almost died from this fasting and self-torture, and after five years he concluded that the end of suffering lay in changing the mind but that ascetic practices only weakened the mind.

Gautama left his ascetic companions, who ridiculed him for his "weakness," walked down to a river and had his first bath in five years, and sat down under an expansive banyan tree (the Indian fig tree) to rest in the cool shade. (Asceticism was regarded as a kind of purifying heat by ancient Indians.) Gautama was then offered a refreshing meal by a rich woman who offered a special meal once a year to the spirit of that tree. Clean, refreshed, and reinvigorated by food, Gautama was vibrantly awake as night fell. He sat up meditating all through the night; as the night progressed, his mind examined the world and its workings, and he came to understand more and more the fundamental causes for all that happens. Shortly before the dawn he attained the key insights for understanding and then eliminating suffering, but not, according to legendary tradition, before the demon Mara (Death) and his daughters Greed, Lust, and Anger did all in their powers to prevent his grasping the truth.

Gautama summarized the truth to which he "woke up" during this Great Awakening as the Four Noble Truths, which succinctly express the entire system of Buddhist thought. The religious way of life to which the Four Noble Truths lead is often called the Middle Way—it is the way of life that is in between the normal human life of sensation, desire, and action, on the one hand, and harsh asceticism, on the other. The Middle Way involves the moderate asceticism of renunciation, celibacy, and the Buddhist monastic way of life as opposed to the much more rigorous asceticism of Indian groups such as the Jains. The whole philosophy, which the Buddha taught to others, and the religious way of life to which those ideas lead is referred to in Buddhism as the Dharma. (The root sense of *dharma* for Hindus is "religious law" or "religious good deeds leading to a good afterlife"; Dharma, for Buddhists, has a broader meaning.)

Buddha's Four Noble Truths are these:

1. Suffering dominates our experience.
2. The cause of suffering is desire or craving.
3. It is possible to extinguish suffering by extinguishing its cause, thereby attaining *nirvana* (*nirvana* originally referred to a fire's going out; the Buddha's idea was to let the fire of desire go out by depriving it of its normal fuel).
4. The Noble Eightfold Path leads to the extinction of desire—that is, it leads to nirvana.

The Noble Eightfold Path consists of pursuing the following eight ideals:

1. *Right views*—the intellectual conviction that the Four Noble Truths are "the Truth"
2. *Right resolve*—the decision to act according to the Four Noble Truths
3. *Right speech*—having words be governed by the Five Moral Precepts of right conduct: do not harm

any living being (ahimsa); do not take what is not given to you; do not speak falsely; do not drink intoxicating drinks; do not be sexually unchaste

4. *Right conduct*—having deeds, like words, be governed by the Five Moral Precepts
5. *Right livelihood*—conducting oneself ethically even in earning a living; hence such occupations as farming, soldiering, prostitution, and tavern-keeping are disallowed
6. *Right effort*—following the path with all one's heart and energy by renouncing the world and becoming a monk or nun
7. *Right mindfulness*—a form of meditation that eventually produces "wisdom"; wisdom undermines desire because the wise person no longer sees his or her own self as particularly important in the world
8. *Right concentration*—a form of meditation that uses trances to make the nonrational and unconscious layers of the person completely calm and tranquil

Buddhism claims that desire is extinguished and nirvana attained when steps 7 and 8 of the path have been perfected—that is, when the person on the path has the wisdom to see that he or she is just one more sentient being among many and is no more valuable or important than any other (this removes the natural instinct to fight for success and even survival) and when "concentration meditation" has stilled all the powerful impulses and drives that condition every sentient being's mind. A person who has reached this nirvana of desire simply looks at his or her own condition at any given moment as "what is" and does not wish it to be otherwise, is not driven to improve it, does not envy anyone else, and does not suffer (physical pain may be present, but the person who has reached nirvana is dissociated from it and simply sees it as one more fact of the situation of the moment). Nirvana is a happy, friendly state (in which the Buddha lived for 45 years after his Awakening), but it is not an "altered state" of consciousness and certainly not a paradise or any kind of heavenly world.

Since in Buddhist thought the essential element of action is the desire to get something for oneself, a person who has extinguished desire no longer performs actions, even if his or her body may be going through the motions. In other words, such a person accumulates no karma and has escaped the round of samsara. For Buddhists this nirvana amounts to gaining moksha. As for the question of what comes after the devotee escapes the cycle of rebirth, the Buddha told his followers that the question could not be answered and was pointless anyway. Such a question "tends not to edify"; that is, it does not contribute to the one important goal. The only important thing a person can do in life is deal with suffering.

Dressed in a simple yellow robe, with begging bowl in hand, Gautama wandered through the plain of the Ganges, speaking with everyone (regardless of social class) and attracting disciples to a growing community (called the Sangha) of monks walking the Path. He taught many sermons (the Sutras) and laid down the Rules specifying many details of the monks' daily life (the Vinaya, analogous to the much later Rule of St. Benedict). Resisting at first, Buddha eventually acquiesced to demands that women be allowed to renounce the world and pursue the path and its advanced meditations on a full-time basis as nuns. Buddhist history states that while the Buddha lived, it was relatively easy to accomplish the nirvana of desire and suffering and that a great number of disciples actually did so.

At last, 80 years old and enfeebled, the Buddha was invited by a poor blacksmith to a meal. According to legend, the food included tainted mushrooms, but Gautama ate the meal rather than offend his host. Later in the day the Buddha had severe pains, and he knew death was near. Calling his disciples together, he gave them this parting message: "Be ye lamps unto yourselves. Be a refuge to yourselves. Hold fast to the truth as to a lamp. Look not for refuge to anyone beside yourselves." The Buddha had instructed that his body be burned. His followers, according to legend, quarreled over possession of his ashes, which were divided into eight parts and ensconced in shrines called *stupas*. There are now stupas all over South Asia. In spite of the Buddha's emphasis on correct understanding and on changing oneself through one's own efforts, his followers developed a profound affection for him and were very attached to him. After his death (even to some extent during his life) many of his followers saw him as a true holy man and believed that mere contact with him would somehow benefit them. What the Buddha taught is a philosophy, but the movement we call Buddhism is a religion.

The Buddha, the Dharma he taught, and the Sangha, the community of Buddha's followers, are regarded by Buddhists as the Three Precious Jewels. People did, and still do, officially become members of the Sangha by publicly declaring that they "take shelter in the Buddha, take shelter in the Dharma, and take shelter in the Sangha." As in the Jain religion, the majority of the community are laypeople who live in the world until they sense the time is right to take the sixth step of the path, right effort, and become a monk or a nun. (In some Buddhist countries, lay Buddhists often make short retreats to a monastery for instruction from the monks and practice in meditation.) In addition to restricting their speech, conduct, and livelihood by the Five Moral Precepts, they cultivate the virtues of generosity, friendliness, and compassion. Only people with great amounts of good karma ever hear the Buddhist teachings; people with even better accumulations of karma understand those teachings when they hear them; people with more good karma actually reach the path; and only those with more good karma possess the courage and determination actually to become a monk or a nun. In the end one does not want any karma at all, good or bad, but whatever good karma a lay Buddhist accumulates will help carry that person further along the Path in this or a future life.

Buddhists who became monks or nuns donned the yellow (or orange) robe worn by all renouncers in India except the Jains (who wore white if they wore anything). Unlike their Hindu and Jain counterparts—who usually lived alone or in small assemblies without any Rule—Buddhist renouncers created the world's first monastic communities, in which people pursuing spiritual goals lived together under strict rules. Often the Buddhists lived in caves that rich lay Buddhists had cut into the sides of mountains or rock cliffs. Their only possessions were their sandals, robe, and begging bowl. They ate only one meal a day and ate only what they had begged as a handout. Periodically all the monks in a given area recited together all the rules of monastic life, and anyone who had violated any rule was required to make a public confession. Four sins warranted permanent expulsion from the community: fornication, stealing, murder, and making false claims of one's spiritual attainments. Large parts of the day were given over to the two kinds of meditation, and monks who had accomplished nirvana were known as *arhats* ("worthy ones").

The Buddha was a critic of all religious and philosophical thinkers who came before him in India. He censured the *Vedas* and the rites of the Brahmins, considered the *Upanishads* wrong about brahman, and thought Mahavira's religion of ascetic purification futile. The Buddha took an agnostic stance on what really might lie beyond this world; he claimed that we, as finite, conditioned beings, had no way of knowing anything about infinite, unconditioned beings. He thought that anyone, regardless of social status, could gain nirvana, but he did not try to change Indian society. Though Sudras and women were admitted to Buddhist monasteries, those monasteries tended to mirror the structures and habits of the larger Indian society.

As with Mahavira, there is great uncertainty about exactly when the man who became the Buddha died. Buddhists have traditionally taught that he died in 526 B.C.E. Modern, non-Buddhist historians believed for many decades that 481 B.C.E. was a more accurate date. Current historical scholarship is energetically reconsidering this date and pushing it down toward 400 B.C.E. Whatever the exact dates of Gautama Buddha and his contemporary Mahavira, both lived and taught in eastern India as powerful new kingdoms were in the process of turning into the Mauryan Empire (inaugurated about 320 B.C.E.).

The Mauryan Empire and Its Aftermath, 320 B.C.E.—300 C.E.

The Aryan invaders of India had established 16 major kingdoms and tribal oligarchies in northern India, stretching from modern Pakistan to Bengal. Then a new invader appeared over the mountains of the northwest, preparing the way for the establishment of the first Indian empire. Celebrated in the legends of East and West alike, his name was Alexander. Continuing his conquest of the Persian Empire (see Chapter 3), Alexander the Great in 326 B.C.E. brought his phalanxes into the easternmost Persian province in the Indus valley, defeating local Punjabi rulers. When his weary troops refused to advance further eastward into the Ganges plain, Alexander constructed a fleet and explored the Indus to its mouth. From there he returned overland to Babylon while his fleet skirted the coast of the Arabian Sea and reached the Persian Gulf.

After Alexander's death in 323 B.C.E., the empire he had built so rapidly quickly disintegrated, and within two years his domain in the Punjab had completely disappeared. He had, however, opened routes between India and the West that would remain in use during the following Hellenistic and Roman periods, and by destroying the petty states in the Punjab, he facilitated—and perhaps inspired—the conquests of India's own first emperor.

Chandragupta Maurya, India's First Emperor

A new era began in India in 321 B.C.E., when Chandragupta Maurya seized the state of Magadha in the Ganges valley. Chandragupta conquered northern

The Mauryan Empire

326 B.C.E.	Alexander the Great invades India
321 B.C.E.	Chandragupta seizes Magadha
305 B.C.E.	Chandragupta defeats Seleucus
268–233 B.C.E.	Reign of Ashoka
c. 185 B.C.E.	Brahmin-led revolt against last Maurya emperor

India and founded the Mauryan dynasty, which endured until about 185 B.C.E. At its height the empire included all the subcontinent except the extreme south.

India's first empire reflected the imperial vision of its founder. Chandragupta created an administrative system of remarkable efficiency. He was also a brilliant general. In 312 B.C.E. Seleucus, the general who had inherited the major part of Alexander the Great's empire, crossed the Indus in an attempt to regain his predecessor's Indian conquests. But in 305 B.C.E. Chandragupta soundly defeated him, and Seleucus ceded all territories east of Kabul to the Indian monarch in return for an alliance and 500 war elephants.

Life in the Mauryan Empire

Seleucus's ambassador to the court of Chandragupta, whose name was Megasthenes, wrote a detailed account of India, fragments of which have survived. They give a fascinating picture of life in the empire. Chandragupta's capital, Pataliputra (known today as Patna), covered 18 square miles and was probably the largest city in the world. Outside its massive wooden walls was a deep trench used for defense and the disposal of sewage.

The remarkably advanced Mauryan Empire was divided and subdivided into provinces, districts, and villages whose headmen were appointed by the state. The old customary law, preserved and administered by the Brahmin priesthood, was superseded by an extensive legal code that provided for royal interference in all matters. A series of courts, ranging from the village court presided over by the headman to the emperor's imperial court, administered the law. So busy was Chandragupta with the details of his highly organized administration that, according to Megasthenes, he had to hear court cases during his daily massage.

Two other factors struck Megasthenes as important in the administration of the empire. One was the professional army, which he reports was an enormous force of 700,000 men, 9000 elephants, and 10,000 chariots. The other was the secret police, whose numbers were so large that the Greek writer concluded that spies constituted a separate class in Indian society. Chandragupta, fearing conspiracies, was said to have lived in strict seclusion, attended only by women who cooked his food and in the evening bore him to his apartment, where they lulled him to sleep with music.

Of course, the historian cannot take literally the details or the numbers in Megasthenes' account. They were impressionistic and designed to create certain effects on his audience at home. Ambassadors had limited knowledge of and exposure to the daily lives of kings, and stories of rulers and their female companions are often myths based on hearsay and conjecture. Furthermore, the counts of armies, especially of one's enemies, tended to be inflated. Nonetheless, it is clear that Megasthenes was impressed by the urban development, political organization, and military force of Chandragupta's empire.

Another source of information on Chandragupta's reign is a remarkable book, the *Arthashastra*, or *Treatise on Material Gain*, written by Kautilya as a guide for the king and his ministers. Kautilya, said to be Chandragupta's chief adviser, exalted royal power as the means of establishing and maintaining "material gain," meaning political and economic stability. The great evil, according to the *Arthashastra*, is anarchy, such as had existed among the small warring states in northern India. To achieve the aims of statecraft, Kautilya argued, a single authority is needed who will employ force when necessary.

The *Arthashastra* is an early example of a whole genre of literature, sometimes called "mirrors for princes," that provided advice to monarchs on the best and most effective ways to rule. Later examples are found in the Middle East and Europe—for example, the medieval Persian work of Qai Qaus and that of the Renaissance author Machiavelli. Machiavelli, like Kautilya, would advocate deception or unscrupulous means to attain desired ends. The *Arthashastra* remains in print today and has been translated into many languages. Modern leaders have been known to consult its pages.

The Mauryan state also controlled and encouraged economic life. Kautilya's treatise, which is thought to reflect much actual practice, advises the ruler to "facilitate mining operations," "encourage manufacturers," "exploit forest wealth," "provide amenities" for cattle breeding and commerce, and "construct highways both on land and on water." Price controls are advocated because "all goods should be sold to the people at favorable prices," and foreign trade should be subsidized: "Shippers and traders dealing in foreign goods should be given tax exemptions to aid them in making profits." Foreign trade did flourish, and in the bazaars of Pataliputra were displayed goods from southern India, China, Mesopotamia, and Asia Minor. Agriculture, however, remained the chief source of wealth. Irrigation and crop rotation were practiced, and Megasthenes states that there were no famines. In theory, all land belonged to the state, which collected one-fourth of the produce as taxes.

Ashoka, India's Greatest King

Following Chandragupta's death, his son and grandson expanded the Mauryan Empire southward into the Deccan peninsula. His grandson, Ashoka (d. 233 B.C.E.), the most renowned of all Indian rulers, how-

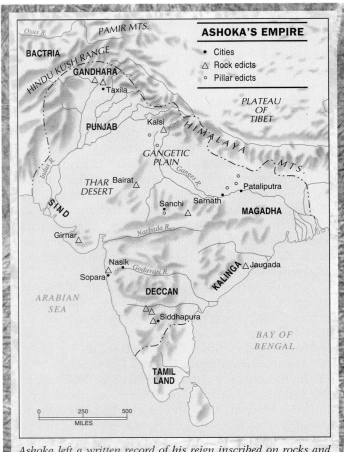

ASHOKA'S EMPIRE
- Cities
- △ Rock edicts
- ○ Pillar edicts

Ashoka left a written record of his reign inscribed on rocks and stone pillars all over the Mauryan Empire.

ever, was more committed to peace than to war. His first military campaign was also his last; the cruelty of the campaign horrified him, and he resolved never again to permit such acts of butchery. Ashoka converted to Buddhism and became a dedicated proponent of nonviolence (ahimsa). The story of Ashoka's horror at the carnage of war is similar in some ways to the account of Yudhishthira in the *Mahabharata*, which also relates a king's remorse in the aftermath of battle.

Throughout his empire, Ashoka had his edicts carved on rocks and stone pillars. They remain today as the oldest surviving written documents of India and are especially valuable for appreciating the spirit and purpose of Ashoka's rule. For example, they contain his conception of the duty of a ruler:

> *He shall . . . personally attend the business . . . of earth, of sacred places, of minors, the aged, the afflicted, and the helpless, and of women. . . . In the happiness of his subjects lies his happiness.[1]*

Although Ashoka made Buddhism India's state religion, he did not persecute the Brahmins and Hindus but proclaimed religious toleration as an official policy:

> *The king . . . honors every form of religious faith . . . ; whereof this is the root, to reverence one's own faith and never to revile that of others. Whoever acts differently injures his own religion while he wrongs another's.[2]*

Ashoka was a successful propagator of his faith. He supported the building of temples and stupas all over his empire, and the remains of many are still standing. He sent Buddhist missionaries to various lands—the Himalayan regions, Tamil Land (India's far south), Sri Lanka (Ceylon), Burma, and even as far away as Syria and Egypt, transforming Buddhism from a small Indian sect to an aggressive missionary faith. Modern Indians revere his memory, and the famous lion on the capital of one of his pillars has been adopted as the national seal of the present Indian republic.

Fall of the Mauryan Empire

Almost immediately after Ashoka's death in 233 B.C.E., the Mauryan Empire began to disintegrate. The last emperor was assassinated about 185 B.C.E. in a palace revolution led by a Brahmin priest. Once again the subcontinent was politically fragmented. Northern India was overrun by a series of invaders, and the south broke free from northern control.

The sudden collapse of the powerful Mauryan state and the grave consequences that ensued have provoked much scholarly speculation. Some historians have believed that the fall of the Mauryans can be traced to a hostile Brahmin reaction against Ashoka's patronage of Buddhism. Others believe that Ashoka's inclination toward nonviolence curbed the military ardor of his people and left them vulnerable to invaders. More plausible explanations for the fall of the Mauryan state take into account the transportation and communications problems facing an empire that spanned most of the Indian subcontinent, the difficulty of financing a vast army and bureaucracy, and the intrigues of discontented regional groups within the empire.

In fact, one might argue that political division is a more natural state for large multiethnic, multilingual landmasses with diverse terrain; empires that endure and unite vast expanses of territory are the exception. No one person could directly rule all of the subcontinent; like the later Roman and Ottoman Empires elsewhere, the Mauryan kingdom survived through a combination of talented leadership, economic success, flexible rule, and delegated authority.

Bactrian Greeks and Kushans

The Mauryan Empire was the first of two successful attempts to unify India in ancient times. The second—the work of the Gupta dynasty (c. 320–550

C.E.)—will be described in Chapter 12. In the five centuries between these two eras of imperial splendor, a succession of foreign invaders entered from the northwest and added new racial and cultural elements to the Indian scene.

The first of the new invaders of India were Greeks from Bactria. They were descendants of the soldiers settled there by Alexander the Great to serve his empire in the East. After Alexander, Bactria continued as a province of the Seleucid Empire, a bastion against the attacks of nomadic tribesmen from the north and a center for trade with India to the southeast. The decline of the Seleucid Empire allowed the Bactrian Greeks to establish an independent kingdom about 245 B.C.E.

In 183 B.C.E., two years after the death of the last Mauryan emperor of India, the fourth Bactrian king, Demetrius, crossed the Hindu Kush mountains as Alexander had done 150 years earlier and occupied the northern Punjab. From his base at Taxila, Demetrius and his successors ruled Bactria and the entire Punjab (modern Afghanistan and northern Pakistan).

The Greeks in India established the farthest outpost of Hellenism in the Hellenistic Age. Demetrius and his successors came closer than any Hellenistic ruler to realizing Alexander's supposed goal of a union of races. Their cities were not artificial Greek enclaves in a hostile land, like Alexandria in Egypt and Antioch in Syria. The Indian peoples were enrolled as citizens, a bilingual coinage was issued bearing Greek inscriptions on one side and Indian on the other, and at least one king, Menander, became a Buddhist.

But soon after 150 B.C.E. Bactria was overrun by nomadic tribesmen. Thereafter, Greek rule in the northern subcontinent steadily declined until the last remnants disappeared late in the first century B.C.E. Hordes of nomadic peoples, migrating out of central Asia, replaced the Greeks in Bactria and northwestern India. First to arrive were the Indo-European Scythians, who had been pushed out of central Asia by other Indo-European nomads known in Chinese sources as the Yueh-chih. In their turn, the Yueh-chih occupied Bactria, and about 40 C.E. they crossed the Hindu Kush and conquered the Punjab. The Kushans, as the Yueh-chih were called in India, expanded eastward to the middle Ganges valley and southward perhaps as far as the borders of the Deccan.

In contrast to the highly centralized Mauryan Empire, the Kushan state was more like a loose federation—its kings were overlords rather than direct rulers—yet it gave northern India two centuries of peace and prosperity. The Kushan kingdom acted as a hub for trade routes linking India, China, and the West. Its greatest ruler, Kaniska (fl. c. 120 C.E.), produced a multicultural coinage that employed Chinese, Greek, Persian, Hindu, and Buddhist devices.

Kaniska gained fame as a patron of the arts and of a new form of Buddhism called Mahayana.

Emergent Hinduism and Buddhism, 200 B.C.E.—300 C.E.

Hinduism and Buddhism were not static or fixed in time; they were evolving during the classical era. In the years 200 B.C.E. to 300 C.E. the religion called Hinduism was formulating a synthesis and meeting the challenge of Buddhism. Buddhism in turn split into two distinct strands of interpretation. These developments were set in the context of an Indian social order that was wedded to village life, caste hierarchies, and a household based on the extended family.

Village, Caste, and Family

In the Later Vedic Age, the three pillars of traditional Indian society—the autonomous village, caste, and the joint or extended family—were established. India has always been primarily agricultural, and its countryside is still a patchwork of villages. The ancient village was made up of joint families governed by a headman and a council of elders. Villages enjoyed considerable autonomy; the raja's government hardly interfered at all as long as it received its quota of taxes.

As noted earlier, Hindu society came to be divided into four classes, or *varnas*—Brahmins (priests), Kshatriyas (nobles), Vaishyas (commoners), and Shudras (workers or servants)—known in the West as the *caste system*. Within the framework of these four varnas (or castes) society was perceived as divided into thousands of subgroups, or *jatis* (literally, "species"), each with a special social, occupational, or religious character. For example, occupational groups of merchants or shopkeepers formed many jatis within the Vaishya caste. Those whose occupations were the most menial and degrading—scavengers, sweepers (who remove human waste), and tanners (because they handle the carcasses of dead animals)—also formed numerous jatis but were perceived as outside and beneath the people of the four varnas. These outcasts were called Untouchables because their touch was considered defiling to members of the other castes.

The third pillar of Indian society was the three-generation household, a patriarchal system. In these households seniority brought status to both men and women. Sons were subordinate to their fathers, and young wives were subordinate to their mothers-in-law. When a woman married, she went from the house of her father to the house of her husband's father. Children were considered the property of the father, not the mother. When the patriarch died, his authority was transferred to his eldest son, but his property was divided equally among all his sons. Women were subordinate to men and required a male protector: father, husband, brother, or son. They could not inherit property, nor could they participate in sacrifices to the gods; their presence at the sacrifice was considered a source of pollution.

The emphasis placed on communal interests rather than on the individual is a common denominator of the three pillars of Indian society. Thus Indian society has always been concerned with stability, respect for elders, and family and group solidarity.

The Hindu Synthesis

Hinduism is not one single doctrine. It is an array of highly diverse beliefs that include the various texts of the Vedic Age, pre-Aryan Indian practices, and an evolving set of deities and rituals. Essential to Hinduism are the beliefs in the cycle of birth, death, and

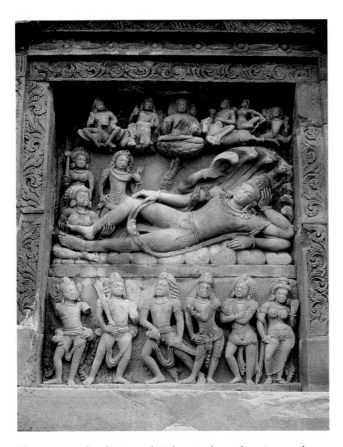

The serene and reclining god Vishnu is shown here in a sculpture from a sixth-century c.e. Hindu temple. Beneath Vishnu are the five Pandavas, heroes of the Mahabharata, *and their shared wife, Draupadi. Draupadi, along with Sita, stands as a model of Hindu womanhood: virtuous, honorable, and strong.*

rebirth (samsara) and a society structured by caste. Beings may be born as humans in various jatis or as lesser creatures, depending on their actions in the previous life. A believer who accumulates good actions ascends in the hierarchy of beings in subsequent births and may ultimately escape rebirth and be absorbed into brahman.

Three Traditions of Worship and Theology: Vishnu, Shiva, and Devi

The Brahmin priests incorporated Upanishadic thought into their teaching. In doing so they gave the caste system additional religious support by linking it to karma and the process of reincarnation. The priests made individual salvation, now a conspicuous part of Indian religion, dependent on the uncomplaining acceptance of one's position at birth and the performance of one's dharma, which varied by caste. In this schema, a person was born into a caste and died in that caste. Marriage outside one's caste was forbidden. Of course, in practice, as in all religious systems, social reality did not always match normative religious ideals. Marriages did cross caste lines, and some groups did apparently change caste over time.

The Upanishadic doctrine of salvation by absorption of the individual soul into brahman, however, was too intellectual and remote for the average person to grasp fully. Thus devotion to personal savior gods also emerged, becoming an important element in Hinduism. This devotion centered on anthropomorphic deities with rich personalities and long histories.

The major Vedic gods gradually faded into the background, and three basically monotheistic gods emerged as paramount in Hinduism: Vishnu, Shiva, and Devi, the Goddess (sometimes called Kali). Brahma, the personification of brahman, never acquired the standing and popular following achieved by these other three, a position they continue to maintain. Vishnu, Shiva, and Devi evolved from Vedic and indigenous Indian origins, and each came to be regarded by one or several different traditions as the uniquely supreme and holy God, creator of the universe. The theologies of Vishnu and Shiva were already well developed by about 200 B.C.E.; that of the Goddess was not fully developed until some time later. As with all great theological traditions, the theologies of these gods did not remain static and fixed over the ensuing centuries.

In the old Vedic pantheon of the Aryans, Vishnu was a relatively minor god associated with the sun. He then developed into a pacific father-god, comforter, and savior who works continuously for the welfare of humanity. "No devotee of mine is lost" is Vishnu's promise. His followers believe that he has appeared in nine major "descents" in human form to save the world from disaster. (A predicted tenth descent has yet to happen.) Two of Vishnu's incarnations are described in the great Indian epics, as Krishna in the *Mahabharata* and as Rama, the hero of the *Ramayana*. Rama saves the human race from the oppressions of a great demon, rules for many years in the city of Ayodhya, and then returns to the "City of the Gods," resuming the form of Vishnu.

Shiva, the other great popular god of classical and modern Hinduism, evolved from a minor Aryan Vedic god who was the guardian of healing herbs but whose arrows also brought disease. It is possible that another prototype of Shiva was a pre-Aryan fertility god who was worshipped in the cities of the Indus civilization. Shiva is often associated with phallic symbols. His spouse, Parvati, is the earliest expression in the Brahmin texts of a powerful female goddess who was eventually recognized as a separate deity in her own right (under other names) and elevated to the status of a unique supreme and holy divinity, the eternal source and end of the universe.

Shiva's followers believe he is superior to the gods Brahma and Vishnu. He personifies the cosmic force of change that destroys in order to build anew; he is often depicted with a necklace of skulls. Some representations show Shiva as the Lord of Dancers; the rhythm of his dance is that of a world continuously forming, dissolving, and re-forming. He also exemplifies another major characteristic of Hinduism, the reconciliation of extremes: violence and passivity, eroticism and asceticism. Shiva is portrayed as remaining unmoved in meditation for years on end. When he emerges from his meditations, however, he is often lustful and violent.

As noted, Shiva's wife, Parvati (followed by Vishnu's wife, Lakshmi), marked the first appearance in Hinduism of a powerful female divinity. Archaeological and other evidence suggests that goddesses were worshipped in India from the time of the Indus valley civilization. But only toward the Gupta period did fully developed theologies of a supreme Goddess, Devi (the word *devi* simply means "goddess"), begin to appear. As with the development of Shiva and Vishnu, the development of Devi involved the fusion of numerous local deities into a single complex figure. The Goddess presents two faces to the world: she is a tender mother to her devotees and a ferocious warrior to those who threaten her devotees. Called "Mother" or "Bestower of Food" (Annapurna) in her benevolent moods, she can also be "the Black One" (Kali), wearing a necklace of the skulls of her victims, or Durga, a many-armed warrior riding on the back of a lion to do battle with demons when angry. As the creative power of the universe (similar to the Vedic idea of brahman), she is referred to as Shakti ("Power," "Creative Energy"), and theologies focused on Devi as the Supreme Being of the universe are referred to as Shaktism.

As mentioned earlier, there is no centralized authority in Hinduism. The resulting "flexibility" makes Hinduism seem extremely complicated to outsiders

Vishnu and his consort, Lakshmi, recline upon the serpent Shesha floating on the waters of creation. Emerging out of Vishnu's navel is a lotus which serves as a throne for the god Brahma, who creates the world.

Lakshmi, Vishnu's consort and goddess of prosperity, beauty, and precious things, emerged from the foam of the ocean. This statuette was found half a world away in the ruins of ancient Pompeii in Italy, thus demonstrating the extent of trade in Indian cultural objects and ideas in the first century C.E.

Most Hindus today are devotees of either Vishnu or Shiva and their respective incarnations. But animals (especially the cow), vegetation, water, and even stones are also worshipped by some as symbols of the divine. Over time literally thousands of deities, demigods, and lesser spirits came to form the Hindu pantheon, the world's largest.

Because the authority to teach normative ideas in Hinduism was vested in the Brahmins as a class, Hinduism is probably the world's most flexible religion. Brahmins were present in villages and towns throughout the subcontinent, and many local ideas and practices were "normalized" as "compatible with the *Vedas.*" Hinduism possesses no canon, such as the Bible or the Qur'an; no single personal founder, such as Christ or Muhammad; and no precise body of authoritative doctrine. Hindu beliefs vary dramatically, but people remain "Hindu" as long as they observe the rules of their caste. Depending on one's intellectual and spiritual needs and capacities, Hinduism offers transcendental philosophies or devotional adherence to a savior god such as Vishnu. From its earliest origins, it has exhibited an unusual organic quality of growth and adaptation and is, by definition, a religious synthesis of highly diverse ritual and belief.

The Epics

The *Mahabharata,* composed in verse, contains over 75,000 stanzas, the longest work of literature in the world. It tells the tale of an all-encompassing war between rival sets of cousins, the Pandavas and the Kauravas. They are fighting for the throne of the Bharata kingdom, in the upper Ganges plain in the region of modern Delhi. But this great battle, lasting 18 days, was ultimately construed as a cosmic struggle between virtue and evil, a battle to set the world right.

As in the Greek *Iliad*'s account of the Trojan War, the *Mahabharata* presents a dramatic tale of heroism, vengeance, and sacrifice in which the gods directly intervene in the affairs of men. In the great Indian epic, however, it is duty that must govern the actions of kings; only through war will the proper order of the universe be restored. When the war is over and the victorious Pandavas view the horrendous slaughter of their sons, cousins, teachers, and friends, Yudhishthira, the intended king, is so shocked and horrified by the carnage that he refuses to accept the throne and wishes to retreat into the forest. Eventually, however, he is persuaded to become king. It is not his own desires or wishes that Yudhishthira must follow but his duty.

The *Mahabharata* was shaped and embellished over time. It was incorporated into royal sacrificial ritual, and a long succession of priestly editors added

who are used to more highly defined religious traditions. One aspect of this flexibility is that many versions of the theology and mythology of these deities are mixed together. For example, worshippers of Shiva often recognize Vishnu as an important and exalted creature fashioned by Shiva but who in no way rivals Shiva's divine supremacy. Worshippers of Vishnu often fit Shiva into their theology in similar ways. They also eventually included the Buddha as one of Vishnu's incarnations, and in modern times some have incorporated the Christians' Jesus into these theologies. Today many Hindus worship Jesus as a divine incarnation, but they do so as Hindus in Hindu ways and are not Christian converts.

many long passages on religious duties, morals, and statecraft. One of the most famous additions is the *Bhagavad-Gita* ("The Lord's Song"), a philosophical dialogue that stresses the performance of duty (dharma) and the overcoming of passion and fear. It is still the most treasured piece in Hindu literature. *Dharma*, whose broad meaning is "moral law" and is often translated as "virtue," had by this time replaced the earlier Vedic term *rita*, which, as noted earlier, originally referred to customary and cosmic law.

The dialogue in the *Bhagavad-Gita* takes place between Arjuna, the greatest warrior of the Pandava brothers, and Krishna, an incarnation of the god Vishnu who takes human form and acts as Arjuna's charioteer. Arjuna is shaken by the prospect of killing his kinsmen. But Krishna, who gradually reveals himself as no ordinary charioteer, instructs Arjuna that he must give up worldly desire and personal attachment and devote himself to discipline and duty. In so doing he will be able to attain freedom, overcome despair, and act according to his dharma, fulfilling his role in the cosmic struggle. Krishna tells Arjuna:

> *"Knowledge is obscured*
> *by the wise man's eternal enemy*
> *which takes form as desire,*
> *an insatiable fire, Arjuna.*
> *The senses, mind, and understanding*
> *are said to harbor desire;*
> *with these desire obscures knowledge*
> *and confounds the embodied self.*
> *Therefore, first restrain*
> *your senses, Arjuna,*
> *then kill this evil*
> *that ruins knowledge and judgment."3*

The universal appeal of Arjuna's internal struggle and Krishna's advice has made the *Bhagavad-Gita* a world classic; it has been translated into many languages. Once Arjuna realizes that he is receiving advice from a god, he wants to know more. He asks Krishna to reveal himself in all his majesty. Krishna obliges the unwitting Arjuna by giving him a "divine eye"; but Arjuna is unnerved by the terrible vision of world-devouring time, of the whole universe inscribed in the god's body. He expresses his awe, and Krishna takes mercy on him and reverts to his human form.

The other great Hindu epic, the *Ramayana*, has been likened to the Greek *Odyssey*. It recounts the wanderings of the banished prince Rama and his faithful wife Sita's long vigil before they are reunited and Rama gains his rightful throne. In the course of time, priestly editors transformed this simple adventure story into a book of devotion. Rama, like Krishna in the *Bhagavad-Gita*, was an incarnation of the great god Vishnu. He was viewed as the ideal ruler: truly virtuous, mighty, a man who exemplifies "proper conduct and is benevolent to all creatures. Who is learned, capable, and a pleasure to behold."4 Sita emerged as the perfect woman, devoted and submissive to her husband. Her words were memorized by almost every Hindu bride:

> *Car and steed and gilded palace,*
> *vain are these to woman's life;*
> *Dearer is her husband's shadow*
> *to the loved and loving wife.*

In the *Ramayana*, Sita is abducted by the demon Ravana, thus launching another cosmic battle between the forces of good and evil. Rama, though victorious, is dishonored because Ravana had touched his wife and taken her to his palace. He feels compelled to repudiate Sita; her abduction is viewed as a rape even though she rejected Ravana's advances. One of the most moving scenes of the *Ramayana* is that in which the loyal Sita proposes to immolate herself (sati) rather than live separated from her lord. The gods save her from the flames, thus allowing Rama honorably to take her back. But years later, wagging tongues revive the question of her "tainted" virtue, and the heroine is once again prompted to prove her purity. The figure of Sita endures as an emblem of ideal Hindu womanhood. In the Indian nationalist struggles of the twentieth century, Sita served as a symbol of femininity and of the nation itself.

Counting Time

There are many ways to understand a civilization: through its art, its buildings, its political systems, its religions, its gender relations. One interesting way to envision a people is to examine its imaginings of time. Past societies have counted time in diverse ways, and those ways then shape the people's myths. Christians and Muslims, for example, trace their histories from a creation that includes the first man, Adam. Then each faith begins counting time from the life of its particular savior or prophet, Jesus and Muhammad, respectively. Of the three great religious traditions that emerged earlier in India, Jainism and Buddhism also focus on the lives of particular holy men who taught the way of Enlightenment. But the belief in reincarnation, shared by Hindus, Buddhists, and Jains, makes Indian notions of time radically different from those of traditions in which humans have only one lifetime. In the Indian traditions, humans can and will have thousands of lifetimes. The question "What comes after death?" is intimately linked to the imagining of time.

Hindu civilization is unique among ancient world civilizations in its crafting of a particularly grand and elaborate scheme for counting time. There

The *Ramayana:* The Trial of Sita

After Rama rescues Sita from her captor, the demon Ravana, he is overjoyed to see her but tormented by the shame of knowing she was touched by another. The doubt thus cast upon her virtue forces him to repudiate her. Devastated at this rejection by her lord, Sita nevertheless proudly answers in her own defense and demands that a pyre be built on which she can immolate herself. The ideas of sexual purity and honor expressed here are not limited to the society of classical India. They are common in many traditional societies and continue to influence gender relations in the present day.

Rama speaks to his beloved: Oh illustrious Princess, I have re-won thee and mine enemy has been defeated on the battlefield; I have accomplished all that fortitude could do; my wrath is appeased; and the insult and the one who offered it have both been obliterated by me. . . . As ordained by destiny the stain of thy separation and thine abduction by that fickle-minded titan has been expunged by me, a mortal. . . . [But] a suspicion has arisen, however, with regard to thy conduct, and thy presence is as painful to me as a lamp to one whose eye is diseased! Henceforth go where it pleaseth thee, I give thee leave, O Daughter of Janaka. O Lovely One, the ten regions are at thy disposal; I can have nothing more to do with thee! What man of honor would give rein to his passion so far as to permit himself to take back a woman who has dwelt in the house of another? Thou hast been taken into Ravana's lap and he has cast lustful glances on thee; how can I reclaim thee, I who boast of belonging to an illustrious House [family]?. . . .

Sita replies: Why dost thou address such words to me, O Hero, as a common man addresses an ordinary woman? I swear to thee, O Long-Armed Warrior, that my conduct is worthy of thy respect! It is the behavior of other women that has filled thee with distrust! Relinquish thy doubts since I am known to thee! If my limbs came in contact with another's it was against my will, O Lord, and not through any inclination on my part; it was brought about by fate. That which is under my control, my heart, has ever remained faithful to thee. . . . If despite the proofs of love that I gave thee whilst I lived with thee, I am still a stranger to thee, O Proud Prince, my loss is irrevocable. . . . Raise a pyre for me, O Saumitri, this is the only remedy for my misery! These unjust reproaches have destroyed me, I cannot go on living! Publicly renounced by mine husband, who is insensible to my virtue, there is only one redress for me, to undergo the ordeal by fire!

From *The Ramayana of Valmiki,* trans. Hari Prasad Shastri, Vol. 3 (London: Shanti Sadan, 1970), pp. 336–337.

---

are many Indian creation myths, and these stories merged and shifted over time. One common notion of the creation and destruction of the universe is that time is counted in eras *(mahayugas).* Just as individuals die and then are reborn, at the end of each era the world dissolves and then reemerges to begin a new era. Each era consists of one complete cycle of four ages: the Golden Age (1,440,000 human years), in which all beings are good and all life is comfortable; the Age of Trey (1,080,000 human years), in which some evil appears along with some suffering and difficulty in life; the Age of Deuce (720,000 human years), in which there is more evil, pain, and suffering; and the Age of Dissolution (360,000 human years), in which evil, pain, and distress predominate in human life. Before and after each age are "twilight periods" of varying length that altogether add another 720,000 years to the length of a whole cycle.

This vast expanse of human time, however, is nothing compared to the life of the god Brahma. One thousand mahayugas make up only one day in his existence, which lasts for 100 years of 360 days each; and as each Brahma dies, a new one is born from an egg that grows within brahman. In this Hindu cosmology, there have already been billions of Brahmas. According to certain ancient Hindu texts, the world is currently in an Age of Dissolution; in other words, we are approaching the end of a mahayuga and the halfway point in the current day of the current Brahma.

Theravada and Mahayana Buddhism

Buddhism reached a great peak of influence and power in India in the third century B.C.E. It maintained a lofty and important position for several hundred years after that and survived in India until it was exterminated in the thirteenth century C.E. in the aftermath of the Muslim invasions. One reason for its enduring presence in India for over 1600 years was that it rejuvenated itself powerfully with an expansive, liberal "Great Vehicle" *(Mahayana)* movement that began to flower about 100 B.C.E. Mahayana Buddhism stressed that pious Buddhists should imitate the Buddha directly by trying to relieve others' suffering with the message of the Dharma. They should do this rather than merely seek their own personal beatitude as arhats.

Whereas the arhat was the ideal Buddhist in the earlier Sangha, the Mahayana argued that the ideal Buddhist was a *bodhisattva,* a person who will eventually become a Buddha, someone who will spread the light of the Dharma. The ideal bodhisattva, according to the Mahayana, is a Buddhist saint who so zealously seeks to eliminate the sufferings of others that, going beyond the example even of Gautama, he postpones his own entry into the final nirvana (that is, one's final death after accomplishing nirvana) in order to act as a compassionate and loving helper to all others who are still suffering within samsara. The Mahayana movement criticized the older forms of Buddhism as a "Lesser Vehicle" *(Hinayana)* because, it said, the ideal of the arhat was a selfish one. Further, said the Mahayana, older forms of Buddhism were mired in a literal-minded sort of Buddhist philosophy, whereas the Mahayana was "sophisticated" and truly profound. One school of older Buddhism continued to thrive in India, Theravada, the so-called Doctrine of the Elders.

The Brahmins launched a countermovement in the second century B.C.E. that picked up several important elements of Buddhism's appeal. The Brahmin countermovement flowered as "Hinduism," and this new "Hinduism" played a major role in giving rise to the Mahayana Buddhist rejuvenation. Brahmins and their followers gradually won back political and economic support from Buddhists, but Buddhism survived in India until the thirteenth century.

Both the older Theravada and the newer Mahayana Buddhism spread outside of India and thrived in all parts of Asia. Buddhism was brought to Sri Lanka by missionaries sent there by the Mauryan emperor Ashoka around 250 B.C.E. After 100 B.C.E. Buddhists spread the Dharma beyond the boundaries of the subcontinent into China and central, western, and southeastern Asia. In those areas it took permanent root, establishing Buddhist societies, states, and monasteries that function to this day. Today the older form of Buddhism survives only in Sri Lanka and Southeast Asia, and the Mahayana is absent there; Mahayana survives in Tibet, Korea, Japan, and China. The translation of the very numerous books of the Buddhist scriptures from Sanskrit into Chinese took place during the second, third, and fourth centuries C.E., an intellectual achievement as fascinating as it is staggering. A small revival of Buddhism occurred in Maharashtra, India, in the 1930s when the Untouchable leader Dr. B. R. Ambedkar led a mass conversion of Untouchables to Buddhism so that they might escape the oppression of Hindu Untouchability.

Buddhist Sculpture and Architecture

Indian thought and art would have a profound effect on the Western world. The most lasting Western influence on India in the Classical Age was the influence of Greek art on Buddhist sculpture. Before the Kushan period, Indian artists were influenced by the

This seated Buddha from Gandhara shows Hellenistic influence in the modeling of the clothing, features, and, hair; the elongated earlobes, heavy-lidded eyes, mark on the forehead, knot of hair, and expression of deep repose are Indian.

Seated Buddha, from Gandhara, Pakistan. Kushan period, 2nd–3rd century. Dark gray schist, H. 36″ × W. 22 ½″. Seattle Art Museum, Eugene Fuller Memorial Collection, 33.180. Photo: Paul Macapia.

Buddha's prohibitions against idolatry, and they refrained from portraying the Buddha in human form. His presence was indicated by symbols only, such as his footprints, his umbrella, or the tree under which he attained Enlightenment. Beginning in the first century C.E., however, the Buddha himself was portrayed in numerous statues and reliefs. Most of these early Buddha figures come from Gandhara, the center of the Kushan Empire and the earlier Greco-Bactrian kingdom.

The primary inspiration for this Gandharan Buddhist art came from Mahayana Buddhism, which viewed the Buddha as a savior. This devotional form of Buddhism needed images for worship, and figures of the Buddha as a bodhisattva savior, as well as of many bodhisattva saints, were produced in large numbers. Mahayana Buddhism and Greco-Buddhist images of the Buddha, both of which developed in the Kushan Empire, spread together throughout eastern Asia.

A second inspiration for Gandharan art came from Greece. Apparently Hellenistic sculptors and craftsmen migrated to Gandhara via the central Asian trade routes. The result was an execution of Indian themes through the use of Greek artistic techniques.

The magnificent buildings of the Mauryan emperors have disappeared. All that remain are Buddhist stupas, the dome-shaped monuments that were used as funeral mounds to enshrine the relics of the Buddha and Buddhist saints or to mark a holy spot. Originally made only of earth, more elaborate mounds were later fashioned out of earth faced with brick and surrounded by railings and four richly carved gateways of stone. On top of the dome was a boxlike structure surmounted by a carved umbrella, the Indian emblem that symbolizes the Buddha's princely birth. As centuries passed, the low dome was heightened in some areas into a tall, tapered structure more like a tower. Later, when Buddhism spread to other countries, the stupa type of architecture went along. Its gateway was widely copied, and the stupa itself may have been the prototype of the multi-storied Buddhist pagodas that are common in East Asia today.

South India

Like many other regions of the globe, India can be divided culturally into north and south. Although the south was often dominated by northern conquerors, in general its civilizations developed in a fashion distinct from those of the north. Before the rise of the Gupta Empire in the fourth century C.E., the vast tableland of South India—the Deccan—and its fertile coastal plains remained outside the main forces of political change in the north, except for the 150 years of Mauryan imperial rule. The Dravidian peoples of this area, with their dark skin and small stature, differed in appearance, language, and culture from the Aryan-speaking peoples of the north. Gradually, however, as Brahmin priests and Buddhist monks infiltrated the south, Hinduism and Buddhism were grafted onto the existing Dravidian culture.

Politically, the south remained divided into numerous warring states. Prominent among them were three well-developed Tamil (an old Dravidian language) kingdoms in the southern third of the Deccan peninsula. Under the patronage of some of these kings, the Tamil language developed a classically exquisite literature in the first few centuries of the Common Era. This tradition, known as the Sangam ("Academy") tradition, was based in the old city of Madurai in Tamil Nadu ("Tamil Land"), and it produced several anthologies of poetry, several unique epics, and a superb handbook of language and poetics. Love was an important theme in the Tamil poetry:

> *As a little white snake*
> *with lovely stripes on its young body*
> *troubles the jungle elephant*
>   *this slip of a girl*
>   *her teeth like sprouts of new rice*
>   *her wrists stacked with bangles*
> *troubles me.*[5]

By the first century B.C.E., Tamil Nadu had become an intermediary in the maritime trade extending eastward to the East Indies and westward to the Hellenistic kingdoms. Indeed, a major factor that distinguishes South India from North India is the former's orientation toward the sea. On the east and west coasts of southern India, ports developed that became important entrepots for the East-West trade

Sanchi is a third-century B.C.E. site in central India that contains Buddhist monastic complexes and large stupas like this one with its carved gateway and umbrella-like summit decoration. Such stupas, supposed to contain relics of the Buddha, were built and patronized by King Ashoka.

and important points of cultural contact with foreign states and peoples.

The Meeting of East and West: Networks of Exchange

In the centuries immediately preceding and following the birth of Christ, the great civilizations of the world—Indian, Chinese, and Roman—were connected by a complex network of commercial, intellectual, and diplomatic exchanges. Although these contacts began to decline in the third century C.E., they were never entirely cut off. Travelers and monks from China visited the holy sites in India, the monsoons carried merchants to and fro across the Indian Ocean, and the goods and ideas of the East continued to enhance and alter the societies of the Mediterranean world.

Beyond the Indian Frontiers

The era of Mauryan hegemony coincided with the rule of the Han dynasty in China and the Roman Empire in the West. These empires provided the commercial anchors in a chain of intercommunicating states that stretched across Eurasia from the Pacific to the Atlantic. While Rome experienced the prosperous years of the Pax Romana during the first and second centuries C.E., Indian merchants supplied goods to the Roman entrepots in the Middle East. South Asian ports acted as staging points for the Chinese silk and Indian cottons in demand in the West. Indian traders exchanged textiles for African gold and ivory and traded rice, oils, precious woods, jewels, and spices in the ports of the Arabian Sea.

After Alexander's death, India maintained trade contacts with the Seleucid and Ptolemaic kingdoms of the Hellenistic Age over two routes, one by land and the other by sea. The most frequented route was the caravan road that extended from Asia Minor and Syria, crossed Mesopotamia, and then skirted the Iranian plateau to either Bactra or Kandahar before crossing the Hindu Kush to reach Taxila in South Asia. The sea route that linked the Eastern and Western worlds extended from China and Southeast Asia across the Bay of Bengal to India and Sri Lanka and thence across the Indian Ocean to the Red Sea ports or to the head of the Persian Gulf. From those two waterways, goods then proceeded overland and via the Mediterranean to the Middle East and into Africa and Europe.

The courts of kings and seats of imperial power were great points of consumption for the goods of the East-West trade. The Mauryan and Kushan kings developed the trade passing through northern India in order to provide the foreign commodities that em-

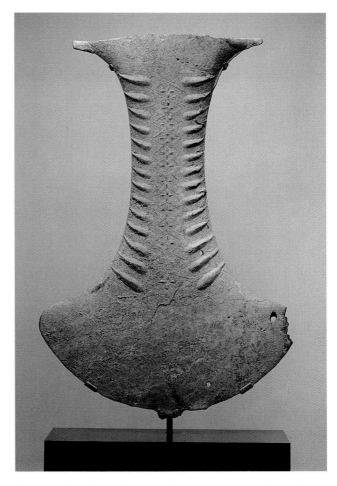

South and Southeast Asia were famous for metalworking. Bronze objects used for practical and ceremonial purposes were widely traded throughout the Indian Ocean region.

Vessel in the Form of an Ax. Bronze. The Metropolitan Museum of Art, Purchase, George McFadden Gift and Edit Perry Chapman Fund, 1993. (1993.525) Photograph by Bruce White © 1993 The Metropolitan Museum of Art.

bellished their palace life. The Roman appetite for luxury goods from India and Southeast Asia—ivory, pearls, spices, dyes, and cotton—greatly stimulated that trade. Rulers vied to control and tax this lucrative commerce.

But no monarch, however great, could maintain control over the whole vast expanse of territory crossed by these trade routes. There were always middlemen. The Parthians, whose kingdom extended from the Euphrates to the borders of Bactria, levied heavy tolls on the caravan trade. The Kushans acted as middlemen for the Chinese silk trade, selling the silk to the Parthians and later to Western merchants coming by sea to India. The Sabaean Arabs of southwestern Arabia seized the Red Sea route at Aden and were in control of much of the Mediterranean world's overseas trade with India. From Aden, the Sabaeans sent Indian goods north by caravan to Petra, which grew rich as a distribution point to Egypt via Gaza and to the north via Damascus.

Discovery Through Maps

The World, Including India, According to Ptolemy, c. 150 C.E.

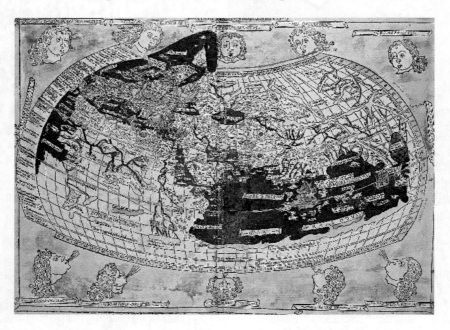

Ptolemy (90–168 C.E.) is well known for his contributions to mathematics and astronomy, but he was also a famous geographer. His work illustrates the fact that people's notions of the world come both from within and from without. South Asian society is a case in point. Indians have apparently been producing maps for more than 2000 years. But with the exception of a few incised potsherds and ancient sculptures, no known examples of distinctively Indian cartography survive from the period covered in this chapter. Later Indian cartography, such as an eleventh-century Jain cosmological map carved in stone, suggests what earlier Indian images of the cosmos may have looked like. (Such images were often markedly different from those produced by Western cartographers.) But at present all we have are out-

siders' visions of India, such as the second-century world map of Ptolemy, whose geographical vision remained influential into the sixteenth century.

Ptolemy's *Geography* described four systems of map projection. His description of the world, as seen in this reconstruction, drastically shortens the Indian peninsula from north to south. It imagines an unknown land south of the Indian Ocean, which is depicted as landlocked. Ptolemy's vision of the world spread with copies of his maps along the land and seaborne trade routes linking the Roman world and India. Ultimately it affected the mapmaking of Indian cartographers. The influence of Ptolemy's geography is just one instance of the bilateral exchange of culture and ideas that accompanied the flow of trade in this era.

So great was the demand and so lucrative the trade in Indian goods that the Roman emperor Augustus Caesar broke the hold of the Parthian and Arab middlemen on the Eastern trade, establishing direct commercial connections by sea with India. By 1 B.C.E. he had gained control of the Red Sea, forcing the Sabaeans out of Aden and converting the city into a Roman naval base. Ships were soon sailing from Aden directly to India across the Arabian Sea, blown by the monsoon winds.

From May to October the monsoon blows from the southwest across the Arabian Sea; between No-

vember and March the countermonsoon blows from the northeast. Thus direct round-trip voyages, eliminating middlemen and the tedious journey along the coasts, could be made in eight months. Strabo, a Greek geographer during the time of Augustus, stated that 120 ships sailed to India every year from Egyptian ports on the Red Sea.

When Augustus became head of the Roman world, the Tamil and Kushan rulers sent him congratulatory embassies. At least nine other embassies from India visited the Roman emperors, and Roman-Indian trade flourished. Indian birds (particularly talking parrots, costing more than human slaves) became the pets of wealthy Roman ladies, and Indian animals (lions, tigers, and buffaloes) were used in the wild beast shows of Roman emperors. In view of these contacts, we can understand why Ptolemy's second-century map of the world shows considerable knowledge of the geography of India.

During the first century C.E., when Roman-financed ships reached the rich markets of southern India and Sri Lanka, Christianity may have accompanied them. Indian Christians today claim that their small group of about 2 million was founded by St. Thomas, one of Jesus' original 12 disciples, who may have sailed to India about 50 C.E. Thus the trade routes carried more than goods. They bore travelers, envoys, pilgrims, and missionaries. In an era when the Buddhist philosophy of India was spreading east and south into China and Southeast Asia, the Christian philosophy spawned in the Middle East was carried across the seas to India. Although Christian proselytizing met with very limited success in India, Buddhism made remarkable progress as it spread beyond the boundaries of the subcontinent.

The Balance of Trade

The balance of trade between East and West from ancient times until the early modern era tended to favor the East. As noted in Chapter 5, although Western trade with the East grew immensely in the first two centuries C.E., Roman exports such as wool, linen, glass, and metalware to the East did not match in value Rome's imports of silk, spices, perfumes, gems, and other luxuries. To make up the difference, gold and silver had continually to be exported to Asia. The discovery of large hoards of Roman coins in India seems to support claims that the Romans had to pay cash for some significant portion of their Indian goods.

Beginning in the third century, contacts between the East and the West gradually declined. India entered a period of change and transition after the Mauryan Empire fell, the Kushan Empire in northeast India collapsed, and the Han dynasty in China was overthrown. At the Western end of the trade routes, the Roman Empire's power was also circumscribed and the hegemony of the Romans challenged. These political upheavals disrupted cultural and commercial interchange but did not eliminate it entirely.

Conclusion

During India's formative age, three major religions were evolving on the subcontinent. Hinduism became the dominant social and religious force in India, with its notions of dharma allocated by caste.

Jainism fostered the notion of ahimsa (nonviolence), which would play a powerful role in the twentieth-century Indian independence movement. Buddhism challenged the Brahmin order and spread beyond the frontiers of India, ultimately to become a world religion. The great bulk of Indian thought seeks not to challenge the existing social order but to explain and justify it; duty (dharma) dominates. Individual rights and desires in this world are ideally overshadowed by the requirements of eternal salvation, and freedom means escape from the cycle of birth, death, and rebirth.

India is today the heir of one of the longest-living civilizations in the world. By the beginning of the third century C.E., this civilization had produced a set of religious, philosophical, and literary traditions that endures to the present day. Television broadcasts of the *Ramayana* and the *Mahabharata* have been enormously successful in India in recent years. In India, Rama and Sita remain as significant models for the virtuous male and female. Although the caste system has been challenged by the nation-state politics of modern India, it remains an essential element of Hindu identity: shaping social convention, determining political allegiance, and providing a framework for the practice of religion.

Suggestions for Reading

Romila Thapar, *A History of India*, Vol. 1 (Penguin, 1966), is an old standard for ancient India; a more recent one is Herman Kulke and Dietmar Rothermund, *A History of India* (Routledge, 1986). Stanley A. Wolpert, *A New History of India*, 5th ed. (Oxford University Press, 1997), is a brief but comprehensive history of ancient and modern India. Still valuable as an introduction to all aspects of pre-Islamic Indian civilization is A. L. Basham, *The Wonder That Was India*, rev. ed. (Sedgwich & Johnson, 1967); see also William W. Tarn, Frank Lee Holt, and M. C. J. Miller, *The Greeks in Bactria and India*, 3rd ed. (Ares, 1984); Mortimer Wheeler, *The Indus Civilization*, 3rd ed. (Cambridge University Press, 1968); and Emil Lengyel, *Asoka the Great: India's Royal Missionary* (Watts, 1969).

The standard geographical work is Joseph Schwartzberg, ed., *A Historical Atlas of South Asia*, 2nd ed. (Oxford University Press, 1992). On seafaring and India's trade, see Kenneth MacPherson, *The Indian Ocean* (Oxford University Press, 1998), and C. G. Simkin, *The Traditional Trade of Asia* (Oxford University Press, 1968). Robert E. Wheeler, *Rome Beyond the Imperial Frontiers* (Greenwood, 1972), is a study of Rome's trade with the East. See also L. Boulnois, *The Silk Road* (Allen & Unwin, 1963).

Edward Conze, *A Short History of Buddhism* (Allen & Unwin, 1980), is a good introduction. See also Edward J. Thomas, *The Life of Buddha as Legend and History* (Routledge, 1975); Richard H. Robinson, Willard L. Johnson, and Sandra A. Wawrytko, *The Buddhist Religion: A Historical Introduction*, 4th ed. (Wadsworth, 1996); T. W. Rhys Davids, trans., *Buddhist Suttas* (Dover, 1969); and John S. Strong, *The Experience of Buddhism* (Wadsworth, 1995).

On Hinduism, Basham's *Wonder That Was India* provides a good introduction; a concise treatment is Thomas Hopkins, *The Hindu Religious Tradition* (Dickenson, 1971); more informed by recent scholarship is Gavin Flood, *An Introduction to Hinduism* (Cambridge University Press, 1996); still good in many ways is Robert C. Zaehner, *Hinduism* (Oxford University Press, 1966). See also Ainslie Embree, ed., *Sources of Indian Tradition*, Vol. 1 2nd ed., (Columbia University Press, 1988); Wendy O'Flaherty, *Hindu Myths* (Penguin, 1975); and Padmini Sathianadhan Sengupta, *Everyday Life in Ancient India*, 2nd ed. (Oxford University Press, 1957). Also recommended are Pratima Bowes, *The Hindu Religious Tradition* (Routledge, 1978), a forceful statement of Hindu dynamic creativity until the Middle Ages; and Sarvepali Radhakrishnan, *The Hindu View of Life* (Allen & Unwin, 1980). W. Theodore de Bary, ed., *Sources of Indian Tradition* (Columbia University Press, 1958), contains a wide range of important texts with illuminating introductions.

On Indian literature, see *The Rig-Veda*, trans. Wendy O'Flaherty (Penguin, 1986); *Upanishads*, trans. Patrick Olivelle (Oxford University Press, 1996); and *The Laws of Manu*, trans. George Bühler (Dover, 1969). For the *Mahabharata*, see J. A. van Buitenen, ed. and trans., *The Mahabharata*, 3 vols. (University of Chicago Press, 1973–1978), and the theatrical adaptation by Jean-Claude Carrière, *The Mahabharata* (Harper & Row, 1985). The scholarly edition of the *Ramayana* is Robert P. Goldman et al., trans., *The Ramayana of Valmiki: An Epic of Ancient India*, 7 vols. (Princeton University Press, 1984–1998). See also Nigel Frith, *The Legend of Krishna* (Schocken, 1976). Tamil literature can be sampled in A. K. Ramanujan, trans., *The Interior Landscape: Love Poems from a Classical Tamil Anthology* (Indiana University Press, 1975); and R. Parthasarathy, *The Cilappatikāram* (Columbia University Press, 1993).

On Indian art, see Benjamin Rowland, *The Art and Architecture of India: Buddhist, Hindu, Jain*, 3rd ed. (Penguin, 1970); John Marshall, *The Buddhist Art of Gandhara* (Cambridge University Press, 1960); Heinrich Zimmer, *The Art of Indian Asia* (Princeton University Press, 1960); and W. G. Archer, *The Loves of Krishna in Indian Painting and Poetry* (New York: Grove Press, n.d.).

Suggestions for Web Browsing

Itihaas: Chronology—Ancient India
http://www.itihaas.com/ancient/index.html

> *Lengthy chronology of ancient India, 2700 B.C.E. to 1000 C.E.; most entries include subsites with text and images.*

India
http://www.dc.infi.net/~gunther/india/medieval.html

> *Site discussing the history, sites and monuments, and classical texts of India, 600 B.C. to 1256 C.E.*

Jainism
http://www.cs.colostate.edu/~malaiya/jainhlinks.html

> *Extensive site discusses the principles, traditions, and practices of Jainism and includes numerous related links.*

The Buddhist Age, 500 B.C.E. to 319 C.E.
http://www.stockton.edu/~gilmorew/consorti/1cindia.htm#religdone

> *Text and images detail Buddha's life, the Four Truths, and the evolution of Buddhism. Related links offer analyses of Buddhist texts and a lengthy list of primary texts.*

Hinduism
http://www.bcca.org/~cvoogt/Religion/hindu.html

> *Web page offering a number of sites about Hinduism, including a discussion of Veda, the Vedic culture, and its meaning in today's world, and excerpts from the* Bhagavad-Gita *and the* Rig-Veda.

The *Ramayana*: An Enduring Tradition
http://www.maxwell.syr.edu/maxpages/special/ramayana/

> *The* Ramayana *is one of the most important literary and oral texts of South Asia. This extensive site from Syracuse University offers both a short and complete story of Rama, history, images, and maps.*

Notes

1. Quoted in Vincent Smith, *The Oxford History of India* (Oxford: Oxford University Press, 1958), p. 131.
2. Quoted in Charles Drekmeier, *Kingship and Community in Early India* (Stanford, Calif.: Stanford University Press, 1962), p. 175.
3. *The Bhagavad-Gita*, trans. Barbara Stoler Miller (New York: Bantam, 1986), pp. 46–47.
4. *The Ramayana of Valmiki*, Vol. 1, trans. Robert P. Goldman (Princeton, N.J.: Princeton University Press, 1984), p. 121.
5. From *The Interior Landscape: Love Poems from a Classical Tamil Anthology*, trans. A. K. Ramanujan (Bloomington: Indiana University Press, 1975), p. 54.

The Middle Ages

After the "fall" of Rome, the great classical tradition was carried on for another thousand years without interruption in Constantinople, or "New Rome." Until it fell in 1453 the Byzantine Empire acted as a buffer for western Europe, staving off attack after attack from the east and projecting its civilization throughout eastern Europe and Russia.

The culminating series of attacks, resulting in the collapse of the empire, was launched by the adherents of Islam—a dynamic way of life developed by the followers of Muhammad, an eloquent prophet who instilled in his people a vital sense of their destiny to rule in the name of Allah. With unbelievable swiftness the followers of the Prophet became rulers of the Near East, swept across North Africa and surged into Spain, and expanded eastward to the frontiers of China.

The Muslims, the great middlemen of medieval times, shuttled back and forth across vast expanses, trading the wares of East and West and acting as the conveyors of culture, including their own. Throughout most of the Middle Ages the East outshone the West even as Constantinople and Baghdad outdazzled in material magnificence and intellectual and artistic triumphs the capitals of western Europe.

In Europe, after the decline of the Roman Empire, a painful search for stability began. Centuries of confusion followed until Charlemagne established a new "Roman" empire. This ambitious experiment was premature, however, and after its collapse a new system had to be created—one that would offer at least a minimum of security, political organization, and law enforcement. Under this system, called feudalism, the landed nobility acted as police force, judiciary, and army. Crude as it was, feudalism served to mitigate the chaos that followed the fall of Charlemagne's empire.

Yet the feudal system was inherently rural and rigid, and by the eleventh century new forces were at work. Shadowy outlines of new kingdoms—Germany, England, France, and Spain—began to emerge under the direction of vigorous monarchs. Europe went on the offensive, ejecting the Muslims from the southern part of the Continent, breaking Muslim control of the Mediterranean, and launching crusades to capture Jerusalem from the "infidels." The closed economy of the feudal countryside gave way before the revival of trade and communications, the growth of towns, the increased use of money as a medium of exchange, and the rise of a new class in society—the bourgeoisie.

Amidst all of this change, the greatest stabilizing force in Europe during the medieval period was the church. With the authority that stemmed from its vital spiritual service, the church provided the nearest approach to effective and centralized supervision of European life. The church was also the chief patron of poets and artists; its monasteries were repositories for precious manuscripts, and it fostered a new institution of learning—the university.

At the same time that Europe was experiencing dynamic cultural growth, sub-Saharan Africa was undergoing similar transformations. Indeed, Africans had created vibrant civilizations centuries before Europeans ventured beyond their coastal water. Africa gave birth to some of the earliest civilizations, Egypt and Nubia. Africans, however, lived in a variety of social and political systems, ranging from small-scale communities in which families met most of their own needs to large kingdoms, with hereditary rulers, elaborate bureaucracies, and extensive trading networks.

During the ten centuries commonly referred to as the Middle Ages in the West, great civilizations in India and China experienced their greatest flowering. In Gupta India the government was stable, and science and the arts flourished. Under the rule of the T'ang and Sung dynasties, Chinese life was enriched by notable creativity. Later, Mongol conquerors, beginning with Genghis Khan, put together the largest empire in the world, stretching west from China as far as Russia and Mesopotamia. Influenced greatly by China, the proud and independent Japanese developed a unique culture pattern characterized best by the *samurai*, the knight, and *bushido*, the code of the warrior.

The two American continents also created civilizations long before European explorers ventured across the Atlantic. As with their African counterparts, the American civilizations followed a sequence similar to that experienced in Eurasia. Agriculture became more diversified and with its increasing food surpluses was capable of supporting large cities, highly skilled crafts, expanding commerce, complex social structures, and the emergence of powerful states.

Just as theologians through the centuries have fought to under-stand Christ's message, so too have artists struggled to capture his image. This powerful mosaic of Christ at the Church of Chora in Istanbul was created in the first part of the fourteenth century. Its beauty and spirituality speak to all: believers and nonbelievers alike.

Christianity and the New Christian Romes

Byzantium, Eastern Europe, and Russia, 325–1500

Chapter Contents

At the same time that Caesar Augustus was laying the foundations of Rome's imperial greatness, Christianity was emerging in the distant Roman province of Judea. The contrast between the grandeur, power, and arrogance of the Romans and the poverty, idealism, and humility of the early Christians could not have been more dramatic.

Three centuries later, despite Diocletian's reforms, the western part of the Roman Empire faced extinction. Throughout the Mediterranean basin, Christianity flourished, especially in the East. After 325 the empire survived in Byzantium as a new, self-proclaimed Christian Rome, the "Second Rome."

Until the fifteenth century, the Byzantines first cooperated and after the eighth century competed in all areas with the Catholic Church, which gained strength after Rome "fell." Rome and Constantinople split eastern Europe into Roman Catholic and Orthodox zones in their combative missionary work, establishing the bases for centuries of Christians killing Christians. When the Ottoman Turks took Constantinople in 1453, the Russians proclaimed the new Christian Rome to be Moscow, the "Third Rome," the arena for the playing out of God's divine plan, the end of the world, and the second coming of Christ. The Russians affirmed that Moscow was the Third Rome, and there would be no other.

After Diocletian, ambitious Christian leaders ruled through the powerful fusion of Roman political, social, and military precedents with symbolism and

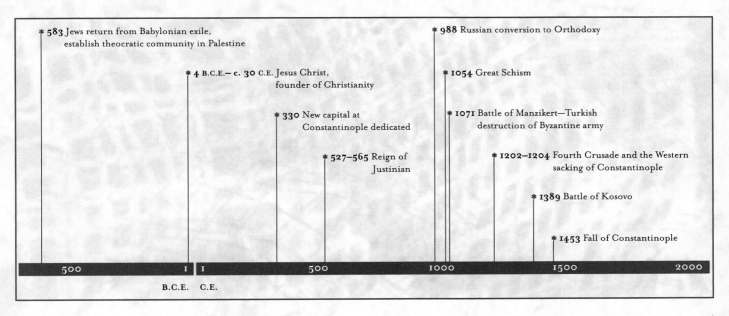

- **583** Jews return from Babylonian exile, establish theocratic community in Palestine
- **4** B.C.E.– c. **30** C.E. Jesus Christ, founder of Christianity
- **330** New capital at Constantinople dedicated
- **527–565** Reign of Justinian
- **988** Russian conversion to Orthodoxy
- **1054** Great Schism
- **1071** Battle of Manzikert—Turkish destruction of Byzantine army
- **1202–1204** Fourth Crusade and the Western sacking of Constantinople
- **1389** Battle of Kosovo
- **1453** Fall of Constantinople

| 500 | I | I | 500 | 1000 | 1500 | 2000 |

B.C.E.   C.E.

Christianity. Not until the development of modern political ideologies after the French Revolution did a more potent combination of theories and symbols help governments motivate and dominate their people.

The Rise and Triumph of Christianity

Following the conquests of Alexander the Great in the Near East, the Ptolemies and then the Seleucids ruled Palestine. After the Jews returned from exile in Babylonia in 538 B.C.E. (see Chapter 2), they created in Palestine a theocratic community based on God's law as recorded by Moses in the *Torah* and contained in the *Pentateuch*, the first five books of the Old Testament. Later they added to this record the teachings of the prophets and the writings of priests and scholars.

Jewish Foundations

Jewish religious life centered on the Temple at Jerusalem, which echoed with the cry "Hallelujah" ("Praise Yahweh") in thanksgiving for Yahweh's gracious dealings with his people. The most powerful figure there was the high priest, who was assisted by the Sanhedrin, the high court for the enforcement of the law. Since there was no distinction between civil and religious law, the jurisdiction of the Sanhedrin covered all aspects of Jewish life.

Jewish groups outside Palestine were linked by spiritual bonds to the Temple and to a law they be-

The Rise of Christianity

4 B.C.E.	Birth of Jesus Christ
c. 30 C.E.	Execution of Jesus Christ
c. 33	Paul begins spreading Christian doctrine
40–70	Writing of the Gospels
c. 65	Peter and Paul executed in Rome
325	Council of Nicaea
340–430	Great church fathers: Jerome, Ambrose, Augustine
440–461	Pontificate of Leo I, the Great
1054	Great, final schism between the Eastern and Western Church

lieved to be divinely inspired. But the Jews of the Diaspora, those who could not return to Palestine after the Babylonian exile, met in local *synagogues* (from the Greek word for "assembly") for public worship and instruction in the Scriptures. Eventually, the synagogue became the heart of Judaism, and it influenced the forms of worship in the Christian churches and the Muslim mosques.

During the Hellenistic Age, Greek influences were constantly at work among the Jews. Most Jews outside Palestine spoke Greek, and a Greek translation of the Hebrew Scriptures, called the *Septuagint* (from the Latin for "seventy"), was produced in Alexandria in the third century B.C.E. Greek influences, however, contributed to factionalism among the Jews in Judea. A radical, extremely pious group came to blows with the aristocratic pro-Greek Sadducees, as they came to be called, who were favored by the Seleucid rulers of Palestine.

In 168 B.C.E this internal conflict gave the Seleucid king, Antiochus IV, an opportunity to intervene and attempt to Hellenize the Jews. He ordered their Temple dedicated to the worship of Zeus. Viewing this decree as a desecration, the Jews rebelled. Under the leadership of Judas Maccabaeus, they rededicated the Temple to Yahweh and in 142 B.C.E. won their independence from the Seleucids. Although Judas and his immediate successors took the title of high priest, later members of the family claimed to be kings. In time these rulers became worldly and corrupt; factionalism flared up again, resulting in persecution and bloodshed.

It was in the midst of a civil war that the Roman legions first made their appearance. Pompey, who was then completing his pacification of Asia Minor and Syria, took advantage of the plea for assistance from one of the factions and ended the civil war in 63 B.C.E. He made Judea subject to the Roman governor of Syria. Eventually, Herod the Great, a half-Jewish, half-Arab leader from Edom, just south of Judea, rose to power as a tool of the Romans. Appointed by Mark Antony, Herod served as king of Judea from 37 to 4 B.C.E. He erected a magnificent palace, a theater, and a hippodrome, and he rebuilt the Temple on a lavish scale. To the Jews, however, Herod remained as a detested usurper who used Judaism as a matter of expediency.

Soon after Herod's death, Judea became a minor Roman province ruled by governors called *procurators*. The best-known procurator was Pontius Pilate, who ruled from 26 to 36 C.E. and under whose government Jesus was crucified. The Jews themselves remained unhappy and divided under Roman domination. For centuries the prophets had taught that God would one day, when righteousness prevailed, create a new Israel under a God-anointed leader, the Messiah. Many Jews lost hope in a political Messiah and an earthly kingdom and instead conceived of a spiritual Messiah who would lead all the righteous, including the resurrected dead, to a spiritual kingdom.

Development of Jewish Religious Thought

Through centuries of suffering, captivity, and subjugation, the Jews had been taught by a succession of prophets and priests to hold their covenant with Yahweh and to safeguard their religious inheritance. In the centuries just preceding and following the birth of Christ, the Sadducees, Pharisees, and Essenes pursued that inheritance in different ways. These theological complexities mirrored cultural, social, and economic differences within the Jewish community.

The aristocratic Sadducees, who controlled the office of high priest, stood for strict adherence to the Torah. The more numerous Pharisees believed that with divine guidance, human beings could modify and amend the law. They accepted belief in personal immortality and the kingdom of heaven. From their ranks came the *rabbis*, scholars who expounded the law and applied it to existing conditions. The "oral law" developed by the Pharisees became the core of the later *Talmud*, the great commentary on Jewish law that laid down a detailed code of daily living for Jews. After the destruction of the Temple and the end of the high priesthood, the rabbinical schools of the Pharisees ensured that Judaism would endure.

The discovery of the Dead Sea Scrolls in 1947 added to modern knowledge of the Essenes, the probable base of the Christian faith. While exploring caves around the desolate western shore of the Dead Sea, two Bedouin boys came across several clay jars containing long manuscripts wrapped in linen. Many more scrolls were later found in other caves. Nearby were the ruins of a monastery built by the Essenes, a militant communal group, "to separate themselves," as the scrolls state, "from the abode of perverse men." Occupied between the second century B.C.E. and 68 C.E., the monastery was destroyed by the Romans during the great Jewish revolt of 66–70 C.E. (see p. 174). Prior to its destruction, the Essenes hid their manuscripts in the caves. Some scrolls are portions of the Old Testament dating from the first century B.C.E. The scrolls that describe the Essene sect in that era have been said to constitute "a whole missing chapter of the history of the growth of religious ideas between Judaism and Christianity."[1]

The Essenes' founder, a shadowy figure known as the Righteous Teacher, suffered persecution and perhaps martyrdom late in the second century B.C.E. His followers considered themselves the true remnant of God's people, preached a "new covenant," and awaited the time when God would destroy the pow-

The partially unrolled Thanksgiving Scroll, one of the Dead Sea Scrolls, preserved at the Hebrew University in Jerusalem, is composed of religious hymns that poetically develop the Essenes' theological doctrines.

ers of evil and inaugurate his kingdom. Similar views concerning the transition from the "Old Age" to the "New Age" were held by many other Jews and later by Christians. Some scholars have attached much significance to common elements in the beliefs and practices of the Essenes and the early Christians. John the Baptist, who baptized Jesus and whom Jesus viewed as the herald of a message from God, may have been a member of the Essene sect.

The Life and Teaching of Jesus

Whatever its parallels with the Essene sect, including baptism and communal meals, the Jewish sect that became Christianity bears the unmistakable imprint of the personality of its founder, Jesus of Nazareth. According to the biblical accounts pieced together from the four Gospels, he was born in Bethlehem during Herod's reign; therefore, he must have been born by the time of Herod's death in 4 B.C.E. rather than in the year that traditionally begins the Christian or Common Era, 1 C.E. After spending the first years of his adult life as a carpenter in the village of Nazareth, Jesus began a three-year mission, preaching love for one's fellow human beings and urging people to turn away from sin because "the kingdom of heaven is near" (Matthew 4:17).

Reports of Jesus' teaching and his "mighty works" miracles such as casting out demons, healing the sick, raising the dead, and walking on water spread among the Jews as he and his 12 apostles traveled from village to village in Palestine. When he came to Jerusalem to observe the feast of the Passover, huge crowds greeted him enthusiastically as the promised Messiah. But Jesus preached a spiritual, not an earthly, kingdom, and when some of the radicals saw that he had no intention of leading a nationalistic movement against the Romans, they turned against him. Other attacks on him were as much social and political as theological. His enemies included the moneylenders, whom he had denounced; the Pharisees, who resented his repudiation of their minute regulations of daily behavior; the people who considered him a disturber of the status quo; and some who saw him as a blasphemer of Yahweh.

Betrayed by Judas, one of his apostles, Jesus was condemned by the Sanhedrin for blasphemy "because he claimed to be the Son of God" (John 19:7). Before the procurator Pontius Pilate, however, Jesus was charged with treason for claiming to be the king of the Jews:

> *"Are you the king of Jews?" he [Pilate] asked him. . . . Jesus answered, "My kingdom does not belong to this world; if my kingdom belonged to this world, my followers would fight to keep me from being handed over to the Jews. No, my kingdom does not belong here. . . . You say that I am a king. I was born and came into the world for this one purpose, to speak about the truth. Whoever belongs to the truth listens to me." (John 18:33–38)*

Pilate was a professional Roman official. He wanted to maintain the calm and ordered province so desired by his masters in Rome. The theological controversy did not matter to him, but the possibility of massive civil disorder did. Jesus was condemned to the death that Rome inflicted on enemies of the state: crucifixion after a brutal whipping.

The End of the Jewish Polity, 66–70 C.E.

In the generation after Jesus' crucifixion, a group of ardent Jewish nationalists, known as Zealots, called for the use of force to drive the Romans out of "God's land." The atmosphere had been poisoned by incidents such as the following, reported by the contemporary Jewish collaborationist historian Josephus:

> *The people had assembled in Jerusalem for the Feast of Unleavened Bread [Passover], and the Roman cohort stood on guard over the Temple colonnade, armed men always being on duty at the feasts to forestall any riot-ing by the vast crowds. One of the soldiers pulled up his garment and bent over indecently turning his backside towards the Jews and making a noise as indecent as his attitude. This infuriated the whole crowd, who noisily appealed to Cumanus [the procurator] to punish the soldier, while the less restrained of the young men and the naturally tumultuous section of the people rushed into battle, and snatching up stones hurled them at the soldiers. Cumanus, fearing the whole population would rush at him, sent for more heavy infantry.[2]*

In 66 C.E. violence erupted into war after the Zealots massacred a small Roman garrison at Jerusalem. After a five-month siege of Jerusalem in 70 C.E., Titus, son of the emperor Vespasian, laid waste to most of the city. Only a small part of the Temple complex, what came to be called the "Wailing Wall," remained standing. It was later prophesied that a third Temple would be erected there when the Messiah came. The Dome of the Rock, a mosque built by the Muslims, has occupied the site since the eighth century C.E. The wholesale destruction of Jerusalem in 70 C.E. marked the end of the Hebrew state, although the fortress of Masada near the Dead Sea held out for two more years. The Jewish dream of an independent homeland was to remain unrealized for almost 19 centuries, until the State of Israel was proclaimed in 1948.

The Work of Paul

With Jesus' death it seemed as though his cause had been exterminated. No written message had been left behind, and his few loyal followers were disheartened. Yet his martyrdom gave impetus to the new religion he inspired. Word soon spread that Jesus had been seen alive after his crucifixion and had spoken to his disciples, giving them solace and reassurance. At first there were few converts in Palestine, but the Hellenized Jews living in foreign lands, in contact with new ideas and modes of living, were less firmly committed to traditional Jewish doctrines. The new faith first made real headway among the Jewish communities in such cities as Damascus, Antioch (where its followers were first called "Christians" by the Greeks), Corinth, and Rome.

The followers of Jesus, like their master, had no thought of breaking away from Judaism. They sought only to pursue the inheritance of their faith spiritually and ethically. Because they adhered to the requirements of the Jewish law, their new message did not easily attract non-Jews. Paul removed this obstacle through his more liberal and cosmopolitan preachings. Because of his influence, he has been called the second founder of Christianity.

Born Saul, of Jewish ancestry but a Roman citizen by birth, and raised in the cosmopolitan city of Tarsus, in Asia Minor, Paul possessed a wide knowledge of Greek culture. He was also a strict Pharisee who considered Christians to be traitors to the sacred law and took an active part in their persecution. One day about 33 C.E., while traveling to Damascus to squelch the Christian community there, Saul had an experience that changed his life. He explained:

As I was traveling and coming near Damascus, about midday a bright light suddenly flashed from the sky around me. I fell to the ground and heard a voice saying to me, "Saul, Saul! Why do you persecute me?" "Who are you, Lord?" I asked. "I am Jesus of Nazareth, whom you persecute," he said to me. The men with me saw the light but did not hear the voice of the one who was speaking to me. I asked, "What shall I do, Lord?" and the Lord said to me, "Get up and go into Damascus, and there you will be told everything that God has determined for you." (Acts 22:6–10)

Saul, henceforth known by the Roman name Paul, turned from being a persecutor into the greatest of Christian missionaries.

Paul taught that Jesus was the Christ (from the Greek *Christos*, "Messiah"), the Son of God, and that he had died to atone for the sins of all people. Only faith in the saving power of Jesus Christ was necessary for the salvation of Jews and Gentiles (non-Jews) alike. Adherence to the complexities of the Jewish law was unnecessary.

A man is put right with God only through faith in Jesus Christ, never by doing what the Law requires. . . . So there is no difference between Jews and Gentiles, between slaves and freemen, between men and women; you are all one in union with Christ Jesus. (Galatians 2:16, 3:28)

After covering 8000 miles teaching and preaching, Paul was put to death in Rome about 65 C.E., the same year as Peter, founder of the church at Rome during the reign of Nero. By this time Christian communities had been established in all important cities in the East and at Rome. Paul performed a very important service to these infant communities of believers by instructing them, either through visits or letters, in the fundamental beliefs of the new religion. He served as an authority by which standardization of belief could be achieved.

Reasons for the Spread of Christianity

The popular mystery religions that the Romans had embraced from Greece and the Near East during the troubled last century of the Republic gave spiritual

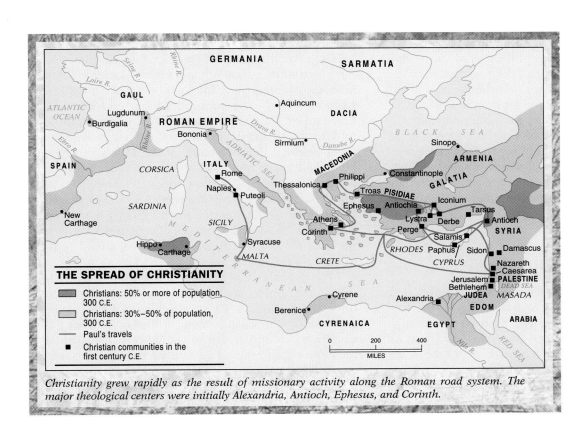

Christianity grew rapidly as the result of missionary activity along the Roman road system. The major theological centers were initially Alexandria, Antioch, Ephesus, and Corinth.

satisfaction not provided by Rome's early ritualistic forms of worship. These mystery religions included the worship of the Phrygian Cybele, the Great Mother *(Magna Mater);* the Egyptian Isis, sister and wife of Osiris; the Greek Dionysus, called Bacchus by the Romans; and the Persian sun-god Mithras, the intermediary between humans and Ahura-Mazda, the great Lord of Light, whose sacred day of worship was called Sunday and from whose cult women were excluded. Common to all the mystery religions were the notions of a divine savior and the promise of everlasting life.

Followers of these mystery cults found Christian beliefs and practices familiar enough to convert easily to the new faith. But Christianity had far more to offer than the mystery religions did. Its founder was not a creature of myth, like the gods and goddesses of the mystery cults, but a real person whose lofty ethical teachings were preserved in detail in a unique record, the New Testament, which also included accounts of his death and resurrection as the divine incarnation of God. Shared with the Jews was the concept of a single omnipotent God, the jealous yet loving God of the Hebrew Scriptures, now the God of all humanity. Moreover, Christianity was a dynamic, aggressive faith. It upheld the equality of all people—rich and poor, slave and freeborn, male and female. Women were among Jesus' audiences, and Paul's letters give much evidence of women active in the early church. One of Jesus' helpers was Mary Magdalene, the repentant prostitute. According to the so-called Gnostic Gospels, which the church declared heretical in the early fourth century and ordered destroyed, "Christ loved her more than all the disciples."[3]

Christianity taught that God, the loving Father, had sent his only Son to atone for human sins and offered a vision of immortality and an opportunity to be "born again," cleansed of sin. Its converts were bound together by faith and hope, and they took seriously their obligation of caring for orphans, widows, and other unfortunates. The courage with which they faced death and persecution impressed even their bitterest enemies.

Persecution of the Christians

The Roman government tolerated any religion that did not threaten the safety or tranquillity of the empire. Christianity, however, was perceived as a subversive danger to society and the state. Christians as monotheists refused to offer sacrifice to the state cults on behalf of the emperor—not even a few grains of incense cast upon an altar. Offering sacrifice to the state cults was considered an essential patriotic rite uniting all Roman subjects in common loyalty to the imperial government. For Christians, however, there was only one God: they could sacrifice to no others. In the eyes of many Roman officials, this attitude branded them as traitors.

To the Romans, the Christians were a secret antisocial group forming a state within a state—"walling themselves off from the rest of mankind," as a pagan writer observed. Many were pacifists who refused to serve in the army, and all were intolerant of other religious sects and refused to associate with pagans or take part in social functions that they considered sinful or degrading.

During the first two centuries after Jesus' crucifixion, persecution of Christians was sporadic and local, such as that at Rome under Nero. But during the late third and fourth centuries, when the empire was in danger of collapse, three organized efforts were launched to suppress Christianity throughout the empire. By far the longest and most systematic campaign against the Christians, who now comprised perhaps one-tenth of the population, was instigated by the emperor Diocletian from 303 to 311. He stringently imposed the death penalty on anyone who refused to sacrifice to Roman gods. But the inspired defiance of the Christian martyrs, who seemed to welcome death, could not be overcome. "The blood of the martyrs is the seed of the church" became a Christian rallying cry.

Official Recognition and Acceptance

In 311 the emperor Galerius recognized that persecution had failed and issued an edict of toleration making Christianity a legal religion in the East. Two years later Constantine and Lucinius granted Christians freedom of worship throughout the empire. Why Constantine did this is a question historians continue to debate. His Christian biographers assert that the night before a decisive battle at the Milvian Bridge, he looked to the night sky and saw a cross with the words *"Hoc vinces"* ("By this, conquer") written on it. The next day, after a night in which Christ appeared in his dreams, Constantine led his troops to victory, raising the cross as his symbol. Thereafter, Constantine and his mother, Helena, remained deeply committed to Christianity.

It is probable that his decision to move the political capital from Rome to the East to escape the traditions and factions of Rome also played a role in his embrace of Christianity, along with the fact that the Christians, at 20 percent of the empire, constituted the most organized and galvanized part of the population. His actions at the Council of Nicaea (see p. 179) as a self-proclaimed "thirteenth apostle" showed that the Christian Church was to be his state church. He waited until just before his death to be baptized, and all of his successors but one were Christian.

This colossal head of Constantine captures the emperor's vision of himself as a man in close contact with God.

The sole exception was Julian the Apostate (361–363), a military hero and scholar who had been raised a Christian but then renounced his faith and sought to revive paganism. But Julian did not persecute the Christians, and his efforts to revive paganism failed.

The emperor Theodosius I (379–395) made Christianity the official religion of the empire. Henceforth paganism was persecuted, and even the Olympic Games were suppressed. One famous victim of this persecution *by* Christians was the philosopher Hypatia, who in 415 was killed by a Christian mob in Alexandria. By the age of 25 she had become famous throughout the eastern half of the empire as a lecturer on Greek philosophy. Her popularity and beauty aroused the resentment of Cyril, the archbishop of Alexandria, who had already led a mob in destroying the homes and businesses of the city's Jews. He now incited the mob to abduct Hypatia. She was dragged into a nearby church and hacked to death.

Church Organization

Viewing the present world as something that would end quickly with the imminent second coming of Christ and the last judgment of the living and the dead, the early Christians saw no need to build a formal religious bureaucracy. But after it became clear that the second coming would not be immediate, a church organization emerged to manage the day-to-day business of defining, maintaining, and spreading the faith.

At first there was little or no distinction between laity and clergy. Traveling teachers visited Christian communities, preaching and giving advice. But the steady growth in the number of Christians made necessary special church officials who could devote all their time to religious work, clarifying the body of Christian doctrine, conducting services, and collecting money for charitable purposes.

The earliest officials were called *presbyters* ("elders") or *bishops* ("overseers"). By the second century the offices of bishop and presbyter had become distinct. Churches in villages near the main church, which was usually located in a city, were administered by *priests* (a term derived from *presbyter*), who were responsible to a bishop. Thus evolved the *diocese*, a territorial administrative division under the jurisdiction of a bishop. The bishops were recognized as the direct successors of the apostles and, like them, the guardians of Christian teaching and traditions.

A number of dioceses made up a *province*. The bishop of the most important city in each province enjoyed more prestige than his fellows and was known as an *archbishop* or *metropolitan*. The provinces were grouped into larger administrative divisions called *patriarchates*. The title of *patriarch* was applied to the bishop of such great cities as Rome, Constantinople, and Alexandria.

The bishop of Rome rose to a position of preeminence in the hierarchy of the church. At first only one of several patriarchs, the Roman bishop gradually became recognized as the leader of the church in the West and was given the title of *pope*, from the Greek word for "father." Many factors explain the emergence of the papacy at Rome. As the largest city in the West and the capital of the empire, Rome had an aura of prestige that was transferred to its bishop. After political Rome had fallen, religious Rome remained. When the empire in the West collapsed in the fifth century, the bishop of Rome emerged as a stable and dominant figure looked up to by all. The primacy of Rome was fully evident during the pontificate of Leo I, the Great (440–461), who provided both the leadership that saved Italy from invasion by the Huns and the major theoretical support for papal leadership of the church, the Petrine theory. This doctrine held that since Peter, whom Jesus had made leader of the apostles, was the first bishop of Rome, his authority over all

This World or the Other World

Six years after Alaric's sacking of Rome in 410, Rutilius Namatianus, a man still faithful to his pagan past, retired as prefect of the city of Rome and returned by sea to his home in Romanized Gaul. Passing a Christian monastery on the shore, he recalls that a young man of great promise, because of some "madness," had left "the lands and company of men" to become a monk and was now "buried here alive."

And in the middle of the water rises
The isle of Gorgon, with the Pisan coast
On one side, that of Cyrnos on the other.
And opposite, a rock that held for me
A memory of lately suffered loss:
A man of my own city, buried here
Alive; a youth of noble ancestors
And matching them in marriage and estate.

At least, he was. A madness came upon him
To leave the lands and company of men
And go to exile and ignominy
Among the shades. Poor, superstitious fool,
To think uncleanliness is godliness
And bring more savage torments on himself
Than heaven in its anger could devise.

Paulinus of Nola (c. 355–431) provides an answer to Rutilius's anguished question "Why!" The governor of a Roman province before he was 30, Paulinus gave up his post and his vast estates in Gaul, Spain, and Italy to become a humble Christian priest at Nola, in Italy.

Not that they beggared be in mind, or brutes,
That they have chosen their dwelling place afar
In lonely places: but their eyes are turned
To the high stars, the very deep of Truth.
Freedom they seek, an emptiness apart
From worthless hopes: din of the marketplace,
And all the noisy crowding up of things,
And whatsoever wars on the divine,
At Christ's command and for His love, they hate;
By faith and hope they follow after God,
And know their quest shall not be desperate,
If but the Present conquer not their souls

With hollow things: that which they see they spurn
That they may come at what they do not see,
Their senses kindled like a torch, that may
Blaze through the secrets of eternity.
The transient's open, everlastingness
Denied our sight; yet still by hope we follow
The vision that our minds have seen, despising
The shows and forms of things, the loveliness
Soliciting for ill our mortal eyes.
The present's nothing: but eternity
Abides for those on whom all truth, all good,
Hath shone, in one entire and perfect light.

From Peter D. Arnott, *The Romans and Their World* (New York: St. Martin's Press, 1970), p. 310; and Helen Waddell, *Medieval Latin Lyrics* (London: Constable, 1929), p. 35.

Christians was handed on to his successors at Rome. The church in the East, insisting on the equality of all the apostles, never accepted the Petrine theory. In the West, the Roman Catholic Church served as the "midwife" of Europe as the next stage of history emerged from the ruins of classical Rome.

Pagan writers saw imperial Rome's fall as the consequence of abandoning ancient gods. St. Augustine (354–430), at the time bishop of Hippo in *The City of God*, argued against this point of view and asserted that history unfolds according to God's design. Rome's fall was part of the divine plan, "the necessary and fortunate preparation for the triumph of the heavenly city where man's destiny was to be attained." The Christians, against whom Diocletian launched his most savage attacks, survived, prospered, and laid their claim to the future. They spread their doctrines along the Roman communications links, established their command posts in the Roman administrative centers, and converted Roman citizens to their faith.

Foundations of Christian Doctrine and Worship

While the administrative structure of the church adapted to changing conditions in the West, a combination of theologians and churchly politicians defined and systematized Christian beliefs, sometimes by arbitrary means. This process of fixing Christian doctrine, or *dogma*, began with Paul, who stressed Jesus' divinity and explained his death as an atonement for the sins of all humanity.

In time, differences of opinion over doctrinal matters caused many controversies. One of the most important was over a belief called Arianism. At issue was the relative position of the three persons of the Trinity: God the Father, God the Son, and God the Holy Spirit. The view that Father and Son were equal was vigorously denied by Arius (256–336), a priest from Alexandria. He believed that Christ logically could not fully be God because he was not of a substance identical with God and, as a created being, was not coeternal with his creator. The controversy became so serious that in 325 the emperor Constantine convened the first ecumenical church council to resolve the problem. This Council of Nicaea was the first of nine "world" councils in early church history. With Constantine presiding, the council branded Arian belief a *heresy*—an opinion or doctrine contrary to the official teaching of the church—and Christ was declared to be of the same substance as God, uncreated and coeternal with him. This mystical concept of the Trinity, essential to the central Christian doctrine of the *incarnation*—God becoming man in Christ—received official formulation in the Nicene Creed. However, Arius's views found acceptance among the Germans, and his version of the doctrine of the Trinity was adopted throughout Europe and North Africa.

The liturgy of the early churches was plain and simple, consisting of prayer, Scripture reading, hymns, and preaching. Early Christians worshiped God and sought salvation through individual efforts. Following the growth of church organization and proclamation of official dogma, however, the church came to be viewed as the indispensable intermediary between God and humans. Without the church, the individual could not hope for salvation.

The development of the church's dogma owed much to the church fathers of the second through fifth centuries. Since most of them were intellectuals who came to Christianity by way of Neo-Platonism and Stoicism, they maintained that Greek philosophy and Christianity were compatible. Because reason (*logos* in Greek) and truth came from God, "philosophy was a preparation," wrote Clement of Alexandria (d. 215), "paving the way toward perfection in Christ," the latest and most perfect manifestation of God's reason. Thus Christianity was viewed as a superior philosophy that could supersede all pagan philosophies and religions.

In the West three church fathers stood out. The scholarship of Jerome (340–420) made possible the church-authorized translation of the Bible into Latin. In a revised form, it is still the official translation of the Roman Catholic Church. Jerome, who was canonized for his work, also justified Christian use of the literature and learning of the classical world. Why should not the Christian take what was good from the pagans, he argued, since the Hebrews had taken "spoil" from Egypt when they fled from Egyptian bondage (Exodus 3:22)?

Another of the church fathers, St. Ambrose (340–397), resigned his government post to become bishop of Milan, where he employed his great administrative skills to establish a model bishopric. By criticizing the actions of the strong emperor Theodosius I and forcing him to do public penance, Ambrose was the first to assert the church's superiority over the state in spiritual matters.

St. Augustine was the most important of all the church fathers. At the age of 32, as he relates in his *Confessions,* one of the world's great autobiographies, he found in Christianity the answer to his long search for meaning in life. Before, he had shared the doubts of men "who rush hither and thither, to this side or that, according as they are driven by the impulse of erratic opinion." Now, "by the pity, mercy, and help of God," he had come to anchor in Christianity. "What man shall teach another to understand this?" Augustine asked. No one can teach him; he must come to it on his own after much travail: "This must be asked of you, sought in you, knocked for at you; thus only shall it be received, thus shall it be found, thus shall it be opened to us."[4] Here Augustine echoes the views expressed by many church fathers, that "Christians are not born but made." He blended classical logic and philosophy with Christian belief to lay the foundation of much of the church's theology.

The Regular Clergy

The secular clergy moved through the world (*saeculum*) administering the church's services and communicating its teachings to the laity. But another type of clergy also arose: the regular clergy, so called because they lived by a rule (*regula*) within monasteries. These monks sought seclusion from the distractions of this world in order to prepare themselves for the next. In so doing, they helped preserve and spread the heritage of the classical world along with the faith.

The monastic way of life was older than Christianity, having existed among the Essenes. Christian ascetics, who had abandoned worldly life to live as hermits, could be found in the East as early as the third century C.E. They pursued spiritual perfection by denying their physical feelings, torturing themselves, and fasting. In Syria, for example, St. Simeon Stylites sat for 33 years atop a 60-foot-high pillar. A disciple then beat his record by three months.

In a more moderate expression of asceticism, Christian monks in Egypt developed a monastic life in which, seeking a common spiritual goal, they lived together under a common set of regulations. St. Basil (330–379), a Greek bishop in Asia Minor, drew up a rule based on work, charity, and a communal life that still allowed each monk to retain most of his independence. The Rule of St. Basil became the standard system in the eastern church.

In the West the work of St. Benedict (c. 480–543) paralleled St. Basil's efforts in the East. About 529

Benedict led a band of followers to a high hill between Rome and Naples, named Monte Cassino, where they erected a monastery on the site of an ancient pagan temple. For his monks Benedict composed a rule that gave order and discipline to western monasticism. Benedictine monks took three basic vows—of poverty, chastity, and obedience to the *abbot,* the head of the monastery. The daily activities of the Benedictine monks were closely regulated: they participated in eight divine services, labored in fields or workshops for six or seven hours, and spent about two hours studying and preserving the writing of Latin antiquity at a time when illiteracy was widespread throughout western Europe. Benedictine monasticism was to be the most dynamic civilizing force in medieval Europe between the sixth and twelfth centuries.

Women played an important role in monastic Christianity. In Egypt an early-fifth-century bishop declared that 20,000 women—twice the number of men—were living in desert communities as nuns. In the West several fourth-century biographies of aristocratic women describe how they turned their villas and palaces into monasteries for women of all classes and remained firmly in control of their institutions. These communities became famous for their social and educational services, in addition to providing a different way of life for women who sought alternatives to the usual pattern of marriage, motherhood, and subordination to men.

Byzantium: The Shining Fortress

Constantine the Great had carefully selected the site of his new Roman capital in 325. He chose a site on the frontier of Europe and Asia, dominating the waterway connecting the Mediterranean and Black Seas and protected on three sides by cliffs. The emperors fortified the fourth side with an impenetrable three-wall network. In the first two centuries Visigoths, Huns, and Ostrogoths unsuccessfully threatened the city. In the seventh, eighth, and ninth centuries first Persians, then Arab forces, and finally Bulgarians besieged but failed to take Constantinople. The fortress city withstood all assaults, with the exception of the Fourth Crusade, until 1453.

Constantinople survived more than a thousand years because of the security and wealth provided by its setting. The city was a world trade center that enjoyed the continuous use of a money economy—in contrast to the barter system found in the West after the fifth century. Its wealth and taxes supported a strong military force and financed an effective gov-

	Byzantium
325	Constantine the Great establishes capital in Constantinople (city dedicated May 11, 330)
361–363	Reign of Julian the Apostate
527–565	Reign of Justinian
c. 590	Slavic invasions begin
610–641	Heraclius saves Constantinople, defeats Persians
674–678; 717	Arab seiges of Constantinople
842-1071	Golden Age of Byzantium
1071	Byzantine defeat at Manzikert
1096	First Crusade
1204	Fourth Crusade; Byzantium disappears until 1261
1354	Turks begin to settle in Europe
1453	Fall of Constantinople, end of East Roman Empire

ernment. The city built excellent sewage and water systems that permitted an extremely high standard of living. Food was abundant, with grain from Egypt and Anatolia and fish from the Aegean. Constantinople could feed a million people at a time when it was difficult to find a city in Europe able to sustain more than 50,000.

Unlike Rome, Constantinople had several industries producing luxury goods, military supplies, hardware, and textiles. Until Justinian's reign (527–565), all raw silk had been imported from China, but after silkworms were smuggled out of China about 550 C.E., silk production flourished and became a profitable state monopoly. The state paid close attention to business, controlling the economy through a system of guilds to which all tradesmen and members of professions belonged; setting wages, profits, work hours, and prices; and even organizing bankers and doctors into compulsory corporations.

This security and wealth encouraged an active political, cultural, and intellectual life. The widespread literacy and education among men and women of various segments of society would not be matched in Europe until eighteenth-century Paris. Whether in its Latin, Roman phase, which lasted to the seventh century, or in its Greek, Byzantine phase, which continued to 1453, the empire remained a shining fortress, attracting both invaders and merchants.

The Latin Phase

The eastern capital had to fight for its life against the same invaders who eventually brought down the Roman Empire in the West. However, the dream of reclaiming the Mediterranean basin and reestablishing the empire to its former glory did not die until the end of the reign of Justinian. Aided by his forceful wife, Theodora, and a corps of competent assistants, he made long-lasting contributions to Byzantine and Western civilization but gained only short-term successes in his foreign policy.

In the 520s and 530s Justinian carried out a massive project of urban renewal throughout the empire after earthquakes devastated much of his realm. He strengthened the walls defending Constantinople and built the monumental Hagia Sophia, which still stands. Forty windows circle the base of its dome, producing a quality of light that creates the illusion that the ceiling is floating.

Justinian also reformed the government and ordered a review of all Roman law. This project led to the publication of the Code of Justinian, a digest of Roman and church law, texts, and other instructional materials that became the foundation of modern Western law. Following Constantine's example, he saw himself as the thirteenth apostle and participated actively in the religious arguments of his day.

Justinian's expensive and ambitious projects triggered massive violence among the political gangs of Constantinople, the circus crowds of the Greens and the Blues.[5] Since ancient times, competing factions formed groups throughout the Mediterranean, push-

Hagia Sophia remains intact today, and visitors can share the awe of the Russians who visited the structure in the tenth century and said, "We knew not whether we were in heaven or on earth."

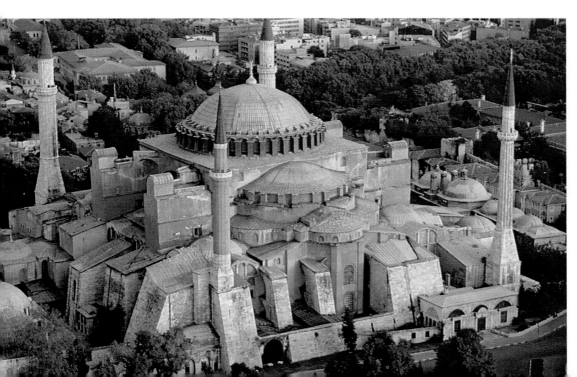

Hagia Sophia (Church of the Holy Wisdom) in Constantinople is considered the architectural masterpiece of the Byzantine Empire. The crowning glory of the church, built during Justinian's reign, was its huge dome, abutted at both ends by a half-dome. The mosaics, painted over when the Ottomans captured the city in 1453, have now been partially restored. The four minarets were added in the fifteenth century.

Discovery Through Maps

A Sixth-Century Map: The Madaba Mosaic

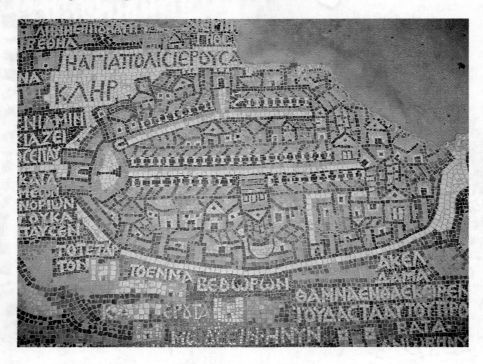

During the first part of Justinian's reign a series of earthquakes shattered buildings around the eastern Mediterranean. The emperor, who had a full treasury, embarked on a massive reconstruction program that adhered to a classical style that was copied all over the empire, even in places that had not suffered from natural disasters. One of the most impressive results of this architectural explosion was Hagia Sophia Church in Constantinople (see p. 181). Another, more subtle but equally revealing, was the Madaba mosaic map, found in present-day Jordan.

Just as Hagia Sophia spoke volumes about the wealth and power of the Christian church, this map, roughly 50 feet by 18 feet, gives remarkable detail about the eastern part of the empire. More than 150 places in present-day Israel, Jordan, Saudi Arabia, Syria, Lebanon, and part of Egypt—the area of the 12 biblical tribes, or the boundaries of Canaan promised to Abraham—are identified, along with an accurate portrayal of the roads, rivers, deserts, seas, and mountains of the region. Unlike modern maps, which are constructed with a north-south orientation, this map points to the east—toward the altar. The importance of a town can be seen by the way it is described—a small town is depicted as having a small church, whereas the unique qualities of the larger places such as Jerusalem are given more elaborate representations.

There are also other details, such as precise illustrations of places mentioned in the Bible, palm trees to indicate oases, and points at which to cross rivers on foot or by ferry boat. It is obvious that the mosaic map profited from the accounts of travelers. The care with which the unique qualities of various sites are illustrated shows that the map had more than just a decorative function: it was also to be used by Christians making pilgrimages—both those from the West and locally.

ing for their own economic, social, and religious goals. Much like contemporary urban gangs, they moved about in groups and congregated at public events. Arguments over the nature of the Trinity divided the Blues and Greens and sparked fights in the streets. A general dislike of Justinian's wife, Theodora, the daughter of a circus animal trainer—a background that made her a virtual untouchable in polite society—provided another point of contention. Her enemies believed that she behaved in an outrageous manner, espoused a heretical variant of Christianity, and had too much control over her husband.

In Constantinople the circus took place in the Hippodrome, a structure that could hold 80,000 spectators. It served as the location for contests of various types, such as chariot races, and the Blues and the Greens could usually be found backing opposing drivers. Usually, the gangs neutralized each other's efforts. In 532, however, the Blues and the Greens joined forces to try to force Justinian from the throne. The so-called Nika rebellion, named after the victory cry of the rioters, almost succeeded. We know from Procopius's *Secret Histories* that Justinian was on the verge of running away until Theodora stopped him and told the frightened emperor:

> I do not choose to flee. Those who have worn the crown should never survive its loss. Never shall I see the day when I am not saluted as empress. If you mean to flee, Caesar, well and good. You have the money, the ships are ready, the sea is open. As for me, I shall stay.[6]

Assisted by his generals, the emperor remained and bloodily put the rebellion down.

Justinian momentarily achieved his dream of reestablishing the Mediterranean rim of the Roman Empire. To carry out his plan to regain the half of the empire lost to the Germanic invaders, Justinian first had to buy the neutrality of the Persian kings who threatened not only Constantinople but also Syria and Asia Minor. After securing his eastern flank through diplomacy and bribery, he took North Africa in 533 and the islands of the western Mediterranean from the Vandals.

The next phase of the reconquest was much more exhausting. Like warriors before and after him, he had a difficult time taking the Italian peninsula. He gained his prize from the Ostrogoths after 20

years, but at the cost of draining his treasury and destroying Rome and Ravenna. Ironically, the people against whom he fought had as great a love for Roman institutions and traditions as Justinian did. His generals also reclaimed the southern part of Spain from the Visigoths, but no serious attempt was ever made to recover Gaul, Britain, or southern Germany.

By a decade after Justinian's death, most of the reconquest had been lost. The Moors in Africa, Germanic peoples across Europe, and waves of nomadic tribes from Asia threatened Byzantium's boundaries. Ancient enemies such as the Persians, who had been bribed into a peaceful relationship, returned to threaten Constantinople when the money ran out, setting in motion a half-century-long battle. In addition, the full weight of the Slavic migrations came to be felt. Peaceful though they may have been, the primitive Slavs severely strained and sometimes broke the administrative links of the state. Finally, the empire was split by debates regarding Christian doctrine. The stress of trying to maintain order under these burdens drove two of Justinian's successors insane.

Heraclius: The Empire Redefined

Salvation appeared from the west when Heraclius (610–641), the Byzantine governor of North Africa, returned to Constantinople in 610 to overthrow the mad emperor Phocas (602–610). When Heraclius

The old Roman tradition of the Mediterranean as "Mare Nostrum" ("Our Sea") died hard for Justinian. Twenty years of fighting allowed one last glimmer of the old days, but exhausted his army and his treasury. A half century after his reign, the western holdings would be lost, and the East Roman Empire would be redefined around an Anatolian, not a Mediterranean, base.

This mosaic from the Church of San Vitale at Ravenna, Italy, features the empress Theodora and her attendants.

arrived in the capital, conditions were so bad and the future appeared so perilous that he considered moving the government from Constantinople to Carthage in North Africa.

The situation did not improve soon for the Byzantines. The Persians marched seemingly at will through Syria, took Jerusalem—capturing the "true cross"—and advanced into Egypt. The loss of Egypt to the Persians cost Constantinople a large part of its grain supply. Two fierce Asiatic invaders, the Avars and the Bulgars, pushed against Byzantium from the north. Pirates controlled the sea lanes, and the Slavs cut land communication across the Balkans. Facing ultimate peril, the emperor abandoned the state structure of Diocletian and Constantine.

Heraclius instituted a new system that strengthened his armies, tapped the support of the church and the people, and erected a more efficient, streamlined administration. He determined that the nucleus of the empire would be Anatolia (Asia Minor, the area of present-day Turkey) and that the main source of fighting men for his army would be the free peasants living there rather than mercenaries. Instead of the sprawling realm passed on by Justinian, Heraclius designed a compact state and an administration conceived to deal simultaneously with the needs of government and the challenges of defense.

This system, the *theme* system, had been tested when Heraclius ruled North Africa. Acting on the lessons of the past four centuries, he assumed that defense was a constant need and that free peasant soldiers living in the *theme* ("district") they were defending would be the most effective and efficient force. He installed the system in Anatolia, and his successors then spread it throughout the empire over the next two centuries. Heraclius's scheme provided sound administration and effective defense at half the former cost.[7] As long as the *theme* system, with its self-supporting, landowning, free peasantry endured, Byzantium remained strong. When the *theme* system and its free peasantry were abandoned in the eleventh century, the empire became weak and vulnerable.

Heraclius fought history's first holy war, what Muslims would later call a *jihad*, to reclaim Jerusalem. During the 620s he applied some of the lessons of Hannibal's mobile warfare to attack Persian strength and took the enemy heartland. In 626 Heraclius stood ready to strike the final blow and refused to be drawn away by the Avar siege of Constantinople. He defeated the Persians at Nineva, marched on to Ctesiphon, and finally—symbolic of his victories—reclaimed the "true cross" and returned it to Jerusalem in 630.

He was unable to savor his victory for long, because the Muslims' advance posed an even more dangerous threat to Byzantium. They took Syria and Palestine at the battle of Yarmuk in 636. Persia fell in 637, Egypt in 640. A millennium of Greco-Roman rule in the eastern Mediterranean ended in a mere five years. Constantinople's walls and the redefined Byzantine state withstood the challenge, enduring two sieges in 674–678 and 717. Both times the capital faced severe land and naval attack. The Byzantines triumphed by using new techniques such as Greek fire and germ warfare. Greek fire was the medieval equivalent of napalm. It caught fire on contact with water and stuck to the hulls of the Arabs' wooden ships. At the same time, the Byzantines faced the serious threats of the Bulgarians—continuing their four-century-long pressure on Constantinople—and the Slavs. Heraclius's successors built on his strong foundations by extending the *theme* system and protecting the free peasants—a source of taxes and soldiers.

Iconoclasm and Schism

From Constantine on, the Byzantine emperors played active roles in calling church councils to debate the questions concerning the nature of Christ and his relationship with the Father and the Holy Spirit. In a Caesaropapist structure, an Orthodox Christian doctrine had to be established as a base to deal with both the secular and spiritual opponents of Constantinople. During times of war, such as the Persian invasions during Heraclius's reign, the combined force of church and state provided great strength. At other times, as in the eighth century, when arguments raged between Rome and Constantinople over the use of icons and the propagation of their particular branches of the faith, the emperor's mixing in matters of faith hurt the East Roman state.

When Constantinople faced a three-sided invasion from the Arabs, Avars, and Bulgarians in 717, another powerful leader, Leo the Isaurian (717–741), came forward to turn back the invaders. Over the next decade Leo rebuilt the areas ruined by war and strengthened the *theme* system. He reformed the law, limiting capital punishment to crimes involving treason. He increased the use of mutilation—a less extreme option than execution—for a wide range of common crimes.

Leo took seriously his role as religious leader. He vigorously persecuted heretics and Jews, decreeing that the latter group must be baptized. In 726 he launched a theological crusade against the use of *icons*, pictures and statues of religious figures such as Christ and the saints. He was concerned that icons played too prominent a role in Byzantine life and that their common use as godparents, witnesses at weddings, and objects of adoration went against the Old Testament prohibition of the worship of graven images. Accordingly, the emperor ordered the army to destroy icons. The destruction of the icons caused a violent reaction in the western part of the empire, especially in the monasteries. The government

The Byzantine navy coupled its prowess in battle with the secret and powerful weapon known as Greek fire, depicted here in a fourteenth-century manuscript illumination.

responded by mercilessly persecuting the *iconophiles* ("icon lovers"). The eastern part of the empire, centered in Anatolia, supported destruction of icons *(iconoclasm)*. By trying to remove what he saw to be an abuse, Leo split his empire in two and drove a deeper wedge between the church in Rome and the church in Constantinople.

In Byzantium the religious conflict over destruction of the icons had far-reaching cultural, political, and social implications. Pope Gregory II condemned iconoclasm in 731. Leo's decision to attack icons stressed the fracture lines that had existed between East and West for the past four centuries, typified by the linguistic differences between the Latin West and Greek East.[8] As Leo's successors carried on his religious and political policies, Pope Stephen II turned to the north and struck an alliance with the Frankish king, Pepin, in 754. This was the first step in a process that a half century later would lead to the birth of the Holy Roman Empire and the formal political split of Europe into East and West.

There was a brief attempt under the regent, later empress, Irene (797–802), in 787, to restore icons. In 797 she gained power after having her son, the rightful but incompetent heir, blinded in the very room in which she had given him life. She then became the first woman to rule the empire in her own name. She failed to win widespread support for her pro-icon policies; nor could she put together a marriage alliance with the newly proclaimed western emperor, Charlemagne, a union that would have brought the forces of East and West together. As Irene spent the treasury into bankruptcy, her enemies increased. Finally, in 802 they deposed her and sent her into exile on the island of Lesbos.[9]

The iconoclastic controversy and Irene's ineptitude placed the empire in jeopardy once again. Her successor, Nicepherus (802–811), after struggling to restore the bases of Byzantine power, was captured in

The empress Irene, the only woman to rule the Byzantine Empire in her own right, attempted in 787 to restore icons. In 802 she was deposed and exiled to Lesbos.

battle with the Bulgarians in 811. Khan Krum beheaded Nicepherus in July and turned his skull into a drinking mug. The iconoclasts had made a comeback, but this phase of image-breaking lacked the vigor of the first, and by 842 the policy was abandoned.

The clash over the icons marked the final split between East and West. Eastern emperors were strongly impressed by Islamic culture, with its prohibition of images. The emperor Theophilus (829–842), for example, was a student of Muslim art and culture, and Constantinople's painting, architecture, and universities benefited from the vigor of Islamic culture. This focus on the East may have led to the final split with the West, but, by the middle of the ninth century, it also produced an East Roman state with its theological house finally in order and its borders fairly secure.

Byzantium's Golden Age, 842–1071

For two centuries, a period coinciding roughly with the reign of the Macedonian dynasty (867–1056), Byzantium enjoyed political and cultural superiority over its western and eastern foes. Western Europe staggered under the blows dealt by the Saracens, Vikings, and Magyars, and the Arabs lost the momentum that had carried them forward for two centuries. Constantinople enjoyed the relative calm, wealth, and balance bequeathed by the *theme* system and promoted by a series of powerful rulers. The time was marked by the flowering of artists, scholars, and theologians as much as it was by the presence of great warriors.

During this Golden Age, Constantinople made its major contributions to eastern Europe and Russia. Missionaries from Constantinople set out to convert the Bulgarians and Slavic peoples in the 860s and in the process organized their language, laws, aesthetics, political patterns, and ethics as well as their religion. But these activities did not take place without competition. Conflict marked the relationship between the Byzantine and Roman churches. A prime example of this conflict was the competition between Patriarch Photius and Pope Nicholas I in the middle of the ninth century.

Photius excelled both as a scholar and as a religious leader. He made impressive contributions to universities throughout the Byzantine Empire and worked to increase Orthodoxy's influence throughout the realm. Nicholas I was Photius's equal in ambition, ego, and intellect. They collided over the attempt to convert the pagan peoples, such as the Bulgarians, caught between their spheres of influence.

Khan Boris of Bulgaria—who was as cunning and shrewd as Photius and Nicholas—saw the trend toward conversion in Europe that had been develop-

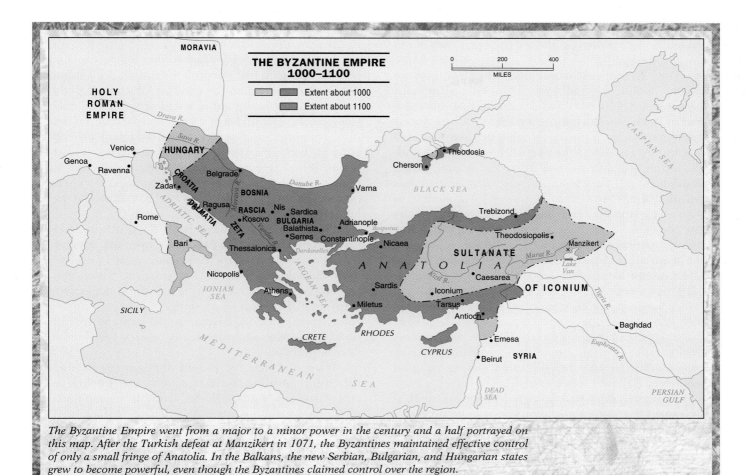

The Byzantine Empire went from a major to a minor power in the century and a half portrayed on this map. After the Turkish defeat at Manzikert in 1071, the Byzantines maintained effective control of only a small fringe of Anatolia. In the Balkans, the new Serbian, Bulgarian, and Hungarian states grew to become powerful, even though the Byzantines claimed control over the region.

ing since the sixth century and realized the increased power he could gain with church approval of his rule. He wanted his own patriarch and church and dealt with the side that gave him the better bargain. From 864 to 866 Boris changed his mind three times over the issue of which holy city to turn to. Finally, the Byzantines gave the Bulgarians the equivalent of an autonomous (independent) church, and in return, the Bulgarians entered the Byzantine cultural orbit. The resulting schism proclaimed between the churches in 867 set off a sputtering sequence of Christian warfare that continued for centuries.[10]

The work of the Byzantine missionary brothers Cyril and Methodius was more important than Bulgarian ambitions or churchly competition. The men were natives of Thessalonica, a city at the mouth of the Vardar-Morava water highway that gave access to the Slavic lands. Versed in the Slavic language, the two led a mission to Moravia, ruled by King Rastislav. He no doubt wanted to convert to Orthodoxy and enter the orbit of distant Constantinople in order to preserve as much independence for his land as he could in the face of pressure from his nearby

powerful German neighbors. Cyril and Methodius carried the faith northward in the vernacular. Cyril adapted Greek letters to devise an alphabet for the Slavs, and the brothers translated the liturgy and many religious books into the Slavic language. Although Germanic missionaries eventually converted the Moravians, the work of Cyril and Methodius profoundly affected all of the Slavic peoples.

Byzantium continued its military as well as its theological dynamism. Arab armies made repeated thrusts, including one at Thessalonica in 904 that led to the loss of 22,000 people. But during the tenth century a decline in Muslim combativeness, combined with the solidity of Byzantine defenses, brought an end to that chapter of conflict. Basil II (963–1025), surnamed *Bulgaroctonus*, or "Bulgar slayer," stopped Bulgarian challenges for more than a century at the battle of Balathista in 1014. At the same time, the Macedonian emperors dealt from a position of strength with western European powers, especially where their interests clashed in Italy. Western diplomats visiting the Byzantine court expressed outrage at the benign contempt with which the eastern emperors treated them. But the attitude merely reflected Constantinople's understanding of its role in the world.

The Byzantines continued their sometimes violent political traditions. Emperor Romanus Lecapenus I (920–944) was overthrown by his sons, and in the eleventh century succession to the throne degenerated into a power struggle between the civil and military aristocracies. Yet through all the political strife, the secular and theological universities flourished, and the emperors proved to be generous patrons of the arts. Basil I (867–886) and Leo VI (886–912) oversaw the collection and reform of the law codes. Leo, the most prolific lawgiver since Justinian, sponsored the greatest collection of laws of the medieval Byzantine Empire, a work that would affect jurisprudence throughout Europe. Constantine VII Porphyrogenitus (912–959) excelled as a military leader, lover of books, promoter of an encyclopedia, and surveyor of the empire's provinces. At a time when scholarship in western Europe was almost nonexistent, Constantinople society featured a rich cultural life and widespread literacy among men and women of different classes.

The greatest contribution to European civilization from Byzantium's Golden Age was the preservation of ancient learning, especially in the areas of law, Greek science and literature, and Platonic and Aristotelian philosophy. Whereas in the West the church maintained scholarship, the civil servants of Byzantium perpetuated the Greek tradition in philosophy, literature, and science. Byzantine monasteries produced many saints and mystics but showed little interest in learning or teaching about this would.

Decline and Crusades

Empires more often succumb to internal ailments than to external takeovers. This was the case with the Byzantine Empire. As long as Constantinople strengthened the foundations laid by Heraclius—the *theme* system and reliance on the free soldier-peasant—the empire withstood the military attacks of the strongest armies of the time. When the Byzantine leaders abandoned the pillars of their success, the state succumbed to the slightest pressure.

Inflation and ambition ate away at the Heraclian structure. Too much money chased too few goods during the Golden Age. Land came to be the most profitable investment the rich could make, and the landowning magnates needed labor. Rising prices meant increased taxes. The peasant villages were collectively responsible for paying taxes, and the rising tax burden overwhelmed them. In many parts of the empire, villages sought relief by placing themselves under the control of large landowners, thus taking themselves out of the tax pool and lowering the number of peasant-soldiers. Both the state treasury and the army suffered as a result.

Until Basil II, the Macedonian emperors had tried to protect the peasantry through legislation, but the trend could not be reversed. Even though the free peasantry never entirely disappeared and each free person was still theoretically a citizen of the empire, economic and social pressures effectively destroyed the *theme* system. An additional factor contributing to the empire's decline was the growth of the church's holdings and the large percentage of the population taking holy orders, thus becoming exempt from taxation.

For 50 years following Basil II's death in 1025, the illusion that eternal peace had been achieved after his devastation of the Bulgarians in 1014 encouraged the opportunistic civil aristocracy, which controlled the state, to weaken the army and neglect the provinces. The next time danger arose, no strong rulers appeared to save Byzantium—perhaps because no enemies massed dramatically outside the walls of Constantinople.

Instead, a new foe moved haphazardly through the empire. Around the sixth century the first in a series of Turkish bands migrated from the region north of China to southwestern Asia. These nomads converted to Islam and, moving westward, fought first with and then against the Persians, the Byzantines, and the Arabs. When the Seljuq Turk leader Alp Arslan (the "Victorious Lion") made a tentative probe into the empire's eastern perimeter near Lake Van in 1071, the multilingual mercenary army sent out from Constantinople fell apart even before fighting began at Manzikert. With the disintegration of the army, the only thing that could stop the Turks' march for the next decade was the extent of their own ambition and energy.

Byzantium lost the heart of its empire, and with it the reserves of soldiers, leaders, taxes, and food that had enabled it to survive for four centuries. From its weakened position, the empire confronted Venice, a powerful commercial and later political rival. By the end of the eleventh century the Venetians had achieved undisputed trading supremacy in the Adriatic and turned their attention to the eastern Mediterranean. The Byzantines also faced the challenges of the Normans, led by Robert Guiscard, who took the last Byzantine stronghold in Italy.

In 1081 a politically astute family, the Comnenians, claimed the Byzantine throne. In earlier times, with the empire at its strongest, these new rulers might have accomplished great things. But the best they could do in the eleventh and twelfth centuries was to play a balance-of-power game between East and West. In 1096 the first crusaders appeared, partly in response to the Council of Clermont, partly in response to the lure of gold and glory (see Chapter 8).

Alexius Comnenus (1081–1118) had appealed to Pope Urban II for help against the Turks, but he did not bargain on finding a host of crusaders, including the dreaded Normans, on his doorstep. Alexius quickly got the crusaders across the Straits of Bosporus and Dardanelles, where they won some battles that allowed the Byzantines to reclaim land lost in the previous 15 years.[11]

Subsequent crusades, however, did not bring good relations between East and West, whose churches had excommunicated each other in 1054. The envy and hatred and frustration that had been building up for some time finally erupted during the Fourth Crusade. The Venetians had control of the ships and money for this crusade and persuaded the crusaders to attack the Christian city of Zadar in Dalmatia—a commercial rival of Venice and Constantinople—before going on to the Holy Land. Venice wanted a trade monopoly in the eastern Mediterranean more than a fight with the Muslims. Constantinople itself was paralyzed by factional strife, and for the first time an invading force captured the city, laying it waste. A French noble described the scene:

> *The fire . . . continued to rage for a whole week and no one could put it out. . . . What damage was done, or what riches and possessions were destroyed in the flames, was beyond the power of man to calculate. . . . The army . . . gained much booty; so much, indeed, that no one could estimate its amount or its value. It included gold and silver, table-services and precious stones, satin and silk, mantles of squirrel fur, ermine and miniver, and every choicest thing to be found on this earth. . . . So much booty had never been gained in any city since the creation of the world.[12]*

The Venetians made sure they got their share of the spoils—such as the bronze horses now found at St. Mark's Cathedral in Venice—and played a key role in placing a new emperor on the throne. The invaders ruled Constantinople until 1261. The Venetians put a stranglehold on commerce in the region and turned their hostility toward the Genoese, who threatened their monopoly.

The empire's last two centuries under the final dynasty, the Paleologus (1261–1453), saw the formerly glorious realm become a pawn in a new game. Greeks regained control of the church and the state, but there was precious little strength to carry on the ancient traditions. Byzantine coinage, which had retained its value from the fourth through the eleventh centuries, fell victim to inflation and weakness. The church, once a major pillar to help the state, became embroiled in continual doctrinal disputes. Slavic peoples such as the Bulgarians and the Serbs under Stephen Nemanja (1168–1196) and Stephen Dushan (1331–1355), who had posed no danger to the empire

The Crusades, viewed from the western perspective as an epoch of bravery, were for the Byzantines and the Arabs a time of barbaric invasions. The crusaders not only failed in the long term to reclaim the Holy Land but also failed to stem the Islamic advance. By the sixteenth century, Turkish forces would be threatening Vienna.

in its former strength, became threats. After Mongol invasions in the thirteenth century destroyed the exhausted Seljuq Turks, a new more formidable foe—the Ottoman or Osmanli Turks—appeared.

The Ottomans were one of the groups of elite warriors, the *ghazis*, on the northwestern frontier of Anatolia. They participated in the complex political and diplomatic relations in the Aegean area in the wake of the Fourth Crusade and were ready to take advantage of the weakened Byzantine Empire. Blessed after 1296 with a strong line of male successors and good fortune, the Ottomans rapidly expanded their power through the Balkans. They crossed the Straits into Europe in 1354 and moved up the Vardar and Morava valleys to take Serres (1383), Sofia (1385), Niš (1386), Thessalonica (1387), and finally Kosovo from the South Slavs in 1389.

The Turks' overwhelming infantry and cavalry superiority gave them their military victories. But their administrative effectiveness, which combined strength and flexibility, solidified their rule in areas

As the Turks patiently advanced in the Balkans in the 1380s, the usually feuding Slavs finally united at the battle of Kosovo. After a long day of valiant fighting, which saw both the Turkish Sultan and the Serbian king die, the Ottomans emerged victorious—with control of the Balkans for the next five centuries. For the Balkan Slavs, especially the Serbs, the memory of the battle of Kosovo would be passed from generation to generation to be used by politicians in the 1990s as a tragedy to unite a people for a better day.

they conquered. In contrast to the Christians, both Roman and Byzantine, who were intolerant of theological differences, the Turks allowed monotheists or any believers in a "religion of the book" (the Bible, Torah, or Qur'an) to retain their faith and be ruled by a religious superior through the *millet* system, a network of religious ghettos.

In response to the Ottoman advance, the West mounted a poorly conceived and ill-fated crusade against the Turks. The confrontation at Nicopolis on the Danube in 1396 resulted in the capture and slaughter of 10,000 knights and their attendants. Only the overwhelming force of Tamerlane (Timur the Magnificent), a Turco-Mongol ruler who defeated the Ottoman army in 1402, gave Constantinople and Europe some breathing space.

The end for Constantinople came in May 1453. The last emperor, Constantine XI, and his force of 9000, half of whom were Genoese, held off 160,000 Turks for seven weeks. Finally, with the help of Hungarian artillerymen, the Turks breached the once im-penetrable walls of the depopulated city. After 1123 years, the shining fortress fell.[13]

Eastern European and Russian Romes

Following in the wake of the Germanic tribes' westward march, the dominant people of eastern Europe, the Slavs, spread from the Pripet marshes west to the Elbe, east to the Urals, north to Finland, and south to the Peloponnesus. As they settled throughout eastern and central Europe from the sixth through the ninth centuries, they absorbed most of the original inhabitants of the region. This mixing of peoples produced the resulting blends of nations that make up the present-day complexity of eastern Europe and Russia.

The geography of eastern Europe contributed to the diversity of the region's population. The climatic extremes range from arctic cold to Mediterranean

Eastern Europe and Russia

c. 700–1014	First Bulgarian Empire
865–870	Bulgarian conversion to Orthodoxy
867	First "Russian" attack on Constantinople
862–867	Cyril and Methodius's mission to the Moravians
c. 900	Serb conversion to Orthodoxy
925	First Croat state, conversion to Catholicism
988	Russian conversion to Orthodoxy
988–1240	Kiev Rus'
1169–1389	Serbian Empire
1197–1393	Second Bulgarian Empire
1220–1242	Mongol invasions in Russia and eastern Europe
1240–1480	Mongol domination of Russia
1300s–1400s	Reemergence of Wallachia and Moldavia
1389	Battle of Kosovo
1450–1468	Albanian state under Skanderbeg
1462–1505	Reign of Ivan III, the Great

mildness. The soil varies from the rich topsoil of the Ukraine and the Danubian plain to the rocky dryness of the Dinaric Alps. Waterways include both the scenic though commercially useless rivulets of Greece and the broad and powerful Vistula and Danube Rivers. Some of the lands have no access to the sea; others, such as Greece, are blessed with fine harbors. The particular scope of climate, soil, and water access dictated the economic possibilities of each nation.

Like that of eastern Europe, Russia's history is largely a product of its geography. The vast expanse of land combined with a comparatively small population has made the domination of the peasants by the landed interests—both individuals and state—one of the continuing themes in Russian history. Russia's difficulty in gaining access to the sea has had important economic and cultural consequences, stunting the growth of a merchant class and encouraging the formation of an inward-looking population.

Russia's waterways have played a key role in the development of the country. The rivers, which flow north or south across the land, have served as thoroughfares for trade and cultural exchange as well as routes for invasion. Unconnected to the western European region, the rivers dictated a line of communication that led early Russian traders to Constantinople rather than to the West. The Volkhov and Dnieper network tied together the Varangians (also known as the Vikings) and the Greeks through Russia, while the Volkhov and Volga system reached toward central Asia.

Russian historians stress that the interaction of the forest and steppe zones must be considered in order to understand the country. The forest provided protection, a means to make a living through fur-trapping and honey-gathering, and a chance to escape the pressures of the central authorities. The extremely rich topsoil of the steppe zone provided agricultural wealth, political control, and a grass-lined highway for nomadic invaders. Where the two come together is where much of early Russian history took place. It is within this geographical framework that the Russian nation developed, with the arrival—six centuries B.C.E.—of Asiatic tribes following the steppe belt and crossing Russian territory.

The Peoples of Eastern Europe

From the sixth through the ninth centuries the Slavs hunted and traded—usually forest products such as furs, honey, and wax. They also farmed, using the "slash and burn" method of cutting down the forests, tilling the land until it was exhausted, and then moving on. With the exception of the Bulgarians, they formed themselves into male-dominated peasant tribal units, based on blood relations. The clan elders chose from their ranks a leader who would meet with other clan leaders to elect a person to coordinate activities throughout the district. From the ranks of the clan would come the local officials, priests, and tax and military payments.

Compared to the wealth and sophistication of the Byzantines, the Slavs' economic and social lives were primitive, and their political and military structures were weak. Outsiders—Byzantines, Germans, Magyars, Mongols, or Turks—often ruled the various Slavic groups. Each outside ruler imposed a distinctive set of cultural, economic, political, and social traits on the Slavic group it dominated. The rulers' religion was the key means through which these distinctive traits were imposed, leading to tragic divisions in the Slavic peoples, such as those that erupted in Bosnia and Herzegovina in the 1990s.

Eastern Europeans who found themselves in the Roman sphere—the Poles, Czechs, Slovaks, Hungarians, Slovenes, and Croats—joined a cultural community that stretched from the Bug River to the Straits of Gibraltar to Iceland. Common threads uniting this

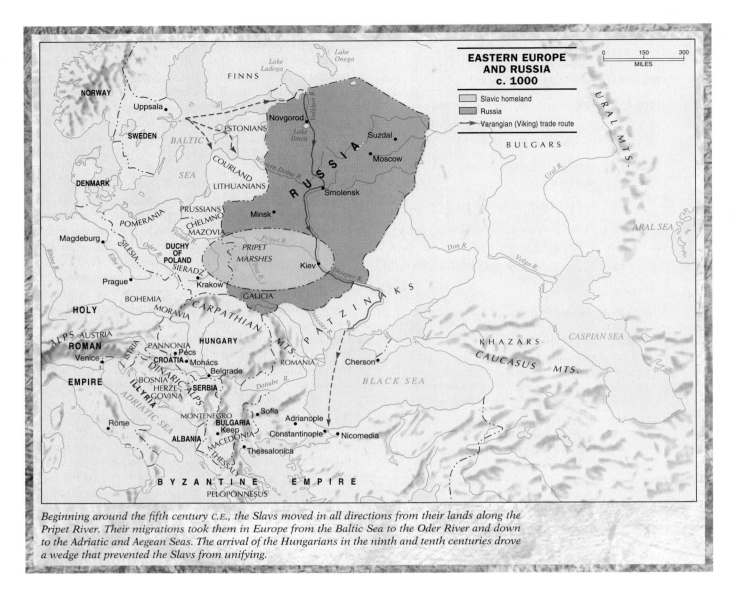

Beginning around the fifth century C.E., the Slavs moved in all directions from their lands along the Pripet River. Their migrations took them in Europe from the Baltic Sea to the Oder River and down to the Adriatic and Aegean Seas. The arrival of the Hungarians in the ninth and tenth centuries drove a wedge that prevented the Slavs from unifying.

community were the Latin language and a belief in papal authority. German monks and priests carried the Roman faith to this area, and they were followed and sustained by a Germanic population movement, the *Drang nach Osten* ("drive to the east"). Hungary, Bohemia, and Poland experienced a golden age of cultural and economic development in the fourteenth century, when their originating dynasties—respectively, the Arpad, Premysl, and Piast dynasties—died out and were replaced by new political and cultural elites. Universities were established in Prague (1348), Krakow (1364), and Pecs (1369), and scholars in those schools partook of the humanist movement of the fifteenth century.

The Hungarians were defeated by the Ottoman Empire at Mohacs (1526), and their land was divided into three zones, the larger part controlled directly by the Turks. Despite this, people in the Roman Catholic orbit shared in the great formative developments of Western civilization: the Renaissance, the Reforma-

tion, the Scientific Revolution, the Capitalist Revolution, the Enlightenment, the French Revolution, and the Industrial Revolution. They also participated directly in the classic developmental process of western Europe of feudalism, the development of the modern state system, and the growth of pluralistic society.

Eastern Europeans who came into the Byzantine, Orthodox orbit during the ninth and tenth centuries—the Bulgarians, Serbs, Montenegrins, Romanians, and Russians—heard the liturgy in their native language, worshiped under a decentralized religious structure, and remained culturally separated from western Europe. These Orthodox Christians lived at various times under the domination of the Mongols or the Turks, two despotic Asiatic powers that permitted the practice of the Orthodox religion but controlled political behavior. The combination of Byzantine autocracy and oriental despotism led to the growth of authoritarian states that did not encourage the pluralistic societies and multifaceted creativity found in western Europe. In fact, before the imposition of Ottoman control, each of the Balkan people would have a moment of glory—the two Bulgarian Empires, the Serbs under Stephen Nemanja and Stephen Dushan—in which it would create its own image of Byzantium. However, in Russia a formidable civilization emerged that by the fifteenth century claimed to be the Third Rome.

Kiev Rus'

In the sixth century C.E. the eastern Slavs began moving out of the area near the Pripet marshes. The various clans went as far north as the White Sea, as far east as the Urals, and to the region south of Kiev. (Kiev Rus' describes the Kievan phase of Russian history, especially the introduction of a stronger Ukrainian historiographical tradition. The apostrophe is for a diacritical mark in the writing of the word Rus' in Russian and Ukrainian.) To the north, around Lake Ilmen, the Slavs established a number of trading towns such as Novgorod, from which they founded other trading bases. By the ninth century they had accumulated sufficient wealth to attract the attention of the Varangians, who came down from the Baltic to dominate the trading routes, especially those going from the Dvina to the Dnieper to Constantinople.

Russian history is said to begin with the entry of the Varangians into eastern Slavic affairs in the 860s. One of the key controversies in Russian history revolves around the question of the Varangians' role. Did they impose themselves on the Slavs and form them into their first political units, or were the Varangians invited in by the already sophisticated, though feuding, Slavic tribes? The so-called Norman controversy can best be addressed by noting that the Slavs, like most other Europeans, fell under the wave of the northern invaders but within two generations assimilated them and incorporated their capabilities.

The Varangian Oleg (c. 882–913) established his seat of government at Kiev, at the transition point between the forest and steppe zones. During the tenth century Oleg and Sviatoslav (964–972) created a state that was the equal of contemporary France. Oleg took control of both Kiev and Novgorod and, with the strength gained, launched an attack on Constantinople. Sviatoslav carried Kievan power to the Danube and the lower Volga. He fell victim to the knives of Asiatic invaders, the Patzinaks. However, he left a state strong enough to endure almost a decade of internal power struggles.

The most important ruler in the Kievan phase of Russian history was Vladimir, who overcame his brothers to dominate his country from 980 to 1015. Vladimir learned his political lessons dealing with the Byzantines, and he consolidated his power in Kiev. At first he based his rule on the pagan party and erected statues to gods such as Perun (the god of thunder) and Volos (the god of wealth). He made peace with the Volga Bulgars to the east and worked with the Byzantines against the Bulgarians in pursuit of his diplomatic and political goals.

Vladimir acknowledged the fact that the nations surrounding him were converting to one organized religion or another: the Poles and Hungarians to Roman Catholicism, the Khazars to Judaism, the Volga Bulgars to Islam, and the Bulgarians to Orthodoxy. His grandmother, the shrewd and skillful Olga, had accepted Orthodox Christianity from Constantinople in 956, as had other members of his family. During the 980s Vladimir sent observers to judge the various religious alternatives. According to the *Russian Primary Chronicle*, they visited Hagia Sophia at Constantinople in 988 and were impressed with the power and wealth of the city. The observers recommended that Vladimir choose the Orthodox faith.

The story, though interesting, ignores the many concrete advantages Vladimir derived from his decision. As part of the negotiation package, Vladimir agreed to help the Byzantine emperor Basil against his enemies. In return he would receive the hand of the emperor's sister in marriage upon converting to Orthodoxy. After a successful campaign, Basil delayed in carrying out his part of the bargain. Vladimir moved quickly to make his point and marched into the Crimea and took the Byzantine city of Cherson. The Kiev-Byzantine arrangements were finally carried out in 990. Vladimir, now a member of the Byzantine royal family, brought his country into the Byzantine, Orthodox orbit. Even before "becoming a saint," the *Chronicle* tells us, he destroyed the pagan statues, converted his many concubines to nuns, and forced his people to become Christians.[14] Eventually the Russians gained their own church, received their own metropolitan, and adapted Byzantine ritual, theology, and monastic practices to their own use. They also applied Byzantine governmental theories to their own social hierarchy.

After Vladimir, few great monarchs ruled during the Kievan period of Russian history. Instead, political fragmentation began to intensify. During the reign of Yaroslav the Wise (1019–1054), the Kievan state reached its high point, and it was the cultural and economic equal of any government in Europe. Yaroslav undertook major building projects, revised the law code, and promoted the growth of the church. He formed a dynastic alliance with Henry I of France. Unfortunately, Kiev did not long maintain its prestigious position. Yaroslav introduced a principle of succession based on the *seniority* system, passing the rule of Kiev from brother to brother in a given generation before the next generation would have its chance. This practice is in contrast with the Western one of *primogeniture*, under which rule is handed

The Acceptance of Christianity

Russia's conversion to Orthodoxy was a fundamental step in the division of Europe between East and West. This excerpt from the *Russian Primary Chronicle* explains how the decision was made.

6494 (986). Vladimir was visited by Volga Bulgars of Mohammedan [Muslim] faith.... Then came the Germans, asserting that they came as emissaries of the Pope.... The Jewish Khazars heard of these missions, and came themselves.... Then the Greeks sent to Vladimir a scholar....

6495 (987). Vladimir summoned together his vassals and the city elders, and said to them, "Behold, the Volga Bulgars came before me urging me to accept their religion. Then came the Germans and praised their own faith; and after them came the Jews. Finally the Greeks appeared, criticizing all other faiths but commending their own, and they spoke at length, telling the history of the whole world from its beginning...."

... The Prince and all the people chose good and wise men to the number of ten, and directed them to go first among the Volga Bulgars and inspect their faith. The emissaries went their way, and when they arrived at their destination they beheld the disgraceful actions of the Volga Bulgars and their worship in the mosque; then they returned to their own country. Vladimir then instructed them to go likewise among the Germans, and examine their faith, and finally to visit the Greeks. They thus went into Germany, and after viewing the German ceremonial, they proceeded to Tsargrad [Constantinople], where they appeared before the Emperor....

Thus they returned to their own country, and the Prince called together his vassals and the elders. Vladimir then announced the return of the envoys who had been sent out, and suggested that their report be heard. He thus commanded them to speak out before his vassals. The envoys reported, "When we journeyed among the Volga Bulgars, we beheld how they worship in their temple, called a mosque, while they stand ungirt. The Volga Bulgar bows, sits down, looks hither and thither like one possessed, and there is no happiness among them, but instead only sorrow and a dreadful stench. Their religion is not good. Then we went among the Germans, and saw them performing many ceremonies in their temples; but we beheld no glory there. Then we went on to Greece, and the Greeks led us to the edifices where they worship their God, and we knew not whether we were in heaven or on earth. For on earth there is no such splendor or such beauty, and we are at a loss how to describe it. We only know that God dwells there among men, and their service is fairer than the ceremonies of other nations...." Then the vassals spoke and said, "If the Greek faith were evil, it would not have been adopted by your grandmother Olga, who was wiser than all other men." Vladimir then inquired where they should all accept baptism, and they replied that the decision rested with him....

By divine agency, Vladimir was suffering at that moment from a disease of the eyes, and could see nothing, being in great distress. The Princess declared to him that if he desired to be relieved of this disease, he should be baptized with all speed, otherwise it could not be cured.... The Bishop of Kherson, together with the Princess' priests, after announcing the tidings, baptized Vladimir, and as the Bishop laid his hand upon him, he straightway received his sight. Upon experiencing this miraculous cure, Vladimir glorified God, saying, "I have now perceived the one true God." When his followers beheld this miracle, many of them were also baptized.

From *The Russian Primary Chronicle*, trans. Samuel H. Cross, in *Harvard Studies and Notes in Philology and Literature*, Vol. 12 (Cambridge, Mass.: Harvard University Press, 1953), pp. 183–213 passim. Reprinted by permission.

down to the eldest son of the ruler. Within two generations, the seniority system led to the political breakup of Kiev, although the city maintained its theoretical superiority within Russia.

Kiev also came under attack from both east and west and suffered as well from the economic decline of Constantinople. Under Vladimir Monomakh (1113–1125), Kiev reemerged briefly as a center of power, but a half century of decline soon followed. Competing centers arose at Suzdal; Galicia, where the local aristocracy dominated; Vladimir, where the prince emerged all-powerful; and Novgorod, where the assembled citizens—the *veche*—were the major force. Even before the Mongols totally destroyed the city in 1240, Kiev's era of prominence was effectively over.

Novgorod, Moscow, and the Mongols

For more than two centuries, from 1240 to 1480, Mongols dominated Russia, and during that time much of the land was cut off from contact with the outside world. During this period a new center of power, Moscow, emerged to serve for most of the time as collector of tribute for the Mongol court. New internal markets developed, and the Orthodox church, unhampered by the Mongols, grew in strength and influence. The Russian city of Novgorod also managed to carry on despite the oriental overlord.

Novgorod had come under the control of the Varangians in the ninth century, but in 997 the citizens received a charter granting them self-government, and for the next five centuries this *veche* elected its own rulers. The city boasted an aggressive and prosperous merchant class, which exploited the region from the Ural Mountains to the Baltic Sea and held its own against German merchants from the Baltic area. Novgorod was the equal of most of the cities found along the Baltic and North Seas. In the middle of the thirteenth century, Alexander Nevsky, the prince of Novgorod, led his fellow citizens in struggles to repel the Teutonic Knights and the Swedes. A few years later he showed exceptional diplomatic skill in paying homage to the Mongols, even though they had halted 60 miles outside the city and left Novgorod untouched. At a time when the rest of Russia suffered mightily under the first phase of Mongol domination, the *veche*-elected oligarchy continued to rule Novgorod.

The city's wealth and traditions permitted the *veche* to rule. The citizens elected their princes and forced them to sign a contract setting out what they could and could not do. In the words of a typical document between ruler and city, the citizens could show their prince "the way out" if he failed to live up to the terms of his agreement. The prince could act as a leader of Novgorod only when he remained within the city's limits. The city's method of government permitted the rise of class divisions that led to more than 20 major outbreaks of violence in the thirteenth and fourteenth centuries. Changes in trade routes in the fifteenth century led to a decline in Baltic commerce, and Novgorod came to depend on Moscow for its grain supply. That dependence, in addition to the class conflict, weakened Novgorod, and in 1478 Moscow absorbed the town.

The obscure fortress town of Moscow, first mentioned in the records in 1147, came to be the core of the new Russia. Even before the Mongol invasion, a large number of Slavs moved toward the north and east, and this migration continued for centuries as that frontier offered opportunities for the oppressed. Moscow was well placed along a north-south river route in a protective setting of marshes and forests.

One of Alexander Nevsky's sons, Daniel, founded the Grand Duchy of Moscow, and he and subsequent rulers inherited Nevsky's ability to get along with the Mongols. As the Moscow princes skillfully acknowledged their inferior position to the Mongol khans,

who sought tribute and recruits, the Muscovites improved their political position in relation to the other Russians by attempting to monopolize the tax collection function for the Mongols, with notable success. In addition, at the beginning of the fourteenth century they made sure that the seat of the Russian Orthodox Church would be in Moscow, a reflection of the city's prestige.[15]

In the first century after the Mongol invasion, the Muscovite princes showed a great deal of ambition and ability, albeit in a sometimes unattractive way. For example, during his reign (1328–1341) Ivan I Kalita (whose surname means "moneybags"), greatly increased the wealth and power of his city by aggressive tax collection practices.

On the surface, the fourteenth century appeared to be a time of decline, of Mongol domination and gains by the European states at Russian expense along the western boundary. The reality, however, was that Russia was laying foundations for its future with Moscow as the country's religious and political center. In 1380 Dmitri Donskoi (1359–1389) defeated the Mongols at Kulikovo. Although Mongol strength was far from broken, the Russian victory had great symbolic significance.

Civil war and invasions threatened the Moscow-based country throughout the fifteenth century. Finally, Ivan III (1462–1505) made major strides to build the modern Russian state. He took Novgorod and two years later ceased acknowledging Mongol domination. He then began to advance toward the south and east against the Turks and Mongols, setting in motion a drive that lasted for centuries.

In developments of considerable symbolic importance, the Russians embraced many elements of the Roman tradition. Ivan III married the niece of the last East Roman emperor, an alliance arranged by the pope. Russians espoused the theory that Moscow was the Third Rome, the logical successor to Constantinople as the center of Christianity. In 1492 (the year 7000 in the Orthodox calendar and the beginning of a new millennium), the Muscovite metropolitan, Zosima, stated that Ivan III was "the new Emperor Constantine of the new Constantinople Moscow." Zosima for the first time called Moscow an imperial city. Philotheus of Pskov expounded the theory of Third Rome in full detail in the 1520s.[16] Ivan began to use the title *tsar* ("caesar") and adopted the Roman two-headed eagle as the symbol of the Russian throne.

Ivan opened the doors to the West ever so slightly. He established diplomatic relations with a number of European powers. He brought in Italian technicians and architects such as Aristotele Fieravanti and Pietro Antonio Solari to work on the churches, palaces, and walls of the Kremlin—the vastly expanded site of the original fortress that was the center of the town three

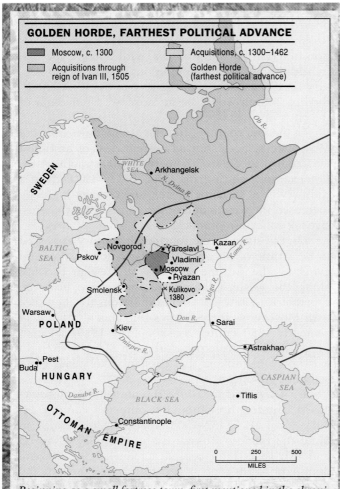

GOLDEN HORDE, FARTHEST POLITICAL ADVANCE

- Moscow, c. 1300
- Acquisitions through reign of Ivan III, 1505
- Acquisitions, c. 1300–1462
- Golden Horde (farthest political advance)

Beginning as a small fortress town, first mentioned in the chronicles in the mid-twelfth century, Moscow grew rapidly by 1500. Thanks to clever and sometimes brave leaders, an ambitious citizenry, and the Orthodox Church, Moscow endured the Mongol occupation to emerge as the self-proclaimed "Third Rome."

centuries earlier. The Italian artistic tradition had no lasting cultural impact on Russia, but use of Italian artists nonetheless signified an awareness of the West. In recognition of the need to establish a standing army, Ivan began the difficult process of building up a modern state structure and increased restrictions on the Russian peasants. During the fifteenth century Ivan was the equal of his western European colleagues Henry VII of England and Louis XI of France. After three centuries, the Russians were back in touch with Europe.[17]

Conclusion

The Christians grew from a small and despised band of believers whose leader had been crucified to be-

come the most notable survivors of the West Roman Empire. Their spiritual message spread rapidly through the crisis-ridden Mediterranean world after the second century and came to be the foundation for powerful forces. By the sixth century the foundations for the papacy's spiritual and political power had been laid in the West. Pope Leo the Great acquired the moral leadership of the West by successfully protecting Rome from the Huns. Political fragmentation after 476 allowed the papacy to achieve independence and laid the groundwork for the doctrine of the supremacy of the church over the state in spiritual matters, a theory implied by St. Augustine in *The City of God*. The church would serve as the frame on which modern Europe would emerge, weaving together Greco-Roman culture and the strengths of the Germanic peoples, their institutions, and their values.

In the East, Constantine had proclaimed Constantinople the first Christian capital and himself the "thirteenth apostle." For the next 1200 years, after the decline of the Roman Empire in the West, Byzantium preserved and enlarged the heritage of Western civilization, Christianized much of eastern Europe, and held off Persian and Arab assaults. During its millennium of existence the eastern empire enjoyed eight centuries of economic, intellectual, political, and military dominance. Perhaps its longest-lasting effect was on the Slavs, especially the Russians.

From the fourth through the ninth centuries, as the Slavs moved to their new homelands, they came under the influence of dominant outside forces. In Russia and the Balkans, Byzantine patterns and traditions shaped their lives. To the north the Roman Catholic faith, carried by the Germans, helped define national characteristics.

After its initial Kievan phase, in which Vladimir made the choice to follow East Roman precedents, the Russians remained under Mongol domination even when Russia's political and religious center moved to Moscow. When the Russians regained their independence in the fifteenth century, they redefined their polity in Roman and Christian terms, claiming the legacy of the fallen city of Constantinople.

The Christian faith, with its origins in spirituality, humility, and love and its founder who preached a heavenly kingdom, played a historical role not foreseen by its earliest adherents. Christianity fueled a spiritual and secular force based in Rome that would serve as the bridge between the classical and modern worlds. In the East powerful emperors in Constantinople and Moscow used Orthodox Christianity to buttress their own power. It matters little whether the politicians of Rome, Constantinople, and Moscow were pious or hypocritical in governing their new

Christian realms. Their embrace of Christ's message profoundly altered the form, if not the substance, of Christianity.

Suggestions for Reading

J. H. Hexter, *The Judaeo-Christian Tradition*, 2nd ed. (Yale University Press, 1995), is a brief but valuable survey of the evolution of ancient Judaism and Christianity. On the late ancient history of the Jews, see Elias Bickerman, *From Ezra to the Last of the Maccabees: Foundations of the Post-Biblical Judaism* (Schocken, 1949), and D. S. Russell, *The Jews from Alexander to Herod* (Oxford University Press, 1967).

Since their discovery a half century ago, the Dead Sea Scrolls have been the subject of much academic intrigue and infighting. Access to them has been limited, but finally Martin Abegg and Edward Cook used computer technology to reconstruct the bits and fragments that were available, and the results can be found in Michael Owen Wise, ed., with Martin G. Abegg and Edward Cook, *The Dead Sea Scrolls: A New Translation* (Harper/SanFrancisco, 1996). Another version, Geza Vemez, ed., *The Complete Dead Sea Scrolls in English* (Allen Lane, 1997), is impressive but incomplete.

Howard Clark Kee and Carter Lindberg, *Understanding the New Testament*, 5th ed. (Prentice Hall, 1997), is highly recommended. See also Edgar J. Goodspeed, *A Life of Jesus* (Greenwood, 1950); Michael Grant, *Saint Paul* (Scribner, 1976); and Rudolf Karl Bultmann, *Primitive Christianity in Its Contemporary Setting* (Meridian, 1956), on the beginnings of Christianity. J. W. C. Wand, *A History of the Early Church to A.D. 500*, 4th ed. (Methuen, 1975), and Henry Chadwick, *The Early Church* (Penguin, 1969), are excellent surveys of the first five centuries of church history. For a look at Jesus as a social critic and the "Jewish Socrates," see John D. Crossan, *Jesus: A Revolutionary Biography* (HarperCollins, 1994). See also Cyril Richardson, *Early Christian Fathers* (Macmillan, 1970); the superb biography by Peter Brown, *Augustine of Hippo* (University of California Press, 1969); Harold B. Mattingly, *Christianity in the Roman Empire* (Norton, 1967); Ramsay MacMullen, *Paganism in the Roman Empire* (Yale University Press, 1981), and *Christianizing the Roman Empire* (Yale University Press, 1984); and Charles N. Cochrane, *Christianity and Classical Culture: A Study of Thought and Action from Augustus to Augustine* (Galaxy, 1960). On early monasticism, see Helen Waddell, trans., *The Desert Fathers* (University of Michigan Press, 1957), and Peter Brown, *The Making of Late Antiquity* (Harvard University Press, 1978). See also Eusebius, *The History of the Church from Christ to Constantine* (Penguin, 1994). Ramsay MacMullen gives a thorough treatment of the spread of Christianity after 100 in *Christianizing the Roman Empire (100–400)* (Yale University Press, 1984), and Judith Herrin covers the early stages of the church's growth from the perspective of Constantinople in *The Formation of Christendom* (Princeton University Press, 1987).

Two works by Arnold Hugh Martin Jones, *The Decline of the Ancient World* (Longman, 1977), and *The Later Roman Empire, 284–602: A Social, Economic, and Administrative Survey*, 2 vols. (Johns Hopkins University Press, 1986), are indispensable. An excellent short introduction to Byzantium is Steven Runciman's classic, *Byzantine Civilization* (Meridian, 1969). Joan M. Hussey, *The Byzantine World* (Greenwood, 1982), is clear and lively. For an exhaustive treatment of life in Byzantium, see *The Cambridge Medieval History*, Vol. 4 (Cambridge University Press, 1966, 1967). George Ostrogorsky, *History of the Byzantine State* (Rutgers University Press, 1957), provides the best institutional overview. John W. Barker, *Justinian and the Later Roman Empire* (University of Wisconsin Press, 1966); Robert Browning, *Justinian and Theodora* (Praeger, 1971); and Glanville Downey, *Constantinople in the Age of Justinian* (University of Oklahoma Press, 1968), give complementary analyses of the sixth century. Joan M. Hussey, *The Orthodox Church in the Byzantine Empire* (Oxford University Press, 1986), is the best introduction in English to the development of the eastern variant of Christianity. Romilly Jenkins, *Byzantium: The Imperial Centuries* (Vintage, 1969), is a beautifully written treatment of medieval Byzantium. Francis Dvornik, *The Photian Schism: History and Legend* (Rutgers University Press, 1970), and *The Slavs in European History and Civilization* (Rutgers University Press, 1970), address the matters of conversion. Charles M. Brand, *Byzantium Confronts the West, 1180–1204* (Harvard University Press, 1968), and Donald E. Queller, ed., *The Latin Conquest of Constantinople* (Wiley, 1971), describe the tragedy of the Crusades for Byzantium and complement Steven Runciman's three-volume *History of the Crusades* (Penguin, 1965). Donald Nicol, *The Last Centuries of Byzantium* (St. Martin's Press, 1972), discusses the empire in its state of weakness. The best treatment of Byzantium at its peak is Michael Agold, *The Byzantine Empire, 1025–1204* (Longman, 1985).

D. Talbot Rice, *Art of the Byzantine Era* (Oxford University Press, 1962), gives a competent overall assessment of the eastern empire's aesthetics. Andre Grabar, *Byzantium* (Thames & Hudson, 1966), is a beautifully illustrated and thorough discussion of art and architecture before 600. Harry J. Magoulias, *Byzantine Christianity: Emperor, Church, and the West* (Wayne State University Press, 1982), and Timothy Ware, *The Orthodox Church* (Penguin, 1993), are two sophisticated surveys.

George Vernadsky, *Kievan Russia*, 2nd ed. (Yale University Press, 1973), is detailed and authoritative. G. Fedotov, *The Russian Religious Mind: Kievan Christianity, the Tenth to the Thirteenth Centuries* (HarperTorchbooks, 1975), notes the impact of Orthodoxy on Russian civilization. The works cited in notes 6, 12, and 14 (see p. 198) are useful primary readings. John Fennell, *The Crisis of Medieval Russia, 1200–1304* (Longman, 1983), and Robert O. Crummey, *The Formation of Muscovy, 1304–1613* (Longman, 1987), are two first-rate analyses of the first phases of Russian history. Oscar Halecki, *Borderlands of Western Civilization* (Ronald Press, 1952), gives the outlines of eastern European history, especially the northern region. For samples of primary sources, see Serge A. Zenkovsky, ed., *Medieval Russia's Epics, Chronicles, and Tales* (Penguin, 1994).

Suggestions for Web Browsing

Byzantium Studies on the Internet
http://www.bway.net/~halsall/byzantium.html
Byzantine Art
http://www.bway.net/~halsall/images.html

This site includes many images of icons, monasteries, Ravenna, and Hagia Sophia; it details Byzantine life in Jerusalem and offers links to related Web sites.

Historical Tour of Jerusalem: Byzantine Period
http://gurukul.ucc.american.edu/TED/hpages/jeruselum/byzantin.htm

Short history of Jerusalem, from 324 to 638 C.E., including an image and discussion of the Madaba mosaic showing the Jerusalem Gate.

Women in Byzantium
http://www.wooster.edu/ART/wb.html

Extensive bibliography of primary and secondary sources regarding women in Byzantium.

Byzantium Through Arab Eyes
http://www.fordham.edu/halsall/source/byz-arabambas.html

An original account of a mission to Constantinople by an Arab ambassador in the late tenth century.

Notes

1. Edmund Wilson, *The Scrolls from the Dead Sea* (New York: Oxford University Press, 1955), p. 60.
2. Josephus, *The Jewish War*, trans. G. A. Williamson (Baltimore: Penguin, 1970), p. 136.
3. Mary Kinnear, *Daughters of Time: Women in the Western Tradition* (Ann Arbor: University of Michigan Press, 1982), p. 55.
4. St. Augustine, *Confessions* 13.38, trans. E. B. Pusey.
5. Alan Cameron, *Circus Factions: Blues and Greens at Rome and Byzantium* (Oxford: Clarendon Press, 1976), pp. 310–311.
6. Procopius of Caesarea, *History of the Wars*, Vol. 1, 24:36–38, trans. S. R. Rosenbaum, in Charles Diehl, *Theodora: Empress of Byzantium* (New York: Ungar, 1972), pp. 87–88.
7. George Ostrogorsky, *History of the Byzantine State*, trans. Joan M. Hussey (New Brunswick, N.J.: Rutgers University Press, 1957), pp. 86–90.
8. Andreas N. Stratos, *Byzantium in the Seventh Century*, Vol. 1, trans. Marc Oglivie-Grant (Amsterdam: Hakkert, 1968), pp. 37–39.
9. Romilly Jenkins, *Byzantium: The Imperial Centuries, A.D. 610–1071* (New York: Vintage Books, 1969), pp. 90–104.
10. Francis Dvornik, *The Photian Schism: History and Legend* (New Brunswick, N.J.: Rutgers University Press, 1970).
11. For an eastern perspective, see Amin Maalouf, *The Crusades Through Arab Eyes* (New York: Schocken, 1985).
12. Geoffrey de Villehardouin, *The Conquest of Constantinople*, in M. R. B. Shaw, *Chronicles of the Crusades* (Baltimore: Penguin, 1963), pp. 79, 92.
13. Steven Runciman, *The Fall of Constantinople* (Cambridge: Cambridge University Press, 1965).
14. *The Russian Primary Chronicle*, trans. Samuel H. Cross and O. P. Sherbowitz-Wetzor (Cambridge: Mediaeval Academy of America, 1953), pp. 110–118.
15. John Fennell, *The Crisis of Medieval Russia, 1200–1304* (London: Longman, 1983).
16. Robert O. Crummey, *The Formation of Muscovy, 1304–1613* (New York: Longman, 1987), p. 135.
17. Donald Treadgold, *The West in Russia and China*, Vol. 1 (Cambridge: Cambridge University Press, 1973), pp. 2–4.

The bejeweled front cover of the Lindau Gospels, a work dating from the third quarter of the ninth century, is an example of Carolingian art. The Celtic–Germanic metalwork tradition has been adapted to the religious art produced during the era of Charlemagne. The main clusters of semiprecious stones adorning the gold cover have been raised so that light can penetrate beneath them to make them glow.

The Church in the Middle Ages

Religion and Learning in Medieval Europe, 500–1500

As we have seen in Chapter 4, the Roman Empire in the third and fourth centuries became increasingly unable to provide political stability, economic security, and social confidence to its people. The newly organized church gradually emerged as one of the mainstays of order and authority.

The Church in the Early Middle Ages

In addition to offering comfort and hope in times of great challenge, the Christian Church steadily established its authority as a powerful institution exercising growing political, economic, and social strength.

The Early Medieval Papacy, 600–1000

Chapter 7 examined the growth in the authority of the bishops of Rome, the popes. Often the early popes were looked to for political as well as spiritual guidance in troubled times. During the pontificate of Gregory I, the Great (590–604), the papacy aggressively began to assert its political as well as spiritual authority. After his election as pope, Gregory assumed the task of protecting Rome and its surrounding territory from the Lombard threat. Gregory was the first pope to act as actual ruler of a part of what later became the Papal States.

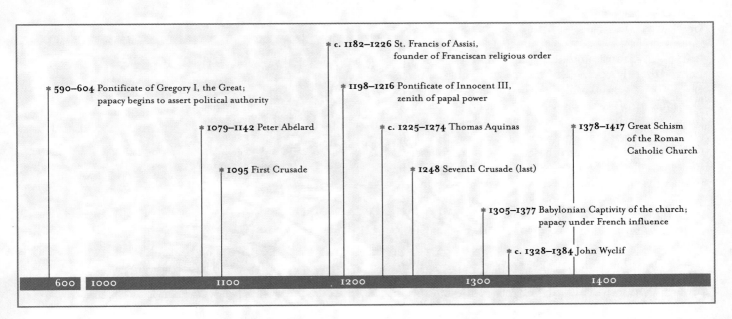

* **c. 1182–1226** St. Francis of Assisi, founder of Franciscan religious order

* **590–604** Pontificate of Gregory I, the Great; papacy begins to assert political authority

* **1198–1216** Pontificate of Innocent III, zenith of papal power

* **1079–1142** Peter Abélard

* **c. 1225–1274** Thomas Aquinas

* **1378–1417** Great Schism of the Roman Catholic Church

* **1095** First Crusade

* **1248** Seventh Crusade (last)

* **1305–1377** Babylonian Captivity of the church; papacy under French influence

* **c. 1328–1384** John Wyclif

| 600 | 1000 | 1100 | 1200 | 1300 | 1400 |

Gregory also laid the foundation for the papal machinery of church government. The pattern of church government that Gregory established in England—bishops supervised by archbishops, who reported to the pope—became standard.

The task of establishing papal control of the church and extending the pope's temporal authority was continued by Gregory's successors. In the eighth century English missionaries transferred to Germany and France the pattern of papal government they had known in England; the Donation of Pepin, a sizable grant of territory in Italy given to the pope by the Merovingian king (see Chapter 9), greatly increased the pope's temporal power by creating the Papal States.

Missionary Activities of the Church

The early Middle Ages was a period of widespread missionary activity. By spreading Christianity, missionaries aided in the merging of Germanic and Roman cultures. One of the earliest Christian missionaries was Ulfilas (c. 311–383), who spent 40 years among the Visigoths and translated most of the Bible into Gothic. Missionary activities in Ireland resulted in the founding of numerous monasteries; in the late sixth and seventh centuries a large number of monks from these Irish monasteries went to Scotland, northern England, the kingdom of the Franks, and even Italy as missionaries to renew the faith and erase the effects of worldly corruption. Irish monks also eagerly pursued scholarship, and their monasteries became storehouses for priceless manuscripts.

The Preservation of Knowledge

After the fall of Rome, learning did not entirely die out in western Europe; the knowledge of the classical world was preserved through the efforts of a number of concerned intellectuals. Seeing that the ability to read Greek was quickly disappearing, the sixth-century Roman scholar Boethius determined to preserve Greek learning by translating all of Plato and Aristotle into Latin. Unjustly accused of treachery by the emperor, Boethius was thrown into prison, where he wrote *The Consolation of Philosophy* while awaiting execution; this work became a medieval textbook on philosophy.

Cassiodorus, a contemporary of Boethius, devoted most of his life to the collection and preservation of classical knowledge. By encouraging the monks to copy valuable manuscripts, he was instrumental in making the monasteries centers of learning. Following his example, many monasteries established *scriptoria*, departments concerned exclusively with copying manuscripts.

During the early Middle Ages most education took place in the monasteries. In the late sixth and seventh centuries, when the effects of the barbarian invasions were still being felt on the Continent, Irish monasteries provided a safe haven for learning. There men studied Greek and Latin, copied and preserved manuscripts, and, in illuminating them, produced masterpieces of art. The *Book of Kells* is a surviving example of their skill.

An outstanding scholar of the early Middle Ages, the Venerable Bede (d. 735) followed the Irish tradition of learning in a northern English monastery. Bede's most famous work, the *Ecclesiastical History of the English People*, remains one of the most important sources for early British history.

Church Dominance, 1000–1300

During the High Middle Ages the church became more involved in the structure of society and, of necessity, more concerned with temporal affairs. Eventually the church overcame its conflicts with secular powers and emerged as a dominant political as well as spiritual force in European life.

Monastic Reform

A religious revival, often called the "medieval reformation," began in the tenth century and reached full force in the twelfth and thirteenth centuries. The first far-reaching manifestation of the revival was the reformed Benedictine order of monks at Cluny, in present-day France, founded in 910. The ultimate goal of the Cluniac reformers was to free the entire church from secular control and subject it to papal authority. Some 300 Cluniac houses were freed from lay control, and in 1059 an attempt was made to rid the papacy itself of secular interference by the creation of the college of cardinals, which elected the pope.

Monastic Reform and the Investiture Controversy

910	Benedictine monastery at Cluny founded
1059	College of cardinals founded
1073–1085	Pontificate of Gregory VII; struggle over lay investiture
1077	Emperor Henry IV begs forgiveness at Canossa
1091–1153	St. Bernard of Clairvaux, founder of the Cistercian religous order

Even the papacy was affected by the call for reform. The most aggressive advocate of church reform in the High Middle Ages was Pope Gregory VII (1073–1085), who claimed unprecedented power for the papacy. In 1075 Gregory VII formally prohibited lay investiture (bestowal of the symbols of the churchman's office by a secular official such as a king) and threatened to excommunicate (expel from the Roman Catholic Church) any layman who performed it. This act virtually declared war against Europe's rulers, as lay investiture had been employed since the emperor Constantine's time. The climax to the struggle occurred in Gregory's clash with the German emperor Henry IV (see Chapter 9).

Late in the eleventh century a second wave of monastic reform produced several new orders of monks, among which were the Cistercians. The Cistercian movement received its greatest impetus from the efforts of St. Bernard of Clairvaux, also in present-day France (1091–1153). This order's abbeys were situated in solitary places, and their strict discipline emphasized fasts and vigils, manual labor, and a vegetarian diet. Their churches contained neither stained glass nor statues, and Bernard denounced the beautification of churches in general as unnecessary distraction.

The Papacy's Zenith: Innocent III

Under Innocent III (1198–1216) a new type of administrator-pope emerged and papal power reached its zenith. Unlike Gregory VII and other earlier reform popes, who were monks, Innocent and other great popes of the late twelfth and thirteenth centuries were lawyers trained in the newly revived and enlarged church, or canon, law.

So successful was Innocent III in asserting his temporal and spiritual supremacy that many states formally acknowledged they were subordinate to the pope. In the case of King John of England, a struggle developed over the election of the archbishop of Canterbury, and Innocent placed England under interdict (see below for definition) for five years and excommunicated John. Under attack from his barons, John capitulated to Innocent by becoming his vassal (subordinate), receiving England back as a fief (feudal estate), and paying him an annual monetary tribute. Innocent forced Philip Augustus of France to take back as his queen the woman he had divorced with the consent of the French bishops. As for the Holy Roman Empire, Innocent intervened in a civil war between rival candidates for the throne, supporting first one and then the other. Innocent finally secured the election of his ward, the young Hohenstaufen heir Frederick II, who promised to respect papal rights.

At Canossa, the penitent Henry IV pleads with Abbot Hugh of Cluny and Countess Matilda of Tuscany to intercede with Pope Gregory VII to rescind Henry's excommunication.

Church Administration

The universality and power of the church rested not only on a systematized, uniform religious creed but also on the most highly organized administrative system in the West. Special emissaries called *legates*, whose powers were superior to those of the local churchmen, carried the pope's orders throughout Europe.

The church was ahead of secular states in developing a system of courts and a body of law. Canon law was based on the Scriptures, the writings of the church fathers, and the decrees of church councils and popes. But the papacy's chief weapons to support its authority were spiritual penalties. The most powerful of these was excommunication. A person who was excommunicated was deprived of the sacraments of the church and condemned to hell.

Interdict was also a powerful instrument. Excommunication was directed against individuals, but interdict suspended all public worship and withheld most sacraments in the realm of a disobedient ruler. Pope Innocent III successfully applied or threatened the interdict 85 times against disobedient kings and princes.

Heresy

Heresy, the belief in doctrines officially condemned by the church, once again became a concern in the High Middle Ages. Numerous spiritual ideas flourished particularly in the newly revived towns, where changing social and spiritual needs went largely unheeded by old-style churchmen. This fertile ground produced many heresies, among which the Albigensian and Waldensian were major ones.

The Cathari ("pure") or Albigensians—so called because Albi in southern France was an important center—regarded the world as the battleground for the opposing forces of good and evil. They denounced many activities of the state and the individual, even condemning marriage for perpetuating the human species in this sinful world. The Albigensians rejected the church as an institution because it too was a part of the earth and thereby inherently evil.

The Waldensians derived their name from Peter Waldo, a merchant of Lyons who gave his wealth to charity and founded a lay order, the Poor Men of Lyons, to serve the needs of the people. He had parts of the New Testament translated into French, believed that laymen could preach the Gospel, and denied the effectiveness of the sacraments unless administered by worthy priests.

For ten years Innocent III tried to reconvert these heretical groups. Unsuccessful, he instigated a crusade against the prosperous and cultured French region of Toulouse where the Albigensians were attacked in 1208. The crusade began with horrible slaughter to the cry of "Kill them all—God will know his own." Soon the original religious motive was lost in a selfish rush to seize the wealth of the accused. In time the Albigensian heresy was destroyed, along with its flourishing culture of southern France, and the Waldensians were scattered.

In 1233 a special papal court called the Inquisition was established to cope with the rising tide of heresy and to bring about religious conformity. Those accused were tried in secret without the aid of legal counsel. Those who confessed and renounced heresy were "reconciled" with the church on performance of penance. Those who did not voluntarily confess could be tortured. If torture failed, the prisoners could be declared heretics and turned over to the secular authorities, usually to be burned at the stake.

Franciscans and Dominicans

As a more positive response to the spread of heresy and the conditions that caused it, Innocent III approved the founding of the Franciscan and Dominican orders of *friars* ("brothers"). Instead of living in remote monasteries, the friars of these orders moved among the people, ministering to their needs, preaching the Gospel, and teaching in the schools.

The Franciscans were founded by St. Francis of Assisi (c. 1182–1226), who rejected riches and spread the gospel of poverty and Christian simplicity. Love of one's fellow human beings and all God's creatures, even "brother worm," was basic in the Rule of St. Francis, which was inspired by Jesus' example.

The second order of friars was founded by St. Dominic (1170–1221), a well-educated Spaniard who had fought the Albigensians in southern France. There he decided that to combat the strength and zeal of its opponents, the church should have champions who could preach the Gospel with the dedication of the apostles. The friar-preachers of Dominic's order dedicated themselves to preaching as a means of maintaining the doctrines of the church and of converting heretics.

The enthusiasm and sincerity of the friars in their early years made a profound impact on an age that had grown increasingly critical of the worldliness of the church. But after they took charge of the Inquisition, became professors in the universities, and served the papacy in other ways, the friars lost much of their original simplicity. Yet their message and zeal had done much to provide the church with moral and intellectual leadership at a time when such leadership was badly needed.

The Crusades

The Crusades, a series of campaigns that began toward the end of the eleventh century, were a remarkable expression of European self-confidence and expansion in the High Middle Ages. The church was instrumental in beginning these efforts to recapture the Holy Land from Muslim control. But by the conclusion of the crusading era, the church, and the papacy in particular, had suffered a serious loss of prestige largely because of its actions related to the crusading movement.

The Call for Crusades

For hundreds of years peaceful pilgrims had been traveling from Europe to worship at the birthplace of Jesus. But during the eleventh century Christian pilgrims to the Holy Land became especially concerned when the Seljuk Turks, new and fierce converts to Islam, took over Jerusalem from the more tolerant Abbasid Muslims.

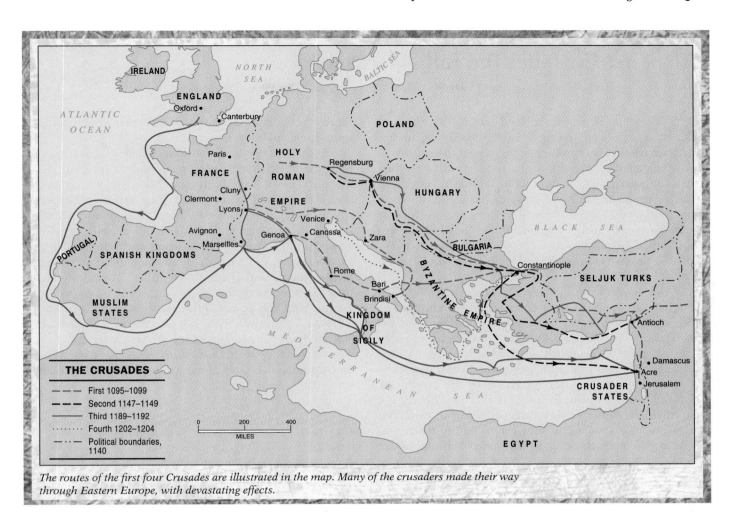

The routes of the first four Crusades are illustrated in the map. Many of the crusaders made their way through Eastern Europe, with devastating effects.

In 1095 Pope Urban II proclaimed the First Crusade to regain the Holy Land. Preaching at the Council of Clermont in that year, he called on Christians to take up the cross and strive for a cause that promised not merely spiritual rewards but material gain as well. Following Urban's appeal, there was a real and spontaneous outpouring of religious enthusiasm. The word *crusade* itself is derived from "taking the cross," after the example of Christ.

The Crusading Expeditions

From the end of the eleventh century through the thirteenth, seven major crusades, as well as various small expeditions, warred against the Muslims, whom the crusaders called Saracens. The First Crusade, composed of feudal nobles from France, parts of Germany, and Norman Italy, marched overland through eastern Europe to Constantinople. Expecting the help of skilled European mercenaries against the Seljuks, the emperor Alexius Comnenus was shocked when confronted by a disorderly mob of crusaders and quickly directed them out of Constantinople to fight the Turks. This First Crusade was the most successful of the seven; with not

more than 5000 knights and infantry, it overcame the resistance of the Turks, who were no longer united. It captured Jerusalem and a narrow strip of land stretching from there to Antioch, which became known as the Latin Kingdom of Jerusalem, and over which crusaders and Islamic armies continued to battle until the region was finally retaken by the Muslims in 1291.

The fall of Jerusalem in 1187 to the Muslims, reinvigorated under the leadership of Saladin, the sultan of Egypt and Syria, provoked the Third Crusade in 1189. Its leaders were three of the most famous medieval kings—Frederick Barbarossa of Germany, Richard the Lion-Hearted of England, and Philip Augustus of France. Frederick drowned in Asia Minor, and, after many quarrels with Richard, Philip returned home. Saladin and Richard remained to fight but finally agreed to a three-year truce and free access to Jerusalem for Christian pilgrims.

The Fourth Crusade (1202–1204) was a disaster from a religious perspective. No kings answered the call of Pope Innocent III, and the knights who did participate were unable to pay the Venetians the agreed-on transport charges. The Venetians persuaded the crusaders to pay off their debts by capturing the Christian

The First Crusade: The Fall of Jerusalem

This selection describes the fall of Jerusalem during the First Crusade in 1099, as witnessed by the author, a Frankish knight.

During this siege, we suffered so badly from thirst that we sewed up the skins of oxen and buffaloes, and we used to carry water in them for the distance of nearly six miles. We drank the water from these vessels, although it stank, and what with foul water and barley bread we suffered great distress and affliction every day, for the Saracens used to lie in wait for our men by every spring and pool, where they killed them and cut them to pieces; moreover they used to carry off the beasts into their caves and secret places in the rocks.

Our leaders then decided to attack the city with engines, so that we might enter it and worship at our Saviour's Sepulchre.... On Friday at dawn we attacked the city from all sides but could achieve nothing, so that we were all astounded and very much afraid, yet, when that hour came when our Lord Jesus Christ deigned to suffer for us upon the cross, our knights were fighting bravely on the siege tower.... All the defenders fled along the walls and through the city, and our men went after them, killing them and cutting them down as far as Solomon's Temple, where there was such a massacre that our men were wading up to their ankles in enemy blood.

At last, when the pagans were defeated, our men took many prisoners, both men and women, in the Temple. They killed whom they chose, and whom they chose they saved alive. After this our men rushed round the whole city, seizing the gold and silver, horses and mules, and houses full of all sorts of goods, and they all came rejoicing and weeping from excess of gladness to worship at the Sepulchre of our Savior Jesus, and there they fulfilled their vows to him. Next morning they went cautiously up on to the Temple roof and attacked the Saracens, both men and women, cutting off their heads with drawn swords. No-one has ever seen or heard of such a slaughter of pagans, for they were burned on pyres like pyramids, and no-one save God alone knows how many there were.

From Rosalind Hill, ed., *Gesta Francorum* (London: Nelson, 1962). Reprinted by permission of Oxford University Press, Oxford.

town of Zara on the Adriatic coast, which had long proved a successful rival to Venetian trading interests. Then, in order to eliminate Byzantine commercial competition, the Venetians pressured the crusaders to attack Constantinople itself. After conquering and sacking the great city, the crusaders set up the Latin Empire of Constantinople and forgot about recovering the Holy Land.

The thirteenth century produced other crusading failures. The boys and girls participating in the Children's Crusade of 1212 fully expected the waters of the Mediterranean to part and make a path from southern France to the Holy Land, which they would take without fighting, but instead thousands of them were sold into slavery by the merchants of Marseilles. The Seventh Crusade was the last major attempt to regain Jerusalem; the crusading movement ended in 1291 when Acre, the last stronghold of the Christians in the Holy Land, fell to the Muslims.

The Crusader States

Four crusader states, with the kingdom of Jerusalem dominant, were established along the eastern Mediterranean coast as a result of the crusading movement. By the time Jerusalem fell to Saladin in 1187, however, only isolated pockets of Christians remained, surrounded by Muslims. The crusader states were able to cling to survival only through frequent delivery of supplies and manpower from Europe.

The crusader states were defended primarily by three semimonastic military orders: the Templars, or Knights of the Temple, so called because their first headquarters was on the site of the old Temple of Jerusalem; the Hospitalers, or Knights of St. John of Jerusalem, who were founded originally to care for the sick and wounded; and the Teutonic Knights, exclusively a German order. Combining monasticism and militarism, these orders served to protect all pilgrims and to wage perpetual war against the Muslims.

Significance of the Crusades

Even though the Crusades failed to achieve their permanent objective, they were more than mere military adventures. Much of the crusading fervor carried over to the European efforts against the Muslims in Spain and the Slavs in eastern Europe. The Crusades crucially weakened the Byzantine Empire and accelerated its fall. And although the early Crusades strengthened the moral leadership of the papacy in Europe, the misadventures of the later Crusades, together with the church's preaching of Crusades against Christian heretics and political opponents,

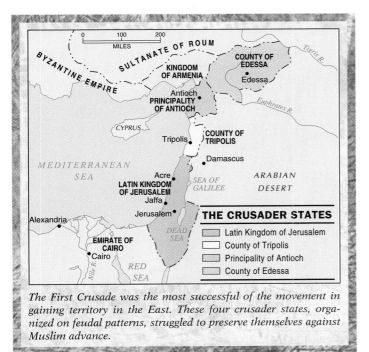

The First Crusade was the most successful of the movement in gaining territory in the East. These four crusader states, organized on feudal patterns, struggled to preserve themselves against Muslim advance.

weakened both the crusading ideal and respect for the papacy.

Contact with the East through the crusading movement widened the scope of many Europeans, ended their isolation, and exposed them to an admirable civilization. And the Crusades did influence the reopening of the eastern Mediterranean to Western commerce, a factor that in itself had an effect on the revival of cities and the emergence of a money economy in the West.

Thought and Culture During the High Middle Ages

In addition to a decline in the general level of education, interest in intellectual matters decreased rapidly in the period following the fall of the Roman Empire and the establishment of the early Germanic kingdoms. And even among the intellectual community that did survive, a controversy raged over the value of studying subjects not directly pertinent to the church. A significant effort to revitalize learning and the arts had been undertaken by Charlemagne (768–814), and his efforts produced what has become known as the Carolingian Renaissance. Charlemagne's efforts to increase literacy and preserve the arts met with great success, but the weakness of later Carolingian rulers somewhat limited the lasting results of his reform.

The Revival of Learning

Prior to the twelfth century, most schools in Europe were under the control and direction of the church.

But when the schools run by monasteries started limiting admissions to students who were preparing for careers in the church, an important development in education took place. Students interested in professions outside the church increasingly sought to attend schools administered by cathedrals. Although still dominated by churchmen and centered around a religion-focused curriculum, the cathedral schools gradually expanded their subject offerings to attract students intending to pursue secular careers.

Interest in studying the classical literature of pagan Greece and Rome further broadened the curriculum. Much of this interest can be attributed to increasing European contacts with the Arab world, through the crusading movement and also through increasing commercial activity. The rebirth of classical learning in the twelfth century produced unprecedented numbers of students flocking to the schools.

Origin of European Universities

The development of professional studies in law, medicine, and theology led to the rise of universities, which soon eclipsed the monastic and cathedral schools as organized centers of learning. Originally the word *university* meant a group of persons possessing a common purpose. The term referred to a guild of learners, both teachers and students, similar to the craft guilds, with their masters and apprentices. In the thirteenth century the universities had no campuses and little property or money, and the masters taught in hired rooms or religious houses. If the university was dissatisfied with its treatment by the townspeople, it could move elsewhere. The earliest universities—at Bologna, Paris, and Oxford—were not officially founded, but in time popes or kings granted them and other universities charters of self-government. These charters gave legal status to the universities and rights to the students, such as freedom from the jurisdiction of town officials.

Scholasticism

Most medieval thinkers did not think of truth as something to be discovered by themselves; they saw it as already existing in authoritative Christian and pagan writings of antiquity. By employing reason (through the use of logic or dialectic), scholars of the twelfth and thirteenth centuries attempted to understand and express truth through this logical process of explanation. Since this task was carried out largely in the schools, these scholars are known as Scholastics, and the intellectual method they produced is called Scholasticism.

Each scholar formed his own judgments and sought to convince others. This activity led to much debate on a range of subjects. Most famous was the argument over universals known as the nominalist-realist controversy. This philosophical controversy

Discovery Through Maps
The Hereford Map, c. 1290

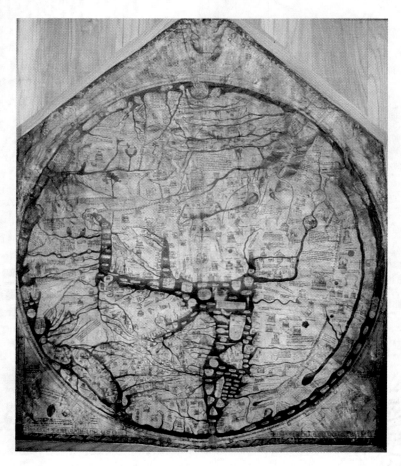

The Hereford Map, the largest of its kind to have remained in excellent condition for 700 years, is now preserved in the cathedral of Hereford, England. It is thought that this map was copied in large detail from another, older map, which was in turn copied from a Roman map perhaps dating to the first century of the Common Era. The entire skin of a calf had to be specially prepared for the writing and illustration of the Hereford Map. Calfskin prepared in this special manner is called *vellum*, from the Latin word for "calf."

The map bears an inscription by its author, Richard of Haldingham and Lafford, in the bottom right corner. Such inscriptions are very unusual on medieval maps. Names and descriptions on the map are written in Latin and in the Norman dialect of French. The circle of the world is surrounded by the ocean. At the center of the world is the holy city of Jerusalem, for it was often thought in the Middle Ages that Jerusalem's religious significance indicated its centrality in the world. Mesopotamia is represented at the top of the Hereford Map, in keeping with medieval custom sanctioned by the church. Note the representation of the Tower of Babel (Turrus Babblus) to the immediate "north" of Palestine, and Paradise placed at the very top of the map. To the right of Palestine is Egypt, which the mapmaker has included in Asia.

Experts think that mapmakers in the late Middle Ages probably did not know as much about geography as sailors and merchants engaged in overseas trade and commerce and may have lagged in their geographical knowledge by as much as 200 years. Such a lag would perhaps explain the lack of a more accurate depiction of Africa and Europe.

The Hereford Map may have been originally intended as a decorative background for an altar. That might account for much of the Christian symbolism displayed on the map and even its basic orientation. Another possibility is that the map was intended to be a teaching device to aid a largely illiterate and provincial populace in understanding both the world and the Christian faith. The Hereford mapmaker was a teacher as well as a cartographer, explaining the world as he illustrated it.

centered on the question of whether universal ideas—beauty, truth, and justice, for example—had a reality other than what existed in people's minds as abstract notions. The realists held that these universal ideas did have a reality, but the nominalists believed that the universal ideas were nothing more than names *(nomina)* used to identify abstract concepts.

The Contribution of Abélard

The extreme and often sterile views of nominalists and realists frustrated the brilliant Peter Abélard (1079–1142), a popular teacher at the cathedral school of Notre Dame in Paris. Abélard's great contribution to medieval thought was an approach called *conceptualism*, his solution to the nominalist-realist controversy. Abélard believed that universals, while existing only in the mind as thoughts or concepts, are nevertheless valid (real) since they are the product of observing the similar qualities that exist in a particular class of things. Thus by observing many chairs and sitting in them, we arrive at the universal concept "chair."

In addition to redefining the purpose of Scholastic thought, Abélard perfected Scholastic method. Like others before him, Abélard emphasized the importance of understanding. However, Abélard's predecessors had begun with faith; Abélard started with doubt. One must learn to doubt, he insisted, for doubting leads to inquiry, and inquiry leads to the truth.

Women and Learning in the High Middle Ages

In the early Middle Ages, and especially after the eighth century, the convents of Europe served as centers of learned activity for a select group of aristocratic and middle-class women who pursued an intellectual life as well as one devoted to religion. But outside of the convents, a life devoted to scholarship was almost impossible for a medieval woman; the church taught that a woman should be either a housewife or a virgin in service to her God, and rarely was it possible for a woman to write, compose, or create in such a society.

Nevertheless, intellectual achievements by some exceptional medieval women were possible. One such remarkable woman was Hildegard of Bingen (1098–1179), the leader of a community of Benedictine nuns in Germany. Hildegard wrote a mystical work describing her visions, which she began to receive at the age of 42. She was also a skilled composer, writing many hymns for her nuns to sing. She wrote a morality play and also several scientific works, which cataloged nearly 500 plants, animals, and stones, assessing their medicinal value.

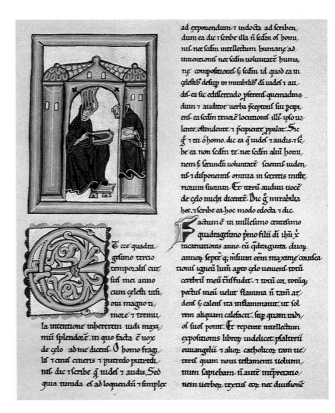

Hildegard's Vision, from Scrivas *by Hildegard of Bingen, c. 1142–1152. Hildegard, a remarkable scholar, musician, and mystic, is shown in this illustrated manuscript receiving divine inspiration while a scribe awaits her words.*

New Knowledge and the Task of Reconciliation

In the twelfth century Western scholars flocked to Spain and Sicily to translate Muslim editions of classical literature. As a result of these translations a great number of new ideas, particularly in science and philosophy, were introduced to Western scholars. Algebra, trigonometry, and Euclid's *Geometry* became available, and Arabic numerals, including the symbol for zero, made possible the decimal system of computation. Physics was based on Aristotle's theory of four elements (water, earth, air, and fire) and on his theories of dynamics—doctrines that took centuries to disprove. Chemistry was also based on Aristotelian concepts, mixed with magic and alchemy. Like Muslim alchemists, Europeans tried in vain to convert base metals into gold and silver and to obtain a magic elixir that would prolong life; in both cases the attempts did much to advance true findings in the field of chemistry.

Because of the emphasis on authority and the influence of the church, the medieval atmosphere was not conducive to free scientific investigation. An exception to this subservience to authority was the English Franciscan Roger Bacon (1214–1292), who introduced the notion of "experimental science" and boldly criticized the deductive "logic chopping" used by Scholastic thinkers. Bacon never doubted the authority of the Bible or the church—his interest lay only in natural science—yet his superiors considered him dangerous because of his criticism of Scholastic thought.

By the thirteenth century learned Muslim commentaries on the medical works of Galen and Hippocrates and on Aristotle's biology were available in the West. This knowledge, coupled with new discoveries and improved techniques, made medieval doctors more than just barbers who engaged in bloodletting. Yet the overall state of medical knowledge and practice was, by current standards, still primitive.

As his writings became known, Aristotle became "the philosopher" to medieval students, and his authority was generally accepted as second only to that of the Scriptures. But because the church's teachings were considered infallible, Aristotle's ideas, as well as those of other great thinkers of antiquity, had to be reconciled with religious dogma. Using logical approaches, the Scholastic thinkers of the thirteenth century undertook this task of reconciliation.

Scholasticism reached its high point with Thomas Aquinas (c. 1225–1274). In *Summa Theologica* this brilliant Italian Dominican dealt with the great problems of theology, philosophy, politics, and economics. Aquinas's goal was to reconcile Aristotle with church dogma—in other words, the truths of natural reason with the truths of faith. There can be no real contradiction, he argued, since all truth comes from God. In case of an unresolved contradiction, however, faith won out because of the possibility of human error in reasoning.

The Decline of Scholasticism

The assumption that faith and reason were compatible was vigorously denied by two Franciscan thinkers, Duns Scotus (d. 1308) and William of Occam (d. c. 1349), who elaborated on Aquinas's belief that certain religious doctrines are beyond discovery by the use of reason. They argued that if the human intellect could not understand divinely revealed truth, it could hope to comprehend only the natural world and should not intrude on the sphere of divine truth.

After the thirteenth century, Scholasticism increasingly lost influence, for its adherents were obsessed with theological subtleties, discouraged independent thought, and in general lost touch with reality. But it should be remembered that the Scholastics sought to compile and then to interpret the vast body of Christian and pagan knowledge left to them by an earlier civilization. In terms of their needs and objectives—an intelligible and complete synthesis of faith, logic, and science—the Scholastics were extremely successful.

The theologian Thomas Aquinas was influenced by Aristotle (lower left) and Plato (lower right) as well as early Christian thinkers, shown above him, The Islamic philosopher Averroës is illustrated as vanquished at his feet.

Arts and Letters in the Middle Ages

Throughout the Middle Ages, Latin served as an international language. This common tongue provided much of the cohesion of the era, for virtually all the crucial communications of the church, governments, and schools were in Latin. Not all Latin dealt with religious and philosophical subjects; the poetry of twelfth- and thirteenth-century students, known as Goliardic verse, proclaimed the pleasures of the good life.

Vernacular Literature: Dante and Chaucer

By the twelfth century, more literature in the vernacular, or native, tongues began to appear, with the epic

Interior view of the Cathedral of St. Pierre at Angoulème, a typical example of Romanesque architecture. The cathedral's ribbed-groin vaults are derived from the Roman intersecting vaults. As shown in the drawing, the ribbed vault is made up of arches that span the sides of a square bay, with groin vaults crossing diagonally from corner to corner.

as the earliest form. The greatest of the French epics, known as *chansons de geste* ("songs of great deeds"), is the late-eleventh-century *Song of Roland,* which tells of the heroic deeds and death of Count Roland in the Pyrenees as he defended the retreat of Charlemagne's army. The great Spanish epic *Poema del Mio Cid* is a product of the twelfth century. These stirring epic poems, with their accounts of prowess in battle, mirror the warrior virtues of early chivalry—the code of conduct developed by the nobility to bring some sophistication and culture to their social conduct.

The vernacular was also used by two of the greatest writers of the period, Dante and Chaucer. Combining a profound religious sense with a knowledge of Scholastic thought and the Latin classics, the Italian Dante Alighieri (1265–1321) wrote the *Divine Comedy,* an allegory of medieval man (Dante) moving from bestial earthliness (hell) through conversion (purgatory) to a spiritual union with God (paradise).

In the *Canterbury Tales,* Geoffrey Chaucer (c. 1340–1400), revealed a cross section of contemporary English life, customs, and thought through personality profiles and stories told by 29 religious pilgrims who assembled in April 1387 at an inn before journeying to the shrine of St. Thomas à Becket at Canterbury.

Medieval Architecture and Sculpture

In the eleventh century a tremendous architectural revival occurred, marked by a return to building in stone rather than in wood, as had been common during the early Middle Ages. At a much later date the term *Romanesque* came to be applied to this new style because, like early Christian architecture, it was based largely on Roman models. Although details of structure and ornamentation differed with locality, the round arch was a standard Romanesque feature. Romanesque cathedrals emphasized symmetry, massive stone walls, small windows, and plain interiors.

In the twelfth and thirteenth centuries Gothic architecture replaced the older Romanesque style. The architects of the Gothic-style cathedral developed vaults with pointed rather than round arches. These vaults replaced the heavy barrel vault and, combined with the use of flying buttresses to distribute weight more evenly, allowed the use of large stained-glass windows set into the walls. The light loftiness of the Gothic interiors was a welcome improvement over the dark, somber interiors of the Romanesque churches.

Most Romanesque and Gothic sculpture served an architectural function by being carved into the

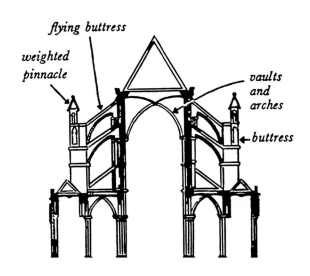

The effect of the fully developed Gothic style, as shown in this interior view of Amiens Cathedral, is one of awesome but ordered intricacy. The drawing is a cross section of the cathedral. Vaults, arches, buttresses, and weighted pinnacles were important structural elements in the Gothic style of architecture.

total composition of a church. To use sculpture to the best architectural advantage, the artist often distorted the subject to achieve a particular effect. Like sculpture, medieval painting in the form of stained-glass windows was an integral part of the architecture.

What the cathedral was to religious life, the castle was to everyday living. Both were havens, and both were built to endure. The new weapons and techniques of siege warfare, which the crusaders brought back from the Holy Land, necessitated more massive castles. By the thirteenth century castle building in Europe had reached a high point of development. The towers were rounded, and bastions stood at strategic points along the walls. The castle as a whole was planned in such a skillful manner that if one section was taken by attackers, it could be sealed off from the remaining fortifications. Whole towns were fortified in the same way, with walls, watchtowers, moats, and drawbridges.

Toward the end of the Middle Ages there was less need for fortified towns and castles. At the same time, the wealth from the revival of trade and increased industry encouraged the development of secular Gothic architecture. Town halls and guildhalls, the residences of the rich, and the chateaux of the nobility all borrowed the delicate Gothic style from the cathedrals.

Decline of the Medieval Church, 1300–1500

The period of the papacy's greatest power—the twelfth and thirteenth centuries—reached its apex with the pontificate of Innocent III, who exerted his influence over kings and princes without challenge. The church then seemed unassailable in its prestige, dignity, and power. Yet that strength soon came under new attack, and during the next two centuries the process of disintegration accelerated.

Decline of the Church

1294–1303	Pontificate of Boniface VIII
1302	*Unam Sanctam*
1305–1377	Popes at Avignon; Babylonian Captivity of the church
1378–1417	Great Schism of the Roman Catholic Church
1414	Council of Constance

Pope Boniface VIII, *Unam Sanctam*

Unam Sanctam (1302), written to Philip IV of France by Pope Boniface VIII, is one of the most extreme statements of papal superiority and one of the final assertions of the temporal power of the church in an age growing more distant from effective political power exercised by the pope.

We are compelled, our faith urging us, to believe and to hold—and we do firmly believe and simply confess—that there is one holy catholic and apostolic church, outside of which there is neither salvation nor remission of sins. . . . In this church there is one Lord, one faith and one baptism. . . . This church, moreover, we venerate as the only one, the Lord saying through His prophet: "Deliver my soul from the sword, my darling from the power of the dog." He prayed at the same time for His soul—that is, for Himself the Head—and for His body—which body, namely, he called the one and only church on account of the unity of the faith promised, of the sacraments, and of the love of the church. . . . Therefore of this one and only church there is one body and one head—not two heads as if it were a monster:—Christ, namely, and the vicar of Christ, St. Peter, and the successor of Peter. . . . We are told by the word of the gospel that in this His fold there are two swords,—a spiritual, namely, and a temporal. . . . Surely he who denies that the temporal sword is in the power of Peter wrongly interprets the word of the Lord when He says: "Put up thy sword in its scabbard." Both swords, the spiritual and the material, therefore, are in the power of the church; the one, indeed, to be wielded for the church, the other by the church; the one by the hand of the priest, the other by the hand of kings and knights, but at the will and sufferance of the priest. One sword, moreover, ought to be under the other, and the temporal authority to be subjected to the spiritual. . . . *Indeed we declare, announce and define, that it is altogether necessary to salvation for every human creature to be subject to the Roman pontiff.* The Lateran, Nov. 14, in our 8th year. As a perpetual memorial of this matter.

From Ernest F. Henderson, ed. and trans., *Select Historical Documents of the Middle Ages* (London: Bell, 1912), pp. 435–437.

Papal power was threatened by the growth of nation-states, which challenged the church's temporal power and authority. Rulers opposed papal interference in state matters. In addition, the papacy was criticized by reformers, who had seen earlier reform movements transformed from their original high-minded purposes to suit the ambitions of the popes, and by the bourgeoisie, whose pragmatic outlook fostered growing skepticism, national patriotism, and religious self-reliance. During the fourteenth and fifteenth centuries, these challenges to papal authority were effective, and papal influence rapidly declined.

Boniface VIII

Pope Boniface VIII (1294–1303) was an outspoken advocate of papal authority. When Boniface boldly declared in the papal bull *Unam Sanctam* (1302) that "subjection to the Roman pontiff is absolutely necessary to salvation for every human creature," King Philip IV of France demanded that the pope be brought to trial by a general church council. In 1303 Philip's henchmen broke into Boniface's summer home at Anagni to arrest him and take him to France to stand trial. Their kidnapping plot was foiled when the pope was rescued by his friends. Humiliated, Boniface died a month later, perhaps from the shock and physical abuse he suffered during the attack.

The Avignon Papacy

But Philip's success was as complete as if Boniface had actually been dragged before the king to stand trial. Two years after Boniface's death, a French archbishop was chosen pope. Taking the title of Clement V, he never went to Rome but instead moved the papal headquarters to Avignon in southern France, where the papacy remained under French influence from 1305 to 1377. During this period, the so-called Babylonian Captivity of the church, papal prestige suffered enormously. Most Europeans believed that Rome was the only suitable capital for the church. Moreover, the English, Germans, and Italians accused the popes and the cardinals, the majority of whom were now also French, of being instruments of the French king.

The Avignon papacy gave support to critics who were attacking church corruption, papal temporal claims, and the apparent lack of spiritual dedication. Increasing their demands for income from England, Germany, and Italy and living in splendor in a newly built fortress-palace, the Avignon popes expanded the papal bureaucracy, added new church taxes, and collected the old taxes more efficiently. These actions provoked denunciation of the wealth of the church and a demand for its reform.

The Great Schism of the Roman Catholic Church

When the papacy paid attention to popular opinion and returned to Rome in 1377, it seemed for a time that its fortunes would improve, but the reverse proved true. In the papal election held the following year, the college of cardinals elected an Italian pope. A few months later the French cardinals declared the election invalid and elected a French pope, who returned to Avignon. The church was now in an even worse state than it had been during the Babylonian Captivity. During the Great Schism (1378–1417), as the split of the church into two allegiances was called, there were two popes, each with his college of cardinals and capital city, each claiming universal sovereignty, each sending forth papal administrators and taxing Christians, and each excommunicating the other. The nations of Europe gave allegiance as their individual political interests prompted them.

The Great Schism continued after the original rival popes died, and each camp elected a replacement. Doubt and confusion caused many Europeans to question the legitimacy and holiness of the church as an institution.

The Conciliar Movement

Positive action came in the form of the Conciliar Movement. In 1395 the professors at the University of Paris proposed that a general council, representing the universal church, should meet to heal the schism. A majority of the cardinals of both factions accepted this solution, and in 1409 they met at the Council of Pisa, deposed both popes, and elected a new one. But neither of the two deposed popes would give up his office, and the papal throne now had three claimants.

The intolerable situation necessitated another church council. In 1414 the Holy Roman Emperor assembled at Constance the most impressive church gathering of the period. By deposing the various papal claimants and electing Martin V as pope in 1417, the Great Schism was ended and a single papacy was restored at Rome.

Failure of Internal Reform

The Conciliar Movement represented a reforming and democratizing influence in the church. But the movement was not to endure, even though the Council of Constance had decreed that general councils were superior to popes and that they should meet at regular intervals in the future. Taking steps to preserve his position, the pope announced that to appeal to a church council without having first obtained papal consent was heretical. Together with the inability of later councils to bring about much-needed reform

and with lack of support for such councils by secular rulers, the restoration of a single head of the church enabled the popes to discredit the Conciliar Movement by 1450. Not until almost a century later, when the Council of Trent convened in 1545, did a great council meet to reform the church. But by that time the church had already irreparably lost many countries to Protestantism.

As the popes hesitated to call councils to effect reform, they failed to bring about reform themselves. The popes busied themselves not with internal problems but with Italian politics and patronage of the arts. The issues of church reform and revitalization were largely ignored.

Wyclif and Hus

Throughout the fourteenth century the cries against church corruption became louder at the same time that heretical thoughts were being publicly voiced (see Chapter 14). In England, a professor at Oxford, John Wyclif (c. 1320–1384), attacked not only church abuses but also certain of the church's doctrines. Wyclif taught that the church should be subordinate to the state, that salvation was primarily an individual matter between humans and God, that transubstantiation—the belief that a miracle actually occurs during the Mass, by which bread and wine actually are transformed into Jesus' body and blood—as taught by the church was false, and that outward rituals and veneration of relics were idolatrous. He formed bands of "poor priests," called Lollards, who spread his views, and he provided the people with an English translation of the Bible, which he considered the final authority in matters of religion. Although Wyclif's demands for reform did not succeed, the Lollards spread a more radical version of Wyclif's ideas until the movement was driven underground early in the next century.

In Bohemia, where a strong reform movement linked with the resentment of the Czechs toward their German overlords was under way, Wyclif's doctrines were popularized by Czech students who had heard him lecture at Oxford. In particular, his beliefs influenced John Hus (c. 1369–1415), a preacher in Prague and later rector of the university there. Hus's attacks on the abuses of clerical power led him to conclude that the true church was composed of a universal priesthood of believers and that Christ alone was its head.

Alarmed by Hus's growing influence, the church excommunicated him. Summoned to the Council of Constance to stand trial for heresy, Hus was promised safe conduct. But he refused to change his views, and the council ordered him burned at the stake. This action made Hus a martyr to the Czechs, who rebelled against both the German emperor and the church. In the sixteenth century the remaining Hussites merged with the Lutheran movement in frustration with a church deaf to their protests.

Conclusion

Religion was largely molded and directed by the church throughout most of the Middle Ages. Through the growing strength of the papacy and because of the timely reform influences originating in the monastic orders, the power of the church as a religious and political force increased steadily in the High Middle Ages. But through a combination of corruption and misuse of power by church officials, the generally negative impact of the crusading movement, the assertiveness of monarchs and the growth of nationalistic interests in the states of Europe, and reforming sentiment within the church itself, the church in the later Middle Ages fell from its position as the sole source of religious authority and as a political power able to rival European nation-states.

Arts and learning in the early Middle Ages were almost completely in the hands of the church, which deserves credit for preserving the learning of antiquity in the dark ages of disorder and invasion. Religious themes and styles continued to dominate medieval literary work until vernacular literature, inspired by such creative forces as Dante and Chaucer, became an acceptable and popular form of expression near the end of the Middle Ages.

Suggestions for Reading

For good general surveys on the church and theology in the Middle Ages, see David Knowles, *The Evolution of Medieval Thought* (Helicon Press, 1962), and *Christian Monasticism* (McGraw-Hill, 1969). See also Gerd Tellenbach, *The Church in Western Europe from the Tenth to the Early Twelfth Century* (Cambridge University Press, 1993); Ian Stuart Robinson, *The Papacy, 1073–1198* (Cambridge University Press, 1990); Stephen E. Ozment, *The Age of Reform, 1250–1550* (Yale University Press, 1980); and Jaroslav J. Pelikan, *The Christian Tradition: Vol. 3. The Growth of Medieval Theology* (University of Chicago Press, 1978).

C. H. Lawrence, *Medieval Monasticism: Forms of Religious Life in Western Europe in the Middle Ages* (Longman, 1984); Malcolm Lambert, *Medieval Heresy: Popular Movements from the Gregorian Reform to the Reformation*, 2nd ed. (Blackwell, 1992); and Geoffrey Barraclough, *The Medieval Papacy* (Norton, 1968), are good examinations. Also see Archibald R. Lewis, *Nomads and Crusaders*, A.D. *1000–1368* (Indiana University Press, 1991); Jonathan Riley-Smith, ed., *The Oxford History of the Crusades* (Oxford University Press, 1997), Malcolm Billings,

The Cross and the Crescent (Sterling, 1987); Amin Maalouf, *The Crusades Through Arab Eyes* (Schocken, 1985); and Malcolm C. Barber, *The Trial of the Templars* (Cambridge University Press, 1993). Also excellent is David Nirenberg, *Communities of Violence: Persecution of Minorities in the Middle Ages* (Princeton University Press, 1996).

See John A. Burrow, *The Ages of Man: A Study in Medieval Writing and Thought* (Oxford University Press, 1989), for an outstanding review of medieval literature, as well as Judith M. Bennett, *Women in the Medieval English Countryside: Gender and Household in Brigstock Before the Plague* (Oxford University Press, 1989); Georges Duby, *The Age of Cathedrals: Art and Society, 980–1420* (University of Chicago Press, 1981); and Nancy G. Siraisi, *Medieval and Early Renaissance Medicine* (University of Chicago Press, 1990). See also C. H. Haskins, *The Rise of Universities* (Cornell University Press, 1965), and Gordon Leff, *Paris and Oxford Universities in the Thirteenth and Fourteenth Centuries: An Institutional and Intellectual History* (Wiley, 1968).

Good accounts of later church history are Ozment's *Age of Reform;* Gordon Leff, *Heresy in the Middle Ages*, 2 vols. (Barnes & Noble, 1967); Kenneth B. McFarlane, *John Wycliffe and the Beginnings of English Nonconformity* (Penguin, 1972); and Matthew Spinka, *John Hus: A Biography* (Princeton University Press, 1968).

Suggestions for Web Browsing

Medieval Studies
http://www.georgetown.edu/labyrinth/Virtual_Library/ Medieval_Studies.html

The WWW Virtual Library for Medieval Studies, a part of the Labyrinth project at Georgetown University, offers numerous links categorized by national cultures and by artistic genre.

Medieval Women Home Page
http://www.media.mcmaster.ca/mw2.htm

Interdisciplinary exploration of the life of women in the late Middle Ages.

Women Writers of the Middle Ages
http://www.millersv.edu/~english/homepage/duncan/medfem/ medfem.html

A collection of both secular and religious works authored by medieval women.

Medieval Science Page
http://members.aol.com/McNelis/medsci_index.html

A great site for anyone interested in medieval medicine and astronomy.

Gregorian Chant Home Page
http://silvertone.princeton.edu/chant.html/

Medieval Gregorian chant is sung, and its music theory is discussed.

Avignon Papacy, 1305–1378
http://www.humnet/cmrs/faculty/geary/instr/students/pope.htm

A very complete site dealing with the Babylonian Captivity of the church. Both literary and artistic materials are presented.

An English view of the battle of
Agincourt. The English victory at
Agincourt, like those at Crécy and
Poitiers, are attributed in part to
the well-disciplined English
longbowmen.

The Birth of Europe
Politics and Society in the Middle Ages

Chapter Contents

T he absence of the political unity and military security once provided by the Roman Empire was increasingly obvious in the fourth and fifth centuries in western Europe. As the centralization of the old Roman order collapsed and Germanic chieftains seized what lands and rights they could, very slowly the civilization of Rome evolved into a culture that melded Roman and Germanic institutions into a distinctly European pattern of life.

A New Empire in the West

In the blending of Roman and Germanic customs and institutions, the Franks played a particularly important role. Not only was the kingdom of the Franks the most enduring of the early Germanic states established in the West, but it became, with the active support of the church, the first significant kingdom of Europe that attempted to replace the Roman Empire in the West.

The Kingdom of the Franks Under Clovis

Before the Germanic invasions of the fourth century, the Franks lived close to the North Sea; late in the fourth century they began to move south and west into Roman Gaul. By 481 they occupied the northern part of Gaul as far south as the old Roman city of Paris, and in that same year Clovis I of the Merovingian dynasty became ruler of one of the small Frankish kingdoms. By the time of his death in 511, Clovis had united the Franks into a single kingdom that stretched south to the Pyrenees.

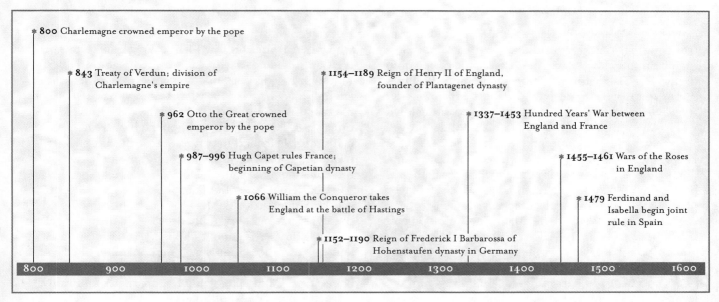

800 Charlemagne crowned emperor by the pope

843 Treaty of Verdun; division of Charlemagne's empire

962 Otto the Great crowned emperor by the pope

987–996 Hugh Capet rules France; beginning of Capetian dynasty

1066 William the Conqueror takes England at the battle of Hastings

1152–1190 Reign of Frederick I Barbarossa of Hohenstaufen dynasty in Germany

1154–1189 Reign of Henry II of England, founder of Plantagenet dynasty

1337–1453 Hundred Years' War between England and France

1455–1461 Wars of the Roses in England

1479 Ferdinand and Isabella begin joint rule in Spain

| 800 | 900 | 1000 | 1100 | 1200 | 1300 | 1400 | 1500 | 1600 |

The Merovingians and the Carolingians

481–511   Clovis unites Franks; beginning of Merovingian dynasty

714–741   Charles Martel mayor of the palace

732   Charles defeats Muslims at Tours

741–768   Pepin the Short mayor of the palace

751   Pepin crowned king of the Franks; beginning of Carolingian dynasty

768–814   Reign of Charlemagne

800   Charlemagne crowned emperor by the pope; beginning of Carolingian Empire

814–840   Reign of Louis the Pious

843   Treaty of Verdun divides Carolingian Empire

Clovis was an intelligent manipulator of alliances and a cunning diplomat who also used religion for political gain. He was converted to Christianity perhaps through the influence of his Christian wife, was baptized together with his whole army, and then became the only Orthodox Christian ruler in the West, since the other Germanic tribes were either still pagan or followers of Arian Christianity (the heresy that maintained that Jesus was not equal to the Father and thereby not completely divine). This conversion of the Franks to Roman Christianity ultimately led to a close alliance of the Franks and the papacy.

Decline of the Merovingians, Rise of the Carolingians

Clovis's sons and grandsons extended Frankish control south to the Mediterranean and east into Germany. But quickly the Merovingian dynasty began to decay. The Germanic tradition of treating the kingdom as personal property and dividing it among all the king's sons resulted in constant and bitter civil wars. Most important, Merovingian kings proved themselves incompetent and ineffectual. Soon the Frankish state broke up into three separate kingdoms; in each, power was concentrated in the hands of the chief official of the royal household, the mayor of the palace, a powerful noble who hoped to keep the king weak and ineffectual. The Merovingian rulers became puppets—"do-nothing kings."

The kingdom of the Franks gained strength when Charles Martel became mayor of the palace (or the king's court) in 714. His military skill earned him the surname Martel, "the hammer." Charles was respon-sible for introducing a major innovation in European warfare. To counteract the effectiveness of the quick-striking Muslim cavalry, Charles recruited a force of professional mounted soldiers. He rewarded his soldiers with land to enable each of them to support a family, equipment, and war horses. With such a force, now aided by their use of the stirrup, Charles Martel won an important victory over the Muslim cavalry at Tours in 732.

Charles's son, Pepin the Short (741–768), legalized the power already being exercised by the mayors of the palace by requesting and receiving from the pope a decision that whoever exercised the actual power in the kingdom should be the legal ruler. In 751 Pepin was elected king by the Franks; the last Merovingian was sent off to a monastery, and the Carolingian dynasty came to power. In 754 the pope reaffirmed the election of Pepin by personally anointing him as king of the Franks.

Behind the pope's action was his need for a powerful protector against the Lombards, who had conquered the Exarchate of Ravenna (the center of Byzantine government in Italy) and were demanding tribute from the pope. Following Pepin's coronation, the pope secured his promise of armed intervention in Italy and his pledge to give the Exarchate to the papacy, once it was conquered. In 756 a Frankish army forced the Lombard king to withdraw, and Pepin gave Ravenna to the pope. The so-called Donation of Pepin made the pope a temporal ruler over the Papal States, a strip of territory that extended diagonally across northern Italy.

The alliance between the Franks and the papacy affected the course of politics and religion for centuries. It furthered the separation of the Roman from the Greek Christian Church by giving the papacy a dependable Western ally in place of the Byzantines, previously its only protector against the Lombards.

Charlemagne: Enlightened Conqueror

Under Pepin's son Charlemagne (Charles the Great), who ruled from 768 to 814, the Frankish state and the Carolingian dynasty reached the height of power. Although he was certainly a successful warrior-king, leading his armies on yearly campaigns, Charlemagne also tried to provide an effective administration for his kingdom. In addition, he had great appreciation for learning; his efforts at furthering the arts produced a revival in learning and letters known as the Carolingian Renaissance.

Charlemagne sought to extend his kingdom southward against the Muslims in Spain. He crossed the Pyrenees and eventually drove the Muslims back to the Ebro River and established a frontier area known as the Spanish March, centered near Barcelona. French immigrants moved into the area, later called Catalonia, giving it a character culturally distinct from the rest of Spain.

Charlemagne: A Firsthand Look

Einhard was the emperor Charlemagne's secretary and biographer. The following is an excerpt from Einhard's *Life of Charlemagne*.

Charles was large and strong, and of lofty stature, though not disproportionately tall (his height is well known to have been seven times the length of his foot); the upper part of his head was round, his eyes very large and animated, nose a little long, hair fair, and face laughing and merry. Thus his appearance was always stately and dignified, whether he was standing or sitting; although his neck was thick and somewhat short, and his belly rather prominent; but the symmetry of the rest of his body concealed these defects. His gait was firm, his whole carriage manly, and his voice clear, but not so strong as his size led one to expect. His health was excellent, except during the four years preceding his death, when he was subject to frequent fevers; at the last he even limped a little with one foot. Even in those years he consulted rather his own inclinations than the advice of physicians, who were almost hateful to him, because they wanted him to give up roasts, to which he was accustomed, and to eat boiled meat instead. In accordance with the national custom, he took frequent exercise on horseback and in the chase, accomplishments in which scarcely any people in the world can equal the Franks. He enjoyed the exhalations from natural warm springs, and often practiced swimming, in which he was such an adept that none could surpass him; and hence it was that he built his palace at Aix-la-Chapelle, and lived there constantly during his latter years until his death. He used not only to invite his sons to his bath, but his nobles and friends, and now and then a troop of his retinue or bodyguard, so that a hundred or more persons sometimes bathed with him. . . .

. . . Charles was temperate in eating, and particularly so in drinking, for he abominated drunkenness in anybody, much more in himself and those of his household; but he could not easily abstain from food, and often complained that fasts injured his health. He very rarely gave entertainment, only on great feast-days, and then to large numbers of people. His meals ordinarily consisted of four courses, not counting the roast, which his huntsmen used to bring in on the spit; he was more fond of this than of any other dish. While at table, he listened to reading or music. . . .

. . . Charles had the gift of ready and fluent speech, and could express whatever he had to say with the utmost clearness. He was not satisfied with command of his native language merely, but gave attention to the study of foreign ones, and in particular was such a master of Latin that he could speak it as well as his native tongue; but he could understand Greek better than he could speak it. He was so eloquent, indeed, that he might have passed for a teacher of eloquence. He most zealously cultivated the liberal arts, held those who taught them in great esteem, and conferred great honors upon them. He took lessons in grammar of the deacon Peter of Pisa, at that time an aged man. Another deacon, Albin of Britain, surnamed Alcuin, a man of Saxon extraction, who was the greatest scholar of the day, was his teacher in other branches of learning. The King spent much time and labor with him studying rhetoric, dialectics, and especially astronomy; he learned to reckon, and used to investigate the motions of the heavenly bodies most curiously, with an intelligent scrutiny. He also tried to write, and used to keep tablets and blanks in bed under his pillow, that at leisure hours he might accustom his hand to form the letters; however, as he did not begin his efforts in due season, but late in life, they met with ill success.

From Samuel Epes Turner, trans., *Life of Charlemagne by Einhard* (Ann Arbor: University of Michigan Press, 1960), pp. 50–57.

Charlemagne conquered the Bavarians and the Saxons, the last of the independent Germanic tribes, on his eastern frontier. Even farther to the east, the empire's frontier was continually threatened by the Avars, Asiatic nomads related to the Huns, and the Slavs. In six campaigns Charlemagne nearly eliminated the Avars and then set up his own military province in the Danube valley to guard against any future advances by eastern nomads. Called the East March, this territory later became Austria. Like his father Pepin, Charlemagne was involved in Italian politics. The Lombards resented the attempts of the papacy to expand civil control in northern Italy. At the request of the pope, Charlemagne attacked the Lombards in 774, defeated them, and named himself their king.

One of the most important events in Charlemagne's reign took place on Christmas Day, 800. In the previous year the Roman nobility had removed the pope from office, charging him with corruption. But Charlemagne came to Rome and restored the pope to his position. At the Christmas service, as Charlemagne knelt before the altar, the pope placed a crown on his head while the congregation shouted: "To Charles Augustus crowned of God, great and pacific Emperor of the Romans, long life and victory!"

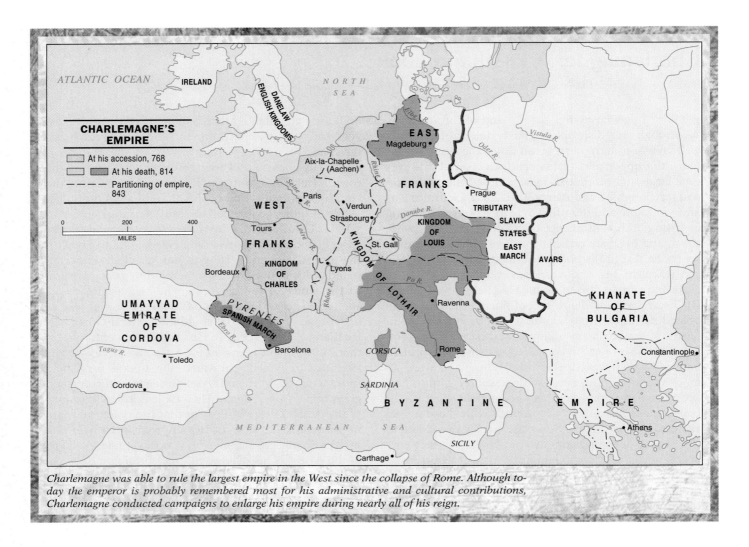

Charlemagne was able to rule the largest empire in the West since the collapse of Rome. Although to-day the emperor is probably remembered most for his administrative and cultural contributions, Charlemagne conducted campaigns to enlarge his empire during nearly all of his reign.

This ceremony demonstrated that the memory of the Roman Empire still survived as a meaningful tradition in Europe and that there was a strong desire to reestablish political unity. In fact, Charlemagne had named his capital at Aix-la-Chapelle (Aachen) "New Rome" and contemplated taking the title of emperor in an attempt to revive the idea of the Roman Empire in the West.

The extent of Charlemagne's empire was impressive. His territories included all of the western area of the old Roman Empire except Africa, Britain, southern Italy, and the majority of Spain. Seven defensive provinces, or marches, protected the empire against hostile neighbors.

The Carolingian territories were divided into some 300 administrative divisions, each under a count (*graf*) or, in the marches along the border, a margrave (*markgraf*). In addition, there were local military officials, the dukes. In an effort to supervise the activities of local officials, Charlemagne issued an ordinance creating the *missi dominici*, the king's envoys. Pairs of these itinerant officials, usually a bishop and a lay noble, traveled throughout the realm to check on the local administration. So that the *missi* were immune to bribes, they were chosen from men of high rank, they were frequently transferred from one region to another, and no two of them were teamed for more than one year.

Charlemagne's Legacy

Charlemagne is considered one of the most significant figures of early European history. He extended Christian civilization in Europe, set up barriers to prevent invasions of the Slavs and Avars, and created a state in which law and order were again enforced after three centuries of disintegration. His patronage of learning began a cultural revival that later generations would build on, producing a European civilization distinct from the Byzantine to the east and the Muslim to the south.

Charlemagne's empire was not long-lived, however, for its territories were too vast and its nobility too divisive to be held together after the dominating personality of its creator was gone. Charlemagne had no standing army; his foot soldiers were essentially the old Germanic war band summoned to fight by its war leader. The king did not have a bureaucratic administrative machine comparable to that of Roman times. The Frankish economy was agricultural and localized, and there was no system of taxation adequate to maintain an effective and permanent administration. Under Charlemagne's weak successors, the empire collapsed in the confusion of civil wars and devastating new invasions. Progress toward a centralized and effective monarchy in Europe ended with Charlemagne's death.

When he died in 814, Charlemagne was succeeded by his only surviving son, Louis the Pious, a well-meaning but ineffective ruler. Louis, in accordance with Frankish custom, divided the kingdom among his three sons, and bitter rivalry and warfare broke out among the brothers even before Louis died in 840.

In 843 the three brothers met at Verdun, where they agreed to split the Carolingian lands among themselves. Charles the Bald obtained the western part of the empire and Louis the German the eastern; Lothair, the oldest brother, retained the title of emperor and obtained an elongated middle kingdom, which stretched 1000 miles from the North Sea to central Italy.

The Treaty of Verdun contributed to the shaping of political problems that continued into the twentieth century. Lothair's middle kingdom soon collapsed into three major parts: Lorraine in the North; Burgundy; and Italy in the South. Lorraine included Latin and German cultures and, although it was divided in 870 between Charles and Louis, the area was disputed for centuries. Lorraine became one of the most frequent battlegrounds of Europe.

Europe Under Attack

During the ninth and tenth centuries, coinciding with the collapse of the Carolingian Empire, western Europe came under attack by Scandinavians from the North and Muslims from the South, while the Magyars, a new band of Asiatic nomads, conducted destructive raids on central Europe and northern Italy. Christian Europe was hard pressed to repel these warlike newcomers, who were more threatening to life and property than the Germanic invaders of the fifth century.

From bases in North Africa, Muslim adventurers in full command of the sea plundered the coasts of Italy and France. In 827 they began the conquest of Byzantine Sicily and southern Italy. From forts erected in southern France they penetrated far inland to attack merchant caravans in the Alpine passes. What trade still existed between Byzantium and western Europe, except for that undertaken by Venice and several other Italian towns, was now al-

This gold bust of Charlemagne was made in the fourteenth century and is housed now in the treasury of the Palace Chapel of Charlemagne in Aachen, Germany. The reliquary bust contains parts of the emperor's skull.

most totally cut off, and the Mediterranean Sea came under almost complete Muslim control.

The most widespread and destructive raids, however, came from Scandinavia. Swedes, Danes, and Norwegians—collectively referred to as Vikings—began to move south. Overpopulation and a surplus of young men are possible reasons for this expansion, but some scholars suggest that these raiders were defeated war bands expelled from their homeland by the emergence of strong royal power. The Vikings had developed seaworthy ships capable of carrying 100 men, powered by long oars or by sail when the wind was favorable. Viking sailors had also developed expert sailing techniques; without benefit of the

This wooden animal head dating from the early ninth century is the terminal of a post of a buried Viking ship found at Oseberg, in southern Norway. The carving combines realistic details with the imaginative use of abstract geometric patterns derived from metalwork.

compass, they were able to navigate by the stars at night and the sun by day.

The range of Viking expansion reached as far as North America to the west, the Caspian Sea to the east, and the Mediterranean to the south. Between 800 and 850 Ireland was raided repeatedly. Many monasteries, the centers of the flourishing Irish Celtic culture, were destroyed. The Icelandic Norsemen ventured on to Greenland and, later, to North America. Other raiders traveled the rivers of Russia as merchants and soldiers of fortune and founded the nucleus of a Russian state. Danes raided Britain and the shores of Germany, France, and Spain. By 840 they had occupied most of Britain north of the Thames. They devastated northwest France, destroying dozens of abbeys and towns. Unable to fend off the Viking attacks, the weak Carolingian king accepted the local Norse chieftain as duke of a Viking state, later called Normandy. Like Viking settlers elsewhere, these Northmen, or Normans, became Christian converts and eventually played an important role in shaping the future of medieval Europe.

Feudalism

Europe's response to the invasions of the ninth and tenth centuries was not uniform. By 900 the Viking occupation of England had initiated a strong national reaction, which soon led to the creation of a united British kingdom. Germany in 919 repelled the Magyar threat through the efforts of a new and able line of kings who went on to become powerful European monarchs. But Viking attacks on France accelerated the trends toward political fragmentation. Since the monarchy could not hold together its vast territory, small independent landowners surrendered both their lands and their personal freedoms to the many counts, dukes, and other local lords in return for protection and security. The decline of trade further strengthened the position of the landed nobility, whose large estates, or manors, sought to become economically self-sufficient. In addition, the nobility became increasingly dependent on military service rendered by a professional force of heavily armed mounted knights, many of whom still lived in the house of their noble retainers in return for their military service.

In most parts of western Europe, where an effective centralized government was entirely absent, personal safety and security became the primary concerns of most individuals. Historians have used the term *feudalism* to apply to the individual and unique political and social patterns resulting from political decentralization and the resulting attempts to ensure personal security.

Feudalism can be described as a system of rights and duties in which political power was exercised locally by private individuals rather than through the bureaucracy of a centralized state. In general, western European feudalism involved three basic elements: (1) a personal element, called *lordship* or *vassalage*, by which one nobleman, the *vassal*, became the follower of a stronger nobleman, the *lord*; (2) a property element, called the *fief* or *benefice* (usually land), which the vassal received from his lord to enable him to fulfill the obligations of being a vassal; and (3) a governmental element, the private exercise of governmental functions over vassals and fiefs.

Theoretical Feudal Hierarchy

In theory, feudalism was a vast hierarchy. At the top stood the king, and all the land in his kingdom belonged to him. He kept large areas for his personal use (royal or crown lands) and, in return for the military service of a specified number of mounted knights, invested the highest nobles—such as dukes and counts (in Britain, earls)—with the remainder. Those nobles, in turn, in order to obtain the services of the required number of mounted warriors owed to the king, parceled out large portions of their fiefs to lesser nobles. This process, called *subinfeudation*, was continued in theory until the lowest in the scale of vassals was reached—the single knight whose fief was just sufficient to support one mounted warrior.

By maintaining the king at the head of this theoretical feudal hierarchy, this custom kept the traces of monarchy intact. Although some feudal kings were little more than figureheads who were less powerful than their own vassals, the tradition of monarchy was retained.

Relation of Lord and Vassal: The Contract

Personal bonds between lord and vassal were sometimes formally recognized. In the ceremony known as *homage*, the vassal knelt before his lord, or *suzerain*, and promised to be his "man." In the *oath of fealty* that followed, the vassal swore on the Bible or some other sacred object that he would remain true to his lord. Next, in the ritual of *investiture*, a lance, a glove, or even a clump of dirt was handed to the vassal to signify his jurisdiction over the fief. As his part of the contract, the lord was usually obliged to give his vassal protection and justice. In return, the vassal's primary duty was military service. In addition, the vassal could be obliged to assist the lord in rendering justice in the lord's court. At certain times, as when the lord was captured and had to be ransomed, the lord also had the right to demand special money payments, called *aids*.

The Early Medieval Economy: Manorialism

The economy of the early Middle Ages reflected the localism and self-sufficiency of life that resulted from an ineffective central government in Europe. The economic and social system based on the manors, the great estates held by the nobles, was referred to as *manorialism*.

The manor usually varied in size from one locality to another; a small one might contain only about a dozen households. Since the allotment of land to each family averaged about 30 acres, the smallest manors probably had about 350 acres of land suitable for farming, not counting meadows, woods, wasteland, and the lord's *demesne*—the land reserved for the lord's use alone. A large manor might contain 50 families in a total area of 5000 acres.

The center of the manor was the village, in which the thatched cottages of the peasants were grouped

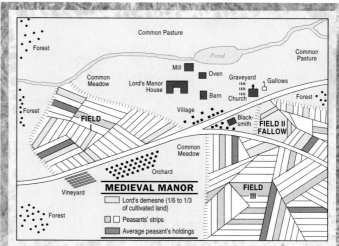

The manor, the self-contained economic unit of early medieval life, operated on a system of reciprocal rights and obligations based on custom. In return for protection, strips of arable land, and the right to use the nonarable common land, the peasant paid dues and worked on the lord's demesne. Under the three-field system, one-third of the land lay fallow so that intensive cultivation did not exhaust the soil.

together along one street. Around each cottage was a space large enough for a vegetable patch, chicken yard, haystack, and stable. An important feature of the landscape was the village church, together with the priest's house and the burial ground. The lord's dwelling might be a fortified house or a more modest dwelling.

Distribution of the Land

Every manor contained arable and nonarable land. Part of the arable land was reserved for the lord and was cultivated for him by his serfs; the remainder was held by the villagers. The nonarable land, consisting of meadow, wood, and wasteland, was used in common by the villagers and the lord.

From one-sixth to one-third of the arable land was given over to the lord's demesne. The arable land not held in demesne was allotted among the villagers under the open-field system, whereby the fields were subdivided into strips. The strips, each containing about an acre, were separated by narrow paths of uncultivated land. The serf's holding was not all in one plot, for all soil throughout the manor was not equally fertile, and an attempt was made to give each of the villagers land of the same quality. Each tenant was really a shareholder in the village community, not only in the open fields but also in the meadow, pasture, wood, and wastelands.

Wooded land was valuable as an area to graze pigs, the most common animal on the manor. Tenants could also gather dead wood in the forest, but cutting down green wood was prohibited unless authorized by the lord.

Medieval Farming Methods

It is difficult to generalize about agricultural methods, because differences in locality, fertility of soil, crop production, and other factors resulted in a variety of farming approaches. Farming as practiced in northwestern Europe was characterized by some common factors. The implements the peasants used were extremely crude; the plow was a cumbersome instrument with heavy wheels, often requiring as many as eight oxen to pull it. (By the twelfth century the use of plow horses had become common.) Other tools included crude harrows, sickles, beetles for breaking up clods, and flails for threshing.

Inadequate methods of farming soon exhausted the soil. The average yield per acre was only 6 to 8 bushels of wheat, one-fourth the modern yield. In classical times farmers had learned that soil planted continually with one crop rapidly deteriorated. As a counteraction they employed a two-field system: half of the arable land was planted while the other half lay fallow to recover its fertility. Medieval farmers learned that wheat or rye could be planted in the autumn as well as in the spring. As a result, by the ninth century they were dividing the land into three fields, with one planted in the fall, another in the spring, and the third left lying fallow. This system not only kept more land in production but also required less plowing in any given year.

Under the manorial system, women of the aristocracy exercised great authority. Often the lord of the manor's wife was placed in charge of managing the manor's accounts and storehouses. She often stood in for her husband in his absence and supervised the peasants and even the courts of justice.

Peasant women usually had to endure backbreaking labor. Peasant women cooked, cleaned, made clothing, maintained the animals, milked cows, made butter and cheese, brewed ale and beer, and nurtured the gardens. Women assisted the men during planting and harvesting seasons and with any seasonal or special projects endorsed by the lord. The sexes were treated fairly equally on the lower social levels in the Middle Ages—there was not much difference in the demanding lifestyle all had to endure.

Administration of the Manor

Although the lord might live on one of his manors, each manor was usually administered by such officials as the steward, the bailiff, and the reeve. The steward was the general overseer who supervised the business of all his lord's manors and presided over the manorial court. It was the bailiff's duty to supervise the cultivation of the lord's demesne; collect rents, dues, and fines; and inspect the work done by the free peasants (freemen) and the nonfree peasants (serfs). The reeve was the "foreman" of the villagers, chosen by them and representing their interests.

Freemen often lived on the manor, although they constituted only a small portion of its population. Freemen were not subject to the same demands as the serfs. The freeman did not have to work in the lord's fields himself but could send substitutes. Serfs, however, were bound to the manor and could not leave without the lord's consent. Serfdom was a hereditary status; the children of serfs were attached to the soil, just as their parents were.

The lord of the manor was bound by custom to respect certain rights of his serfs. So long as they paid their dues and services, serfs could not be evicted from their hereditary holdings. Although a serf could not appear in court against his lord or a freeman, he could appeal to the manor court against any of his fellows. To the serfs, the manor was the center of their very existence, but to the lord, the manor was essentially a source of income and subsistence.

The Life of the Peasants

On the manors of the Middle Ages, the margin between starvation and survival was narrow, and the life of the peasant was not easy. Famines were frequent; warfare was a constant threat; and grasshoppers, locusts, caterpillars, and rats repeatedly destroyed the crops. Men, women, and children alike had to toil long hours in the fields.

Home life offered few comforts. The typical peasant dwelling was a cottage with mud walls, clay floor, and thatched roof. The fire burned on a flat hearthstone in the middle of the floor; unless the peasant was rich enough to afford a chimney, the smoke escaped through a hole in the roof. The window openings had no glass and were stuffed with straw in the winter. Furnishings were meager, usually consisting of a table, a kneading trough for dough, a cupboard, and a bed, often either a heap of straw or a box filled with straw, which served the entire family. Pigs and chickens wandered about the cottage continually; the stable was often under the same roof, next to the family quarters.

The peasants, despite their hard, monotonous life, enjoyed a few pleasures. Wrestling was popular, as were cockfighting, a crude type of football, and fighting with quarter-staves, in which contestants stood an excellent chance of getting their heads

Both peasant men and women toiled in the fields. Here women reap with sickles, while behind them a man binds the sheaves.

bashed in. Dancing, singing, and drinking were popular pastimes, especially on the numerous holy days and festivals promoted by the church.

The High Middle Ages, 1000–1300

The High Middle Ages witnessed the full development of earlier medieval civilization. In this era European monarchies struggled to emerge from the decentralized feudal organization. The church rose to great heights of power and authority. The revival of trade and the rebirth of towns altered the economy of Europe and sped the end of manorialism. And this period gave birth to developments in art, architecture, and literature that stand as some of the most significant achievements in European civilization.

Feudalism was a system founded on the decentralization of authority; the king was often no more than a figurehead in the feudal order. But gradually the monarchs of most European states sought to increase their powers at the expense of their feudal nobility. Through such efforts, several of which took centuries to bear results, national monarchies began to take form on the European continent.

The Capetians and the Beginnings of France

In France, by the beginning of the tenth century, more than 30 great feudal princes were vassals of the king, but they gave him little or no support. When the last Carolingian, Louis the Sluggard, died in 987, the nobles elected one of their number, Hugh Capet, count of Paris, as his successor. The territory that Hugh Capet (987–996) actually controlled was a small feudal county, the Île-de-France, extending from Paris to Orléans. The royal lands were surrounded by many large duchies and counties, such as Flanders, Normandy, Anjou, and Champagne, which were fiercely independent.

The major accomplishment of the first four Capetian kings was their success at keeping the French crown within their own family and at slowly expanding their influence. With the support of the church, the Capetians cleverly arranged for the election and coronation of their heirs. For 300 years the House of Capet never lacked a male heir.

The reign of the fifth Capetian king, Louis VI (1108–1137), known as "the Fat," saw an expansion of Capetian strength. Determined to crush the barons who defied royal authority, he captured their castles and in many cases tore them down. Louis made his word law in the Île-de-France, established a solid

Nation-Building in France

987–996	Reign of Hugh Capet
1108–1137	Reign of Louis VI
1180–1223	Reign of Philip II Augustus
1226–1270	Reign of Louis IX
1285–1314	Reign of Philip IV, the Fair

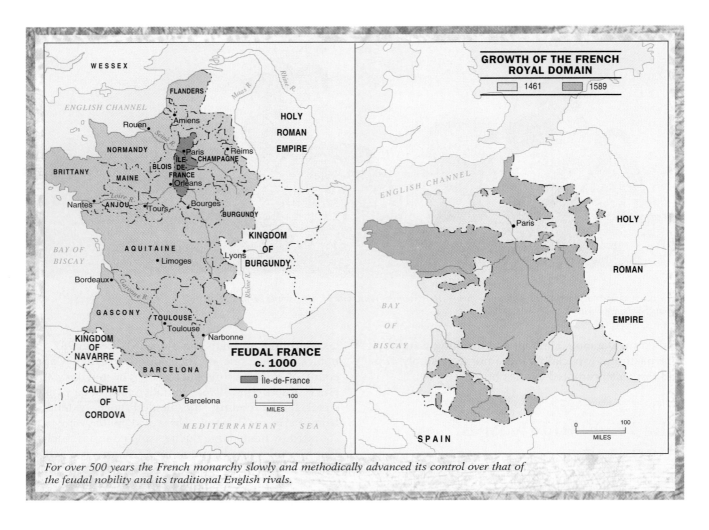

WESSEX

ENGLISH CHANNEL

FLANDERS

HOLY
ROMAN
EMPIRE

Rouen • Amiens

NORMANDY • Paris • Reims
ÎLE- CHAMPAGNE
DE-
BLOIS FRANCE

BRITTANY
MAINE • Orléans

ANJOU • Tours • Bourges

Nantes •
BURGUNDY

AQUITAINE
KINGDOM
OF
BURGUNDY

BAY OF
BISCAY • Limoges Lyons •

Bordeaux •

GASCONY

KINGDOM
OF
NAVARRE • Toulouse

TOULOUSE • Narbonne

BARCELONA

CALIPHATE
OF
CORDOVA • Barcelona

MEDITERRANEAN   SEA

**FEUDAL FRANCE
c. 1000**
Île-de-France
0   100
MILES

**GROWTH OF THE FRENCH
ROYAL DOMAIN**
1461   1589

ENGLISH CHANNEL

• Paris

HOLY

ROMAN

EMPIRE

BAY
OF
BISCAY

SPAIN

0   100
MILES

*For over 500 years the French monarchy slowly and methodically advanced its control over that of
the feudal nobility and its traditional English rivals.*

base from which royal power could be extended, and increased the prestige of the monarchy so much that the great duke of Aquitaine agreed to marry his daughter Eleanor to Louis's son. Unfortunately, Eleanor's behavior so scandalized Louis's pious son that the marriage was annulled, and Aquitaine passed to Eleanor's second husband, Henry II of England.

Philip II Augustus

The first great expansion of the royal domain was the work of Philip II Augustus (1180–1223). Philip's great ambition was to seize from the English kings the vast territory they held in France. He made little progress against Henry II, except to encourage his sons, Richard the Lion-Hearted and John, to revolt. Philip took Normandy, Maine, Anjou, and Touraine from John, and by doing so he tripled the size of the French royal domain.

Philip also greatly strengthened the royal administrative system by devising new agencies for centralized government and tapping new sources of revenue, including a money payment from his vassals

instead of military service. Salaried officials, called bailiffs, were given military, political, and judicial responsibilites by the king. Special administrative departments were established: the *parlement*, a supreme court of justice; the chamber of accounts, or royal treasury; and the royal or privy council, a group of advisers who assisted the king in the conduct of the daily business of the state.

After the brief reign of Philip II's son Louis VIII, France came under the rule of Louis IX (1226–1270), better known as St. Louis. Louis's ideal was to rule justly, and in so doing he became one of the most beloved kings of France. The king believed himself responsible only to God, who had put him on the throne to lead his people out of a life of sin. Just, sympathetic, and peace-loving, Louis IX convinced his subjects that the monarchy was the most important agency for ensuring their happiness and well-being.

Height of Capetian Rule
Under Philip IV

The reign of Philip IV, known as Philip the Fair (1285–1314), culminated three centuries of Capetian rule. The opposite of his saintly grandfather, Philip was a man of violence and cunning. Aware that anti-Semitism was growing in Europe in the wake of the Crusades, he expelled the Jews from France and confiscated their possessions.

Philip's need for money also brought him into conflict with the last great medieval pope. Boniface VIII refused to allow Philip to tax the French clergy and made sweeping claims to supremacy over secular powers. But Philip IV would not tolerate papal interference, and the result was the humiliation of Boniface, a blow from which the influence of the medieval papacy never recovered. In domestic affairs, the real importance of Philip's reign lay in the king's ability to increase the power and improve the organization of the royal government. Philip's astute civil servants, recruited mainly from the middle class, sought to make the power of the monarch absolute.

Philip enlarged his feudal council to include representatives of the third "estate" or class, the townspeople. This Estates-General of nobles, clergy, and burghers was used to obtain popular support for Philip's policies, including the announcement of new taxes. Philip did not ask the Estates-General's consent for his tax measures, and thus this body did not acquire a role in decisions affecting taxation.

England to 1300

After the Romans withdrew from England in the fifth century, Germanic tribes known as Angles and Saxons invaded the island of Great Britain and divided it among more than a dozen tribal kingdoms, and the overlordship of the island was held in turn by the different rulers. (Soon after their arrival, the Angles and Saxons intermixed to become essentially one tribal group, the Anglo-Saxons.) In the ninth century the kingdom of Wessex held the dominant position. Its king, Alfred the Great (871–899), was confronted with the task of turning back the Danes, who overran all the other English kingdoms. Alfred defeated the Danes and forced them into a treaty whereby they settled in the region called the Danelaw and accepted Christianity.

Alfred's successors were able rulers who conquered the Danelaw and created a unified English monarchy. Danes and Saxons intermarried, and soon most differences between the two peoples disappeared. After 975, however, the power of the central government lagged. In 1016 the Anglo-Saxons were again overrun by the Danes, and King Canute of Denmark extended his rule to include England and Norway.

Canute proved to be a wise and civilized king and was well liked by his Anglo-Saxon subjects because he respected their rights and customs. But Canute's

Nation-Building in England

871–899	Alfred the Great rules Wessex
1016–1035	Reign of Canute
1066	Battle of Hastings
1066–1087	Reign of William the Conqueror
1154–1189	Henry II begins Plantagenet dynasty
1189–1199	Reign of Richard I, the Lion-Hearted
1199–1216	Reign of John I
1215	Magna Carta
1272–1307	Reign of Edward I

empire fell apart after his death in 1035, and in 1042 the English crown was secured by the Anglo-Saxon Edward the Confessor. Although noted for his devotion to religion, Edward was a weak ruler who had little control over the powerful earls who had taken over most of the king's authority in their territories.

William the Conqueror and the Norman Conquest

Edward the Confessor died without an heir, and immediately William, duke of Normandy, claimed the English throne based on a questionable hereditary right and on the assertion that Edward had promised him the crown. An outstanding statesman and soldier, William as duke of Normandy had subdued his rebellious vassals and established an effective centralized feudal state.

William and his army of 5000 men crossed the English Channel to enforce the Norman claim to the English throne. On October 14, 1066, the duke's mounted knights broke through the English infantry at Hastings, and William became king in England, where he began to introduce the Norman style of feudal organization. The new king retained some land as his royal domain and granted the remainder as fiefs to royal vassals called *tenants-in-chief*. In return for their fiefs, the tenants-in-chief provided William with a number of knights to serve in the royal army. From all the landholders in England, regardless of whether they were his immediate vassals, William exacted an oath that they would "be faithful to him against all other men." Both the tenants-in-chief holding fiefs directly from the king and the lesser vassals owed their first allegiance to William.

In line with his policy of controlling all aspects of the government, William redesigned the *witan*, the

Discovery Through Maps

The Danelaw: When Half of England Was Viking

As part of the Treaty of Wedmore, a boundary was drawn across England from London to Mersey. South of this line the laws and customs would be those of the English, under the rule of the king of Mersey. The land to the north and east of this line would be under Viking rule, with Scandinavian laws and customs. This Viking part of England became known as the Danelaw.

Although the Danelaw was brought back under English control within 50 years, Scandinavian cultural influences continued to be important there for many generations. Even today there are vestiges of the time when this area was distinct from England. The strongest reminder is modern English: the words, phrases, and grammar rules of Anglo-Saxon were altered by speakers of Old Norse, the tongue of the Vikings, and more than 600 loan words—including *egg*, *knife*, and *die*—entered the English language. Dialects in the Danelaw developed differently from those in other parts of the island, and even today the residents of the old Danelaw lands pride themselves on the distinctions in their manner of speaking. Arts and crafts were influenced as well, typified by the merging of Norse and Anglo-Saxon design in the Anglo-Norse cross and the design of gravestones.

The Bayeux tapestry, a woolen embroidery on linen, dates from the eleventh century. Over 230 feet long, it depicts events in the Norman conquest of England in 1066, accompanied by a commentary in Latin and surrounded by a decorative border portraying scenes from fables and everyday life.

council that had elected and advised the Anglo-Saxon kings. The new Norman ruler changed its title to the great council—the *Curia Regis,* or king's court—and converted it into a body composed of his tenants-in-chief. The great council met as a court of justice for the great barons and as an advisory body in important matters.

William also dominated the English church. He appointed bishops and abbots and required them to provide military service for their lands. Although he permitted the church to retain its courts, he denied them the right to appeal cases to the pope without his consent. Nor could the decrees of popes and church councils circulate in England without royal approval.

William II, who succeeded his father in 1087, was an ineffective king who inspired several baronial revolts before being shot in the back—accidentally, it was said—while hunting. Succeeding him was his brother, Henry I (1110–1135), a more able monarch who easily put down the only baronial revolt that challenged him.

Although the great council occasionally met to advise Henry, a small permanent council of barons grew in importance. From it, specialized branches of government gradually appeared. The *exchequer,* or court of accounts, supervised the collection of royal revenue and greatly expanded with the revival of a money economy. The well-trained "barons of the exchequer" also sat as a special court to try cases involving revenue.

ENGLAND: THE DOMINIONS OF HENRY II, c. 1180

- Inheritance
- Suzerainty
- Acquisitions by marriage to Eleanor of Aquitaine
- French royal domain

Henry's claims to lands in England and France threatened to absorb the kingdom of France. Note the sizable territory claimed by the king through marriage to Eleanor of Aquitaine, once wife of the French king.

Henry II

Almost 20 years of civil war followed Henry's death. But the monarchy was strengthened by Henry's grandson, Henry II (1154–1189), the founder of the Plantagenet, or Angevin, dynasty. As a result of his inheritance (Normandy and Anjou) and his marriage to Eleanor of Aquitaine, the richest heiress in France, Henry's possessions extended from Scotland to the Pyrenees. Henry's great military skill and restless energy were important assets to his reign. He quickly recaptured the lands of his grandfather and began rebuilding the power of the monarchy in England.

Henry's chief contribution to the development of the English monarchy was to increase the jurisdiction of the royal courts at the expense of the feudal courts. His efforts produced significant results. Itinerant justices on regular circuits were sent out once each year to enforce the "King's Peace." Henry's courts also used the jury system to settle private lawsuits; circuit judges handed down quick decisions based on evidence sworn to by a jury of men selected because they were acquainted with the facts of the case.

Henry's judicial reforms stimulated the growth of the common law—one of the most important factors in unifying the English people. The decisions of the royal justices became the basis for future decisions made in the king's courts and became the law common to all English people.

Thomas à Becket

Although Henry strengthened the royal courts, he was not as successful in regulating the church courts. When he appointed his trusted friend Thomas à Becket archbishop of Canterbury, the king assumed that the cleric could easily be persuaded to cooperate, but Becket proved stubbornly independent in upholding the authority of the church courts over the king's. After a number of disagreements in which Becket defended the independence of the English church from royal authority, Henry was reputed to have remarked that he would be relieved if someone would rid England of the troublesome Becket. Responding to this angry remark, four knights went to Canterbury and murdered Becket before the high altar of the cathedral. Popular outrage over this murder destroyed Henry's chances of reducing the power of the church courts.

The Successors of Henry II

Henry's many accomplishments were marred by the mistakes of his successors. Having no taste for routine

A detail from the Carrow Psalter depicts the murder of Thomas à Becket by the knights of Henry II in Canterbury Cathedral. One knight has broken his sword over the archbishop's head.

The Martyrdom of Thomas Becket, Carrow Psalter, MS W. 34 f. 15v. The Walters Art Gallery, Baltimore.

tasks of government, Richard the Lion-Hearted (1189–1199) spent only five months of his ten-year reign in Britain, which he regarded as a source of money for his overseas adventures. Richard's successor, his brother John (1199–1216), was an inept and cruel ruler whose unscrupulousness cost him the support of his barons, at the time he needed them most, in his struggles with the two ablest men of the age, Philip II of France and Pope Innocent III. As feudal overlord of John's possessions in France, Philip declared John an unfaithful vassal and his claims to lands in France illegitmate. John only feebly resisted, and after losing more than half his possessions in France, he became involved in a struggle with Innocent III that ended in John's complete surrender. In the meantime the king alienated the British barons, who rebelled and in 1215 forced him to agree to the Magna Carta, a document that bound the king to observe all feudal rights and privileges. Although in later centuries people looked back on the Magna Carta as one of the most important documents in the history of political freedom, to the English nobility of John's time the Magna Carta did not appear to break any new constitutional ground. It was essentially a feudal agreement be-

tween the barons and the king, the aristocracy and the monarchy. Two great principles were contained in the charter: the law is above the king, and the king can be compelled by force to obey the law of the land.

The Origins of Parliament

The French-speaking Normans commonly used the word *parlement* (from *parler*, "to speak") for the great council. Anglicized as *parliament*, the term was used interchangeably with *great council* and *Curia Regis*. Modern historians, however, generally apply the term to the great council only after 1265, when its membership was radically enlarged. Parliament first became truly influential during the reign of Edward I (1272–1307), one of England's most outstanding monarchs. Beginning with the so-called Model Parliament of 1295, Edward followed the pattern of summoning representatives of shires and towns to meetings of the great council. In calling parliaments, Edward had no intention of making any concession to popular government; rather, he hoped to build popular consensus to support his own policies.

Early in the fourteenth century the representatives of the knights and the townsmen, called the Commons, adopted the practice of meeting separately from the lords. This resulted in the division of Parliament into what came to be called the House of Commons and the House of Lords. Parliament, particularly the Commons, soon discovered its power as a major source of revenue for the king. It gradually became the custom for Parliament to exercise this power by withholding its financial grants until the king had redressed grievances, made known by petitions. Parliament also presented petitions to the king with the request that they be recognized as statutes (laws drawn up by the king and his council and confirmed in Parliament). Gradually, Parliament assumed the right to initiate legislation through petition.

Expansion Under Edward I

Edward I was the first English king who was determined to be master of the whole island of Great Britain—Wales, Scotland, and England. In 1284, after a five-year struggle, English law and administration were imposed on Wales, and numerous attempts were made to conquer the Scots, who continued to offer Edward serious resistance up to the time of his death.

The Reconquista and Medieval Spain

Unification in Spain took a different course from that in either France or England. Customary rivalry between the Christian feudal nobles and

Edward I at a session of Parliament. Edward was the first monarch to give real standing to the institution of Parliament and to expand it to include representatives of the shires and boroughs.
Windsor Castle, Royal Library; © Her Majesty Queen Elizabeth II.

royal authority was complicated by another element: religious fervor. Unification of Christian Spain was not thought possible without the expulsion of the Muslims, with their foreign religion and culture.

During the long struggle to drive the Muslims from Spain, patriotism blended with fierce religious devotion. This movement became known as the *Reconquista*—the reconquest of Spain from Muslim control. As early as the ninth century, northern Spain became caught up in religious zeal centering around the shrine at Santiago de Compostela, reputed to be the burial site of the apostle St. James. In 1212 at Las Navas de Tolosa, the Christian Spaniards achieved a decisive victory over the Muslims. A few years later they captured first Cordova and Seville. The conquest of Seville effectively doubled the territory of the Spanish kingdom. From the end of the thirteenth century, when the Reconquista slowed, until the latter part of the fifteenth century, Muslim political control

was confined to Granada. Until the fifteenth century, the Christian victors usually allowed their new Muslim subjects to practice their own religion and traditions. Muslim traders and artisans were protected because of their economic value, and Muslim culture—art in particular—was often adapted by the Christians.

Disunity in Germany and Italy

When the last Carolingian ruler of the kingdom of the East Franks, Louis the Child, died in 911, the great German dukes elected the weakest of their number to hold the title of king. But an exceptionally strong ruler inherited the throne in 936—Otto the Great (936–973), duke of Saxony and founder of the Saxon dynasty of kings. Otto attempted to gain control of the great dukes by appointing his own relatives and favorites as their rulers. As an extra precaution he appointed counts as supervising officials who were directly responsible to the king.

Through alliance with the church, Otto constructed a stronger German monarchy. The king promised protection to the bishops and abbots and granted them a free hand over their vast estates; in return the church furnished the king with the advisers, income, and troops that he lacked. Otto himself appointed German bishops and abbots; since their offices were not hereditary, he expected that their first obedience was to the king.

Otto also ended the Magyar invasions, thereby enhancing his claim that the king, not the dukes, was the true defender of the German people. In 955 Otto crushed a Magyar army at Lechfeld. The surviving Magyars settled in Hungary, and by 1000 they had accepted Christianity.

Otto the Great wanted to establish a German empire, modeled after Roman and Carolingian examples. The conquest and incorporation of the Italian peninsula into that empire were Otto's primary objectives. He proclaimed himself king of Italy, and in 962 he was crowned emperor by the pope, whose Papal States were threatened by an Italian duke. No doubt Otto thought of himself as the successor of the imperial Caesars and Charlemagne; in fact, his empire later became known as the Holy Roman Empire. But Otto also needed the imperial title to legitimize his claim to Lombardy, Burgundy, and Lorraine, which had belonged to the kingdom of Lothair, the last to hold the title of emperor. Otto and his successors became deeply involved in Italian politics and sometimes preoccupied with Italy to the neglect of their German subjects. The negative effects of the German obsession with Italy were apparent in the reign of Otto III (983–1002), who promoted "the renewal of the Roman Empire." Ignoring Germany, the

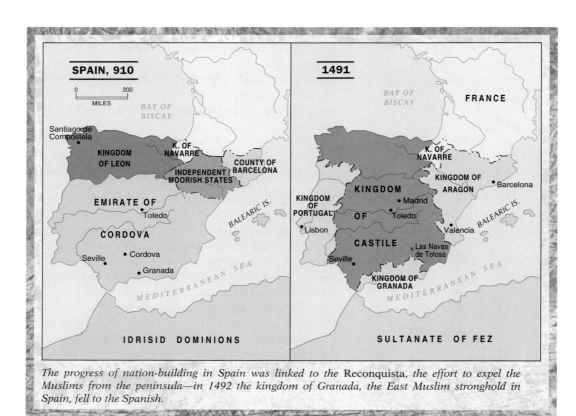

The progress of nation-building in Spain was linked to the Reconquista, *the effort to expel the Muslims from the peninsula—in 1492 the kingdom of Granada, the East Muslim stronghold in Spain, fell to the Spanish.*

real source of his power, he made Rome his capital, built a palace there, and styled himself emperor of the Romans.

Despite the distractions in Italy, the Saxon rulers were the most powerful in Europe. They had permanently halted Magyar advances and, by utilizing the German church as an ally, reduced feudal fragmentation in their homeland. They also fostered economic progress. German eastward expansion had begun, and the Alpine passes had been freed from Muslim control and made safe for Italian merchants.

The Salian Emperors

The Saxon kings were succeeded by the Salian dynasty, which ruled from 1024 to 1125 and whose members also tried to establish a centralized monarchy. Under the emperor Henry IV (1056–1106) the monarchy reached the height of its power, but it also experienced a major reverse. The revival of a powerful papacy led to a bitter conflict with Henry, centering on the king's right to appoint church officials who were also his most loyal supporters. This disagreement between state and church culminated in Henry's begging the pope's forgiveness at Canossa in 1077. This conflict, the Investiture Controversy, resulted in the loss of the

monarchy's major sources of strength: the loyalty of the German church, now transferred to the papacy; the support of the great nobles, now openly rebellious and insistent on their "inborn rights"; and the chief material base of royal power, the king's lands, which were diminished by grants to nobles who would stay loyal to the monarchy only if such concessions were made.

The Holy Roman Empire

962	Otto the Great crowned emperor by the pope
1056–1106	Reign of Henry IV
1152–1190	Frederick I Barbarossa begins Hohenstaufen dynasty
1212–1250	Reign of Frederick II
1273	Election of Rudolf of Habsburg as German emperor
1356	Golden Bull
1493–1519	Reign of Maximilian I

The Holy Roman Empire, in its infancy in 1000, was united under the Saxon's emperors, but unity was challenged by strong and independent feudal nobles opposed to the emperor's efforts to rule other than in name only.

The second emperor of the new Hohenstaufen dynasty, Frederick I Barbarossa ("Redbeard"), who ruled from 1152 to 1190, also sought to force the great nobles to acknowledge his overlordship. To maintain his hold over Germany, Frederick needed the resources of Italy—particularly the income from taxes levied on the wealthy northern Italian cities. Encouraged by the papacy, these cities had joined together in the Lombard League to resist him. Frederick spent about 25 years fighting intermittently in Italy, but the final result was failure: opposition from the popes and the Lombard League was too strong. Frederick did, however, succeed in marrying his son to the heiress of the throne of the kingdom of Naples and Sicily.

Barbarossa's grandson, Frederick II (1212–1250), was a remarkable individual. Orphaned at an early age, Frederick was brought up as the ward of Innocent III, the most powerful medieval pope. With the pope's support, Frederick was elected emperor in 1215, one year before Innocent's death. Frederick sacrificed Germany in his efforts to unite Italy under

his rule. He transferred crown lands and royal rights to the German princes in order to win their support for his Italian wars. Born in Sicily, he remained devoted to the southern part of his empire. He shaped his kingdom there into a vibrant state. Administered by paid officials who were trained at the University of Naples, which he founded for that purpose, his kingdom was the most centralized and bureaucratic in Europe.

As long as he lived, this brilliant monarch held his empire together, but it quickly collapsed after his death in 1250. In Germany his son ruled ineffectively for four years before dying, and soon afterward Frederick's descendants in Sicily were executed when the count of Anjou, brother of Louis IX of France, was invited by the pope to annihilate what remained of what he called the "viper breed of the Hohenstaufen."

The Holy Roman Empire never again achieved the brilliance it had enjoyed during the reign of Frederick Barbarossa. Later emperors usually did not try to interfere in Italian affairs, and they ceased going to Rome to receive the imperial crown from the pope. In German affairs the emperors no longer even attempted to assert their authority over the increasingly powerful nobles.

Revival of Trade and Towns

Even though manorialism sought to secure economic self-sufficiency, an increase in trade and commercial activity in Europe was obvious before the tenth century. A northern trading zone, centered on Flanders, extended from the British Isles to the Baltic Sea. By 1050 Flemish artisans were producing woolen cloth of fine quality and in great demand. Baltic furs, honey and forest products, and British tin and raw wool were exchanged for Flemish cloth. From the south by way of Italy came oriental luxury goods—silks, sugar, and spices.

Trade Routes and Trade Fairs

The opening of the Mediterranean to European trade was instrumental in increasing trade and commerce. In the eleventh century Normans and Italians broke the Muslim hold on the eastern Mediterranean, and the First Crusade revived trade with the Near East. The easiest route north from the Mediterranean was to Marseilles and up the Rhône valley. Early in the fourteenth century an all-sea route connected the Mediterranean with northern Europe via the Strait of Gibraltar. The old overland route from northern Italy

A fifteenth-century illustration of the fair of Lendit, held every June in a field outside Paris. Here the bishop of Paris gives his blessing to the fair.

through the Alpine passes to central Europe was also reused.

Along the main European trade routes, lords set up fairs, where merchants and goods from Italy and northern Europe met. During the twelfth and thirteenth centuries the fairs of Champagne in France functioned as the major clearinghouse for this international trade.

Factors in the Revival of Towns

The resurgence of trade in Europe was a prime cause of the revival of towns; the towns arose because of trade, but they also stimulated trade by providing greater markets and by producing goods for the merchants to sell. Rivers were also important in the development of medieval towns; they were natural highways on which articles of commerce could be easily transported.

Another factor contributing to the rise of towns was population growth. In Britain, for example, the population more than tripled between 1066 and 1350. The reasons for this rapid increase in population are varied. The ending of bloody foreign invasions and, in some areas, the stabilization of feudal

society were contributing factors. More important was an increase in food production brought about by the cultivation of wastelands, clearing of forests, and draining of marshes.

Medieval towns were not large by modern standards. Before 1200 no European town contained 100,000 inhabitants, and a town of 20,000 was considered very large. Since the area within the walls was at a premium, towns were more crowded than the average modern city. Shops were even built on bridges, and buildings were erected to seven or more stories. Each additional story of a house often projected over the street, so that it was often possible for persons at the tops of houses opposite one another to touch hands. Streets were crowded, narrow, and noisy.

Merchant and Craft Guilds

In each town the merchants and artisans organized themselves into guilds. There were two kinds of guilds: merchant and craft. The merchant guild ensured a monopoly of trade within a given locality. All foreign merchants were supervised closely and made

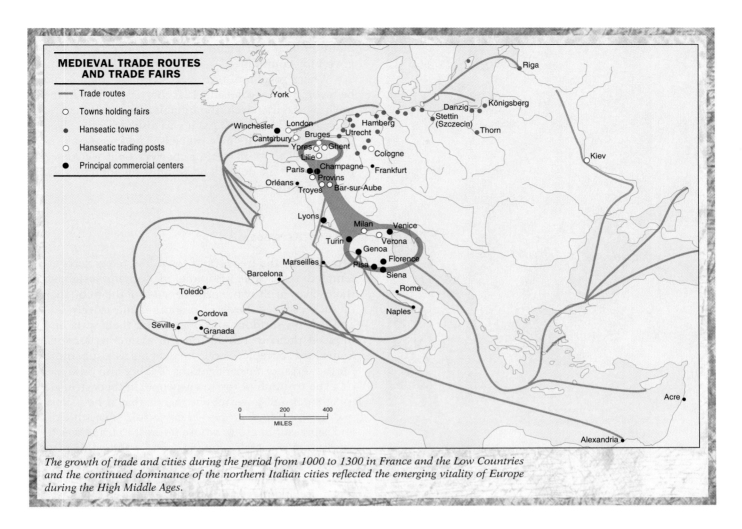

MEDIEVAL TRADE ROUTES AND TRADE FAIRS

— Trade routes
○ Towns holding fairs
● Hanseatic towns
○ Hanseatic trading posts
● Principal commercial centers

The growth of trade and cities during the period from 1000 to 1300 in France and the Low Countries and the continued dominance of the northern Italian cities reflected the emerging vitality of Europe during the High Middle Ages.

to pay tolls. Disputes among merchants were settled at the guild court according to its own legal code. The guilds also tried to ensure that the customers were not cheated: they checked weights and measures and insisted on a standard quality for goods. To allow only a legitimate profit, the guild fixed a "just price," which was fair to both producer and customer.

With the increase of commerce in the towns, artisans and craftspeople in each of the medieval trades—weaving, cobbling, tanning, and so on—began to organize as early as the eleventh century. The result was the craft guild, which differed from the merchant guild in that membership was limited to artisans in one particular craft.

The general aims of the craft guilds were the same as those of the merchant guilds: the creation of a monopoly and the enforcement of trade rules. The guild restricted the number of its members, regulated the quantity and quality of the goods produced, and set prices. It also enforced regulations to protect the consumer from poor workmanship and inferior materials.

The craft guild differed from the merchant guild in its recognition of three distinct classes of workers: apprentices, journeymen, and master craftsmen. The apprentice was a youth who lived at the master's house and was taught the trade thoroughly. Although the apprentice received no wages, all his physical needs were supplied. Apprenticeship commonly lasted seven years. When the apprentice's schooling was finished, the youth became a journeyman. He was then eligible to receive wages and to be hired by a master. At about age 23, the journeyman sought admission into the guild as a master. To be accepted he had to prove his ability. Some crafts demanded the production of a "master piece," for example, a pair of shoes that the master shoemakers would find acceptable in every way.

The guild's functions stretched beyond business and politics into charitable and social activities. A guild member who fell into poverty received aid from the guild. The guild also provided financial assistance for the burial expense of its members and looked after their dependents. Members attended social

A guild master judges the work of two craftsmen, a mason and a carpenter.

meetings in the guildhall and periodically held processions in honor of their patron saints.

Acquiring Urban Freedom

The guilds played an important role in local government. Both artisans and merchants were subject to the feudal lord or bishop in whose domain the city stood. The citizens of the towns came to resent their overlord's collecting tolls and dues as though they were serfs. The townspeople demanded the privileges of governing themselves—of making their own laws, administering their own justice, levying their own taxes, and issuing their own coinage. The overlord resisted these demands for self-government, but the towns were able to win their independence in various ways.

One method was to become a *commune*, a self-governing town. The merchant guilds took the lead in acquiring charters of self-government for the towns. Sometimes a charter had to be won by revolt; in other circumstances it could be purchased, for a feudal lord was always in need of money. By 1200 the Lombard towns of northern Italy, as well as many French and Flemish towns, had become self-governing communes.

Where royal authority was strong, a town could be favored as "privileged." In a charter granted to the town by the monarch, the inhabitants won extensive financial and legal powers. It was also generally given the right to elect its own officials. The king was usually willing to grant such a charter, for it weakened the power of the nobles and won for the monarch the support of the townspeople.

The Bourgeoisie

Attracted by the freedom of town life, many serfs attempted to escape from the manor and establish themselves in a town. Partly because of the frequency of such escapes, lords of manors came to rely less and less on serfdom and often freed their serfs and induced them to remain on the manor as tenants. Some lords accepted money payments as a substitute for the serf's former obligations of labor and produce.

The triumph of the townspeople in their struggle for greater self-government meant that a new class had evolved in Europe—a powerful, independent, and self-assured group whose interest in trade was to revolutionize social, economic, and political history. The members of this class were called burghers and came to be known as the *bourgeoisie*. Kings began to rely more and more on them in combating the power of the feudal lords, and their economic interests gave rise to an early capitalism.

The Later Middle Ages, 1300–1500

Europe saw many changes during the later Middle Ages, some constructive, some disastrous. Distructive wars and suffering produced by disease and famine took a massive toll on the population. At the same time, political and cultural changes that would have lasting effects on European civilization were under way.

The Black Death and Economic Depression

The twelfth and thirteenth centuries had been an era of growth, but in the fourteenth and fifteenth centuries the economy leveled off and then stagnated. By 1350 the Continent was in the grips of a great economic depression, which lasted almost a century.

Henry Knighton, "The Devastation of England"

The plague raged throughout England and was especially harsh in London, where nearly two-thirds of the residents perished. The following account was written by Henry Knighton, a clergyman in Leicester, who was a boy in 1348 but who had an abundance of direct information.

Then the grievous plague penetrated the seacoasts from Southampton, and came to Bristol, and there almost the whole strength of the town died, struck, as it were, by sudden death; for there were few who kept their beds more than three days, or two days, or half a day; and after this the fell death broke forth on every side with the course of the sun. There died at Leicester in the small parish of St. Leonard more than 380; in the parish of Holy Cross, more than 400; in the parish of St. Margaret of Leicester, more than 700; and so in each parish a great number. Then the bishop of Lincoln sent through the whole bishopric, and gave general power to all and every priest, both regular and secular, to hear confessions, and absolve with full and entire episcopal authority except in matters of debt, in which case the dying man, if he could, should pay the debt while he lived, or others should certainly fulfill that duty from his property after his death. Likewise, the pope granted full remission of all sins to whoever was absolved in peril of death, and every one could choose a confessor at his will. . . . And there were small prices for everything on account of the fear of death. For there were very few who cared about riches or anything else; for a man could have a horse, which before was worth 40 *s.*, for 6 *s.* 8 *d.* . . . Sheep and cattle went wandering over fields and through crops, and there was no one to go and drive or gather them, so that the number cannot be reckoned which perished in the ditches and hedges in every district, for lack of herdsmen; for there was such a lack of servants that no one knew what he ought to do. . . . Wherefore many crops perished in the fields for want of some one to gather them; but in the pestilence year, as is above said of other things, there was such abundance of grain that no one troubled about it. . . .

From Edward Potts Cheyney, ed., *Readings in English History Drawn from the Original Sources* (Boston: Ginn, 1908), pp. 255–256.

One symptom of economic stagnation was social unrest and tension. Common working people, many of whom resented the restrictions of the guild system, organized themselves to protect their interests against the guild masters and rich merchants. Peasant unrest in Britain and France erupted into full-scale revolts.

A major cause of the slump was the arrival in Europe of the Black Death, a bubonic plague from Asia carried by fleas on rats. The Black Death struck Europe in 1347 and intermittently thereafter for the next two centuries, decimating and demoralizing society. It is estimated that about one-third of the European population was wiped out. Hardest hit were the towns; within five years the population of Florence, for example, fell from 114,000 to about 50,000. Coupled with the devastation wrought by the Black Death was the destruction and death caused by the Hundred Years' War between France and England.

By 1450 the effects of economic depression and stagnation had begun to ease. A period of great economic expansion was at hand, promoted by a new style of strong monarchy and stimulated by European geographical discovery and expansion over the face of the globe.

The Progress of Late Medieval Politics

The late Middle Ages witnessed the accession of strong monarchs in several of the emerging nation-states of Europe, all of whom put national political and economic interests ahead of submission to papal power. These monarchs sought to break forever the power of the papacy and the feudal nobility in their countries. Some succeeded in doing so; others met with less than total success.

Germany: The Early Habsburgs

After the fall of the Hohenstaufens, Germany lapsed more and more into political disunity. In 1273 the imperial crown was given to the weak Count Rudolf (1273–1291) of the House of Habsburg, a name derived from Habichtsburg ("Castle of the Hawk"), the family's home in northern Switzerland. During the remainder of the Middle Ages, the Habsburgs had amazing success in territorial acquisition; Rudolf himself acquired Austria through marriage, and thereafter the Habsburgs ruled their holdings from Vienna.

At first, victims of the plague were laid to rest in coffins. Later as the plague raged through Europe, mass burials were the only way to keep up with the rapidly increasing number of dead.

In 1356 the German nobility won another significant victory in their efforts to avoid the creation of a powerful monarchy. The Golden Bull, a document that served as the political constitution of Germany until early in the nineteenth century, established a procedure by which seven German electors—three archbishops and four lay princes—chose the emperor. The electors and other important princes were given rights that made them virtually independent rulers, and the emperor could take no important action without the consent of the imperial feudal assembly, the Diet, which met infrequently.

From 1438 until 1806, when the Holy Roman Empire disintegrated, the Habsburgs held the imperial crown almost without interruption. Maximilian I (1493–1519) helped make the Habsburgs the most important royal family in sixteenth-century Europe by marrying Mary of Burgundy, heiress of the rich Low Countries, and by marrying his son to the heiress of Spain.

Inspired by the accomplishments of other contemporary European monarchs, Maximilian attempted to strengthen the monarchy. His program for a national court system, army, and taxation was frustrated by the German princes who insisted on guarding what they called "German freedom." The emperor continued to be limited in power; nor was the empire successful in establishing an imperial treasury, an efficient central administration, or a standing army.

Spain: Ferdinand and Isabella

In 1479 Isabella of Castile and Ferdinand of Aragon began a joint rule that united the Iberian peninsula except for Granada, Navarre, and Portugal. The "Catholic Majesties," the title the pope conferred on Ferdinand and Isabella, set out to establish effective royal control in all of Spain. The Holy Brotherhood, a league of cities that had long existed for mutual protection against unruly nobles, was taken over by the crown, and its militia was used as a standing army and police force. The powerful and virtually independent military orders of knights, which had emerged during the Reconquista, were also brought under royal control.

"One King, One Law, One Faith"

Ferdinand and Isabella believed that the church should be subordinate to royal government. By tactful negotiations the Spanish sovereigns induced the pope to give them the right to make church appointments in Spain and to establish a Spanish court of Inquisition largely free of papal control.

In this romantic Flemish tapestry, Ferdinand and Isabella reign in splendor, attended by richly costumed courtiers and ladies-in-waiting.

The Spanish Inquisition confiscated the property of most Jews and Muslims and terrified the Christian clergy and laity into accepting royal absolutism as well as religious orthodoxy. Although the Inquisition greatly enhanced the power of the Spanish crown, it also caused many people to flee Spain and the threat of persecution. About 150,000 Spanish Jews, mainly merchants and professional people, fled to the Netherlands, England, North Africa, and the Ottoman Empire. Calling themselves Sephardim, many of these exiles retained their Spanish language and culture into the twentieth century.

Another manifestation of Spanish absolutism, defined by Isabella herself as "one king, one law, one faith," was the intentional neglect of the *Cortes* of Castile and Aragon. These representative assemblies, having emerged in the twelfth century, never were allowed by the monarchy to take an effective position as legislative bodies.

One of the most dramatic achievements of the Catholic Majesties was the conquest of Granada in 1492, the same year that Columbus claimed the New World for Spain. Before Ferdinand died in 1516, a dozen years after Isabella, he seized the part of Navarre that lay south of the Pyrenees. This acquisition, together with the conquest of Granada, completed the unification of the Spanish nation-state.

Results of Spanish Unification

Royal absolutism and unification, coupled with the acquisition of territory in the New and Old Worlds, made Spain the strongest power in sixteenth-century Europe. But centuries of fighting against the Muslims left a legacy of hatred and excessive national pride. Religious fervor was generated as a means to an end, and the result was a heritage of religious bigotry and the end of the tolerance, intellectual curiosity, and sense of balance that had been characteristic of Muslim culture in Spain. Spanish contempt for the Muslims fostered scorn for many activities in which the "unbelievers" had engaged, especially commerce and agriculture. This attitude hampered Spanish development in subsequent centuries.

Crisis in England and France

Nation-making in both England and France was greatly affected by the long conflict that colored much of both nations' history during the fourteenth and fifteenth centuries. In both lands the crisis of war led to a temporary resurgence of the feudal nobility at the expense of the king. But increasing anarchy and the continuing misery of war stimulated nationalistic feelings and a demand for strong rulers who could guarantee law and order. By the late fifteenth century the English and French kings were able to resume the task of establishing the institutions of the modern nation-state.

The Hundred Years' War

The Hundred Years' War had its origins in a fundamental conflict between the English and the French monarchies. The English kings wanted to regain the large holdings in France that had been theirs in the days of Henry II. But the French kings were determined not only to keep what had been taken from John of England but also to expand their holdings. Their ultimate goal was a centralized France under the direct rule of the monarchy at Paris.

Another cause was the clash of French and English economic interests in Flanders. This region was falling more and more under French control, to the frustration of both the English wool growers who supplied the great Flemish woolen industry and the English king, whose income came in great part from duties on wool.

The immediate excuse for open conflict was a dispute over the succession to the French throne. In 1328, after the direct line of Capetian succession ended, Philip VI of the House of Valois assumed the throne. But the English king, Edward III, maintained that he was the legitimate heir, and warfare resulted. Interrupted by several peace treaties and a number of truces, the devastating Hundred Years' War stretched from 1337 to 1453.

The first years of warfare witnessed impressive English victories. At the naval battle of Sluys (1340) the English gained command of the English Channel and thus were able to send their armies to France at will. England won a series of great battles—at Crécy (1346), Poitiers (1356), and Agincourt (1415), where the French lost some 7000 knights, including many great nobles, and the English only 500. In the aftermath of Agincourt, large portions of France fell to the English.

The English armies were much more effective than those of the French. With no thought of strategy, the French knights charged the enemy at a mad gallop and then engaged in hand-to-hand fighting. But the English had learned more effective methods. Their greatest weapon was the longbow. Six feet long and made of special wood, the longbow shot steel-tipped arrows that were dangerous at 400 yards and deadly at 100. The usual English plan of battle called for the knights to fight dismounted. Protecting them was a forward wall of bowmen just behind a barricade of iron stakes planted in the ground to slow the enemy's cavalry charge. By the time the French cavalry reached the dismounted knights, the remaining few French were easily killed.

English military triumphs stirred English pride and what we now think of as nationalism—love of country, identification with it, and a sense of difference from (and usually superiority to) others. However, nationalism was stirring in France also. The revival of French patriotism is associated with Joan of Arc, who inspired a series of French victories. Moved by inner voices that she believed divine, Joan persuaded the timid French ruler, Charles VII, to allow her to lead an army to relieve the besieged city of Orléans. Clad in white armor and riding a white horse, she inspired confidence and a feeling of invincibility in her followers, and in 1429 Orléans was rescued from what had seemed certain conquest. Joan was ultimately captured by the enemy, found guilty of bewitching the English soldiers, and burned at the stake. But the martyrdom of the Maid of Orléans seemed a turning point in the long struggle. Also, France's development of a permanent standing army and the greater use of gunpowder began to transform

the art of war. English resistance crumbled as military superiority now turned full circle; the English longbow was outmatched by French artillery. Of the vast territories they had once controlled in France, the English retained only Calais when the war ended in 1453.

Aftermath of the War in England

The Hundred Years' War exhausted England and fueled discontent with the monarchy in Parliament and among the common people. Richard II (1377–1399), the last Plantagenet king, was unstable, cruel, power-hungry, and firm in his belief that the king should oversee the lives and property of his subjects. His seizure of the properties of Henry, the duke of Lancaster, led to a revolt in which Henry was victorious.

Henry IV established the Lancastrian dynasty, which ruled England from 1399 to 1461. The king was given the support of Parliament, which had deeply resented Richard's autocratic reign and was determined that its authority should not again be ignored. Hard pressed for money to suppress revolts at home and to carry on the war in France, the Lancastrian kings became more and more financially dependent on Parliament.

A fifteenth-century portrait of Joan of Arc in battle dress. After leading the French to victory at Orléans in 1429, she was captured by the English, tried and convicted of witchcraft and heresy, and burned at the stake in 1431. The French king, Charles VII, whose kingdom she had helped save, did nothing to rescue her.

Baronial rivalry to control both Parliament and the crown flared up during the reign of the third Lancastrian king, Henry VI (1421–1471). When Henry went completely insane in 1453, the duke of York, the strongest noble in the kingdom, became regent. Two years later full-scale civil war broke out between the House of York and the supporters of the Lancastrians. The struggle became known as the Wars of the Roses; the white rose was the symbol of the Yorkists, and the red rose that of the House of Lancaster. In 1461 the Yorkists succeeded in having their leader, Edward IV, crowned king. Within ten years Edward was able to subdue the nobles and win the support of the English middle class, who saw a strong monarchy as the only alternative to anarchy. Edward's power became practically absolute.

The leadership of the House of York ended in 1483 when Edward IV died, leaving two young sons as his heirs. Their uncle bribed and intimidated Parliament to declare his nephews illegitimate and to give him the throne as Richard III. The two boys were imprisoned in the Tower of London, where they were secretly murdered. The double murder caused the kingdom to suspect the involvement of King Richard, and support grew for the claim of Henry Tudor to the throne. Henry defeated Richard in battle at Bosworth Field in 1485 and thereby became Henry VII, the first of the Tudor dynasty.

Henry VII and the Tudor Dynasty

During Henry VII's reign (1485–1509), the English monarchy reclaimed the support of the people. Henry's attention to the domestic affairs of the kingdom, his efficient administration, and his vigorous efforts to increase royal revenues strengthened the monarch's hold on power and his popularity with the commoners. The "new monarchy" in England restored order, promoted trade at home and abroad, and provided a sense of security. The king won the support of the people of middle rank, the burghers and landed gentry, who provided the basis of his power. Henry VII always worked through Parliament, where his wishes were generally honored.

France After the Hundred Years' War

The Hundred Years' War left France with a new national consciousness and royal power that was stronger than ever. In 1438 Charles VII established effective influence over the church in France by decreeing that it should be controlled by a council of French bishops whose appointment was to be regulated by the monarch. Furthermore, the *taille*, a land tax voted during the war to support a standing army, became permanent, making the king financially inde-

Henry Tudor, who ruled England as Henry VII, was the first of the Tudor line. His victory over Richard III in Bosworth Field in 1485 ended the rule of the House of York.

pendent of the Estates-General. Financial matters were kept firmly under royal control.

After the war, the astute and ruthless Louis XI (1461–1483) continued the process of consolidating royal power. A tireless worker completely lacking in scruples, Louis XI earned himself the epithet the "universal spider" because of his constant intrigues. In his pursuit of power he used any weapon—violence, bribery, treachery—to obtain his ends. The "spider king" devoted his reign to restoring prosperity to his nation and to reducing the powers of the noble families still active and ambitious after the long war. Like Henry VII in England, Louis XI was one of the "new monarchs" who worked for the creation of a subject-sovereign relationship in their kingdoms, replacing the old feudal ties of personal fidelity.

Conclusion

During the period known as the early Middle Ages (500–1000), the focus of European civilization shifted from the Mediterranean to France. The conversion of Clovis to Christianity and the subsequent Frankish alliance with the papacy united the most energetic of the Germanic tribes with the greatest existing force for civilization in western Europe, the church. The foundation of a new Europe was established by Charlemagne, but his empire depended too heavily on the forceful personality of its founder and did not survive his successors.

After the Carolingian collapse, feudal systems of organization evolved to meet the turbulent conditions of the time. Manorialism became the economic system through which most of the population provided for its needs. Self-sufficiency and economic isolation provided the most secure means of survival. But the expansion of trade and commerce and the revival of urban life altered the traditional isolation of the manor and helped bring about economic expansion.

The High Middle Ages (1000–1300) and later Middle Ages (1300–1500) witnessed significant change and political development in all the states of Europe. In England, William the Conqueror secured a unified kingdom in 1066, and later kings made progress in keeping the nobility under control and in building the machinery of royal administration. In France, each of the many counties and duchies that constituted the feudal kingdom had to be subordinated and brought within the framework of royal authority. It took the French kings three centuries to accomplish what William the Conqueror had done in one generation.

The political evolution of both England and France was affected by the Hundred Years' War. In England, the power of Parliament was increased, and the upsurge in the power of the nobility led to the Wars of the Roses, which ended finally with the accession of the Tudor dynasty; in France, royal power was consolidated under Louis XI, and his abilities in government made possible further progress in national unification.

Nation-making in Spain was unique, since the ambitions of the monarchy were combined with the religious fervor of a Crusade. In the mid-eleventh century the Christian Spanish states began the Reconquista in earnest, but not until the end of the fifteenth century was the task completed. In Germany, the kings dissipated their energies by seeking to establish an empire that encompassed Italy and Sicily. In the later Middle Ages Germany remained divided and weak; there national unification would not be achieved until the nineteenth century.

Suggestions for Reading

Robert Bartlett, *The Making of Europe: Conquest, Colonization, and Cultural Change, 950–1350* (Princeton University Press,

1993); Harry S. L. B. Moss, *The Birth of the Middle Ages, 395–814* (Oxford University Press, 1962); and Richard W. Southern, *The Making of the Middle Ages* (Yale University Press, 1992), are excellent surveys of the early Middle Ages. Margaret Deanesly, *History of Early Medieval Europe from 476 to 911* (Barnes & Noble, 1959); John Hine Mundy, *Europe in the High Middle Ages, 1150–1309*, 2nd ed. (Addison-Wesley, 1991); Malcolm C. Barber, *The Two Cities: Medieval Europe, 1050–1320* (Routledge, 1992); and Joseph R. Strayer, *Western Europe in the Middle Ages*, 3rd ed. (Waveland, 1991), are also excellent. On Frankish history, see Suzanne Wemple, *Women in Frankish Society: Marriage and the Cloister, 500–900* (University of Pennsylvania Press, 1981), and Peter Munz, *Life in the Age of Charlemagne* (Capricorn, 1971). See also Friedrich Heer, *Charlemagne and His World* (Macmillan, 1975). Johannes Brondsted, *The Vikings* (Penguin, 1965); Gwyn Jones, *A History of the Vikings* (Oxford University Press, 1991); and Gabriel Turville-Petre, *The Heroic Age of Scandinavia* (Greenwood, 1976), are outstanding works on Viking society.

For economic and social history, see "The Agrarian Life of the Middle Ages" in *The Cambridge Economic History of Europe*, Vol. 1, 2nd ed. (Cambridge University Press, 1967); Georges Duby, *Rural Economy and Country Life in the Medieval West* (University of South Carolina Press, 1968); George G. Coulton, *The Medieval Village* (Johns Hopkins University Press, 1991); Robert Fossier, *Peasant Life in the Medieval West* (Blackwell, 1988); and Eileen Power, *Medieval People* (Smith, 1993), all worthwhile accounts of rural life and the manorial system. See also Frances Gies and Joseph Gies, *Women in the Middle Ages* (HarperPerennial, 1980), *Life in a Medieval Village* (HarperPerennial, 1991), *Marriage and Family in the Middle Ages* (Harper Perennial, 1989), and *A Medieval Family: The Pastons of Fifteenth-Century England* (HarperCollins, 1998). Other good studies are Georges Duby, *Medieval Marriage* (Johns Hopkins University Press, 1991); Barbara A. Hanawalt, *Growing Up in Medieval London* (Oxford University Press, 1993); Marjorie Rowling, *Life in Medieval Times* (Perigee, 1979); Shulamith Shahar, *Childhood in the Middle Ages* (Routledge, 1992); Tania Bayard, ed., *A Medieval Home Companion: Housekeeping in the Fourteenth Century* (HarperCollins, 1992); David Herlihy, *Opera Muliebria: Women and Work in Medieval Europe* (McGraw-Hill, 1990), and Georges Duby, *The Three Orders* (University of Chicago Press, 1981).

On Germany in the Middle Ages, see Geoffrey Barraclough, *The Origins of Modern Germany* (Capricorn, 1963), and Robert E. Herzstein, ed., *The Holy Roman Empire in the Middle Ages: Universal State or German Catastrophe?* (Heath, 1966). Peter Munz, *Frederick Barbarossa: A Study in Medieval Politics* (Cornell University Press, 1969), and Thomas Curtis van Cleve, *The Emperor Frederick II of Hohenstaufen, Immutator Mundi* (Oxford University Press, 1972), are interesting biographies. See also Franz Bäuml, *Medieval Civilization in Germany* (Praeger, 1969).

On French history, see Robert Fawtier, *The Capetian Kings of France: Monarchy and Nation, 987–1328* (St. Martin's Press, 1969); John Bell Henneman, ed., *The Medieval French Monarchy* (Krieger, 1973); and Margaret Wade Labarge, *Saint Louis* (Macmillan, 1968). G. O. Sayles, *The Medieval Foundations of England* (Barnes, 1968), and Christopher N. L. Brooke, *From Alfred to Henry Third, 871–1272* (Norton, 1961), are valuable surveys on English history. See also Frank Merry Stenton, *Anglo-Saxon England*, 3rd ed. (Oxford University Press, 1971), the standard account; D. P. Kirby, *The Making of Early England* (Schocken, 1968); and Edmund King, *Medieval England, 1066–1485* (Salem House, 1989).

Joseph F. O'Callaghan, *A History of Medieval Spain* (Cornell University Press, 1983), and J. H. Elliot, *Imperial Spain, 1469–1716* (Penguin, 1963), are standard works. See also

Gabriel Jackson, *The Making of Medieval Spain* (Harcourt Brace, 1972); Ramon Menendez Pidal, *The Cid and His Spain* (Cass, 1971); and Felipe Fernandez-Armesto, *Ferdinand and Isabella* (Taplinger, 1975).

On the later Middle Ages, see Robert S. Gottfried, *The Black Death: Natural and Human Disaster in Medieval Europe* (Free Press, 1983); Christopher Allmand, *The Hundred Years' War* (Cambridge University Press, 1988); Denys Hay, *Europe in the Fourteenth and Fifteenth Centuries,* 2nd ed. (Addison-Wesley, 1989); Edward Potts Cheyney, *The Dawn of a New Era, 1250–1453* (HarperTorchbooks, 1966); Robert E. Lerner, *The Age of Adversity: The Fourteenth Century* (Cornell University Press, 1967); and Daniel Waley, *Later Medieval Europe: From St. Louis to Luther* (Longman, 1985).

Suggestions for Web Browsing

Medieval Studies
http://www.georgetown.edu/labyrinth/Virtual_Library/
    Medieval_Studies.html
   The WWW Virtual Library for Medieval Studies, a part of the Labyrinth project at Georgetown University, offers numerous links categorized by national cultures and by artistic genre.

Netserf: The Internet Connection for Medieval Resources
http://netserf.cua.edu
   A comprehensive site for resources on many aspects of medieval history, from archaeology and art to law and philosophy.

Internet Medieval Sourcebook
http://www.fordham.edu/halsall/book.html
   Extremely helpful site containing original course materials from medieval authors and secondary sources dealing with a large variety of medieval subjects.

Middle Ages
http://www.learner.org/exhibits/middleages/
   This site, under the direction of the Annenberg/CBS Project, features information and exhibits illustrating what daily life was really like during the Middle Ages.

Medieval Women
http://www.georgetown.edu/labyrinth/subjects/women/
    women.html
   Site details the individual lives and works of medieval women, including Hildegard of Bingen; women rulers and creators; and the impact of the Crusades on women, in addition to numerous general resources.

Women Writers of the Middle Ages
http://www.fordham.edu/halsall/source/byz-arabambas.html
   Site offers biographies and images and includes an extensive bibliography.

World of the Vikings
http://www.viking.org/viking.html
   This well-indexed site provides links to almost everything there is to know about these medieval seafarers—their everyday life, their travels, their influence.

The Plague
http://www.brown.edu/Departments/Italian_Studies/dweb/
    plague/plague.html
   Offers links detailing the origins, causes, effects, and literary influence of the Black Death.

The Dome of the Rock, a Muslim edifice from the seventh century, is built above the Temple Mount in Jerusalem, the site of Solomon's Temple. According to tradition, the site is also the place where Muhammad ascended into heaven on his "Night Journey." Intricate mosaic decoration covers the outer walls of the building.

Islam

From Its Origins to 1300

Chapter Contents

Arabia was the birthplace of the Islamic religion; and the Arabic language was the "tongue of the angels," since God chose to reveal himself through that vehicle to Muhammad, the prophet of the faith. Arabia became the center of the Islamic world and the source of renewal and inspiration for the faithful believers throughout an expanding Islamic Empire.

One of history's most dynamic movements began in the Arabian peninsula, an area of deserts, high temperatures, and exposed frontiers. The geographical conditions encouraged nomadic tribes and strong individualism, not large, settled civilizations with overbearing governments. Much of the interior of Arabia remained isolated, but the peninsula was crossed by trade routes that brought commerce, religious influences, and sometimes military domination from the world beyond. From out of this region between Asia, Europe, and Africa emerged Muhammad, to whom Allah chose to speak.

Muhammad became the prophet of a religion that shaped every aspect of individual and community life: from diet to politics, from family relations to law, from prayer to conquest. Within one century, the power of Islam would be felt from the Indian Ocean to the Atlantic; it would transfigure age-old religious, intellectual, and political patterns.

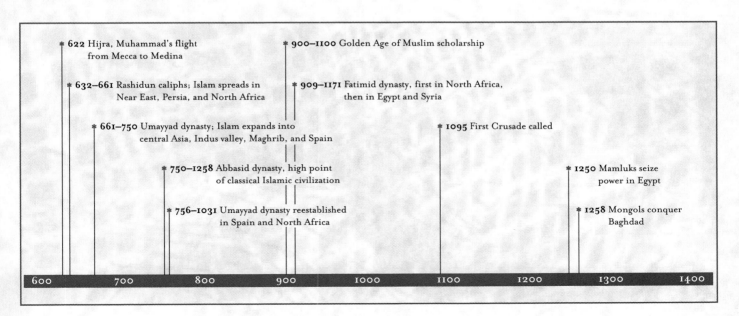

622 Hijra, Muhammad's flight from Mecca to Medina

632–661 Rashidun caliphs; Islam spreads in Near East, Persia, and North Africa

661–750 Umayyad dynasty; Islam expands into central Asia, Indus valley, Maghrib, and Spain

750–1258 Abbasid dynasty, high point of classical Islamic civilization

756–1031 Umayyad dynasty reestablished in Spain and North Africa

900–1100 Golden Age of Muslim scholarship

909–1171 Fatimid dynasty, first in North Africa, then in Egypt and Syria

1095 First Crusade called

1250 Mamluks seize power in Egypt

1258 Mongols conquer Baghdad

600　700　800　900　1000　1100　1200　1300　1400

Arabia Before the Prophet

The Arabian peninsula is one-third the size of the continental United States. Most of its land is desert; rainfall is scarce, vegetation is scant, and very little of the land is suitable for agriculture. Arabia before the birth of Muhammad was a culturally isolated and economically underdeveloped region. In the relatively more fertile southwestern corner of the peninsula, however, several small Arab kingdoms once flourished in the area now known as Yemen. The most notable of these early kingdoms, Saba' (the biblical Sheba), existed as early as the eighth century B.C.E. and lasted until the third century C.E., when it was taken by the Himyarites from the south.

Aided by the domestication of the camel and the expanding trade in frankincense and spices, these kingdoms became prosperous; they formed part of a commercial network of kingdoms within and beyond the Arabian peninsula. In the north of Arabia, several kingdoms were able to establish contacts with the Byzantine and the Persian (Sassanid) Empires as early as the fifth century C.E. Among the most notable of these small kingdoms were Nabataea in northwestern Arabia, which dominated Arabian trade routes until the Romans annexed the kingdom in the second century C.E., and the realm of the Lakhmids in the northeast, whose prominence was greatest around 250 to 600 C.E., until the kingdom was destroyed by the Sassanids. But in the interior of Arabia, a vast desert dotted sparsely with oases, a nomadic life based on herding was the only successful existence.

The Bedouin

The desert nomads, or *Bedouin*, lived according to ancient tribal patterns; at the head of the tribe was the male elder, or *shaykh*, elected and advised by the heads of the related families comprising the tribe. These men claimed authority based on family connections and personal merit. Tribes tended to be made up of three-generation families employing a gendered division of labor. The Bedouin led a precarious existence, moving their flocks from one pasture to the next, often following set patterns of migration. Aside from maintaining their herds, these nomads traded animal products for goods from the settled areas. They also relied on plunder from raids on settlements, on passing caravans, and on one another.

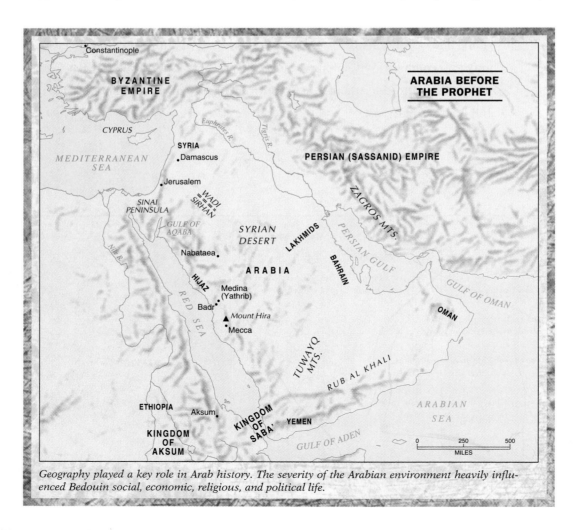

Geography played a key role in Arab history. The severity of the Arabian environment heavily influenced Bedouin social, economic, religious, and political life.

Their nomadic existence, its hardships, and the beauty of the desert landscape are all celebrated in the poetry of pre-Islamic Arabia.

The Bedouin enjoyed a degree of personal freedom unknown in more agrarian and settled societies. They developed a code of ethics represented in the word *muru'a,* or "manly virtue." Far from being abrasive and rough, men proved *muru'a* through grace and restraint, loyalty to obligation and duty, a devotion to do what must be done, and respect for women. The tribe shared a corporate spirit, or *'asabiyya,* which reflected the shared interests and honor of the tribe.

Although Bedouin society was patriarchal (dominated by the senior males), women enjoyed a great degree of independence. They engaged in business and commerce and could sometimes wed men of their own choosing. However, as in all traditional agricultural societies, women were under the protection of men, and the honor of the tribe was vested in the sexual honor of the women. The relative freedom of the Bedouin sprang from the realities of life in the desert, as did their values and ethics. One rule of conduct was unqualified hospitality to strangers. A nomad never knew when the care of a stranger might be essential to provide the necessary water and shade to save his or her own life.

The Bedouin of the seventh century did not have a highly structured religious system. They apparently looked at life as a brief time during which to take full advantage of daily pleasure. Ideas of an afterlife were not well defined or described. The Bedouin were animists; they worshipped a large number of gods and spirits, many of whom they believed to inhabit trees, wells, and stones. Each tribe had its own gods, sometimes symbolized by sacred stones.

The Bedouin of the Arabian interior led a relatively primitive and isolated existence, but it was not in their herding camps that the message of Islam was first spoken. In the Arabian cities along the trade routes, the people came into contact with traders and travelers who brought a complex mix of artistic, religious, and philosophical influences. Among these were the monotheistic beliefs of Judaism and Christianity. Some parts of Arabia were greatly influenced by the neighboring and more highly sophisticated cultures of Byzantium, Sassanid Persia, and Ethiopia. It was out of this more urban and commercial context that the early Islamic state would emerge.

Early Mecca

On the western side of the Arabian peninsula, along the Red Sea, is a region known as the Hijaz, or "barrier." The Hijaz extends along the western coastal plain from Yemen in the south to the Sinai peninsula in the north. One of the oases in the Hijaz is Mecca, set among barren hills 50 miles inland from the sea. This site had several advantages: Mecca possessed a well (the Zamzam) of great depth, and two ancient caravan routes met there. One route ran from Africa through the peninsula to Iran and central Asia, and another, a southeast-northwest route, brought the spices of India and Southeast Asia to the Mediterranean world.

A second significant advantage for Mecca was its importance as a religious sanctuary. An ancient temple, an almost square structure built of granite blocks, stood near the well of Mecca. Known as the *Ka'ba* ("cube"), this square temple contained the sacred Black Stone. According to tradition, the stone, probably a meteorite, was originally white but had become blackened by the sins of all those who touched it. Later Muslim historians would attribute the building of the Ka'ba to the prophet Abraham or even to Adam. The Ka'ba itself was draped with the pelts of sacrificial animals and supposedly held the images and shrines of 360 gods and goddesses. For centuries the Ka'ba had been a holy place of annual pilgrimage for the Arab tribes and a focal point of Arabic culture and ritual practice. As a pilgrimage site, it also brought prestige and wealth to the tribes who controlled the city of Mecca.

By the sixth century, Mecca was controlled by the Quraysh tribe, whose rulers organized themselves into an aristocracy of merchants and wealthy businessmen. The Quraysh engaged in lucrative trade with Byzantium and Persia, as well as with the southern Arabian tribes and the kingdom of Aksum across the Red Sea in what is now Ethiopia. In addition, a number of annual merchant fairs, such as one usually held at nearby Ukaz, were taken over by the Quraysh to extend the economic influence of Mecca. The Quraysh were also concerned with protecting the religious shrine of the Ka'ba, in addition to ensuring that the annual pilgrimage of tribes to the holy place would continue as a source of revenue for the merchants of the city.

Muhammad, Prophet of Islam

Into this environment at Mecca was born a man who would revolutionize the religious, political, and social organization of his people. Muhammad (c. 570–632) came from a family belonging to the Quraysh. An orphan, he suffered the loss of both his parents and his grandfather, who cared for him after his parents' death. He was then raised by his uncle, Abu Talib, a prominent merchant of Mecca. His early years were spent helping his uncle in the caravan trade. Even as a young man, Muhammad came to be admired by his fellow Meccans as a sincere and honest person, who earned the nickname al-Amin, "the trustworthy." When he was

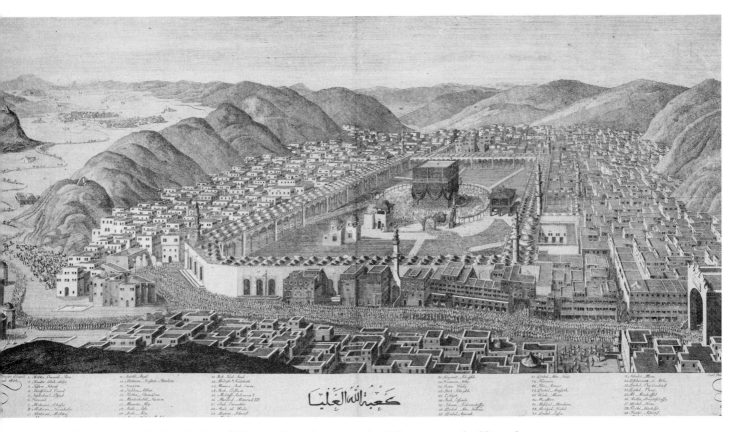

كعبة الله العليا

This engraving depicts the city of Mecca with, at its center, the Ka'ba, a square building of stone draped with black cloth that became the focal point of Muslim worship. Each year Muslims make the pilgrimage to celebrate their unity and to worship at this most sacred shrine of Islam. The site itself has been greatly expanded, and the number of pilgrims has dramatically increased since the time of the prophet Muhammad.

about 25 years old, he accepted employment from a wealthy widow, Khadija, whose caravans traded with Syria. He later married Khadija and began to take his place as a leading citizen of Mecca. Muhammad's marriage to Khadija was a long and happy one that produced two sons, who both died as infants, and two daughters. The younger, Fatima, would play an important role in the future of the fledgling Islamic state.

The Early Islamic State

622	The Hijra, Muhammad's migration from Mecca to Medina
630	The Prophet returns and takes control of Mecca, Ka'ba consecrated to Allah
632	Death of the Prophet
632–661	Rule of the first four caliphs: Abu Bakr, Umar, Uthman, Ali
638	Muslim armies take Jerusalem
651	Defeat of the Sassanids in Persia

Biographies of the Prophet, written after his death by his followers, describe him as a handsome, large man with broad shoulders and black, shining eyes, a man who was reserved and gentle but possessed of impressive energy. Tradition relates that Muhammad was an introspective man. Often he would escape from Meccan society, which he considered too materialistic and irreligious, and spend long hours alone in a cave on nearby Mount Hira. During these hours of meditation, Muhammad searched for answers to the metaphysical questions that many thoughtful people have pondered. Muhammad's meditations sometimes produced nearly total mental and physical exhaustion. During one such solitary meditation, Muhammad heard a call that was to alter history. This initial communication from heaven came in the form of a command:

> *Recite! In the name of your Lord, who created all things, who*
> *created man from a clot [of blood].*
> *Recite! And your Lord is Most Bounteous*
> *Who teaches by the Pen,*
> *teaches man that which he would not have otherwise known.* (Qur'an 96:1–5)

The collected revelations given to Muhammad are known as the *Qur'an* (or *Koran*), an Arabic word meaning "recitation" or "reading." The revelations that continued to come over the next 20 years or so were sometimes terse and short, at other times elaborate and poetic. The early revelations did not immediately persuade Muhammad that he was a messenger of God. In fact, his first reactions were fear and self-doubt. Anxious about the source and nature of his revelations, he sought the comfort and advice of Khadija.

As the revelations continued, Muhammad was persuaded that he had been called to be a messenger of divine revelation. He began to think of himself and his mission as one similar to those of prophets and messengers who had preceded him in announcing the existence of the one God, Allah. Allah, *"the* God," was the same God worshipped by the Christians and Jews, but Allah had now chosen Muhammad to be his last and greatest prophet to perfect the religion revealed earlier to Abraham, Moses, the Hebrew prophets, and Jesus. The religion Muhammad preached is called *Islam,* which means "submission" to the will of God. The followers of Islam are called *Muslims,* those who submit to God's law.

Muhammad's Message and Its Early Followers

At first Muhammad had little success in attracting followers in Mecca. The early message Muhammad brought to the Arabs was strong and direct: that Allah was one and majestic, all-powerful and demanding of the faith of his followers. Furthermore, Allah decreed that his followers be compassionate, ethical, and just in all their dealings:

> *In the name of Allah, the most Beneficent, the Most Merciful*
> *by the night as it enshrouds*
> *by the day as it illuminates*
> *by Him Who created the male and female*
> *indeed your affairs lead to various ends.*
> *For who gives [of himself] and acts righteously, and conforms to goodness,*
> *We will give him ease.*
> *But as for him who is niggardly deeming himself self-sufficient and rejects goodness,*
> *We will indeed ease his path to adversity.*
> *Nor shall his wealth save him as he perishes*
> *for Guidance is from Us*
> *and to Us belongs the Last and First.* (Qur'an 92:1–14)

Muhammad was able to win the early support of some of his relatives and close friends. His first converts were his wife, his cousin Ali, and Abu Bakr, a leading merchant of the Quraysh tribe who was highly respected for his integrity. Abu Bakr remained the constant companion of the Prophet during his persecution and exile and later succeeded him as the leader of Islam. But opposition to Muhammad's message was very strong, especially from Mecca's leading citizens. Many thought Muhammad was an ambitious poet attempting to pass on his own literary creations as the word of God. Others believed him to be possessed by demons. Muhammad challenged the status quo; his strong monotheism threatened the polytheistic beliefs of Mecca and the people who obtained their income from the pilgrims to the Ka'ba. Many of Muhammad's early converts were among the poorest of the city's residents, and Mecca's leading citizens feared the possibility of social revolution.

Since Muhammad was himself a member of the Quraysh tribe, its leaders first approached his uncle Abu Talib to persuade his nephew to stop preaching. Next they tried to bribe Muhammad with the promise of a lucrative appointment as an official. When he rejected such offers, actual persecution of Muhammad's converts began, and the Quraysh attempted a commercial and social boycott of the Prophet's family. During this time of trial, Abu Talib and Khadija both died, and Muhammad's faith and resolution were greatly tested. But inspired by the spirit and example of earlier prophets such as Abraham and Moses, who were also tested and persecuted, Muhammad persevered in his faith and continued his preaching.

The Hijra

To the north of Mecca is the city of Medina, which was then called Yathrib. The residents of Medina were somewhat familiar with monotheistic beliefs, in part because of the Jewish community in residence there. While visiting Mecca, some pilgrims from Medina judged Muhammad to be a powerful and influential mediator and invited him to come to Medina to settle differences among that city's tribal chiefs. As opposition to his message increased in Mecca, Muhammad sent some of his followers to take up residence in Medina in order to escape persecution. Finally, Muhammad and Abu Bakr fled Mecca when it became known that the Quraysh intended to kill the Prophet. They were followed, but escaped, the story goes, by hiding in a narrow cave whose entrance was quickly covered by a spider's web. The Quraysh pursuers saw the web and passed on, thinking that the cave had been abandoned for a long time.

The *Hijra* (or *Hegira*), Muhammad's "migration" from Mecca to Medina, took place in September in the year 622. The event was such a turning point in the history of Islam that 622 is counted as year 1 of the Islamic calendar. It marked the beginning of the Islamic state. In Medina, the Prophet met with entirely different circumstances from those in his birthplace. Muhammad's leadership turned Medina (*Madinat al-Nabi,* the "City of the Prophet") into the major center of power in the Arabian peninsula.

This Turkish manuscript illustration depicts one of the incidents said to have occurred during the Hijra. As the Prophet and his companion, Abu Bakr, were fleeing Mecca for Medina, one of their pursuers was thrown from his horse. Muhammad forgave the man for persecuting him, and Abu Bakr presented him with a written pardon. The Prophet, as in this illustration, is often shown veiled and with a halo of fire.

The Community at Medina

Muhammad was received in Medina as a leader and a spiritual visionary. There, he and his followers set about the establishment of the Muslim *umma* (community). This new community established relations with the Medinan tribes, including the Jewish and Christian residents. Those who did not choose to accept Muhammad's faith were allowed to continue their way of life, since Christians and Jews were thought to be "people of the Book" to whom God had made himself known through earlier prophets. Ultimately, however, the Prophet's new polity came into conflict with some of the Jewish tribes of Medina and expelled them. This conflict illustrates the tension between the expansionist political policies and generally tolerant religious policies of the new state.

Muhammad and his followers became steadily more aggressive in their attempts to win converts to Islam. The word *jihad*, meaning "struggle," was ap-

plied to the early efforts of the *umma* to win converts and conquer territory. Military encounters with the opponents of Islam began in 624, with the battle of Badr. Muhammad defeated a stronger Quraysh troop from Mecca, and the victory reinforced the resolve of the new religion's followers. Succeeding battles established the Muslims as the dominant force in Arabia, and a truce with Mecca was arranged, under which the Muslims could visit the holy city.

Return to Mecca

In 630 Muhammad returned to take control of the city of Mecca and to cleanse the Ka'ba of idols. The temple itself, together with the Black Stone, was preserved as the supreme religious center of Islam and rededicated to the One God, Allah. It is to this shrine that all devout Muslims, if able, make pilgrimage during their lifetime. Muhammad urged unbelievers and his old enemies to accept Islam and become part of the *umma.* By 632 almost all of the Arabian peninsula had (at least nominally) accepted Islam, and Muhammad had even sent ambassadors to the neighboring Byzantine and Persian Empires to announce the new religion and encourage converts. Clearly, Muhammad did not regard Islam as a religion solely of the Arabs. Like Christianity, and unlike Judaism, Islam was a universal religion with a missionary spirit.

The Death of Muhammad

Muhammad died on June 8, 632, in Medina. Muslims at first refused to accept his death but were reassured by Abu Bakr, who recited this verse from the Qur'an: "Muhammad is only a messenger: many are the messengers who have died before him; if he dies, or is slain, will you turn back on your heels?" (3:144).

Muhammad had no surviving son and had not designated a successor. On the day of his death, his close companions solved the question of leadership of the faithful by agreeing on the election of Abu Bakr, who became the first successor, or *caliph* (from the Arabic *khalifa*). Abu Bakr could not really replace Muhammad, the last prophet. However, as caliph, he was regarded as the head of the Islamic *umma;* he combined the roles of religious leader and head of state. Abu Bakr and his three successors in the office, Umar, Uthman, and Ali, are often referred to as the *Rashidun,* the "Rightly Guided" caliphs.

The significance of Muhammad to the birth and growth of Islam is impossible to overestimate. The Prophet and his message inspired his followers to create and work for the betterment of a society united by the Islamic faith. Ideally, tribal loyalties were replaced by loyalty to the *umma* and faith in the One God, who chose to speak to his people in their own language through a messenger who was also one of their own.

Soon after Muhammad's death, his followers began to collect and codify his teachings and actions. The result of their efforts was the *hadith,* or reports of the sayings and activities of Muhammad. The hadith have become an important source of values and ethical paths of behavior for the Islamic world. The *sunna,* the custom or practice of the Prophet, is grounded in the hadith and serves as a pattern for a model way of life to be imitated by the faithful.

Islamic Faith and Law

Islam places great emphasis on the necessity of obedience to God's law in addition to faith. The Qur'an is the fundamental and ultimate source of knowledge about Allah. This holy book contains both the theology of Islam and the patterns of ethical and appropriate conduct to which a Muslim must subscribe. Included in the Qur'an are some basic concepts that the Islamic community holds in common as fundamental to the faith.

The Qur'an

Muslims believe that the Qur'an contains the actual word of God as it was revealed to Muhammad through divine inspiration. These revelations to the Prophet took place over a period of more than 20 years. Before Muhammad's death, many of these messages were written down. Muhammad himself began this work of preservation, and Abu Bakr, as caliph, continued the process by compiling revelations that up to that time had been memorized by the followers and passed on by word of mouth. A complete written text of the Qur'an was produced some years after Muhammad's death, with particular care taken to eliminate discrepancies and record only one standard version. This "authorized" edition was then transmitted to various parts of the new Islamic Empire and used to guide the faithful and assist in the conversion of unbelievers. The text of the Qur'an has existed virtually unchanged for nearly 14 centuries.

This Qur'an leaf from the eighth or ninth century illustrates the formality and elegance of the Kufic form of Arabic calligraphy. In various styles, calligraphy served as a major decorative art form throughout the Islamic world; it was both art and worship.

Islamic manuscript, 8th–9th century. Purchase F30.60. Freer Gallery of Art and Arthur M. Sackler Gallery, Smithsonian Institution.

The Qur'an

The Qur'an is one of the most significant of all religious works and one of the world's most beautiful works of literature. The following is a selection celebrating God's creation, from sura 23, titled "The Believers." It illustrates Islam's connection, through the prophets Moses and Jesus, to the sacred texts and beliefs of Judaism and Christianity. But it also points out the Islamic doctrine that God has no son.

In the name of Allah, the Beneficent, the Merciful.
Successful indeed are the believers
Who are humble in their prayers,
And who shun vain conversation,
And who are payers of the poor-due;
And who guard their modesty—
Save from their wives or the [slaves] that their right
*   hands possess, for then they are not blameworthy,*
But whoso craveth beyond that, such are transgres-
*   sors—*
And who are shepherds of their pledge and their
*   covenant, and who pay heed to their prayers.*
These are the heirs
Who will inherit Paradise. There they will abide.
Verily We created man from a product of wet earth;
Then placed him as a drop [of seed] in a safe lodg-
*   ing;*
Then fashioned We the drop a clot, then fashioned
*   We the clot a little lump, then fashioned We the*
*   little lump bones, then clothed the bones with*
*   flesh, and then produced it as another creation.*
*   So blessed be Allah, the Best of Creators!*
Then lo! after that ye surely die.
Then lo! on the Day of Resurrection ye are raised
*   [again].*
And We have created above you seven paths, and We
*   are never unmindful of creation.*
And We send down from the sky water in measure,
*   and We give it lodging in the earth, and lo! We are*
*   able to withdraw it.*
Then We produce for you therewith gardens of date-
*   palms and grapes, wherein is much fruit for you*
*   and whereof ye eat;*
And a tree that springeth forth from Mount Sinai
*   that groweth oil and relish for the eaters.*
And lo! in the cattle there is verily a lesson for you.
*   We give you to drink of that which is in their bel-*
*   lies, and many uses have ye in them, and of them*
*   do ye eat;*

And on them and on the ship we are carried.
Then We sent Moses and his brother Aaron with Our
*   tokens and a clear warrant*
Unto Pharaoh and his chiefs, but they scorned
*   [them] and they were despotic folk.*
And they said: Shall we put faith in two mortals like
*   ourselves, and whose folk are servile unto us?*
So they denied them, and became of those who were
*   destroyed.*
And We verily gave Moses the Scripture, that haply
*   they might go aright.*
And We made the son of Mary and his mother a
*   portent, and We gave them refuge on a height,*
*   a place of flocks and water-springs.*
O ye messengers! Eat of the good things, and do
*   right. Lo! I am Aware of what ye do.*
And lo! this your religion is one religion and I am
*   your Lord, so keep your duty unto Me.*
Say: In Whose hand is the dominion over all things
*   and He protecteth, while against Him there is no*
*   protection, if ye have knowledge?*
They will say: Unto Allah [all that belongeth]. Say:
*   How then are ye bewitched?*
Nay, but We have brought them the Truth, and lo!
*   they are liars.*
Allah hath not chosen any son, nor is there any
*   God along with Him; else would each God have*
*   assuredly championed that which he created,*
*   and some of them would assuredly have over-*
*   come others. Glorified be Allah above all that*
*   they allege.*
Knower of the invisible and the visible! and exalted
*   be He over all that they ascribe as partners [unto*
*   Him]!*

From Marmaduke William Pickthall, *The Meaning of the Glorious Koran: An Explanatory Translation* (London: Unwin Hyman/HarperCollins). Reprinted by permission.

The Qur'an was intended to be recited aloud; anyone who has listened to the chanting of the Qur'an can testify to its beauty, melody, and power. Much of the power of the Qur'an comes from the experience of reciting, listening, and feeling the message. The Qur'an is never to be translated from the Arabic for the purpose of worship because it is believed that translation distorts the divine message. But over time, the Qur'an was indeed translated into many languages to facilitate scholarship and the spread of the Islamic message. As Islam spread, so too did the Arabic language. Arabic replaced many local languages as the language of administration, and gradually, some of the conquered territories adopted Arabic as the language of everyday use. The Qur'an remains the basic document for the study of Islamic theology, law, social institutions, and ethics. It forms the core of Muslim scholarship, from law and grammatical inquiry to scientific and technical investigation.

The Tenets of Islamic Faith

Monotheism is the central principle of Islam. Muslims believe in the unity or oneness of God; there is no other God but Allah, and this belief is proclaimed five times daily as the believers are called to prayer with these words:

> God is most great. I testify that there is no God but Allah. I testify that Muhammad is the Messenger of Allah. Come to prayer, come to revelation, God is most great! There is no God but Allah.

Allah is the one and only God, unchallenged by other false divinities and unlike all others in the strength of his creative power. All life—all creation—is the responsibility of Allah alone. His nature is described in many ways and through many metaphors:

> Allah is the light of the heaven and the earth. . . . His light is as a niche wherein is a lamp. The lamp is in a glass. The glass is as it were a shining star. [The lamp is] kindled from a blessed tree, an olive neither of the East nor of the West, whose oil would almost glow forth [of itself] though no fire touched it. Light upon light, Allah guided unto His light whom He will. And Allah speaketh to mankind in allegories, for Allah is Knower of all things.
>
> [This lamp is found] in houses which Allah hath allowed to be exalted and that His name shall be remembered therein. Therein do offer praise to Him at noon and evening. (Qur'an 24:35–36)

Islam also recognizes the significance and the contributions of prophets who preceded Muhammad. From the beginnings of human history, Allah has communicated with his people either by the way of these prophets or by written scriptures:

> Lo! We inspire thee as We inspired Noah and the Prophets after him, as We inspired Abraham and Ishmael and Isaac and Jacob and the tribes, and Jesus and Job and Jonah and Aaron and Solomon and as We imparted unto David the Psalms. (Qur'an 4:164)

Twenty-eight such prophets are mentioned in the Qur'an as the predecessors of Muhammad, who is believed to have been Allah's final messenger. Muhammad is given no divine status by Muslims; in fact, Muhammad took great care to see that he was not worshipped as a god.

The creation of the universe and all living creatures within it is the work of Allah; harmony and balance in all of creation were ensured by God. In addition to humans and other creatures on the earth, angels exist to protect humans and to pray for forgiveness for the faithful. Satan, "the Whisperer," attempts to lead people astray, and mischievous spirits called *jinn* can create havoc for believers and unbelievers alike.

These illustrations from a sixteenth-century Persian manuscript depict scenes from the lives of the prophets: Jesus multiplying the loaves and fishes, and the staff of Moses transformed into a dragon.

Noah's Ark. Islamic manuscripts often depict the prophets with halos of fire.

Men and women are given a special status in the pattern of the universe. They can choose to obey or to reject Allah's will and deny him. Allah's message includes the belief in a Day of Resurrection when people will be held responsible for their actions and rewarded or punished accordingly for eternity. The Qur'an graphically describes heaven and hell. Those who have submitted to Allah's law—the charitable, the humble, and the forgiving—and those who have preserved his faith shall dwell in the Garden of Paradise, resting in cool shade, eating delectable foods, attended by "fair ones with wide, lovely eyes like unto hidden pearls," and hearing no vain speech or recrimination but only "Peace! Peace!" This veritable oasis is far different from the agonies of the hell that awaits sinners, the covetous, and the erring. Cast into a pit with its "scorching wind and shadow of black smoke," they will drink boiling water and suffer forever.

The Five Pillars

Islam is united in the observance of the Five Pillars, or five essential duties that all Muslims are required to perform to the best of their abilities. These obligations are accepted by Muslims everywhere and thus serve further to unite the Islamic world. The first obligation is a basic *profession of faith,* by which a believer becomes a Muslim. The simple proclamation *(shahada)* is repeated in daily prayers. Belief in the One God and imitation of the exemplary life led by his Prophet are combined in the profession of faith.

Prayer (salat) is said five times a day, when Muslims are summoned to worship by the *muezzin,* who calls them to prayer from atop the minaret of the mosque *(masjid,* "place of prostration"). During prayer Muslims face Mecca and in so doing give recognition to the birthplace of Islam and the unity of the Islamic community. Prayer can be said alone, at work, at home, or in the mosque.

A Muslim is required to give *alms (zakat)* to the poor, orphans, and widows and to assist the spread of Islam. The payment of alms is a social and religious obligation to provide for the welfare of the *umma.* Muslims are generally expected to contribute annually in alms a percentage (usually 2.5 percent) of their total wealth and assets.

Muslims are requested to *fast (sawm)* during the holy month of Ramadan, the ninth month of the Islamic lunar calendar. From sunrise to sunset, adult Muslims in good health are to avoid food, drink, tobacco, and sexual activity. Finally, every Muslim able to do so is called to make a *pilgrimage (hajj)* to Mecca at least once in his or her lifetime, in the twelfth month of the Islamic year. The focus of the pilgrimage is the Ka'ba and a series of other sites commemorating events in the lives of the prophets Muhammad and Abraham. The *hajj* emphasizes the unity of the Islamic world community and the equality of all believers regardless of race or class.

Islamic Law

Islam is a way of life as well as a religion, and at its heart is the *Sharia,* the law provided by Allah as a guide for a proper life. The Sharia is based on the Qur'an and hadith; it gives the believers a perfect pattern of human conduct and regulates every aspect of a person's activities. God's decrees must be obeyed even if humans are incapable of understanding them, since the Sharia is greater than human reason. Those who study, interpret, and administer the Sharia are called *ulama,* "those who know." These men emerged, in the era after the Prophet's death, as religious scholars and leaders who administered the institutions of worship, education, and law. But there is no priesthood in Islam; all believers are equal members of the community.

Islamic law, then, permeates all aspects of human conduct and all levels of activity, from private and personal concerns to those involving the welfare of the whole state. The Sharia became the universal law of the Islamic lands. In practice it worked in conjunction with the decrees of rulers and with customary laws that varied from region to region. Family law, set forth in the Qur'an, is based on earlier Arab tribal patterns. Islamic law emphasizes the patriarchal nature of the family and society. Marriage is expected of every Muslim man and woman unless physical infirmity or financial inability prevents it. Muslim men can marry non-Muslim women, preferably Christians or Jews, since they too are "people of the Book," but Muslim women are forbidden to marry non-Muslim men. This law reflects the notion, common in traditional societies, that the children "belong" to the father and his family. Thus the children of a Muslim father and non-Muslim mother would be Muslims. The Qur'an had the effect of improving the status and opportunities of women, who could contract their own marriages, keep and maintain their own dowries, and manage and inherit property (unlike many Western Christian women at that time).

The Qur'an allows Muslim men to marry up to four wives, but only if each wife is treated with equal support and affection. Many modern-day Muslims interpret the Qur'an as encouraging monogamy. Polygamy, in any case, is not required; it is a practice that may have arisen to provide protection and security in early societies, where women may have outnumbered men because of the toll of constant warfare.

Islamic law is considered to be God's law for all humankind, not only for the followers of Islam. Non-Muslim citizens of the Islamic state were called *dhimmis;* they received protection from the state and paid an extra head tax called the *jizya.* The Sharia courts were open to *dhimmis,* who could also appeal to juridical authorities, such as rabbis or priests, within their own communities. Islamic law designated certain dress markers for *dhimmis* and forbade them from corrupting Muslims (with wine, for example) and from ostentatious religious displays.

Thus in addition to its theology, Islam offers to its believers a system of government, a legal foundation, and a pattern of social organization. The Islamic *umma* was and is an excellent example of a theocratic state, one in which power ultimately resides in God, on whose behalf political, religious, and other forms of authority are exercised. Ideally, the role of the state is to serve as the guardian of religious law. Islamic monarchs ruled in the name of Allah and called on the Sharia law to legitimize their rule. Of course, as the Islamic state evolved, some rulers were more pious than others. Some came into conflict with the *ulama* over matters of law. But all Muslim kings, like all Christian kings in this era, claimed to be defenders of their faith.

The Early Islamic Dynasties

661	Umayyad dynasty established; Damascus becomes capital
680	Muhammad's grandson Husayn killed by Umayyads at Karbala in Iraq
711	Tariq ibn Ziyad invades Spain from North Africa
750	Abbasids defeat the Umayyads and establish a new dynasty
756	Umayyads set up a new dynasty in Spain; Córdoba later becomes capital
786–809	Reign of Abbasid caliph Harun al-Rashid
909–1171	Fatimid Shi'ite dynasty in North Africa, Egypt, and Syria
1055	Seljuk Turks gain control of Baghdad but leave Abbasid caliph in place
1095	First Crusade mobilized
1250	Mamluk kingdom established in Egypt, will endure until 1517
1258	Mongols conquer Baghdad and kill Abbasid caliph, ending Abbasid dynasty

The Spread of Islam

The Islamic state expanded very rapidly after the death of Muhammad through remarkable successes in the form of military conquest and conversion. Immediately after the Prophet's death in 632, Caliph Abu Bakr continued the effort to abolish polytheism among the Arab tribes and also to bring all of Arabia under the political control of Medina. The Muslim polity succeeded in strengthening its power throughout the Arabian peninsula and even began to launch some exploratory offensives north toward Syria.

Expansion Under the First Four Caliphs

Under the first four caliphs (632–661), Islam spread rapidly. The wars of expansion were aided by the devotion of the faithful to the concept of *jihad.* Muslims are obliged to extend the faith to unbelievers and to defend Islam from attack. The original concept of *jihad* did not include aggressive warfare against non-Muslims, but Muslims whose interpretation of the Qur'an allowed them such latitude sometimes waged

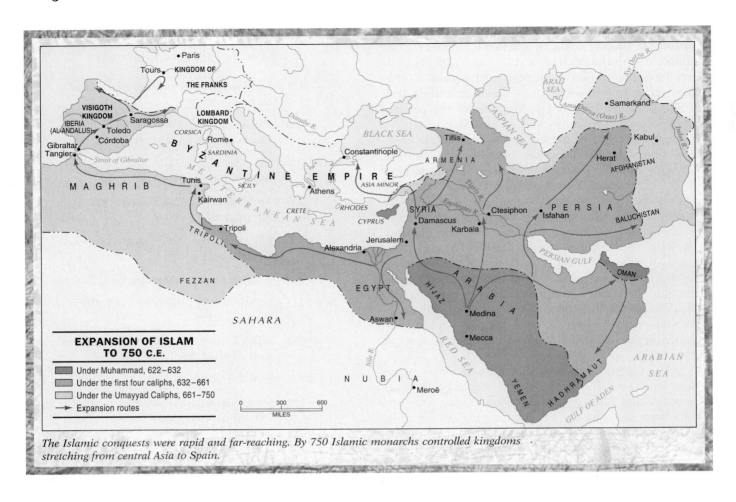

EXPANSION OF ISLAM TO 750 C.E.

▨ Under Muhammad, 622–632
▨ Under the first four caliphs, 632–661
▨ Under the Umayyad Caliphs, 661–750
→ Expansion routes

The Islamic conquests were rapid and far-reaching. By 750 Islamic monarchs controlled kingdoms stretching from central Asia to Spain.

"holy war." *Jihad* was responsible in part for Islam's early conquests beyond the Arabian peninsula.

Political upheavals occurring outside of Arabia also aided the Islamic cause. Early Muslim triumphs in the Near East can be accounted for in part by the long series of wars waged between the Byzantine and Persian (Sassanid) Empires to the north, which left both sides exhausted and open to conquest. In addition, the inhabitants of Syria and Egypt, alienated by religious dissent and resenting the attempts of the Byzantine Empire to impose its brand of Christianity on the population, sought freedom from Byzantine rule. The Arabs combined use of camels for long distance travel and swift horses for the attack was extremely effective. In 636 Arab armies conquered Syria and occupied the city of Damascus. Jerusalem was taken in 638. The Muslims then won Iraq from the Persians and in 651 defeated the last Sassanid ruler, thereby ending the 400-year-old Persian Empire. Most of Egypt had fallen with little resistance by 646, and raids had begun into the lands the Muslims called the Maghrib, in North Africa west of Egypt and north of the Sahara. Within 30 years of Muhammad's death, Islam had become the dominant faith of a vast empire connecting western Asia with the Mediterranean and Africa. This area possessed a cer-

tain cultural unity under Islam, but it was politically divided.

The new Islamic territories were governed with remarkable efficiency and flexibility. The centralization of authority typical of effective military organization aided in the incorporation of new peoples. Unbelievers in the conquered territories became increasingly interested in the new religion and accepted Islam in great numbers. In addition to the power of the religious message of Islam, the imposition of a head tax on all non-Muslims and some restrictions on unbelievers' holding political office encouraged many to become converts. Accounts of the coercive imposition of Islam on conquered peoples are inexact: Jews and Christians outside Arabia enjoyed toleration because they worshipped the same God as the Muslim, and many non-Muslims were active participants in the Islamic state and prospered financially and socially.

Islam was and remains one of the most effective religions in overcoming the potential barriers of race and nationality. In the early days of the spread of Islam, apart from a certain privileged position allowed Arabs and the Prophet's earliest supporters, distinctions were mostly those of economic and political rank. The new religion converted and included peoples of many ethnic origins and cultures. This egalitarian ideal of Islam undoubtedly aided its rapid and successful expansion.

Defining the Community

All Muslims shared belief in the unity of God and the practice of the Five Pillars. But Islamic civilization, like other traditions, was marked by debate and conflict over the interpretation of the law. As Islamic law was codified and as the Islamic state expanded, four main schools of legal interpretation emerged. Scholars struggled with questions of faith and reason, just as their Christian counterparts did. Inspired in part by the spiritual thought and practices of India, Islam also developed a set of mystical traditions that challenged the orthodoxy of the *ulama*. In the political realm, not long after the death of the Prophet, the new Islamic state underwent a crisis that split the community over the question of political authority.

Islam's first three caliphs—Abu Bakr (632–634), Umar (634–644), and Uthman (644–656)—were chosen in consultation with the elders and leaders of the Islamic community, setting a pattern for selecting the caliph exclusively from the Quraysh tribe of Mecca. When Uthman was assassinated by a fellow Muslim, the ensuing struggle for power ultimately split the community into two major divisions, Sunni and Shia. The Shi'ites believed that only descendents of the Prophet could command authority in the Islamic state. Because Muhammad had no surviving sons, his bloodline passed through his grandsons, the sons of his daughter Fatima and her husband Ali, the fourth caliph. Thus for the Shi'ites, the first three caliphs before Ali had been usurpers. Ali and his descendents were the only legitimate heads of the community, *imams*, who were believed to have a special knowledge of the inner meaning of the Qur'an. The Sunnis, rather than insist on a caliph who was a direct descendant of the Prophet, accepted the first three caliphs and upheld the principle that the caliph owed his position to the consent of the Islamic community. The Sunnis argued that they followed the *sunna* of the Prophet, the patterns of behavior modeled on Muhammad's life.

The Shi'ites (or Shia) did not refute the validity of the *sunna*, but they insisted on the Qur'an as the sole and unquestioned authority on the life and teachings of the Prophet. Though originally an Arab party, the Shia in time became a more widespread Islamic movement that stood in opposition to the ruling Umayyad dynasty. That the Shia remained, in general, a minority and opposition party in part explains the evolution of its doctrine of opposition to political authorities. Notwithstanding the several major Shi'ite dynasties in Islamic history, Sunni Muslims have remained numerically dominant. Some 85 percent of the modern world's Muslims are Sunnis, although large Shi'ite communities exist, particularly in Iran, Iraq, and Lebanon.

Umayyad Rule

Ali and his followers were opposed first by Muslims under the leadership of Muhammad's widow and favorite wife Aisha, daughter of Abu Bakr, and later by the forces of Muawiya, the governor of Syria and a relative of the third caliph. The power struggle for leadership in the Muslim community thus erupted into civil war. In 661, after Ali was assassinated, Muawiya proclaimed himself caliph, made Damascus his capital, and founded the Umayyad dynasty, which lasted until 750. In this manner the Umayyads made the caliphate in fact, although never in law, a hereditary office rather than one chosen by election.

The Umayyads expanded the borders of Islam, but not with the spectacular successes of the years immediately after Muhammad's death. The Umayyads held Cyprus, Rhodes, and several Aegean islands, which served as bases for naval attacks on the Byzantine Empire. The Byzantines successfully defended Constantinople against persistent Umayyad attacks, and the Islamic advance toward eastern Europe was checked for the first time. The Umayyads established garrisons in central Asia to further their conquests northward across the Oxus River and southwest into India. Westward across North Africa, Umayyad armies were eventually victorious. The Berbers, a nomadic tribal people inhabiting the Maghrib, initially resisted stubbornly but eventually converted to Islam. The Berbers then aided the Umayyad armies in expanding across the Strait of Gibraltar into the weak Visigoth kingdom in Spain. General Tariq ibn Ziyad led an army across the strait into Spain in 711 (according to legend, the name *Gibraltar* is derived from Jabal Tariq, or "Mountain of Tariq"). After the kingdom of the Visigoths swiftly crumbled, the Muslims were able to make conquests throughout the Iberian peninsula, which they called *al-Andalus*.

The Muslims in Spain seem never to have had serious intentions of expanding their territorial holdings across the Pyrenees into what is now France, but they did engage in seasonal raids to the north. One such raiding party was defeated by Charles Martel near Tours in 732 in a battle that later Europeans exaggeratedly portrayed as a decisive blow to Muslim expansion in Europe. But the Byzantines indeed delivered such a blow: in 717 the Byzantine emperor, Leo III, won a major victory over the Muslims that halted the Umayyad advance into eastern Europe. To the east the Umayyads successfully extended their rule into central Asia; by the middle of the eighth century they could claim lands as far east as

The Early Islamic Conquests

Traditional Western historiography used the rhetorics of medieval Christian writers to portray the early Islamic conquests as sweeping and brutal. The following two excerpts from the Arabic chronicle of al-Tabari (839–923) suggest that wisdom, mercy, and rhetorics of intimidation all played a role in the early Islamic conquests. The Qur'an enjoined mercy as well as warfare, and Abu Bakr's rules of war suggest that the wise conqueror did not kill the citizens and livestock of the lands he wished to rule.

Abu Bakr on the Rules of War (632)

Oh People! I charge you with ten rules; learn them well!

Do not betray, or misappropriate any part of the booty; do not practice treachery or mutilation. Do not kill a young child, an old man, or a woman. Do not uproot or burn palms or cut down fruitful trees. Do not slaughter a sheep or a cow or a camel, except for food. You will meet people who have set themselves apart in hermitages; leave them to accomplish the purpose for which they have done this. You will come upon people who will bring you dishes with various kinds of food. If you partake of them, pronounce God's name over what you eat. You will meet people who have shaved the crown of their heads, leaving a band of hair around it. Strike them with the sword. Go, in God's name, and may God protect you from sword and pestilence..

The Arab general Khalid ibn al-Walid's letters to the Persians offer mercy in exchange for submission, but they follow up that offer with a challenge.

Letters to the Persians (633)

In the name of God, the Merciful and the Compassionate.

From Khalid ibn al-Walid to the kings of Persia.

Praise be to God who has dissolved your order, frustrated your plans, and split your unanimity. Had he not done this to you, it would have been worse for you. Submit to our authority, and we shall leave you and your land and go by you against others. If not, you will be conquered against your will by men who love death as you love life.

In the name of God, the Merciful and the Compassionate.

From Khalid ibn al-Walid to the border chiefs of Persia.

Become Muslim and be saved. If not, accept protection from us and pay the jizya. If not, I shall come against you with men who love death as you love to drink wine.

From Bernard Lewis, *Islam,* Vol. 1 (Oxford: Oxford University Press, 1987), pp. 213–214.

Turkestan and the Indus valley. To celebrate the enduring power of Islam in the 690s the Umayyads built the Dome of the Rock in Jerusalem on the site of the Jewish Temple. This sacred shrine is built around an enormous rock where, according to tradition, God asked Abraham to sacrifice his son Isaac. A monumental building, it reflected the power of the dynasty and its god; its interior is decorated with Qur'anic inscriptions. The Dome of the Rock has endured to the present day and has become a major site of struggle over Muslim and Jewish claims to the city they both consider holy.

The mainstay of the Umayyad dynasty's power was the ruling class, composed of an Arab military aristocracy. The Arabs formed a privileged class greatly outnumbered by non-Arab converts to Islam. Many of these converted peoples had cultures much more highly developed than that of the Arabs, and the economic and cultural life of this Islamic empire came to be dominated by these non-Arab Muslims, called *mawali,* or "affiliates." Because they were not Arab by birth, they were treated to a certain extent as citizens of inferior status. They were granted fewer privileges and received less from the spoils of war than the Arabs. Resentment grew steadily among some of the non-Arab Muslims who objected to their inferior status as a violation of the Islamic laws advocating equality. Eventually the resentment of the *mawali* and the opposition of the Shi'ites, who had been forced from power on the accession of Muawiya, helped bring about the downfall of the Umayyads.

Hostility to the Umayyads was also inflamed in 680 when an Umayyad troop massacred Husayn, the second son of Ali, and his followers at Karbala in Iraq. The killing of the grandson of the Prophet was an affront to the Islamic community. The event introduced the theme of martyrdom in Shi'ite tradition around which opposition party unity could be mobilized. To this day, a "passion play" commemorating

Husayn's death is a dramatic and important element in Shi'ite ceremonial in many communities.

The Abbasid Era, Zenith of Classical Islamic Civilization

A new dynasty, the Abbasid, was founded when a rebel army, with Shi'ite support, defeated the Umayyads. The first Abbasid caliph was Abu al-Abbas, a descendant of Muhammad's uncle Abbas. His dynasty ruled most of the Muslim world from 750 to 1258 and built the city of Baghdad in 762 as a symbol of its wealth, power, and legitimacy. The Abbasids owed their initial support and successes in part to the discontent of the non-Arab Muslims, many of whom had become prominent leaders in Islam's cities.

The fall of the Umayyad dynasty marked the end of Arab domination within Islam. The Arab "aristocracy" had led the forces of conquest during the great period of Islamic expansion, but over time, as the new dynasties established themselves, the dominant status previously held only by Arab soldiers was shared with non-Arab administrators, merchants, and scholars.

Traditional Arab patterns of tribal organization and warfare gave way to patterns of military organization and governance based on the imperial traditions of the conquered lands. The new Abbasid polity fostered economic prosperity, the growth of town life, and the promotion of the merchant class. The Abbasid caliph forecast that Baghdad would become the "most flourishing city in the world"; indeed, it rivaled Constantinople for that honor, situated as it was on the trade routes linking East and West. Furthermore, Abbasid patronage of scholarship and the arts produced a rich and complex culture far surpassing that in western Europe.

The founding of the new capital at Baghdad shifted Islam's center of gravity to the province of Iraq, whose soil, watered by the Tigris and Euphrates Rivers, had nurtured the earliest civilizations. Here the Abbasid caliphs set themselves up as potentates in the traditional style of the ancient East (particularly Persia) so that they were surrounded by a lavish court that contrasted sharply with the simplicity of the lifestyle of the Prophet and the first caliphs. One historian described the amazement of the Byzantine envoys who, on entering the Abbasid court, found a magnificent tree of silver and gold, with singing birds, also of silver and gold, perched in its leaves. The Abbasids were also great patrons of scholarship; in Baghdad they founded one of the great medieval libraries, the House of Wisdom.

The Abbasid dynasty marked the high point of Islamic power and civilization. The empire ruled by the Abbasid caliphs was greater in size than the Roman Empire at its height; it was the product of an expansion during which the Muslim state assimilated peoples, customs, cultures, learning, and inventions on an unprecedented scale. This Islamic empire, in fact, drew from the resources of the entire known world.

Abbasid power, however, did not go unchallenged, even in the Muslim world. While the Abbasids ruled in Baghdad, rival dynasties established their sovereignty in other areas that had been incorporated into the Islamic state during the early conquests. Members of the deposed Umayyad dynasty established a new dynasty in Muslim Spain in 756 and eventually set up a glorious court in Córdoba, famous for its scholarship and patronage of the arts. In Egypt the Fatimids established a Shi'ite ruling house and developed a formidable navy that dominated the eastern Mediterranean. To bolster their legitimacy, the Fatimids claimed descent from the Prophet's daughter, Fatima, hence the name of the dynasty. They, too, founded a new and glorious capital at Cairo, where they established al-Azhar, the famous institution of Islamic learning that has attracted scholars from throughout the Muslim world since the tenth century. Thus the eighth to the twelfth centuries were not only the period of the classical glory of the Islamic state but also an era during which rulers in three different Muslim capitals all claimed the title "caliph." This political division stood in contrast to the Islamic world's civilizational unity, which was based on the universal Sharia law and the spread of the Arabic language.

Trade, Industry, and Agriculture

From the eighth century to the twelfth, the Muslim world enjoyed enormous prosperity. In close contact with three continents, merchants from the Islamic lands could move goods back and forth from China to western Europe and from Russia to central Africa. The absence of tariff barriers within the empire and the tolerance of the caliphs, who allowed non-Muslim merchants and craftsmen to reside in their territories and carry on commerce with their home countries, further facilitated trade. The presence of such important urban centers as Baghdad, Cairo, and Córdoba stimulated trade and industry throughout the Muslim world; the courts of the monarchs were great consumers of textiles, foodstuffs, arts, and crafts.

The cosmopolitan nature of Baghdad was evident in its bazaars, which contained goods from all over the known world. There were spices, minerals, and dyes from India; gems and fabrics from central Asia; honey, furs, and wax from Scandinavia and Russia; and ivory and gold from Africa. Muslim trade increased with Southeast Asia, and a large Muslim trading community established itself in the Chinese

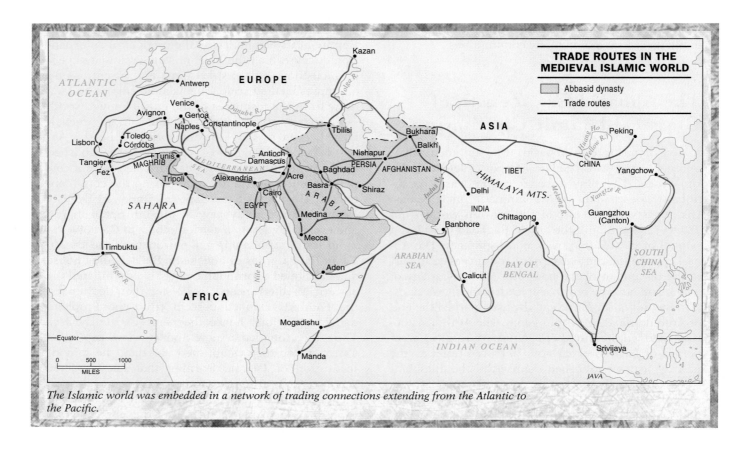

TRADE ROUTES IN THE MEDIEVAL ISLAMIC WORLD

☐ Abbasid dynasty
— Trade routes

The Islamic world was embedded in a network of trading connections extending from the Atlantic to the Pacific.

port of Guangzhou (Canton). One bazaar in Baghdad specialized in goods from China, including silks, musk, and porcelain. In the slave markets Muslim traders bought and sold Scandinavians, Mongolians from central Asia, and Africans. Joint-stock companies flourished along with branch banking organizations, and checks (an Arabic word) drawn on one bank could be cashed with commercial agents throughout this vast network of traders.

Muslim textile industries turned out excellent cottons (muslins) and silks. The steel of Damascus and Toledo, the leather of Córdoba, and the glass of Syria became internationally famous. Notable also was the art of papermaking, learned from the Chinese. Under the Abbasids, vast irrigation projects in Iraq increased cultivable land, which yielded large crops of fruits and grains. Wheat came from the Nile valley, cotton from North Africa, olives and wine from Spain, wool from eastern Asia Minor, and horses from Persia.

By the tenth century Islam was also making inroads into Africa south of the Nile and the Maghrib. Trade routes through the Sahara brought spices, leather work, and eventually slaves from the south to the northern coast, and in return caravans from the north brought luxury goods, salt, and the Islamic re-

ligion to the early African kingdoms of Ghana and Mali. Commercial agents and missionaries carried Islam along the sea routes to central and southeastern African ports such as Mogadishu and Manda and to South and Southeast Asia.

The Spectacular Reign of Harun al-Rashid

Just as the Abbasid caliphate was the most celebrated Islamic dynasty, so the rule of Harun al-Rashid (786–809), hero of the tales of *The Arabian Nights,* was the most spectacular of the Abbasid reigns. A contemporary of Charlemagne, who had revived the idea of a Roman Empire in the West (see Chapter 9), Harun was surely the more powerful of the two and the ruler of the more advanced culture. The two monarchs were on friendly terms, based on self-interest. Charlemagne wanted to exert pressure on the Byzantine emperor to recognize his new imperial title. Harun saw Charlemagne as an ally against the Umayyad rulers of Spain, who had broken away from Abbasid dominion. The two emperors exchanged embassies and presents. The Muslim sent the Christian rich fabrics, aromatics, and even an elephant named Abu-Lababah, meaning "the father of

 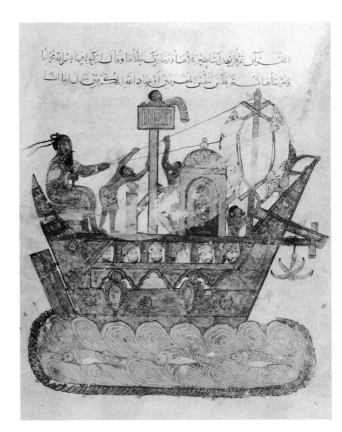

In the Muslim world, merchants transported goods by both land and sea. Camels carried merchants and goods on the overland routes, as shown in this manuscript illumination from the thirteenth century (above left). Sound vessels with space for both passengers and cargo, like the Indian ship depicted in this Iraqi manuscript from 1238 (above right), and reliable navigation techniques facilitated the sea trade.

intelligence." Another gift, an intricate water clock from Baghdad, seems to have been regarded as miraculous in the West.

Relations between the Abbasid caliphate and the Byzantine Empire were never very cordial, and conflicts often broke out along the shifting borders that separated Christian and Muslim territories. Harun al-Rashid once responded to a communiqué from the Byzantine emperor with the following answer:

> *In the name of God, the Merciful, the Compassionate. From Harun, Commander of the Faithful, to Nicepherus, the dog of the Greeks, I have read your letter, you son of a she-infidel, and you shall see the answer before you hear it.*

This response was followed up with Abbasid raids on Byzantine possessions in Asia Minor.

In the days of Harun al-Rashid, Baghdad's wealth and splendor equaled that of Constantinople, and its chief glory was the royal palace. With its annexes for officials, the harem, and eunuchs, the caliph's residence occupied one-third of the city of Baghdad. The caliph's audience chamber was the setting for an elaborate ceremonial, which mirrored that of the Byzantines and Persians. Such court ceremonial was designed to impress the Abbasid citizens with the justice, power, and magnificence of the caliph and to intimidate foreign envoys.

Challenges to Abbasid Authority

In the tenth century a movement of migration and conquest out of central Asia began that would have a dramatic impact on the political and cultural configuration of the central Islamic lands. By the early eleventh century Turkish peoples had moved from central Asia into the Abbasid lands, where, over time, they converted to Islam. One group, the Seljuks, after annexing most of Persia, gained control of Baghdad in 1055 and subjugated Iraq. Subsequently, they conquered Syria and Palestine at the expense of the Fatimids and proceeded to take most of Asia Minor from the Byzantines. The Seljuks permitted the Abbasids to retain nominal authority, in part to secure political legitimacy for their reign, but they themselves ruled the state. By the time of the First

Crusade in 1095, which was provoked in part by the Seljuk advances, the Abbasid dynasty had lost much of its power and status in the Islamic world.

Seljuk dominance of much of the old Abbasid Empire was later challenged by the arrival of Turco-Mongol invaders from the northeastern steppes of central Asia. Early in the thirteenth century Genghis Khan succeeded in uniting the animistic, tribal horsemen of Mongolia and conquering much of China and Russia; he and his successors moved on to eastern and central Asia (see Chapter 12) and ultimately conquered Persia and Iraq. In 1258 a grandson of Genghis Khan captured Baghdad and had the caliph executed. Unlike the Seljuks, the Mongols were contemptuous of the caliph and felt no need to preserve an Abbasid successor as a figurehead to secure their legitimacy. Not only did the Abbasid dynasty come to an end, but so did most of the vast irrigation system that had supported the land. The dynasty established there by the Mongols survived for almost a century, but the Mongol invaders were eventually acculturated and absorbed into the local population.

Egypt was "saved" from the Mongol advance by the Mamluks (1250–1517). The Fatimids had been replaced by one of their own commanders, Salah al-Din, who established a new dynasty, the Ayyubids (1169–1252). Famed in the West as Saladin, it was Salah al-Din who took Jerusalem from the crusaders. The Ayyubids were in turn overthrown by their own elite "slave" guard, called *mamluks*. *Mamluk* literally means "slave," but these men were not slaves in the sense of people of low status who did menial tasks. Taken as captives or purchased as young men in the slave market, they were trained in the military and political arts to serve their commanders. They were converted to Islam and hence could not be held as true slaves. Indeed, they often wielded great power and wealth. After overthrowing the Ayyubids and founding their own ruling group, they formed the elite military caste of Egypt. It was the Mamluks who stopped the Mongol advance in Syria and later ejected the last of the crusaders in 1291. They ruled in Egypt and Syria until 1517, claiming the title "Protector of the Holy Places" as a result of their governance of Mecca, Medina, and also Jerusalem, the three holy cities of Islam.

Islamic Culture

The attainments of the Muslims in the intellectual and artistic fields can be attributed not only to the genius of the Arabs but also to the peoples who embraced Islam in Persia, Iraq, Turkey, Syria, Egypt, North Africa, and Spain. Muslim learning benefited both from Islam's ability to absorb other cultures and from the native talents of the Islamic peoples. Under Abbasid rule a great synthesis of culture and scholarship emerged, strands of which were then transmitted by traveling scholars, traders, and missionaries throughout the known world from the Mediterranean to the Indian Ocean.

The cosmopolitan spirit permeating the Abbasid dynasty supplied the tolerance necessary for a diversity of ideas, so that the science, philosophies, and literatures of ancient Greece and India alike received a cordial reception in Baghdad. Under Harun al-Rashid and his successors, the writings of Aristotle, Euclid, Ptolemy, Archimedes, Galen, and other great Greek philosophers and scientific writers were translated into Arabic. This knowledge, together with the teachings of the Qur'an, formed the basis of Muslim learning, which was in turn transmitted to scholars in Europe and Asia. In addition to being valuable transmitters of learning, Muslim scholars made many original contributions to science and the arts

Advances in Medicine

The years between 900 and 1100 can be regarded as the golden age of Muslim learning. This period was particularly significant for its medical advances. Muslim students of medicine were by all measures far superior to their European contemporaries. Muslim cities had excellent pharmacies and hospitals, where physicians received instruction and training. Muslim scholars perfected surgical techniques, figured out the mode for the spread of the plague, and described the course of many diseases.

Perhaps the greatest Muslim physician was the Persian Abu Bakr Muhammad al-Razi (d. 925), better

Husayn ibn Ishaq's Book of the Ten Treatises on the Eye *shows the Islamic scientist's outstandingly accurate understanding of the anatomy of the eye. Written in the tenth century, the work was still standard in the thirteenth century, when the copy shown here was made.*

known in the West as Rhazes. Chief physician in Baghdad, he wrote more than 100 medical treatises in which he summarized Greek medical knowledge and added his own clinical observations. His most famous work, *On Smallpox and Measles*, is the first clear description of the symptoms and treatment of these diseases.

The most influential Muslim medical treatise is the vast *Canon of Medicine*, in which the great scholar Ibn Sina, or Avicenna (d. 1037), systematically organized all Greek and Muslim medical learning. In the twelfth century the *Canon* was translated into Latin. It was so much in demand in the West that it was issued 16 times in the last half of the fifteenth century and more than 20 times in the sixteenth, and it continued in use until the modern era.

Progress in Other Sciences

Muslim physicists were also highly creative scientists. Al-Hasan ibn al-Haytham, or Alhazen (d. 1038), of Cairo, developed optics to a remarkable degree and challenged the theory of Ptolemy and Euclid that the eye sends visual rays to its object. The chief source of all medieval Western writers on optics, Alhazen interested himself in optical reflections and illusions and examined the refraction of light rays through air and water.

Although astronomy continued to be strongly influenced by astrology, Muslim astronomers built observatories, recorded their observations over long periods, and achieved greater accuracy than the Greeks in measuring the length of the solar year and in calculating eclipses. Interest in alchemy—the attempt to change base metals into precious ones and to find the magic elixir for the preservation of human life—produced the first chemical laboratories and caused attention to be given to the value of experimentation. Muslim alchemists prepared many chemical substances (sulfuric acid, for example) and developed methods for evaporation, filtration, sublimation, crystallization, and distillation. The process of distillation, invented around 800, produced what was called *al-kuhl* ("the essence"), or alcohol, a new liquor that brought its inventors great honor in some circles.

In mathematics the Muslims were indebted to the Hindus as well as to the Greeks. From the Hindus came arithmetic, algebra, the zero, and the nine signs known in the West as Arabic numerals. From the Greeks came the geometry of Euclid and the fundamentals of trigonometry, which Ptolemy had established. Two Muslim mathematicians made significant contributions: al-Khwarizmi (d. c. 844), whose *Arithmetic* introduced Arabic numerals and whose *Algebra* first employed that mathematical term, and Omar Khayyám (d. c. 1123), the mathematician, astronomer, and poet whose work in algebra went beyond quadratics to cubic equations. Other Islamic scholars developed plane and spherical trigonometry.

In an empire that straddled continents, where trade and administration made an accurate knowledge of lands imperative, the science of geography flourished. The Muslims added to the geographical knowledge of the Greeks, whose treatises they translated, by producing detailed descriptions of the climate, manners, and customs of many parts of the known world. Developments in mapping went hand in hand with the progress of Arab seafaring, which aimed at exploiting commercial possibilities along the seaborne routes of trade.

Islamic Literature and Scholarship

To Westerners, Islamic literature may seem somewhat alien. Early Western literary styles tried to emphasize restraint and simplicity, but Muslim writers have long enjoyed literature that makes use of elegant expression, subtle combinations of words, and fanciful and even extravagant imagery.

Westerners' knowledge of Islamic literature tends to be limited to *The Arabian Nights* and the poetry of Omar Khayyám. The former is a collection of often erotic tales told with a wealth of local color. Although it professedly covers different facets of life at the Abbasid capital, the story is in fact often based on life in medieval Cairo. *The Arabian Nights* took the literary influences of India and Persia, combined them with conventions of Arabic literature, and passed them on to the West, where they can be seen in the works of Chaucer and Boccaccio. These tales present an interesting combination of the courtly and the vulgar. The fame of Omar Khayyám's *Rubáiyát* is due at least in part to the musical (though rather free) translation of Edward FitzGerald. The following stanzas indicate the poem's beautiful imagery and gentle resignation:

A Book of Verses underneath the Bough,
A Jug of Wine, a Loaf of Bread—and Thou
*   Beside me singing in the Wilderness—*
Oh, Wilderness were Paradise enow!

Some for the Glories of This World; and some
Sigh for the Prophet's Paradise to come;
*   Ah, take the Cash, and let the Credit go,*
Nor heed the rumble of a distant Drum! . . .

The Moving Finger writes; and, having writ,
Moves on: nor all your Piety nor Wit
*   Shall lure it back to cancel half a Line,*

Nor all your Tears wash out a Word of it.
And that inverted Bowl they call the Sky,
Whereunder crawling coop'd we live and die,
*   Lift not your hands to It for help—for It*
As impotently moves as you or I.[1]

Discovery Through Maps

An Islamic Map of the World

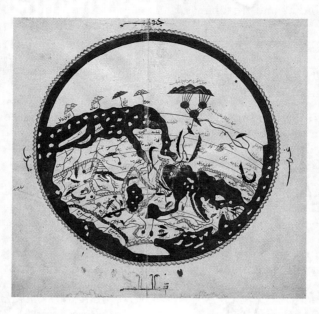

Which way is up? We tend to take the orientation of maps for granted, with north as up. For example, American world maps often depict the United States at the center and north at the top. But not all maps make those same assumptions. The world map of al-Idrīsī, an Arab geographer, is a case in point. Al-Idrīsī's map is oriented, as was common in Arab maps of his time, with south at the top. It is centered on the world of his own experience, the sacred city of Mecca in Arabia and the civilized realm of the Mediterranean. The map includes several distinctive features typical of this type of medieval map. The world is shown as an island encircled by a world sea. The extent of Africa is unknown; it is depicted as a giant mass occupying the upper half of the map. The Americas are not included at all.

Al-Idrīsī was born in Morocco in 1100. Educated in Córdoba, he began his travels as a youth and ended up at the cosmopolitan court of King Roger of Sicily around 1138. There the king asked him to construct a world map complete with written commentary. In collaboration with other scholars, al-Idrīsī crafted the map, which was engraved on silver, around the year 1154. Although the original is lost, there are various manuscript versions of al-Idrīsī's world map, one of which is shown here. The Arab scholar's map was very influential and widely copied in Europe and Asia for centuries after his death in 1165. Al-Idrīsī's map suggests one type of medieval worldview, and his life confirms the notion that cartographers were a valuable commodity in the Afro-Eurasian courts of the time.

Turn the map upside down and see if you can identify the Mediterranean Sea, the Arabian Peninsula, and the Maghrib.

The same rich imagery characterizes much Islamic prose, but *The Arabian Nights* and the *Rubáiyát* merely hint at the breadth and diversity of Islamic literature. As the first important prose work in Arab literature, the Qur'an set the stylistic pattern for all Arabic writers. With classical Arabic then "fixed" in the Qur'an, Muslim writers, spurred on by the generosity of the Islamic kings, produced a great corpus of literature. Arabic and then Persian were the languages of high culture. Poetry contests were a standard of the early Islamic courts, where the poets who contrived the most beautiful or wittiest verses received honors and rich rewards. Poetry was also used for satire. Poets used pointed verse to wound or defame their rivals, and kings used the talents of their poets to send insulting messages to their enemies.

Muslim philosophy, essentially Greek in origin, was developed and modified by Islamic scholars. Like the medieval Christian philosophers (see Chapter 8), Muslim thinkers were largely concerned with

Ibn Sina's Path to Wisdom

Ibn Sina, the famous Muslim philosopher who died in 1037, recorded the progress of his education. His dilligence, but not his pride, might in some ways serve as a model for modern students. As a young boy, Ibn Sina began his education in religion and the sciences. He remembers himself as a determined and independent student who had little patience with or respect for some of his teachers. By the time he was 16, his education was already far-reaching. Ibn Sina was raised in Bukhara, an important center of Islamic learning in central Asia. There, he writes:

I was put under teachers of the Qur'an and of letters. By the time I was ten I had mastered the Qur'an and a great deal of literature, so that I was marvelled at for my aptitude. . . . My father sent me to a certain vegetable-seller who used the Indian arithmetic, so that I might learn it from him. Then, there came to Bukhara a man called Abu 'Abd Allah al-Natili who claimed to be a philosopher; my father invited him to stay in our house, hoping I would learn from him also. I had already occupied myself with Muslim jurisprudence, attending Isma'il the Ascetic; so I was an excellent enquirer, having become familiar with the methods of expostulation and the techniques of rebuttal according to the usages of the canon lawyers. . . . Whatever problem he [al-Natili] stated to me, I showed a better mental conception of it than he. So I continued until I had read all the strightforward parts of Logic with him; as for the subtler points, he had no acquintance with them. From then onwards I took to reading texts by myself; I studied the commentaries, until I had completely mastered the science of Logic. Similarly with Euclid I read the first five or six figures with him, and thereafter undertook on my own account to solve the entire remainder of the book. . . . I now occupied myself with mastering the various texts and commentaries on natural science and metaphysics, until all the gates of knowledge were open to me. Next I desired to study medicine, and proceeded to read all the books that have been written on this subject. Medicine is not a difficult science, and naturally I excelled in it in a very short time, so that qualified physicians began to read medicine with me. I also undertook to treat the sick, and methods of treatment derived from practical experience revealed themselves to me such as baffle description. At the same time I continued between whiles to study and dispute on law, being now sixteen years of age.

From A. J. Arberry. *Aspects of Islamic Civilization* (Ann Arbor: University of Michigan Press, 1967), pp. 136–137.

reconciling Aristotelian rationalism and religion. Some sought to harmonize Platonism, Aristotelianism, and Islam. The philosopher Ibn Sina (980–1037) sought to extract what was purely Aristotelian from later additions and to articulate the truths of Islam in terms of Aristotelian logic. His work had a profound effect on Islamic philosophy and was widely read in the West, where it was translated into Latin in the twelfth century.

Another great Islamic philosopher, Ibn Rushd, or Averroës (d. 1198), lived in Córdoba, where he was the caliph's personal doctor. He is famous for his marvelous commentaries on Aristotle. Ibn Rushd rejected the belief in the ultimate harmony between faith and reason along with all earlier attempts to reconcile Aristotle and Plato. He argued that parts of the Qur'an were to be taken metaphorically, not literally. But most human beings, according to Ibn Rushd, were unable to understand either philosophy or the metaphorical meanings of the Qur'an.

In contrast, Moses Maimonides, Ibn Rushd's contemporary who was also born in Muslim Spain, sought, in his still influential *Guide to the Perplexed,* to harmonize Judaism and Aristotelian philosophy. St. Thomas Aquinas, who in the next century undertook a similar project for Christianity, was influenced by these earlier attempts to reconcile faith and reason.

Islamic historiography found its finest expression in the work of Ibn Khaldun of Tunis (d. 1406), who has been called the "father of sociology." Ibn Khaldun wrote a large general history dealing particularly with human social development, which he held to be the result of the interaction of society with the physical environment. He delineated guidelines for the writing of history and ridiculed earlier historical writing, saying it was often full of stupid or thoughtless errors. Ibn Khaldun defined history in this manner:

It should be known that history, in matter of fact, is information about human social organization, which itself is identical with world civilization. It deals with such conditions affecting the nature of civilization as, for instance, savagery and sociability, group feelings, and the different ways by which one group of human beings achieves superiority over another. It deals with royal authority and . . . with the different kinds of gainful occupations and ways of making a living, with the sciences and crafts that human beings pursue as part of their activities and efforts, and with all the other institutions that originate in civilization through its very nature.[2]

Ibn Khaldun conceived of history as an evolutionary process, in which societies and institutions change continually. He traveled widely in the Islamic world, serving as a judge and scholar in the courts of the Mamluks and other rulers. When he beheld the city of Cairo, he described it as a pinnacle of Islamic civilization, full of shops, gardens, scholars, and institutions of higher learning.

The Sufis

As Islamic civilization produced traditions of scholarship and philosophy, it also produced a tradition of mysticism that came to be a significant factor in the spread of Islam throughout the world. The Arabic word *tasawwuf*, "mysticism," is related to the word *suf*, for the coarse woolen clothes some of the early mystics wore. The early *Sufis* were lone ascetics who practiced physical and spiritual discipline in order to transcend the material world and gain a special kind of closeness to Allah. Later, Sufi orders were founded, where the devotees practiced rules of discipline, followed the path shown them by a spiritual master or *shaykh*, divorced themselves to some extent from the community, and developed rituals that ranged from the simple to the elaborate. There are many similarities between some of the Sufi orders and the medieval monastic orders of Christian Europe. To be a Sufi, however, one does not need to join a spiritual order; many Sufis live and work in the community. What is essential to Sufism is the belief in following a path of discipline that leads to mystical communion with Allah.

The early Muslim mystics expressed their desire for union with God in a language of love, longing, and ecstasy. This longing came to be embodied in the mystical poetry of Sufis like the famous Jalal al-Din Rumi (1207–1273), who compared the Sufi to a man "drunk with God." The *dhikr*, collective repetition of the name of God, sometimes accompanied by rhythmic movements and breathing, became part of Sufi practice as a way of both glorifying God and transcending the distractions of the body and the world. In their quest for communion with God, the Sufis also ran afoul of Islamic orthodoxy, because their beliefs and practices were sometimes considered extreme or blasphemous.

In the ninth century, Sufis began systematically to write down the ways of the path. Communion with God meant the losing of self, however briefly. That losing or merging of self with God smacked of polytheism to many members of the *ulama*. Thus the Sufis were accused of claiming to be divine and of believing they were above the law. In 922 al-Hallaj, a famous teacher and Sufi in Baghdad, was executed for blasphemy after he claimed "I am the Truth." Al-Hallaj had also alienated the authorities by claiming that the *hajj*, the pilgrimage to Mecca, was not necessary, because the Sufi could pursue the pilgrimage to God from his own room. The pathos of the death of al-Hallaj is graphically described in the words of his servant, Ibrahim ibn Fatik, who wrote that al-Hallaj asked Allah to forgive those who were preparing to kill him:

> *Then he was silent. The Headsman stepped up and dealt him a smashing blow which broke his nose, and the blood ran onto his white robe. The mystic al-Shibli, who was in the crowd, cried aloud and rent his garment, and Abu Husayn al-Wasiti fell fainting, and so did other famous Sufis who were there, so that a riot nearly broke out. Then the executioners did their work.[3]*

Al-Hallaj gave the Sufi community in Baghdad a martyr. But in the end, the message of Sufism was too powerful and compelling for Islamic orthodoxy to ignore. Sufis were very effective in spreading the message of Islam beyond its Middle Eastern heartlands. In South and Southeast Asia, Sufi asceticism and belief in mystical communion found resonances in the ascetic and mystical practices of those areas and aided the conversion of non-Muslims to Islam. By the end of the Abbasid era, Sufism had been brought into the mainstream of Islamic thought as a result of its widespread appeal and through the systematic efforts of scholars like al-Ghazali (1058–1111), who legitimized the Sufi way as an acceptable path toward God. Sufism remains a powerful tool in the spread of Islam. In the United States today, Rumi's poetry remains popular, and American college students may get their first taste of Islam through the words of Sufi masters.

Art and Architecture

Religious attitudes played an important part in shaping Islamic art. Because the Prophet warned against idols and their worship, there was a prohibition against pictorial representation of human and animal figures; that prohibition, however, was not always obeyed. The effect of this injunction was to encourage the development of stylized and geometrical designs. Islamic art, like other artistic traditions, borrowed extensively to forge a new and unique synthesis. Artists and craftspeople followed chiefly Byzantine and Persian models, but central Asian, South Asian, and African motifs were also integrated into Islamic styles.

The Muslims excelled in the fields of architecture and the decorative arts. That Islamic architecture can boast of many large and imposing structures is not surprising; monumental building was a natural extension of the power and glory of the Islamic dynasts who wanted to celebrate their own power and glorify God. In time, original styles of building evolved; the great mosques embody such typical features as domes, arcades, and minarets, the slender towers from which the faithful are summoned to prayer. The horseshoe arch is another graceful and familiar feature of Muslim architecture.

On the walls and ceilings of their buildings, the Muslims gave full rein to their love of ornamentation and beauty of detail. The Spanish interpretation of the Islamic tradition is particularly delicate and elegant. A superb artistic example of the sophistication and wealth of the Muslim world is the Alhambra, built between 1248 and 1354 by Muslim kings in Granada, Spain. Some authorities consider it the apogee of Muslim architecture.

Restricted in their subject matter, Muslim craftspeople conceived beautiful patterns from flowers and geometrical figures. The Arabic script, one of the most graceful ever devised, was often used as a decorative motif. Muslim decorative skill also found expression in such fields as carpet and rug weaving, brass work, and the making of steel products inlaid with precious metals.

Conclusion

The great power of Islam's message enabled the fragmented Arab tribes to unify and expand across three continents in an astoundingly brief period. During the reigns of the first four caliphs and the century of dominance by the Umayyad dynasty, great gains were made in conquering new territories and peoples. But the Umayyad dynasty was based on a ruling hierarchy of Arabs, and the resentment of the non-Arab Islamic community helped establish the Abbasid dynasty in a new caliphate in Baghdad. The Abbasid Empire provided the security, patronage, and institutional framework for a great cultural synthesis. Its capital at Baghdad was also a major center in an expanding network of international trade.

During the early Abbasid period Islam reached new heights of geographical expansion and cultural achievement, extending from Spain to eastern Asia. As in all traditional empires of the time, agriculture provided the base for the economy of the Abbasid state. Its unparalleled prosperity evolved from a combination of successful agriculture, trade, and industry. But the Abbasids were not able to maintain an integrated empire; despite its relative religious unity, the great empire broke up into smaller Muslim states.

Muslims made many significant contributions in science, literature, and philosophy. Muslim intellec-

The ultimate stage of refinement of Moorish architecture, which combines Spanish and Islamic elements, is the Alhambra in Granada, the last Islamic stronghold in Spain during the Middle Ages. Slender, rhythmically spaced columns and arches covered with an intricate design of molded stucco frame the Court of the Lions, the most luxurious portion of the palace.

tual life was in large part the product of a genius for synthesizing varying cultural traditions, and the diffusion of this knowledge was a tremendous factor in the rediscovery of classical learning and the emergence of the Renaissance in Europe.

Islam remains an extremely powerful force in the world. The Islamic community today is made up of leading industrialized societies as well as nations just emerging from colonialism. The message of faith and unity under Islam is a powerful influence that will continue to play a significant part in world politics. Islam faces the new era as one of the world's most influential religious and social forces. Present-day

Muslims still derive great meaning from the teachings of Muhammad and the community he and his disciples constructed.

Suggestions for Reading

Major scholarly surveys are Marshall Hodgson, *The Venture of Islam: Conscience and History of a World Civilization*, 3 vols. (University of Chicago Press, 1974), and Albert Hourani, *A History of the Arab Peoples* (Warner, 1992). See also Philip K. Hitti, *The Arabs: A Short History* (Regnery, 1996), an excellent abridgment of a scholarly general history; and H. A. R. Gibb, *Mohammedanism: A Historical Survey*, 2nd ed. (Oxford University Press, 1969). See also the clear introduction to Islam by John L. Esposito, *Islam: The Straight Path*, 3rd ed. (Oxford University Press, 1998); and C. Brockelmann, *History of the Islamic Peoples* (Capricorn, 1948).

W. Montgomery Watt, *Muhammad: Prophet and Statesman* (Oxford University Press, 1974), is a brief account of the Prophet's life and teachings. See also Maxime Rodinson, *Mohammed* (Vintage, 1974); Karen Armstrong, *Muhammad: A Biography of the Prophet* (HarperCollins, 1992); Frederick Mathewson Denny, *An Introduction to Islam*, 2nd ed. (Macmillan, 1996); and Martin Lings, *Muhammad: His Life Based on the Earliest Sources* (Inner Traditions International, 1983). For an interpretation and translation of the Qur'an, see Marmaduke William Pickthall, ed., *The Meaning of the Glorious Koran: An Explanatory Translation* (Knopf, 1993). For primary source selections in translation, see James Kritzeck, *Anthology of Islamic Literature* (Meridian, 1975). John Renard, *Islam and the Heroic Image* (University of South Carolina Press, 1994), is an excellent introduction to heroic Muslim personalities.

On the early development of Islam, see Fred Donner, *The Early Islamic Conquests* (Princeton University Press, 1981); J. J. Saunders, *History of Medieval Islam* (Routledge, 1990); and Dominique Sourdel, *Medieval Islam*, trans. J. Montgomery Watt (Routledge, 1983). For an evaluation of the Umayyad period and its importance, see G. R. Hawting, *The First Dynasty of Islam* (Southern Illinois University Press, 1986).

On the impact of the Crusades, see Malcolm Billings, *The Cross and the Crescent* (Sterling, 1987); Amin Maalouf, *The Crusades Through Arab Eyes* (Schocken, 1985); and Francesco Gabrieli, *Arab Historians of the Crusades* (University of California Press, 1969).

Reynold A. Nicholson, *A Literary History of the Arabs* (Cambridge University Press, 1969), traces the growth of Arab thought and culture through its literature, as does H. A. R. Gibb, *Arabic Literature*, 2nd ed. (Oxford University Press, 1974). See also Philip K. Hitti, *Makers of Arab History* (Torchbooks, 1964), and D. Talbot Rice, *Islamic Art* (Praeger, 1974).

Suggestions for Web Browsing

Internet Islamic History Sourcebook: Muhammad and Foundations
http://www.fordham.edu/halsall/islam/islamsbook .html Muhammad and Foundations—to 632 C.E.

Extensive on-line source for links about the early history of Islam, including a biography of Muhammad and the many aspects of Islam, including the role of women.

Islam and Islamic History in Arabia and the Middle East: The Message
http://www.islamic.org/Mosque/ihame/Sec1.htm
Islam and Islamic History in Arabia and the Middle East: The Golden Age
http://www.islamic.org/Mosque/ihame/Sec7.htm

Extensive site details the origins of Islam and provides information and images about Muhammad, the Hijra, the Qur'an, Arabic writing, science and scholarship, Arabic literature, and Arabic numerals.

The Qur'an
http://islam.org/mosque/arabicscript/1/1.htm
The entire text of the Qur'an, with audio.

Islamic and Arabic Arts and Architecture
http://www.islamicart.com/

A rich and attractively designed general site, with information and images regarding architecture, calligraphy, and textiles. Includes a glossary of terms and names of important artists and architects. A subsite offers a portfolio of shrines and palaces including the Ka'ba, the Mosque of the Prophet Muhammad, the Dome of the Rock, and the Alhambra.

Notes

1. *Rubáiyát of Omar Khayyám*, trans. Edward FitzGerald, stanzas 12, 13, 71, and 72.
2. Ibn Khaldun, *The Muqaddimah: An Introduction to History*, Vol. 1, trans. Franz Rosenthal (London: Routledge & Kegan Paul, 1958), p. 71.
3. John Williams, ed., *Islam* (New York: Braziller, 1962), p. 142.

Cattle played a vital role in the political, economic, social, and religious life of many African cultures. This picture is of a Nuer cattle camp in the modern nation of Sudan.

The African Genesis

African Civilizations to 1500

Chapter Contents

At the same time that other world civilizations were experiencing dynamic cultural growth, sub-Saharan Africa was undergoing similar transformations. Northern Africa had given birth to some of the earliest civilizations, Egypt and Nubia. But the peoples of the entire continent developed a variety of social and political systems, ranging from small-scale communities in which families and lineages met most of their own needs to large kingdoms with hereditary rulers, elaborate bureaucracies, and extensive trading networks.

The image of Africa as a collection of societies that were isolated, unchanging, and unaware of developments in other parts of the world is erroneous. African cultures emerged from their own experiences and traditions; adapted to changing situations; adopted new ideas, innovations, and technologies; and developed extensive relations with one another through trade, diplomacy, migration, and marriage. They created interregional networks to exchange goods such as salt, iron, and pots, and they traded with other continents. The trans-Saharan trade linked West Africa to the Mediterranean; the Indian Ocean trade tied East Africa to Arabia, Persia, and Asia; and the Red Sea served as a bridge connecting Ethiopia to the Mediterranean and the Indian Ocean.

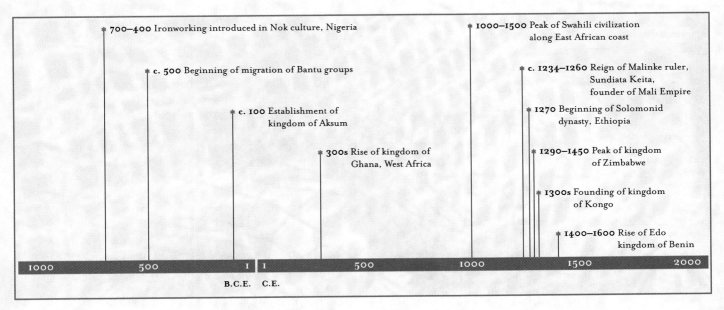

700–400 Ironworking introduced in Nok culture, Nigeria

c. 500 Beginning of migration of Bantu groups

c. 100 Establishment of kingdom of Aksum

300s Rise of kingdom of Ghana, West Africa

1000–1500 Peak of Swahili civilization along East African coast

c. 1234–1260 Reign of Malinke ruler, Sundiata Keita, founder of Mali Empire

1270 Beginning of Solomonid dynasty, Ethiopia

1290–1450 Peak of kingdom of Zimbabwe

1300s Founding of kingdom of Kongo

1400–1600 Rise of Edo kingdom of Benin

1000   500   I   I   500   1000   1500   2000

B.C.E.   C.E.

The African Environment

Ignorance of African geography and environment has contributed greatly to prevailing misconceptions about African culture and history. Many Americans, for instance, have thought of the continent as an immense "jungle." In reality, more than half of the area south of the Sahara consists of grassy plains, known as *savanna*, whereas "jungle," or tropical rain forests, takes up just 7 percent of the land surface.

Physical Environment

The most habitable areas have been the savannas, their grasslands and trees favoring both human settlement and long-distance trade and agriculture. The northern savanna, sometimes called the Sudan (not to be confused with the modern nation of Sudan), stretches across the continent just south of the central desert, the Sahara. Other patches of savanna are interspersed among the mountains and lakes of East Africa and another belt of grassland that runs east and west across southern Africa, north and east of the Kalahari Desert.

Between the northern and southern savannas, in the region of the equator, is dense rain forest. Although the rain forest is lush, its soils are poor because torrential rains cause soil erosion and intense heat leaches the soil of nutrients and burns off humus or organic matter that is essential for soil fertility. The rain forests also harbor insects that carry deadly diseases. Mosquitoes transmit malaria and yellow fever, and the tsetse fly is a carrier of sleeping sickness to which both humans and animals such as horses and cattle are susceptible.

Because of Africa's often harsh and fragile environments, Africans accumulated sophisticated knowledge of what food crops to grow in particular areas and how to manage their environments and sustain a living from marginal or poor soils. Permanent cultivation was a luxury that few African farmers were able to practice. A more prevalent approach in sparsely populated areas was shifting, or "slash and burn," cultivation. Farmers knew that they could stay on a piece of land for a few growing seasons before soils were exhausted. Thus every growing season they would clear land with iron hoes and machetes and fertilize it by burning natural vegetation such as brush and tree leaves for ash. Usually after two to three years, a family had to move on and start the cycle in another area. Shifting agriculture was especially necessary in the rain forests, where, as noted, heavy rainfall and high temperatures produced very poor soils.

Farmers also relied on other strategies, such as bush fallow and intercropping. Bush fallow means letting a field rest for a number of years to restore its fertility before cultivating it again. Intercropping in-volves growing plants that complement each other side by side. For instance, legumes such as peanuts and beans were introduced because they converted nitrogen from the air and spread it to other plants.

General Cultural Patterns

Although African societies are remarkably diverse, they often have common values, belief systems, and aesthetic styles that are reflected in their family and kinship relations and political, economic, religious, and cultural institutions.

Africans place great importance on family and kinship ties. The primary unit of social organization is the extended family, which includes not only parents and children but also a network of wives and relatives—grandparents, aunts, uncles, and cousins. Relations within families are based on descent patterns. Most African societies are patrilineal, with descent traced through the father to his sons and daughters who belong to their father's kin group. When a woman married, she became part of her husband's kin group and usually no longer shared in the economic resources of her father's group.

About 15 percent of African societies are matrilineal, in which descent is passed through the mother's side of the family through a mother's brother. In matrilineal societies, when a man married, he usually went to live at his wife's family homestead and had to work for her family for a number of years. In these societies women lived with their own kin and had at least some independent access to economic resources such as land. Many of the matrilineal societies are found in forest areas with poor soils. Because farming required large numbers of laborers, an advantage of matrilineal relationships is that they can bring together a wide network of families who can contribute laborers to agricultural production.

Families also played an important role in decisions about marriages. Marriage was not solely a private issue between a bride and a groom but was a uniting of two larger groups, such as families or clans. Strict rules stipulated whether a person could marry outside a clan or lineage. Marriage was typically accompanied by an exchange of *bridewealth*, the husband's payment of money, goods, services, or cattle to his new wife's family. Bridewealth gave a husband certain domestic rights—to establish a homestead with his wife, to use his bride's labor in his household and fields, and to attach their offspring to his kinship group. Bridewealth also cemented a social relationship between a husband and his wife's family. If a wife could not bear children or deserted her husband, her parents had to return the bridewealth. This gave the wife's family a vested interest in preserving the marriage.

Another characteristic of African societies is that they accepted *polygyny*, a man's marrying more than one wife. Although a minority of men actually took a second wife, polygyny was seen as a necessity because of high infant mortality, the need for more manpower in farming, and the desire to express status and wealth.

The family household was the foundation for building larger identities and communities—one's *lineage* contained people who could trace their descent to a common ancestor, and one's *clan* contained many lineages or people who shared kinship. Within a society, lineages and clans could be used to mobilize people for self-defense and work parties, to allocate rights to land, to raise bridewealth, and to perform religious rituals. African societies also contained groups of people who were not bound by kinship and who created larger social identities. These were secret societies that often guarded medicines, performed ritual activities, and organized defense and cohorts of people of roughly the same age who had gone through rites-of-passage ceremonies such as circumcision.

The lineage and clan also provided the basis for political units, ranging from the most basic to the largest kingdoms. Many African societies were formed without chiefs, rulers, or centralized political institutions and operated at the village level. These are known as "stateless" societies. Authority was usually vested in a group of elders or senior members of families and lineages who conferred to work out approaches to common concerns such as deciding when to plant and to harvest, whether to move or migrate, and how to resolve disputes within a community or handle conflicts with other communities. In these egalitarian societies, reaching a consensus was an essential part of the decision-making process.

Other African societies developed slowly into chiefdoms and kingdoms that incorporated larger populations, featured elaborate hierarchies and extensive bureaucracies, and engaged in long-distance trade with other states. Even though kingdoms could be made up of many lineages or clans, they were usually dominated by one. These kingdoms were governed by hereditary rulers who wielded religious as well as political power. However, their tendencies to abuse their power were often held in check by councils and courts.

Women played influential roles in decision making. Some states had women rulers, and the king's mother (the queen mother), his wife (the queen), and his sisters were often powers behind the throne. On occasion women served as officials and advisers, religious leaders, and even soldiers. Women were prominent in religious rituals, serving as priestesses, healers, and diviners.

Work within communities was carried out by families and kinship groups. However, specific tasks were usually determined by sex and age. Women were primarily responsible for maintaining the homestead, cultivating the fields, preparing the food, and running local markets, while men took the lead in building houses, constructing paths and roads, clearing fields, raising livestock, hunting, and conducting long-distance trade. Work parties consisting of agemates of one or both sexes could be mobilized for communal tasks such as harvesting and planting, clearing fields, weeding, threshing, and housebuilding. Although men usually controlled technological advances such as ironworking and blacksmithing, there were exceptions to this practice. Among the Pare of eastern Africa, women were given the responsibility for gathering and smelting iron.

An important aspect of the African heritage was its value system, which shaped all aspects of life. Paramount were a profound awareness of human interdependence and an appreciation for communal harmony and unity within the family and the larger society. The African conception of land ownership, for instance, stressed that individuals had the right to cultivate untilled land but that they could not sell or rent the land to others or pass it on to their children. Land was held in trust by the larger community.

Religion permeated the everyday experiences of Africans and was an integral part of their social and political life. Specific religious beliefs and institutions varied from society to society, but several tenets were shared. Most African societies had a belief in a high god or creator that was usually remote and rarely concerned with the everyday affairs of humans. Therefore, Africans were more directly engaged with other divinities, such as nature and ancestral spirits that maintained an active interest in the affairs of the living and could intercede for humans with the high god. Political leaders were often imbued with ritual authority to approach the ancestors, who provided legitimacy to the moral order and reinforced political authority.

As individuals and as communities, Africans were concerned with identifying the causes of illness and disasters such as drought, crop failures, and plagues. One way of explaining misfortune was that the high god or the ancestors were unhappy with the actions of humans. Thus people sought the goodwill of the ancestors with prayers and ritual offerings and sacrifices at shrines. Africans also attributed misfortune to witches, who wielded evil powers and inflicted suffering on people. Those afflicted by witchcraft appealed to specialists such as diviners to diagnose the sources of evil and provide remedies for them.

Some African religious systems were extremely complex, with elaborate priesthoods and cults. The Yoruba traditionally had four levels of spiritual beings. At the top was the supreme being, Oludumare, who was served by his subordinate gods on the second level. The secondary gods had their own priests, who presided over temples and shrines. Then came the ancestors, known as Shango. Finally, there were

Many African religious ceremonies featured masked male dancers. In this photo of the Dogon people of West Africa, the masked dancers performing at a funeral ceremony are driving the spirit of the dead person from its home. The dancers also act out the Dogon myth explaining how death entered the world through the disobedience of young men.

the nature spirits found in the earth, mountains, rivers, and trees.

Like the ancient Mayas in Central America, Africans were remarkably skilled and sensitive artists, particularly in sculpture, which they used to record historical events. They carved expertly in wood, ivory, and soapstone. They also fashioned statues from baked clay and cast them in bronze. An innovative technique was the *cire perdue* (lost wax) technique, which involved making a cast of the object in wax, covering it with clay, and then melting the wax and replacing it with molten bronze. The famous bronze statuary of Benin, which drew on a long tradition of metalworking in the region of present-day Nigeria, compares in craftsmanship and beauty with the best work of the European Renaissance. Other specific artistic traditions, producing naturalism and symbolism in a rich tapestry of styles, flourished in many African cultures.

The Peopling of Africa

Africa was the cradle of humankind. Dating back to 4 million years ago, the fossil remains of the earliest hominid forms, such as *Australopithecus afarensis* and *Homo habilis,* have been found exclusively in the grasslands and woodlands of eastern and southern

Africa (see Chapter 1). Likewise, the earliest skeletal remains of *Homo erectus* have been found near Lake Turkana in East Africa. The tools it used bear a remarkable similarity to the tool kit of *H. erectus* in Asia and Europe. This evidence, as well as the trail of fossil evidence, leads to the conclusion that *H. erectus* spread to southern, western, and northern Africa and then migrated out of Africa through the Arabian peninsula to the Near East, Europe, and Asia.

Early African Civilizations

10,000–6000 B.C.E.	Aquatic Age
c. 4000 B.C.E.	Domestication of food crops in central Sudan
c. 3100 B.C.E.	Beginning of unification of Upper and Lower Egypt
c. 3000 B.C.E.	Sahara region begins changing into desert
c. 730 B.C.E.	Kushite conquest of Egypt
c. 700 B.C.E.	Spread of knowledge of iron-working from Egypt to Kush

The earliest fossil evidence for *Homo sapiens* also comes from eastern and southern Africa. However, this evidence has not resolved the debate whether *H. sapiens* originated on the African continent and spread to other continents or whether it developed independently elsewhere. However, recent testing involving mitochondrial DNA supports the argument for an African origin for *H. sapiens*. Because mitochondrial DNA is passed on only through a mother to her offspring, it is not affected by gene mixing from both parents. Thus by comparing mitochondrial DNA samples from individuals around the world and calculating the rate of mutations, geneticists have traced human ancestors back to a hypothetical "Eve," a woman they believe lived in East Africa some 200,000 years ago.

During the late Stone Age, human communities in Africa were small bands of foragers who based their existence on hunting wild animals and gathering wild plants. Their technology was relatively simple but effective. Small bands of hunters, armed with bows and arrows with stone barbs treated with poisons, tracked down and killed the small and large game that roamed the plains of Africa. While hunting was conducted by men, gathering was mainly carried out by women. With a tool kit of digging sticks, gourds, and carrying bags, they "collected a variety of wild fruits, nuts, and melons, and dug up edible roots and tubers from the ground."[1] For many small groups, hunting and gathering satisfied all their dietary requirements and remained a preferred way of life long after the invention of agriculture.

Foraging groups added more protein to their diets by fishing in rivers and lakes and gathering shellfish. This was done by groups along the Nile River 15,000 to 20,000 years ago. From 10,000 B.C.E. to 6000 B.C.E, the northern half of Africa went through a wet phase known as the Aquatic Age. The region that is now the Sahara was actually a savanna of grassland and woodland, with an abundance of rivers and lakes. Lake Chad, for instance, formed part of a large inland sea. By fashioning bone harpoons and fishnets, people lived off the rich aquatic life. Around 3000 B.C.E. an extended dry phase set in and the vast barren area that we know now as the Sahara began to form. This dry period was likely a major stimulus for the invention of agriculture in West Africa as communities began experimenting with crop agriculture to supplement their diets. They began growing barley, wheat, and flax with simple tools such as digging sticks and wooden hoes.

In the past it was widely assumed that sub-Saharan African communities acquired agriculture by diffusion from Nile civilizations, but more recent scientific investigations have shown that plant domestication began independently in four regions: the Ethiopian highlands, the central Sudan, the West African savanna, and the West African forests. In all cases African farmers adapted crops suited to particular environments that were tested over long periods of

Before the Sahara became a desert, the region was home to pastoralists who herded cattle, sheep, and goats. On a plateau at Tassili n-Ajjer in the central Sahara, these pastoralists left an impressive array of wall paintings depicting their lifestyles and the wild animals that roamed the region. In this painting from the Tassili frescoes, women ride oxen as their community migrates to a new settlement.

time. For instance, around 3000 B.C.E. in the grasslands of the Ethiopian highlands, farmers began cultivating teff (a tiny grain), finger millet, *noog* (an oil plant), sesame, and mustard. In the forests they planted *ensete* (a bananalike plant) and coffee. Around 1000 B.C.E. wheat and barley were imported from across the Red Sea. In the central Sudan agricultural communities producing sorghum, millet, rice, cowpeas, and groundnuts began appearing as far back as 4000 B.C.E. In the West African forests, oil palms, cowpeas, and root crops such as yams were produced.

Africans also began to use domesticated animals about the same time as they adopted agriculture. The earliest evidence of livestock is from the western Egyptian desert about 8000 B.C.E. Cattle, sheep, goats, and pigs were introduced from western Asia to

Egypt and North Africa and then spread much later to western, eastern, and southern Africa. Because these animals were vulnerable to diseases carried by the tsetse fly in the rain forests, they thrived primarily in the savannas and woodland areas with less rainfall.

The other major breakthrough for sub-Saharan African cultures was the introduction of ironworking. Although bronze and copper toolmaking had developed in western Asia, the technology had not spread to sub-Saharan Africa. This was not the case with iron technology, which reached sub-Saharan Africa by two routes. The first was from Egypt to Nubia in the seventh century B.C.E. and then southward to other parts of Africa. Iron technology also appeared in West Africa about the same time, apparently brought south across the Sahara by Berbers, in contact with Phoenician or Carthaginian traders.

Two of the earliest centers of iron smelting were at Meroë, in the Nubian kingdom of Kush, and Nok, situated on the Jos plateau in central Nigeria. Located on the Nile River in a region rich in iron ore deposits, Meroë became well known in the fourth century B.C.E. for iron smelting and making iron tools and weapons that were key to the kingdom's success. Huge iron slag heaps still exist around the ruins of Meroë.

Archaeologists have dated ironworking sites at Nok from 700 to 400 B.C.E. Although some contend that ironworking was an independent invention at Nok, other ironmaking sites of about the same time period have recently been identified in Mauritania, southern Mali, and central Nigeria. Nevertheless, it is clear that Nok had one of the earliest ironworking sites. The Nok workers' preheating techniques and their ability to produce steel with a high carbon content were equal to those of Egypt and Rome. The Nok population included ironsmiths, craftspeople, and artists, who produced terra-cotta sculptures of remarkable realism that were strikingly similar to later art forms among the Yoruba kingdoms of Ife and Benin.

Iron production in most African societies usually took place in the dry months when rain and floods were not disruptive and agriculture was less intensive. Because their products were highly valued and could be exchanged for animals and food, ironworking specialists were persons of wealth and status. Magical, ritual, and spiritual powers were often attributed to them. In some societies the ironworking craft assumed such ritualistic significance that the furnaces were hidden in secluded places. African furnaces in the 900s were capable of generating higher temperatures than those in Europe before the 1700s.

Ironworking allowed African societies to make the leap from stone to metal tools. Iron tools such as hoes, knives, sickles, spear heads, and axes made a

significant difference in clearing forests and thick vegetation for agriculture, in hunting, and in waging war. When combined with the introduction of agriculture and pastoralism, the knowledge of ironworking contributed to population growth, craft specializations, trade between communities, and more complex political and economic systems. Ironworking also spurred migrations such as the spread of Bantu groups throughout eastern, central, and southern Africa.

Bantu Dispersion

One of the striking features of many African societies from central to eastern to southern Africa is that their languages (called Niger-Congo) and cultures have many similarities. How these societies—known as Bantu ("people")—came to spread over this vast area is a question that has long vexed scholars.[2]

Authorities generally agree that the original homeland for Bantu speakers was an area in present-day Cameroon near the Nigerian border. However, they are still not sure what prompted Bantu groups to start migrating from their homeland. One explanation relates to environmental changes—as the Sahara region dried up, small groups were forced to move

This stylized terra-cotta head, dating from about 500 B.C.E., is an outstanding example of a sculpture from the Nok culture of central Nigeria. The head, which has a human face, was probably used for religious purposes.

southward in search of new areas to farm and fish. Another explanation is that the acquisition of iron-working gave Bantu groups access to iron tools that they could use in clearing the thicker vegetation of the forest regions.

Using archaeological and linguistic data, historians have had some success in reconstructing the complex movements of Bantu groups. Around 500 B.C.E, bands of Bantu began slowly moving out of their original homeland. These Bantu groups had common lifestyles—they lived in scattered homesteads and villages and farmed root crops, foraged for food, and fished. One stream moved south into the equatorial rain forests of west central Africa and settled in present-day Angola and Namibia. Their agriculture relied heavily on root crops and cultivating palm trees. The other stream moved east and eventually settled in the area east of Lake Victoria in East Africa. There they came into contact with Cushitic-speaking peoples that had migrated from the Ethiopian highlands. The Bantu adopted their mixed farming practices—growing cereal crops such as millet and sorghum and herding cattle, sheep, and goats.

From that point, wherever Bantu groups migrated, they searched for areas that had enough summer rainfall to support cereal cultivation and their animal herds. As soils were not rich and could not support farmers for long periods, Bantu groups practiced slash-and-burn agriculture. The need to move on after two or three years in an area may explain why some Bantu groups, after spreading throughout East Africa, migrated southward, along tributaries of the Congo River, through the equatorial rain forest to present-day southern Congo and Zambia, where they settled in the savannas and woodland areas. Others migrated south, crossing the Zambezi and Limpopo Rivers by the fourth century of the Common Era.

As Bantu communities moved into eastern and southern Africa, they also acquired knowledge of ironworking and adopted new food crops such as the banana and the Asian yam, brought to Africa by sailors from Malaysia and Polynesia who settled on the island of Madagascar several thousand years ago. The banana in particular became a staple food and a source of mash for beer in the moist regions of Africa.

Throughout their migrations, Bantu societies came into contact with hunting and gathering groups. Although some scholars have portrayed the Bantu as a superior culture that overwhelmed hunting and gathering groups, recent scholarship has shown that the relationship was complex and not one-sided. At the same time that Bantu were practicing agriculture and pastoralism, they relied on foraging for subsistence and turned to hunting and gathering bands for assistance and knowledge of

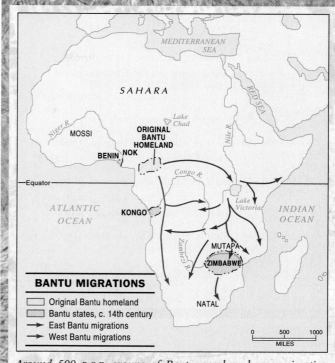

Around 500 B.C.E. groups of Bantu speakers began migrating from west central Africa and establishing farming and pastoral communities in eastern, central, and southern Africa.

local conditions. In addition, hunters and gatherers married into Bantu groups or attached themselves to Bantu groups for periods of time.

Ethiopia and Northeastern Africa

Situated along and inland from Africa's Red Sea coast, Ethiopia has been one of Africa's most enduring and richest civilizations. Indeed, the region between the Nile River and the Red Sea had been recognized as a major source of trade goods several thousand years before the kingdom of Ethiopia came into existence. To the Egyptians the area was known as the Land of Punt, and from the Fifth Dynasty (c. 2494–2345 B.C.E.) on, Egypt's rulers regularly sent expeditions to trade for frankincense, myrrh, aromatic herbs, ebony, ivory, gold, and wild animals. The Egyptian queen Hatshepsut's funerary temple recorded a major expedition that she sent to Punt around 1470 B.C.E. However, historians have not been able to pinpoint Punt's location precisely or reconstruct the inner workings of its political system.

Around 800 B.C.E. traders from Saba', a kingdom on the southwestern Arabian peninsula, crossed the Red Sea, first founding trading settlements on the Eritrean coast and later a kingdom, Da'amat. The Sabaeans tapped into the ivory trade in the interior

Aksum and Ethiopia

c. 800 B.C.E.	Sabaean traders establish trading settlements on the Eritrean coast
320–350 C.E.	Reign of Ezana, king of Aksum
c. 350	Aksum conquers Kush
700–800	Aksum's control of Red Sea trade ended by Persian and Muslim forces
c. 1185–1225	Reign of Lalibela, emperor of the Ethiopian Zagwe dynasty; beginning of construction of rock churches
c. 1314–1344	Reign of Amde-Siyon, emperor of Ethiopia
1434–1468	Reign of Zara Yakob, emperor of Ethiopia

highlands, but because they were also proficient at farming in arid environments, they interacted well with farming communities of the coastal interior. The Sabaean language was similar to the Semitic languages spoken in the area, and a language called Ge'ez evolved that became the basis for oral and written communication of the elites.

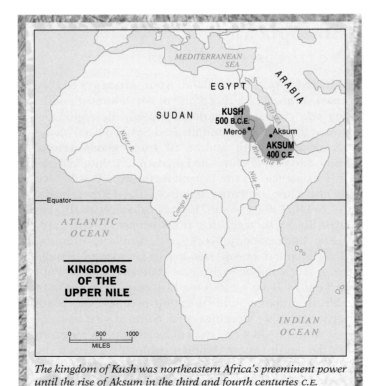

The kingdom of Kush was northeastern Africa's preeminent power until the rise of Aksum in the third and fourth centuries C.E.

By the start of the Common Era, a new state, Aksum, emerged to dominate the Red Sea trade. Taking advantage of its location between the Mediterranean and the Indian Ocean, Aksum developed extensive trading ties with Ptolemaic Egypt and the Roman Empire as well as Asia as far as Sri Lanka and India. Aksum also controlled trade with its interior, exporting ivory and exotic items such as tortoise shells and rhinoceros horns and even slaves in exchange for cloth, glassware, and wine. Aksum's capital, also called Aksum, was a major entrepot for the trade with the interior, while its bustling seaport, Adulis, prospered as the middleman for trade between the Mediterranean and the Indian Ocean. Monsoon winds dictated the rhythm of Indian Ocean trade. After July, when the summer monsoon winds were favorable, Adulis's traders set forth on their journeys. They returned in October when the prevailing winds reversed direction.

By the third and fourth centuries C.E., Aksum was at its zenith as a trading power, conquering its rival, Meroë, on the Nile, and replacing Rome as the dominant trading power on the Red Sea. Aksum minted its own coins with Greek inscriptions, something that only a handful of other states, such as Persia and Rome, were doing.

Aksum's best-known ruler was Ezana (320–350), who converted to Christianity toward the end of his reign, about the same time as the Roman emperor Constantine the Great. Some historians contend that Ezana conveniently converted to strengthen trading relations with the Greek-speaking world. Two Syrian brothers, Frumentius and Aedisius, have been credited with winning over Ezana to the Christian faith. Shipwrecked on the Red Sea coast, the brothers were brought to Aksum's royal court as slaves when Ezana was a child. Frumentius became an influential figure in the royal court, serving as main adviser to Ezana's mother, the queen regent. Following Ezana's conversion, Frumentius was chosen Aksum's first bishop, and Christianity was made the official state religion. Subsequently, the head of the Ethiopian church (abuna) was traditionally chosen by Coptic church leaders in Egypt, even after Muslims gained control over Egypt.

Although Aksum's court language remained Greek, Ge'ez assumed a new prominence as the language of the Ethiopian church. The Old and New Testaments were translated into Ge'ez, which, much like Latin in the Catholic Church, became the primary language of literature and the liturgy. Several centuries after Ezana's conversion, a group of Syrian monks called the Nine Saints played a major role in spreading Christianity among rural people. The Nine Saints were known for their belief in the Monophysite doctrine, which held that Christ's human and divine qualities were inseparable.

The key to Aksum's continued prosperity was maintaining control over Red Sea trade. In the early sixth century Aksum invaded Yemen to protect its trading interests as well as a Christian community persecuted by Jews. However, the Aksumites' influence in the Arabian peninsula ended later in the century when a Persian expeditionary force ousted them. Then, in the eighth century, Islamic expansion totally removed Aksum as a trading force in the Red Sea. Aksum's rulers were forced to migrate to the central highlands of the interior, where their rule continued to be plagued by conflict and warfare. There they mixed with a Cushitic-speaking people, the Agaw, who were assimilated into Aksum's political elite and also converted to Christianity.

This new nobility formed the core of the new Zagwe dynasty that took over in the mid-twelfth century. The Zagwes stressed their continuity with the Aksumite political order by claiming that they were descendants of Moses and encouraging the faithful to make pilgrimages to Jerusalem and Palestine. In this regard, the most enduring cultural expressions of the Zagwe dynasty were its churches, the most famous of which are the 11 awe-inspiring rock-hewn cathedrals of Roha, commissioned by the legendary Emperor Lalibela (c. 1185–1225). These impressive architectural feats, with ornate decorations and intricate workmanship, drew on Byzantine, Greek, and Roman motifs.

Lalibela's reign was the high point of Zagwe rule. His successors were unable to maintain the kingdom, and a new dynasty, the Solomonids, assumed power in 1270. Like the Zagwes, the Solomonid emperors (each known as *negus,* or "king of kings") legitimized their rule by claiming a direct tie to the Aksumite past. In their royal chronicle, the *Kebre Negast* ("Glory of the Kings"), they gave an epic account of their dynasty's direct descent from the Old Testament's King Solomon. The tale related how Makeda, the queen of Sheba (Saba') had visited Solomon to learn his techniques of rule. Instead, Solomon had seduced Makeda, who bore him a son, Menelik. When Menelik later visited his father's court, he tricked Solomon and spirited the Ark of the Covenant out of Israel to Ethiopia. This story was interpreted as a sign of the covenant God was establishing with Ethiopia. Thus to the kings of the Solomonid dynasty it was an article of faith that they were directly descended from Solomon.

To avoid the same fate as the Zagwes, the Solomonid rulers set strict rules to ensure orderly successions. To insulate royal princes from palace infighting and forming alliances with nobles in the countryside, the first Solomonid emperor, Yikunno-Amlak, took the bold step of placing the princes in a remote retreat, Mount Geshen (the "mountain of the kings"). The princes lived a comfortable but monastic existence, totally isolated from the outside world. Many of them followed an ascetic life, absorbed in religious issues and gaining reputations as accomplished writers of Ge'ez poetry and composers of sacred music. When an emperor died without a designated heir, the princes provided a pool of candidates for the throne.

The first Solomonid rulers concentrated on consolidating their rule over the central highlands of Ethiopia

Ethiopia's Emperor Lalibela oversaw the construction of 11 churches carved out of red volcanic rock at Roha. Shaped in the form of a Greek cross, the Church of St. George was an impressive architectural feat. Workers chipped away at the stone until they reached 40 feet down and then molded the church and hollowed out its interior.

A characteristic art form of Ethiopia is wall murals. In this painting the bishop of Aksum confers a blessing on the emperor of Ethiopia at the Cathedral of St. Mary of Zion. When Zara Yakob became emperor in 1434, he chose to be crowned in Aksum because he wanted to link the monarchy with the historical prestige of that kingdom.

and refrained from carrying out aggressive wars of expansion. These goals changed dramatically during the reign of Emperor Amde-Siyon (c. 1314–1344), who conquered territories to the west and toward the coast and who led his armies against Muslim principalities to the south and east. Amde-Siyon's campaigns against the Muslims were aimed not only at securing control of trade routes but also at putting pressure on the Muslim rulers of Egypt to allow the Coptic church to send a new bishop to Ethiopia. Amde-Siyon was so successful in vanquishing his opponents that an Arab historian reported, "It is said that he has ninety-nine kings under him, and that he makes up the hundred."[3] The powers of the Ethiopian monarchy were at their greatest during the reign of Zara Yakob (1434–1468), who resurrected the tradition of kings' being crowned at the ancient capital of Aksum. He fended off Muslim rivals, stamped out doctrines threatening Christianity, strengthened the Ethiopian church, and reorganized the bureaucracy. He also initiated a tentative alliance with the pope against the Muslims.

Within his immediate environs Zara Yakob ruled as an absolute monarch, surrounded by hundreds of courtiers and servants. To consolidate his rule, he dismissed provincial governors and replaced them with his own daughters and other female members of his family. When he held audiences at his court, he was positioned behind a curtain and communicated through a royal spokesman. When he traveled about his kingdom, his subjects had to avert their eyes on the penalty of death.

Because of the conquests of emperors such as Amde-Siyon and Zara Yakob, Ethiopia's rulers had to govern a diverse kingdom of many ethnic, linguistic, and religious backgrounds. They achieved this goal through the feudal relationships they established with their nobles and by promoting the expansion of the Ethiopian church. Until Gondar was designated as the capital in the seventeenth century, Ethiopian emperors did not have a centralized bureaucracy or a fixed capital for more than a few decades at a time. Rather they created a mobile court of family members, high officials, soldiers, priests, and retainers that moved regularly around the kingdom. This mobile court allowed the emperor to show off his power as well as encourage trade with outlying regions and to collect tribute from all his subjects. Mobile courts encamped in areas for up to four months, but they put such a strain on local resources that they were not encouraged to return for many years.

The emperor had to be constantly on guard against potential revolts against his authority. Although he allowed local rulers to remain in power, he strategically placed military garrisons around the kingdom. Moreover, because all land was owned by the emperor, he had the power to grant *gults*, or fiefs, to nobles for their loyalty and to soldiers who distinguished themselves in his service. The emperor could dismiss nobles as easily as he could create them.

In return the landholders had to pay tribute to the emperor and to contribute soldiers to his army. The emperor also imposed taxes on imports and exports. The nobles lived off the taxes or tribute—such as grain, labor service, or cattle—they collected from peasant farmers. Tribute cattle were called "burning" because the cows were branded or "touched with fire" before they were handed over. Peasants were also expected to support any soldiers living in their area.

The Ethiopian church became an extension of the Solomonid rulers, who renewed it and actively promoted its expansion throughout the empire. Clerics, who had previously led ascetic lives more concerned with their personal salvation, were now expected to play active roles in spreading the Christian faith. Priests recruited from monasteries were commissioned to establish churches and evangelize in newly conquered territories. Emperors also granted the church extensive estates and sponsored monastic schools. The schools, mostly for boys, primarily attracted students from families of the priesthood and

Emperor Zara Yakob's Coronation and His Concern for the Church

This fifteenth-century ruler of Ethiopia pulled the central administration together after a long period of feudal decentralization. His several daughters assisted in the task by taking over provincial governments.

When our King Zara [Yakob] went into the district of Aksum to fulfil the law and to effect the coronation ceremony according to the rites followed by his ancestors, all the inhabitants, including the priests, came to meet him and welcomed him with great rejoicing; the chiefs and all the soldiers of Tigre were on horseback carrying shield and lance, and the women, in great numbers, gave themselves up, according to the ancient custom, to endless dancing. When he entered the gates of the town the King had on his right and left the governors of Tigre and Aksum who, according to custom, both waved olive branches. . . . After arriving within the walls of Aksum the King had gold brought to him which he scattered as far as the city gate on the carpets spread along his route. This amount of gold was more than a hundred ounces. . . .

On the twenty-first of the month of Ter [January 16] the day of the death of our Holy Virgin Mary, the coronation rite was carried out, the King being seated on a stone throne. This stone, together with its supports, is only used for the coronation. There is another stone on which the King is seated when he receives the blessing, and several others to the right and left on which are seated the twelve chief judges. There is also the throne of the metropolitan bishop.

While at Aksum the Emperor made a number of regulations for the church.

During his stay at Aksum our King regulated all the institutions of the church and ordered that prayers which had up to that time been neglected should be recited each day at canonical hours. For this purpose he convened a large number of monks and founded a convent, the headship of which he entrusted to an abbot with the title of Pontiff of Aksum, who received an extensive grant of land called Nader. The King accomplished this work through devotion to the Virgin Mary and to perpetuate his own memory and that of his children and his children's children. He summoned some catechists and presented to the church a great number of ornaments and a golden ewer, revived all the old traditions, spread joy in these places, and returned thence satisfied.

Zara Yakob also founded churches and regulated religious affairs in other provinces.

Arriving in the land of Tsahay in Amhara, he went up a high and beautiful mountain, the site of which he found pleasing; at the top of this mountain and facing east he found a wall which had been raised by his father, King Dawit, with the intention of erecting a shrine. His father, however, had not had the time to complete the work, in the same way that the ancient King David, who planned to build a temple to the Lord, could not accomplish his task which was completed by his son Solomon. Our king Zara Yaqob fulfilled his father's intention by building a shrine to God on the west of the mountain. Everyone, rich and poor alike and even the chiefs, were ordered to carry the stones with the result that this edifice was speedily erected. They embellished this locality, which underwent a great transformation; two churches were built there, one called Makana Gol and the other Dabra Negwadgwad. The King attached to them a certain number of priests and canons to whom he gave grants of land. He also founded a convent and placed in it monks from Dabra Libanos, whom he endowed in a similar manner.

From Richard K. Pankhurst, ed., *The Ethiopian Royal Chronicles* (Oxford: Oxford University Press, 1967), pp. 34–36.

the royal elite. Although these policies may have revived the church, they also made the church intimately identified with imperial power and unable to develop deep roots among the common people.

This was a period of the blossoming of the arts in which priests played a leading role. They produced innumerable biblical translations, theological treatises, biographies of saints, historical chronicles, illuminated manuscripts, and mural paintings.

Zara Yakob's reign was a high point in the Ethiopian kingdom's history. His successors did not have the skills to hold the kingdom together, and the Solomonid dynasty went into a decline. Provincial officials and nobles seized on the weakness of the emperor to refrain from paying taxes and build up their own power. The Oromo, a pastoral people, began challenging Ethiopian control of the highland areas, and Muslims stopped sending tribute. Muslim states also grew restive. Under the military leadership of Ahmad al-Ghazi Ahmad Gran, the state of Adal launched a holy war against the Christian kingdom in 1527 that continued until 1543 when Ahmad was killed in battle.

Empires of the Western Sudan

The savanna of the western Sudan has been characterized by the long-standing trans-Saharan trade between the western savanna and the Mediterranean coast. Large camel caravans made regular trips across the dangerous desert carrying North African salt in exchange for West African gold. To the Berbers who organized these caravans, the bend of the Niger River offered a secure watering and resting place. Here they found people who had conducted local trade for centuries before the caravans came, who knew the savanna well, and who could acquire gold from distant places. Their resulting control of the lucrative gold and salt trade brought great accumulations of wealth and was a key factor in the rise of major West African kingdoms.

Before the formation of these kingdoms, there was already a thriving interregional trade among the savanna communities. Archaeological evidence shows that in the ninth century B.C.E. some savanna communities began harnessing the floodwaters of the Niger River and started raising livestock and cultivating cereals. They formed settlements of 800 to 1000 people. That the villages they lived in were unwalled and in open areas is an indication that relations between communities were mostly peaceful and cooperative. However, between 600 and 300 B.C.E. the pattern changed as villages erected walls and retreated to more remote and defensible sites—an indication that they were responding to external threats, possibly from nomadic Berbers that roamed the Sahara and occasionally raided savanna societies.

West African Sudanic Kingdoms

c. 250 B.C.E.	Jenne-jeno on Niger River settled
c. 100–40 B.C.E.	Camel introduced to trans-Saharan trade
c. 900 C.E.	State of Kanem founded
1000–1200	Hausa city-states founded
1076	Almoravid attack on Ghana
c. 1200–1235	Reign of Sumaguru, Sosso king
1300–1400	Rise of kingdom of Oyo
1307–1337	Reign of Mansa Musa in Mali
1352	Visit of Berber geographer Ibn Battuta to Mali
1464–1492	Reign of Sunni Ali, Songhai emperor
1493–1528	Reign of Askia Muhammad, Songhai emperor
1591	Morocco invades Songhai

One of the earliest urban settlements, Jenne-jeno, was begun around 250 B.C.E. Situated on an inland delta of the Niger River, Jenne-jeno was ideally located because it was surrounded by water during the rainy season and was much safer for trade than other settlements. Over time, Jenne-jeno became an interregional trade center for farmers, herders, and fishermen that long predated any involvement in the trans-Saharan trade. Jenne-jeno exported food via the Niger to points to the east.

Although the Sahara was not easy to traverse, it was not impenetrable. As early as 1000 B.C.E. Carthaginians, Romans, and perhaps Greeks began establishing several routes across the Sahara for their horse- and ox-drawn chariots. One route stretched from Libya and Tunisia through the Fezzan, while the other connected Morocco to Mauritania. Trade declined with the collapse of the Roman Empire in the fourth century C.E. but was revived several centuries later, first by the Byzantine Empire and then by Arabs.

The camel, introduced from the Middle East in the first century B.C.E., became the main conveyor of goods in the trans-Saharan trade. As pack animals camels had several advantages over horses and oxen. Carrying loads of 250 to 300 pounds, camels could travel extended distances with little water. However, they were slow and inefficient. Averaging about 20 to 30 miles a day, they took about two months to cross the Sahara. Moreover, attendants had to load and unload their cargo once or twice each day, and much of the provisions were used to feed attendants. What-

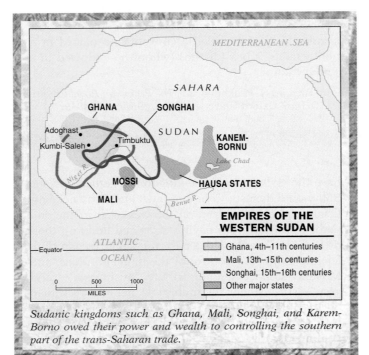

Sudanic kingdoms such as Ghana, Mali, Songhai, and Karem-Borno owed their power and wealth to controlling the southern part of the trans-Saharan trade.

ever the camel's liabilities, its introduction boosted the volume of trade. The camel remained an essential part of the trans-Saharan trade until the twentieth century, when it was replaced by the automobile.

Ghana

The earliest of the Sudanic kingdoms, first known as Aoukar or Wagadu, later took the name of its war chief, Ghana (not to be confused with the modern nation of the same name). It arose on the upper Niger during the fourth century C.E. as a loose federation of village-states, inhabited by Soninke farmers. This set a pattern for future kingdoms of the savanna as a lineage or a clan asserted its authority over other groups.

The introduction of ironworking allowed the Soninke farming communities to form larger political systems. In the face of drier conditions, they applied iron tools to improving agricultural production and devised iron swords and spears to conquer neighboring groups. They also used these weapons to fend off Saharan nomads who grazed their animals in the Sahel (the southern fringe of the Sahara) and occasionally raided Soninke communities.

By about 800 C.E. Ghana had established itself as a powerful kingdom able to exact tribute from vassal states in the region. Although agricultural production contributed to Ghana's wealth, it was the expanding trans-Saharan trade with Europe and the Mediterranean world that gave Ghana even more influence. From their strategic position on the upper Niger River, the Soninke were well positioned as middlemen to barter the salt produced from the Taghaza

Introduced from the Middle East in the first century B.C.E., *the camel was the main transporter of goods in the trans-Saharan trade between North Africa and the West African savanna.*

salt mines in the Sahara, the gold coming from Bambuk, and kola nuts and slaves captured from areas south of the savanna.

Ghana's king controlled the supply of gold within his kingdom and claimed every gold nugget coming into the country, leaving ordinary citizens the right to buy and sell only gold dust. The king was reputed "to own a gold nugget so large that he could tether a horse to it." In addition, taxes were levied on every load of goods entering and leaving the country.

Ghana's gold was actually mined in Bambuk, a region eight days' journey to the west of Ghana's capital, Kumbi-Saleh, from the beds of the Senegal and Faleme Rivers. Ghana's rulers did not have direct control over Bambuk, and the persons who worked the goldfields jealously guarded information about where and how they produced the gold. They devised a strategy for negotiating with Mande traders without actually coming into direct contact with them. Al Masudi, a noted Arab traveler, described this "silent trade" around 950:

> They have traced a boundary which no one who sets out to them ever crosses. When the merchants reach this boundary, they place their wares and cloth on the ground and then depart, and so the people of the Sudan come bearing gold which they leave beside the merchandise and then depart. The owners of the merchandise then return, and if they are satisfied with what they have found, they take it. If not, they go away again, and the people of the Sudan return and add to the price until the bargain is concluded.[4]

Traders avidly sought salt from the trans-Saharan trade because it was a crucial element in diets and a preservative for foods and skins. It was also a scarce commodity in savanna communities. A certain amount of salt could be extracted from vegetable matter or from soil, but not enough to satisfy the requirements of savanna communities. However, in the Sahara there were large salt deposits, the best known at Taghaza, in the middle of the Sahara, about a three-week journey from both Mediterranean and Sudanese trading centers. Salt was quarried in huge 200-pound slabs, loaded on camels, and transported to trading centers like Timbuktu, where they were distributed to other places.

Another item that featured in the trade was kola nuts, which were primarily grown in the forest areas to the south of the savanna. Used to quench thirst, kola nuts were consumed mainly in the drier savanna. They did not become a major staple of the trans-Saharan exchange.

Slaves were the final component of the trans-Saharan trade. Although slavery was an established practice in some, though not all, sub-Saharan African societies, it took many shapes and forms. A common practice was for a family to send a family member—usually a child or a young adult—to serve in another household to pay off a debt or some other obligation (such as compensation for a crime) or to raise food in times of famine. In those cases, slaves were integrated into a master's family. Servile status could be of limited duration, and the slave would be sent back home as soon as the debt was repaid.

With centralized kingdoms such as Ghana and, later, Mali, slaves were bought and sold in trading transactions and were called on to perform a variety of roles—as servants, farm laborers, porters, traders, and soldiers. Most household slaves were women and children; slave women were often selected as marriage partners or concubines because a man did not have to pay bridewealth for them. Their children had all the rights of free persons.

Slave warriors had a privileged status; they could serve in high capacities as military officers, administrators, and diplomats in a king's court. Slave soldiers were the mainstays of armies and were used in raids to kidnap and capture more slaves. Most slaves were kidnapped or captured in raids on weaker communities by the stronger savanna states, especially in the forest region to the south. Muslim law enjoined Muslims from enslaving other Muslims, but this was not always observed when raiding parties were sent out.

Although savanna kingdoms created their own internal trade in slaves, the trans-Saharan slave trade was fueled primarily by demands from North African Mediterranean states. Slaves were typically taken in caravans, where they were exchanged for salt and horses. In Senegambia in the mid-fifteenth century, 9 to 14 slaves could fetch one horse, while in Kanem-Bornu a horse would cost 15 to 20 slaves. In later centuries some slaves, especially those sold in Libya, were traded on to the eastern Mediterranean, the Italian peninsula, and other southern European areas. From the eighth century, when the trade was initiated, to the early twentieth century, an estimated 3.5 to 4 million slaves were taken across the Sahara.[5]

The 1200-mile journey across the desert was as perilous as the trans-Atlantic slave trade's infamous Middle Passage. Many slaves lost their lives to the harsh conditions. The majority of slaves were women who worked as domestic servants in royal households and courts or were designated as concubines. Male slaves were pressed into service in the salt mines and as caravan porters, agricultural labor, and soldiers. Because many slaves were manumitted or died of diseases and because so few children were born in captivity, there was a constant demand for more slaves to be sold on the market.

To reconstruct the histories of the Sudanic kingdoms, historians draw heavily on the accounts of Arab geographers, travelers, holy men, and scholars. One Arab chronicler, al-Bakri, described Ghana at its peak in 1067. He noted that the army was some 200,000 strong, with many contingents wearing chain mail. The king, who had not converted to Islam, was considered divine and able to intercede with the gods. He appointed all officials and served as supreme judge. His government was organized under ministers, with one responsible for his capital, Kumbi-Saleh. Princes of tributary states were held hostage at his court. When the king appeared in public, he was surrounded by highborn personal retainers holding gold swords, horses adorned with gold cloth blankets, and dogs wearing gold collars.

Ghana's capital, Kumbi-Saleh, was situated on the edge of a crop-growing area and had 15,000 to 20,000 residents. The capital was really two towns, 6 miles apart. One was a large Soninke village, in which the king and his retinue lived. Close to the village was a sacred grove where traditional religious cults were practiced. The other town was occupied by Muslim merchants. The merchants' town had 12 mosques, two-story stone houses, public squares, and a market. Besides the traders, the town was also home to religious and legal scholars. Ghana's king relied on literate Muslims as treasurer, interpreters, and counselors. However influential the Muslims were, Ghana's king had to make sure that his own religious leaders were regularly consulted and that he participated in shrine and other religious activities. The first king to convert to Islam did not do so until after the Almoravid invasion.

Following Ghana's conquest of Adoghast, a Sanhaja Berber trading center, Sanhaja Berbers had rallied around an Islamic revivalist movement called the Almoravid and attacked Ghana in 1076. Although it is still a subject of debate whether the Almoravid attack was a full-scale invasion or a series of raids, Ghana had to give up Adoghast and its dominance over trade. Ghana's dominance over the gold trade was further weakened when the Bure goldfield opened up on the Niger River.

Mali

In the early thirteenth century Ghana's rule was ended by an uprising led by Sumaguru (c. 1200–1235) of the Sosso, who were related to the Soninke. Oral traditions characterize Sumaguru as a tyrant who wielded magical powers over his people. Sumaguru was overthrown in 1235 by Sundiata of the Malinke Keita clan, who forged an alliance of Malinke clans and chiefdoms for that purpose. Lengthy wars followed in which Sundiata's army defeated and killed Sumaguru and routed the Sosso. Sundiata's army then embarked on campaigns of conquest throughout the territory that had been Ghana.

Eventually Sundiata's Malinke created a vast empire called Mali that stretched from the Atlantic south of the Senegal River to Gao on the middle

Niger River. Mali gained control of the desert gold trade and the gold-producing regions of Wangara and Bambuk. When gold replaced silver in 1252 as the main currency in Europe, West Africa became Europe's leading supplier of gold. Several tons of gold were produced annually. Two-thirds of it was exported, while the rest was kept for conspicuous display by Mali's ruling elites.

The kingdom of Mali was at the height of its power and prosperity during the reign of Sundiata's nephew, Mansa (king) Musa (1307–1337). Musa was perhaps the most widely known sub-Saharan African ruler throughout western Asia and Europe. He was a great soldier who consolidated his kingdom's control over a vast domain. Malian and Arab merchants carried on trade with the Mediterranean coast, particularly with Algeria, Tunisia, Egypt, and the Middle East.

Mansa Musa ruled over a state more efficiently organized than the relatively crude European kingdoms of the time. On the north and northeast were loosely held tributary kingdoms of diverse populations, including some Berbers. To the south were more closely controlled tributary states, under resident governors appointed by the king. Elsewhere, particularly in the cities, such as Timbuktu, provincial administrators governed directly in the king's name and at his pleasure. Mali's central government included ministries for finance, justice, agriculture, and foreign relations.

A devout Muslim, Musa lavishly displayed his wealth and power on a pilgrimage he took to Mecca in 1324–1325. His retinue included thousands of porters and servants and a hundred camels bearing loads of gold. In Egypt he spent so lavishly and gave away so much gold that its value in that country plummeted and did not recover for a generation:

> *This man spread upon Cairo the flood of his generosity. . . . So much gold was current in Cairo that it ruined the value of money. Let me add that gold in Egypt had enjoyed a high rate of exchange up to the moment of their arrival. But from that day onward, its value dwindled. That is how it has been for twelve years from that time, because of the great amounts of gold they brought to Egypt and spent there.*[6]

When he returned to his kingdom, Musa brought along an architect who designed mosques in Gao and Timbuktu as well as an audience chamber for Musa's palace. Musa sent students to study at Islamic schools in Morocco. They returned to found Qur'anic schools, the best known of which was at Timbuktu.

Mansa Musa's pilgrimage also caught the attention of Muslim scholars. Among them was the Berber geographer and traveler Ibn Battuta, who visited Mali in 1352 during the reign of Musa's brother,

Mansa Sulayman (1336–1358). Battuta's account is one of the key sources for understanding the kingdom of Mali. He was favorably impressed by Mali's architecture, literature, and institutions of learning but was most laudatory about its law and justice, which guaranteed that no person "need fear brigands, thieves, or ravishers" anywhere in the vast domain. Battuta praised the king's devotion to Islam but was disappointed that so many subjects of Mali were not Muslims. He noted also that the unveiled women were attractive but lacking in humility. He was astounded that they might take lovers without arousing their husbands' jealousy and might discuss learned subjects with men. Battuta was describing the trading center of Walata. He might have been equally impressed with other Malian trading cities, including Adoghast, Kumbi-Saleh, Gao, and Timbuktu.

As Mali's empire grew, Islam became an important unifying element among the political and commercial elite. Key agents for the spread of Islam were Mande traders known as Dyula or Wangara, who settled in towns and villages along the main trade routes that connected every section of western Africa. Although they were largely responsible for the trade in such items as gold and kola nuts, they were Muslim teachers as well. Wherever they went, they became the lifeblood of small Muslim communities, establishing Qur'anic schools and arranging for the faithful to make pilgrimages to Mecca. Although at this time Muslims were not actively converting people in the countryside, they did so in the region known as Senegambia. Despite the devoutness of kings like Musa and the presence of Muslim traders in many areas, Islam was mainly a religion of court and commerce. Most people in the countryside were faithful to their traditional religious beliefs. Even kings and chiefs who were Muslims had to pay homage to traditional religious rituals.

After Mansa Musa's death, his successors found the large empire increasingly difficult to govern. They were plagued by dynastic disputes, raids by desert nomads such as the Tuaregs and Sanhaja, and the restlessness of tributary states. One of the rebellious states was Songhai, centered around the bend of the Niger. Songhai had been in existence for many centuries before it was absorbed into the Malian Empire in the thirteenth century, and its principal city, Gao, was an entrepot for trade with the Maghrib and Egypt. Before the end of the fifteenth century, Songhai had won its independence, and within another century it had conquered Mali.

Songhai

Songhai became the largest of the Sudanic empires, reaching its zenith during the reigns of Sunni Ali (1464–1492) and Askia Muhammad (1493–1528).

Discovery Through Maps
The Catalan Atlas

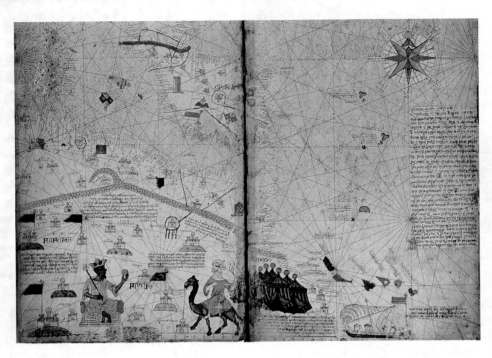

The Catalan Atlas of 1375 was probably drawn by Abraham Cresques (1325–1387), one of a group of Jewish cartographers residing on the Mediterranean island of Majorca. The Catalan Atlas was done for their patron, King Pedro III of Aragon, who presented it to Charles V of France in 1381.

The Catalan Atlas was a *portolano,* or sea chart; it featured radiating *rhumb lines* that noted compass directions. Because the atlas was designed for mariners, it was more concerned with coastlines and harbors and showed detailed knowledge of the Mediterranean and Black Seas. Land areas, by contrast, included very few features. The atlas's depiction of Asia drew heavily from Marco Polo's travels a half century before, and the description of the West African Sudan relied on contacts with a group of Moroccan Jews who had intimate knowledge of the trans-Saharan trade.

One of the 12 leaves of the atlas covered West Africa and featured three inscriptions. The first marked a gap in the Atlas Mountains through which traders passed on their way to the lands south of the Sahara. The inscription reads: "Through this place pass the merchants who travel to the land of the Negroes of Guinea." The second inscription is of a Tuareg trader mounted on a camel: "All this region is occupied by people who veil their mouths; one only sees their eyes. They live in tents and have caravans of camels. There are also beasts called Lemp from the skins of which they make fine shields." The cartographer clearly believed that the inhabitants of the Sudan

were Muslims, as evidenced by the domes that identified Muslim centers such as Timbuktu and Gao. Finally there is the depiction of Mali's king, Mansa Musa, who is holding a huge gold nugget as he awaits the arrival of the Tuareg trader. The inscription beside him reads: "This Negro lord is called Musa Mali, lord of all the Negroes of Guinea. So abundant is the gold which is found in his country that he is the richest and most noble king in all the land." A half century before the Catalan map was drawn, Mansa Musa had lavishly displayed his wealth on a pilgrimage to Mecca. In Egypt he spent lavishly and gave away great quantities of gold. The story of his pilgrimage had such an impact on the Arab and European worlds that they gave an exaggerated prominence to Mansa Musa as a ruler and his kingdom as a source of gold.

Some of the geographical details on the map are wrong. For instance, the mapmaker placed a large lake that does not exist in the middle of the Sudan below the figure of Mansa Musa. One river (the Senegal) is shown flowing out of this lake into the Atlantic, while another river (the Niger) flows eastward and eventually connects to the Nile.

The Catalan Atlas was designed to encourage Europeans to establish commercial ties with other parts of the world. To Europeans, who were seeking sources to finance their trade with India, China, and the Spice Islands, establishing direct contact with the goldfields of the West African Sudan was a tantalizing prospect that the Catalan Atlas encouraged.

Mali, as Described by Ibn Battuta

Ibn Battuta (1304–1368) was a famous Muslim traveler in the Near and Far East, as well as in Africa. He was the only medieval commentator who visited every land under Muslim rule.

The sultan of Mali is Mansa Sulayman, *mansa* meaning sultan, and Sulayman being his proper name. He is a miserly king, not a man from whom one might hope for a rich present. He held a banquet in commemoration of our master [the sultan of Morocco] to which the commanders, doctors, judge and preacher were invited, and I went along with them. Reading desks were brought in and the Koran was read through, then they prayed for our master and also for Mansa Sulayman. When the ceremony was over, I went forward and saluted Mansa Sulayman. The judge, the preacher, and Ibn al-Faquih told him who I was and he answered them in their tongue. They said to me "The sultan says to you 'Give thanks to God,'" so I said, "Praise be to God and thanks under all circumstances."

When I withdrew the sultan's hospitality gift was sent to me. Ibn al-Faquih came hurrying out of his house barefooted, and entered my room saying "Stand up; here comes the sultan's gift to you." So I stood up thinking that it consisted of robes of honour and money, and lo! it was three cakes of bread, and a piece of beef fried in native oil, and a calabash of sour curds. When I saw this I burst out laughing and thought it a most amazing thing that they could be so foolish. . . .

On certain days the sultan holds audiences in the palace yard, where there is a platform; this they call the *pempi*. It is carpeted with silk and has cushions placed on it. Over it is raised the umbrella, which is a sort of pavilion made of silk, surmounted by a bird in gold, about the size of a falcon. The sultan comes out of a door in a corner of the palace, carrying a bow in his hand and a quiver on his back. On his head he has a golden skull-cap bound with a golden band. His usual dress is a velvety red tunic, made of the European fabrics called *mutanfas*. The sultan is preceded by his musicians who carry gold and silver guimbris

[two-stringed guitars], and behind him come three hundred armed slaves. He walks in a leisurely fashion . . . and even stops from time to time. On reaching the *pempi*, he stops and looks around the assembly, then ascends it in the sedate manner of a preacher ascending a mosque-pulpit. As he takes his seat the drums, trumpets, and bugles are sounded. Three slaves go out at a run to summon the sovereign's deputy and the military commanders, who enter and sit down. Two saddled and bridled horses are brought, along with two goats, which they hold to serve as a protection against the evil eye.

The negroes are of all people the most submissive to their king and most abject in their behavior before him. They swear by his name, saying *Mansa Sulayman ki* [the Emperor Sulayman has commanded]. If he summons any of them while he is holding an audience in his pavilion, the person summoned takes off his clothes and puts on worn garments, removes his turban and dons a dirty skull-cap, and enters with his garments and trousers raised knee-high. He goes forward in an attitude of humility and dejection, and knocks the ground hard with his elbows, and stands with bowed head and bent back listening to what he says. If anyone addresses the king and receives a reply from him, he uncovers his back and throws dust over his head and back, for all the world like a bather splashing himself with water. . . . Sometimes one of them stands up before him and recalls his deeds in the sultan's service, saying, "I did so-and-so on such a day" or "I killed so-and-so." Those who have knowledge of this confirm his words, which they do by plucking the cord of the bow and releasing it with a twang.

From Rhoda Hoff, ed., *Africa: Adventures in Eyewitness History* (New York: Walck, 1963), pp. 11–12.

Sunni Ali is remembered for his military exploits. His armies ventured out on constant campaigns of conquest, largely to the west along the Niger in what had been Mali's heartland, and captured the trading centers of Timbuktu, Walata, and Jenne-jeno.

After Sunni Ali died, his son ruled for a few months before Askia Muhammad, who came from Sunni Ali's slave officer corps, deposed him. Askia Muhammad set about consolidating and reorganizing the whole empire. Although his armies seized control of the Taghaza saltworks in the Sahara, their

attempts to expand control over the Hausa states to the east were not successful.

Askia Muhammad created a centralized bureaucracy to manage finances, agriculture, and taxation, appointed administrators (usually relatives) to oversee newly created provinces, and built up a professional army featuring a cavalry of chain-mailed horsemen and an enlarged fleet of canoes, which constantly patrolled the Niger.

Unlike Sunni Ali, a former Muslim who expelled Muslim scholars from Timbuktu, Askia Muhammad

The Sankore mosque is the oldest surviving mosque in West Africa. Its pyramidlike minaret rises above the city of Timbuktu, the center of Islamic culture in the kingdom of Mali.

became their benefactor. During his reign Timbuktu, Jenne-jeno, and Walata achieved recognition as centers of Islamic scholarship. The Sankore mosque in Timbuktu became so renowned that a contemporary Arab traveler noted that more profits were being made from selling books and manuscripts there than from any other trade.

Like Mansa Musa, Askia Muhammad made a much publicized pilgrimage to Mecca. Traveling in 1497 with a large group of pilgrims, he brought thousands of gold pieces, which he freely distributed as alms to the poor and used to establish a hostel in Mecca for pilgrims from the western Sudan. Muhammad was not just expressing his faith; he was also drumming up trade with Songhai and shoring up his credentials with Muslims throughout his far-flung empire. On his return trip he won the recognition of the Egyptian caliph, an important distinction for any Muslim ruler.

Although a son deposed Askia Muhammad in 1528 and the kingdom was weakened by internal rivalries, Songhai remained a savanna power until 1591, when Morocco's King Ahmad al-Mansur launched an invasion of Songhai to prevent European rivals from gaining access to Sudanese gold. Taking offense at Songhai's refusal to pay a tax on salt from the Taghaza mines, al-Mansur sent a contingent of 4000 mercenaries to secure control over the Sudanic goldfields. Many died in the harsh march across the Sahara, but the survivors, armed with arquebuses (guns mounted on a forked staff) and muskets, proved superior to the spears, swords, and bows and arrows of Songhai's soldiers. Although Morocco's impact was fleeting, Songhai was not able to recover, and the empire fragmented into many smaller kingdoms.

Kanem-Bornu and the Hausa States

In the central Sudan, which stretches from the bend of the Niger to Lake Chad, the Muslim kingdoms of Kanem and Bornu and the Hausa city-states were the dominant political actors. Kanem, which lay to the northeast of Lake Chad, had been formed around 900 C.E. when groups of nomadic pastoralists unified and established the Sayfuwa dynasty. In the Sayfuwas' as in other Sudanic states, power and wealth were based on control of the Saharan trade. The main trade route cut through the central Sahara to the Fezzan and on to Tripoli and Egypt. Because Kanem was too far away from any sources of gold, its rulers exported ivory, ostrich feathers, and especially war captives from societies to the south. In return Kanem received horses that its rulers used to create a cavalry that fueled further raiding. Under Mai (king) Dunama Dibalemi (1210–1248), Kanem boasted a cavalry of 40,000 horsemen.

In the fourteenth century one of Kanem's tributary states, Bornu, became a power in its own right, organizing its own trade and refusing to pay tribute to Kanem. During this period Kanem's rulers were challenged by another clan and by the deterioration of their pasturage. About 1400 the Sayfuwa dynasty decided to move its capital from Njimi to Bornu, where they gained access to new trading networks. At first they paid tribute to Bornu, but during the sixteenth century Kanem's leaders gradually took over and began carrying out raids over an extensive area. Their rule was based on tribute and their ability to tax peasants and levy customs on trade. They established good relations with the Ottoman rulers of Tripoli and imported firearms and contracted Turkish mercenaries to train Bornu's army.

To the west of Kanem and Bornu a group of Hausa city-states had been founded by nomadic cattle-keepers and farmers between 1000 and 1200. A common feature of Hausa villages was wooden stockades for protection. When villages grew into larger towns, they were also surrounded by large walls.

The Hausa city-states became important political and economic forces in the fifteenth century, at the same time as Islam became an important part of the trading and merchant class and the political elite. All of the Hausa states were centralized, with a king and council making decisions. They relied on cavalries to maintain their power and to raid for the slaves who labored on the large royal farms. To undermine lineages who were contesting for power, the rulers of Kano appointed slaves to important state offices, as treasurer, and as palace guards. Kano was noted for its textiles, dyed cloth, and leatherwork. Other significant Hausa city-states were Katsina, an important terminus for the trans-Saharan trade; Zazzau, a supplier of slaves to Hausa states and to North Africa; and Gobir, which traded with Songhai and Mali. However, some of the Hausa states still had to pay tribute to Songhai to the west and Kanem and Bornu to the east. The Hausa states usually coexisted peacefully, although Kano and Katsina carried on a periodic war for almost a century.

West African Forest Kingdoms

Between the savanna grasslands and the Atlantic was forest land. Some of the forests were extensions of the savannas and were suitable for extensive human settlements; closer to the coast were rain forests that required considerable energy to clear for settlement and cultivation. The rain forests were also the home of the tsetse fly, the carrier of sleeping sickness, which prevented the herding of highly susceptible livestock.

Most forest societies were built around villages and small chiefdoms sustained by agriculture and hunting. Root crops such as yams and later cassava were the main staples. Although they did not approach the same size as the savanna empires, some of these small chiefdoms merged and formed vibrant kingdoms.

In southwestern Nigeria a Yoruba city-state, Ife, emerged around the eleventh century C.E. According to oral traditions, the Yoruba god of the sky, Olorun, had sent a founding ancestor, Oduduwa, to establish Ife. Anyone who subsequently made a claim to the kingship of Ife or other Yoruba states had to trace descent from Oduduwa.

To the southeast of Ife was the Edo kingdom of Benin, which rose to prominence in the fifteenth and sixteenth centuries. Benin's prosperity was based not only on commerce with the Hausa states, trading food, ivory, and kola nuts for copper and possibly salt, but also on the strength of its fishing communities on the Niger delta.

Benin was ruled by hereditary kings, known as *obas,* who maintained large, well-trained armies. Advising the king was the *ozama,* a council composed of hereditary leaders who represented the main Edo lineages. They acted as a restraint on the *oba's* powers until a thirteenth-century *oba* named Ewedo undermined the *ozama's* powers by creating a court of men who were not members of the royal elite and who were given nonhereditary titles.

Benin remained a minor state until the rule of Oba Ewuare, who usurped the throne by killing his younger brother in 1440. He took over in a period of instability following the conquest of Benin by a neighboring state. Ewuare ensured that his line would succeed him by arranging that his heir be added to the *ozama* council.

Noted for his magical and healing powers, Ewuare was famous for rebuilding the capital, surrounded by a wall and featuring a broad avenue. He constructed an extensive royal palace that provided quarters for his family as well as for advisers, guilds of craftsmen, and servants. All of his freeborn subjects were expected to spend a period in the service of the palace. During Ewuare's three decades of rule, his armies expanded Benin's borders, conquering some 200 towns and extending Benin's influence far to the north and to coastal regions to the east and west. However, Ewuare and his successors did not tightly control their empire. Although *obas* placed loyal officials in subject territories, they gave local rulers autonomy as long as they paid tribute on a regular basis.

The Yoruba kingdoms of Benin and Ife were noted for their bronze, brass, and copper castings dating from the twelfth to the fifteenth centuries. This photo is of a brass casting of an Ife oni *(ruler) and was probably used in a funeral ceremony.*

Other states developed along the forest fringe of the northern savanna. Most of them profited from the long-distance Saharan trade through the Hausa states to the north, but all remained relatively isolated from Sudanic culture. In the Niger River region, the kingdom of Oyo emerged in the fourteenth century. The kings *(alafins)* of Oyo presided over a complex of palace councils, subkings, secret organizations, and lineage organizations at the village level. The *alafins'* wealth was built on their control of a slave labor force that they placed on royal farms. Oyo's rise as a regional power was due to its cavalry, assembled with horses traded from the savanna. Because horses did not survive in the tsetse-infested forests, the cavalry was most effective in the open savannas to the southwest of Oyo.

All of these forest states are noted for their artistic achievements. Yoruba artisans created sculptures in bronze, copper, brass, and terra-cotta. Most of these artworks were used in religious contexts, as funereal pieces placed in tombs to honor ancestors and in temples. These objects showed continuity with the artistic styles of earlier civilizations such as the Nok culture of central Nigeria.

Swahili City-States in East Africa

The East African or Swahili coast has also been part of a much wider economic network, the Indian Ocean trading system, for the past 2000 years. However, unlike the trans-Saharan trade, which opened up extensive trade to the south of the desert, trade along the East African coast, with some exceptions, did not have the same impact on the East African interior until the nineteenth century.

The historical and cultural development of the East African coast was intimately linked to the creation of a coastal culture that dates to 100 B.C.E. to 300 C.E. with the arrival of Bantu-speaking communities along the coast north of the Tana River. They took advantage of the fertile soils and forests along the coast to pasture their animals and to raise a great variety of food crops. They also found the creeks, rivers, lagoons, mangrove swamps, and seas ideal for fishing. Although Bantu farmers relied on subsistence agriculture and fishing, they began to expand their local and regional trading contacts and eventually linked up with merchants from the Arabian peninsula and the Persian Gulf.

The language that evolved on the coast and islands was Swahili, which was based on a Bantu language spoken on the Kenyan coast. Indeed, the word *Swahili* is taken from an Arabic word *sawahil*, meaning "coast." As the language evolved, it adopted Arabic loan words.

Trade between the coastal Swahili city-states and Indian Ocean trading partners was regulated by monsoon winds that blow in a southwesterly direction between November and March and in a northeasterly direction between April and October.

The earliest known record of the East African trade is *The Periplus of the Erythrean Sea*, a navigational guide written in Greek around the first century C.E. The *Periplus* chronicles shipping ports of the Red Sea and the Indian Ocean and identifies a string of market towns on the "Azanian" (East African) coast that actively participated in the Indian Ocean trade, especially with Arabia. The most important was a port named Rhapta. Market towns exported such goods as ivory, rhinoceros horn, copra, and tortoise shells in exchange for iron tools and weapons, cloth, glass, and grain.

The Indian Ocean trade continued between 300 and 1000, but it was given a great stimulus by the spread of Islam and the settling of Muslims from Arabia and the Persian Gulf along the East African coastline. Muslims intermixed with African communities and helped expand trading links with the Arab world. An Arab traveler described this trade on a visit to the "land of Zanj" (the East African coast) in 916:

The land of Zanj produces wild leopard skins. The people wear them as clothes, or export them to Muslim countries. They are the largest leopard skins and the most beautiful for making saddles. . . . They also export tortoise-shell for making combs, for which ivory is likewise used. . . . There are many wild elephants in this land but no tame ones. The Zanj do not use them for war or anything else, but only hunt and kill them for their ivory. It is from this country that come tusks weighing fifty pounds and more. They usually go to Oman, and from there are sent to China and India.[7]

Arab boats or dhows made the Indian Ocean trade possible. They had the ability to cross the Indian Ocean three times as fast as a camel could cross the Sahara, and they could carry a thousand times as much. The dhows' lateen sails made it possible for sailors to take advantage of seasonal monsoon winds in the Indian Ocean that blow in a southwesterly direction between November and March and northeasterly between April and October. As with the Red Sea trade, the monsoon winds governed the trading calendar. It took about a month for a dhow to make the 2000-mile journey from East Africa to the Persian Gulf, and the traders had to carry out their business according to the favorable winds or they could not transport their goods at all. Along the East African coast itself, however, it was possible to move between the islands at most times of the year.

Swahili civilization flourished between 1000 and 1500, when perhaps as many as 100 city-states, many of them on offshore islands, sprang up along the 1800-mile stretch from Mogadishu to Sofala on the Mozambique coast. Most were short-lived, but some—such as Malindi, Pemba, Pate, Mombasa, Mafia, and Kilwa—thrived for centuries.

Kilwa had the advantage of a good supply of fresh water and several natural harbors that could handle large ships. But it became the wealthiest of the city-states because of its near monopoly over gold exported from the Zimbabwe interior. Kilwa's merchants claimed a sphere of influence over the East African coast from Kilwa southward to Sofala on the Mozambique coast, where they established an outpost to facilitate the gold trade with Africans from the interior.

The Swahili city-states were never part of an empire, nor were they dominated by any one of the city-states. Indeed, they usually competed fiercely with one another. At times one city might exact tribute from its neighbors or a number of states might federate in time of war. However, commercial competition made such cooperation difficult to maintain and curtailed political expansion on the African mainland, where kingdoms like Great Zimbabwe played one coastal city against another.

Within the city-states, political institutions were controlled exclusively by a Muslim commercial elite.

The Arab dhow was the primary transporter of trade goods in the Indian Ocean. The dhow's lateen sails made it possible to navigate the monsoon winds that dictated the direction of trade at different times of the year.

Although they provided the capital, skills, and boats for their piece of the Indian Ocean trade, they always remained in the shadow of the Indian Ocean trading powers. Most of the Swahili commercial elite were descendants of Arabs and Africans. However, they often claimed that they were descendants of Shirazi Persians. This connection is highly unlikely. Because the Persian Empire had once been an Indian Ocean trading power, Swahili elites probably manufactured a connection to the Persians who settled along the coast many centuries earlier.

The governments of the city-states were usually headed by monarchs or sultans, assisted by merchant councils and advised by holy men or royal relatives. Although the sultans were typical Muslim rulers in most respects, the common order of succession was according to matrilineal rules. When a sultan died at Kilwa, Pate, or any of numerous other cities, the throne passed to one of the head queen's brothers.

As the Muslim Middle East became the commercial center of Eurasia, the maritime trade of the Swahili cities figured significantly in the commercial networks of three continents. Gold, ivory, and slaves were the main exports. Other products commonly exported were hides and skins, rhinoceros horns, spices, and grain, in exchange for cloth, beads, porcelain, incense, glass, cloth, and perfume. Kilwa became the major port for gold sent through Egypt to Europe. Iron ore, exported from Malindi and Mombasa, supplied the iron industries of India. Slaves were shipped to the Arabian peninsula and Cambay, the capital of Gujarat, in India. There they served as domestic slaves or, as in southern Iraq, as laborers draining marshes. Mangrove tree poles were exported throughout the southern Persian Gulf as materials for house construction.

In the early 1400s a Chinese fleet under the command of admiral Zheng He visited Swahili towns such as Malindi and Mombasa, bearing porcelain, silks, lacquerware, and fine art objects and exchanging them for ivory, rhinoceros horns, incense, tortoise shell, rare woods, and exotic animals such as ostriches, zebras, and giraffes. Zheng He's ships also took back African envoys, who stayed at the Chinese court for several years.

Swahili civilization was an urban culture that reflected a well-entrenched hierarchy dominated by the commercial elite. Some towns, such as Mombasa and Lamu, were densely settled; in others, settlements were dispersed. The towns were the preserves of the commercial elite, who lived in houses made of wood and coral blocks. Some of the homes were two or three stories high and reflected the wealth, status, and rank of their owners. Most towns also had a central mosque, a Qur'anic school, a marketplace, a palace, and government buildings.

With the exception of the most loyal household slaves, the Swahili traders were the only ones who

In the early 1400s the Chinese commissioned seven expeditions to visit all the lands of the Indian Ocean to promote trade. A Chinese fleet under the command of admiral Zheng He visited some of the Swahili towns and took back several envoys from Malindi who brought along a giraffe as a gift to the Chinese court in 1414. The presentation of this giraffe was memorialized in a tapestry.

lived inside the walled cities. Most slaves slept outside the city in houses with mud walls and palm-matted roofs. They came into the city to work every day. Because the towns were not self-sufficient, they relied on the farmers and fishermen on the mainland for foodstuffs and meat.

Swahili masons and craftsmen were celebrated for building ornate stone and coral mosques and palaces, adorned with gold, ivory, and other wealth from nearly every major port in southern Asia. Perhaps because it borrowed architectural styles from the Middle East, Kilwa impressed the famous Muslim scholar-traveler Ibn Battuta in 1331 as the most beautiful and well-constructed city he had seen anywhere. Archaeological excavations have confirmed this evaluation, revealing the ruins of enormous palaces, great mansions, elaborate mosques, arched walkways, town squares, and public fountains. The Husuni Kubwa palace and trade emporium at Kilwa, built on the edge of an ocean cliff, contained over 100 rooms, as well as an eight-sided bathing pool in one of its many courtyards.

Kingdoms of Central and Southern Africa

By the third century C.E. central and southern Africa had been settled by migrating groups of Bantu farmers who lived in scattered homesteads or small villages and subsisted on cereal crops and animal herds.

Around 1000 C.E. some of these societies began to grow in size and complexity. This was very evident south of the Zambezi River, where states formed with ruling elites that displayed their wealth through their cattle herds. They accumulated cattle through a variety of means—raids, tribute, death dues, court fines, and bridewealth exchanges for marriages. Cattle exchanges through marriages and loans gave ruling families the opportunity to establish broader social and political networks with other powerful families. Cattle herds also financed their participation in regional trading networks and links with the Indian Ocean economy.

A common feature of the ruling elites of these new states was that they built walls, dwellings, palaces, and religious centers made of stone. Throughout present-day eastern Botswana, northern South Africa, eastern Mozambique, and Zimbabwe, archaeologists have identified more than 150 political centers. An early state was Mapungubwe, situated south of the Limpopo River. Mapungubwe's rulers lived in stone residences on a hilltop, while commoners lived in their traditional settlements in the surrounding valley. The elites maintained their privileged status through their control over cattle herds, the trade in such metals as tin, copper, iron, and gold, and the hunting of elephants for ivory. Tin, copper, and iron were traded regionally, but ivory and gold were designated primarily for the expanding trade with the Indian Ocean coast. Mapungubwe peaked during the thirteenth century, but its main settlement had to be abandoned soon thereafter because farmers were not able to sustain production when a climatic changed produced a colder, drier environment.

Mapungubwe's successor was Great Zimbabwe ("houses of stone"), centered on a well-watered plateau north of the Limpopo. Its grandeur as a state is symbolized by its imposing granite structures, left after its rulers were forced to move northward to the

Constructed in the thirteenth century by the Muslim sultans of Kilwa, the Great Mosque was built from coral blocks. In the mosque's center, its arches supported a domed ceiling.

Zambezi. Extending over 60 acres and supporting about 18,000 residents, the complex at Great Zimbabwe contained many structures built over several centuries. At its center was a large complex of stoneworks where the political and religious elite lived. The most impressive structure was the Great Enclosure, which likely served as the royal family's main residence. Over 800 feet in circumference, the Great Enclosure was built without mortar and featured massive freestanding walls 12 feet thick and 20 feet high. Undoubtedly, Great Zimbabwe's rulers intended their monumental architecture to enhance their power and prestige among their subjects.

Zimbabwe's king presided over an elaborate court and administration. His key advisers included the queen mother and a ritual sister, a half-sister who was appointed when a king was installed. She had to give her consent to decisions made by the royal council before they could be enacted, she kept the ritual medicines that protected the well-being of the king, and she had considerable input into the choice of a new king.

Zimbabwe's rulers combined political and sacred power. Great Zimbabwe contained a rainmaking shrine, where its rulers prayed for abundant rainfall. On a nearby hillside was a temple where they prayed and offered sacrifices to the high god Mwari and the ancestors to ensure the fertility of the land and the prosperity of the people. Within the temple were placed stone sculptures of birds with human attributes. The birds played symbolic roles as God's messengers, mediating between God and man and the spirits of royal ancestors.

Great Zimbabwe's political elite based their power on their vast cattle herds as well as the control of regional trade, particularly copper and gold. The principal sources of gold were located on the plateau west of Great Zimbabwe. Women and children were responsible for mining most gold, which they did during the dry season, when they could take time off from their farming responsibilities. They sank narrow shafts as deep as 100 feet, brought the ore to the surface, crushed it, and sifted out the gold in nearby streams. Although some of the gold was fashioned into ornamental bangles and jewelry for Zimbabwe's rulers, most of the gold was transported as a fine powder for the external trade with the coastal Swahili cities, especially Kilwa, whose prosperity depended on its ties to Zimbabwe. Besides gold, ivory and animal skins were traded for glass beads, Indian cloth, ceramic vessels from Persia, and blue-and-white porcelain from China.

Great Zimbabwe's zenith was between 1290 and 1450. A common explanation for its sudden collapse is environmental degradation. The land could no longer support large numbers of people living in a

The Great Enclosure was Great Zimbabwe's most impressive structure and likely served as the royal family's main residence. Over 800 feet in circumference, the Great Enclosure was built without mortar and featured massive, freestanding granite walls 12 feet thick and 20 feet high.

concentrated area. However, this interpretation is not supported by data showing that rainfall actually increased around that time. A more likely explanation for the kingdom's decline is the rise to prominence of two of its former tributary states: Torwa to the northwest and Mutapa to the north.

Oral tradition relates that Mutapa's founder was Nyatsimbe Mutota, who Great Zimbabwe's rulers had sent north to search for an alternative source of salt. He founded the Mutapa kingdom in the well-watered Mazoe valley south of the Zambezi River. By 1500 Mutapa's ruler, the *mwene mutapa* ("conqueror"), and his army held sway over a vast part of the upper Zimbabwe Plateau. The *mwene mutapa* did not adopt the stone building traditions of Great Zimbabwe. Instead, he lived in a palace complex within a wooden palisade. With his family, military, bureaucracy, and representatives of tributary chiefdoms, he ruled over a federation of tributary states through governors that he appointed. They paid tribute in the form of agricultural produce, iron, cattle, and especially gold, which was still the mainstay of the trade with the East African coast.

Another notable kingdom in west central Africa was Kongo, located in a fertile agricultural area near the Atlantic coast at the mouth of the Congo River. It was formed in the fourteenth century when a petty prince named Wene led a migration, married into the local ruling family, and began developing a loose federation of states. Wene took the title of *Manikongo* ("lord of Kongo"). However, as kings of Kongo centered their political rule at their capital, Mbanza Kongo, they developed a centralized state. By the time the Portuguese arrived in the late fifteenth century, Kongo had already developed a sophisticated political system. The king, who had a professional army resident at his capital, appointed officials, usually close relatives, as his provincial administrators. The Kongo kingdom also controlled interregional trade, exchanging its cloth, woven from fibers of the raffia palm, for salt and seashells from neighboring societies.

Conclusion

By 1500 C.E. Africans had successfully adapted to the harsh challenges of Africa's environment by creating a diverse range of communities and states. Critical turning points in the histories of African cultures occurred with the introduction of agriculture, herding, and ironworking. These developments spurred population growth, migrations, craft specialization, trade between communities, and more complex political and economic systems. Most Africans in 1500 still lived in scattered homesteads and small communities

and earned their livelihoods from farming, herding, and hunting. However, because of trading relations with one another and with other continents, Africans began to establish kingdoms and empires in all parts of the continent. Egypt, Kush, Aksum, Ethiopia, Ghana, Mali, Oyo, Benin, and Great Zimbabwe are some of the major civilizations that dominated eras of Africa's history.

While Africans created their own distinct cultures and traditions, they carried on vigorous commercial, technological, and intellectual exchanges with the cultures of the Indian Ocean region, Europe, the Near East, and Asia, largely through Muslim intermediaries. The kingdom of Aksum became a major Red Sea power, serving as a bridge between the Mediterranean and the Indian Ocean. The Swahili city-states on the East African coast and the states of the Zimbabwe Plateau carried on extensive relations with Indian Ocean trading networks. West African savanna kingdoms created the most extensive trading network through their position overseeing trade between North Africa, the savanna, and forest regions to the south.

Although most Africans remained faithful to their traditional religious beliefs and practices, many in certain areas converted to Christianity and Islam. Ethiopia's rulers firmly established Christianity as their kingdom's state religion, and some rulers and traders in the West African savanna, in northeastern Africa, and along the Swahili coast adopted Islam. However, until the eighteenth century Islam remained primarily a religion of court and commerce in sub-Saharan Africa.

Suggestions for Reading

The best detailed coverage of African history can be found in two multivolume series, each containing chapters by leading scholars: *The Cambridge History of Africa* and *The UNESCO General History of Africa.* This chapter has drawn on vols. 1–3 of the former and vols. 1–4 of the latter. Among other general surveys of African history are Robert W. July, *Precolonial Africa: An Economic and Social History* (Scribner, 1975) and *A History of the African People*, 4th ed. (Waveland Press, 1992); Roland Oliver and J. D. Fage, *A Short History of Africa*, 4th ed. (Facts on File, 1989); Philip Curtin et al., eds., *African History: From Earliest Times to Independence*, 2nd ed. (Longman, 1995); Kevin Shillington, *History of Africa* (St. Martin's Press, 1995); Elizabeth Isichei, *A History of African Societies to 1870* (Cambridge University Press, 1997); and Joseph Harris, *Africans and Their History*, 2nd ed. (Penguin, 1998). The best general reference works on early African history are John Middleton, ed., *Encyclopedia of Africa South of the Sahara*, 4 vols. (Scribner, 1997), and Joseph Vogel, *Encyclopedia of Precolonial Africa: Archaeology, History, Languages, Cultures, and Environment* (AltaMira Press, 1997). General works that examine Africa's history with a disciplinary focus are Ralph Austen, *African Economic History: Internal Development and External Dependency* (Heinemann, 1987), and James Newman, *The Peopling* of Africa: A Geographic Interpretation (Yale University Press, 1995). A general introduction to early African urbanization is R. W. Hull, *African Cities and Towns Before the European Conquest* (Norton, 1976).

Studies on African archaeology and the African Iron Age include Thurstan Shaw, *The Archaeology of Africa: Foods, Metals, and Towns* (Routledge, 1993) and *Nigeria: Its Archaeology and Early History* (Thames & Hudson, 1978); J. Desmond Clark, *From Hunters to Farmers: The Causes and Consequences of Food Production in Africa* (University of California Press, 1984); Randi Haaland and Peter Shinnie, *African Iron Working, Ancient and Traditional* (Oxford University Press, 1985); Peter Schmidt, *The Culture and Technology of African Iron Production* (University Press of Florida, 1996) and *Iron Technology in East Africa: Symbolism, Science, and Archaeology* (Indiana University Press, 1997); Roland Anthony Oliver and Brian M. Fagan, *Africa in the Iron Age, c. 500 B.C. to A.D. 1400* (Cambridge University Press, 1975); Roland Anthony Oliver, *The African Experience* (HarperCollins, 1991); David W. Phillipson, *African Archaeology*, 2nd ed. (Cambridge University Press, 1993); Christopher Ehret and Merrick Posnansky, eds., *The Archaeological and Linguistic Reconstruction of African History* (University of California Press, 1982); Graham Connah, *African Civilizations: Precolonial Cities and States in Tropical Africa* (Cambridge University Press, 1987); and Eugenia Herbert, *Iron, Gender, and Power: Rituals of Transformation in African Societies* (Indiana University Press, 1993).

On Nubia and Ethiopia, see William Y. Adams, *Nubia: Corridor to Africa* (Princeton, 1977); Mohammed Hassen, *The Oromo of Ethiopia: A History, 1570–1860* (Red Sea Press, 1994); Steven Kaplan, *The Beta Israel (Falasha) in Ethiopia: From Earliest Times to the Twentieth Century* (New York University Press, 1994); Yuri M. Kobishchanov, *Axum* (Pennsylvania State University Press, 1979); Stuart C. Munro-Hay, *Aksum: An African Civilization of Late Antiquity* (Edinburgh University Press, 1991); Tadesse Tamrat, *Church and State in Ethiopia, 1270–1527* (Oxford University Press, 1972); Richard K. Pankhurst, *A Social History of Ethiopia: The Northern and Central Highlands from Early Medieval Times to the Rise of Emperor Tewodros II* (Red Sea Press, 1992); and Harold Marcus, *A History of Ethiopia* (University of California Press, 1994).

General works on West Africa include A. G. Hopkins, *An Economic History of West Africa* (Longman, 1973), and J. F. Ajayi and Michael Crowder, eds., *History of West Africa*, 3rd ed., Vol. 1 (Longman, 1985). The Sudanic kingdoms of West Africa are treated in Nehemia Levtzion, *Ancient Ghana and Mali* (Methuen, 1973); George Brooks, *Landlords and Strangers: Ecology, Society, and Trade in Western Africa, 1000–1630* (Westview Press, 1993); and E. W. Bovill, *The Golden Trade of the Moors* (Oxford University Press, 1968). The Sundiata epic of the Malian Empire is recorded in D. T. Niane, *Sundiata: An Epic of Old Mali* (Longman, 1995). An excellent study on Muslim scholars in the Sudan is Elias Saad, *Social History of Timbuktu: The Role of Muslim Scholars and Notables, 1400–1900* (Cambridge University Press, 1983). Two important collections of primary documents on West Africa are Nehemia Levtzion, *Medieval West Africa Before 1400: Ghana, Takrur, Gao (Songhay), and Mali as Described by Arab Merchants and Scholars* (Markus Wiener, 1998), and Said Hamdun and Noel Q. King, eds., *Ibn Battuta in Black Africa* (Markus Wiener, 1997).

The East African coast and Swahili city-states are well covered in Christopher Ehret, *An African Classical Age: Eastern and Southern Africa in World History, 1000 B.C. to A.D. 400* (University Press of Virginia, 1998); John Middleton, *The World of the Swahili: An African Mercantile Civilization* (Yale University Press, 1992); Ali Mazrui and I. B. Sharif, *The Swahili: Idiom and Identity of an African People* (Africa World Press, 1994); Derek Nurse and Thomas G. Spear, *The Swahili: Reconstructing*

the History and Language of an African Society, 800–1500 (University of Pennsylvania Press, 1985); Randall Pouwels, *Horn and Crescent: Cultural Change and Traditional Islam on the East African Coast, 800–1900* (Cambridge University Press, 1987); B. A. Ogot and J. A. Kieran, eds., *Zamani: A Survey of East African History*, 2nd ed. (Longman, 1974); G. S. P. Freeman-Grenville, *The East African Coast* (Oxford University Press, 1962); John Sutton, *A Thousand Years of East Africa* (Thames & Hudson, 1990); and H. Neville Chittick, *Kilwa: An Islamic City on the East African Coast* (British Institute in Eastern Africa, 1974).

A record of the earliest written documentation on the Swahili coast is G. W. B. Huntington, ed., *The Periplus of the Erythrean Sea* (Haklyt Society, 1980). Chinese contacts with East Africa are examined in Louise Levathes, *When China Ruled the Seas: The Treasure Fleet of the Dragon Throne, 1405–1433* (Oxford University Press, 1996), and Teobaldi Filesi, *Le Relazioni della Cina con l'Africa nel Nedio-Evo* (Giuffre, 1975).

The best general studies on early central and southern African history are David Birmingham, ed., *History of Central Africa to 1870* (Cambridge University Press, 1981), and Martin Hall, *The Changing Past: Farmers, Kings, and Traders in Southern Africa* (Philip, 1987). The kingdom of Great Zimbabwe is extensively treated in D. N. Beach, *The Shona and Zimbabwe, 900–1850* (Heinemann, 1980); Peter Garlake, *Great Zimbabwe* (Thames & Hudson, 1973); Thomas N. Huffman, *Symbols in Stone: Unravelling the Mystery of Great Zimbabwe* (Witwatersrand University Press, 1987) and *Snakes and Crocodiles: Power and Symbolism in Ancient Zimbabwe* (Witwatersrand University Press, 1996); and Joseph Vogel, *Great Zimbabwe: The Iron Age in South Central Africa* (Garland, 1994). Richard Elphick, *Kraal and Castle: Khoikhoi and the Founding of White South Africa* (Yale University Press, 1977), remains the classic study of Khoikhoi history. Detailed studies of central and eastern African states are Jan Vansina, *Paths in the Rainforest: Toward a History of Political Tradition in Equatorial Africa* (Currey, 1990); Joseph Miller, *Kings and Kinsmen: Early Mbundu States in Angola* (Clarendon Press, 1976); and David Schoenbrun, *A Green Place, a Good Place: Agrarian Change, Gender, and Social Identity in the Great Lakes Region to the 15th Century* (Heinemann, 1998).

Suggestions for Web Browsing

Internet African History Sourcebook
http://www.fordham.edu/halsall/africa/africasbook.html

Extensive on-line source for links about the history of ancient Africa, including the kingdoms of Ghana, Mali, and Songhai.

Art of Benin
http://www.si.edu/organiza/museums/africart/exhibits/beninsp.htm

Site of the Smithsonian Institution's National Museum of African Art displays art objects from the kingdom of Benin before Western dominance.

Great Zimbabwe
http://www.mc.maricopa.edu/academic/cult_sci/anthro/lost_tribes/zimbabwe/intro.html

A 23-slide series, with commentary, that will take you through the ruins of Great Zimbabwe in southern Africa.

Notes

1. Kevin Shillington, *History of Africa* (New York: St. Martin's Press, 1989), p. 10.

2. The latest synthesis of research on Bantu migrations is Jan Vansina, "A Slow Revolution: Farming in Subequatorial Africa," *Azania*, 29–30 (1994–1995), pp. 15–26.

3. Al Omari, quoted in Tadesse Tamrat, "The Horn of Africa: The Solomonids in Ethiopia and the States of the Horn of Africa," in D. T. Niane, ed., *UNESCO General History of Africa: Africa from the Twelfth to the Sixteenth Century* (Berkeley: University of California Press, 1984), p. 435.

4. Joseph Vogel, *Encyclopedia of Precolonial Africa: Archaeology, History, Languages, Cultures, and Environment* (Walnut Creek, CA: AltaMira Press, 1997), p. 490.

5. Ralph Austen, "Slave Trade: Trans-Saharan Trade," in Seymour Drescher and Stanley Engerman, eds., *A Historical Guide to World Slavery* (Oxford: Oxford University Press, 1998), p. 368.

6. Al Omari, quoted in Vogel, *Encyclopedia of Precolonial Africa*, p. 492.

7. Al Masudi, quoted in G. S. P. Freeman-Grenville, *The East African Coast* (Oxford: Oxford University Press, 1962), pp. 15–17.

The Growth and Spread of Asian Culture, 300–1300

Before and After the Mongol Conquests

Chapter Contents

The millennium between 300 and 1300 was a time of preservation, consolidation, and innovation for the ancient Asian civilizations. Some earlier values and institutions were reaffirmed so effectively that characteristic Hindu and Chinese culture patterns have endured until today despite frequent invasions of both homelands. Alongside that cultural continuity, however, emerged new syntheses combining the cultural patterns of the indigenous peoples with those of new waves of invaders. Each civilization produced significant contributions to the world's common culture. India made remarkable advances in mathematics, medicine, chemistry, textile production, and literature, and Buddhism continued its dramatic spread to East and Southeast Asia. China excelled in political organization, scholarship, and the arts, at the same time producing such revolutionary technical inventions as printing, gunpowder, and the mariner's compass. Maritime trade flourished as Arab, Jewish, and Indian traders crisscrossed the Indian Ocean to the west of the subcontinent while Indian and Southeast Asian traders plied the waters to the east as far as China and Japan.

Growth in the old Asian centers led naturally toward outward cultural diffusion and a varied exchange of goods, philosophies, literatures, and fashions with bordering civilizations. In Southeast Asia these arose from increasing contacts with India and China through trade, missionary efforts, colonizing, and conquest. First Korea and then Japan imported cultural bases from China. Similarly,

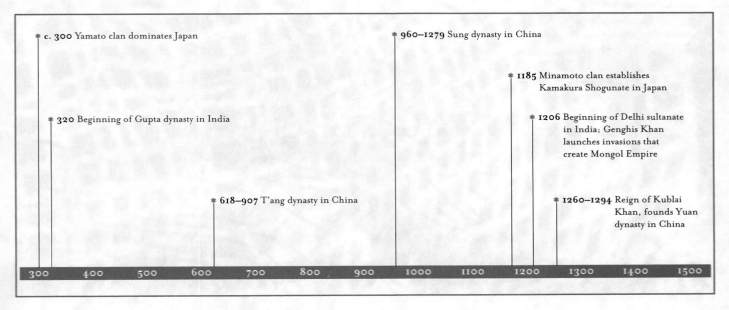

- c. 300 Yamato clan dominates Japan

- 320 Beginning of Gupta dynasty in India

- 618–907 T'ang dynasty in China

- 960–1279 Sung dynasty in China

- 1185 Minamoto clan establishes Kamakura Shogunate in Japan

- 1206 Beginning of Delhi sultanate in India; Genghis Khan launches invasions that create Mongol Empire

- 1260–1294 Reign of Kublai Khan, founds Yuan dynasty in China

300 400 500 600 700 800 900 1000 1100 1200 1300 1400 1500

nomads of central Asia—Turks, Uighurs, Mongols, and numerous other steppe peoples—engaged in a vigorous exchange with China and India (often assimilating the cultural patterns of those civilizations) as merchants, subjects, or conquerors. Their states, culminating in the great Mongol Empire of the thirteenth and fourteenth centuries, facilitated the passing of those influences to the peoples of the Middle East and Europe.

India's Politics and Culture

India's cultural renaissance culminated in the fourth and fifth centuries as the Gupta dynasty emerged and attempted to recapture the territorial and cultural grandeur of the Mauryas. The Gupta era marks the end of what has been termed India's Classical Age. Its monarchs gained control over northern India while fostering traditional religions, Sanskrit literature, and indigenous art. Hindu and Buddhist culture also spread widely throughout Southeast Asia in this period.

The Gupta state began its rise in 320 with the accession to power of Chandra Gupta I (not related to his earlier Mauryan namesake). His son Samudra Gupta (c. 335–375) and grandson Chandra Gupta II (c. 376–414) were successful conquerors, extending the boundaries of an original petty state in Maghada until it included most of northern India, from the Himalayas to the Narmada River and east to west from sea to sea. Within this domain the Gupta monarchs developed a political structure along ancient Mauryan lines, with provincial governors, district officials, state-controlled industries, and an imperial secret service. This centralized system, however, was effective only on royal lands, which were much less extensive than in Mauryan times. With a smaller bureaucracy, the Gupta rulers depended on local authorities and communal institutions, raising revenues primarily through tribute and military forces by feudal levy.

Marriage alliances aided the Guptas' rise to power. Chandra Gupta I married a princess from the powerful Licchavi clan; his coins show the king and his queen, Kumaradevi, on one side and a lion with his queen's clan name on the other. Chandra Gupta II gave his daughter, Prabhavati Gupta, in marriage to

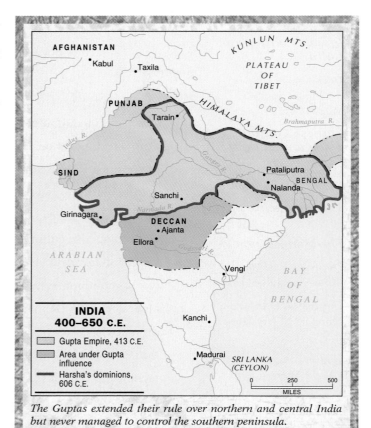

The Guptas extended their rule over northern and central India but never managed to control the southern peninsula.

Gupta India

320	Accession of Chandra Gupta I
c. 335–375	Reign of Samudra Gupta
c. 376–414	Reign of Chandra Gupta II
510	Huns seize northwest India; Gupta Empire collapses

Rudrasena II, king of the powerful Vakataka dynasty in central India. Rudrasena died after a short reign, and his wife then took control of his kingdom for about 20 years as regent for her minor sons. The two kingdoms remained closely tied even after her death.

Peace and stable government under the later Guptas increased agricultural productivity and foreign trade. Flourishing commerce with Rome in the last decades of the fourth century brought a great influx of gold and silver into the Gupta Empire. Indian traders were also active in Southeast Asia, particularly in Burma, Vietnam, and Cambodia, where they contributed to emerging civilizations. India's resulting prosperity was reflected in great public buildings and in the luxuries of the elite, particularly at the Gupta court.

Although the Gupta rulers generally favored Hinduism, they practiced religious pluralism, patronizing and building temples for Hindus, Buddhists, and Jains. The Brahmins provided the Guptas with religious legitimacy, and the Guptas rewarded them with significant grants of land. Hinduism dominated the subcontinent. The Hindu revival of this period brought a great upsurge of devotion to Vishnu and Shiva. This religious fervor was reflected in a series of religious books, the *Puranas,* which emphasized the compassion of the personal gods. The *Puranas* are a collection of myths, philosophical dialogues, ritual prescriptions, and dynastic genealogies; their tales of the gods were popular.

Fa-Hsien: A Chinese Buddhist Monk in Gupta India

Fa-Hsien is an important source on India around 400 C.E. A Buddhist monk, he left China as a pilgrim to India in search of Buddhist texts and was gone for 14 years. When he returned, he translated various Indian works and wrote the account of his travels. Fa-Hsien's story and long arduous journey on foot illustrate both the spread of Buddhism from India to China and the draw that the Indian heartland had on Buddhists abroad. Here he describes Pataliputra (modern Patna), where Ashoka once reigned. The festival illustrates the amalgamation of Buddhist and Hindu ritual and suggests the joyous nature of some urban religious celebrations. Fa-Hsien's account of hospitals gives us some insight into the quality medical care available even to the poor.

By the side of the tower of King Ashoka is built a monastery belonging to the Great Vehicle [Mahayana Buddhism], very imposing and elegant. There is also a temple belonging to the Little Vehicle [Theravada Buddhism]. Together they contain about 600 or 700 priests; their behavior is decorous and orderly. . . . Of all the kingdoms in Mid-India, the towns of this country are especially large. The people are rich and prosperous; they practice virtue and justice. Every year on the eighth day of the second month, there is a procession of images. On this occasion, they construct a four-wheeled [vehicle], and erect upon it a tower of five stages, composed of bamboos lashed together, the whole being supported by a center post resembing a large spear with three points, in height twenty-two feet or more. So it looks like a pagoda. They then cover it with fine white linen, which they afterward paint with gaudy colors. Having made figures of the *devas* [gods], and decorated them with gold, silver, and glass, they place them under canopies of embroidered silk. Then at the four corners [of the car] they construct niches in which they place figures of Buddha in a sitting pos-

ture, with a Bodhisattva [a Buddha in the making] standing in attendance. There are perhaps twenty cars thus prepared and differently decorated. During the day of the procession both priests and laymen assemble in great numbers. There are games and music, whilst they offer flowers and incense. . . . Then all night long they burn lamps, indulge in games and music, and make religious offerings. Such is the custom of all those who assemble on this occasion from the different countries round about. The nobles and householders of this country have founded hospitals within the city, to which the poor of all countries, the destitute, cripples, and the diseased may repair. They receive every kind of requisite help gratuitously. Physicians inspect their diseases, and according to their cases order them food and drink, medicine or decoctions, everything in fact that may contribute to their ease. When cured they depart at their convenience.

From Samuel Beal, ed., *Buddhist Records of the Western World,* translated from the Chinese of Hiuen Tsiang (629) (Delhi: Oriental Books, 1969), pp. lvi–lvii.

Among their legends, for example, is a recounting of the deeds of the goddess Durga and her fight against the buffalo demon. By promoting the devotional Hinduism reflected in these tales, the Gupta monarchs gained great favor among all classes of their subjects.

Much of our knowledge of Gupta society comes from the journal of a Chinese Buddhist monk, Fa-Hsien, who traveled in India for 14 years at the opening of the fifth century. Fa-Hsien was primarily interested in Buddhism in India, but he did occasionally comment on social customs. He reported the people to be happy, relatively free of government oppression, and inclined toward courtesy and charity. He mentions the caste system and its associations with purity and impurity, including "untouchability," the social isolation of a lowest class that is doomed to menial labor.

Gupta Art and Literature

Indian art of the Gupta period depicts a golden age of classical brilliance, combining stability and serenity with an exuberant love of life. The Gupta artistic spirit is well expressed in the 28 monasteries and temples at

Ajanta, hewn out of a solid rock cliff and portraying in their wall frescoes not only the life of Buddha but also life in general: lovers embracing, beds of colorful flowers, musicians, and dancers. These sculptures reveal the beauty of the human form, attesting to the notion of Gupta artists that the divine is not separate from the human, nor the spirit from the body. The various incarnations of Vishnu and the deeds of the goddess Durga were also common subjects of Gupta sculpture.

The Gupta era was also a golden age for literature, written in Sanskrit, the ancient language of the Brahmins. Authors supported by royal patronage poured forth a wealth of sacred, philosophical, and dramatic poetic and prose works, including fables, fairy tales, and adventure stories featuring a wide range of characters—thieves, courtesans, hypocritical monks, and strange beasts. The *Panchatantra* is a manual of political wisdom employing animal tales to advise the king on proper rule. A most renowned literary figure of this era was India's greatest poet and dramatist, Kalidasa, who wrote (apparently) at the court of Chandra Gupta II. His best-known work in the West is *Shakuntala,* a great drama of lovers separated by adversity for many years and then by chance reunited. The play is full of vivid imagery and a loving sympathy for nature.

Gupta Scholarship and Science

The Gupta era brought a great stimulus to learning. Brahmin traditions were revitalized, and Buddhist centers, which had spread after the Mauryan period, were given new support. The foremost Indian university, founded in the fifth century, was at Nalanda. Accomplishments in science were no less remarkable than those in art, literature, scholarship, and philosophy. The most famous Gupta scientist was the astronomer-mathematician Aryabhatta, who lived in the fifth century. He elaborated (in verse) on quadratic equations, solstices, and equinoxes, along with the spherical shape of the earth and its rotation. Other Hindu mathematicians of this period popularized the use of a special sign for zero, passing it on later to the Arabs. Mathematical achievements were matched by those in medicine. Hindu physicians sterilized wounds, prepared for surgery by fumigation, performed cesarean operations, set bones, and were skilled in plastic surgery. They used drugs then unknown in the West, such as chaulmoogra oil for leprosy, a treatment still used in the twentieth century. With these accomplishments in pure science came many effective practical applications by Gupta craftsmen, who made soap, cement, superior dyes, and the finest tempered steel in the world.

New Political Configurations

Gupta hegemony began to collapse in the second half of the fifth century with an invasion of the Huns from the north and a long war for succession. After 497 Guptas ruled only in parts of northern India. In 510 the Huns—who had already successfully invaded Persia and Europe—seized northwestern India, which once again became attached to a central Asian empire. Hun rule did not endure, but it helped prompt the migration of more central Asian tribesmen into India and precipitated a period in which India was generally divided into regional kingdoms rather than more expansive empires like that of the Guptas. The central Asian tribesmen also intermarried with local populations to produce a class of fighting aristocrats known as Rajputs. These fierce warriors carved out kingdoms among the Hindu states of northern India.

In the seventh century the unity of northern India was revived for a short while by Harsha, a strong Hindu leader. In six years he reconquered much of what had been the Gupta Empire, restoring order and partially reviving learning. However, Harsha failed in his bid to conquer the Deccan, and no ruler would again do so until 1206. Harsha left no heir when he died in 647, and regional kingdoms again prevailed.

The period of the regional kingdoms was not a sterile one. In this era the great Hindu philosopher Shankara (c. 788–820) brilliantly argued a nondualist mystical philosophy based on the Upanishads; regional literatures, especially in Tamil in the south, flourished; and Brahmins and Buddhist monks continued to carry their religious and cultural ideas to Southeast Asia and China. Their crucial role in the "Indianization" of Southeast Asia is reflected in the great temples there. It is also reflected in the Chinese sources that note 162 visits of Buddhist monks from the fifth to the eighth centuries.[1]

The Chola kingdom on India's southwestern coast played a significant role in the commercial and cultural exchange with Southeast Asia as well. Chola rulers in the eleventh century exchanged embassies with China, Sumatra, Malaya, and Cambodia; Chola fleets took Sri Lanka (Ceylon) and challenged the power of the Southeast Asian kingdom of Shrivijaya. When a Chola king conquered Bengal, he ordered the defeated princes to carry the holy water of the Ganges River to his new capital to celebrate his victory.

Muslims in India

The prophet Muhammad founded an Arab Muslim state in Arabia in the seventh century; soon the Arab conquerors had defeated the Sassanids in Persia and Muslim armies arrived at the boundaries of the Indian subcontinent. In 712 an Arab force seized Sind, a coastal outpost in northwestern India, an early signal of the Muslim invasions to come 30 years later. Other Muslim states were established across the northern mountains in Persia and central Asia.

In the year 1000 the Muslim sovereign Mahmud of Ghazni launched a series of campaigns into northwestern India. He gained a reputation as a destroyer for his 17 campaigns, over the course of 25 years, that devastated northern India. One notable episode during these campaigns was Mahmud's destruction of Shiva's large temple complex in Gujarat and the slaughter of its defenders who, according to legend, numbered 50,000 men. These campaigns of pillage rather than conquest made Mahmud a name that to the present day evokes powerful emotions among Hindus. Mahmud is also known for the famous scholars at his court, among them Firdawsi, who wrote the great epic Persian poem the *Shahnamah*, and al-Biruni, author of a major history of India. When Mahmud died, it was more than a century before new Muslim armies attacked the subcontinent.

The date 1206 stands out as the next significant marker of Muslim conquest in India. In the same year that the Mongol Genghis Khan mobilized his campaigns of conquest and expansion, the general Qutb ud-Din Aibak seized power as sultan at Delhi. Qutb ud-Din had been a commander in the army of the Afghan ruler Muhammad of Ghur, who seized Delhi from the Rajputs in 1192. Qutb ud-Din founded a new dynasty and was followed on the throne by his son-in-law, Iltutmish,

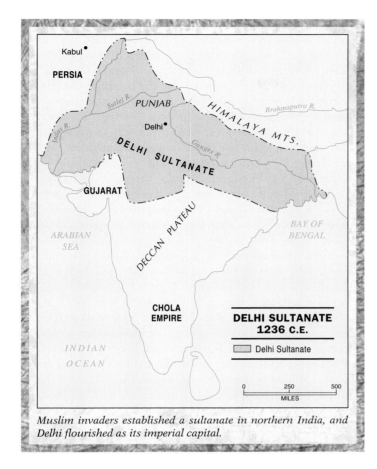

Kabul
PERSIA
Sutlej R.
PUNJAB
HIMALAYA MTS.
Brahmaputra R.
Indus R.
Delhi
Ganges R.
DELHI SULTANATE
GUJARAT
DECCAN PLATEAU
BAY OF BENGAL
ARABIAN SEA
INDIAN OCEAN
CHOLA EMPIRE

DELHI SULTANATE 1236 C.E.
Delhi Sultanate

0   250   500
MILES

Muslim invaders established a sultanate in northern India, and Delhi flourished as its imperial capital.

little power at this time, he was still a source of Islamic legitimacy for South Asian Muslim rulers. Less than 30 years later the Abbasid caliphate would fall prey to the Mongol descendants of Genghis Khan.

At the peak of its power in the thirteenth century, the Delhi Sultanate held not only the north but also part of the Deccan Plateau in the south. When Sultan Ala ud-Din invaded the Deccan, he called himself the "Second Alexander," a title that was emblazoned on his coins. The Delhi Sultanate also managed to ward off the Mongol invaders who seized the Punjab, thus avoiding the fate of Persia and Iraq. Delhi under the sultanate emerged as a great imperial capital. Patrons of the arts, builders of splendid monuments, and proponents of philosophy, the Delhi sultans held an uneasy rule over the majority Hindu populace. By the middle of the fourteenth century, they had lost control of the south (upon the rise of the Vijayangar Empire in 1346) and were hard pressed by various Hindu and Muslim challengers. Although experiencing brief periods of revival, the regime continued to decline internally before it was destroyed by the Turco-Mongol Timur (Tamerlane) in 1398. Timur's army wrought such destruction in Delhi that in his autobiography he denied responsibility and blamed the slaughter on his soldiers.

Muslim rule in India brought some cultural integration as local lords and warriors were incorporated into the new Muslim court. Some Hindus found emotional appeal in the Muslim faith, which had no caste system, or sought to lighten their taxes and qualify for public service by converting to Islam. Others formed new religious groups synthesizing aspects of Hinduism and Islam—for example, Sikhism. Another typical example of cultural integration was the

and by the latter's daughter, who ruled for three years. Iltutmish had himself formally consecrated in 1229 as sultan of Delhi by a representative of the Abbasid sultan in Baghdad. Even though the Abbasid sultan wielded

India is famous for its rock-carved temples. This is the Kailasanatha Temple at Ellora, dedicated to Shiva and dating to approximately 765 C.E.

spread of Urdu, a spoken Indian language incorporating Persian, Arabic, and Turkish words.

Cultural synthesis, however, could not eliminate Hindu-Muslim contention over polytheism, religious images, and closed castes. Many aristocratic Hindu leaders desperately resisted Islam, often suffering cruel persecution. Unlike the Mongol invaders in the Middle East who became Islamized and adopted the high culture of the Persian courts, the Muslim invaders of the subcontinent assimilated only certain aspects of Hindu civilization. Religion and caste remained significant barriers to assimilation, and the Delhi Sultanate remained a Muslim military-administrative class that ruled over a predominantly Hindu, caste-divided population. The same would be true for the Muslim Mughuls who ruled over India in a later age (see Chapter 17).

Chinese Continuity: T'ang and Sung

Like India, China was also divided into north and south and experienced an invasion of conquerors from beyond its northern frontiers toward the year 1300. In contrast with India and medieval Europe, however, China achieved both political and cultural continuity between the sixth and thirteenth centuries. Political unity was attained briefly under the Sui dynasty (589–618), consolidated under the T'ang (618–907), and maintained precariously under the Sung (960–1279). Despite periods of internal disruption, this political system, re-created from Han precedents, survived repeated invasions and civil wars. Its stability resulted from a common written language; an ancient family structure, guided by mature and conservative-minded matriarchs; an enduring Confucian tradition; and a Chinese elite of scholar bureaucrats who shared power while contending for dominance. Their efforts promoted a flowering of Chinese culture during the expansionist T'ang period, when China was the largest state in the world, and during the ensuing economic prosperity of the Sung.

Before the T'ang Dynasty

Following the fall of the Han Empire in 220, China suffered three centuries of disorder and division. Various nomadic peoples, mainly Huns (Hsiung-nu) and Turks (Yueh-chih), pillaged northern China, setting up petty states. These states were administered mostly by Chinese, and the invaders gradually absorbed Chinese culture. Central and southern China escaped these intrusions and enjoyed relative prosperity and population growth, both resulting from an influx of northern émigrés, in addition to increasingly productive rice cultivation. This growing economy supported a series of political regimes at Nanking, all maintaining classical traditions and the idea of a united state ruled by a "son of heaven." Such a ruler was responsible for maintaining the harmony between humans and nature; he was empowered by his knowledge and practice of right conduct.

During turbulent times in the fourth century, the old Confucian ideal of a balanced social order was challenged by the rapid spread of Buddhism in China. It provided comfort in times of crisis. Its promise of salvation (particularly for common people), its special appeal to the natural compassion of women, its offer of monastic security to men in troubled times, and its long incubation within Chinese culture all ensured its popularity. Although challenged by native Taoism (which adopted many of its ideas), scorned by some Confucian intellectuals, and periodically persecuted by rulers jealous of its strength, Buddhism ultimately won adherents among its critics, especially among the monarchs of the north, including the Sui emperors. They patronized Buddhism by building splendid temples and generously endowing monasteries. From the fourth to the ninth centuries Buddhism interacted with Chinese religious and philosophical traditions to create a complex new synthesis of ideas and art.

The two Sui monarchs, tempered in the rough frontier wars of the north, reconquered all of China, ending nearly four centuries of political fragmentation. They established an imperial military force and a land-based militia, centralized the administration, and revived a civil service recruited through an examination system. They also started building a waterway, which would later become the famous Grand Canal, to link the rice-growing Yangtze basin with northern China. However, their unpredictable cruelty, oppression, and conscription of labor for the

T'ang and Sung China

618–907	T'ang dynasty
c. 692–712	Reign of Empress Wu
713–756	Cultural flowering under Emperor Hsuan-tsung
960–1279	Sung dynasty
1005, 1042	Sung sign treaties of subordination with Khitan Mongols
1115	Sung court flees south to escape invading Jürchen; Chin dynasty established in north

canal led to a great rebellion that ended the dynasty; nevertheless, the Sui emperors deserve much credit for later T'ang successes.

Political Developments Under the Rising T'ang Dynasty, 618–756

During the early T'ang period to 756, China attained a new pinnacle of glory. The first three emperors subjugated Turkish central Asia, made Tibet a dependency, and conquered Annam (northern Vietnam). Along with territorial expansion came great economic, social, and cultural advances. Ironically, these gains resulted largely from the emperors' commitment to Confucianism, with its deference to civilian over military values.

This era of growth and grandeur was marked by the extraordinary reign of the able Empress Wu, a concubine of the second and third emperors, who controlled the government for 20 years after the latter's death, torturing and executing her political opponents but also firmly establishing the T'ang dynasty. She greatly weakened the old aristocracy by favoring Buddhism and strengthening the examination system for recruiting civil servants. Moreover, she decisively defeated the Koreans, making Korea a loyal vassal state. Largely because she was a woman and a usurper, she found little favor with some Chinese historians and politicians, who emphasized her vices, particularly her many favorites and lovers. Her overthrow in 712 ended an era of contention and ushered in a new age of cultural development in the long reign of Emperor Hsuan-tsung (713–756).

T'ang rulers perfected a highly centralized government, utilizing a complex bureaucracy organized in specialized councils, boards, and ministries, all directly responsible to the emperor. Local government functioned under 15 provincial governors, aided by subordinates down to the district level. Military commanders supervised tribute collections in semi-autonomous conquered territories. Officeholders throughout the empire were, by the eighth century, usually degree-holders from government schools and universities who had qualified by passing the regularly scheduled examinations. These scholar-bureaucrats were steeped in Confucian conservatism but were more efficient than the remaining minority of aristocratic hereditary officials. One notable T'ang institution was a nationalized land register, designed to check the growth of large estates, guarantee land to peasants, and relate their land tenure to both their taxes and their militia service. Until well into the

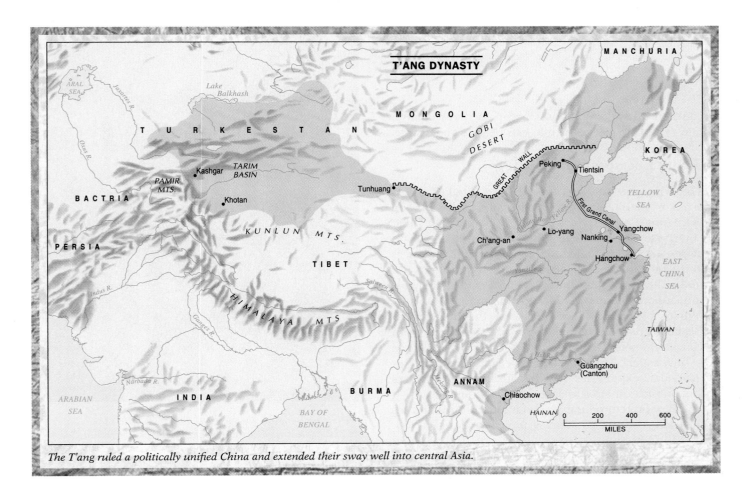

The T'ang ruled a politically unified China and extended their sway well into central Asia.

Empress Wu, the only woman to rule China in name as well as in fact. A royal concubine to two emperors, she usurped the imperial throne and assumed the special title of "Holy Mother Divine Imperial One." As a young girl, Wu studied music and the Chinese classics; as empress, she sponsored the writing of biographies of famous women.

eighth century, when abuses began to show, the system worked to merge the interests of state and people.

T'ang Economy and Society

The T'ang economy was carefully regulated. The government maintained monopolies on salt, liquor, and tea, using licensing in an attempt to prohibit illicit enterprises. In conducting its business, it issued receipts, which circulated among merchants and were antecedents of the paper money that came into use under the Sung. The state also built roads and canals to facilitate commerce. Perhaps the most technically remarkable of these projects was the magnificent Grand Canal, stretching some 650 miles between Hangchow and Tientsin, a great waterway for trade and transport. Other typical government enterprises included post houses and restaurants for travelers and public granaries to ensure against famine.

Economic productivity, both agricultural and industrial, rose steadily during the early T'ang period. The introduction of tea and wet rice from Annam turned the Yangtze area into a vast irrigated food bank and the economic base for T'ang power. More

food and rising population brought increasing manufactures. Chinese techniques in the newly discovered craft of papermaking, along with iron casting, porcelain production, and silk processing, improved tremendously and spread west to the Middle East.

Foreign trade and influence increased significantly under the T'ang emperors in a development that would continue through the Sung era. Chinese control in central Asia facilitated trade along the old overland silk route; but as porcelain became the most profitable export and could not be easily transported by caravan, it swelled the volume of sea trade through Southeast Asia. Most of this trade left from southern ports, particularly from Guangzhou (Canton), where more than 100,000 aliens—Indians, Persians, Arabs, and Malays—handled the goods. Foreign merchants were equally visible at Ch'ang-an, the T'ang capital and eastern terminus of the silk route.

Although largely state-controlled and aristocratic, T'ang society was particularly responsive to new foreign stimuli, which it swiftly absorbed. A strongly pervasive Buddhism, a rising population, and steady urbanization fostered this cross-cultural exchange. Many city populations exceeded 100,000, and four cities had

During the T'ang era, foreign trade and travel affected the character of Chinese art, while technological advances in ceramics led to the development of fine porcelain. Chinese porcelain then became a highly prized trade good. This glazed earthenware figure depicts a Bactrian camel from west central Asia.

more than a million people; the capital at Ch'ang-an was the largest city in the world. Merchants clearly benefited from this exchange, but despite their wealth, merchants were still considered socially inferior. They often used their wealth to educate their sons for the civil service examination, thus promoting a rising class of scholar-bureaucrats. The latter, as they acquired land, gained status and power at the expense of the old aristocratic families. Conditions among artisans and the expanding mass of peasants improved somewhat, but life for them remained hard and precarious.

In the early T'ang era, elite women had been considered sufficiently equal socially to play polo with men. By the eighth century, however, T'ang legal codes had imposed severe punishments for wifely disobedience or infidelity to husbands. New laws also limited women's rights to divorce, inheritance of property, and remarriage as widows. Women were, however, still active in the arts and literature. Although some wielded influence and power at royal courts, many were confined to harems, a practice without precedent in Chinese traditions. This subordinate position was only partly balanced by the continued high status and authority of older women within the families.

T'ang Literature, Scholarship, and the Arts

A fresh flowering of literature occurred during the early T'ang period. It followed naturally from a dynamic society, but it was also greatly furthered by the development of papermaking and the invention, in about 600, of block printing, which soon spread to Korea and Japan. Movable type, which would later revolutionize Europe, was little used in East Asia during this period because Chinese writing was done in characters representing whole words. Printing helped meet a growing demand for the religious and educational materials generated by Buddhism and the examination system.

T'ang scholarship is best remembered for historical writing. Chinese of this period firmly believed that lessons from the past could be guides for the future. As an early T'ang emperor noted, "By using a mirror of brass, you may . . . adjust your cap; by using antiquity as a mirror you may . . . foresee the rise and fall of empires."[2] In addition to universal works, the period produced many studies of particular subjects. History itself came under investigation, as illustrated by *The Understanding of History*, a work that stressed the need for analysis and evaluation in the narration of events.

Writers produced works of all types, but poetry was the accepted medium, composed and repeated by emperors, scholars, singing courtesans, and common people in the marketplaces. T'ang poetry was marked by ironic humor, deep sensitivity to human feeling, concern for social justice, and a near-worshipful love of nature. Three of the most famous

among some 3000 recognized poets of the era were Po Chu, Tu Fu, and Li Po. The last, perhaps the greatest of them all, was an admitted lover of pleasure, but he could pinpoint life's mysteries, as in the following poetic expression of a statement by the Taoist philosopher Chuang Tzu (fl. c. 369–286 B.C.E.):

> *Chuang Tzu in a dream*
> *became a butterfly,*
> *And the butterfly became*
> *Chuang Tzu at waking.*
> *Which was the real—the*
> *butterfly or the man?*[3]

The T'ang literary revival was paralleled by movements in painting and sculpture. The plastic arts, dealing with both religious and secular subjects, became a major medium for the first time in China. Small tomb statues depicted both Chinese and foreign life with realism, verve, and diversity. These figures—warriors, servants, and traders—were buried with the dead and believed to serve them in the afterlife. Religious statuary, even in Buddhist shrines, showed strong humanistic emphases, often juxtaposed with the naive sublimity of Buddhas carved in the Gandaran (Greek Hellenistic) style of northwestern India. Similar themes were developed in T'ang painting, but the traditional preoccupation with nature prevailed in both the northern and southern landscape schools. The most famous T'ang painter was Wu Tao-tzu, whose landscapes and religious scenes were produced at the court of the emperor Ming Huang in the early eighth century.

In the T'ang dynasty, earthenware models of people and objects, like this one of traders with a bullock and cart, were buried with the dead. Such objects were believed to be useful in the afterlife.
Bullock and cart, T'ang Dynasty, 7th–8th century. Pottery with green and brown glazes, H. 16" × L. 20 1/4". Seattle Art Museum, Eugene Fuller Memorial Collection, 37.17. Photo: Paul Macapia.

Fashions in female beauty change from place to place and over time. Around the sixth century, slim elegant earthenware figures of Chinese females showed the influence of dress styles from central Asia and Persia. By the early-seventh-century T'ang dynasty, foreign fashions were all the rage among the upper classes. In the eighth century, however, the slim female and tight wraps gave way to voluptuous female figures (again depicted in earthenware images) in loose gowns. These figures are thought to be modeled after Yang Guifei, the hefty favorite concubine of T'ang emperor Hsuan-tsung (713–756). Yang Guifei is represented in various artworks from the T'ang court. T'ang China is not the only place and era in world history where the ample woman, rather than her gaunt sister, represented health, prosperity, and sexuality—the height of feminine beauty.

T'ang Decline

After the middle of the eighth century, T'ang China began an era of decline. The Uighur Turks gained control of Mongolia. Meanwhile, as the fiscal system weakened under attack from various vested interests, military governors took over control of outlying provinces. One of them, a former court favorite named An Lu-shan, marched on Ch'ang-an in 755; he was a protégé of the emperor's favorite concubine, Yang Guifei. The aged emperor Hsuantsung, while fleeing for his life from the capital, was forced by his troops to approve the execution of Yang Guifei, who had dominated his court. According to legend, he died of sorrow less than a month later.

An Lu-shan's rebellion was put down after seven years, but the ensuing disruption was so extensive that the late T'ang emperors never recovered their former power. Following a breakdown of the old land registration system, revenues declined and peasants rebelled against rising taxes. Falling revenues brought deterioration of the state education establishment and a corresponding drop in administrative efficiency. The government further alienated some groups by seizing Buddhist property and persecuting all "foreign" religions. At the capital, weak emperors lost their authority to eunuchs who had originally been only harem servants. Finally, in 907, a military commander killed all the eunuchs and deposed the last T'ang emperor.

Political Developments During the Sung Era, 960–1279

Even as the T'ang dynasty ended, it prepared a way for the Sung. South China, under T'ang rule, had developed an expanding economy. The T'ang collapse permitted a commercial expansion that in turn generated much of the Sung's remarkable cultural achievement, but not before China endured a period of disruptions. For a half century after the fall of the T'ang dynasty, China experienced political division, at times approaching anarchy. During this period of five dynasties in the north and ten kingdoms in the south, attacks by "barbarian" raiders from the north alternated with internal conflicts among contending warlords. One military leader of the northern Chou staged a palace coup and founded the Sung line in 960. He and his successor reunited the country, although certain frontier provinces and the tributary areas held by T'ang rulers were never regained.

Although they were northern conquerors, the early Sung emperors soon abandoned their military aggressiveness in order to win economic support in the south. Most of the remaining aristocratic officials were replaced by military officers or their sons, as soon as they could qualify for office in a newly regenerated educational and examination system. Within a half century these former soldiers had been absorbed into a Confucian scholar-bureaucracy that became an even more powerful elite than had prevailed under the T'ang. In the process, state policy became concentrated on civilian concerns rather than foreign affairs.

Lacking an effective military and plagued with internal bureaucratic dissension, Sung ministers faced continuous threats along their northern and western frontiers. Their weak defenses provoked raids and invasions from neighboring kingdoms, notably that of the Khitan Mongols (907–1127). When their military efforts failed, the Sung ministers turned to diplomacy, ultimately agreeing, in 1005 and 1042, to pay tribute in silk and silver for peace and protection while acknowledging Sung subordination to the Khitan ruler. The process was repeated a century later when a nomadic people from Manchuria, the Jürchen (1115–1234), destroyed the Khitan regime, established the Chin ("golden") dynasty, and invaded the northern Sung territories, taking the capital at K'ai-feng. The Sung court fled in panic to Nanking and later set up a new capital at Hangchow, thus bringing to an inglorious end the Sung effort to govern a united China. After a decade of indecisive war, a treaty in 1141 stipulated new tribute levies of silk and silver on the Sung. It also prescribed that the Chin monarch be addressed as "lord" and the Sung emperor as "servant" in all official communications. The subordination of the Sung was thus formalized in language and in goods.

Along with such troubles, the Sung rulers faced an ambiguous situation at home. The country experienced unprecedented economic and cultural ad-

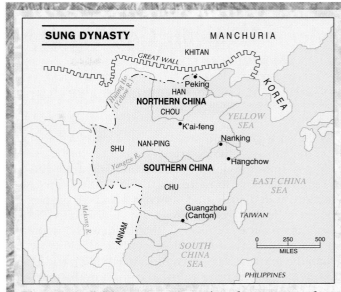

The Great Wall did not protect Sung China from invasions from the north. The Khitan Mongols from central Asia and the Jürchen nomads from Manchuria in turn attacked and subordinated the Sung.

vances, particularly after being reduced to only southern China, and turned increasingly toward oceanborne commerce. But this dearly purchased prosperity brought many internal problems. Spreading affluence encouraged selfish individualism and weakened loyalties among all classes. Paying tribute and suffering tax evasion by the wealthy, the state experienced mounting budgetary deficits, while rising taxes produced peasant unrest. In the late eleventh century, even before the country was divided, the emperor called on an eminent statesman, Wang An-shih, to meet this crisis. Wang sponsored a program that enforced state-controlled interest rates on agricultural loans, fixed commodity prices, provided unemployment benefits, established old-age pensions, and reformed the examination system by stressing practical rather than literary knowledge. Although these measures brought some improvements, they evoked fanatical opposition from scholars, bureaucrats, and moneylenders. In the next generation most of the reforms were rescinded.

The humiliating treaty with the Chin in 1141 was followed by a period of steeper political decline, particularly under the "dim-witted" emperor Ning-tsing (1194–1224) and his lecherous successor Li-tsung (1224–1264). Intrigues of court women paralyzed the central government; high taxes, official injustice, and criminal disorder destroyed public morale; and Mongol armies, moving against the Chin, foreshadowed an inevitable and fast-approaching disaster.

Memorial on the Crop Lands Measure

Wang An-shih wrote this proposal in 1069. It was presented by a government commission to Emperor Shen-tsung, who applied it first in a few provinces. Later it was extended to other areas. The proposal aims in part to relieve farmers from having to take loans at high rates and having to pay loans back in times of bad harvests. Note how the proposal points out abuses and tries to redress them; it ends by invoking the memory of past kings who ruled benevolently, thus urging the current monarch to do the same.

The cash and grain stored in the Ever-Normal and the Liberal-Charity granaries of the various circuits, counting roughly in strings of cash and bushels of grain, amount to more than 15,000,000. Their collection and distribution are not handled properly, however, and therefore we do not derive full benefit from them. Now we propose that the present amount of grain in storage should be sold at a price lower than the market price when the latter is high; and that when the market price is low, the grain in the market should be purchased at a rate higher than the market price. We also propose that our reserves be made interchangeable with the proceeds of the land tax and the cash and grain held by the Fiscal Intendants, so that conversion of cash and grain may be permitted whenever convenient.

With the cash at hand, we propose to follow the example set by the crop loan system in Shensi province. Farmers desirous of borrowing money before the harvest should be granted loans, to be repaid at the same time as they pay their tax, half with the summer payment and half with the autumn payment. They are free to repay either in kind or in cash, should they prefer to do so if the price of grain is high at the time of repayment. In the event disaster strikes, they should be allowed to defer payment until the date when the next harvest payment would be due. In this way not only would we be prepared to meet the distress of famine, but, since the people would receive loans from the government, it would be impossible for the monopolistic houses to exploit the gap between harvests by charging interest at twice the normal rate.

Under the system of Ever-Normal and Liberal-Charity granaries, it has been the practice to keep grain in storage and sell it only when the harvest is poor and the price of grain is high. Those who benefit from this are only the idle people in the cities.

Now we propose to survey the situation in regard to surpluses and shortages in each circuit as a whole, to sell when grain is dear and buy when it is cheap, in order to increase the accumulation in government storage and to stabilize the prices of commodities. This will make it possible for the farmers to go ahead with their work at the proper season, while the monopolists will no longer be able to take advantage of their temporary stringency. All this is proposed in the interests of the people, and the government derives no advantage therefrom. Moreover, it accords with the idea of the ancient kings who bestowed blessings upon all impartially and promoted whatever was of benefit by way of encouraging the cultivation and accumulation of grain.

From *Sources of Chinese Tradition*, comp. W. Theodore de Bary, Wing-tsi Chan, and Burton Watson (New York: Columbia University Press, 1963), pp. 475–476.

Sung Economic and Social Conditions

Economic efficiency was certainly Sung China's redeeming strength. Although the government maintained some monopolies and taxed trade moderately, it built great water-control projects, aided intensive agriculture, and otherwise loosened control over individual enterprise. Consequently, rice production doubled within a century after 1050, and industry grew rapidly, pouring out the finest silk, lacquer wares, and porcelain for home and foreign markets. Sung economic advances were furthered by such technical innovations as water clocks, paddleboats, seagoing junks, the stern post rudder, and the mariner's compass. It was also in this era that the Chinese developed the first explosive projectile weapons. The resulting commercial expansion prompted banks to depend on paper currency and specialized commercial instruments. Trade with the outside world, formerly dominated by foreigners, was taken over by the Chinese, who established trading colonies throughout East Asia.

The Sung economic revolution exerted tremendous foreign influence abroad. Paper money, dating from the eleventh century in the south, was soon copied in the Khitan state and issued by the Chin government in 1153; its use then spread steadily in all directions. Other Sung economic innovations appeared quickly along the Asiatic coast from Japan and Korea to the East Indies, where Chinese merchants were immigrant culture carriers. Sung technology also spread to India, the Middle East, and

This scroll painting is attributed to the Sung dynasty emperor-artist Hui-tsung but may have been produced by an artist in his court. It portrays richly dressed palace women beating and preparing silk. An ineffectual ruler, Hui-tsung is best remembered as a painter, calligrapher, and patron of the arts.

Court Ladies Preparing Newly Woven Silk, Emperor Huizong (attributed to), r. 1101–1125. Chinese; Northern Song Dynasty, early 12th century. Handscroll; ink, color and gold on silk. 27.0 × 145.3 cm. Museum of Fine Arts, Boston, Chinese and Japanese Special Fund.

even Europe. From China, Europe acquired metal horseshoes, the padded horse collar, and the wheelbarrow. Chinese mapping skills, along with the compass and the stern post ship rudder, helped prepare the way for Europe's age of expansion. Later, gunpowder and movable type, both pioneered in Sung China, arrived in Europe via Asian intermediaries.

Profound and rapid change brought many tensions to Sung society. Some arose from urban expansion in a population that swelled from 60 to 115 million, a percentage increase of more than twice the world average. Crowded living and rising economic competition undermined the family, weakened old values, and lessened loyalty to the state. Before the Mongol threat in the thirteenth century, people in the south tended to feel safe from nomad attack, but they were increasingly concerned about their personal freedom, social advancement, psychological satisfaction, and amusement. Social changes during the Sung era, however, did little to affect the class structure. Merchants, no matter how wealthy, could not replace the dominant scholar-bureaucrats, who continued to hold power and land.

Although lower-class women gained the freedom to conduct some businesses and court women continued to exercise power indirectly, Sung affluence and competition helped erode Buddhist compassion and revive the Confucian doctrine of rigid male dominance. Particularly among the elite classes, these changes brought new restrictions for most women. Usually betrothed by their fathers, they lived in near-servile status within their husbands' families, producing children and providing social decoration. The binding of little girls' feet, as preparation for this sterile adult life, became common under the Sung, as

did female infanticide, restriction on remarriage of widows, and harsh legal penalties, including death, for violating the accepted code of prescribed wifely conduct.

Sung Philosophy, Literature, and Art

The rapidly changing Sung society was reflected in a personalizing of philosophy, literature, and art. Writers explored the lives of individual subjects. Artists, while remaining interested in nature, depicted its beauty in more varied styles, all involving greater attention to objectivity and employing a lighter touch than was typical of the T'ang era. Serious thinkers turned increasingly toward humane as opposed to political morality, despite the lingering Confucian influence.

A prevailing social insecurity and the political debate over Wang An-shih's humanitarian reforms led to major philosophical dissension. Most reformers claimed that their proposals were based on Confucian principles, but the reforms were nevertheless strongly opposed by the majority of Confucian scholars, who were part of the established bureaucracy. Buddhist and Taoist spokesmen generally opposed the government, increasing the conflict. Thus the fragile compromise between Buddhism and Confucianism achieved during the T'ang period was placed under severe strain. Ultimately, these problems were resolved by a new compromise known as Neo-Confucianism, which was to become the intellectual foundation for Chinese thought until the twentieth century.

Chu Hsi (1130–1200), the greatest of the Neo-Confucian synthesizers, was a brilliant scholar and

A painting from the Sung dynasty showing the poet Li Po in repose. Li Po's poetry is renowned for its exquisite imagery, rich allusions, and beautiful cadence.

respected commentator on the Confucian classics. His teaching sought to reconcile the mystical popular faiths of Buddhism and Taoism with Confucian practicality. Like his near-contemporary in Europe, St. Thomas Aquinas, Chu Hsi synthesized faith and reason; but unlike Aquinas, Chu's highest priority was disciplined reason. He believed that people are naturally neither good nor bad but are inclined either way by experience and education. The universe, according to Chu, is a self-generating and self-regulating order to which humans may adjust rationally. Faith and custom, however, are necessary supports for reason and proper training.

Chu Hsi contended that self-cultivation required the extension of knowledge, best achieved by the "investigation of things." As a consequence, Neo-Confucianism was accompanied by significant advances in the experimental and applied sciences. Chinese doctors, during the period, introduced inoculation against smallpox. Their education and hospital facilities far surpassed anything in the West. In addition, there were notable achievements in astronomy,

chemistry, zoology, botany, and cartography. Sung algebra was also the most advanced in the world.

Sung aesthetic expression was more secular and less introspective than that during the earlier era of Buddhist influence. This outlook encouraged versatility; as during the later European Renaissance, the universal man—public servant, scholar, poet, or painter—was the ideal. The most famous female Chinese poet, Li Ch'ing-chao (b. 1181), whose work was enthusiastically promoted by her scholar husband, wrote her uniquely personalized verse in the southern Sung period. Another well-known poet of nature and gardens was the traveling scholar-bureaucrat and reporter Fan Changda (1126–1193). Historical and philosophical works reflected the main literary interests of the time, but the traditional love of nature was still displayed in landscape painting, which reached a peak under the Sung. Artists gave more attention to detail and were therefore more precisely naturalistic than T'ang painters, although the latter were often more imaginative.

The Emergence of Japan

The rise of Japan after the sixth century was part of a much larger process in which a number of new fringe cultures developed rapidly in the shadows of the old major civilizations. In Europe, Africa, southeastern and central Asia, Korea, and Japan, these civilizations

Ma Yüan, Bare Willows and Distant Mountains. Ma Yüan was one of the two leading painters of the southern Sung dynasty, the other was Hsia Kuei. Their style of landscape painting, known as the Ma-Hsia school, followed a prescribed formula: a foreground, a middle ground, and a far ground, each separated by mist, which gave the paintings a light, ethereal quality. The delicate tranquillity of this small fan painting is disturbed only by the red seals placed there by a Ming collector.

Ma Yuan, Chinese, active 1190–1235; Southern Song Dynasty, *Bare Willows and Distant Mountains.* Round fan mounted as album leaf; ink and light color on silk, 23.8 × 24.2 cm. Museum of Fine Arts, Boston. Special Chinese and Japanese Fund.

Japan

were able to appropriate the cultural values and commodities of the more highly developed civilizations and integrate them with their own cultural patterns. In its early evolution, for example, Japan borrowed much from China, but this cultural raw material was mixed and reworked into a new Japanese pattern.

Geographical, Ethnic, and Historical Backgrounds

Much that is distinctive in Japanese culture has resulted from geographical conditioning, which provided harsh challenges but maximum national secu-

rity. The inland sea surrounded by the islands of Kyushu, Shikoku, and Honshu, with their lush and beautiful sheltered plains, was the center of Japanese civilization until the twelfth century. Yet even this area, along with the other 3000 islands of the archipelago, has frequently experienced earthquakes and typhoons. Location was the most important early factor in Japan's evolution; approximately 200 miles of water separate the highly populated islands from the mainland. Isolated as they were during their early history, the Japanese were secure enough to experiment with new ways while retaining a deep attachment to their land and its traditional culture.

Ethnically, the Japanese are of mixed origins, a result of many prehistoric migrations from the mainland, by way of Korea and Southeast Asia, through the island chain to the south. The resulting common ethnic community was predominantly Mongoloid, though darker than Asian mainland types. The language was derived from the basic Altaic family of northern Asia, which also produced Mongol and Korean variations. As the Japanese population expanded and moved north, after the third century C.E., it began exterminating and absorbing the Ainu, a people of less developed culture, who had first occupied the area. This process has continued into the modern era.

In ancient times numerous small warring states, each ruled by a hereditary chieftain who claimed

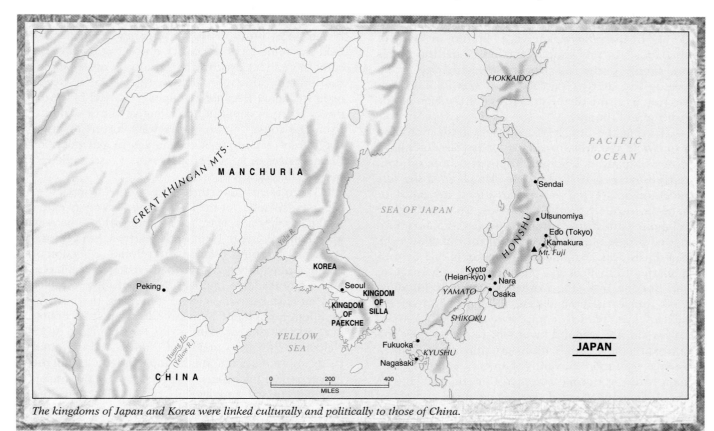

The kingdoms of Japan and Korea were linked culturally and politically to those of China.

descent from a tribal deity, occupied the mountainous Japanese islands. According to Japanese folklore, one of these chieftains named Jimmu ("Divine Warrior"), a descendant of the sun goddess, began the current line of Japanese emperors in 660 B.C.E. Current scholarship places the date later, after migrants from the southern Korean state of Paekche began conquering western Kyushu in the third century C.E. One of their leaders, a fighting queen called Jingo, began a process of unification, with diplomatic and military support from Paekche. During this "tomb period" of war and confusion, which lasted through the fourth century, the Yamato clan emerged as the ruling power in Kyushu, then advanced its conquests east and north, ultimately attacking the Ainu in Honshu.

Early Japanese society resembled others in transition from nomadism to a settled way of life. Dependent on peasant agriculture and centered in villages, it was organized in clans on a kinship basis. Years of war and conquest, however, divided the clans along class lines; members of the top clans enjoyed special privileges, wielded political power, and collected taxes. These nobles constituted a military aristocracy, famous for its archery, iron swordplay, horsemanship, and a code stressing courage, discipline, honor, and pride. Despite this military emphasis, early Japanese society was largely matriarchal, as evidenced by the raising of children in the wives' families, the relative social equality of women, their frequent queenly roles, and the prevalence of female deities in the religion known as Shinto, or "Way of the Gods." In this simple worship of natural forces and family spirits, war leaders served as priests and priestesses; later, as Yamato power grew, Shinto concentrated on the divine ancestress of the clan as the protector of the state.

During the first few centuries of the Common Era, while the Yamato clan extended its domain in central Japan, its chieftain imposed tribute on conquered native clan leaders. He also claimed the title of emperor, forcing vassals to attend his court or send hostages from their families. Continued close relations with Korea through the sixth century promoted progress and awareness of the outside world. Buddhism was introduced into Japan in 552 by missionaries from Paekche. They brought an image of the Buddha from the Korean king, some Buddhist texts, and a recommendation of the new faith as "excellent" but "hard to comprehend." At first Yamato rulers did not respond favorably, but soon they embraced the new faith, with its accompanying Chinese values, even more fervently than contemporary German tribes in Europe accepted Christianity. Thus as the sixth century ended, Japan had about completed its period of early transition and was ready to assume its role as a civilized Asian state.

The Taika Reforms

The first long step in this direction came in 645, when the emperor's government imposed a sweeping program of change, embodied in legal edicts known as the Taika reforms. The new policy was a direct result of rising interest in Korean and Chinese culture, which began after 552 with migrating Korean Buddhists. The Korean influx was markedly increased by refugees after Paekche was absorbed by the neighboring kingdom of Silla in 663. Because Silla had been an ally of China for years, the Japanese feared an attack from the victors in Korea and saw a need to strengthen their defenses. These concerns, along with the expanding Korean influence, generated interest in reforms to protect the country.

The new program was revealed in 645 as the Yamato regime deliberately established a centralized absolutism modeled on T'ang China. A group of young Japanese, including eight Paekchean scholars recently returned from China, seized power to proclaim a new order, hailing the Yamato ruler as *Tenno*, or "Heavenly Emperor." The resulting Taika ("Great Change") reforms asserted the absolute authority of the monarch at the expense of the former clan chieftains. The reformers also established a centralized bureaucracy, a legal code, a tightly controlled provincial system, a standing army, and a land tax similar to that of the T'ang.

From the beginning, differences between Japanese and Chinese societies required drastic adjustments. Most positions in the Japanese bureaucracy, held by members of the old clan nobility, quickly became hereditary. Recruitment through an examination system, after the Chinese model, never developed in Japan. Because the newly asserted power of direct taxation could not be effective at any distance from the court, the emperors were forced to grant tax-exempt estates to some nobles in payment for their services or support. Such estates also tended to become hereditary.

The reforms nevertheless had a great impact on Japanese society, not the least being the construction of Japan's first city, Nara, as a capital where the new ways could flourish. Built in the early eighth century, Nara was carefully planned as a miniature version of Ch'ang-an, with broad streets, imposing new palaces, and many Buddhist edifices. Some of these temples and monasteries still survive as among the best remaining examples of T'ang architectural style. Scholars, priests, and artisans from the mainland were welcomed at Nara. Carriers of Chinese culture found ready apprentices among the Japanese, including the first Japanese historians, who recorded, in Confucian contexts, myths and legends of the past that supported the emperor's right to his throne as a descendant of the sun goddess.

The Great Buddha at Nara, Japan. This 1200-year-old bronze image is Japan's largest Buddha. Its face is approximately 16 feet long. Such Buddhas are dramatic evidence of Buddhism's successful spread into East Asia.

A New Japanese Order: The Heian Period, 794–1185

A re-created Japanese cultural and political system, part traditional, part Chinese, part imperial, and primarily feudal, came into being during the Heian period. In 794 a Confucian-trained emperor built a new capital at Heian-kyo (now called Kyoto and modeled, like Nara, on Ch'ang-an) to free himself from the growing political power of the Buddhist clergy; here the imperial court remained for over a thousand years, until 1868. During the next three and a half centuries, "peace and tranquillity" (a literal translation of *Heian-kyo*) generally characterized Japanese life. The era of Chinese-inspired reforms was over. Imperial authority weakened, and a court aristocracy flourished without much political power. What was left of central government came under the domination of the Fujiwara family, and local lords in the provinces became virtually independent.

By the tenth century the Fujiwara family was accepted as the source of hereditary regents, who ruled the country for figurehead emperors, a system continued, in various forms, to the present. Fujiwara Michinaga, who held dominion over the court from 995 to 1027, was the brother of two empresses and the father of four, the uncle of two emperors, the grandfather of two more, and the great-grandfather of another. Controlled by such a web of family connections and influence, the Heian court functioned in accordance with its own stately rhythms. The sacred emperor performed his ceremonial duties, some Shinto and some Buddhist. Fujiwara women, as imperial consorts, produced future emperors. Monarchs were pressured to retire to Buddhist monasteries when their male heirs, usually as little boys, were old enough to perform the prescribed rituals. As maternal uncles or grandfathers of the child-sovereigns, Fujiwara regents managed affairs until the emperors matured and abdicated in turn.

While the Fujiwara, the puppet emperors, and effete court nobles played their formal roles at Heian-kyo, political power was shifting toward the provinces, where local lords were becoming independent governors and military commanders. Some of the strongest and most adventurous lords organized campaigns against the Ainu, seizing and colonizing territories with their followers. A network of feudal relationships, linking land grants with pledges of personal loyalty and service, developed among these provincial nobles and their subordinates, often completely outside imperial authority. The *bushi* (warrior) lords and their mounted *samurai* retainers generated a primitive value system, the Code of *Bushido*, which stressed courage, endurance, discipline, and loyalty unto death. The long-range effect of the Bushido tradition among Japanese men was recognized by many American soldiers in World War II.

Culture of the Heian Period

The court at Heian-kyo produced an artificial culture, largely imported from China. Behind this facade of Chinese traditions and aristocratic pretensions, however, the Japanese by the tenth century had developed a cultural perspective quite distinct from China's. Although also nature lovers, the Japanese were much less scholarly than the Chinese and more moved by intuitive preferences for balance, restraint, delicate precision, and economy. Indeed, "cultivation of the little" has been identified as a characteristic Japanese culture trait, which may have resulted from people living closely together on small secluded islands.

Perhaps the most obvious signs of Chinese influence were the temples. Generally, they followed the characteristic T'ang style and were adorned lavishly with both imported and Japanese statues of the Buddha, executed in bronze or wood and showing the typical benign expression of the Gandaran school. Surviving temples include the Horyuji at Nara and the Phoenix Hall of the Byodoin at Uji, not far from Kyoto. The latter features perfect symmetry, extravagant decoration, and striking contrasts of white and bright red. Although symbolizing the Buddhist paradise, it also expresses the Japanese penchant for harmony between a subject and its natural setting. The hall stands beside a pond, its reflection creating an inverse picture of the building in the water.

Painting developed from Chinese models but, like architecture, soon showed a distinctive Japanese

A fine example of architecture during the Heian period in Japan is Phoenix Hall, near the modern city of Kyoto. The building shows the influence of Chinese style.

flavor. Buddhist themes predominated at first, but later artists chose subjects drawn from everyday life. The new Japanese style, known as *Yamato-e*, was noted for its use of bright colors and for filling in finely sketched outlines. It was often used in decorating sliding doors and screens, but it was most commonly seen in picture scroll illustrations for literary works.

Heian literature, while reflecting clearly the aristocratic life of its setting, was even more independent of Chinese influence than the other arts. Most Japanese intellectuals were men, trained to write in Chinese characters that could not easily express Japanese syllables or thought. Upper-class Japanese women were not as well educated in Chinese and therefore wrote in a phonetic script, expressing Japanese sensitivities in poems, diaries, and novels. These works contained analyses of personal feeling that had no precedents in Chinese literature. The finest example is undoubtedly *The Tale of Genji*, a long novel by Lady Murasaki (c. 978–1031), who depicted her narrow court life with great psychological profundity and aesthetic appreciation for human emotion. As Lady Murasaki explained in the words of her hero, Genji, an author does not write only to tell a story but also to express an "emotion so passionate that he can no longer keep it shut up in his heart" or "let it pass into oblivion."[4]

Well before Lady Murasaki, in the early eighth century, the countryside beyond Heian-kyo had begun producing its own literature. The *Manyoshu*, a collection of some 4000 poems, reflects a fresh outpouring of the native Japanese spirit in treating the old religion, the brevity of life, love of nature, and appreciation of friends. These short poems have never been surpassed in equating natural phenomena and human emotion, clinching each point in typical Japanese fashion with a twist of thought at the end of a set syllabic sequence.

The Kamakura Shogunate

Cultural development continued past the thirteenth century in directions set during the Heian era, but the Fujiwara regency disintegrated much sooner as the result of warfare among the noble clans. In 1185, after a long struggle still celebrated in Japanese historical fiction, movies, and television, a clique dominated by the Minamoto clan emerged victorious. Its leader, an outstanding soldier-statesman named Yoritomo, forced

A portrait of Lady Murasaki, courtier and author of the romantic novel The Tale of Genji, *the great classic of Japanese literature.*

the emperor to grant him the title of *shogun* ("supreme commander") and established a capital at Kamakura. Subsequent shoguns paid utmost respect to the emperors and governed at a discreet distance from the imperial court at Heian-kyo. Nevertheless, the shoguns, not the emperors, were the real rulers of Japan.

The Kamakura Shogunate was a superfeudal order, designed to control an earlier one created by the Fuji-wara court. It employed constables and stewards in every province but still relied on a complex web of personal obligations among local aristocrats and their common adherence to the Code of Bushido. The prevailing values were extended to women, who were now expected to bear hardships with Spartan endurance, to fight and, if necessary, to die beside their husbands. Their lives became much harder, but they could hold

A thirteenth-century wooden statue of Minamoto Yoritomo, Japan's first shogun.

The artistic style of the Kamakura period in Japan emphasized strength and realism, as is evident in this battle scene. The scroll is from a series illustrating the Heiji Monogatari, *an epic narrative describing the rise and fall of the Taira clan, rivals of the Minamoto, the eventual victors and founders of the Kamakura Shogunate. The* Heiji Monogatari *chronicles events from the winter of 1159–1160 when the Taira temporarily defeated the Minamoto.*

Battle Scene, Kamakura period, 14th century. Section of handscroll mounted as a hanging scroll; ink, color, and touches of gold paint on paper, H. 14" × W. 17 1/4". Seattle Art Museum, Eugene Fuller Memorial Collection, 48.173. Photo: Paul Macapia.

the rights of a vassal and inherit property under the code. Kamakura noblewomen were often successful administrators. One of the ablest was Masako, Yorimoto's widow, also known as the "nun-shogun," who became the power behind the next ruler after her husband died.

The Mongol Impact

Debate continues over what sparked the Mongol invasions: population pressure, military capability, or the inspiration of an ambitious warlord. Regardless of cause, the impulse of the Mongols altered the course of history for much of the world. In the second half of the thirteenth century, a militaristic and well-organized Mongol horde moved out of central Asia to attack China, India, the Middle East, and Europe. The Mongols, horse- and sheep-raising nomads and formidable mounted warriors, spread terror among their enemies and conquered cities and trade routes on the way to establishing a world empire. Beginning with their great conqueror, Genghis Khan

(1162–1227), they claimed that they were destined by "heaven" to subdue all peoples. The greatest of all the khans repeated this injunction as an order to his successors. They responded using their unprecedented organizational skills to launch large-scale military operations throughout Eurasia. They seized Persia, toppled the Islamic Abbasid caliphate in Baghdad, established their rule in Russia and China, and sacked the imperial city of Delhi in India.

In China and the Middle East, the invaders were assimilated into the well-established cultures they conquered. In the subcontinent the invaders were ultimately turned back. And in Russia they established *khanates* (territories ruled by khans) that would endure down to the early modern era. The Mongols have often been represented as destroyers par excellence, sacking cities, disrupting trade, and building towers of the heads of their conquered foes. But holding sway in old and new imperial cities in Eurasia, the Mongols also fostered trade and diplomatic activity, patronized the arts, promoted religious tolerance, and provided security and postal service on the

The Mongols

1162–1227	Genghis Khan establishes Mongol Empire in central Asia
1229–1241	Reign of Ögedei; Mongols take northern China and Russia
1258	Mongol Hülegü takes Baghdad, ends Abbasid caliphate
1260–1294	Rule of Great Khan Kublai, who establishes Yuan dynasty in China
c. 1275	Marco Polo arrives at Kublai's court

roads of a series of interlinked kingdoms extending from China to Europe.

Nomads of Central Asia

The Mongols were part of an old and developing nomadic tradition on the steppes of central Asia. Prior to their conquests, they had ranged widely there, pitching their black felt tents, pasturing their animals, and fighting the elements much like other peoples who had terrorized settled Eurasian populations since the fourth century B.C.E. Their chiefs contended to be the "first among equals," their decisions were made by councils of warriors, and their women enjoyed a high degree of freedom, respect, and influence. It was a proud tradition and one that Genghis

Khan ordered maintained, a charge honored in Mongol law into the fourteenth century.

Mongol society on the steppes fostered a mixture of values, combining primitive superstitions and the fierce ruthlessness of fighting men with a crude democratic equality. The ruling khans held almost unlimited authority, but criminal penalties were enforced equally regardless of one's status. Polygamy was practiced among the warriors, but not all marriages were polygamous, and marital fidelity was enforced equally for men and women. Wives sometimes rode and fought beside their husbands; in a harsh environment where raiding and warfare were common, women as well as men had sometimes to defend the hearth and livestock. But usually Mongol women, as in most traditional societies, confined their activities to domestic affairs. In addition to caring for children, they milked the mares and made all clothing. They were also responsible for many tasks required by their nomadic life, such as breaking camp, loading the ox wagons, and driving animals on the march. There was a gendered division of labor, but within its context women were honored and afforded a rough approximation of social equality.

As was true of their central Asian predecessors, the Mongols held military advantages in their superior cavalry tactics and mobility. Once the conquests began, their disadvantages were that their numbers were relatively few and that they had to depend on the bureaucratic skills of the conquered peoples to run their empire. This situation changed steadily as civilization spread on the steppes of central Asia after the sixth century. Over time the Mongol conquerors were sedentarized and acquired the languages, religions,

Two views of Mongols as seen by their contemporaries. Left is a Persian miniature showing Mongols preparing food at their tents. Right is a Chinese painting of a mounted Mongol archer.

cultural patterns, and administrative skills of the civilizations they conquered.

An earlier precedent for invasions out of central Asia came from the Turkic peoples, who had figured in Eurasian history for a thousand years before the emergence of the Mongols. Originating in the Altai Mountains, near the Orkhon River north of Tibet, they had begun attacking northwestern China in the third century C.E. and continued to be mentioned in Chinese annals as the Yueh-chih, a branch of the Hsuing-nu (Hun) frontier barbarians. As some Turks began living in cities after 500, they were noted for their skills as ironworkers. According to the Chinese, in the sixth century the Turks produced the first written language among the peoples of central Asia; the oldest surviving Turkish records date from 200 years later, by which time the Turks had established their first steppe empire.

Between the sixth and eighth centuries, Turkic and Chinese regimes competed for control of the steppes. With Chinese support, the first Turkish Empire emerged in 552 and extended its dominion over much of central Asia. Internal dissension caused it to split briefly into eastern and western khanates, followed by submission of the eastern khanate to China and ultimately conquest under the early T'ang emperors. Later, as the T'ang regime weakened, a revived Turkish Empire dominated the steppes (684–734), only to succumb again to internal weaknesses. Although maintaining many old tribal institutions, these states had central bureaucracies and appointed provincial officials, as did many petty Turkic monarchies in border areas.

During and after their imperial experiments, the Turks absorbed and transmitted much of the culture from their more advanced neighbors. Trade, religion, and warfare facilitated the process. Eastern Turks borrowed early from China, adopting Buddhism and converting their western kinsmen in far distant Ferghana. After the eighth century, when the Abbasid caliphate brought Islam to the steppes, Turkic invaders launched conquests in the Middle East and India. There were several waves of migration and conquest, lasting into the fifteenth century, out of central Asia and into the settled territories of Eurasia. Such incursions most often brought short-term disaster to occupied regions, but they effected a great synthesis of peoples and cultures and ultimately led to the establishment of Turkic regimes from India to the Middle East (see Chapter 17).

For more than five centuries before the Mongol conquests, this process had been growing in intensity. Westward and to the north of the Chinese frontiers, a series of large states, partially urbanized but still containing nomadic or seminomadic populations, rose and fell. Among them were the Uighur Empire of the ninth century and the Tangut state. Both of these regimes prospered by providing protection and transport for the overland trade with China, which continued to grow. For many peoples of central Asia—Turks, Uighurs, Tanguts, Tibetans, Mongols, and a host of

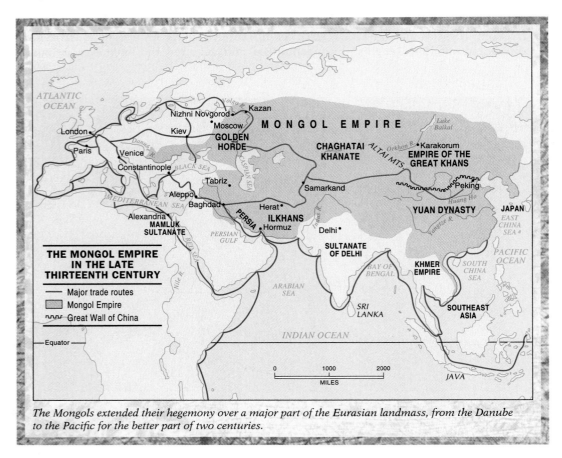

The Mongols extended their hegemony over a major part of the Eurasian landmass, from the Danube to the Pacific for the better part of two centuries.

others—trade, especially the silk trade, was one of many stimuli that turned their attention toward the outside world in the thirteenth century.

Formation of the Mongol Empire

At the opening of the thirteenth century, the Mongols began their whirlwind campaign of conquests and empire building. Within less than a century they had subdued most populations from the Pacific to the Danube, terrorized the rest, and gained luxuries beyond their imaginings. The Mongols also established what has been called the *Pax Mongolica*, which permitted more trade and travel across Eurasia than the world would see again until the seventeenth century. This was the largest empire ever known, comparable in geographical area only to the twentieth-century Soviet Union.

Like all large empires in an era of primitive transportation and communications, however, when it extended far beyond its central administrative centers it began to weaken even as it was being formed and extended. Like the Roman, Mauryan, and Abbasid Empires, the Mongol Empire required the delegation of authority, shared power, and reliance on provincial governors with considerable autonomy to keep it intact. It is also the case, as demonstrated by the reign of Aurangzeb in India, that empires are difficult to hold together once they expand past the distance that a ruler's army can march in a single campaign season. Thus empires like the Mongol are exceptional and notable for the fact that they did not collapse quickly.

Mongol successes, against such great odds, owed much to the guiding genius who launched his people into history. The son of a minor Mongol chief, he was born around 1162 and named Temüjin, or "Man of Iron." When Temüjin's father was killed by enemies, the young warrior was forced into a lonely exile on the steppe, where he nursed his ambitions though barely managing to survive. Using cunning, courage, brutality, and patience through subsequent years, he gathered followers, persevering through tribal wars and forming a new confederacy. Ultimately, a convocation of all the tribes in 1206 recognized him as Genghis Khan, "Oceanic Ruler" of the Mongols.

During the first stage of empire building, to 1241, the Mongols concentrated on the steppe and its less developed border areas. Genghis subordinated the Uighur and Tangut, conquered the Chin capital in northern China, seized Turkestan and Afghanistan, and invaded Persia. After his death in 1227, the campaigns halted and the Mongol forces reassembled in Mongolia to elect Genghis's designated successor, his son Ögedei (1229–1241). Under the new khan the Mongols seized northern China, occupied Russia, and invaded eastern Europe. When Ögedei died, the succession to the khanate was contested. During that time his widow ruled as regent; again in 1248 there was a period of female rule after Güyük Khan died.

In their second phase of conquest the Mongols extended their domain into every civilized area of Eurasia, but as the empire grew larger, its unity became increasingly harder to maintain. Between 1251 and 1259, during the reign of the Grand Khan Möngke, a grandson of Genghis Khan, Mongol armies conquered eastern Tibet (1252) and Korea (1258) while the horde led by Möngke's brother, Hülegü, toppled the Abbasid caliphate, absorbing every subsidiary state in Persia, Palestine, and Syria. Unlike the Seljuk Turks before them, who had also conquered Baghdad but retained the Abbasid caliph to legitimize their rule, the Mongols killed the caliph in 1258, thus effectively ending the classical era of Islamic rule. Hülegü's campaign reflected the newly cosmopolitan nature of the Mongol army; it included a contingent of Chinese catapult operators. Hülegü also had Chinese physicians at his court.

The end of Möngke's reign marked a climax in Mongol expansion. In 1260 the Mongol tide was stopped by the Mamluk army in Syria. This defeat was followed by bloody contention among rival Mongol khans. Kublai Khan (1260–1294) emerged as dominant, but after 1264 the empire broke up into four parts under only nominal central administration: China under Kublai, where he established the Yuan dynasty; the Chaghatai khanate in western Turkestan; the Golden Horde in Russia and the western steppe area; and Hülegü's line, the Ilkhans, in Persia and Iraq. Some Mongol advances occurred when Kublai, another grandson of Temüjin, completed the conquest of southern China and major areas of Southeast Asia in the 1270s and 1280s, but attempted naval attacks against Japan (1281) and Java (1293) were complete failures.

Because they were so few in number, the Mongols often relied on terror to control conquered peoples, particularly during the early conquests. One of Genghis Khan's "old guard" is supposed to have suggested that all of northern China be depopulated and the land used for pasturage. The Mongols were especially noted for abuses by their official envoys, traveling with rapacious entourages through subdued territories. Mongol commanders also regularly imposed mass murder, torture, and resettlement on resisting populations. In Baghdad, for example, Hülegü, Möngke's younger brother, was said to have executed hundreds of thousands of men, women, and children, sparing only some skilled craftsmen and Christian victims of the Muslims, whom he hoped to recruit as allies. The accompanying destruction of the irrigation system almost ruined Mesopotamian agriculture. Such ruthless policies were modified somewhat by Möngke, who issued reforms aimed at lessening Mongol excesses and restoring economic productivity. Yet even under more benign Mongol rule, the population in Kublai's China dropped, according to some figures, from 100 million to less than 70 million.

A Mamluk Officer in Hülegü's Camp

After the Mongols seized the Abbasid capital in Baghdad, the khan, Hülegü, marched on Syria and Egypt. The Muslim Mamluk regime based in Cairo managed to stop the troops at the battle of Ayn Jalut, but the Mongol advance terrified populace and palace alike. In these scenes, al-Sarim, an officer of the Mamluk king, visits the enemy camp while it is laying seige to Aleppo and describes the khan. In effect, al-Sarim became a member of the Mongol's court, but he retained his Mamluk loyalties. Note the roles that honor and magnanimity play in these encounters and the deference granted to the khan's wife. Mongol women often held positions of great influence and sometimes ruled as regents for their minor sons.

When he sent for me and I appeared before him, I saw before me a king of majestic demeanor, high distinction, and great dignity, of short stature, with a very flat nose, a broad face, a loud voice, and compassionate eyes. The ladies sat at his side with the lady Doquz Khatun sitting at his left. . . .

Hülegü asks al-Sarim to bring his Mamluk lord, al-Malik al-Ashraf, to see him, and al-Sarim does so. The Mamluk chief stands terrified before the Mongol khan.

Doquz Khatun looked at al-Malik al-Ashraf and then looked toward Hülegü and said, "This is a fine young man and the knight of the Muslims. That is how kings should be." Then Hülegü looked back at her smiling and said, "Yet we are the kings before whom these kings stand on foot, humbled and in fear of our power." While all this was happening, al-Malik al-Ashraf stood in front of Hülegü, not knowing what fate would do with him. Then Hülegü raised his head and said, "Ashraf, choose what gift you will." And al-Malik al-Ashraf kissed the ground three times. Al-Sarim said: "Ask him to give you the tower of the Citadel [of Aleppo] in which are your mother, and two sisters, your daughters, the wives of the kings, and the daughters and wives of al-Malik al-

Nasir. If you do not ask for this tower now, on this very night the Mongols will capture the Citadel of Aleppo and the womenfolk of the Muslim kings will become slave-girls of this lady Doquz Khatun." Al-Malik al-Ashraf asked, "Will he not kill me?" I answered, "The Mongols do not kill those who are with them as guests."

So al-Malik asked Hülegü for the tower.

This angered Hülegü, who looked downward and said, "Ask for something else." But al-Malik al-Ashraf remained silent. Then Doquz Khatun looked at King Hülegü and said to him, "Are you not ashamed? A man like this king asks you for that tower and you refuse it to him. By God, if he had asked me for Aleppo, I would not have refused it for he is the knight of the Muslims." Hülegü said, "But I only refused it to him for your sake, so that the daughters and wives of the kings may be your slaves." Then she said, "I declare them free before Almighty God and for the sake of Malik al-Ashraf." Thereupon Hülegü granted al-Malik al-Ashraf what he asked, and al-Malik al-Ashraf kissed Hülegü's hand three times.

From Bernard Lewis, ed. and trans., *Islam*, Vol. 1 (Harper & Row, 1974), pp. 89–96 passim.

The Mongol Imperial Structure

Although they were three generations beyond nomadism, Mongol rulers of the mid-thirteenth century were forced to learn quickly how to organize and operate the largest imperial state that had ever existed. Its ethnic diversity was demonstrated at Möngke's court, where official communications had to be prepared in many languages, including Persian, Uighur, Chinese, Tibetan, Arabic, and Tangut. For this complex imperial structure, the methods of the steppes were obviously no longer effective and had to be integrated with those of more experienced conquered bureaucrats.

The ultimate base of authority in the sprawling Mongol territories was military power. Its nucleus was a cavalry force of potentially 130,000 Mongols. For campaigns, the Mongol horsemen were augmented by larger forces, including infantry and siege troops, recruited from the native peoples. Many came as part of the tribute payments from submitting monarchs. Like other conquerors, the Mongols incorporated local war-

riors and governors into their military and administrative systems as long as these men were willing to submit to Mongol rule. Mongol persuasion and diplomacy were effective enough to draw large contingents, who performed well under precise Mongol discipline and organization and shared in the booty of further conquests. Thus the Mongols who conquered northern China in 1241 used more than 97,000 Chinese conscripts, and Hülegü's host before Baghdad numbered 300,000 soldiers. These numbers, of course, are taken from contemporary sources and cannot necessarily be taken literally. Estimates of the size of armies (even today) are often exaggerated to instill fear or inspire awe.

Central administration and internal stability reached a developmental climax in the notable reforms of Möngke's reign. The original empire, divided among descendants of Temüjin's four sons, with one recognized as supreme, was pulled closer together under Möngke's regime. Although he conducted a cruel purge of suspected opponents, Möngke revised the law code of Genghis Khan to accommodate native cultural differences and meet practical needs. He minted coins, issued paper currency, collected taxes in money, and perfected a census system as a basis for taxes and military service. His decrees lessened abuses in the famous Mongol courier service and the thousands of post stations that now radiated in all directions from the capital at Karakorum. To support military operations, his state industries mined ores and produced arms. Other measures regularized trade tolls, improved roads, and provided for the safety of travelers, especially merchants. These reforms encouraged support from subject peoples, many of whom were now employed in the khan's service.

Despite the complex Mongol regimes in Mongolia, Russia, the Middle East, and China, much government within the empire continued to be conducted by vassal monarchs, such as those in Bulgaria or Siam. These subordinate rulers were required to proclaim their submission publicly, leave hostages with the khans, pay annual tribute, and provide troops for military campaigns. A Mongol agent, assigned to the court of each dependent monarch and supported by an occupying military force, approved all policies before they were implemented. In return, tributary rulers who served the khans loyally were guaranteed political security, honored publicly, and rewarded with lavish gifts.

China Under the Mongols

During the reign of Kublai as Grand Khan (1260–1294), China gained new significance in the Mongol system. Although Kublai successfully maintained his titular authority over the subkhanates, he moved his capital from Karakorum to Peking; proclaimed himself the founder of a new Chinese dynasty, the Yuan; and turned attention primarily to his Chinese territories. This new emphasis on the eastern end of the empire contributed directly to the decentralization of Mongol power after Kublai's succession.

For much of our knowledge about China in this era, we are indebted to the Venetian traveler Marco Polo. As a youth he had accompanied his father and uncle, two Venetian merchants who journeyed eastward to Kublai's court, arriving there about 1275. Polo served the khan about 17 years as a trusted administrator before returning home. His fabulous story, dictated to a fellow prisoner of war in Genoa, reported the wondrous world of Cathay (China)—its canals, granaries, social services, technology, and such customs (strange to much of Europe) as regular bathing. His detailed descriptions of the wealth of the khan's court are awe-inspiring. It is no wonder that Polo's contemporaries considered him a braggart and a colossal liar. Polo's account, like many histories, is an interesting mix of fact and fantasy based on impressionistic observations and

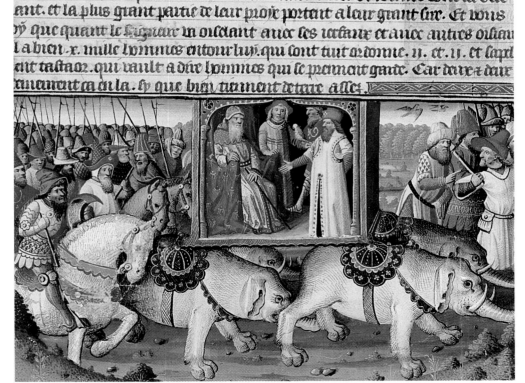

A manuscript illumination from Marco Polo's journal depicts the Great Khan riding in a palanquin (an enclosed litter) borne by elephants. Kublai used this mode of travel because he was afflicted with gout. The artist seems not to have been very familiar with elephants, since these look rather like a cross between a boar and a dog.

Marco Polo on Mongol Military Prowess

One of the most famous of world travelers, the Venetian Marco Polo here describes the battle order and provisions of the Mongol army under Kublai Khan. Of course, there is always a fine line between myth and reality in such accounts, and we cannot take literally Marco Polo's account of ten-day rides sustained by the blood of a warrior's mount. Like other observers, however, Polo was impressed with the stamina of the Mongol warriors and astounded at their horsemanship. He calls the Mongol troops "Tartars."

You see, when a Tartar prince goes forth to war, he takes with him, say, one hundred thousand horses. Well, he appoints an officer to every ten men, one to every hundred, one to every thousand, and one to every ten thousand, so that his own orders have to be given to ten persons only, and each of these ten persons has to pass the orders only to another ten, and so on; no one having to give orders to more than ten. And every one in turn is responsible only to the officer immediately over him; and the discipline and order that comes of this method is marvelous, for they are a people very obedient to their chiefs. Further, they call the corps of one hundred thousand men a *Tuc;* that of ten thousand they call a *Toman;* the thousand they call *Miny;* the hundred *Guz;* the ten *On.* And when the army is on the march they have always two hundred horsemen, very well mounted, who are sent a distance of two marches in advance to reconnoitre, and these always keep ahead. They have a similar party detached in the rear, and on either flank, so that there is a good lookout on all sides against a surprise. When they are going on a distant expedition they take no gear with them except two leather bottles for milk, a little earthenware pot to cook their meat in, and a little tent to shelter them from rain. And in case of great urgency they will ride ten days on end without lighting a fire or taking a meal. On such an occasion they will sustain themselves on the blood of their horses, opening a vein and letting the blood jet into their mouths, drinking till they have had enough, and then staunching it.

They also have milk dried into a kind of paste to carry with them; and when they need food they put this in water, and beat it up till it dissolves, and then drink it. It is prepared in this way: they boil the milk, and when the rich part floats on the top they skim it into another vessel, and of that they make butter; for the milk will not become solid till this is removed.

Then they put the milk in the sun to dry. And when they go on an expedition, every man takes some ten pounds of this dried milk with him. And of a morning he will take a half pound of it and put it in his leather bottle, with as much water as he pleases. So, as he rides along, the milk paste and the water in the bottle get well churned together into a kind of pap, and that makes his dinner.

When they come to an engagement with the enemy, they will gain the victory in this fashion. They never let themselves get into a regular medley, but keep perpetually riding round and shooting into the enemy. And as they do not count it any shame to run away in battle, they will sometimes pretend to do so, and in running away they turn in the saddle and shoot hard and strong at the foe, and in this way make great havoc. Their horses are trained so perfectly that they will double hither and thither, just like a dog, in a way that is quite astonishing. Thus they fight to as good purpose in running away as if they stood and faced the enemy, because of the vast volleys of arrows that they shoot in this way, turning round upon their pursuers, who are fancying that they have won the battle. But when the Tartars see that they have killed and wounded a good many horses and men, they wheel round boldly, and return to the charge in perfect order and with loud cries: and in a very short time the enemy are routed. In truth they are stout and valiant soldiers, and inured to war. And you perceive that it is just when the enemy sees them run, and imagines that he has gained the battle, that he has in reality lost it; for the Tartars wheel round in a moment when they judge the right time has come. And after this fashion they have won many a fight.

From *The Travels of Marco Polo* (New York: Grosset & Dunlap, 1931), pp. 79–81.

probably prompted by the desire to entertain as well as inform a specific audience, but his descriptions, particularly of trade goods, are meticulous.

Yuan China strongly resembled the picture presented under earlier dynasties, with some exceptions. The country was governed mainly by foreigners: Mongols at the top, other peoples of central Asia on the next rung, northern Chinese in lower positions, and southern Chinese almost completely excluded from of-

fice. Kublai retained the traditional ministries and local governmental structure. Generally, Mongol law prevailed, but the conquerors were often influenced by Chinese legal precedents, as in the acceptance of brutal punishments for loose or unfaithful women. Most religions were tolerated unless they violated Mongol laws. According to Polo, the state insured against famine, kept order, and provided care for the sick, the aged, and the orphaned. To the awed Venetian, the

Yuan state appeared fabulously wealthy, as indicated by the khan's 12,000 personal retainers, bedecked in silks, furs, fine leathers, and sparkling jewels.[5]

In its cultural preferences, the Yuan court reverted to Chinese traditions. At first, Taoism and Confucianism were subordinated to Buddhism, but both revived during Kublai's reign. Chinese drama remained popular, influenced somewhat by the dance of central Asia. Interest in drama encouraged the development of classical Chinese opera, a combination of singing, dancing, and acting, which reached maturity in the Yuan period. Some of the most influential Chinese painters were also producing at this time, and the novel emerged as a reflection of Chinese concerns. An example is *Romance of the Three Kingdoms*, a long and rambling tale set in late Han times but written in the fourteenth century.

Pax Mongolica: Relinking East and West

During the century of the Mongol Peace, when much of Eurasia was unified to some degree and pacified by Mongol armies, East and West were in closer communication than ever before, even in Han and Roman times. Hosts of missionaries, traders, and adventurers continued to journey to and from Asia, Africa, and Europe, taking advantage of the security provided by the Pax Mongolica and hoping to benefit from the prosperity and patronage of the Mongol courts. These travelers describe the opulence of the Mongol courts, especially the gold brocade used to make court garments and to line the insides of the spectacular Mongol reception tents, some of which could hold over a thousand men.

Even before the Polos, Christian missionaries had proceeded eastward, encouraged by hopes of converting the Mongols and, more important, gaining allies against the Muslims. John of Plano Carpini, dispatched by Pope Innocent IV, visited the Great Khan in 1246 but failed to convert the ruler or enlist him as a papal vassal. In fact, the khan sent him home with a letter demanding that Europe's monarchs submit to him and that the pope attend the khan's court to pay homage. Later, a Flemish Franciscan, William of Rubruck, visited Möngke's court in 1254 and 1255 and met with similar results; but another Franciscan, John of Monte Corvino, attracted thousands of converts between his arrival in Peking in 1289 and his death in 1322. Meanwhile, Mongol religious toleration had drawn Nestorian Christians into central Asia and Buddhists into the Middle East.

In addition to the missionaries, swarms of other people responded to the Mongol interest in foreign knowledge and goods. One was Guillaume Boucier, a Parisian architect, who trekked to Karakorum, where he constructed a palace fountain capable of dispensing four different alcoholic beverages. Other adventurers, equally distinct, moved continuously on the travel routes. Between 1325 and 1354, Ibn Battuta, the famous Muslim globe-trotter from Morocco, visited Constantinople, every Middle Eastern Islamic state, India, Sri Lanka, Indonesia, and China. In Hangchow he encountered a man from Morocco whom he had met before in Delhi. Some travelers went the opposite way. Rabban Sauma, a Nestorian monk from central Asia, traveled to Paris; and a Chinese Christian monk from Peking, while in Europe as an envoy from the Persian khan to the pope, had audiences with the English and French kings.

Eurasian traders—Persians, Arabs, Greeks, and western Europeans—were numerous and worldly-wise travelers. They were enticed by Mongol policies that lowered tolls in the commercial cities and provided special protection for merchants' goods. A Florentine document, published about 1340, described conditions on the silk route as

> *perfectly safe whether by day or night. . . . Whatever silver the merchants carry . . . the lord of Cathay takes from them . . . and gives . . . paper money . . . in exchange . . . and with this money you can readily buy silk and whatever you desire to buy and all the people of the country are bound to receive it.*[6]

Land trade between Europe and China, particularly in silk and spices, increased rapidly in the fourteenth century. The main western terminals were Nizhni Novgorod, east of Moscow, where the China caravans made contact with merchants of the Hanseatic League, a coalition of German merchant companies; Tabriz, in northeastern Persia, which served as the eastern terminal for Constantinople; and the Syrian coastal cities, where the caravans met Mediterranean ships, mostly from Venice.

Expanding land trade along the old silk route did not diminish the growing volume of sea commerce. Indeed, the Mongol devastation of Middle Eastern cities provided a quick stimulus, particularly to the spice trade, which was partly redirected through the Red Sea and Egypt to Europe. Within a few decades, however, the Mamluk monopoly in Egypt drove prices up sharply, and the European demand for cheaper spices helped revive overland trade. By now, however, the southern sea route was thriving for other reasons. The Mongol conquest of China had immediately opened opportunities to Japanese and Malayan sea merchants, causing a modest commercial revolution. Later, after the government in China stabilized and became involved in the exchange, the volume of ocean trade between northeastern Asia and the Middle East surpassed that of Sung times.

The Mongol Legacy

Although their conquests were often accompanied by horrifying slaughter and wrought considerable havoc, Mongol control also promoted stability. The

Discovery Through Maps

Gog and Magog in the Ebstorf Mappamundi

Maps depict more than geographical observations; they tell us the beliefs and imaginings of the people who produce them and reflect the point of view of the mapmaker. Historically, when people lacked a clear picture of far-off lands, they employed fantastic stories to describe what lay beyond their own known world. Like myths and folktales, maps from different eras illustrate some of the ways that societies have imagined apparently "strange" or "foreign" lands. We have seen that there was considerable commercial and intellectual exchange among Europe, India, China, and central Asia in the years 300–1300 C.E. Nonetheless, the "Orient" remained a mysterious place in the imagination of many Westerners, a sometimes frightening place inhabited by strange creatures.

The thirteenth-century Ebstorf Mappamundi (map of the world), discovered in a Benedictine monastery in Germany, presents a geographical vision that combines Christian historiography, geographical observation, biblical mythology, the legends of Alexander the Great, and ancient tales of beastlike races inhabiting the "ends of the earth." It incorporates the idea of Gog and Magog, the homelands of apocalyptic destroyers, drawn from the New Testament (Revelation 20:7–8), into the description of the territory of northeastern Asia, the Mongol territory to the north of the Caucasus Mountains. On medieval Christian maps Gog and Magog were equated with barbarian races, with the Ten Lost Tribes of Israel, and with the armies of the Anti-Christ. According to legend, these ferocious peoples had been trapped by Alexander the Great, who built a great wall to contain them; they would break out at the end of time and overwhelm civilized societies. On the Ebsdorf map the people of Gog and Magog are tribes of savages who are shown eating human body parts and drinking blood. They are walled off in the far northeast of the world. Their identification with the Tartars suggests the fear of Turco-Mongol invaders that pervaded the mapmaker's society in the thirteenth century. Given the striking success of the Mongols' conquests in this era, it is no wonder that they came to be associated with Gog and Magog. Gog and Magog also appear on the twelfth-century Islamic world map of al-Idrīsī (see Chapter 10).

Mongols encouraged trade and borrowed freely from old established civilizations, while their commercial contacts spread knowledge of explosives, printing, medicine, shipbuilding, and navigation to the West. In the Middle East they furthered art, architecture, and historical writing. To China they brought Persian astronomy and ceramics, plus sorghum, a new food from India. The Mongol era also saw great commercial and population growth in Japan and Southeast Asia. Not least important was a new awareness of the wider world, which the Mongols gave to a Europe on the brink of global exploration.

While creating the largest empire in history and decisively affecting Eurasian history, like other conquerors the Mongols could not create an enduring unified empire. Logistic realities and the diverse territories conquered and cultures absorbed meant that the Mongol polity had of necessity to be divided in various ways. The Yuan regime declined rapidly after Kublai's death as the economy became more oppressive and the Mongol aristocracy weakened. A great rebellion, beginning in southern China, ultimately ended the dynasty. After the Chinese reconquered most of Mongolia and Manchuria, many northern Mongols reverted to nomadism. Others, on the western steppes, were absorbed into Turkic states.

Genghis Khan himself may have had the last word on the fleeting glory of empires. According to the Mongol history, written in Persian, of Rashid al-Din, Genghis had this to say about success and memory:

> *"After us, our posterity will wear garments of sewn gold, partake of fatty and sweet delicacies, sit well-formed horses, and embrace beauteous wives. [But] they will not say '[all] these things our fathers and brothers collected,' and they will forget us in this great day."*[7]

Conclusion

During the centuries following the collapse of Rome in the West, significant cultural revivals occurred in Asia. First India and then China experienced golden ages when old political structures were restored and social systems were revitalized in accordance with traditional values. In India the Gupta era brought a lasting synthesis of Hindu thought, along with notable advances in painting, architecture, literature, drama, medicine, and the physical sciences. China perfected its administrative structure while further developing its characteristic Confucian philosophy, poetry, landscape painting, and practical technology. Each civilization served as a culture bank, preserving and extending knowledge.

Over the centuries, cultural diffusion gained increasing momentum throughout Eurasia. From both India and China, goods and cultural patterns spread through migrations, invasions, missionary activities, and trade to Southeast Asia, Japan, the Asian steppes, and Europe. The result was a third wave in the civilizing process. The first wave had washed over the Near East before 500 B.C.E.; the second brought great empires in China, India, and the Mediterranean basin; the third dramatically affected the evolution of civilizations in Southeast Asia and Japan while contributing significantly to the emergence of another in western Europe.

Steppe nomads played an increasingly important role in this period of Eurasian history. Many remained nomad warriors, attacking and pillaging the high civilizations on their frontiers. Others adopted civilized ways, shifting from herding to farming, living in cities as craftspeople or traders, and assimilating the high courtly cultures of the conquered peoples. The steppe peoples in turn brought their military ethos, tactics, and modes of organization to the cities of China and Persia. This development was climaxed by the Mongols, who developed a vast network of imperial cities connected by trade routes and fostering an expansive exchange of goods, embassies, ideas, and cultural patterns that in turn created a medieval "world system" in the era "before European hegemony."[8]

Suggestions for Reading

Two standard treatments of the Gupta era are Sir Percival Spear, *India: A Modern History*, rev. ed. (University of Michigan Press, 1972), and R. C. Majumdar and A. D. Pulsaker, eds., *The Classic Age*, Vol. 3 of *The History and Culture of the Indian Peoples* (Bharatiya Vidya, 1954). Reliable and informative recent surveys include Hermann A. Kulke, *A History of India* (Routledge, 1998); Tej Ram Sharma, *The Political History of the Imperial Guptas* (Concept, 1989); and Stanley Wolpert, *A New History of India*, 5th ed. (Oxford University Press, 1997). Steven Warshaw, *India Emerges* (Diablo, 1987), is a concise and readable paperback for the student and general reader. B. H. Gokhale, *Samudra Gupta* (Asia, 1962), is an interesting biography. A special treatment of women is A. S. Altekar, *The Position of Women in Hindu Civilization*, 3rd ed. (Sundar Lal Jam/Motilal Banarsidass, 1962). For a well-illustrated account of Indian influences on the art of neighboring countries, see Benjamin Rowland, *The Art and Architecture of India* (Penguin, 1971).

Among the best general histories of China for the T'ang and Sung periods are William Scott Morton, *China: Its History and Culture* (Lippincott/Crowell, 1980); Witold Rodzinzki, *A History of China*, 2 vols. (Pergamon, 1979); and Charles O. Hucker, *China's Imperial Past* (Stanford University Press, 1975). John K. Fairbank, *The United States and China*, 4th ed. (Harvard University Press, 1983), is a highly readable treatment that goes well beyond the scope of its title to give a brief survey of Chinese history. Others deserving mention are Wolfram Eberhard, *A History of China* (University of California Press, 1977); John Meskill, *An Introduction to Chinese Civilization* (Heath, 1973); Raymond Dawson, *Imperial China* (Hutchinson, 1972); and Hilda Hookham, *A Short History of China* (St. Martin's Press, 1970). A readable paperback is Steven Warshaw, *China Emerges* (Diablo, 1987).

For complete coverage of Chinese technology and engineering, see Joseph Needham, *Science and Civilization in China* (Cambridge University Press, 1954) and *Clerks and Craftsmen in China and the West* (Cambridge University Press, 1970). See also Robert Temple, *The Genius of China* (Simon & Schuster, 1989). A new and comprehensive work on Chinese painting is *Three Thousand Years of Chinese Painting* (Yale University Press, 1998); Esther Yao, *Chinese Women Past and Present* (Idle House, 1987), provides complete coverage of social conditions and important personalities.

The T'ang historical background is ably presented in Arthur F. Wright, *The Sui Dynasty* (Knopf, 1978), and in Woodbridge Bingham, *The Founding of the T'ang Dynasty* (Octagon, 1975). Arthur F. Wright and Dennis Twitchett provide special insights in *Perspectives on the T'ang* (Yale University Press, 1973). The significance of the T'ang examination system is depicted in David McMullen, *State and Scholars in T'ang China* (Cambridge University Press, 1988). A classic study of T'ang decline is Edwin G. Pulleyblank, *The Background of the Rebellion of An Lu-shan* (Greenwood, 1955). Charles Hartman, *Han Yu and the T'ang Search for Unity* (Princeton University Press, 1986), describes the famous philosopher's efforts to synthesize meaning from traditional values during the late T'ang troubles.

Interesting and revealing special studies of the Sung period include Jing-shen Tao, *Two Sons of Heaven* (University of Arizona Press, 1988); Winston W. Lo, *An Introduction to the Civil Service System of Sung China* (University of Hawaii Press, 1987); and Thomas H. C. Lee, *Government, Education, and the Examinations in Sung China, 960–1278* (St. Martin's Press, 1985). Other excellent special studies are James M. Hargett, *On the Road in Twelfth Century China* (Steiner Verlag, 1989), and Richard L. Davis, *Court and Family in Sung China* (Duke University Press, 1986).

George B. Sansom, *A History of Japan*, 3 vols. (Stanford University Press, 1958–1963), is still the best exhaustive work in English. Also valuable are John K. Fairbank et al., *East Asia: Tradition and Transformation* (Houghton Mifflin, 1989); Eric Tomlin, *Japan* (Walker, 1973); Mikiso Hane, *Japan: A Historical Survey* (Scribner, 1972); and Edwin Reischauer, *Japan: The Story of a Nation* (Knopf, 1970). Other noteworthy surveys include R. H. P. Mason, *A History of Japan* (Tuttle, 1987), and Steven Warshaw, *Japan Emerges* (Diablo, 1987). Three penetrating special studies of early Japan are Wontack Hong, *Relationship Between Korea and Japan in the Early Period* (Ilsimsa, 1988); Jonathan E. Kidder, *Early Buddhist Japan* (Praeger, 1972); and Peter Judd Arensen, *The Medieval Japanese Daimyo* (Yale University Press, 1979). Rose Hempel, *The Golden Age of Japan* (Rizzoli, 1983), is a study of Japanese art and architecture in the Heian period.

For a scholarly study of the Turkic peoples, including the Mongols, see Peter Golden, *An Introduction to the History of the Turkic Peoples* (Harrassowitz, 1992). Luc Kwanten, *Imperial Nomads: A History of Central Asia, 500–1500* (University of Pennsylvania Press, 1979), is a superb study of the nomadic steppe peoples, including Turks, Uighurs, Uzbeks, and Mongols. It has been ably augmented by two later works on Mongol life and conquests: David Morgan, *The Mongols* (Blackwell, 1986), and Thomas T. Allsen, *Mongol Imperialism* (University of California Press, 1987). Other standard treatments of the Mongol impact are Rene Grousset, *The Empire of the Steppes* (Rutgers University Press, 1970); Eustace D. Phillips, *The Mongols* (Praeger, 1969); John J. Saunders, *History of the Mongol Conquests* (Barnes & Noble, 1971); and Bertold Spuler, *The Mongols in History* (Praeger, 1971). Paul Ratchnevsky, *Chingiz Khan: His Life and Legacy* (Blackwell, 1993), is a good updated social biography of the great conqueror. See also Adam Kessler, *Empires Beyond the Great Wall: The Heritage of Genghis Khan* (Natural History Museum of Los Angeles County, 1992).

An excellent study of networks of trade and communication in the Mongol era is Janet Abu-Lughod, *Before European Hegemony: The World System, A.D. 1250–1350* (Oxford University Press, 1989). Thomas Allsen looks at the textile trade of the Mongol era in *Commodity and Exchange in the Mongol Empire* (Cambridge University Press, 1997). A sound treatment of the Pax Mongolica is presented in G. F. Hudson, *Europe and China* (Gordon, 1976). On early relations between the Chinese and the Mongols, see H. D. Martin, *The Rise of Genghis Khan and the Conquest of North China* (Octagon, 1971). Charles Halperin, *Russia and the Golden Horde* (Indiana University Press, 1987), looks at the Mongol impact on Russia. Two works by L. Olschki, *Marco Polo's Precursors* (Johns Hopkins University Press, 1943) and *Marco Polo's Asia* (University of California Press, 1960), provide complete accounts of the long-range trade leading to Polo's mission. A readable biography is Henry Hart, *Marco Polo, Venetian Adventurer* (University of Oklahoma Press, 1967). Frances Wood, *Did Marco Polo Go to China?* (Westview, 1996), is a provocative look at the famous traveler.

The best recent accounts of the Yuan regime in China are Elizabeth E. West, *Mongolian Rule in China* (Harvard University Press, 1989); Morris Rossabi, *Kublai Khan: His Life and Times* (University of California Press, 1987); and John D. Langlois, *China Under Mongol Rule* (Princeton University Press, 1981). On Persia in this era, see David Morgan, *Medieval Persia, 1040–1797* (Longman, 1988), and Richard Frye, *Islamic Iran and Central Asia, 7th–12th Centuries* (Variorum, 1979).

Suggestions for Web Browsing

Itihaas: Chronology—Medieval India
http://www.itihaas.com/medieval/index.html

Extensive chronology of medieval India, 1000 C.E. to 1756 C.E.; most entries include subsites with text and images.

Medieval India
http://www.dc.infi.net/~gunther/india/medieval.html

Site discussing the history, sites and monuments, and classical texts of medieval India, 600 B.C.–1526 C.E.

Chinese Empire
http://www.wsu.edu:8080/~dee/chempire/chempire.htm

Chinese history from 256 B.C.E. to 1300 C.E., with details about philosophy and culture.

Ancient Japan
http://www.wsu.edu:8080/~dee/ancjapan/ancjapan.htm

Web site on ancient Japan includes political, religious, and cultural history, details about women and women's communities, and a portfolio of art from the era.

Empires Beyond the Great Wall: The Heritage of Genghis Khan
http://www.pinc.com/khan/khan.html

A rich site offering a biography of Genghis Khan and information about the history and culture of the Mongol Empire.

Notes

1. Hermann Kulke and Dietmar Rothermund, *History of India*, 3rd ed. (London: Routledge, 1998), p. 147.
2. Quoted in H. H. Gowen and H. W. Hall, *An Outline History of China* (New York: Appleton, 1926), p. 117.
3. *The Works of Li Po*, trans. Shigeyoshi Obata (New York: Dutton, 1950), no. 71.

4. Quoted in Ryusaku Tsunoda et al., eds., *Sources of Japanese Tradition* (New York: Columbia University Press, 1958), pp. 181–182.

5. Marco Polo, *Tht Travels of Marco Polo* (New York: Grosset & Dunlap, 1931), pp. 30, 133–149.

6. Quoted in G. F. Hudson, *Europe and China* (Boston: Beacon Press, 1931), p. 156.

7. Thomas Allsen, *Commodity and Exchange in the Mongol Empire* (Cambridge: Cambridge University Press, 1997), p. 12.

8. This system is lucidly outlined in Janet Abu-Lughod, *Before European Hegemony: The World System, A.D. 1250–1350* (Oxford: Oxford University Press, 1989), which delineates the networks of exchange characterizing this era.

The Cliff Palace of the Anasazi,
Mesa Verde National Park,
Colorado, is among the important
Anasazi ruins to be found in the
southwestern United States.

The Americas
to 1492

At the same time that medieval Europe was experiencing dynamic cultural growth and Africa south of the Sahara was undergoing its own rich evolution, the Americas were creating their own civilizations half a globe away. The American civilizations followed a social sequence similar to that experienced in Africa and Eurasia. Agriculture became more diversified, and as food supplies increased, the culture became more and more able to support large cities, highly skilled crafts, expanding commerce, complex social structures, and the emergence of powerful states.

What is unique about the development of the American civilizations is their having evolved in complete isolation from the rest of the world. The most noteworthy were the civilizations of the Mayas in Yucatán and Guatemala, the Aztecs in central Mexico, and the Incas in Peru. The Mayas are especially famous for their mathematics, solar calendar, and writing system, which has only recently been deciphered. The Aztecs and Incas conquered large populations and governed extensive states. Each civilization produced distinctive customs, values, art, and religion, much of which have become part of the Latin American heritage.

Spanish adventurers who invaded these civilizations were repelled by Amerindian religious sacrifices but astonished by the wealth, grandeur, technical efficiency, urban populations, and institutional complexity they saw in Mesoamerica and Peru. For example, Tenochtitlán, the Aztec capital, with its 150,000

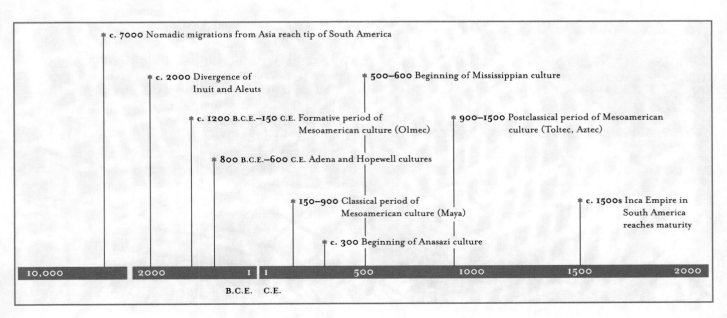

- ✳ **c. 7000** Nomadic migrations from Asia reach tip of South America
- ✳ **c. 2000** Divergence of Inuit and Aleuts
- ✳ **500–600** Beginning of Mississippian culture
- ✳ **c. 1200** B.C.E.–**150** C.E. Formative period of Mesoamerican culture (Olmec)
- ✳ **900–1500** Postclassical period of Mesoamerican culture (Toltec, Aztec)
- ✳ **800** B.C.E.–**600** C.E. Adena and Hopewell cultures
- ✳ **150–900** Classical period of Mesoamerican culture (Maya)
- ✳ **c. 1500s** Inca Empire in South America reaches maturity
- ✳ **c. 300** Beginning of Anasazi culture

| 10,000 | 2000 | I | I | 500 | 1000 | 1500 | 2000 |

B.C.E.   C.E.

inhabitants, was larger and probably cleaner than any European city of its time. Yet this high level of social accomplishment had been attained without iron, draft animals, an alphabet, or known contacts with other high civilizations.

To the north, hundreds of Amerindian tribes developed diverse social patterns, languages, and economic pursuits as they adapted to the differing environmental challenges they faced. Around 3000 B.C.E. Amerindians in the southwestern part of present-day Florida founded villages along the coast in which they enjoyed a rich diet of fish, shellfish, grains, and berries and adhered to a sophisticated religious system that included the burial of the dead in funeral mounds. Recent archaeological finds indicate that still earlier, in the present-day state of Washington, Amerindians founded villages with their own unique cultures and economic activities.

Because of the complex and immense land-mass—3000 miles across and 5000 miles from north to south—in which they found themselves, the Amerindians to the north never attained the centralized power or wealth of the Mayas, Aztecs, and Incas. However, they left behind a rich legacy of archaeological sites that indicate their sophistication and flexibility. Unfortunately, in their diversity lay conflict, and the Amerindians were often their own worst enemy.

Origins of Americans and Their Cultures

All American cultures can be traced back to nomadic migrations from Asia to Alaska, across the Bering Strait land bridge. During the Pleistocene epoch, coinciding with the last great ice age, humans established themselves in Siberia, where they built subterranean shelters and hunted mammals. The most recent ice advance, beginning some 65,000 years ago, locked up immense amounts of global water and lowered sea levels, creating a land bridge that enabled Paleolithic hunters to follow their quarry into the New World, as the Americas came to be known. As

increasing global temperatures melted the ice and raised water levels, the bridge slowly disappeared, around 10,000 years ago, after an estimated 30,000 years of sporadic human migrations. From Alaska those generations of early Amerindian peoples moved east and south, reaching southern Mexico by 20,000 years ago, Chile some 2500 years later, and the tip of South America by about 7000 B.C.E. Over this protracted period they split into eight major ethnolinguistic groups and hundreds of subgroups and adapted to numerous physical environments.

The development of agriculture in the Mexican highlands, along the Peruvian coastal plain, and in what is now the southwestern United States caused a profound modification of Amerindian culture after 7000 B.C.E. Not only did this development occur considerably later than in the Near East, but the plants that were domesticated were also different from those in other parts of the world. Wheat, barley, and rye did not exist in the New World; instead, the Amerindians domesticated squash, beans, fruits, and peppers. They also domesticated animals—not the cattle, sheep, or horses of the Old World, but alpacas and llamas in the Andes. The major agricultural impact came with the cultivation of maize (corn), shortly before 5000 B.C.E., in the Tehuacán valley of Mexico. From this center, maize culture spread widely. After 1000 B.C.E. it became the staple food for hundreds of societies, from the Mississippi valley to the Argentine pampas. Although the resulting sociopolitical impact was slow, it was decisive; the Aztec and Inca Empires, which so awed the Spanish *conquistadores* after 1500, were based largely on maize economies.

Beyond these mature civilizations, cultural levels varied widely among more than 75 million Amerindians at the end of the fifteenth century. Some cultures, like that of the famous Mound Builders of the Mississippi valley, borrowed heavily from Mexico; Cahokia, an obvious capital and trade center near contemporary St. Louis, Missouri, housed approximately 10,000 people during the thirteenth century. Less complex peasant cultures north of the Rio Grande ranged from the Pueblo of the southwest to the large Iroquois Confederacy of the eastern woodlands. In South America, protocivilizations had risen along the north coast and near the mouth of the Amazon. Simpler peasant societies developed on Caribbean islands, in the South American pampas, and in Chile. Most other Amerindians—probably a majority of them—were still hunters and gatherers. These included the Eskimos, Mesolithic seminomads of the Pacific Northwest; jungle tribes such as the Jivaro of the upper Amazon; and the peoples of Tierra del Fuego, at the southern tip of South America.

Despite their isolation, Amerindian cultures, including the mature civilizations, followed a pattern of development similar to those in Eurasia and

New World Civilizations

2500s B.C.E.–400s C.E.	Olmec
300s–900s C.E.	Mayas
900s–1200s C.E.	Toltecs
1100s–1500s C.E.	Incas
1300s–1500s C.E.	Aztecs

Africa. This phenomenon has been described as "parallel invention." New World societies had evolved certain customs, such as the wearing of ear or lip plugs. They were also limited by their dependence on maize cultivation, with its special demands, as well as by their lack of iron, horses, other common domesticated animals, and an alphabet. Yet they differed little from Old World cultures in their progression from Paleolithic hunting and food-gathering to Mesolithic semifixed communities to Neolithic food production and settled communal life and thence to urban centers and the emergence of political states. They also displayed common traits with other civilizations in their theocratic systems, sun cults, and human sacrifices. Like the African cultures, they were in transition from matriarchal to patriarchal institutions, although further advanced in this process. Finally, a common belief in divine monarchy among Aztecs and Incas was also typical of many other peoples in the ancient riverine civilizations of the Old World.

Emerging Civilizations in Mesoamerica

The term *Mesoamerica* applies to Mexico and Central America, home to a matrix of related cultures. The region varies greatly in geomorphology, climate, and vegetation. Two mountain ranges run through northern Mexico to join a central highland block in the region of the Valley of Mexico. The Pacific coastal region is relatively narrow while that on the Atlantic side is wide. The north and west have dry lands with sparse vegetation; the south and east are marked by tropical rain forests and savannas.

Despite these physical differences, the early Mesoamerican cultures were unified by their economic interdependence, since no one region was self-sufficient. They shared a complex calendar, hieroglyphic writing, bark paper, deerskin books, team games played with balls of solid rubber, chocolate bean money, widespread upper-class polygamy, large markets, and common legends (a popular one featured a god-man symbolized by a feathered serpent).

To facilitate our study of developing Mesoamerican culture, we may conveniently divide its history into three main periods: formative (to 150 C.E.), classical (150–900), and postclassical (900–1492).

The Formative Period

For a millennium after 1500 B.C.E., Mesoamerican villages evolved steadily toward larger urban communities. They fostered the development of pottery making, weaving, feather working, and masonry. As population increased and a more complex division of labor evolved, priests came to dominate governments, but merchants enjoyed social status as they conducted trade among the temple cities. In time the common culture, known as the Olmec, centered in five geographical areas. One was in the Oaxaca region of western Mexico; another was in the inland Valley of Mexico; a third straddled the present Mexican-Guatemalan border; and a fourth (the later Mayan) arose in the southern highlands and lowlands of Yucatán, Honduras, and Guatemala. The fifth and at the time most significant area spread over some 125 miles of the eastern Mexican coast and its hinterlands, near present-day Veracruz. It was largely parent to the others.

Since 1920 this Olmec culture, revealed through archaeological remains, has astounded experts by its revealed wealth, technical efficiency, and artistic sensitivity. Among many Olmec sites, the oldest, at San Lorenzo, had great stone buildings and pyramids, dating from 1200 B.C.E. The culture is perhaps best known for its colossal heads and its fine jade carving, featuring jaguars. It had already attained maturity when San Lorenzo was destroyed by invaders about 900 B.C.E.; another ceremonial center at La Venta, in Tabasco, assumed leadership until it collapsed six centuries later.

Scattered throughout the Olmec heartland were some 350,000 people, living in relatively sparsely

A magnificent monumental stone head from the Olmec Center at San Lorenzo. Some scholars have suggested that these massive heads are portraits of rulers.

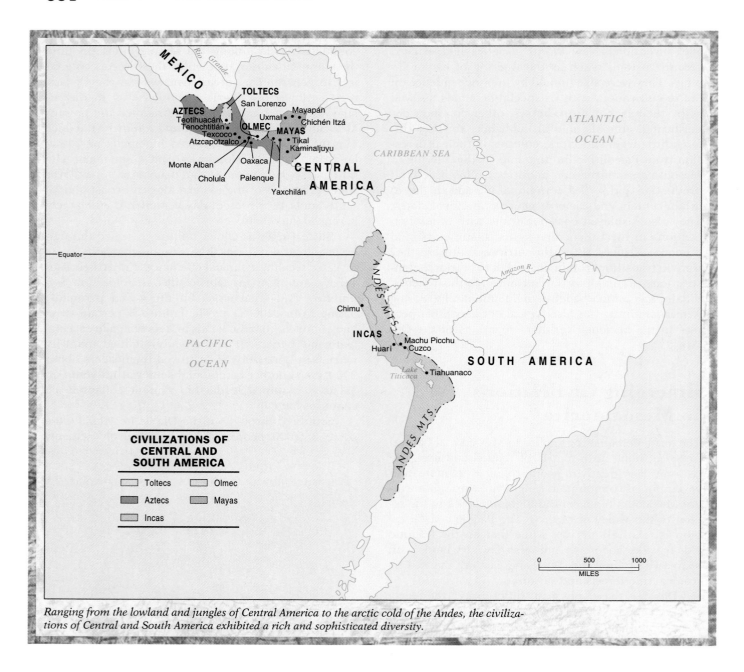

CIVILIZATIONS OF
CENTRAL AND
SOUTH AMERICA

☐ Toltecs ☐ Olmec

☐ Aztecs ☐ Mayas

☐ Incas

Ranging from the lowland and jungles of Central America to the arctic cold of the Andes, the civilizations of Central and South America exhibited a rich and sophisticated diversity.

populated ceremonial trading centers and their supporting villages. Labor and stone for the massive construction projects, jade for carving, luxury goods, raw materials for the crafts, and food were brought to the centers often from distant places. These goods were probably not the spoils of conquest; Olmec society left little evidence of war or violence, although military operations would have been conducted to protect trading missions. Merchants were bestowed a social status second only to the ruling priestly classes, which governed by enjoying respect and exploiting fear rather than relying on force. The general theocratic orientation is reflected most clearly in the great temple mounds; in the huge stone conical pyramid at

La Venta, rising some 100 feet; and in the characteristic carved statuary that represented Olmec cultism.

Olmec influence permeated most of Mesoamerica. A few independent Olmec centers may have been established in central Mexico, but it was probably more common for a number of Olmec priests and traders to live among native populations, conducting religious rites and arranging for the transport of goods to the homeland. Such enclaves were typical of regions as distant as the Pacific coast of Central America. In other places, such as the Oaxaca valley to the west, the southwestern Mexican highlands, or the southern Mayan regions, Olmec influence was more indirect, possibly resulting from trade or Olmec marriage into local elites. By such varied means, Olmec foundations were laid for the religion, art, architecture, and characteristic ball games—and possibly for the calendars, mathematics, and writing systems—of later Mesoamerican civilizations, including the Mayan and the Aztec.

The Classical Period in Northern Mesoamerica

After the fall of La Venta, Olmec prestige waned, but high civilizations continued to flourish. By the second century C.E., development had progressed to a point of florescence known as the classical period, which would last until the tenth century. This was literally a golden age, when written communication, complex time reckoning, a pantheon of gods, interregional trade, and a 40-fold population increase over the Olmec period affected most of Mesoamerica. Hundreds of communities raised great buildings, decorated them with beautiful frescoes, produced pottery and figurines in large quantities, and covered everything with sculptures. Although classical Mayan culture of the Yucatán lowlands is perhaps best known, we will begin our look at the classical period by viewing other notable northern sites in the Valley of Mexico and Oaxaca.

Teotihuacán, in the northeastern valley, generated the most notable classical culture outside of Yucatán. At its peak about 500 C.E., it was the sixth largest city in the world, with a population of 125,000 to 200,000. Three and a half miles long and nearly 2 miles wide, it was laid out in a grid of sorts and paved with a plaster floor on which clusters of impos-

ing edifices were erected. This ceremonial center is dominated by the temple-pyramids dedicated to the moon and the sun. The first pyramid was truncated to provide for a temple with a broad step ascending from a wide rectangular court. Running south is a long ceremonial axis, and adjacent to it the Pyramid of the Sun. Also truncated, it measures 650 feet at the base and rises in four terraces to 213 feet above the valley floor. The interior contains more than a million cubic yards of sun-dried bricks, and the exterior was once faced entirely with stone. As with other pyramids throughout Mesoamerica, these structures, with their ceremonial staircases, led to temples at the summit where rites and sacrifices were offered to the gods.

Teotihuacán was noted for its specialized craftspeople, who came from all over Mexico and occupied designated quarters of the city. Its streets were studded with bustling markets, where all types of goods were available from foreign as well as local sources. This wealth permitted a governing elite of priests, civil officials, military leaders, and merchants to enjoy great luxury. Over other states, including some among the lowland Mayas, Teotihuacán exerted a powerful influence, arising mainly from its cultural reputation, social connections, and commercial advantages. When necessary, it used its formidable military power to enforce trade and tribute agreements.

Another impressive classical center in Mexico was located at Monte Alban in the Oaxaca valley. In 200 B.C.E. it already had a population of 15,000, and its fortifications dominated the valley. In Teotihuacán's era, this concentration of temples, pyramids, and shrines was a theocratic state, still drawing

The colossal Pyramid of the Sun rose above the metropolis of Teotihuacán. Measuring 650 feet at its base and 213 feet high, the structure is more than four times larger than the Great Pyramid of Cheops in Egypt.

tribute from adjacent hill settlements and a valley population of over 75,000 people. Although developed on a smaller scale than Teotihuacán, Monte Alban produced a similar pattern of external trade, class differentiation, elaborate religious architecture, artistic creativity, writing, and time reckoning. It derived most of its art styles from Teotihuacán and some from the Mayas but synthesized both in its own traditions. Politically, it remained independent through the classical era, although its elite sought the luxury goods and favor of Teotihuacán.

Classical Mayan Civilization

While Teotihuacán and Monte Alban flourished, Mayan peoples farther south in Yucatán and Guatemala produced the most splendid cultural achievements of the classical era and perhaps of Amerindian societies in any time. Artistic and intellectual activity rose to new heights in more than 100 Mayan centers, each boasting temples, palaces, observatories, and ball courts. Although it borrowed from Teotihuacán before the latter's decay in the eighth century C.E., Mayan civilization subsequently cast a brilliant light over the whole of Mesoamerica.

The earliest Mayas are thought to have migrated from the northwest coast of California to the Guatemalan highlands during the third millennium B.C.E. From that homeland, Yucatec- and Cholian-speaking peoples settled the northern and central lowlands, respectively, between 1500 B.C.E. and 100 C.E. Mayan villages developed steadily, many becoming ceremonial centers by the start of the Common Era. In the highlands, Kaminaljuyu had by then developed architecture and primitive writing under the influence of Oaxaca and Teotihuacán. But in the early classical period, before 550 C.E., Tikal, in the central lowlands, assumed Mayan leadership as it traded with Teotihuacán and allied itself with Kaminaljuyu. The fall of Teotihuacán brought temporary confusion, soon followed by the glorious renaissance of the late classical era at Tikal, Palenque, Yaxchilán, Uxmal, and other Mayan centers.

Mayan communities were supported by productive economies, based on agriculture but heavily involved in handicrafts and long-distance trade. In soil sometimes nearly barren, with some exceptions in the highlands, Mayan farmers used intensive agriculture, clearing, irrigating, and terracing to raise squash, chili peppers, and many other crops, including maize—which supplied 80 percent of their food. Mayan metalwork, cotton cloth, and chipped stone implements were traded widely, carried in large dugout canoes along the rivers and the Atlantic coast. Exchange was facilitated by the use of common

goods as media of exchange, including cocoa beans, polished beads, salt, and lengths of cotton cloth.

Mayan society in this period was a bewildering mixture of old and new. An ancient kinship system prevailed among all classes, with lands assigned and controlled by the clans. Matriarchal values persisted, as indicated by some queens who retained power and influence. Women were generally respected, held some legal rights, and did some of the most important work, such as weaving. The shift toward patriarchy, however, was definite and unmistakable, as was indicated in priorities accorded men in most social situations, such as being served first by women at meals. A more fundamental change involved the rise of social classes. Hereditary male nobles and priests were in most positions of authority and power, but craftspeople and merchants enjoyed more privileges and status than was formerly believed by experts on Mayan society. Slaves did most of the hard work, particularly in the continuous heavy construction of ceremonial buildings. They were also subject to religious sacrifice, although this was far less common than among the Aztecs later.

Each Mayan center was governed by a hereditary priest-king, usually considered to be a descendant of a god. He was assisted by a council of priests and nobles. His government levied taxes, supervised local government in outlying villages, and administered justice. It also was responsible for conducting foreign relations and making war. This last point is worth

A high-caste Mayan woman working at the loom. One end of the loom is attached to the woman's waist; the other is fastened to a tree trunk. Weaving was considered a noble occupation.

stressing. The Mayas were not very successful in large-scale military operations because their armies were drawn mainly from the nobility and therefore limited in size. Nevertheless, they were equal to other Mesoamericans in their warlike propensities; they could wield their stone-bladed weapons as ferociously as the Aztecs. Indeed, as time passed and cities vied for supremacy, warfare became increasingly common. In the process, some centers remained independent, but most joined loosely organized leagues, based on common religious traditions, royal marriages, or diplomatic alignments.

Religion permeated all phases of Mayan life. Like the later Aztecs, the Mayas saw life as a burden and time as its measure, and they deified many natural phenomena, particularly the heavenly bodies, as powers to be appeased by human pain and suffering. Public bloodletting was part of normal ritualistic worship. Human sacrifice, usually accomplished by decapitation, was common, although not obsessive, and war to obtain prisoners for sacrifice was sometimes waged. The dominance of religion over everyday life is further illustrated by the general interpretation of law as religious principle and taxation as religious offerings. Economic value derived as much from the religious sanctity of a thing as from its material utility or scarcity. Moreover, education was aimed primarily at training priests; reading and writing were considered necessary religious skills, and mathematics and astronomy were valued mainly because they were required in scheduling ceremonies honoring the gods. Despite their many intellectual accomplishments, the Mayas were far more ritualistic than scientific.

The two most significant achievements of the Mayas were their calendar and their writing system. Neither of these was original, but both were more efficient than those of earlier Mesoamerican peoples. The Mayan astronomers, using only naked-eye observation, far surpassed their European contemporaries. Their constant scanning of the heavens allowed the Mayas to perfect a solar calendar with 18 months of 20 days each and a five-day period for religious festivals. Using an ingenious cyclical system of notation known as the "long count," they dated events of the distant past for accurate record keeping and the scheduling of astronomical observations. Their notational mathematics, based on 20 rather than 10 as in the decimal system, employed combinations of dots and bars in vertical sequences, to indicate numbers above 20. For nonnumerical records, they combined pictographic and glyphic symbols, which have recently been deciphered sufficiently to reveal specific historic events and their human dimensions.

These remarkable accomplishments in mathematics, astronomy, and writing were more than matched by the magnificent Mayan art and architecture. The plaza of each Mayan community was marked by at least one pyramid, topped by a temple. The one at Tikal towered to 229 feet, 16 feet higher than the Pyramid of the Sun at Teotihuacán. With their terraced sides and horizontal lines, Mayan pyramids demonstrated a prevailing sense of proportion. The highly stylized sculpture decorating their terraces is regarded by some authorities as the world's finest, even though the Mayan sculptors accomplished their intricate carving with only stone tools. The Mayas also developed mural painting to a high level of expression. Even their lesser arts, such as weaving, ceramics, and jewelry making, reveal a greater aesthetic sense, subtlety of design, and manipulative skill than similar work in numerous other high civilizations.

The Postclassical Era in Mesoamerica

Mesoamerica's classical artistic florescence ended during the eighth and ninth centuries. The causes, not yet fully uncovered, have been generally attributed to overpopulation, internal struggles, and fierce Chichimec invasions from the North. Amid the accompanying disturbances, urban populations dwindled, and most of Teotihuacán's residents scattered in all directions, even into the Mayan lands. But there was no complete collapse; trade continued on a large scale, and the expanded use of writing indicated more social complexity and interstate competition, which contributed to intensified political conflict. Consequently, the age produced a new cultural mode, with heavier emphases on militarism, war, and gods thirsting for human blood. Among many smaller but thriving city-states, in addition to the dying Teotihuacán, were the Mayan polities of Tikal, Chichén Itzá, and Mayapán. Farther north, the Oaxacan centers were still flourishing after the tenth century, as were Atzcapotzalco, Xochicalio, and Cholula, with its colossal pyramid.

The Toltecs

Most prominent of all these centers was Tollan, the Toltec capital. Toltec history is unclear before 980, when Topiltzin, a legendary king, founded the city and created a new power in the Valley of Mexico. His subjects were a mixture of Chichimecs and former urbanites of the area, who may have served for a while as peacekeepers in the north. Over the next two centuries the city became a great urban complex of 120,000 people, a hub of trade, and the center of an evolving Toltec confederacy, which assumed the leading role formerly played by Teotihuacán. Meanwhile,

Tollan's future was shaped by a struggle for power between Topiltzin and his enemies. The king had early adopted the Teotihuacán god Quetzalcoatl, who opposed human sacrifice; but followers of the traditional Toltec war-god, Tezcatlipoca, ultimately rebelled and forced Topiltzin into exile. The victorious war cult took over, steadily expanding its hegemony, by conquest and trade, into an empire stretching from the Gulf of Mexico to the Pacific, including some Mayan cities of the south.

The tumultuous political conditions of the early postclassical period finally brought disaster to the Toltecs. Failing crops and internal dissension caused great outward migrations from Tollan and abandonment of the capital at the end of the twelfth century. Shortly after, the city was burned by Chichimecs. For two centuries thereafter, Mesoamerica was a land of warring states and constantly forming and dissolving federations. Some cultural continuity, however, was maintained by peoples in the Oaxaca valley, notably the Zapotecs, whose culture was as old as the Olmec. Although they struggled constantly with neighboring peoples for supremacy and survival, the Zapotecs produced towns, temples, ball courts, and art, which helped preserve Mesoamerican traditions for later times.

As Toltec militarism spread from central to southern Mexico, it left the less developed Mayan highlands relatively undisturbed but brought decline and reorientation to the old lowland centers, such as Tikal. Severe droughts also drove migrants into northern Yucatán, where a developing cistern technology provided more water. At Chichén Itzá, in the tenth century, a cosmopolitan Mexican-Mayan military elite established tributary hegemony and maintained a trading network, by land and sea, throughout the southern region. From the early thirteenth into the fifteenth century, Mayapán was a fortified center, defended by Mexican mercenaries and maintaining leverage over subkingdoms by holding hostages from dependent royal families. Trade continued to grow, along with population, among the postclassical Mayas; but art, cultural pursuits, and even architecture deteriorated. The Spaniards were later to describe the Mayan people as fiercely independent, bloodthirsty, and, like the Aztecs, inclined to sacrifice war captives' hearts on their gods' altars.

The Aztecs

Arising in the confusion of the late postclassical era, the Aztec Empire, in less than two centuries, came to dominate central Mexico from coast to coast. Cortés and his Spanish adventurers were utterly amazed by the monumental architecture, teeming markets, and dazzling wealth of the Aztec capital at Tenochtitlán; they did not realize that Aztec culture, despite its material prosperity and political power, was a relatively recent and somewhat crude version of earlier and more mature civilizations. The Aztecs, like the

This deer effigy vessel, which comes from the Toltec culture is an example of the only glazed pottery produced in the ancient Americas. The pottery, known as "plumbate ware" although it does not contain lead, was imported from non-Toltec artisans located on the Pacific coast near the Mexico-Guatemala border and traded to all major Toltec sites. Incised on each side of the deer's body is a spear thrower. The head and legs are hollow, with openings on the bottom.

Deer Effigy, Vessel, Mexico. "Plumbate" earthenware. The Saint Louis Art Museum. Gift of Morton D. May.

Discovery Through Maps

Toltec Map of a Mayan City

This map of a Mayan city from the Temple of the Warriors in Chichén Itzá, in present-day Yucatán, provides a number of details of life in Mesoamerica. On its surface, it is a portrayal of a scouting party of Toltecs observing the town from their boats. They are the ultimate outsiders, seemingly ignored by the people on land and even by the fish, crabs, and turtles of the river.

But there is more than just the normal earthly plant, animal, and human life in this map. To the upper right is the god Quetzalcoatl (the Feathered Serpent), not a distant abstraction but a presence in everyday life, a factor to be acknowledged and sacrificed to, who may choose one group over the other.

By the middle of the ninth century, the Mayan civilization went into a decline for reasons that are still uncertain. What we do know is that the Toltecs came down from Mexico and filled the power vacuum. The Toltecs' base was near present-day Mexico City, and they dominated Central America between the tenth and twelfth centuries. That this is a Toltec map can be seen by the fact that the warriors attributed their success to the Cloud Serpent, Mixcoatl, and his son Quetzalcoatl, who occupies a place of honor in this map. The militaristic Toltecs ruled through a series of armed orders, like those depicted in the boats. They were eventually supplanted by the Aztecs.

Toltecs before them, retained much of their old barbarism while freely borrowing from their neighbors and victims. The most significant example of this borrowing was their hydraulic agriculture. It was the major factor by which they increased population in the Valley of Mexico to more than a million people, living in some 50 city-states.

The Aztecs' story really begins with the founding of the capital at Tenochtitlán; their earlier history is

quite obscure. They evidently migrated from the north into central Mexico some time before 1200. For a while they were dominated by other peoples, including the Toltecs. About 1325 they settled on an island in Lake Texcoco (the site of present-day Mexico City), later connecting their new town to the mainland by causeways. In its later days Tenochtitlán was an architectural wonder. The Aztecs built a dam to control the lake level, completed a freshwater aqueduct, and created floating artificial islands where irrigated fields supplied food for the capital. Within the imperial metropolis, beautiful avenues, canals, temples, and monuments symbolized increasing Aztec power, particularly after the early fifteenth century.

The Aztec Empire began assuming a recognizable form about that time. During the early decades at Tenochtitlán, the Aztecs had fought as tributaries of Atzcapotzalco, the dominant city-state in the valley. In 1370 they accepted a king of assumed Toltec lineage. For decades they won victories and prospered in concert with their overlords, but in 1427 they rebelled, forming a "triple alliance" with nearby Texcoco and Tlacopán, which defeated Atzcapotzalco and became the major power in the region. For the Aztecs, these events brought great change. Internally, they shifted power from the old clan leaders to a rising military aristocracy. Externally, they started a series of conquests and trading agreements. Thus arose a new imperial order, shared at first by the other two allies but increasingly dominated by Tenochtitlán. The reigns of the Aztec kings Itzcoatl (1427–1440) and his nephew, Montezuma I (1440–1468), ushered in this new era of rising centralism and expansion. It was still in progress under the ninth monarch, Montezuma II (1502–1520), at the time of the Spanish conquest.

As the empire expanded, so did the state-controlled economy. Its base was agricultural land, particularly anchored floating plots installed on the lake after the 1430s. Most were built by the government. Some were allotted to the clans (calpulli) for distribution to families. Others were developed as estates for the monarch and the nobility; the latter were worked by resident tenants under government supervision. Rising agricultural production supported not only the engineering, dredging, stonework, and carpentry required for heavy construction but also a plethora of crafts, turning out weapons, cloth, ceramics, featherwork, jewelry, and hundreds of other goods. Porters from distant places backpacked over mountains to the markets of the valley. A later Spanish observer reported that the great market at Tlateloco, serving Tenochtitlán, attracted 25,000 people daily.

Conquest and accumulating wealth modified the ancient social structure. The old calpulli developed into city wards, identified largely by occupational specialties. By 1500 most calpulli families were headed by men. Women could inherit property and divorce their husbands but were confined mostly to household tasks, except for midwives, healers, and prostitutes. Kinship still promoted social cohesion, but class status provided major incentives. The appointed nobility (pipiltin), along with the priests, held both power and social status, but they were burdened with heavy responsibilities. Moreover, they held appointed rather than hereditary posts, although they could inherit property. Commoners could be made nobles by performing superior service, particularly in war. Craftspeople and merchants paid taxes but were exempt from military service; some long-distance merchants (pochteca) served the government as diplomats or spies in foreign states. Peasants worked their plots and served in the army; nonmembers of calpulli were tenants. Their lot was hardly better than that of the numerous slaves, except for the latter's potential role as ceremonial sacrifice victims.

Official documents of the period and other written accounts focus mainly on Mesoamerican social and political elites and conditions in the imperial capitals. However, recent archaeological studies throw fresh light on the lives of the Aztec common people and conditions in the provinces. Surveys of settlement patterns show that Aztec society experienced one of the most significant population explosions of premodern times. In the Valley of Mexico, the heartland of the Aztec Empire, population increased from 175,000 in the early Aztec period (1150–1350) to almost 1 million in the late period (1350–1519). This pattern of growth was duplicated elsewhere in the empire. To cope with this population explosion, the environment was altered: farmers built dams and canals to irrigate cropland, constructed terraced stone walls on hillsides to form new fields, and drained swamps outside Tenochtitlán to create raised fields (chinampas), and with these changes emerged new villages and towns.

Excavations of rural sites near modern Cuernavaca disclose that provincial society was much more complex than previously thought. Commoners evolved a thriving marketing system whereby craft goods produced in their homes were exchanged for a variety of foreign goods. Houses at these sites were small, built of adobe brick walls supported on stone foundations. These houses were furnished with mats and baskets and had a shrine with two or three figurines and an incense burner on one of the walls. In this region the household production of cotton textiles was the major craft. All Aztec women spun and wove cloth, which provided garments, constituted the most common item of tribute demanded by the state, and served as currency in the marketplaces for obtaining other goods and services. In addition to textiles, some residents made paper out of the bark of the wild fig tree, used to produce books of picture-writing and to burn in ritual offerings.

According to written sources, Aztec commoners were subject to the nobles, who possessed most of the land and monopolized power in the polity. But new archaeological excavations show that the commoners were relatively prosperous and enterprising people whose market system operated largely beyond state control. "There is no evidence to suggest that nobles controlled craft production or exchange. The people of the provinces managed to achieve a degree of economic success through channels unconnected to the state and unreported in the official histories of the Aztecs."[1]

The Aztec polity included subordinated allies and 38 provinces. The latter were taxed directly; most of the former paid tribute in some form; and all were denied free foreign relations. This polyglot empire was headed by a hereditary despot, the proclaimed incarnation of the sun-god. His household was more lavish than many in Europe and swarmed with servants. A head wife supervised the concubines and scheduled their assignments, but Aztec queens rarely engaged in court intrigues or offered advice to the emperor, for he usually ruled without concern for other opinions. He was assisted in his official duties by a chief minister and subordinate bureaucracies for war, religion, justice, treasury, storehouses, and personnel. The capital and each province were administered directly by governors, most of whom were descended from former kings. They collected taxes, held court, arranged religious ceremonies, regulated economic affairs, and directed police activities. In addition, urban guilds, villages, and tribes had their own local officials. Vassal states were governed under their own laws but observed by resident Aztec emissaries. This whole system was defended by a large military organization, comprising allied forces, local militias, and an imperial guard of elite troops.

Aztec religion developed from the worship of animistic spirits, symbolizing natural forces seeking balance while in constant conflict. A pessimistic obsession with human futility also dominated the Aztec worldview, perpetuating the common Mesoamerican belief that the gods required human blood to sustain life. Thus as they assembled their empire, the Aztecs came to envision their sun deity, Uitzilopochtli, as a bloodthirsty war god with an appetite for warriors captured in battle. In every city, the Aztecs built pyramids, topped by its two temples to the sun deity and Tlaloc, god of rain. Here they honored Uitzilopochtli in great public ceremonies, when bloodstained priests at the high altars tore out the living hearts of victims and held them up, quivering, to the sun. One such ceremony in 1487 lasted four days and accounted for 80,000 victims. The need for such victims forced continuing conquests and later weakened the state as it faced the Spanish threat.

Comparing the Aztecs and Mayas with the Romans and Greeks can be an interesting theoretical exercise. The Aztec calendar, mathematics, and writing were derived mainly from Mayan sources, somewhat the way that Roman philosophy and science were based on Greek models. Although Aztec culture spawned skilled sculptors, painters, and craftspeople who produced in great numbers, they lacked the imagination of the Mayas, whom they indirectly

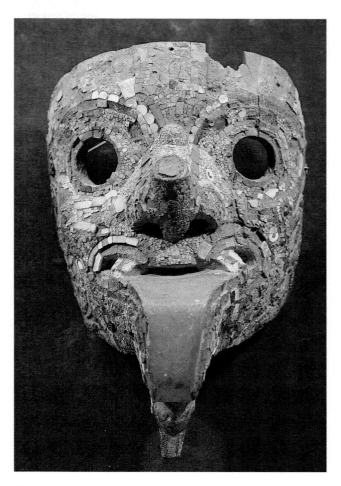

Xototl, the Aztec god of death, depicted as a skeleton. In Aztec religion, the benevolence of the gods was ensured through human sacrifice.

copied, just as Roman artists largely imitated their Greek predecessors. Similarly, both Roman and Aztec cultures were characterized by respect for discipline, practicality, directness, and force. Each was highly skilled in engineering, as attested, for example, by their aqueducts and other feats for furnishing copious amounts of water to their respective capitals. They also shared a militaristic ethos and powerful standing armies.

The Inca Empire

Both the Mayan and Aztec states were less complex than the great Inca Empire in the Andean highlands of South America. Upon reaching full maturity in the early 1500s, it extended 3500 miles between Ecuador and Chile, including almost impassable mountain ranges that separate the upper Amazon forests from the Pacific. The empire contained at least 10 million people in 200 ethnolinguistic groups. It was six times the size of France. The capital, Cuzco, which had an estimated 200,000 inhabitants, was governed in a more centralized way than any city in Europe at the time. The Incas produced fine art and architecture, and were superb engineers, but their major achievement was imperial organization. In this respect they compared favorably with the Romans and the Chinese.

Although it rose very rapidly just before the Spanish conquest, Inca civilization evolved from ancient cultural foundations. Ceremonial and commercial centers had existed on the Peruvian coastal plain well before the Common Era. About 600 C.E. cities began rising in the highlands of the interior. During the next two centuries, tributary kingdoms drew together formerly isolated ceremonial centers of the Peruvian highlands. Some of the resulting states exercised control over the plain, along with territories in what are now Bolivia and Chile. Two kingdoms had capitals at Huari and Tiahuanaco, south central Peru. When these states collapsed in the tenth century, they were succeeded by independent agrarian towns, which were nearly consumed by continuous warfare. A completely different situation developed along the northern coast, where the kingdom of Chimu fostered a high civilization, marked by extensive irrigation, rising population, centralized government, public works, high craft production, widespread trade, and an expanding tributary domain. This polity was conquered and its culture absorbed by the Incas in 1476.

Amid ruthless struggles in the highlands, the Incas created their state in the late medieval era. According to their own legends, these "children of the sun" settled the Valley of Cuzco, in the heartland of the Andes, about 1200 C.E., having migrated from the south, possibly from the region of Tiahuanaco. During the next hundred years they were a simple peasant people, organized by kinship in clans *(ayllu),* living in villages, and worshipping their an-

An Aztec "calender stone," which once stood on the platform of the Great Pyramid at Tenochtitlan.

cestors. To strengthen their unity and better protect themselves in constant wars for survival, they formed a monarchy, developed their military, and began taking over territory near Cuzco. In this competition they were only moderately successful during the reigns of the first seven kings, to the early fifteenth century.

Like the Aztec state at almost the same time, the Inca polity began a climactic period of rapid development with a memorable series of rulers. Viracocha (d. 1438), the eighth emperor, turned his ragtag army into a formidable fighting machine, conquered adjoining territories, and instituted a divine monarchy, with his lineage accepted as descendants of the sun-god. His son, Pachacuti (1438–1471), a reformer, religious leader, and builder, has been called "the greatest man ever produced by the American race."[2] He began arduous campaigns to the north and south, notably against Chimu. Topa Yupanqui (1471–1493), Pachacuti's son and successor, who commanded the Inca armies after 1463, completed the annexation of Chimu and extended the empire south into central Chile. The next emperor, Huayna Capec (1493–1527), completed the subjugation of Ecuador, put down rebellions, and attempted to impose order, although the empire was seething with internal discontent when the Spaniards arrived in 1532.

Despite internal problems, intensified by the steep slopes and harsh weather of the Andes, the Incas demonstrated rare technical skills in fashioning their civilization in difficult and often dangerous circumstances. They were master engineers, carrying water long distances by canals and aqueducts, building cities high in the Andes, and constructing networks of roads along the coast and through the

Machu Picchu, a natural fortress on a narrow ridge between two mountains, was built by the Incas probably after 1440. When the last Inca ruler died, the fortress was abandoned and lost until its rediscovery in 1911.

mountains, along with suspension bridges and interconnecting valley roadways. All were designed to knit together a vast region that in the Inca Empire covered some 380,000 square miles.

Recent excavations have revealed new evidence about the Incas' sophisticated knowledge of canals and irrigation systems. Canals are difficult to construct: if the slope is too narrow, the canal silts up; if it is too steep, its sides erode. Inca engineers devised different canal shapes to control the water's speed and prevent its velocity from ruining the canal. One "intervalley" canal carried water to a city from 60 miles away; it was only one of many networks, involving thousands of feeder canals, that stretched for hundreds of miles. These hydraulic techniques have been described as deserving to stand with Egypt's pyramids and China's Great Wall as among the world's greatest engineering feats. With irrigation canals constructed far removed from the water's source, the Incas farmed 40 percent more land than is achieved today. But if skills fail, land can quickly return to desert conditions. We have yet to learn what caused the destruction or abandonment of these canal systems—was it human or environmental agencies, or both?

Hydraulic feats were matched by sophisticated organizational skills. To link the empire together, Inca leaders established a communication service, using state-built roads, runner-messengers, rest houses, and smoke signals. Governing by means of a divide-and-rule technique, they appealed wherever possible to traditional prejudices among conquered peoples, perpetuating feuds, courting native leaders, settling colonies of subjects among their enemies, and generally provoking disunity among potentially rebellious areas. They also relied on a common official language and the cult of divine monarchy to unify their own people, particularly the elite. Every part of their system was fitted together in a highly disciplined and integrated whole. Before the Incas, few other states had succeeded so effectively in regimenting millions of people over such great distances and against such formidable obstacles.

Like all civilized peoples, the Incas faced the problem of population expansion and a limited food supply. They solved it well enough to support large military, bureaucratic, and priestly establishments by developing what economists call a command economy. They used no money, no credit, and very little trade beyond local barter. The state planned all economic operations and kept all accounts. Government assigned to families the land to be worked; local family heads, under government supervision, directed workers who produced the crops and saw that harvests were brought to state warehouses. Labor taxes provided work done on public projects, the nobles' estates, and royal lands. A similar approach was used in manufacturing, with craftspeople producing in local guilds, noble households, and palace workshops.

Thanks to the extremely dry Peruvian climate, fine intact examples of early Mesoamerican textiles have survived. This embroidered mantle from the central coast of Peru is from the late intermediate period (c. 1000–1400). Rows of geometric human figures, embroidered in reversals of red and yellow, adorn a sheer tan cotton backing. Miniature human figures fill the interstices between the rows of the large figures.

From its storehouses, the government distributed goods to individuals, to the military, and to government projects. In the process, it built roads, operated hospitals, and maintained schools. All property, even the nobles' land, was state-owned and assigned, except for distinctly personal possessions, including some luxury goods owned by the privileged classes.

This state-controlled economy functioned by way of a precisely defined class structure, built on the lingering kinship tradition. Commoners were kept loyal and disciplined by identifying the state with their ancient *ayllus*. Inca nobles maintained respect because they were all related directly or indirectly to the royal lineage and therefore shared the divine mandate to rule. They held the highest positions in government, the army, and the priesthood. A notch lower were lesser aristocrats and nobles among conquered peoples, who held local offices, up to subgovernors in the provinces. The two upper classes made up a privileged elite. Trained in special schools, they were identified by luxuries in food, dress, and housing. They were also exempted from taxes and cruel punishments. At the third level were common workers. They were generally confined to their villages; their work was prescribed; their dress and food were restricted; and government checked even the cleanliness of their houses. Commoners were thus little better off than the lowest class of slaves, who were taken as war captives and assigned to serve the upper classes.

The shift from kinship toward class division was accompanied by a decline of matriarchal values. Upper-class women shared some social status with their husbands, and all women could inherit property when they were widowed; but they were generally subordinated and exploited. Indeed, a fifteenth-century royal decree prohibited women from testifying in court because they were by nature "deceitful, mendacious, and fainthearted."[3] Female commoners worked in the fields, while women of all classes were expected to keep house, mind the children, and serve the needs of men. Many were concubines or surplus wives, the number depending on the husbands' wealth and status. The most beautiful and intelligent young girls were drafted as "chosen women." Some would become "virgins of the sun," serving as nuns and weavers in the temple workshops; others would become concubines of the emperor or nobles; a few would be sacrificed. All were honored as servants of the state.

All authority in the Inca state originated with the hereditary divine emperor, who exercised the power of life and death over all his subjects. He was usually aloof, even with his own immediate family, although he might, if he chose, delegate authority to the queen (his full sister after 1438) or take advice from his mother. With its thousands of servants and concubines, his court was a magnificent display of wealth and power. It was also the locus of a central government that included agencies for rituals (religion), war, treasury, accounts, and public works. The chief ministers were advisers to the Imperial Council, consisting of the emperor and four viceroys, who governed the four provinces. Each province, about the size of New York State, was divided into approximately 40 districts, under subgovernors and their assistants. Authority in the districts was further subdivided, ultimately into units of ten families. Officials at each level reported regularly to superiors and were subject to frequent inspections. This system regulated every aspect of life, including labor, justice, marriage, and even morals.

The power of the ruler depended largely on an excellent military system, which featured compulsory service. Instructors in the villages trained peasant boys for the army; the most promising were marked for advancement when they were called to active service in their twenties. They served for two years before retiring to the labor reserve and militia. The army was organized in units of 10, 50, 100, 1000, and 10,000, under officers who held complete authority over subordinates. A combat force of 200,000, with support units, was always under arms. It was supplied from military storehouses throughout the country and garrisoned in mighty stone fortresses, each with independent water sources. Troops from these centers ruthlessly suppressed any resistance to the regime.

A second base for Inca authority was religion. As the empire grew, its priests appropriated the gods of conquered peoples and included them in a vast pantheon, headed by the Inca sun-god. For example, the virgins of the sun, with their ceremonies and temples, evolved from an earlier moon goddess cult among matrilinear societies. War victims would on occasion be sacrificed to the sun, as would some children of "chosen women." In later times the servants of an emperor, as well as his favorite concubines, were sent with him, at his death, to serve him in the hereafter. To emphasize the emperors' divinity and symbolize the state's continuity, dead emperors were mummified, seated on thrones in their sacred palaces, and attended by living servants, wives, and priests. On public occasions these grotesque figures were paraded before the people, who bowed before them in reverence. Such ceremonies were conducted by a clerical establishment of 4000 priests in the capital and many scores of thousands more throughout the country.

There was a remarkable exception to this religious mind-set in the person of the emperor Pachacuti. A highly successful military leader who largely laid the empire's foundation by consolidating the area around Cuzco and annexing the rich Titicaca basin, this multitalented innovator established Quechua as the administrative language (it is today the most widely spoken Indian language in the Americas), reformed the calendar, introduced methods of terracing the hillsides and extending irrigation, and created an efficient public service. Although regarded as a direct descendant of the sun-god, Pachacuti asked himself how the sun could be the supreme deity since it never rested but revolved endlessly around the earth. He concluded that the sun was itself a messenger sent by a more powerful being who from his place of rest could illuminate and command the world. This must be the universal Creator, Viracocha ("Lord"), who governed the sun and had brought into being all other deities. And in his honor the emperor constructed a temple in Cuzco. But as in the case of Akhenaton, his conceptual forerunner in Egypt, Pachacuti's nascent monotheism did not prevail; later rulers continued to sacrifice victims to the sun-god—though not to the extent practiced by the Aztecs.

Order and security were dominant values in Inca cultural expression, and neither aesthetic concerns nor philosophical speculation received much attention. As we have seen, religious innovation was given short shrift, and any theorizing was subordinated to the practicalities of a state cult and the morality of

Father Bernabé Cobo, "Pachacuti, the Greatest Inca"

This selection is from Chapter 12 of Father Bernabé Cobo's *History of the Inca Empire*. Cobo relied on Indian legends and contemporary Indian testimony, as well as earlier Spanish writings.

Viracocha Inca left four sons by his principal wife; they were called Pachacuti Inca Yupanqui, Inca Roca, Tupa Yupanqui, and Capac Yupanqui. The first one succeeded him in the kingdom, and concerning the rest, although they were lords and grandees, nothing is said. Pachacuti married a lady named Mama Anahuarque, native to the town of Choco, near Cuzco, and he founded a family that they call Iñaca Panaca. This king was the most valiant and warlike, wise and statesmanlike of all the Incas, because he organized the republic with the harmony, laws, and statutes that it maintained from that time until the arrival of the Spaniards. He injected order and reason into everything; eliminated and added rites and ceremonies; made the religious cult more extensive; established the sacrifices and the solemnity with which the gods were to be venerated, enlarged and embellished the temples with magnificent structures, income, and a great number of priests and ministers; reformed the calendar; divided the year into twelve months, giving each one its name; and designated the solemn fiestas and sacrifices to be held each month. He composed many elegant prayers with which the gods were to be invoked, and he ordered that these prayers be recited at the same time that the sacrifices were offered. He was no less careful and diligent in matters pertaining to the temporal welfare of the republic; he gave his vassals a method of working the fields and taking advantage of the lands that were so rough and uneven as to be useless and unfruitful; he ordered that rough hillsides be terraced and that ditches be made from the rivers to irrigate them. In short, nothing was overlooked by him in which he did not impose all good order and harmony; for this reason he was given the name of Pachacuti, which means "change of time or of the world"; this is because as a result of his excellent government

things improved to such an extent that times seemed to have changed and the world seemed to have turned around; thus, his memory was very celebrated among the Indians, and he was given more honor in their songs and poems than any of the other kings that either preceded him or came after him.

After having shown himself to be so devoted to the sun and having taken the care just mentioned that all worship him in the same way that his ancestors had done, one day Pachacuti began to wonder how it was possible that a thing could be god if it was so subject to movement as the Sun, that it never stops or rests for a moment since it turns around the world every day; and he inferred from this meditation that the Sun must not be more than a messenger sent by the Creator to visit the universe; besides, if he were God, it would not be possible for a few clouds to get in front of him and obscure his splendor and rays so that he could not shine; and if he were the universal Creator and lord of all things, sometimes he would rest and from his place of rest he would illuminate all the world and command whatever he wished; and thus, there had to be another more powerful lord who ruled and governed the Sun; and no doubt this was Pachayachachic. He communicated this thought to the members of his council, and in agreement with them, he decided that Pachayachachic was to be preferred to the Sun, and within the city of Cuzco, he built the Creator his own temple which he called Quishuarcancha, and in it he put the image of the Creator of the world, Viracocha Pachayachachic.

From *History of the Inca Empire*, trans. and ed. Roland Hamilton from the holograph manuscript in the Biblioteca Capitular y Colombina de Sevilla, © 1979. Reprinted by permission of the University of Texas Press.

power—treason and cowardice were considered the worst sins. The Incas had no written records and seem to have lacked even the picture-writing of Mesoamerica. Instead they relied on oral traditions, supplemented by mnemonic devices such as the system of knotted strings called the *quipu*. These oral traditions would have been dealt a lethal blow by the Spanish conquest. "The result is that our knowledge of the intangible features of Inca civilization, literature, laws and so on, is very imperfect, and we are cut off almost completely from those of pre-Inca ones."[4]

The Inca lunar calendar was inaccurate and provided no starting point for the identification of historical events. Although the Incas were excellent craftspeople, capable of producing fine pottery and metalwork in copper and gold, their most striking technical and cultural accomplishments were in engineering and massive architecture. Without using mortar, they fitted immense slabs of stone into temple and fortress walls. This efficiency is still exhibited in existing roads, bridges, terraced fields, and stone fortresses.

The Amerindians of North America

The movies have reinforced the fallacy that all Indians constituted a single type with a common lifestyle. The mounted, warbonneted warrior of the plains has too often been considered the archetype of the "Red Man." Yet early European settlers found the North American Indians as diverse as the Europeans themselves. Two hundred distinct North American languages have been classified, and numerous physical differences in the continent's inhabitants have been identified. Amerindian societies presented a wide spectrum of variation: from small bands of hunter-gatherers and farmers to well-organized states. A similar diversity was found in their arts and crafts; various regions excelled in basketry, metalwork, weaving, sculpture, totem-carving, and boatmaking.

Amerindians north of the Rio Grande did not produce the massive technological and governmental achievements of the Mesoamericans. As Paleolithic and Neolithic societies, their populations were much smaller and consequently did not create large cities, with their complex division of labor and urban way of life. They had survived by hunting and fishing until knowledge of food raising spread north from Mesoamerica. Agriculture's effect on those regions where it could be practiced was the same as elsewhere in the world: more stable settlements in which men cleared the fields and women tended the crops. Marked demographic growth, with accompanying large village or town centers, occurred in the Rio Grande, Ohio, Mississippi, and St. Lawrence valleys.

The Iroquois of the Northeast Woodlands

Europeans arriving in what is now upper New York State found various groups speaking dialects of a common Iroquoian language. They had created a distinctive culture by 1000 C.E. and subsequently formed the League of the Five Nations. They used the metaphor of the longhouse, their traditional communal dwelling, to describe their political alliance: the Mohawk along the Hudson were the "keepers of the eastern door," adjoined in sequence by the Oneida, Onondaga, and Cayuga, with the Seneca "keepers of the western door." When the Tuscarora joined in the early eighteenth century, the confederacy became known as the Six Nations. The warlike Iroquois even-

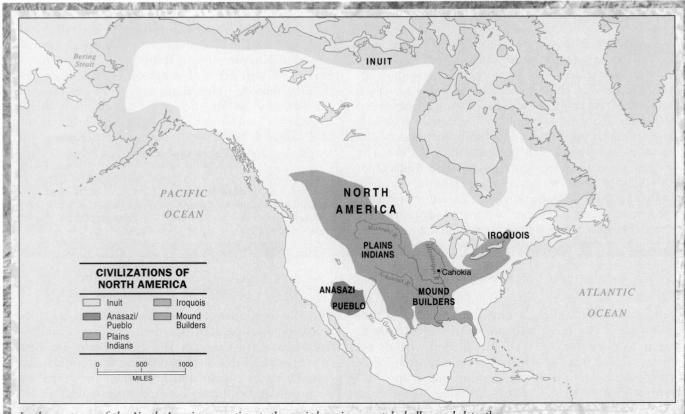

In the vastness of the North American continent, the varied environmental challenges led to the development of hundreds of different Indian tribes—more than 250 alone in the present-day state of California.

tually extended their control from the Great Lakes toward the Atlantic by subjugating the nomadic, food-gathering Algonkian people.

The Iroquois had the advantage of being agriculturists with permanent villages. Some of these had several hundred residents and extensive fields where maize, beans, squash, and tobacco were grown. Weirs were built across streams, and smokehouses preserved joints of game. Related families lived in the longhouses, "long rectangular buildings . . . protected by high wooden palisades. Women played a notable part; they owned the homes and gardens, and, since descent was through the female, chose the leaders. If the men chosen did not give good leadership, they could be replaced."[5]

The Adena and Hopewell Cultures of the Ohio Valley

In the area of present-day Kentucky and Ohio, important Amerindian settlements took root between 800 B.C.E. and 600 C.E. Known generally as the Adena and Hopewell cultures, these Amerindians developed ways of life and social patterns from the Missouri River to the Appalachians and from the Great Lakes to the Gulf of Mexico.

The two groups developed differing ways to construct their homes: the Adena chose to live in circular houses made out of poles and covered with mats and thatched roofs, while the Hopewell built round or oval houses with more protective roofs made of skins, bark from trees, and a combination of thatch and clay. They had a sophisticated view of the after-life, as can be seen in the effort they took to bury their dead. The Adena interred their deceased in vast cone-shaped mounds of earth, sometimes 500 feet around. Sometimes the dead were cremated, and the ashes were placed in the mounds along with all sorts of relics such as carved stone tablets, pipes smoked during religious ceremonies, and jewelry. The Hopewell did the same, but on a larger scale for the more distinguished members of their families.

Along with the impressive burial mounds, archaeologists have found indications of other projects indicating the combined efforts of hundreds of people in addition to a substantial investment of wealth. At Newark, Ohio, for example, the ceremonial site covers 4 square miles. Such enterprises indicate a long period of relative peace, generations remaining in the same place, and a substantial level of wealth. That these took place before the introduction of the planting of corn is significant. Archaeologists think that the Hopewell and Adena cultures survived on a diet of fish, game, nuts, and other plant life. They have also found indications of contacts with tribes across North America. Whether through trading or tribute, the Ohio valley tribes had access to metals and goods found only in the Rocky Mountain area and shells from the Gulf coast. They had mastered the manufacture of tools, pottery, and copper jewelry.

The Mississippian Culture

In the sixth century C.E. another major Amerindian culture made its appearance in the area just east of present-day St. Louis. Archaeologists are still investi-

The Great Serpent Mound in Ohio is a rich repository of the North American Indian life centered in the Adena culture. Active between 500 B.C.E. and 100 C.E., the Indians of the Adena culture had a well-developed village life and traded with other peoples from Canada to the Gulf of Mexico.

gating the origins and extent of this culture from the various burial sites, the most important of which is that at Cahokia, Illinois. Unlike the Adena and Hopewell cultures, the Mississippian culture lived in houses made out of thin pieces of wood (laths) covered with clay—so-called *wattle-and-daub houses*. These took various shapes in the large villages of the area. So influential was this culture that it came to dominate most of the region west of the Mississippi.

The Mississippian peoples benefited from mastering the raising of maize, beans, and squash, and they tied their religion to the planting and harvesting cycles. Their burial mounds took the form of flat-topped pyramids, arranged around a central square. In the most developed regions, fortresslike palisades surrounded the site. The Cahokia complex was constructed over a period of nearly three centuries (c. 900–c. 1150). The centerpiece of the Cahokia site is a pyramid with a base of more than 18 acres, reaching a height of almost 100 feet. This is only one of more than 80 such mounds to be found at Cahokia, a village more than 6 miles long. There was no set burial practice for the Mississippian culture—remains have also been found in cemeteries, in urns, and under the floors of houses.

After the thirteenth century the peoples in the Mississippian culture passed a highly complex religion along from generation to generation—an indication of their stability, continuity, and sophistication. The extent of their wealth enabled them to construct temples filled with ceremonial objects such as large stone scepters and copper plates. Their religion used symbols such as the cross, the sun, arrows surrounded by semicircles, a sunburst, and—most intriguing—an outstretched hand with an eye in the palm. The art that derived from the religion featured portrayals of gods based on animals, rattlesnakes with feathers and wings, and people portrayed as birds. Vessels found at the sites indicate the presence of human sacrifice: jars with human faces painted on them and portrayals of the heads of sacrificed victims. These are indications that not only adults but also infants were given up to the higher deity the Mississippi culture believed controlled their lives.

The Mogollon, Hohokam, and Anasazi Cultures of the Southwest

The southwestern Amerindian cultures lived in the most environmentally challenging part of the continental United States, the dry and rocky regions of present-day Utah, Arizona, New Mexico, and Colorado. In response to their surroundings, they produced the most advanced levels of technology and agriculture. The Mogollon, Hohokam, and Anasazi grew maize, beans, and squash, each group evolving its own techniques. The homes of each group were built out of adobe brick or other techniques of masonry, sometimes on extremely challenging sites. Each group also produced pottery that could rank in beauty with any in the world.

The Mogollon culture lasted almost 1600 years, from around 300 B.C.E. to 1350 C.E. in southwestern New Mexico. Its people built their homes low to the ground along the tops of ridges. Their villages were built around large underground buildings used for religious ceremonies and as pit houses until the eleventh century; thereafter they built these structures at ground level. Because of the constant threat of drought, they developed a diversified economy based on hunting, gathering, and farming. Relatively isolated, they saw little need to change over the centuries.

The Hohokam culture grew along the valleys of the Salt and Gila Rivers. Its architecture was similar to that of the early Mogollon, except the Hohokam built not just ceremonial structures but also their homes inside underground pits. Perhaps learning from the Mesoamerican cultures, the Hohokam constructed an impressive network of canals, some more than 30 miles long, 6 to 10 feet deep, and 15 to 30 feet wide. The existence of these canals proves the existence not only of wealth but also of substantial social organization. The Hohokam also borrowed their religion, their burial practices, and even some of their games from the Mesoamericans.

Deriving from these two cultures was the Anasazi, which appeared around 300 C.E. Of the three cultures, the Anasazi had the most sophisticated and most impressive architecture and the largest area of influence—from the Idaho-Utah border to the Gulf of California. Early on they built their homes in the shape of beehive-shaped domes made out of logs held together by a mudlike mortar. They grew maize and made pottery, like the Mississippian culture, and stored both in warehouselike structures. Around 700 C.E. they took their economic development one step further by beginning the manufacture of cotton cloth. Their technological genius is apparent from their use of two forms of irrigation: runoff by building dikes and terracing hills and subsoil by constructing sand dunes at the base of hills to hold the runoff of the sometimes torrential rains. Their lives revolved around their religion, with ceremonies to placate the gods to hold off storms and to ensure fertility.

The Anasazi are best known today for their architectural accomplishments. Around the eleventh century they began to construct cities, with houses built in the shapes of squares, ells, and semicircles. They used all of the available materials to build these settlements; with wood, mud, and stone, they erected cliff dwellings and the equivalent of terraced apartment houses. One such structure, with some 500 living units, was the largest residential building in the North America until the completion of an apartment

The features on this artifact, thought to be a stabilizer for a spear shaft, illustrate the closeness of the Eskimo (Inuit and Aleut) peoples to their Mongoloid forebears.

house in New York in 1882. The disappearance of the Anasazi around 1300 remains a mystery. It is believed that a combination of a long drought, internecine conflicts, and the arrivals of the Navajo and the Apache led to their demise.

The Navajo, the Apache, the Mandan

Three other groups of Amerindians established their presence before the arrival of Europeans. The Navajo, the largest tribe in the United States, came down from the north to the Southwest sometime in the eleventh century. There they borrowed extensively from the indigenous cultures.

A century or so later, the Apache, who speak a language close to that of the Navajo, arrived and by the end of the 1500s lived in parts of the present states of Arizona, Colorado, and New Mexico. They too were heavily influenced by the cultures present there.

Finally, the Mandan, who based their economy on fur trading and hunting, came to the vast valley of the Missouri River from east of the Mississippi in the late 1300s. They filled in the final empty spaces on the map of North America, and by 1500 Amerindians lived across the length and breadth of what would become the United States, a long time before the New World would be "discovered" by Christopher Columbus.

The Far North: Inuit and Aleuts

The appearance of the Inuit, also known as the Eskimos, is shrouded in controversy. Some observers assert that they descended from ancient seagoing peoples; others believe that they developed their culture in Alaska after the last ice age. They speak much the same language as the Aleuts, whose origins are similarly unclear. It is accepted that the two groups split apart more than 4000 years ago and that they are tied more closely to Asians than the Amerindians are.

The Aleuts stayed largely in the area that is now known as the Alaskan peninsula, the Aleutian Islands, and the far eastern portion of Russia. The Inuit spread along the area south of the Arctic Circle from the Bering Strait across the top of Canada to Greenland. Both peoples lived by hunting and fishing. The Aleuts hunted sea lions, otters, and seals from *kayaks*—small boats made of a wood frame over which skins were stretched. The Inuit showed more flexibility, hunting both sea and land animals, fishing in fresh and salt water. Their diet was based primarily on the caribou, musk-ox, walruses, and whales. They used the kayak too, but supplemented it with canoes and dogsleds. Their greatest accomplishment in seafaring vessels was the *umiak*, from which they harpooned whales.

By about 100 C.E. the Inuit had established large villages; one of the biggest, with around 400 homes, was near Nome, Alaska. To counter the arctic cold, they dug as much as 20 inches into the permafrost to erect their homes, covered with poles and sod. In settlements such as that near Nome, archaeologists have found large structures for the performance of religious rites, led by shamans who claimed to be able to heal diseases and wounds.

Conclusion

Before the coming of the Europeans, the Americas produced a rich variety of highly sophisticated and complex civilizations in response to the varied environmental challenges and opportunities of the Western Hemisphere. Some of these groups made the transition from food hunting to food raising, and some did not.

In Central and South America agriculture supplied the sustenance to support growing populations. This in turn led to the establishment of villages and then cities and finally far-flung states. More food and more wealth also produced leisure and priestly classes who had the time to think about religion, literature, art, architecture, mathematics, and astronomy.

In North America environmental conditions were harsher and did not permit an equivalent accumulation of agricultural surpluses found in Central and South America. Some Indian tribes remained hunter-gatherers. Others established settled villages and complex civilizations, but without the wealth, power, or sophistication of Mesoamerica.

Unfortunately, a combination of European diseases and technology would decimate and subjugate the peoples of the Americas after the fifteenth century. Although they fought bravely against overwhelming odds, the Indians would have to struggle to maintain their cultural identities in the centuries to come.

Suggestions for Reading

A sound in-depth introduction to indigenous cultures in the New World is Alvin M. Josephy, ed., *America in 1492* (Knopf, 1992). See also Robert Wauchope's *Indian Background of Latin American History* (Knopf, 1970). The three following comparative studies are well worth attention: George Collier, ed., *The Inca and Aztec States, 1400–1800* (Academic Press, 1982); Geoffrey W. Conrad and Arthur A. Demarest, *Religion and Empire: The Dynamics of Aztec and Inca Expansionism* (Cambridge University Press, 1984); and Alfred Sundell. *A History of the Aztec and the Maya and Their Conquest* (Collier Books, 1967).

Among the most informative works on pre-Columbian Mesoamerica are Ross Hassig, *War and Society in Ancient Mesoamerica* (University of California Press, 1992); Richard A. Dieh and Janet C. Berlo, eds., *Mesoamerica After the Decline of Teotihuacán* (Dumbarton Oakes, 1989); Michael D. Coe, *Mexico*, 3rd ed. (Thames & Hudson, 1986); and Robert R. Miller, *Mexico* (University of Oklahoma Press, 1989). See also Shirley Gorenstein, *Not Forever on Earth: The Prehistory of Mexico* (Scribner, 1975); Kenneth Pearce, *The View from the Top of the Temple* (University of New Mexico Press, 1984); Jacques Soustelle, *The Olmecs: The Oldest Civilization in Mexico* (University of Oklahoma Press, 1985); and Joseph W. Whitecotton, *The Zapotecs: Princes, Priests, and Peasants* (University of Oklahoma Press, 1984).

For informative studies on the Mayas, see Michael D. Coe, *The Maya* (Thames & Hudson, 1987); Norman Hammond, *Ancient Maya Civilization* (Rutgers University Press, 1982); and John S. Henderson, *The World of the Ancient Maya* (Cornell University Press, 1981). Special insights into the Mayan experience are provided in Jeremy A. Sobloff, *A New Archeology and the Ancient Maya* (Scientific American Library, 1990); Linda Schele and David Friedel, *A Forest of Kings* (Morrow, 1990); and Ralph Witlock, *Everyday Life of the Maya* (Dorset, 1987).

Works that reveal the private as well as the public life of the Aztecs include Jane S. Day, *Aztec: The World of Montezuma* (Robert Rinehart, 1992); Richard Townshend, *The Aztecs* (Thames & Hudson, 1992); Inga Clendinnen, *Aztecs* (Cambridge University Press, 1991); Francis F. Berdan, *The Aztecs* (Chelsea House, 1989); Alfonso Caso, *The Aztecs, People of the Sun* (University of Oklahoma Press, 1988); and Nigel Davies, *The Aztecs* (University of Oklahoma Press, 1989). An older acclaimed work, Burr Cartwright Brundage, *A Rain of Darts* (University of Texas Press, 1972), is still

valuable. For special studies on Aztec political institutions and development, see Susan Gillespie, *The Aztec Kings* (University of Arizona Press, 1989), and Ross Hassig, *Aztec Warfare: Imperial Expansion and Political Control* (University of Oklahoma Press, 1988). For an interesting description of social conditions, see Rudolf van Zantwijk, *The Aztec Arrangement: The Social History of Pre-Spanish Mexico* (University of Oklahoma Press, 1985), and June Nash, "The Aztecs and the Ideology of Male Dominance," *Signs* 4 (1978), pp. 349–362.

On the Incas, Ian Cameron, *Kingdom of the Sun God* (Facts on File, 1990), deserves special attention. Bernabé Cobo, *A History of the Inca Empire* (University of Texas Press, 1979), is still considered sound and complete. Another long-respected anthropological approach to pre-Columbian Andean culture is J. Alden Mason, *Ancient Civilizations of Peru* (Penguin, 1988). It is supplemented by Richard W. Keating, *Peruvian Pre-History* (Cambridge University Press, 1988). Other standard works include Loren McIntyre, *The Incredible Inca and Their Timeless Land* (National Geographic, 1978), and Alfred Metraux, *The History of the Incas* (Schocken, 1970). Excellent depictions of the Inca command economy can be found in Jonathon Haas et al., *The Origin and Development of the Andean State* (Cambridge University Press, 1987); Frank Solomon, *The Native Lords of Quito in the Age of the Incas: The Political Economy of the North-Andean Chieftains* (Cambridge University Press, 1986); and John V. Murra, *The Economic Organization of the Inca State* (JAI Press, 1980).

Suggestions for Web Browsing

Mesoweb, including Illustrated Encyclopedia of Mesoamerica
http://www.mesoweb.com/

Mesoweb is devoted to ancient Mesoamerica and its cultures: the Olmec, Mayas, Aztecs, Toltecs, Mixtecs, Zapotecs, and others.

University of Pennsylvania Museum of Archaeology and Art: Mesoamerica
http://www.upenn.edu/museum/Collections/mesoamerica.html

A history of Mesoamerican culture as reflected by the many artifacts in the university's museum.

National Museum of the American Indian
http://www.si.edu/activity/planvis/museums/aboutmai.htm

Web site of the Smithsonian Institution's National Museum of the American Indian offers a look at one of the finest and most complete collections of items from the indigenous peoples of the Western Hemisphere.

Arctic Studies Center
http://nmnhwww.si.edu/arctic/

Smithsonian Institution site dedicated to the study of Arctic peoples, culture, and environments includes numerous images, as well as audio and video segments of dance and discussion.

Notes

1. Michael E. Smith, "Life in the Provinces of the Aztec Empire," *Scientific American*, September 1997, p. 83.
2. Clements Markham, in Edward Hyams and George Ordish, *The Last of the Incas* (New York: Simon & Schuster, 1963), p. 99.
3. Ibid., p. 88.
4. G. H. S. Bushnell, *Peru* (London: Thames & Hudson, 1960), p. 30.
5. J. Wreford Watson, *Social Geography of the United States* (New York: Longman, 1979), p. 25.

The Transition to Modern Times

So far we have encountered a number of societies that emphasized the group at the expense of the individual—societies such as ancient Egypt or medieval Europe. In other societies, such as classical Greece, individualism counted for more than collectivism. During the period that historians speak of as early modern times, the interests and rights of the individual were again in the ascendant in the West. By the end of the fifteenth century the medieval ideal of universal political unity had been shattered as national monarchies gained supremacy in England, France, and Spain. Despite opposition from popes and nobles, vigorous monarchs in these countries succeeded in their attempts at nation-making—a process that fostered and was in turn supported by a growing national consciousness among the common people.

In the realm of thought, Italian scholars known as humanists discovered in the manuscripts of ancient Greece and Rome the same emphasis on individual freedom that was rapidly gaining momentum in their own day, and with this spirit of individualism sprang up an unashamed delight in the beauties and joys of life. The creative vigor of the Italian Renaissance in literature, thought, and the fine arts surged throughout Europe, resulting in one of the most fruitful epochs in human cultural history.

Carried into the religious sphere, the resurgence of individualism shattered the universal supremacy of the church and gave rise to the religious diversity of the modern Western world. The followers of Luther, Calvin, and Zwingli substituted the authority of the Scriptures for that of the Roman church and interposed no priestly mediator between the individual and God. The Roman church, which launched a vigorous reform movement of its own, nevertheless continued to be a potent force.

The economic structure of western Europe went through a Commercial Revolution in early modern times. The quickening of town life abetted the rise of a new and forceful middle class, whose members were the chief supporters of the system of economic individualism known as capitalism. Furthermore, overseas expansion stimulated trade, increased wealth, and introduced to European markets an abundance of products previously scarce or unknown. The barter economy of the Middle Ages was superseded by one of money, banks, and stock exchanges, and Europe rapidly became the economic center of the world.

For the kingdoms of Europe, the Ottoman conquest of Constantinople in 1453 signaled a catastrophe. However, the Ottomans symbolized a new Muslim world emerging between the eastern Mediterranean and Indonesia. In that vast territory three new empires held sway for centuries. Geographically, this world was centered in Persia, under its Shi'ite Safavid dynasty. Culturally, it was influenced by Persian, Arab, and Byzantine courtly traditions. To the east the magnificent Mughul Empire emerged on the frontiers of Hindu and Confucian polities. Militarily, this Muslim world was dominated by the forces of the Ottoman Empire, far stronger than those of any country in Europe at the time. Warfare often prevailed among these contending states; but they also shared the same Islamic faith, steppe antecedents, and Persian art traditions. They would later be challenged and supplanted by European states also seeking dominion in the midst of a global economic revolution. But in the sixteenth century Asian empires held primacy of place in the contest for world power, controlling the land and seaborne routes of the East-West trade.

For China, geography and demography had dictated that it would be impossible to have the Central Kingdom remain isolated and arrogant into the modern age. The Ming rulers tried their best after their first half century to pursue a conservative policy of noninvolvement with other peoples and succeeded in bringing some stability to China. However, toward the seventeenth century their inability to reform and the arrival of all manner of outsiders—invading forces and merchants alike—spelled an end to their nearly three-century-long run.

Korea and Japan were the two major recipients of the Chinese example and closeness. Korea rested under the immediate gaze of its immense neighbor yet managed to construct a unique and powerful nation. Japan, blessed with its island position, had the unparalleled advantage of picking and choosing the currents and influences it would receive. To the south and southeast a complex mosaic of nations grew, formed from Indian, Chinese, and Muslim influences. Never able to achieve regional dominance, each of them had a moment of hegemony and added to the rich Asian cultural picture.

The Renaissance in Italy and Northern Europe

Renaissance Thought and Art, 1300–1600

Chapter Contents

In Italy during the fourteenth and fifteenth centuries, thinkers and artists began to view the thousand years that had passed since the fall of Rome as the "Dark Ages," a time of stagnation and ignorance, in contrast to their own age, which appeared to them enlightened and beautiful. They called themselves *humanists*—scholars who were dedicated to the recovering, study, and transmission of the intellectual and cultural heritage of Greece and Rome. They exuberantly said that they were participating in an intellectual and artistic revolution sparked by a renaissance ("rebirth") of the values and forms of classical antiquity. Modern historians have accepted the term *Renaissance* as a convenient label for this exciting age of intellectual and artistic revival, which continued through the sixteenth century. But since the Renaissance had deep roots in the Middle Ages, which also made rich contributions to civilization, in what ways can the Renaissance be said to signify a true "rebirth"?

First of all, there was an intensification of interest in the literature of classical Greece and Rome. This Classical Revival, as it is called, was the product of a more worldly focus of interest—a focus on human beings and life as an end in itself rather than as a temporarily occupied stop on the way to eternity. Renaissance scholars searched the monasteries for old Latin manuscripts that had been unappreciated and largely ignored by medieval scholars, and they translated previously unknown works from Greek into Latin, the common language of scholarship. In

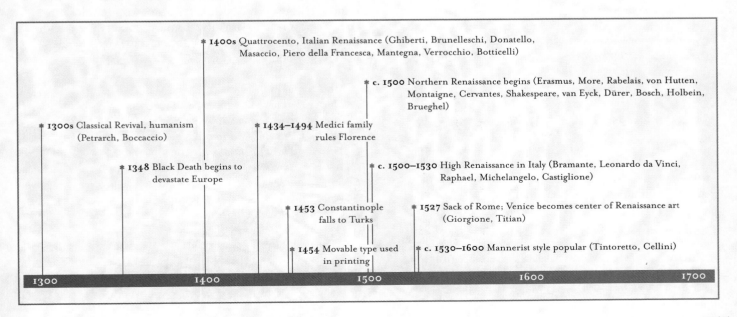

* **1400s** Quattrocento, Italian Renaissance (Ghiberti, Brunelleschi, Donatello, Masaccio, Piero della Francesca, Mantegna, Verrocchio, Botticelli)

* **c. 1500** Northern Renaissance begins (Erasmus, More, Rabelais, von Hutten, Montaigne, Cervantes, Shakespeare, van Eyck, Dürer, Bosch, Holbein, Brueghel)

* **1300s** Classical Revival, humanism (Petrarch, Boccaccio)

* **1434–1494** Medici family rules Florence

* **1348** Black Death begins to devastate Europe

* **c. 1500–1530** High Renaissance in Italy (Bramante, Leonardo da Vinci, Raphael, Michelangelo, Castiglione)

* **1453** Constantinople falls to Turks

* **1527** Sack of Rome; Venice becomes center of Renaissance art (Giorgione, Titian)

* **1454** Movable type used in printing

* **c. 1530–1600** Mannerist style popular (Tintoretto, Cellini)

| 1300 | 1400 | 1500 | 1600 | 1700 |

this manner the humanists greatly added to the quantity of classical literature that had entered the mainstream of Western thought since the Middle Ages. Second, while Renaissance scholars found a new significance in classical literature, artists in Italy were stimulated and inspired by the study and imitation of classical sculpture and architecture.

But the Renaissance was not a mere cult of antiquity, a looking backward into the past. The humanists of the Renaissance were the forefathers of the modern world, enthusiastically widening the horizon of human interests. Renaissance culture exhibited a strong belief in the worth of the individual and the individual's ability to think and act as a free agent. The Renaissance spirit was admirably summed up by the Florentine humanist Leon Battista Alberti when he declared, "Men can do all things if they will."

In some respects every age is an age of transition, but it may be fair to state that the Renaissance marked one of the major turning points in Western civilization. The dominant institutions and thought systems of the Middle Ages were in decline; Scholasticism, church authority, and conformity were constantly questioned. Instead a culture that depended on individualism, on skepticism, and ultimately on science was taking its place.

The Renaissance originated in the cities of central and northern Italy. We shall begin with a description of the new secular interests and values that arose in these urban centers, then note the relationship between these urban interests and the Classical Revival and flowering of art, and conclude with a discussion of the spread of the Renaissance as it crossed the Alps to France, Germany, and England. Ultimately it was in England that the underlying optimism and dynamism of the entire Renaissance period was epitomized by Shakespeare:

> O, wonder!
> How many goodly creatures are there here!
> How beauteous mankind is! O brave new world,
> That has such people in 't![1]

The Italian Renaissance

The culture of the Italian Renaissance was not created in a vacuum. Historians today find a clue to the intellectual and aesthetic changes of the age in economic, social, and political change.

Emergence of the Italian City-States

During the High Middle Ages, a new economy and a new society emerged in western Europe (see Chapter 9). Commerce and a money economy revived, towns arose and became self-governing communes, and townspeople constituted a new middle class, the bourgeoisie. Although Italy had been one of the leaders in these twelfth- and thirteenth-century developments, during the next two centuries the region moved dramatically ahead of the rest of Europe.

During the fourteenth and fifteenth centuries the city-states of northern and central Italy experienced a tremendous growth in population and expanded to become small territorial states. These included the Papal States, where the restored authority of the popes crushed the independence of many little city-states in central Italy. Feudalism had died out in Italy during the twelfth and thirteenth centuries.

Unlike the French nobility, who spent their time participating in the vigorous court life of their fellow nobles, the Italian nobles moved to the cities and joined with the rich merchants to form a patrician ruling class. Together they successfully fought off the intervention of the German emperors Frederick Barbarossa and Frederick II. By 1300 nearly all the land of northern and central Italy was owned by profit-seeking urban citizens who produced for city markets. In the large export industries, such as woolen cloth (it employed 30,000 in Florence), a capitalistic system of production was emerging—the "putting out" system in which the merchant-capitalist retained ownership of the raw material and paid others to work it into the finished product. Additional great wealth was gained from commerce, particularly the import-export trade in luxury goods from the East. So much wealth was accumulated by these merchant-capitalists that they turned to moneylending and banking. From the thirteenth to the fifteenth centuries, Italians monopolized European banking (Florence had 80 banking houses by 1300). It is no wonder that in this prosperous, worldly Italian society, money transformed values and became a new virtue, celebrated in poetry:

> Money makes the man,
> Money makes the stupid pass for bright, . . .
> Money buys the pleasure-giving women,
> Money keeps the soul in bliss, . . .
> The world and fortune being ruled by it,
> Which even opens, if you want, the doors of paradise.
> So wise he seems to me who piles up
> What more than any other virtue
> Conquers gloom and leavens the whole spirit.[2]

These economic and political successes made the Italian upper-class groups strongly assertive, self-confident, and passionately attached to their city-states.

This map illustrates Europe in the time of the Italian and Northern Renaissance, as well as some of the cities which served as centers for artistic and humanist activities during the period.

Literature and art reflected their self-confidence. Poets described them as riding "self-assuredly through the streets"; every major sculptor and painter produced their portraits, sometimes tucked away in corners of religious paintings; and architects affirmed their importance by constructing their imposing palaces—the *palazzi* of the Medici, Rucellai, Pitti, Strozzi, and Pazzi families, for example, still standing in Florence.

Furthermore, the humanists provided them with a justification for their efforts. The humanists' focus on individuals and society, along with their insistent theme of the "dignity of man," was entirely in keeping with the outlook, manners, and accomplishments of the dominant urban groups. These groups embraced new and more secular art and values, both largely alien to the church-dominated culture of the Middle Ages.

Renaissance Patrons

Political leaders and the wealthy merchants, bankers, and manufacturers conspicuously dis-

played their wealth and bolstered their own importance and that of their cities by patronizing artists and humanists. Most of these artists and scholars were provided with governmental, academic, and tutorial posts.

Renaissance artists enjoyed the security and protection offered by their patrons and the advantage of working exclusively on commission. Artists knew where their finished work would be displayed—in cathedral, villa, or city square. This situation contrasts with some later periods, when artists painted as they wished and then attempted to sell the work to anyone who would buy it.

Among the most famous patrons were members of the Medici family, champions of the lower classes, who ruled Florence for 60 years (1434–1494). Under their leadership Florence was in name a republic, but the Medici family completely dominated the state. Lorenzo de' Medici, who was the first citizen of Florence from 1469 until his death in 1492, carried on his family's proud

Discovery Through Maps

The Power and Glory of Renaissance Venice

Maps can be designed to illustrate much more than the physical features of the subject; they can also serve as propaganda—a vehicle to enhance the image of a particular city or state. For example, examine this representation of the Italian Republic of Venice in the mid-sixteenth century, painted by Ignazio Danti (1536–1586), a local member of the Dominican order. Danti depicts a sophisticated and glorious metropolis, proud of its wealth and power. Over the city hovers its symbol, the lion, clutching in its paws a scroll acclaiming the past glory of the city and the perpetual prosperity and honor that is its due.

The purpose of this map was not to render geographical assistance but rather to promote the power and glory of its subject city in the hope of attracting commerce—a beautiful and impressive piece of cartographic propaganda.

The classic example of the Renaissance nobleman, statesman, and patron of the arts was the Florentine Lorenzo de' Medici, known as Lorenzo the Magnificent. Under his patronage and guidance, Florence became the leading city of the Italian Renaissance, renowned for the splendor of its buildings and lavish support for the arts.

traditions and added so much luster to Florence that he became known as Lorenzo the Magnificent. When he added up the principal expenditures made by his family between 1434 and 1471 for commissions to artists and architects, as well as for charities and taxes, and it came to the astounding total of 663,755 gold florins, he remarked: "I think it casts a brilliant light on our estate and it seems to me that the monies were well spent and I am very well pleased with this."[3]

The Renaissance popes—with few exceptions as worldly as their fellow citizens—were lavish patrons who made Rome the foremost center of art and learning by 1500. What Pope Nicholas V (1447–1455) said of himself applies to most of the Renaissance popes through the pontificate of Clement VII (1523–1534), who was a member of the Medici family: "In all things I have been liberal: in building, in the purchase of books [the Vatican Library is still one of the world's greatest], in the constant transcription of Greek and Latin manuscripts, and in the rewarding of learned men."

Humanism and the Classical Revival

During the Middle Ages the writers of antiquity had been interpreted within the framework of Christian religion and often cited as authorities to bolster

The popes' building program was in large measure responsible for Rome's superseding Florence as the center of artistic activity during the High Renaissance. The greatest builder, Julius II (1503–1513), commissioned Bramante to begin the new St. Peter's and had Michelangelo paint the Sistine Chapel while Raphael decorated adjoining rooms in the Vatican.

church dogma. Although many aspects of antiquity were avoided because of their disturbingly pagan quality, the clergy did make use of pagan literature that could be interpreted allegorically and given a Christian meaning. Consequently, the true nature of the classical legacy was generally distorted or obscured. But in Italy in the fourteenth and fifteenth centuries there emerged a new spirit of humanism, a movement that sought to recapture the learning and culture of ancient Greece and Rome.

The Classical Revival

In fourteenth-century Italy a new perspective on life began to evolve and a fresh appreciation of classical literature emerged. As successors to a small group of medieval teachers of grammar and rhetoric, the representatives of this new movement called themselves *humanists,* a name derived from the *studia humanitatis,* or "humanistic studies," as Roman authors termed a liberal or literary education. Writing in praise of the *studia humanitatis,* an early Italian humanist identified them as studies that "perfect and adorn man."

Medieval Scholastic education had emphasized logic, science, and professional training in law, medicine, and theology at the expense of the arts, the literary side of the curriculum. Hence the Scholastics had centered their attention on Aristotle's *Logic, Metaphysics,* and scientific writings and on other an-

cient works on astronomy, medicine, and mathematics. The humanists, however, reflecting urban society's interest in the problems and values of human living, reversed this medieval emphasis and called attention to the importance of an education in the humanities—history, grammar, rhetoric, poetry, and moral philosophy. The humanists avoided the sciences because, as Petrarch—the first of the great Italian humanists—wrote:

> They help in no way toward a happy life, for what does it advantage us to be familiar with the nature of animals, birds, fishes, and reptiles, while we are ignorant of the nature of the race of man to which we belong, and do not know or care whence we come or whither we go?[4]

Thus despite the fact that both the humanist and the Scholastic looked to the past and respected its heritage, they differed widely in their choice of the ancient material to be revered.

Humanists and Scholastics also differed in the manner in which they saw themselves in relation to the writers of ancient times. Whereas the Scholastics always felt inferior to the ancients and looked up to them as child to parent or pupil to teacher, humanists saw themselves as equal to the ancients and boldly hailed them as individual to individual and friend to friend. At the beginning of his *Divine Comedy,* Dante describes medieval reliance on the authority of the ancients in allegorical terms: Dante (symbolizing medieval man) is lost in the "dark wood" that is this life until he is rescued by Virgil (a favorite medieval symbol of ancient wisdom), who thereafter guides him along the right path. "Losing me," Virgil is made to say to Dante, "ye would remain astray."

The noticeably different attitude of the humanists was expressed by Niccoló Machiavelli (1469–1527), a Florentine politician, diplomat, and political theorist. In his strictly secular and realistic treatise on politics, *The Prince* (1513), Machiavelli wrote of his regard for classical learning: "I enter the ancient courts of the men of antiquity. Received with affection by them, . . . I do not hesitate to hold conversation with them and to inquire the reason for their actions. They, in their humanity, reply to me."[5] It was in this spirit that Petrarch wrote his *Letters to Ancient Authors,* addressing Homer, Plato, Cicero, and others in familiar terms and sharing with them his own thoughts and experiences. This feeling of equality with ancient authors was also behind the humanists' practice of filling their own writings with apt quotations from the classics. The humanists' purpose, however, differed from that of the Scholastics, who also quoted extensively from the ancients. As the French humanist Montaigne explained in his essays, he quoted the ancients not because he agreed with them but because they agreed with him.

Petrarch and Boccaccio

The "father of humanism" is a title given to Francesco Petrarca, better known as Petrarch (1304–1374), by later Italian humanists because he was the first to play a major role in making people conscious of the attractions of classical literature. Distressed by the condition of society in fourteenth-century Italy—political and social unrest, the decline of the church, the shortcomings of Scholasticism—and resentful of being forced by his father to study law at Bologna, Petrarch found consolation and escape in the literature of ancient Rome. As he explained later in his *Letter to Posterity,* "In order to forget my own time I have constantly striven to place myself in spirit in other ages." And in the same vein, "Nothing that we suffer but has happened to others before us."

In 1327 he met and fell in love with Laura. Little is known of Laura other than that she was married. Inspired by his love for her, Petrarch wrote sonnets that show him to be one of the greatest lyric poets of all time. His portrayal of Laura represents a fresh approach. Earlier poets had woven about their heroines an air of courtly love and religious idealization, which made the characters quite unreal. Petrarch's Laura was a flesh-and-blood creature whom all readers could recognize as human. Petrarch praised her

A miniature portrait of Petrarch from his illuminated manuscript of Remedies Against Fortune. *In keeping with a classical tradition, Petrarch composed many letters—which he edited for publication—that were in effect literary essays expressing his own attitudes and humanistic concerns.*

chastity, which had withstood his advances. And even though he wrote that she had "mocked, despised, scorned" him "with an air of haughty disdain," he forever viewed her as an ennobling influence on his life.

The ancient writers' attitude toward life struck a sympathetic chord in Petrarch. In *On the Secret Conflict of My Cares,* Petrarch has an imaginary conversation with St. Augustine that forcibly brings out the conflict between his new worldly interests and those of traditional Christianity. St. Augustine accuses Petrarch of pursuing false goals: "What are you doing, poor little man? What are you dreaming?" Petrarch concludes that although St. Augustine's arguments cannot be refuted, he will not renounce his chosen path: "The care of mortal things must come first in mortal minds."

This inner conflict between Petrarch's concern for "mortal things" and his loyalty to the traditional Christian ideal of self-denial and otherworldliness exemplifies the transitional position Petrarch, and humanism, occupied in Western culture. He could not accept a lessening of an individual's importance or a reduction of one's mental horizons. Thus he condemned the rigidity and empty logic of Scholasticism and the narrow limits of medieval education. He took as his motto a line from the Roman dramatist Terence: "I am a man, and nothing human do I consider alien to myself." Petrarch was not a careful scholar and never learned Greek, yet he gave humanism its first great impetus.

Another celebrated early humanist was the Florentine Giovanni Boccaccio (1313–1375), who began his career as a writer of poetry and romances. In 1348 the horrible Black Death struck—it wiped out nearly two-thirds of Florence's population. Boccaccio used this event to establish the setting of his masterpiece, the *Decameron.* To escape the pestilence, his characters—three young men and seven young women—seek seclusion in a country villa, where they while away the time telling stories. Boccaccio injected the hundred tales of the *Decameron,* based on medieval *fabliaux* and chivalric romances, with a new and different spirit. Recounted by sophisticated city-dwellers, the tales satirize the follies of knights and other medieval types and clearly express the contempt that had developed for the old and by then dying ideals of feudalism. Many tales are bawdy and even scandalous—a charge Boccaccio sought to refute:

> *Some of you may say that in writing these tales I have taken too much license, by making ladies sometimes say and often listen to matters which are not proper to be said or heard by virtuous ladies. This I deny, for there is nothing so unchaste but may be said chastely if modest words are used; and this I think I have done.[6]*

The *Decameron* offers a wealth of anecdotes, portraits of flesh-and-blood characters, and vivid (although one-sided) glimpses of Renaissance life.

Zeal for the Study of Greek Literature

Petrarch had tried without success to learn Greek. Not until Greek scholars arrived in Italy from Constantinople were competent instructors available. Manuel Chrysoloras, the first of these scholars, came to Venice in 1393, sent by the Byzantine emperor to secure help against the Turks. Three years later he was invited to Florence, where he remained for three years as a teacher of Greek language and literature. Leonardo Bruni (1370–1444) tells how he took this opportunity to throw himself enthusiastically into the study of Greek.

Chrysoloras the Byzantine, a man of noble birth and well versed in Greek letters, brought Greek learning to us. When his country was invaded by the Turks, he came by sea, first to Venice. The report of him soon spread, and he was cordially invited and besought and promised a public stipend, to come to Florence and open his store of riches to the youth. I was then studying Civil Law, but . . . I burned with love of academic studies, and had spent no little pains on dialectic and rhetoric. At the coming of Chrysoloras I was torn in mind, deeming it shameful to desert the law, and yet a crime to lose such a chance of studying Greek literature; and often with youthful impulse I would say to myself: "Thou, when it is permitted thee to gaze on Homer, Plato and Demosthenes, and the other poets, philosophers, orators, of whom such glorious things are spread abroad, and speak with them and be instructed in their admirable teaching, wilt thou desert and rob thyself? Wilt thou neglect this opportunity so divinely offered? For seven hundred years, no one in Italy has possessed Greek letters; and yet we confess that all knowledge is derived from them. How great advantage to your knowledge, enhancement of your fame, increase of your pleasure, will come from an understanding of this tongue? There are doctors of civil law everywhere; and the chance of learning will not fail thee. But if this one and only doctor of Greek letters disappears, no one can be found to teach thee." Overcome at length by these reasons, I gave myself to Chrysoloras, with such zeal to learn, that what through the wakeful day I gathered, I followed after in the night, even when asleep.

From Henry Osborn Taylor, ed., *Thought and Expression in the Sixteenth Century*, Vol. 1 (New York: Macmillan, 1920), pp. 36–37.

The *Decameron* closed Boccaccio's career as a creative artist. Largely through the influence of Petrarch, whom he met in 1350, Boccaccio gave up writing in Italian and turned to the study of antiquity. He began to learn Greek, composed an encyclopedia of classical mythology, and went off to monasteries in search of manuscripts. By the time Petrarch and Boccaccio died, the study of the literature and learning of antiquity was growing throughout Italy.

The search for manuscripts became a mania, and before the middle of the fifteenth century, works by most of the important Latin authors had been found. The degree of difference between humanist and Scholastic is indicated by the ease with which the early humanists recovered the "lost" Latin literary masterpieces: they were found close at hand in monastic libraries, covered by the undisturbed dust of many centuries. The books had always been there; what had been largely lacking was an appreciative audience of readers. In addition to these Latin works, precious Greek manuscripts were brought to Italy from Constantinople after it fell to the Turks in 1453.

Civic Humanism

For the humanists of the fifteenth century—the "civic humanists," as they are called—humanism became the foundation of a course of study designed not for pure contemplation, as it was for Petrarch, but as an educational program outlining what was relevant and useful in the classics for the leaders of the Italian city-states. One of them warned against letting literature "absorb all the interests of life. . . . For the man who surrenders himself entirely to the attractions of letters or speculative thought perhaps follows a self-regarding end and is useless as a citizen or prince." Whereas Petrarch wrote of the "much sweetness and charm" he found in the writings of his "dear friend" Cicero "when the difficulties of life are pressing on me so sharply and inexorably," the civic humanists honored Cicero more for his emphasis on moral philosophy and rhetoric (the art of persuasion) and his commitment to public affairs. They found the ancient historians, notably Livy and Plutarch, especially valuable. "The careful study of the past," wrote one of the humanists, "enlarges our foresight in contemporary affairs."

Revival of Platonism

During the late fifteenth century many humanists gravitated to Platonic and Neo-Platonic philosophy as a result of both their lack of interest in the Aristotelian emphasis on natural science and their search for a classical philosophy that stressed moral purpose and religious and even mystical values. A factor in this revival was the study of Plato in the original Greek, particularly at Florence where Cosimo de' Medici, one of the great patrons of the Renaissance, founded the informal club that came to be known as the Platonic Academy. Its leader, Marsilio Ficino (1433–1499), who always kept a candle burning before a bust of Plato, made the first complete Latin translation of Plato's works.

Ficino sought to synthesize Christianity and Plato, much as St. Thomas Aquinas had done with Aristotle. In his principal work, appropriately titled *The Platonic Theology*, Ficino viewed Plato as essentially Christian and Plato's "religious philosophy" as a God-sent means of converting intellectuals. He coined the expression "Platonic love" to describe an ideal, pure love, and this concept found its way into Renaissance literature and art.

Ficino's disciple, Pico della Mirandola (1463–1494), was driven by an insatiable appetite for knowledge. In addition to Latin and Greek, he learned Hebrew and Arabic in order to read everything he possibly could. At age 23 he announced to the world that he knew everything and invited all interested scholars to join him in Rome (expenses paid) for a public debate on 900 theological and philosophical propositions. (The pope considered some propositions heretical and forbade the debate.) As an introduction to his list of propositions, Pico composed "Oration on the Dignity of Man," an essay that remains one of the most glowing tributes to the human race in all Renaissance writing. With youthful exuberance he wrote, "There is nothing to be seen more wonderful than man. . . . To him it is granted to have whatever he chooses, to be whatever he wills."

Aristotelianism

Despite its great attraction for many humanists, Platonism still had a powerful rival in Aristotelianism. Concerned chiefly with natural science, logic, and metaphysics, Aristotelian commentators continued to dominate teaching in the Italian universities.

The most influential Aristotelians were the Latin Averroists, followers of the Muslim philosopher Averroës (see Chapter 10). The Averroists followed Aristotle in teaching that matter is eternal and in denying the immortality of the soul. Since such views were contrary to the biblical story of creation and the belief in personal immortality, the Averroists advocated the doctrine of "double truth"—a truth in philosophy need not be valid in religion.

By the fifteenth century the University of Padua had become the center of Aristotelianism, which reached its peak in the next century. By championing a secular rationalism that kept philosophy separate from theology, its followers maintained an environ-

Pico della Mirandola, the brilliant humanist who was recognized as a genius. (This medal was produced in the year following his death.) Before he died at age 31, he had been influenced by the fiery sermons of Savonarola, the puritanical reformer of society and the church. In 1494, the year Pico died, Savonarola gained control of Florence and ruled it for four years as the Kingdom of God.

ment necessary for the triumph of scientific thought in the seventeenth century. Some of the pioneers of that "scientific revolution" (see Chapter 21) were connected with Padua. Copernicus studied there before publishing his *Revolutions of the Heavenly Spheres* in 1543; the anatomist Vesalius, whose revolutionary *Fabric of the Human Body* appeared in the same year, was a professor there; and the astronomer and physicist Galileo lectured there early in the next century. Ironically, the experimentalism that Aristotelianism encouraged was destined to overthrow Aristotle's own theories in physics and other fields of science.

Evaluation of Humanism

In the meantime, the humanists continued to downgrade science as sterile, and they did not teach it in the schools they established. Their educational goal, which is still the goal of a liberal education, was the cultivation of the mind both for individual happiness and for equipping a person to play a worthy role in society.

To the humanists we owe the modern ideal of the well-rounded person, the versatile, accomplished, socially assured citizen of the world. Called by the humanists the *uomo universale* ("complete man"), such a person was the subject of eagerly read books on correct social behavior that were produced during the Renaissance.

The most famous book on Renaissance manners, published in 1528, was *The Courtier* by Baldassare

Castiglione (1478–1529), which was soon translated into French, German, English, and Spanish and which established a model for the Renaissance gentleman. To Castiglione good manners and social skills were essential to the ideal courtier because women now played a freer and more active role in polite society, to which they added such feminine refinements as music and dancing.

In the judgment of a modern feminist historian "There was no renaissance for women . . . during the Renaissance."[7] In truth, there were a good number of Renaissance women who were highly educated, read the classics in Greek and Latin, painted with great skill, and produced literature of merit. Most of these women were the daughters and wives of privileged aristocrats, and educational opportunities were provided them so that they would make better companions and conversationalists for their husbands. Many talented women lacked access to further training or patronage necessary to pursue a professional career—a path in life that was not yet considered proper for a woman of high status, whether she possessed extraordinary talent or not.

The courtier must please the ladies as well as the prince; he must master the social graces. But Castiglione's central idea was that a courtier's true worth was more in keeping with his strength of character and excellence of intellect than with his hereditary social position. Well read in the classics but no isolated scholar, the courtier should be a well-rounded individual, capable in the arts of both war and peace.

Reviving the ancient ideal of a healthy mind in a sound body, Renaissance educators and writers stressed the importance of exercise and sports and took their inspiration from ancient Greek examples of leisure—running, track and field events, and wrestling. But not every sport was thought acceptable: in 1531 an English author of a book on manners wrote that football (in reference to a game much like the modern sport of rugby) ought to be avoided by all gentlemen because there is in it "nothing but beastly furie and exstreme violence; whereof precedeth hurte, and consequently rancour and malice do remaine."[8]

Although we owe the humanists a debt of gratitude for reintroducing Latin and Greek literature into the mainstream of Western thought, theirs was otherwise a closed culture whose boundaries had been set by ancient Greece and Rome. Their course was to re-travel old ground, not to explore uncharted territory. The humanists resented the centuries separating them from the golden days of antiquity. Unfortunately, this viewpoint resulted in their dislike of the best works (Dante excepted) produced in the Middle Ages.

The cult of classical letters gave rise to another defect. By the late fifteenth century the humanists' passion for writing Latin prose in imitation of Cicero's graceful, eloquent, and polished style had become a dangerous obsession. One famous humanist, who was also a cardinal of the church, even hesitated to read St. Paul's epistles for fear they might corrupt his Latin style. A reaction in favor of the native language resulted; Castiglione and Machiavelli, for example, chose to write in the vernacular, Italian.

The humanist men of letters contributed nothing new to philosophy or to science and did little or no original thinking. Nevertheless, they did contribute indirectly to the coming scientific revolution. Their search for Roman and Greek manuscripts resulted in the recovery of more ancient scientific writings than were available to medieval scholars. These were at hand later when the interests of scholars turned decisively toward science. (Copernicus's heliocentric theory of planetary motion, for example, came from his reading of ancient authors.) Furthermore, modern critical scholarship began with the humanists' emphasis on verified facts. They compared manuscripts in order to eliminate errors and establish authentic texts. In their writings they exposed historical myths and eliminated supernatural causes. This critical and objective outlook would be of great value in later scientific research.

Italian Renaissance Art

Outside Italy during the fourteenth and fifteenth centuries, there was a continuation of "Gothic" art—in painting and sculpture, the same emphasis on realistic detail; in architecture, an elaboration of the Gothic style.

Fourteenth- and fifteenth-century Italy, however, saw innovations that culminated in the classic High Renaissance art of the early sixteenth century. All

Major Artists of the Italian Renaissance

c. 1266–1337	Giotto: *Life of the Virgin, Life of St. Francis, Life of St. John the Baptist*
1401–1428	Masaccio: *Tribute Money, Trinity, St. Peter*
1447–1510	Botticelli: *Judith and Holofernes, St. Sebastian, Birth of Venus*
1452–1519	Leonardo da Vinci: *Adoration of the Magi, The Last Supper, La Gioconda* (Mona Lisa)
1475–1564	Michelangelo: Ceiling of the Sistine Chapel, *Moses, Pietà, David*
c. 1477–1576	Titian: *The Venus of Zerbine, The Allegory of Marriage, Venus and Adonis*

these were the products of a new society centered in rich cities, the humanist spirit in thought and religion, and a revived interest in the classical art of Greece and Rome.

Transitional Period in Painting

The greatest figure in the transitional painting of the fourteenth century was the Florentine painter Giotto (c. 1266–1337), who it was said "achieved little less than the resurrection of painting from the dead." While earlier Italian painters had copied the unreal, flat, and rigidly formalized images of Byzantine paintings and mosaics, Giotto observed from life and painted a three-dimensional world peopled with believable human beings dramatically moved by deep emotion. He humanized painting much as Petrarch humanized thought and St. Francis, whose life was one of his favorite subjects, humanized religion. Giotto initiated a new epoch in the history of painting, one that expressed the religious piety of his lay patrons and their delight in images of everyday life.

Quattrocento Painting, Sculpture, and Architecture

The lull in painting that followed Giotto's death in 1337, during which his technical innovations were retained but the spirit and compassion that make him one of the world's great painters were lost, lasted until the beginning of the *quattrocento* (Italian for "four hundred," an abbreviation for the 1400s). In his brief lifetime the Florentine Masaccio (1401–1428) completed the revolution in technique begun by Giotto. As can be seen in his few surviving paintings, Masaccio largely mastered the problems of perspective, the anatomical naturalism of flesh and bone, and the modeling of figures in light and shade *(chiaroscuro)* rather than by Giotto's sharp line. Masaccio was also the first to paint nude figures (Adam and Eve, in his *Expulsion from Eden*), thus reversing the trend of Christian art, which since its beginnings in late Roman times had turned its back on the beauty of the human form. Masaccio died in debt in Rome, having received few commissions in Florence. Apparently, his work was too austere and short on elegance to attract many patrons.

Inspired by Masaccio's achievement, most quattrocento painters constantly sought to improve technique. This search for greater realism culminated in such painters as Andrea Mantegna (1431–1506) and Piero della Francesca (c. 1420–1492). Mantegna's painting of the dead body of Christ lying on a marble slab clearly shows the results of his lifelong study of perspective. His group portrait of the family of his chief patron, the Gonzaga duke of Mantua, is done "in the grand manner" and reflects the self-assurance of the Renaissance elite.

Masaccio, Expulsion from Eden. *Masaccio's mastery of perspective creates the illusion of movement as the angel drives Adam and Eve from Paradise.*

Piero della Francesca's approach to painting was scientific and intellectual. His zeal to reduce perspective to a mathematical science—he wrote a book on the subject—led him to neglect motion. The figures in his *Discovery and Proving of the True Cross*, showing Constantine's mother, Helena, discovering the cross used for Christ's crucifixion, are as still as if hewn out of marble. Piero's restrained, undramatic, unemotional, and mathematically precise paintings bring to mind the abstract painting of our own time.

Whereas Masaccio's successors in the second half of the fifteenth century were intent on giving their figures solidity and resolving the problem of three-dimensional presentation, the Florentine Sandro Botticelli (1447–1510) proceeded in a different direction, abandoning the techniques of straightforward representation of people and objects. Botticelli used a sensitive, even quivering line to stir the viewer's imagination and emotion and to create a mood in keeping with his more subtle and sophisticated poetic vision. This unconventional artist was associated with the Platonic Academy at Florence, where the Christian faith was fused with pagan mythology. Thus although his *Birth of Venus* depicts the goddess of love rising from the sea, there is little that is human or material about her ethereal figure. Like the Virgin Mary, she has become the symbol of a higher kind of love—divine love. The allegory is reinforced by making the winds that blow Venus onto the shore look like Christian angels.

Progress was also being made in sculpture, and it, like painting, reached stylistic maturity at the beginning of the quattrocento. Like the humanists, the sculptors found in ancient Rome the models they were eager to imitate; they too saw what seemed related to their own experience and aspirations.

In his second pair of bronze doors for the baptistery in Florence, Lorenzo Ghiberti (1378–1455) achieved the goal he had set for himself: "I strove to imitate nature as closely as I could, and with all the perspective I could produce." These marvels of relief sculpture, which resurrected the form and spirit of Roman sculpture and architecture and drew from Michelangelo the declaration that they were worthy to be the gates of paradise, depict skillfully modeled human figures—including some classically inspired nudes—which stand out spatially against architectural and landscape backgrounds.

Although Ghiberti was a superb craftsman, he was less of an innovator than his younger contemporary in Florence, Donatello (1386–1466), who visited Rome to study the remains of antique sculpture. Divorcing sculpture from the architectural background it had in the Middle Ages, Donatello produced truly freestanding statues based on the realization of the human body as a functional, coordinated mechanism of bones, muscles, and sinews, maintaining itself against the pull of gravity. His *David* was the first bronze nude made since antiquity, and his equestrian statue of the army commander Gattamelata, clad in Roman armor, was the first of its type done in the Renaissance. The latter clearly reveals the

Botticelli, The Birth of Venus. *The last great Florentine painter of the early Renaissance, Botticelli did most of his best work for Lorenzo de' Medici and his court. In* The Birth of Venus, *Botticelli blends ancient mythology, Christian faith, and voluptuous representation.*

After winning the commission to design the bronze doors for the baptistery in Florence, Ghiberti spent most of his life making the 28 panels for the doors. This panel illustrates the biblical story of Joseph.

influence of classical models and was probably inspired by the equestrian statue of the emperor Marcus Aurelius in Rome.

More dramatic than either of these equestrian statues is that of the Venetian general Bartolomeo Colleoni, the creation of Andrea del Verrocchio (1435–1488). A versatile Florentine artist noteworthy as a sculptor, a painter, and the teacher of Leonardo da Vinci, Verrocchio designed the statue of Colleoni to permit one of the horse's forelegs to be unsupported—a considerable achievement. The posture and features of the famous general dramatically convey the supreme self-confidence and even arrogance of Renaissance public figures.

Renaissance architecture, which even more than sculpture reflects the influence of ancient Roman models, glorifies the worldly success of its patrons. It began with the work of Filippo Brunelleschi (1377–1446). As a youth Brunelleschi accompanied Donatello to Rome, where he employed measuring stick and sketchbook to master the principles of classical architecture. Returning to Florence, Brunelleschi constructed there the uncompleted dome of the cathedral, the first dome to be built since Roman times. Although strongly influenced by classical architecture, Brunelleschi's buildings in Florence,

which include churches and palaces, were not just copies of Roman models. Employing arcades of Roman arches, Roman pediments above the windows, and Roman columns and other decorative motifs, Brunelleschi re-created the Roman style in a fresh and original manner. So began the Renaissance style of architecture that, with many modifications, has lasted to the present time.

The High Renaissance, 1500–1530

By the time of the High Renaissance in Italy, when painting, sculpture, and architecture all reached a peak of perfection, the center of artistic activity had shifted from Florence to Rome. The popes were lavish patrons, and the greatest artists of the period worked in the Vatican at one time or another. It did not seem inconsistent to popes and artists to include representations of pagan mythological figures in the decorations of the papal palace, and so the Vatican became filled with secular as well as religious art.

The great architect of the High Renaissance was Donato Bramante (1444–1514) from Milan. Bramante's most important commission came in 1506 when Pope Julius II asked him to replace the old basilica of St. Peter, built by the emperor Constan-

In Verrocchio's equestrian statue of the condottiere *(professional soldier) Bartolomeo Colleoni, the spirit of the military leader is captured in the face, which is individual and very human, rather than classical.*

Donatello, David. *"The questing genius of Donatello led him in many directions and established him, both for his contemporaries and for all time, as the dominant sculptor of his century."*[9]

tine, with a monumental Renaissance structure. Bramante's plan called for a centralized church in the form of a Greek cross surmounted by an immense dome. His design for St. Peter's exemplifies the spirit of High Renaissance architecture—to approach the monumentality and grandeur of Roman architecture. In Bramante's own words, he would place "the Pantheon on top of the Basilica of Maxentius." Bramante died when the cathedral was barely begun, and it was left to Michelangelo and others to complete the work. Michelangelo's dome influenced the design of most major domes until the beginning of the twentieth century.

The painters of the High Renaissance inherited the solutions to such technical problems as perspective space from the quattrocento artists. But whereas the artists of the earlier period had been concerned with movement, color, and narrative detail, painters in the High Renaissance attempted to eliminate nonessentials and concentrated on the central theme of a picture and its basic human implications. By this process of elimination, many High Renaissance painters achieved a "classic" effect of seriousness and serenity and endowed their work with idealistic values.

Leonardo da Vinci, Raphael, and Michelangelo

The great triad of High Renaissance painters consists of Leonardo da Vinci, Raphael, and Michelangelo. An extraordinary man, Leonardo da Vinci (1452–1519) was brilliant in a variety of fields: engineering, mathematics, architecture, geology, botany, physiology, anatomy, sculpture, painting, music, and poetry. Unfortunately, because he loved the process of experimentation more than seeing all his projects through to completion, few of the projects Leonardo started were ever finished.

A superb draftsman, Leonardo was a master of soft modeling in light and shade and of creating groups of figures perfectly balanced in a given space. But in addition to an advanced knowledge of technique, what makes Leonardo one of the great masters is his deep psychological insight into human nature. As he himself expressed it, "A good painter has two chief objects to paint, man and the intention of his soul."

One of Leonardo's most famous paintings is *La Gioconda,* known as the Mona Lisa, a portrait of a woman whose enigmatic smile captures an air of tenderness and humility. Another is *The Last Supper,* a study of the dramatic impact of Christ's announcement to his disciples, "One of you will betray me." When he painted this picture on the walls of the refectory of Santa Maria delle Grazie in Milan, Leonardo was experimenting with the use of an oil medium combined with plaster, which unfortunately was unsuccessful. The painting quickly began to disintegrate and has had to be repainted several times.

The second of the great triad of High Renaissance painters was Raphael (1483–1520). By the time he was summoned to Rome in 1508 by Pope Julius II to aid in the decoration of the Vatican, Raphael had

Da Vinci, La Gioconda. *Leonardo da Vinci was a painter, sculptor, architect, inventor, scientist, writer, and musician. His portrait of Mona Lisa, perhaps the most famous portrait ever painted, seems to express the artist's feelings about the mystery of human existence.*

St. Peter's Basilica, Rome. After Michelangelo took charge of the construction of the basilica, he modified Bramante's original plan. For the dome Bramante had planned a stepped hemisphere similar to the dome of the Pantheon. Michelangelo redesigned the dome to add a high drum and strongly projecting buttresses accented by double columns. Later a long nave was added to the front of the church, giving it the form of a Latin, rather than a Greek, cross.

absorbed the styles of Leonardo and Michelangelo. His Stanze frescoes in the Vatican display a magnificent blending of classical and Christian subject matter and are the fruit of careful planning and immense artistic knowledge. Raphael possessed neither Leonardo's intellectuality nor Michelangelo's power, but his work has an appealing serenity, particularly evident in his lovely portraits of the Madonna (Mary, the mother of Jesus). Most critics consider him the master of perfect design and balanced composition.

The individualism and idealism of the High Renaissance have no greater representative than Michelangelo Buonarroti (1475–1564). Stories of this stormy and temperamental personality have helped shape our definition of a genius. Indeed, there is something almost superhuman about both Michelangelo and his art. His great energy enabled him to paint for Julius II in four years the entire ceiling of the Vatican's Sistine Chapel, an area of several thousand square yards, and his art embodies a superhuman ideal. With his unrivaled genius for rendering

Leonardo da Vinci, The Last Supper. *In early Renaissance art, architecture sometimes overpowered the figures, but here the architectural details are subordinate to the figures. The main opening in the rear wall, for example, acts as a halo for Christ's head.*

Raphael, Madonna of the Chair. *Along with Michelangelo and da Vinci, Raphael is recognized as one of the three masters of the High Renaissance. Raphael combined the qualities of the other two artists to create a style that is lyrical and dramatic.*

the human form, he devised a wealth of expressive positions and attitudes for his figures in scenes from Genesis. Their physical splendor is pagan, but their spirit is Christian. The *Creation of Adam* depicts God, with the unborn Eve under his left arm, instilling the divine spark of the soul into the body of Adam.

Michelangelo considered himself first and foremost a sculptor, and this *uomo universale*, who also excelled as poet, engineer, and architect, was undoubtedly the greatest sculptor of the Renaissance. The glorification of the human body, particularly the male nude, was Michelangelo's great achievement. Fired by the grandeur of such newly discovered pieces of Hellenistic sculpture as the Laocoön group and strongly influenced by Platonism with its dualism of body and soul, he displayed the classical influence in such works as his *David*. This masterpiece, commissioned in 1501 when he was 26, expressed his idealized view of human dignity and majesty. Succeeding Bramante as chief architect of St. Peter's in 1546, Michelangelo designed the great dome and was still actively creative as a sculptor when he died, almost in his ninetieth year, in 1564. He had long outlived the High Renaissance.

The Venetian School

Following the sack of Rome in 1527 during the Italian Wars, the rich trading city of Venice became the center of art. This wealthy, sophisticated urban center produced a secular rather than a devotional

Michelangelo, David. *To Michelangelo, the Florentine painter, sculptor, poet, and architect, sculpture was the noblest of the arts. The large marble statue of the biblical David was commissioned in 1501 to stand in Florence as a symbol of the city, its government, and its culture.*

school of painting. Most Venetian artists were satisfied with the here and now; though they sometimes painted Madonnas, they more often painted wealthy merchants and proud doges (magistrates), attired in rich brocades, jewels, and precious metals. The sensuousness of the Venetian painting of this period is evident in the artists' love of decoration, rich costumes, striking nude figures, and radiant light and color. It has been said that whereas earlier painting consisted of drawing and coloring, at Venice color and light became paramount ingredients of painting.

The first master of the Venetian High Renaissance was Giorgione (1477–1510), who like Botticelli rejected the quattrocento concern to be scientific and realistic and substituted a delicate and dreamily poetic lyricism. Common to all of his paintings is a mood of languor and relaxation that is called *Giorgionesque.* The lyrical grace of his *Sleeping Venus,* for example, is devoid of erotic overtones. His paintings are fanciful idylls that have no narrative content—

they tell no story. Viewers are left free to extract their own meaning from them.

The paintings of Titian (c. 1477–1576), who was probably born in the same year as his friend Giorgione but outlived him by 65 years, are less subtle and poetic. His Venuses, for example, are buxom Venetian models—mature, opulent, and sex-conscious. During his long working life he proved himself the master of every kind of subject ranging from religion to pagan mythology and including portraits of royalty and the self-satisfied upper class, for which he was most famed among his contemporaries. With his robust sensuousness and view of all things in terms of light and color, Titian is the type-figure of the Venetian painter, and his work has influenced many generations of modern painters.

Mannerism: The "Anti-Renaissance" Style

In 1494 the French king Charles VIII crossed into Italy with an army of 40,000 men and inaugurated the Italian Wars that lasted until 1559 and turned Italy into a battleground for the powerful new monarchies of France and Spain. While Italians were losing control of their destiny, Machiavelli in *The Prince* lamented his native land as being "more a slave than the Hebrews, more a servant than the Persians, more scattered than the Athenians; without head, without government; defeated, plundered, torn asunder, overrun; subject to every sort of disaster."[10]

In 1527 the unruly army of Charles V, Spanish king and German emperor, sacked Rome, the major center of High Renaissance patronage and culture, and its many artists, writers, and scholars fled the city.

Such unsettling developments, added to the Protestant and Catholic Reformations (see Chapter 15), produced a radical change of outlook on life. The earlier optimistic emphasis on the dignity of man was replaced by a pessimistic belief in man's evil nature—one of the basic assumptions in Machiavelli's *Prince.* Michelangelo, who as we noted had outlived the High Renaissance, expressed a similar pessimism in the tortured figures of his late sculptures and his painting *The Last Judgment* which was painted on a wall of the Sistine Chapel in the 1530s after the sack of Rome and more than 40 years after his glorious *Creation of Adam* on the ceiling. "Led by long years to my last hours," Michelangelo wrote, "too late, O world, I know your joys for what they are. You promise a peace which is not yours to give."

From about 1530 to the end of the sixteenth century, Italian artists responded to the stresses of

Parmigianino, Madonna with the Long Neck. *Parmigianino's smooth, elongated, languid figures embody an ideal of unearthly beauty and perfection that bears little resemblance to real human beings. Characteristic of Mannerist painting are huge discrepancies in scale, here shown by the tiny figure of the prophet beside the gigantic column.*

the age in a new style called Mannerism. Consciously revolting against the classical serenity and poise of High Renaissance art, Mannerist artists sought to express their own inner vision—often, like Michelangelo in his later years, their doubts and indecisions—in a manner that evoked shock in the viewer.

Typical are the paintings of Parmigianino, who returned to his native Parma from Rome after it was sacked, and the Venetian Tintoretto. Parmigianino's *Madonna with the Long Neck* (1535) shows no logic of structure. One cannot tell whether the distorted figure of the Madonna is seated or standing. Her cloak billows out in defiance of gravity, and her child seems to be slipping off her lap. The prophet in the

background, standing beside a gigantic and purposeless column, is absurdly tiny.

Contemporaries of Tintoretto (1518–1594) had good reason to call him "the thunderbolt of painting." His *Abduction of the Body of St. Mark*, depicting the legend that three Venetians stole the body of their patron saint from Alexandria during a storm, replaces the harmony, proportion, balance, and idealized reality of the High Renaissance with dramatic force and movement, violent contrast in light and color, imbalanced composition, and crowded figures in uneasy and agitated poses. The upholders of the pure classical tradition who opposed the innovations of the Mannerists considered Tintoretto's work to be marred by careless execution and eccentric taste. One of them wrote that "had he not abandoned the beaten track but rather followed the beautiful style of his predecessors, he would have become one of the greatest painters seen in Venice."

The outstanding Mannerist sculptor was the braggart Benvenuto Cellini (1500–1571). Both his sculpture and his famous *Autobiography* reflect his violent and corrupt age's rejection of artistic and moral standards. (He boasts of the number of

Tintoretto, Abduction of the Body of St. Mark. *The leading proponent of the Mannerist style in Venice, Tintoretto combined strong use of light and shade with a gift for dramatic storytelling.*

Cellini, Saltcellar of Francis I. *The utilitarian purpose of the condiment dish is subordinate to its lavish decoration. Neptune, god of the sea, guards the boat-shaped salt container while a personification of Earth watches over the pepper. Figures around the base represent the four seasons and the four parts of the day. The intricacy of the design is a showcase of the sculptor's virtuosity.*

personal enemies he has killed and quotes a pope as excusing him on the ground that "men like Benvenuto, unique in their profession, stand above the law.") His work, like the gold cup decorated with enamel and precious stones now in the Metropolitan Museum of Art in New York, consists largely of similar elegant, showy trifles, which Michelangelo described as "snuff-box ornaments."

Mannerist architects developed the Jesuit style, named for the new Jesuit Order that first sponsored it in its Gesù (Jesus) Church in Rome (c. 1575). The classical components of Renaissance architecture were manipulated to achieve anticlassical effects. Columns and pilasters were paired for greater richness, curved lines ending in volutes replaced straight lines, and statues were often fixed to upper stories and roofs. The parts were arranged to form a climax in the center and fused into one complex pattern.

Tintoretto's *Abduction of the Body of St. Mark* pictures both the old architecture and the new. In the left background is a typical Renaissance building with its repetition of the same pattern; the whole is no greater than the sum of its parts. To the rear is a Jesuit-style structure whose effect is much more than the sum of its parts—to leave out any part would destroy its essential unity.

The Mannerist Jesuit style prefigures the fully developed baroque architecture of the seventeenth cen-

tury, just as the Mannerist style of Tintoretto—and El Greco (d. 1614) in Spain a generation later—prefigures baroque painting (see Chapter 15). There is no clear dividing line between the Mannerism of the sixteenth century and the baroque of the seventeenth.

Renaissance Music

In contrast to the simple single-voiced, or monophonic, music—called plainsong or Gregorian chant—of the early Middle Ages, the later medieval composers of church music wrote many-voiced, or polyphonic, music. Polyphony often involved a shuttling back and forth from one melody to another—musical counterpoint. By the fifteenth century as many as 24 voice parts were combined into one intricately woven musical pattern. The composers of the High Renaissance continued to produce complicated polyphonic music but in a calmer and grander manner. Compared with the style of his predecessors, that of the Flemish composer Josquin des Prés (c. 1440–1521), the founder of High Renaissance music, "is both grander and more simple . . . and the rhythms and forms used are based on strict symmetry and mathematically regular proportions. Josquin handled all technical problems of complicated constructions with the same ease and sureness one finds in the drawings of Leonardo and Raphael."[11] Also

Gesù Church, Rome. The Mannerist Jesuit style in architecture is characterized by a deliberate contradiction of classical rules and a conscious effort to produce an effect of discord and strain rather than harmony and repose, the ideals of Renaissance style.

during the sixteenth century, instruments such as the violin, spinet, and harpsichord developed from more rudimentary types.

The Renaissance in Italy stimulated various new forms of secular music, especially the madrigal, a love lyric set to music. Castiglione in *The Courtier* insists that the ability to sing, read music, and play an instrument was essential for gentlemen and ladies. In addition to the Italian madrigal, French *chansons* and German *Lieder* added to the growing volume of secular music.

The Northern Renaissance

The Italian Renaissance had placed human beings once more in the center of life's stage and infused thought and art with humanistic values. In time these stimulating ideas current in Italy spread to other areas and combined with developments particular to the other countries of Europe to produce a French Renaissance, an English Renaissance, and so on.

Throughout the fifteenth century the enrollment records of Italian universities listed hundreds of northern European students. Though their chief interest was the study of law and medicine, many were influenced by the intellectual climate of Italy with its new enthusiasm for the classics. When these students returned home, they often carried manuscripts—and later printed editions—produced by classical and humanist writers. By this time Scholasticism had declined into uncreative repetition and logical subtleties, and both literate laymen and devout clergy in the north were ready to welcome the new outlook of humanism.

The Influence of Printing

Very important in the diffusion of the Renaissance and later in the success of the Reformation was the

Major Figures in the Northern Renaissance

c. 1395–1441   Jan van Eyck (painter): *Man with the Red Turban, Wedding Portrait*

c. 1466–1536   Desiderius Erasmus (humanist and scholar): *The Praise of Folly, Handbook of the Christian Knight*

1471–1528   Albrecht Dürer (painter): *Adam and Eve, The Four Apostles, Self-Portrait*

1478–1535   Sir Thomas More (humanist and diplomat): *Utopia*

c. 1483–1553   François Rabelais (writer): *Gargantua* and *Pantagruel*

1488–1523   Ulrich von Hutten (humanist and poet)

1547–1616   Miguel de Cervantes (writer): *Don Quixote*

1564–1616   William Shakespeare (playwright and poet): *Julius Caesar, Romeo and Juliet, King Lear*

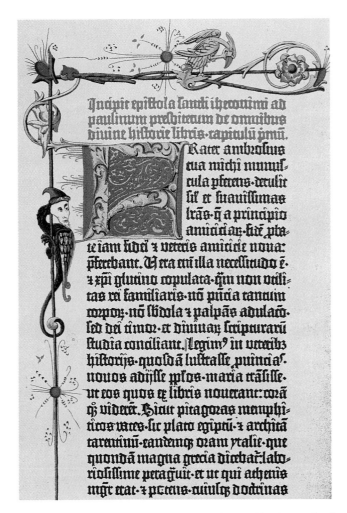

Facsimile copy of a page from the Gutenberg Bible, the Book of Genesis. With the development of printing, learning was no longer the private domain of the church and those few persons wealthy enough to own hand-copied volumes.

invention of printing in Europe. The essential elements—paper and block printing—had been known in China since the eighth century. During the twelfth century the Spanish Muslims introduced papermaking to Europe; in the thirteenth Europeans, in close contact with China (see Chapter 12), brought knowledge of block printing to the West. The crucial step was taken in the 1440s at Mainz, Germany, where Johann Gutenberg and other printers invented movable type by cutting up old printing blocks to form individual letters. Gutenberg used movable type to print papal documents and the first printed version of the Bible (1454).

Soon all the major countries of Europe possessed the means for printing books. In 1465 two Germans brought printing to Italy, and within four years the works of eight classical authors (including Cicero, Livy, Virgil, Pliny, and Caesar) had been printed there. In all of Europe during the remainder of the century an estimated 40,000 titles were published. It is said that the prices of books sank to one-eighth of their former cost, thus placing books within the reach of many people who formerly had been unable to buy them. In addition, pamphlets and controversial tracts soon began to circulate, and new ideas reached a thousand times more people in a relatively short span of time. In the quickening of Europe's intellectual life, it is difficult to overestimate the effects of the printing press. Without printing it is doubtful that a German writer at the end of the fifteenth century could have made the exaggerated boast that "once upon a time Germany was poor in wisdom, power, and wealth; now it is not only equal to others in glorious work, but surpasses loquacious Greece, [and] proud Italy."

Erasmus and Northern Humanism

The intellectual life of the first half of the sixteenth century was dominated by the Dutch humanist Desiderius Erasmus (c. 1466–1536). Although born in Rotterdam, he passed most of his long life elsewhere—in Germany, France, England, Italy, and especially Switzerland. The most influential and cosmopolitan of the northern humanists, he corresponded with nearly every prominent writer and thinker in Europe and personally knew popes, emperors, and kings. He was *the* scholar of Europe, and his writings were eagerly read everywhere.

Perhaps the most famous and influential work by Erasmus was *The Praise of Folly*, a satire written in 1511 at the house of the English humanist Sir Thomas More. Folly, used in the Middle Ages as a synonym for human nature, is described by Erasmus as the source not only of much harmless enjoyment in life but also of many things that are wrong and need correcting. A historian has described the work in these words:

> *At first the book makes kindly and approving fun of the ways of action and the foibles and weaknesses of mankind. It is not mordant, only amused. But gradually from fools innocent and natural and undebased, it passes to those whose illusions are vicious in their setting and results.*[12]

Among such are merchants ("they lie, swear, cheat, and practice all the intrigues of dishonesty"), lawyers ("they of all men have the greatest conceit of their own abilities"), Scholastic philosophers ("that talk as much by rote as a parrot"), and scientists ("who esteem themselves the only favorites of wisdom, and look upon the rest of mankind as the dirt and rubbish of the creation"). Most roughly handled are the clergy, in particular monks ("impudent pretenders to the profession of piety") and popes, cardinals, and bishops ("who in pomp and splendor have almost equaled if not outdone secular princes"). Although his satire is indeed harsh, Erasmus was himself balanced, moderate, and intolerant only of bigotry, ignorance, greed, and violence.

The Praise of Folly illustrates a significant difference between the northern humanists and their Italian predecessors. Most Italian humanists—the civic humanists—spoke to and for the upper-class elements in their city-states. They urged political leaders to become more statesmanlike, businessmen to become more generous with their wealth, and all to become more moral. They did not dissent or speak out in opposition; in urging the elite groups to assume their responsibilities, they were actually trying to defend, not condemn, them. Italian humanism "centered on the liberality or parsimony of princes, on the moral worth of riches, and on the question of how to define true 'nobility.'"[13] By contrast, the northern humanists, like Erasmus in *The Praise of Folly*, spoke out against a broad range of political, social, economic, and religious evils. They faced reality and became ardent reformers of society's ills.

The northern humanists also went further than the Italians in broadening their interest in ancient literature to include early Christian writings—the Scriptures and the works of the church fathers. This led them to prepare new and more accurate editions of the Scriptures (Erasmus's Greek edition of the New Testament became famous and was used by Martin Luther, the founder of Protestantism) and to compare unfavorably the complexities of the church

Portrait of Erasmus by Hans Holbein the Younger. Erasmus's scholarly achievements include a Greek edition of the New Testament and editions of the writings of St. Jerome and other early church fathers. Erasmus is best known, however, for his popular works, especially The Praise of Folly.

in their own day with the simplicity of early Christianity. Since they held that the essence of religion was morality and rational piety—what Erasmus called the "philosophy of Christ"—rather than ceremony and dogma, it is not surprising that the church became a major target of their reforming zeal.

Sir Thomas More's *Utopia*

The most significant figure in English humanism was Sir Thomas More (1478–1535), a good friend of Erasmus. More is best known for his *Utopia*, the first important description of an ideal state since Plato's *Republic*. In this extraordinarily realistic work, More criticized his age through his portrayal of a fictitious sailor who contrasts the ideal life he has seen in Utopia (the "Land of Nowhere") with the harsh

Humanism in the North: Erasmus, *The Praise of Folly*

In 1521 Martin Luther, a respected German friar, broke with the Catholic Church, triggering the so-called Protestant Reformation. Luther and his followers were reacting against abuses and corruption in the Catholic system. Many other Catholics chose to stay true to the church while speaking out against its foibles and follies at the time. One was Desiderius Erasmus. This learned churchman and humanist criticized many of his fellow Catholics for losing sight of the true purpose of Christian life, which he believed to be the imitation of Christ. Monks, priests, intellectuals—all were fair targets for Erasmus's keen mind and satirical pen. In this selection, Erasmus addresses his readers through the voice of Folly.

As for the theologians, perhaps it would be better to pass them over in silence, "not stirring up the hornets' nest," and "not laying a finger on the stinkweed," since this race of men is incredibly arrogant and touchy. For they might rise up en masse and march in ranks against me with six hundred conclusions and force me to recant. And if I should refuse, they would immediately shout "heretic." For this is the thunderbolt they always keep ready at a moment's notice to terrify anyone to whom they are not very favorably inclined. . . .

In all these there is so much erudition, so much difficulty, that I think the apostles themselves would need to be inspired by a different spirit if they were forced to match wits on such points with this new breed of theologians. Paul could provide a living example of faith, but when he said, "Faith is the substance of things to be hoped for and the evidence of things not seen," his definition was not sufficiently magisterial. So too, he lived a life of perfect charity, but he neither distinguished it nor defined it with sufficient dialectical precision in the first epistle to the Corinthians, chapter 13. . . .

Almost as happy as the theologians are those men who are commonly called "religious" and "monks"— though both names are quite incorrect, since a good part of them are very far removed from religion and no one is encountered more frequently everywhere you go. I cannot imagine how anything could be more wretched than these men, if it were not for the many sorts of assistance I give them. For even though everyone despises this breed of men so thoroughly that even a chance meeting with one of them is considered unlucky, still they maintain a splendid opinion of themselves. First of all, they consider it the very height of piety to have so little to do with literature as not even to be able to read. Moreover, when they roar out their psalms in church like braying asses (counting their prayers indeed, but understanding them not at all) . . .

Now what shall I [Folly] say about those who find great comfort in soothing self-delusions about fictitious pardons for their sins, measuring out the times in purgatory down to the droplets of a waterclock, parceling out centuries, years, months, days, hours, as if they were using mathematical tables? Or what about those who rely on certain little magical tokens and prayers thought up by some pious impostor for his own amusement or profit? They promise themselves anything and everything: wealth, honor, pleasure, an abundance of everything, perpetual health, a long life, flourishing old age, and finally a seat next to Christ among the saints, though this last they don't want for quite a while yet—that is, when the pleasures of this life, to which they cling with all their might, have finally slipped through their fingers, then it will be soon enough to enter into the joys of the saints. Imagine here, if you please, some businessman or soldier or judge who thinks that if he throws into the collection basket one coin from all his plunder, the whole cesspool of his sinful life will be immediately wiped out. He thinks all his acts of perjury, lust, drunkenness, quarreling, murder, deception, dishonesty, betrayal are paid off like a mortgage, and paid off in such a way that he can start off once more on a whole new round of sinful pleasures.

From Desiderius Erasmus, *The Praise of Folly*, trans. Clarence H. Miller (New Haven, Conn.: Yale University Press, 1979).

conditions of life in England. More's denunciations centered on the new acquisitive capitalism, which he blamed for the widespread insecurity and misery of the lower classes. More felt that governments

are a conspiracy of the rich, who, in pretence of managing the public, only pursue their private ends, . . . first, that they may, without danger, preserve all that they have so ill acquired, and then, that they may engage the poor to toil and labor for them at as low rates as possible, and oppress them as much as they please.[14]

In Utopia, by contrast, no one is in want because the economy is planned and cooperative and because property is held in common. Utopia is the only true commonwealth, concludes More's imaginary sailor:

In all other places, it is visible that while people talk of a commonwealth, every man only seeks his own wealth: but there, where no man has any property, all men zealously pursue the good of the public. . . . In Utopia, where every man has a right to every thing, they all know that if care is taken to keep the public stores full, no private man can want any thing; for among them there is no unequal distribution, so that no man is poor, none in necessity; and though no man has anything, yet they are all rich; for what can make a man so rich as to lead a serene and cheerful life, free from anxieties; neither apprehending want himself, nor vexed with the endless complaints of his wife?[15]

More was the first of the modern English socialists, but his philosophy should not be considered a forerunner of modern socialism. His economic outlook was a legacy from the Middle Ages, and his preference for medieval collectivism over modern economic individualism was consistent with his preference for a church headed, in medieval style, by popes rather than by kings. This view prompted Henry VIII, who had appropriated the pope's position as head of the Church of England, to execute More for treason.

Rabelais's *Gargantua and Pantagruel*

One of the best-known French humanists was François Rabelais (c. 1483–1553). A brilliant, if coarse, lover of all life from the sewers to the heavens, Rabelais is best remembered for his novel *Gargantua and Pantagruel*. Centering on figures from French folklore, this work relates the adventures of Gargantua and his son Pantagruel, genial giants of tremendous stature and appetite, to whom were credited many marvelous feats.

With much burlesque humor—hence the term *Rabelaisian*—Rabelais satirized his society while putting forth his humanist views on educational reform and inherent human goodness. He made powerful attacks on the abuses of the church and the shortcomings of Scholastics and monks, but he also had no patience with overzealous Protestants. What Rabelais could not stomach was hypocrisy and repression, and for people guilty of these offenses he reserved his strongest criticism. He bid his readers to flee from that

rabble of squint-minded fellows, dissembling and counterfeit saints, demure lookers, hypocrites, pretended zealots, tough friars, buskin-monks, and other such sects of men, who disguise themselves like masquers to deceive the world. . . . Fly from these men, abhor and hate them as much as I do, and upon my faith you will find yourself the better for it. And if you desire . . . to live in peace, joy, health, making yourselves always merry, never trust those men that always peep out through a little hole.[16]

Ulrich von Hutten: German Humanist and Patriot

One of the outstanding German humanists was Ulrich von Hutten (1488–1523). His idealism combined a zeal for religious reform and German nationalist feelings. This member of an aristocratic family, who wanted to unite Germany under the emperor, led a tumultuous life as a wandering Greek scholar and satirist. He supported Luther as a rallying point for German unity against the papacy, to which he attributed most of his country's ills. Hutten reflected the tensions and aspirations of the German people in the early years of the Protestant revolt against the papacy (see Chapter 15).

Montaigne's Essays

The last notable northern humanist was the French skeptic Michel de Montaigne (1533–1592). At age 38, he gave up the practice of law and retired to his country estate and well-stocked library, where he studied and wrote. Montaigne developed a new literary form and gave it its name—the *essay*. In 94 essays he set forth his personal views on many subjects: leisure, friendship, education, philosophy, religion, old age, death. He did not pretend to have the final answer to the subjects he discussed. Instead, he advocated open-mindedness and tolerance—rare qualities in the sixteenth century, when France was racked by religious and civil strife.

Montaigne condemned the empty scholarship and formalism into which humanism and humanistic education had largely degenerated by the end of the sixteenth century. "To know by heart is not to

Michel de Montaigne, author of the Essays. *Montaigne retired from the business world while in his thirties to reflect on and write about humanity's problems.*

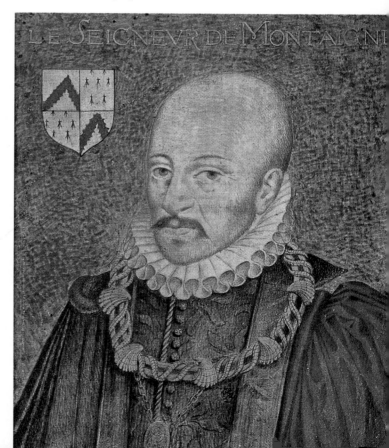

LE SEIGNEVR DE MONTAIGNE

know; it is to retain what we have given our memory to keep," he wrote. He added:

> Our tutors never stop bawling into our ears, as though they were pouring water into a funnel; and our task is only to repeat what has been told us. I should like the tutor to correct this practice. . . . I want him to listen to his pupil speaking in his turn.[17]

Montaigne's final essay, "Of Experience," which developed the thought that "when reason fails us we resort to experience," is an acknowledgment of the shortcomings of humanism and a foreshadowing of the coming triumph of science.

Cervantes's *Don Quixote*

In the national literatures that matured during the northern Renaissance, the transition from feudal knight to Renaissance courtier finds its greatest literary expression in a masterpiece of Spanish satire, *Don Quixote de la Mancha*, the work of Miguel de Cervantes (1547–1616). By Cervantes's time, knighthood had become an anachronism, though its accompanying code of chivalry still retained its appeal. It remained for a rationalist like Cervantes to expose the inadequacies of chivalric idealism in a world that had acquired new and intensely practical aims. He did so by creating a sad but appealing character to serve as the personification of an outmoded way of life.

Don Quixote, the "knight of the woeful countenance," mounted on his "lean, lank, meagre, drooping, sharp-backed, and raw-boned" steed Rozinante, sets out in the Spanish countryside to right wrongs and uphold his lady's honor and his own. In his misadventures he is accompanied by his squire, the much less gallant but infinitely more realistic Sancho Panza, whose peasant wisdom and hard-grained common sense serve as a contrast to the impracticality of his master's chivalric code. Tilting at windmills, mistaking serving wenches for highborn ladies and inns for castles, and lamenting the invention of gunpowder as depriving brave knights of a chance to win immortality, Don Quixote is, on the surface at least, a ridiculous old man whose nostalgia for the "good old days" is a constant source of grief to him. But the story represents a superb satire directed against the outworn ideology of the Middle Ages; in particular, it laughed the ideal of chivalric romance into the world of make-believe.

And *Don Quixote* is still more. Cervantes instilled in his main character a sadness born in large measure of the author's own career of frustrated hopes and ambitions. As a result, Don Quixote becomes more than a romantic lunatic; he serves to embody the set of ideals that each of us would like to see realized but that we must compromise in a world in which we must often serve other interests.

Title page from the 1605 English translation of Don Quixote *by Cervantes. In its parody of chivalric romances,* Don Quixote *represents a great change from the outworn concepts of the Middle Ages to the ideology of a newer age, one much more complex and practical.*

Secular Drama

Like Greek drama, medieval drama developed out of religious ceremonies. A complete divorce of church and stage did not occur until the middle of the fifteenth century, when the Renaissance era of drama began in Italian cities with the performance of ancient Roman comedies. In the following century appeared the *commedia dell'arte*, reflections of everyday life in vulgar and slapstick fashion, usually improvised by the players from a plot outline.

As secular dramas grew in popularity, theaters were built as permanent settings for their presentations. Great ingenuity was shown in the design of elaborate, realistic stage scenery as well as in lighting and sound effects. Theaters embodying these innovations only gradually appeared outside Italy. Not until 1576 was the first public theater erected in London; three years later a similar theater was constructed in Madrid.

Imitating the ancient models they admired, French and Italian writers followed what they believed were the rigid conventions of the classical drama and to a large extent catered to the tastes of the aristocracy. By contrast, Spanish and English playwrights created a theatrical environment that was at once more socially democratic, more hospitable to national themes, and less concerned with classical models.

William Shakespeare

The reign of Queen Elizabeth I (1558–1603) climaxed the English Renaissance and produced such a galaxy of talented writers that one would have to go back as far as Athens in the fifth century B.C.E. to find an age as rich with literary genius. Strongly influenced by the royal court, which served as the busy center of intellectual and artistic life, these writers produced works that were intensely emotional, richly romantic, and often wildly extravagant in spite of all their poetic allusions to classical times.

The supreme figure in Elizabethan literature and perhaps in all Western literature is William Shakespeare (1564–1616). His rich vocabulary and poetic imagery were matched by his turbulent imagination. He was a superb lyric poet, and numerous critics have judged him the foremost sonnet writer in the English language.

Shakespeare wrote 37 plays—comedies, histories, tragedies, and romances. His historical plays reflected the patriotic upsurge experienced by the English after the defeat of the Spanish Armada in 1588. For his comedies, tragedies, and romances, Shakespeare was content in a great majority of cases to borrow plots from earlier works. His great strength lay in his creation of characters—perhaps the richest and most diversified collection conceived by the mind of one man—and in his ability to translate his knowledge of human nature into dramatic speech and action. Today his comedies still play to enthusiastic audiences: *The Taming of the Shrew, As You Like It, A Midsummer Night's Dream,* and *The Merchant of Venice* are but a few. But it is in his tragedies that the poet-dramatist runs the gamut of human emotion and experience.

Shakespeare possessed in abundance the Renaissance concern for human beings and the world around them. Hence his plays deal first and foremost with the human personality, passions, and problems. In such works as *Romeo and Juliet, Measure for Measure,* and *Troilus and Cressida,* the problems of love and sex are studied from many angles. Jealousy is analyzed in *Othello,* ambition in *Macbeth* and *Julius Caesar,* family relationships in *King Lear,* and a man's struggle with his own soul in *Hamlet.* Shakespeare's extraordinary ability to build every concrete fact and action on a universal truth makes his observations as applicable today as when they were first presented at

the Globe Theater. Small wonder that next to the Bible, Shakespeare is the most quoted of all literary sources in the English language.

Northern Painting

Before the Italian Renaissance began to influence the artistic circles of northern Europe, the painters of the Low Countries—modern Belgium, Luxembourg, and the Netherlands—had been making significant advances on their own. Outstanding was the Fleming Jan van Eyck (c. 1395–1441), whose work has been called the "full flowering of the spirit of the late Middle Ages," for he continued to paint in the realistic manner developed by medieval miniaturists. Van Eyck also perfected the technique of oil painting, which enabled him to paint with greater realism and attention to detail. In his painting of the merchant Arnolfini and his wife, for example, he painstakingly gives extraordinary reality to every detail, from his own image reflected in the mirror in the background to individual hairs on the little dog in the foreground.

Jan van Eyck, Wedding Portrait. *The painting of a merchant named Arnolfini and his pregnant bride is extraordinary for its meticulously rendered realistic detail. Van Eyck painted exactly what he saw—he "was there," as his signature on the painting says (Johannes de Eyck fuit hic). The painting is also filled with symbolism; the dog, for instance, stands for marital fidelity.*

Jan van Eyck, The Arnolfini Portrait, 1434. NG 186. © National Gallery, London.

The first German painter to be influenced deeply by Italian art was Albrecht Dürer (1471–1528) of Nuremberg. Dürer made more than one journey to Italy, where he was impressed both with the painting of the Renaissance Italians and with the artists' high social status—a contrast with northern Europe, where artists were still treated as craftsmen, not men of genius. His own work is a blend of the old and the new; thus his engraving *Knight, Death, and the Devil* fuses the realism and symbolism of the Gothic with the nobility of Verrocchio's equestrian statue of Colleoni. In his own lifetime and after, Dürer became better known for his numerous engravings and woodcuts, produced for a mass market, than for his paintings.

Another famous German painter, Hans Holbein the Younger (1497–1543), chiefly painted portraits and worked abroad, especially in England. His memorable portraits blend the realism and concern for detail characteristic of all northern painting with Italian dignity.

Two northern painters who remained completely isolated from Italian influences were Hieronymus Bosch (1480–1516) and Pieter Brueghel the Elder

The first German painter influenced by the Italian style was Albrecht Dürer. His engraving The Knight, Death, and the Devil *is typical of his combination of the new style (the knight on his charger echoes Verrocchio's statue of Colleoni) with medieval Gothic realism and subject matter.*

Albrecht Dürer, *The Knight, Death and the Devil*, 1513. Engraving, 9 11/16" × 7 9/16". The Brooklyn Museum of Art, New York. Gift of Mrs. Horace OP. Havemeyer.

(c. 1525–1569). Brueghel retained a strong Flemish flavor in his portrayal of the faces and scenes of his native land. He painted village squares, landscapes, skating scenes, and peasants at work and at leisure just as he saw them, with a reporter's eye for detail.

Very little is known about the Dutch master Bosch other than that he belonged to one of the many puritanical religious sects that were becoming popular at the time. This accounts for his most famous painting, *The Garden of Delights*, a triptych whose main panel is filled with innumerable naked men and women reveling in the sins of the flesh. The smaller left panel, by contrast, depicts an idyllic Garden of Eden, while the right panel portrays a nightmarish hell filled with frenzied sinners undergoing punishment. Bosch was a stern moralist whose obsession with sin and hell reflects the fears of his contemporaries, which contributed to the religious movement to be described in the next chapter—the Reformation.

Conclusion

In the Middle Ages people had thought and acted primarily as members of a community—a manor, a guild, or, above all, the universal community represented by the Roman Catholic Church. But gradually individuals began to attach importance to themselves and to develop an interest in worldly things for their own sake. This new individualistic and secular spirit, the period in which it became prominent, and the ways in which it manifested itself in art, literature, and learning, are called the Renaissance.

The change took place earliest in the cities of fourteenth- and fifteenth-century Italy, and its intellectual and artistic aspects were linked to the practical activities of Renaissance civic life. Its intellectual manifestation, known as humanism—a movement that sought to recapture the learning and culture of ancient Greece and Rome—resulted in a revival of classical literature and learning; it led citizens to seek out and imitate what was relevant and useful in the classics. Scholars eagerly searched for ancient manuscripts and introduced the literature of Greece and Rome into contemporary life. Italian humanists also laid the foundation for modern scholarship. Thus they helped prepare the way for modern science, even though they themselves generally avoided the subject.

Artists, too, reflected the new human-centered view of the world. The extent to which the Italian Renaissance sculptors, architects, and painters succeeded remains one of the glories of Western civilization. But the "anti-Renaissance" art called Mannerism, which arose during the last two-thirds of the sixteenth century after the peak of perfection had been reached in the High Renaissance, has also of late received much favorable attention. Long dismissed as the "grotesque Renaissance" and described as "variations on ugliness," in the twentieth century the appearance of such styles as surrealism and expressionism led to a new understanding and appreciation of Mannerism. The Mannerist period is also regarded as one of invention and exploration out of which arose the baroque style of the seventeenth century.

In the sixteenth century the stimulating ideas current in Italy spread beyond the Alps and combined with local developments to produce renaissances in France, England, and elsewhere. Although influenced by Italian models, thought and art beyond the Alps also developed in distinctive ways. These developments included the invention of printing from movable type, the impact of the reforming zeal of the northern humanists on society, some of the great classics of European national literature, and achievements in painting that blended late medieval Gothic realism with Italian Renaissance dignity.

Suggestions for Reading

Margaret Aston, *The Fifteenth Century: The Prospect of Europe* (Norton, 1979); Peter Burke, *The Italian Renaissance: Culture and Society in Renaissance Italy* (Princeton University Press, 1987); and Jonathan W. Zophy, *A Short History of Renaissance and Reformation Europe*, 2nd ed. (Prentice Hall, 1998), are first-rate introductions to the Renaissance period.

Jacob Burckhardt, *The Civilization of the Renaissance in Italy*, 2 vols. (Torchbooks, 1958), first published in 1860, inaugurated the view that the Italian Renaissance of the fourteenth and fifteenth centuries was a momentous turning point in the history of Western civilization. The editors of this edition maintain that Burckhardt's major interpretations remain valid. For other excellent interpretations, see John Hale, *The Civilization of Europe in the Renaissance* (Touchstone, 1994); De Lamar Jensen, *Renaissance Europe: Age of Recovery and Reconciliation*, 2nd ed. (Heath, 1992); and Lisa Jardine, *Worldly Goods: A New History of the Renaissance* (Bantam, 1996).

Several excellent accounts dealing with the individual Italian city-states include Giovanni Tabacco, *The Struggle for Power in Medieval Italy* (Yale University Press, 1990); David Waley, *The Italian City Republics* (Addison-Wesley, 1988); John Norwich, *A History of Venice* (Vintage, 1989); and Charles Stinger, *The Renaissance in Rome* (Indiana University Press, 1985). Christopher Hibbert, *Florence: The Biography of a City* (Norton, 1993), focuses on the Renaissance period and serves as a guidebook as well as a history. See also Melissa Bullard, *Lorenzo il Magnifico: Image and Anxiety, Politics and Finance* (Oxford University Press, 1994); Christopher Hibbert, *Florence* (Morrow, 1990); and Alison Brown, *The Medici in Florence: The Exercise of Language and Power* (Penguin, 1992).

Paul O. Kristeller, *Renaissance Thought: The Classic, Scholastic, and Humanist Strains* (Torchbooks, 1961), and Paul O. Kristeller and Michael Mooney, eds., *Renaissance Thought and Its Sources* (Columbia University Press, 1979), are both excellent introductions. See also E. B. Fryde, *Humanism and Renaissance Historiography* (Harvard University Press, 1983); Roberto Weiss, *The Renaissance Discovery of Classical Antiquity*

(Blackwell, 1988); Donald R. Kelley, *Renaissance Humanism* (Twayne, 1991); Charles Edward Trinkaus, *The Scope of Renaissance Humanism* (Indiana University Press, 1983); and Brian P. Copenhaver, *Renaissance Philosophy* (Oxford University Press, 1992). Katharina M. Wilson, ed., *Women Writers of the Renaissance and Reformation* (University of Georgia Press, 1987), is an excellent study of a neglected subject. See also Paul F. Grendler, *Schooling in Renaissance Italy* (Johns Hopkins University Press, 1989); Nicholas Mann, *Petrarch* (Cornell University Press, 1984); and Margaret F. Rosenthal and Catherine R. Stimpson, *The Honest Courtesan: Veronica Franco, Citizen and Writer in Sixteenth-Century Venice* (University of Chicago Press, 1992). Sebastian de Grazia, *Machiavelli in Hell* (Princeton University Press, 1989), is an excellent biography.

Frederick Binkerd Artz, *From the Renaissance to Romanticism: Trends in Style in Art, Literature, and Music, 1300–1830* (University of Chicago Press, 1962), is a good overall view of the arts. Also recommended are Peter Murray and Linda Murray, *The Art of the Renaissance* (Thames & Hudson, 1985), and Michael Levey, *Early Renaissance* (Penguin, 1978) and *High Renaissance* (Penguin, 1975), which contain many illustrations of paintings; see also Lorne Campbell, *Renaissance Portraits: European Portrait-Painting in the 14th, 15th, and 16th Centuries* (Yale University Press, 1991); Joachim Poeschke, *Donatello and His World: Sculpture of the Italian Renaissance* (Abrams, 1993); Norman E. Land, *The Viewer as Poet: The Renaissance Response to Art* (Pennsylvania State University Press, 1994); and John White, *Art and Architecture in Italy, 1250–1400*, 3rd ed. (Yale University Press, 1993). Bernard Berenson, *Italian Painters of the Renaissance* (Cornell University Press, 1980), and Rudolf Wittkower, *Architectural Principles in the Age of Humanism* (Norton, 1971), are two classics of art history. See also Roberta J. M. Olsen, *Italian Renaissance Sculpture* (Thames & Hudson, 1992); Charles Seymour Jr., *Sculpture in Italy, 1400–1500* (Yale University Press, 1994); and David Thompson, *Renaissance Architecture: Patrons, Critics, Luxury* (St. Martin's Press, 1993).

On the northern Renaissance, see Charles G. Nauert Jr., *Humanism and the Culture of Renaissance Europe* (Cambridge University Press, 1995); Elaine V. Beilin, *Redeeming Eve: Women Writers of the English Renaissance* (Princeton University Press, 1987); Lisa Jardine, *Erasmus, Man of Letters* (Yale University Press, 1993); Max M. Reese, *Shakespeare: His World and His Work* (Oxford University Press, 1980); Jeffrey Chips Smith, *German Sculpture of the Later Renaissance, c. 1520–1580: Art in an Age of Uncertainty* (Princeton University Press, 1994); and Carl C. Christensen, *Art and the Reformation in Germany* (Yale University Press, 1979).

Suggestions for Web Browsing

Renaissance Art
http://online.anu.edu.au/ArtHistory/renart/pics.art/Part1.html

One of the very best and most comprehensive sites for reproductions of the major paintings, works of sculpture, and architecture from the Renaissance. An amazing resource of the study of Renaissance art.

WebMuseum, Paris: Italian Renaissance (1420–1600)
http://www.hipernet.ufsc.br/wm/paint/tl/it-ren/

A useful site for anyone interested in the art of the Italian Renaissance, especially the work of Leonardo da Vinci, Raphael, and Michelangelo.

Florence in the Renaissance
http://www.mega.it/eng/egui/epo/secrepu.htm

A history of the Florentine Republic, with details about the city's influence on Renaissance culture.

Sistine Chapel
http://christusrex.org/www1/sistine/0-Tour.html

Photo collection depicting all facets of the Sistine Chapel, including 18 images of Michelangelo's ceiling.

Michelangelo
http://www.michelangelo.com.br/

Featuring the works of the artist beautifully illustrated and annotated. An outstanding site.

The Louvre
http://www.paris.org/Musees/Louvre

Web site for one of the world's greatest museums offers many paths to some of the most beautiful Renaissance art in existence.

Image Gallery: Renaissance
http://www.lycos.com/cgi-bin/
   pursuit?que...&fs=parent&cat=image_gallery

This site displays the greatest works of Renaissance art by artist. A very comprehensive collection.

Creative Impulse: Renaissance
http://history.evansville.net/renaissa.html

The University of Evansville's outstanding series of sites on Western civilization includes this compendium of art, history, and descriptions of daily life and culture. Includes one of the very best compilations of other sites dealing with the Renaissance.

Medieval and Renaissance Fact and Fiction
http://www.angelfire.com/mi/spanogle/medieval.html

A useful guide to Web resources for students interested in the history, culture, and literature of the Renaissance.

Northern Renaissance Art Web
http://pilot.msu.edu/~cloudsar/nrweb.html

A collection of links for exploring the artists and literature of the northern Renaissance.

Notes

1. *Tempest*, act 5, scene 1, lines 182–185.
2. Quoted in Lauro Martines, *Power and Imagination: City-States in Renaissance Italy* (New York: Knopf, 1979), p. 83.
3. Quoted in ibid., p. 243.
4. Quoted in John Herman Randall Jr., *The Making of the Modern Mind* (Boston: Houghton Mifflin, 1976), p. 213.
5. Letter to Francesco Vettori; see Allan H. Gilbert, *The Letters of Machiavelli* (New York: Capricorn Books), p. 142.
6. Richard Addington, trans., *The Decameron of Giovanni Boccaccio* (New York: Garden City, 1949), p. 559.
7. Joan Kelly, quoted in Bonnie S. Anderson and Judith Zinsser, *A History of Their Own: Women in Europe from Prehistory to the Present*, Vol. 1 (New York: Harper & Row, 1988), p. xvii.
8. Sir Thomas Elyot, *The Book of the Governor*, quoted in Eugene F. Rice, *The Foundations of Early Modern Europe, 1460–1559* (New York: Norton, 1970), p. 88.
9. Eric Newton, *European Painting and Sculpture*, 4th ed. (New York: Penguin, 1956), pp. 139–140.
10. Allan H. Gilbert, trans., *Machiavelli:* The Prince *and Other Works* (Chicago: Packard, 1941), p. 177.
11. Frederick Binkerd Artz, *From the Renaissance to Romanticism: Trends in Style in Art, Literature, and Music, 1300–1830* (Chicago: University of Chicago Press, 1962), p. 102.
12. Henry Osborn Taylor, ed., *Thought and Expression in the Sixteenth Century*, Vol. 1 (New York: Macmillan, 1920), p. 175.
13. Martines, *Power and Imagination*, p. 208.
14. From the 1684 translation by Gilbert Burnet, in *Introduction to Contemporary Civilization in the West: A Source Book*, Vol. 1 (New York: Columbia University Press, 1946), p. 461.
15. Ibid., p. 460.
16. Quoted in Taylor, *Thought and Expression*, pp. 328–329.
17. Montaigne, "Of the Education of Children," in Donald M. Frame, trans., *The Complete Works of Montaigne* (Stanford, Calif.: Stanford University Press, 1957), p. 112.

The transition from papal religious domination in the thirteenth century to control by kings and states brought with it a pandemic of violence that touched all ages, classes, and nations. That Pieter Brueghel the Elder understood the nature of his times can be seen when he placed the biblical account of the Death of the Innocents (Matthew 2:16) in the context of sixteenth-century Europe. By placing Herod's order to kill all children under the age of 2 in a contemporary setting, Brueghel captured the mindless slaughter justified by the political and religious zealots of his age.

The Christian Reformations and the Emergence of the Modern Political System

Faith and State in Europe, 1517–1648

Chapter Contents

When the men and women of the late Middle Ages who lived north of the Mediterranean and west of Russia had occasion to think about the world outside their villages, they believed they lived in Christendom. By the middle of the seventeenth century, people living in that part of the world referred to it as Europe. The change from Christendom to Europe, from a community based on faith to an allegiance imposed by the state, brought with it much death, suffering, and destruction in the 150 years after Luther first made his stand at Wittenberg. Not until the twentieth century would Europeans experience greater carnage.

This transition from the medieval to the modern world brought with it the first national liberation struggle—the Dutch; new banks, insurance companies, and stock markets—the rise of modern capitalism; the first modern, elite cadre dedicated to redefining the truth and imposing it throughout the world—the Jesuits; and the Habsburgs' attempt to eradicate not only the Bohemians but also their civilization after 1620—the first modern genocide. The faithful knew that the Almighty had moved in the life of his people since the world had begun, but in this century and a half kings and clerics used the name of God to justify the slaughter of anyone who opposed them. Not since the Crusades had the Christians gone to battle with such bloodthirsty results. Then it was against the so-called infidel. Now it would be against each other, until finally in 1648 the Europeans grew tired of the combat and sought refuge in the rules of the modern state system and absolutist kings.

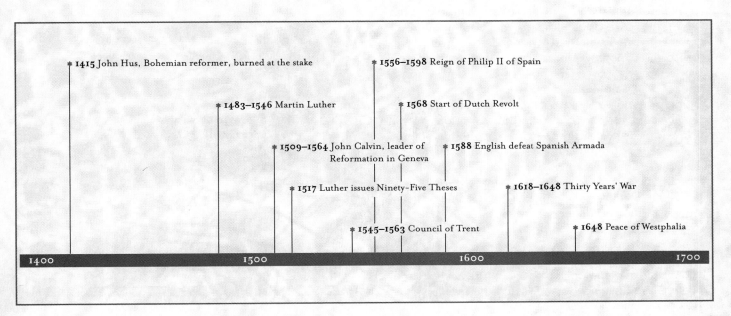

* **1415** John Hus, Bohemian reformer, burned at the stake

* **1556–1598** Reign of Philip II of Spain

* **1483–1546** Martin Luther

* **1568** Start of Dutch Revolt

* **1509–1564** John Calvin, leader of Reformation in Geneva

* **1588** English defeat Spanish Armada

* **1517** Luther issues Ninety-Five Theses

* **1618–1648** Thirty Years' War

* **1545–1563** Council of Trent

* **1648** Peace of Westphalia

1400   1500   1600   1700

This chapter traces the tortured path of the transition between the age of faith and the age of the state. Faith is the believer's link with God, an individual and mystical force. The state is an artificial creation: an institution erected by human beings that has a monopoly over the right to tax and use force within a defined boundary. The tragic mixture of the faith of an individual such as Martin Luther and the blunt instrument that is the modern state is the subject of this chapter.

The Protestant Reformation in Germany

Luther had no intention of setting the spark that launched this century and a half of conflict. Born in 1483, the son of an ambitious and tough Thuringian peasant turned miner and small businessman, he was raised by his parents under a regime of Christian love and the attendant harsh physical discipline that would affect his way of dealing with the world after 1521. Like many young boys of his time, he enjoyed the sometimes earthy and profane humor of his peasant society. Unlike many of his friends, he, like St. Augustine, distrusted his passionate nature and became obsessed with fear of the devil and an eternity in hell. Until 1517, Luther's pursuit of his salvation was an intensely personal one, with little regard to the larger context of discontent in which he lived.

The Context for Change

As we saw in Chapter 8, the plague, famine, and warfare of the fourteenth and fifteenth centuries brought Europe brutally down from the mountaintop of the High Middle Ages. Institutions such as the papacy and the established nobilities suffered greatly. The Roman Catholic Church's prestige plummeted after Philip the Fair's kidnapping of Pope Boniface and the split between Rome and Avignon—with even, for a time, three popes. Almost continuous warfare destroyed a large part of the nobility of western Europe, and the new nobles created to replace the old warriors were more often bureaucrats than soldiers. The plague and its periodic, dreadful visitations would for centuries keep Europe from reaching its population levels of around 1300. Fewer people meant a tax loss for the various kings, and those people who survived found themselves able to move more easily from the former feudal contracts to become wage laborers in the countryside or workers and artisans in the cities. All of these factors contributed to a potentially explosive situation.

Crisis and change were not new in Europe. But the means of communicating the nature and extent of the crisis and change was new, and the result was the

force of mobilized public opinion. The printing presses since their European introduction in the mid-fifteenth century had already spewed out 6 million publications in more than 200 European towns. There were more and better-educated people with a thirst to read these books, which dealt largely with religious themes. Although 90 percent of the population remained rural, cities increased considerably in size and number, swelled by the people coming from the countryside to make a living. And in the cities in the north of Europe, lending libraries were established to make books available to those who could not buy them.

Life in these cities became increasingly difficult as the social problems of urban growth outran the resources of the Catholic Church to deal with them. Many a city-dweller was a peasant who had just arrived and was cut off from his family and village. Such a person would try to adjust to the strange and new ideas and gasped to see his pocketbook emptied as the Catholic Church charged its fees, the feudal nobles claimed their tolls, and the entrenched interests blocked his chances of getting work. The country

Religious Reforms and Reactions

1415	John Hus, Bohemian reformer, burned at the stake
1437–1517	Cardinal Ximenes, carried out reforms of Spanish Catholic Church
c. 1450	Revival of witchcraft mania in Europe
1452–1498	Savonarola, attempted religious purification of Florence
1483–1546	Martin Luther
1484–1531	Ulrich Zwingli, leader of Swiss Reformation
1491–1556	Ignatius Loyola, founder of Society of Jesus (Jesuits)
1509–1564	John Calvin, leader of Reformation in Geneva
1515–1582	St. Teresa of Avila, founder of Carmelite religious order
1517	Luther issues Ninety-Five Theses
1521	Luther declared an outcast by the Imperial Diet at Worms
1534–1549	Pontificate of Paul III
1545–1563	Council of Trent
1561–1593	Religious wars in France

Discovery Through Maps

The Road to Eternity

In the fifteenth and sixteenth centuries, Christians, such as Martin Luther, lived in an environment characterized by disorder and death. As Europe struggled out of the disaster of the recurring plagues, wars, and the breakdown of law and order, life was a tenuous thread between birth and judgment.

Flemish artist Jan van Eyck (d. 1441) did most of his work during the first half of these tumultuous times. In his paintings he made a breakthrough from the formulaic elegance and unnecessary complications of the Gothic style to go to the heart of the human condition. In his travels about Europe he witnessed the fragility of life in the towns where the plague had just made its reappearance, in the bodies of people killed by highway robbers, and in the joy of the birth of a child and the tragedy of the all-too-often death of its mother.

In this altarpiece entitled *The Last Judgment*, painted by van Eyck, we see the only cartography that mattered to believers—the vertical distances between heaven and hell at the Last Judgment. Here, in the upper portion, we have those judged or yet to be judged. Below, pictured in agonizing detail, is hell in all of its awful terror.

As Luther was concerned with his soul, traumatized by his lustful impulses, so too were other Europeans who knew—from paintings such as this—what awaited them on their final journey through time.

Jan van Eyck, *The Last Judgment* (one of two panels), tempera and oil on canvas, transferred from wood. 22¼" × 7¾". The Metropolitan Museum of Art, Fletcher Fund, 1933. Photograph © 1998 The Metropolitan Museum of Art.

person faced a society of grasping merchants, suspicious craftspeople, and poor townsfolk, and more often than not the newcomer would end up among the other starving and out-of-work ex-peasants outside city walls.

The beginning of the sixteenth century marked the end of the relatively favorable situation women had enjoyed in the Middle Ages. The new emphasis on wage labor and competition from men limited their opportunities for outside work. They could get some part-time employment as field laborers, but it paid very little. They also continued to face male resentment against their entry into the economy and nearly complete exclusion from craft guilds. Their bargaining power was further limited because they outnumbered men in most cities, a situation that helped flood the job market while limiting them in finding security with husbands. Later in the century the number of single women rose even more noticeably when thousands were widowed in religious wars.

A sure indicator of the tortured nature of the era was the witchcraft mania that spread over Europe. The idea of witches as agents of evil had been present in the pre-Christian era but had weakened by the end of the thirteenth century. Its revival after 1450 was sudden and fanatical. Accused witches were usually tried in religious courts, both Catholic and, later, Protestant, where many were tortured until they confessed. Over 100,000 of these unfortunates were prosecuted, and many were executed by strangling, drowning, burning, or beheading. Seven out of ten victims were women, nearly half of them widows; most were old and eccentric. Punishment was justified by their alleged alliance with the devil and their threat to the true faith. Supposedly, they had gone over to Satan's side because women were portrayed as being weak and innately evil, as indicated by the biblical account of Eve's role in corrupting Adam. Throughout history, a time of uncertainty has always encouraged the search for scapegoats.

Economic dislocation accompanying the development of capitalism, even this early, added to the crisis of the time, especially among the peasantry. A new global economy brought high rates of inflation and shifting trade routes. The decline of the importance of the Hanseatic League, the Mediterranean, and the routes connecting the two hurt the economy of central Europe. Further, the shifting of work to laborers in the surrounding villages—cottage industry—ruined many old guild industries while swelling the ranks of the urban unemployed. Large-market agriculture weakened the peasants' traditional rights, subjected them to rents beyond their resources, and drove them from the land into the towns, where they joined the idle and the impoverished. The poor and out-of-work often directed their anger against the Catholic Church because it was a visible source of authority and it was rich. The profit motive overshadowed the church's canon law, which stressed compassion and a "just price."

Political Conditions

If Luther's search for salvation had taken place at a time only of social and economic distress, he would have remained just another agonized Christian in his own quest. At the beginning of the sixteenth century, the modern state system was in its formative stages, and the political currents of his time gave Luther's message a powerful medium of expression across central Europe after 1517.

The papacy's political power had been in a continual decline since the thirteenth century. In the cities north of the Alps and east of France, local elites fought both the Catholic clergy and the excluded lower classes for political control. In the country, nobles, local clergy, cities, and state rulers were often engaged in many-faceted political struggles. Kings and their lesser-titled feudal counterparts in the German states competed for supremacy within their realms with the popes and their major political allies of the Habsburg dynasty. The main issues here involved control of taxes and fees, the courts, the law, public support, and military power, but significant economic interests were also at stake. The Catholic Church owned vast properties and collected fortunes in tithes, fees, and religious gifts, controlling by some estimates between a fifth and a fourth of Europe's wealth—all coveted by secular rulers, who hoped to increase their wealth by taking over the church's functions and property.

In the first half of the sixteenth century, the Habsburgs, personified by Charles V, ruled a global empire. Because of fortunate marriage alliances and convenient deaths of competitors in the previous two generations, Charles was king of Spain and its world empire, Bohemia, and Hungary; sovereign over the Netherlands, Burgundy, Austria, Styria, Milan, Naples, and Sicily; and titular head of the Holy Roman Empire. But his far-flung holdings and conflicts with the Turks and the French left him little time to look after the church. The empire, including 2000 independent lesser nobles, 66 autonomous cities, over 100 imperial counts, and 30 secular princes, was loosely governed by the Imperial Diet, which functioned primarily to protect the independence of the princes and cities. With its 70 quasi-independent bishoprics and its close ties with the emperor, the church was naturally an object of resentment within the Diet.

The Catholic establishment faced even more serious political difficulties with the new independent monarchies of western Europe. During the fifteenth century, English, French, and Spanish rulers began freeing themselves from traditional restrictions and gaining independence from the papacy. In Spain, Charles V's maternal grandparents, Ferdinand and Isabella, made taxation of the church a major revenue source and the Inquisition a political tool for removing enemies of the monarchy. French kings by the mid-fifteenth century had won the right of clerical appointment and used it to control their church. In England the Tudor dynasty after 1485 co-opted the nobility and raised new revenues; the break with Rome under Henry VIII would climax a long and bitter struggle between English kings and the papacy over appointments and church incomes.

No longer able to prevail over secular rulers by its religious authority alone, the papacy fared badly in an era of power politics in foreign relations. Free Italian cities, such as Venice and Florence, had helped generate the new balance of power diplomacy, but it soon involved the peninsula in a desperate struggle between the Habsburg and Valois (French) dynasties that lasted from the 1490s to 1559. The Papal States became a political pawn. The papacy's weaknesses were exploited by the troops of Charles V when they sacked Rome in 1527.

Wyclif, Hus, and the Humanists

Before 1517, political notions were not an important part of Luther's life. The confusion and corruption in the Catholic Church affected him far more. As one of his century's finest theologians, he knew that it had taken seven councils and eight centuries to arrive at an agreed-on definition of Christianity and that thereafter the church had fought continuously against heretics—people who disagreed with that prescribed definition of the faith. Adding to the theological disputes during and after the fourteenth century was a widespread argument about the role and pretensions of the papacy. There were also German and Dutch mystics who sought direct spiritual communion with God outside the Catholic Church's hierarchy.

Theologians in England and Bohemia during the 1300s advanced the issues Luther would advocate more than a century later. John Wyclif (1328–1384), the son of a minor Yorkshire nobleman, studied at Balliol College, Oxford, and stayed on there as a professor. He gained a solid foundation in mathematics and optics, but his major contribution lay in theology. Wyclif lived and worked at a time of the weakened Catholic Church and rejected the French-dominated papacy and the popes' desire to exercise power inside England. Strongly influenced by the writings of St. Augustine, Wyclif emphasized the primacy of the Bible in the life of a Christian. He believed that God directly touched each person and that the role of the popes was of minor importance. In fact, the kings had a higher claim on their subjects' loyalty, and the monarchs themselves were accountable only to God, not the pope. Wyclif believed that the church itself, and not the Catholic hierarchy, is the true community of believers. He even went so far as to question the validity of some of the sacraments. Toward the end of his life, Wyclif was attacked by the papacy, and after his death he was declared a heretic. In 1428 his remains were taken from consecrated ground and burned, and his ashes were thrown into a river. In the church's eyes, this act condemned his soul to perpetual wandering and suffering and destroyed the possibility that Wyclif's followers could preserve any parts of his body as relics.

But the influence of Wyclif's writings took root in England through a group he helped organize called the "poor priests," later known as the Lollards. The Welshman William Tyndale (1494–1536) encountered Wyclif's ideas at Oxford and later at Cambridge during his study of Hebrew, Greek, and Latin. He began a translation of the Bible into English but was unable to publish it in England during the 1520s. He went to Germany, where he found a publisher and also met Luther. For the rest of the decade he continued his work of translation and tried to send his published New Testament to England. His books arrived before Henry VIII's creation of the new Protestant Church, and the bishop of London ordered around 18,000 copies to be burned. Finally, he was imprisoned in Antwerp in 1535, was found to be a heretic, and was strangled and burned on the orders of Charles V in 1536. The following year Parliament decreed that an English Bible be published and placed in each church. That text, supervised by one of his colleagues, was essentially the same as Tyndale's translation. In a certain sense, the seeds that Wyclif had planted bore fruit.

The Englishman deeply influenced events in Bohemia and the rest of central Europe. Bohemian students studying at Oxford took his writings back to Prague in the late fourteenth century, where they were translated by John Hus (c. 1370–1415), an im-

poverished but brilliant student at the Charles University in Prague. In 1402, after rising to become the dominant figure at his university, he began to give sermons in the Czech language that soon attracted groups as large as 3000 people to the Bethlehem Chapel. He preached that the Bible is the only source of faith and that every person has the right to read it in his own language. Like Wyclif, Hus preached against clerical abuses and the claim of the church to guarantee salvation. This message became more explosive because it was linked with his criticism of the excesses of the German-dominated church at a time of a growing Czech nationalist movement. In his preaching he openly acknowledged his debt to Wyclif and refused to join in condemning him in 1410. Hus was later excommunicated and called to account for himself at the Council of Constance in 1415. Even though he had been given the assurance of safe passage, he was seized and burned at the stake as a heretic, and his ashes were thrown into the Rhine. His death led to the Hussite wars (1419–1437) in which the Czechs withstood the crusades preached against them. The Bohemians maintained their religious reforms until their defeat by the Habsburgs in the Thirty Years' War.

During the fifteenth century, humanist reformers believed that abuses in the Catholic Church resulted largely from misinterpretation of Scripture by late medieval Scholastic philosophers and theologians. The Scholastics had seen reason as God's greatest gift, permitting man to understand the nature of good and evil. For example, St. Thomas Aquinas, perhaps the best-known Scholastic, tried in his *Summa Theologica* to reconcile Aristotle's logic with church teaching. Unfortunately, during Luther's time Scholastic logic was employed to rationalize many ritualistic and mechanical paths to salvation: good works earned credits against sins; popes could dispense grace through indulgences; the clergy were direct representatives of God and therefore only they could minister the sacraments. These and other similar propositions all reinforced the idea that salvation required services from the Roman Church and the clergy more than piety or faith.

Northern humanists like Erasmus ridiculed later Scholasticism as pedantic; other critics, such as the Augustinian monks, saw the Scholastics as presumptuous and worldly. Following the teachings of St. Augustine, they believed man to be such a depraved sinner that he could be saved not through "good works" but only through personal repentance and faith in God's mercy. Augustinians accepted only Scripture as religious truth; they denied emphatically that the clergy held the keys to heaven; and they condemned all changes from the early primitive church, including veneration of relics, celibacy of the clergy, priests as intermediaries, the necessity of most sacraments, and the infallibility of the pope. They believed that faith was more important than the Scholastics' manipulated power of reason.

Martin Luther found great comfort in the teachings of the humanists and the Augustinians. After four years of law study at Erfurt University, young Martin disappointed his father by entering an Augustinian monastery at age 22, following what was to him a miraculous survival in a violent thunderstorm. Even as a monk, however, Luther was tormented by what he saw as his sinful nature and the fear of damnation. Then, in his mid-thirties, he read St. Paul's Epistle to the Romans and found freedom from despair in the notion of justification by faith:

> *Then I grasped that the justice of God is that righteousness by which through grace and sheer mercy God justifies us through faith. Thereupon, I felt myself to be reborn and to have gone through open doors into paradise.[1]*

As an Augustinian, Luther entered into abstract religious debates that became more spirited because of the widespread problems of the church in central Europe. Critics' doctrinal arguments came to be tied to complaints that the church hierarchy, particularly at the highest levels, had been seriously infected by the lust for power, profit, and sensual pleasures, at the expense of spiritual concerns. Each critic had his list of specific abuses, but most agreed that some priests were so ignorant that they could not read the Scriptures or conduct the Mass; others, even some popes, took mistresses, fathered children, and paid money for forgiveness; and many clergymen, despite their vows of poverty, lived extremely well, enjoying fine wines, rich foods, and superb art. These elements of corruption had been present for centuries, but Luther was still shocked by what he saw when he made a journey to Rome.

The buying and selling of church offices and charging fees to give comfort through a variety of theologically questionable ceremonies to superstitious parishioners angered the critics. A very profitable venture was the sale of supposedly sacred relics, including reputed bones of the saints, vials of mystically preserved blood from Christian martyrs, and other items such as shrouds and pieces of the true cross. There were so many pieces of the "true cross," one critic remarked, that a navy could well be built from them.

The practice that outraged Luther and brought him openly to oppose the Roman Catholic Church was the sale of indulgences. Theoretically, these were shares of surplus grace, earned by Christ and the saints and available for papal dispensation to worthy souls after death. Originally, indulgences were not sold or described as tickets to heaven. By the sixteenth century, however, papal salesmen regularly peddled them as guarantees of early release from purgatory.

Luther's Stand

There are moments in history when the actions of a single person will link all of the prevailing and contrasting currents of an era into an explosive mixture. In Wittenberg on October 31, 1517, Martin Luther issued his celebrated Ninety-Five Theses, calling for public debate on issues involving indulgences and other related theological questions.[2] The ensuing controversy, which soon raged far beyond Wittenberg, split all of western Christendom and focused and strengthened the social, economic, and political contradictions of the time. Luther's act and its repercussions affected not only the German princes and the Holy Roman Emperor but all other states in Europe as well.

Conditions in Germany help explain the impact of Luther's protest, but his powerful personality is also a compelling factor. His immediate adversary in 1517 was a Dominican monk named Johan Tetzel, commissioned by the pope to sell indulgences. This was part of a large undertaking by which Leo X hoped to finance completion of St. Peter's Cathedral in Rome. Tetzel used every appeal to crowds of the country people around Wittenberg, begging them to aid their deceased loved ones and repeating the slogan "A penny in the box, a soul out of purgatory."[3] Luther and many other Germans detested Tetzel's

This map illustrates the geographical patterns of the Protestant Reformation. Lutheranism spread through German-speaking areas along the Baltic Sea but rarely crossed the Rhine River. The spread of Calvinism defies linguistic explanations.

In this sixteenth-century satirical engraving, Johan Tetzel, mounted on a donkey, blessed by the dove of peace, and aided by angels, arrives to sell indulgences. He was reputed to have said that "as soon as coin in coffer rings, the soul to heaven springs."

methods and his Roman connections. The reformer also rejected Tetzel's Dominican theology, which differed from Augustinian beliefs.

Luther's statements were soon translated from Latin into German and published in all major German cities. They denied the pope's ability to give salvation and declared that indulgences were not necessary for a contrite and repentant Christian. The resulting popular outcry forced Tetzel to leave Saxony, and Luther was almost immediately hailed as a prophet, directed by God to expose the pope and a grasping clergy. His message was so well received because it combined a passionate loyalty to religious traditions and a pragmatic acceptance of social change. It satisfied those who wanted a return to simple faith; it also appealed to those, like the humanists, who fought church abuses and irrationality. Luther's message also provided an outlet for German resentment against Rome, and it gave encouragement to princes seeking political independence.

At first, however, Luther proceeded cautiously, as a reformer rather than a revolutionary. Despite such caution, he was soon in trouble. Although Rome was not immediately alarmed, the Dominicans levied charges of heresy against their Augustinian competitor. Having already begun his defense in a series of pamphlets, Luther continued in 1519 by debating the eminent theologian John Eck (1486–1543) at Leipzig. There Luther denied the infallibility of the pope and church councils, declared the Scriptures to be the sole legitimate doctrinal authority, and proclaimed that salvation could be gained only by faith. The next year, Luther was excom-

municated by the pope. Charles V, only recently crowned emperor and aware of Luther's growing following among the princes, afforded the rebellious monk an audience before the Imperial Diet at Worms in 1521, where Luther publicly refused to recant any of his stated principles. The Diet finally declared him an outcast. But by this time his message had spread by the 300,000 copies of his 30 works printed between 1517 and 1520, and he was a German hero.

Soon afterward, as he left Worms, Luther was secretly detained for his own protection in Wartburg Castle by Elector Frederick of Saxony, his secular lord. When the pope issued a decree requiring that he renounce his heretical views, Luther burned the document—unlike the unfortunate Hus, who himself was

Martin Luther and the Wittenberg Reformers, *by Lucas Cranach the Younger. That Martin Luther (left) and other Protestant reformers did not suffer the same fate as John Hus a century earlier was largely due to the political support of rulers such as the Elector Frederick of Saxony (center).*

Lucas Cranach the Younger, German, 1515–1586, Martin Luther and the Wittenberg Reformers (1926.55) c. 1543, oil on panel, 27⅞ × 15⅝ in. (72.8 × 39.7 cm.) The Toledo Museum of Art; Toledo, Ohio; Purchased with funds from the Libbey Endowment, Gift of Edward Drummond Libbey.

Martin Luther at the Diet of Worms

In April 1521, Emperor Charles V called the Imperial Diet into session to hear Luther's defense of statements against church teachings and the papal authority. Luther's refusal to recant resulted in his being put under an imperial ban aimed at enforcing the pope's bull of excommunication.

Most Serene Lord Emperor, Most Illustrious Princes, Most Gracious Lords . . . I have thought and written in simplicity of heart, solely with a view to the glory of God and the pure instruction of Christ's faithful people. . . .

Your Imperial Majesty and Your Lordships; I ask you to observe that my books are not all of the same kind.

There are some in which I have dealt with piety in faith and morals with such simplicity and so agreeably with the Gospels that my adversaries themselves are compelled to admit them useful, harmless, and clearly worth reading by a Christian. . . . If I should begin to recant here, what, I beseech you, should I be doing but condemning, alone among mortals, that truth which is admitted by friends and foes alike, in an unaided struggle against universal consent?

The second kind consists in those writings levelled against the papacy. . . . If then I recant these, the only effect will be to add strength to such tyranny, to open not the windows but the main doors to such blasphemy, which will thereupon stalk farther and more widely than it has hitherto dared. . . .

The third kind consists of those books which I have written against private individuals. . . . But it is not in my power to recant them, because that recantation would give that tyranny and blasphemy an occasion to lord over those whom I defend and to rage against God's people more violently than ever. . . .

And so, through the mercy of God, I ask Your Imperial Majesty, and Your Illustrious Lordships, or anyone of any degree, to bear witness, to overthrow my errors, to defeat them by the writings of the Prophets or by the Gospels; for I shall be most ready, if I be better instructed, to recant any error, and I shall be the first in casting my writings into the fire. . . .

Thereupon the Orator of the Empire, in a tone of upbraiding, said that this answer was not to the point, and that there should be no calling into question of matters on which condemnations and decisions had before been passed by Councils. He was being asked for a plain reply, without subtlety or sophistry, to this question: Was he prepared to recant, or no?

Luther then replied: Your Imperial Majesty and Your Lordships demand a simple answer. Here it is, plain and unvarnished. Unless I am convicted of error by the testimony of Scripture or (since I put no trust in the unsupported authority of Pope or of councils, since it is plain that they have often erred and often contradicted themselves) by manifest reasoning I stand convicted by the Scriptures to which I have appealed, and my conscience is taken captive by God's word, I cannot and will not recant anything, for to act against our conscience is neither safe for us, nor open to us.

On this I take my stand. I can do no other. God help me. Amen.

From Henry Bettenson, ed., *Documents of the Christian Church* (New York: Oxford University Press, 1963), pp. 280–283.

---

burned for lack of a protector for having said many of the same things a century earlier.

At Wartburg Luther set his course for life as he began organizing an evangelical church distinct from Rome. He also translated the Bible from Latin into German and composed the sermons that would be repeated in hundreds of Lutheran pulpits all over Germany and Scandinavia. Soon he was able to leave Wartburg. He took off his clerical habit in 1523 and two years later married a former nun, Katherine von Bora, who bore him six children, raised his nieces and nephews, managed his household, secured his income, entertained his colleagues, and served as his supportive companion.

As his church grew and sustained its independence, Luther became more confident and strident, pouring verbal abuse on his enemies in 156 works published between 1530 and 1535. His attacks against Jews, Catholics, and even other Protestants became increasingly violent and vulgar in his old age. He died in 1546, pleased to see his church firmly established but disappointed by its meager spiritual accomplishments.

The Lutheran Church

Although he denounced much of the formality and ritual of the Catholic Church, Luther spent much of his time after the Diet of Worms building a new church for his followers. It reflected his main theological differences with Rome but kept many traditional ideas and practices. These were not always dictated by Luther or by the Protestant rulers among the princes; in many cases former Catholic congregations organized themselves into Lutheran churches and influenced secular authorities to go along. Luther was protected by Elector Frederick, who was above all a practical politician.

The fundamental principle of the Lutheran creed was that salvation occurred through faith, that Christ's sacrifice alone could wash away sin. This departed from the Catholic doctrine of salvation by faith and good works, which required conformance to prescribed dogma and participation in rituals. Along with the Lutheran emphasis on faith went belief in an all-powerful and all-knowing God beyond the rational understanding of depraved human sinners. A Christian, according to Luther, could experience God and gain salvation only through personal faith in Christ and the revealed word of the Scriptures.

Following these basic tenets, Lutheranism rejected much of the Catholic ritual. It abandoned all sacraments not mentioned in the New Testament, retaining only baptism and the Eucharist. The Catholic Mass became the Lutheran Communion, involving all who attended services and requiring no priestly blessing to transform the bread and wine into Christ's body and blood, which in Lutheran theory automatically "coexisted" with the wafer and the wine. Other changes included church services in German instead of Latin, an emphasis on preaching, the abolition of monasteries, and the curtailment of formal ceremonies foreign to the personal experiences of ordinary people.

The Lutheran Church claimed to be a "priesthood of all believers" in which each person could receive God directly or through the Scriptures. This required accurate translation of the Bible from Greek and Roman sources, a humanist achievement that Luther hailed, but he saw no absolute need for clerical mediation between a Christian and God. Ordained clergymen and lay members were equally responsible for keeping the faith, helping others, and saving their own souls. Luther saw a clerical hierarchy as at best a necessary evil. Having denied papal infallibility and Catholic clerical privileges, he followed the same principles in dealing with his own hardworking and often impoverished preachers.

Luther's ideas on marriage and Christian equality promised women new opportunities, which were only partly realized. He stressed the importance of wives as marriage partners for both the clergy and the laity. Contrary to Catholic doctrine, he even condoned divorce in cases of adultery and desertion. During the 1520s his views drew numerous women, including his own wife, to Wittenberg, where they found refuge from monasteries or Catholic husbands. Some Lutheran women became wandering preachers, but they evoked protests from male ministers and legal prohibitions from many German municipal councils, including those of Nuremberg and

Augsburg. Although teaching that women were equal to men in opportunities for salvation and in their family roles, in his later writings Luther described them as subordinate to their husbands and not meant for the pulpit.

Despite his prejudices against hierarchies, Luther established a church organization as well as a doctrine. Each congregation was charged with disciplining its members in the faith and maintaining schools, with approved catechisms (summaries of religious principles), for the moral and religious education of children. At first each congregation conducted its own affairs, but by the late 1520s Luther saw a need for a governing bureaucracy to maintain unity of faith and combat ignorance of the Scriptures. This led to a central committee in Saxony whose members visited and instructed the congregations. Ultimately, each of the four Saxon districts was put under a superintendent. This Saxon system became the model for subsequent Lutheran state churches in Germany and Scandinavia.

More than has been commonly realized, this early Lutheranism was a religion of resignation and suffering. Luther believed that the end of the world was near at hand, a time when the devil would reign supreme before the day of final judgment. In this "end-time," Christians would be required to endure the most intense miseries as testimony of their faith. They would resist when that faith was threatened, but in other ordinary secular affairs they were obliged to obey authority. Thus Lutheranism recognized two main human spheres of human obligation: the first and highest was to God; the other involved a subordinate loyalty to earthly governments, which also existed in accordance with God's will.

The Political Orientation and Effects of Lutheranism

Luther's idea of "two kingdoms," one of God and one of the world, fit well with contemporary political conditions, winning him support from German and Scandinavian rulers while wedding his movement to dynastic nationalism. Although he was sincere in his anticipation of the end-time, he was also aware of the need to protect his church, which he achieved by political cooperation with the elector of Saxony and other German Protestant princes. Under pressure in the 1530s he even wrote and spoke for armed resistance in what he regarded as holy causes. Thus the Lutheran political orientation helped shape emerging national monarchies.

Because his church depended on Saxon electors to protect him from execution and to give him money, Luther was naturally inclined to identify his religion with secular authority. He was also innately conservative, fearful of "the mob" and full of genuine respect for divinely appointed rulers. Although his pleas for equal treatment of children diminished the practice of primogeniture and fragmented Protestant states, Luther strongly supported their rulers. He accepted state churches that enforced the true faith, advocated government efforts to punish idleness while aiding the deserving poor, and favored mercantilist control of the economy to effect communal welfare and enhance state power.

Luther's political orientation was more clearly revealed in 1522 and 1523 during a rebellion of German knights. Seeing themselves ruined by decaying manorialism, these lesser nobles sought an alliance with the emperor against their common enemies: Rome, the princes, and the free cities. Led by ultra-nationalists such as Ulrich von Hutten and Franz von Sickingen, they attacked the archbishop of Trier while proclaiming their Lutheranism. When Lutheran support was not forthcoming, the rebellion was quickly crushed. Luther took no part in the struggle but was embarrassed by opponents who claimed his religion threatened law and order.

A better example of Luther's political and social conservatism was provided by a general revolt of peasants and discontented townsmen in 1524 and 1525. Encouraged by Lutheran appeals for Christian freedom, the rebels drew up petitions asking for religious autonomy. One group, led by a former Luther ally, Thomas Muntzer (1489–1525), proclaimed that direct revelation was superior to biblical authority. Other demands called for ending serfdom, tithes, enclosure of common lands, excessive rents, high taxes, and harsh punishments. At first Luther expressed sympathy for the requests, particularly for each congregation's right to select its own pastor. Then, as violence erupted throughout central Germany in April and May 1525, imperial and princely troops crushed the rebel armies, killing an estimated 90,000 insurgents. Luther had advised rebel leaders to obey the law as God's will; when they turned to war, he penned a virulent pamphlet, *Against the Thievish and Murderous . . . Peasants.* In it he called on the princes to "knock down, strangle, . . . stab, . . . and think nothing so venomous, pernicious, or Satanic as an insurgent."[4] By this policy he guaranteed his princely support but lost his earlier appeal to the lower classes in country and town.

His alliance with German princes and city councils marked a turning point in the Lutheran political orientation and in its rising success. After this time Lutheran pamphleteers placed heavier emphasis on discipline in church and society. Luther posed as a religious adviser to rulers and often told them what they wanted to hear, as when he approved Philip of Hesse's bigamous marriage. Converted rulers often accepted his advice to their own disadvantage, as when they refused Catholic benefices for their sons or willed away their family lands among many quarreling heirs. In the main, however, Lutheranism aided state-building by ending the Catholic dominance of law, courts, and revenues while providing popular religious support for government. In return Lutheranism was favored by numerous patrician urban oligarchies and by a coterie of Protestant princes. Often the benevolent authorities were women, such as Elizabeth, duchess of Brunswick (1510–1558). These earthly lords provided Luther with respect, political concessions, and security from Catholic persecution. Without them, his life and his movement would have been doomed.

This dependence was soon very evident as the movement precipitated a struggle for religious control in Germany between the emperor and the Lutheran princes. When Catholics sought to impose conformity in Imperial Diets during the late 1520s, Lutheran leaders drew up a formal protest (hence the appellation *Protestant*). After this Augsburg Confession (1530) was rejected, the Lutheran princes organized for defense in the Schmalkaldic League. Because Charles V was preoccupied with the French and the Turks, open hostilities were minimized, but a sporadic civil war dragged on until after Luther's death in 1546. It ended at the Peace of Augsburg in 1555, when the imperial princes were permitted to choose between Lutheranism and Catholicism in their state churches, thus increasing their independence of the emperor. In addition, Catholic properties confiscated before 1552 were retained by Lutheran principalities, which provided a means for financing their policies. Although no concessions were made to other Protestant groups, such as the Calvinists, this treaty shifted the European political balance against the empire and the church.

Outside Germany, Lutheranism furnished a religious stimulus for developing national monarchies in Scandinavia. There as in Germany, rulers welcomed not only Lutheran religious ideas but also the chance to acquire confiscated Catholic properties. They were especially glad to have ministers preaching obedience to constituted secular authority. In Sweden, Gustavus Vasa (1523–1560) used Lutheranism to lead a successful struggle for Swedish independence from Denmark. In turn, the Danish king, who also ruled Norway, issued an ordinance in 1537 establishing the national Lutheran Church, with its bishops as salaried officials of the state. Throughout eastern Europe, wherever there was a German community, the Lutheran church spread—for a brief time even threatening the supremacy of the Catholic Church in Poland and Lithuania.

The Protestant Reformation in England

England was affected by the crises and changes of the fourteenth and fifteenth centuries along with the rest of Europe. And English theologians such as John Wyclif played an active role in the intellectual and theological debates of the High Middle Ages and after. During the fifteenth century, as on the Continent, there was an active underground church, the Lollards, in which laypeople, especially women, played an important role. Unlike central Europe, England was one of the new "Atlantic states" characterized by national monarchies, centralized authority, and greater independence from the papacy. The Tudor dynasty adapted itself to the new conditions after the Hundred Years' War with France and the devastating Wars of the Roses, which depopulated the traditional nobility. During this time of difficult transition it was necessary that each king and queen raise a strong and healthy heir to ensure the continuity of the Tudor dynasty and the strength of England.

Henry VIII (1509–1547) became the heir to the English throne when his brother, Arthur, died in 1502. It had not been expected that he would be king, and his education ran to that of a true Renaissance man: he showed talent in music, literature, philosophy, jousting, hunting, and theology. Not only did he become the king of England on his father's death in 1509, but he also soon married the woman who had been his brother's wife, thus continuing the dynastic alliance with Spain. Henry was a devout Roman Catholic who gained the title "Defender of the Faith" from the pope for a pamphlet he wrote denouncing Luther and his theology. But as one of the strongest kings in a century of powerful monarchs (Charles V, Philip II, Francis I, Sultan Suleiman, Ivan IV, and eventually Henry's own daughter, Elizabeth I), he knew that his primary duty was to ensure his dynasty's continuity and with it his nation's well-being.

Henry's immediate problem in the 1520s was the lack of a male heir. After 11 years of marriage, he had only a sickly daughter and an illegitimate son. His queen, Catherine of Aragon (1485–1536), after four earlier pregnancies, gave birth to a stillborn son in 1518, and by 1527, when she was 42, Henry had concluded that she would have no more children. His only hope for the future of his dynasty seemed to be a new marriage with another queen. This, of course, would require an annulment of his marriage to Catherine. In 1527 he appealed to the pope, asking for the annulment.

Normally, the request would probably have been granted; the situation, however, was not normal. Because she had been the wife of Henry's brother, Arthur, Catherine's marriage to Henry had necessitated a papal dispensation, based on her oath that the first marriage had never been consummated. Now Henry professed concern for his soul, tainted by living in sin with Catherine. He also claimed that he was being punished, citing a passage in the Book of Leviticus that predicted childlessness for the man who married his dead brother's wife. The pope was sympathetic and certainly aware of an obligation to the king, who had strongly supported the church. However, granting the annulment would have been admission of papal error, perhaps even corruption, in issuing the dispensation. Added to the Lutheran problem, this would have doubly damaged the papacy.

A more formidable problem for Henry was Catherine. She was a cultured Spanish woman, a respected consort, and a devoted wife, who had successfully conducted a war against Scotland when he was campaigning in France and had borne their failured attempts to produce a son with admirable Christian patience. Henry recognized her strong character in his daughter, Mary (1516–1558), whom he appointed princess of Wales and heir apparent in the absence of a prince. As late as the mid-1520s, he sought Catherine's companionship and her counsel. Henry soon learned, however, that Catherine would never accept an annulment, and he was afraid she might lead a rebellion against him. As the aunt of Charles V, whose armies occupied Rome in 1527, she was also able to exert considerable pressure on the pope.

Despite these difficulties, Henry could hope for success in his appeal to the pope. He was vigorous, handsome, and popular. Any conflict with Rome was in accord with national pride, often expressed in traditional resentment against Roman domination. Late medieval English kings had challenged the popes over church appointments and revenues. More than a century and a half before Luther, Oxford professor John Wyclif had denounced the false claims of popes and bishops. In more recent times, English Christian humanists, such as Sir Thomas More, had criticized the artificialities of Catholic worship. Thus when the pope delayed a decision, Henry was relatively secure in his support at home.

The Political Reformation

During the three years after 1531, when Catherine saw him for the last time, Henry took control of affairs. Sequestering his daughter and his banished wife in separate castles, he forbade them from seeing each other. He also intimidated the clergy into proclaiming him head of the English church "as far as the law of Christ allows," extracted from Parliament the authority to appoint bishops, and designated his willing tool, Thomas Cranmer (1489–1556), as archbishop of Canterbury. In 1533 Cranmer pronounced Henry's marriage to Catherine invalid, at the same time that he legalized his union with Anne Boleyn, a lady of the court who was carrying his unborn child, the future Elizabeth I. Cruelly, Henry even forced his daughter Mary to accept him as head of the church and admit the illegality of her mother's marriage—by implication acknowledging her own illegitimacy. Parliament also ended all payment of revenues to Rome. Now, having little other choice, the pope excommunicated Henry, making the breach official on both sides.

Amid a marked anti-Catholic campaign in the 1530s, Henry secured the Anglican establishment, which became an engine for furthering royal policies, with his henchmen controlling every function, from the building of chapels to the wording of the liturgy. Former church revenues, including more than 40,000 pounds sterling per year from religious fees alone, poured into the royal treasury. In 1539 Parliament completed its seizure of monastery lands and the wealth of pilgrimage sites such as Canterbury Cathedral, selling some for revenue and dispensing others to secure the loyalties of crown supporters. Meanwhile, Catholics suffered. Dispossessed nuns, unlike monks and priests, could find no place in the new church and were often reduced to despair. One, the famous "holy maid of Kent," who dared to rebuke the king publicly, was executed, as were other Catholic dissidents including former chancellor Sir Thomas More and the saintly Bishop Fisher of Rochester. And later there were Protestant martyrs. Perhaps the most notable was Anne Askew, a woman of Lincolnshire, who was tried before a church court for heresy and so confounded her judges that she became a legend. She was nevertheless burned in 1546, a year before Henry died.

The new Anglican Church, however, brought about little change in doctrine or ritual. The Six Articles, Parliament's declaration of the new creed and ceremonies in 1539, reaffirmed most Catholic theology except papal supremacy. Henry, in his later years, after the decapitation of Anne Boleyn on charges of adultery in 1536 (ironically, the year of the death of Catherine of Aragon), grew increasingly suspicious of popular Protestantism, which built on the centuries-old bases established by Wyclif and others and was spreading into England and Scotland from the Continent. He refused to legalize clerical marriage, which caused great hardships among many Anglican clergymen, including some bishops, and their wives.

Henry finally gained a male heir with his third wife, Jane Seymour, who died giving birth to Edward VI in 1537. His final three wives reflected the religious politics of the time. He married the homely Anne of Cleves in 1539 to consolidate an alliance with Lutheran princes but divorced her the next year. His fifth wife, Catherine Howard, was put forward by the party displeased by the rapid pace of the English Reformation, but she was decapitated two years later in 1542 on charges of adultery. The sixth, Catherine Parr, was sympathetic to the reformers and narrowly escaped the king's displeasure by humbly appealing to his vanity.

The Turmoil of Extremes

In the decade after Henry's death, religious fanaticism brought social and political upheaval. For six

Holbein's portrait of Henry VIII, painted in 1542, shows a man sure of himself in his royal setting. He had by this time broken with Rome, married six times in pursuit of a legitimate male heir, and turned England into a major naval power. What the portrait does not show is all of the suffering and discord he left in his wake.

years during growing political corruption, extreme Protestants ruled the country and dominated the frail young king, Edward VI (1547–1553). When Edward died in 1553, Mary Tudor came to the throne and strove to restore Catholicism until her death in 1558.

In Edward's reign the government was controlled by the Regency Council, dominated first by the duke of Somerset and then after 1549 by his rival, the duke of Northumberland. While the council members furthered their own ambitions, many parishes were engulfed by a wave of radical Protestantism, which weakened religious traditions. Foreign refugees contributed to the unrest, although many were led by English sympathizers like Catherine Willoughby, duchess of Suffolk, and other Protestant court ladies. Starting slowly under Somerset and moving faster under Northumberland, the government sought political support by courting the religious dissidents. It repealed the Six Articles, permitted priests to marry, replaced the Latin service with Cranmer's English version, and adopted the Forty-Two Articles, an embodiment of extreme Protestantism. Such policies frightened Catholics, but there were only two religious burnings, neither involving Catholics.

Harsh persecutions of Protestants marked the reign of Mary Tudor. Although known in Protestant history as "Bloody Mary," the new queen possessed many admirable qualities, including dignity, intelligence, compassion, and a strong moral sense, but she was handicapped by a religious obsession and by her hopeless love for her Catholic husband, Philip II, king of Spain, who married her in 1554, courteously abandoned her soon after, and returned only once, briefly, to ask her aid in furthering his diplomacy. At first successful in putting down rebellion, Mary squandered her early popularity by imposing her will on a divided people. This involved restoring the Catholic church service, proclaiming papal authority, forging a Spanish alliance, and burning 300 Protestants, including Cranmer and two other bishops. Most victims, however, were of the middle and lower classes; 55 of these were women, and two were blind girls. Mary died pitifully, rejected by her husband and people but unmoved from her determined hope to save English Catholicism. Leaving no heir, she was compelled to name Elizabeth, her half-sister, as her successor.

The Protestant Reformation in Switzerland, France, and the Rhine Valley

A very different variety of church reforms took place in Switzerland, France, and the Rhine valley. The leaders of these reforms were conscious of the state, but not dominated by it, as the Anglicans were. Like the Lutherans, they were also concerned for the salvation of their souls, but in a much more doctrinal and often vindictive way. Calvinism was the most popular and the most conservative of these, but there were many others, including multiple forms of Anabaptism. All of them went farther than Lutheranism and Anglicanism in rejecting Catholic dogma and ritual. They were also marked by their fanaticism in pursuing objectives. Generally, they were opposed to monarchy, but their position did not become very apparent until they were deeply involved in religious wars after 1560, when they often found themselves under attack by both the Catholics and the Lutherans.

Popular Protestantism arose early in Switzerland, where many of the same conditions found in Germany favored its growth. During the late medieval period the country prospered in the growing trade between Italy and northern Europe. Busy Swiss craftsmen and merchants in such cities as Zurich, Bern, Basel, and Geneva suffered under their Habsburg overlords and by papal policies, particularly the sale of indulgences. In 1499 the Confederation of Swiss Cantons won independence from the Holy Roman Empire and the Habsburgs. To many Swiss this was also a first step in repudiating outside authority.

The Swiss Reformation began in Zurich, shortly after Luther published his theses at Wittenberg. It was led by Ulrich Zwingli (1484–1531), a scholar, priest, and former military chaplain, who persuaded the city council to create a regime of clergymen and magistrates to supervise government, religion, and individual morality. Zwingli agreed with Luther in repudiating papal in favor of scriptural authority. He simplified services, preached justification by faith, attacked monasticism, and opposed clerical celibacy. More rational than Luther, he was also more interested in practical reforms, going beyond Luther in advocating additional grounds for divorce and in denying any mystical conveyance of grace by baptism or communion; both, to Zwingli, were only symbols. These differences proved irreconcilable when Luther and Zwingli met to consider merging their movements in 1529.

As Zwingli's influence spread rapidly among the northern cantons, religious controversy separated north from south, rural from urban areas, and feudal overlords, both lay and ecclesiastical, from towns within their dominions. When in the 1520s Geneva repudiated its ancient obligations and declared its independence from its local bishop and the count of Savoy, the city became a hotbed of Protestantism, with preachers swarming in from Zurich. Zwingli was killed in the resulting religious war of 1531; the fighting ended quickly in a peace that permitted each Swiss canton to choose its own religion.

John Calvin

Hoping to ensure the dominance of Protestantism in Geneva after the religious wars, local reformers invited John Calvin (1509–1564) to Geneva. Calvin arrived from Basel in 1536. His preaching ultimately won enough followers to make his church the official religion. From Geneva the faith spread widely in all directions after the early 1540s.

Calvin was an uncompromising French reformer, a formidable foe of the ungodly but a caring colleague and minister to humble believers. His mother had died while he was still a child. He had been partly alienated from his father, and a friend of the family sent him to the University of Paris when he was 12. There he began studying theology but later transferred to Orléans, where he took up law. He read some humanist writings, talked to Lutherans, experienced a personal conversion, broke with the church (1534), was suspected of heresy by the authorities, and ultimately fled to Basel. There in 1536 he published the first edition of his *Institutes of the Christian Religion*, an extremely influential theological work that transformed the general Lutheran doctrines into a profoundly rational legal system based around the concept of predestination. It also earned Calvin his invitation to Geneva.

His original plan for a city government there called for domination by the clergy and banishment of all dissidents. This aroused a storm of opposition from both Anabaptists—who believed in adult baptism and separation of church and state—and from the more worldly portion of the population, and Calvin was forced into exile. At Strasbourg he associated with other reformers who helped him refine his ideas and urged him to take a wife. In 1539 he married Idellete de Bures, a sickly widow with two children. She came back to Geneva with him in 1541, when his party regained power. Henceforth, as Protestant refugees packed the city, Idellette managed Calvin's household, took in friends and refugees, nursed him through frequent headaches, tried unsuccessfully to bear his children, and left him bereft when she died in 1549.

Calvin's second regime at Geneva after 1541 involved a long struggle with the city council. His proposed ordinances for the Genevan Church gave the clergy full control over moral and religious behavior, but the council modified the document, placing all appointments and enforcement of law under its jurisdiction. Although recognizing the Bible as supreme law and the *Institutes* as a model for behavior, it did not always act on recommendations from the Consistory, Calvin's supreme church committee. For the next 14 years Calvin fought against public criticism and opposition in the council. He gradually increased his power, however, through support from a stream of Protestant refugees who poured into the city. His influence climaxed after a failed "revolt of the godless" in 1555. From that year until his death in 1564, he dominated the council, ruling Geneva with an iron hand, within the letter but not the spirit of the original ordinances.

Particularly in that later period, the Consistory apprehended violators of religious and moral law, sending its members into households to check every detail of private life. Offenders were reported to secular magistrates for punishment. Relatively light penalties were imposed for missing church, laughing during services, wearing bright colors, dancing, playing cards, or swearing. Religious dissent, however, brought much heavier punishment. The council frequently approved Consistory recommendations by banishing offenders for blasphemy, mild heresies, adultery, or suspected witchcraft. Magistrates sometimes used torture to obtain confessions and often executed heretics, averaging more than a dozen annually as early as the 1540s. Michael Servetus (1511–1553), a Spanish theologian-philosopher and refugee from the Catholic Inquisition, was burned for heresy because he had denied the doctrine of the Trinity.

Calvinism and Its Impact

Before 1555 Calvinism was not a major Protestant movement; indeed, the Peace of Augsburg made no concessions to Calvinist regimes. Yet even that early, when it had gained official status only in Switzerland and the quasi-French state of Navarre, Calvinism exerted its own special appeal and unique impact. Although it shared with Lutheranism a strong dislike of Scholastic theology and a stringent dogmatism, it also perpetuated Calvin's respect for rational precision and his belief in education, along with his will to aggressive resistance whenever the danger of political suppression outweighed his natural inclination to cooperate with secular authorities. Such typical ambiguities between Calvinism and Lutheranism led to differences in theology and politics that helped generate a gulf between the two that has never been bridged.

These differences in theology were subtle but distinct. Calvin accepted Luther's insistence on justification by faith; like Luther, he saw Christian life as a constant struggle against the devil, and he expected a coming divine retribution, an end-time, when God would redress the evils increasing on every side. Calvin also agreed with Luther in seeing God's power as a relief for human anxiety and a source of inner peace. Both reformers believed man to be totally depraved, but Calvin placed greater emphasis on this point, at the same time emphasizing God's immutable will and purpose. If Calvinism, to human minds, seemed contradictory in affirming man's sinful nature and his creation in God's image, this only proved that God's purposes were absolutely beyond human understanding. For depraved humans God required faith and obedience, not understanding.

God's omnipotence was Calvin's cardinal principle. He saw all of nature as governed by a divinely ordained order, discernible to man but governed by laws that God could set aside in effecting miracles as he willed. Carried to its logical conclusion, such ideas produced Calvin's characteristic doctrine of predestination. Since God is all-powerful and all-knowing, he must also know who are to be saved and who are to be damned eternally. The human purpose, then, is not to win salvation, for this has already been determined, but to honor God. Calvin did not profess to know absolutely who were God's chosen, but he believed that some tests might be at least partly successful in identifying the elect: a moral life, a public

John Calvin on God's Omniscience and Predestination

This selection from Calvin's most famous work summarizes one of the two most significant points in his theology. The other was justification by faith.

Of the Eternal Election, by Which God Has Predestined Some to Salvation, and Others to Destruction.

The predestination by which God adopts some of the hope of life, and adjudges others to eternal death, no man who would be thought pious ventures simply to deny; but it is greatly cavilled at, especially by those who make prescience its cause. We, indeed, ascribe both prescience and predestination to God; but we say that it is absurd to make the latter subordinate to the former. When we attribute prescience to God, we mean that all things always were, and ever continue, under his eye; that to his knowledge there is no past or future, but all things are present, and indeed so present, that it is not merely the idea of them that is before him (as those objects are which we retain in our memory), but that he truly sees and contemplates them as actually under his immediate inspection. This prescience extends to the whole circuit of the world, and to all creatures. By predestination we mean the eternal decree of God, by which he determined with himself whatever he wished to happen with regard to every man. All are not created on equal terms, but some are preordained to eternal life, others to eternal damnation; and, accordingly, as each has been created for one or other of these ends, we say that he has been predestined to life or to death. This God has testified, not only in the case of single individuals; he has also given a specimen of it in the whole posterity of Abraham, to make it plain that the future condition of each nation was entirely at his disposal. . . .

We say, then, that Scripture clearly proves this much, that God by his eternal and immutable counsel determined once for all those whom it was his pleasure one day to admit to salvation, and those whom, on the other hand, it was his pleasure to doom to destruction. We maintain that this counsel, as regards the elect, is founded on his free mercy, without any respect to human worth, while those whom he dooms to destruction are excluded from access to life by a just and blameless, but at the same time incomprehensible judgment. In regard to the elect, we regard calling as the evidence of election, and justification as another symbol of its manifestation, until it is fully accomplished by the attainment of glory. But as the Lord seals his elect by calling and justification, so by excluding the reprobate either from the knowledge of his name or the sanctification of his Spirit, he by these marks in a manner discloses the judgment which awaits them. I will here omit many of the fictions which foolish men have devised to overthrow predestination. There is no need of refuting objections which the moment they are produced abundantly betray their hollowness. I will dwell only on those points which either form the subject of dispute among the learned, or may occasion any difficulty to the simple, or may be employed by impiety as specious pretexts for assailing the justice of God.

From "Institutes of the Christian Religion," in Harry J. Carroll et al., eds., *The Development of Civilization* (Glenview, Ill.: Scott, Foresman, 1970), pp. 91–93.

---

profession of faith, and participation in the two sacraments of baptism and communion.

In Calvin's grand scheme, as laid out precisely in the *Institutes*, his church served to aid the elect in honoring God and preparing the elect for salvation. As communities of believers, congregations were committed to constant war against Satan. They also functioned to spread the Word (Scripture), educate youth, and alleviate suffering among the destitute. Ministers of the church were responsible for advising secular authorities on religious policies and resisting governments that violated God's laws. Within the church, ministers were elected by congregations, under the guidance of experienced pastors, convened in official sessions. Each congregation was required to live by central doctrines but permitted variations in

ritual and ceremony arising from local traditions. Regional elected *synods*, or councils, decided common policies and judged alleged violations by individual churches.

Calvin was particularly ambivalent in his views on government. He believed that all rulers were responsible to God and subject to God's vengeance. But throughout the 1540s, when he was hoping to gain the support of monarchs, he emphasized the Christian duty of obedience to secular authorities. Even then, however, he advised rulers to seek counsel from church leaders, and he ordered the faithful, among both the clergy and the laity, to disregard any government that denied them freedom in following Christ. Although willing to support any political system that furthered the true faith, Calvin always preferred rep-

By the 1560s most of the Rhône valley in France had fallen under Calvinist domination. This painting illustrates a Protestant service in Lyons, France, in 1564. Note that men and women are separated and the believers are seated according to their importance in the town.

resentative government. Later, as a surging Calvinism faced widespread royal opposition, this prejudice remained as a distinct threat to absolute monarchy.

Another ambiguity in Calvin's social thought involved his attitude toward women. Unlike Catholic theologians, he did not cast women in an inferior light. In his mind men and women were equally full of sin, but they were also equal in their chances for salvation. As he sought recruits, Calvin stressed women's right to read the Bible and participate in church services, a promise that attracted women to his movement. At the same time he saw women as naturally subordinate to their husbands in practical affairs, including the conduct of church business. Without female patron saints or priestly confessors, they were now expected to seek protection and moral discipline from their spouses.

Before the Peace of Augsburg, Calvinism made its greatest gains in France, the reformer's own homeland. His message there attracted numerous ambitious nobles and many members of the urban middle classes, who had begun to feel alienated from both church and state. Missionaries from Geneva recruited thousands of these people in a national system of congregations and synods. A large proportion were women, who worked diligently, not only converting their husbands and families but also founding religious schools, nursing the sick, and aiding the poor. Many educated aristocratic women also promoted the growth of Calvinism. One of them was Margaret of Angoulême, queen of Navarre (1492–1549) and sister of the French king. She often petitioned her brother on behalf of Protestantism and kept reformers at her court, where Calvin was sheltered at one time. Her daughter Jeanne d'Albret (1528–1572), who became queen in 1549, established Calvinism in Navarre. Calvinism also enlisted many French dissident nobles, particularly among the Bourbons, who hoped to use Calvinist support in claiming the French throne. They were part of the aristocratic Huguenot (French Calvinist) clique that included Admiral de Coligny, Jeanne d'Albret, and the Bourbon prince, Louis of Conde.

Calvinism made gains elsewhere but did not win political power. In Italy the duchess of Ferrara copied the Navarre church service for her private chapel while harboring Calvinist refugees; Zofia Olesnicka, the wife of a Polish noble, endowed a local Calvinist church. Strasbourg in the 1530s was a free center for Protestant reformers such as Matthew Zell and his

Margaret of Navarre, a supporter of Protestantism, was the author of the Heptameron, *a collection of tales modeled on Boccaccio's* Decameron.

wife, Katherine, who befriended many Calvinist preachers, including Martin Bucer, a missionary to England during the reign of Edward VI. In the same period John Knox spread the Calvinist message in Scotland. Such efforts, however, were most significant in preparing for later aggressive action.

Anabaptism and the Protestant Sects

Even more extreme than Calvinism were many divergent Protestant splinter groups, each pursuing its own "inner lights." Some saw visions of the world's end, some advocated a Christian community of shared wealth, some opposed social distinctions and economic inequalities, some—the Anabaptists—repudiated infant baptism as a violation of Christian responsibility, and some denied the need for any clergy. Most of the sects emphasized biblical literalism and direct emotional communion between the individual and God. The majority of them were indifferent or antagonistic to secular government; many favored pacifism and substitution of the church for the state.

Women were prominent among the sects. They were usually outnumbered by men, but female sect members in the sixteenth century were marked by their biblical knowledge, faith, courage, and independence. They helped found religious communities, wrote hymns and religious tracts, debated theology, and publicly challenged the authorities. Some preached and delivered prophecies, although such activities were soon suppressed by male ministers. More women than men endured torture and suffered martyrdom. Their leadership opportunities and relative freedoms in marriage, compared to women of other religions, were bought at a high price in hardship and danger.

Persecution of the sects arose largely from their radical ideas, but Catholics and other Protestants usually cited two revolutionary actions. Some radical preachers took part in the German peasants' revolt of the 1520s and shared in the savage punishments that followed. In 1534 a Catholic army besieged Münster, a German city near the southern Netherlands, where thousands of recently arrived Anabaptist extremists had seized control and expelled dissenters. Facing its desperate fate, the regime of saints confiscated property, institutionalized polygamy, and planned to convert the world. John of Leyden, a former Dutch tailor who claimed divine authority, headed a terrorist regime during the final weeks before the city fell. Its defenders suffered horrible tortures and executions.

Among the most damaging charges against the Münster rebels was their reputed sexual excesses and the dominant role played by women in this immorality. Such charges were mostly distortions. The initiation of polygamy, justified by references to the Old Testament, was a response to problems arising from a shortage of men, hundreds of whom had fled the city. Many other men were killed or injured in the fighting. Thus the city leaders required women to marry so that they could be protected and controlled by husbands. Most Anabaptist women accepted the requirement as a religious duty. Although some paraded through the streets, shouting religious slogans, the majority prepared meals, did manual labor on the defenses, fought beside their men, and died in the fighting or at the stake. Most of the original Münster women, however, fiercely resisted forced marriage, choosing instead jail or execution.

For more than a century, memories of Münster plagued the Protestant sects. They were almost immediately driven underground throughout Europe. Their persecution continued long after they had abandoned violence. In time they dispersed over the Continent and to the New World as Mennonites, Quakers, and Baptists, to name only a few denominations. For obvious reasons, voices of the radicals were among the first raised for religious liberty. Their negative experience with governments made them even more suspicious of authority than the Calvinists were. In both the Netherlands and England, they participated in political revolutions and helped frame the earliest written demands for constitutional government, representative institutions, and civil liberties.

Two Edicts Issued by the Elders of Münster

In mid-1534 the Anabaptist regime in the German city of Münster reached its most extreme, as reflected to some extent by these decrees relating to private life and public behavior.

Although all of us in this holy church of [Münster], in whose hearts the law and the will of God are inscribed by the finger of God . . . should readily fulfill them, we, twelve elders of the nation, shall nevertheless summarize them briefly in a list in order that the new state may be protected so that each one may see what to do and what not to do. . . .

The Scripture directs that those who are disobedient and unrepentant regarding several sins shall be punished with the sword:

1. Whoever curses God and his holy Name or his Word shall be killed (Lev. 24).
2. No one shall curse governmental authority (Ex. 22, Deut. 17), on pain of death.
3. Whoever does not honor or obey his parents (Ex. 20, 21) shall die.
4. Servants must obey their masters, and masters must be fair to their servants (Eph. 6).
5. Both parties who commit adultery shall die (Ex. 20, Lev. 20, Matt. 5).
6. Those who commit rape, incest, and other unclean sexual sins should die (Ex. 22, Lev. 20). . . .
7. Avarice is the root of all evil (I Tim. 6).
8. Concerning robbery, you shall not steal (Ex. 20, Deut. 27): Cursed be he who narrows his neighbor's boundary.
9. Concerning fraud and overcharging (I Thess. 4): The Lord will judge this.
10. Concerning lying and defamation (Wisd. [of Sol.] 1): A lying mouth destroys a soul.
11. Concerning disgraceful speech and idle words (Matt. 12): Men must account for every idle word they speak, on the Day of Judgment.
12. Concerning strife, disputes, anger, and envy (Gal. 5, I John 4): Whoever hates his brother is a murderer.
13. Concerning slander, murmuring, and insurrection among God's people (Lev. 19): There shall be no slanderer or flatterer among the people.

. . . Whoever disobeys these commandments and does not truly repent, shall be rooted out of the people of God, with ban and sword, through the divinely ordained governmental authority.

The elders of the congregation of Christ in the holy city of [Münster], called and ordained by the grace of the most high and almighty God, desire that the following duties and articles be faithfully and firmly observed by every Israelite and member of the house of God.

1. What the Holy Scriptures command or prohibit is to be kept by every Israelite at the pain of punishment.
2. Everybody is to be industrious in his vocation and fear God and his ordained government. Government authority does not carry the sword in vain, but it is the avenger of evildoers. . . .
6. Every day from seven to nine o'clock in the morning and from two to four o'clock in the afternoon, six elders are to sit in the market at the appointed place and settle all differences with their decisions. . . .
9. In order to keep the proper order concerning the administration of good, the food-masters are every day to prepare dishes of the kind as was hitherto customary for the brothers and sisters. These are to sit modestly and moderately at separate tables. They must not demand anything apart from what is served to them. . . .
30. A baptized Christian is not to converse with any arriving person or pagan stranger and is not to eat with him, lest there arise the suspicion of treacherous consultation. . . .

From Lowell H. Zuck, ed., *Christian and Revolution* (Philadelphia: Temple University Press, 1975), pp. 95–97.

The Catholic Counter-Reformation

The era of the Protestant Reformation was also a time of rejuvenation for the Roman Catholic Church. This revival was largely caused by the same conditions that had sparked Protestantism. Many sincere and devout Catholics had recognized a need for reform through-out the fifteenth century, and they had begun responding to the abuses in their church before Luther acted at Wittenberg. Almost every variety of reform opinion developed within the Catholic Church. Erasmus, More, and other Christian humanists provided an impetus for Luther but refused to follow him out of the Catholic Church. In a category of his own was Savonarola (1452–1498), a Dominican friar, ardent puritan, and mystic, who ruled Florence during the last four years before his death. This "Catholic Calvin" consistently invoked the wrath of God on worldly living and sinful luxuries, criticizing the pope and the clergy in terms more caustic than Luther's. At the other extreme, on the side of the establishment, was Cardinal Ximenes (1437–1517) in Spain, who carried out his own Reformation by disciplining the clergy, encouraging biblical studies, and instilling a new spirit of dedication into the monastic orders.

After the Protestant revolt began, the primary Catholic reformer was Pope Paul III (1534–1549). Coming into office at a time when the church appeared ready to collapse, Paul struggled to overcome the troubled legacy of his Renaissance predecessors and restore integrity to the papacy. Realizing that issues raised by the Protestants would have to be resolved and errors corrected, he attacked the indifference, the corruption, and the vested interests of the clerical organization. In pursuing these reforms he appointed a commission, which reported the need for correcting such abuses as the worldliness of bishops, the traffic in benefices (church appointments with guaranteed incomes), and the transgressions of some cardinals. Their recommendations led Paul to call a church council, an idea that he continued to press against stubborn opposition for more than ten years.

When Paul died in 1549, he had already set the Roman Church on a new path, although his proposed church council had only begun its deliberations. Perhaps his greatest contribution was his appointment of worthy members to the college of cardinals, filling that body with eminent scholars and devout stewards of the church. As a result of his labors, the cardinals elected a succession of later popes who were prepared, intellectually and spiritually, to continue the process of regeneration.

New Troops for the Faith

The spirit of reform was reflected in a number of new Catholic clerical orders that sprang up in the early sixteenth century. Among these were the Theatines, a body of devoted priests who worked to regenerate faith among the clergy. The Capuchins, a revived Franciscan brotherhood, became known for preaching and ministering to the poor and the sick. Societies of women also furthered reform. Some of these, such as the Sisters of the Common Life and the Beguines, continued their work of charity and nursing among the poor from the medieval period into the sixteenth century. The Ursuline order of teaching nuns, founded by St. Angela Merci (1474–1540), educated girls in morality and the faith. Even more renowned were the Carmelites, founded by St. Teresa of Avila (1515–1582), whose determination and selfless devotion became legendary. She inspired mystical faith and reforming zeal in written works, such as *Interior Castle* and *The Ladder of Perfection.* Her Carmelite nuns were models of Christian

The devotional works and personal example of St. Teresa of Avila, mystic and visionary, inspired the rebirth of Spanish Catholicism. In 1970 she was proclaimed a doctor of the church, the first woman to be so honored. The sculpture here, The Ecstasy of St. Teresa *(1645–1652), is by the Italian baroque artist Giovanni Bernini.*

charity and compassion who helped restore the pride and integrity of the church.

The most significant of the new orders was the Society of Jesus, whose members are known as Jesuits. It was founded by Ignatius Loyola (1491–1556), a Spanish nobleman and former soldier. While recovering from battle wounds in 1521, he experienced a religious vision similar to the one that transformed Luther. Loyola then became a wandering pilgrim, a self-styled religious teacher, and the author of *Spiritual Exercises,* a work of great psychological insight and Christian inspiration. In 1524 he launched his society at the University of Paris; 16 years later Pope Paul gave it official authorization.

Organized along military lines, with Loyola as general and the pope as commander in chief, the Jesuits were an army of soldiers, sworn to follow orders and defend the faith. As preachers, teachers, confessors, organizers, diplomats, and spies, they took the field everywhere, founding schools and colleges, serving as missionaries on every continent, and working their way into government wherever possible. Their efforts were probably most responsible for the decided check that Protestantism received after the 1560s. They zealously defended Catholicism in France and may be accurately credited with saving Poland and southern Germany for the church. Jesuit missions overseas also helped Spain and Portugal develop their empires. Jesuits played prominent roles after the Council of Trent in reinforcing uniformity and discipline on the church as it faced the Protestant challenge.

The Council of Trent

Pope Paul's reform initiatives were given impetus by the great multinational church council, the first since 1415, which met in three sessions between 1545 and 1563 in the northern Italian city of Trent. Devoting much attention to the external struggle against Protestantism, the council also sought to eliminate internal abuses by ordering changes in church discipline and administration. It strictly forbade absenteeism, false indulgences, selling church offices, and secular pursuits by the clergy. Bishops were ordered to supervise their clergies—priests as well as monks and nuns—and to fill church positions with competent people. The Council of Trent also provided that more seminaries be established for educating priests while instructing the clergy to set examples and preach frequently to their flocks.

Rejecting all compromise, the Council of Trent retained the basic tenets of Catholic doctrine, including the necessity of good works as well as faith for salvation, the authority of church law and traditions, the sanctity of all seven sacraments, the use of only Latin in the Mass, and the spiritual value of indulgences, pilgrimages, veneration of saints, and the cult of the Virgin. The council also strengthened the power of the papacy. It defeated all attempts to place supreme church authority in any general council. When the final session voted that none of its decrees were valid without papal approval, the church became more than ever an absolute monarchy.

The full significance of Trent became evident after the 1560s, when the Catholic reaction to Protestantism acquired new vigor and militancy. Having steeled itself within, the church and its shock troops, the Jesuits, went to war against Protestants and other heretics. The new crusade was both open and secret. In Spain, Italy, and the Netherlands, the Inquisition more than ever before became the dreaded scourge of Protestants and other heretics. Jesuit universities trained scholars and missionaries, who served as both priests and organizers in Protestant countries, such as England. Many died as martyrs, condemned by Protestant tribunals; others suffered similar fates, meted out by pagan authorities in America or Asia. Consequently, Protestantism made no more significant gains in Catholic lands after Trent. Indeed, the geographical scope of Catholicism expanded, particularly overseas.

In this uncompromising and bloody conflict of faiths, women on the Catholic side were both unappreciated heroines and victims. Out of 41 heretics executed in Spain during 1559, some 26 were women. Other Catholic women in Protestant lands faced frustrating problems; some dispossessed nuns, with no place to go were the most stubborn holdouts against secularizing the monasteries. An order of Jesuit nuns became quite active, though it never received papal approval. Their efforts, however, alarmed church leaders. The Council of Trent reaffirmed the prohibition against women preachers; after Trent, the church forced the Ursulines into convents. Catholic prejudice against the female orders is best illustrated by the ordeal of St. Teresa, who struggled for years and was even brought before the Inquisition before her Carmelites were approved.

Impact on the Arts: Mannerism, Baroque, and Rococo

There was no cultural uniformity across Europe from 1500 to 1650, a period of religious and political unrest. By then the Renaissance spirit was beginning to be transformed in Italy but was reaching a climax elsewhere in Europe. Each aspect of the Protestant Reformation had its particular view on the nature and purpose of art. The Counter-Reformation, after the Council of Trent, also polarized European thought and produced spectacular cultural developments. Sometimes reviving religious sensitivities were accompanied by perplexing uncertainties. In other instances lingering Renaissance values coexisted with Protestant Puritanism to fit a middle class and not a noble set of tastes. Such incongruities were indications of a cultural transition, like that in political and social affairs, between medieval and early modern times.

In art and architecture the post-Renaissance transition was reflected in a new style called Mannerism (see Chapter 14). Mannerist painters rejected Renaissance balance and harmony by defying perspective, using asymmetrical designs, and creating bizarre lighting effects. Perhaps the greatest of them was El Greco (1547–1614), who was born in Crete,

The Arts

1472–1553	Lucas Cranach
c. 1525–1569	Pieter Brueghel the Elder
1547–1614	El Greco
1557–1612	Giovanni Gabrieli
1557–1640	Peter Paul Rubens
c. 1564–c. 1638	Pieter Brueghel the Younger
c. 1565–1609	Michelangelo da Caravaggio
1573–1631	John Donne
1598–1680	Giovanni Bernini
1600–1660	Baroque era in art
1606–1669	Rembrandt van Rijn
1608–1674	John Milton

studied in Italy, and settled in Spain. He is known for his imaginative but morbidly ascetic treatment of religious themes, using *chiaroscuro* (strong contrasts of light and shade). Andrea Palladio (1518–1580) exemplified the style in architecture with his Villa Rotonda near Venice, which displays an exaggerated magnificence in its grouping of four identical temple facades on the sides of a square-domed building.

Like art and architecture, trends in music reflected the transition of the era. Both in Italy and in the north, music developed new complexities in keeping with a spirit of gaiety and respect for aesthetic beauty. This was evident in the increase of chordal writing, in the great expansion of tonal ranges, and in the emergence of new secular forms, like the chanson and the madrigal, which often had poetic lyrics. At the other extreme, church music also became very popular. Protestant hymn writing and singing were given high priorities by the reformers. Luther's hymn "A Mighty Fortress Is Our God" is only one example; many others were composed by women, who found this religious outlet when they were prohibited from preaching. Catholic church music was also revolutionized after the Council of Trent ruled that it be less complex and more appealing. The new spirit, simple but emotionally powerful, was well expressed in the masses of Giovanni Palestrina (1525–1594), who has been called the first Catholic church musician.

After about 1600 European culture generated a new artistic style, the baroque. Taken literally, the term means "irregular" and is generally applied to the dynamic and undisciplined artistic creativity of the seventeenth century. At first the baroque style

grew out of the Catholic pomp and confidence accompanying the Roman Reformation. Later as the style spread north it became popular at royal courts, where it symbolized the emerging power of the new monarchies. Wherever it showed itself, the baroque approach was likely to exhibit power, massiveness, or dramatic intensity, embellished with pageantry, color, and theatrical adventure. Without the restraints of the High Renaissance or the subjectiveness of Mannerism, it sought to overawe by its grandeur.

Baroque painting originated in Italy and moved north. One of its Italian creators was Michelangelo da Caravaggio (c. 1565–1609), whose bold and light-bathed naturalism impressed many northern artists. The Italian influence was evident in the works of Peter Paul Rubens (1557–1640), a well-known Flemish artist who chose themes from pagan and Christian literature, illustrating them with human figures involved in dramatic physical action. Rubens also did portraits of Marie de' Medici and Queen Anne, at the

El Greco, The Dream of Philip II. *The characteristic art of the seventeenth century was a consciously anti-Renaissance style called Mannerism, which reached its greatest achievements in the works of El Greco, "the Greek." Born in Crete and trained first as a painter of icons, El Greco traveled to Venice and Rome, where he studied the works and techniques of the Italian Renaissance masters. He settled finally in Toledo, Spain. His works combine elements of the Byzantine tradition and Italian Renaissance and Mannerist styles, infused with the intense emotional spiritualism of the Spanish Counter-Reformation.*

French court of Louis XIII. Another famous baroque court painter was Diego Velázquez (1599–1660), whose canvases depict the haughty formality and opulence of the Spanish royal household. A number of Italian women were successful baroque painters, including Livonia Fontana (1552–1614), who produced pictures of monumental buildings, and Artemesia Gentileschi (1593–1652), a follower of Caravaggio.

While the baroque style was profoundly affecting most of Europe, the Dutch were perfecting their own unique artistic genre. It grew directly from their pride in political and commercial accomplishments, emphasizing both the beauty of local nature and the solidity of middle-class life. Dutch painting was sober, detailed, and warmly soft in the use of colors, particularly yellows and browns. Almost every town in the Netherlands supported its own school of painters who helped perpetuate the local traditions. Consequently, many competent artists arose to meet the demand for this republican art.

Only a few painters among hundreds can be cited here. The robust Frans Hals (1580–1666) em-

Frans Hals, Malle Babbe *(c. 1650). Hals's technique consisted of economical brushwork, using a few vigorous strokes. The work has the immediacy of a sketch, but in reality it was done with careful precision over a period of hours, not minutes.*

Peter Paul Rubens, Descent from the Cross. *The muscular figures convey a sense of both physical power and passionate feeling. The elements of the work combine to form a composition of tremendous dramatic force.*

ployed a vigorous style that enabled him to catch the spontaneous and fleeting expressions of his portrait subjects. He left posterity a gallery of types, from cavaliers to fishwives and tavern loungers. His most successful follower, whose works have often been confused with those of Hals, was Judith Leyster (1609–1660), a member of the Haarlem painters guild with pupils of her own. Somewhat in contrast, Jan Vermeer (1632–1675) exhibited a subtle delicacy. His way of treating the fall of subdued sunlight on interior scenes has never been equaled.

Towering above all the Dutch artists, and ranking with the outstanding painters of all time, was Rembrandt van Rijn (1606–1669). While reflecting the common characteristics of his school, he produced works so universally human that they not only expressed Dutch cultural values but also transcended them. His canvases show tremendous sensitivity, depicting almost every human emotion except pure joy. This omission arose partly from his own troubled consciousness and partly from his republican, Calvinist environment. Nevertheless, his work furnished profound insights into the human enigma. He has been called the "Dutch Baroque da Vinci."

Baroque architecture, like painting, was centered in Italy, from whence it permeated western Europe. The most renowned architect of the school in the sev-

Rembrandt van Rijn, Self-Portrait. *The Dutch artist Rembrandt was one of the most gifted painters of all time. His self-portrait, painted late in his life, perfectly captures the simple dignity and quiet resignation of age.*

clined many writers toward religious subjects. In England this trend continued into the next century and was augmented by a flood of political tracts during the civil war. Religious concerns were typical of the two most prominent English poets, John Donne (1573–1631) and John Milton (1608–1674). Milton's magnificent poetic epic *Paradise Lost* was planned in his youth but not completed until 1667. French literature during the early 1600s was much less memorable. The major advance came in heroic adventure novels, pioneered by Madeleine Scudéry (1608–1701). Most other French writers, influenced by the newly formed French Academy, were increasingly active in salon discussions but were more concerned with form than with substance.

Baroque art and literature somewhat ambiguously expressed the values of this time. In keeping with the prevailing social atmosphere of warring states and their famous rulers, the baroque style emphasized power and grandeur, along with the heroic and the bizarre. But despite its masculine values, the baroque style glorified women in the abstract, at a time when ordinary women were losing social status. This apparent contradiction might be explained by the dominant contemporary roles of famous queens, powerful female regents, and aristocratic salon hostesses.

enteenth century was Giovanni Bernini (1598–1680). He designed the colonnades outside St. Peter's Basilica, where his plan illustrates the baroque style in the use of vast spaces and curving lines. After Bernini, hundreds of churches and public buildings all over Europe displayed the elaborate baroque decorativeness in colored marble, intricate designs, twisted columns, scattered cupolas, imposing facades, and unbalanced extensions or bulges. Stone and mortar were often blended with statuary and painting; indeed, it was difficult to see where one art left off and the other began.

The seventeenth century also brought baroque innovations in music. New forms of expression moved away from the exalted calmness of Palestrina and emphasized melody, supported by harmony. Instrumental music, particularly for the organ and violin, gained equal popularity for the first time with song. Outstanding among baroque innovations was opera, which originated in Italy at the beginning of the century and quickly conquered Europe. The new form combined many arts, integrating literature, drama, music, and painting in elaborate stage settings.

Literature of the baroque age before 1650 showed a marked decline from the exalted heights of the northern Renaissance. Even before 1600, however, Puritanism and the Counter-Reformation in-

Wars of Religion and Emergence of the Modern State System

After the 1560s, religious fanaticism, both Protestant and Catholic, combined with pragmatic politics to form a combustible mixture. Sometimes religious conflict caused the reshaping of the old political system to justify movements against royal authority. More often it popularized centralized monarchies, whose rulers promised to restore order by wielding power. Despite pious declarations, kings and generals in this period conducted war with little regard for moral principles; indeed, as time passed they steadily subordinated religious concerns to dynastic ambitions or national interests. This change, however, came slowly and was completed only in 1648 after Europe was thoroughly exhausted by the human suffering and material destruction of religious wars.

Although it ended a short war in Germany, the Peace of Augsburg (1555) failed to end politicoreligious conflict. Even before Calvin died in 1564, his movement was spreading rapidly in France, Scotland, Germany, Poland, Bohemia, and Hungary. The Council of Trent launched a formidable counteroffensive, led by the Jesuits and supported by the Spanish and Austrian Habsburgs, against all Protestants.

Religious and Political Wars

1556–1598	Reign of Philip II of Spain
1558–1603	Reign of Elizabeth I of England
1568	Revolt in the Netherlands
1571	European forces defeat Turks at Lepanto
1572	Massacre of St. Bartholomew's Eve in Paris
1581	Dutch United Provinces declare independence from Spain
1585–1642	Cardinal Richelieu (holds power in France, 1624–1642)
1587	Dutch Republic formed
1588	English defeat Spanish Armada
1589–1616	Reign of Henry IV of France, beginning of Bourbon dynasty
1598	Edict of Nantes guarantees Protestant rights in France
1611–1632	Reign of Gustavus Adolphus in Sweden
1618–1648	Thirty Years' War
1648	Peace of Westphalia

England narrowly avoided the religious civil wars that ended the Valois line in France, the Spanish Netherlands exploded in religious rebellion, and the militant Catholic Reformation suppressed Protestantism in eastern Europe. For decades the politics of religion dominated politics within every European state.

The Spanish Habsburgs' Drive for Dominance

Although it was a relatively small, underdeveloped, and sparsely populated country of 8 million people, Spain under Philip II (1556–1598) was considered the strongest military power in Europe. Seven centuries of resistance against the Arabs during the Reconquista (see Chapter 9) had formed a chilvalric nobility that excelled in the military arts, if not business. This tradition, in addition to the promise of empire, saw the rigidly disciplined Spanish infantry absorb neighboring Portugal and then fan out around the world as *conquistadores* and bring back silver in seemingly unlimited quantities from America. Working in tandem with the army was the Spanish church, with its courts of the Inquisition, which

had earlier banished the Jews and were now being used to eliminate the Moors and Spanish Protestantism. Yet an overworked and overextended bureaucracy and a weak financial, communications, and industrial infrastructure placed the victories gained by the army and the church on a weak foundation.

Philip willingly took on the Habsburgs' global burdens of maintaining Catholic orthodoxy, fighting the Turks, and imposing his will on his troublesome European neighbors. This responsibility was part of Philip's inheritance from his father, Charles V, whose long reign ended in 1556 when he abdicated his imperial throne and entered a monastery. At that time Charles split his Habsburg holdings. His brother Ferdinand, who had governed Austria, Bohemia, and Hungary for Charles, acquired official control of these lands when he was elected Holy Roman Emperor in 1558. Philip received Naples, Sicily, Milan, the Netherlands, Spain, and a vast overseas empire, which was much more lucrative than his father's imperial domain in Germany. Indeed, the division of Habsburg lands appeared to be a blessing for Philip, allowing him to shed his father's worrisome "German problem" and concentrate more effectively on his Spanish realm.

Philip was an obedient, hardworking son and took his father's advice very seriously. A slightly built, somber, and stolid man, he was almost completely absorbed by his awesome official obligations. Charles had warned him about becoming too intimate with subordinates and particularly against trusting or depending on women. Philip heeded this advice. Although he was involved briefly with mistresses, none of them influenced his judgment or policies. The same could be said about his four wives: Maria of Portugal, Mary of England, Elizabeth of France, and his niece, Anne of Austria, all of whom he married for political reasons. Except for Mary, they bore his children but ate at his table only during official banquets. Elizabeth was his favorite, as were her daughters, to whom he wrote notes of tender and loving concern. However, such revelations of his inner feelings were very rare.

Philip made skillful use of his role as defender of the Catholic faith. Although the church owned half the wealth of the country and used the Inquisition to wipe out Protestant and Muslim "heresies," Philip used church policies to enforce Spanish traditions, arouse patriotism, increase his popularity, and strengthen the state. He was by no means a tool of the papacy; indeed, like his father, he defied more than one pope, carefully weighing the costs of papal proposals, particularly military ones, against their benefits. He denied the pope jurisdiction over Spanish ecclesiastical courts, ignored objectionable papal decrees, defied the Council of Trent on clerical appointments in Spanish territories, and fought the Je-

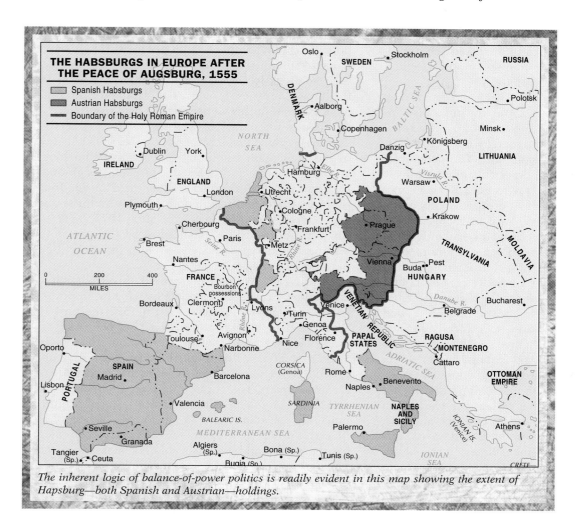

THE HABSBURGS IN EUROPE AFTER
THE PEACE OF AUGSBURG, 1555

- Spanish Habsburgs
- Austrian Habsburgs
- Boundary of the Holy Roman Empire

The inherent logic of balance-of-power politics is readily evident in this map showing the extent of Hapsburg—both Spanish and Austrian—holdings.

suits when they challenged his authority. Though a dedicated Catholic and an opponent of heresy, Philip saw the church as an arm of his government and expected its cooperation in return for his support.

Throughout his long reign Philip tried with only moderate success to be an absolute monarch. His councilors, appointed as advisers more than as administrators, submitted most decisions for his resolution. In the Escorial, the cold and somber palace he built north of Madrid, he labored endlessly, reading and annotating his councilors' documents. His attention was directed mainly to Castile, where he nearly achieved complete mastery, issuing royal edicts as law and using the Cortes (the traditional assembly of estates) as a device for measuring public opinion rather than as a legislative body. But such pretensions of centralized government were without much meaning in other parts of Spain. There, as well as in the Netherlands and Italy, proud noble families dominated the assemblies, jealously guarding their privileges and often opposing royal viceroys. They were aided by the weight of tradition, by poor communications, and—in the eastern Spanish kingdoms of Aragon and Catalonia—by the fact that those regions

were so poor it was not worth the effort for Philip to impose strict, centralized rule.

The backward Spanish sociopolitical system caused Philip many economic problems. Tax-exempt nobilities, comprising under 2 percent of the people, owned 95 percent of nonchurch land; the middle classes, overtaxed and depleted by purges of Jews and *Moriscos* (Spanish Muslims), were diminished; and the peasants were so exploited that production of food, particularly grains, was insufficient to feed the population. The use of arable lands for the nobles' sheep runs aggravated the situation. State regulation of industry and trade further limited revenues and forced primary reliance on specie from America, which ultimately brought ruinous inflation. When his income failed to meet expenses, Philip borrowed at rising interest rates. In 1557 and 1575 he had to suspend payments, effectively declaring national bankruptcy.

Revolt of the Netherlands

Philip's centralized rule encouraged some unity in Spain; the Netherlands, with its own traditions, was immediately suspicious of its foreign king. His efforts to enforce Catholic conformity provoked resistance, which ultimately led to the first successful rebellion against a major European monarchy.

This outcome could have been expected. The Netherlands ("Low Countries") at the time also included modern Belgium, Luxembourg, and small holdings along 200 miles of a marshy northern coast, an area not open to easy conquest. The geography promoted strong local nobilities but also relatively independent peasants and townsmen. Even in medieval times cities were centers of rapidly expanding commerce; of the 300 walled towns in 1560, some 19 had populations over 10,000 (England had only three or four that size), and Antwerp was the commercial hub of northern Europe. A resulting independent spirit found early expression in the Reformation, first with Lutheranism, then with Anabaptism, and finally with Calvinism after the 1550s. Charles V had suppressed Protestantism and sporadically burned heretics, but his status as a native son allowed him to preserve a precarious political stability before 1556.

Charles's heavyset, hard-riding daughter, Margaret of Parma (1522–1586), was Philip's first regent for the Netherlands. Like her father, she was also a native of the region who understood her subjects. She was an able administrator, but Philip wasted this asset by ordering her to combat heresy with the Inquisition, a policy that drove the leading nobles from her council and brought increasingly threatening popular protests. For years Philip ignored Margaret's frantic appeals for leniency before finally permitting her to dismiss the hated Cardinal Granville from her government. Despite this belated concession, public clamor against the execution of Protestants continued; the so-called Calvinist Fury in 1566 terrorized Catholics and desecrated 400 churches.

Although the public reaction to these Calvinist outrages provided new support for Margaret, Philip was unimpressed. He dispatched the duke of Alva to the Netherlands with 10,000 Spanish troops, a great baggage train, and 2000 camp followers. Alva removed Margaret from her regency and clamped a brutal military dictatorship on the country. By decree he centralized church administration, imposed new taxes, and established a special tribunal, soon dubbed the Council of Blood, to stamp out treason and heresy. During Alva's regime between 1567 and 1573, at least 8000 people were killed, including the powerful counts of Egmont and Horne. Women and children were often victims. In 1568 one woman was executed because she had refused to eat pork, and an 84-year-old woman whose son-in-law had aided a heretic was condemned at Utrecht. In addition to such atrocities the Catholic terror deprived 30,000 people of their property and forced 100,000 to flee the country.

By 1568 Alva's excesses had provoked open rebellion, led by William of Orange (1533–1584), nicknamed William the Silent. He was a wealthy noble, with holdings in Germany and France as well as in the Low Countries provinces of Holland and Brabant. Born of Lutheran parents, he had been raised a Catholic at the court of Charles V. He had served Charles as an official before 1556 and participated in the abdication ceremony that made Philip king. William only reluctantly became a rebel. His gradual ideological transformation is illustrated by his four marriages. The first two, before 1561, were for status and convenience; the last two, after 1577, were to Charlotte de Bourbon and Louise de Coligny, both leading Huguenots who served him as committed partners in a religious cause.

Until 1579 William persevered through terrible adversities. Constant early defeats left him impoverished and nearly disgraced, but in 1572 the port of Brielle fell to his privateers, the "sea beggars," an event that triggered revolts throughout the north. Soon thereafter William cut the dikes near Zeeland, mired down a weary Spanish army, and forced Alva's recall to Spain. The continuing war was marked by savage ferocity, such as the sack of Antwerp by mutinous Spanish soldiers (1576). At the Spanish siege of Maestricht (1579), women fought beside their men on the walls, and Spanish soldiers massacred the population, raping women first before tearing some limb from limb in the streets. That same year in the Pacification of Ghent, Catholics and Protestants from the 17 provinces united to defy Philip, demand the recall of his army, and proclaim the authority of their traditional assembly, the States General.

Unfortunately for the rebel cause, this unity was soon destroyed by religious differences between militant northern Calvinists and Catholic southerners, particularly the many powerful nobles. The Spanish commander Alexander Farnese exploited these differences by restoring lands and privileges to the southern nobles. He was then able to win victories that induced the ten southern provinces to make peace with Spain in 1579. The Dutch, now alone, proclaimed their continued resistance to Spanish persecution and in 1581 declared their independence from Spain. They persisted after William was assassinated in 1584, while the Spanish continued their war on heresy, hanging, butchering, burning, and burying alive Protestants who would not renounce their faith. This cruelty lasted until a truce was negotiated in 1609.

Religious Wars in France

Although frustrated in the Netherlands, Philip did not face his father's French problem. By the Treaty of Cateau-Cambrésis in 1559, France gave up claims in

Italy and the Netherlands. This humiliating surrender to the Habsburgs marked a definite turning point in French history. With its government bankrupt, its economy nearly prostrate, and its people disillusioned, France lost its leverage in foreign affairs as internal dissension encouraged by Philip wasted the country during the next four decades.

Beneath the prevailing religious contention was another bitter struggle between the haves and the have-nots. High prices, high rents, and high taxes drove the lower classes to riot and rebel against urban oligarchies, noble landlords, and government tax collectors. The social unrest continued sporadically throughout the sixteenth century. It brought no improvement of conditions for suffering peasants and town artisans, but it did badly frighten the wealthy nobles, merchants, and bankers, whose mildly divergent interests were unified by threats from below.

By the 1560s Calvinism had become a major outlet for the frustrations of the discontented. Although outlawed and persecuted earlier, the movement grew rapidly during the decade. It converted approximately 15 percent of the population, most of whom were of the lower urban middle class; however, the leadership came mainly from the nobility, 40 to 50 percent of whom accepted Calvinism. Their motives varied; although many were sincerely religious, most pursued political ends. Even among lesser nobles Calvinism promised military employment, political prominence, and a way for redirecting popular discontent. The movement's potential popular support was particularly appealing to contenders for the throne among the high nobility. In 1559 the Huguenots held a secret synod in Paris that drew representatives from 72 congregations and a million members. Admittedly a distinct minority, they were well organized, with articulate spokesmen and competent military leadership.

Religion and the politics of the high nobility were closely joined after 1559, when King Henry II died, leaving the crown to his sickly 15-year-old son, who became Francis II. The young queen was Mary Stuart (later Mary, queen of Scots), whose uncles, the brothers Guise, assumed control of the government. Their most ambitious opponent was Antoine de Bourbon, a prince by blood and the husband of Jeanne d'Albret, the Calvinist queen of Navarre. The Montmorency family was also opposed to the Guises and was in the process of turning Protestant. Faced with this challenge, the Guises naturally claimed to be champions of the Catholic cause.

Francis died in 1560 and was succeeded by his 9-year-old brother, Charles IX. The real power behind the throne, however, was his mother, Catherine de' Medici. She was a most able woman, single-minded, crafty, ready to use any means but also open to compromise, and determined to save the throne for one of her three sons, none of whom had produced a male heir. Exploiting the split between the Guises and their enemies, she assumed the regency for Charles. She then attempted through reforms of the church to reconcile the differences between Catholics and Protestants. In this endeavor she was unsuccessful, but she retained her tenuous control, using every political strategy, including a squadron of highborn women who solicited information by seducing powerful nobles.

Religious war erupted in 1561; supported by substantial Spanish financial and military interventions, it lasted through eight uneasy truces until 1593. Fanaticism evoked the most violent and inhumane acts on both sides, as destructive raids, assassinations, and torturous atrocities became commonplace. Catherine maneuvered through war and uneasy peace, first favoring the Guises and then the Bourbons. In 1572, fearing that the Huguenots were gaining supremacy, she projected a Guise plot that resulted in the murder of some 10,000 Huguenots in Paris. This Massacre of St. Bartholomew's Eve was a turning point in decisively dividing the country. The final "war of the three Henries" in the 1580s involved Catherine's third son, Henry III, who became king upon the death of Charles IX in 1574. The king's rivals were Henry of Guise and the Protestant Henry of Navarre. When the other two Henries were assassinated, Henry of Navarre proclaimed himself king of France in 1589. Spain would have little to fear from France for the next half century.

Elizabethan England, 1558–1603

For most of the sixteenth century, Spain built its European foreign policies on the base of an English alliance. Despite Henry's breaking his marriage with Catherine of Aragon, the Spanish ambassadors did not give up their efforts to keep England in their camp. For the better part of his reign, Philip had to deal with England's most outstanding monarch, Elizabeth I.

Elizabeth, a superb imagemaker, projected the picture of a country united behind a national church even as her government suppressed Catholicism, put down a northern rebellion, and avoided serious troubles with Scotland or Ireland. Elizabeth dealt with potential dangers from the great Catholic powers, Spain and France, by playing them against each other. Such successes were the natural result of her wisdom and courage. This image only partly reflected reality. The "Protestant Queen" privately detested Protestantism. Her support for Scottish and Dutch rebels violated her fervent inner belief in absolute monarchy. Her celebrated coy approach in encouraging but ultimately denying prospective royal suitors, despite the diplomatic advantages of the practice, often ran counter to her emotional inclinations, throwing her into rages against her advisers.

She was almost incapable of making lasting decisions. But unlike Catherine de' Medici, she had learned from Tudor politics to compromise and discount personal attachments. Consequently, England became her family and her primary interest. She was especially skilled at judging people, dealing with foreign diplomats in their own language, and projecting charisma in public speeches. With these talents she was able to bring the English people a new sense of national pride. In fact, in contrast to France, England seemed to have achieved relative peace and prosperity in the second half of the sixteenth century.

Elizabeth's earliest immediate danger emerged in Scotland, where Mary of Guise was regent for her daughter Mary Stuart, queen of both France and Scotland. French troops in Scotland supported this Catholic regime. Because Mary Stuart was also a direct descendant of Henry VII of England, she was a leading claimant for the English throne and a potential rallying symbol for Catholics who hoped to reestablish their faith in England. These expectations were diminished in 1559 when a zealous Calvinist named John Knox (1505–1572), fresh from Geneva, led a revolt of Scottish nobles. Aided by English naval forces, which Elizabeth delayed and only reluctantly approved, the Scots broke religious ties with Rome, established a Presbyterian (Calvinist) state church, and drove out the French soldiers. Temporarily, Elizabeth had averted disaster.

Another serious problem loomed in Ireland, where Spanish and papal emissaries used old grievances over taxes and religion to arouse uprisings against English rule. James Maurice, an Irish leader in the southwest, began a series of revolts in 1569. Eight years later the pope helped raise troops and money for Maurice on the Continent. An expedition in 1579 to aid the Irish rebels was ruthlessly suppressed, but fighting dragged on for four more years. In 1601 a more serious Irish rebellion, aided by 3000 Spanish troops, cost Elizabeth a third of her revenues up to her death in 1603. Although never directing a successful Irish policy, she managed to escape catastrophe by stubborn persistence.

Her innate pragmatism was most beneficial in quieting English sectarian strife. She despised Puritans and favored rich vestments for the clergy, but she thoroughly understood the practical necessity of securing Protestant political support. Moving firmly but slowly, Elizabeth re-created a nominal Protestant national church but one similar to her father's. It confirmed the monarch as its head, recognized only baptism and communion as sacraments, rejected relic veneration, conducted services in English, and avoided other controversial Protestant tenets. It also retained the old organization, under bishops and archbishops, along with much of the Catholic ritual.

This "Elizabethan compromise" in religion was acceptable to most of the English people.

The queen's policy lessened religious controversy and persecution but failed to end either completely. Nonconformists attacked the establishment in sermons and pamphlets; some, like the Presbyterian minister Thomas Cartwright, were jailed by church courts. Catholics faced more severe persecution and were therefore even more determined and daring. A network of Jesuit priests operated throughout the country, particularly in the north and west, secretly conducting Masses and working with a Catholic political underground. Women played prominent roles among dissidents of both extremes. Protestants, like the duchess of Suffolk and Lady Russell, steadily pressured the queen; Catholic women were the most effective allies of the Jesuits, as evidenced by Margaret Clitherow, who died under torture in 1586 rather than deny her faith.

While dealing with this internal dissension, Elizabeth faced a serious danger from abroad. In 1568 Mary Stuart was forced into exile by her Protestant subjects and received in England by her royal cousin. Although kept a virtual prisoner, she became involved in a series of Catholic plots, which appeared even more dangerous after the pope excommunicated Elizabeth in 1570. Philip of Spain aided the plotters but still hoped to enlist Elizabeth's cooperation in helping him create a Catholic hegemony in Europe.

Despite all her troubles, Elizabeth's reign showed marked economic improvement. By careful financial management, her governments reduced debt and improved the national credit. A new coinage helped make London the financial center of Europe after the collapse of Antwerp. Monopolies granted to joint-stock companies promoted foreign trade and brought specie into the country. Parliamentary acts of 1563 and 1601 standardized laws governing conditions for artisans and relief of the poor. Such positive actions, along with an economy expanding with foreign trade, stimulated agriculture, manufacturing, coal mining, and shipbuilding. By the end of Elizabeth's reign in 1603, England was the most prosperous state in Europe.

If Philip had not assumed the burden of Catholic Orthodoxy, fighting the Turks, and dominating Europe, he could have left well enough alone and compromised with the Dutch, taken pleasure in the self-destructive French civil wars, and continued a patient long-term policy toward England. But he did not have that luxury. His responsibilities and sense of Spain's power drove him to take military action.

The Spanish Bid for Supremacy

Philip's earlier wars against Turkey promoted his image as the Catholic champion, boosted Spanish morale, and revived the traditional national pride in defending the faith. When Cyprus, the last Christian stronghold in the eastern Mediterranean, fell to the Turks in 1570, Philip responded to the pope's pleas and formed a Holy League to destroy Turkish naval power. Spanish and Venetian warships, together with smaller squadrons from Genoa and the Papal States, made up a fleet of over 200 vessels, which drew recruits from all over Europe. In 1571 the Holy League's fleet and the Turkish navy clashed at Lepanto, off the western coast of Greece. The outcome was a decisive victory for Christian Europe; Ottoman sea power would never again be a major threat to Christendom, and Spain could deploy its resources to northwest Europe.

Philip's diplomatic efforts, particularly his marriage to Mary Tudor in 1558, his next marriage to Isabel of Valois in 1560, and his clumsy efforts to court Queen Elizabeth, brought no lasting influence over English or French policies. Indeed, English captains were preying on Spanish shipping in the Atlantic, and Dutch privateers, with English and Huguenot support, were diminishing the flow of vital supplies to northern Europe. In 1580, after nine years of frustration in the Netherlands, Philip launched the first phase of his new offensive policy, using military force to validate his claim to the Portuguese throne. As king of Portugal he gained control of the Portuguese navy and Atlantic ports, where he began assembling an oceangoing fleet, capable of operations against the Dutch and English in their home waters.

Tensions increased in 1585 when Philip signed an alliance with the Guises and sent troops into France. To prevent such an outcome, Elizabeth had been encouraging assorted French dukes to think that she might turn Catholic and marry one of them. She was now especially fearful of a Franco-Spanish invasion from the Netherlands. To delay it she sent token military forces to the Dutch and French Protestants, in addition to the financial aid she was already providing. By 1586 Philip's policies were about to precipitate a major war.

Philip's last hope for an easy solution to his problems was dashed in 1587. Pressed by the pope and the English Catholic exiles, he had tried for years to use Mary Stuart to overthrow Elizabeth, regain England for Catholicism, and seize control of the country, but Mary's complicity in a plot against Elizabeth's life was discovered. Elizabeth, reluctantly convinced that Mary alive was more dangerous than Philip's final frustration, finally signed the death warrant. Mary's execution confirmed Philip's earlier decision that England had to be conquered militarily. In pursuing this end, Philip planned a "great enterprise," an invasion of England blessed by the pope.

The Spanish strategy depended on a massive fleet, known as the Invincible Armada. It was ordered to meet a large Spanish army in the southern Nether-lands and land this force on the English coast. But in 1588, when the Armada sailed for Flanders, Dutch ships blocked the main ports, preventing the convoying of troops to the Spanish galleons, which could not enter shallow waters. Philip's project was then completely ruined when the smaller and more maneuverable English ships, commanded by Sir Francis Drake, defeated the Armada in the English Channel. A severe storm, the famed "Protestant wind," completed the debacle. After a long voyage around Scotland, the Armada limped back to Spain, having lost a third of its ships. Contrary to English expectations, defeat of the Armada brought no immediate shift of international power. While Spain built new ships and successfully defended its sea lanes, neither side gained dramatic victories. All the major combatants were exhausted, a factor that largely explains the Bourbons' acquisition of the French crown and continued Dutch independence through the 1590s. Lingering war brought new opportunities for France and the Netherlands but only a strength-draining stalemate for England and Spain.

The Balance Sheet of Spanish Failure

During the last decade of Philip's life, his multiple failures foreshadowed the decline of his country. He

An English view of the Spanish Armada shows the pope and the devil plotting the Spanish invasion of England. The engraving is dated 1620.

encountered rebellion in Aragon, quarreled with Pope Clement VIII over recognizing the Bourbons, and sent two more naval expeditions against England, both of which were scattered by storms. In 1598 he gave the southern Netherlands to his favorite daughter, Isabel, and her husband, Archduke Albert, an Austrian Habsburg. Then, before he died in 1598, Philip had to make peace with France. He left Spain bankrupt for the third time during his reign, having wasted the country's considerable resources and sacrificed its future to his dynastic pride. The same poor judgment was even more pronounced in his successor, Philip III (1598–1621), who was lazy, extravagant, and also frivolous. His henchmen increased the already prevalent graft and inefficiency.

Elizabeth experienced similar difficulties. Sea raids on Spanish shipping continued and returned some profits, yet all the grand projects failed, including a fiasco in 1596 when an English naval force, commanded by the earl of Essex, plundered Cadiz but missed the Spanish treasure fleet. Land campaigns in France and the Netherlands, in addition to a continuing rebellion in Ireland, depleted Elizabeth's carefully husbanded resources. When asked for grants, Parliament insisted on debating constitutional questions and hearing Puritan demands for reform of the church. While the old queen grew crotchety, muttering about cutting off heads, the country needed peace. But peace did not come until a year after her death in 1603.

The Dutch, meanwhile, were stumbling toward independence, fearing the advancing Spanish tide in the south, pleading for English or French Protestant aid, and stubbornly persevering. Their declaration of 1581, while displaying what could be interpreted later as democratic rhetoric, reflected more concern for aristocratic privilege and national survival. After failing to find a suitable French or English monarch, the Dutch created a republic in 1587 and held on to sign a truce with Spain in 1609. As time passed, their growing maritime trade and naval power guaranteed their security.

The post-Armada stalemate was most beneficial to war-torn France. With the death of the last Valois claimant in 1589, the Bourbon Protestant king of Navarre was proclaimed king of France as Henry IV. This act threw the Catholic Holy League into a fanatical antiroyalist frenzy and encouraged Philip's military intervention in France to support his daughter's claim to the throne. But English aid and Henry's willingness to turn Catholic led to Philip's withdrawal and the Peace of Vervins in 1598. To pacify the Huguenot minority Henry then issued the Edict of Nantes, which guaranteed the Huguenots some civil and religious rights while permitting them to continue holding more than a hundred fortified towns. Henry thus achieved peace, but the French economy was prostrated, and powerful Protestant armed forces within the country challenged royal authority.

The Thirty Years' War: The Austrian Habsburgs' Quest for Central European Hegemony

By 1600 Spain's golden age had ended, but the religious and political strife of dynasties and nations would continue with even greater intensity. Despite the weakening of Spain, some nations still feared a Habsburg resurgence from the Vienna throne, while other dynasties sought to win more territories and power. Moreover, the increasing number of Calvinists and proponents of the Catholic Counter-Reformation were still looking toward a complete victory for "true religion" in central Europe. Now in the early 1600s they faced severe economic depression, along with intensified conflict in every sphere of human relations. It was a time of disruption and frustration, and a deepening sense of crisis gripped the Continent.

The first few decades of the century brought a marked decline to the European economy, even before the advent of open warfare. Prices continued to fall until about 1660, reversing the inflation of the 1500s. International trade declined, as did Spanish bullion imports from Central and South America. Heavy risks on a falling market caused failures among many foreign trading companies; only the larger houses, organized as joint-stock companies, were able to survive. European industry and agriculture also fell on hard times; urban craftspeople saw their wages drop, and peasants faced increasing exploitation.

Tensions accompanying economic depression added to those arising from continuing religious differences. Calvinism was becoming a formidable force, having become official in Scotland and the Netherlands while achieving an uneasy toleration in France. It was also spreading in eastern Europe and Germany. In England, soon after James of Scotland succeeded Elizabeth, both Anglicans and the more radical sects feared the southward march of Scottish Presbyterianism. A similar tension prevailed in the Dutch Republic, where a militant movement for Calvinist uniformity strove to wipe out all other churches. But the most dangerous area was in Germany, which had directly experienced an increasingly militant Counter-Reformation since the Peace of Augsburg.

Although absolute monarchy was already a recognizable ideal and a dominant trend in the early seventeenth century, every royal house from England to Russia was insecure. The usual threat was posed by nobles defending their traditional privileges. In England and the Netherlands, however, where commercial development was most advanced, nobles tended to support central authority against the urban commercial classes. Theoretical opposition to absolutism, based on monarchs' contractual responsibilities to their subjects, had gained some widespread popularity during the early religious wars. It was particularly common among radical Protestants, but the same theme had even been expressed among extreme royalists, such as the French Guises who opposed Henry IV.

France best illustrates developing absolutism during the period. Henry IV and his hardheaded chief minister, the duke of Sully (1560–1641), produced a balanced budget and a treasury surplus in little more than a decade. At the same time, Henry ended the nobles' control of hereditary offices and council seats. This royalist centralization was temporarily disrupted in 1610 when Henry was assassinated, but the queen, Marie de' Medici (1573–1642), served as regent for her young son Louis XIII until 1617. Like her distant relative Catherine, Marie had survived a tragic marriage to play a dominant role in French affairs. Her peace policy toward Spain and her successful defenses, both military and diplomatic, kept the Huguenots and the great nobles in check, thus securing the succession. Meanwhile, she negotiated a marriage between Louis and the Habsburg princess Anne of Austria.

When he was 15, the new king seized power from his mother. For the next 13 years, after he restored her to his council, they continued their duel for power. Marie favored a pro-Spanish and Catholic policy; Louis, following the advice of his famous minister, Cardinal Richelieu (1585–1642), saw the Habsburgs and the papacy as the main threats to French interests. Richelieu finally prevailed, and Marie was banished in 1631, after which she continued to conspire with Spain and the French Catholic party. Inside France, Richelieu worked relentlessly to increase the king's power. He organized a royal civil service, restricted the traditional courts, brought local government under royal agents *(intendants)*, outlawed dueling, prohibited fortified castles, stripped the Huguenots of their military defenses, and developed strong military and naval forces.

Absolutism elsewhere in Europe was moving in the same general direction but with less success. The Swedish Vasa dynasty, supported by a strong national church and an efficient army, was building an empire involving Finland, the Baltic states, parts of Poland, and Denmark. In Germany many of the princes, particularly the Hohenzollerns of Brandenburg, hoped to become independent absolute monarchs. As was true of earlier Habsburgs, the Holy Roman Emperor Ferdinand II (1619–1637) struggled to concentrate his control over Austria, Hungary, and Bohemia, while extending his limited authority in Germany at the expense of the princes. Other rulers, including those in England, Spain, Russia, and

The power behind the throne of Louis XIII. Cardinal Richelieu was chiefly responsible for the direction of the government, including France's involvement in the Thirty Years' War.

Phillipe de Champaigne, c. 1637. Cardinal Richelieu. NG 1449. © National Gallery, London.

Poland, faced determined local opposition as they sought to centralize power.

This political contention within states was accompanied by rising international tensions. Although the European power balance in 1618 resembled that of the 1500s, it was much less fixed. The Habsburgs still evoked counteralliances, but their vulnerability was now greater, not only because Spain was weakening but also because other states—France, the Netherlands, and Sweden—were growing more powerful. Under these circumstances European revolt against Habsburg dominance became almost inevitable. A general awareness of the coming conflagration was perhaps the most important single source of European insecurity.

The Habsburgs' High Tide to 1630: The Bohemian and Danish Phases of the Thirty Years' War

The Thirty Years' War, fought between 1618 and 1648, was a culmination of all these related religious and political conflicts. Almost all of western Europe except England was involved and suffered accordingly. Wasted resources and manpower, along with disease, further checked economic development and curtailed population expansion. Germany was hit particularly hard, suffering population declines in some areas. Despite the terrible devastation, neither Protestantism nor Catholicism won decisively. What began as a religious war in Bohemia and the German principalities turned into a complex political struggle involving the ambitions of northern German rulers, the expansionist ambitions of Sweden, and the efforts of Catholic France to break the "Habsburg ring."

Despite the general decline of Habsburg supremacy in Spain, the early years of the war before 1629, usually cited as the Bohemian and Danish phases, brought a last brief revival of Habsburg prospects. The new Habsburg emperor, Ferdinand II, who had been raised by his mother as a fanatical Catholic, was determined to intensify the Counter-Reformation, set aside the Peace of Augsburg, and literally wipe out Protestantism in central Europe. For a time he almost succeeded.

Ferdinand's succession came amid severe political tension. Spreading Calvinism, in addition to the aggressive crusading of the Jesuits, had earlier led to the formation of a Protestant league of German princes in 1608 and a Catholic counterleague the next year. The two had almost clashed in 1610. Meanwhile, the Bohemian Protestants had extracted a promise of toleration from their Catholic king, the earlier Holy Roman Emperor Rudolf II (1576–1612). In 1618 the Bohemian leaders, fearing that Ferdinand would not honor the promise, threw two of his officials out a window after heated discussions—an incident known as the "defenestration of Prague." When Ferdinand mobilized troops, the Bohemians deposed him and offered their throne to Frederick, the Protestant elector of the Palatinate, in western Germany.

In the short Bohemian war that followed, Frederick was quickly overwhelmed. At the urging of his wife, Elizabeth, the daughter of James I of England, Frederick had reluctantly accepted the Bohemian crown. But while he and Elizabeth held court in Prague, no practical military support came from England, the Netherlands, or the Protestant German princes. Ferdinand, in contrast, deployed two superb armies, one from Spain and the other from Catholic Bavaria. In 1620 Frederick's meager forces were scattered at the battle of the White Mountain, near Prague. Afterward, the hapless Bohemian monarch and his queen fled the country, ultimately settling at The Hague, in the Netherlands, where they continued to pursue their lost cause. Ferdinand gave their lands to Maximillian of Bavaria, distributed the holdings of Bohemian Protestant nobles among Catholic aristocrats, and proceeded to stamp out Protestantism in Bohemia. Of the some 3.2 million Bohemians in 1618, mostly Protestants, all that remained 30 years later were less than a million people, all Catholics.

War began again in 1625 when Christian IV (1588–1648), the Lutheran king of Denmark, invaded Germany. As duke of Holstein and thus a prince of the empire, he hoped to revive Protestantism and win a kingdom in Germany for his youngest son. Christian was luckier than Frederick had been in attracting support. The Dutch reopened their naval war with Spain, England provided subsidies, and the remaining independent German Protestant princes, now thoroughly alarmed, rose up against the Catholics and the emperor. All of these renewed efforts were in vain. Ferdinand's new general, Albert von Wallenstein, defeated the Protestants in a series of brilliant campaigns. By 1629 Christian had to admit defeat and withdraw his forces, thus ending the Danish conflict with another Protestant debacle.

Their successful campaigns of the 1620s gave the Habsburgs almost complete domination in Germany. Using the army raised by Wallenstein in Bohemia, Ferdinand reconquered the north. In 1629 he issued his famous Edict of Restitution, restoring to the

By the simplicity and starkness of his portrayal, the French artist Jacques Callot captured, in a series of 24 etchings, the senseless tragedy of the Thirty Years' War. The dangling bodies in this plate dramatized the tenuousness of life in turbulent times.

Catholics all properties lost since 1552. This step seemed to be only the first step toward eliminating Protestantism completely and creating a centralized Habsburg empire in Germany.

The Swedish and French Phases and the Balance of Power, 1630–1648

Fearing the Counter-Reformation and the growing Habsburg power behind it, threatened European states resumed the war in 1630. As it rapidly spread and intensified, religious issues were steadily subordinated to power politics. This was evidenced by the phases of the conflict usually designated as the Swedish (1630–1635) and the French (1635–1648), because these two countries led successive anti-Habsburg coalitions. Ultimately, their efforts were successful. By 1648 the Dutch Republic had replaced Spain as the leading maritime state and Bourbon France had become the dominant European land power.

Protestant Swedes and French Catholics challenged Ferdinand's imperial ambitions for similar political reasons. Although Gustavus Adolphus (1611–1632), the Swedish king, wanted to save German Lutheranism, he was also determined to prevent a strong Habsburg state on the Baltic from restricting his own expansion and interfering with Swedish trade. A similar desire to liberate France from Habsburg encirclement motivated Cardinal Richelieu. He offered Gustavus French subsidies, for which the Swedish monarch promised to invade Germany and permit Catholic worship in any lands he might conquer. Thus the Catholic cardinal and the Protestant king compromised their religious differences in the hope of achieving mutual political benefits.

Gustavus invaded Germany in 1630 while the Dutch attacked the Spanish Netherlands. With his mobile cannons and his hymn-singing Swedish veterans, Gustavus and his German allies won a series of smashing victories, climaxed in November 1632 at Lützen, near Leipzig, where Wallenstein was decisively defeated. Unfortunately for the Protestant cause, Gustavus died in the battle. Meanwhile, a Dutch army in Flanders advanced toward Brussels, where Philip II's aging daughter Isabella was still governing. Aware of her subjects' desperate need for peace, Isabella began negotiations, but the news from Lützen raised Habsburg hopes in Vienna and Madrid. Subsequently, Isabella was removed, a Spanish army was dispatched to Germany, and Wallenstein was mysteriously murdered. This Habsburg flurry brought no significant victories but led to the compromise Peace of Prague in 1635 between the emperor and the German Protestant states.

The situation now demanded that France act directly to further its dynastic interests. Thus a final French phase of the war began when Richelieu sent French troops into Germany and toward the Spanish borders. He also subsidized the Dutch and Swedes while recruiting an army of German Protestant mercenaries. France continued limiting Protestantism within its borders but gladly allied with Protestant states against Spain, Austria, Bavaria, and their Catholic allies. The war that had begun in religious controversy had now become pure power politics, completing the long political transition from medieval to modern times.

Sweden's warrior-king Gustavus Adolphus is portrayed here at the battle of Breitenfeld in 1631.

Hardships in a German Town During the Thirty Years' War

This account of disaster and suffering by a refugee from Calw, who returned to find his "beloved town" in "ashes and rubble," illustrates the terrible havoc experienced by ordinary German people during the conflict.

During the pillage of Calw by Croat Imperial troops in September [1634] I never totally forsook my flock and only sought to escape from falling into the hands of the enemy. I joined a band of women and children soon amounting to more than 200 people. Like ants we scurried over hills and rocks. The beneficial influence of Heaven helped us continuously throughout this time. If we had bad weather we would have fared even worse than we did.

After it became known that the town [Calw, in Württemberg] had been burnt down, we escaped to Aichelberg, a rough place. We had agreed among ourselves where each of us should hide but since our presence had been betrayed to the enemy, we were barely able to escape a quarter of an hour before we would have been totally ruined. At this the enemy became angry and vented his wrath upon the richest peasant in the place, who after hideous torture was burnt along with his house. . . .

Since the enemy was also active in these parts, . . . we decided to make an attempt to ask the victor for mercy. But to our further consternation we had to flee once again into the hills where no one could readily follow us. From there we wandered around, divided into smaller bands, and on the 15 September alone with my nephew John Joshua and son Gottlieb I hid in the deep Lauterback valley near the stream in a barn on the fields. We spent the night calmly and also the next one.

Since our lodging was moved to another barn where a certain Peter Schill, whom I must praise for his great honesty among the wood-folk, provided us with food and drink, our lack of caution led us back to Gernsbach where we scarcely avoided falling into the net of the enemy. As we lived scattered about all the secret places on Obertsrot, Hilpertsau, Reichtal, Weissenbach, Langenbrand and elsewhere, the hue and cry was raised after us and huntsmen were hired who knew the forests to track us down with their dogs. We saw them in the distance and became heartily dispirited, but also took a serious warning from the event.

I finally arrived at a peasant's place where the wife was nearing her childbirth, and I had a sleepless night since three hours before dawn I had climbed over the peaks of the hills, gone through hill and dale and eventually arrived back at my own vineyard where I had placed my little son Ehrenreich, and in which farm we now spent our exile. I found my little son much weakened and unable to stand cold and hunger. The Lord took him and released his spirit into the freedom of Heaven on the 20 September. But shortly before this I had already left. We were called back in a letter from our friends, since everything, as far as the times allowed, was back in order, which accorded with the enemy's own best interest.

When I saw my beloved town of Calw in ashes and rubble—it was however not the first time that I had seen a town in ruins—I felt a cold shudder and I brooded repeatedly on that which I neither can nor wish to repeat now. What struck me most deeply was that long ago I had already prophesied the calamity, and that my prophecy had now come true in as much as it had also included me.

From Gerhard Benecke, ed., *Germany in the Thirty Years' War* (London: Edward Arnold, 1978). Reprinted by permission of Hodder & Stoughton, Ltd.

For 13 more years the seemingly endless conflict wore on. France's allies, the Swedes and northern Germans, kept Habsburg armies engaged in Germany, while French armies and the Dutch navy concentrated on Spain. In 1643 the French won a decisive battle at Rocroi, in the southern Netherlands. Next they moved into Germany, defeating the imperial forces and, with the Swedes, ravaging Bavaria. When Richelieu died in 1642, he had already unleashed forces that would make the Bourbon dynasty supreme in Europe.

For all practical purposes the war was over, but years of indecisive campaigning and tortuous negotiations delayed the peace. The French held to rigid demands, despite the deaths of Richelieu in 1642 and Louis XIII in 1643. Richelieu's protégé, Cardinal Mazarin (1602–1661), continued to conduct diplomacy for Queen Anne, now ruling as regent for her son, the future Louis XIV. In the past she had been lazy, indiscreet, and suspected of conspiring with her Spanish relatives, but she now consistently supported her minister's hard line through budget crises and popular unrest. French intransigence was partially nullified, however, by a conciliatory Swedish approach after Queen Christiana, the daughter of Gustavus Adolphus, succeeded to the throne in 1644. A horde of peace emissaries met that year at Westphalia. Even then Spain and France could reach no

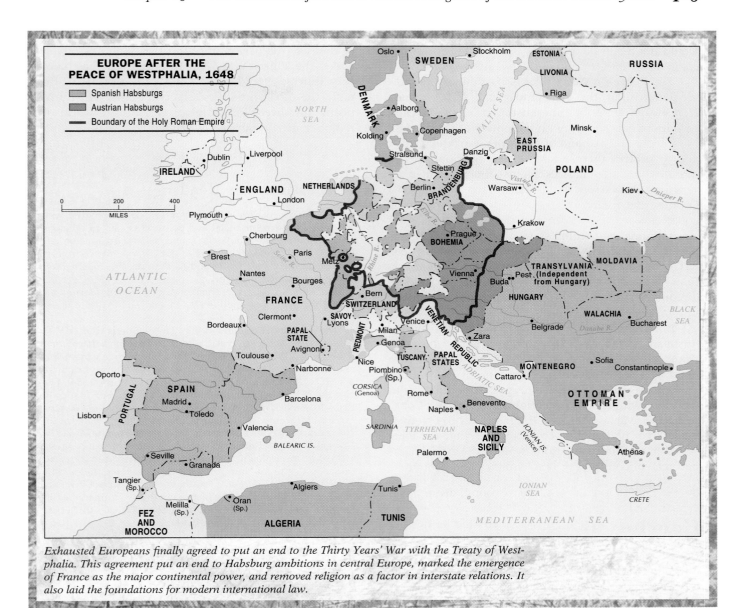

Exhausted Europeans finally agreed to put an end to the Thirty Years' War with the Treaty of Westphalia. This agreement put an end to Habsburg ambitions in central Europe, marked the emergence of France as the major continental power, and removed religion as a factor in interstate relations. It also laid the foundations for modern international law.

agreement, but a settlement for the empire was finally completed in 1648.

The Peace of Westphalia

The Peace of Westphalia is among the most significant pacts in modern European history. It ended Europe's torturous journey to the doubtful comforts of the modern state system. Even so, it did not yet establish universal peace; the war between France and Spain lasted another 11 years, ending only at the Peace of the Pyrenees in 1659.

The peace agreement at Westphalia signaled a victory for Protestantism and the German princes while almost dooming Habsburg imperial ambitions: France moved closer to the Rhine by acquiring Alsatian territory, Sweden and Brandenburg acquired

lands on the Baltic, and the Netherlands and Switzerland gained recognition of their independence. The emperor was required to obtain approval from the Imperial Diet for any laws, taxes, military levies, and foreign agreements—provisions that nearly nullified imperial power and afforded the German states practical control of their foreign relations. Their German religious autonomy, as declared at Augsburg, was also reconfirmed, with Calvinism now permitted along with Lutheranism. In addition, Protestant states were conceded all Catholic properties taken before 1624.

In its religious terms the treaty ended the dream of reuniting Christendom. Catholics and Protestants now realized that major faiths could not be destroyed. From such intuitions a spirit of toleration would gradually emerge. Although religious uniformity could be imposed within states for another century, it would not again be a serious issue in European foreign affairs until the end of the twentieth century.

The Peace of Westphalia is particularly notable for confirming the new European state system. Henceforth states would customarily shape their policies in accordance with the power of their neighbors, seeking to expand at the expense of the weaker and to protect themselves—not by religion, law, or morality, but by alliances against their stronger adversaries. Based on the works of the Dutch jurist Grotius, the treaty also instituted the international conference as a means for registering power relationships among contending states, instituted the principle of the equality of all sovereign states—as seen today in the General Assembly of the United Nations—and put into practice the tools of modern diplomacy such as extraterritoriality and diplomatic immunities.

Both Spain and Austria were weakened, and the Austrian Habsburgs shifted their primary attention from central to southeastern Europe. German disunity was perpetuated by the autonomy of so many of the microstates. France emerged from this time as the clear winner, the potential master of the Continent. The war also helped England and the Netherlands. No matter the condition of the surviving states, their future relations would be based on the pure calculus of power, both military and economic.

Conclusion

In many ways the Protestant Reformation and Catholic Counter-Reformation helped create the modern world. By breaking the religious monopoly of European Catholicism, Lutheranism and Anglicanism assisted the growth of northern European national monarchies. Later the puritan values and "work ethic" of Calvinism helped justify the activities of the middle classes. By the 1570s the Catholic Counter-Reformation had checked the spread of Protestantism, and the Roman Church emerged strengthened to protect and advance itself in Europe and carry its message around the globe.

The century and a half after Luther's stand at Wittenberg was an era of wrenching change for Europe. At the opening of the period most people were still imbued with the medieval concern for salvation, which gave meaning to the religious issues of the Protestant Reformation and Catholic Counter-Reformation. In the century after the Peace of Augsburg (1555), the nature of state competition changed. Initially long and exhaustive religious wars and civil wars dominated the Continent. Later secular political concerns became increasingly evident. But whether the wars were for faith or for state, or a combination of the two, the period until the Treaty of Westphalia ended the Thirty Years' War was the bloodiest century Europe would endure until the twentieth. Finally, the modern political structure emerged. Europeans now lived, for better or worse, in a world of nation-states dominated by secular concerns.

Suggestions for Reading

Steven B. Ozment, *The Age of Reform* (Yale University Press, 1980), is excellent for social and political as well as religious topics. Among older but still sound general treatments are Hans J. Hillerbrand, *The World of the Reformation* (Scribner, 1973), and the classic by Roland H. Bainton, *The Reformation of the Sixteenth Century*, rev. ed. (Beacon Press, 1985). On the impact of John Hus, see Thomas A. Fudge, *The Magnificent Ride: The First Reformation in Hussite Bohemia* (Ashgate Press, 1998).

The general background of the Reformation is covered well in Steven E. Ozment, *Protestants: The Birth of a Revolution* (Doubleday, 1992). Criticism of the church by northern humanists is ably described in John Huizinga, *Erasmus and the Age of the Reformation* (Princeton University Press, 1984). See also the debate between the humanists and the Scholastics in Erika Rummel, *The Humanist-Scholastic Debate in the Renaissance and Reformation* (Harvard University Press, 1988). On social conditions in the Reformation era, see R. Po-chin Hsia, *The German People and the Reformation* (Cornell University Press, 1988). The Protestant urban movement in microcosm is treated in Susan C. Karent-Nunn, *Zwickau in Transition, 1500–1547: The Reformation as a Force for Change* (Ohio State University Press, 1987). The sad plight of women in the era is treated in Susan Cahn, *The Industry of Devotion* (Colgate University Press, 1987); Mary E. Wiesner, *Working Women in Renaissance Germany* (Rutgers University Press, 1986); and Retha M. Warnicke, *Women of the English Renaissance and Reformation* (Greenwood, 1983).

The old standard biography by Roland H. Bainton, *Here I Stand: A Life of Martin Luther* (Abingdon-Cokesbury, 1950), is still moving and interesting. For an interesting contrast, compare Erik H. Erikson, *Young Man Luther* (Norton, 1962), and also Mark U. Edwards, *Luther's Last Battles* (Cornell University Press, 1983), which presents a portrait of an aging, prejudiced, and politically motivated reformer. The reformer's personal struggles are vividly depicted in Heiko A. Oberman, *Luther: Between God and the Devil* (Yale University Press, 1989). On the political and social implications of Lutheranism, see Paula Fichtner, *Protestantism and Primogeniture in Early Modern Germany* (Yale University Press, 1989); Abraham Friesen, *Thomas Muentzer, a Destroyer of the Godless* (University of California Press, 1990); and William J. Wright, *Capitalism, the State, and the Lutheran Reformation: Sixteenth-Century Hesse* (Ohio University Press, 1988).

Ulrich Gabler gives a thorough background of Ulrich Zwingli's place in history in his *Huldrych Zwingli: His Life and Work* (Clark, 1995). William J. Bouwsma, *John Calvin* (Oxford University Press, 1988), is a scholarly portrayal of Calvin's human side, emphasizing his inner conflict against the humanistic trend of his time. Another competent study, based on primary materials, is George R. Potter and Mark Greengrass, *John Calvin* (St. Martin's Press, 1983). See also T. H. L. Parker, *John Calvin* (Lion, 1987); Alexandre Ganoczy, *The Young Calvin* (Westminister, 1987); and François Wendel, *Calvin* (Baker,

1996). Rewarding special studies of Calvinism include Mark Greengrass, *The French Reformation* (Blackwell, 1987); Jane Dempsey Douglas, *Women, Freedom, and Calvin* (Westminister, 1985); and Willem Balke, *Calvin and the Anabaptist Radicals* (Eerdmans, 1981). Calvin's political orientation is also thoroughly explored in Ralph C. Hancock, *Calvin and the Foundations of Modern Politics* (Cornell University Press, 1989). A useful handbook for understanding Calvin's contributions is T. H. L. Parker, *Calvin: An Introduction to His Thought* (John Knox Press, 1995).

The context for the English Reformation is provided by Richard H. Britnell in *The Closing of the Middle Ages: England, 1471–1529* (Blackwell, 1997). Two solid and informative accounts of English society and the Anglican Reformation are J. J. Scarisbrick, *The Reformation and the English People* (Blackwell, 1984), and Robert S. Feuerlicht, *The Life and World of Henry VIII* (Crowell-Collier, 1970). See also Peter Lake and Maria Dowling, *Protestantism and the National Church in the Sixteenth Century* (Croom Helm, 1987). G. J. R. Parry, *A Protestant Vision* (Cambridge University Press, 1987), is a thoughtful interpretation of William Harrison's Puritan theology. See also Caroline Litzenberger, *The English Reformation and the Laity: Gloucestershire, 1540–1580* (Cambridge University Press, 1998). On the roles played by Tudor women, see Margaret P. Hannay, *Silent but for the Word* (Kent State University Press, 1985), and Carolly Erickson, *Bloody Mary* (Doubleday, 1978). Paul Hogrife has also produced two volumes on the subject: *Tudor Women* (Iowa State University Press, 1975) and *Women of Action in Tudor England* (Iowa State University Press, 1977).

On the "left wing" of Protestantism, see Peter C. Clasen, *Anabaptism: A Social History* (Cornell University Press, 1972), and E. Belfort Bax, *The Rise and Fall of Anabaptism* (Kelley, 1970). A good recent treatment of Anabaptism is a collection of essays edited by James M. Stayer, *The Anabaptists and Thomas Münzer* (Kendall Hunt, 1980).

John C. Olin places the Catholic response in perspective in *The Catholic Reformation: From Savonarola to Ignatius Loyola* (Fordham University Press, 1993). Nicholas S. Davidson, *The Counter-Reformation* (Blackwell, 1987), and Michael A. Mullett, *The Counter-Reformation and the Catholic Reformation in Early Modern Europe* (Methuen, 1984), are among the recent works on the Catholic revival. A sympathetic Catholic account is in P. Janelle, *The Catholic Reformation* (Bruce, 1963). Also worth noting is James Brodrick, *The Origin of the Jesuits* (Greenwood, 1971).

Two excellent overall surveys of this Reformation period are Robert Bireley, *Religion and Politics in the Age of the Counter-Reformation* (University of North Carolina Press, 1981), and Helmut G. Koenigsberger, *Early Modern Europe, 1500–1789* (Longman, 1987). See also Trevor Henry Aston, ed., *Crisis in Europe, 1560–1660* (Harper Torchbooks, 1974), and Perez Zagoren, *Rebels and Rulers, 1500–1660* (Cambridge University Press, 1982). Helga Mobius, *Women of the Baroque Age* (Schram, 1984), provides good detail, particularly on women painters, but is less scholarly and more superficial in its generalizations.

Four sound studies of Spain during the period are John Lynch, *Spain Under the Habsburgs*, Vol. 1, *Empire and Absolutism, 1516–1598* (New York University Press, 1984); Reginald Trevor-Davis, *The Golden Century of Spain, 1501–1621* (Greenwood, 1984); Robert James Weston Evans, *The Making of the Habsburg Monarchy, 1550–1700* (Oxford University Press, 1984); and Henry A. F. Kamen, *The Golden Age of Spain* (Humanities Press, 1988). John H. Elliott, *Spain and Its World* (Yale University Press, 1989), is a collection of excellent previously published essays. The classic treatment of the Armada is Garrett Mattingly, *The Armada* (Houghton Mifflin, 1988). Of the spate of books that appeared to commemorate the four

hundredth anniversary of the legendary battle, Peter Kemp, *The Campaign of the Spanish Armada* (Facts on File, 1988), is perhaps the most readable. Peter Pierson, *Commander of the Armada* (Yale University Press, 1989), is a biography of the ill-fated Spanish admiral Medina Sidonia.

The best-known account of the Dutch rebellion is Pieter Geyl, *The Revolt of the Netherlands* (Barnes & Noble, 1958). Noel G. Parker, *The Dutch Revolt* (Cornell University Press, 1977), and John C. Cadoux, *Philip of Spain and the Netherlands* (Archon Books, 1969), are two excellent older studies. For background of the rebellion, see Jonathan I. Israel, *The Dutch Republic and the Hispanic World, 1606–1661* (Oxford University Press, 1986), and James D. Tracy, *Holland Under Habsburg Rule* (University of California Press, 1990). Simon Schama, *The Embarrassment of Riches: An Interpretation of Dutch Culture in the Golden Age* (Knopf, 1987), and Charles R. Boxer, *The Dutch Seaborne Empire* (Penguin, 1989), depict the republic's problems at the apex of its struggle for power and wealth. The social backgrounds are treated in Sherrin Marshall, *The Dutch Gentry, 1500–1650: Family, Faith, and Fortune* (Greenwood, 1987). See also J. L. Price, *Culture and Society in the Dutch Republic During the Seventeenth Century* (Columbia University Press, 1974). Cicely V. Wedgewood, *William the Silent* (Norton, 1968), is a superb biography. See also Guido Marnef, *Antwerp in the Age of Reformation* (Johns Hopkins University Press, 1996).

French society and politics during the whole era are ably treated in Robert Briggs, *Early Modern France, 1560–1715* (Oxford University Press, 1977), and Mack P. Holt, ed., *Society and Institutions in Early Modern France* (University of Georgia Press, 1991). Henry Heller, *Iron and Blood: Civil Wars in Sixteenth-Century France* (McGill-Queen's University Press, 1991), and George D. Balsama, *The Politics of National Despair* (University of Washington Press, 1978), describe the catastrophic religious wars. This tragic time is also reflected in Frederick J. Baumgartner's readable biography, *Henry II, King of France* (Duke University Press, 1988). Robert M. Kingdon presents a Catholic view in *Myths About the Saint Bartholomew's Day Massacres, 1572–1576* (Harvard University Press, 1988). On the early seventeenth century, see Victor L. Tapie, *France in the Age of Louis XIII and Richelieu* (Cambridge University Press, 1984). The best biographies for this later period are A. Lloyd Moote, *Louis XIII* (University of California Press, 1989); Ruth Kleinman, *Anne of Austria* (Ohio State University Press, 1985); and Elizabeth Warwick's two controversial but interesting studies, *Louis XIII: The Making of a King* (Yale University Press, 1986) and *The Young Richelieu* (University of Chicago Press, 1983). The role of French Protestantism in both eras is clearly depicted in George A. Rothrock, *The Huguenots: A Biography of a Minority* (Nelson Hall, 1979).

An outstanding survey of English social history is J. A. Sharpe, *Early Modern England: A Social History, 1550–1760*, 2nd ed. (Arnold, 1997). On the growing social and political awareness of English women in the sixteenth and seventeenth centuries, see Katherine A. Henderson and Barbara McManus, *Half Humankind: Contexts and Texts of the Controversy About Women in England, 1540–1640* (University of Illinois Press, 1985), and Mary Prior, ed., *Women in English Society, 1500–1800* (Methuen, 1985).

Excellent general interpretations of Elizabethan England are presented in Arthur Bryant, *The Elizabethan Deliverance* (St. Martin's Press, 1982), and David B. Quinn and A. N. Ryan, *England's Sea Empire, 1550–1642* (Allen & Unwin, 1983). A creditable but less creative work that gives broad coverage of Elizabethan experience is Stephen White-Thomson, *Elizabeth I and Tudor England* (Bookwright Press, 1985). Other biographies worth consulting include Anne Somerset, *Elizabeth I* (Knopf, 1991); Jasper G. Ridley, *Elizabeth: The Shrewdness of Virtue* (Viking, 1988); Allison Plowden, *Elizabeth Tudor and*

Mary Stuart (Barnes & Noble, 1984); and J. Mary Wormald, *Mary, Queen of Scots* (Philip & Son, 1988). For studies of Elizabethan politics and diplomacy, see Joel Hurstfield, *Elizabeth I and the Unity of England* (Harper Torchbooks, 1967); Charles Wilson, *Queen Elizabeth and the Revolt of the Netherlands* (University of California Press, 1970); and a pair of companion volumes by Richard B. Wernham, *Before the Armada: The Emergence of the English Nation, 1485–1588* (Norton, 1972) and *After the Armada: Elizabethan England and the Struggle for Western Europe*, rev. ed. (Oxford University Press, 1984). A noteworthy special work on Elizabethan women is Susan Cahn, *The Transformation of Women's Work in England, 1500–1600* (Columbia University Press, 1987).

For discussion of the baroque artistic style in its historical setting, see Michael Kitson, *The Age of Baroque* (Haslyn, 1966), and Victor L. Tapie, *The Age of Grandeur: Baroque Art and Architecture* (Praeger, 1961). Three excellent relevant biographies are Henry Bonnier, *Rembrandt* (Braziller, 1968); Christopher White, *Rembrandt and His World* (Viking, 1964); and Andrew M. Jaffe, *Rubens and Italy* (Cornell University Press, 1977). On Mannerism, see Arnold Hauser, *Mannerism* (Knopf, 1965), and Linda Murray, *The High Renaissance and Mannerism* (Oxford University Press, 1977).

A good new study of the Thirty Years' War is Ronald Asch, *The Thirty Years' War: The Holy Roman Empire and Europe, 1618–1648* (St. Martin's Press, 1997), which adds to, but does not replace, Cicely V. Wedgewood's classic *The Thirty Year's War* (Anchor Books, 1961). Joseph Polisensky discusses the byproducts of the war in *War and Society in Europe, 1618–1648* (Cambridge University Press, 1978). Michael Roberts, *Sweden's Age of Greatness* (St. Martin's Press, 1973), gives good coverage of both the political and military events in this conflict.

Suggestions for Web Browsing

Internet Medieval History Sourcebook: Protestant and Catholic Reformations
http://www.fordham.edu/halsall/sbookly.html#Protestant Reformation

http://www.fordham.edu/halsall/sbookly.html#Catholic Reformation

Extensive on-line source for links about the Protestant and Catholic Reformations, including primary documents by or about precursors and papal critics, Luther, and Calvin and details about the Reformations themselves.

Martin Luther
http://www.wittenberg.de/e/seiten/personen/luther.html

This brief biography of Martin Luther includes links to his Ninety-Five Theses and images of related historical sites.

Tudor England
http://tudor.simplenet.com/

Site detailing life in Tudor England includes biographies, maps, important dates, architecture, and music, including sound files.

Lady Jane Grey
http://users.wantree.com.au/~halligan/ladyjane/index.html

A biography of the woman who would be queen of England for nine days and a general history of the time.

Peace of Westphalia
http://www.yale.edu/lawweb/avalon/westphal.htm

Complete text of the peace treaties that together made up the Treaty of Westphalia (1648), which ended the Thirty Years' War.

Notes

1. Quoted in Roland H. Bainton, *Here I Stand: A Life of Martin Luther* (New York: Abingdon-Cokesbury Press, 1950), p. 54.
2. Luther probably never posted his theses on the church door at Wittenberg. See H. G. Halle, *Luther* (New York: Doubleday, 1980), pp. 177–178.
3. Quoted in Heiko A. Oberman, *Luther: Between God and the Devil* (New Haven, Conn.: Yale University Press, 1982), p. 190. See also pp. 187–188.
4. Quoted in Harold Grim, *The Reformation Era* (New York: Macmillan, 1968), p. 17.

Marketplace at Antwerp.
*In the sixteenth century, Antwerp
was the leading city in international commerce. As many
as 500 ships a day docked in its
bustling harbor, and as many as
1000 wagons arrived each week
carrying the overland trade.*

The Global Impact of European Expansion and Colonization, 1492–1660

Chapter Contents

During the fifteenth century Europe began a process of unprecedented expansion, affecting all areas of the world but most decisively the Americas and Africa. This was actually part of a worldwide development of civilizations, encompassing those of the Aztecs, the Incas, Africans, the western Europeans, and the Japanese, as well as others around the Eurasian fringes. The process was furthered by improved navigational technology and the resulting expansion of trade that encouraged long sea voyages by Arabs, Japanese, and Chinese. But only the Europeans succeeded in linking all the continents in a new global age, when their sea power, rather than land-based armies, would become a determining force in empire building.

European successes overseas were obviously related—both as cause and as effect—to salient trends in the European transition from medievalism. The Crusades and the Renaissance stimulated European curiosity; the Reformation produced thousands of zealous missionaries seeking foreign converts and refugees seeking religious freedom; and the monarchs of emerging sovereign states sought revenues, first by trading with the Orient and later by exploiting new and less developed worlds. Perhaps the most permeating influence was the rise of European capitalism, with its monetary values, profit-seeking motivations, investment institutions, and consistent impulses toward economic expansion. Some historians have labeled this whole economic transformation the Commercial

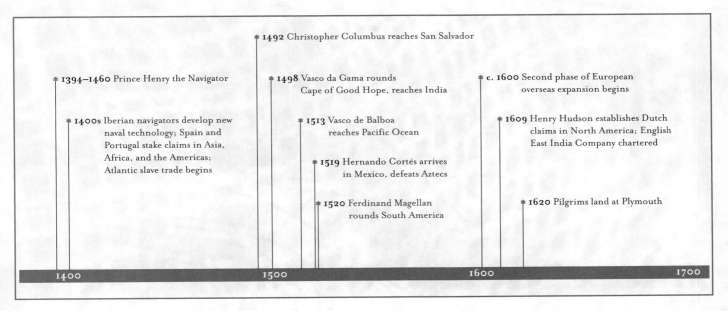

* **1492** Christopher Columbus reaches San Salvador

* **1394–1460** Prince Henry the Navigator

* **1498** Vasco da Gama rounds Cape of Good Hope, reaches India

* **c. 1600** Second phase of European overseas expansion begins

* **1400s** Iberian navigators develop new naval technology; Spain and Portugal stake claims in Asia, Africa, and the Americas; Atlantic slave trade begins

* **1513** Vasco de Balboa reaches Pacific Ocean

* **1609** Henry Hudson establishes Dutch claims in North America; English East India Company chartered

* **1519** Hernando Cortés arrives in Mexico, defeats Aztecs

* **1520** Ferdinand Magellan rounds South America

* **1620** Pilgrims land at Plymouth

1400   1500   1600   1700

Revolution. Others have used the phrase to refer to the shift in trade routes from the Mediterranean to the Atlantic. Interpreted either way, the Commercial Revolution and its accompanying European expansion helped usher in a modern era, largely at the expense of Africans and Amerindians.

Europe's Commercial Revolution developed in two quite distinct phases. The second and climactic one, after 1600, was centered in the Netherlands, England, and to some extent France. It fostered a maritime imperialism based more on trade and finance than the more directly exploitative systems of Portugal and Spain during their earlier "golden age" in the first phase.

The Iberian Golden Age

The two Iberian states launched the new era in competition with each other, although neither was able to maintain initial advantages over the long term. Portugal lacked manpower and resources required by an empire spread over three continents. Spain wasted its new wealth in continuous wars while neglecting to develop its own economy. In 1503 Portuguese pepper cost only one-fifth as much as pepper coming through Venice and the eastern Mediterranean.[1] Within decades gold and silver from the New World poured into Spain. Iberian bullion and exotic commodities, flowing into northern banks and markets, provided a major stimulus to European capitalism. This early European impact abroad also generated

great cultural diffusion, promoting an intercontinental spread of peoples, plants, animals, and knowledge that the world had never seen before. But it also destroyed nascent Amerindian states and began a weakening of those in Africa at a time when civilizations were approaching maturation in both places.

Conditions Favoring Iberian Expansion

A number of conditions invited Iberian maritime expansion in the fifteenth century. Muslim control over the eastern caravan routes, particularly after the Turks took Constantinople in 1453, brought rising prices in Europe. At the same time the sprawling Islamic world lacked both unity and intimidating sea power, and China, after 1440, had abandoned its extensive naval forays into the Indian Ocean. These conditions encouraged Portugal and Spain to seek new sea routes to the East, where their centuries-old struggle with Muslims in the Mediterranean might be continued on the ocean shores of sub-Saharan Africa and Asia (and where they also drained the wealth from ports of those distant lands).

During the 1400s Iberian navigators became proficient in new naval technology and tactics. Having adopted the compass and the astrolabe, they learned to tack against the wind, thus partly freeing themselves from hugging the coast on long voyages, particularly when sailing home from West Africa. The Iberians, especially the Portuguese, were also skilled cartographers and chartmakers. But their main advantages lay with their ships and naval guns. The stormy Atlantic required broad bows, deep keels, and complex square rigging for driving and maneuvering fighting ships. Armed with brass cannons, such ships could sink enemy vessels without ramming or boarding at close range. They could also batter down coastal defenses. Even the much larger Chinese junks could not match the maneuverability and firepower of European ships.

A strong religious motivation augmented Iberian naval efficiency. Long and bitter wars with the Moors had left the Portuguese and Spanish with an obsessive drive to convert non-Christians or destroy them in the name of Christ. Sailors with Columbus recited prayers every night, and Portuguese seamen were equally devout. Every maritime mission was regarded as a holy crusade.

For two centuries Iberians had nursed their religious prejudices against Muslims by hoping for a new Christian crusade in concert with Ethiopia. The idea originated with twelfth-century crusaders in the Holy Land; it gained strength later with Ethiopian migrants at Rhodes, who boasted of their king's prowess against the infidels. Thus arose the myth of "Prester John," a mighty Ethiopian monarch and potential European ally against Mongols, Turks, and

---

Spanish Exploration and Expansion

1470–1541	Francisco Pizarro
1474–1566	Bartolomé de Las Casas
1479	Treaty of Alcacovas
1494	Treaty of Tordesillas
1509–1515	Alfonso de Albuquerque serves as eastern viceroy of Portugal
1510–1554	Francisco de Coronado
1510	Portuguese acquire Goa, in India
1531	Pizarro defeats Incas in Peru
c. 1550	Spanish introduce plantation system to Brazil
1565	St. Augustine founded, first European colony in North America

Using ships like these broad-beamed carracks, the Portuguese controlled much of the carrying trade with the East in the fifteenth and sixteenth centuries.

Muslims. In response to a delegation from Zara Yakob, the reigning emperor, a few Europeans visited Ethiopia after 1450. These and other similar contacts greatly stimulated the determination to find a new sea route to the East, which might link the Iberians with the legendary Ethiopian king and bring Islam under attack from two sides.

This dream of war for the cross was sincere, but it also served to rationalize more worldly concerns. Both Spain and Portugal experienced dramatic population growth between 1400 and 1600. The Spanish population increased from 5 to 8.5 million; the Portuguese more than doubled, from 900,000 to 2 million, despite a manpower loss of 125,000 in the sixteenth century.[2] Hard times in rural areas prompted migration to cities, where dreams of wealth in foreign lands encouraged fortune seeking overseas. Despite the obvious religious zeal of many Iberians, particularly among those in holy orders, a fervent desire for gain was the driving motivation for most migrants.

The structures of the Iberian states provided further support for overseas expansion. In both, the powers of the monarchs had been recently expanded and were oriented toward maritime adventure as a means to raise revenues, divert the Turkish menace, spread Catholic Christianity, and increase national unity. The Avis dynasty in Portugal, after usurping the throne and alienating the great nobles in 1385, made common cause with the gentry and middle classes,

who prospered in commercial partnership with the government. In contrast, Spanish nobles, particularly the Castilians, were very much like Turkish aristocrats, who regarded conquest and plunder as their normal functions and sources of income. Thus the Portuguese and Spanish political systems worked in different ways toward similar imperial ends.

Staking Claims

During the late fifteenth century both Portugal and Spain staked claims abroad. Portugal gained a long lead over Spain in Africa and Asia. But after conquering Grenada, the last Moorish state on the Iberian peninsula, and completely uniting the country, the Spanish monarchs turned their attention overseas. The resulting historic voyage of Columbus established Spanish claims to most of the Western Hemisphere.

The man most responsible for the brilliant exploits by the Portuguese was Prince Henry (1394–1460), known as "the Navigator" because of his famous observatory at Sagres, where skilled mariners planned voyages and recorded their results. As a young man in 1411, Henry directed the Portuguese conquest of Ceuta, a Muslim port on the Moroccan coast, at the western entrance to the Mediterranean. This experience imbued him with a lifelong desire to divert the West African gold trade from

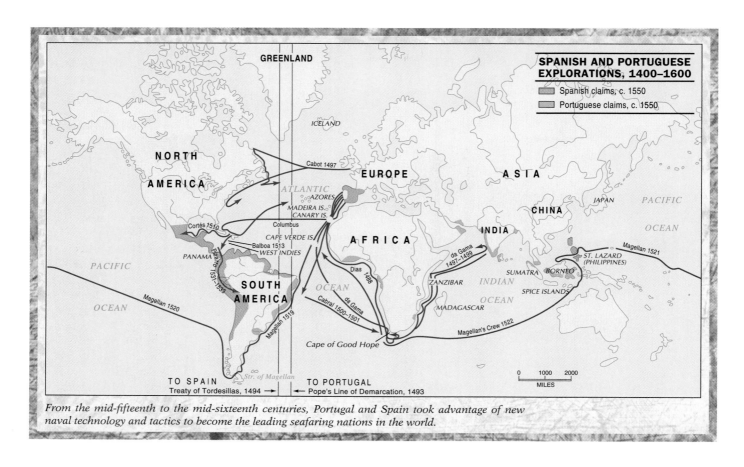

From the mid-fifteenth to the mid-sixteenth centuries, Portugal and Spain took advantage of new naval technology and tactics to become the leading seafaring nations in the world.

Muslim caravans to Portuguese ships. He also shared the common dream of finding Ethiopian Christian allies against the Turks. Such ideas motivated him for 40 years as he sent expeditions down the West African coast, steadily charting and learning from unknown waters.

Before other European states began extensive explorations, the Portuguese had navigated the West African coast to its southern tip. Henry's captains claimed the Madeira Islands in 1418 and the Azores in 1421. They had explored the Senegal River by 1450 and then traced the Guinea coast during the next decade. After Henry's death in 1460 they pushed south, reaching Benin in the decade after 1470 and Kongo, on the southwest coast, in 1482. Six years later Bartolomeu Dias rounded southern Africa, but his disgruntled crew forced him to turn back. Nevertheless, King John II of Portugal (1481–1495) was so excited by the prospect of a direct route to India that he named Dias's discovery the "Cape of Good Hope."

Spain soon challenged Portuguese supremacy. The specific controversy was over the Canary Islands, some of which were occupied by Castilians in 1344 and others by Portuguese after the 1440s. The issue, which produced repeated incidents, was ultimately settled in 1479 by the Treaty of Alcacovas, which recognized exclusive Spanish rights in the Canaries but

banned Spain from the Madeiras, the Azores, the Cape Verdes, and West Africa. Spanish ambitions were thus temporarily frustrated until Columbus provided new hope.

Christopher Columbus (1451–1506), a Genoese sailor with an impossible dream, had been influenced by Marco Polo's journal to believe that Japan could be reached by a short sail directly westward. Although he underestimated the distance by some 7000 miles and was totally ignorant of the intervening continents, Columbus persistently urged his proposals on King John of Portugal and Queen Isabella of Spain, who was captivated by Columbus's dream and became his most steadfast supporter until her death in 1504. Having obtained her sponsorship, Columbus sailed from Palos, Spain, in three small ships on August 3, 1492. He landed on San Salvador in the West Indies on October 12, thinking he had reached his goal. In three more attempts he continued his search for an Asian passage. His voyages touched the major Caribbean islands, Honduras, the Isthmus of Panama, and Venezuela. Although he never knew it, he had claimed a new world for Spain.

Columbus's first voyage posed threats to Portuguese interests in the Atlantic and called for compromise if war was to be averted. At Spain's invitation the pope issued a "bull of demarcation,"

An engraving that shows Columbus landing at Hispaniola. Columbus made four voyages to the New World but died believing that the islands he explored were off the coast of China.

establishing a north-south line about 300 miles west of the Azores. Beyond this line all lands were opened to Spanish claims. The Portuguese protested, forcing direct negotiations, which produced the Treaty of Tordesillas (1494). It moved the line some 500 miles farther west. Later explorations showed that the last agreement gave Spain most of the New World but left eastern Brazil to Portugal.

The Developing Portuguese Empire

Through the first half of the sixteenth century, the Portuguese developed a world maritime empire while maintaining commercial supremacy. They established trading posts around both African coasts and a faltering colony in Brazil, but their most extensive operations were in southern Asia, where they drove Muslims from the Indian Ocean and dominated the spice trade of the East Indies.

Two voyages at the turn of the sixteenth century laid the foundations for the Portuguese Empire in America and the Orient. In 1497 Vasco da Gama (1469–1524) left Lisbon, Portugal, in four ships, rounding the Cape of Good Hope after 93 days on the open sea. While visiting and raiding the East African ports, da Gama picked up an Arab pilot, who brought the fleet across the Indian Ocean to Calicut, on the western coast of India. When he returned to Lisbon in 1499, da Gama had lost two ships and a third of his men, but his cargo of pepper and cinnamon returned the cost of the expedition 60 times over. Shortly afterward Pedro Cabral (1468–1520), commanding a large fleet on a second voyage to India, bore too far west and sighted the east coast of Brazil. The new western territory was so unpromising that it

was left unoccupied until 1532, when a small settlement was established at São Vicente. In the 1540s it had attracted only some 2000 settlers, mostly men, although a few Portuguese women came after the arrival of the lord protector's wife and her retinue in 1535. The colony served mostly as a place to send convicts in the sixteenth century. By 1600 it had only 25,000 European residents.

Brazil was neglected in favor of extensive operations in the Indian Ocean and Southeast Asia. The most striking successes there were achieved under Alfonso de Albuquerque, eastern viceroy from 1509 to 1515. He completed subjugation of the East African sultanates and established fortified trading posts in Mozambique and Zanzibar. After a decisive naval victory over an Arab fleet (1509), Albuquerque captured Hormuz, thus hampering Arab passage from the Persian Gulf. In 1510 the Portuguese acquired Goa on the west coast of India; it became a base for aiding Hindus against Indian Muslims and conducting trade with the interior. The next year a Portuguese force took Malacca, a Muslim stronghold in Malaya, which controlled trade with China and the Spice Islands, through the narrow straits opposite Sumatra.

Although dominant in Indonesia, the Portuguese were mostly supplicants on the Asian mainland. They acquired temporary influence in Laos and Cambodia but were expelled from Vietnam and enslaved in Burma. Their arrogance and violence caused them to be banished from Chinese ports in 1522 and 1544. The Chinese gave them strictly regulated trading rights in Macao in 1557; from then until they were expelled at the end of the Ming dynasty, the Portuguese in China conformed to the law, serving as traders, advisers, and missionaries. In Japan after the 1540s they prospered by selling guns to the warring *daimyo* (feudal barons). Jesuit missionaries converted thousands of Japanese. But as Japan approached political unity, conditions for Europeans grew steadily worse until all Europeans were forced out in the 1630s.

Long before this expulsion the Portuguese Empire had begun to decline. It did not have the special skills or fluid capital required by a global empire and had become dependent on the bankers and spice brokers of northern Europe for financing. This deficiency was magnified by Albuquerque's failure to recruit women from home who might have produced a Portuguese governing elite in the colonies. To make matters worse, the home population dropped steadily after 1600. Thus the relatively few Portuguese men overseas mated with local women. Most were concubines, prostitutes, or slaves—regarded generally as household pets or work animals. These conditions contributed largely to a decided weakening of morale, economic efficiency, and military power. After the turn of the seventeenth century the Portuguese lost ground to the Omani Arabs in East Africa, the Spanish in the Philippines, and the Dutch in both hemispheres. Despite a mild later revival, their empire never regained its former glory.

The Growth of New Spain

While Portugal concentrated on Asian trade, Spain won a vast empire in America. Soon after 1492, Spanish settlements sprouted in the West Indies, most notably on Hispaniola and Cuba. By 1500, as the American continents were recognized and the passage to Asia remained undiscovered, a host of Spanish adventurers—the *conquistadores*—set out for the New World. From the West Indies they crossed the Caribbean to eastern Mexico, fanning out from there in all directions, toward Central America, the Pacific, and the vast North American hinterlands.

In Mexico the Spaniards profited from internal problems within the Aztec Empire. In the early 1500s unrest ran rampant among many recently subdued tribes, who were forced to pay tribute and furnish sacrificial victims for their Aztec overlords. Montezuma II, the Aztec emperor, professed a fear that the Spaniards were followers of the white-skinned and bearded Teotihuacán god, Quetzalcoatl, who had been exiled by the Toltecs because he forbade human sacrifice and had promised a return from across the sea to enforce his law. Whether this was Montezuma's true belief or not, the legend probably added to the widespread resentment already verging on rebellion.

In 1519 Hernando Cortés (1485–1574) arrived from Cuba with 11 ships, 600 fighting men, 200 servants, 16 horses, 32 crossbows, 13 muskets, and 14 mobile cannons. Before marching against the Aztec capital, he destroyed his ships to prevent his men from turning back. In a few battles the Spanish horses, firearms, steel armor, and tactics produced decisive victories. Exploiting the Quetzalcoatl legend and the Aztec policy of taking sacrificial victims, Cortés was able to enlist Amerindian allies. As the little army marched inland, its members were welcomed, feasted, and given Amerindian women, including daughters of chiefs, whom Cortés distributed among his men. One woman, Malinche, later christened Doña Marina, became a valuable interpreter as well as Cortés's mistress and bore him a son. She helped save him from a secret ambush at Cholula; it had been instigated by Montezuma, who otherwise delayed direct action as Cortés approached Tenochtitlán, accompanied by thousands of Amerindian warriors.

In that city of more than 150,000 people, Cortés became a guest of Montezuma, surrounded by a host of armed Aztecs. Undaunted, Cortés implemented his preconceived plan and seized the Amerindian ruler in the man's own palace. Malinche then informed Montezuma, as if in confidence, that he must cooperate or die. The bold scheme worked temporarily, but soon the Aztecs rebelled, renounced their emperor as a traitor, stoned and killed him when he tried to pacify them, and ultimately drove a battered band of terrified Spaniards from the city in the narrowest of

An illustration from the Codex Azacatitlán of the Spanish arriving in Mexico. Standing next to Cortés is Malinche, the Aztec woman who served as his interpreter.

Cortés Meets Montezuma

After arriving in Tenochtitlán, Cortés wrote this famous report in a long letter to Charles V, the Spanish monarch. Such descriptions of fabulous wealth in the New World were major causes of Spanish adventuring overseas.

The next day after I had arrived in this city, I left, and having gone half a league, I reached another causeway, leading out into the lake a distance of two leagues to the great city of Temixtitan, which stands in the midst of the said lake. This causeway is two lances broad, and so well built that eight horsemen can ride abreast; and, within these two leagues, there are three cities, on one and the other side of the said highway, one called Mesicalsingo, founded for the greater part within the said lake, and the other two, called Niciaca, and Huchilohuchico, on the other shore of it, with many of their houses on the water.

The first of these cities may have three thousand families, the second more than six thousand, and the third four or five thousand. In all of them, there are very good edifices, of houses and towers, especially the residences of the lords and chief persons, and the mosques or oratories, where they keep their idols. These cities have a great trade in salt, which they make from the water of the lake, and from the crust of the land which is bathed by the lake, and which they boil in a certain manner, making loaves of salt, which they sell to the inhabitants in the neighbourhood.

I followed the said causeway for about half a league before I came to the city proper of Temixtitan. I found at the junction of another causeway, which joins this one from the mainland, another strong fortification, with two towers, surrounded by walls, twelve feet high with castellated tops. This commands the two roads, and has only two gates, by one of which they enter, and from the other they come out. About one thousand of the principal citizens came out to meet me, and speak to me, all richly dressed alike according to their fashion; and when they had come, each one in approaching me, and before speaking, would use a ceremony which is very common

amongst them, putting his hand on the ground, and afterwards kissing it. . . . There is a wooden bridge, ten paces broad, in the very outskirts of the city, across an opening in the causeway, where the water may flow in and out as it rises and falls. This bridge is also for defence, for they remove and replace the long broad wooden beams, of which the bridge is made, whenever they wish; and there are many of these bridges in the city, as Your Highness will see in the account which I shall make of its affairs.

Having passed this bridge, we were received by that lord, Montezuma, with about two hundred chiefs, all barefooted, and dressed in a kind of livery, very rich, according to their custom, and some more so than others. They approached in two processions near the walls of the street, which is very broad, and straight, and beautiful, and very uniform from one end to the other, being about two thirds of a league long, and having, on both sides, very large houses, both dwelling places, and mosques. Montezuma came in the middle of the street, with two lords, one on the right side, and the other on the left, one of whom was the same great lord, who, as I said, came in that litter to speak with me, and the other was the brother of Montezuma, lord of that city Iztapalapan, whence I had come that day. All were dressed in the same manner, except that Montezuma was shod, and the other lords were barefooted. Each supported him below his arms, and as we approached each other, I descended from my horse, and was about to embrace him, but the two lords in attendance prevented me, with their hands, that I might not touch him. . . .

From *Hernando Cortés, His Five Letters of Relation to the Emperor Charles V*, in Harry J. Carroll et al., eds., *The Development of Civilizations*, Vol. 1 (Glenview, Ill.: Scott, Foresman, 1970), pp. 56–57.

---

escapes. Later, having regrouped and gained new Amerindian allies, Cortés wore down the Aztecs in a long and bloody siege during which some Spanish prisoners were sacrificed in full view of their comrades. Finally, after fearful slaughter, some 60,000 exhausted and half-starved defenders surrendered. Most tribes in central Mexico then accepted Spanish rule; many who resisted were enslaved.

Tenochtitlán, rebuilt as Mexico City, became the capital of an expanding Spanish empire. *Conquistadores* steadily penetrated the interior, but the fierce

Mayas of Yucatán and Guatemala were not subdued until the 1540s. By then settlements had been established throughout Central America. The first colony in North America was founded at St. Augustine, on Florida's east coast, in 1565. Meanwhile, numerous expeditions, including those of Hernando de Soto (1500–1542) and Francisco de Coronado (1510–1554), explored what is now California, Arizona, New Mexico, Colorado, Texas, Missouri, Louisiana, and Alabama. Spanish friars established a mission at Santa Fe in 1610, providing a base for

Antonio Pigafetta, "Magellan's Last Fight"

This firsthand account, recorded by an Italian crew member, describes the skirmish with inhabitants of the Philippine island of Mactan, where Magellan was killed in April 1521.

On Friday the 26th of April, Zula, the chief of this island of Mactan, sent one of his sons to present two goats to the Captain, and to tell him that [he would send him everything that he had promised but that he could not send it] because of the other chief, Cilapulapu, [who] did not want to obey the king of Spain, [and asked] that on the following night he send him but one boatload of men to help him and fight him. The Captain General decided to go there with three boats. And for a long time the others begged him not to go there, but like a good captain, he did not want to abandon his allies. At midnight sixty men armored with cuirasses and sallers left with the Christian king, the prince and some of the chieftains in twenty or thirty boats. And three hours before daylight they reached Mattan. . . . When day came, our men leaped into the water up to their thighs, forty-nine of them, and thus they waded more than two bowshots before they came to dry land. . . . When they arrived on land, these people had made three sections of more than one thousand and fifty persons. And as soon as they realized that [Magellan's men] were coming, two sections attacked their flanks, and the other their front. When the Captain saw this, he divided his men into two groups and thus they began to fight. The musketeers and the bowmen shot from a distance for almost a half hour in vain, able only to penetrate the shields made of thin planks that they carried on their arms. The Captain shouted to cease firing, but they did not cease firing. [When the natives saw that we were firing muskets without any result] they cried out determined to stand firm. And when the muskets were fired, they shouted all the louder and would not keep still, but jumped hither and yon, covered with their shields shooting so many arrows and hurling bamboo lances, charred pointed stakes, stones and mud at the Captain that he could scarce defend himself. When the Captain saw this he sent some men to burn their houses to frighten them. And when they saw their houses burning they were all the more fierce, and they killed two of our men near the houses, and twenty or thirty burned. And so great a number came upon us that they pierced the right leg of the Captain with a poisoned arrow, wherefor he ordered that they gradually retreat, and they would follow them, and six or eight remained with the Captain. These people aimed only at their legs because they were not covered with armor. And they had so many spears, darts and stones that [Magellan's soldiers] could not withstand them, and the artillery of the fleet was so far away that it could not help them. And our men withdrew to the shore, fighting all the while, even up to their knees in water, and they recovered their own spears four or five times in order to throw them at us. They recognized the Captain and so many assailed him that twice they knocked his sallet from his head. And he, like a good knight, continued to stand firm with a few others, and they fought thus for more than an hour and refused to retreat. An Indian threw his bamboo spear into his face and he immediately killed him with his own spear and it remained in [the Indian's] body. And the Captain tried to draw his sword and was able to draw it only half way, because he had been wounded in the arm with a spear. When our men saw this they turned their backs and made their way to the ships, still pursued with lances and darts until they were out of sight, and they killed [the Europeans'] guide.

From Paula S. Paige, trans., *The Voyage of Magellan: The Journal of Antonio Pigafetta* (Englewood Cliffs, N.J.: Prentice Hall, 1969). Used by permission of the publisher and the William L. Clements Library.

later missions. All these new territories, known as New Spain, were administered from Mexico City after 1542.

The viceroyalty of Mexico later sponsored colonization of the Philippines, a project justified by the historic voyage of Ferdinand Magellan (1480–1521). Encouraged by the exploits of Vasco de Balboa (1479–1519), who had crossed Panama and discovered the Pacific Ocean in 1513, Magellan sailed from Spain in 1520, steered past the ice-encrusted straits at the tip of South America, and endured a 99-day voyage to the Philippines, where he was killed by inhabitants of Mactan Island. Only one of Magellan's five ships completed this first circumnavigation of the world, but the feat established a Spanish claim to the Philippines. It also prepared the way for the first tiny settlement of 400 Mexicans at Cebu in 1571. By 1580, when the capital at Manila had been secured against attacking Portuguese, Chinese, and Moro fleets, the friars were beginning conversions that would reach half a million by 1622. The colony prospered in trade with Asia but remained economically dependent on annual galleons from Mexico. Here as in Mexico, Spanish males, as a tiny elite, spawned a mixed-race population in liaisons with Filipino and Chinese women.

The Development of Spanish South America

As in Mexico, the Spanish exploited unique opportunities in their process of empire building in Peru. Just as they arrived, the recently formed Inca state was torn by a bitter civil war between two rival princes. This war, which soon destroyed nearly every semblance of imperial unity, was also a major factor in the surprisingly easy triumph of a handful of Spanish freebooters over a country of more than 10 million people, scattered through Peru and Ecuador in hundreds of mountain towns and coastal cities.

Francisco Pizarro (1470–1541), the son of an illiterate peasant, was the conqueror of Peru. After two earlier exploratory visits, he landed on the northern coast in January 1531 with a tiny privately financed army of 207 men and 27 horses. For more than a year he moved south, receiving some reinforcements as he plundered towns and villages. Leaving a garrison of 60 soldiers in a coastal base, he started inland in September 1532 with a Spanish force of fewer than 200. About the same time, word came that Altahualpa, one of the contending princes, had defeated the other in battle. Pizarro now posed as a potential ally to both sides. At Cajamarca he met and captured Altahualpa, slaughtering some 6000 unarmed retainers of the Inca monarch. He next forced Altahualpa to fill a room with silver and gold, including the imperial throne. Then, having collected the ransom, Pizarro executed his royal prisoner and proclaimed Manco, the young son of Altahualpa's dead brother, as emperor. Thus upon arriving in Cuzco with their puppet ruler, the Spaniards were welcomed as deliverers and quickly secured tentative control of the country.

For two more decades political anarchy reigned in Peru, while *conquistadores* fought, explored, and plundered. Manco, after suffering terrible indignities from the Spaniards, led a rebellion that lasted for 26 years after his final defeat and execution in 1544. The period was marked by an obsessive Spanish rape of the country, along with cruel persecution of its Amerindian population, and by ruthless contention, involving every degree of greed and brutality, among the conquerors. Meanwhile, marauding expeditions moved south into Chile and north through Ecuador into Colombia. Expeditions from Chile and Peru settled in Argentina, founding Buenos Aires. *Conquistadores* and Amerindian women produced a new *mestizo* (Spanish-Indian) population in Paraguay. Despite this dynamic activity, there was no effective government at Lima, the capital, until the end of the sixteenth century.

Along with brutality, Spaniards in the postconquest era also demonstrated unprecedented fortitude and courage. Pizarro's Spaniards were always outnumbered in battle. They faced nearly unendurable torments, including scorching heat, disease-carrying insects, air too thin for breathing, and cold that at times could freeze a motionless man into a lifeless statue. Amid the terrible hardships of this male-dominated era, both Amerindian and Spanish women played significant roles. As in Mexico, Amerindian women were camp-following concubines; like them, some Spanish women prepared food, bore children, and when necessary fought beside the men. Some women were present on all the pioneering ventures, and others were direct participants in the terrible sacrifices of the civil wars.

By 1600 the two viceroyalties of Mexico and Peru were well established, governing over 200 towns with a Spanish and mestizo population of 200,000. Nevertheless, the empire was already in decline. Peruvian silver, the main source of Spanish wealth, was either running out or requiring very expensive mining operations; the Amerindian labor force was depleted, and African slaves were both scarce and expensive. Spain's deteriorating home economy and waning sea power presented even more serious problems.

Iberian Systems in the New World

European expansion overseas after the fifteenth century brought revolutionary change to all the world's peoples, but the Iberian period before 1600 was unique in its violence and ruthless exploitation. Not only were highly organized states destroyed in the New World, but whole populations were wiped out by European diseases, shock, and inhumane treatment. This tragic catastrophe was accompanied by a decided change in the racial composition of Iberian America as an influx of African slaves, along with continued Spanish and Portuguese immigration, led to a variegated racial mixture, ranging through all shades of color between white and black. Fortunately, the Amerindian population began recovering in the mid-1600s, and their cultures, combining with Iberian and African, formed a new configuration, to be known later as Latin American.

The General Nature of Regimes

Iberian regimes in America faced serious problems. Their vast territories, far greater than the homelands, contained nearly impassable deserts, mountains, and jungles. Supplies had to be moved thousands of miles, often across open seas. Communications were difficult, wars with indigenous peoples were

The arrival of the Spanish and Portuguese in America led to a mixing of three cultures: European, African, and Amerindian. This painted wooden bottle, done in Inca style and dating from about 1650, shows the mix. The three figures are an African drummer, a Spanish trumpeter, and an Amerindian official.

frequent, and disease was often rampant. Such conditions help explain, if not justify, the brutality of Iberian imperialism.

With all their unique features, Iberian overseas empires were similar to Roman or Turkish provinces: they were meant to produce revenues. In theory, all Spanish lands were the king's personal property. The Council of the Indies, which directed the viceroys in Mexico City and Lima, advised him on colonial affairs. The highborn Spanish viceroys were aided (and limited) by councils *(audiencias)*, made up of aristocratic lawyers from Spain. Local governors, responsible to the viceroys, functioned with their advisory councils *(cabildos)* of officials. Only the rich normally sat in such bodies; poor Spaniards and mestizos had little voice, even in their own taxation. Most taxes, however, were collected by Amerindian chiefs *(caciques)*, still acting as rulers of Amerindian peasant villages.

Portuguese Brazil was less directly controlled than the Spanish colonies. It languished for years under almost unrestricted domination of 15 aristocratic "captains" who held hereditary rights of taxing, disposing lands, making laws, and administering justice. In return, they sponsored settlement and paid stipulated sums to the king. This quasi-feudal administration was abandoned in 1548. When Philip II became king of Portugal in 1580, he established munic-ipal councils, although these were still dominated by the hereditary captains.

Iberian Economies in America

Both the philosophies and the structures of the Iberian states limited colonial trade and industry. Most Spanish and Portuguese immigrants were disinclined toward productive labor. With few exceptions, commercial contacts were limited to the homelands; Mexican merchants fought a steadily losing battle to maintain independent trade with Peru and the Philippines. Local trade grew modestly in supplying the rising towns, some crafts developed into large-scale industrial establishments, and a national transport system, based on mule teams, became a major Mexican industry. So did smuggling, as demand for foreign goods rose higher and higher.

Agriculture, herding, and mining silver, however, were the main economic pursuits. The early gold sources soon ran out, but silver strikes in Mexico and Peru poured a stream of wealth back to Spain in the annual treasure fleets, convoyed by warships from Havana to Seville. Without gold to mine, many Spanish aristocrats acquired abandoned Amerindian land, raising wheat, rice, indigo, cotton, coffee, and sugarcane. Cattle, horses, and sheep were imported and bred on ranches in the West Indies, Mexico, and Argentina. Brazil developed similar industries, particularly those related to sugar, livestock, and coffee. Iberian economic pursuits in America were potentially productive, revealing numerous instances of initiative and originality, but they were largely repressed by bureaucratic state systems.

Before 1660, plantations were not typical for agriculture in Iberian America, although they were developing in certain areas. Portugal had established sugar plantations on its Atlantic islands (Madeiras, Cape Verde, and São Tomé) before introducing the system into Brazil around 1550. The Spanish tried plantations in the Canaries, later establishing them in the West Indies, the Mexican lowlands, and Central America and along the northern coasts of South America. Even in such areas, which were environmentally suited for intensive single-crop cultivation, it was not easy to raise the capital, find the skilled technicians, and pay for the labor the system required.

The perpetual labor problem was solved primarily by the use of Amerindians, but African slaves were imported early and were coming in greater numbers by the late sixteenth century. Some 75,000 slaves were in the Spanish colonies by 1600; more than 100,000 more arrived in the next four decades. In Brazil, slave importing boomed after 1560, with annual figures surpassing 30,000 in the early 1600s. Some slaves were brutally oppressed as laborers in the mines, and others sweated on Spanish or Brazil-

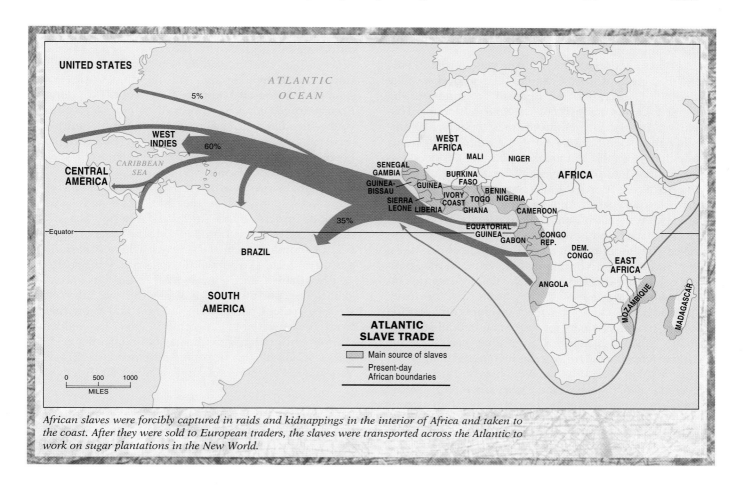

African slaves were forcibly captured in raids and kidnappings in the interior of Africa and taken to the coast. After they were sold to European traders, the slaves were transported across the Atlantic to work on sugar plantations in the New World.

ian plantations, but they were the exceptions during this period. Slaves were also teamsters, overseers, personal servants, and skilled artisans. Particularly in the Spanish colonies, a good many earned their freedom, attaining a social status higher than that of Amerindian peasants. Free blacks, both men and women, operated shops and small businesses. Prostitution was understandably common among black and mulatto women, a profession encouraged by the sexual exploitation of female slaves as concubines and breeders.

Iberian Effects on Amerindian Life

The Spanish and Portuguese brought terrible disaster to most Amerindians. Having seen their gods mocked and their temples destroyed, many accepted Christianity as the only hope for survival, as well as salvation, while toiling for their Iberian masters. Some died from overwork, some were killed, and others simply languished as their cultures disintegrated. The most dangerous adversity was disease—European or African—to which Amerindians had no immunities.

Epidemics arrived with Columbus and continued throughout the sixteenth century. Smallpox on Hispaniola in 1518 left only 1000 Amerindians alive

there. Cortés carried the pox to Mexico, where it raged while he fought his way out of Tenochtitlán. From Mexico the epidemic spread through Central America, reaching Peru in 1526. It killed the reigning emperor and helped start the civil war that facilitated Pizarro's conquest. Following these smallpox disasters in the 1540s and 1570s, a wave of measles, along

Amerindian slaves work a Spanish sugar plantation on the island of Hispaniola. Spanish treatment of the Amerindians was often brutal.

with other successive epidemics, continued depleting the population.

Depopulation of Amerindians was caused in part by their enslavement, despite disapproval by the Catholic Church and the Spanish government. The worst excesses came early. Original settlers on Hispaniola herded the gentle Arawaks to work like animals; they soon became extinct. A whole indigenous population of the Bahamas—some 40,000 people—were carried away as slaves to Hispaniola, Cuba, and Puerto Rico. Cortés took slaves before he took Tenochtitlán; other Amerindians, captured in Panama, were regularly sent to Peru. Before Africans arrived in appreciable numbers, the Portuguese organized "Indian hunts" in the forests to acquire slaves.

Another more common labor system in the Spanish colonies was the *encomienda*. This system was instituted in Mexico by Cortés as a way of using Amerindian caciques to collect revenues and provide labor. It was similar to European feudalism and manorialism, involving a grant that permitted the holder *(encomiendero)* to take income or labor from specified lands and the people living on them. Many *encomienderos* starved and lashed their Amerindian laborers, working men and women to exhaustion or renting them to other equally insensitive masters. Amerindian women on the *encomiendas* were generally used as sex slaves by the owners and the caciques, who served as overseers. Abuses became so widespread and Amerindian complaints so insistent that the system was slowly but steadily abandoned after the 1550s.

The change resulted largely from efforts by the Dominican friar Bartolomé de Las Casas (1474–1566), who protested the cruel treatment of Amerindians and persuaded Charles V that they should hold the same rights as other subjects. These led to the New Law of 1542, which ended existing *encomiendas* upon the death of their holders, prohibited Amerindian slavery, and gave Amerindians full protection under Spanish law. Most of these provisions, however, were rescinded when the law evoked universal protest and open rebellion in Peru. Although later governors gradually eliminated *encomiendas*, many Amerindians were put on reservations and hired out as contract laborers under the direction of their caciques and local officials *(corrigodores)*. This practice eliminated some of the worst excesses of the *encomiendas*, but corrupt officials often exploited their wards, particularly in Peru.

Such physical hardships were matched by others of a psychological nature, which were almost equally damaging to Amerindians. The Spaniards insisted on forcing Christian conversion even while they raped and destroyed, as Pizarro did before executing Altahualpa. Except when they used Amerindian authorities to support their regimes, the Spaniards went out of their way to insult, shame, and degrade their unfortunate subjects. In the new social milieu, Amerindians were constantly reminded of their lowly status, unworthy of human consideration. Cortés, for example, passed off Malinche to one of his captains; Pizarro forced Manco, while still an ally, to give his young Inca queen to the conqueror. Such indignities, repeated by the hundreds among both Spanish and Portuguese, left many Amerindians demoralized to the point of utter despair.

Their distress was alleviated to some extent by missions, established by the Dominican and Jesuit religious orders. These afforded Amerindians the most effective protection and aid. Las Casas led the way in founding such settlements, where Amerindians were shielded from white exploitation, instructed in Christianity, and educated or trained in special skills. The prevailing philosophy in the missions stressed patient persuasion, "as rain and snow falls from heaven, not ... violently ... like a sudden shower, but gradually, with suavity and gentleness."[3] Large mission organizations developed in Brazil, Venezuela, Paraguay, and upper California. But even

Moved by the simplicity and gentle nature of the Amerindians, Bartolomé de Las Casas launched a vigorous campaign to ensure their protection. His Apologetic History of the Indies *(1566) is an indictment of the Spaniards' harsh treatment of the Amerindians.*

the Amerindians protected by the missions died rapidly in this alien way of life.

Although most Amerindians were demoralized by their misfortunes, some resisted. In Yucatán and Guatemala, where the Mayas did not believe the Spaniards were gods, bloody fighting lasted until the 1540s. About that time a revolt on the Mexican Pacific coast was put down with great difficulty by the Spaniards. As the silver mines opened in northern Mexico into the 1590s, the Chichimecs, relatives of the Apaches, conducted a border war, using horses and captured muskets. In Peru an Inca rebellion, led first by Manco, was subdued only in 1577. The most stubborn resistance came from the Araucanians of southern Chile, who fought the Spaniards successfully until the close of the sixteenth century.

The full Iberian impact on Amerindian culture is difficult to assess, although there can be no denying that it was disastrous. A conservative estimate of Amerindian population losses puts the proportion at 25 percent during the era to 1650, but some recent figures place losses much higher, up to 95 percent of the pre-1492 total of 100 million.[4] Signs of mental deterioration were also evident in prevalent alcoholism, which began among Amerindians shortly after the conquest. The social ills of many Amerindians in Latin America have endured, arising from their cultural alienation in a modern world not of their own creation.

Spanish Colonial Society and Culture

Spanish colonial society was stratified but somewhat flexible. A small elite of officials and aristocrats contended over politics, policy toward subject peoples, and foreign trade. Merchants and petty officials were on a lower social level but above mestizos, mulattos, and *zambos* (Indo-Africans). Amerindians were considered incompetent wards of the home government, and African slaves were legally designated as beneath the law, but there were numerous individual exceptions. Many Amerindians went from their rural homes to the towns, mines, or haciendas; some caciques enjoyed wealth and privilege; and a few established Amerindian families retained their nobility as early Spanish allies. Similarly, some African slaves were craftspeople, overseers, or privileged personal servants; others acquired freedom and became prosperous merchants; still others escaped slavery, organized free communities, and successfully defended their independence.

Women in Spanish America played ambiguous roles, reflecting the traditional ideal of male superiority mitigated by a dynamic society. They were excluded from male contacts throughout childhood, educated in cloistered schools to become wives and mothers, married in their teens to further family interests, and legally subordinated to their husbands. Those who did not marry, particularly women of the upper classes, usually entered convents. There was, however, another side to the story. Spanish law guaranteed a wife's dowry rights, a legal protection against the squandering of her wealth, and leverage to limit her husband's activities. The courts recognized separations and at times even granted annulments in cases of wife abuse. Women, particularly widows, operated businesses and held public office. Some were wealthy, powerful, and even cruel *encomienderas,* supervising thousands of workers. Whatever their special roles, Iberian matrons defended religion, sponsored charities, dictated manners, and taught their children family values. They civilized the empires conquered by their men.

Both the unique environment and the mix of peoples shaped Spanish colonial culture toward a new distinctive unity. From southwestern Europe came its aristocratic government, disdain for manual labor, a preference for dramatic over precise expression, and ceremonial Catholic Christianity. From Amerindian traditions came characteristic foods, art forms, architecture, legends, and practical garments like the poncho and serape, as well as substantial vocabulary. From Africa came agricultural knowledge, crafts, and animal husbandry. By 1650 this characteristic colonial culture was being preserved in its own universities, such as those at Lima and Mexico City, both founded more than a century earlier.

The Portuguese Impact on Africa

Unlike the Spanish in America, the Portuguese came to Africa as traders rather than settlers. Their original goal was to find a way around Muslim middlemen who controlled the trans-Saharan caravan trade and to gain direct access to the fabled goldfields of West Africa. Muslim kingdoms of the Sudan, such as Mali, Kanem-Bornu, and the Hausa states, dominated trade in the West African interior and were reluctant to open up their trade to Europeans. When Portugal sent envoys to Mali in the late fifteenth century, the king of Mali claimed that he had never heard of the king of Portugal. Therefore, the Portuguese concentrated their efforts on establishing commercial bases along the West African coast.

The Portuguese in West Africa

Africa was not of primary importance to the Portuguese, especially after they opened up sea routes to Asia. Thus they selectively established links with African states where they could trade for goods of

The Portuguese and Africa

1482	Portuguese establish Fort Elmina on Gold Coast; Portuguese reach kingdom of Kongo
1506–1543	Reign of Nzinga Mbemba, king of Kongo
1506	Portuguese seize Sofala
1571	Portuguese establish colony of Angola
1607	King of Mutapa kingdom signs treaty with Portugal
1698	Portuguese driven from East African coast by Omani Arabs

value such as gold, which could be traded anywhere in the world, and slaves, which were initially taken to southern Portugal as laborers. The first bases of operation for Portuguese seafarers were at Cape Verde, Arguin, and Senegambia. The latter two places afforded opportunities to trade with African states that had trading links with the Sudanic kingdoms.

The Portuguese finally located a place close to a source of gold when they arrived on the Gold Coast (present-day Ghana) in 1471. There they found Akan states carrying on a vigorous trade to the north through Muslim Dyula traders. In a short time the Portuguese crown established a profitable relationship with Akan leaders, exchanging copper, textiles, and later cowrie shells for gold. From their fort at Elmina ("the mine"), established in 1482, the Portuguese exported close to a ton of gold annually for the next half century.

The Portuguese also initiated contacts with the kingdom of Benin, located in the forests of southwestern Nigeria. The kings of Benin, called *obas*, had governed their land since the eleventh century. When the Portuguese arrived, Benin possessed a formidable army and was at the peak of its power. Edo, the walled capital, was a bustling metropolis with wide streets, markets, and an efficient municipal government. The huge royal palace awed Europeans who chanced to see it, although the Portuguese—and later the Dutch—were generally prohibited from living in the city. The few European visitors who gained entrance were amazed by Benin's metalwork, such as copper birds on towers, copper snakes coiled around doorways, and beautifully cast bronze statues. Portuguese visitors were occasionally invited to attend court, and the obas sent emissaries to Lisbon. In the early 1500s the oba Ozuola admitted Catholic missionaries to the kingdom. Although they converted several of Ozuola's sons and high-ranking officials, their influence ended at Ozuola's death.

Portugal believed that it could manipulate Benin's rulers to extend Portuguese trade over a much wider area, but the obas did not regard trade with the Portuguese as a vital necessity and did not allow them to establish a sizable presence in the kingdom. The obas controlled all transactions, and Portuguese traders duly paid taxes, observed official regulations, and conducted business only with the obas' representatives.

The Portuguese traded brass and copper items, textiles, and cowrie shells for pepper, cloth, beads, and slaves. Because Benin did not have access to sources of gold, the Portuguese took the slaves from Benin and traded them for gold with the Akan states, which needed laborers for clearing forests for farmland. However, in 1516, Benin decided to curtail the slave trade and offered only female slaves for purchase.

This saltcellar from Benin depicts a Portuguese sailor sighting land from the crow's nest of his ship.

Although effectively limited in Benin, Portuguese traders operated among nearby coastal states, where they gained some political influence. They were particularly successful in the small kingdom of Warri, a Niger delta vassal state of Benin. Shortly after 1600 the Warri crown prince was educated in Portugal and brought home a Portuguese queen. Warri supplied large numbers of slaves, as did other nearby states, which were now competing fiercely with one another. Before long even Benin would accept dependence on the trade in order to control its tributaries and hold its own against Europeans.

The Portuguese and the Kongo Kingdom

Farther south, near the mouth of the Congo River, the Portuguese experienced their most intensive involvement in Africa. Portuguese seafarers found the recently established Kongo kingdom of several million people, ruled by a king who was heavily influenced by the queen mother and other women on his royal council. Kongo's king, Nzinga Nkuwu, saw the Portuguese as a potential ally against neighboring African states. In the 1480s he invited the Portuguese to send teachers, technicians, missionaries, and soldiers. His son, Nzinga Mbemba (1506–1543), who converted to Catholicism in 1491, consolidated the control of the Catholic faction at his court, making Portuguese the official language and Catholicism the state religion. He encouraged his court to adopt European dress and manners while changing his own name to Don Afonso. Many friendly letters subsequently passed between him and King Manuel of Portugal.

This mutual cooperation did not last long. While the Portuguese were prepared to assist Afonso's kingdom, their desire for profits won out over their humanitarian impulses. Portuguese traders, seeking slaves for their sugar plantations at São Tomé and Principe, ranged over Kongo. By 1530 some 4000 to 5000 slaves were being taken from Kongo annually. No longer satisfied with treaty terms that gave them prisoners of war and criminals, they ignored the laws and bought everyone they could get, thus creating dissension and weakening the country. Driven to despair, Afonso wrote to his friend and ally Manuel: "There are many traders in all corners of the country. They bring ruin. . . . Every day, people are enslaved and kidnapped, even nobles, even members of the King's own family."[5] Such pleas brought no satisfactory responses. For a while Afonso tried to curb the slave trade; he was shot by disgruntled Portuguese slavers while he was attending Mass. Afonso's successors were no more successful, and Portuguese slavers operated with impunity throughout Kongo and in neighboring areas.

The Portuguese crown also turned its attention to the Mbundu kingdom to the south of Kongo. In 1520 Manuel established contact with the Mbundu king, Ngola. However, when the Portuguese government agreed to deal with Ngola through Kongo, São Tomé slavers were given a free hand to join with Mbundu's rulers to attack neighboring states. Using African mercenaries known as *pombeiros* equipped with firearms and sometimes allied with feared Jaga warriors, the slavers and their allies began a long war of conquest. In the last stages of this war they met the stubborn resistance of Queen Nzinga of Mbundu, a former ally who finally broke with the Portuguese and rallied her kingdom against them.

In 1571 the Portuguese crown issued a royal charter to establish the colony of Angola, situated on the Atlantic coast south of the Kongo kingdom. Although Portugal had ambitious plans to create an agricultural colony for white settlement and to gain control over a silver mine and the salt trade in the interior, Angola was never a successful venture. Few settlers immigrated, and Angola remained a sleepy outpost, consisting of a handful of Portuguese men, even fewer Portuguese women, a growing population of Afro-Portuguese, and a majority of Africans. The colony functioned primarily as a haven for slavers. By the end of the sixteenth century 10,000 slaves were flowing annually through Luanda, Angola's capital.

The Portuguese in East Africa

Portuguese exploits in East Africa were similar to those in Kongo and Angola. The African states of the east were much weaker than those in West Africa. The Swahili city-states along the coast north of the Zambezi River were divided and militarily impotent. They were tempting targets for Portuguese intervention because they were strategically well located for trade with Asia.

Although the Swahili people scorned the bad manners, unclean habits, and tawdry trade goods of the Portuguese, they had been prosperous and peaceful for so long that they could not effectively defend themselves against a ruthless Portuguese naval force that plundered from Kilwa to Mombasa. At Mombasa Portuguese sailors broke into houses with axes, looted, and killed before setting the town afire. The sultan of Mombasa wrote to the sultan of Malindi: "[They] raged in our town with such might and terror that no one, neither man nor woman, neither the old or the young, nor even the children, however small, was spared to live."[6]

To control commerce the Portuguese built fortified stations from which they attempted to collect tribute and maintain trade with the interior. An early station at Mozambique became the main port of call for vessels on the Asia route. In the 1590s the

Afonso Appeals to the King of Portugal

This is an excerpt from a long letter, written by a Kongo schoolboy who was a scribe for Don Afonso, the converted and disillusioned king of Kongo. The rest of the letter, dated October 5, 1514, contains many more complaints against Portuguese treachery and villainy.

We ask your Highness to demand of Fernão de Melo why he imprisoned our Dom Francisco, and why he did not allow him to proceed on your Highness' ships to the place we sent him, out of love—for your Highness had sent word that we should despatch 20 or 30 youths of our kin. And we sent our son to your Highness, so that he could present all the slaves and goods we were remitting—and Fernão de Melo did not wish to let him go, but kept him there on his island, with a stick in his hand, making him beg for the love of God—and likewise our nephews—for which reason we are keenly sorrowful. And as to the flesh, we feel much pain, because he is the fruit of our loins; but as to the soul, it grieves us not, for we sent our son to search for the things of God and learn them, and thus all the travails of the world that visit him, while he searches for the faith of our Lord Jesus Christ and learns it, we take to be blessings, and suffer them for the love of our Lord God, for He will ever remember us.

And now we beg of your Highness that, for the love of our Lord Jesus Christ, that you will not forsake us, nor allow the loss of the fruits of Christianity growing in our kingdom—for we can do no more, and have but one mouth to preach and instruct. We have already married, and all the nobles near us have been married—but those who are afar off do not want to be married, because of the evil examples they see every day, and they do not wish to obey us. So we ask your Highness to help us, so that we can make them get married. And if your Highness does not wish to help us in the spiritual realm, we will kiss your royal hands and ask that you send us five or six ships to take us and our sons and relatives, so that we will not witness so great a perdition. . . .

We shall not write more to your Highness because we would have need of a whole ream of paper to relate all the imbroglios that occur here, but Dom Pedro will give your Highness a detailed account of everything. And if anything in this letter be badly written, we ask pardon, because we do not know the styles of Portugal. And we write this with one of our schoolboys, for we do not dare to use any of the [Portuguese] men who are here, for those who best know how to write are guilty of one misdeed or another.

We would kiss the royal hands of your Highness if you would write a letter, on your own behalf, to the *Moynebata* Dom Jorge, and another to the *Moinepanguo*, who are the principal lords in our kingdom, in which your Highness would thank them for being good Christians, and also send them two priests, in addition to those sent to us, so that in their own churches they can say mass, hear confessions, and teach all the things pertaining to God's service. Your Highness should realize that these two lords live a good 80 or 90 leagues distant from us, and each of them has his own church wherein to see God. In both places we have put two schoolboys to teach them [the lords], and their sons and relatives. In this way we have begun the work there and may reap a great harvest. So now let your Highness see if you can complete it, for our powers are thinly spread out and that is all that we can do—but if they can have priests, to say mass to them and confess them, it will be of great merit and they will be strengthened.

From William H. McNeill and Mitsuko Iriye, eds., *Modern Asia and Africa* (New York: Oxford University Press, 1971), pp. 68–71.

Portuguese built a fort at Mombasa, hoping to intimidate other cities and support naval operations against Turks and Arabs in the Red Sea. Such efforts diminished the coastal trade but failed to achieve any military objectives. When Omani Arabs drove the Portuguese from the Swahili coast in 1698, a proverb captured Swahili sentiment: "Go away, Manuel [the king of Portugal], you have made us hate you; go, and carry your cross with you."[7]

On the southeast coast the Portuguese were lured by the gold trade with the Zimbabwean plateau. The Portuguese seized Sofala in 1506, diminishing the role of Muslim traders and positioning themselves as the middlemen for the gold trade with the coast. After establishing trading settlements along the Zambezi River at Sena and Tete, the Portuguese developed a close relationship with the Karanga kingdom of Mutapa, which received Portuguese traders and Catholic missionaries. This relationship soured when the king of Mutapa ordered a Jesuit missionary to be killed in 1560. In the 1570s the Portuguese retaliated by sending several expeditionary forces up the Zambezi to take over the gold mines. These adventures ended disastrously as drought, disease (especially

Discovery Through Maps

Sebastian Munster's Map of Africa

Born in Hesse, Germany, and educated at Heidelberg University, Sebastian Munster (1489–1552) established a reputation as a professor of Hebrew and mathematics at Heidelberg long before involving himself in mapmaking. A master of Latin and Greek as well as Hebrew, he published a Hebrew Bible and dictionary before settling in 1529 at Basel, the home of Switzerland's oldest university and a center of geographers and cartographers.

Munster became involved in maps through his interest in Ptolemy (90–168 C.E.), the celebrated astronomer, geographer, and mathematician of Alexandria, Egypt, whose theories about the universe influenced the European and Arab worlds for many centuries. Around 1400 Ptolemy's *Guide to Geography* was published in Florence as the first atlas of the world. Drawing on his linguistic skills, Munster translated his own version of Ptolemy's *Geography* from Greek into German and published four editions of it between 1540 and 1552.

Ptolemy's volume shaped Munster's views when he began creating his own atlas of the world. First published in 1544, Munster's *Cosmographia Universalis* went through 46 editions and was translated into six languages over the next century. It was the first collection to feature individual maps of Europe, Asia, the Americas, and Africa.

Munster's map of Africa relied not only on Ptolemy but also on Portuguese and Arab sources. However, it still contained many errors. Like the Catalan Atlas, Munster's map showed a mountain chain stretching across much of North Africa. The source of the Nile was identified far to the south. Based on the assumption that the Senegal and Niger Rivers in West Africa were connected, a river was shown flowing westward to the Atlantic.

The *Cosmographia* was also a descriptive geography, providing an accompanying narrative and drawings of prominent figures, the customs and manners of societies, and the products, animals, and plants of regions. Munster's Africa map showed a lone human figure that bore no resemblance to Africans and a large elephant at the southern end of the continent. His rendering of Africa conformed to Dean Swift's satirical lines:

So Geographers in Africa-Maps
With Savage-Pictures fill their Gaps;
And o'er unhabitable Downs
Place Elephants for want of Towns.

malaria), and African resisters decimated the Portuguese forces.

However, a series of internal rebellions and wars with neighboring states later forced Mutapa's rulers to turn to the Portuguese for assistance. In 1607 they signed a treaty that ceded control of the gold mines to the Portuguese. For the rest of the century the Portuguese regularly intervened in Mutapa's affairs until the forces of Mutapa and a rising power, Changamire, combined to expel the Portuguese from the Zimbabwean plateau.

Along the Zambezi River the Portuguese crown granted huge land concessions (prazos) to Portuguese settlers (prazeros) who ruled them as feudal estates. Over time, the prazeros loosened their ties with Portugal's officials and became virtually independent. In the absence of Portuguese women, prazeros intermarried with Africans and adopted African culture.

Ethiopia also attracted Portugal's attention. The tale of Prester John, the mythical Ethiopian Christian monarch who held the Muslims at bay, had long captivated Portugal's monarchs. Thus they responded positively when the Ethiopian empress Eleni made diplomatic overtures in 1513. However, a projected alliance was not completed for many years. In 1541 some 400 Portuguese musketeers helped the Ethiopian army defeat a Muslim army that had almost taken over the kingdom. The following year Muslim forces rallied and defeated a Portuguese force, killing its commander, Christopher da Gama, Vasco's son. Although the Ethiopians later pushed the Muslims out, Portuguese involvement with Ethiopia remained at a low level.

For the rest of the sixteenth century the primary European presence in Ethiopia was that of Catholic priests. Ultimately, a Spanish Jesuit delegation won favor with the Ethiopian royal family and secretly converted Emperor Susenyos (1604–1632). However, the zealous policies of Bishop Alphonso Mendez, head of the mission after 1625, led to rebellion and the emperor's abdication. Mendez tried to Catholicize the Ethiopian orthodox faith by reordaining Ethiopian priests, reconsecrating the churches, and banning circumcision. Susenyos's son, Fasilidas, responded by expelling the Jesuits. Ethiopia's rulers retreated from direct contacts with Europe and concentrated on consolidating their hold over the country.

The Portuguese impact on Africa was not as immediately disastrous as Spanish effects on the New World. The Portuguese did not have the manpower or arms to dictate the terms of trade with most African states. However, they did inflict severe damage in Kongo, Angola, Zimbabwe, and the Swahili city-states. Their most destructive involvement was the slave trade. By the end of the sixteenth century the Portuguese had moved an estimated 240,000 slaves from West and Central Africa; 80 percent were transported after 1575. These trends foreshadowed much greater disasters for African societies in the seventeenth and eighteenth centuries as the Atlantic slave trade expanded.

Beginnings of Northern European Expansion

European overseas expansion after 1600 entered a second phase, comparable to developments at home. As Spain declined, so did the Spanish Empire and that of Portugal, which was tied to Spain by a Habsburg king after 1580 and plagued with its own developing imperial problems. These conditions afforded opportunities for the northern European states. The Dutch between 1630 and 1650 almost cleared the Atlantic of Spanish warships while taking over most of the Portuguese posts in Brazil, Africa, and Asia. The French and English also became involved on a smaller scale, setting up a global duel for empire in the eighteenth century.

The Shifting Commercial Revolution

Along with this second phase of expansion came a decisive shift in Europe's Commercial Revolution. Expanding foreign trade, new products, an increasing supply of bullion, and rising commercial risks created new problems, calling for energetic initiatives. Because the Spanish and Portuguese during the sixteenth century had depended on quick profits, weak home industries, and poor management, wealth flowed through their hands to northern Europe, where it was invested in productive enterprises. Later it generated a new imperial age.

European markets after the sixteenth century were swamped with a bewildering array of hitherto rare or unknown goods. New foods from America included potatoes, peanuts, maize (Indian corn), tomatoes, and fish from Newfoundland's Grand Banks. In an era without refrigeration, imported spices, such as pepper, cloves, and cinnamon, were valued for making spoiled foods palatable. Sugar became a common substitute for honey, and the use of cocoa, the Aztec sacred beverage, spread throughout Europe. Coffee and tea from the New World and Asia would also soon change European social habits. Similarly, North American furs, Chinese silks, and cottons from India and Mexico revolutionized clothing fashions. Furnishings of rare woods and ivory and luxurious oriental carpets appeared more frequently in the homes of the wealthy. The use of American tobacco became almost a mania among all classes, further contributing to the booming European market.

Imported gold and, even more significant, silver probably affected the European economy more than all other foreign goods. After the Spaniards had looted Aztec and Inca treasure rooms, the gold flowing from America and Africa subsided to a respectable trickle; but 7 million tons of silver poured into Europe before 1660. Spanish prices quadrupled, and because most new bullion went to pay for imports, prices more than tripled in northern Europe. Rising inflation hurt landlords who depended on fixed rents and creditors who were paid in cheap money, but the bullion bonanza ended a centuries-long gold drain to the East, with its attendant money shortage. It also increased the profits of merchants selling on a rising market, thus greatly stimulating northern European capitalism.

At the opening of the sixteenth century, Italian merchants and moneylenders, mainly Florentines, Venetians, and Genoese, dominated the rising Atlantic economy. The German Fugger banking house at Augsburg also provided substantial financing. European bankers, particularly the Fuggers and the Genoese, suffered heavily from the Spanish economic debacles under Charles V and Philip II. As the century passed, Antwerp, in the southern Netherlands, became the economic hub of Europe. It was the center for the English wool trade as well as a transfer station, drawing southbound goods from the Baltic and Portuguese goods from Asia. It was also a great financial market, dealing in commercial and investment instruments. The Spanish sack of the city in 1576 ended Antwerp's supremacy, which passed to Amsterdam and furthered Dutch imperial ventures.

Meanwhile, northern European capitalism flourished in nearly every category. Portuguese trade in Africa and Asia was matched by that of the Baltic and the North Atlantic. Northern joint-stock companies pooled capital for privateering, exploring, and commercial venturing. The Dutch and English East India companies, founded early in the seventeenth century, were but two of the better-known stock companies. In England common fields were enclosed for capitalistic sheep runs. Throughout western Europe, domestic manufacturing, in homes or workshops, was competing with the guilds. Large industrial enterprises, notably in mining, shipbuilding, and cannon casting, were becoming common. Indeed, the superiority of English and Swedish cannons caused the defeat of the Spanish Armada and Catholic armies in the Thirty Years' War.

The Dutch Empire

By 1650 the Dutch were supreme in both southern Asia and the South Atlantic. Their empire, like that of the Portuguese earlier, was primarily commercial; even their North American settlements specialized in fur trading with the Indians. They acquired territory where necessary to further their commerce but tried

Dutch Exploration and Expansion

1576	Sack of Antwerp; Amsterdam becomes commercial hub of Europe
1595	First Dutch fleet enters East Indies
1609	Henry Hudson explores Hudson River
1621	Dutch form West India Company
1624	Dutch found New Amsterdam on Manhattan Island
1641	Dutch drive Portuguese out of Malacca

to act pragmatically in accordance with Indian cultures rather than by conquest. Unlike the Spanish and the Portuguese, the Dutch made little attempt to spread Christianity.

Systematic Dutch naval operations ended Iberian imperial supremacy, beginning in 1595 when the first Dutch fleet entered the East Indies. Dutch captains soon drove the Portuguese from the Spice Islands. Malacca, the Portuguese bastion, fell after a long siege in 1641. The Dutch also occupied Sri Lanka and blockaded Goa, thus limiting Portuguese operations in the Indian Ocean. Although largely neglecting East Africa, they seized all Portuguese posts on the west coast north of Angola. Across the Atlantic, they conquered Brazil, drove Spain from the Caribbean, and captured a Spanish treasure fleet. Decisive battles off the English Channel coast near Kent (1639) and off Brazil (1640) delivered final blows to the Spanish navy. What the English began in 1588, the Dutch completed 50 years later.

Trade with Asia, the mainstay of the Dutch Empire, was directed by the Dutch East India Company. Chartered in 1602 and given a monopoly over all operations between South Africa and the Strait of Magellan, it conserved resources and tended to eliminate costly competition. In addition to its trade and diplomacy, the company sponsored explorations of Australia, Tasmania, New Guinea, and the South Pacific. With a capital concentration larger than that of most states, it could easily outdistance its European rivals.

The Dutch Empire in the East was established primarily by Jan Pieterszoon Coen, governor-general of the Indies between 1618 and 1629 and founder of the company capital at Batavia in northwestern Java. At first he cooperated with local rulers in return for a monopoly over the spice trade. When this involved him in costly wars against local sultans as well as their Portuguese and English customers, Coen determined to control the trade at its sources. In the ensuing numerous conflicts and negotiations, which out-

Batavia (present-day Djakarta), on the island of Java, became the headquarters of the Dutch East India Company when the Dutch ousted the Portuguese and took command of the East Indies trade in the seventeenth century.

lasted Coen, the Dutch acquired all of Java, most of Sumatra, the spice-growing Moluccas, and part of Sri Lanka. They began operating their own plantations, supplying pepper, cinnamon, sugar, tea, tobacco, and coffee to a fluctuating world market.

Although commercially successful in Asia, the Dutch were not able to found flourishing colonial settlements. Many Dutchmen who went to the East wanted to make their fortunes and return home; those willing to stay were usually mavericks, uninterested in establishing families but instead pursuing temporary sexual liaisons with female slaves or servants. For a while after 1620 the company experimented with a policy of bringing European women to the Indies, but such efforts were abandoned when the venture failed to enlist much interest at home or in the foreign stations. Consequently, the Dutch colonies in Asia, as well as those in Africa, the Caribbean, and Brazil, remained primarily business ventures with little racial mixing, compared with the Iberian areas.

After resuming war with Spain in 1621, the Dutch formed their West India Company, charged with overtaking the diminishing Spanish and Portuguese holdings in West Africa and America. The company wasted no time. It soon supplanted the Portuguese in West Africa; by 1630 it had taken over the slave trade with America. After driving the Spanish from the Caribbean, the Dutch invited other European planters to the West Indies as customers, keeping only a few bases for themselves. The company then launched a successful naval conquest of Brazil, from the mouth of the Amazon south to the San Francisco River. In Brazil the Dutch learned sugar planting, passing on their knowledge to the Caribbean and applying it directly in the East Indies.

Dutch settlements in North America never amounted to much because of the company's commercial orientation. In 1609 Henry Hudson (d. 1611), an Englishman sailing for the Dutch, explored the river named for him and established Dutch claims while looking for a northwest passage. Fifteen years later the company founded New Amsterdam on Manhattan Island; over the next few years it built a number of frontier trading posts in the Hudson valley and on the nearby Connecticut and Delaware Rivers. Some attempts were made to encourage planting by selling large tracts to wealthy proprietors *(patroons)*. Agriculture, however, remained secondary to the fur trade, which the company developed in alliance with the Iroquois tribes. This arrangement hindered settlement; in 1660 only 5000 Europeans were in the colony.

The French Empire

French exploration began early, but no permanent colonies were established abroad until the start of the seventeenth century. The country was so weakened by religious wars that most of its efforts, beyond fishing, privateering, and a few failed attempts at settlement, had to be directed toward internal stability. While the Dutch were winning their empire, France was involved in the land campaigns of the Thirty Years' War. Serious French empire building thus had to be delayed until after 1650, during the reign of Louis XIV.

Early French colonization in North America was based on claims made by Giovanni da Verrazzano (1485–1528) and Jacques Cartier (1491–1557). The first, a Florentine mariner commissioned by Francis I in 1523, traced the Atlantic coast from North Carolina to Newfoundland. Eleven years later Cartier made one of two voyages exploring the St. Lawrence River. These French expeditions duplicated England's claim to eastern North America.

British and French Exploration and Colonization

1485–1528	Giovanni da Verrazzano
1491–1557	Jacques Cartier
1497–1498	John Cabot establishes English claims in North America
1567–1635	Samuel de Champlain
1605	French establish base at Port Royal, in Nova Scotia
1607	First English colony in North America founded at Jamestown
1627	British conquer Quebec
1629	Puritans settle near Boston
1632–1635	English Catholics found colony of Maryland
1642	Montreal established

French colonial efforts during the sixteenth century were dismal failures. They resulted partly from French experiences in exploiting the Newfoundland fishing banks and conducting an undeclared naval war in the Atlantic against Iberian treasure ships and trading vessels after 1520. In 1543 Cartier tried and failed to establish a colony in the St. Lawrence valley. Other such failures included a French colony in Brazil, terminated by the Portuguese (1555–1557), and an aborted Huguenot settlement in Florida (1562–1564). No more serious efforts were made until 1605, when a French base was established at Port Royal, on Nova Scotia. It was meant to be a fur-trading center and capital for the whole St. Lawrence region. Mapping of the coast was immediately begun, but the site was temporarily abandoned when its fur monopoly was canceled by the French government. The fort was restored after 1610, but it barely survived attacks by Amerindians and the English.

Three years after the founding of Port Royal, Samuel de Champlain (1567–1635), who had been an aide to the governor of the Nova Scotia colony, acted for a French-chartered company in founding Quebec on the St. Lawrence. The company brought in colonists, but the little community was disrupted in 1627 when British troops took the town and forced Champlain's surrender. Although the fort was returned to France by a treaty in 1629, when Champlain came back as governor, growth was slowed by the company's emphasis on fur trading, the bitterly cold winters, and skirmishes with Indians. Only a few settlers had arrived by Champlain's death in 1635, and just 2500 Europeans were in Quebec as late as 1663. Nevertheless, Montreal was established in 1642, after which French trapper-explorers began penetrating the region around the headwaters of the Mississippi.

An early drawing shows the arrival of the first French colonists in North America, brought by Cartier on his third voyage in 1541, against a map of the St. Lawrence estuary. The colony soon failed. (The map is drawn so that north is at the bottom of the drawing rather than at the top.)

Elsewhere the French seized opportunities afforded by the decline of Iberian sea power. They acquired the isle of Bourbon (Réunion) in the Indian Ocean (1642) for use as a commercial base. In West Africa they created a sphere of commercial interest at the mouth of the Senegal River, where they became involved in the slave trade with only slight opposition from the Dutch. Even more significant was the appearance of the French in the West Indies. They occupied part of St. Kitts in 1625 and acquired Martinique and Guadeloupe ten years later. Because the sugar boom was just beginning, the French islands would soon become very profitable. However, fierce attacks by warlike Caribs limited economic development in this era before 1650.

The English Empire

In terms of power and profit, English foreign expansion before 1650 was not impressive. Like French colonialism, it was somewhat restricted by internal political conditions, particularly the poor management and restrictive policies of the early Stuart kings, which led to civil war in the 1640s. A number of circumstances, however, promoted foreign ventures. The population increased from 3 to 4 million between 1530 and 1600, providing a large reservoir of potential indentured labor; religious persecution encouraged migration of nonconformists; and surplus capital was seeking opportunities for investment. Such conditions ultimately produced a unique explosion of English settlement overseas.

During the sixteenth century English maritime operations were confined primarily to exploring, fishing, smuggling, and plundering. English claims to North America were registered in 1497 and 1498 by two voyages of John Cabot, who explored the coast of North America from Newfoundland to Virginia but found no passage to Asia. For the next century English expeditions sought such a northern passage, both in the East and in the West. All of them failed, but they resulted in explorations of Hudson Bay and the opening of a northeastern trade route to Russia. From the 1540s English captains, including the famous John Hawkins of Plymouth, indulged in sporadic slave trading in Africa and the West Indies, despite Spanish restrictions. Subsequent raids against Spanish shipping by English "sea dogs," like Sir Francis Drake, helped prepare for the later dramatic defeat of the Armada.

After failures in Newfoundland and on the Carolina coast, the first permanent English colony in America was founded in 1607 at Jamestown, Virginia. For a number of years the colonists suffered from lack of food and other privations, but they were saved by their dauntless leader, Captain John Smith (1580–1631), whose romantic rescue by the Indian princess Pocahontas (1595–1617) is an American legend. Jamestown set a significant precedent for all English colonies in North America. By the terms of its original charter, the London Company, which founded the settlement, was authorized to supervise government for the colonists, but they were to enjoy all the rights of native Englishmen. Consequently, in 1619 the governor called an assembly to assist in governing. This body would later become the Virginia House of Burgesses, one of the oldest representative legislatures still operating.

Shortly after the founding of Jamestown, large-scale colonization began elsewhere. In 1620 a group of English Protestants known as Pilgrims landed at Plymouth. Despite severe hardships, they survived, and their experiences inspired other religious dissenters against the policies of Charles I. In 1629 a number of English Puritans formed the Massachusetts Bay Company and settled near Boston, where their charter gave them the rights to virtual self-government. From this first enclave, emigrants moved out to other areas in present-day Maine, Rhode Island, and Connecticut. By 1642 more than 25,000 people had migrated to New England, laying the foundations for a number of future colonies. Around the same time (1632–1635), a group of English Catholics, fleeing Stuart persecution, founded the Maryland colony. These enterprises firmly planted English culture and political institutions in North America.

Life in the English settlements was hard during those first decades, but a pioneering spirit and native colonial pride was already evident. Food was scarce, disease was ever-present, and Amerindians were often dangerous. Yet from the beginning, and more than in other European colonies, settlers looked to their future in the new land because they had left so little behind in Europe. Most were expecting to stay, establish homes, make their fortunes, and raise families. The first Puritans included both men and women; a shipload of "purchase brides" arrived in 1619 at Jamestown to lend stability to that colony. This was but the first of many such contingents, all eagerly welcomed by prospective husbands. In addition, many women came on their own as indentured servants.

Anglo-American colonial women faced discrimination but managed to cope with it pragmatically. They were legally dependent on their husbands, who controlled property and children; a widow acquired these rights, but it was not easy to outlive a husband. Hard work and frequent pregnancies—mothers with a dozen children were not uncommon—reduced female life expectancies. Nevertheless, many women developed a rough endurance, using their social value to gain confidence and practical equality with their husbands, although some did this more obviously than others. This independent spirit was revealed by Anne Hutchinson (1591–1643), who left

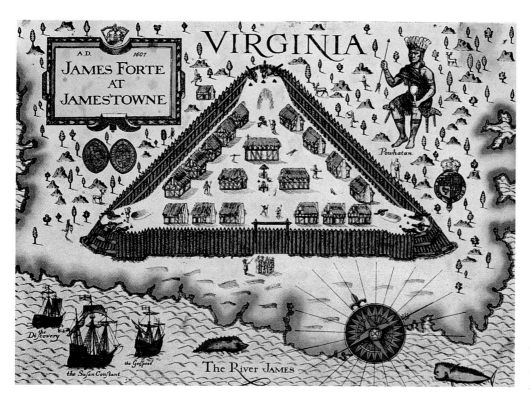

View of Jamestown in 1607 drawn by John Hull. Surrounded by water on three sides, the marshy peninsula on the James River seemed easy to defend and thus an ideal location for the Jamestown fort. By 1614 there were "two faire rowes of howses" protected by a palisade.

Massachusetts and founded a dissenting religious settlement in Rhode Island. Another freethinker was Anne Bradstreet (c. 1612–1672), who wrote thoughtful poetry, although painfully aware that men considered her presumptuous.

The English government considered the rough coasts and wild forests of North America less important in this period than footholds in the West Indies and Africa, where profits were expected in planting and slave trading. Therefore, a wave of English migrants descended on the West Indies after the Dutch opened the Caribbean. In 1613 English settlers invaded Bermuda, and by the 1620s others had planted colonies on St. Kitts, Barbados, Nevis, Montserrat, Antigua, and the Bahamas. Tobacco planting was at first the major enterprise, bringing some prosperity and the promise of more. The white population expanded dramatically, especially on Barbados, which was not subject to Carib Indian attacks. There the English population increased from 7000 to 37,000 in seven years. As yet, however, there were few African slaves on the English islands, although some were already being imported for the sugar plantations.

Meanwhile, English slaving posts in West Africa were beginning to flourish and English adventurers were starting operations in Asia. Captain John Lancaster took four ships to Sumatra and Java in 1601, returning with a profitable cargo of spices. His voyage led to the founding of the British East India Company, which was chartered in 1609. But expansion outside of the Caribbean was difficult because

the Dutch were uncooperative. In the Moluccas, for example, they drove out the English in the 1620s, after repeated clashes. The English fared better in India. By 1622 the British East India Company had put the Portuguese out of business in the Persian Gulf. Subsequently, the English established trading posts on the west coast of India at Agra, Masulipatam, Balasore, and Surat. The station at Madras, destined to become the English bastion on the east coast, was founded in 1639.

Conclusion

Between 1450 and 1650, the era of the early Commercial Revolution, Europeans faced west toward a new world and initiated a new age of oceanic expansion. In the process they stimulated capitalistic development, found a sea route to Asia, became more familiar with Africa, began colonizing America, and proved the world to have a spherical surface. For most of the period Spain and Portugal monopolized the new ocean trade and profited most from exploiting American wealth, following precedents set by earlier Eurasian empires. Only after 1600, when leadership shifted toward the Dutch, French, and English, did European colonialism show signs of developing in new directions.

Overseas expansion exerted a tremendous effect on European culture and institutions. Spain's political predominance in the sixteenth century was

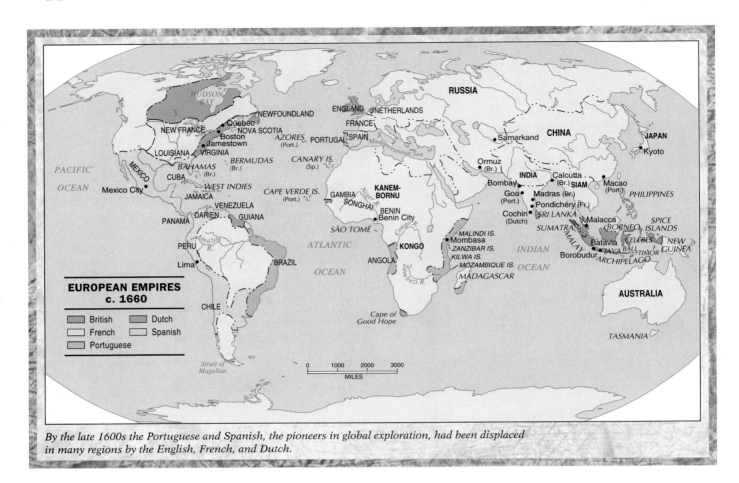

**EUROPEAN EMPIRES
c. 1660**

- British
- French
- Portuguese
- Dutch
- Spanish

By the late 1600s the Portuguese and Spanish, the pioneers in global exploration, had been displaced in many regions by the English, French, and Dutch.

largely bought with American treasure, and Spain's quick decline was mainly caused by the influx of American bullion, which inflated Spanish money and discouraged Spanish economic development. Northern European capitalism, developing in financial organization, shipbuilding, metalworking, manufacturing, and agriculture, brought a new vitality to northern economies in response to Spanish and Portuguese purchasing power. Economic advantages also contributed to Protestant victories in the Thirty Years' War. This first age of the Commercial Revolution increased northern European confidence and initiative in preparation for later world dominance.

In the New World the European impact was both dramatic and tragic. Spanish *conquistadores* and Portuguese captains nearly destroyed native peoples and subjected most of the survivors to terrible hardships, indignities, cultural deprivations, and psychological injuries. The plight of Latin American peasants today began in Spanish and Portuguese imperial policies of the sixteenth century. Yet the balance sheet is not all negative. The Spanish and Portuguese in America generated a new cultural synthesis, blending European, Amerindian, and African elements to produce a richness and variety not present in any of

the parent cultures. This integration was largely accomplished by racial mixing, which created a new Latin American stock in the Western Hemisphere.

The European impact on Africa was less apparent at the time but perhaps more damaging in the long run than what happened to the Amerindians of Latin America. When the Portuguese began exploring the African coastline, they were more concerned with scoring quick profits through gold exports than with establishing stable, long-term relationships with African states. Moreover, with the exception of Angola or landed estates along the Zambezi River, the Portuguese did not have the manpower or resources to conquer or influence the political affairs of African states. However, as the Atlantic slave trade increased, the Portuguese and leaders of African states became bound up in a destructive process that would reach its tragic climax in the next few centuries.

In Asia the European impact before 1650 was mixed. Sri Lanka and the Spice Islands of the Malay archipelago, which were vulnerable to sea attack, came under domination, direct or indirect, and were exploited by the Portuguese and the Dutch. Elsewhere in Asia the European influence was present but less obvious. The Portuguese were run out of

China twice before they came to respect Chinese law, and other Europeans fared worse. All were ultimately excluded from Japan. Southern India was not entirely open, as the Portuguese found by the end of the period. In the main, Turks, Arabs, Chinese, Japanese, Thais, and Vietnamese felt superior to Europeans and were usually able to defend their interests with effective action.

Suggestions for Reading

An excellent work, which covers the whole subject of European exploration and colonization, is Geoffrey V. Scammell, *The First Imperial Age: European Overseas Expansion, 1400–1700* (Unwin Hyman, 1989). See also the two classic studies, Charles E. Nowell, *The Great Discoveries and the First Colonial Empires*, rev. ed. (Greenwood, 1982), and Samuel Eliot Morison, *The European Discovery of America*, in two volumes: *The Northern Voyages* (Oxford University Press, 1971) and *The Southern Voyages* (Oxford University Press, 1974). A briefer but still reliable and interesting volume along the same lines is Samuel Eliot Morison, *The Great Explorers* (Oxford University Press, 1978). A number of other surveys are well worth consulting: Geoffrey V. Scammell, *The World Encompassed: The First European Maritime Empires, c. 800–1650* (University of California Press, 1981); Louis B. Wright, *Gold, Glory, and Gospel* (Atheneum, 1970); Daniel Devine, *The Opening of the World: The Great Age of Maritime Exploration* (Putnam, 1973); and Daniel J. B. Boorstin, *The Discoverers* (Random House, 1985).

For more pointed analyses of early European imperialism, see Carlo M. Cipolla, *Guns, Sails and Empires*, rev. ed. (Sunflower University Press, 1985); William H. McNeil, *Plagues and People* (Doubleday, 1977); Eric R. Wolf, *Europe and the People Without History* (University of California Press, 1982); and Nicholas Canny and Anthony Pagden, *Colonial Identity in the Atlantic World* (Princeton University Press, 1989).

Two time-tested secondary sources on the Iberian New World are H. Hering, *A History of Latin America* (Knopf, 1968), and Stanley J. Stein and Barbara H. Stein, *The Colonial Heritage of Latin America* (Oxford University Press, 1970). To these may be added a number of excellent later studies: Tzvetan Todorov, *The Conquest of America* (Harper & Row, 1984); Lyle N. McAlister, *Spain and Portugal in the New World, 1492–1700* (University of Minnesota Press, 1984); and Mark A. Burkholder, *Colonial Latin America* (Oxford University Press, 1989). For penetrating studies of Latin American social conditions, see two edited collections by Louisa Hoberman and Susan M. Socolow, *Cities and Society in Colonial Latin America* (University of New Mexico Press, 1986) and *The Countryside in Colonial America* (University of New Mexico Press, 1996). The complex issues relating to slavery and plantations are ably identified and evaluated in W. R. Aykroyd, *Sweet Malefactor: Sugar, Slavery, and Human Society* (Heinemann, 1967); Eric Williams, *From Columbus to Castro*, rev. ed. (Random House, 1984); and Herbert S. Klein, *African Slavery in Latin America and the Caribbean* (Oxford University Press, 1988). On the ambiguous status of women, see Ann M. Pescatello, *Power and Pawn: The Female in Iberian Families* (Greenwood, 1976), and Asuncion Lavin, ed., *Latin American Women* (Greenwood, 1978).

A general overview of Spanish empire building in America is provided in Colin M. MacLachlan, *Spain's Empire in the New World* (University of California Press, 1988). Three earlier works are also worth attention: Oskar H. K. Spate, *The Spanish*

Lake (University of Minnesota Press, 1979); J. H. Parry, *The Spanish Seaborne Empire* (Knopf, 1971); and Charles Gibson, *Spain in America* (Harper Torchbooks, 1968). Gianni Granzotto, *Christopher Columbus* (University of Oklahoma Press, 1988), reveals the world of Columbus and a personalized account of his exploits. Other works on Columbus and his voyages are David Henige, *In Search of Columbus: The Sources for the First Voyage* (University of Arizona Press, 1991); Joseph Schnaubelt and Frederick Van Fleteren, *Columbus and the New World* (Long, 1998); and John Yewell, Chris Dodge, and Jan De Surey, *Confronting Columbus: An Anthology* (McFarland, 1992).

On the whole subject of Spanish campaigns in the New World, William H. Prescott, *The Conquest of Mexico* (Bantam, 1964) and *The Conquest of Peru* (Mentor, 1961), are readable abridgments of memorable and dramatic historical classics. See also Frederick A. Kirkpatrick, *The Spanish Conquistadores* (Meridian, 1962); Ross Hassig, *Mexico and the Spanish Conquest* (Longman, 1994); and James Muldoon, *The Americas in the Spanish World Order: The Justification for Conquest in the Seventeenth Century* (University of Pennsylvania Press, 1994). Luis Martin, *Daughters of the Conquistadores* (Southern Methodist University Press, 1989), documents the significant role of women in the grueling process, and Nathan Wachtel, *Vision of the Vanquished* (Barnes & Noble, 1977), shows the Amerindians' views of their new masters. On the Spanish conquest of Mesoamerica, see Inga Clendinnen, *Ambivalent Conquest: Maya and Spaniard in Yucatán, 1517–1570* (Cambridge University Press, 1989); Kenneth Pearce, *The View from the Top of the Temple* (University of New Mexico Press, 1984); T. R. Fehrenbach, *Fire and Blood: A History of Mexico* (Da Capo, 1995); Jon M. White, *Cortés and the Downfall of the Aztec Empire* (Carrol & Graf, 1989); Maurice Collis, *Cortés and Montezuma* (Clark, 1994); and Hugh Thomas, *Conquest: Montezuma, Cortés, and the Fall of Old Mexico* (Simon & Schuster, 1993). Good coverage of the Spanish campaigns in Peru is provided in Bernabé Cobo, *History of the Inca Empire* (University of Texas Press, 1979); Ian Cameron, *The Kingdom of the Sun God* (Facts on File, 1990); Susan Ramirez, *The World Upside Down: Cross-Cultural Contact and Conflict in Sixteenth-Century Peru* (Stanford University Press, 1996); and Rafael Gabai, *Francisco Pizarro and His Brothers: The Illusion of Power in Sixteenth-Century Peru* (University of Oklahoma Press, 1997).

For more focused treatments of the colonial development of New Spain, see Peggy K. Liss, *Mexico Under Spain* (University of Chicago Press, 1984), and James M. Lockhart, *Spanish Peru, 1532–1600* (University of Wisconsin Press, 1968). On political, economic, and social conditions, see Jonathan I. Israel, *Race, Class, and Politics in Colonial Mexico* (Oxford University Press, 1975); Leslie B. Simpson, *The Encomienda in New Spain*, 3rd ed. (University of California Press, 1982); Ross Hassig, *Trade, Tribute, and Transportation in the Sixteenth-Century Political Economy of the Valley of Mexico* (University of Oklahoma Press, 1985); and William I. Sherman, *Forced Native Labor in Sixteenth-Century Central America* (University of Nebraska Press, 1979). The following works effectively depict the racial and cultural synthesis in colonial Mexico: Colin MacLachlan and James E. Rodriguez, *The Forging of the Cosmic Race* (University of California Press, 1980); S. L. Cline, *Colonial Culhacán, 1580–1600: A Social History of an Aztec Town* (University of New Mexico Press, 1986); Jacques Lafaye, *Quetzalcoatl and Guadalupe: The Formation of Mexican National Consciousness* (University of Chicago Press, 1987); and Edward Murguca, *Assimilation, Colonialism, and the Mexican American People* (University Press of America, 1989).

Three respected works on Portuguese exploration and colonization are Samuel Eliot Morison, *Portuguese Voyagers to America in the Fifteenth Century* (Octagon, 1965); Charles R.

Boxer, *Four Centuries of Portuguese Expansion* (University of California Press, 1969); and Malyn Newitt, *The First Portuguese Colonial Empire* (Humanities Press, 1986). On the Portuguese in Asia, see Gerald R. Crone, *The Discovery of the East* (St. Martin's Press, 1972); K. M. Matthew, *History of Portuguese Navigation in India* (South Asia Books, 1987); and Charles R. Boxer, *The Christian Century of Japan* (University of California Press, 1974). On Portugal's policies in America, see E. Bradford Burns, *A History of Brazil* (Columbia University Press, 1970), and Dagmar Schaeffer, *Portuguese Exploration in the West and the Formation of Brazil, 1450–1800* (Brown, 1988). For Portugal's impact on Africa, see Malyn Newitt, *Portuguese Settlement on the Zambesi* (Longman, 1973). An interesting and informative biography is Elaine Sanceau, *Henry the Navigator* (Archon Books, 1969).

For the best treatment of developing African culture during the era of European expansion, see works cited in Chapter 11, particularly Robert W. July, *A History of the African People* (Scribner, 1980). The calamities accompanying Portuguese policies in west central Africa are graphically described in John Thornton, *Kingdom of the Kongo* (University of Wisconsin Press, 1983), and Anne Hilton, *The Kingdom of Kongo* (Oxford University Press, 1985). On early slavery and the slave trade, see Barbara Solow, ed., *Slavery and the Rise of the Atlantic System* (Cambridge University Press, 1991); Charles R. Boxer, *Race Relations in the Portuguese Colonial Empire*, rev. ed. (Greenwood, 1985); and Patrick Manning, *Slavery and African Life* (Cambridge University Press, 1990).

A good survey of Dutch imperial development is Charles R. Boxer, *The Dutch Seaborne Empire* (Penguin, 1989). See also Charles R. Boxer, *The Dutch in Brazil* (Archon Books, 1973); Pieter Geyl, *The Netherlands in the Seventeenth Century* (Barnes & Noble, 1961); and Charles Wilson, *The Dutch Republic* (McGraw-Hill, 1968).

A sound treatment of French colonialism in America is William J. Eccles, *France in America* (Michigan State University Press, 1990). See also John Hopkins Kennedy, *Jesuit and Savage in New France* (Archon Books, 1971), and George W. Wrong, *Rise and Fall of New France* (Octagon Books, 1970).

Angus Calder, *Revolutionary Empire* (Dutton, 1981), is a sweeping study of expanding English culture from the fifteenth to the eighteenth century. Barry Coward, *The Stuart Age* (Longman, 1984), deals effectively with expansion but also provides significant English economic, social, and political backgrounds. See also John Bowle, *The Imperial Achievement* (Little, Brown, 1974), and William Abbot, *The Colonial Origins of the United States* (Wiley, 1975). Carl Bridenbaugh, *Vexed and Troubled Englishmen* (Oxford University Press, 1968), provides a penetrating analysis of perspectives among English colonists. For excellent special studies, see Alden T. Vaughn, *Captain John Smith and the Founding of Virginia* (Little, Brown, 1975);

Grace Woodward, *Pocahontas* (University of Oklahoma Press, 1980); and Cyril Hamshere, *The British in the Caribbean* (Harvard University Press, 1972).

Suggestions for Web Browsing

Age of Discovery
http://www.win.tue.nl/cs/fm/engels/discovery/#age

An excellent collection of resources that includes text, images, and maps relating to the early years of European expansion.

Internet Medieval History Sourcebook: Exploration and Expansion
http://www.fordham.edu/halsall/sbook1z.html

Extensive on-line source for links about Western exploration and expansion, including primary documents by or about da Gama, Columbus, Drake, and Magellan.

Columbus Navigation Home Page
http://www1.minn.net/~keithp/

Extensive information regarding the life and voyages of Christopher Columbus.

Internet African History Sourcebook
http://www.fordham.edu/halsall/africa/africasbook.html

Extensive on-line source for links about African history, including primary documents about the slave trade and by people who opposed it, supported it, and were its victims.

Notes

1. Daniel J. B. Boorstin, *The Discoverers* (New York: Random House, 1985), p. 178.
2. Colin McEvedy and Richard Jones, *Atlas of World Population History* (New York: Penguin, 1978), pp. 100–103.
3. Quoted in H. Hering, *A History of Latin America* (New York: Knopf, 1968), p. 173.
4. For the conservative estimate, see McEvedy and Jones, *Atlas of World Population*, pp. 272–273. For the higher estimate, see Patrick Manning, *Slavery and African Life* (New York: Cambridge University Press, 1978), p. 31.
5. Quoted in David Killingray, *A Plague of Europeans* (New York: Penguin, 1973), p. 20.
6. Quoted in Robert Rotberg, *A Political History of Tropical Africa* (New York: Harcourt Brace, 1965), pp. 85–86.
7. Quoted in John Middleton, *The World of the Swahili: An African Mercantile Civilization* (New Haven, Conn.: Yale University Press, 1992), pp. 46–47.

Islam shares the story of Adam and Eve with Christianity and Judaism, with certain variations. In this Persian manuscript Adam rides a dragonlike serpent and Eve rides a peacock; these two beasts facilitated the entrance of Iblis [Satan] into the Garden of Eden.

Detail. Freer Gallery of Art and Arthur M. Sackler Gallery Archives Smithsonian Institution.

The Islamic Gunpowder Empires, 1300–1650

Chapter Contents

By the fourteenth century the waves of migration and conquest out of central Asia that had established the Mongol Empire and altered the political configurations of the Islamic world were mostly over. Late in that century a new conqueror called Timur began a campaign that ravaged northern India, Persia, Iraq, and Anatolia; but his empire was not enduring. In the fifteenth and sixteenth centuries, however, three great Turkic empires gained preeminence in the old Mongol and Byzantine domains. The Ottoman, Safavid, and Mughul Empires flourished on the bases of preexisting civilizations, Turco-Mongol military organization, and enhanced firepower; in the process they also crafted a new cultural synthesis. These empires are sometimes called the "gunpowder empires" because, like their European counterparts, they incorporated gunpowder weaponry into their traditional military systems. All three formed parts of a vast trading network reaching from the Pacific to the Atlantic. At the same time that the Ming Chinese (see Chapter 18) were launching voyages that reached the East African coast, the Ottoman Turks were building an empire in the eastern Mediterranean that in the sixteenth century would dominate the region and challenge the Portuguese in the Indian Ocean.

Europeans were active in Asia during this period but exerted relatively little influence. Awed by the wealth and power of Muslim empires, they were generally held in disdain by Asian elites, who considered their own cultures superior. Akbar, the great Mughul emperor, referred to the "savage Portuguese" at his court,[1]

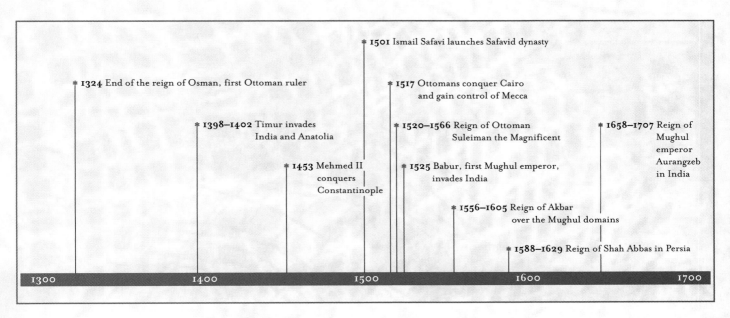

* **1501** Ismail Safavi launches Safavid dynasty

* **1324** End of the reign of Osman, first Ottoman ruler

* **1517** Ottomans conquer Cairo and gain control of Mecca

* **1398–1402** Timur invades India and Anatolia

* **1520–1566** Reign of Ottoman Suleiman the Magnificent

* **1658–1707** Reign of Mughul emperor Aurangzeb in India

* **1453** Mehmed II conquers Constantinople

* **1525** Babur, first Mughul emperor, invades India

* **1556–1605** Reign of Akbar over the Mughul domains

* **1588–1629** Reign of Shah Abbas in Persia

| 1300 | 1400 | 1500 | 1600 | 1700 |

Ottoman sultans regarded European envoys as suppliants, and the Safavid shah kept English merchants waiting for weeks while he attended to more important matters.

These were the dominant Asian empires that aspired to world power in this era. They would later be challenged and supplanted by European states also seeking dominion in the midst of a global economic revolution. But in the sixteenth century Asian empires held primacy of place in the contest for world power, controlling the land and sea routes of the East-West trade.

New Polities in Eurasia

For the kingdoms of Europe, the Ottoman conquest of Constantinople in 1453 signaled a catastrophe: the end of the Eastern Roman Empire and a disruption in established commercial patterns. Preachers and writers in Europe depicted the Ottoman victories as a type of divine punishment for the sins of Christendom. Even more significant, the Ottomans symbol-ized a new Muslim world emerging between the eastern Mediterranean and Southeast Asia. In that expansive territory, the three new empires held sway for centuries. Geographically, this world was centered in Persia, under its Shi'ite Safavid dynasty. Culturally, it was influenced by Persian, Arab, and Byzantine courtly traditions. To the east, the magnificent Mughul Empire emerged on the frontiers of Hindu and Confucian polities. Militarily, this Muslim world was dominated by the forces of the Ottoman Empire, which were far more formidable than those of any country in Europe at the time. War often raged among these contending states. Nevertheless, they shared the Islamic faith, common steppe antecedents, and Persian art traditions.

Background: The Steppe Frontier

After the mid-fourteenth century, tumultuous conditions in central Asia helped generate the Muslim empires to the south. The fragmented Mongol Empire left the steppe politically divided into states that dis-

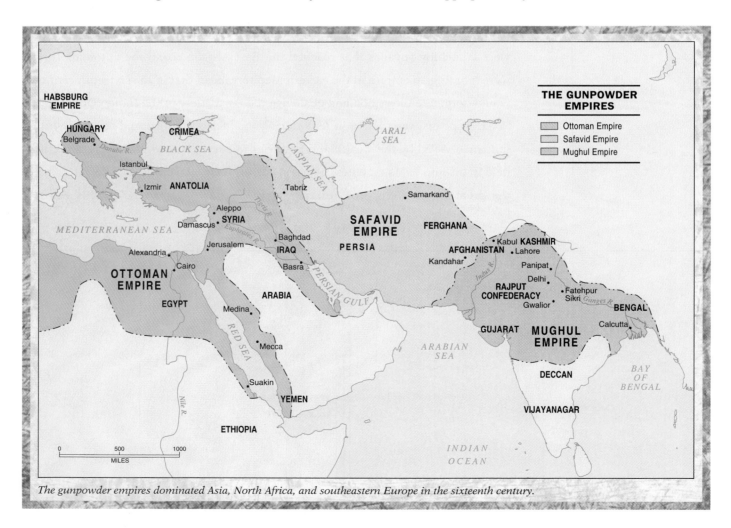

The gunpowder empires dominated Asia, North Africa, and southeastern Europe in the sixteenth century.

solved and re-formed in new combinations. While the old khanates survived for a while, war was almost continuous along the southern steppe frontier, from the Crimea to China.

The continuing steppe influence was well illustrated by the quick rise and collapse of the Timurid Empire at the close of the fourteenth century. Timur the Lame, the "Tamerlane" celebrated in Western literature, who claimed descent from Genghis Khan, rose to power during the 1370s as an *emir* (commander) in the Chaghatai khanate of central Asia. In his quest to restore the original Mongol Empire, Timur led whirlwind campaigns through the western steppe, the Crimea, Persia, and Anatolia. He crushed Ottoman resistance and carted the defeated Ottoman sultan, Bayezid I, off across Anatolia in a cage, subjecting him to ridicule. Timur terrorized northern India and was planning to invade Ming China when he died in 1405. But once Timur's army withdrew, the leaders who had submitted to him were less likely to comply with his demands. A conqueror's real domains were those from which he could collect taxes and levy troops.

For more than a century after Timur had resurrected the spirit of Genghis Khan, a dream of universal empire lingered in the minds of his descendants, real or imagined, among the many Turco-Mongol rulers in northern Persia and Transoxiana to its east. The Ottoman sultans, who had established their hegemony in Asia Minor before Timur's time and only barely survived his onslaught, were not direct heirs of his traditions, but they too aspired to the conquests and prestige of Genghis Khan and Alexander the Great. Russia and particularly northern India, where Muslim regimes took hold after Timur's armies devastated Delhi in 1398, were also sites of a renewed struggle for power.

Drastic change marked the steppe frontier after the late fifteenth century as populations settled around cities and firearms moderated the advantages of tribal cavalry. Indeed, the Uzbeks, who seized most of Transoxiana in this era, were among the last steppe conquerors. Like their predecessors, they were integrated into the courtly cultures of the lands they conquered. But long after the Uzbek conquest, old nomadic traditions continued to shape the rituals and military ethos of Turco-Mongol dynasties.

This miniature painting depicts the envoy of Timur at the court of the Ottoman sultan Bayezid I. The sultan is surrounded by his courtiers, with pages to his right and janissaries, arquebusiers, and officials in the foreground. Bayezid looks imposing, but he was defeated and killed by Timur.

The Ottoman Empire

The most powerful of the new Muslim empires was that of the Ottoman Turks. Centered in Anatolia, its military might cast long shadows over southeastern Europe, western Asia, and North Africa. In the middle of the sixteenth century the Ottoman patrimony stretched from Hungary to Ethiopia and from the borders of Morocco to Arabia and Iraq.

The origin myth of the Ottomans suggests the unique role that both the central Asian warrior traditions and Sufi Islam played in the legitimation of kingship. The founder of the Ottoman line was called Osman. According to legend, he was a valiant young warrior, fighting as a Seljuk subordinate on the frontiers of the Byzantine Empire in the late thirteenth century. Osman had, as a warrior must, a good horse, a strong arm, and a loyal companion. He fell in love

The Ottomans

c. 1281   Osman establishes the Ottoman dynasty

1453   Ottomans capture Constantinople

1517   Sultan Selim conquers Cairo, becomes Protector of the Holy Cities

1520–1566   Reign of Suleiman the Magnificent, Ottoman Golden Age

with the daughter of a revered Sufi *shaykh* and asked for her hand in marriage. Her father refused; but that night the *shaykh* dreamed that he saw the moon descending on his sleeping daughter, merging into her breast. From this union grew a huge and imposing tree that spread its branches over many lands and many flowing streams. When he awoke, the *shaykh* decided to approve the marriage.

Dreams play an important role in Middle Eastern literatures, and many kings took the interpretation of dreams seriously. The legend of the *shaykh's* dream linked the warrior tradition to the mystical religious authority of the Sufis, thus legitimizing Osman's rule. His dynasty, like the tree, did endure and expand to control many and prosperous territories. As the dynasty grew more powerful, the Ottomans also falsified a genealogy linking them to the prophet Muhammad. This Ottoman claim, like Timur's claim to be a descendent of Genghis Khan, also lent an aura of legitimacy to their rule. The Ottomans were not the first or the last family to imagine for themselves illustrious ancestors. Osman's line was spectacularly successful; it ruled for over six centuries, from the late thirteenth century until World War I.

Osman's successors won independence from their Seljuk Turk overlords and gradually conquered the surrounding principalities. They had gained control over most of Asia Minor when Timur's army invaded Anatolia, defeated the Ottomans, and forced a half century of internal restoration. Then two remarkable sultans resumed the Ottoman conquests.

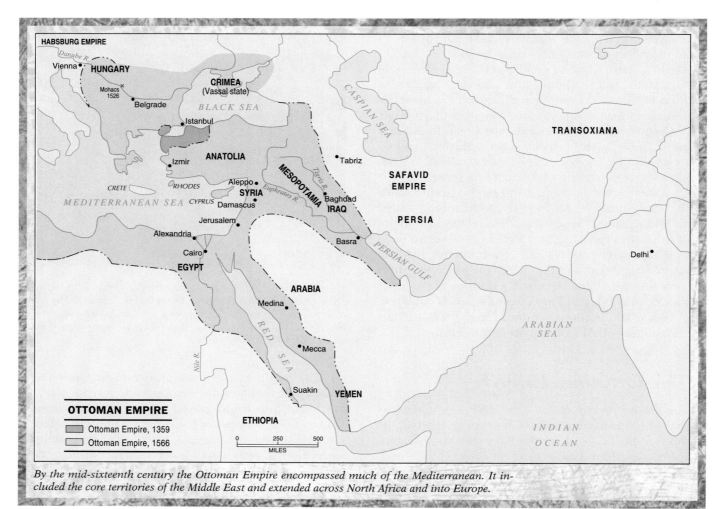

By the mid-sixteenth century the Ottoman Empire encompassed much of the Mediterranean. It included the core territories of the Middle East and extended across North Africa and into Europe.

Discovery Through Maps

The World Map of Piri Reis

Western historiography has highlighted Europeans' "discovery" of the New World. But the Age of Discovery produced many visions of the world, only some of which were preoccupied with the Americas. Ottoman cartographers were interested in the Americas, although Ottoman ambitions for conquest were directed primarily eastward to Asia. Mapping in this era was intimately associated with the objectives of merchants and sailors, and the most famous of Ottoman cartographers was a skilled sea captain named Piri Reis. Like other members of the Ottoman military-administrative class, Piri Reis was a man of diverse talents. In 1517, when his sovereign, Sultan Selim, conquered Cairo, Piri Reis presented him with a parchment map of the world, only part of which survives. The segment reproduced here shows the Atlantic Ocean, the western shores of Africa and Europe, and the eastern shores of South and Central America. Piri Reis map incorporates elaborate illustrations of ships, kings, wildlife, and mythical creatures. It depicts strange tales (like the sailors who landed on a whale's back, mistaking it for an island, at top left) and gives nautical distances. The cartographer provided a list of 20 Western and Islamic sources he consulted, including a map of Christopher Columbus. Piri Reis's map suggests the currents of shared knowledge that linked the scholars, merchants, and sailors of Asia, Africa, and Europe at this time. The boundaries of scholarship were fluid, and learned men eagerly sought out new information. Cartographers like Piri Reis benefited from and contributed to the knowledge assembled by peoples of many nations and religions.

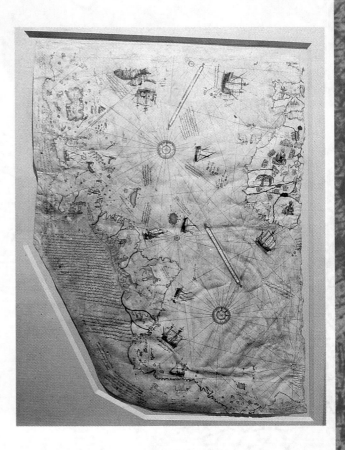

For the sailor or merchant, any map that was more accurate, regardless of its provenance (Portuguese, Ottoman, Christian, Muslim), was a tool for ensuring a more successful and safer journey.

The first, Mehmed II (second reign 1451–1481), took Constantinople, Romania, and the Crimea. The second, Selim I (1512–1520), annexed Kurdistan, northern Iraq, Syria, and Egypt. Mehmed's conquests terrorized European Christendom and brought the Ottoman state considerable wealth and prestige. The sultan repopulated Constantinople, now called Istanbul, using a combination of tax breaks and forced population transfers. The declining but intrepid old warrior was planning new campaigns when he died.

Mehmed's son, Bayezid II, acquired further territories and built up a powerful fleet. Then Selim's conquest of Egypt and Arabia brought added prestige: control of another great imperial capital, Cairo, and

claim to the title Custodian of the Holy Cities (Mecca and Medina), coveted by all Muslim monarchs. It also gave him control over the wealth and grain of Egypt and all the Mediterranean outlets of the eastern trade in spices, textiles, and jewels. Under Selim, the Ottoman navy dominated the eastern Mediterranean.

Ottoman power increased under Selim's only son, Suleiman (1520–1566). This determined campaigner soon became the most feared ruler among a generation of monarchs that included Henry VIII of England, Francis I of France, and Charles V of Spain. Suleiman's estimation of his own supremacy is illustrated in a letter to the French monarch in which Suleiman claimed glorious and elaborate titles but addressed Francis simply as "King."

Suleiman extended all his borders, particularly those touching Habsburg lands in Europe. After taking Belgrade in 1521 and the island of Rhodes from the Knights of St. John in 1522, he invaded Hungary in 1526 with 100,000 men and 300 artillery pieces. At Mohacs the Turks won an overwhelming victory, slaughtering thousands of Hungarian nobles and their king. Hungary was then integrated into the Ottoman Empire. Suleiman continued threatening Habsburg interests and European commerce in the Mediterranean. Meanwhile, his forces took Iraq from the Safavids, thus acquiring access to the Persian Gulf. This monarch, who built the great wall around Jerusalem that is still standing today, claimed to be "Lord of the two lands and two seas." His conquests provoked conflicts with the Portuguese in the Red Sea and Indian Ocean. The Portuguese imagined taking Mecca to chastise the "heathen" Ottomans, but no such attack ever materialized.

Suleiman responded harshly to challenges to his authority. He executed his own favorite son and a grandson who rebelled against him. The sultan lived amid pomp and splendor exceeding that of Louis XIV's France. An army of servants awakened, bathed, dressed, and entertained him. At meals, each course was served on silver, gold, and fine porcelain, while a physician stood by, ready to minister instantly against poisoning. In the hours between waking and sleeping, Suleiman met with advisers and petitioners, read, or listened to music. For amusement he watched wrestling matches and listened to court poets and jesters. Trained in the fine art of goldsmithing, Suleiman also wrote poetry and had a keen interest in maps. Foreign ambassadors, such as those from the French king or Habsburg emperor, had to prostrate themselves before the sultan, an indication of the perceived balance of power. European observers commented on the intimidating nature of a visit to Suleiman's court where thousands of massed troops would stand for hours in absolute silence. In Europe he was known as Suleiman the Magnificent; in the Ottoman Empire he was called Suleiman the Lawgiver.

The Empire Under Suleiman

Suleiman governed the mightiest state of his day. Extending from Poland to Yemen and from Persia to Tripoli, it included 21 provinces and many linguistic and ethnic groups, such as Magyars, Armenians, Bosnians, Albanians, Greeks, Tartars, Kurds, Arabs, Copts, and Jews. "Multiculturalism," often thought of

Terms Integral to the Ottoman Empire

Bey:	Ottoman provincial governor
Darwish:	a Sufi
Devshirme:	special Ottoman levy of non-Muslim boys destined for the janissary corps and palace service
Dhimmi:	non-Muslim subject of a Muslim state
Emir:	commander (same as amir)
Janissaries:	Ottoman elite infantry corps armed with gunpowder weapons
Jizya:	special head tax charged to non-Muslim subjects of Muslim states
Kadi:	(same as qadi) Islamic judge; member of the ulama
Pasha:	Ottoman military commander (governor) of high rank
Sharia:	Islamic law
Sipahi:	Ottoman "feudal" cavalry
Timar:	a type of military "fief" assigned to members of the Ottoman "feudal" cavalry in return for military service
Ulama:	Muslim religious authorities; men versed in the religious sciences and the law

An illuminated tughra *of Sultan Suleiman. The* tughra *was the sultan's signature, used to validate imperial documents and mark coinage. It included the sultan's name and his father's name and designated the sultan as "eternally victorious." The palace employed hundreds of artists, including the designers who fashioned and illuminated such beautiful* tughras.

Tughra, (calligraphic emblem) of Suleiman the Magnificent, Sultan of Turkey (1520–1566); from an imperial edict. Ink, colors, and gold on paper. The Metropolitan Museum of Art, Rogers Fund, 1938. (38.149.1) Photograph © 1986 The Metropolitan Museum of Art.

as a twentieth-century concept, was in fact typical of the various large agrarian empires of this age. Economically, Suleiman's empire was nearly self-sufficient, with expanding production and flourishing trade. It produced grain surpluses that gave the Ottomans considerable leverage in the Mediterranean region, where grain shortages were endemic. The Ottoman dominions produced annual revenues greater than those available to any contemporary European monarch.

Power in such a far-flung empire could never be absolute. The sultan delegated authority to local governors and to his top military-administrative officials *(pashas)*. Rule in distant provinces, like Egypt, was more flexible and less direct. Conquered lands closer to the capital were given to Ottoman "fief" holders *(sipahis)*, who were expected to bring cavalry contingents for military campaigns. At other times they lived on their lands *(timars)*, administering local affairs, collecting taxes, and keeping order. Unlike European feudal lords, they were not usually local residents and were often away in distant wars. Provincial governors *(pashas* or *beys)* were drawn from the higher-ranking Ottoman commanders. All members of this governing class were thus heavily dependent on the sultan, who might suddenly change their assignments or cancel their holdings. By Suleiman's reign, the political power of the *sipahis* over their *timars* had been partly usurped by the sultan's central bureaucracy. It functioned under a *vizir,* or chief minister, with a host of subordinate officials. The top officials met regularly as the sultan's council *(divan)* to advise the ruler, but his word was law and he might even execute his own ministers.

The Ottomans developed a unique "slave" *(kul)* system that was a major factor in their success. The system was based on a levy *(devshirme)* of boys from the non-Muslim subjects of the empire; it functioned as a special type of "human tax" on the Balkan provinces. These boys were brought to the capital, converted to Islam, and taught Turkish. Most of them went to the *janissaries,* the famed elite Ottoman infantry corps that was armed with gunpowder weapons. They formed the backbone of the formidable Ottoman armies. The smartest and most talented of the boys, however, were sent to the palace to be educated in literature, science, the arts, religion, and military skills. These boys, when they reached maturity, were given the highest military and administrative posts in the state. Ideally, the *kul* system provided the state with a group of expert administrators who, because they had been separated from their families and homes, would remain loyal to the sultan, to whom they owed everything. These "slaves," rather than occupying the lowest level of the social order, controlled much of the wealth and power in

European writers and their audiences were fascinated by the Ottoman harem and often depicted it in exaggerated erotic terms. This engraving from a seventeenth-century French history of the Ottoman palace imagines the sultan taking his bath attended by naked harem women. In fact, this image is pure fantasy; both sexuality and reproduction in the harem were tightly controlled.

Ottoman society. Many of the buildings they endowed are still standing today.

Western literature has produced an exotic, erotic image of the Ottoman sultan's *harem* (the sacred area of the palace, or of any home, forbidden to outsiders). But much of this image is a myth produced by the overactive imaginations or hostile sentiments of European men inspired by the prospect of several hundred women in one household. In fact, sexuality in the palace was tightly controlled. Like women in other traditional patriarchal societies, most Ottoman women had to work in the fields and towns. Only the women of the elite classes could be fully veiled and secluded. In the palace, the harem women were arranged in a rigid hierarchy much like that of the

Evliya Çelebi, "An Ottoman Official's Wedding Night"

Marriages in the Ottoman administrative system were often arranged to link powerful families, consolidate wealth, and secure loyalty. Love matches were also made, but sometimes officials were forced into marriages at the sultan's command. That was the fate of Melek Ahmed Pasha, who after the death of his beloved first wife was forced to marry the elderly and intransigent Fatma Sultan, daughter of Sultan Ahmed I. This passage, in which Ahmed tells his tale of woe to the chronicler Evliya Çelebi, suggests that marriage to a princess, however prestigious, could be burdensome. It also illustrates the consumption of goods by royal households and the power and status of royal women, who could supersede the wishes of influential men.

As soon as I entered the harem, having uttered a *besmele* [invocation of God's name], I saw her. Now I am supposed to be her husband, and this is our first night—she ought to show me just a little respect. She just sat there stock still, not moving an inch. I went up and kissed her hand.

"Pasha," she says, "welcome."

"God be praised that I have seen my sultan's smiling beauty," say I, and I shower her with all sorts of self-deprecating flatteries. Not once does she invite me to sit down. And she puts on all kinds of virginal airs, as though she weren't an ancient crone who has gone through twelve husbands!

The first pearl from her lips is this: "My dear pasha, if you want to get along with me, whether you are present at court or absent in some government post, my expenses are 15 purses each and every month. Also I owe my steward, Kermetçi Mustafa Agha, 100 purses: pay my debt in the morning. And every year I get six Marmara boatloads of firewood . . . ." (She continued with a long list of expenses.)

Now her stewardess and treasuress and ladies in waiting and, in short, 300 or more women came to kiss my hand and stand there in rows. "Well, my dear pasha, these are my servants of the interior. I also have as many

or more manumitted slave girls on the exterior. Together with children and dependents, they total 700 souls. You will provide all of them with their annual stipend of silk and gauze and brocade and broadcloth. And you will pay the annual stipend of my halberdiers and cooks and gardeners and coachmen and eunuchs and *begs*, as well as those serving them, numbering 500 people. And if you don't—well, you know the consequence!"

Melek Ahmed replied: "I swear by God, my sultan," say I, "that I have just returned from the Transylvania campaign. I am a vizir who fights the holy war. In that campaign I had 7,000 men to feed. I spent 170,000 goldpieces and 600 purses. I even had to sell quite a lot of equipment and arms and armor and helmets and to borrow money from the janissary corps. . . . I am unable to bear such expenses."

After this "wedding night" Melek prayed for death and complained that he had been asked to "feed the state elephant." He vowed never to see Fatma Sultan again.

From Robert Dankoff, trans., *The Intimate Life of an Ottoman Statesman, Melek Ahmed Pasha (1588–1662), as Portrayed in Evliya Çelebi's Book of Travels* (Albany: State University of New York Press 1991), pp. 260–263.

men; each was paid according to her rank. Most of the women were not destined for the sultan's bed; instead they were married to the sultan's officers to create further ties of loyalty to the palace. A select few were chosen to bear the sultan's heirs.

The harem women wielded power because of their wealth, their connections, and their proximity to the sultan. The most powerful among them was the sultan's mother (the *valide sultan*), not his wife. The *valide sultans* participated actively (although behind the scenes) in court politics. Petitioners, including pashas, applied to these high-ranking women to intercede on their behalf with the sultan. Some *valide sultans* even served a diplomatic function, corresponding with European rulers like the Venetian doge, Catherine de' Medici in France, and Queen Elizabeth in England.

Religion was an integral part of government and society. But as in other Muslim lands, the religious authorities *(ulama)* did not run the government; they were subordinated to the state and the sultan. The

grand mufti, as head of the Islamic establishment, was also the chief religious and legal adviser to the sultan. The sultan approved religious appointments and might dismiss any religious officer, including the grand mufti. A corps of learned religious scholars represented the sultan as judges *(kadis)*, dispensers of charities, and teachers. Non-Muslims were regarded as inferior but were granted a significant degree of legal and religious toleration through government arrangements with their religious leaders, who were responsible for their civil obedience.

Non-Muslim subjects *(dhimmis)* lived under their own laws and customs, pursuing their private interests within limits imposed by Islamic law and Ottoman economic needs. For tax purposes, Ottoman society was divided between taxpaying subjects and the military-administrative class. The non-Muslim subjects, as in other Islamic lands, had to pay an additional head tax.

In the Ottoman system, proximity to the sultan was the primary avenue to power, and membership in the royal household or military class brought with it the highest status in society. But pashas, palace women, muftis, and members of the palace staff jockeyed for positions of power and formed alliances to advance their own interests. Harem politics, illustrated in Suleiman's reign by the contending influences of his mother and his wife, have often been blamed for weakening the Ottoman state. In fact, however, the factors that compromised Ottoman power were much more complex. Continued conquests produced serious communication and transportation problems, and long wars and failure to pay the troops on time caused rebellions in the ranks. Religious contention, provoked by the rise of the Shi'ite Safavids in Persia, also threatened the empire.

Another important factor in Ottoman politics was the fact that the eldest son had no automatic claim to the throne. The sultan's sons thus contended to succeed him, sometimes producing extended periods of interregnum. That was the case with Bayezid II, whose sons got tired of waiting for him to die and launched a civil war to determine who would sit on the throne in his stead. Once a prince established himself as sultan, he would often have his brothers executed, a grim task designed to ensure the stability of the state and avoid further struggles. A wise prince would try to gain the favor of the janissary corps, for their support might make or break him.

Artistic Production

Ottoman success resulted in a vigorous cultural renaissance, most evident in monumental architecture and decorative tile work. Mehmed II rebuilt his decaying capital, from sewers to palaces. His monumental Fatih Mosque and great Topkapi Palace, with its fortress walls, fountains, and courtyards, were models of the new Ottoman style, which was influenced by the Byzantine artistic tradition. The palace was divided into three courts that reflected Ottoman concepts of power and space. The outer court was for public affairs, as well as stable and kitchen facilities. The second court provided a dividing line between the public and private life of the sultan. There the sultan met with diplomats and built his library. The inner court was reserved for the sultan and his intimates, a place for relaxation and privacy. Suleiman surpassed Topkapi's splendor with the beautiful and elegant Suleimaniye, his own mosque and mausoleum. These were but three architectural wonders among thousands scattered throughout the empire.

In addition, the period was marked by wondrous productions in the realms of decorative arts. Calligraphy could take the form of birds or boats in official documents. Elaborate calligraphy and stunning painted tiles decorated Ottoman mosques and buildings. For example, Suleiman added luminous tiles to the Dome of the Rock in Jerusalem. Ottoman high

An engraving of the sixth emperor of the Turks, Sultan Murad III (r. 1574–1595).

culture also produced a great outpouring of scholarship and literature, mostly following Persian traditions but reflecting a unique Ottoman synthesis. Poets and historians vied for the attentions—and rewards (silver, sable furs, robes of honor, even houses)—of the sultan. Both often signed themselves as humble beggars or "slaves" of the sultan. Some achieved remarkable rank and success; others left the palace disheartened and poor.

Challenges to Ottoman Supremacy

Beginning in Suleiman's reign, cheap silver from the Americas and a population increase led to rising inflation, rebellions, and military mutinies, all of which weakened the government. None of the eight sultans who followed Suleiman before 1648 could duplicate

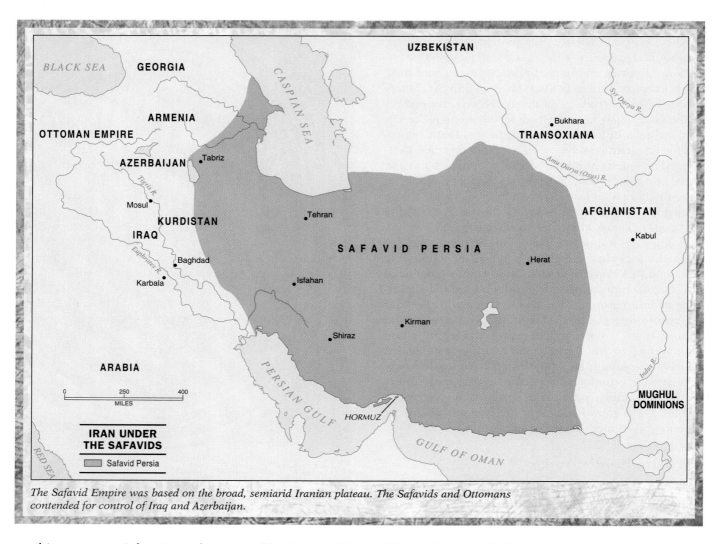

The Safavid Empire was based on the broad, semiarid Iranian plateau. The Safavids and Ottomans contended for control of Iraq and Azerbaijan.

his successes. Selim II was known as "the drunkard"; another sultan gained notoriety by having 19 of his brothers killed on his accession. Increasingly, the sultans did not themselves lead their troops into battle. Other problems plaguing Suleiman's successors were losses to the Russians and Habsburgs in Europe, stalemated wars with Persia, and the end of Ottoman naval supremacy in the Red Sea. Nonetheless, the period between 1566 and 1650 should be viewed as one of reorganization and retrenchment rather than decline. The Ottoman Empire was adjusting to newly emerging global configurations of power and commerce, and Ottoman armies still managed to gain important victories in this era, notably the reconquest of Iraq by Murad IV (1623–1640) in 1638.

With Suleiman's death the Ottoman Empire passed its zenith, but it remained a significant contender for power in the Euro-Asian sphere well into the eighteenth century. It dominated the overland trade with Asia, thus contributing decisively to European maritime expansion. Moreover, the sultans moderated Portuguese domination of the Indian Ocean, ultimately aiding the Dutch and English seaborne empires in the East while humbling their Habsburg rivals in Europe.

The Safavid Empire in Persia

The Safavid dynasty had its origins in an Islamic Sufi (mystical) order founded by Safi al-Din (c. 1252–1334). One of Safi's descendants, Shah Ismail (1501–1524), gathered an army of devoted followers and began a series of campaigns that united Persia, conquered Iraq, and posed a formidable challenge to the Ottomans on their eastern frontiers. Ismail was only 14 when he seized his first territories. Although such precocity may seem unusual today, it was common enough in this era for the sons of powerful men to be trained to fight and rule while still boys.

Ismail was not only a successful military commander; he was also the head of a Shi'ite Muslim sect. Contemporary accounts portray him as a charismatic leader whose army thought him invincible. They followed him into battle crying "Shaykh, Shaykh!" The Safavid troops wore red headgear with 12 folds to commemorate the 12 Shi'ite imams (descendants of the prophet Muhammad); because of this headgear they were called "redheads."

Ismail angered the Ottoman sultan by sending missionaries and agitators to stir up the sultan's

The Coming of Ismail Safavi Foretold

Histories and legends of famous leaders and religious figures often recount the ways in which the coming of these men was predicted or foretold. In this selection, from an anonymous Persian manuscript, the story is told of a Sufi mystic named Dede Mohammad. This Sufi, or *darwish*, while returning from a pilgrimage to Mecca, becomes separated from his caravan in the desert. Dying of thirst, he is rescued by a mysterious youth who takes him to a magnificent encampment in a flowering plain. There he sees a veiled prince, whom he does not realize is the Twelfth Imam, a descendant of the Prophet revered by the Shi'ite Muslims. In this vision, the Twelfth Imam girds and sends forth the young Ismail Safavi, thus legitimizing his reign to the Shi'ites.

After his rescue, Dede Mohammad . . . walked by the young man's side, until they came to a palace, whose cupola outrivaled the sun and moon. . . . Golden thrones were arranged side by side, and on one of the thrones a person was seated whose face was covered by a veil. Dede Mohammad, placing his hand on his breast, made a salutation, whereupon an answer to his salutation came from the veiled one, who having bidden him be seated, ordered food to be brought for him. The like of this food he had never seen in his life before. . . . As soon as he had finished his repast, he saw that a party of men had entered, bringing a boy of about fourteen years of age, with red hair, a white face, and dark grey eyes; on his head was a scarlet cap. . . . The veiled youth then said to him, "Oh! Ismail, the hour of your 'coming' has now arrived." The other replied: "It is for your Holiness to command." . . . His Holiness, taking his belt three times lifted it up and placed it on the ground again. He then, with his own blessed hands, fastened on the girdle and taking [Ismail's] cap from his head, raised it and then replaced it. . . . His Holiness then told his servants to bring his own sword which, when brought, he fastened with his own hands on the girdle of the child. Then he said, "You may now depart." [The Arab youth then guided Dede Mohammad back to his caravan, and the Sufi asked his guide who the veiled prince was.] He replied, "Did you not know that the prince you saw was no other than the Lord of the Age?" When Dede Mohammad heard this name he stood up and said: "Oh! youth, for the love of God take me back again that I may once more kiss the feet of His Holiness, and ask a blessing of him, perchance I might be allowed to wait on him." But the youth replied: "It is impossible. You should have made your request at first. You cannot return. But you can make your request where you will, for His Holiness is everywhere present and will hear your prayers."

From E. Dennison Ross, "The Early Years of Shah Ismail," *Journal of the Royal Asiatic Society* (1896), pp. 328–331.

subjects on the Ottoman eastern frontiers. He also launched a sometimes violent campaign to convert the Sunni Muslims of his domain to Shi'ite Islam. Because Persia had been predominantly Sunni, he had to import Shi'ite scholars and jurists from the Arab lands, like Syria and Iraq. Under the Safavid shahs, Persia became overwhelmingly Shi'ite, as it is today.

Power is acquired not only on the field of battle but also in the arenas of reputation and diplomacy. Legends grew up around the youthful leader Ismail because of his many and rapid conquests. He was also supposed to have received the secret knowledge of the Safavi mystical order, passed down from his brother as he lay dying. Hence he had a powerful aura of both political and religious legitimacy. European rulers, including the Portuguese king and the pope, were inspired by the accounts of Ismail's victories and the rumors of his quasi-divine prowess. Hoping that the Safavids would help them defeat the Ottomans, who were Sunni Muslims, they sent envoys to the young shah. Ismail had some interest in exploring possibilities with European powers, but he was apparently more interested in European artillery and defeating the Ottomans than in a Christian-Shi'ite alliance.

Rulers used envoys to intimidate, placate, or try to gain information about foreign powers. The Portuguese, for example, thought of the Safavids as barbarians. Their envoy to Ismail was instructed to brag to the Safavids about the fine Portuguese horses, table service, and women. When in 1510 Ismail defeated Shaibani Khan, the Uzbek ruler in central Asia, he had the Khan's skull gilded and made into a drinking cup. He sent an envoy with the grisly trophy, along with a taunting message, to the Ottoman sultan, Bayezid II. Of course, being an envoy in this era was often dangerous, especially for the bearers of rude messages. The Ottoman sultans often imprisoned Safavid envoys, and messengers to the Safavid court were sometimes detained or abused. When Ismail sent another arrogant message to the Mamluk sultan in Egypt (before the Ottoman conquest), the latter was so enraged that he sponsored a poetry contest to see which of his poets could write the most insulting reply in verse. But he did not harm Ismail's messenger because he was afraid of a Safavid invasion.

The Ottomans were intimidated by Ismail's early successes. In 1514, however, they soundly defeated Ismail's forces on the frontier between Anatolia and Persia. This victory is often attributed to the fact that the Ottomans had more and better gunpowder weaponry. Demoralized, Ismail withdrew to his palace, having lost his reputation for invincibility. After his death, the Safavids fought a series of long wars against the Ottomans to the west and the Uzbeks to the east.

None of his successors wielded the same charismatic religious power as Ismail. They were kings, not *shaykhs* (holy men), even though Ismail's son Tahmasp still claimed the headship of the Safavid order. Still, the next hundred years of Safavid rule were characterized by a consolidation of state power, lavish patronage of the arts, and an exploration of diplomatic and commercial relations with Europe. European merchants visited the shah's court, trying to gain access to the coveted Iranian silk trade, but they met with little success. Tahmasp ruled for half a century (1524–1576), despite having to contend with foreign invasions, religious factionalism, and power struggles among the tribal leaders. The Safavids, with the aid of European renegades, developed their gunpowder weaponry but never to the same extent as the Ottomans. Nor did they imitate the elaborate "slave"-based hierarchy and infantry corps (janissaries) that became the basis for Ottoman success. In Persia, the tribal leaders and their cavalry-based militaries retained their position of power.

The Reign of Abbas the Great

The reign of Shah Abbas (1588–1629) is considered a "golden age" of Safavid power, comparable to that of Suleiman in the Ottoman Empire. Ascending the throne at the age of 17, Abbas ultimately became a pragmatic politician, a wise statesman, a brilliant strategist, and a generous patron of the arts. During his reign, Persia acquired security, stability, and a reputation for cultural creativity, symbolized by the shah's splendid new capital at Isfahan.

Abbas directed much of his attention to the threat posed by an Ottoman-Uzbek alliance, which had almost destroyed his country. He held his holy men in political check but labored to project an image of Shi'ite piety. He reorganized his government and army, creating a personal force of "slaves" of the royal household. This force acted as a counterweight to the ambitious and often unruly tribal chiefs. Within the army, Abbas increased his artillery and musket forces, relying less on traditional cavalry. During the 1590s he slowly recovered territory lost by his less adept predecessors.

Persia prospered under Abbas. The government employed thousands of workers, and the palace was a great consumer of luxury goods, foodstuffs, and other commodities. Government monopolies, particularly in silk, promoted various crafts. Hundreds of new roads, bridges, hostels, and irrigation projects promoted agriculture, encouraged trade, and swelled urban populations. These projects also enhanced the prestige of the ruler. Contemporaries noted that a person could travel from one end of the empire to another in safety, without fear of bandits. That was a significant claim in an age when merchants traveled at their own risk, often with large retinues of armed guards.

A commercial agreement with the British subsequently led to the forcible ejection of the Portuguese from Hormuz, in the Persian Gulf, a most significant development that permitted direct export of Persian silk to Europe by sea, thus avoiding Ottoman tolls on the overland routes. The silk trade was so lucrative that merchants on both sides conspired to get the shipments through, even when the Safavids and the Ottomans were at war. Persia was an important center in the networks of East-West trade. Its silk was in such demand in Europe that Venetian, French, and other traders would wait in the Syrian entrepots for the caravans of Persian silk to come in. They negotiated with local agents, trying to outbid each other for the rights to purchase each incoming load. One Venetian observer stated that a merchant would willingly pluck out his own eye to triumph over a competitor.

Persia at this time was one of the primary cultural centers of the world. It was a conduit to the West not only for the goods but also for the spiritual and literary influences of India. Meanwhile, Sufi Muslim missionaries traveled to South and Southeast Asia, transmitting their own ideas and bringing a synthesis of mystical ideas and practices back to the Islamic heartlands. Persia's fine arts—ceramics, tapestries, and carpets—were eagerly sought from Alexandria to Calcutta. Persian literary forms, particularly the exquisite imagery of Persian poetry, were imitated at both the Ottoman and Mughul courts, even by the rulers themselves. Persian painters explored realist styles and erotic themes. They were recruited abroad, as were two émigrés, Khwaja Abdus Samad and Mir Sayyid Ali, who founded the famous Mughul school of painting in India.

Major Middle Eastern courts housed large workshops of artists, sometimes numbering in the hundreds. The Safavid shahs paid their painters to produce lavish manuscripts like the *Epic of Kings (Shahnamah)*, a long rhyming poem by Firdawsi. Ismail commissioned a wondrous illustrated version of the *Shahnamah* that was not finished in his lifetime. When the Ottomans conquered the Persian capital of Tabriz, they carried back many of the Safavid artists as a valuable part of the booty.

Persian architecture, with its jewel-like colors, intricate geometric and floral patterns, luxurious gardens, and artificial streams, exerted considerable in-

A school scene from a Safavid manuscript painted around 1540 at Tabriz. Not all miniatures were devoted to the exploits of kings or legendary heroes. More mundane matters like education, building projects, and funerals were also sometimes depicted. This scene illustrates some of the beauty, color, and style of Safavid painting.

Mir Sayyid-Ali, Safavid dynasty, 16th century. Freer Gallery of Art and Arthur M. Sackler Gallery Archives, Smithsonian Institution.

fluence on the architecture of the Islamic world. Abbas made the capital at Isfahan a showcase for these artistic and architectural talents. One of the largest cities of its time, Isfahan had a million inhabitants. Its public life centered around a broad square (used for assemblies and polo matches), the palace compound, a huge bazaar, and the main mosque. Five hundred years later the beauty of Abbas's surviving monuments still inspires awe in visitors.

The Mughul Empire in South Asia

The Safavid and Ottoman states were contemporaries of the mighty Mughul Empire in India. It too was ruled by a Turkic dynasty. But unlike the Ottoman sultans and Safavid shahs, the Mughuls ruled a population that was predominantly Hindu rather than Muslim. That fact marked the Mughul Empire indelibly and helped craft its distinctive character.

The Mughuls

1525	Babur invades India
1556–1605	Reign of Akbar, Mughul Golden Age
1632	Shah Jahan commissions the Taj Mahal
1658–1707	Reign of Aurangzeb, reasserts Islamic orthodoxy

Origins

The Ottoman Empire emerged out of a warrior principality in what is now Turkey, and the Safavid Empire was established by a Sufi boy-king who commanded both political and religious authority in Persia. The origin of the Mughul Empire was different from these; one might say it was founded by a determined prince in search of a kingdom.

Miniatures were not painted solely for artistic expression; they also suggested relationships. In this Mughul painting of Shah Jahangir and the Safavid Shah, Jahangir's artist portrayed his master as big and powerful, dominating his rather puny-looking Safavid rival. The monarchs stand on the globe, but Jahangir's lion is much more imposing than Abbas's lamb. The angels supporting the rulers' halo show the influence of European art motifs on Mughul imagery.

Mughal painting, c. 1620. (F45.9a) Freer Gallery of Art and Arthur M. Sackler Gallery Archives, Smithsonian Institution.

The establishment of the Mughul Empire was not the first instance of Muslim contact with the diverse but predominantly Hindu population of India. Muslim merchants and Sufi mystics had traveled to India from the Islamic heartlands for many centuries. From the seventh century onward Muslim rulers extended the frontiers of Islam eastward to the borders of South Asia. Then a Turkic warrior, Mahmud of Ghazna (c. 971–1030), gained control of Khurasan in western Persia and Afghanistan and seized control of northern India. He destroyed the Hindu temple of Shiva in Gujarat. Muslim sultanates were established on the west coast of India, and the Muslim Delhi Sultanate ruled in the thirteenth and fourteenth centuries until Timur's invasion. Thus by the sixteenth

century, much of South Asian society had become familiar with Islamic culture and political power.

India is a land of many peoples, many languages, and diverse terrain. At the beginning of the sixteenth century it was politically fragmented. The Delhi Sultanate, having spawned a number of independent contending Muslim states, had been partially resurrected under the Lodi Afghan dynasty. The Rajput Confederacy held sway in the northwest, the Vijayangar Empire controlled much of southern India, and a string of commercial city-states held sway along the southwestern coast. Although many rulers had aspired to unite the entire subcontinent, that goal remained daunting.

Early in the sixteenth century a new conqueror cast his eye on India. The adventurous Turco-Mongol ruler of Kabul, Babur, "the Tiger" (1483–1530), was a descendant of both Timur and Genghis Khan. Babur did not begin his career in India. He inherited the Afghan principality of Ferghana and twice conquered the Timurid capital at Samarkand before losing everything to the Uzbeks. He and his troops finally seized the throne of Kabul in 1504.

Babur is a striking historical figure because, unlike many rulers of his time, he compiled his memoirs.

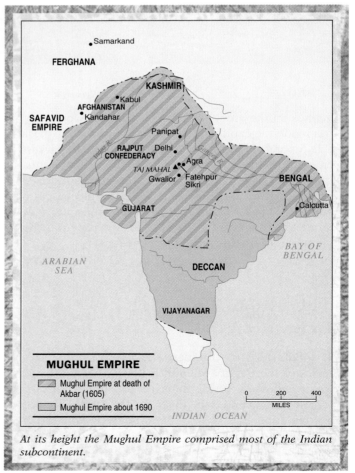

At its height the Mughul Empire comprised most of the Indian subcontinent.

Babur, conqueror of northern India, surveying the spectacular rock-cut Hindu sculptures at Urwa fortress in Gwalior, from an illustrated manuscript of Babur's memoirs. Babur ordered these sculptures defaced.

They are a tale of triumphs and losses that reveal Babur as a straightforward narrator who built gardens wherever he went, paid careful attention to geography, was solicitous of his mother, and seemed to enjoy good wine and a good fight. He also loved to compose and declaim poetry. Babur's memoirs tell of rhinoceros hunts and military relations. He notes, rather ruefully, that he had sworn to give up drink when he reached the age of 40 but now felt compelled to drink out of anxiety because he was already 39. Armed with Turkish artillery, this intrepid warrior mobilized an invasion in 1525, winning decisive battles against the Afghan Sultanate at Delhi and the Rajput Confederacy. Babur was not impressed with Indian culture. He

criticized native dress, religion, and the failure of Indians to have running water in their gardens.

> *Hindustan is a place of little charm. There is no beauty in its people, no graceful social intercourse, no poetic talent or understanding, no etiquette, nobility or manliness. . . . There are no good horses, meat, grapes, melons, or other fruit. There is no ice, cold water, good food or bread in the markets.*[2]

Like many travelers, Babur tended to find his own culture superior to those of other peoples. He did, however, admire the Indian systems of numbers, weights, and measures and the country's vast array of craftsmen. Speaking as a prospective ruler, he could not help but remark that "the one nice aspect of Hindustan [India] is that it is a large country with lots of gold and money."[3] When Babur died, soon after the conquest, the hard-living and thoughtful ruler had laid the foundations for a Mughul empire that would dominate most of the subcontinent and endure into the eighteenth century.

Babur was succeeded by his able but erratic son Humayun. After ten years of rule during which he expanded Mughul domains, Humayun was overthrown by his vassal Sher Khan. He then fled to the Safavid court of Tahmasp in Persia. The Safavid shah welcomed Humayun. It was always useful for monarchs of the time to shelter in their courts the sons or rivals of neighboring kings. Such refugees could prove useful; they gave rulers leverage against their enemies. Rulers also demanded that vassals send their sons to reside at court; it was a practical way to ensure the loyalty of subordinates.

In 1555 Shah Tahmasp helped Humayun regain his kingdom, no doubt presuming that Humayun would prove a significant ally on the Safavids' eastern frontiers. But Humayun died shortly thereafter in a fall down his library steps, perhaps a fitting end for a learned man but a rather ignominious one for a warrior.

The Reign of Akbar

Humayun's son Akbar (1556–1605) was 14 years old when he succeeded his father, about the same age as Shah Ismail when he commenced his reign. During a half century of rule Akbar united northern India, advanced against the sultanates in the south of the subcontinent, and presided over a glorious courtly culture. Akbar ruled an empire more populous than those of the Ottoman sultan and the Persian shah; Mughul subjects numbered between 100 and 150 million.

Unlike Ismail, Akbar did not immediately consolidate his power. Initially, he was controlled by a regent. As often happens when a prince comes to power at an early age, powerful men in the court used the prince's youth to advance their own influence and objectives. By the age of 20, however, Akbar took charge and began a determined campaign of conquest that would continue into his old age.

This Mughul potentate was the counterpart of Suleiman in the Ottoman Empire and Shah Abbas in Safavid Persia. His reign is associated with military might, prosperity, and patronage of the arts at a spectacular level. At 13 Akbar led troops in battle; in his thirties he challenged an enemy commander to personal combat; in late middle age he still hunted wild animals with sword and lance. Akbar's concern for morality and social justice was indicated by his advice to a son: "Avoid religious persecution; be strong but magnanimous; accept apologies, sincerely given."[4]

A significant aspect of Akbar's reign is that he adapted the Islamic state to the conditions of ruling a non-Muslim population. In so doing, he promoted cultural synthesis, incorporated Hindus into the inner workings of government, and showed himself to be a pragmatic monarch. He married a number of Rajput princesses and made alliances with Hindu families, taking the men into his service. The mother of his heir, Jahangir, was a Hindu. He also abolished the *jizya,* the special head tax on non-Muslims. This decision may seem like a simple matter, but the *jizya* was a standard of Islamic rule and had been institutionalized in the Sharia Islamic law. By abolishing it, Akbar gave notice to his Hindu subjects that they were granted a more equitable position vis-à-vis the Muslims, who constituted the ruling class.

Akbar also stopped taxing Hindu pilgrims, financed the construction of Hindu temples, and forbade Muslims to kill or eat the cow, which was sacred to Hindus. These measures alienated the *ulama* (the Muslim religious authorities) and the diverse Muslim elite of Turks, Afghans, Mongols, and Persians but won new support among the majority. Akbar, however, also initiated certain measures designed to force Hindu practice into compliance with Islamic law; he issued decrees outlawing Hindu child marriages and *suttee* (the self-burning of widows), two reforms that violated Hindu traditions.

Akbar's tolerance in public administration was matched by his pursuit of knowledge and personal explorations of various religious faiths. He was devoted to certain Sufi *shaykhs* and launched at his court a "house of worship," a forum for religious discussion to which he invited Muslims, Christians, Jews, Jains, Hindus, and Zoroastrians. In 1582 Akbar proclaimed a new cult, the *Din-i Ilahi,* or "Divine Faith," which centered on Akbar himself and was highly influenced by Zoroastrianism. The new creed gained few adherents, but it further antagonized the *ulama* and demonstrated Akbar's religious eclecticism.

The Mughul State and Its Culture

One of the great accomplishments of the Mughul Empire was its establishment of a highly organized and intrusive central administration. In many ways like that of the Ottomans, it was designed to produce a consistent supply of taxes and troops for the government and to manage distant provinces. Akbar's military administrators, about two-thirds of whom were foreign-born Muslims, were organized in military ranks and paid salaries according to the number of soldiers they commanded. Promotion for these military administrators, who were called *mansabdars,* was ideally based on merit. Their ranks were open to Hindus, and their positions were not hereditary like those of European nobles. Like the Ottoman *kul* system, the *mansabdar* system was designed to produce loyalty to the state. Officials, in turn, were now made more dependent on the emperor. Like the Ottomans and Safavids, Akbar drew conquered foes into his service as long as they offered their submission. In this way he took advantage of the military expertise of defeated commanders.

In the early seventeenth century the Mughul Empire was the wealthiest state in the world, with revenues ten times greater than those of France. Cities were numerous and large by European standards. Akbar's capital at Agra, for example, housed 200,000 people—twice the population of contemporary London. In the towns and villages, many industries flourished, particularly cotton textiles, which were exported to most of Asia and Africa. The majority of subjects were Hindu peasants. One-third to one-half of their produce, paid in land taxes, supported the army and kept the administrative elite in considerable luxury.

The early Mughul period saw a new Hindu-Muslim cultural synthesis, well illustrated in literature. Beginning with Babur, each emperor considered himself a poet, a scholar, and a collector of books. Akbar himself could not read, but he founded a great library housing over 20,000 illustrated manuscripts. The Mughuls used their wealth to patronize the arts. Their literature was cosmopolitan, reflected a fresh originality, and was expressed in a variety of languages, including Turkish, Persian, Hindi, Arabic, and Urdu (an Indo-Persian fusion).

Despite the Muslim prohibition of representational figures, human or animal, painting developed rapidly as an art in the early Mughul period. Akbar had studied art as a child under Abdus Samad and Mir Sayyid Ali, two Safavid court painters whom Humayan brought to Kabul and later took to India. Akbar's royal studio employed over a hundred artists, mostly Hindus, who created works of great variety including miniatures of courtly life and large murals for Akbar's palaces.

The royal studio produced beautiful illustrated manuscripts requiring many painters and many years to complete. Foremost among these is the spectacular *Hamzanamah,* which includes 1400 illustrations on cloth. Akbar also sponsored illustrated versions of Babur's memoirs and of the great Sanskrit epics the *Mahabharata* and the *Ramayana*. The Mughul school of painters under Jahangir, Akbar's son, produced wonderful animal and bird imagery, developed new strains of sensual and realist representation, and expertly incorporated motifs of European painting into Mughul art.

The most imposing symbols of Mughul glory are to be seen in architecture. Fusing Persian and Indic styles, it featured the lavish use of mosaics, bulbous domes, cupolas, slender spires, lofty vaulted gateways, and formal gardens, all carefully harmonized. Akbar's major building project was his palace complex at Fatehpur Sikri. Akbar wanted to build his new palace on a site dedicated to a famous Sufi holy man, Shaykh Salim Chishti. But Fatehpur Sikri became a monument to man's vanity and lack of planning. Akbar's court abandoned the complex (which took 15 years to build) after only 14 years because the water supply was inadequate. But visitors still marvel at the red sandstone blocks of the monumental fortress, which were hewn so precisely that they needed no fasteners or mortar.

Akbar's son Jahangir and his grandson Shah Jahan continued the tradition of monumental building. The latter replaced Akbar's sandstone buildings at Delhi with new ones of marble. At Agra Shah Jahan erected the famous Taj Mahal, a tomb for his favorite wife, Mumtaz Mahal, who died while giving birth to her fifteenth child. This elaborate tomb, set in beautiful gardens, took over 20 years to build. Its luminous white marble, beautiful tracery of semiprecious stones, and elegant lines make the Taj Mahal one of the best-known buildings in the world today.

Akbar's Successors: Contesting the Hindu-Muslim Synthesis

Like most empires, the Mughul polity fared best when its administration was relatively tolerant, its treasury full, and its military successful. Jahangir (1605–1627) and Shah Jahan (1628–1658) continued Akbar's policies of relative tolerance. Jahangir was learned and artistically sensitive, but he was also a wastrel, a drunkard, and a drug addict, without the strength to make decisions or conduct policy. He lost Kandahar to the Persians. Shah Jahan launched three unsuccessful campaigns to retake Kandahar, a disastrous thrust into central Asia, four costly invasions of the Deccan, and an extravagant expedition to oust a Portuguese enclave on the Indian coast. To compensate for these military expeditions, Shah Jahan had to raise land taxes, thus oppressing the peasantry.

The tension between Mughul tolerance and Muslim rule culminated in the seventeenth century with Akbar's great-grandsons, Dara Shikoh and Aurangzeb (1658–1707). Dara Shikoh took Akbar's tolerance one step further. He was a devoted Sufi and wrote his own mystical works; he also studied Hindu mysticism. In the end this prince's attempt to find a middle

In 1632 the Mughul emperor, Shah Jahan, commissioned the building of the resplendent Taj Mahal as a memorial to his late wife. Tall minarets surround a central dome, and a reflecting pool perfectly mirrors the white marble building, one of the glories of Mughul architecture.

ground between Islam and Hinduism provoked a violent response from the empire's Muslims and from his brother, Aurangzeb. Dara Shikoh was his father's favorite, but in the battle to succeed Shah Jahan, Aurangzeb was victorious. Charging his brother with apostasy, Aurangzeb marched him through the streets of Delhi in humiliation and had him executed.

Both Sufi orders and the *ulama* opposed the ecumenicalism of Akbar and Dara Shikoh. When Aurangzeb gained the throne, he was determined to restore Sunni orthodoxy to the Mughul dominions. He reimposed the *jizya* and enforced the Sharia with a vengeance. Many Hindu temples were destroyed during his reign, and his intolerance and rigid orthodoxy weakened the Mughul hold on its diverse Hindu populations.

The Mughul Social Order

As already noted, Mughul society comprised a series of hierarchies based on a Hindu majority and a predominantly Muslim ruling class. The vast majority of the populace, as in China, the Middle East, and Europe, consisted of illiterate peasants who provided the bulk of the empire's revenue through agricultural taxes. Wealth was an important factor in determining status, but it was not the primary factor. A merchant could be very wealthy but could not achieve the same status as a member of the elite military-administrative class. Among Hindus, status was intimately linked to caste.

Mughul society, like most societies, was also patriarchal; it allocated family, religious, and political dominance to men. This system of male dominance is often attributed to Islam, but patriarchy predated Islam in India, as it did in the Middle East. In general, it would be more accurate to say that Islam both reinforced preexisting patriarchal structures and improved the position of women by forbidding female infanticide and granting women inheritance rights. In India under Islamic rule, the position of women derived from a synthesis of Hindu custom and Islamic law. Despite Akbar's reform-minded decrees, *suttee* and child marriages continued. Formal education of females, as in most societies, was practically nonexistent, except in a few affluent or learned families.

These practices must, of course, be understood in their temporal and social contexts. In Hindu society, as in Muslim society, in which marriage is considered a preferred state (especially for women), early marriage age acted to prevent the girl's sexual purity from being compromised or questioned. By social convention, women needed male protectors, and when a woman married, she left the protection of her father or brother and became part of her husband's household. By placing herself on her hus-

The birth of a prince in the Mughul harem. This unusual scene shows the numerous female attendants of the princely court and suggests the ceremonial significance of such an event.

Birth of a Prince from an illustrated manuscript of the Jahangir-nama, Bishndas (Attributed to), Northern India, Mughal, about 1620. Opaque watercolor on paper, 24.1 × 17 cm. Museum of Fine Arts, Boston, Francis Bartlett Donation of 1912 and Picture Fund.

band's funeral pyre, a Hindu woman gained honor in the eyes of the community. She also escaped the dilemma of being left without a protector (especially if she had no sons) and becoming a social burden.

As for female education, we should remember that the overwhelming majority of people, in all the world civilizations of this era, were illiterate. Only certain of the elites could read, and even many people of rank, like Akbar, were illiterate. Men's and women's roles were considered complementary, not equal. Because men were expected to perform the political, religious, and administrative tasks that required literacy, formal education tended to be reserved for men.

Networks of Trade and Communication

The gunpowder empires emerged in a set of interconnected regions that were in turn imbedded in even more extensive networks of trade and communication. The primitive nature of transport and communications technology limited the flow of goods, knowledge, and information. But all three circulated in ways that might seem surprising, given that the only ways to get from one place to another were on foot, on animal-back, or aboard oared and sailing vessels. Despite these limitations, scholars traveled from one court to another, enjoying the patronage of Ottoman, Safavid, or Mughul kings and sharing literary, artistic, and legal traditions. The royal courts consumed prodigiously and supported the exchange of goods and culture on a grand scale. Mehmed II had his portrait painted by the famous Italian painter Bellini. Babur brought Persian artists into India, and the Safavid court imported Arab jurists. Rulers in all three empires drank from Chinese porcelain cups.

The Ottoman, Safavid, and Mughul Empires derived most of their income from agriculture. But trade was their second source of wealth. None of these empires invented the trading routes. Rather, they emerged and expanded across a set of well-established commercial networks linking urban centers. They inherited these networks from their predecessors and competed with rival kingdoms to monopolize goods and collect commercial taxes. To understand how these empires worked, we must abandon the notion of modern boundaries that are marked, fixed, and defended. Rulers could not control frontiers absolutely; instead they defended and taxed key routes, fortresses, and cities. The porous nature of borders encouraged tax evaders. If officials demanded high taxes along one route, merchants might shift to another route. If taxes were collected by the camel-load, merchants stopped their beasts outside of town and repacked in order to have fewer loads.

In this context of flexible boundaries, trading communities developed that facilitated the flow of goods from one place to another. Although the Ottomans fought long wars with both Christian states in Europe and Muslim competitors in Persia and Egypt, trade among these regions was seldom squelched for long. The furs of Muscovy flowed south into the empire and the gold of Africa came north. Jewish merchants traded copper to Arab merchants who sold it to South Asian traders in return for cotton, jewels, and spices.

Many great trading centers were scattered throughout the territories of the gunpowder empires. Babur described the emporium of Kabul, located between Persia and India, as receiving merchant caravans of 15,000 or 20,000 pack animals carrying slaves, textiles, sugar, and spices. Kabul channeled the trade of China and India westward in exchange for goods coming eastward from the Ottoman and Safavid realms.

The merchants in turn served an information function. Because communication technologies were so limited, rulers used travelers of all sorts to gain knowledge about the rest of the world. Scholars, Sufis, traders, envoys, and spies all served this purpose. Monarchs used envoys as spies, and their rivals tried to control information by keeping visiting envoys sequestered and by intimidating them with military displays. Response to another ruler's challenge could never be swift because it was often months or years before a monarch received a reply or news about his envoy's fate.

Outside these channels of communication, relations between the gunpowder empires and European or East Asian states were still quite limited. Only the Ottomans had resident consuls from some of the European states in their capital. In this era the balance of trade was tipped very much in favor of the East, with eastern goods flowing into Europe and cash flowing back. European imports, with the exception of certain kinds of textiles, were negligible by comparison.

Conclusion

In the three and a half centuries before 1650, Europe still lagged behind Asia in many respects. No European state, not even the polyglot empire of Charles V, could compare in manpower and resources with the realms of Suleiman or Akbar. Europeans were impressed by the resources and taxation capabilities of the Ottoman governing system. Opportunities for minorities and toleration for dissenting religions were greater in the Muslim countries than in Europe. Asian cities were usually better planned, more tastefully adorned with works of art, and even better supplied with water and with sewage disposal.

Europe's advantages, which began to be more apparent after the beginning of the seventeenth century, were most evident in the realm of technology, specifically in the production of field artillery and ocean-going ships. These technical assets helped certain of the European states gain leverage in a new age, when powerful states would depend on strategic control of sea lanes and world markets. But in the period from 1300 to 1650 it was the gunpowder empires that tended to dominate, using their resources and militaries to become the great imperial powers of that age.

Suggestions for Reading

On Inner Asia and Turkic groups, see Peter Golden, *An Introduction to the History of the Turkic Peoples* (Harrassowitz, 1992). Luc Kwanten, *A History of Central Asia: Imperial Nomads, 500–1500* (University of Pennsylvania Press, 1979), is an illuminating study of a subject long neglected in standard texts. See also David Morgan, *The Mongols* (Blackwell, 1986). More on the steppe background for other civilizations in this period can be found in Gavin Hambly, ed., *Central Asia* (Delacorte, 1969); William H. McNeil, *Europe's Steppe Frontier* (University of Chicago Press, 1964); and John Joseph Saunders, *The Muslim World on the Eve of Europe's Expansion* (Prentice Hall, 1966). The Saunders work also presents coverage of high Muslim civilizations in southern Asia. On Timur and his times, see Beatrice Manz, *The Rise and Fall of Tamerlane* (Cambridge University Press, 1989).

The Ottoman Golden Age is ably depicted in Halil Inalcik, *The Ottoman Empire* (Praeger, 1973); Norman Itkowitz, *The Ottoman Empire and the Islamic Tradition* (University of Oklahoma Press, 1980); Stanford Shaw, *A History of the Ottoman Empire*, 2 vols. (Cambridge University Press, 1976); and M. A. Cook, ed., *A History of the Ottoman Empire to 1730* (Cambridge University Press, 1976). On Sultan Suleiman, see Metin Kunt and Christine Woodhead, eds., *Süleyman the Magnificent and His Age* (Longman, 1995). The harem is covered in Leslie P. Peirce, *The Imperial Harem* (Oxford University Press, 1993). On Ottoman artistic production, see Esin Etil, *The Age of Sultan Suleyman the Magnificent* (Abrams, 1987). A captivating and revealing biography is Franz Babinger, *Mehmed the Conqueror and His Time* (Princeton University Press, 1978); a primary source on the subject is Tursun Beg, *The History of Mehmed the Conqueror*, trans. Halil Inalcik and Rhoads Murphey (Bibliotheca Islamica, 1978). For effects of the Ottomans on Europe, see Paul Coles, *The Ottoman Impact upon Europe* (Harcourt Brace, 1968); C. Max Kortepeter, *Ottoman Imperialism During the Reformation* (New York University Press, 1972); and Peter Sugar, *Southeastern Europe Under Ottoman Rule, 1354–1804* (University of Washington Press, 1977).

On medieval Persia, see Ann Lambton, *Continuity and Change in Medieval Persia* (Persian Heritage Foundation, 1988), and David Morgan, *Medieval Persia, 1040–1479* (Longman, 1988). See also Roger Savory, *Iran Under the Safavids* (Cambridge University Press, 1980). Coverage in English of the Safavid period is still limited; an old standard is Percy M. Sykes, *A History of Persia* (Gordon, 1976), first published in 1938.

The standard popular survey of Indian history, with brief coverage of the Mughul period, is Stanley A. Wolpert, *A New History of India*, 5th ed. (Oxford University Press, 1997). The Mughul system is ably described in John F. Richards, *The Mughul Empire* (Cambridge University Press, 1996); Douglas E. Streusand, *The Formation of the Mughal Empire* (Oxford University Press, 1990); Shireen Mooson, *The Economy of the Mughal Empire* (Oxford University Press, 1987); and Neelan Chandler, *Socio-Economic History of Mughal India* (Discovery, 1987). For studies of individual emperors, see A. S. Beveridge, *The History of Humayun* (B. R. Publishers, 1989), and Bamber Gascoigne, *The Great Moghuls* (Harper & Row, 1971). A well-known biography of Akbar is J. M. Shelat, *Akbar* (Bharatiya Bidya Bhavan, 1964). See also Michael Naylor Pearson, *The Portuguese in India* (Cambridge University Press, 1988); Charles R. Boxer, *The Portuguese Seaborne Empire, 1415–1825* (Knopf, 1969); and A. J. R. Russell-Wood, *The World on the Move: The Portuguese in Africa, Asia, and America, 1415–1808* (New York: St. Martin's Press, 1992).

On networks of trade, see K. N. Chaudhuri, *Asia Before Europe* (Cambridge University Press, 1990); Michael Naylor Pearson, *Merchants and Rulers in Gujarat* (University of California Press, 1976); and James Tracy, *The Rise of Merchant Empires: Long-Distance Trade in the Early Modern World, 1350–1750* (Cambridge University Press, 1990), which, however, bypasses the Ottoman Empire entirely. All of these works focus on South Asia. For a broader study, see Philip Curtin, *Cross-Cultural Trade in World History* (Cambridge University Press, 1992). On Mediterranean and Persian Gulf trade, see Eliyahu Ashtor, *Levant Trade in the Later Middle Ages* (Princeton University Press, 1983); Robert S. Lopez, *Medieval Trade in the Mediterranean World*, trans. Irving W. Raymond (Columbia University Press, 1990), a collection of documents; Daniel Goffman, *Izmir and the Levantine World, 1550–1650* (University of Washington Press, 1990); and Niels Steensgaard, *The Asian Trade Revolution of the Seventeenth Century* (University of Chicago Press, 1973).

Suggestions for Web Browsing

Islam and Islamic History in Arabia and the Middle East
http://www.islamic.org/Mosque/ihame/Sec11.htm
http://www.islamic.org/Mosque/ihame/Sec12.htm
http://www.islamic.org/Mosque/ihame/Sec13.htm

Related sites detailing the enormous legacy of the early Islamic civilization, a history of Mongol destruction and Mamluk victory, and the rise of the Ottoman Empire.

Ottoman Page
http://www.xnet.com/ottoman/

Site dedicated to classical Ottoman history, 1300–1600, offering numerous links to other sites.

Topkapi Palace
http://www.ee.bilkent.edu.tr/~history/topkapi.html

A guide to Topkapi Palace, with numerous images of the palace rooms and grounds and its phenomenal artifacts, including portraits of the sultans, manuscripts, clothing, porcelains, and armaments.

Internet Islamic History Sourcebook: The Persians
http://www.fordham.edu/halsall/islam/islamsbook.html

Links to a variety of documents detailing the rise and spread of the Safavid Empire.

Mughul Monarchs
http://rubens.anu.edu.au/student.projects/tajmahal/mughal.html

A detailed introduction to the Mughul dynasty and the city of Agra, whose images emphasize the superb architecture of the time.

Notes

1. Vincent A. Smith, *Akbar, the Great Mogul*, 2nd ed. (Mystic, Conn.: Verry, 1966), p. 522.
2. Zahiruddin Muhammad Babur, *Baburnama*, trans. and ed. Wheeler Thackston (New York: Oxford University Press, 1996), pp. 350–351.
3. Ibid., p. 351.
4. Quoted in Bamber Gascoigne, *The Great Moghuls* (New York: Harper & Row, 1971), p. 128.

Sesshu, details from Birds and Flowers in a Landscape. *Painter and Zen priest Sesshu (c. 1420–1506) is one of the leading figures in Japanese art. Two of six panels, this formal, balanced, and complex work shows the influence on Japanese art of the landscape painting of China's Sung dynasty.*

(Detail) Attributed to Sesshu, Japan, 1420–1506. Muromachi period. *Birds and Flowers in a Landscape.* Six-fold screen, ink and color on paper, 173.4 × 378 cm. © The Cleveland Museum of Art, Purchase from the J. H. Wade Fund, 1961.204.

Ming China and National Development in Korea, Japan, and Southeast Asia, 1300–1650

Chapter Contents

Chinese historians from the beginning wrote the history of their country as a series of consecutive dynastic waves—as one dynasty would exhaust itself, another would form in the yin-yang dialectic of ocean and earth. Sometimes the change from one dynasty to the next would be brutal and ugly, but the underlying rhythm of China seemed undisturbed. The sheer vastness of the subcontinent, ranging from the arctic cold of Manchuria to the equatorial lushness of Malaysia, with its diverse populations, could be seen as pale imitations of the Central Kingdom. Ming China, viewed from the West during the period between 1300 and 1650, fits the image of the Central Kingdom—sublimely independent and superior to all outside forces.

But that image is not accurate. Throughout its history, China did not develop in a vacuum. It has been shaped by its neighbors, just as it has shaped its neighbors. A vast network of roads and sea lanes promoted the movement of people, plants and animals, technologies, thoughts, and institutions. The Chinese genius made itself felt in the synthesis the underlying civilization made with each of these outside influences. This capacity to co-opt potentially destructive forces kept Chinese civilization alive and fresh until the eighteenth century. Whether it was from the nomadic tribes continually pressuring from the north, the Indian missionaries coming into China from the west, or the trade and resources coming from the south, China profited.

The noun *China* is used to indicate the actual territory ruled by the central government at a given time. More important is the adjective *Chinese,* which applies to the region dominated by the culture and civilization of China—a much larger area.

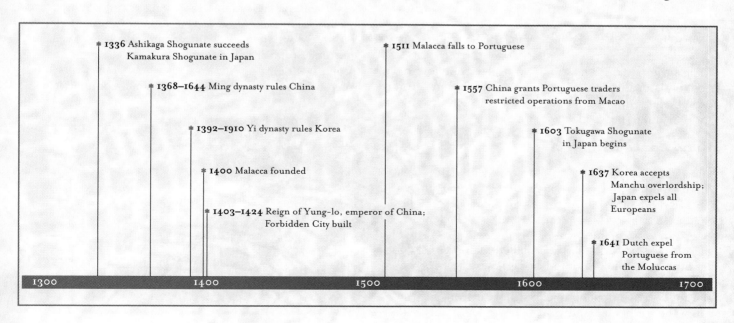

* **1336** Ashikaga Shogunate succeeds Kamakura Shogunate in Japan

* **1368–1644** Ming dynasty rules China

* **1392–1910** Yi dynasty rules Korea

* **1400** Malacca founded

* **1403–1424** Reign of Yung-lo, emperor of China; Forbidden City built

* **1511** Malacca falls to Portuguese

* **1557** China grants Portuguese traders restricted operations from Macao

* **1603** Tokugawa Shogunate in Japan begins

* **1637** Korea accepts Manchu overlordship; Japan expels all Europeans

* **1641** Dutch expel Portuguese from the Moluccas

1300   1400   1500   1600   1700

The Chinese civilization deeply affected the development of Korea, which was under direct Chinese rule for four centuries; Vietnam, which was under Chinese central power for more than a millennium; Japan, which was a cultural satellite for three centuries; and Mongolia, central Asia, Tibet, and Southeast Asia for varying lengths of time. This chapter discusses the development and mutual influences of China, Korea, Japan, and Southeast Asia during what in Europe was known as the late Middle Ages.

China: Political Recovery and the Ming Dynasty

The Mongol-imposed Yuan regime declined rapidly after Kublai's death in 1294 (see Chapter 12). Taxation became more oppressive, and peasant discontent grew. In addition, there were not enough Mongols to carry on the actual governing of the country, so they had to trust foreigners to oversee the Chinese officials. Even Marco Polo had earlier worked for a while in that capacity. Further, the traditionally nomadic Mongol soldiers—the only ones permitted to bear arms—did not take well to serving in permanent posts and lost much of their toughness and discipline. In the 39 years after Kublai's death and the installation of the last Mongol sovereign in 1333, the disorder that prevailed can be seen in the fact that there were eight emperors on the throne. Rising inflation stemming from the higher prices accompanying the expansion of trade and bureaucratic breakdown weakened the base of Yuan power. Finally, a peasant-nationalist rebellion sparked by famine began in southern China in 1352. Sixteen years later the Chinese put an end to the foreign dynasty.

One of the new leaders was a young Buddhist monk, Chou Yuan-Chang, who would rule under the name of Hung-wu. The Ming era, which he began, lasted to 1644. Although the Ming were perhaps less memorable then the earlier Han or T'ang, they stabilized the government and defended their homeland against invasion for the better part of three centuries. For most of the era the country prospered and fostered cultural creativity. Generally, however, the emperors followed pre-Mongol models, except for resisting innovation and trying to block out foreign influences.

The Early Ming Era

The new dynasty showed some potential for creativity before the early fifteenth century. Hung-wu (1368–1398) was aided by his able consort, the legendary Empress Ma, in establishing an efficient Chinese regime. Hung-wu's son, known as Yung-lo (1403–1424), further strengthened the regime and moved the capital back to Peking. These first two emperors restored the examination system and the traditional law, harshly punishing violators but respecting the rights of individuals, even Mongols who

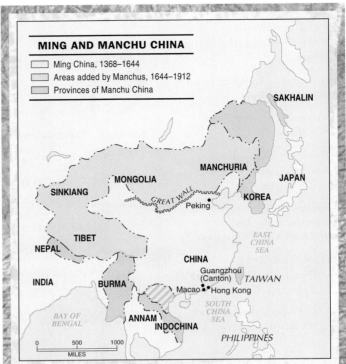

After the first two Ming emperors consolidated and expanded their rule, the rest of the dynasty remained content with the extent of their realm. The Manchus, who would take power in the second half of the seventeenth century, would greatly expand the Central Kingdom.

accepted Ming rule. Hung-wu and Yung-lo also initiated a degree of local autonomy and fostered traditional education while keeping firm control of national government and the military. In addition, they carried on vast economic reconstruction projects: reforestation, water projects, and repopulation.

Policy in the first two reigns reflected a definite interest in the wider world. Both emperors fought successful campaigns against the Mongols, and Yung-lo forcibly reannexed Annam. The Ming government encouraged foreign trade with Japan, Southeast Asia, and India, officially promoting cotton production, introduced earlier from the West, as a new staple export. Yung-lo regularly sent diplomatic and commercial

Ming China

1368–1398	Reign of Hung-wu
1405–1433	Naval expeditions led by Cheng Ho
1472–1529	Wang Yang-ming, philosopher
1644	Founding of Manchu dynasty
1683	Fall of Taiwan

missions to neighboring states and encouraged Chinese migration into the Malay Archipelago. In 1405 Yung-lo set in motion a series of naval expeditions led by Cheng Ho that ended in 1433. With some ships exceeding 500 tons and carrying crews of 700, the Chinese flotillas visited Sumatra, India, the Persian Gulf, Aden, and East Africa. There they exchanged porcelains and pottery for ivory, ostrich feathers, and exotic animals, such as zebras and giraffes. China had already penetrated the Indian Ocean while Portuguese captains were still cautiously exploring the Atlantic coast of Morocco. After the last voyage, Chinese emperors never again sponsored such pathbreaking journeys, but instead rested content within their own Central Kingdom.

Thereafter the Ming emperors were more concerned about recovering the past than pioneering the future. They rallied support by using popular prejudices against the Mongols and the Chinese elite who had served the foreign oppressors. In the process they tried to build a welfare state, funded by heavily taxing the wealthy people who had not supported them and managed by former peasants and tradesmen, instead of the old scholar-bureaucrats. Despite their attempts at some change, the emperors perpetuated many old bureaucratic sources of corruption and weakness. The excesses of court eunuchs, male children sold by their parents to be castrated for court service, continued. Eunuchs had served as court advisers and servants since the Chou dynasty. Continuing destructive Mongol raids, compounded by Japanese pirate attacks along the coast, brought other problems. Consequently, economic revival remained only moderate, population stayed low, and revenues declined while expenditures rose.

The Ming tendency to perpetuate misfortune by clinging to tradition is well illustrated by the declining status of women in this era. This trend had been steady under the Sung and Yuan dynasties, but it reached a new low under the Ming. Foot binding, for example, was most common in the Ming period, when middle-class families hoping to be accepted into the governing elite emulated it. Similarly, legal recognition of concubinage encouraged a traffic in young virgins from poor families. Concubine brokers bought them and then supplied wealthy merchants and officials. Another indication of the new social atmosphere is provided by the increase in suicides and self-mutilations among widows seeking to show grief or prove their loyalty to dead husbands. By the mid-seventeenth century, 8600 Ming widows killed themselves, compared with 359 under the Yuan and 150 under the Sung.

Ming Society and Culture in the Sixteenth Century

As time passed, Chinese rulers became even more resistant to innovation. Yet this inflexibility, so common

Portrait of Hung-wu, the first emperor of the Ming dynasty.

among a long line of "do nothing" emperors, generated an aura of stability through most of the 1500s, when Chinese culture was a model for East Asia. Sixteenth-century European visitors were impressed by Chinese courtesy, respect for law, confidence, and stately ceremonies. They saw material prosperity in the bustling markets, stone-paved roads, and beautiful homes of Ming officials. The elaborate Ming examination system, with its proclaimed principle of advancement on merit, often evoked favorable surprise. But European commentators were perhaps most lavish in praising Chinese justice; one concluded that China was "one of the best-governed" countries "in the entire world."[1] Such recognized superiority, along with the resulting Chinese satisfaction, was a major obstacle to progress in the later Ming period.

The Ming respect for learning was most evident in the production of vast multivolume collections, including 1500 local histories and a dry but famous medical work, *The Outline of Herb Medicine*, which took 30 years to complete. In this spirit, during the reign of Yung-lo there was an attempt to create an enormous library containing all of the works of

Polygamy in a Ming Household

This selection reveals the kind of competition and petty jealousy that could develop in a middle-class family with multiple wives.

Now that she was the favorite, Lotus became more and more intent on having her own way. She was never at peace. . . . One day, in a bad mood over nothing, she upbraided her maid Plum. . . . That morning she had risen earlier than usual to help Moon, the principal wife, get ready for a funeral. She had been so tired she took a nap, and was just going back to her own suite. On her way there she ran into Jade, the third wife.

"Why are you looking so worn out?" Jade asked.

"Don't ask me! I had to get up early," Lotus replied, then added, "Sister, where are you coming from?"

"I stopped at the kitchen."

"Did the one there tell you anything?"

"No, not that I can think of."

. . . She and Jade sat down and passed some time doing needlework. After finishing the tea and cakes Plum and Chrysanthemum set out, they decided to play a game of chess. But no sooner had their game become exciting than Hsi-men was announced and entered the room. . . .

When Jade asked about Moon, Hsi-men said she would be coming later in the sedan chair and that he had sent two servant boys to meet her. He sat down next to them and asked, "What were your stakes in this game?"

"Oh, we were just playing for the fun of it," Lotus answered.

"Then let me challenge you each to a game. Whoever loses forfeits a tael of silver to pay for a party."

"But we don't have any money with us," Lotus objected.

"Never mind. You can give me a hairpin as security."

First he played with Lotus and she lost. He began to reset the pieces for a game with Jade, but Lotus suddenly tipped over the board, causing the chessmen to fall in a jumble. Then she ran out of the room and into the garden.

Hsi-men chased her and found her picking flowers. "What a spoilsport! You run away because you lost, my lovable little oily-mouth," he called to her, panting. . . .

Their diversions were soon interrupted by Jade who called, "Moon has just returned. We'd better go."

Lotus broke loose from Hsi-men and said she would talk to him more later. Then she hurried after Jade to pay her respects to Moon.

Moon asked them, "What makes you two so merry?"

"Lotus lost a tael of silver playing chess with the master, so she will have to host a party tomorrow," Jade answered. "You must come."

Moon smiled and Lotus soon took her leave. She rejoined Hsi-men in the front suite and had Plum light some incense and draw a hot bath so that later they could amuse themselves like a couple of fish.

Although Moon was Hsi-men's principal wife, her ill-health usually kept her from fulfilling all the duties of the mistress of the house. Grace, the second wife, performed most of the social duties such as paying visits and receiving guests, and handled the household budget. Snow, the fourth wife, took charge of the servants and was the chief cook. Wherever Hsi-men was in the house, if he wanted something to eat or drink, he would send his request to Snow via one of the maids of the lady he was visiting.

From the novel *Chin P'ing Mei* (1610), in Patricia B. Ebrey, ed., *Chinese Civilization and Society: A Sourcebook* (New York: Macmillan, 1981), pp. 167–168.

ancient Chinese literature and an encyclopedia on which more than 3000 scholars worked. There were, however, more dynamic intellectual developments, encouraged by the increased printing of books and by the growth of education in private academies preparing students for public examinations. A pragmatic influence against orthodox Neo-Confucianism was provided by the soldier, poet, and philosopher Wang Yang-ming (1472–1529), who taught that knowledge is intuitive and thought is inseparable from action.

Some Ming literature deviated from classical poetic styles. Written in colloquial language, novels describe ordinary life, often including explicit pornography. Three of the best-known novels date from the sixteenth century. *Monkey* is a rollicking semisatirical tale about a Buddhist monk traveling to India with his pig and a monkey, which had led an earlier human life. The partly pornographic *Chin P'ing Mei* recounts a pharmacist's romantic adventures. Perhaps the best-read work is *All Men Are Brothers*, the story of an outlaw band, like Robin Hood's merry men, who robbed the rich to help the poor. Travel literature and adventures found great acceptance among the merchant classes.

Playwrights from the south dominated Chinese drama, which had a golden age of its own during the Ming period. Plays ran sometimes to ten acts, developing intricate plots and subplots with unexpected endings. Music became more prominent on the stage as solos, duets, and even entire choirs alternated with the spoken word in performances.

Ming artists and architects produced great quantities of high-quality works but generally lacked originality. The horizontal lines of the Forbidden City, the imperial family's area of temples and palaces, dating from 1403 to 1424, illustrate the period's values of acceptance, balance, and formalism. In Ming painting, slight exceptions from the norm are found in the free naturalistic landscapes of Shen Chou (1427–1509) and his most talented pupil, Wen Cheng-ming (1470–1559). The great later Ming painter Tung Ch'i-ch'ang (1555–1636) was noted for the formal discipline of his brush strokes. By far the period's major artistic achievement was its porcelains, decorated in "Ming blue" under the glaze. They were copied unsuccessfully from Japan to Holland but were prized everywhere, especially in the sultan's court at the Topkapi Palace in Istanbul.

Porcelain vase featuring the distinguishing blue underglaze of the Ming dynasty.

Prunis Vase (Meiping) with Blossoming Lotus: Fahug Ware. Porcelain with polychrome glazes, H. 37.5 cm. China, Jiangxi Province, Jingdezhen kilns, late 15th century, Ming dynasty. The Cleveland Museum of Art, 1994, Bequest of John L. Severance, 42.716.

Ming Decline

Despite many signs of early vigor, the Ming regime steadily weakened after the middle of the fifteenth century. This decline resulted largely from dynamic changes that the emperors and their courtiers tried to ignore while restricting foreign contacts. Ultimately, the government was beset with serious difficulties on every side, and its own decadence prevented it from responding to the challenges. In the later years of the Ming, eunuchs controlled most of the state power and were content to play the competing clans one against the other. The traditional scholar-bureaucrats found themselves frozen out of their usual positions of influence and pursued their interests through a series of secret societies.

Economic and social signs of decline were particularly evident in the late 1500s. Population had expanded rapidly, from less than 75 million in 1400 to over 150 million.[2] This rising human flood swelled the number and size of market towns, particularly in the heavily populated south. The overflow of determined emigrants poured into Indonesia and the Philippines. Trade expanded voluminously within the country, and smuggling increased along the coasts, despite desperate government attempts to prevent it. Portuguese traders, banned in 1517, were permitted restricted operations from Macao after 1557. Soon

This subtle work, Whispering Pines on a Mountain Path, *painted by Tang Yin (1470–1523) embodies the artistic ideals of the Ming dynasty.*

A sixteenth-century engraving of Macao shows Portuguese ships anchored at the port.

foreign foods, goods, and money, especially Spanish silver, disrupted the economy and contributed to inflation. These changes drew the gentry and peasants into the towns, away from rising land taxes. They became prosperous but discontented members of a middle class that was increasing even faster than the burgeoning general population. Urban unrest and inflation were only two of the converging problems facing later Ming emperors. Technical progress lagged, and production failed to supply the rising population.

Corruption, waste, conservatism, and bureaucratic inertia prevailed at every level of government and especially in the military. The armed forces had doubled in size by the end of the sixteenth century, but they were badly equipped and generally poorly led. The army suffered a serious drop in morale as disorder increased throughout the country: hordes of pirates ravaged the coasts, while Mongol attacks brought near-anarchy along the Great Wall. There was an almost complete breakdown in confidence in the battles with the Japanese, who used gunpowder weapons against Chinese swords and spears in the 1590s. Japanese assaults on Korea, however, were rebuffed.

Local governors and commanders, rather than the imperial government, were largely responsible for limited successes in dealing with these misfortunes. One such leader in southwestern China was the famous female general Ch'in Liang-yu, whose troops put down local rebellion and restored order. Known for her bravery and strength of character, she was also a refined woman who wrote elegant poetry. The central administration meanwhile nearly ceased to function. Most emperors were prisoners of the highly formalized system and puppets of their eunuch ministers, who generally pursued their own interests in directing policies increasingly frivolous and unrealistic.

Until about 1650 China seemed to influence Europe more than Europe influenced China, but the Western impact, viewed in historical perspective, was perhaps greater than it appeared at the time. Its most visible signs were the Portuguese ships and traders at

Macao, the few Portuguese artillerymen employed against the Manchus, and the Jesuit advisers in Peking, who followed Father Matteo Ricci to the Ming court after 1601. The Jesuits were not very successful missionaries, converting only some 100,000 Chinese, a tiny fraction of the population. But Jesuit treatises on the practical sciences, such as medicine, shipbuilding, and metal casting, were widely read and highly valued. Even more lasting effects came with European trade and Western food crops, which helped weaken Chinese values and expand an increasingly contentious population.

In the summer of 1644, after attempting to kill his oldest daughter and succeeding only in cutting off her arm, the last Ming emperor, Ch'ung-cheng (1627–1644), hanged himself in his imperial garden, leaving a pitiful note to indicate his shame in meeting his ancestors. An insurgent government had already formed to the west in Szechwan, another rebel army was approaching Peking, and only a few Portuguese mercenaries and some imperial guards remained nominally loyal. But neither of the Chinese countermovements would succeed. As the Ming regime collapsed, Manchu forces crossed the northern borders. By 1683 a Manchu emperor controlled the whole country.

Korea: The Restless Satellite

Korea, China's northeastern satellite, clung resolutely to its own identity. It had survived for centuries by periodically accepting tributary status under Chinese emperors and adapting imported Chinese culture, much of which it passed on to Japan. The country had been united again by the founder of the Koryo dynasty (918–1392), who gave Korea its name. Koryo kings adopted the Sung Chinese imperial bureaucratic structure as well as its examination system. They were particularly zealous in promoting Neo-Confucian learning. Korean presses, using movable type, were printing scholarly treatises by the eleventh century. The government also organized many basic industries, for which it imported Chinese technology.

As in the past, however, little was done for the common people. While popular unrest and aristocratic contentions prevailed, the Mongols overran the country and dominated it until 1368. Korean monarchs became virtual puppets of Yuan emperors. The nation was then divided between those who courted the conquerors and those who resented the heavy Yuan taxes and manpower levies.

The Beginning of the Yi Dynasty

When the Yuan regime was overthrown in China, Korean military leaders seized power, dispossessing the old landed aristocrats of the Koryo establishment

Discovery Through Maps

A Korea-Centered View of the World

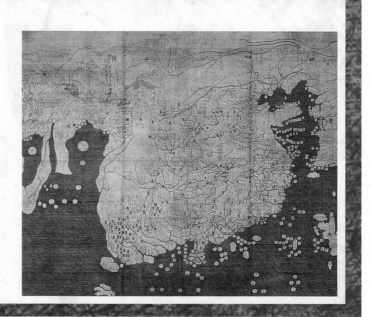

By the way they portray their homeland in relation to their neighbors, mapmakers make a statement about their love of their country and their capacity to see themselves from an accurate perspective.

Unlike modern mapmakers, who are constrained through centuries of observations, satellite photos, and projections to render accurately the comparative sizes of the recorded landmasses, the Korean mapmaker centuries ago faced no limits in his presentation. Korea assumes continental dimensions in this map, and Japan shrivels away to a distant, puny archipelago. Thus, the cartographer served his countrymen with a reassuring, if false, image of Korea's strength.

and redistributing their lands among scholar-bureaucrats who supported the rebellion. In 1392 the military leader Yi Song-gye was recognized as the first king of the new Yi dynasty, which lasted until 1910.

Like the Ming rulers to whom they paid tribute, early Yi monarchs carried out a revolution against elitists of the old regime. They created a new land register, abolished feudal relations in the armed forces, eliminated many Buddhist privileges, made Confucianism the state religion, and created a new bureaucracy made up of military leaders and scholars. In foreign affairs the new dynasty began territorial expansion into Manchuria and conducted successful operations against Japanese coastal pirates.

Improved communications, better agricultural techniques, and new inventions in the crafts brought rising economic productivity. The manufacture of cotton cloth, learned from China, also stimulated trade. Such economic growth increased the number of craftspeople and merchants, although most were employed in government monopolies.

The early Yi promised more than they delivered. In less than a century a new centralized administration entrenched a class of privileged Neo-Confucian bureaucrats who were as corrupt, inefficient, and overbearing as those in Ming China. With their growing power came higher taxes and service requirements for common people, most of whom were peasant tenants, and more than a third were still slaves. These conditions touched off popular uprisings, which the government brutally suppressed.

As in China, the Neo-Confucian revival brought more difficulties for women. Up through the tenth century they had enjoyed near-equality with men

King Sejong of Korea (1419–1450), a member of the Yi dynasty. During his reign Korea reached the height of cultural achievements, and the modern boundaries of the country were fixed. Sejong is also credited with the creation of the Korean phonetic, or Han'gul, alphabet.

This stoneware wine pitcher from the twelfth-century Koryo dynasty of Korea features a celadon glaze and inlaid white and black slip.

in property, inheritance, and marriage rights. Silla rulers had often been women. After the Koryo period, however, new laws severely restricted women's legal rights and prohibited them from participating in games, attending feasts, appearing in public unveiled, or even walking alone outside their homes.

The early Yi period brought a mild upsurge of cultural expression, particularly in literature. Treatises produced by the scholarly ruling class were often dull, but some showed genuine respect for rational learning. These scholarly efforts helped promote practical curricula in the academies, a Korean alphabet, and the development of metal-casted type for printing. Government presses published an increasing number of works in various literary forms. Some of these were prose compositions on mundane subjects, but poetry, stressing love of nature, personal grief, and romantic love, became quite popular. Many lyric poets were women. Less initiative was evident in the other arts, however. Painting, jewelry, calligraphy, sculpture, and architecture generally followed Chinese models, resulting in many creditable works, though most lacked originality. Only in ceramics did the Koreans equal the Chinese.

The end of the Ming era brought troubled times to Korea. Factionalism plagued the government, as too many bureaucrats competed for too few positions. Then, as Ming protective power waned, the Japanese invaded in 1592 with a force of 200,000 soldiers supported by 9000 sailors. The invaders hoped

to use Korea as a base against China. Disaster was temporarily averted by Korean armored "tortoise boats," which cut supply lines of the invading forces. In 1597 the Japanese tried again, unsuccessfully, to take Korea. Deliverance was not assured until the death of Hideyoshi, the Japanese shogun, in 1598. The seven years of war diminished Korea's wealth and inflicted terrible hardships on its people. King Kwang-haegun (1608–1623) made determined efforts to rebuild the country, but they came too late.

After aiding Ming China in war against the Manchus, Korea was invaded, ultimately defeated, and forced to accept Manchu overlordship in 1637. Thousands of Koreans, held hostage by the Manchus, suffered great cruelty and privation before they could be ransomed. Many Korean families rejected female members who had been sexually violated and therefore dishonored.

Japan: From Feudal Conflicts to the Tokugawa Shogunate

The disastrous fate of Ming China was not repeated in Japan as it was in Korea. During the fifteenth century the Japanese central government lost almost all of its power to great local lords, the *daimyo*, who fought among themselves for control of the country. Their wars actually stimulated the economy and temporarily opened Japan to foreign influences. Later Japan isolated itself, not from a sense of superiority or a desire to ignore the outside world, but in order to achieve political stability.

The End of Central Power

The rising daimyo, strangely enough, prepared the way for their own decline. Greatly weakened by resisting Mongol invasions in 1274 and 1281, the Kamakura government faced an uprising against the shogun in favor of the emperor. For some 60 years Japan was caught up in civil strife as supporters of the emperor and the shogun claimed authority, each supported by contending forces. In 1336 the dominant force proclaimed the Ashikaga Shogunate the successor to the Kamakura, but the new regime soon lost control of its vassals. The daimyo in time assumed complete authority over each of their lands, not only raising armies but also taxing and issuing laws.

By the late 1400s their sporadic fighting had become protracted and full-scale. When civil war broke out between rival Ashikaga houses in 1467, more than 250,000 men were soon in combat around Kyoto. Intensified by the use of firearms, the conflagration spread throughout the country and lasted, with brief lapses, for over a century; it reduced the number of daimyo from roughly 260 in 1467 to 45 in 1580.

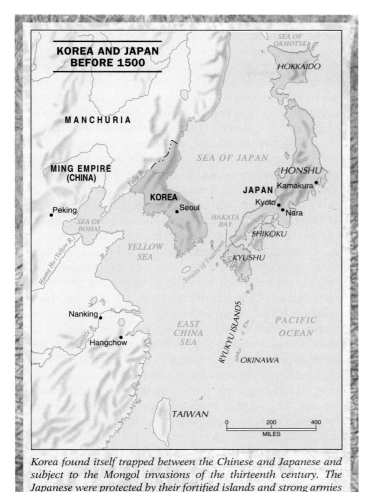

Korea found itself trapped between the Chinese and Japanese and subject to the Mongol invasions of the thirteenth century. The Japanese were protected by their fortified islands and strong armies and maintained control over Kyushu, Shikoku, and Honshu.

Along with political instability, the period brought economic growth and dynamic social change. The daimyo were so occupied with their wars that they were forced to be more lenient with merchants who paid taxes and with some peasants who served in mercenary armies. Needing weapons, supplies, and money, the daimyo sought to foster trade, build towns, and encourage industry. Agricultural production also continued to rise, as it had done since the thirteenth century. Rising food production increased population, spurred city growth, and encouraged social mobility. Despite such spotty prosperity, many common laborers and peasants worked hard for an insecure existence. These conditions spurred the growth of mystical religions, such as Zen Buddhism and other evangelical cults, which stressed street preaching, congregational worship, and salvation in the next world.

The interests that impelled the daimyo toward trade with China and Korea led them as well toward Europeans. Because Portuguese captains could best supply efficient firearms and help foster profitable enterprises, the daimyo competed for Portuguese fa-

vor. After 1544 various daimyo concluded commercial agreements with the Portuguese, who took over most trade with the mainland, exchanging Japanese silver and copper for Chinese silks. After 1580 Portuguese operations transformed Nagasaki from a tiny fishing village to one of the largest ports in Asia, while the Spanish, English, and Dutch could be found in the ports of Hirado, Nagoya, and Kyushu.

Behind the traders came the missionaries, who were generally welcomed by daimyo eager to establish commercial contacts. Francis Xavier began preaching near Kyoto in 1549; by 1600 he and his Jesuit brothers had converted 300,000 Japanese, including some influential daimyo of Kyushu. The Jesuits worked closely with Portuguese merchants, sometimes acting as commercial agents among the local potentates.

The Tokugawa Shogunate

Between 1560 and 1598 two powerful warlords, Oda Nobunaga and his able commander Toyotomi Hideyoshi, gained control over the daimyo. Nobunaga in 1573 set aside the last of the Ashikaga shoguns, put down the Buddhist military orders, and drove the powerful Mori family from central Japan. Hideyoshi, who succeeded to the regency in 1584, completed the conquest of the daimyo. This former peasant without formal education and training in the higher forms of Japanese culture was extraordinarily intelligent, as could be seen in his military and political policies.

In his pursuit of a strong central power he disarmed the populace and ended all feudal grants of political authority. He made all levels sacrifice for the "greater good." As the feudal lords lost their power, the peasants were tied to the earth and forced to turn over two-thirds of their harvest to the state. Hideyoshi turned increasingly to the merchant classes, which he favored, for both support and taxes. To solidify his control, he separated the warrior samurai from the local landed interests and nationalized their service. With this base thus fortified in the decade after 1590, Hideyoshi warred against Korea and China, hoping to gain Christian support for a religious crusade. When these hopes were not realized and his campaigns failed, he began sporadic persecution of Christians, executing 26 of them in 1597.

After Hideyoshi died in 1598, the country lapsed again into civil war. Within a few years, however, Hideyoshi's former ally in eastern Japan, Tokugawa Ieyasu, became the strongest warlord. He won the decisive battle of Seikigahara in 1600 and soon had himself appointed shogun. Although his son Hidetada succeeded him in 1605, Ieyasu continued to exercise the real power until his own death in 1616. Seven years later his grandson Iemitsu became shogun, holding the office until 1651. By that time the Tokugawa Shogunate was firmly established; it would shape Japanese culture for the next two and a half centuries. The shoguns always remained the subjects of the emperor. They ruled with the aid of a council and had the responsibility to maintain order throughout all of Japan. They also commanded the unified forces of the country should a foreign threat occur, carried on relations with foreign powers, and generally decided the issues of war and peace.

Ieyasu, shrewd, patient, and ruthless, was one of the most successful rulers in Japanese history. Conditioned by the cruel uncertainties of the civil wars, he was both modest and unprincipled. To obtain favor with Nobunaga, he murdered his own wife and compelled a son to commit suicide. He won many battles by treachery. Yet his personal philosophy extolled self-criticism, quiet patience, and humble bearing. Above all, he displayed an iron determination to achieve political security for himself, his family, and his country.

The Tokugawa government was a model of efficient centralized feudalism. As in the past, the emperor symbolized national unity while the shogun held the real power over the fiscal and military affairs. The daimyo remained as local governors, paying tribute to the capital, but bureaucratic regulations and inspections increasingly limited their powers. From the beginning, all were required to attend court, leaving close relatives as hostages when they were at home. This system, so similar to that of the Muslim empires, was much more successful. A major weakness, however, was the government's conservative response to a rapidly expanding economy.

Economic and Social Changes: The Western Factor

Political stability and government projects led directly to a burgeoning Tokugawa economy before the end of Iemitsu's reign. An official system of levees, canals, and dams provided drainage and irrigation for new arable lands; another government network of roads, post houses, and messengers brought agricultural products to flourishing towns. Various industries, especially cotton cloth manufacturing, provided a mass of consumer goods for exchange. Although foreign trade was limited after Ieyasu's time, its regulated flow from the port of Osaka made that city into a great financial center.

Tokugawa society was a medley of contrasts. Along with its expanding economy came a great swelling of population, which would rise by 32 percent during the seventeenth century, from 22 to 29 million.[3] Much of this rising human tide would congregate in cities such as Osaka, Kyoto, Edo (Tokyo), and other castle towns of the earlier warring states. There a rising merchant class began to supersede the old daimyo lords and their fighting retainers, the samurai. Members of the latter class were still honored as they rode the social momentum of the recent civil wars, but they had been reduced to an ornamental petty aristocracy of state mercenaries. Lacking real purpose or practical judgment and addicted to their own amusement, many became indebted to moneylenders and merchants, who profited from samurai misfortunes. Perhaps the two least favored groups were peasants and aristocratic women. The former were still heavily taxed, recruited for labor services, and subject to heavy discipline in their villages. The latter, unlike middle-class women, were victims of the prevailing Neo-Confucian code, which relegated wives to an inferior status as untrustworthy wards of their fathers and husbands.

The early Tokugawa period brought a rapid increase and then a dramatic end to most European influence. At first Ieyasu tolerated Christianity in the hope of maintaining good relations and foreign trade. In his own pursuit of trade Ieyasu issued more than 300 patents permitting Japanese to trade in the first third of

As a defense measure, the Tokugawa government outlawed the building of bridges across major rivers. Thus the rivers were crossed by palanquin, *an enclosed litter that men bore on their shoulders by means of poles. Or one might cross the river on the back of a human porter.*

Ando Hiroshige, c. 1832. Abe River near Fuchu, woodblock print. Honolulu Academy of Arts, Gift of James A. Michener, 1978 (17,235).

Father Xavier's Difficulties as a Missionary in Sixteenth-Century Japan

This is from one of Father Xavier's letters, written in 1549 to friends in India. Note references to recent wars of the daimyo.

I went on with Joam Fernandez to Amanguchi. . . . The city contains more than ten thousand households. . . . We found many here, both of the common people and of the nobility, very desirous to become acquainted with the Christian law. We thought it best to preach twice a day in the streets and cross roads, reading out parts of our book, and then speaking to the people about the Christian religion. Some of the noblemen also invited us to their houses, that they might hear about our religion with more convenience. They promised of their own accord, that if they came to think it better than their own, they would unhesitatingly embrace it. Many of them heard what we had to say about the law of God very willingly; some, on the other hand, were angry at it, and even went so far as to laugh at what we said. So, wherever we went through the streets of the city, we were followed by a small crowd of boys of the lowest dregs of the populace, laughing at us and mocking us with some such words as these: "There go the men who tell us that we must embrace the law of God in order to be saved, because we cannot be rescued from destruction except by the Maker of all things and by His Son! There go the men who declare that it is wicked to have more than one wife!"

. . . We had spent some days in this office of preaching, when the king, who was then in the city, sent for us and we went to him. He asked us wherever did we come from? why had we come to Japan? And we answered that we were Europeans sent thither for the sake of preaching the law of God, since no one could be safe and secure unless he purely and piously worship God and His Son Jesus Christ, the Redeemer and Saviour of all nations. Then the king commanded us to explain to him the law of God. So we read to him

a good part of our volume; and although we went on reading for an hour or more, he listened to us diligently and attentively as long as we were reading, and then he sent us away. We remained many days in the city, and preached to the people in the streets and at the cross roads. Many of them listened to the wonderful deeds of Christ with avidity, and when we came to His most bitter death, they were unable to restrain their tears. Nevertheless, very few actually became Christians.

Finding, therefore, that the fruit of our labours was small, we went on to Meaco, the most famous city in all Japan. We spent two months on the road, and passed through many dangers, because we had to go through countries in which war was raging. I say nothing of the cold of those parts, nor of the roads so infested by frequent robberies. When we arrived at Meaco, we waited for some days that we might obtain leave to approach the king, and ask of him to give us permission to publish the divine law in his kingdom. But we found all ways of access to him altogether closed. And as we discovered that the edicts of the king were generally thought little of among the princes and rulers, we laid aside our design of obtaining from him any such licence, and I determined to sound and try the minds and dispositions of the people themselves, so as to find out how disposed that city was to receive the worship of Christ. But as the people were under arms, and under the pressure of a severe war, I judged that the time was most inopportune for the preaching of the Gospel. . . .

From William H. McNeill and Mitsuko Iriye, eds., *Modern Asia and Africa* (New York: Oxford University Press, 1971), pp. 15–17.

the seventeenth century. The ships ranged from 300 to 800 tons in size and ventured to Taiwan, China, and the Strait of Malacca. Quarters for Japanese sailors were erected in Manila, Haiphong, Phnom Penh, and Indonesia. Despite the arrogance of Spanish Franciscan missionaries, he also tried to negotiate a commercial agreement with the Spanish, but they refused to admit Japanese ships into Philippine or Mexican ports. Ieyasu was also alienated by the desperate intrigues of recently arrived Dutch and English merchants, who consistently outmaneuvered his own merchants. Finally, in 1635 he forbid all Japanese to go abroad, on pain of death.

At the same time, in 1612, 1613, and 1614 Ieyasu issued edicts prohibiting Christianity. Thousands of

loyal Japanese Christians suffered martyrdom during succeeding years, hundreds being crucified. A climax came in 1637 when a popular revolt, led by some Christian daimyo, was put down. Japan then expelled all Europeans except for one regulated Dutch station at Nagasaki. In 1639 he cut all relations with Portugal and Spain. When in 1640 the Portuguese negotiators ignored his order and came back to Nagasaki, he burned their vessels, executed 61 of them, and sent the 13 crew members back to Macao. The Chinese were also limited to their own quarters in Nagasaki after 1635. Ieyasu saw the Christians and the foreigners as disturbers of the public order he was bound by his role as shogun to uphold.

Cultural Expressions

As with the European Renaissance, which was a unique variation on its classical heritage, Japanese culture in this period continued to accent its peculiar identity within Chinese forms. It also expressed the curious duality of Japanese society: a striving for calm serenity and a contrasting lusty vitality, as shown in explicit literature, massive architecture, and brilliant color. Although often obscured by tradition, these latter characteristics became increasingly evident in the Tokugawa era.

During the late Ashikaga period, Zen Buddhism spread from the great monasteries to impress thought and art with respect for things elegantly simple. Its best-known expressions were flower arranging, landscape gardening, and the famous tea ceremony, with its accented restraint and quiet contemplation. Zen also influenced painting as artists strove through the discipline of their brush strokes and the austerity of their subject matter to demonstrate that "less is more" in artistic creativity. The most enduring literary vehicle of the period was the Noh, a traditional form of lyric drama that combined stately mimetic dancing, music, and song. All such pursuits continued to be popular, particularly among the elite, into the Tokugawa era.

The era of political unification, however, brought new cultural emphases. In his mania for discipline, Ieyasu promoted Neo-Confucianism at his court, hoping to achieve emancipation from Buddhist thought. Similarly, the Momoyama period in Japanese art, the age from Nobunaga to Iemitsu, was often marked by ostentation and flamboyance, resembling in its own contexts the contemporary European baroque. It was most obvious in architecture, particularly in massive stone castles. Hideyoshi's famous fortress at Osaka, for example, had 48 towers; the base of the central tower was 75 feet high, and the main structure rose another 102 feet. Within the castles, other arts were displayed in wild profusion, featuring woodcarving, sliding doors, folding screens, and brilliantly colored walls. Paintings were often grandiose, in keeping with the pretensions of the castle lords. To this showy melange early haiku poetry, with its 17-syllable verses, added its own version of traditional sensitivity and measured elegance.

The Competing States of Southeast Asia

Situated on the main sea route between East Asia and the Indian Ocean and divided geographically into diverse subregions, Southeast Asia had long been an area of contending states. Most of the region had managed to escape prolonged, direct Mongol occupation. Although much of the culture came from elsewhere in Asia, particularly from India and China, each country was fiercely committed to its own interests. This nationalism frequently involved war in defense of independence or attempted conquest of neighboring states, which were usually held in contempt.

As Southeast Asia approached the modern era after 1300, difficulties increased with the weakening of the influence of the Khmer and the decline of the civilization of Angkor. The Mongols, who temporarily received tribute from the mainland and parts of Java, seriously disrupted all existing governments. Throughout there were ruinous petty wars, often based on Hindu-versus-Buddhist conflicts, each of which suffered individually under Muslim expansion. Finally, Muslim regimes replaced many traditional Hindu states in Indonesia, which also felt the effects of European empire building, first by the Portuguese and then by the Dutch. Before 1650, however, the total European impact on the mainland was negligible.

Burma and the Thais

In the first millennium of the Common Era, the region of present-day Burma remained an ethnically diverse region under Chinese domination divided into a number of small principalities. Around 1050 a process of political unification began under the Burmese, a group of people who moved to the south from the Tibetan frontier. This movement was shattered by the Mongol invasions of the 1280s. The process of unification recommenced after 1287, culminating in the dominance of the Tongoo kingdom in the fifteenth and sixteenth centuries.

Advancing to the south during the Mongol invasions were the Thais, a group of people from Yunnan already strongly influenced by Chinese culture and civilization. Once in Indochina the Thais also absorbed the richness of the Indian civilization. In the middle of the thirteenth century, during the Sukhothai kingdom (1220–1349), they founded a series of strong settlements in Indochina, displacing the indigenous Khmer and Burmese populations. The Sukhothai were later overthrown by the Ayutthaya kingdom, which lasted from 1350 to 1782 and had periods of regional dominance. After the Mongol withdrawal, a strong Thai state rose to fill the vacuum and came to control the greater part of Indochina by 1394.

Under King Bayinnaung in the 1550s and 1560s Burma briefly absorbed Laos and conquered Siam (Thailand) with an army estimated at 500,000, the largest ever assembled in Southeast Asia. Bayinnaung's capital at Pegu was a nucleus of Buddhist culture, a thriving commercial center, and the site of

The region of Southeast Asia served as an arena for the interaction of Chinese, Indian, and Arab cultures, whether in the powerful states of Siam or in the islands of the Philippine Archipelago.

his wondrous palace, which was roofed in solid gold. But his successor wasted resources in unsuccessful invasions of Siam. Later the Thai state gained supremacy, humbling Cambodia and Burma after 1595 and profiting from commercial alliance with the Dutch.

Vietnam

During the fifteenth century Vietnam completely overshadowed its neighbors. Rulers of the early Le dynasty after 1428 drove out the Chinese and absorbed Champa while threatening Laos, Cambodia, and Burma. These three nations were all in decline; indeed, Burma had broken into a number of feudal domains. A slight exception to the general trend was the little Thai polity under King Trailock (1448–1488), who was partly successful in creating an efficient army and establishing a civil administra-

tion. By the end of the fifteenth century the Vietnamese, along with the Thais, momentarily controlled the Indochinese peninsula.

Indonesia

Islam expanded into Indonesia in a gradual and generally peaceful manner and achieved a great success in the fourteenth and fifteenth centuries. Sufi Muslim missionaries were drawn to the area by the expanding India-China trade, particularly when Chinese interests waned in the decade after 1424. Many local rulers embraced Islam to gain independence from the great Hindu state of Madjapahet on Java; others sought a share of Indian commerce. The Muslims built on the framework of the Madjapahet maritime empire, which extended throughout the island chain from Sumatra to Bali. The trading power easily accepted and dealt with foreigners, among them the large number of Chinese who immigrated and large number of merchants from Egypt, Persia, Arabia, and western India. These Muslims mixed easily with the populations of the port cities. As the power of the Javan empire weakened, the influence of Islam grew. Muslim sailors—either pirates or traders, depending on the circumstances—came to control the various straits between the islands and set up their own states.

The indigenous population came quite naturally to adopt Islam, as the local princely families intermarried with the Muslims in alliances bringing the power and legitimacy of the first to the wealth of the second. An especially strong point in the mass conversion to Islam in the sixteenth century came in the former Hindu areas: the equality of all people as taught by Muhammad pleased the local people caught in the chains of the caste system. At the same time, the Islamic clerics adapted their faith to some of the local customs and beliefs. From this base in Indonesia, Islam spread throughout present-day Malaysia, the Moluccas, and the Philippines. Only Bali remained relatively untouched by the Islamic advance.

The rising Muslim commercial center of Malacca, on the Malay coast opposite Sumatra, best illustrates the entry of Islam into Southeast Asia. Founded in 1400 under the protection of China, its rulers became Muslims, won independence from Siam, and built a Muslim empire of commercial vassal states in the region. Before 1511, when it fell to the Portuguese, Malacca was the busiest port in Asia, linking China and the Moluccas with India and Africa. Its growing success paralleled Muslim expansion through western Indonesia to the Philippines in the sixteenth century.

Arrival of the Europeans

In Southeast Asia, mainland governments generally maintained their independence against the Europeans. Portuguese missionaries, at first active in Vietnam, were expelled by the end of the period. Portuguese traders and mercenary soldiers served everywhere, but they were usually controlled. Some were enslaved in Burma; only in weakened Cambodia and Laos did they acquire significant political influence. By the seventeenth century the Portuguese were giving way to the Dutch, who courted the Vietnamese in only partially successful efforts to monopolize trade with Siam and Burma.

Well before 1650 Europeans were becoming very active in Indonesia. The Portuguese tried to use Malacca as a base for dominating trade in the region, but Muslim confederacies forcefully ejected them from Java and Sumatra and limited their operations in the Moluccas. In the late 1500s Portugal was allied with Spain when the latter acquired a foothold in the Philippines. The Spanish established a colonial capital at Manila and converted the country to Christianity. But the Spanish presence failed to protect the Portuguese from European competition.

Dutch newcomers quickly took control of the Moluccas and expelled the Portuguese in 1641. Soon after, the Dutch concluded a long war in Java by forcing upon the sultans a treaty that guaranteed a Dutch commercial monopoly in return for native political autonomy. Thereafter, Dutch plantation agriculture began undermining Indonesian economies. By the second half of the century the Dutch had replaced the Muslims as the most powerful merchants in the region. From then on, Europe's demands for the spices and riches of the region would be satisfied by the merchants of Amsterdam.

Conclusion

The geography and demographics of China had dictated that it would be impossible to maintain a Central Kingdom, isolated and arrogant, for long. The Ming tried their best after their first half century to pursue a conservative policy of noninvolvement with other peoples and succeeded in bringing some stability to China. However, toward the seventeenth century their inability to reform and the arrival of all manner of outsiders—invaders and merchants alike—spelled an end to their nearly three-century-long run.

Korea and Japan were the two major recipients of the Chinese example and closeness. Korea rested under the immediate gaze of its immense neighbor yet managed to construct a unique and powerful nation. Japan, blessed with its island position, had the unparalleled advantage of picking and choosing the currents and influences it would receive. To the south and southeast, a complex mosaic of nations grew, formed from Indian, Chinese, and Muslim influences. Never able to achieve regional dominance, each of them had a moment of hegemony and remained to add to the rich and varied cultural picture that Asia remains.

Suggestions for Reading

Among the best general histories of China are William Scott Morton, *China: Its History and Culture* (McGraw-Hill, 1982); Witold Rodzinzki, *A History of China*, 2 vols. (Pergamon, 1979); and Charles O. Hucker, *China's Imperial Past* (Stanford University Press, 1975). Others deserving mention are Wolfram Eberhard, *A History of China* (University of California Press, 1977); John Meskill, *An Introduction to Chinese Civilization* (Heath, 1973); Raymond Dawson, *Imperial China* (Hutchinson, 1972); and Hilda Hookham, *A Short History of China* (St. Martin's Press, 1970). A recent readable paperback is Steven Warshaw, *China Emerges* (Diablo, 1987). For complete coverage of Chinese technology and engineering, see Joseph Needham, *Clerks and Craftsmen in China and the West* (Cambridge University Press, 1970). Esther Yao, *Chinese Women Past and Present* (Idle House, 1987), provides complete coverage of social conditions and important personalities.

Morton's *China: Its History and Culture* provides excellent broad coverage of the Ming era. See also a special study by Albert Chan, *The Glory and Fall of Ming China* (University of Oklahoma Press, 1982). Ray Huang, *1587, A Year of No Significance* (Yale University Press, 1981), is noteworthy for its penetrating case study of late Ming weaknesses. A commendable special study of the early Ming period is Bruce Swanson, *The Eighth Voyage of the Dragon: A History of China's Quest for Sea Power* (Naval Institute, 1982). Other scholarly but readable treatments of the Ming era are available in the Hucker, Dawson, and Hookham works cited earlier.

On Korea, see Carter J. Eckert et al., *Korea, Old and New* (Harvard University Press, 1990); Andrew C. Nahm, *Introduction to Korean History and Culture* (Hollym International, 1993); and James Palais, *Politics and Policy in Traditional Korea* (Council of East Asian Studies, 1991). Yung-Chung Kim, *Women of Korea* (Ewha Women's University, 1979), provides a readable and informative treatment of the period.

George B. Sansom, *A History of Japan*, 3 vols. (Stanford University Press, 1958–1963), is still the best exhaustive work in English. Also valuable are John K. Fairbank, *East Asia: Tradition and Transformation* (Houghton Mifflin, 1973); Eric Tomlin, *Japan* (Walker, 1973); Mikiso Hane, *Japan: A Historical Survey* (Scribner, 1972); and Edwin Reischauer, *Japan: The Story of a Nation* (Knopf, 1970). Noteworthy recent surveys include R. H. P. Mason, *A History of Japan* (Tuttle, 1987), and Steven Warshaw, *Japan Emerges* (Diablo, 1987). Rose Hempel, *The Golden Age of Japan* (Rizzoli, 1983), is the only recent study of Japanese art and architecture in the Heian period. A number of other well-known books are recommended for the period before 1650: Mikiso Hane, *Pre-Modern Japan and Modern Japan* (Westview, 1986); Edwin O. Reischauer and Albert Craig, *Japan: Tradition and Transformation* (Houghton Mifflin, 1989); Chie Nakane, *Tokugawa Japan* (University of Tokyo Press, 1990); John W. Hall et al., *Japan Before Tokugawa* (Yale University, 1981); and William S. Martin, *Japan: Its History and Culture* (McGraw-Hill, 1984). Conrad Totman, *Japan Before Perry* (University of California Press, 1981), which devotes much attention to the early modern period, is well organized despite an awkward periodization framework. Stuart Fewster, *Japan from Shogun to Superstate* (St. Martin's Press, 1988), is informative. Two excellent biographies that mirror the time are Mary Elizabeth Berry, *Hideyoshi* (Harvard University Press, 1982), and Conrad Totman, *Tokugawa Ieyasu* (Heian International, 1983). Mary R. Beard, *The Force of Women in Japanese History* (Public Affairs Press, 1953), is still a reliable source. See also Neil Pedlar, *The Imported Pioneers: Westerners Who Helped Build Modern Japan* (St. Martin's Press, 1991).

Anthony Reid, *Southeast Asia in the Age of Commerce, 1450–1680* (Yale University Press, 1988), supplies brilliant coverage of separate cultures and attempts a synthesis of the whole in terms of affecting Western commercialism. Two older general works are well worth examining: George Coedes, *The Making of Southeast Asia*, 2nd ed. (Allen & Unwin, 1983), and Steven Warshaw, *Southeast Asia Emerges* (Diablo, 1987). In addition, the following standard surveys are still useful: John F. Cady, *Southeast Asia* (McGraw-Hill, 1964); George Coedes, *The Indianized States of Southeast Asia* (East-West Center, 1968); D. G. H. Hall, *A History of Southeast Asia* (St. Martin's Press, 1964); and B. R. Pearn, *An Introduction to the History of Southeast Asia* (Longman, 1963). The best regional treatments may be found in Michael Aung-Thwin, *Pagan: The Origins of Modern Burma* (University of Hawaii Press, 1985); David K. Wyatt, *Thailand: A Short History* (Yale University Press, 1983); David P. Chandler, *A History of Cambodia* (Westview, 1992); Joseph Buttinger, *Oragon Defiant* (Praeger, 1972); Barbara W. Andaya, *A History of Malaysia* (Macmillan, 1985); and John David Legge, *Indonesia* (Prentice Hall, 1965).

Suggestions for Web Browsing

Imperial China: The Ming
http://www.fordham.edu/halsall/eastasia/
    eastasiasbook.html#Imperial China

Map and images pertaining to the Ming dynasty, 1368–1644; a part of the Internet East Asian History Sourcebook.

Exploring Japanese Feudalism
http://www.variable.net/hidden/japan/introduction.html

Site explores in depth the history of Japanese feudalism, including Japan's founding myth, the warrior ethic, and the establishment of the shogunate.

Masterpieces of the Kyoto National Museum
http://www.kyohaku.go.jp/

Numerous images, with descriptions, of the artworks of Japan, Korea, and China.

History of Korea
http://socrates.berkeley.edu/~korea/koryo.html
http://socrates.berkeley.edu/~korea/choson.html

Text and images documenting the Koryo and Choson dynasties of Korea.

Notes

1. Quoted in G. F. Hudson, *Europe and China* (Boston: Beacon Press, 1931), p. 244.
2. Colin McEvedy and Richard Jones, *Atlas of World Population History* (New York: Penguin, 1978), p. 171.
3. Ibid., p. 181.

Epilogue

Into the Third Millennium

This ninth edition of *Civilization Past & Present* takes us beyond the two thousandth anniversary of the birth of Christ and therefore into the third millennium of the Christian era. In the Bible, the *millennium* related to the prophecy of Christ's reign on earth for 1000 years, envisioned as an era of happiness and good government. Associated with any such era is the concept of an ideal society, or *utopia*. We have referred to some of these in the pages of this book: Plato's *Republic*, Thomas More's *Utopia*, and Francis Bacon's *New Atlantis*.

In contrast to these earlier works about societies where everything is fundamentally good, twentieth-century literature also produced a number of *dystopias*, where things are basically bad. They include Aldous Huxley's *Brave New World* and its disillusionment with Western materialism, George Orwell's *Nineteen Eighty-Four* with its nightmare vision of a future totalitarian state controlled by "Big Brother," and Jacques Ellul's *Technological Society*, where moral and social values are subordinated to the overarching demands of "technique," and human beings have become appendages of mechanistic processes.

What are we to make of this? Is our society fundamentally good and getting better or bad and getting worse? Because we live in a highly complex period of history, although the moral guidelines may still seem straightforward, our social behavior has been anything but simple. At the beginning of the 1990s there was much talk about a "new world order," but few believe that it ushered in any "golden age." Yet if we cannot expect to live in a utopia, the challenge of the twenty-first century is to make sure at least that our actions do not become dystopian. To employ a salutation that reflects our times: "Take care."

"I am like a man standing between two worlds. I look both forward and backward." So spoke the Italian "father of humanism," Francesco Petrarch, who has been described as the "hinge of the door" between two very different societies: the Middle Ages, with its emphasis on faith and collective values, and the Renaissance, with its humanist concerns and focus on individual values. Is it possible that we too are in the midst of a societal shift of historic proportions, one that will become increasingly apparent as we move forward in the coming decades? To determine whether we are also situated at another "hinge of the door," let us emulate Petrarch by looking both backward at our recent past and forward into the emerging shape of the third millennium.

The Twentieth Century in Retrospect

As we leave the twentieth century, we have the opportunity to look back at its evolution, the description of which occupies nearly a quarter of the pages of the ninth edition of *Civilization Past & Present*. It was probably the most tumultuous and creative—and certainly the most populous—century in recorded history. Perhaps its unique characteristic has been to create what the American statesman Wendell Willkie in the 1940s described as "One World" and Marshall McLuhan later termed the "global village"—observations vividly corroborated in photographs of our beautiful but finite planet taken from space. Its decades were responsible for *globalizing* communication networks, air routes, weather systems, scientific and medical discoveries, trade and finance, travel and tourism, sports and movies, and a host of computerized technologies. Sadly, they also witnessed warfare and carnage on a global scale, as well as unprecedented despoliation of our planetary environment. The Chinese have a benediction that they traditionally regarded as something of a curse: "May you live in interesting times." It has indeed been an "interesting" century.

Along with *global*, our language makes increasing use of a number of related terms that give a distinctive quality to our times, terms such as *systemic*, *holistic*, *interconnected*, and *interacting*. Nationalism and independence remain powerful divisive forces in the world, as is seen in the continuation of tragic microconflicts and political devolution around the world. But at the same time in today's increasingly integrated world we find an unprecedented emphasis on internationalism and interdependence in the activities of transnational corporations and intergovernmental agencies. It remains to be seen which force, the centrifugal or the centripetal, will dominate in the next century.

Scientific and Technological Change

More scientists and technologists have worked in the past hundred years than in all previous centuries combined. Together they have revolutionized our understanding of the planet's basic structure and processes. Some of the major scientific breakthroughs occurred early in the century with Planck's quantum mechanics, Einstein's relativity theory, and Heisenberg's uncertainty principle; later decades saw the development of systems and chaos theories. Advances in biology, especially in molecular biology and the significance of the DNA code, have opened the way to genetic engineering in plants and animals, cloning, and the treatment of various human diseases.

Atomic fission created the nuclear age by releasing vast new energy sources for civilian and military purposes. But this has proved to be a two-edged sword. On the one hand, nuclear power gives promise of a seemingly endless source of energy that might be employed, for example, to desalinate ocean waters on a massive scale. On the other hand, atomic bombs destroyed urban populations in Hiroshima and Nagasaki, and an explosion in a nuclear power plant wreaked havoc in Chernobyl and far beyond. Meanwhile, a continuing problem is the safe disposal of ever-growing amounts of spent radioactive nuclear fuel.

A quantum leap in the technological evolution of humanity occurred with the invention of heavier-than-air machines to move into the third, or vertical, dimension, thereby ushering in the space age. This new control capability has had unprecedented global consequences for transportation, politics, and the peace equation and has propelled us in turn into exploring and understanding outer space. And with the invention of computer technology, we now network in the information age and through cyberspace. Electronics enables the factoring and dissemination of an incredible amount of data at the speed of light. Millions of computer terminals make possible the complex activities of large and small businesses, governments, universities, and schools. In short, the computer provides the informational sinews of a global economy and all segments of society.

Political Change

The past century was marked by tensions and competition in two areas: nationalism and ideology. World War I was largely a struggle between competing national ambitions; World War II witnessed a struggle to the death among liberal democracy, fascism, and communism. As the century waned, we again saw nationalist struggles break out in Europe, Asia, and Africa.

For decades after World War II, millions of people living on either side of the Iron Curtain suffered the trauma of the Cold War between antagonists equipped with trillions of dollars' worth of nuclear weapons—a conflict that, by desire or mishap, could have plunged the planet into the holocaust of World War III. In the early 1990s the Cold War ended with the tearing down of the Berlin Wall and the signing of new disarmament agreements. These years also saw the dismantling of the Soviet Union itself. In the ensuing period, marked by regional upheavals such as the Persian Gulf War, conflict in the former Yugoslavia, and genocidal tragedies in central Africa, Americans wondered how long their country, as the only remaining superpower, must bear the primary responsibility for policing the world.

To create a new international institution for advancing peace, the United States and its allies had founded the United Nations, together with a number of specialized agencies to work toward new global economic and social standards and improve health and education in the developing countries. Because of the threat of mutual annihilation posed by nuclear weapons, new means for controlling conflict had to be devised. One such technique was to empower the UN with the role of peacekeeper—a role it has found difficult to fulfill.

Probably the most far-reaching political change since 1945 was the dismantling of colonial empires and their replacement by large numbers of new nation-states in Asia, Africa, and the Middle East. All too often their respective roads to independence and economic viability proved rocky, thereby threatening global stability. Their problems underscored a potentially dangerous threat to all societies, namely, an increasing disparity in living standards between the rich industrial countries and the impoverished developing countries.

Economic Change

Throughout the past century, in times of peace and war alike, national economies continued to expand. Industrialization triumphed in the developed countries of the world. Its success was accompanied by the advent of the "consumer society" and the extension of the "welfare state." Notable, too, was the creation of a truly global economic market, spearheaded by the transnational corporations of these nations. Their penetration into developing countries stimulated the governments of East Asia to establish market economies geared to emulate, on a massive scale, the developed nations' industrial processes and manufacturing of consumer goods. East Asia, led by China, became the world's fastest-growing economic region.

However, in attempting to modernize their economies, many countries in Africa and Latin America embarked on ambitious programs largely financed by borrowing from wealthier nations' financial institutions. The result was a debt crisis; in the 1981–1990 period, interest payments alone became larger than the total debt of developing countries at the beginning of that decade. Meanwhile, the failure of state-controlled economies in the former Soviet Union and other socialist countries in eastern Europe led to wholesale shifts to market economies. These shifts were so abrupt and so lacking in transitional strategy that they caused enormous economic suffering and social unrest.

After decades of unprecedented growth, the economies of the developed world ran into major problems. Postwar expansion enabled governments to embark on publicly funded programs that created the welfare state. In the 1990s, skyrocketing public debt brought into question the affordability and even the value of retaining this welfare state. How to handle the national debt and its implications for maintaining existing standards in education, health, and social assistance became major issues in the United States and other democracies.

Social Change

The greatest population explosion in history occurred in the twentieth century. Concurrent with this demographic explosion was the mass migration to cities on every continent. Urban dynamics also found expression in two other major social movements: universal free public education and universal suffrage. Increasing dependence on specialized skills and scientific knowledge translated into a fundamental need for effective systems of education. The expansion of educational opportunities for women, especially at the postsecondary level, was part of the drive toward gender parity in society.

The urban explosion and way of life were certain to strengthen a globally oriented type of society, given the continuous communication exchanges among all cities. The city is also the center of what has been called the mass society. Here, too, we encounter widespread socioeconomic tensions. In addition, the dynamics of social change gave voice in the 1960s to a counterculture: rebellion, particularly among the young, against traditional values and the materialism of an acquisitive society. The century had produced a volatile global society.

The Twenty-First Century in Prospect

Let us extrapolate from our present experiences to project foreseeable issues of fundamental importance for our new century. The basic issues we have examined throughout the pages of *Civilization Past & Present* will simultaneously affect global society and the future prospects of our various ways of life. They derive logically from the experiences and behavior of the twentieth century and are intermixed with both promises and perils. In what follows, we set forth these doubled-edged issues in the form of *challenges* confronting all peoples.

Sustaining the Natural Environment

All species depend for survival on the planet's resources, derived from its water, soil, and air. Hence it is logical that ecologists and philosophers alike are discussing whether we humans own the earth and its resources or have the right only to act as its stewards. According to the Haida Indians, "We do not inherit the earth from our fathers; we borrow it from our children." Poets and painters describe its beauty by word and brush; societies are organized on its land. Governments seek to control specific parcels of territory and adjacent waters. Economists devise means to account for its wealth; from time immemorial men and women have labored to sustain their families by harvests from the soil and seas, while technologists invent ever more effective means to obtain and consume the planet's resources.

As a consequence of all these activities, our species' relationship to its global environment has shifted from simple adaptation to progressively more powerful usage and exploitation. Today we see about us the consequences of this exploitation; tomorrow will confront us with prospects and problems challenging human ingenuity to preserve the planet and its myriad inhabitants. In the decades ahead we shall have to cope with at least six major environmental issues.

1. *The population explosion will continue to exert ecological pressures.* To appreciate the magnitude of this issue, we should put it into historical perspective. After hundreds of thousands of years of high birth and death rates, genus *Homo* reached the 1.6 billion mark in 1900. Half a century later, the number rose to

2.5 billion, and it took only another 37 years for it again to double. By 2000 C.E. it had reached 6.25 billion. The planet's human population had virtually quadrupled in one century.

This demographic increase is already slowing down from the twentieth century's unparalleled rate of growth, and some of the developed countries are reaching a steady state. But other regions, including Southeast Asia, sub-Saharan Africa, and Latin America, continue to have such rapid growth that the planet's aggregate numbers could still reach 10 billion by the middle of the twenty-first century and conceivably exceed 12 billion by its end.

2. *Demographic pressures are accelerating the diminution of nonrenewable resources, such as minerals and fossil fuels, and the destruction of many renewable resources.* Fishing stocks in the North Atlantic have become so depleted that scientists warn they may never return to previous levels. Rain forests in Amazonia are being destroyed at the rate of thousands of hectares daily to create new grazing lands that serve, among other purposes, to raise beef for fast-food outlets in the United States. This destruction is doing critical harm to the earth's atmosphere since the rain forests are its principal producers of oxygen. They are also the chief repository of animal species and plants whose daily destruction represents the permanent loss of potential sources of pharmaceutical material for our medicines. In 1998 a global assessment based on more than two decades of field studies found at least one in eight plant species in the world—and nearly one in three in the United States—threatened by extinction. Meanwhile, the current destruction of plants, "the building blocks of our food," continues at an accelerating pace.[1]

3. *Gases released by the use of refrigerants and aerosols have depleted the atmosphere's ozone layer.* This depletion, observed over both the Antarctic and Arctic latitudes, has increased the incidence of skin cancers in numerous countries, and experts predict that a substantial loss of ozone "could have catastrophic effects on human and livestock health and on some life forms at the base of the marine food chain."[2]

4. *Slow but significant atmospheric warming is likely to occur.* Caused by the emission of greenhouse gases, such as carbon dioxide, methane, and chlorofluorocarbons, this could either enhance or impede agriculture. It might be of benefit in cold regions where the growing season is short, but it would reduce crop yields in tropical and subtropical areas where certain crops are already growing near their limit of heat tolerance. In fact, National Oceanic and Atmospheric Administration reported that the 1990s had been the hottest decade on record. Were global warming to precipitate a swelling of the oceans and a

melting of polar ice, the results could be catastrophic. Higher sea levels could claim low-lying farmland, such as in Bangladesh and parts of Florida, or even entirely submerge islands in the Indian Ocean and elsewhere.

5. *The lower atmosphere is likely to become increasingly polluted from smog and other harmful substances.* Although this problem is now being alleviated in most developed countries, it will continue to endanger the health of urban populations in the developing nations where economies, such as the Chinese, are rapidly industrializing with little concern for protecting the environment.

6. *All countries will have to carry large economic burdens resulting from environmental problems.* To the long-standing problems of water pollution, depletion of groundwater, and proliferation of hazardous wastes and toxic chemicals must be added two more: acid rain and desertification. Acid rain has threatened lakes and forests over large areas of North America and Europe. Meanwhile, deserts have been advancing on every continent, the worst situation occurring in Africa's Sudano-Sahelian zones. Caused by increasing human population, cattle overgrazing, cultivation of cash crops on unsuitable rangelands, and deforestation, the degradation of land to desert-like conditions has grown at an annual rate of 6 million hectares, while 21 million more hectares provide no economic return.[3]

In an effort to avert any potential environmental disaster, 135 governments held an "Earth Summit" at Rio de Janeiro in June 1992. There they agreed to protect endangered species and act on global warming and adopted an agenda for economic development within a sustainable environment. But most of the recommendations were nonbinding, and when they gathered again in Kyoto in 1998 to confer on protecting the global climate, participants admitted that little had been accomplished. Then, in what seemed a backward step to environmentalists, they agreed that international audits of each country's performance on reducing carbon emissions would not begin until 2008. They also accepted the principle of "carbon trading," giving each country a quota for the amount of carbon dioxide it is allowed to release into the atmosphere each year.

Our ultimate ability to survive as a species depends squarely on our planet's continued environmental viability. And for the first time in history that viability is now in question.

Balancing Population and Resources

The past century's population explosion resulted from two interrelated components: mortality and fertility. The major cause for the spectacular jump in global population has been the rapid fall in death rates as a result of medical advances and increased life expectancy. Birthrates have not declined proportionately, nor have they declined evenly among regions. In this century the populations of the developed nations will reach a steady state, but those of the developing world will continue so as to become about nine times that of the developed world by 2050, in large part because of the high percentage of children who have yet to reproduce. Population control depends in large measure on ethical and religious considerations and on political will. An international population conference held in Cairo in 1994 showed how difficult it will be to mobilize sufficient political consensus to make a substantial difference in reducing global population growth.

The relationship between global population and resources is worsened by the inverse ratio between increasing human numbers and diminishing arable space on which to feed them. In 1000 B.C.E. the planet's estimated 50 million people had available roughly 3 square kilometers per person. A millennium later saw that figure reduced to 0.8 square kilometer, while in 1000 C.E. the earth's 265 million people had little more than half a square kilometer apiece. Since 1500, space per person has been shrinking drastically. If and when global population reaches 11.6 billion later in the twenty-first century, it will be constricted to 0.013 square kilometer per person. Each square would have to provide living space, operate factories, and grow food for 78 persons. But since that area includes polar ice caps, mountain ranges, and deserts, an estimated 200 people would then have to squeeze themselves and their support systems into each habitable square kilometer.[4]

Can the growing human population continue to feed itself? Experts are divided. The optimists—economists and some agricultural scientists—argue that the earth can produce more than enough food for the expected population in 2050 because of technological innovation and continued investment of human capital. Thus the Green Revolution, with its combination of high-yielding hybrid seed, chemical pesticides, and improved water supply, has enabled Asian and Latin American agriculture to keep pace with population growth in the aggregate—although per capita food production declined in Africa. The pessimists, led by environmentalists, regard the situation as a catastrophe in the making. Feeding a growing population can only be done by intensifying farming practices, which, as with the Green Revolution, run counter to ecologically sound aspects of traditional agriculture and cause massive damage by depleting water tables, increasing salinity, reducing soil fertility, and reducing biodiversity.[5] A third position regards the other two as extremist. The real problem lies in the maldistribution of resources and wealth, and this will continue to be the case until developing countries have greater access to resources and acquire greater freedom of economic initiative.

In the past, the prosperous people of the developed nations thought they could insulate themselves from the poverty and problems in the rest of the world. But developments in recent decades have made the rich and the poor nations mutually vulnerable. Besides their environmental interconnectedness and global population pressures, strains between their respective economic standards will have to be addressed. At present, some 70 percent of the world's income is produced and consumed by 15 percent of its people. Conversely, living standards in Latin America are lower than in the 1970s, and in Africa they have fallen to 1960s levels. We are confronted with a "growing mismatch between where the world's riches, technology, good health, and other benefits are to be found, and where the world's fast-growing new generations, possessing few if any of those benefits, live. A population explosion on one part of the globe and a technology explosion on the other is not a good recipe for a stable international order" because it leads to the crisis posed by the "revolution of rising expectations" among both the haves and the have-nots.[6]

Affecting developed and developing nations alike, the fulfillment of these expectations depends on availability of resources, a high level of employment, and continuing growth of a consumer society. Environmentalists warn that present rates of resource consumption cannot continue indefinitely and that we should already be cutting back for the sake of future generations. This warning strikes at the heart of the free enterprise system as we know it today. The concept of growth has always been considered essential to the structure and behavior of this system, which historically has made spectacular gains producing goods and services and raising living standards. But this growth ethos always assumes that abundant physical resources and energy can continue to satisfy all future requirements, whatever the scale. The new century will test that basic assumption as never before.

Social Changes and Challenges

At the international level, we will have to recognize that in an interdependent world, people everywhere must be treated as equals. Global acceptance of nondiscrimination is critical as population and resource problems build and regions of the developed world cry out for help. Realistic responses will require not only aid and rehabilitation assistance to poorer societies at critical times but also willingness by the richer economies to share a larger proportion of their own resources for the others' long-term development. Given the growing mutual vulnerability of the two great segments of the planet's people, such cooperation will be indispensable in this century to make them mutually viable.

A related factor affecting all nations will be the massive movement of people. Migration has been a phenomenon throughout history, but its present scale is made unique by the speed of the process combined with the density of existing settlements. Among the many millions of migrants are refugees fleeing from political conflicts and civil wars, and these flows will pose mounting social and ethical questions as developed societies formulate their immigration policies.

Another kind of perennial migration is taking place on every continent: from the countryside to the cities, a phenomenon that began in ancient Mesopotamia and made possible the first urban civilization. Today the world is urbanizing as never before, with cities increasing by 170,000 people daily. In 1950 London and New York were the only megacities with populations of 8 million or more. In 2015 there will be 33 megacities, 27 of them in the developing world. The ten largest will range from Mexico City (28.7 million) to Tokyo (18.8 million).[7]

Many chapters in this book attest to the key role of the city in advancing cultural and economic development. The pace of societal advancement can be expected to accelerate as a result of global urbanization. Indeed, the city has been described as a hotbed of creative innovation where key intellectual spillovers occur across a variety of enterprises concentrated in the urban environment.[8] To optimize its unique role, however, tomorrow's city must reform and reorganize itself. It will not be enough to get rid of the *barrios* that surround Latin American cities or rebuild the decaying cores of America's older urban centers. The push of highways, automobiles, and real estate developments into the open country has produced a formless urban sprawl; there is need to return—in concept—to the pedestrian scale of the small town with its familiar individuality. Paradoxically, because all cities will be interconnected in tomorrow's communication superhighway so as to function as components of the global village, "the smallest neighborhood or precinct must be planned as a working model of the larger world."[9] The corporate will of its citizens, aiming at self-knowledge, self-government, and self-actualization, needs to be embodied in the city. In such a social environment, "education will be the center of their activities . . . [while] the city itself provides a vivid theater for the spontaneous encounters and challenges and embraces of daily life."[10]

We can expect social change to continue to be marked by "liberation" movements. These are characterized by "rights" that their proponents insist must be recognized as fundamental. One ongoing movement relates to racial and ethnic rights, a second to women's rights. Female emancipation remains a long and difficult struggle around the world. Suffrage was won by most women of the West early in the twentieth century, but their attempts to gain commensurate economic and social rights continue to be protracted, with their gains too often circumscribed or only begrudgingly yielded. "Coming out of the closet" is a familiar phrase associated with a third broad movement: the right of homosexuals to disclose their sexual orientation without being ostracized or denied rights to full economic and social parity.

Related to these broad social changes will be the need to advance the role of education on a global scale. After decades of international efforts to eradicate illiteracy, over a billion adults still cannot read or write, and over 100 million children of primary school age are not able to attend school every year.[11] These problems exist primarily in the developing world, where in the past 30 years the educational gap with the industrialized nations has increased. A close correlation exists among national levels of education, the status of women, and fertility rates. When education is widely available to women, average family size drops sharply, birthrates decline to socially manageable proportions, and health and living standards improve.[12]

In the developed countries, the dynamics of widespread technological change will require the continuing educational upgrading of the workforce, with technical and professional programs geared to both training and retraining. In other words, education is likely to be regarded as a lifelong process for all citizens—not only because of the demands of economies to remain competitive in the global economy but also because of the need for altering and enriching our understanding of why and how the world community is changing and what the privileges and accompanying responsibilities of world citizenry entail.

A historic change is occurring in the accumulation of knowledge and the ability of our educational system to assimilate information and deliver it effectively. Until modern times, humanity suffered from an overall paucity of knowledge, and acquiring knowledge entailed much rote learning at school. Today, in sharp contrast, a plethora of information—and misinformation—bombards us from all directions or is readily accessible from data banks. In fact, we seem to be suffering progressively from information overload and run the risk as societies of becoming so complex as to become dysfunctional.

Before World War II, T. S. Eliot had asked:

Where is the Life we have lost in living?
Where is the wisdom we have lost in knowledge?
Where is the knowledge we have lost in
*   information?*[13]

His question seems more relevant now than ever. Are today's world citizens controlled by the dictates of the computer and data bank, or are they being empowered to use the new technology creatively so as to solve problems and set meaningful goals? There is much experimentation these days in educational theory and pedagogy as educators recognize that fundamental change is essential if our schools are to cope with tomorrow's many challenges.

Throughout recorded history, human striving and aspirations have been essential elements of problem solving. As the twenty-first century unfolds, what is new is not the existence of problems but humanity's more acute awareness of them and of an impending need to solve them. What is also unique for our times is that these major problems and the challenges they present are truly global in dimension. If they are great, so too are the numbers of people in every society who are deeply concerned about the future prospects of life on earth. This unprecedented awareness bodes well for a creative collective response.

Lest we become complacent, however, we have to ask ourselves: How much lead time do we have to make and then implement critical decisions for a global-scale civilization that is changing at an accelerating rate? The most intelligent planning can be thwarted by sociocultural inertia, by an inherent resistance to basic changes. A large, complex society can be likened to a supertanker whose size and momentum prevent it from coming to a stop for many miles. To pursue this analogy, those concerned about the future have no intention of trying to halt society in its tracks. Even if that were possible, any sudden stop could prove catastrophic. Rather they seek to alert society to be ready to change course. This requires not only charting viable alternative routes but also making sure that all concerned are fully alerted to the need for a change of direction and will accept the new destination. The critical factors here are awareness and timing, because setting a new course cannot wait for the storm that could engulf us if unprepared. We must develop contingency plans well in advance and be ready to act on them.

Suggestions for Reading

Because of the present-day and future orientation of materials in this Epilogue, you may want to consult a broad body of periodicals and journals to obtain up-to-date information regarding developments in the various segments of global culture. The Internet is a readily available and rapidly increasing source of new information in these areas—environmental, economic, political, social, scientific, technological, literary, and aesthetic (architecture, the arts, and music).

A useful introduction to what we may anticipate in the decades ahead as a global community, with its interlinked opportunities and constraints, is set forth lucidly in Paul Kennedy's *Preparing for the Twenty-First Century* (HarperCollins, 1993). This book might be read in conjunction with "A Special Moment in History" (*Atlantic Monthly*, May 1998), in which it is argued that the planet's fate will be determined in the next few decades through our technological, lifestyle, and population choices.

An important and influential assessment of the relationship of ecological and economic factors in a global context was produced in 1987 by the UN Commission on Environment and Development in *Our Common Future* (also known as the "Brundtland Report"); the commission was mandated by the General Assembly to "propose long-term environmental strategies for achieving sustainable development by the year 2000 and beyond." For an annual updating of progress toward a sustainable society, see the Worldwatch Institute Reports, *State of the World*. Consult *Planet Earth: Problems and Prospects* (McGill-Queen's University Press, 1995) for sections on climatic change, world hunger and health, animal impoverishment, and environmental toxicology. A special issue of *Scientific American* (September 1989), titled "Managing Planet Earth," also deals with major threats and challenges.

The powerful impetus provided by contemporary technological innovations in shaping and altering society is discussed from a number of vantage points in Merritt R. Smith and Leo Marx (eds.), *Does Technology Drive History? The Dilemma of Technological Determinism* (MIT Press, 1996); among its topics are technological determinism in American culture, technological momentum, the political and feminist dimensions of technological determinism, and rationality versus contingency in the history of technology. How systems' behavior affects the relationship of technology and society is discussed in Paul A. Alcorn's *Social Issues in Technology* (Prentice Hall, 1997). A *Newsweek Extra* (Winter 1997–1998) explores the power of invention and how an explosion of discoveries has changed our lives in the ways we work, live, fight, and heal.

The accelerating role of transnational corporations and the globalization of national economies have resulted in a large number of studies. These include Richard O'Brien, *Global Financial*

Integration: The End of Geography (Council on Foreign Relations Press, 1992); Richard Barnet and John Cavanagh, *Global Dreams: Imperial Corporations and the New World Order* (Simon & Schuster, 1994); and Jerry Mander and Edward Goldsmith (eds.), *The Case Against the Global Economy—and a Turn Toward the Local* (Sierra Club Books, 1996). The World Bank has published a number of monographs, including *Global Economic Prospects and the Developing Countries* (1993) and *Workers in an Integrating World* (1995). See also United Nations Development Program, *World Development Report, 1992* (Oxford University Press, 1992).

A major overhaul of trends in historiography, past and present, has been undertaken by Joyce Appleby, Lynn Hunt, and Margaret Jacob in *Telling the Truth About History* (Norton, 1994); they provide a fair forum to the advocates of postmodernism but defend with telling arguments the relevance and intellectual integrity of their discipline. In *The Culture of Hope: A New Birth of the Classical Spirit* (Free Press, 1995), Frederick Turner charges the "postmodern cultural establishment" with being philosophically empty and failing to give a satisfying answer to the question of the proper role of the arts in our society. But he revives the vision of a hope-oriented culture in the current convergence of science, art, and religion.

Notes

1. William R. Stevens, *Toronto Globe and Mail*, April 9, 1998.
2. World Commission on Environment and Development, *Our Common Future* (New York: Oxford University Press, 1987), p. 33.
3. Ibid., p. 128.
4. John Kettle, "Population Jump Puts the Squeeze on Space," *Toronto Globe and Mail*, April 23, 1998.
5. Gita Sen, "World Hunger, Livelihoods, and the Environment," in *Planet Earth: Problems and Prospects* (Montreal: McGill-Queen's University Press, 1995), pp. 67–81.
6. Paul Kennedy, *Preparing for the Twenty-First Century* (New York: HarperCollins, 1993), p. 331.
7. "Habitat II," United Nations Conference on Cities, Istanbul, June 1996.
8. Jane Jacobs, *The Economy of Cities* (New York: Vintage Books, 1970); Jane Jacobs, *Cities and the Wealth of Nations: Principles of Economic Life* (New York: Random House, 1984).
9. Lewis Mumford, *The City in History: Its Origins, Its Transformations, and Its Prospects* (New York: Harcourt Brace, 1961), p. 573.
10. Ibid.
11. United Nations Development Program, *Human Development Report, 1992* (New York: Oxford University Press, 1992), p. 2.
12. Kennedy, *Preparing for the Twenty-First Century*, pp. 339–343.
13. T. S. Eliot, choruses from "The Rock," in *The Complete Poems and Plays, 1909–1950* (New York: Harcourt Brace, 1971), p. 96.

Credits

Chapter 1

4 Des & Jen Bartlett/Bruce Coleman; **7** John Reader/Science Photo Library/Photo Researchers, NY; **8** John Reader/Science Photo Library/Photo Researchers, NY; **13** Courtesy of James Mellaart, London; **16R** Art Resource, NY; **16M** Art Resource, NY; **16R** Giraudon/Art Resource, NY; **17** © Adam Woolfitt/ Woodfin Camp & Associates, Inc., New York.

Chapter 2

20 SCALA/Art Resource, NY; **24** Kassite Map of Nippur, Hilprecht Collection of Near Eastern Antiquities, Friedrich-Schiller-Universitäåt Jena, Germany; **26** SCALA/Art Resource, NY; **27** Hirmer FotoArchiv, Munich; **30** Pair Statue of Mycerinus and Queen Kha-merer-nebty II, Egypt, Dynasty IV, Giza, Valley Temple of Mycerinus. Museum of Fine Arts, Boston, Harvard-Museum Expedition, 11.1738; **31** © The British Museum, London; **32** Black Star; **34** © The British Museum, London; **35** © The British Museum, London; **36** Hirmer FotoArchiv, Munich; **37L** Fragment of a head of King Sesostris III. The Metropolitan Museum of Art, Carnarvon Collection, Gift of Edward S. Harkness, 1926 (26.7.1394). All rights reserved. The Metropolitan Museum of Art; **37R** © Bildarchiv Preussischer Kulturbesitz, Berlin, 1999. Photo by Margarete Büsing. Staatliche Museen zu Berlin-Ägyptisches Museum; **44** © The British Museum, London; **46** Erich Lessing/ Art Resource, NY; **48** Museo Nazionale, Naples.

Chapter 3

52 Claudia Parks/The Stock Market; **55** © Michael Holford Photographs; **56** Hirmer FotoArchiv, Munich; **57** Art Resource; **60** Art Resource; **63** © The British Museum, London; **67** Courtesy of The Manchester Museum, The University of Manchester; **73** AKG London; **75B** Robert Frerck/Odyssey Productions, Chicago; **75T** Robert Frerck/Odyssey Productions, Chicago; **76L** Kouros, Statue of a youth, c. 610–600 B.C.E. The Metropolitan Museum of Art, New York. Fletcher Fund, 1932. (32.11.1). Photograph © 1993 The Metropolitan Museum of Art; **76M** SCALA/Art Resource, NY; **76R** SCALA/Art Resource, NY; **77** SCALA/Art Resource, NY; **81** Erich Lessing/Art Resource, NY.

Chapter 4

86 Steve Vidler/Leo de Wys Inc.; **90** SCALA/Art Resource, NY; **91** SCALA/Art Resource, NY; **102B** Alinari/Art Resource, NY; **102T** Nimatallah/Art Resource, NY; **104** Bedroom from the Villa of P. Fannius Synistror, Roman Pompeii, 1st century B.C.E. The Metropolitan Museum of Art, Rogers Fund, 1903 (03.14.13). Photograph by Schecter Lee. Photograph © 1986 The Metropolitan Museum of Art; **105** SCALA/Art Resource, NY; **106** SCALA/Art Resource, NY; **111L** © Michael Holford Photographs; **111R** SCALA/Art Resource, NY; **115** SCALA/Art Resource, NY.

Chapter 5

120 Don Hamilton; **122** Christie's Images, Ltd. 1999; **123** Academia Sinica, Taipei; **125** Musée Cernushi, Paris; **127** Corbis/Bettmann; **132L** Laurie Platt Winfrey, Inc.; **132R** Christie's Images, Ltd. 1999; **134** Bronze cowrie-container decorated with weaving scene on lid, unearthed in 1955. The Chinese Exhibition, Nelson Gallery-Atkins Museum, Kansas City, Missouri; **135** Robert Harding Picture Library; **136** Brocade mitten with the characters: Yen Nien Yi Shou, 1st–2nd century A.D. (Eastern Han) Unearthed in 1959 from a site at Niya, Minfeng county in Sinkiang. The Chinese Exhibition, Nelson Gallery-Atkins Musueum, Kansas City, Missouri; **137** Vault Map Collection, Library of Congress.

Chapter 6

140 *Adoration of the Bodhi Tree*, India, Amaravati Satavahana period, 2nd century. Stone relief, 80 × 57.1 cm. The Cleveland Museum of Art, Purchase from the J. H. Wade Fund, 1970.43; **143** © MacQuitty International Collection, London; **144** Pakistan National Museum; **144** Pakistan National Museum; **156** AKG London; **157** British Library/e.t. archive, London; **58** Museo Nazionale, Naples; **161** Seated Buddha, from Gandhara, Pakistan. Kushan period, 2nd-3rd century. Dark gray schist, H. 36" × W. 22½". Seattle Art Museum, Eugene Fuller Memorial Collection, 33.180. Photo: Paul Macapia; **162** Prithwish Neogy; **163** Vessel in the Form of an Ax. Bronze. The Metropolitan Museum of Art, Purchase, George McFadden Gift and Edit Perry Chapman Fund, 1993. (1993.525) Photograph by Bruce White © 1993 The Metropolitan Museum of Art; **164** © Michael Holford Photographs.

Chapter 7

170 Erich Lessing/Art Resource, NY; **173** The "Thanksgiving Scroll" before opening, Dead Sea Scroll. Israel Museum, Jerusalem. The Shrine of the Book; **177** Photo by Duane Preble. Museo dei Conservatori, Rome; **181B** © 95 Harvey Lloyd/The Stock Market; **181T** Marvin Trachtenberg; **182** AKG London; **184** SCALA/Art Resource, NY; **185** The Granger Collection, New York; **186** © The British Museum, London; **189** Bibliothèque nationale de France, Paris; **190** Roger-Viollet/ Gamma Liaison.

Chapter 8

200 The Pierpont Morgan Library/Art Resource, NY; **203** AKG London; **208** The Cathedral Churck of the Blessed Virgin Mary and St. Ethelbert in Hereford, England; **209** Giraudon/Art Resource, NY; **210** SCALA/Art Resource, NY; **211** Marburg/Art Resource, NY; **212** Archives Photographiques, Paris.

Chapter 9

216 Battle of Agincourt, 1415, English with Flemish illuminations St. Alban's Chronicle (late 15th century). Lambeth Palace Library, London, UK/Bridgeman Art Library, London/New York; **222** Universitets Oldsaksamling, Oslo; **221** Art Resource, NY; **225** The British Library, London; **228** Giraudon/Art Resource, NY; **230** The Martyrdom of Thomas Becket, Carrow Psalter, MS W. 34f. 15v. The Walters Art Gallery, Baltimore; **231** Edward I in Parliament, MS 1113. The Royal Collection © 1999 Her Majesty Queen Elizabeth II; **234** Bibliothèque nationale de France, Paris; **236** Master, carpenter and stonemason, 1482. Roy 15 EII f.265. Des Proprietez des Choses/British Library, London, UK/Bridgeman Art Library, London/New York; **238** Bibliothèque Royale Albert, Brussels; **239** Institut Amatller d'Art Hispanic; **240** Giraudon/Art Resource, NY; **241** Portrait of Henry VII by English School (16th century), T31778. Phillips, The International Fine Art Auctioneers, UK/Bridgeman Art Library, London/New York.

Chapter 10

244 Color Day Productions/The Image Bank; **248** The British Library, London; **250** Edinburgh University Library; **251** Islamic manuscript, 8th–9th century. Purchase F30.60. Freer Gallery of Art and Arthur M. Sackler Gallery, Smithsonian Institution; **253L** Courtesy of the Spencer Collection, The New York Public Library, Aster, Lenox and Tilden Foundation; **253R** Qisas al-Anbiya, Moses turns staff into a dragon. Spencer Persian Manuscript, 46, folio 82. Courtesy of the Spencer Collection, The New York Public Library, Aster, Lenox and Tilden Foundation; **254** Qisas al-Anbiya, Jesus performs miracle of loaves. Spencer Collection 46, folio 152v. Courtesy of the Spencer Collection, The New York Public Library, Aster, Lenox and Tilden Foundation; **261L** Bibliothèque nationale de France, Paris; **261R** Bibliothèque nationale de France, Paris; **262** National Library, Cairo; **264** © The Bodleian Library, Oxford, England; **267** SuperStock.

Chapter 11

270 © Betty Press/Woodfin Camp & Associates, Inc.; **274** © Sarah Errington/The Hutchison Library, London; **275** © Erich Lessing/Art Resource, New York ; **276** National Museum, Lagos, Nigeria; **279** © Georg Gerster/Photo Researchers; **280** Marc/Evelyn Berheim/ Woodfin Camp & Associates, New York; **283** Bibliothèque nationale de France, Paris; **286** Bibliothèque nationale de France, Paris; **288** Werner Forman Archive/Art Resource, New York; **290** © Dirk Bakker; **291** AKG London; **292** The National Palace Museum, Republic of China; **293** Marc/Evelyn Berheim/ Woodfin Camp & Associates, New York; **294** Robert Aberman/Werner Forman Archive/ Art Resource, New York.

Chapter 12

298 *Krishna Battling the Horse Demon*, Keshi, Terracotta. The Metropolitan Museum of Art, Purchase, Florence and Herbert Irving Gift, 1991. (1991.300) Photograph by Bruce White, Photograph © 1994 The Metropolitan Museum of Art; **303** Robert Ivey/Ric Ergenbright Photography; **306L** Shaanxi Provincial Museum, Xian; **306R** © The British Museum,

London; **307** Bullock and cart, T'ang Dynasty, 7th–8th century. Pottery with green and brown glazes, H. 16" × L. 20¼". Seattle Art Museum, Eugene Fuller Memorial Collection, 37.17. Photo: Paul Macapia; **308** Courtesy of The Schloss Collection, The Bowers Museum of Cultural Art, Santa Ana, CA **311** *Court Ladies Preparing Newly Woven Silk*, Emperor Huizong (attributed to), r. 1101–1125. Chinese; Northern Song Dynasty, early 12th century. Handscroll; ink, color and gold on silk, 27.0 × 145.3 cm. Museum of Fine Arts, Boston, Chinese and Japanese Special Fund; **312L** Tokyo National Museum; **312R** Ma Yuan, Chinese, active 1190–1235; Southern Song Dynasty, *Bare Willows and Distant Mountains*. Round fan mounted as album leaf; ink and light color on silk, 23.8 × 24.2 cm. Museum of Fine Arts, Boston. Special Chinese and Japanese Fund; **315** Black Star; **316** © Kyodo News Service; **317B** Courtesy of Kyoryokukai, The Tokyo National Museum; **317T** Kodansha Ltd., Tokyo; **318** *Battle Scene*, Kamakura period, 14th century. Section of handscroll mounted as a hanging scroll; ink, color, and touches of gold paint on paper, H. 14" × W. 17¼". Seattle Art Museum, Eugene Fuller Memorial Collection, 48.173. Photo: Paul Macapia; **319L** Bibliothèque nationale de France, Paris; **319R** Victoria & Albert Museum, London/Art Resource, NY; **323** Bibliothèque nationale de France, Paris; **326** Special Collections, The New York Public Library.

Chapter 13

330 Randy G. Taylor/Leo de Wys, Inc., New York; **333** Werner Forman/Art Resource, NY; **335** Enrique Franco Torrijos; **336** Museo Nacional de Antropologia, Mexico City; **338** Deer Effigy, Vessel, Mexico. "Plumbate" earthenware. The Saint Louis Art Museum. Gift of Morton D. May; **339** Library of Congress; **341L** SCALA/Art Resource, NY; **342L** Werner Forman Archive/Art Resource, New York; **342R** Ewing Krainen; **343** Lee Boltin; **347** Mark C Burnett, Ohio Historical Society, Columbus/Photo Researchers; **349** Museum of Anthropology and Ethnography in St. Petersburg FL.

Chapter 14

354 Victor Boswell/National Geographic Society Image Collection; **358L** SCALA/Art Resource, New York; **358R** SCALA/Art Resource, New York; **360** © Erich Lessing/Art Resource, New York; **362** © The British Museum, London; **364** © Erich Lessing/Art Resource, New York; **365** SCALA/Art Resource, NY; **366** Alinari/Art Resource, NY; **367L** Alinari/Art Resource, NY; **367R** Alinari/Art Resource, NY; **368L** SCALA/Art Resource, New York; **368R** Art Resource; **369B** SCALA/Art Resource, NY; **369T** SCALA/Art Resource, NY; **370** SCALA/Art Resource, NY; **371L** © Erich Lessing/Art Resource, New York; **371R** Cameraphoto/Art Resource, New York; **372** Kunsthistorisches Museum, Vienna; **373** SCALA/Art Resource, New York; **374** AKG London; **375** Reunion des Musées nationaux; **377** Giraudon/Art Resource, New York; **378** The History of Don Quixote, London, 1620 (t.p.) Special Collections, The New York Public Library; **379** Jan van Eyck, The Arnolfini Portrait, 1434. NG 186. © National Gallery, London; **380** Albrecht Dürer, *The Knight, Death and the Devil*, 1513. Engraving, 9¹¹⁄₁₆" × 7⅜". The Brooklyn Museum of Art, New York. Gift of Mrs. Horace O. Havemeyer, 54.35.6.

Chapter 15

384 © Erich Lessing/Art Resource, New York; **387** Jan van Eyck, *The Last Judgment* (one of two panels), tempera and oil on canvas, transferred from wood. 22¼" × 7¾". The Metropolitan Museum of Art, Fletcher Fund, 1933. Photograph © 1998 The Metropolitan Museum of Art; **391L** Lutherhalle, Wittenberg, Germany; **391R** Lucas Cranach the Younger, German, 1515-1586, *Martin Luther and the Wittenberg Reformers* (1926.55) c. 1543, oil on panel, 27⅞ × 15⅝ in. (72.8 x 39.7 cm.) The Toledo

Museum of Art; Toledo, Ohio; Purchased with funds from the Libbey Endowment, Gift of Edward Drummond Libbey; **397** Erich Lessing/Art Resource, NY; **400** Photo Francois Martin, Geneva. Document BPU; **401** Giraudon/Art Resource, NY; **403** SCALA/Art Resource, NY; **405** SCALA/Art Resource, NY; **406L** SCALA/Art Resource, NY; **406R** *Malle Babbe*, Style of Frans Hals, c. 1650. The Metropolitan Museum of Art, Purchase, 1871 (71.76) All rights reserved. The Metropolitan Museum of Art; **407** English Heritage as Trustees of Iveagh Bequest, Kenwood; **413** © The British Museum, London; **415** Philippe de Champaigne, c. 1637. *Cardinal Richelieu*. NG 1449. © National Gallery, London; **416** Print Collection, Miriam and Ira D. Wallach. Division of Art, Prints and Photographs, the New York Public Library, Astor, Lennox and Tilden Foundations.

Chapter 16

424 Musées royaux des Beaux-Arts de Belgique, Bruxelles-Koninklijke Musea voor Schone Kunsten van Belgie, Brussel; **427** Portuguese Carracks off a Fortified Coast, c. 1520 by Joachim Patinir. National Maritime Museum, London, UK/Bridgeman Art Library, London/New York; **430** Bibliothèque nationale de France, Paris; **434** © The British Museum, London; **436** Hispanic Society of America, New York; **438** The British Museum, London/Werner Forman Archive; **442** Sebastian Münster, Cosmographia, 1540. Vault Map Collection, Library of Congress; **445** The Huntington Library, Art Collections, and Botanical Gardens-San Marino, CA/SuperStock; **447** © A.H. Robins Co. Courtesy Doneiler's Custom Photography.

Chapter 17

452 Detail. Freer Gallery of Art and Arthur M. Sackler Gallery Archives, Smithsonian Institution; **455** The British Library, London; **457** Weltkarte des Piri Reis, 1513; Istanbul, Topkapi Serail-Museum. AKG London; **458** Tughra (calligraphic emblem) of Süleyman the Magnificent, Sultan of Turkey (1520–1566); from an imperial edict. Ink, colors and gold on paper. The Metropolitan Museum of Art, Rogers Fund, 1938. (38.149.1) Photograph © 1986 The Metropolitan Museum of Art; **459** Title page of Baudier's Histoire...empereur des Turcs, 1631. Department of Rare Books and Special Collections, Princeton University Library; **461** Hulton Getty/Liaison Agency; **465** Mir Sayyid-Ali, Safavid dynasty, 16th century. Freer Gallery of Art and Arthur M. Sackler Gallery Archives, Smithsonian Institution; **466** Mughal painting, c. 1620. (F45.9a) Freer Gallery of Art and Arthur M. Sackler Gallery Archives, Smithsonian Institution; **467** The British Library, London; **469** S. Vidler/SuperStock; **470** Birth of a Prince from an illustrated manuscript of the Jahangir-nama, Bishndas (Attributed to), Northern India, Mughal, about 1620. Opaque watercolor on paper, 24.1 × 17 cm. Museum of Fine Arts, Boston, Francis Bartlett Donation of 1912 and Picture Fund.

Chapter 18

474 (Detail) Attributed to Sesshu, Japan, 1420–1506. Muromachi period. Birds and Flowers in a Landscape. Six-fold screen, ink and color on paper, 173.4 × 378 cm. © The Cleveland Museum of Art, Purchase from the J. H. Wade Fund, 1961.204; **477** © Wan-go H. C. Weng, Lyme, NH; **479L** National Palace Museum, Taipei Taiwan; **479R** Prunis Vase (Meiping) with Blossoming Lotus: Fahug Ware. Porcelain with polychrome glazes, H. 37.5 cm. China, Jiangxi Province, Jingdezhen kilns, late 15th century, Ming dynasty. The Cleveland Museum of Art, 1994, Bequest of John L. Severance, 42.716; **481T** Courtesy of the History of Cartography Project. By permission of Ryukoku University Library, Kyoto, Japan; **481B** Korean Cultural Center; **482** National Museum of Korea, Seoul; **484** Ando Hiroshige, c. 1832. *Abe River near Fuchu*, woodblock

print. Honolulu Academy of Arts, Gift of James A. Michener, 1978 (17,235).

Chapter 19

492 Hyacinthe Rigaud (1659–1743), *Louis XIV, King of France, Portrait in royal costume*. Oil on canvas, 277 × 194 cm—Inv. 7492. Louvre, Dpt. des Peintures, Paris, France. © Photograph by Erich Lessing/Art Resource, New York; **496** Giraudon/Art Resource, NY; **497** © Photo RMN-D. Arnaudet/G.B; **497** © Photo RMN-D. Arnaudet/G.B; **503** Danish Royal Collection at Rosenborg Castle, Copenhagen; **506** Central Naval Museum, St. Petersburg; **508L** Alinari/Art Resource, NY; 510 Corbis/Bettmann; **518** AKG London; 521 Art Resource, New York; **522** Giraudon/Art Resource, NY.

Chapter 20

528 Jan Steen (1626–1679), *Fishmarket of Leiden*. Stadelsches Kunstinstitut, Frankfurt am Main. Photo: © Ursula Edelmann, Frankfurt am Main; **531** Johannes Blaeu, Toonneel der Steden, 1652. Map of Amsterdam. Library of Congress; **532** Aelbert Cuyp, SK-A-2350, A senior merchant of the Dutch East India Company, presumably Jacob Mathieusen and his wife; in the background the fleet in the roads of Batavia. Rijksmuseum, Amsterdam; **534** Nimatallah/Art Resource, NY; **540** © Michael Holford Photographs; **542** Rembrandt, SK-C-6, The syndics: the sampling officials of the Amsterdam drapers' guild. Rijksmuseum, Amsterdam.

Chapter 21

550 SCALA/Art Resource, NY; **553** The British Library, London; **554** Art Resource; **556** Jacques Louis David/Bulloz; **557** Herman Verelst, Portrait of John Locke. By Courtesy of The National Portrait Gallery, London **559** Corbis/Bettmann; **560** John Opie, Portrait of Mary Wollstonecraft Godwin, c. 1797. Courtesy of the National Portrait Gallery, London; **565** By kind permission of the Earl of Harrowby, Sandon Hall, Stafford, England; **566** From Clark, An Album of Methodist History, Abingdon Press; **570** © Sovfoto/Eastfoto; **573** Austrian National Library, Vienna; **574** © Collection of The New-York Historical Society.

Chapter 22

584 Giraudon/Art Resource, NY; **587** Giraudon/Art Resource, New York; **589** Bulloz; **592** Bulloz; **594** Giraudon/Art Resource, NY; **595** Giraudon/Art Resource, NY; **599** © Erich Lessing/Art Resource, NY; **603** NYPL, Astor, Lenox, and Tilden Foundations, Prints Division; **609R** The Royal Collection © 1999 Her Majesty Queen Elizabeth II.

Chapter 23

614 The Newark Museum/Art Resource, New York; **619** Werner Forman Archive/Art Resource, New York; **621** Library of Congress; **622** Pierpoint Morgan Library/Art Resource, NY; **623** G. Weidenfeld and Nicholson; **624** Peter Newarks' Historical Pictures; **626** *Birth in a Harem*, late 18th century. Los Angeles County Museum of Art, gift of Edwin Binney, 3rd collection of Turkish art; **628** Selim III, Sultan of Turkey (1761–1808) Duchateau, 1792, engraved by Nutter. Mary Evans Picture Library, London; **631** Victoria & Albert Museum, London/Art Resource, New York; **632** Victoria & Albert Museum, London; **635** National Maritime Museum, London; **638** Christie's Images, Ltd. 1999.

Chapter 24

646 Detail. Claude Monet, *The Gare Saint-Lazare*, 1877. Oil on canvas, 80.33 cm × 98.11 cm. Courtesy of the Fogg Art Museum, Harvard University Art Museums, Bequest from the Collection of Maurice Wertheim, Class of 1906. Photo: David Mathews. © President and Fellows of Harvard College, Harvard University; **648** © The British Museum, London; **649** Mansell Collection; **653** Gustav Dore and Blanchard Jerrold, London: A Pilgrimage, Grant & Co. London, 1872; **656** Courtesy Fried Krupp GmbH (Historisches Archiv Fried. Krupp AG); **658** James Reynolds, Geological Map, 1849 NO. 946 (5) By Permission of the British Library, London; **659** Corbis/Bettmann; **661** P833.167. From the Collections of Henry Ford Museum & Greenfield Village; **662** Pear's Soap Ad (African Girl), Illustrated London News, 1899. Mary Evans Picture Gallery; **664L** Bibliothèque nationale de France, Paris; **664R** Thomas Phillips, Portrait of George Gordon Byron, 6th Baron Byron, 1835. Courtesy of the National Portrait Gallery, London; **666** Corbis/Bettmann.

Chapter 25

670 Giraudon/Art Resource, NY; **675** Library of Congress; **76** Bibliothèque nationale de France, Paris; **679** AKG London; **681** © The British Museum, London; **682** Mansell Collection; **684** Roger Viollet/Gamma Liaison; **685** © Sovfoto; **687** Mansell Collection; **688L** Weidenfeld & Nicholson Ltd.; **689** Memphis Brooks Museum of Art, Memphis, TN; Memphis Park Commission Purchase 46.2; **692** George Caleb Bingham, *The Jolly Flatboatmen in Port*, 1857. The Saint Louis Art Museum, Purchase.

Chapter 26

696 Die Proklamierung des Deutschen Kaiserreiches am 18. Januar 1871 im Spiegelsaal von Versailles (Friedrichsruher Fassung). Gemälde von Anton von Werner, 1885. Oil on canvas, 167 × 202 cm. Friedrichsruh, Bismarck-Museum, bildarchiv preussischer kulturbesitz, Berlin; **698** Liaison Agency; **703** Bibliothèque nationale de France, Paris; **708** © Sovfoto; **711** Museum of London; **712** Mansell Collection; **713** Library of Congress; **715** The Granger Collection, New York; **718** Giraudon/Art Resource, NY; **719T** Claude Monet, French, 1840–1926, *Water Lilies*,1906. Oil on canvas, 87.6 × 92.7 cm., Mr. & Mrs. Martin A. Ryerson Collection, 1933.1157. © 1999, The Art Institute of Chicago. All rights reserved. **719B** van Gogh, Vincent. *The Starry Night*. (1889) Oil on canvas, 29 × 36¼" (73.7 × 92.1 cm). The Museum of Modern Art, New York. Acquired through the Lillie P. Bliss Bequest. Photograph © 1999 The Museum of Modern Art, New York; **720** Pablo Picasso, *Les Demoiselles d'Avignon*, Paris (June–July 1907). Oil on canvas, 243.9 × 233.7 cm. The Museum of Modern Art, New York. Acquired through the Lillie P. Bliss Bequest, Photograph © 1999 The Museum of Modern Art, New York. © 2000 Estate of Pablo Picasso/Artists Rights Society (ARS), New York; **721** Poster for L'arroseur arrosé for Cinématographe Lumière, designed by Auzolle, 1896. Cliché J.- L. Charmet.

Chapter 27

724 W. Wellner in Lushige Blatter. Courtesy Mary Evans Picture Library; **727** Map of Liberia (9 out of 20) from the American Colonization Society Collection. G8882.C6 1830.A8 ACS 2. Library of Congress, Geography and Map Division, Washington, DC; **728** Roger Viollet/Gamma Liaison; **729L** The British Library, London; **730** Mary Evans Picture Library, London; **732L** Africana Museum JPL; **732R** Corbis/Hulton Deutsch; **733** Culver Pictures, Inc.; **737** Roger Viollet/Gamma Liaison; **738** Roger Viollet/Gamma Liaison; **741** Delacroix, Eugene (1798–1860) *The Massacre of Chios, Greek families waiting for death or slavery*. Oil on canvas, 1824. Louvre, Department of Paintings, Paris. © Erich Lessing/Art Resource, New York; **742** Mary Evans Picture Library; **743** The Ottoman Gazette Kalem; **745** Roger Viollet/Gamma Liaison; **746** Corbis/Bettmann; **747** Brown Brothers.

Chapter 28

752 *Canton factories*, M3156. Oil on glass, post 1780. Peabody Essex Museum, Salem, MA. Photo by Mark Sexton; **755** *Castas, De mestizo y española, castiza*. Museo National de Historia; **757** Instituto Nacional de Bellas Artes; **759** From W. H. Russell, A Visit to Chile, 1890; **765** Tz'u-hsi, Empress Dowager of China, 1835–1908, Photographs Freer Gallery of Art and Arthur M. Sackler Gallery Archives, Smithsonian Institution; **767** *Puck*, August 15, 1900. Courtesy of American Heritage; **768** Mariners' Museum, Newport News, Virginia. Carl. H. Boehringer Collection; **769** Keystone-Mast Collection (Ku58130) UCR/California Museum of Photography, University of California, Riverside; **772** Mary Evans Picture Library.

Chapter 29

778 SCALA/Art Resource, NY; **780L** Culver Pictures, Inc.; **781** Culver Pictures, Inc.; **782** Culver Pictures, Inc.; **784** Corbis/Hulton Deutsch; **786** Historical Photos/Stock Montage, Inc.; **787** Corbis/Bettmann; **789** Roger Viollet/Gamma-Liaison; **790** The Granger Collection, New York; **793** Hulton Getty/Liaison Agency.

Chapter 30

798 © 1999 Artists Rights Society (ARS), New York/ADAGP, Paris; **802** Corbis/Bettmann; **806** Corbis/Bettmann; **807** The Trustees of the Imperial War Museum, London; **809** The Trustees of the Imperial War Museum, London; **811** Brown Brothers; **818L** Historical Photos/Stock Montage, Inc.; **818R** Corbis/Bettmann; **821** Corbis/Bettmann; **823** Corbis/Bettmann; **825** © 2000 Estate of Pablo Picasso/Artists Rights Society (ARS), New York. Giraudon/Art Resource, NY; **828** Corbis/Bettmann; **830** Corbis/Bettmann; **832** Dali, Salvador. *The Persistence of Memory* (Persistance de la mémoire). 1931. Oil on canvas, 9½ × 12" (24.1 × 33 cm). The Museum of Modern Art, New York. Given anonymously. Photograph © 1999 The Museum of Modern Art, New York. © 2000 Artists Rights Society (ARS), New York; **834** Art Resource, NY; **835** The Museum of Modern Art/Film Stills Archive, NY.

Chapter 31

838 Corbis/Bettmann; **841T** Corbis/Bettmann; **841B** Corbis/Hulton Deutsch; **846** Corbis/Underwood; **849** © Sovfoto; **852** © Sovfoto; **855** Erich Lessing/Art Resource, NY; **856T** Corbis/Bettmann; **865B** Corbis/Bettmann; **858** bpk Berlin, Nationalgalerie; **860** Popperfoto; **861** Wiener Library, London; **862** Kulturgeschichtliches Museum, Osnabruck (c) Auguste Moses-Nussbaum and Shulamit Jaari. © 2000 Artists Rights Society (ARS), New York/VG Bild-Kunst, Bonn.

Chapter 32

868 The End of the Ottoman Empire, Turkey 1908–1938. A History in Documentary Photographs by Jaques Benoist-Méchin. Published by Swan; **874** Culver Pictures, Inc.; **876** Corbis/Bettmann; **880** Margaret Bourke-White /Life Magazine/Time Warner, Inc.; **881** AP/Wide World Photos, Inc.; **885**

Corbis/Bettmann; **886** Hulton Getty/Liaison Agency; **888** Corbis/Bettmann; **891** © Cosmic Illusion Productions, Amsterdam; **892** Werner Forman Archive/Art Resource, NY; **893** Roger Viollet/Gamma Liaison; **894** Africana Museum JPL; **896** Corbis/Bettmann; **897L** Corbis/Bettmann; **897R** Corbis/Paul Almasy.

Chapter 33

904 Corbis; **909** National Archives; **911** National Archives; **912** Corbis/Bettmann; **913** Corbis/Bettmann; **918** Corbis/Bettmann; **919** British Information Service, London; **921** AKG London; **922** Corbis/Bettmann; **923** Cloth Map Collection, Library of Congress; **925** © Archive Photos; **926** Franklin D. Roosevelt Library; **928** Corbis/Bettmann.

Chapter 34

934 Corbis/Reuters; **937** Corbis/Bettmann; **941** Consulate General of Germany; **942** Corbis/Hulton Deutsch; **943** © Sovfoto; **945** Gschwind, Fortune, 1954, Time Inc.; **946** Corbis/Bettmann; **948** John Olson/LIFE Magazine © Time Inc.; **950** Corbis/Bettmann; **954** © Sovfoto/Eastfoto; **955** © Sovfoto/Eastfoto; **957** Corbis/Bettmann; **961** AP/Wide World Photos, Inc.; **962** Corbis/Bettmann; **963** Popperfoto; **964** Corbis-Reuters; **967** Wade Goddard-SYGMA .

Chapter 35

970 Corbis/AFP; **973** Corbis/Wolfgang Kaehler; **975** Harry S. Truman Library; **976** Corbis/Bettmann; **978** Roland Freeman/Magnum Photos; **979** AP/Wide World Photos, Inc.; **981** Kyodo News; **983** Courtesy French Ministry of Finance; **986** Peter Jordan/Gamma-Liaison; **987** Steve McCurry/Magnum Photos; **990** Contifoto/Sygma; **992** Along Reininger/Contact Press/Woodfin Camp.

Chapter 36

994 Greenpeace action against Indian Nuclear Test, Taj Mahal, Agra, India. © Greenpeace/Morgan; **998** © Sovfoto/Eastofoto; **999** AP/Wide World Photos, Inc.; **1000** Corbis/Reuters; **1005** © Bartholomew/Liaison; **1006** © Robert Nickelsberg/The Gamma Liaison Network; **1011** © Dirck Halstead/The Gamma Liaison Network; **1016** Corbis/Reuters; **1017** © Stephen Ferry/Liaison Agency; **1021** Hulton Getty/Liaison Agency; **1024** Namibie, 1966. Edimedia, Paris; **1026** Corbis/Reuters; **1029** AP/Wide World Photos, Inc.

Index

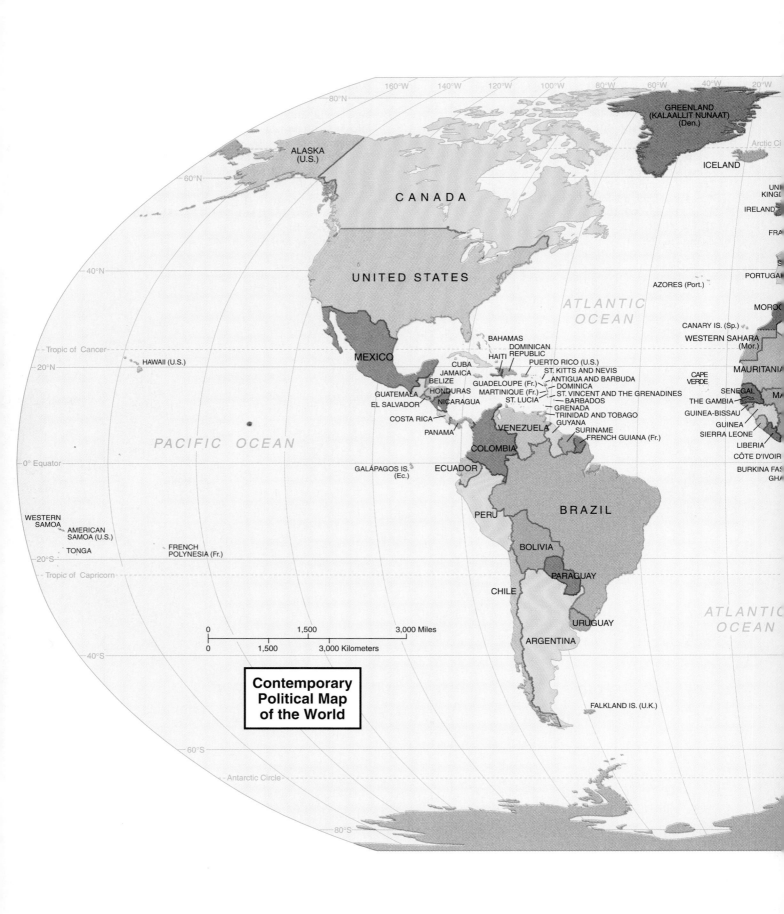

Contemporary
Political Map
of the World